England

David Else, Oliver Berry, Fionn Davenport, Martin Hughes,
Sam Martin, Etain O'Carroll, Becky Ohlsen

Contents

Destination England

Welcome to England, a 1000-year-old nation packed with history, and right in the spotlight on the world stage today. The English people often take their own country for granted, but whether you're from far-flung regions or just exploring your own backyard, a closer look reveals a feast of delights to make your head spin – from Hadrian's Wall in the north to Canterbury Cathedral in the south, from high culture in the Tate galleries to high energy at Old Trafford, from the ancient megaliths of Stonehenge to the space-age domes of the Eden Project.

This astounding variety is the key to enjoying travel in England. There really is something for everyone, whether you're eight or 80, visiting for a week or a month, travelling solo or in a group, with friends, your kids or your grandma.

London – quite rightly – is a major magnet, while England's other cities have flourished, with stunning new buildings, tempting bars and restaurants, and some of the finest museums in the world. After dark, the cutting-edge clubs, top-class theatre and formidable live music can't fail to provide a string of nights to remember. And then there's the great English countryside: wild mountains, rolling hills, pristine beaches, rocky islands, woodland floors decked with bluebells and gorse-clad moors dropping down to the sea.

Along with these gems, England's top drawcard is its compact geography. In a country that takes just eight hours to travel end to end, you're never far from the next castle, the next national park or the next relaxed lunch in a friendly village pub. The choice is endless, and we've hand picked the best to produce this book. Use it as a guide – to steer you from place to place – and mix it with making your own discoveries. You won't be disappointed.

DAVID RYAN

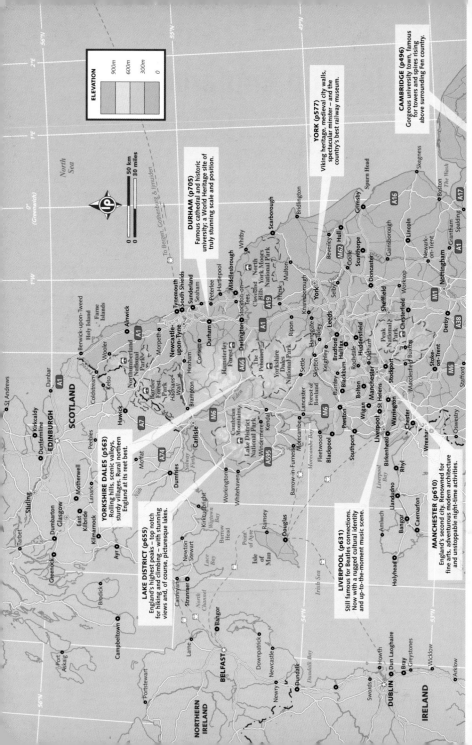

ELEVATION

900m
600m
300m
0

North Sea

To Bergen, Gothenburg & Ijmuiden

50 km
30 miles

DURHAM (p705)
Famous cathedral and historic university; a World Heritage site of truly stunning scale and position.

YORK (p577)
Viking heritage, medieval city walls, spectacular minster – and the country's best railway museum.

CAMBRIDGE (p496)
Gorgeous university town, famous for towers and spires rising above surrounding Fen country.

YORKSHIRE DALES (p563)
Rolling hills, scenic valleys, sturdy villages. Rural northern England at its best best.

LAKE DISTRICT (p655)
England's highest peaks – top notch for hiking and climbing – with stunning views and, of course, picturesque lakes.

LIVERPOOL (p631)
Still famous for Beatles connections. Now with a rugged cultural identity and up-to-the-moment music scene.

MANCHESTER (p610)
England's second city. Renowned for fine arts, adventurous modern architecture and unstoppable night-time activities.

SCOTLAND

SCOTLAND

NORTHERN IRELAND

IRELAND

North Channel

Irish Sea

Liverpool Bay

Morecambe Bay

Solway Firth

The Wash

Isle of Man

St Andrews
Dunfermline
Kirkcaldy
EDINBURGH
Peebles
Dunbar
Coldstream
Kelso
Hawick
Moffat
Dumfries
Kirkcudbright
Newton Stewart
Stranraer
Cairnryan
Portstewart
BELFAST
Downpatrick
Newry
Newcastle
Dundalk
DUBLIN
Dun Laoghaire
Bray
Greystones
Wicklow
Arklow
Howth
Swords

Tarbet
Greenock
Dumbarton
Glasgow
East Kilbride
Kilmarnock
Lanark
Motherwell
Stirling
Ayr
Brodick
Campbeltown
Port Askaig

Berwick-upon-Tweed
Holy Island
Farne Islands
Alnwick
Wooler
Morpeth
Newcastle-upon-Tyne
Tynemouth
South Shields
Sunderland
Seaham
Peterlee
Hartlepool
Hexham
Brampton
Corbett
Durham
Stockton-on-Tees
Middlesbrough
Darlington
Whitby
Scarborough
Bridlington
Spurn Head
Skegness
Boston
Spalding
Grantham
Newark-on-Trent
Lincoln
Gainsborough
Grimsby
Hull
Beverley
Scunthorpe
Goole
Doncaster
Worksop
Chesterfield
Derby
Nottingham
Stoke-on-Trent
Stafford
Oswestry
Wrexham

Northumberland National Park
Border Forest Park
Hadrian's Wall
Kielder Forest
Cumbrian Mountains
Lake District National Park
Windermere
Kendal
Barrow-in-Furness
Morecambe
Fleetwood
Blackpool
Southport
Lancaster
Forest of Bowland
Settle
Skipton
Keighley
Ilkley
Harrogate
Knaresborough
Ripon
Thirsk
York
Selby
Leeds
Bradford
Halifax
Huddersfield
Rochdale
Oldham
Sheffield
Buxton
Macclesfield
Peak District National Park
Yorkshire Dales National Park
North York Moors National Park
Malton
Pickering
Hamsterley Forest

Carlisle
Workington
Whitehaven
Preston
Blackburn
Burnley
Bolton
Wigan
St Helens
Warrington
Manchester
Stockport
Liverpool
Birkenhead
Chester
Rhyl
Llandudno
Bangor
Caernarfon
Holyhead
Amlwch

Ramsey
Douglas
Point of Ayre
Burrow Head
Laxe Bay
Luce Bay
Wigtown Bay

Carnryan
Lame
Dundalk Bay

Eden
Nith
Ouse
Trent
Ouse

The Pennines
A66
A1
A19
A66
M6
A74
A7
A1
A595
A16
A17
A1
A38
M1
M6
M62
M6

North Sea
56°N
55°N
54°N
53°N
56°N
49°N
2°E
1°E
0° (Greenwich)
1°W
2°W

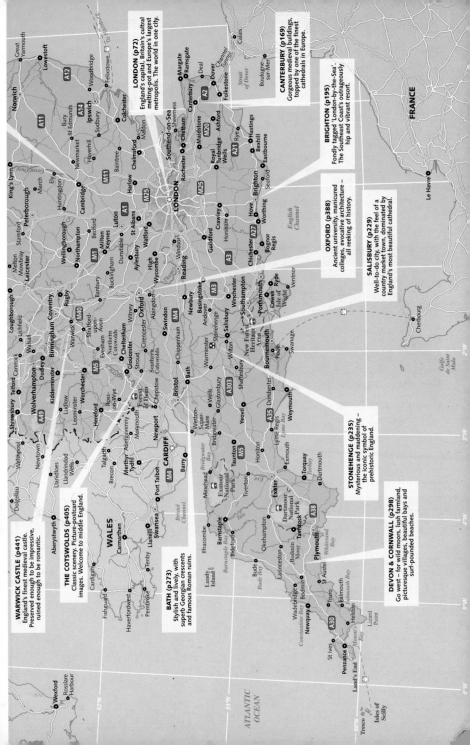

WARWICK CASTLE (p441)
England's finest medieval castle. Preserved enough to be impressive, ruined enough to be romantic.

THE COTSWOLDS (p405)
Classic scenery. Picture-postcard images. Welcome to middle England.

BATH (p273)
Stylish and lively, with superb Georgian crescents and famous Roman ruins.

DEVON & CORNWALL (p298)
Go west – for wild moors, lush farmland, picturesque villages, beautiful bays and surf-pounded beaches.

STONEHENGE (p235)
Mysterious and maddening – the iconic symbol of prehistoric England.

SALISBURY (p229)
Well-to-do city, with the feel of a country market town, dominated by England's most beautiful cathedral.

OXFORD (p388)
Ancient university, manicured colleges, evocative architecture – all reeking of history.

BRIGHTON (p195)
Fondly tagged 'London-by-the-Sea'. The Southeast Coast's outrageously hip and vibrant resort.

CANTERBURY (p169)
Gorgeous medieval buildings, topped by one of the finest cathedrals in Europe.

LONDON (p72)
England's capital, Britain's cultural melting-pot and Europe's largest metropolis. The world in one city.

WALES

CARDIFF

LONDON

FRANCE

ATLANTIC OCEAN

English Channel

It may be a small nation, but England boasts an astounding collection of historic towns and cities, and a vast array of impressive castles and stately homes. Any list has to start with **London** (p72), with towers, palaces, bridges, squares, museums and monuments from every period since the Bronze Age. Evocative ruins? Don't miss **Warwick Castle** (p441). If you like historic buildings with the roof on, visit **Blenheim Palace** (p400), the mother of all stately homes. Visit **Canterbury** (p169) or **Salisbury** (p229), with their simply beautiful cathedrals; **Winchester** (p207), capital of near-mythical King Alfred; or **Bath** (p273), with superb Georgian crescents and Roman remains. Travel even further back in time to **Stonehenge** (p235), *the* iconic symbol of ancient England, while nearby **Avebury Stone Circle** (p244) is still overwhelming after 5000 years.

... or Cambridge (p496)

Wander through gorgeous university towns with evocative architecture, such as Oxford (p388) ...

Look out across England's capital city from Tower Bridge (p108)

MANFRED GOTTSCHALK

Watch the changing of the guards at Buckingham Palace (p101)

CHRIS MELLOR

Head to York for its spectactular minister (p579)

Explore the ruins at Rievaulx Abbey (p599)

GRANT DIXON

England's cities are confident and buzzing with energy, with plenty of attractions to keep you enthralled and entertained. Head west to **Bristol** (p261), a hotbed of musical innovation with nightlife to match, or north to re-born **Birmingham** (p429) for big-name clubs, groundbreaking arts venues, top theatre and classical music. Chill out in **Leeds** (p553), with its sleek entertainment and shopping to die for – 'Knightsbridge of the North' is no idle claim. **London** (p72) gets top billing under Rich History, but it's very much a city of the present too – with more clubs, pubs, shows and venues than even the Londoners can visit in a lifetime.

RICHARD I'ANSON

See the Yellow Submarine in Liverpool (p631), a city still famous for Beatles connections

MARK DAFFEY

Feel the youth and energy of Manchester (p610)

Take in the old and the new in Bath (p273)

JAN STROMME

NEIL SETCHFIELD

Mix with the hip crowd in happening Brighton & Hove (p195)

Experience Liverpool's vibrant drinking and entertainment scene (p639)

RICHARD I'ANSON

JONATHAN SMITH

Get to know the locals in London's pubs (p133)

Catch a gig at one of London's innumerable music venues (p136)

NEIL SETCHFIELD

Spend a few days in London, and you feel unbearably cramped. But jump on a train, or drive a few hours, and you'll quickly be far from the madding crowd, enjoying England's wonderful coast and countryside. Come face to face with the elements on the wild coast of **Northumberland** (p720), or for a more gentle landscape, go to the limestone dales of **Derbyshire** (p472).

ANDREW MARSHALL & LEANNE WALKER

Don't miss the coastal paths and open spaces of Cornwall (p325)

Visit the Cotswolds (p405) for classic English scenery

BRYN THOMAS

PAUL BIGLAND

Head to the South Downs (p203) for rolling hills and chalk cliffs

MICHELLE LEWIS

Check out the picture-postcard views
in Devon (p302)

EOIN CLARKE

Climb England's highest peaks in the
Lakes District National Park (p655)

Commune with the wildlife, like these puffins on the Farne Islands (p722) off the shore of
Northumberland

GRAHAM BELL

To work up a sweat or just amble about, the national parks of England offer endless walking and cycling opportunities: check out the **New Forest** (p217) or **Dartmoor** (p317). For surfing, head for **Newquay** (p343). Then reach for the spas. Our favourites include **Shambhala Healing Retreat** (p288) for soothing massage and spiritual regeneration on the slopes of the suitably mystical Glastonbury tor, and **Ardencote Manor** (p444) not far from Stratford-upon-Avon, where no doubt Shakespeare, with his fondness for the absurd, would have delighted in seaweed baths and aromatherapy facials.

CHRIS MELLOR

Walk through gentle countryside in the Peak District National Park (p478)

Test your climbing skills in the Exmoor National Park (p291)

MARK DAFFEY

Cycle through North York Moors National Park (p596) – but don't forget to stop and take in the views

GRANT DIXON

Getting Started

Here's a handy slogan to keep in mind while you're planning your trip: travel in England is easy. Granted, it may not be totally effortless, but it's a breeze compared to many parts of the world. In this compact country you're never far from the next town, the next national park, the next pub or the next impressive castle on your hit list of highlights.

WHEN TO GO

Anyone spending time in England will soon sympathise with the locals' obsession with weather (see the boxed text p45). Generally, temperatures are mild and rain showers can fall any time; the key word is *changeable* – the weather can be bad one minute, great the next. Summer (June to August) normally gets the most sunshine, but there'll be cloudy days too. Conversely, winter (November to February) may enjoy fantastic clear spells between bouts of snow, while spring (March to May) or autumn (September to October) can sometimes produce the best weather of the year. There are also wide variations over distance: southern England might be chilly, while the north enjoys a heat wave. Be prepared for anything and you won't get a surprise.

For more weather facts and figures, see the climate charts on p736.

With all that in mind, May to September is undoubtedly the best period to travel in England. July and August are the busiest months (it's school holiday time), especially in coastal towns, national parks, and historical cities such as Oxford, Bath and York. April and October are marginal, but can be a good opportunity to avoid crowds, although some hotels and attractions close from mid-October to Easter, and Tourist Information Centres (TICs) have limited opening times.

For winter visits, London and the big cities are an exception – they're busy all the time and there's such a lot to see that the weather is immaterial. Besides, you're almost as likely to have a damp day in June as you are in January.

COSTS & MONEY

If you're a global traveller, whatever your budget, you'll know that England is expensive compared to many other countries. But don't let that put you off. If funds are tight you'll still have a great trip with some forward planning, a bit of shopping around and a modicum of common sense. There's a lot of stuff that's cheap or good value, and a lot more that's completely free. The following will give you some guidelines; for more details see the Directory and Transport chapters.

DON'T LEAVE HOME WITHOUT...

Travel in England is not like crossing the Sahara or exploring the Amazon. Anything can be bought as you go. Our advice is to take only what you absolutely need, which may include the following:

- a rain jacket
- comfortable shoes (the sort your granny would call 'stout')
- a small day-pack for sightseeing (and for carrying that rain jacket when the sun shines)
- a taste for beer that isn't icy cold
- listening skills and a sense of humour

HOW MUCH?

B&B
£20 per person

CD
£12

The Times (newspaper)
50p

Restaurant meal
£15 per person

Coffee:
£2 in Starbucks, 50p in a basic café

LONELY PLANET INDEX

Litre of petrol
80p

Litre of bottled water:
20p to £1

Pint of beer
£2.25

Souvenir T-shirt
£10

Takeaway fish and chips
£4

Backpackers in London need £40 a day for bare survival. Dorm beds cost at least £15, basic sustenance about £10 per day, and transport around town £5 unless you prefer to hoof it. If your purse strings aren't so short, bargain London hotels are about £50 to £75 per person. Past that price band, there are more choices: around £100 gets you something pretty decent. On top of food and bed, extras might include a pint in a pub (£2.50), entrance to a club (£5 to £10, up to £20 at weekends), and admission fees to museums and galleries (work on £10 to £20 a day, though many places don't charge).

Out of London, costs drop. Shoestringers will need around £30 per day to cover hostels and food. Mid-rangers will be fine on £50 to £75 per day: allow around £20 to £30 for a B&B, £10 to £15 for lunch, snacks and drinks, and £10 to £20 for an evening meal. Admission fees are the same for everyone – work on £10 per day.

Travel costs depend on your transport choice. Roughly speaking, train travel costs about £25 per 100 miles. Long-distance buses cost about half that. For car drivers, allow £10 per 100 miles for fuel, plus parking (and hire charges if necessary).

TRAVEL LITERATURE

There's nothing like a decent travelogue to set the mood for your own trip. The choice of books about travel in England can be daunting, so here's a list of our favourites to inspire you, add an extra dimension to your planning or help you dig under the English skin a little when you're on the road.

- *Notes from a Small Island* by Bill Bryson is incisive and perceptive. This American author really captures the spirit of England. When he pokes fun he's spot on, so the locals don't mind.
- *The Kingdom by the Sea* by Paul Theroux provides more keen observations from another cousin across the pond, although without Bryson's sense of fondness. Published 20 years ago, but still worth a read.
- *Lights Out for the Territory* by Iain Sinclair is a darkly humorous, entertaining and acerbic exploration of 1990s London, taking in – among other things – Jeffrey Archer's penthouse and an East End gangster funeral.
- *Park and Ride* by Miranda Sawyer is a wry and minutely observed 2001 sojourn through English suburbia, the land of never-ending home improvements and keeping up appearances.
- *Two Degrees West* by Nicholas Crane describes a walk in a perfectly straight line (two degrees west of the Greenwich meridian) across England, wading rivers, cutting through towns, sleeping in fields and meeting an astounding selection of real people along the way.
- *Crap Towns*, edited by Sam Jordison and Dan Kieran, describes the 50 worst places to live in the country – as voted by their own residents. It's vitriolic, but shouldn't be taken *too* seriously. There are some real surprises too – Brighton, Winchester and Liverpool, for example – but that's because some towns that are bad for locals are still great for visitors. Maybe read it *after* your trip.

HALF PRICE FOR KIDS

Most museums and historic sites in England charge half price (or thereabouts) for children, so we have only given adult prices throughout this book (unless the kids' price is significantly more or less than half price). Likewise, we have just quoted adult rates for hostels and campsites; children usually pay about 50% to 75% of this. In hotels, children get similar discounts – and may even go free of charge if they share a parent's room.

TOP TENS
MUST-SEE MOVIES

Predeparture planning is no chore if it includes a trip to the cinema or a night on the sofa with a DVD and a bowl of popcorn. Our parameters for an 'English' film? Anything about England. Anything which gives a taste of history, scenery or peculiar cultural traits. For reviews of these and other cinematic gems, see p51.

- *Brief Encounter* (1945)
  Director: David Lean
- *Passport to Pimlico* (1949)
  Director: Henry Cornelius
- *Secrets & Lies* (1996)
  Director: Mike Leigh
- *Sense & Sensibility* (1996)
  Director: Ang Lee
- *Brassed Off* (1996)
  Director: Mark Herman

- *The Full Monty* (1997)
  Director: Pater Cattaneo
- *East is East* (1999)
  Director: Damien O'Donnell
- *Shakespeare in Love* (1999)
  Director: John Madden
- *Billy Elliot* (2000)
  Director: Stephen Daldry
- *Bend it like Beckham* (2002)
  Director: Gurinda Chadha

RAVE READS

Travel broadens the mind. Especially if you read before you go. For a taste of life in England, try a few of these novels – from past classics to contemporary milestones. For more details on these and other great books, see p49.

- *Pride & Prejudice* (1813)
  Jane Austen
- *Oliver Twist* (1837)
  Charles Dickens
- *Wuthering Heights* (1847)
  Emily Brontë
- *The Trumpet Major* (1895)
  Thomas Hardy
- *The Rainbow* (1915)
  DH Lawrence

- *Waterland* (1983)
  Graham Swift
- *High Fidelity* (1995)
  Nick Hornby
- *Bridget Jones's Diary* (1996)
  Helen Fielding
- *White Teeth* (2000)
  Zadie Smith
- *Small Island* (2004)
  Andrea Levy

FAVOURITE FESTIVALS & EVENTS

For entertainment or attractions to weave your travels around, here's a list of our 10 favourite festivals and events. For more ideas, see p738.

- Jorvik Viking Festival
  (York) February
- University Boat Race
  (London) March
- Brighton Festival
  (Brighton) May
- Bath International Music Festival
  (Bath) May
- Trooping the Colour
  (London) June

- Glastonbury Festival
  (Somerset) June
- Mardi Gras Pride in the Park
  (London) June/July
- International Flying Display
  (Farnborough) July
- Notting Hill Carnival
  (London) August
- Reading Festival
  (Reading) August

INTERNET RESOURCES

The Internet is a wonderful planning tool for travellers, and there are millions of sites about England. Before plunging into the cyber-maze, try these for starters:

Able to Go (www.abletogo.com) Excellent listings for visitors with mobility difficulties.

Backpax (www.backpaxmag.com) Cheerful info on budget travel, visas, activities and work.

BBC (www.bbc.co.uk) Immense and invaluable site from the world's best broadcaster.

i-UK (www.i-uk.com) Official site for all UK matters – business, study and travel.

Independent Hostels (www.independenthostelguide.co.uk) Hostels in England and beyond.

Lonely Planet (www.lonelyplanet.com) Loads of travel news, a bit of merchandise, and the legendary Thorn Tree bulletin board.

UK Student Life (www.ukstudentlife.com) Language schools and courses, plus where to go outside study time.

VisitBritain (www.visitbritain.com) A great first call for all tourism information.

Itineraries

CLASSIC ROUTES

CAPITAL HIGHLIGHTS
One to Two Weeks / London to Oxford

With so many places to visit in England, however long you stay you'll always be spoilt for choice. But what a choice!

Top of the list just has to be **London** (p72), England's irrepressible capital, brimming with energy and spectacle. From here, go west to **Winchester** (p207), ancient capital of England, or to **Salisbury** (p229), with its beautiful cathedral. Then aim for mysterious **Stonehenge** (p235), England's most famous prehistoric site. **Avebury's stone circle** (p244) is bigger than Stonehenge, and nearby Silbury Hill adds yet more mystic aura. Carry on to Georgian **Bath** (p273), renowned for grand architecture, and Roman remains.

Return to London from Bath or, if you have time, carry on: from Bath you can saunter through the quintessentially English countryside of the **Cotswolds** (p405) to reach **Oxford** (p388), another city steeped in history, with manicured colleges, stunning architecture, great pubs and even a link with new all-English hero Harry Potter. Return to London by train or Quidditch broomstick to complete this capital highlights circuit.

Without stopping much you could do this circuit in a couple of days. But with pauses to drink in the history (not to mention the occasional beer in a country pub), a week is better for the first half of the circuit, and two weeks ideal for the whole 300-mile (480km) loop.

ENGLAND'S GREEN & PLEASANT LAND

**Two to Four Weeks /
London to the Lake District**

'Did these feet in ancient times walk upon England's pastures green?' mused English poet and visionary William Blake. Who knows. But *your* feet certainly can stroll through the meadows or stride across the mountains in England's countryside today.

Begin the journey in the **New Forest** (p217), England's most recently opened national park, for a spot of walking, cycling or horse-riding, or simply relaxing in country pub gardens. Then strike out west through **Dartmoor National Park** (p317) into Devon and Cornwall, which tempt with wild moors, grassy hills, and a beautiful coast of cliffs and sandy beaches.

Next stop, the **Cotswolds** (p405) provide classic English countryside: neat fields, clear rivers, grassy valleys and endless pretty villages with cottages and churches of honey-coloured Cotswold stone – all glowing contentedly whenever the sun is out.

From here travel through the **Marches** (p353), the often-overlooked rural landscape between Wales and the cities of the English Midlands, to reach the foot of the Pennine Hills, 'the backbone of England'. Here you'll discover the limestone valleys of the **Peak District** (p478), the dark peaty moors around **Haworth** (p561), made famous by Brontë novels, and the delightful **Yorkshire Dales** (p563), home of Wensleydale cheese.

The trip ends on a high – in the glorious mountains of the **Lake District** (p655), home to Scaféll Pike (England's highest point) and many other summits, welcoming valleys and the picturesque Lakeland scenery immortalised by Wordsworth.

Free from urban life, this is a tour to recharge your batteries, replenish your soul and fill your lungs with fresh air. The whole trip is around 600 miles (around 1000km), and could easily take a month. Do lots of walking or cycling, and it might be double that. Cherry-pick a little and it'll take two or three weeks.

THE GRAND TOUR

**One to Two Months /
London to Cambridge (the long way)**

Begin this extensive tour in **London** (p72), then aim for **Winchester** (p207), **Salisbury** (p229) and the national park **New Forest** (p217), taking time for a ferry hop across to the **Isle of Wight** (p221). For a coastal scene of a different sort, from London you could head to hip and happening **Brighton** (p195) and the hills of the **South Downs** (p203), or marvel at the cathedral in **Canterbury** (p169), before tracking across country via prehistoric **Stonehenge** (p235) to reach the Georgian city of **Bath** (p273). Take a short loop to **Wells** (p282), or a longer jaunt into rural **Dorset** (p246) and **Devon** (p302).

Retrace your path to **Bristol** (p261), then travel through the scenic **Cotswolds** (p405) to historic **Oxford** (p388). From here journey into the Midlands to savour scenic towns like **Stow-on-the-Wold** (p414), spectacular **Warwick Castle** (p441) and Shakespeare's birthplace **Stratford-upon-Avon** (p445). Continue north to **Chester** (p625), **Liverpool** (p631) and **Manchester** (p610) – cities ancient and modern – followed by a complete change of scenery in the **Lake District** (p655) and a journey back in time along **Hadrian's Wall** (p715) to enjoy recently restyled-to-the-hilt party town **Newcastle-upon-Tyne** (p696).

Then it's time to head south, via **Durham** (p705) and its World Heritage–listed cathedral, and the heather-clad **North York Moors** (p596), pausing for breath (or fish and chips) at the jolly resort of **Whitby** (p602) or the ancient Viking capital of **York** (p577). Then it's back on the road – maybe stopping to sample the shopping in **Leeds** (p553) or the nightlife in **Nottingham** (p465) – to end your tour with a final flourish in beautiful **Cambridge** (p496).

This energetic pack-it-in loop is about 900 miles (about 1400km), or 1200 miles (1900km) with the longer options, and takes about a month. If you don't want to rush, just leave out a few places.

ROADS LESS TRAVELLED

NEW ENGLAND
Seven to 10 days / Bristol to Manchester

'I don't want to change the world, I'm not looking for a new England'. So sang urban troubadour Billy Bragg. He'd have found it here, in the once down-at-heel but now revitalised English cities.

Kick off in **Bristol** (p261), once a poor cousin to grand neighbour Bath, but today a city with fierce pride, rich historic legacy and a music scene that rivals hip northern outposts. Next stop, **Birmingham** (p429), formerly famous for hideous 1960s architecture, today simply oozing transformation – renovated waterside, energised museums and space-age shopping centre. Nearby is **Nottingham** (p465), famous for men in tights, but renowned today for some very merry nightlife. If hitting the dance floor isn't your thing, relax in the city's great pubs, including one of the oldest in the country.

But don't dawdle. Sup your pint. We're off again – this time to fashionable **Leeds** (p553), Yorkshire's shopping heaven, the Knightsbridge of the North. Retail not your thing? Head for **Liverpool** (p631) instead. The Beatles may be done to death, but there's a rich and genuine musical heritage here, not to mention a rather famous football team.

And to finish, where else? **Manchester** (p610), England's second city and a long-time hotbed of musical endeavour, with a thriving arts and club scene, galleries a go-go, fine dining, dramatic new architecture and – oh yes – another well-known football team.

In theory you could do this 330-mile (530km) urban odyssey in five days, but England's cities may tempt you to linger longer. Better allow at least a week. Ten days would be even better. Don't say we didn't warn you...

CINDERELLA ENGLAND   10 to 14 days / Suffolk to Northumberland

Some of England's best-known national parks and natural beauties are mentioned under Classic Routes. This jaunt takes you through slightly less frequented (but no less scenic) countryside.

Surprisingly near London sit the tranquil counties of **Suffolk** (p510) and **Norfolk** (p521). Here the coastline is dotted with picturesque harbours, shingle beaches, salt marshes, bird reserves and the occasional old-fashioned seaside resort. Inland you'll find rivers and lakes, pretty villages and endless miles of flat countryside – perfect for a gentle bicycle ride.

Then cruise across the even flatter fens of **Cambridgeshire** (p496) and head north to reach the bumpy hills and peaceful countryside of the **Yorkshire Wolds** (p572). Nearby is the **North York Moors National Park** (p596), with heather-covered hills and charming coastline; the massive flocks of seabirds nesting at **Bempton Cliffs** (p577) are one of England's top wildlife spectacles.

Inland lie the **North Pennines** (p684), the part of 'England's backbone' between the Yorkshire Dales and Hadrian's Wall. Sometimes overlooked in favour of these famous neighbouring landmarks, this is the place for dramatic hiking or enjoying the old pubs and cosy B&Bs in sturdy hill-country towns such as **Alston** (p690).

On the other side of the Roman Wall is **Northumberland National Park** (p727) where the wild and empty big-sky landscapes of the Cheviot Hills give a taste of the Scottish mountains just over the border. To finish your journey, it's a short trip down to the **Northumberland coast** (p720) an area famous for its beaches and castles, not to mention its delicious crab sandwiches.

If you don't stop much, you could see these 'hidden' areas in a week, covering about 400 miles (about 650km). But allow two weeks or more if you plan to wear your hiking boots or want to relax over tea and cake, or a pie and a pint, and catch a little local flavour off the beaten track.

TAILORED TRIPS

ENGLAND FOR KIDS

Are we nearly there yet? Follow this suggested route and you soon will be.

Start at **Origins** (p523) in Norwich, an interactive museum with hands-on opportunities to flood the fens. Then head to **London** (p72), where the scope of kid-friendly attractions is mesmerising, and north to **Warwick Castle** (p441), decayed just enough to be picturesque. Knights in armour? You bet. And those of a ghoulish disposition can creep around the dungeons.

It's a short distance, but a leap across centuries, to the **National Space Centre** (p461) near Leicester, where highlights include interactive cosmic myths, interplanetary travel displays, zero-gravity toilets and germ-devouring underpants. We know why kids love it. And it *is* rocket science.

Hungry after crossing the galaxy? No problem. Next stop is **Cadbury World** (p439) near Birmingham, a lip-smacking exploration of chocolate production and consumption. Just make sure all those samples settle in tiny tummies before you reach **Alton Towers** (p455), England's most popular theme park, with a stomach-churning selection of vertical drops and plunging roller coasters.

And to finish, limber up the brain cells at **Explore** (p263), Bristol's interactive science museum, bursting with hands-on exhibits and lots of action for inquisitive children.

SLOWLY FLOWS THE THAMES

Follow England's best-known river from picture-postcard countryside to the heart of the capital. You can travel by car, train or bike, or walk the whole way on the Thames Path, and even sample a few sections by boat.

Start at the source of the Thames, a damp patch near the honey-stoned town of **Cirencester** (p406) – once the second-largest city in Roman Britain. A trickle soon becomes a stream, then a river, as you follow the Thames through the fields and villages of the **Cotswolds** (p405) to **Oxford** (p388) – famous for its university and a good place to hire a boat.

Keep on downstream through **Dorchester-on-Thames** (p401) and the **Chiltern Hills** (p151), then past **Reading** (p158) to charming **Henley-on-Thames** (p403), which is the site of the nation's favourite regatta.

The Thames then runs past **Windsor Castle** (p154), royal residence since AD 850; **Runnymede** (p157), where the Magna Carta was signed; and **Hampton Court Palace** (p117), once home to Henry VIII and today well known for its maze, before it flows into the heart of London.

NORTHERN EXPOSURE

Here's one for grease monkeys and fans of large-scale machinery. This is a tour through northern England's great industrial heritage.

Start, appropriately, at **Ironbridge Gorge** (p375), the crucible of the Industrial Revolution, the Silicon Valley of the 18th century and a World Heritage site today, boasting 10 fascinating museums. Then travel to **Stoke-on-Trent** (p454) and the Wedgwood Story Visitor Centre, where space-age robots create fine bone china, and to **Derby** (p472), where the Royal Crown Derby factory provides more ceramic insights and the Industrial Museum is heaven if you're into trains or – especially – aero-engines.

If china isn't your cup of tea, head for Manchester's **Museum of Science & Industry** (p615), revelling in the glory of the industrial age, with large-scale exhibitions including machinery from the cotton mills that made the city great.

Just over the Pennines, Sheffield's prodigious industrial heritage is the subject of the excellent **Kelham Island Museum** (p549), where highlights include a working steam engine the size of a house. Nearby, kid-friendly **Magna** (p552) celebrates heavy industry and hands-on high technology, while the **National Coal Mining Museum** (p560) near Leeds is fascinating for everyone.

Last stop. All change please. York's **National Railway Museum** (p582) is an award-winning mix of heritage, nostalgia and sheer gargantuan scale. It's the perfect place to go loco.

ENGLAND FOR GROWN-UPS

Forget about work. Turn off the phone, leave behind the kids (if you have them), take your best friend or lover (if you have one), and indulge. This is not an arduous journey; this is a voyage of comfort, a transport of delight.

Limber up for the journey at **Chewton Glen Hotel & Country Club** (p221), a world-class spa resort on the edge of the New Forest, then relax at the **Royal Crescent Hotel** (p278), Bath's top place to stay, oozing charm at the grandest of grand addresses. Choose a room and hang up the 'Do Not Disturb' sign.

Then it's a mere chauffeur-driven hop to **Whatley Manor** (p241), Cotswold mansion turned stylish hotel, where contemporary art contrasts with wood panelling and crystal chandeliers.

Need a break from all that seclusion? How about a night at the opera? Put on the ritz at Buxton's gorgeously restored **Opera House** (p481), then match it with a room at the **Old Hall Hotel** (p482), a grand establishment whose former guests include Mary, Queen of Scots.

For more regal flavours, head for the 14th-century **Langley Castle** (p718), near Hadrian's Wall, which has four-poster beds and no medieval privations whatsoever. One of the rooms even has a big sunken bathtub.

The Authors

DAVID ELSE
Coordinating Author

David's knowledge of England comes from a lifetime of travel around the country, often by foot and bike – a passion which started at university, when heading for the hills was always more attractive than visiting the library. Originally from London, David slowly trekked northwards, via Wiltshire, Bristol and Derbyshire – interspersed with exile in Wales and long spells in Africa – to his present base in Yorkshire. A full-time travel writer, David has authored about 20 guidebooks including Lonely Planet's *Britain* and *Walking in Britain*. He also likes journeys by train, bus, car or canoe – and is still rarely seen in libraries.

My Favourite Day

It's 7am. I drink a cup of tea – English Breakfast, naturally – then go straight down to the River Thames. This is my favourite time in London; early in the morning on a sunny day. I cross Westminster Bridge to the South Bank, and walk past 1000-year-old Lambeth Palace and new-millennium symbol the London Eye, later getting views of St Paul's Cathedral and the Tower of London. Icons, I love 'em. Next, a boat down to Greenwich and long lunch in an old pub near the *Cutty Sark*, before walking it off with a mooch around the National Maritime Museum and a stroll through two hemispheres. Just before rush hour, the Docklands Light Railway gives a bargain-priced bird's-eye view of London and a quick ride back to the heart of the city.

BECKY OHLSEN
The Midlands, Eastern England

Becky has studied and practised the English language for 32 years, though her accent remains depressingly American. After roughly a decade strapped to her desk as a copy editor of the alternative press, she was seized with the urge to ramble, and ramble she did, spending a year underneath an enormous backpack on a quest to explore every nook and cranny of Europe. Given her fondness for warm beer, green hills, yellow journalism and tiny cars, it's no surprise she got hooked on England almost instantly. Several visits later, she's decided the Peak District is her favourite part, with London a close second.

ETAIN O'CARROLL
Wessex, The Marches, The Cotswolds

Etain's first childhood trips to England consisted of seemingly endless architectural tours of stately homes and castle ruins punctuated with visits to what then seemed like exotic motorway service stations. It sowed the seeds of a deep appreciation of the wonderful buildings and countryside in southern England, and work on this edition led back to many old haunts in the glorious villages and winding country lanes of Wessex, the Marches and the Cotswolds. Etain now lives and works in Oxford as a travel writer and photographer and has published with a variety of magazines and papers.

OLIVER BERRY
Cumbria, Devon & Cornwall
Oliver graduated from University College London with a degree in English and now works as a freelance writer. Having moved to Cornwall at the tender age of one, he has spent the last twenty-six years trying to find excuses for wandering along the county's beaches and clifftops; writing a guidebook is the best one yet. Oliver has received several awards for his writing including *The Guardian* Young Travel Writer of the Year.

SAM MARTIN
The Southeast Coast, Home Counties
Sam's first encounter with England was as a two-year-old, when his family moved to London from the States. He lived there for five years, etching lasting images of Rupert Bear and Punch & Judy upon his memory before returning to the States and settling in Texas. There he quickly lost his English accent under the withering criticism of his fellow eight-year-olds. Sam has travelled through England many times since, even selling Nepali T-shirts at Camden Market to get stateside again. He now lives Austin, Texas, with his wife and two sons. Sam is a full-time writer and has contributed to Lonely Planet's *USA* and *San Antonio, Austin & The Hill Country*.

MARTIN HUGHES
London
Martin Hughes was born and bred in Dublin where, as an adult, he dithered for five years between journalism and public relations before ditching both and shifting to the brighter lights of London. After a year of very odd jobs, he took off on a three-year Grand Tour of the world, popping back to London each summer to raise funds. He eventually settled in Melbourne, Australia, where he works as a freelance journalist and travel writer. He still earns a crust from London, where he returns at least twice a year for cultural catch-ups and assignments.

FIONN DAVENPORT Northeast England, Northwest England, Yorkshire
Dublin born and bred, Fionn was separated from England by what is little more than a big polluted puddle, but for years he had no clue what England was really like. As far as he was concerned, Ireland had the monopoly on wild scenery and friendliness and England was really just London and its outer suburbs. When he crossed the puddle to write the first edition, he wasn't expecting much. He couldn't have been more wrong. He's worked on every edition since, and returns to Ireland preaching England's stunning beauty to the wholly surprised. Maybe that puddle is a lot bigger than he thought.

CONTRIBUTING AUTHOR

Dr Caroline Evans wrote the Health chapter. Having studied medicine at the University of London, Caroline completed general practice training in Cambridge. She is the medical adviser to Nomad Travel Clinic, a private travel-health clinic in London, and is also a GP specialising in travel medicine. Caroline has acted as expedition doctor for Raleigh International and Coral Cay expeditions.

Snapshot

As we were writing this book in 2004, England was a country in crisis. Was it the economy? International politics? Environmental degradation? No. It was football. The national team returned defeated from the European championships. And so, a nation mourned. Not just the die-hard fans. Everyone. A million flags were sadly taken down. Even people normally unaware of the beautiful game were drawn into deep discussions about the referee's eyesight or the captain's skills on the penalty spot.

Then along came tennis at Wimbledon and the part-time supporters forgot about David Beckham and started cheering Tim Henman instead. That's the way it goes: the English are sport mad – but it really helps if the English players are actually winning.

And if it's not sport, what else do the English talk about? In the early years of the 21st century, what are the hot topics in the pubs, clubs and drawing rooms of England?

The invasion of Iraq is a biggie. There's still considerable resentment about the Labour government obediently backing the American invasion, and cartoonists still depict Tony Blair as George Bush's poodle. 'It had to be done', says Tony. But while we might agree that Saddam Hussein was an evil dictator and a threat to world peace, if that's reason enough to go marching into counties and deposing their leaders, there's surely a long list of other candidates due the same treatment. And has the 'war against terrorism' made the world a safer place? We're not sure.

It's not just global security. On many other matters, the people of England seem disillusioned with their government. After the Conservative era of Mrs Thatcher, Labour came to power on a tsunami of popularity in the mid-1990s and cruised to victory again in 2001. But promises of ethical foreign policy and a green transport strategy now ring hollow as realpolitik has inevitably taken hold: English companies still sell armaments around the world, and even if millions of pounds are invested in improving transportation, most of the money seems to go on widening motorways.

The disillusionment was reflected in a swing away from Labour during elections for local councils and the European parliament in June 2004. Perhaps it was a rap on the knuckles. Perhaps it's more serious. But with the next general elections due by 2006 at the latest, all the parties are gearing up for a serious battle.

And what will they be arguing about? Britain in Europe, for one. Suspicion of all matters 'continental' seems to be a particularly English trait, whether it be the introduction of the euro, the enlargement of the European Union (EU) or the policies of the European Parliament. In the minds of most people they're all lumped under the same diabolical banner anyway, a fact not missed by the fledgling UK Independence Party – its single policy to withdraw Britain from the EU earned it considerable public support and a lot of votes at the '04 elections.

Back in the bars and drawing rooms, discussion about European expansion rolls into concerns about asylum seekers. For the desperate people who leave impoverished parts of the world, England seems a land of endless jobs and welfare services, and many go to extraordinary lengths to get here, hiding for days in transport containers, or hanging underneath the trains that trundle through the Channel Tunnel – sometimes with fatal results.

FAST FACTS

Population: 51 million

Size: 50,000 sq miles (130,000 sq km)

Inflation: 2.7%

Unemployment: 2.3%

Number of monarchs since William the Conqueror: 40

Number of ships launched by the Queen: 16

Proportion of preteen children with computer or TV in their bedroom: 67%

Proportion of preteen children getting less sleep than they need: 20%

Average household weekly cost of alcohol consumed at home: £6

Average household weekly cost of fruit and vegetables: £5.50

Average number of credit cards per person: 2

Average outstanding credit-card debt per person: £5000

For those who make it, there's not much of a welcome. Asylum seekers, economic migrants, refugees, foreigners, terrorists: they're all the same, according to the headlines in xenophobic (and high-circulation) newspapers. The message is uncompromising: these foreigners are destroying the English way of life and need to be kept out. Britain's immigration laws may be less emotional, but they're increasingly stringent – if you're escaping a brutal government, there's a chance you can stay; if you're here because you're poor, you'll be sent packing pretty soon.

Meanwhile, on the home front, the state of the nation's public services – health and education – is another big issue in England today. Performance-related 'league tables', a concept introduced by the Conservatives and continued by the Labour government, may encourage some schools and hospitals to excel, while politicians from both parties claim their policies mean more choice. But they miss the point: the punters don't want to choose between Hospital A and Hospital B. They want to go to a place nearby, and they simply want it to be good.

Perhaps this general air of disillusionment and disappointment is why election turn-outs have been dropping steadily since the 1960s (although a postal ballot in 2004 pushed figures up again). The people of England are tired of politicians, or simply don't trust them – whatever their hue. A constant complaint is that Parliament seems out of touch. It's a telling indictment that more people vote in TV talent shows than they do for their own political leaders, which in turn is a symptom of England's ever-growing obsession with fame and celebrity.

The popular newspapers feature celebrities on a daily basis, while dedicated magazines such as *Hello* and *Heat* sell half a million copies every week. And we all lap up the stories of the famous-for-being-famous, and love to see pictures of these happily tanned and starched people – even though their actual skills seem limited to kicking a ball, singing a jolly tune or looking good in tight trousers.

Why are the celebs everywhere? Maybe it's because they saw the great unwashed stealing their limelight. It all started with *Big Brother* – ground-breaking in its day, but now tired and sordid. Critics say the show dumbed down to chase ratings. Producers say the introduction of seminaked mud-wrestling and group showers was sheer coincidence. In truth, 'reality' TV is so contrived it makes the soaps look ad-libbed (but then maybe that's just the quality of the soaps). Whatever, millions still tune in and sit on the edge of their seat each evening to see what happens next.

And that brings us nicely back to football. With the World Cup of 2006 looming on the horizon, it won't be long before we all catch football fever once again, and the world's problems will be forgotten. The English will dust off the flags, dig out the face paint and come together to support the national team. Let's hope we get further than the quarter-finals this time.

History

It may be on the edge of Europe, but England was never on the sidelines of history. For thousands of years, invaders and incomers alike have arrived, settled and made their mark. The result is England's fascinating mix of landscape, culture and language – a dynamic pattern that shaped the nation and continues to evolve today.

For many visitors, this rich historic legacy is England's main attraction; everything from Stonehenge to Hadrian's Wall, via Canterbury Cathedral, the Tower of London, hundreds of castles and an endless line of kings and queens. Even if you're no fan of dates and dynasties, English history will certainly dominate your travels, so the bare essentials in this chapter will just as certainly help you enjoy it.

FIRST ARRIVALS

Human habitation in England stretches back at least 400,000 years, although exact dates depend on your definition of 'human'. Ice Ages came and went, sea levels rose and fell, and the island now called Britain was frequently joined to the European mainland. Hunter-gatherers crossed the land bridge, moving north as the ice melted and retreating to warmer climes when the glaciers advanced again.

Around 4000 BC a group of migrants arrived from Europe. What made them different was their use of stone tools; instead of having to hunt and keep moving, they could settle in one place and start farming – most notably in open chalky hill areas like Salisbury Plain and the South Downs. Alongside the fields these early settlers built burial mounds, but perhaps their most enduring legacies are the great stone circles of Avebury and Stonehenge, still clearly visible today, and described on p244 and p235.

IRON & CELTS

Move on a millennium or two, and it's the Iron Age. Better tools meant trees were felled and more land was turned to farming, laying down a patchwork pattern of fields and small villages that still exists in parts of rural England today.

A History of Britain by historian and TV star Simon Schama is an incisive and highly accessible three-volume set, putting events from 3000 BC to AD 2000 in a modern context.

The Isles: A History by Norman Davies provides much-acclaimed and highly readable coverage of the past 10,000 years in England within the broader history of the British Isles.

ENGLAND? BRITAIN? WHAT'S IN A NAME?

The country of England, along with Wales and Scotland, is part of the state of Great Britain. Three countries in one might seem a strange set-up, and visitors are sometimes confused about the difference between England and Britain – as are a lot of English people. But getting a grip on this basic principle will ease your understanding of English history and culture, and make your travel more enjoyable too.

And just for the record, the United Kingdom (UK) consists of Great Britain, Northern Ireland and some semiautonomous islands such as the Isle of Man. The island of Ireland consists of Northern Ireland and the Republic of Ireland (also called Eire). The British Isles is a geographical term for the whole group of islands that make up the UK and the Republic of Ireland. Got all that? Good.

TIMELINE	4000 BC	55 BC
	Neolithic migrants arrive from Europe. Stonehenge built	Roman invaders under Julius Caesar make forays into southern England

Sarum by Edward Rutherford is a truly mammoth novel, covering the stories of five fictional families through about 10,000 years of English history – from the building of Stonehenge and Salisbury Cathedral, right up to the 1980s.

As landscapes altered, this was also a time of cultural change. The Celts, a people who originally migrated from Central Europe, had settled across much of the island of Britain by around 500 BC, absorbing the indigenous people. A Celtic-British population developed – sometimes known as the 'ancient Britons' – divided into about 20 different tribes, including the Cantiaci (in today's county of Kent), the Iceni (today's Norfolk) and the Brigantes (northwest England). You noticed the Latin-sounding names? That's because the tribal tags were first handed out by the next arrivals on England's shores…

ENTER THE ROMANS

Think of the Romans, and you think of legions, centurions and aqueducts. They were all here, as Britain and much of Europe came under the power (or the yoke, for those on the receiving end) of the Classical Period's greatest military empire.

Julius Caesar, the emperor everyone remembers, made forays into England from what is now France in 55 BC. But the real Roman invasion happened a century later when Emperor Claudius led a ruthless campaign which resulted in the Romans controlling pretty much everywhere in southern England by AD 50. It wasn't all plain sailing though: some locals fought back. The most famous freedom fighter was warrior-queen Boudicca, who led an army as far as Londinium, the Roman port on the present site of London.

However, opposition was mostly sporadic and no real threat to the legions' military might. By around AD 80 the new province of Britannia (much of today's England and Wales) was firmly under Roman rule. And although it's tempting to imagine noble natives battling courageously against occupying forces, in reality Roman control and stability was probably welcomed by the general population, tired of feuding chiefs and insecure tribal territories.

London is another epic from Edward Rutherford, this time a novel (or rather around 50 separate mini-novels, each set in a key historical era) about England's capital from the Roman invasion to the Blitz of WWII. Exhaustive and exhausting, but great for a sense of each period.

HADRIAN DRAWS A LINE

North of Britannia was the land the Romans called Caledonia (one day to become Scotland). This proved a harder place to find a fan club, and in AD 122 Emperor Hadrian decided rather than conquer the wild Pict tribes, he'd settle for keeping them at bay. So a barricade was built across northern England – between today's Carlisle and Newcastle. For nearly 300 years it marked the northernmost limit of the Roman Empire, and today Hadrian's Wall is one of England's best-known historic sites (see p715).

EXIT THE ROMANS

Settlement by the Romans in England lasted almost four centuries, and intermarriage was common between locals and incomers (many from other parts of the empire, including today's Belgium, Spain and Syria – rather than Rome itself) so that a Romano-British population evolved, particularly in the towns, while indigenous Celtic culture remained in rural areas.

Along with stability and wealth, the Romans introduced another cultural facet – a new religion called Christianity, after it was recognised by Emperor Constantine in AD 313. But by this time, although Romano-British

LEGACY OF THE LEGIONS

To control the territory they'd occupied, the Romans built castles and garrisons across England. Many of these developed into towns, later to be called 'chesters' and today remembered by names such as Winchester, Manchester and Colchester. The Romans are also well known for the roads they built – initially so the legions could march quickly from place to place, and later so that trade could develop. Wherever possible the roads were built in straight lines (because it was efficient, not – as the old joke goes – to stop the ancient Britons hiding round corners), and included Ermine St between London and York, Watling St between London and Chester, and the Fosse Way between Exeter and Lincoln. Many ruler-straight Roman roads are still followed by modern highways today, and in a land better known for old lanes and turnpike routes winding through the landscape, they clearly stand out in the atlas.

culture was thriving in what we now call England, back in its Mediterranean heartland the Empire was already in decline.

It was an untidy finale. The Romans were not driven out by the ancient Britons (by this time, Romano-British culture was so established there was nowhere for the 'invaders' to go 'home' to). In reality, Britannia was simply dumped by the rulers in Rome, and the colony slowly fizzled out of existence. But historians are neat folk, and the end of Roman power in England is generally dated at AD 410.

THE EMERGENCE OF ENGLAND

When Roman power faded, England went downhill. Trade declined, Romano-British towns were abandoned, and rural areas became no-go zones as local warlords fought over fiefdoms. Not inappropriately, the next few centuries are called the Dark Ages.

The vacuum didn't go unnoticed and once again a bunch of pesky continentals invaded. Angles and Saxons – Teutonic tribes from northern Europe – advanced across the former Roman turf. They moved fast, and quickly overcame the Celts and what remained of Romano-British culture, so that by the late 6th century the country now called England was almost 100% Anglo-Saxon. So thorough was the invasion that even today much of the English language is Anglo-Saxon in origin, many place names have Anglo-Saxon roots, and the very term 'Anglo-Saxon' has become a (much abused and factually incorrect) byword for 'purely English'.

On the religious front, the Anglo-Saxons were pagans, and their invasion forced Celtic culture and the Christian religion to the edges of the British Isles – to Wales, Scotland and Ireland. The pope of the time, Gregory, decided this was a poor show, and in AD 597 sent missionaries to England to revive interest in Christianity. One holy pioneer was St Augustine, who successfully converted Angles in Kent, and some good-looking specimens were sent to Rome as proof – giving rise to Pope Gregory's famous quip about Angles looking like angels.

Meanwhile in northern England another missionary called St Aidan was even more successful. With faith and fervour, he converted the entire populations of the Anglo-Saxon kingdoms of Mercia and Northumbria, and still had time to establish a monastery at Lindisfarne which can still be seen today (see p724).

DID YOU KNOW?

The Romans were settled in Britain for almost 400 years. That's longer than European settlement in Australia or North America in our own era.

Missionary St Augustine revives interest in Christianity among the Anglo-Saxons

Vikings conquer and occupy east and northeast England, making Yorvik (today's York) their capital

THE VIKING ERA

Just as Christianity was getting a grip, England was once again invaded from the European mainland. This time, Vikings appeared on the scene.

It's another classic historical image: blonde Scandinavians, horned helmets, big swords, square-sailed longboats, raping and pillaging. School history books give the impression that Vikings turned up, killed everyone, took everything, and left. There's *some* truth in that, but in reality many Vikings settled for good, and their legacy is still evident in parts of northern England – in the form of place names, local dialect and even the traces of Nordic DNA in some of today's inhabitants.

The main wave of Vikings from Denmark conquered east and northeast England in AD 850, making Yorvik (today's York) their capital, then spread across central England until they were confronted by the Anglo-Saxon armies of Alfred the Great – the king of Wessex, and one of English history's best-known characters.

The battles which followed were seminal to the foundation of the nation-state of England, but they didn't all go Alfred's way. For a few months he was on the run, wading through swamps, hiding in peasant hovels, and famously burning cakes. It was the stuff of legend, which is just what you need when the chips are down. By 886, Alfred had garnered his forces and pushed the Vikings back to the north.

Thus England was divided in two: north and east was Viking 'Danelaw', while south and west was Anglo-Saxon territory. Alfred was hailed as king of the English – the first time the Anglo-Saxons truly regarded themselves as a united people.

Alfred's son and successor was Edward the Elder. After more battles, he gained control of the Danelaw, and thus the whole of England. His son, Athelstan, took the process a stage further and was specifically crowned King of England in 927. But it was hardly cause for celebration: the Vikings were still around, and later in the 10th century more raids from Scandinavia threatened the fledgling English unity. Over the following decades, control swung from Saxon (King Edgar), to Dane (King Knut), and back to Saxon again (King Edward the Confessor). As England came to the end of the first millennium AD, the future was anything but certain.

1066 & ALL THAT

When King Edward the Confessor died, the crown passed to Harold, his brother-in-law. That should've settled things, but Edward had a cousin in Normandy called William, who thought *he* should have succeeded to the throne of England.

The end result was the Battle of Hastings in 1066 – the most memorable of dates for anyone who's studied English history – or for anyone who hasn't. William sailed from France with an army of Norman soldiers, the Saxons were defeated, and Harold was killed – according to tradition by an arrow in the eye (see the boxed text p191).

William became king of England, earning himself the prestigious title William the Conqueror. It was no idle nickname. To control the Anglo-Saxons, the Norman invaders built numerous castles, and by 1085–86 the Domesday Book provided a census of the country's current stock and future potential.

927	1066
Athelstan, grandson of King Alfred the Great, crowned first King of England	Battle of Hastings – one in the eye for King Harold

William the Conqueror was followed by William II, but he was mysteriously assassinated during a hunting trip and succeeded by Henry I, another Norman ruler, and the first of a long line of kings called Henry.

In the years after the invasion, the French-speaking Normans and the English-speaking Saxon inhabitants kept pretty much to themselves. A strict hierarchy of class developed, known as the feudal system. At the top was the monarch, below that the nobles (barons, bishops, dukes and earls), then knights and lords, and at the bottom were peasants or 'serfs', effectively slaves.

The feudal system may have established the basis of a class system which still exists in England to a certain extent, but intermarriage was not completely unknown. Henry himself married a Saxon princess. Nonetheless, such unifying moves stood for nothing after Henry's death: a bitter struggle for succession followed, finally won by Henry II who took the throne as the first king of the House – or dynasty – of Plantagenet.

ROYAL & HOLY SQUABBLING

The fight to follow Henry I continued the enduring English habit of competition for the throne, and introduced an equally enduring tendency of bickering between royalty and the church. Things came to a head when Henry II had 'turbulent priest' Thomas Becket murdered in Canterbury Cathedral in 1170 (see the boxed text p171).

Perhaps the next king, Richard I, wanted to make amends for his forebears' unholy sentiments by fighting against Muslim 'infidels' in today's Middle East – then called the Holy Land. Unfortunately, he was too busy crusading to bother about governing England (although his bravery earned him the Richard the Lionheart sobriquet), and after his brother John became king things got even worse. According to legend, it was during this time that a nobleman called Robert of Loxley, better known as Robin Hood, took to hiding in forests, and energetically engaged in a spot of wealth redistribution. For more on this story see the boxed text p468.

PLANTAGENETS PLOUGH ON

In 1215 the barons found King John's erratic rule increasingly hard to swallow, and forced him to sign a document called Magna Carta, limiting the monarch's power for the first time in English history. Although originally intended as a set of handy ground rules, Magna Carta was a fledgling bill of human rights which eventually led to the creation of Parliament – a body to rule the country, independent of the throne. The signing took place at Runnymede, near Windsor and you can still visit the site today (see p157).

The next king was Henry III, followed in 1272 by Edward I – a skilled ruler and ambitious general. During a 56-year reign, he expounded English nationalism and was unashamedly expansionist in his outlook, leading campaigns into Wales and Scotland, where his ruthless activities earned him the title 'hammer of the Scots'.

Edward I was succeeded by Edward II, but the new model lacked the military success of his forebear, and his favouring of personal friends over barons didn't help. Edward failed in the marriage department too,

Medieval Women by Henrietta Leyser looks through a female lens at the period from AD 500 to 1500: a life of work, marriage, sex and children – not necessarily in that order.

A Brief History of British Kings & Queens by Mike Ashley is perfect for an overview: a concise and comprehensive rundown, with time-lines, lists, biographies and family trees. Good for pub-quiz training too.

1337	1348
Start of the Hundred Years' War with France	Arrival of the Black Death – killing more than a third of the country's population

and his rule came to a grisly end when his wife, Isabella, and her lover, Roger Mortimer, had him murdered in Berkeley Castle. (For more gruesome details see p409.)

Next in line was Edward III. Notable events during his reign included the start of the Hundred Years' War with France in 1337 and the arrival of a plague called the Black Death about a decade later, which eventually carried off 1.5 million people – more than a third of the country's population. Another change of king didn't improve things either. Richard II had barely taken the throne when the Peasants' Revolt erupted in 1381. This attempt by commoners to overthrow the feudal system was brutally suppressed, further injuring an already deeply divided country.

HOUSES OF YORK & LANCASTER

Shakespeare's *Henry V* was filmed most recently in 1989 – a superb modern epic, staring English cinema darling Kenneth Branagh as the eponymous king. An earlier film of the same name, staring Laurence Olivier and filmed in 1944 as a patriotic rallying cry during the dark days of WWII, is also worth catching.

The ineffectual Richard II was ousted in 1399 by a powerful baron called Henry Bolingbroke, who became Henry IV – the first monarch of the House of Lancaster.

Henry IV was followed, neatly, by Henry V, who decided it was time to stir up the dormant Hundred Years' War. He defeated France at the Battle of Agincourt and the patriotic tear-jerker speech he was given by Shakespeare ('cry God for Harry, England and St George') has ensured his pole position among the most famous English kings of all time.

Still keeping things neat, Henry V was followed by Henry VI. His main claim to fame was overseeing the building of great places of worship (King's College Chapel in Cambridge, Eton Chapel near Windsor), interspersed with great bouts of insanity.

When the Hundred Years' War finally ground to a halt in 1453, you'd have thought things would be calm for a while. But no. The English forces returning from France threw their energies into another battle – a civil conflict dubbed the War of the Roses.

Briefly it went like this: Henry VI of the House of Lancaster (whose emblem was a red rose) was challenged by Richard, Duke of York (proud holder of a white-rose flag). Henry was weak and it was almost a walkover for Richard, but Henry's wife, Margaret of Anjou, was made of sterner mettle and her forces defeated the challenger. But it didn't rest there. Richard's son Edward entered with an army, turned the tables, drove out Henry, and became King Edward IV – the first monarch of the House of York.

DARK DEEDS IN THE TOWER

Life was never easy for the guy at the top. Edward IV hardly had time to catch his breath before facing a challenger to his own throne. Enter scheming Richard Neville, Earl of Warwick, who liked to be billed as 'the kingmaker'. In 1470 he teamed up with the energetic Margaret of Anjou to shuttle Edward into exile and bring Henry VI back to the throne. But a year later Edward IV came bouncing back himself – to kill Warwick, capture Margaret, and have Henry snuffed out in the Tower of London. Result.

Although Edward IV's position seemed secure, he ruled for only a decade before being succeeded by his 12-year-old son, now Edward V. But the boy-king's rule was even shorter than his dad's. In 1483 he was mysteriously murdered, along with his brother, and once again the Tower of London was the scene of the crime.

1381	1459–71
Richard II confronted by the Peasants' Revolt	War of the Roses

With the 'little princes' dispatched, this left the throne open for their dear old uncle Richard. Whether he was the princes' killer is still the subject of debate, but his rule as Richard III was short-lived. Despite another famous Shakespearean soundbite ('A horse, a horse, my kingdom for a horse'), few tears were shed when he was tumbled from rule in 1485 by Henry Tudor.

MOVES TOWARDS UNITY

There hadn't been a Henry on the throne for a while, and this new incumbent, Henry VII, harked back to the days of his namesakes with a skilful reign. After the York-vs-Lancaster War of the Roses, his Tudor neutrality was important. He also diligently mended fences with his northern neighbours by marrying off his daughter to James IV of Scotland, thereby linking the Tudor and Stewart lines.

Matrimony may have been more useful than warfare for Henry VII, but the multiple marriages of his successor, Henry VIII, were a very different story. Fathering a male heir was his problem – hence the famous six wives – but the pope's disapproval of divorce and remarriage led to a split with the Roman Catholic Church.

Henry became head of the Protestant Church of England and followed this up by 'dissolving' many monasteries – more a blatant land takeover than a struggle between church and state. Authority was further exerted over Wales, effectively a colony since the days of Edward I, with the Acts of Union (1536–43) formally tying the two countries.

THE ELIZABETHAN AGE

Henry VIII died in 1547, succeeded by his son Edward VI, then by daughter Mary I, but their reigns were short. So, unexpectedly, the third child, Elizabeth, came to the throne.

As Elizabeth I, she inherited a nasty mess of religious strife and divided loyalties, but after an uncertain start she gained confidence and turned the country round. Refusing marriage, she borrowed from biblical imagery and became known as the Virgin Queen – perhaps the first English monarch to create a cult image. It paid off. Her 45-year reign was a period of boundless English optimism characterised by the writings of William Shakespeare and Christopher Marlowe, the defeat of the Spanish Armada, the expansion of trade, and the global explorations of English seafarers Walter Raleigh and Francis Drake.

Meanwhile, Elizabeth's cousin Mary (daughter of Scottish King James V, and a Catholic) had become known as Mary Queen of Scots. She'd spent her childhood in France and had married the French dauphin (crown prince), thereby becoming queen of France as well. Why stop at two? After her husband's death, Mary returned to Scotland, and ambitiously claimed the English throne as well – on the grounds that Elizabeth I was illegitimate. But Mary's plans failed; she was imprisoned and forced to abdicate in favour of her son (a Protestant, who became James VI of Scotland).

Mary escaped to England and appealed to Elizabeth for help. Bad move. It could have been a rookie error; she might have been advised by courtiers with their own agenda. Either way, Mary was not surprisingly seen as a security risk and imprisoned once again. In an uncharacteristic display of indecision, before finally ordering her execution, Elizabeth

The 1955 film version of Shakespeare's *Richard III*, staring Laurance Olivier and John Gielgud, is now available on DVD; a great choice for the award-winning drama of its time, and a view of this turbulent period in history.

Six Wives: the Queens of Henry VIII by David Starkey and based on a popular TV history series, is an accessible modern study of this turbulent period.

This time the Bard gets his own movie. *Shakespeare in Love* is unashamedly romantic, undoubtedly modern and unrepentantly funny: a fabulous romp through backstage Elizabethan London.

1509–47

Rule of Henry VIII; marries six times and dissolves monasteries

1558

Elizabeth I comes to throne: enter stage right playwright William Shakespeare and exit due west Walter Raleigh and Francis Drake

RULING THE ROOST

A glance at England's tempestuous history clearly shows that life was never dull for the folk at the top. Despite immense power and privilege, the position of monarch (or, perhaps worse, *potential* monarch) probably ranks as one of history's least safe occupations. English kings have died in battle (eg an arrow through the eye for Harold), been beheaded (Charles I), been murdered by a wicked uncle (Edward V) or been knocked off by their queen and her lover (Edward II). Below is a brief overview of the past 1200 years. As you visit the castles and battlefields of England, having this basic grasp of who ruled when should make your visit much more rewarding.

Saxons & Danes
Alfred the Great 871–99
Edward the Elder 899–924
Athelstan 924–39
Edmund I 939–946
Eadred 946–955
Eadwig 955–959
Edgar 959–975
Edward the Martyr 975–79
Ethelred II (the Unready) 979–1016
Knut 1016–35
Harold I 1035-1040
Harthacanute 1035–1042
Edward the Confessor 1042–66
Harold II 1066

Normans
William I (the Conqueror) 1066–87
William II 1087–1100
Henry I 1100–35
Stephen 1135–54

House of Plantagenet
Henry II 1154–89
Richard I (the Lionheart) 1189–99
John 1199–1216
Henry III 1216–72
Edward I 1272–1307
Edward II 1307–27
Edward III 1327–77
Richard II 1377–99

House of Lancaster
Henry IV (Bolingbroke) 1399–1413
Henry V 1413–22
Henry VI 1422–61 & 1470–71

House of York
Edward IV 1461–70 & 1471–83

Edward V 1483
Richard III 1483–85

House of Tudor
Henry VII 1485–1509
Henry VIII 1509–47
Edward VI 1547–53
Mary I 1553–58
Elizabeth I 1558–1603

House of Stuart
James I 1603–25
Charles I 1625–49

Protectorate (Republic)
Oliver Cromwell 1649–58
Richard Cromwell 1658–59

Restoration
Charles II 1660–85
James II 1685–88
Mary II 1688–94
William III (of Orange) 1688–1702
Anne 1702–14

House of Hanover
George I 1714–27
George II 1727–60
George III 1760–1820
George IV 1820–30
William IV 1830–37
Victoria 1837–1901

Houses of Saxe-Coburg & Windsor
Edward VII 1901–10
George V 1910–36
Edward VIII 1936
George VI 1936–52
Elizabeth II 1952–

1644–49	1721–42
English Civil War between king's royalists forces (Cavaliers) and Oliver Cromwell's parliamentarians (Roundheads)	Robert Walpole is Britain's first prime minister

held Mary under arrest for 19 years, moving her frequently from house to house, so that today England has many stately homes (and even a few pubs) claiming 'Mary Queen of Scots slept here'.

UNITED & DISUNITED BRITAIN

When Elizabeth died in 1603, despite a bountiful reign, one thing the Virgin Queen failed to provide was an heir. She was succeeded by her closest relative, James, the safely Protestant son of the murdered Mary. He became James I of England and VI of Scotland, the first English monarch of the House of Stuart (Mary's time in France had Gallicised the Stewart name). Most importantly, James united England, Wales and Scotland into one kingdom for the first time in history – another step towards British unity, at least on paper.

But James' attempts to smooth religious relations were set back by the anti-Catholic outcry that followed the infamous Guy Fawkes Gunpowder Plot, a terrorist attempt to blow up Parliament in 1605. The event is still celebrated every 5 November, with fireworks, bonfires and burning effigies of Guy himself.

Alongside the Catholic–Protestant rift, the divide between king and Parliament continued to smoulder. The power struggle worsened during the reign of the next king, Charles I, and eventually degenerated into the Civil War of 1644–49. The antiroyalist forces were led by Oliver Cromwell, a Puritan who preached against the excesses of the monarch and established church, and his army of parliamentarians (or Roundheads) was pitched against the king's forces (the Cavaliers) in a war that tore England apart – although fortunately for the last time in history. The war ended with victory for the Roundheads, the king executed, and England declared a republic – with Cromwell hailed as 'Protector'.

THE RETURN OF THE KING

By 1653 Cromwell was finding parliament too restricting and he assumed dictatorial powers, much to his supporters' dismay. On his death in 1658, he was followed half-heartedly by his son, but in 1660 parliament decided to re-establish the monarchy – as republican alternatives were proving far worse.

Charles II (the exiled son of Charles I) came to the throne, and his rule, 'the Restoration', saw scientific and cultural activity bursting forth after the straitlaced ethics of Cromwell's time. Exploration and expansion was also on the agenda. Backed by the army and navy (modernised, ironically, by Cromwell), colonies stretched down the American coast, while the East India Company set up headquarters in Bombay, laying foundations for what was to become the British Empire.

The next king, James II, had a harder time. Attempts to ease restrictive laws on Catholics ended with his defeat at the Battle of the Boyne by William III, the Protestant king of Holland, better known as William of Orange. Ironically, William was married to James' own daughter Mary, but it didn't stop him doing the dirty on his father-in-law.

William and Mary both had equal rights to the throne and their joint accession in 1688 was known as the Glorious Revolution. Lucky they were married or there might have been another civil war.

Elizabeth, directed by Shekhar Kapur (1998) and staring Cate Blanchett, covers the early years of the Virgin Queen's rule – as she moves from novice princess to commanding monarch – a time of forbidden love, unwanted suitors, assassination attempts, intrigue and death.

DID YOU KNOW?

Charles I wore two shirts on the day of his execution, to avoid shivering and being thought cowardly.

What the Tudors & Stuarts Did for Us by popular TV presenter and historian Adam Hart-Davis covers great achievements and innovations in this key period of English history.

1799–1815	1837
Napoleonic Wars – key battles: Trafalgar (1805) and Waterloo (1815)	Queen Victoria comes to the throne; rest of the 19th century seen as Britain's 'Golden Age'

UNITED COUNTRY, EXPANDING EMPIRE

In 1694 Mary died, leaving William as sole monarch. He died a few years later and was followed by his sister-in-law Anne. During her reign, in 1707, the Act of Union was passed, finally linking the countries of England, Wales and Scotland under one parliament – based in London – for the first time in history.

Anne died without an heir in 1714, marking the end of the Stuart line. The throne passed to distant (but still safely Protestant) German relatives – the House of Hanover – but by this time, struggles for the throne seemed a thing of the past; Hanoverian kings increasingly relied on parliament to govern. As part of the process, from 1721 to 1742 a senior parliamentarian called Robert Walpole effectively became Britain's first prime minister.

Meanwhile, the British Empire – which, despite its title, was predominantly an *English* entity – continued to grow in Asia and the Americas, while claims were made to Australia after James Cook's epic voyage in 1768. The Empire's first major reverse was the American War of Independence (1776–83), forcing England to withdraw from the world stage for a while.

This gap was not missed by French ruler Napoleon; he threatened to invade England and hinder British power overseas, before his ambitions were curtailed by navy hero Nelson and military hero Wellington at the famous battles of Trafalgar (1805) and Waterloo (1815).

THE INDUSTRIAL AGE

While the Empire expanded abroad, at home Britain had become the crucible of the Industrial Revolution. Steam power (patented by James Watt in 1781) and steam trains (launched by George Stephenson in 1830) transformed methods of production and transport, and the towns of the English Midlands became the first industrial cities.

At the same time, medical advances allowed a sharp population increase, but the rapid change from rural to urban society caused great dislocation. For many, poverty and deprivation were the adverse side-effects of Britain's economic blossoming.

Nevertheless, by the time Queen Victoria took the throne in 1837, Britain's fleets dominated the seas, and Britain's factories dominated world trade. The rest of the 19th century was seen as Britain's Golden Age (for some people, it still is) – a period of confidence not seen since the days of the last great queen, Elizabeth I.

Victoria ruled a proud nation at home, and great swathes of territories abroad, from Canada through much of Africa and India to Australia and New Zealand – trumpeted as 'the Empire on which the sun never sets'. In a final move of PR genius, the queen's chief spin doctor and most effective prime minister, Benjamin Disraeli, had Victoria crowned Empress of India. She'd never even been there, but the British simply loved the idea.

The times were optimistic, but it wasn't all tub-thumping jingoism. Disraeli and his successor William Gladstone also introduced social reforms to address the worst excesses of the Industrial Revolution. Education became universal, trade unions were legalised and the right to vote was extended to commoners. Well, to male commoners. Women didn't get the vote for another few decades. Disraeli and Gladstone may have been enlightened gentlemen, but there *were* limits.

1914–18	1926
WWI; Britain at war with Germany	General Strike

DRINKING IN HISTORY

As you travel around England, you can't fail to notice the splendid selection of pub names, often illustrated with attractive signboards. In days gone by, these signs were vital because most of the ale-swilling populace couldn't read. In our more literate times, pub signs are still a feature of the landscape, and remain as much a part of English history as medieval churches or stately homes.

Many pub names have connections to royalty. The most popular is the Red Lion, with over 500 pubs in England bearing this title. It dates from the early 17th century, when King James VI of Scotland became King James I of England. Lest the populace forget his origin, he ordered that the lion, his heraldic symbol, be displayed in public places.

The second-most popular pub name is The Crown, which has more obvious royal connections, while the third-most popular, the Royal Oak, recalls the days of the Civil War when King Charles escaped Cromwell's army by hiding in a tree. (Look hard at most Royal Oak pub signs and you'll see his face peeping out from between the leaves.)

The King's Arms is another popular pub name with clear royal connections, as is the Queen's Head, the Prince of Wales and so on. Less obvious is the White Hart – the heraldic symbol of Richard II, who in 1393 decreed that every pub should display a sign to distinguish it from other buildings. The decree rounded off by saying anyone failing in this duty 'shall forfeit his ale', so many landlords chose the White Hart as a sign of allegiance, and an insurance against stock loss.

Another common pub name is the Rose and Crown. Again, the regal links are obvious, but look carefully at the colour of the rose painted on those signs, especially if you're in the north of England. West of the Pennine Hills it should be the red rose of the House of Lancaster; east of the Pennines it's the white rose depicting the House of York. Woe betide any pub sign that is sporting the wrong colour!

While some pub names crop up in their hundreds, others are far from common, although many still have links to history. Nottingham's most famous pub, Ye Olde Trip to Jerusalem (p469), commemorates knights and soldiers departing for crusades in the Holy Land in the 12th century. Pub names such as the George and Dragon may date from the same era – as a story brought back from the east by returning crusaders. Move on several centuries and pub names such as the Spitfire, the Lancaster or the Churchill recall the days of WWII.

For a more local perspective, the Nobody Inn near Exeter in Devon is said to recall a mix-up over a coffin, the Hit or Miss near Chippenham in Wiltshire recalls a close-run game of village cricket, while the Quiet Woman near Buxton in Derbyshire, with a sign of a headless female, is a reminder of more chauvinistic times.

WORLD WAR I

Queen Victoria died in 1901 and ever-expanding Britain died with her. But at the dawn of the 20th century, when Edward VII ushered in the relaxed new Edwardian era, it wasn't evident that a long period of decline was about to set in.

In continental Europe, things were far from calm. Four restless military powers (Russia, Austro-Hungary, Turkey and Germany) focussed their sabre-rattling on the Balkan states, and the assassination of Archduke Ferdinand at Sarajevo in 1914 finally sparked a clash which became the Great War we now call WWI. When German forces entered Belgium, on their way to invade France, soldiers from Britain and Allied countries were drawn into a vicious conflict of stalemate and horrendous slaughter – most infamously on the killing fields of Flanders and the beaches of Gallipoli.

1939–45	1948
WWII; Britain at war with Germany. Again.	National Health Service founded

By the war's weary end in 1918 over a million Britons had died (not to mention millions more from many other countries) and there was hardly a street or village untouched by death, as the sobering lists of names on war memorials all over England still show. The conflict added 'trench warfare' to the dictionary, and further deepened the huge gulf that had existed between ruling and working classes since the days of the Norman feudal system.

For the soldiers who did return from WWI, disillusion led to questioning of the social order. A new political force – the Labour Party, to represent the working class – upset the balance long enjoyed by the Liberal and Conservative parties, as the right to vote was extended to all men aged over 21 and women over 30.

The Labour Party were elected for the first time in 1923, in coalition with the Liberals, with James Ramsay MacDonald as prime minister. A year later the Conservatives were back in power, but the rankling 'them-and-us' mistrust, fuelled by soaring unemployment, led to the 1926 general strike. When 500,000 workers marched through the streets, the government's heavy-handed response included sending in the army – setting the stage for industrial unrest that was to plague Britain for the next 50 years.

The unrest of the 1920s worsened in the '30s as the world economy slumped and the Great Depression took hold – a decade of misery and political upheaval. Even the royal family took a knock when Edward VIII abdicated in 1936 so he could marry a woman who was twice divorced and, horror of horrors, American. The ensuing scandal was good for newspaper sales and hinted at the prolonged 'trial by media' suffered by royals in more recent times.

The throne was taken by Edward's less-than-charismatic brother George VI and Britain dithered through the rest of the decade, with mediocre and visionless government failing to confront the country's problems.

WORLD WAR II

Meanwhile on mainland Europe, Germany saw the rise of Adolf Hitler, leader of the Nazi party. Many feared another Great War, but Prime Minister Neville Chamberlain met Hitler in 1938 and promised Britain 'peace in our time'. He was wrong. The following year Hitler invaded Poland. Two days later Britain was once again at war with Germany.

The German army moved with astonishing speed, swept west through France, and pushed back British forces to the beaches of Dunkirk in northern France in June 1940. An extraordinary flotilla of rescue vessels turned total disaster into a brave defeat – and Dunkirk Day is still remembered with pride and sadness in Britain every year.

By mid-1940, most of Europe was controlled by Germany. In Russia, Stalin had negotiated a peace agreement. The USA was neutral, leaving Britain virtually isolated. Neville Chamberlain, reviled for his earlier 'appeasement', stood aside to let Winston Churchill lead a coalition government.

Hitler had expected an easy victory, but Churchill's extraordinary dedication (not to mention his radio speeches) inspired the country to resist, and between July and October 1940 Britain's Royal Air Force withstood Germany's aerial raids to win what became known as the Battle of Britain – a major turning point in the war, and a chance for land forces to rebuild their strength. The pendulum swung further as the USA entered the

Birdsong by Sebastian Faulks is partly set in the trenches of WWI. Understated, perfectly paced and severely moving, it tells of love, passion, fear, waste and death, as well as incompetent generals and the poor bloody infantry.

DID YOU KNOW?
Men over 21 and women over 30 voted after WWI, but it wasn't until 1928 that women were granted the same rights as men – despite the opposition of an up-and-coming politician named Winston Churchill.

DID YOU KNOW?
The Normandy landings was the largest military armada in history; over 5000 ships were involved, with hundreds of thousands of troops landed in the space of about four days.

1952	1963
Queen Elizabeth II comes to the throne	The Beatles become household names. Outbreak of incurable Beatlemania.

war to support Britain, while Japan mobilised behind Germany, and by late 1941 Germany was bogged down on the 'eastern front' fighting Russia.

In 1942 German forces were defeated in North Africa, and by 1944 Germany was in retreat. Britain and the USA controlled the skies, Russia's Red Army pushed back from the east, and the Allies were again on the beaches of France as the Normandy landings (D-Day, as it's better remembered) marked the start of the liberation of Europe from the west, and in Churchill's words, 'the beginning of the end of the war'. By 1945 Hitler was dead, and Germany was a smoking ruin. Two atomic bombs forced the surrender of Japan and brought WWII to a dramatic and terrible close.

SWINGING & SLIDING

In Britain, despite the victory, there was an unexpected swing on the political front. An electorate tired of war and hungry for change tumbled Churchill's Conservatives, and voted in the Labour Party, led by Clement Attlee. This was the dawn of the 'welfare state'; key industries (such as steel, coal and railways) were nationalised, and the National Health Service was founded. But rebuilding Britain was a slow process, and the postwar 'baby boomers' experienced food rationing well into the 1950s.

The effects of depleted reserves were felt overseas too, as one by one the colonies became independent, including India and Pakistan in 1947, Malaya in 1957 and Kenya in 1963. People from these ex-colonies – and especially from the Caribbean – were drawn to the mother country through the 1960s. In many cases they were specifically invited, as additional labour was needed to help rebuild post-war Britain. In the 1970s many immigrants of Asian origin arrived, after being forced out of Uganda by dictator Idi Amin.

In the Empire the sun was setting, but Britain's royal family was still going strong. In 1952 George VI was succeeded by his daughter Elizabeth II, and following the trend set by earlier queens Elizabeth I and Victoria, she has remained on the throne for more than 50 years (2002 was her Golden Jubilee), overseeing a period of massive social and economic change.

By the late 1950s, recovery was strong enough for Prime Minister Harold Macmillan to famously remind the British people that they'd 'never had it so good'. Some saw this as a boast for a confident future, others as a warning about difficult times ahead, but most probably forgot all about it because by this time the 1960s had started and grey old England was suddenly more fun and lively than it had been for generations – especially if you were over 10 and under 30. There was the music of the Beatles, the Rolling Stones, Cliff Richard and the Shadows, while cinema audiences flocked to see Michael Caine, Peter Sellers and Glenda Jackson.

Alongside the glamour, business seemed swinging too, but the 1970s brought inflation, the oil crisis and international competition – a deadly combination quickly revealing everything that was weak about Britain's economy, and a lot that was rotten in British society too. The struggle between disgruntled working classes and inept ruling classes was brought to the boil once again; the rest of the decade was marked by industrial disputes, three-day weeks and general all-round gloom – especially when the electricity was cut, as power stations went short of fuel or labour.

Neither the Conservatives under Edward Heath, nor Labour under Harold Wilson and Jim Callaghan, proved capable of controlling the strife.

Windrush – The Irresistible Rise of Multi-Racial Britain by Mike and Trevor Phillips traces the history of Britain's West Indian immigrants – from the first arrivals in 1949 (on the merchant ship *Empire Windrush*) to their descendants living in our own time.

Small Island by Andrea Levy is a novel (and 2004 Orange Prize winner) about a Jamaican couple who settle in 1950s London. The author is of Jamaican origin, and draws on rich family memories of the time.

The Queen's Story by Marcus Kiggell is a royal biography far more studied and serious, and far less gushing, than many similar titles that cover the current monarch's happy and glorious rule.

1979	1982
Mrs Thatcher elected	Britain at war with Argentina over the Falkland Islands

The British public had had enough, and the elections of 1979 returned the Conservatives led by a little-known politician named Margaret Thatcher.

THE THATCHER YEARS

Soon everyone had heard of Mrs Thatcher. Love her or hate her, no-one could argue that her methods weren't dramatic. British workers were Luddites? She fired them. Trade unions archaic? She smashed them. British industry inefficient? She shut it down. Nationalised companies a mistake? She sold them off – with a sense of purpose that made Henry VIII's dissolution of the monasteries seem like a Sunday-school picnic.

And just in case there was any doubt about Mrs Thatcher's patriotism, in 1982 she led Britain into war against Argentina in a dispute over the Falkland Islands, leading to a bout of public flag-waving which hadn't been seen since WWII, or probably since Agincourt.

By economic measures, Mrs Thatcher's policies were mostly successful, but by social measures they were a failure. The new, competitive Britain was also a greatly polarised Britain. Once again a trench formed, but not between the classes; this time it was between the people who gained from the prosperous wave of Thatcherism and those left drowning in its wake – not only jobless, but jobless in a harsh environment. Even Thatcher fans were unhappy about the brutal and uncompromising methods favoured by the 'iron lady', but by 1988 she was the longest-serving British prime minister of the 20th century, although her repeated electoral victories were helped by the Labour Party's total incompetence and destructive internal struggles.

STAND DOWN MARGARET, HELLO TONY

When any leader believes they're invincible, it's time to go. In 1990 Mrs Thatcher was finally dumped when her introduction of the hugely un-popular 'poll tax' breached even the Conservatives' limits of tolerance. The voters regarded Labour with even more suspicion, however, allowing new Conservative leader John Major to unexpectedly win the 1992 election.

Another half-decade of political stalemate followed, as the Conservatives imploded and Labour was rebuilt on the sidelines. It all came to a head in 1997 when 'New' Labour swept to power with a record parliamentary majority. After nearly 18 years of Conservative rule, it really seemed that Labour's victory call ('things can only get better') was true – and some people literally danced in the street when the results were announced.

In turn, this sometimes blurred the distinction between Labour and the Liberal-Democrats, and forced the Conservatives to take a sizable jump to the right.

NEW LABOUR, NEW MILLENNIUM

The election in 2001 was another walkover for Tony Blair and the Labour party, while on the opposition benches the Conservatives replaced John Major with William Hague, a little-loved leader who tried to soften his staid image by wearing a baseball cap. It didn't work and he was soon followed by Ian Duncan-Smith, a more serious contender from the 'Euro-sceptic' right of the party. His rule was shortlived too, and in 2004 the experienced hardliner Michael Howard became Conservative leader.

One Can Only Get Better

One of Us: A Biography of Mrs Thatcher by respected journalist and commentator Hugo Young covers the early life of the 'iron lady' and concentrates on her time in power – showing that her grip on events, and on her own party, wasn't quite as steely as it seemed.

Things Can Only Get Better by John O'Farrell is a witty, self-deprecating story of politics in the 1980s and early '90s – the era of Thatcher and Conservative domination – from a struggling Labour viewpoint. As well as comedy, the author also wrote speeches for Chancellor Gordon Brown.

1990	1997
Mrs Thatcher ousted from her position as leader of the Conservative party	'New' Labour under Tony Blair wins general election, ending 18 years of conservative rule

Meanwhile, Tony Blair remained at the helm of government (2004 was his tenth year as party leader, and seventh as prime minister), if not always in total control, as Labour's rule since the turn of the millennium proved remarkably eventful and frequently doused in controversy. Hot topics included House of Lords reform, where the government's apparent favouritism in the appointment of members led to cries of 'Tony's cronies', and the issues of economic migrants and asylum seekers – the latter addressed by a raft of new rules from the increasingly tough (some would say rough) home secretary David Blunkett.

Of even greater significance was Britain's role in Iraq. Initially, notwithstanding a massive anti-war campaign, there was considerable – if grudging – support from the opposition Conservatives in Parliament and a significant proportion of the public for Tony Blair's decision to back the American invasion. But when weapons of mass destruction (the central premise for the war) were not discovered, and when it became apparent that secret reports indicating this nonexistence were ignored by the government (or not passed to those responsible), then the positions of ministers and the prime minister himself were seriously called into question.

As the Iraq war continued to backfire, newspapers carried reports that Tony Blair had considered resignation (leaving the door open for Chancellor of the Exchequer Gordon Brown – so long the PM-in-waiting – to finally go for the top job) but was persuaded to stay on by loyal ministers. This led to a newfound resolve which translated into mixed success in the local council and European Parliament elections of June 2004: Labour lost some seats, as the public used its vote to register its unhappiness, and the Conservatives and Liberals made gains – the latter party benefiting in no small way from its anti-war stance. But this election also saw the rise of a new force: the United Kingdom Independence Party (UKIP), whose primary aim is to withdraw the country from the European Union, just as a European constitution is launched and a referendum in Britain to accept it (or not) becomes a reality.

Despite the gloom and numerous controversies, opinion polls in mid-2004 showed that Labour was still the most popular party in Britain, and the party most people trusted (or, at least, the one they distrusted least). But more than this, polls also revealed that the people of Britain were unanimous in their desire for major improvements in the social sectors of health and education. In response, in July 2004 chancellor Gordon Brown rolled out a major 'spending review', pledging a massive increase in funds for schools and hospitals, and for other areas such as transport and housing. How would this increase be paid for? Partly by cutting over 100,000 jobs in the civil service, said Mr Brown, and rechannelling a saving of over £20 billion. The Conservatives counterclaimed they would spend even more than Labour on public services, without diminishing the civil service and without increasing tax.

With these promises in mind, during the third quarter of 2004, as the final parts of this book were being written, the eyes and minds of politicians, newspaper editors and the British public (well, probably about half of them) were focused on the next general election, tipped to happen in 2005. It remains to be seen if the voters thought Labour's improvements were sufficient, or simply too little too late.

'Despite the gloom and numerous controversies, opinion polls in mid-2004 showed that Labour was still the most popular party in Britain'

2001	2003
Tony Blair re-elected	Britain joins the US-led invasion of Iraq

The Culture

THE NATIONAL PSYCHE

The English by Jeremy Paxman is an incisive exploration of the English psyche, as befits one of the toughest interviewers on the airwaves.

It's difficult to generalise about an English national psyche or homogenous trait – mainly because there isn't one! Not surprisingly, 'Englishness' has developed through centuries of cultural cherry-picking from history's numerous invaders, and from neighbours in Wales, Scotland and Ireland, as well as from numerous peoples – Russians, West Indians, Somalis, whoever – who have arrived in more recent times. Add the influence of other nations through the global speakeasy of TV and cinema, and you've got a real mixed bag. The English proudly honour traditions introduced by Celtic forbears (maypoles) or German monarchs (Christmas trees), while kids mix their own regional accents with intonations apparently perfected in California or Queensland. Despite the claims of racial supremacists and excitable newspapers, the English are a mongrel race – and many are happy to revel in this diversity.

Nonetheless there's a preconception that the English are reserved, inhibited and stiflingly polite. While this may indeed apply in some parts of England, in general it simply doesn't. Anywhere in the country, if you visit a pub, a nightclub, a football match, a seaside resort, or simply go walking in city parks or on wild open hills, you'll soon come across other English characteristics – uninhibited, tolerant, exhibitionist, passionate, aggressive, sentimental, hospitable and friendly. It hits you like a breath of fresh air.

Having said all that, a major factor still running through English society, even in these egalitarian days, is class. Although the days of peasants doffing their caps to the lord of the manor may be gone, some English people still judge others by their school, accent or family wealth (and how long they've had it), rather than by their skills, intelligence and personality.

On a more positive note, the English have an obsession with hobbies and pastimes. We're not talking about obvious things like football and cricket (although fanatical supporters number in their millions), but about steam fanatics, bird-watchers, train-spotters, model-makers, home improvers, antique hoarders, pigeon fanciers, royal watchers, teapot collectors, ramblers, anglers, gardeners, caravanners and crossword fans. The list goes on, with many participants verging on the edge of complete madness. But it's all great, and England just wouldn't be the same without them.

LIFESTYLE

When it comes to family life, many English people regard the 'Victorian values' of the late 19th century as an idyllic benchmark – a time of perfect morals and harmonious nuclear families, a highpoint from which the country has been sliding ever since. As recently as the 1960s, only 2%

QUEUING FOR ENGLAND

The English are notoriously addicted to queues – for buses, train tickets, or to pay at the supermarket. The order is sacrosanct and woe betide any foreigner who gets this wrong! Few things are more calculated to spark an outburst of tutting – about as publicly cross as most English get – than 'pushing in' at a queue.

The same applies to escalators. If you want to stand still, keep to the right, so people can pass you on the left. There's a definite convention here and recalcitrants have been hung, drawn and quartered (well, at least provoked more tutting) for blocking the path of folk in a hurry.

WHITHER THE WEATHER?

It was Dr Johnson who noted that 'when two Englishmen meet, their first talk is of the weather'. Two centuries later, little has changed: weather is without doubt a national obsession. According to the Meteorological Office – known fondly as the Met Office – weather reports are the third-most-watched television broadcasts, and when BBC Radio 4 proposed cutting the late-night shipping forecast ('warning of gales in North Atlantic; Viking, Forties, good' etc) there was a huge outcry from listeners – most of whom never went anywhere near the sea.

This fascination with the weather is part of a long tradition, and folklore dating back to the mists of time is rich in ways of second-guessing the moods of the elements. If it snows on St Dorothea's day (6 February), we can expect no heavier snowfall. If it rains on St Swithin's day (15 July), we can expect it to continue for the next 40 days. The slightest tinge of a pink cloud and English folk will chant 'red sky at night, shepherd's delight, red sky at morning, shepherd's warning' like a mantra.

But despite this obsession, the weather still manages to keep the English on their toes. A couple of weeks without rain and garden-hose bans are rushed in. A tad too much rain, and low-lying houses are flooded. One autumn some years ago, stretches of railway had to be closed as falling leaves unexpectedly clogged the points. But the excuse everyone remembers came one winter when the railway authorities blamed delays on the 'wrong kind of snow'.

of couples had 'lived in sin' under the same roof before getting married, whereas by 2004 'cohabiting' (there's still not a proper word for it) was perfectly acceptable in most circles; around 60% of couples who marry are already living together, and at any given time about a third of all couples living together are unmarried.

In line with this, the number of nonmarried couples having children has also increased in the last 40 years; while illegitimate children were comparatively rare and a social stigma in the 1960s, today about 40% of births in the UK are to nonmarried couples. The 'pro-family' lobby argues that married couples provide more stability and a better environment for children. But marriage apparently provides no guarantees: currently about one in three ends in divorce.

All the above is about heterosexual marriages of course – it's still not legal for gay or lesbian couples to get hitched. To be precise, it's not illegal either – it's just that gay weddings aren't recognised. This makes it tricky when dealing with matters like pensions and inheritance – as it does for nonmarried straight couples – although the legal situation will change in 2005 when the Civil Partnership Act comes into force. There's still a way to go before total tolerance and full equality is reached though.

It's a similar situation when it comes to race. In most parts of England general tolerance prevails, with commercial organisations and official bodies such as the police trying hard to stamp out discrimination. But bigotry can still lurk close to the surface: far-right political parties won several seats in the local council elections of 2004, and it's not unusual to hear people openly discuss other races in quite unpleasant terms – in smart country pubs as much as rough city bars. And while it's no longer OK for comedians to tell racist jokes on prime-time TV (as it was until the 1980s), this type of humour still goes down well in some quarters.

Along with race, another major issue in England is health. Obesity – especially in the young – is the hot topic on everyone's lips (in a radio interview in mid-2004 former Conservative minister Norman Tebbit famously managed to link it to homosexuality – or as he put it, 'buggery'), while smoking has moved down to No 2. Although smoking is still a major cause of disease, recent studies showed that about 75% of the population does not smoke – the lowest figures since records began, and

DID YOU KNOW?

Compared to the 1950s, there are now 25% fewer marriages per year, but five times as many divorces. For more fascinating figures see www.2-in-2-1.co .uk/ukstats.

probably since Sir Walter Raleigh discovered the Virginias. (Cue old joke: they were in his pocket all the time.) And another study in mid-2004 showed that about 80% of the population would support a total ban on smoking in public places – including pubs and restaurants, hot on the heels of a similar ban in Ireland. Even more interesting, among smokers the figure was still 60%. These people want to be told they should stop.

White Teeth, the moving and witty best-selling debut novel by Zadie Smith, is on one level a story about families living in North London. On other levels it's about friendship, marriage, race, class, immigration and different generations.

POPULATION

England's population is 51 million (which is around 80% of Britain's total 60 million) and growth has been virtually static in recent years – if you don't count the annual influx of about 26 million tourists.

Within England the population picture is fluid too. The North–South divide has existed for centuries, and recent census returns show it's still a very real feature. For example, along the M4 motorway west of London are towns with hi-tech jobs on the rise and less than 1% unemployment. In sharp contrast, economic depression is a major issue in parts of the Midlands and north of England – an 'archipelago of deprivation' according to one report.

Of course, the North–South split is oversimplified and across the country there are pockets of affluence in 'poor' areas, and zones of poverty only a few blocks away from Millionaires Row. But overall, even though the cost of living in London and the southeast is much higher than elsewhere in England (double the price for a beer, 10 times more for a house), people – and the work opportunities that attract them – still seem inexorably drawn to the capital and its environs.

Billy Elliott is yet another film with England's declining industry as backdrop, but also about people rising above it: particularly the son of a hardened coal-miner who strives to becomes a ballet dancer.

Meanwhile, an even more significant migration is under way. In the last decade, over one million people in England have moved from urban to rural areas. A 2004 report from the Countryside Agency says this is four times more than the number moving from north to south. The new country-dwellers seek a better standard of living, and many can work from home via phone and the Internet, while others set up small businesses – especially valuable in rural areas where traditional jobs such as farming are on the wane. But there are downsides too – most notably the rise in rural house prices, which has pushed property beyond the reach of locals and forced *them* to move to the towns which the incomers have just vacated.

SPORT

To check the dates and details of football, cricket, horseracing and numerous other events in England tomorrow, next week or next month, a great start is the sports pages of www.whatson when.com.

The English invented many of the world's most popular spectator sports – or at least laid down the modern rules – including cricket, tennis, rugby and football. Trouble is, the national teams aren't always so good at playing them (as the newspapers continually like to remind us), although recent years have seen some notable success stories. But a mixed result doesn't dull the enthusiasm of the fans. Every weekend, thousands of people turn out to cheer their favourite team, and sporting highlights such as Wimbledon or the Derby keep the entire nation enthralled.

This section gives a brief overview of sports you might see as part of your trip; the regional chapters have more details. For information on participatory sports, see the Outdoor Activities chapter and p734 of the Directory.

Cricket

The rules and terminology of cricket appear arcane, but for aficionados the game provides 'resolute and graceful confrontations within an intricate and psychologically thrilling framework'. OK, the quote is from a cricket fan. Nonetheless, at least one cricket match should feature in your travels around England.

THE SWEET FA CUP

The Football Association held its first interclub knockout tournament in 1871. Fifteen clubs took part, playing for a nice piece of silverware called the FA Cup – then worth about £20.

Nowadays, around 600 clubs compete for this legendary and priceless trophy. It differs from many other competitions in that every team – from the lowest-ranking part-timers to the stars of the Premier League – is in with a chance. The preliminary rounds begin in August, and the world-famous Cup Final is held in May. It's been staged at Wembley for decades, although the current venue is Cardiff's Millennium Stadium.

Manchester United has won the most FA Cup Finals, with 10 victories. But with the English affection for the underdog, public attention always goes to 'giant-killers' – minor clubs that claw their way up through the rounds, unexpectedly beating higher-ranking competitors. The best-known giant-killing event occurred in 1992, when Wrexham, then ranked 24th in Division 3, famously beat league champions Arsenal.

In recent years, the FA Cup has become one competition among many. The Premier League and Champion's League (against European teams) have a higher profile, bigger kudos, and – simply – more money to play with. Perhaps the FA Cup will one day be consigned to history – but what a sweet and glorious history it's been!

One-day games and five-day test matches are played against sides such as Australia and the West Indies at landmark grounds like Lords in London, Edgbaston in Birmingham and Headingley in Leeds. Test match tickets cost £25 to £100 and tend to sell fast. County championships usually charge £10 to £15 – local games cost even less – and rarely sell out.

Football (Soccer)

The English football league has some of the finest teams and players in the world. They're the richest too, with multimillion-pound sponsorship deals for players regularly clinched by powerful agents. The elite English Premier League is for the country's top 20 clubs – including globally renowned Manchester United, Arsenal and Liverpool – while 72 others play in the Championship, League One and League Two (renamed from Divisions 1, 2 and 3 in 2004 – an attempt, say cynics, to make them seem more exciting).

The football season lasts from August to May, so seeing a match can easily be tied into most visitors' itineraries. But tickets are like gold dust, and cost £20 to £50 even if you're lucky enough to find one. If you can't get in to see the big names, tickets for lower division games are cheaper and more easily available.

The England national side has enjoyed mixed fortunes in the last couple of years, although since the World Cup of 2002 and European Championships of 2004 support has never been so strong – with St George's red cross now a firm fan favourite, happily reclaimed from far-right organisations.

Horse Racing

There's a horse race somewhere in England pretty much every day, but the top event in the calendar is **Royal Ascot** in mid-June, when even the queen turns up to put a fiver each way on Lucky Boy in the 3.15. (Actually, she knows her nags, this lady, with 19 Ascot winners to date from the royal stables.) For details about Royal Ascot, see p157.

Other highlights include the **Grand National** steeplechase at Aintree in early April, and **the Derby**, run at Epsom on the first Saturday in June. The latter is especially popular with the masses so, unlike Ascot, you won't see morning suits and grand hats anywhere.

DID YOU KNOW?

The word 'soccer' (the favoured term in countries where 'football' means another game) is derived from 'Association'. The sport is still officially called Association Football, to distinguish it from Rugby Football.

DID YOU KNOW?

At one time, English football was associated with fan violence, but through the 1990s this problem has been seriously tackled. Most football grounds are now good for a family day out.

Rugby

A wit once said that football was a gentlemen's game played by hooligans, while rugby was the other way around. Whatever, rugby is very popular, especially since England's victory in the 2004 World Cup, and it's worth catching a game for the fun atmosphere on the terraces. Tickets cost around £15 to £40 depending on the club's status and fortunes.

There are two variants – rugby union is played more in southern England, rugby league in the north – but there's a lot of crossover. Leicester, Bath and Gloucester are among the better rugby union clubs, while London has a host of good-quality teams (including Wasps and Saracens). In rugby league, teams to watch include the Wigan Warriors, Bradford Bulls and Leeds Rhinos.

The international rugby union calendar is dominated most years by the annual Six Nations Championship (England, Scotland, Wales, Ireland, France and Italy) between January and April.

Tennis

Tennis is widely played at club and regional level, but the best known tournament is the All England Championships – known to all as Wimbledon – when tennis fever sweeps through England in the last week of June and first week of July (give or take a day or so). There's something quintessentially English about the combination of grass courts, polite applause and umpires in boaters, with strawberries and cream devoured by the ton. (That's 27 tonnes of strawberries and 7000 litres of cream annually, to be precise.) England's top player is Tim Henman, the cause of another disease – Henmania.

Tickets for Wimbledon are sold through a public ballot. Send a stamped addressed envelope (or International Reply Coupon) to: PO Box 98, London SW18 5AE, between August and December. Those in luck are contacted in March. If you want to take your chance on the spot, about 6000 tickets are sold each day (but not the last four days). Queuing from around 7am should get you into the ground, though not a seat on Centre Court.

MEDIA

Breakfast need never be boring in England. For such a small country, there's an amazing range of daily newspapers to read over your cornflakes. (For information on the broadcast media, see p741.)

The bottom end of the market is occupied by easy-to-read tabloids, full of sensational 'exclusives' and simplistic political coverage. The *Sun* is a national institution with mean-spirited content and headlines based on outrageous puns – a good combination apparently, as it's Britain's biggest-selling paper, with a circulation around three million, and a readership three times that. The *Mirror*, once the 'paper of the workers', tried to compete head-on with the *Sun* for a while, then rediscovered its left-of-centre, pro-Labour heritage. The *Sport* takes bad taste to the ultimate, with stories of aliens and celebrities (sometimes in the same report), and pictures of seminaked women of improbable proportions.

The *Daily Mail* and *Daily Express* bill themselves as middle-market, but are little different to the tabloids, both thunderously right-of-centre with a steady stream of crime and scare stories about threatening immigrants and rampant homosexuals. Some may find this diet distasteful, but about eight million readers don't.

At the upper end of the market are the broadsheets: the *Daily Telegraph* is right-of-centre and easily outsells its rivals; the *Times* is conservative, Murdoch-owned, thorough and influential; the *Guardian* is left-of-centre

Leap the net to www .wimbledon.org – for everything you need to know about the grassy drama of the All England Championship.

Want to scan the papers on-line? Find them at:
Daily Express – www.express.co.uk
Daily Telegraph – www.telegraph.co.uk
Guardian – www.guardianunlimited .co.uk
Independent – www.independent.co.uk
Mirror – www.mirror.co.uk
Sun – www.the-sun.co.uk
Times – www.the-times.co.uk

and innovative; and the *Independent* lives up to its title. 'Tabloid' and 'broadsheet' have always referred more to substance than actual dimensions, but the distinction is now totally content-based as several serious papers are also issued in handy-to-carry sizes.

Most dailies have Sunday stablemates (the *Sunday Mirror*, *Sunday Express*, *Sunday Telegraph* and so on) and there's also the long-standing liberal-slanted *Observer*. The broadsheets are filled more with comment and analysis than hot news, and on their day of rest the British settle in armchairs to plough through endless supplements; the *Sunday Times* alone comes in 12 different parts, and must destroy a rainforest every issue.

Private Eye is a weekly no-frills satirical publication, with stories to make you laugh (pompous 'pseuds') and cry (government corruption), well worth reading along with more mainstream publications.

RELIGION

The Church of England (or Anglican Church) became independent of Rome in the 16th century at the behest of Henry VIII, and today remains large, wealthy and influential – even in these increasingly secular times. It's traditionally conservative, and predominantly Conservative (the Church has been called 'the Tory Party at prayer'), and it's only since 1994 that women have been ordained as priests. The debate has now moved on to the rights and wrongs of gay clergy.

Although the vast majority of English people write 'C of E' when filling in forms, only about a million attend Sunday services. About 10% of England's population is Roman Catholic. Other groups include Methodists and Baptists, but attendances are down every year at mainstream churches, with evangelical and charismatic churches the only ones attracting growing congregations.

There are around 1.5 million Muslims in Britain – about 3% of the total population. Other faiths include Sikhs, Hindus and Jews (and those druids at Stonehenge). Numbers may be small, but nowadays more non-Christians regularly visit their places of worship than do all the Anglicans, Catholics, Methodists and Baptists combined.

ARTS
Literature

Modern English literature – poetry and prose – starts around 1387 (yes, that's modern in history-soaked England) with Geoffrey Chaucer's classic *The Canterbury Tales*, a collection of fables, stories and morality tales using travelling pilgrims – the Knight, the Wife of Bath, the Nun's Priest and so on – as a narrative hook. For more background see the boxed text p172.

Two centuries later William Shakespeare entered the scene. Still England's best-known playwright (as under Theatre p57), he was pretty good at poems too. The famous line 'Shall I compare thee to a summer's day?' comes from sonnet No 18. In all he penned more than 150.

If you studied Eng Lit at school you'll remember the metaphysical poets of the early 17th century; their vivid imagery and far-fetched conceits or comparisons daringly pushed the boundaries. In *A Valediction: Forbidding Mourning*, for instance, John Donne compares two lovers with the points of a compass. Racy stuff in its day.

Moving on a little, the stars of the 19th century were the Romantic poets. John Keats, Percy Bysshe Shelley and Lord Byron wrote with emotion, exulting the senses and power of the imagination, and were particularly passionate about nature. The best-known Romantic, William Wordsworth, lived in the Lake District, and his famous lines from *Daffodils*, 'I wandered lonely as a cloud', were inspired by a hike in the hills.

The Romantic movement produced a genre called 'literary Gothic'; exemplified by Mary Shelley's *Frankenstein*, which she originally penned

For a lowdown while you're travelling, the *Oxford Literary Guide to Great Britain and Ireland* gives details of writers who immortalised towns, villages and countryside.

Another well-known (though perhaps little-read) poem of the 17th century is John Milton's epic *Paradise Lost*, on the downfall of Adam and Eve. Can be hard-going for mortals, but worth dipping into for a taste of the rich language.

Jane Austen's favoured subjects were the provincial middle classes. Intrigues and passions boiling under the stilted preserve of social convention are beautifully portrayed in *Emma* and *Pride & Prejudice*.

for a private ghost story competition with her husband Percy. This genre was satirised in *Northanger Abbey* by Jane Austen, still one of Britain's best-known and best-loved novelists.

Next came the reign of Queen Victoria and the era of industrial expansion. Novels of the time often took social and political issues as subject matter: in *Oliver Twist*, Charles Dickens captures the lives of young thieves in the London slums; in *Hard Times* he paints a brutal picture of capitalism. Meanwhile, Thomas Hardy's classic *Tess of the D'Urbervilles* deals with the decline of the peasantry, and *The Trumpet Major* paints a picture of idyllic English country life changed by war and encroaching modernity.

Other major figures from this era are the Brontë sisters – Charlotte Brontë's *Jane Eyre* and Anne Brontë's *The Tennant of Wildfell Hall* are classics of passion, mystery and love. Fans still flock to Haworth (p561), their former home, perched on the edge of the wild Pennine moors which inspired so many books.

Of the Brontë family's prodigious output, Emily Brontë's *Wuthering Heights* is the best known – an epic tale of obsession and revenge, where the dark and moody landscape plays as great a role as any human character.

In the 20th century, the pace of English writing increased. WWI made poetic heroes of Rupert Brooke and Wilfred Owen. Brooke's *The Soldier* is romantic and idealistic but Owen's *Dulce et Decorum Est* is harshly cynical about the 'glory' of war. Meanwhile, DH Lawrence produced *Sons and Lovers* and *The Rainbow*, novels set in the Midlands, following the lives and loves of generations, as the country changes from 19th-century idyll to the modern world we recognise today. In 1928, Lawrence pushed his explorations of sexuality further in *Lady Chatterley's Lover*, which was initially banned as pornographic. Torrid affairs are no great shakes today, but the quality of the writing still shines.

Other highlights of the interwar years included EM Forster's *A Passage to India*, about the hopelessness of British colonial rule, and Daphne du Maurier's romantic suspense novel *Rebecca*, set on the Cornish coast. In a different world entirely, JRR Tolkien published *The Hobbit*, trumping it some 20 years later with his awesome trilogy *The Lord of the Rings*.

After WWII, a new breed of writer emerged. George Orwell wrote *Animal Farm* and *Nineteen Eighty-Four*, his closely observed studies of totalitarian rule, while the Cold War inspired Graham Greene's *Our Man in Havana*, in which a secret agent studies the workings of a vacuum cleaner to inspire fictitious spying reports.

As the Pennine moors haunt Brontë novels, so the marshy Cambridge-shire Fens dominate *Waterland* by Graham Swift – a tale of personal and national history, betrayal and compassion, and rated a landmark work of the 1980s.

Another spook of that period was Ian Fleming's full-blooded hero James Bond. He first appeared in 1953 in *Casino Royale*, then swashbuckled through numerous thrillers for another decade. Meanwhile, TH White's *The Once and Future King* covers battles of a different time – the magical world of King Arthur and the knights of the Round Table.

Alongside the novelists, the 20th century was a great time for poets. Big names include WH Auden (*Funeral Blues* is his most popular work thanks to a role in *Four Weddings and a Funeral*) and TS Eliot, who penned the epic *Wasteland*, although he is better know for *Old Possum's Book of Practical Cats* – turned into the musical *Cats* by Andrew Lloyd Webber. Different was the harsh, gritty verse of Ted Hughes, while Roger McGough and friends determined to make art relevant to daily life; their first publication – *The Mersey Sound* – was landmark pop poetry for the streets.

Writers breaking new ground in the 1970s included Martin Amis – just 24 when he wrote *The Rachel Papers*, a witty observation of sexual obsession in puberty. Since then Amis has published 15 books, including *London Fields* and *The Information*, all greeted with critical acclaim and high sales. In contrast, two authors who struggled for recognition initially then hit the jackpot with later works were Sebastian Faulks and Louis de Bernières. Their respective novels *Birdsong*, a perfect study of passion and the horrors of WWI, and *Captain Corelli's Mandolin*, a tale of love, war and life on a Greek island, were massive sellers in the 1990s.

Hot names of early 21st-century English literature include Zadie Smith, who was only 25 when *White Teeth* topped bestseller lists in 2000. She followed it up with the equally hyped, and almost as good, *The Autograph Man*. Another star is Hari Kunzru, who received one of the largest advances in publishing history in 2002 for his debut *The Impressionist*. His second novel *Transmission* was published in June 2004, and rewarded with (mostly) critical acclaim and high sales in the bookstores. Perhaps the most talked-about title of 2004 was *The Curious Incident of the Dog in the Night-time* – a murder mystery narrated by a boy with Asperger's syndrome, with unique and unexpected results.

Helen Fielding's *Bridget Jones's Diary*, a fond look at the heartache of a modern single girl's blundering search for love, epitomised the late-1990s 'chick-lit' genre.

Cinema

In the early years of the 20th century, silent movies from Britain gave the Americans a run for their money, and *Blackmail* by Alfred Hitchcock – still one of England's best-known film directors – launched the British film industry's era of sound production in 1929.

After a decline in film output during WWII, the English film recovery in the 1940s and '50s was led by Ealing studios with a series of eccentric ('very English') comedies such as *Kind Hearts and Coronets*, staring Alec Guinness. More serious box-office hits of the time included *Hamlet*, starring Laurence Olivier (the first British film to win an Oscar in the Best Picture category) and Carol Reed's *The Third Man*. An absolute classic of the era is *Brief Encounter*, directed by David Lean, who went on to make *Lawrence of Arabia* and *Doctor Zhivago*.

Passport to Pimlico is an Ealing Studios film classic, the story of a London suburb declaring independence from the rest of the country.

By the end of the 1960s, British film production had declined again and didn't really pick up until David Puttnam's *Chariots of Fire* won four Oscars in 1981. Perhaps inspired by this success, TV company Channel 4 began financing films for the large and small screen, one of the first being *My Beautiful Laundrette* – a story of multicultural life and love in Mrs Thatcher's England. The following year, Richard Attenborough's big-budget epic *Gandhi* carried off eight Oscars including best director and best picture, while another classic of the 1980s was *Withnail and I*, staring Richard E Grant and Paul McGann.

Chariots of Fire is an inspiring dramatisation of a true story: the progress of two athletes from university to the 1924 Olympics, exploring their friendship and their rivalry.

The 1990s saw another minirenaissance in British film-making, ushered in by *Four Weddings and a Funeral*, featuring US star Andie MacDowell, and introducing Hugh Grant, who played a likable and self-deprecating Englishman. This movie spearheaded a genre of 'Brit flicks', including *Secrets and Lies*, which won the Palme d'Or at Cannes, *Bhaji on the Beach*, a quirky East-meets-West-meets-Blackpool road movie, *Brassed Off*, a gritty northern drama, and *The Full Monty*, which in 1997 became England's most successful film ever.

Other great films of the 1990s include London gangster flick *Lock, Stock and Two Smoking Barrels* – which went on to spawn a host of geezer copycats, and incidentally launched the acting career of former footballer Vinnie Jones (more recently seen, but not heard, in *Gone in 60 Seconds*). In a very different tone, *East is East* is a beautifully understated study of the clash between first- and second-generation Pakistanis in 1970s Manchester. A popular movie that decade was *Notting Hill*, set in a London bookshop, and staring Julia Roberts, with Hugh Grant as a likable and self-deprecating Englishman. Much more enjoyable was *Sense and Sensibility*, with English doyens Emma Thompson (who also wrote the fabulous screenplay) and Kate Winslet as the Dashwood sisters, and Hugh Grant as...a likable and self-deprecating Englishman.

The Full Monty centres on unemployed steelworkers who turn to stripping on stage to raise cash. It's a great film, but the hard truth (six blokes getting their kit off can't solve an economic slump) is heavily glossed over.

A classic of the Brit-flick genre, and a great success of 2000, was *Billy Elliott*, while 2001 saw the release of *Harry Potter and the Philosopher's Stone*, and perfectly understated *Last Orders* – both with nearly exclusively British casts. A year later, critical acclaim was dished out to *Iris*, a heart-wrenching dramatisation of Iris Murdoch's descent into Alzheimer's, starring Judi Dench, Jim Broadbent and Kate Winslet – darlings of the British film industry. In contrast, *About a Boy* was a feel-good movie about a dating ploy leading unexpectedly to fatherly responsibilities, staring the ever-popular Hugh Grant as (you guessed it) a likable and self-deprecating Englishman. Meanwhile, surprise hit *Bend it like Beckham* addressed more fundamental themes: growing up, first love, sex, class, race – and football.

Notable English films of the early 21st century include *Love, Actually* – in which Hugh Grant plays a (yep – likable and self-deprecating) prime minister who falls in love with the tea lady at No 10 Downing Street, and *Shaun of the Dead* – a great horror spoof where the key character fails to notice the walking corpses because most of his neighbours are zombies at the best of times. A return from death (this time for real) is the topic of *Touching the Void*, about English mountaineer Joe Simpson and his survival of an appalling accident in the Andes, which won the UK movie industry's 2004 Bafta award for Best British Film. In 2005, look out for *Hitchhikers Guide to the Galaxy* – already an English cult classic book and radio series – staring Bill Nighy as Slatibartfast and Mos Def as Ford Prefect.

www.screenonline.org.uk – the website of the British Film Institute – has complete coverage of Britain's film and TV industry.

Music

In England you're never short of choice in live music. London has several world-class venues for pop, rock, jazz and classical, while most other cities have concert halls and stadiums for the big names. For live music on a smaller scale, local folk singers or grungy garage bands thrive all over the country. Once again, London has the largest choice, but you can hear great sounds (and some really dire stuff) in pubs and clubs everywhere. Options are more restricted in the countryside – but then you're in the wrong place for bright lights anyway.

POP & ROCK

Since the dawn of the swinging '60s, England has been firmly on the main stage (with access all areas) of pop and rock music. The first big exports were the Beatles, the Rolling Stones, the Who and the Kinks. They were followed in the 1970s by stardust-speckled heroes like Marc Bolan and David Bowie. Other artists of the time included Cream (featuring Eric Clapton), Genesis (initially fronted by Peter Gabriel and later by Phil Collins), Roxy Music (featuring for a while the highly influential Brian Eno and then the

---

BUT IF WE DID...

This section concentrates on pop and rock. We haven't got space to discuss England's many other rich veins of music – jazz, folk, roots, fusion, banghra, R&B, drum'n'bass, dance, techno, chill-out, dub, gospel, urban, hip-hop, eski and so on. But if we did, here are some names we would mention:

Basement Jaxx, Faithless, Prodigy, Mark B & Blade, Ty, Roots Manuva, LTJ Bukem, Roni Size, Goldie, Craig David, Massive Attack, Zero 7, Portishead, Leftfield, Dizzee Rascal, Underworld, Fila Brazillia, the Chemical Brothers, Fatboy Slim, Dillinja, Total Science, Kathryn Williams, Goldfrapp, Paul Oakenfold, Panjabi MC, Rae & Christian, Cassius Henry, Gerard Presencer, Courtney Pine, Jamie Cullum, The Streets, PJ Harvey, Special D, Tricky, Shy FX, Andrew Weatherall, EZ Rollers, Lemon Jelly, Carl Cox, Tom Middleton, Morcheeba, Raghav, Talvin Singh, Nitin Sawhney, Kate Rusby, the Levellers, Nick Drake, Eliza Carthy, Billy Bragg, Jools Holland...

ACE CLUBS

If clubbing floats your boat, the major cities of England have some of the best clubs and late bars in the world, with DJs and theme nights that bring in eager punters from miles around. Of course, London is indisputably the top spot, but Brighton, Bristol, Nottingham, Manchester, Sheffield, Leeds and Liverpool all have large and ecstatic club scenes. Whatever your taste when it comes to clubs or any other kind of entertainment, the best way to find out who's who and what's hot is to check out posters, pick up flyers, or scan the local listing magazines (which are mentioned throughout this book). Then go out and enjoy!

last word in suave, Bryan Ferry), Pink Floyd, Deep Purple, Led Zeppelin, Queen and Elton John – all very different, but all globally renowned, and some, such as Bowie, still bringing out decent material today.

In the late '70s and early '80s self-indulgent dinosaur bands were left floundering in the wake of punk music. It was energetic, anarchic ('here's three chords, now form a band') and frequently tuneless, but punk was great fun and returned pop to grassroots level – at least for a while. The Sex Pistols produced one album and a clutch of (mostly banned) singles, while more prolific were the Clash, the Damned, the Buzzcocks, the Stranglers and the UK Subs (the last are still touring today).

Punk begat 'New Wave' (ie everything that was a bit punky), with leading exponents including the Jam and Elvis Costello; this crossed over with the brief ska revival of the 1980s led by the Specials and tapped into by bands such as the Beat and Madness. Meanwhile, a punk-and-reggae-influenced trio called the Police – fronted by bassist Sting – became one of the biggest names of the decade.

Around this time, heavy metal enjoyed an upsurge, with bands such as Black Sabbath (featuring the currently once-again-famous Ozzy Osbourne) and Judas Priest exporting soulful melodies and intriguing interpretations of established religion to concert halls worldwide.

The ever-changing music of the 1980s also experienced a surge of electronica with the likes of Depeche Mode, Cabaret Voltaire and Human League which overlapped into the New Romantic bands such as Spandau Ballet, Duran Duran, and Culture Club – favouring frills and fringes, and a definite swing of pop's pendulum away from untidy punks. Other big names of that decade included Wham! (a two-piece boy band headed by a bright young fellow called George Michael), Joy Division (who evolved into New Order), the Stone Roses and the Happy Mondays (who epitomised the late-'80s/early-'90s scene in Manchester, England's second city and musical hotbed – see The Madchester Sound on p622), and the painfully morose but curiously engaging Smiths, fronted by Morrissey (also currently enjoying a comeback) – once again, all very different, but all quintessentially English, and all with worldwide followings.

The '90s saw the renaissance of indie bands, with the likes of Blur, Elastica, Suede, Supergrass, The Verve, Pulp, Radiohead and, above all, Oasis reviving the flagging guitar-based format. Heralded as the Britpop revolution, it is largely thanks to these bands that the indie guitar sound remains such a major feature of pop music today – as exemplified by Badly Drawn Boy, Gomez, British Sea Power and The Libertines, while Coldplay, Starsailor and Muse tend towards the more soulful side of the genre.

Halfway through first decade of the 21st century, English pop seems dominated by the likes of faux-indies Busted and ex–Pop Idol Will Young, while The Darkness make glam rock cool again, and bands like The Streets, The Zutons and Keane show that even genuine indie music is also going through a retro phase. On the solo songstress front, Dido

A film about love, betrayal, brass bands, coal-mine closures and the breakdown of society in 1980s England, *Brassed Off* makes you laugh then cry, and shouldn't be missed.

24 Hour Party People is a totally irreverent, suitably chaotic film about the 1990s Manchester music scene – the Hacienda, Factory Records, Joy Division, Happy Mondays, the lot.

remains massively popular, with Amy Winehouse and the very soulful Joss Stone the rising stars of 2004. Despite some quiet periods, leading R&B, dance and garage acts include Ms Dynamite, Jamelia, Mis-Teeq, So Solid Crew and Groove Armada, still fighting the good fight against a relentless onslaught of US imports. Going the other way, should we be proud that England's biggest export of recent times is ex–Take That crooner and Sinatra wannabe Robbie Williams?

CLASSICAL MUSIC & OPERA

See www.bbc.co.uk /proms for full details of dates, tickets and when to sing 'Land of Hope and Glory'.

The country that gave you the Beatles and Oasis is also a hive of classical music, with several professional symphony orchestras, dozens of amateur orchestras, and an active National Association of Youth Orchestras. Such enthusiasm is all the more remarkable given England's small number of well-known classical composers, especially compared with Austria, Germany and Italy.

Key figures include: Henry Purcell, who flourished in the Restoration period, but is still regarded as one of the finest English composers; Thomas Arne, best known for the patriotic anthem 'Rule Britannia'; Edward Elgar, famous for his 'Enigma Variations'; Gustav Holtz, from Cheltenham, who wrote 'The Planets' (everyone knows the Mars, Bringer of War bit); Vaughan Williams, whose London Symphony ends with chimes from Big Ben; and Benjamin Britten, perhaps the finest English composer of the last century, best known for the 'Young Person's Guide to the Orchestra' and the opera *Peter Grimes*. More recently, the works of Sir Michael Tippett, Peter Maxwell Davies, John Tavener and Harrison Birtwhistle have found international fame, while the music of composer William Lloyd Webber has been brought to public attention by his sons Julian and Andrew.

Best-known of all English classical music concert programmes is The Proms (short for 'promenade' – because people used to walk about, or stand, while they listened) – one of the world's greatest music festivals, held from mid-July to mid-September each year at the Royal Albert Hall in London and widely broadcast on radio and TV.

In London, the Royal Opera House in Covent Garden recently enjoyed a multimillion-pound renovation and is bringing in the crowds, while English National Opera's big thing of 2004 was a stunning performance of Wagner's Ring Trilogy, with *Valkyrie* right up there in the lists of top London attractions. Later that year, ENO performed act three of the opera, which includes 'Ride of the Valkyries' (you know, the bit from *Apocalypse Now*), at the Glastonbury festival (p285) – fittingly under gathering storm clouds – proudly sharing the bill with Morrissey and James Brown.

SOUNDS OF SUMMER

If you're a fan of the performing arts, some fine productions are staged outdoors from May to September. Many stately homes put on open-air plays (*Macbeth* at dusk is magic) while purpose-built places such as Regent's Park Theatre (p113) in London and cliff-edge Minack Theatre (p337) in Cornwall always pull in crowds. The best-known music event is Glyndebourne (p195) – a programme of world-class opera in the spectacular setting of a country-house garden.

Summertime also inspires villages, towns and cities across the country to stage arts and music festivals – everything from small-scale weekend shows to massive spectaculars like the Bath International Music Festival (p277), via specialist events like the Three Choirs Festival (held once every three years at the cathedrals of Gloucester, Hereford or Worcester), Buxton Opera Festival (p481) or Whitby Folk Festival (p604). And don't forget pop and rock extravaganzas such as Leeds (p555) and Glastonbury (p285), or the colourful Womad global music gathering (p158) in Reading.

Architecture

One of the many good reasons to visit England is to savour its rich architectural heritage – everything from 5000-year-old Bronze Age burial mounds to the stunning steel-and-glass constructions of the late 20th and early 21st centuries. Perhaps the best-known historical construction is the mysterious stone circle of Stonehenge (p235) in southwest England – top of the highlight hit-list for many visitors. And moving on a few millennia, the Roman occupation of England around 2000 years ago also left an impressive legacy, including grand Fishbourne Palace (p207) in West Sussex and the well-preserved swimming pools and saunas that gave the city of Bath (p275) its name – another major highlight for many visitors.

In much of the 1000 years or so leading up to our own time, English architecture was dominated by two aspects: worship and defence. This gave us the incredibly diverse and truly magnificent collection of cathedrals, minsters, abbeys and monasteries dotted across the country, and an equally diverse collection of castles – from evocative ruins such as Dunstanburgh (p722) on the coast of Northumberland and the finely maintained gargantuan pile of Windsor Castle (p154), to the iconic Tower of London (p107) itself, with walls and moats, battlements and ramparts from every century since the Norman Conquest.

Castles were good for keeping out the enemy, but there were few other benefits of living in a large damp pile of stones, and as times grew more peaceful in England from around the 16th century, the landed gentry started to build fine residences – known simply as country houses. There was a particular boom in the 18th century, and one of the most distinctive features of England's countryside today is the sheer number (not to mention the sheer size) of these grand and beautiful structures.

But it's not all about big houses. Alongside the stately homes, ordinary domestic architecture from the 16th century onwards can also still be seen in rural areas: black-and-white 'half-timbered' houses still characterise counties such as Worcestershire, while brick-and-flint cottages pepper Suffolk and Sussex, and hardy centuries-old farms built with slate or local gritstone are a feature of areas such as Derbyshire and the Lake District.

In our own era, the rebuilding that followed WWII showed scant regard for the overall 'feel' of the cities, or for the lives of the people who lived in them, leaving legacies such as inner-city tower-block housing estates and the 'brutalist' concrete structures of London's South Bank Centre. Perhaps this is why, on the whole, the English are conservative in their architectural tastes, and often resent ambitious or experimental designs, especially when they're applied to public buildings, or when form appears more important than function. But a familiar pattern often unfolds: after a few years of resentment, first comes a nickname (London's new near-spherical City Hall, aka the Greater London Authority Building, was called 'Livingstone's Ball' by some, after London's well-known mayor), then grudging acceptance, and finally – once the locals have got used to it – comes pride and affection for the new building. The English just don't like to be rushed, that's all.

With this attitude in mind, over the last 15 years or so English architecture has started to redeem itself, and many big cities now have contemporary buildings their residents can enjoy. Highlights in London include the spiky MI6 HQ in Vauxhall and the bulging cone of the SwissRE building (already dubbed 'the gherkin') which dominates the financial district. At the same time, architecture continues to be more internationalised as English architects design airports in Germany or Southeast Asia, while Spanish architects design offices in Britain.

DID YOU KNOW?

As well as the grand cathedrals, England has over 12,000 parish churches packed with historical and/or architectural significance.

BUILDING ON SUCCESS

Two men have dominated modern English architecture for the last 30 years: Sir Norman Foster and Lord Richard Rogers.

Foster favours clean designs with flowing lines. Key works include the sinuous and sensuous glass roof for the Great Court of the British Museum (p104); try to visit on a sunny day to catch the crisscross of shadows. And don't miss the Millennium Bridge (p109) between St Paul's and the Tate Modern in London – almost organic in form. The Sage Gateshead concert hall (p703) in Newcastle-upon-Tyne is another splendid recent example of his work. Foster was also one of the architects short-listed to design a building to replace the World Trade Center in New York.

In contrast, the work of Rogers is technical and intricate. Perhaps his best-known work is the Millennium Dome (p116), a tent-like structure with vast curving white fields held aloft by cables and spindly yellow towers. A more recent work is the massive Paddington Basin complex, near the London train station of the same name. Rogers has also worked for Ken Livingstone, Mayor of London, on 20,000 new homes.

Meanwhile, Foster's new project for Mayor Ken is City Hall (Greater London Authority Building), which opened in July 2002. It looks like a tilted beehive, and the glass walls mean you can see everyone inside, hard at work – a deliberate symbol of local government transparency – while at the top there's the spectacular Londoner's Lounge where you can admire the panoramic views and buy a traditional English cappuccino.

Out of London, contemporary architecture is epitomised by Manchester's theatrical Imperial War Museum North (p616), the soaring wood and glass arcs of Sheffield's Winter Gardens (p548), the chic new Bullring (p430) in Birmingham, The Deep aquarium (p573) in Hull, and The Sage Gateshead (p703) in Newcastle.

Painting & Sculpture

For centuries, English art was influenced by the great European movements, and in the days before cameras, portrait-painting was a reliable if unadventurous mainstay for most working artists. Top names include Sir Joshua Reynolds, whose portraits in the 'grand style' include *Lady Anstruther* (which you can see today in London's Tate Britain gallery, p100) and his rival, Thomas Gainsborough, who produced informal works with subjects at ease in a landscape, such as *Mr & Mrs Andrews* (National Portrait Gallery, p97). For more about the rivalry between Reynolds and Gainsborough see the boxed text on p513.

In the 18th century William Hogarth proved to be a breakaway figure from the comfortable world of portraits, producing a series of paintings which satirised social abuses. His most celebrated work is *A Rake's Progress*, displayed today at Sir John Soane's Museum, London (p105).

Two other key figures of the 18th-century English art scene were Joseph Wright, whose interest in science inspired the oddly titled but beautifully executed *An Experiment on a Bird in the Air Pump*, and George Stubbs, whose passion for animal anatomy, particularly horses, is evident in many works at Tate Britain, and in countless prints on countless country pub walls.

Gainsborough's English landscape tradition was continued by John Constable who painted mainly in Suffolk (still billed as 'Constable Country' by the local tourist board). His most famous work is *The Haywain* (National Gallery, p97) – an idyllic rural scene.

Constable's contemporaries include poet, painter and visionary William Blake, and JMW Turner, whose works increasingly subordinated picture details to the effects of light and colour. By the 1840s, Turner's

DID YOU KNOW?

Hogarth helped form the Royal Academy of Arts in 1768, along with Sir Joshua Reynolds, who became its first president. The Royal Academy (p102) is still at the forefront of the British artistic establishment today.

Click on www.saatchi -gallery.co.uk for details of artists, works and exhibitions at one of London's highest-profile galleries of contemporary art.

compositions became almost entirely abstract and were widely vilified. Both artists have rooms dedicated to their work at Tate Britain, and the Turner collection at Petworth House (p207) in West Sussex is exquisite.

In the 20th century, the place of English art in the international arena was ensured by Henry Moore's and Barbara Hepworth's monumental sculptures, Francis Bacon's contorted paintings, and David Hockney's highly representational images of – among other things – dachshunds and swimming pools. Much of Hockney's work can be seen at Salt's Mill gallery in Bradford (his hometown, p559), while Hepworth is forever associated with St Ives in Cornwall (p338).

After WWII, Howard Hodgkin and Patrick Heron developed an English version of American abstract expressionism. At the same time, but in great contrast, Manchester artist LS Lowry was painting his much-loved 'matchstick men' figures set in an urban landscape of narrow streets and smoky factories. A good place to see his work is in The Lowry Centre, Manchester (p616).

In 1956 a young artist called Richard Hamilton crated a photomontage *Just what is it that makes today's homes so different, so appealing?* as a poster for the Whitechapel Art Gallery in London. It launched the pop-art movement in England, which culminated with record covers such as Peter Blake's *Sergeant Pepper's Lonely Hearts Club Band* for the Beatles.

The Whitechapel Art Gallery also helped launch the career of Anthony Caro, a sculptor who works primarily in steel and bronze, with a groundbreaking exhibition in 1963. Since then, Caro has become a highly influential figure, and is considered by many to be England's greatest living sculptor– see www.anthonycaro.org.

Jumping forward a few decades, the contemporary art scene is dominated by the 'Brit pack', a group of artists championed by advertising tycoon Charles Saatchi. These include Rachel Whiteread, who casts commonplace objects in resin; Damien Hirst, whose use of animals, alive and dead, caused outrage; and Tracey Emin, still most famous for *My Bed*, a combination of soiled sheets and 'sluttish detritus'.

Key sculptors of today include Antony Gormley, whose *Angel Of The North* overlooks the city of Gateshead near Newcastle; it's a massive steel construction of a human figure with wings outstretched – although these wings would be more fitting on a 747 than on a heavenly being. Initially derided by the locals, it is now a proud symbol of the northeast.

Theatre

However you budget your time and money, make sure that you see some English theatre as you travel around the country. It easily lives up to its reputation as the finest in the world, and London's West End is the international centre for theatrical arts – whatever New Yorkers say.

But first, let's set the stage with some history. England's best-known theatrical name is of course William Shakespeare, whose plays were first performed in the 16th century at the Globe Theatre. His brilliant plots and sharp prose, and the sheer size of his canon of work (including classics such as *Hamlet* and *Romeo and Juliet*), have turned him into a national icon. (See p445 for more historical information on Shakespeare and the Royal Shakespeare Company.) The Globe has now been rebuilt, (see p109) and today you can see the Bard's plays performed in Elizabethan style – in the round, with no roof, and with 'groundlings' down the front heckling and joining in the bits they know.

Theatres were great fun, and so they were firmly closed as dens of iniquity in Oliver Cromwell's day. But when Charles II returned from exile

DID YOU KNOW?

The *Angel of the North* is one of the most viewed works of art in the world. It stands beside the busy A1 highway and millions of drivers each year can't help but see this huge sculpture. See www .gateshead.gov.uk/angel.

DID YOU KNOW?

England's first theatre was built in 1576 on the northern outskirts of London and was called – rather unimaginatively – 'The Theatre'. Shakespeare's famous Globe Theatre came a little later.

For a sample of Restoration comedy, try to see William Congreve's *The Way of the World* – or at least read a few pages. Full of adultery, gossip and intrigue, it was a huge hit in 1700.

in 1660 he opened the doors again, and encouraged radical Continental practices such as actresses (female roles had previously been played by boys) – an innovation which London audiences loved, along with the humorous plays known as Restoration comedies, which delighted in bawdy wordplay and mockery of the upper classes. The leading lady of the day was Nell Gwyn, who also became Charles II's mistress.

In the 18th century, theatres were built in the larger English cities. The Bristol Old Vic and The Grand in Lancaster date from this time, along with plays such as Oliver Goldsmith's uproarious *She Stoops to Conquer*. Top of the bill was actor David Garrick, who later gave his name to one of London's leading theatres.

The innovation of gas-lighting at London's Drury Lane and Covent Garden theatres set the 19th-century stage for some wonderful shows, including the brilliant comedies of Oscar Wilde – everyone's heard of *The Importance of Being Earnest* (even if they haven't seen it). And the quality continued into the 20th century, with the 1950s a particularly rich era, when Laurence Olivier, John Gielgud and Peggy Ashcroft were at their professional peak.

The postwar years also marked the emergence of new playwrights with new freedoms, such as John Osborne, whose best-known work is *Look Back in Anger*. A contemporary was Harold Pinter, who developed a new dramatic style and perfectly captured the stuttering illogical diction of real-life conversation. In the 1960s and 1970s, plays by Tom Stoppard (*Rosencrantz and Guildenstern are Dead*), Peter Shaffer (*Amadeus*), Michael Frayn (*Noises Off*) and Alan Ayckbourn (*The Norman Conquests*) took the country by storm – and famous English actors such as Helen Mirren, Glenda Jackson, Judi Dench and Tom Courtenay did justice to them on stage.

In the 1990s and early years of the 21st century, big names in English theatre include Brenda Blethyn, Charles Dance, Judi Dench (still!), Ian McKellen, Anthony Sher, Simon Callow, Toby Stephens, Jane Horrocks and Ralph Fiennes, although most perform in stage productions only once or twice a year, combining this with (more lucrative) appearances on the small or silver screen. In London, other stars of the stage these days are the directors, especially Nicholas Hytner at the National, or the writers, like Conor McPherson, while the native actors are sometimes joined visitors from over the pond, as the likes of Madonna, Nicole Kidman, Gwyneth Paltrow, Matthew Perry, Molly Ringwald, Aaron Eckhart, Julia Stiles, Macaulay Culkin and Kevin Spacey have performed in London productions in recent years, exchanging pay-cuts for the genuine cred that only treading West End boards can bestow. (Spacey is now based in London, and contracted to perform in Old Vic productions twice a year.) Some more cues about the capital's current drama scene are given on p135.

And while there's often an urge among producers to stick with the big names and safe (and profitable) productions, the risk and innovation normally more associated with fringe events does sometimes filter through too, making London's theatre arguably more innovative and exciting than it's been since the Restoration, and certainly – according to some critics – since the angry postwar era of Osborne and co.

For many visitors to London, though, the theatres of the West End mean one thing: musicals, from *Jesus Christ Superstar* in the 1970s to *Billy Elliot* in 2004, through *Cats*, *Les Mis*, *Phantom* and all the rest. Many of today's shows are based on the pop lexicon, with singalongs from *We Will Rock You* to *Tonight's the Night*, proving that – just like in Shakespeare's day – we all just like to join in really.

Look Back in Anger launched the careers of playwright John Osborne and actor Alan Bates, with rebellious lead character Jimmy Porter perfectly capturing the spirit of an unhappy and frustrated postwar generation.

Harold Pinter wrote numerous plays, but is probably still best known for his landmark work *The Birthday Party* – a study of sinister figures and shady untold pasts.

DID YOU KNOW?

A London tradition is the 'long run' – plays which are performed for season after season. The record holder is *The Mousetrap* by Agatha Christie; the play has been seen at the St Martin's Theatre for more than 50 years.

Outdoor Activities

As you travel around England, pursuing an outdoor activity is an ideal way to get beyond the beaten track and escape the veneer of major tourist sites. Fresh air is good for your body and soul, of course, and becoming actively involved in the country's way of life is much more rewarding than staring at it through a camera lens or car window.

This chapter concentrates on the most popular and accessible outdoor activities, walking and cycling, which can also open up some of the most beautiful corners of the country. (More formal or organised activities, such as golf and fishing, are covered on p734.) The options are endless – short rambles or long expeditions, conquering mountains or cruising across plains – with something for young and old, and are often perfect for families. Whatever your budget, a walk or ride through the English countryside will almost certainly be a highlight of your visit to the country.

Information

Numerous local walks and cycle rides are described throughout this book, and the start of each regional chapter gives an overview of the best opportunities in that area. For more information and inspiration on any area, your first stop should always be a Tourist Information Centre (TIC). These have racks of free leaflets on local walks and rides, and also sell booklets (for a nominal fee) plus detailed books and maps (around £5) describing everything from half-hour strolls to week-long expeditions. In rural areas, books and maps are also available in local newsagents and outdoor-gear shops. TIC staff can also tell you where to arrange local guides, hire bikes, find repair shops and so on.

WALKING

Perhaps because England is such a crowded place, open spaces are highly valued, and every weekend millions of English people get their boots on and take to the countryside. You could do a lot worse than join them!

Every village and town is surrounded by a web of footpaths, while most patches of open country are crossed by paths and tracks. The options are limitless too. You can walk from place to place in true backpacking style, or base yourself in one interesting spot for a week or so and go out on day walks to explore the surrounding countryside.

The joy of walking in England is due in no small part to the 'right of way' network – public paths and tracks across private property. Nearly all land (including in national parks) in England is privately owned, but if there's a right of way, you can follow it through fields, woods, even farmhouse yards, as long as you keep to the route and do no damage. In some mountain and moorland areas, walkers can also move freely beyond the rights of way, and this is clearly advertised.

The main types of rights of way are footpaths and bridleways (the latter open to horse-riders and mountain-bikers too). You'll also see byways, which due to a quirk of history are open to *all* traffic, so don't be surprised if you're disturbed by off-road driving fanatics.

Where to Walk

Here's a quick rundown of some great walking areas, with everything from gentle hills to high peaks.

The official website of VisitEngland – the country's main tourism promotion body – is www.visitengland.com. Of more use is www .visitbritain.com/uk/out doorbritain with routes, maps, tours and annual walking festivals.

DID YOU KNOW?

England's right of way network has existed for centuries (some paths for millennia), and long, single trails don't exist here. Long-distance routes simply link many shorter paths.

With numerous links and information on many walks, www.ramblers .org.uk is the site of the Ramblers' Association (☎ 020-7339 8500), the country's leading walking organisation.

NORTHERN ENGLAND

In the northwest of the country, the **Lake District** (p655) is the heart and soul of walking in England – a wonderful area of soaring peaks, endless views, deep valleys and, of course, beautiful lakes. There's a great selection of country hotels, B&Bs and campsites too. Good bases include the towns of Ambleside and Keswick, and the village of Patterdale.

Further north, keen walkers love the starkly beautiful hills of **Northumberland National Park** (p727), while the coast is less daunting but just as dramatic. In the park, good bases include Wooler and Bellingham. On the coast, head for Alnmouth or to Bamburgh, near a spectacular castle.

For something a little gentler, the valleys, moors and rolling hills of the **Yorkshire Dales** (p563) are popular walking areas in England. Good bases for walks include the villages of Grassington and Malham. Further north, the dramatic valleys of Wensleydale and Swaledale have more options.

CENTRAL ENGLAND

The gem of central England is the **Cotswold Hills** (p405). This is classic English countryside, with gentle paths through neat fields and mature woodland, past clear rivers flowing down grassy valleys, or pretty villages with churches, farms and cottages of honey-coloured stone. The marvellously named towns of Moreton-in-Marsh, Stow-on-the-Wold and Bourton-on-the-Water all make ideal bases.

SOUTHERN ENGLAND

The emptiest, highest and wildest area in southern England? It's **Dartmoor** (p317), where the rounded hills are dotted with granite outcrops called 'tors' – looking for all the world like abstract sculptures – and the valleys are full of Bronze Age sites and other ancient remains. Good places to base yourself for day walks include Buckfastleigh on the south side of Dartmoor, or Sticklepath on the north side.

Also in the southwest, **Exmoor** (p291) has grassy, heather-covered hills cut by deep valleys and edged by spectacular cliffs, great beaches, quiet villages and busy seaside resorts. The walking opportunities are immense. Good bases include Exford and Simonsbath, while on the coast you can head for Lynton and Lynmouth.

In the deep south lies the **New Forest** (p217). Visitors to England love this name, as the area is more than 1000 years old and there aren't *that* many trees – it's mainly conifer plantation and great open areas of gorse and heath. But apart from these minor details, it's a wonderful place for easy strolls, and the towns of Lyndhurst or Lymington make good bases.

And just over the water is the **Isle of Wight** (p221). If you're new to walking in Britain, or simply not looking for high peaks and wilderness, this is a good first choice. The local authorities have put a lot of effort into footpaths and trails; most are linear and can be done in a day, and you can always get back to your starting point using the island's excellent bus service.

The Ramblers' Association's annually published *RA Yearbook* is an invaluable publication for all walkers – it outlines routes and walking areas, and has handy lists of walker-friendly B&Bs and hostels all over Britain.

For comprehensive coverage of a selection of walking routes and areas, we recommend Lonely Planet's *Walking in Britain*, which also covers places to stay and eat along several long-distance walks.

THERE'S COLD IN THEM THERE HILLS

The English countryside often looks gentle and welcoming, but the weather can turn nasty at any time of year, especially on the high hills or open moors. If you're walking in these areas, it's vital to be well equipped. You should carry (and know how to use) good maps and a compass. If you're really going off the beaten track, leave details of your route with someone. Wear decent footwear. Carry warm and waterproof clothing (even in summer). Make sure you've got some drink, food and high-energy stuff like chocolate. Carrying a whistle and torch – in case of emergency – is no bad thing either.

Long-distance Walks

Many walkers savour the chance of completing one of England's famous long-distance routes. There are hundreds, of which around 10 are official national trails with better signposting and maintenance – so they're ideal for beginners or visitors. You don't have to do them from end to end; you can walk just a section for a day or two or use the route as a basis for loops exploring the surrounding area. Here's a short list of our favourites to get you started.

Coast to Coast Walk (190 miles/306km) The number-one favourite, through three national parks and spectacular scenery, with sea-cliffs, plains, mountains, dales and moors. See p545.

Cotswold Way (102 miles/164km) A fascinating walk through history and classic picture-postcard countryside. See p405.

Cumbria Way (68 miles/109km) A fine hike through Lake District valleys, with top-quality mountain views. See p653.

Hadrian's Wall Path (84 miles/135km) In the footsteps of the legions, follow the Roman Wall as it strides across northern England. See p716.

Pennine Way (256 miles/412km) The grandaddy of them all, along the mountainous spine of northern England. See pp480, 564 and 694.

South West Coast Path (610 miles/976km) A roller-coaster epic past beaches, bays, shipwrecks, seaside resorts, fishing villages and cliff-top castles. See p227.

Thames Path (173 miles/277km) A journey of contrasts beside England's best-known river, from rural Gloucestershire to the heart of London. See p387.

CYCLING

A bike is the perfect transport for exploring back-road England. Once you escape the busy main highways, there's a vast network of quiet country lanes leading through fields and peaceful villages, ideal for touring on a road bike or mountain bike. Off-road riders can go further into the wilds on the many tracks and bridleways that cross England's farmlands, forests and high moors.

The opportunities are endless. Depending on your energy and enthusiasm you can amble along flat lanes, taking it easy and stopping for cream teas, or thrash all day through hilly areas, revelling in steep ascents and swooping downhill sections. You can cycle from place to place, camping or staying in B&Bs (many are cyclist friendly), or you can stay in one place for a few days and go out on rides in different directions.

Access & Rules

Bikes aren't allowed on motorways, but you can cycle on all other public roads, although main roads (A-roads) tend to be busy and should be avoided. Many B-roads suffer heavy motor traffic too, so the best places for cycling are the small C-roads and unclassified roads ('lanes') that cover rural England, especially in lowland areas, meandering through quiet countryside and linking small, picturesque villages.

Cycling is *not* allowed on footpaths, but mountain-bikers can ride on unmade roads or bridleways that are a public right of way. For mountain-biking it's often worth seeking out forestry areas; among the vast plantations, signposted routes of varying difficulty have been opened up for single-track fans.

Where to Cycle

While you can cycle anywhere in England, some areas are better than others. In many popular areas, car traffic can be a problem on summer weekends. This section gives a brief overview. With a map and a sense of adventure, the rest is up to you!

Stroll over to www .nationaltrail.co.uk and www.countryside.gov .uk/nationaltrails for full details on England's national trail options.

DID YOU KNOW?

Many routes are served by baggage-carrying services. For about £5 to £10 per day, your pack will be delivered to your next B&B while you walk unencumbered. See www.carrylite.com, www.cumbria.com/pack horse and www.pikedaw .freeserve.co.uk/walks.

The Cyclists' Touring Club (☎ 0870 873 0060), the UK's leading recreational cycling and campaigning body, has a comprehensive website at www.ctc .org.uk with a cycle-hire directory and mail-order service for maps and books.

SUSTRANS & THE NATIONAL CYCLE NETWORK

Anyone riding a bike through England today will almost certainly come across the National Cycle Network, a web of roads and paths that spreads across Britain, on target to cover 10,000 miles (over 16,000km) by 2005. Strands of the network pass through the heart of busy cities and are aimed at commuters or school kids, while other sections follow some of the most remote roads in the country and are perfect for touring.

The whole scheme is the brainchild of Sustrans (derived from 'sustainable transport'), a campaign group barely taken seriously way back in 1978 when the network idea was first announced. But the growth of cycling, coupled with near-terminal car congestion, has earned the scheme lots of attention – not to mention £40 million in government funding. The eventual goal is to have the network pass within 2 miles of half the homes in Britain.

Most of the network keeps to quiet country lanes, while traffic-free sections make use of old roads and former railways, as well as purpose-built cycle paths. Where the network follows city streets, cyclists normally have their own lane, separate from motor traffic.

Several long-distance touring routes have been designed, using the most scenic sections of the National Cycle Network (and a few less-than-scenic sections through some towns, it has to be said). Other features include a great selection of sculptures and works of art to admire along the way. In fact, the network is billed as the country's largest outdoor sculpture gallery. The whole scheme is a re-sounding success and a credit to the visionaries who persevered against inertia all those years ago.

NORTHERN ENGLAND

The **North York Moors** (p597) offer exhilarating off-road rides, while the **Yorkshire Dales** (p564) is great for cycle touring. Some routes can be strenuous, but the scenery is superb and it's all well worth the effort. It's no accident that many of England's top racing cyclists come from this area – the Pennine Hills make an excellent training ground.

The Guide to the National Cycle Network describes 30 one-day rides throughout Britain. For off-roading, get Where to Mountain Bike in Britain, or see www.wheretomtb .com.

CENTRAL ENGLAND

Derbyshire's **Peak District** (p480) is a very popular cycling area, although the hills are quite steep in places. More leisurely options are excellent cycle routes cutting through the landscape along disused railways – dramatic and effortless at the same time. The **Cotswolds area** (p406) is another good place, with lanes through farmland and quaint villages. From the western side of the hills you get fantastic views over the Severn Valley, but you wouldn't want to go up and down this escarpment too often! The **Marches** (p355), where England borders Wales, are another rural delight, with good quiet lanes and some off-road options in the hills.

EASTERN ENGLAND

This area (p494) is great for easy pedalling: Norfolk, Suffolk and parts of Lincolnshire are generally low-lying and flat, with lanes winding through farmland and picturesque villages, past rivers, lakes and welcoming country pubs.

Anyone planning a cycle tour in England should visit www.sustrans .org.uk, site of Sustrans (☎ 0845 113 0065), originators of the National Cycle Network.

SOUTHERN ENGLAND

Cornwall and **Devon** (p301) are beautiful, and enjoy the best of the English climate, but the rugged landscape makes for tough pedalling. **Somerset** (p282), **Dorset** (p246) and **Wiltshire** (p228) have more gentle hills (plus a few steep valleys to keep you on your toes) and a beautiful network of quiet lanes, making it perfect for leisurely cycle touring. In Hampshire, the ancient woodland and open heath of the **New Forest** (p217) is especially good for on-road and off-road rides, while in Sussex the **South Downs** (p163) have numerous mountain-bike options.

Environment

England is the largest of the three nations within the island of Britain, with Scotland to the north and Wales to the west. Further west lies the island of Ireland. Looking south, France is just 20 miles away across the narrowest part of the English Channel.

THE LAND
Geologically at least, England is part of Europe, on the edge of the Eurasian landmass, separated from the mother continent by the shallow English Channel. (The French are not so proprietorial, and call it La Manche, the sleeve.) When sea levels were lower, England was *physically* part of Europe, and today – despite some misgivings on the part of anti-Europeans – the Channel Tunnel means the island is linked to the mainland once again.

England is not a place of geographical extremes. There are no Himalayas or Lake Baikals here. But there's plenty to keep you enthralled, and even a short journey can take you through a surprising mix of landscapes. Southern England is fairly flat or dotted with small hills, covered in a mix of countryside, towns and cities. East Anglia is almost entirely low and flat, while the Southwest Peninsula has granite outcrops, rich pastures and wild moors – Devon cream is world-famous – with a rugged coast and sheltered beaches that make it a favourite holiday destination.

In the north of England, farmland remains interspersed with towns and cities, but the landscape is noticeably more bumpy. A line of large hills called the Pennines (fondly tagged 'the backbone of England') run from Derbyshire to the Scottish border, and includes the peaty plateaus of the Peak District, the wild moors around Haworth (immortalised in Brontë novels), the delightful valleys of the Yorkshire Dales and the frequently windswept but ruggedly beautiful hills of Northumberland.

Perhaps England's best-known landscape is the Lake District, a small but spectacular cluster of hills and mountains in the northwest, where Scaféll Pike (a towering 978m) is England's highest peak.

WILDLIFE
For a small country, England has a diverse range of plants and animals. Many native species are hidden away, but there are some undoubted gems, from woods carpeted in shimmering bluebells to a stately herd of deer in the mountains. Having a closer look will enhance your trip enormously.

Animals
In farmland and woodland areas, a favourite English mammal is the black-and-white striped badger, while on riverbanks the once-rare otter

DID YOU KNOW?

The Fens of Lincolnshire will be among the first parts of England to be submerged when predictions about global warming and rising oceans are realised.

Wild Britain: A Traveller's Guide by Douglas Botting has excellent advice on exploring England's outback.

COMPARING COVERAGE

Statistics can be boring, but these essential area measurements may be handy for planning or perspective as you travel around:

England: 50,000 sq miles (130,000 sq km)   **UK:** 95,000 sq miles (246,000 sq km)
Britain: 88,500 sq miles (230,000 sq km)   **British Isles:** 123,000 sq miles (319,000 sq km)

If you want some comparisons, France is about 550,000 sq km, Texas 690,000 sq km, Australia seven million sq km and the USA over nine million sq km.

is slowly making a comeback. Common birds include the robin, with its red breast and cheerful whistle, and the yellowhammer, with its 'little-bit-of-bread-and-no-cheese' song. The warbling cry of a skylark is a classic, but now threatened, sound of the English countryside.

Also look out for brown hares, another increasingly rare species – related to rabbits, but much larger with longer legs and ears. Males who battle for territory in early spring are, of course, as 'mad as a March hare'.

Other woodland mammals include the small white-spotted fallow deer and the even smaller roe deer. Red foxes are very widespread and have adapted well to a scavenging life in country towns, and even in city suburbs. Grey squirrels (introduced from North America) have also proved very adaptable, to the extent that native red squirrels are severely endangered.

If you're hiking in the moorlands, birds you might see include the red grouse and the curlew with its elegant curved bill. Golden plovers are beautifully camouflaged, while lapwings are just show-offs with spectacular aerial displays.

One of England's finest wildlife spectacles occurs on the coastal cliffs in early summer, particularly in Cornwall or Yorkshire; countless thousands of guillemots, razorbills, kittiwakes and other breeding sea birds fight for space on crowded rock ledges, and the air is thick with their sound.

Plants

In the chalky hill country of southern England and the limestone areas further north (such as the Peak District and Yorkshire Dales), the best place to see wild flowers are the fields that evade large-scale farming – many erupt with great profusions of cowslips and primroses in April and May. Some flowers prefer woodland, and the best time to visit is also April and May, before the leaf canopy is fully developed so sunlight can break through to encourage plants such as bluebells – a beautiful and internationally rare species.

Another classic English plant is gorse: you can't miss the swathes of this spiky bush in heathland areas, most notably the New Forest in southern England. Legend says that it's the season for kissing when gorse blooms – luckily its vivid yellow flowers show year-round.

In contrast, the blooming season for heather is quite short. On the Pennine moors of northern England, and on Dartmoor in the south, the wild hill country is covered in a riot of purple in August and September; one of the finest areas to see this is the North York Moors (see p596).

NATIONAL PARKS

Way back in 1810, poet and outdoors-lover William Wordsworth suggested that the Lake District should be 'a sort of national property, in which every man has a right'. More than a century later it became a national park (although quite different from Wordsworth's vision), along with Dartmoor, Exmoor, Norfolk & Suffolk Broads, Northumberland, North York Moors, Peak District and Yorkshire Dales. Two more parks, the New Forest and the South Downs, are in the process of being created.

SEA LIFE

Two seal species frequent English coasts; the larger grey seal is more often seen than the mis-named common seal. Dolphins, porpoises, minke whales and basking sharks can all be seen off the western coasts, especially from about May to September when viewing conditions are better – as long as you go with someone who knows where to look!

ENGLAND'S WORLD HERITAGE SITES

World Heritage Sites are places of great environmental or cultural significance. There are around 700 sites globally, of which about 25 are in the UK. England's include the following:

Bath Georgian city (p273)
Blenheim Palace (p400)
Canterbury Cathedral sites (p169)
Derwent Valley Mills (p476)
Dorset & East Devon Coast (p246)
Durham Castle & Cathedral (p705)
Greenwich Maritime sites (p115)
Hadrian's Wall (p715)
Ironbridge Gorge (p375)

Kew Royal Botanic Gardens (p117)
Liverpool Commercial Centre & Waterfront (p631)
Saltaire (p559)
Stonehenge & Avebury (p235 & p244)
Fountains Abbey & Studley Royal Water Garden (p589)
Tower of London (p107)
Westminster Palace & Westminster Abbey (p99)

It's an impressive total, but the term 'national park' can cause confusion. First, they are not state-owned: nearly all land is private, belonging to farmers, companies, private estates and conservation organisations. Second, they are not wilderness areas, as in many other countries. In England's national parks you'll see roads, railways, villages and even towns.

Despite these apparent anomalies, national parks still contain vast tracts of wild mountain and moorland, rolling downs and river valleys, and other areas of quiet countryside, all ideal for long walks, cycle rides, easy rambles, sightseeing or just lounging around. To help you get the best from the parks, they all have information centres, and various recreational facilities (trails, car parks, campsites etc) are provided for visitors.

See p66 for the best activities and features of the national parks

For more details on World Heritage Sites, in the UK and globally, see the following:

www.icomos.org/uk/

www.wcmc.org.uk/whin/

www.culture.gov.uk /historic_environment /World_Heritage.htm

ENVIRONMENTAL ISSUES

With England's long history of human occupation, it's not surprising that the country's appearance is almost totally the result of people's interaction with the environment. The most dramatic environmental changes in rural areas came after WWII, when a drive to be self-reliant in food and timber meant new farming methods, which changed the landscape from a patchwork of small fields to a scene of vast prairies, as walls were demolished, trees felled, ponds filled, wetlands drained and – most notably – hedgerows ripped out.

In most cases the hedgerows were a few metres wide, a dense network of bushes, shrubs and trees that stretched across the countryside, protecting fields from erosion, supporting a varied range of flowers and providing shelter for numerous insects, birds and small mammals. But in the rush to improve farm yields, thousands of miles of hedgerows have been destroyed since 1950. And the destruction continues – since 1984 another 25% of hedgerows have disappeared. However, farmers are now encouraged to maintain and 'set aside' such areas as havens for birds.

Of course, environmental issues are not exclusive to rural areas. In England's towns and cities, topics such as air pollution, light pollution, levels of car use, road building, airport construction, public-transport provision, household-waste recycling and so on are never far from the political agenda. Some might say they're not near enough to the top of the list, and the main political parties certainly show lack of real engagement, but apathy abounds in most areas; for example, the Green Party enjoyed only modest increased support in the council elections of 2004.

DID YOU KNOW?

Although the land in national parks is not owned by the state, large sections of several national parks are owned by the National Trust (NT) – one of the largest charities in Britain – but the NT has no formal link with park administrative bodies.

National Park	Features	Activities	Best Time to Visit	Page
Dartmoor	wild heath, marshy moorland: Dartmoor ponies, deer, otter, badger, rabbit, buzzard, peregrine falcon, sheep	hiking, horse-riding	May-Jun (wild flowers in bloom)	p317
Exmoor	craggy sea cliffs, sweeping moors: native, wild red deer, Exmoor pony, horned sheep	horse-riding, hiking	Sep (heather in bloom)	p291
Lake District	majestic fells, rugged mountains, glassy lakes: osprey, red squirrel, waterfowl, sparrowhawk, sheep, England's only golden eagles	hiking, cycling, water sports	Sep-Oct (summer crowds have left and autumn colours abound)	p655
New Forest	woodlands and heath: wild pony, otter, owl, Dartford warbler, southern damselfly	walking, cycling, horse-riding	Apr-Sep (wild ponies are grazing)	p217
Norfolk & Suffolk Broads	expansive shallow lakes and marshlands: water lily, wildfowl, otter	walking, boating	Apr-May (birds most active)	p526
Northumberland	spiky moors of autumn-coloured heather and gorse: black grouse, red squirrel and sheep; Hadrian's Wall	walking, climbing, cycling and Roman history	spring (lambs) & Sep (flowering of the heather)	p727
North York Moors	heather-clad moors and deep green valleys punctuated by lonely farms and isolated villages: full of moorland birds like curlew, golden plover and merlin	1400 miles (2300km) of track make this a paradise for walkers and cyclists	Aug-Sep (purple heather in bloom)	p596
Peak District	rolling hills, limestone caverns: jackdaw, kestrel, grouse, rabbit, fox, badger and, of course, sheep	walking, cycling, hang-gliding	Apr-May (newborn lambs everywhere)	p478
Yorkshire Dales	limestone hills and lush valleys (dales) cut through by rugged stone walls and spotted with extravagant houses and the faded, spectral grandeur of monastic ruins	walking, cycling	Apr-May (when lambs just about outnumber visitors)	p563

WILD READING

To further your enjoyment of wildlife-watching, peruse these useful guides:

■ *Wildlife Walks* (published by Think) details walks in wildlife reserves across the country.

■ *Complete Guide to British Wildlife* by N Arlott, R Fitter & A Fitter is highly recommended if you want a single handy volume covering common mammals, birds, fish, plants, snakes, insects and even fungi.

■ *Birds, Trees, Fish* and *Wild Flowers* are part of the Gem series of books. They fit in your pocket, cost only a few pounds and are often sold at Tourist Information Centres.

■ *The Birdwatchers Pocket Guide* by Peter Hayman is highly rated, and frequently carried, by keen (as opposed to obsessive) bird-watchers; it's slim, light, and designed for speedy reference on the move, with clear illustrations and good notes.

■ *Top Birding Spots* by David Tipling covers 400 sites in Britain and Ireland, for those who want more detail about specific destinations.

Meanwhile, back in the country hot environmental issues include farming methods such as irrigation, monocropping, pesticide use and the intensive rearing of cows, sheep and other stock. The results: rivers run dry, fish are poisoned by runoff, and fields consist of one type of grass with not another plant to be seen. These 'green deserts' support no insects, which in turn means populations of some wild bird species dropped by an incredible 70% from 1970 to 1990. It's not a case of wizened old peasants recalling the idyllic days of their forbears; you only have to be over about 30 in England to remember a countryside where birds such as skylarks or lapwings were visibly much more numerous.

But all is not lost. In the face of apparently overwhelming odds, England still boasts a great biodiversity and some of the best wildlife habitats are protected to a greater or lesser extent, thanks to the creation of national parks and similar conservation zones – often within areas privately owned by conservation campaign groups, such as the **Wildlife Trusts** (www .wildlifetrusts.org), **Woodland Trust** (www.woodland-trust.org), **National Trust** (www.national trust.org.uk) and **Royal Society for the Protection of Birds** (www.rspb.org.uk). Many of these areas are open to the public – ideal spots for walking, bird-watching or simply enjoying the peace and beauty of the countryside.

DID YOU KNOW?

Britain's new 'hedgerows' are motorway verges; these long trips of grass and bushes support many small mammals – that's why kestrels are often seen hovering nearby.

Food & Drink

England once boasted a cuisine so undesirable that there's still no English equivalent for *bon appétit*, but these days it's easy to find decent food. For every greasy spoon and fast-food joint, there's a pub or restaurant serving up enticing local specialities – and for even the most budget-conscious of visitors, tasty eating definitely won't break the bank.

To a large extent, food in England has changed thanks to outside influences. For decades most towns have boasted Chinese and Indian restaurants, and in more recent times dishes from Thailand and other countries east of Suez have become available too. Closer to home, pastas, pizzas and Mediterranean specialities are commonplace not only in restaurants, but also in everyday pubs and cafés.

The overall effect of these influences has been the introduction to English restaurants of new techniques (like steaming) and revolutionary ingredients (like crisp fresh vegetables). We've also seen the creation of 'modern British cuisine': even humble bangers and mash rise to new heights when handmade thyme-flavoured sausages are paired with lightly chopped fennel and new potatoes.

And finally – it's official – vegetarianism is no longer weird. Many restaurants have at least a token vegetarian dish (another meat-free lasagne, anyone?), but better places offer more imaginative choices. Vegans will find the going tough, except at dedicated veggie/vegan restaurants – and where possible we recommend good options throughout this book.

STAPLES & SPECIALITIES

For years, the typical English dinner has been roast beef (that's why the French call the English 'les rosbif'). Meat consumption took a bit of a knock in 2000 and 2001 following 'mad cow' scares and the foot-and-mouth outbreak, but good-quality roasts from well-reared cattle now grace menus everywhere once again.

And with the beef comes Yorkshire pudding. It's simply roast batter, but very tasty when properly cooked. In pubs and cafés – especially in northern England – you can buy a big bowl-shaped Yorkshire pudding, filled with meat stew, beans, vegetables or – in these multicultural days – curry.

Another local speciality in northern England is Cumberland sausage – a tasty mix of minced meat and herbs so large it has to be spiralled to fit on your plate. Bring sausage and Yorkshire pud together and you have toad-in-the-hole.

Another classic English meal is takeaway fish and chips. Sometimes it's greasy and tasteless (especially once you get far from the sea), but in towns with salt in the air this deep-fried delight is always worth trying. Yorkshire's coastal resorts are particularly famous for huge servings of cod, while restaurants in Devon and Cornwall regularly conjure up prawns, lobster, oysters, mussels and scallops. Other seafood specialities include Norfolk crab, Northumberland kippers, and jellied eels in London.

Some other English specialities include Melton Mowbray pork pies (motto: 'gracious goodness for over 100 years'); rhubarb (best eaten in a crumble, and currently enjoying a renaissance in gourmet restaurants); and Marmite (a dark and pungent yeast extract traditionally spread on buttered toast, especially great for late-night munchies).

An English speciality you can now buy everywhere – especially in pubs – is the ploughman's lunch. Originally a lump of cheese and a lump of

NAME THAT PASTY

A favourite in southwest England is the Cornish pasty – originally a mix of cooked vegetables wrapped in pastry, now available everywhere in England, and often including meat varieties (much to the chagrin of the Cornish people). Invented long before Tupperware, the pasty was an all-in-one-lunchpack that tin miners carried underground and left on a ledge ready for mealtime. So pasties weren't mixed up, they were marked with owners' initials – always at one end, so the miner could eat half and safely leave the rest to snack on later without it mistakenly disappearing into the mouth of a workmate. And before going back to the surface, the miners traditionally left the last corner of the pasty as a gift for the spirits of the mine known as 'knockers', to ensure a safe shift the next day.

bread which hearty yokels carried to the fields wrapped in a spotted hand-kerchief, this meal has been prettified to include butter, salad, pickled onion and dressings – even a selection of cheeses. You'll also find other variations – farmer's lunch (bread and chicken), stockman's lunch (bread and ham), Frenchman's lunch (brie and baguette) and fisherman's lunch (you guessed it, with fish).

DRINKS

As you travel around England, you should definitely try some traditional beer, also known as real ale. But be ready! If you're used to the amber nectar, a local brew may come as a shock – a warm, flat and expensive shock. This is partly to do with England's climate, and partly with the beer being served by hand pump rather than gas pressure. Most important, though, is the integral flavour: traditional English beer doesn't *need* to be chilled or fizzed. Drink a cheap lager that's sat in its glass for an hour and you'll see it has very little actual taste.

Another key feature is that real ale must be looked after (which is why many pubs don't serve it), so beware of places where the landlord gives the barrels as much care as the cigarette machine. There's nothing worse than a bad pint of real ale – you might as well just have a bottle of Bud.

If beer doesn't tickle your palate, try cider – available in sweet and dry 'scrumpy' varieties. On hot summer days, go for shandy – a mix of beer and lemonade.

Most pubs also offer a good range of wines, but you'll have to search hard for the produce of Denbies, England's major vineyard (www.denbies vineyard.co.uk); their wines are found in good restaurants, with case-loads snapped up by mail-order customers.

> Tipplers' favourite tomes include the annual *Good Beer Guide to Great Britain*, produced by the Campaign for Real Ale, which steers you to the best beers and the pubs that serve them, and the *Good Pub Guide*, which details thousands of fine establishments across the country.

WHERE TO EAT & DRINK

There's a huge choice of places to eat in England, and this section out-lines just some of your options. For details on opening times, see p735. The tricky issue of tipping is covered on p741, while some pointers on restaurants' attitudes to kids are on p736.

For picnics or self-catering, markets can be a great place for food bargains – everything from dented tins of tomatoes for 1p (mmm) to home-baked cakes and organic goat cheese. Farmers markets are a great way for producers to sell good wholesome food direct to consumers, with both sides avoiding supermarkets.

> The Campaign for Real Ale (www.camra.org.uk) promotes the under-standing of traditional British beer – and recommends good pubs that serve it. Look for endorsement stickers on pub windows.

Cafés & Teashops

The traditional English café is nothing like its continental European namesake. Most are basic places serving basic food. And the usual café

THE OLDEST PUB IN ENGLAND?

Studious drinkers are often surprised to learn that the word 'pub', although apparently steeped in history, dates only from the 19th century. But places selling beer have been around for much longer, and the 'oldest pub in England' is a hotly contested title.

One of the country's oldest pubs, with the paperwork to prove it, is Ye Olde Trip to Jerusalem in Nottingham, which was serving ale to departing Crusaders in the 12th century. Other contenders sniff at this newcomer: a fine old hotel called the Eagle & Child in Stow-on-the-Wold (Gloucestershire) claims to have been selling beer since around AD 950, and Ye Olde Fighting Cocks in St Albans apparently dates back to the 8th century – although the 13th is more likely (see p149).

But then back comes Ye Trip with a counter-claim: one of its bars is a cave hollowed out of living rock, and that's more than a million years old.

---

accent is often omitted too; it's pronounced 'caffy', or shortened to 'caff'. Meals like meat pie or omelette with chips cost around £3. Sandwiches, cakes and other snacks are £1 to £2.

Some cafés definitely earn their 'greasy spoon' handle, while others are neat and friendly. Smarter cafés are called teashops, and you might pay a bit extra for extras like twee décor and table service. In country areas, cafés cater for tourists, walkers, cyclists and so on, and in summer they're open every day. Like B&Bs, good cafés are a wonderful institution and always worth a stop.

In most cities and towns you'll find American-flavoured coffee shops and Euro-style café-bars, serving decent lattes and espressos, and bagels or ciabattas rather than beans on toast. Some of these places even have outside chairs and tables – rather brave considering the narrow pavements and inclement weather much of England enjoys.

Restaurants

There are many excellent restaurants in England. London has scores of eateries that could hold their own in major cities worldwide, while places in Bath, Leeds and Manchester can give the capital a fair run for its money (actually, often for rather less money). We've taken great pleasure in seeking out some of the best and best-value restaurants in England, and recommending a small selection throughout this book.

Prices vary considerably across the country, with a main course in a straightforward restaurant around £7 to £10, rising to £15 or £20 at good-quality places. Utterly excellent food, service and surroundings can be enjoyed for £30 to £50.

Pubs & Bars

The difference between pubs and bars is sometimes vague, but generally bars are smarter, larger and louder than pubs, with a younger crowd. Drinks are more expensive too, unless there's a gallon-of-vodka-and-Red-Bull-for-a-fiver promotion – which there often is.

Perhaps the biggest difference is when it comes to food. In recent years pubs in England have become a good-value option, whether you're looking for a toasted sandwich or a three-course meal. Some particularly specialised in excellent food, while maintaining their informal atmosphere – and bingo, the gastro-pub was born.

What makes a good pub? It's often hard to pin down. In our opinion, the best pubs follow a remarkably simple formula – they offer good food and drink, with a welcoming atmosphere – and this is the type of pub that

Like the taste of meat, but don't like the idea of battery pens? Click on www.farmgatedirect.com – a list of lamb, beef, chicken and salmon producers approved by the RSPCA.

Nigella Lawson (www.nigella.com) snatched the culinary crown from Delia Smith (www.deliaonline.com) some time around the turn of the millennium, thanks to a no-nonsense style and outright seduction with recipes like chicken in Coca-Cola.

we have often recommended in this book. But nothing beats the fun of doing your own research, so here are a few more things to look for:

- A choice of beers from local brewers. Classic names include Adnams (eastern England), Aarkells (south, southwest), Black Sheep (north), Fullers (southeast), Greene King (eastern, central, south), Hardys & Hansons (central), Hook Norton (south, midlands), Jennings (northwest), Marstons (south, central, north), St Austel (west), Shepherd Neam (southeast), Timothy Taylor (north), Wadworth (west) and Youngs (southeast).
- Hand-pulled pumps to serve the beer. This means real ale, and a willingness on the part of the landlord to put in extra effort (which often translates into extra effort on food, atmosphere, cleanliness and so on).
- A good menu of snacks and meals, cooked on the premises, not shipped in by the truckful and defrosted in the microwave by untrained staff.

London

CONTENTS

Bet you told your friends you were going to London rather than England didn't you? Such is the lure of the capital that it seems to be a bigger draw than the whole country.

London boggles. Even if you come from a bigger city, you'll experience some culture shock here. The sheer size of it confounds, and travelling on the underground makes it even more difficult to get your bearings. Meanwhile, seven million people race around you. They come from more than 40 different ethnic communities speaking some 300 languages, making it impossible to define a typical Londoner anymore.

Don't get stuck in London (like so many travellers do), but don't be intimidated into an early departure either. This is one of the greatest cities on earth – fascinating, challenging, exciting, stimulating and unforgettable. Oh yeah, and expensive.

Whatever your pleasure, London has it in spades. For sights, a list might start with the iconic London Eye, St Paul's Cathedral, Big Ben, Buckingham Palace and the regalia of Royal London. Culture vultures can swoop on the many galleries and museums of international renown (not forgetting the smaller ones). If it's character you're craving head to the football or the nearest pub. Partygoers will be spoilt for choice with some of Europe's best clubs hosting famous DJs nightly while live music from big international names is never more than a tube ride away.

London can be whatever you want it to be; the key is knowing what you want and going for it.

HIGHLIGHTS

- Exploring almost a millennium of art at the **National Gallery** (p97)
- Soaking in the gravitas of **Westminster** (p98)
- Going to see **live bands** (p136)
- Being astonished at the **British Museum** (p104)
- Getting tipsy in a traditional **West End pub** (p133)

LONDON
★

| ■ TELEPHONE CODE: 020 | ■ POPULATION: 7.2 MILLION | ■ AREA: 607 SQ MILES |

HISTORY

Celts first established themselves around a ford across the River Thames. However, it was the Romans who developed the square mile now known as the City of London (which lies within today's Greater London city – note the small 'c') with a crossing, near today's London Bridge, that served as the hub of their road system. By the end of the 3rd century AD 'Londinium' was almost as multicultural as it is today with 30,000 people of various ethnic groups (albeit all Roman citizens, of course) and temples dedicated to a large number of cults. Parts of London like Aldgate and Ludgate get their names from the gates of the original city walls built by the Romans. Internal strife and relentless barbarian attacks took their toll on the Romans, who abandoned Britain in the 5th century, reducing the conurbation to a sparsely populated backwater.

The Saxons then moved in to the area, establishing farmsteads and villages, and their 'Lundenwic' prospered, becoming a large, well-organised town divided into 20 different wards. As the city grew in importance, it caught the eye of Danish Vikings who launched many invasions and razed the city in the 9th century. The Saxons held on until, finally beaten down in 1016, they were forced to accept the Danish leader Knut (Canute) as King of England, after which London replaced Winchester as its capital. In 1042 the throne reverted to the Saxon Edward the Confessor, whose main contribution to the city was the building of Westminster Abbey.

A dispute over his successor led to what's known as the Norman Conquest (Normans broadly being Vikings with shorter beards). When William the Conqueror won the watershed Battle of Hastings in 1066, he and his forces marched into London where he was crowned king. He built the White Tower (the core of the Tower of London), negotiated taxes with the merchants, and affirmed the city's independence and right to self-government.

The throne passed through various houses in the millennium or so since (the House of Windsor has warmed its cushion since 1910), but royal power has been concentrated in London since the 12th century. From the 12th century to the late 15th century, London politics were largely taken up by a three-way power struggle between the monarchy, the church and city guilds.

The greatest threat to the burgeoning city was that of disease caused by unsanitary living conditions and impure drinking water. In 1348 rats on ships from Europe brought the bubonic plague, which wiped out a third of London's population of 100,000 over the following year.

Violence became commonplace in the hard times that followed. In 1381, miscalculating or just disregarding the mood of the nation, the king tried to impose a poll tax on everyone in the realm. Tens of thousands of peasants marched on London. Several ministers were murdered and many buildings razed before the so-called Peasants' Revolt ran its course. The ringleaders were executed, but there was no more mention of a poll tax (until Margaret Thatcher, not heeding the lessons of history, tried to introduce it in the 1980s).

Despite these setbacks, London was consolidated as the seat of law and government in the kingdom during the 14th century. An uneasy political compromise was reached between the factions, and the city expanded rapidly under the House of Tudor. The first recorded map of London was published in 1558, and John Stow produced the first comprehensive history of the capital in 1598.

The 'Great Plague' struck in 1665 and 100,000 Londoners perished by the time the winter cold arrested the epidemic. Just as the population considered a sigh of relief, another disaster struck.

The mother of all blazes, the Great Fire of 1666, virtually razed the place, destroying most of its medieval, Tudor and Jacobean architecture. One plus was that it created a blank canvas upon which master architect Christopher Wren could build his magnificent churches.

London's growth continued unabated and by 1700 it was Europe's largest city with 600,000 people. An influx of foreign workers brought expansion to the east and south, while those who could afford it headed to the more salubrious environs of the north and west, divisions that still largely shape London today.

Georgian London saw a surge in creativity in architecture, music and art with the likes of Dr Johnson, Handel, Gainsborough and Reynolds enriching the city's culture while Georgian architects fashioned an elegant new metropolis. At the same time the gap between the rich and poor grew ever wider, and lawlessness was rife.

In 1837 the 18-year-old Victoria ascended the throne. During her long reign (1837–1901), London became the fulcrum of the expanding British Empire, which covered a quarter of the earth's surface. The Industrial Revolution saw the building of new docks and railways (including the first underground line in 1863), while the Great Exhibition of 1851 showcased London to the world. The city's population mushroomed from just over two million to 6.6 million during Victoria's reign.

Road transport was revolutionised in the early 20th century when the first motor buses were introduced and replaced the horse-drawn versions that had trotted their trade since 1829.

Although London suffered relatively minor damage during WWI, it was devastated by the Luftwaffe in WWII when huge swathes of the centre and East End were totally flattened and 32,000 people were killed. Ugly housing and low-cost developments were hastily erected in postwar London, and immigrants from around the world flocked to the city and changed its character forever.

The latest major disaster to beset the capital was the great smog on 6 December 1952, when a lethal combination of fog, smoke and pollution descended on the city and killed some 4000 people.

Prosperity gradually returned, and the creative energy that had been bottled up in the postwar years was suddenly unleashed. London became the capital of cool in fashion and music in the 'swinging '60s'.

The party didn't last long, however, and London returned to the doldrums in the harsh economic climate of the 1970s. Recovery began – for the business community at least – under the iron fist of Margaret Thatcher, elected Britain's first woman prime minister in 1979. Her monetarist policy and determination to crush socialism sent unemployment skyrocketing and her term was marked by civil unrest.

London got its first true mayor in 2000 when feisty 'Red' Ken Livingstone swept to victory on the promise that he would lock horns with the central government when it came to doing what was best for

TOP FIVE OLD-FASHIONED LONDON

- **The Ritz** (p120)
- **Fortnum & Mason** (p139)
- **Wallace Collection** (p113)
- **Buckingham Palace** (p101)
- **Inns of Court** (p105)

London. His big plan has been to improve public transport and reduce traffic congestion. Londoners voted for it but weren't too happy when he made moves to fix it. However, even the most cynical locals concede that Ken's controversial 'congestion tax' on vehicles entering central London has reduced the traffic jams, and the mayor has also followed through on his word to get the buses running on time.

ORIENTATION

The city's main geographical feature is the murky Thames, a river that was sufficiently deep (for anchorage) and narrow (for bridging) to attract the Romans here in the first place. It divides the city roughly into north and south.

The 'square mile' of the City of London – the capital's financial district – is counted as one of London's 33 council-run boroughs and is referred to simply as 'the City' (look for the capital 'C'). The M25 ring road encompasses the 607 sq miles that is broadly regarded as Greater London.

London's Underground railway ('the tube') makes this enormous city relatively accessible. The Underground map – now a London icon – is easy to use although geographically confounding. Most of the important sights, theatres, restaurants and even affordable places to stay lie within a reasonably compact rectangle formed by the tube's Circle Line (colour-coded yellow), which encircles central London just north of the river.

Londoners commonly refer to areas by their postcode. The letters correspond to compass directions from the centre of London, approximately St Paul's Cathedral. EC means East Central, W means West and so on. The numbering system after the letters is less helpful: 1 is the centre of the zone but after that it gets confusing.

LONDON

LONDON IN...

Two Days

Start your express tour with a walk around **Westminster** (p98) and its sights. You don't need to visit the sights to soak up the atmosphere. Head to grandiose **Trafalgar Square** (p97), and the **National Gallery** (p97) for a squiz at its sensational collection. Catch a Routemaster, open-backed bus into the heart of the West End and lunch in **Chinatown** (p103). Wander around **Soho** (p103) and **Covent Garden** (p103). On your way to **St Paul's Cathedral** (p106), have a look at **Somerset House** (p103) and stop for a cup of tea on its back terrace. Pull into the first traditional-looking pub you come across, peruse the listings and go and see a band.

Four Days

Visit the **British Museum** (p104), undergo some retail therapy, go to a football match and retire. Head 'sarf' of the river, have a go on the giant wheel, visit Charles Saatchi's 'Trophy Room' of contemporary Britart at the **Saatchi Gallery** (p110) and compare his collection with the fabulous **Tate Modern** (p109). Imagine Shakespeare at the **Globe Theatre** (p109). Get a big dollop of old London at **Borough Market** (p139) before heading to the hulking **Tower of London** (p107) for a history lesson. A riverside pub would be nice.

One Week

With the luxury of a week, go with the flow but try and see the following. **South Kensington** (p111) has three world-class museums and the inimitable **Harrods** (p139). The Victorian Valhalla of **Highgate Cemetery** (p114) is in north London but worth the trip. Don't miss **Portobello Rd Market** (p139) on the weekend. A day out in Greenwich – at the **National Maritime Museum** (p116) and on board **Cutty Sark** (p115) – will be well spent. You don't have to pay the exorbitant admission prices to get a feel for Royal London. Wander over to **Buckingham Palace** (p101) and **Kensington Palace** (p112), and around **St James's Park** (p101) and **Kensington Gardens** (p112). Marvel in outstanding smaller sights like **Sir John Soane's Museum** (p105) and the **Wallace Collection** (p113).

Maps

The *London A–Z* series is a range of excellent maps and hand-held street atlases. Lonely Planet also publishes a *London City Map*. Stanford's bookshop, see Bookshops below, is one of the best travel shops in the world.

INFORMATION
Bookshops

Foyle's (Map pp91-3; ☎ 7437 5660; 113-119 Charing Cross Rd WC2; ✆ Tottenham Court Road) Venerable and respected independent store with a broad range and a version of the old women's books specialist Silver Moon on the top floor.

Borders (Map pp91-3; ☎ 7292 1600; 203 Oxford St W1; ✆ Oxford Circus) Flagship of the huge nonunionising chain.

Waterstone's (Map pp91-3; ☎ 7851 2400; 203-206 Piccadilly W1; ✆ Piccadilly Circus) The best of this book-purveying giant.

Books for Cooks (Map pp82-3; ☎ 7221 1992; 4 Blenheim Cres W11; ✆ Ladbroke Grove) What the label says.

Forbidden Planet (Map pp91-3; ☎ 7836 4179; 179 Shaftesbury Ave; ✆ Leicester Square or Covent Garden) A trove of comics, sci-fi, horror and fantasy literature.

Gay's the Word (Map pp80-1; ☎ 7278 7654; 66 Marchmont St WC1; ✆ Russell Square) Everything from advice on coming out to queer and lesbian literature.

Grant & Cutler (Map pp91-3; ☎ 7734 2012; 55-57 Great Marlborough St W1; ✆ Oxford Circus) The best foreign language store in town.

Helter Skelter (Map pp91-3; ☎ 7836 1151; 4 Denmark St WC2; ✆ Oxford Circus) Biographies, fanzines and rock literature.

Sportspages (Map pp91-3; ☎ 7240 9604; 94-96 Charing Cross Rd WC2; ✆ Leicester Square or Tottenham Court Road) For the inside track on sporting heroes, heroics and help on how to.

Stanfords (Map pp91-3; ☎ 7836 1321; 12-14 Long Acre W C2; ✆ Covent Garden) The grandaddy of travel bookstores.

The Travel Bookshop (Map pp82-3; ☎ 7229 5260; 13 Blenheim Cres W11; ✆ Ladbroke Grove) The latest guidebooks, travel literature and antiquarian gems.

Zwemmer Art & Architecture (Map pp91-3; ☎ 7240 4158; 24 Litchfield St WC2; ✆ Tottenham Court Road) Tomes of fine art here and photography and cinema across the road.

LONDON UNDERGROUND MAP

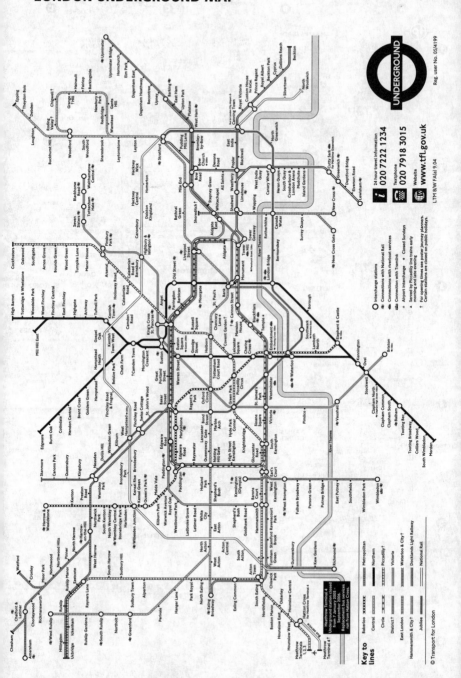

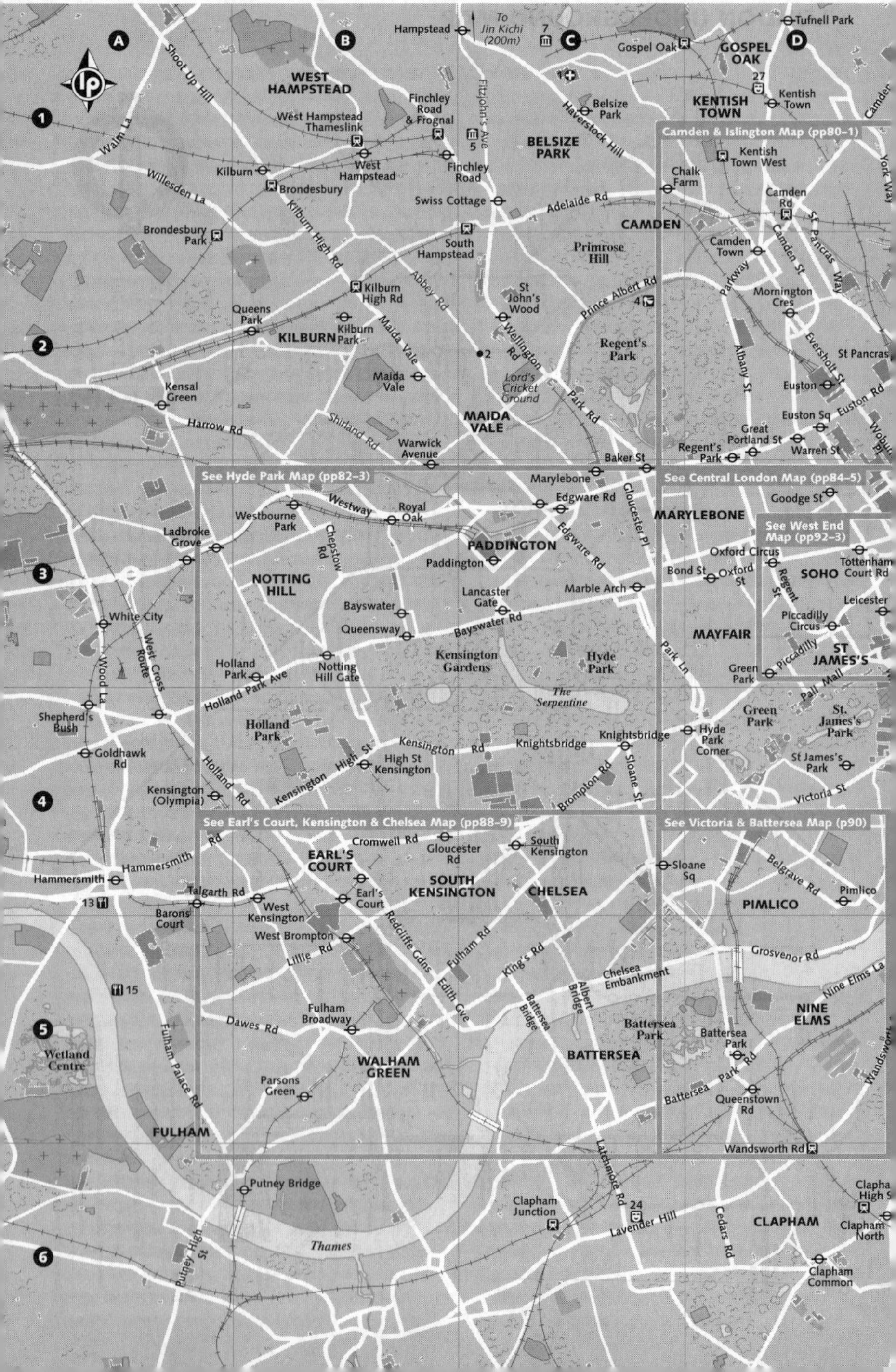
A
B
C
D
1
2
3
4
5
6
To Jin Kichi (200m)
Hampstead
Tufnell Park
Gospel Oak
GOSPEL OAK
WEST HAMPSTEAD
KENTISH TOWN
Kentish Town
Shoot Up Hill
Finchley Road & Frognal
Fitzjohn's Ave
Belsize Park
Haverstock Hill
West Hampstead Thameslink
BELSIZE PARK
Camden & Islington Map (pp80–1)
Walm La
Kilburn
West Hampstead
Finchley Road
Kentish Town West
Willesden La
Brondesbury
Chalk Farm
York Way
Swiss Cottage
Adelaide Rd
Camden Rd
Kilburn High Rd
CAMDEN
Brondesbury Park
South Hampstead
Primrose Hill
Camden Town
Camden St
St Pancras Way
Abbey Rd
Prince Albert Rd
Parkway
Kilburn High Rd
St John's Wood
Mornington Cres
Queens Park
Kilburn Park
Maida Vale
Wellington Rd
KILBURN
Regent's Park
Eversholt St
St Pancras
Albany St
Kensal Green
Maida Vale
Lord's Cricket Ground
Euston
Euston Rd
Park Rd
Harrow Rd
MAIDA VALE
Shirland Rd
Euston Sq
Great Portland St
Warwick Avenue
Regent's Park
Warren St
Baker St
See Hyde Park Map (pp82–3)
Marylebone
See Central London Map (pp84–5)
Goodge St
Westway
Royal Oak
Edgware Rd
Westbourne Park
Chepstow Rd
Edgware Rd
Gloucester Pl
MARYLEBONE
See West End Map (pp92–3)
Ladbroke Grove
PADDINGTON
Paddington
Oxford Circus
Tottenham Court Rd
NOTTING HILL
Bond St
Oxford St
SOHO
Regent St
Lancaster Gate
Marble Arch
Bayswater
Leicester
White City
Queensway
Bayswater Rd
Piccadilly Circus
MAYFAIR
West Cross Route
Wood La
Kensington Gardens
Hyde Park
Park Ln
Piccadilly
ST JAMES'S
Holland Park
Notting Hill Gate
The Serpentine
Green Park
Holland Park Ave
Pall Mall
Shepherd's Bush
Holland Park
Green Park
St. James's Park
Knightsbridge
Hyde Park Corner
Goldhawk Rd
Kensington Rd
Knightsbridge
High St Kensington
Kensington High St
St James's Park
Kensington (Olympia)
Holland Rd
Brompton Rd
Sloane St
Victoria St
See Earl's Court, Kensington & Chelsea Map (pp88–9)
See Victoria & Battersea Map (p90)
Cromwell Rd
Gloucester Rd
South Kensington
EARL'S COURT
Sloane Sq
Hammersmith Rd
Belgrave Rd
Hammersmith
SOUTH KENSINGTON
Earl's Court
CHELSEA
Pimlico
Talgarth Rd
PIMLICO
West Kensington
Barons Court
West Brompton
Redcliffe Gdns
Lillie Rd
Fulham Rd
King's Rd
Grosvenor Rd
Chelsea Embankment
Edith Gve
Albert Bridge
Nine Elms La
Fulham Broadway
Battersea Bridge
Battersea Park
NINE ELMS
Dawes Rd
Wetland Centre
Battersea Park
Fulham Palace Rd
WALHAM GREEN
BATTERSEA
Wandsworth Rd
Battersea Park Rd
Parsons Green
Queenstown Rd
FULHAM
Wandsworth Rd
Putney Bridge
Clapham Junction
Latchmere Rd
Clapham High St
Lavender Hill
Cedars Rd
CLAPHAM
Clapham North
Putney High St
Thames
Clapham Common

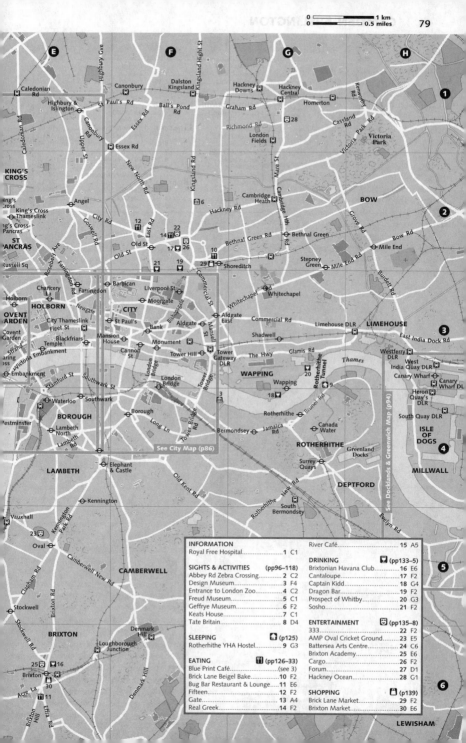

0 ___ 1 km
0 ___ 0.5 miles

E Caledonian Rd · Highbury Gve · Highbury & Islington · Canonbury · Ball's Pond Rd

F Dalston Kingsland · Kingsland High St

G Hackney Downs · Hackney Central · Homerton

H

Caledonian Rd

St Paul's Rd · Canonbury · Upper St · Essex Rd · Graham Rd · Mare St · Kennedy Rd · Victoria Park Rd

KING'S CROSS

King's Cross Thameslink · King's Cross-Pancras · ST PANCRAS · Russell Sq

Canonbury · New North Rd · Essex Rd · Richmond Rd · London Fields · Cambridge Heath · Cambridge Hth · Cassland Rd · Victoria Park · **BOW**

Angel · City Rd · Goswell Rd · Old St · Hackney Rd · Bethnal Green Rd · Bethnal Green · Grove Rd · Bow Rd · Mile End

1
2

Chancery · Farringdon · Barbican · Liverpool St · Moorgate · Commercial St · Whitechapel · Whitechapel · Stepney Green · Mile End Rd · Mile End · Burdett Rd

HOLBORN · Holborn · Newgate · **CITY** · St Paul's · Bishopsgate · Aldgate · Aldgate East · Commercial Rd · Limehouse DLR · **LIMEHOUSE** · East India Dock Rd

COVENT GARDEN · Covent Garden · Strand · Charing Cross · Embankment · Victoria Embankment · City Thameslink · Fleet St · Blackfriars · Temple · Mansion House · Bank · Cannon St · Monument · Tower Hill · Tower Gateway DLR · The Hwy · Glamis Rd · **WAPPING** · Rotherhithe Tunnel · Westferry DLR · West India Quay DLR · Canary Wharf · Canary Wharf DLR · Heron Quay's DLR · South Quay DLR

3

Waterloo · Southwark Bridge · London Bridge · London Bridge · Tower Bridge · Wapping · Brunel Rd · Thames · **ISLE OF DOGS**

BOROUGH · Lambeth North · Lambeth Rd · Borough · Long Ln · Tower Bridge Rd · Bermondsey · Jamaica Rd · Rotherhithe · Canada Water · **ROTHERHITHE** · Greenland Docks · **MILLWALL**

4

See City Map (p86)

LAMBETH · Elephant & Castle · Old Kent Rd · Surrey Quays · **DEPTFORD**

Kennington · Rotherhithe New Rd · South Bermondsey · Evelyn Rd

See Docklands & Greenwich Map (p94)

Vauxhall · Oval · Kennington Park Rd · Camberwell New Rd · **CAMBERWELL**

5

Clapham Rd · Brixton Rd · Stockwell · Stockwell Rd · **BRIXTON** · Denmark Hill · Loughborough Junction · Denmark Hill · Brixton · Acre Ln · Brixton Hill · Effra Rd

LEWISHAM

6

A   B   C   D

INFORMATION
Eastman Dental Hospital...........1 F5
Gay's the Word......................2 E6
STA Travel.........................3 D5

SIGHTS & ACTIVITIES (p114)
Camden Market.....................4 B3

SLEEPING (pp120–3)
Crescent Hotel.....................5 D5
Generator..........................6 E6
Harlingford Hotel..................7 E6
Jenkins Hotel......................8 D5
Zetter Hotel.......................9 H6

EATING (pp131–2)
Afghan Kitchen....................10 H3
Almeida...........................11 H3
Café Delancey.....................12 B3

Diwana............................13 C5
Eagle.............................14 G6
Engineer..........................15 A3
Le Mercury........................16 H2
North Sea Fish Restaurant.........17 E5

DRINKING (pp134–5)
Bar Vinyl.........................18 B3
Crown & Goose.....................19 B3
Medicine Bar......................20 H2
Pembroke Castle...................21 A2

ENTERTAINMENT (pp135–8)
Almeida Theatre...................22 H3
Barfly@the Monarch................23 A2
Cross.............................24 E3
Garage............................25 H1
Jazz Café.........................26 B3
Sadler's Wells....................27 G5

Kentish
Town West

CAMDEN

Chalk
Farm

23

21

Camden
Lock Pl

Camden Rd

Bonny St

Baynes St

Barker Dve

Gloucester Ave

Buck St
4

18

Jamestown Rd

Camden
Town

15

26

Greenland
Rd

Lyme St

**CAMDEN
TOWN**

St Pancras Way

Royal College St

Camley St

Regent's Park Rd

19

Prince Albert Rd

Delancey St

12

Camden High St

Bayham St

Plender St

College Pl

St Pancras
Gardens

Camley
Garden St
Natural Par

Pancras Rd

**London
Zoo**

Mornington
Cres

Crowndale Rd

**Regent's
Park
Barracks**

Granby Tce

**Regent's
Park**

Cumberland Tce

**SOMERS
TOWN**
Drummond
Cres

4

Albany St

Harrington St

Euston
Station

Euston

Brita
Libra

5

**Queen
Mary's
Gardens**

Chester Rd

Chester
Gate

Clarence
Gardens

Robert St

St James
Gardens

William Rd

13

Euston Rd

Euston Sq

**Boating
Lake**

Longford St

Drummond St

6

Outer Cir

Park Square
Gardens

Warren St

**Regent's
Park**
Park Cres

Great
Portland
St

**Fitzroy
Square**

BLOOMSBURY

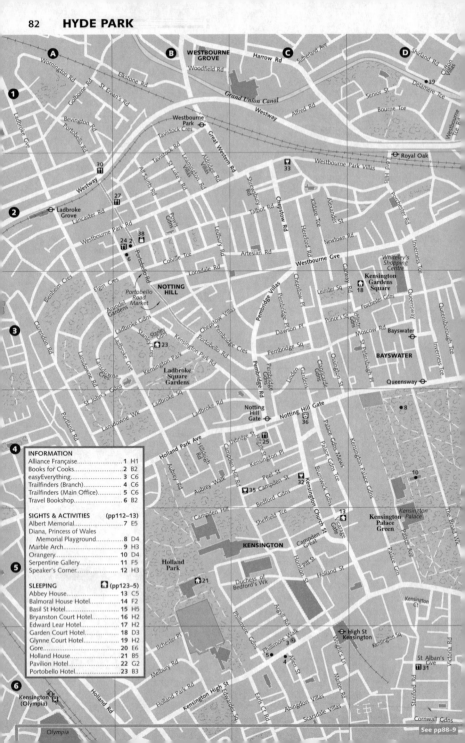

INFORMATION

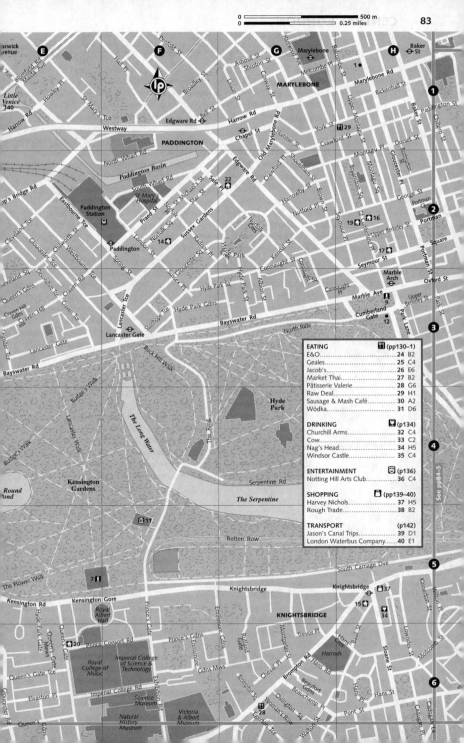

EATING 🍴 (pp130–1)
E&O	**24**	B2
Geales	**25**	C4
Jacob's	**26**	E6
Market Thai	**27**	B2
Pâtisserie Valerie	**28**	G6
Raw Deal	**29**	H1
Sausage & Mash Café	**30**	A2
Wódka	**31**	D6

DRINKING 🍷 (p134)
Churchill Arms	**32**	C4
Cow	**33**	C2
Nag's Head	**34**	H5
Windsor Castle	**35**	C4

ENTERTAINMENT 🎭 (p136)
Notting Hill Arts Club	**36**	C4

SHOPPING 🛍 (pp139–40)
Harvey Nichols	**37**	H5
Rough Trade	**38**	B2

TRANSPORT (p142)
Jason's Canal Trips	**39**	D1
London Waterbus Company	**40**	E1

See pp84–5

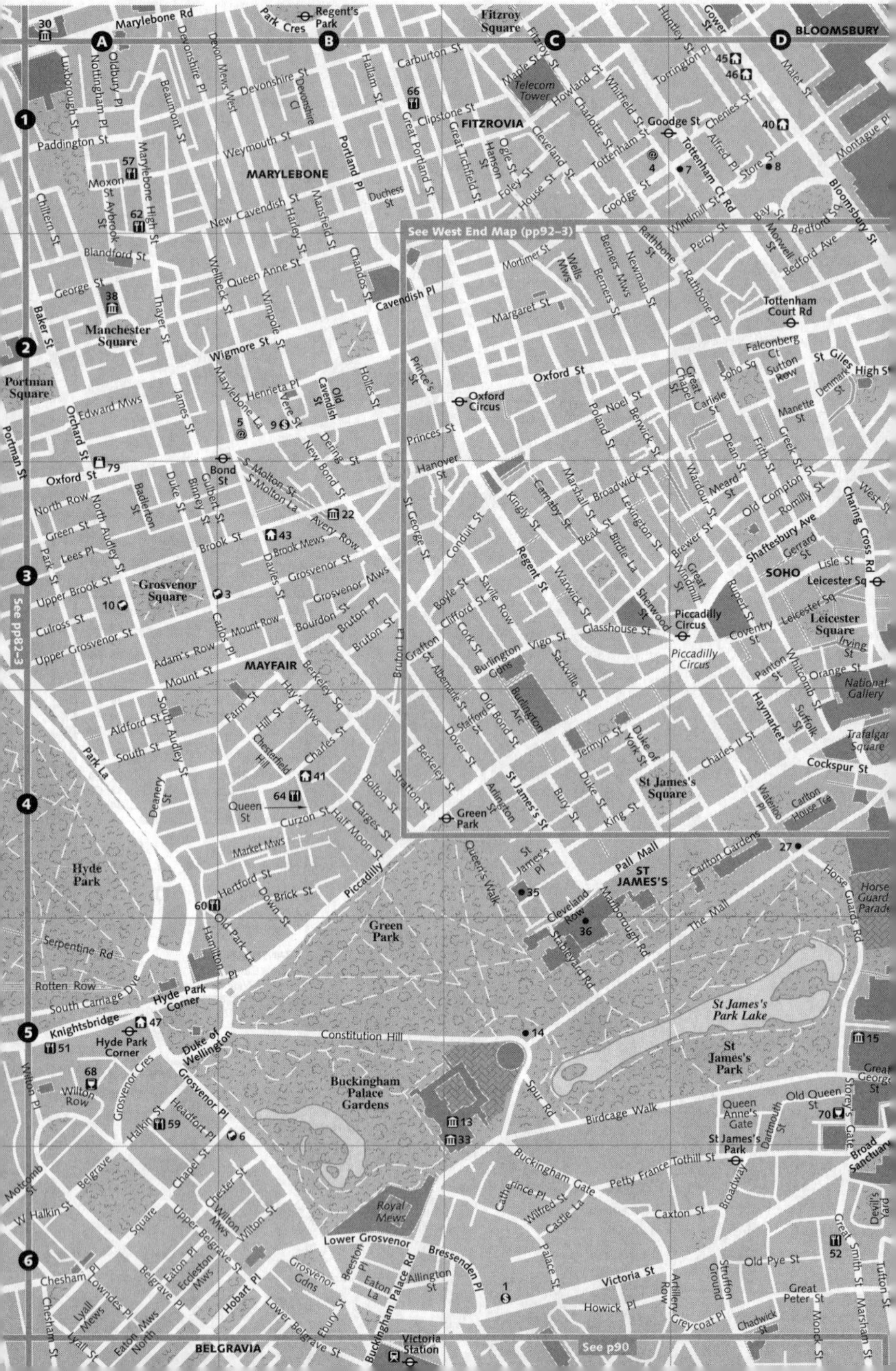

A
B
C
D
1
2
3
4
5
6
BLOOMSBURY
FITZROVIA
MARYLEBONE
MAYFAIR
SOHO
ST JAMES'S
BELGRAVIA
Marylebone Rd
Regent's Park
Park Cres
Fitzroy Square
Telecom Tower
Goodge St
Tottenham Ct Rd
Tottenham Court Rd
Oxford Circus
Bond St
Piccadilly Circus
Leicester Sq
Green Park
Hyde Park Corner
St James's Park
Victoria Station
See West End Map (pp92–3)
See pp82–3
See p90
Luxborough St
Nottingham Pl
Oldbury Pl
Devonshire Pl
Devon Mews West
Devonshire St
Devonshire Cl
Beaumont St
Paddington St
Moxon St
Aybrook St
Chiltern St
Marylebone High St
Weymouth St
New Cavendish St
Harley St
Mansfield St
Portland Pl
Hallam St
Carburton St
Great Portland St
Clipstone St
Great Titchfield St
Hanson St
Ogle St
Foley St
Cleveland St
Howland St
Charlotte St
Whitfield St
Maple St
Fitzroy St
Huntley St
Gower St
Torrington Pl
Chenies St
Alfred Pl
Store St
Malet St
Montague Pl
Bloomsbury Sq
Bloomsbury St
Tottenham St
Goodge St
Windmill St
House St
Duchess St
Blandford St
George St
Baker St
Manchester Square
Thayer St
Welbeck St
Queen Anne St
Wimpole St
Chandos St
Cavendish Pl
Wigmore St
Portman Square
Portman St
Orchard St
Edward Mws
James St
Marylebone La
Henrieta Pl
Vere St
Old Cavendish St
Holles St
Dering St
New Bond St
Oxford St
Bond St
S Molton St
S Molton La
Gilbert St
Binney St
Duke St
Balderton St
North Row
North Audley St
Green St
Lees Pl
Park St
Upper Brook St
Grosvenor Square
Culross St
Upper Grosvenor St
Brook St
Brook Mews
Avery Row
Davies St
Grosvenor St
Grosvenor Mws
Bourdon St
Bruton Pl
Bruton St
Bruton La
Carlos Pl
Mount Row
Adam's Row
Mount St
Berkeley Sq
Hay's Mws
Farm St
South Audley St
Aldford St
South St
Hill St
Chesterfield Hill
Charles St
Park La
Deanery St
Queen St
Curzon St
Half Moon St
Clarges St
Bolton St
Stratton St
Market Mws
Hertford St
Brick St
Down St
Piccadilly
Hyde Park
Serpentine Rd
Rotten Row
South Carriage Dve
Hamilton Pl
Old Park La
Knightsbridge
Wilton Pl
Wilton Row
Grosvenor Cres
Halkin St
Headfort Pl
Grosvenor Pl
Duke of Wellington
Constitution Hill
Buckingham Palace Gardens
Green Park
Queen's Walk
St James's Pl
Pall Mall
Carlton Gardens
Cleveland Row
Marlborough Rd
Stableyard Rd
The Mall
Horse Guards Rd
Horse Guard Parade
St James's Park Lake
St James's Park
Spur Rd
Birdcage Walk
Queen Anne's Gate
Old Queen St
Dartmouth St
Storey's Gate
Great George St
Broad Sanctuary
Buckingham Gate
Petty France
Tothill St
Broadway
Catherine Pl
Wilfred St
Castle La
Caxton St
Palace St
Royal Mews
Lower Grosvenor Pl
Bressenden Pl
Buckingham Palace Rd
Allington St
Beeston Pl
Eaton La
Grosvenor Gdns
Victoria St
Artillery Row
Stufton Ground
Old Pye St
Great Peter St
Howick Pl
Greycoat Pl
Chadwick St
Great Smith St
Marsham St
Monck St
Tufton St
Devil's Yard
Motcomb St
W Halkin St
Belgrave Square
Chapel St
Chester St
Wilton Mws
Wilton St
Upper Belgrave St
Eaton Pl
Eccleston Mws
Hobart Pl
Lower Belgrave St
Ebury St
Chesham Pl
Chesham St
Lowndes Pl
Lyall Mews
Lyall St
Eaton Mws North
Belgrave Pl
Mortimer St
Wells Mws
Berners Mws
Berners St
Newman St
Rathbone St
Rathbone Pl
Percy St
Bay St
Morwell St
Bedford Sq
Bedford Ave
Margaret St
Falconberg Ct
Sutton Row
Soho Sq
St Giles High St
Denmark St
Great Chapel St
Carlisle St
Manette St
Prince's St
Princes St
Hanover St
Noel St
Poland St
Berwick St
Dean St
Frith St
Greek St
Charing Cross Rd
West St
St George St
Conduit St
Kingly St
Carnaby St
Marshall St
Broadwick St
Lexington St
Wardour St
Meard St
Old Compton St
Romilly St
Shaftesbury Ave
Beak St
Birdie La
Brewer St
Great Windmill St
Gerrard St
Lisle St
Regent St
Warwick St
Sherwood St
Rupert St
Leicester Square
Boyle St
Savile Row
Clifford St
Cork St
Glasshouse St
Coventry St
Irving St
Grafton St
Albemarle St
Burlington Gdns
Vigo St
Sackville St
Burlington Arc
Panton St
Whitcomb St
Orange St
National Gallery
Stafford St
Dover St
Old Bond St
Jermyn St
Duke of York St
Haymarket
Suffolk St
Trafalgar Square
Berkeley St
Arlington St
St James's St
Bury St
Duke St
King St
St James's Square
Charles II St
Waterloo Pl
Carlton House Tce
Cockspur St

INFORMATION
American Express.............................. 1 C6
Australian High Commission.............. 2 F3
Canadian High Commission................ 3 A3
Cyberia... 4 C1
easyEverything................................. 5 B2
Irish Embassy................................... 6 B5
STA Travel....................................... 7 D1
STA Travel....................................... 8 D1
Thomas Cook...............................(see 1)
Thomas Cook Branch........................ 9 B2
US Embassy.................................... 10 A3

SIGHTS & ACTIVITIES   (pp96–118)
Banqueting House............................ 11 E5
Big Ben.. 12 E5
Buckingham Palace.......................... 13 C5
Buckingham Palace Ticket Office
    (Summer Only)............................ 14 C5
Cabinet War Rooms.......................... 15 D5
Cenotaph....................................... 16 E5
Central Criminal Court (Old Bailey)..... 17 H2
Dr Johnson's House.......................... 18 G2
Florence Nightingale Museum............ 19 F5
Foreign & Commonwealth Office
    Visitor Centre............................. 20 E5
Gilbert Collection............................ 21 F3
Handel House Museum..................... 22 B3
Hayward Gallery............................. 23 F4
Hermitage Rooms........................(see 21)
Houses of Parliament....................... 24 E6
Imperial War Museum...................... 25 G6
Inns of Court.................................. 26 F1
Institute for Contemporary Arts........ 27 D4

London Aquarium............................ 28 F5
London Eye..................................... 29 F5
London Planetarium.....................(see 30)
Madam Tussaud's............................ 30 A1
New Parliament Building................... 31 E5
No 10 Downing Street...................... 32 E5
Queen's Gallery.............................. 33 C5
Royal Courts of Justice..................... 34 F2
Spencer House................................ 35 C4
St James's Palace............................. 36 C5
Temple Church................................ 37 G3
Wallace Collection........................... 38 A2
Westminster Abbey......................... 39 E6

SLEEPING   🛏 (pp120–6)
Academy Hotel................................ 40 D1
Chesterfield.................................... 41 B4
City of London YHA.......................... 42 H3
Claridges....................................... 43 B3
County Hall Travel Inn Capital........... 44 F5
Hotel Cavendish.............................. 45 D1
Jesmond Hotel................................ 46 D1
Lanesborough................................. 47 A5
Malmaison..................................... 48 H1
Ridgemount Hotel.......................(see 46)
Rookery... 49 H1
St Margaret's Hotel......................... 50 E1

EATING   🍴 (pp126–33)
Boxwood Café................................ 51 A5
Cinnamon Club............................... 52 D6
Club Gascon................................... 53 H1
Dim Sum....................................... 54 H3
Greenery....................................... 55 H1

Konditor & Cook............................. 56 G5
La Fromagerie Café.......................... 57 A1
Mesón Don Felipe........................... 58 G5
Nahm... 59 A5
Nobu... 60 A4
Oxo Tower Restaurant
    & Brasserie................................ 61 G4
Providores..................................... 62 A1
St John.. 63 H1
Tamarind....................................... 64 B4
Tas... 65 G5
Villandry....................................... 66 B1

DRINKING   🍷 (pp133–5)
Cock Tavern................................... 67 H1
Grenadier...................................... 68 A5
Red Lion.. 69 E5
Westminster Arms........................... 70 D5
Ye Olde Cheshire
    Cheese..................................... 71 G2
Ye Olde Mitre................................. 72 G1

ENTERTAINMENT   🎭 (pp135–8)
Fabric... 73 H1
National Film Theatre....................... 74 F4
Purcell Room..............................(see 75)
Queen Elizabeth Hall....................... 75 F4
Royal Festival Hall........................... 76 F4
Royal National Theatre..................... 77 F4
Young Vic..................................(see 56)

SHOPPING   🛍 (pp138–40)
London Silver Vaults........................ 78 F2
Selfridges...................................... 79 A3

CITY (p87)

INFORMATION
American Express.............................. 1 A2

SIGHTS & ACTIVITIES   (pp105–118)
Bank of England Museum.................... 2 B2
Britain at War Experience................... 3 C4
Fashion & Textile Museum.................. 4 C5
Greater London Authority Building....... 5 D4
Guildhall Art Gallery.......................... 6 B2
HMS Belfast.................................... 7 C4
London Dungeon.............................. 8 B4
Monument...................................... 9 B3
Museum of London......................... 10 A2
Old Operating Theatre Museum &
    Herb Garret............................... 11 B4
Shakespeare's Globe & Exhibition........ 12 A4

Southwark Cathedral....................... 13 B4
St Bartholomew-the-Great................ 14 A1
St Mary-le-Bow.............................. 15 A2
Tate Modern.................................. 16 A4

SLEEPING   🛏 (p123)
Great Eastern Hotel......................... 17 C1
St Christopher's Village.................... 18 B5

EATING   🍴 (pp128–9)
Arkansas Café................................ 19 D1
Crussh... 20 C2
Delfina... 21 C5
Fish!.. 22 B4
Konditor & Cook............................. 23 B4
Le Taj... 24 D1

Manze's.. 25 C6
Place Below...............................(see 15)
Sweeting's.................................... 26 A3

DRINKING   🍷 (p134)
Anchor.. 27 B4
George Inn.................................... 28 B4
Jamaica Wine
    House...................................... 29 B3
Market Porter................................ 30 B4

ENTERTAINMENT   🎭 (p136)
Ministry of Sound............................ 31 A6

SHOPPING   🛍 (p139)
Bermondsey Market......................... 32 C6

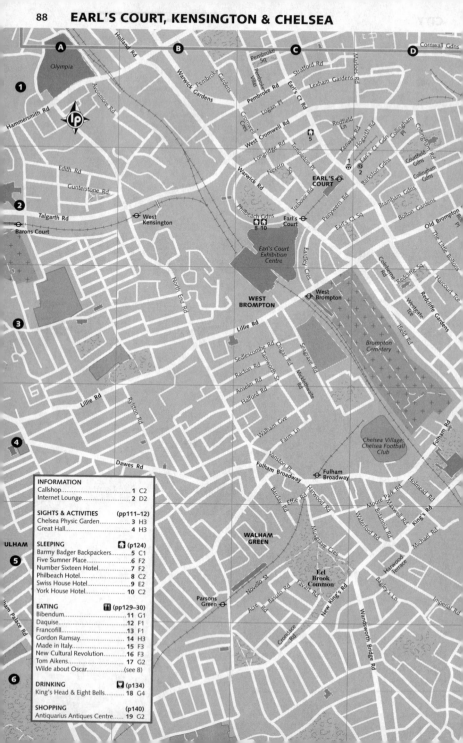

INFORMATION
Callshop	**1**	C2
Internet Lounge	**2**	D2

SIGHTS & ACTIVITIES (pp111–12)
Chelsea Physic Garden	**3**	H3
Great Hall	**4**	H3

SLEEPING (p124)
Barmy Badger Backpackers	**5**	C1
Five Sumner Place	**6**	F2
Number Sixteen Hotel	**7**	F2
Philbeach Hotel	**8**	C2
Swiss House Hotel	**9**	E2
York House Hotel	**10**	C2

EATING (pp129–30)
Bibendum	**11**	G1
Daquise	**12**	F1
Francofill	**13**	F1
Gordon Ramsay	**14**	H3
Made in Italy	**15**	F3
New Cultural Revolution	**16**	F3
Tom Aikens	**17**	G2
Wilde about Oscar	(see 8)	

DRINKING (p134)
King's Head & Eight Bells	**18**	G4

SHOPPING (p140)
Antiquarius Antiques Centre	**19**	G2

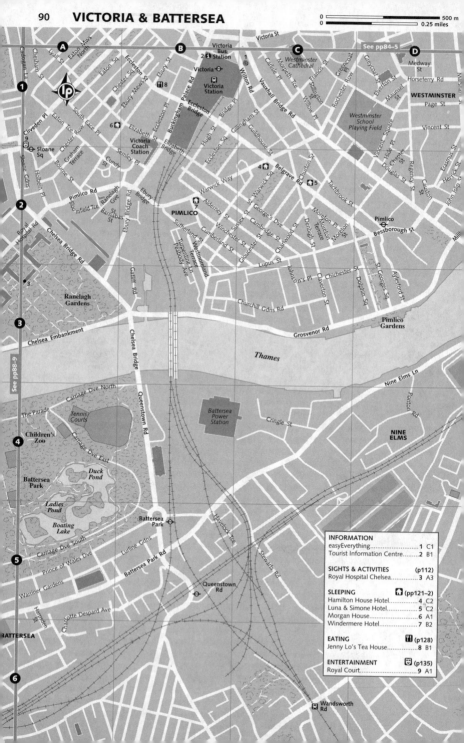

0   500 m
0   0.25 miles

INFORMATION
easyEverything.......................... 1 C1
Tourist Information Centre......... 2 B1

SIGHTS & ACTIVITIES   (p112)
Royal Hospital Chelsea.............. 3 A3

SLEEPING   (pp121–2)
Hamilton House Hotel................ 4 C2
Luna & Simone Hotel................. 5 C2
Morgan House........................... 6 A1
Windermere Hotel..................... 7 B2

EATING   (p128)
Jenny Lo's Tea House................. 8 B1

ENTERTAINMENT   (p135)
Royal Court.............................. 9 A1

0 ____ 500 m
0 ____ 0.25 miles

POPLAR

Ⓐ Ⓑ Poplar DLR Ⓒ Blackwell DLR Ⓓ

❶
West India Quay DLR
6
Cab Sq
Canary Wharf
Canary Wharf DLR
Heron Quay's DLR

Poplar Dock
Blackwall Basin

Blackwall Tunnel (New) Southbound
5 ● Millennium Dome
Blackwall Tunnel (Old) Northbound
North Greenwich

West India Docks

❷
South Quay DLR

Millwall Inner Dock

ISLE OF DOGS

Preston Rd

❸
Millwall Inner Dock
4
Crossharbour & London Arena DLR

Millwall Outer Dock

Mudchute Park

MILLWALL

❹
Thames

Mudchute DLR
Millwall Park

DEPTFORD

Manchester Rd
Island Gardens DLR
Saunders Ness Rd
Pelton Rd

Greenwich Foot Tunnel

❺
See Greater London Map (pp78-9)

13
Old Woolwich Rd
Tusk St
Trafalgar Rd
Maze Hill

INFORMATION	
Tourist Information Centre	**1** C5
SIGHTS & ACTIVITIES	**(pp115–16)**
Cutty Sark	**2** C5
Fan Museum	**3** C6
London Arena	**4** B3
Millennium Dome	**5** D2
Museum in Docklands	**6** A1
National Maritime Museum	**7** C5
Old Royal Navy College	**8** C5
Painted Hall	**9** C5
Queen's House	**10** D5
Royal Observatory	**11** D6
EATING	**🍴 (p132)**
Goddards Ye Olde Pie Shop	**12** C5
DRINKING	**🍺 (p135)**
Trafalgar Tavern	**13** D5

8
University of Greenwich
2 ● ❶ 1
9
Cutty Sark DLR 12
Romney Rd
7 10
Park Vista

Thames St
Creek Rd
Bardsley La
Norman Rd
Roan St

❻
King William Wk
Greenwich Park

3
GREENWICH
11
The Ave

Greenwich & Greenwich DLR
Greenwich High Rd
Tarves Way
Straightsmouth
Ashburnham Pl
Ashburnham

Cultural Centres

Alliance Française (Map pp82-3; ☎ 7723 6439; 1 Dorset Sq NW1; ⊖ Marylebone) Organises French-language classes, and social and cultural events.

British Council (Map pp91-3; ☎ 7930 8466; 10 Spring Gardens, SW1; ⊖ Charing Cross) Can advise foreign students on educational opportunities in Britain.

Emergency

Police/Fire/Ambulance (☎ 999)
Samaritans (☎ 08457 909 090)
Rape & Sexual Abuse Support Centre (☎ 8683 3300)

Internet Access

Cyberia (Map pp84-6; ☎ 7681 4223; 39 Whitfield St W1; ⊖ Goodge Street)

easyEverything (Map pp91-3; ☎ 7233 8456; 9-13 Wilton Rd SW1; ⊖ Victoria; 9-16 Tottenham Court Rd; ⊖ Tottenham Court Road) A chain with branches throughout central London.

Internet Exchange (Map pp91-3; ☎ 7836 8636; 37 The Market WC2; ⊖ Covent Garden) Another ubiquitous chain.

Internet Lounge (Map pp88-9; ☎ 7370 5742; 24A Earl's Court Gardens SW5; ⊖ Earl's Court)

Internet Resources

The Lonely Planet website (www.lonely planet.com) offers a speedy link to many of London's websites. You can also try the following:

BBC London (www.bbc.co.uk/London/whereyoulive)
Evening Standard (www.thisislondon.co.uk)
Time Out (www.timeout.com)
UK Weather (www.met-office.gov.uk)

Laundry

Many hostels and some hotels have self-service washing machines and dryers, and nearly every main street has a laundrette. The average cost to wash and dry a single load is £3. Your lodging will be able to guide you to the nearest laundrette.

Media

The only true London paper is the *Evening Standard*, a jingoistic tabloid that comes out in early and late editions throughout the day. *Metro* is a morning freebie from the same stable, while *Time Out* (£2.20) is the local listing guide par excellence, published every Wednesday.

Medical Services

To find a local doctor or hospital, consult the local telephone directory or call ☎ 100 (toll free). There is always one local chemist that opens 24 hours (see local newspapers or notices in chemist windows). In the event of a dental crisis, phone the **Dental Emergency Care Service** (☎ 7955 2186) weekdays between 8.45am and 3.30pm, or call into **Eastman Dental Hospital** (Map pp80-1; ☎ 7915 1000; 256 Gray's Inn Rd WC1; ⊖ King's Cross St Pancras).

Hospitals with 24-hour accident and emergency units include the following:

Guy's Hospital (Map pp86-87; ☎ 7955 5000; St Thomas St SE1; ⊖ London Bridge)

Royal Free Hospital (Map pp78-9; ☎ 7794 0500; Pond St NW3; ⊖ Belsize Park)

University College Hospital (Map pp80-1; ☎ 7387 9300; Grafton Way WC1; ⊖ Euston Square)

Money

Banks and ATMs abound across central London and most are linked to the international money systems such as Cirrus and Maestro. If you're carrying cash (besides asking for trouble), you won't have a problem changing it over because banks, bureaux de change and travel agents are tripping over themselves to get your business. If you use bureaux de change, make sure to check commission rates *and* exchange rates; some can be extortionate.

There are 24-hour bureaus in Heathrow Terminals 1, 3 and 4 (the one in Terminal 2 opens 6am to 11pm), in Gatwick's South and North Terminals, and at Stansted. The airport bureaus are good value; they charge less than most high-street banks – usually about 1.5% of the transaction value, with a £3 minimum. The following are reliable bureaus (both have outlets at Victoria train station):

American Express (AmEx; Map pp91-3; ☎ 7930 4411; 6 Haymarket SW1; currency exchange ☻ 9am-6pm Mon-Sat, 10am-5pm Sun; ⊖ Piccadilly Circus) Has branches all around town.

Thomas Cook (Map pp84-6; ☎ 7853 6400; 30 St James's St SW1; ☻ 9am-5.30pm Mon, Tue, Thu & Fri, 10am-5.30pm Wed, 9am-4pm Sat; ⊖ Green Park) Also has branches around London.

Post

London post offices usually open from 8.30am or 9am to 5pm or 5.30pm Monday to Friday. Some main ones also open 9am to noon or 1pm Saturday. The **Trafalgar Square post office** (Map pp91-3; GPO/Poste Restante; actually on William IV St) opens 8.30am to 6.30pm Monday to Friday, and 9am to 5.30pm Saturday.

Telephone

CallShop (Map pp88-9; ☎ 7390 4549; ✆ 9am-noon)
Earl's Court Rd (181A Earl's Court Rd SW5; ✦ Earl's Court)
Edgware Rd (189 Edgware Rd; ✦ Edgware Road) A private
company with cheaper international calls than British
Telecom (BT). You can also send and receive faxes.

Tourist Information

Britain Visitor Centre (Map pp91-3; www.visitbritain
.com; 1 Regent St SW1; ✆ 9am-6.30pm Mon-Fri year-
round; 10am-4pm Sat & Sun Oct-late Jun; 9am-5pm Sat,
10am-4pm Sun late Jun-Sep; ✦ Piccadilly Circus) A comprehensive information and booking centre with a map and
guidebook shop, accommodation desk, entertainment and
transport ticket desks, a bureau de change, international
telephones and computer terminals for accessing tourist information on the Internet. It handles walk-in inquirers only,
but there's lots of good information on its website. You can
also get the lowdown on the rest of the British Isles here.

Corporation of London information centre
(☎ 7332 1456; www.cityoflondon.gov.uk; ✆ 9.30am-
5pm daily Apr-Sep, 9.30am-5pm Mon-Fri, 9.30am-2pm Sat
the rest of the year; ✦ St Paul's) In St Paul's Churchyard
EC4, opposite St Paul's Cathedral.

London Line (☎ 09068 663344; per min 60p) A telephone service that will give you the lowdown on events
and attractions.

London Tourist Board & Convention Bureau (www
.londontown.com; Glen House, Stag Pl, London SW1E 5LT)
Send written inquiries here.

Tourist Information Centre (TIC) Victoria train
station (Map p90; ✆ 8am-8pm Mon-Sat, 8am-6pm Sun
Apr-Oct; 8am-7pm Mon-Sat, 8am-6pm Sun Nov-Mar;
✦ Victoria); Waterloo International Terminal (Map pp84-6;
✆ 8.30am-10.30pm; ✦ Waterloo); Liverpool Street station
(Map pp86-7; ✆ 8am-6pm; ✦ Liverpool St); Heathrow
Terminals 1, 2 & 3 (✆ 8am-6pm) The Victoria train station
branch is London's main TIC and handles accommodation
bookings. It can get positively mobbed in the peak season.
TICs are also at Gatwick, Stansted, Luton and London City
airports. You'll also find information desks at Paddington
train station and Victoria coach station.

Travel Agencies

STA Travel Old Brompton Rd (Map pp88-9; European inquiries ☎ 7361 6161, worldwide inquiries ☎ 7361 6262,
tours, accommodation, car hire or insurance ☎ 7361
6160; www.statravel.co.uk; 86 Old Brompton Rd SW7;
✦ South Kensington); Euston Rd (Map pp80-1; 117 Euston
Rd NW1; ✦ Euston) Long-standing and reliable.

Trailfinders (Map pp82-3; long-haul travel ☎ 7938
3939, 1st- & business-class flights ☎ 7938 3444; www
.trailfinders.com; 194 Kensington High St W8; ✆ 9am-
5pm Mon-Wed & Fri, 9am-6pm Thu, 10am-5.15pm Sat;
✦ High Street Kensington) A visa and passport service

(☎ 7938 3848), immunisation centre (☎ 7938 3999),
foreign exchange (☎ 7938 3836) and information centre
(☎ 7938 3303).

DANGERS & ANNOYANCES

Considering its size and the disparities in
wealth, London is remarkably safe and the
closest you'll probably come to robbery is
the daylight variety in tourist areas. That
said, don't take anything for granted and
don't let your guard down too low, particularly in heavily touristed areas.

Take particular care at night. When travelling by tube, choose a carriage with other
people in it and avoid deserted suburban
stations. Solo women travellers should avoid
unlicensed minicabs at night. The drivers are
often unreliable and occasionally dangerous.

Scams

Wherever tourists congregate, you're always
going to get a few scallies trying to part
them and their money, although London's
not nearly as bad as many other capitals.
Scams come and go. At the time of research,
card-cloning was becoming a problem.
Cards can be copied at ATM cashpoints,
and if someone can see your PIN they can
take off with a cloned copy of your card. So
guard your PIN details carefully.

Hotel and hostel touts descend on backpackers at popular tube and mainline stations. Don't accept lifts from them unless
you know exactly where you are going. In
general, if an offer appears too good to be
true, then it probably is.

Some Soho strip clubs and hostess bars are
dodgy, and people should be especially wary
of those that tout for business on the street.

SIGHTS

It's difficult to get your bearings in vast
and sprawling London, and only more
difficult if you're using the geographically
nonsensical tube to get around. Your best
bet is to start in the tourist heart, the West
End, which incorporates familiar names like
Soho, Covent Garden and Bloomsbury. It's
around here you'll find many of London's
finest galleries and museums, its mainstream
entertainment, its funkiest shopping and its
steepest prices. West of here you enter what
you might picture as old-money London,
incorporating the la-di-da neighbourhoods
of Mayfair, St James's and Kensington. This

LONDON FOR FREE

It's possible to savour some of London's greatest sights for free. You won't have to cough up any money to visit the following: the British Museum, National Gallery, National Portrait Gallery, Theatre Museum, Guildhall, Museum of London, Tate Modern, Bank of England Museum, Imperial War Museum, Victoria & Albert (V&A) Museum, National History Museum, Science Museum and the Wallace Collection. Plus, well, stacks of others.

---

is where royalty resides and the cashed-up play. It's also where you will find some outstanding museums. It gets groovier as you head north into the likes of Marylebone and Notting Hill, while to the south is Westminster, Whitehall and the cradle of British democracy.

Across the river from the West End, conveniently called the South Bank, is an area that has been regenerated in the last decade or so and is now home to some of London's most popular attractions, including the London Eye, the Tate Modern and the Saatchi Gallery. Heading anticlockwise over the river again is Britain's financial cockpit, a square mile known simply as the City (note the capital 'C'). St Paul's Cathedral is the main draw for you here. Continuing the loop you'll come upon the reclaimed areas of Hoxton and Shoreditch, new centres of London cool, and then on to Camden and Islington, the ones they replaced.

Trafalgar Square

In many ways Trafalgar Sq is the centre of London, where great rallies and marches have taken place, and the New Year is ushered in by tens of thousands of revellers. It's also here that Londoners congregate to celebrate anything from football victories to the ousting of political leaders. While neglected for many decades, when it was ringed with gnarling traffic and invaded by pesky pigeons, it has undergone a remarkable transformation in recent years and stakes a claim to being one of the world's grandest public places.

It's now easier to appreciate not only the square but also the splendid buildings flanking it: the National Gallery, the National Portrait Gallery and the eye-catching church of St Martin-in-the-Fields. The ceremonial **Pall Mall** runs southwest from the top of the square. To the southwest stands **Admiralty Arch** (erected in honour of Queen Victoria in 1910), beyond which the Mall leads to

Buckingham Palace. The 43.5m-high **Nelson's Column** – upon which the admiral surveys his fleet of ships to the southwest – has stood in the centre of the square since 1843 and commemorates Nelson's victory over Napoleon off Cape Trafalgar in Spain in 1805.

NATIONAL GALLERY

There's an astonishing collection of European paintings at the **National Gallery** (Map pp91-3; ☎ 7747 2885; www.nationalgallery.org.uk; Trafalgar Sq WC2; admission free, temporary exhibition prices vary; ❤ 10am-6pm Thu-Tue, 10am-9pm Wed; ❷ Charing Cross), one of the finest galleries in the world and a destination for some five million visitors each year.

More than 2000 paintings form a continuous time-line, from the Old Masters (1260–1510) in the Sainsbury addition and the Renaissance-influenced West Wing (1510–1600) to the Dutch and Italian-focused North Wing (1600–1700) and East Wing (1700–1900).

The highlights listed in the boxed text (p98) show the cream of the gallery's exhibits, but if you want to know a lot more borrow an audio guide (contribution suggested) from the central hall and simply punch in the number of each painting that catches your eye. Free one-hour guided tours introduce you to a manageable half-dozen paintings at a time, and leave at 11.30am and 2.30pm on weekdays and at 2pm and 3.30pm on Saturday (additional tour at 6.30pm on Wednesday). A **Micro Gallery** (❤ 10am-5.30pm Thu-Tue, 10am-8.30pm Wed), on the 1st floor of the Sainsbury Wing, has interactive screens providing a visual encyclopedia of the collection. The gallery provides activity sheets for kids.

NATIONAL PORTRAIT GALLERY

As much about history as about art, this **gallery** (Map pp91-3; ☎ 7306 0055; www.npg.org.uk; St Martin's Cres WC2; admission free; ❤ 10am-6pm Sat-Wed, 10am-9pm Thu-Fri; ❷ Charing Cross) provides a great

NATIONAL GALLERY HIGHLIGHTS

- *The Arnolfini Portrait* – van Eyck
- *Rokeby Venus* – Velázquez
- *The Wilton Diptych Bathers* – Cézanne
- *Venus and Mars* – Botticelli
- *The Virgin of the Rocks* – da Vinci
- *The Virgin and Child with St Anne and St John the Baptist* – da Vinci
- *The Battle of San Romano* – Uccello
- *The Ambassadors* – Holbein the Younger
- *Equestrian Portrait of Charles I* – Van Dyck
- *Le Chapeau de Paille* – Rubens
- *The Hay Wain* – Constable
- *Sunflowers* – Van Gogh
- *The Water-Lily Pond* – Monet
- *The Fighting Temeraire* – Turner

opportunity to put faces to the famous and infamous names of Britain's past. There is an imaginative calendar of temporary exhibitions, which helps the gallery overcome what used to be a rather staid atmosphere.

Founded in 1856, the gallery houses a primary collection of some 10,000 works from different media (ranging from water colours to electronic art) spread out over five floors. The pictures are displayed roughly in chronological order, starting with the early Tudors on the top floor and descending to contemporary figures on the ground floor, where it seems some of the artists have begun to think that they are more important than the subjects. No court in the land would prosecute fashion designer Zandra Rhodes if she took a sledgehammer to the bust that some chancer made of her.

Since the 1990s the gallery has seen a major revamp with expansions to exhibition spaces and the creation of a café and shop in the basement, while escalators in the new Ondaatje Wing can whisk you up to the **Portrait Restaurant** on the top floor and a splendid view. An **IT Gallery** on the mezzanine above the information desk lets you examine the entire collection digitally. June to September is when to see the entrants in the prestigious national Portrait Award.

Whitehall

Whitehall is the administrative heart of the country and is best explored on foot (see the Whitehall Walking Tour p118).

BANQUETING HOUSE

The **Banqueting House** (Map pp84-6; ☎ 7930 4179; www.hrp.org.uk/webcode/banquet_home.asp; Whitehall; adult/child £4/3; ☉ 10am-5pm Mon-Sat; ⊖ Charing Cross) is the only surviving part of the Tudor Whitehall Palace, which once stretched most of the way along Whitehall but burned down in 1698. Designed by Inigo Jones in 1622, this was England's first purely Renaissance building and looked like no other building in the country at the time. The highlight is the ceiling of the 1st-floor ceremonial hall, which features nine panels painted by Rubens in 1634. A bust outside commemorates 30 January 1649 when Charles I, accused by Cromwell of treason, was executed on a scaffold built against a 1st-floor window here. There's a video account of the house's history.

FOREIGN & COMMONWEALTH OFFICE

The Foreign & Commonwealth Office (FCO) was built in 1872 and restored by Sir George Gilbert Scott and Matthew Digby Wyatt. If you're interested in how Britain projects itself through global diplomacy, there's a **visitor centre** (Map pp84-6; ☎ 7270 1500; Parliament St; admission free; ☉ 10am-4.30pm Mon-Fri; ⊖ Westminster) with audio and visual exhibitions as well as an information technology centre.

CABINET WAR ROOMS

The **Cabinet War Rooms** (Map pp84-6; ☎ 7930 6961; www.iwm.org.uk; King Charles St; adult/child £7/5.50; ☉ 9.30am-6pm May-Sep, 10am-6pm Oct-Apr; ⊖ Westminster) are the bunkers in which the British government took refuge during the hairier moments of WWII. It's a wonderfully evocative and atmospheric museum that has captured the drama and sense of the time with restored and preserved rooms, and an entertaining audio guide. A new **Churchill Museum** was slated to open in 2005 to coincide with the 40th anniversary of the wartime PM's death.

Westminster, Victoria & Pimlico

While the City of London (known simply as 'the City') has always concerned itself with the business of making money, Westminster has been the centre of political power for over a millennium and most of its interesting places are linked with the monarchy, parliament or the Church of England. The area is a remarkable spectacle, a picture of rare architectural cohesion and an awesome display of power, gravitas and historical import.

Pimlico, to the south and southwest, is unfortunate to be clumped with these. It is, by comparison, mind-numbingly bland and would probably disappear in an X-ray. Its only redeeming features are Tate Britain and the view it affords across the river to Battersea Power Station.

Victoria has little to recommend it – there are no attractions and it's best known for coming and going via its huge train and coach stations.

WESTMINSTER ABBEY

One of the most visited churches in Christendom, **Westminster Abbey** (Map pp84-6; ☎ 7222 5152; www.westminster-abbey.org; Dean's Yard SW1; adult/child £7.50/5; ☯ 9am-4.45pm Mon-Fri, 9am-2.45pm Sat, services Sun; ● Westminster) is one of the most sacred and symbolic sites in England and has played an enormous role in the history of the country and the Anglican Church. With the exception of Edward V and Edward VIII, every sovereign has been crowned here since William the Conqueror in 1066, and most of the monarchs from Henry III (died 1272) to George II (1760) were also buried here. As well as being the well from which the Anglican Church draws its inspiration, the abbey is also where the nation commemorates its political and artistic idols. It's difficult to imagine its equivalent anywhere else in the world.

The abbey is a magnificent and arresting sight. Though a mixture of architectural styles, it is considered the finest example of Early English Gothic (1180–1280) in existence. The original church was built during the Dark Ages by the King (later St) Edward the Confessor in the 11th century, who is buried in the chapel behind the main altar. Henry III (r 1216–72) began work on the new building but didn't complete it; the French Gothic nave was finished in 1388. Henry VII's huge and magnificent chapel was added in 1519. Unlike St Paul's, Westminster Abbey has never been a cathedral. It is what is called a 'royal peculiar' and is administered directly by the Crown.

Without in any way belittling its architectural achievements, the abbey is probably more impressive from the outside than within. The interior is chock-a-block with small chapels, elaborate tombs of monarchy and monuments to various luminaries from down the ages. As you might expect, it can get intolerably busy in here and the combination of clutter and crowds can make you wish you were still outside looking in.

That said, there are many highlights inside, including the incongruously ordinary-looking **Coronation Chair**, upon which almost every monarch is said to have been crowned since the late 13th century. The **Henry VII Chapel** is an outstanding example of late perpendicular architecture (a variation of English Gothic) with spectacular circular vaulting on the ceiling. In the **Royal Air Force (RAF) Chapel**, beneath a stained-glass window commemorating the force's finest hour, the Battle of Britain, a plaque marks the spot where Oliver Cromwell's body lay for two years until the Restoration, when it was disinterred, hanged and beheaded.

The octagonal **Chapter House** (admission with/without abbey ticket £1/2.50; ☯ 9.30am-5pm Apr-Sep, 10am-5pm Oct, 10am-4pm Nov-Mar) has one of Europe's best-preserved medieval tile floors. Other museums include a formal royal treasury, the **Pyx Chamber** (admission with/without abbey ticket £1/2.50) and the **Abbey Museum** with death masks of generations of royalty.

There are free lunchtime concerts from 12.30pm to 2pm on Thursday in July and August in the 900-year-old **College Garden** (☯ 10am-6pm Tue-Thu Apr-Sep, 10am-4pm Tue-Thu Oct-Mar), the oldest in England, and accessed through Dean's Yard.

There are 1½-hour **guided tours** (☎ 7222 7110; admission £4; Mon-Sat), leaving several times during the day, and limited **audio tours** (£3). One of the best ways to visit the abbey is to attend a service (evensong 5pm weekdays, 3pm at weekends). Sunday Eucharist is at 11am.

HOUSES OF PARLIAMENT

Comprising the House of Commons and the House of Lords, the **Houses of Parliament** (Map pp84-6; ☎ 7219 4272; www.parliament.uk; Parliament Sq SW1; ● Westminster) are in the Palace of Westminster, built by Sir Charles Barry and Augustus Pugin in 1840 when neogothic style was all the rage. A recent cleaning revealed the soft golden brilliance of the original.

The most famous feature outside the palace is the clock tower, commonly known as **Big Ben**. The real Ben, a bell named after Benjamin Hall, who was commissioner of works when the tower was completed in 1858, hangs inside. If you're very keen, you can apply in writing for a free tour of the clock tower (see the website). Thirteen-ton Ben has rung in the New Year since 1924, and gets its hands and face washed by abseiling cleaners once every five years. The best view of the whole complex is from the eastern side of Lambeth Bridge.

The House of Commons is where members of parliament (MPs) meet to propose and discuss new legislation. Although the national assembly comprises 659 MPs, the chamber has seating for only 437 of them.

When Parliament is in session, visitors are admitted to the **House of Commons Visitors' Gallery**. Expect to queue for at least an hour if you haven't already organised a ticket through your local British embassy. Parliamentary recesses (ie holidays) last for three months over the summer, and a couple of weeks over Easter and Christmas, so it's best to ring in advance to check whether Parliament is in session. Bags and cameras must be checked at a cloakroom before you enter the gallery, and no large suitcases or backpacks are allowed through the airport-style security gate. The **House of Lords Visitors' Gallery** (☎ 7219 3107; admission free; ⊗ from 2.30pm Mon-Wed, from 3pm Thu, from 11am Fri) is also open to outsiders and is as good a place as any for an afternoon nap along with the peers.

The roof of **Westminster Hall**, added between 1394 and 1401, is the earliest known example of a hammer-beam roof and has been described as 'the greatest surviving achievement of medieval English carpentry'.

When parliament is in recess, there are guided **summer tours** (☎ 0870 906 3773; www.parliament.uk; from St Stephen's Entrance, St Margaret St; 75-min

tours £7/5; times change, so telephone or check website) of both chambers and other historic buildings.

WESTMINSTER CATHEDRAL

Completed in 1903, **Westminster Cathedral** (Map p90; ☎ 7798 9064; Victoria St SW1; admission free, donation suggested; ⊗ 7am-7pm; ⊖ Victoria) is the headquarters of the Roman Catholic Church in Britain and the only good example of neo-Byzantine architecture in London. Its distinctive candy-striped redbrick and white-stone tower features prominently on the west London skyline.

The interior is part splendid marble and mosaic and part bare brick; funds dried up and the cathedral was never completed. It features the highly regarded stone carvings of the 14 **Stations of the Cross** (1918) by Eric Gill. For £2 you can take a lift up to the 83m (273ft) tower of the **Campanile Bell** for splendid panoramic views of London, or take an **audio guide** (£2.50).

TATE BRITAIN

The place to see, appreciate and interpret British art from the 16th century to the present, **Tate Britain** (Map pp78-9; ☎ 7887 8008; www.tate.org.uk; Millbank SW1; admission free, temporary exhibitions vary; ⊗ 10am-5.50pm; ⊖ Pimlico) has been spruced up, expanded and rearranged in broadly chronological order. It features works by notables such as William Blake, the Hogarths, Gainsborough, Whistler, Spencer and many more. Adjoining the main building is the quirky **Clore Gallery**, where the bulk of JMW Turner's paintings can be found.

There are free one-hour guided tours, a general tour at 11.30am weekdays, one on Turner and his contemporaries at 2.30pm and 3.30pm weekdays, and a Tate Highlights tour at 3pm Saturday. There are also children's activities throughout the week. The immensely popular **Tate Restaurant** (☎ 7887 8825; ⊗ noon-3pm Mon-Sat, noon-4pm Sun; mains £9-17.50), with an impressive Rex Whistler mural, is open for lunch only.

TATE-A-TATE

If you wish to see both of London's Tate galleries, Britain and Modern, you can easily get between the two in style. The **Tate-to-Tate ferries** – one of which sports a Damien Hirst dot painting – will whisk you from the Millennium Pier at Tate Britain to the Bankside Pier at Tate Modern, stopping en route at the London Eye. Services run 10am to 6pm daily at 40-minute intervals. A three-stop ticket (purchased on board) costs £4.50 (discounts available).

St James's & Mayfair

Mayfair is where high society high fives. Its defining features are silver spoons and old-fashioned razzmatazz. As any Monopoly player knows, it's the most expensive place in London, and if you land here you could go bankrupt. St James's is a mixture of exclusive gentlemen's clubs (the Army & Navy sort as opposed to lap-dancing), historic shops and elegant buildings; indeed, there are some 150 historically noteworthy buildings within its 36 hectares. Despite a lot of commercial development, its matter-of-fact elitism remains pretty much intact.

INSTITUTE FOR CONTEMPORARY ARTS

Renowned for being at the cutting edge is the **Institute for Contemporary Arts** (ICA; Map pp84-6; ☎ 7930 3647; www.ica.org.uk; The Mall SW1; admission varies; ☺ noon-7.30pm; ✆ Charing Cross). In any given week you might see art-house films, dance, photography, art, theatre, music, lectures, multimedia works or book readings. The complex includes a bookshop, gallery, cinema, bar, theatre and café.

ST JAMES'S PARK & ST JAMES'S PALACE

The neatest and most royal of London's royal parks, **St James's Park** (Map pp84-6; The Mall SW1; ✆ St James's Park or Charing Cross) also has the best vistas, including Westminster, Buckingham Palace and St James's Palace. The flowerbeds are spectacular in summer, but it's the lake and waterfowl that make a stroll or a lounge in here so special.

The striking Tudor gatehouse of St James's Palace, the only surviving part of a building initiated by the palace-mad Henry VIII in 1530, is best approached from St James's St to the north of the park. This was the residence of Prince Charles and his sons until they shifted next door to the former residence of the Queen Mother **Clarence House** (1828) after she died in 2002 (and the future king spent £4.6 million reshaping the house to his own design).

SPENCER HOUSE

The ancestral home of Princess Diana's family, **Spencer House** (Map pp84-6; ☎ 7499 8620; www .spencerhouse.co.uk; 27 St James's Pl SW1; adult/child £6/5; ☺ 10.30am-5.45pm Sun Feb-Jul & Sep-Dec; ✆ Green Park) was built in the Palladian style between 1756 and 1766. Although the Spencers moved out in 1927 and the house became offices, an

TOP FIVE GREEN SPACES

- **Hyde Park** (p112)
- **St James's Park** (p101)
- **Hampstead Heath** (p114)
- **Regent's Park** (p113)
- **Kew Gardens** (p117)

£18 million restoration project returned it to its former glory in the 1980s. Visits through the house are by guided tour only. The restored gardens (£3.50) are opened just a few days each summer.

BUCKINGHAM PALACE

The official residence of Queen Elizabeth II, **Buckingham Palace** (Map pp84-6; ☎ 7830 4832, credit-card bookings ☎ 7321 2233; admission £12.50; ☺ 9.30am-4.30pm daily early Aug-late Sep; ✆ St James's Park or Victoria) is at the southwestern end of the Mall.

Built in 1803 for the Duke of Buckingham, it has been the royal family's London home since 1837 when St James's Palace was judged too old-fashioned and unimpressive. Nineteen lavishly furnished staterooms, used by the royals to meet and greet, are open to visitors during part of the summer when HRH takes her holidays in Scotland. The tour includes **Queen Victoria's Picture Gallery** (a full 76.5m long, with works by Rembrandt, Van Dyck, Canaletto, Poussin and Vermeer) and the **Throne Room**, with his-and-hers pink chairs initialled 'ER' and 'P' sitting smugly under what looks like a theatre arch. The Queen has also swung open the gates to part of her backyard, although many people still find the visit distinctly underwhelming.

Changing of the Guard

London's quintessential tourist attraction takes place when the old guard (Foot Guards of the Household Regiment) comes off duty to be replaced by the new guard in the forecourt of Buckingham Palace. If you're dedicated to pomp – and arrive early to get a good vantage point by the rails – you can gape at the soldiers' bright-red uniforms and bearskin hats as they shout and march in one of the world's most famous displays of pageantry. Otherwise, you'll see little more than the backs of heads. The **ceremony** (☎ 0839-123411) takes place at 11.30am daily from April until the end of July and on alternate days for the rest of the year, weather permitting.

Queen's Gallery

This **gallery** (admission £6.50; ☺ 10am-5.30pm) houses changing displays from the extensive Royal Collection of art and treasures, shaped by the tastes of monarchs through the centuries. It was originally designed by John Nash as a conservatory and blown to smithereens by the Luftwaffe in 1940 before being reopened as a gallery in 1962. The exhibition space was greatly expanded in a £20 million renovation project and reopened for the Queen's Golden Jubilee in 2002.

Royal Mews

The **Royal Mews** (Buckingham Palace Rd SW1; admission £5.50; ☺ 11am-4pm Apr-Oct; ⊖ Victoria) provides shelter for the immaculately groomed royal horses and the opulent vehicles the monarchy uses for getting from A to B, including the stunning gold coach of 1762, which has been used for every coronation since that of George III, and the Glass Coach of 1910, used for royal weddings.

HANDEL HOUSE MUSEUM

The house where George Frideric Handel lived and wrote some of his greatest works, including *Messiah*, is now a **museum** (Map pp84-6; ☎ 7495 1685; www.handelhouse.org; 25 Brook St W1K; admission £4.50; ☺ 10am-6pm Tue-Wed, Fri & Sat, 10am-8pm Thu, noon-6pm Sun; ⊖ Bond Street). It has been restored to how it would have looked when the composer lived here – for 36 years until his death in 1759. Visitors can wander through the rooms, see personal belongings and hear recitals of his music.

GREEN PARK

Green Park is less manicured than the adjoining St James's Park, and has trees and open space, sunshine and shade. It was once a duelling ground and served as a vegetable garden during WWII.

West End – Soho to the Strand

No two Londoners ever agree on the exact borders of the West End (more a cultural term than a geographical one), but let's just say it takes in Piccadilly Circus and Tra-

falgar Sq to the south, Oxford St and Tottenham Court Rd to the north, Regent St to the west and Covent Garden and the Strand to the east. A heady mixture of consumerism and culture, the West End is where outstanding museums, galleries, historic buildings and entertainment venues rub shoulders with tacky tourist traps.

PICCADILLY CIRCUS

Piccadilly Circus is home to the popular landmark the **Eros statue** and was named after the stiff collars ('picadils') that were the sartorial staple of a 17th-century tailor who lived nearby. It is a ridiculously busy hub characterised by gaudy neon advertising hoarding (billboards), choking fumes and reliable Tower Records (p140).

London Trocadero

Basically just a huge indoor amusement arcade, the **Trocadero** (Map pp91-3; ☎ 090 6888 1100; www.londontrocadero.com; 1 Piccadilly Circus W1; ☺ 10am-midnight Sun-Thu, 10am-1am Fri & Sat; ⊖ Piccadilly Circus) has six levels of hi-tech, high-cost fun for youngsters, and cinemas, US-themed restaurants and bars for anyone else with nothing better to do. Each ride costs from £3, but you can get discounts on multiple tickets.

PICCADILLY

Piccadilly is home to the quintessential London icons of the Ritz Hotel and Fortnum & Mason department store.

Royal Academy of Arts

Britain's first art school, the **Royal Academy of Arts** (Map pp91-3; ☎ 7300 8000; www.royalacademy .org.uk; Burlington House, Piccadilly W1; admission varies; ☺ 10am-6pm Sat-Thu, 10am-10pm Fri; ⊖ Green Park), used to play second fiddle to the Hayward Gallery (p110). It has created a storm in recent years, however, with perfectly pitched shows ranging from the art of the Aztecs to its popular Summer Exhibitions showcasing the work of contemporary British artists.

Burlington Arcade

Flanking the Royal Academy of Arts, you'll find the curious **Burlington Arcade** (Map pp91-3; 51 Piccadilly W1; ⊖ Green Park), built in 1819 and today a shopping precinct for the well heeled. It is most famous for the Burlington Berties, uniformed guards who patrol the area keeping an eye out for punishable offences such as running, chewing gum or whatever else might lower the arcade's tone.

REGENT STREET

Distinguished by elegant shop fronts, Regent St is where you'll find Hamley's, London's premier toy and game store, and the upmarket department store Liberty (p139).

OXFORD STREET

Oxford St is the zenith of High St shopping, a must or a miss depending on your retail persuasion and eye for style. West towards Marble Arch, you'll find many famous department stores including the incomparable Selfridges (p139).

SOHO

One of the liveliest corners of London, this is the place to come for fun and games after dark. A decade ago it was known mostly for strip clubs and peepshows. The sleaze is still there, of course, but these days it blends with some of London's trendiest clubs, bars and restaurants. West of Soho proper is **Carnaby St**, the epicentre of London's 'swinging '60s'. It subsequently descended into tourist tack, but has lately regained some of its cred.

LEICESTER SQUARE

Pedestrianised Leicester (*les*-ter) Sq is usually heaving with tourists – and inevitably buskers – essentially it feels like somewhere you pass through on the way elsewhere.

CHINATOWN

Lisle and Gerrard Sts form the heart of Chinatown, which is full of verve and unfairly hip Japanese youngsters. Street signs are bilingual and the streets themselves are lined with Asian restaurants. If you're in town in late January or early February, don't miss the sparkles and crackles of Chinese New Year.

COVENT GARDEN

This elegant **piazza** (Map pp91-3; ⊖ Covent Garden), London's first planned square, is a tourist mecca where chain restaurants, souvenir shops, balconied bars and street entertainers vie for the punters' pound. It positively heaves in summer, especially weekends, yet seems unfettered by the fickleness of fashion and is still one of the few parts of London where pedestrians rule.

In the 1630s Inigo Jones converted the former vegetable field into a graceful square that at first housed the fruit and vegetable market immortalised in the film *My Fair Lady*. The area eventually slumped and became home to brothels and coffee houses, but the market was shifted in the 1980s and Covent Garden was transformed into one of the city's grooviest hubs.

London Transport Museum

Tucked into a corner of Covent Garden, this **museum** (Map pp91-3; ☎ 7836 8557; www.ltmuseum .co.uk; Covent Garden Piazza WC2; admission £5.95; ⏰ 10am-6pm Sat-Thu, 11am-6pm Fri; ⊖ Covent Garden) is an unexpected delight, exploring how London made the transition from streets choked with horse-drawn carriages to streets choked with horse-powered cars.

Theatre Museum

This **museum** (Map pp91-3; ☎ 7836 7891; Russell St WC2; admission free; ⏰ 10am-6pm Tue-Sun; ⊖ Covent Garden) is a branch of the Victoria & Albert Museum and displays costumes, artefacts and curiosities relating to the history of British theatre. There are regular programmes and activities for kids.

THE STRAND

Described by Benjamin Disraeli in the 19th century as Europe's finest street, this 'beach' of the Thames – which was built to connect Westminster (the seat of political power) and the City (the commercial centre) – has since lost much of its lustre. It still boasts a few classy hotels and theatres, but today is as well known for the homeless who sleep in its doorways.

Somerset House

The splendid Palladian masterpiece of **Somerset House** (Map pp84-6; www.somerset-house.org.uk; Strand WC2; ⊖ Temple) was designed by William Chambers in 1775 and contains three fabulous galleries: the Courtauld Gallery, the Gilbert Collection and the Hermitage Rooms. Its expansive central courtyard – a car park for civil servants only a few years ago – was returned to its former glory in a millennial make-over and is now one of the most elegant spaces in London, with dancing water fountains, outside tables and all the panache of Paree. It hosts a summer programme of open-air events from music to theatre. Out the back there's a wonderful terrace and café overlooking the Thames, while the Admiralty restaurant (p127) is a little bit special.

The **Courtauld Gallery** (Map pp91-3; ☎ 7848 2526; adult/child £5/free, admission free 10am-2pm Mon; ☺ 10am-6pm) displays some of the Courtauld Institute's marvellous collection of paintings in grand surroundings. There's a wealth of 14th- to 20th-century works, including a roomful of Rubens and Impressionist and post-Impressionist works by Van Gogh, Renoir and Toulouse-Lautrec.

The **Gilbert Collection** (Map pp84-6; ☎ 7240 5782; adult/child £5/free, admission free after 4.30pm; ☺ 10am-6pm) includes such treasures as European silverware, gold snuffboxes and Italian mosaics bequeathed to the nation by London-born American businessman Arthur Gilbert.

The **Hermitage Rooms** (Map pp84-6; ☎ 7845 4630; www.hermitagerooms.co.uk; adult/child £6/free; ☺ 10am-6pm) displays diverse and rotating exhibitions from St Petersburg's renowned (and underfunded) State Hermitage Museum, to which goes a slice of your admission fee.

Royal Courts of Justice

Designed in 1874, the gargantuan melange of Gothic spires, pinnacles and burnished Portland stone of the **Royal Courts of Justice** (Map pp84-6; ☎ 7936 6000; 460 The Strand; ☺ 9am-4.30pm Mon-Fri; ⊖ Temple) is where civil, and usually rather dry, cases are heard.

Bloomsbury

Largely nonresidential, Bloomsbury is a genteel blend of the University of London, beautiful Georgian squares, the British Museum and literary history. **Russell Square**, its very heart, was laid out in 1800 and is London's largest.

Between the World Wars these pleasant streets were colonised by a group of artists and intellectuals known collectively as the Bloomsbury Group, which included the novelists Virginia Woolf and EM Forster, and the economist John Maynard Keynes.

BRITISH MUSEUM

London's most visited attraction – with more than six million punters each year – the **British Museum** (Map pp84-6; ☎ 7636 1555; www.thebritishmuseum.ac.uk; Great Russell St WC1; admission free; ☺ 10am-5pm Mon-Sat, noon-6pm Sun; ⊖ Totten-

ham Court Road or Russell Square) is the largest in the country and one of the oldest and finest in the world, boasting vast Egyptian, Etruscan, Greek, Oriental and Roman galleries among many others. It was started in 1749 in the form of a 'cabinet of curiosities' belonging to Dr Hans Sloane (one of the royal physicians), which he later bequeathed to the country, and has been augmented over the years partly through the plundering of the empire (see Britain & Greece Squabble Over Marbles p105).

You'll need multiple visits to savour even the highlights here, which include a spectacular glass-and-steel roof designed by Norman Foster and opened to the public as the **Great Court** in late 2000. From here, there are nine 50-minute **'eye opener' tours** (tours free; ☺ 11am-3pm Mon-Sat, 1-4pm Sun) to help you decide which part of the collection you want to focus on. Other tours include the 1½-hour **highlights tour** (adult/child £8/5; ☺ 10.30am, 1pm & 3pm Mon-Sat) and a range of **audio guides** (£3.50). The back entrance at Montague Pl is usually quieter than the porticoed main one off Great Russell St. Also, you should calmly consider a guided tour before starting your exploration because the museum's size and scope really are mind-boggling.

Among the many must-sees are the **Rosetta Stone**, discovered in 1799 and the key to deciphering Egyptian hieroglyphics; the controversial **Parthenon Marbles**, which once adorned the walls of the Parthenon in Athens; the stunning **Oxus Treasure** of 7th- to 4th-century BC Persian gold; and the Anglo-Saxon **Sutton Hoo Ship Burial** site. In the Great Court's centre is the **Reading Room**, where Karl Marx wrote *The Communist Manifesto*. Along with the Great Court, the most recent additions to the museum are the **Sainsbury African Galleries**, the restored **King's Library** and the new **Wellcome Gallery of Ethnography**.

Holborn & Clerkenwell

Holborn's most distinctive features are the wonderful Sir John Soane's Museum and the atmospheric Inns of Court, built here to symbolise the law's role as mediator in the traditional power struggle between Westminster and the City. The little pocket of Clerkenwell was for most of the 19th and 20th centuries a dilapidated, working-class area of no interest to anyone but its inhabitants.

BRITAIN & GREECE SQUABBLE OVER MARBLES

Wonderful though it is, the British Museum can sometimes feel like one vast repository for stolen booty. Much of what's on display wasn't just 'picked up' along the way by Victorian travellers and explorers, but stolen, or purchased under dubious circumstances.

Restive foreign governments occasionally pop their heads over the parapet to demand the return of their property. The British Museum says 'no' and the problem goes away until the next time. Not the Greeks, however. They have been kicking up a stink demanding the return of the so-called Parthenon Marbles, the ancient marble sculptures that once adorned the Parthenon. The British Museum, and successive British governments, steadfastly refuse to hand over the priceless works that were removed from the Parthenon and shipped to England by the British ambassador to the Ottoman Empire, the Earl of Elgin, in 1806. (When Elgin blew all his dough, he sold the marbles to the government.) The diplomatic spat continues. Only time will tell who blinks first.

In the 1980s property developers realised the value of such central, tourist-free real estate and Clerkenwell has since been transformed into a glaringly trendy corner of the capital, replete with new pubs, restaurants and clubs.

SIR JOHN SOANE'S MUSEUM

One of the most charming London sights, this ridiculously under-visited **museum** (Map pp91-3; ☎ 7405 2107; www.soane.org; 13 Lincoln's Inn Fields WC2; admission free, tour 2.30pm Sat £3; ☻ 10am-5pm Tue-Sat, 6-9pm 1st Tue of month; ◑ Holborn) is partly a beautiful, bewitching house and partly a small museum representing the taste of celebrated architect and collector extraordinaire Sir John Soane (1753–1837).

The house is largely as it was when Sir John was taken out in a box. It has a glass dome that brings light right down to the basement, a lantern room filled with statuary, rooms within rooms and a picture gallery where each painting folds away when pressed and reveals another one behind. Among his eclectic acquisitions are an Egyptian sarcophagus, ancient vases and works of arts, and the original *Rake's Progress*, William Hogarth's set of cartoon caricatures of late-18th-century London lowlife.

The tour is well worth catching should you be in the neighbourhood on Saturday afternoon; tickets are sold at the museum from 2pm.

INNS OF COURT

Clustered around Holborn to the south of Fleet St are the Inns of Court whose alleys, atmosphere and open spaces provide an urban oasis. All London barristers work from within one of the four Inns, and a roll call of former members would include the likes of Oliver Cromwell and Charles Dickens to Mahatma Gandhi and Margaret Thatcher. It would take a lifetime working here to grasp the intricacies of the arcane protocols of the Inns – they're similar to the Freemasons, and both are 13th-century creations. It's best just to soak up the dreamy atmosphere, relax, and thank your lucky stars you're not one of the bewigged and deadly serious barristers scurrying about.

Lincoln's Inn (Map pp84-6; ☎ 7405 1393; Lincoln's Inn Fields WC2; ☻ grounds 9am-6pm Mon-Fri, chapel 12.30-2.30pm Mon-Fri; ◑ Holborn), largely intact with several original 15th-century buildings, is the most attractive of the bunch with a chapel and pretty landscaped gardens. **Gray's Inn** (Map pp84-6; ☎ 7458 7800; Gray's Inn Rd WC1; ☻ grounds 10am-4pm Mon-Fri, chapel 10am-6pm Mon-Fri; ◑ Chancery Lane) was largely rebuilt after the Luftwaffe levelled it. **Middle Temple** (Map pp84-6; ☎ 7427 4800; Middle Temple Lane EC4; ☻ grounds 10-11.30am & 3-4pm Mon-Fri; ◑ Temple) and **Inner Temple** (Map pp84-6; ☎ 7797 8250; King's Bench Walk EC4; ☻ grounds 10am-4pm Mon-Fri; ◑ Temple), the former being the best preserved, are both part of the Temple complex between Fleet St and Victoria Embankment (see also Temple Church p118).

The City

The City of London, the commercial heart of the capital, is 'the square mile' on the northern bank of the Thames where the Romans first built their walled community two millennia ago. Its boundaries have changed little since, and you can always tell when you're within them because the Corporation of London's coat of arms appears on the street signs.

Less than 10,000 people actually live here, although some 300,000 descend on it each weekday, where they generate almost three-quarters of Britain's entire GDP before nicking back off to wherever it is they live.

St Paul's Cathedral and the Tower of London are also here and a quiet weekend stroll offers a unique opportunity to explore the area's architectural richness, including the many atmospheric alleyways snaking between the modern office towers.

FLEET ST

As twentieth-century London's 'Street of Shame', **Fleet St** (Map pp84-6; ⊖ Blackfriars) was synonymous with the UK's scurrilous tabloids until the mid-1980s when the press barons embraced computer technology, ditched a load of staff and largely relocated to the Docklands. It was here in 1850 that Reuters news agency, the last media outlet to stick with Fleet St, began its service with a loft of carrier pigeons.

CENTRAL CRIMINAL COURT (OLD BAILEY)

Many of Britain's most notorious criminals – and a few Irishmen who were in the wrong place at the wrong time – have been convicted at the Central Criminal Court, better known as the Old Bailey after the street on which it stands. Look up at the great copper dome and you'll see the figure of justice holding a sword and scales in her hands. Oddly, she is *not* blindfolded, which has sparked many a sarcastic comment from those being brought in here.

You can visit the court's **public gallery** (Map pp84-6; ☎ 7248 3277; Newgate St; ⏰ 10.30am-1pm & 2-4pm Mon-Fri).

DR JOHNSON'S HOUSE

Where Samuel Johnson and his assistants compiled the first English dictionary between 1748 and 1759, **Dr Johnson's House** (Map pp84-6; ☎ 7353 3745; www.drjh.dircon.co.uk; 17 Gough Sq EC4; adult/concession £4/3; ⏰ 11am-5.30pm Mon-Sat May-Sep, 11am-5pm Oct-Apr; ⊖ Chancery Lane) is a well-preserved, Georgian building. It's full of prints and portraits of friends and intimates, including Johnson's Jamaican servant, to whom he bequeathed the house in his will.

ST PAUL'S CATHEDRAL

Dominating the City with a dome second in size only St Peter's in Rome, **St Paul's Cathedral** (Map pp86-7; ☎ 7236 4128; www.stpauls.co.uk; admission £6; ⏰ 8.30am-4pm Mon-Sat; ⊖ St Paul's) was built between 1675 and 1710 by Sir Christopher Wren after the Great Fire of 1666. Four other cathedrals on this site, the first dating from 604, preceded it.

The dome is renowned for somehow dodging the bombs during the Blitz of WWII and became an icon of the resilience shown in the capital during the crisis. Outside the cathedral, to the north, is a **monument to the people of London**, a simple and elegant memorial to the 32,000 Londoners who weren't so lucky.

Inside, some 30m above the main paved area, is the first of three domes (actually a dome inside a cone, inside a dome) supported by eight huge columns. The walkway round its base is called the **Whispering Gallery**, because if you talk close to the wall your words will carry to the opposite side 32m away.

This, the **Stone Gallery** and the **Golden Gallery** can be reached by a staircase on the western side of the scrubbed-up southern transept. It is 530 lung-busting steps to the Golden Gallery at the very top, and an unforgettable view of London. But even if that's too much, you can still get terrific city vistas from the lower galleries.

The **Crypt** has memorials to up to 300 military demigods, including Wellington, Kitchener and Nelson, whose body lies below the dome. But the most poignant memorial is to Sir Christopher Wren himself. On a simple slab bearing his name a Latin inscription translates as: 'If you seek his memorial, look about you'.

Audio tours lasting 45 minutes are available for £3.50. **Guided tours** (adult/child £2.50/2) leave the tour desk at 11am, 11.30am, 1.30pm and 2pm (90 minutes). There are organ concerts at St Paul's at 5pm most Sundays. Evensong takes place at 5pm most weekdays and at 3.15pm on Sunday.

GUILDHALL

The **Guildhall** (Map pp86-7; ☎ 7606 3030; Basinghall St EC2; admission free; ⏰ 10am-5pm Mon-Sat, 10am-4pm Sun May-Sep; 10am-5pm Mon-Sun Oct-Apr; ⊖ Bank) sits exactly in the centre of the sq mile and has been the seat of the City's local government for eight centuries. The present building dates from the early 15th century.

You can see the **Great Hall** where the mayor is still elected, a vast empty space with ecclesiastical-style monuments and the shields and banners of London's 12 principal livery companies, which emerged from the guilds of the Middle Ages. Beneath it is London's largest **medieval crypt** (☎ 7606 3030, ext 1463; visited by free guided tour only) with 19 stained-glass windows showing the livery companies' coats of arms.

The **Guildhall Art Gallery** (admission £2.50) holds more than 4000 artworks, primarily of historical import. Only 250 or so are displayed at any one time.

BARBICAN

Tucked into a corner of the City of London where a watchtower (or 'barbican') once stood, the **Barbican** (Map pp86-7; ☎ 7638 4141; Silk St EC2; ⊖ Barbican or Moorgate) is a prime example of a local council making a pig's ear of development.

The plan was to create a modern complex for offices, residences and the arts on a vast bomb site provided by WWII. The result – which was only completed in the early 1980s, by which time the ultramodern plans should have been museum pieces – is a forbidding series of wind tunnels and gloomy high-rise apartments, with an enormous cultural centre hidden somewhere in the middle.

The **Barbican Centre** is the home of the Royal Shakespeare Company (RSC), the London Symphony Orchestra and the London Classical Orchestra. It also houses the Museum of London and the wonderful **Barbican Art Gallery** (☎ 7588 9023; admission £4.50; ⏰ 10am-6pm Mon-Sat, noon-6pm Sun) on Level 3, with some of the best photographic exhibits in London. The programmes are generally first-rate, but it's a hassle finding the complex in the first place, never mind reaching the right spot at the right time.

MUSEUM OF LONDON

Despite its unprepossessing setting in the Barbican (look for gate 7), the **Museum of London** (Map pp86-7; ☎ 7600 0807; www.museumof london.org.uk; London Wall EC2; admission free; ⏰ 10am-5.50pm Mon-Sat, noon-5.50pm Sun; ⊖ Barbican) is one of the city's finest, and is expanding its exhibitions depicting the city's evolution from the ice age to the Internet. Among more than one million objects is a 2000-year-old plaque engraved with the Latin word 'Londiniensium'. It was only discovered in late 2002 and is the earliest known physical proof of the capital's original Roman name.

TOWER OF LONDON

Despite the heaving crowds and all the marketing claptrap, the **Tower of London** (Map pp86-7; ☎ 7680 9004; www.hrp.org.uk; Tower Hill EC3; adult/child £12.50/8; ⏰ 9am-6pm Mon-Sat, 10am-6pm Sun Apr-Oct; 9am-5pm Mon-Sat, 10am-5pm Sun Nov-Mar; ⊖ Tower Hill) is one of the most essential sights to see in London, and a window into a gruesome, fascinating history. It is also one of the city's three World Heritage Sites (joining Westminster Abbey and Maritime Greenwich). Well over two million people visit each year and, even in winter, you should arrive early to commandeer enough space to savour the experience.

To help get your bearings, take the hugely entertaining and free guided tour with any of the Tudor-garbed Beefeaters. Hour-long tours leave every 30 minutes from the Middle Tower between 9am and 3pm Monday to Saturday and from 10am Sunday.

In 1078 William the Conqueror laid the first stone of the White Tower to replace the timber-and-earth castle he'd already built here. By 1285 two walls with towers and a moat were built around it and the medieval defences have barely been altered since. A former royal residence, treasury, mint and arsenal, it became most famous as a prison when Henry VIII moved to Whitehall Palace in 1529 and started dishing out his preferred brand of punishment.

The most striking building is the huge **White Tower**, in the centre of the courtyard, with its solid Romanesque architecture and four turrets, which today houses a collection from the Royal Armouries. On the 2nd floor is the **Chapel of St John the Evangelist**, dating from 1080 and therefore the oldest church in London.

On the small green in front of the church stood the **scaffold**, set up during Henry VIII's reign, where seven people were beheaded, among them Anne Boleyn and her cousin Catherine Howard (his second and fifth wives).

Facing the White Tower to the north is the **Waterloo Barracks**, which now contains the Crown Jewels. On a busy day, you'll be whisked past with hardly time to blink.

On the far side of the White Tower from here is the **Bloody Tower**, where the 12-year-old Edward V and his little brother were held 'for their own safety' and later murdered, probably by their uncle, the future Richard III.

Sir Walter Raleigh did a 13-year stretch here, when he wrote his *History of the World*, a copy of which is on display.

On the patch of green between the Wakefield and White Towers you'll find the latest in the tower's long line of famous ravens, which legend says could cause the White Tower to collapse should they leave. Their wings are clipped in case they get any ideas.

TOWER BRIDGE

When it was built in 1894, London was still a thriving port and Tower Bridge was designed to rise and allow ships to pass through. It is raised electronically these days but you can still see the original steam engines. There are excellent views from the walkways.

For the **Tower Bridge Exhibition** (Map pp86-7; ☎ 7378 1928; www.towerbridge.org.uk; admission £5.50; ✆ 10am-6.30pm Apr-Oct, 9.30am-6pm Nov-Mar; ⊖ Tower Hill), a lift takes you up from the modern visitors' facility in the northern tower where the story of its building is recounted with videos and animatronics.

BANK OF ENGLAND MUSEUM

Guardian of the country's financial system, the Bank of England was established in 1694 when the government needed to raise some cash to support a war with France. It was moved here in 1734 and largely renovated by Sir John Soane. The **museum** (Map pp86-7; ☎ 7601 5545; www.bankofengland.co.uk; Bartholomew Lane EC2; admission free; ✆ 10am-5pm Mon-Fri; ⊖ Bank) traces the history of the bank and bank notes with various interactive technology, and isn't quite as dry as it sounds.

THE MONUMENT

Designed by Christopher Wren to commemorate the Great Fire of 1666, the **Monument** (Map pp86-7; ☎ 7626 2717; Monument St; adult/child £1.50/50p; ✆ 10am-5.40pm; ⊖ Monument) is 60.6m high, the exact distance from its base to the bakery on Pudding Lane east where the blaze began. If you're up to it, 311 tight steps lead to a balcony beneath the gilded bronze urn at the top and a splendid view.

South of the Thames

A little over a decade ago, the southern part of central London was the city's forgotten underside – run-down and offering little for foreign visitors. All that has changed in recent years; even north Londoners are venturing 'sarf' of the river for play and stimulation. Although parts of Bermondsey still look a little dejected, there are pockets of refurbishment and revitalisation, as exemplified by the Design Museum and the brand new Zandra Rhodes' Fashion & Textile Museum. (See To Market, to Market p139.)

BERMONDSEY
Design Museum

The gleaming white **Design Museum** (Map pp78-9; ☎ 7403 6933; 28 Shad Thames SE1; www.designmuseum .org; adult/child £6/4; ✆ 10am-5.45pm; ⊖ Tower Hill) is a must for anyone interested in the evolution of design and all its applications. The 1st floor is dedicated to innovation from around the world, the 2nd concentrates on the practicalities of design, while a relatively new gallery focuses on contemporary design.

Fashion & Textile Museum

Kooky British designer Zandra Rhodes' **Fashion & Textile Museum** (Map pp86-7; ☎ 7403 0222; www.ftmlondon.org; adult/child £6/4; 83 Bermondsey St SE1; ⊖ London Bridge) showcases the best of vintage and modern, local and international fashion plus textile design (as well as thousands of her own pieces, of course) in a cool Mediterranean building.

SOUTHWARK

An important thoroughfare during the Middle Ages, Southwark (suth-erk) is in a transition period, retaining at least some of its working-class gritty edge while a slew of sights and attractions – such as the magnificent Tate Modern – open up along the Thames in Bankside.

HMS Belfast

Launched in 1938, the **HMS Belfast** (Map pp86-7; ☎ 7407 6328; Morgan's Lane, Tooley St SE1; adult/child £6/free; ✆ 10am-6pm Mar-Oct, 10am-5pm Nov-Feb; ⊖ London Bridge) is a large, light cruiser with 16 six-inch guns. It saw much action during WWII and is hugely popular with little boys.

London Dungeon

The **London Dungeon** (Map pp86-7; ☎ 7403 7221; www.thedungeons.com; 28-34 Tooley St SE1; adult/child £14.50/9.75; ✆ 10am-6.30pm Apr-Jun & Sep, 10am-9pm Jul & Aug; ⊖ London Bridge) is long on gore and short on substance. Kids, of course, love it. Beware of touts selling fake tickets.

Britain at War Experience

Designed to educate about the hardships endured, and spirit exemplified, during WWII, the **Britain at War Experience** (Map pp86-7; ☎ 7403 3171; www.britainatwar.co.uk; 64-66 Tooley St SE1; admission £8.50; ☺ 10am-5.30pm Apr-Sep, 10am-4.30pm Oct-Mar) is crammed with fascinating memorabilia from a bombarded London.

Old Operating Theatre Museum & Herb Garret

One of London's most genuinely gruesome attractions is the **Old Operating Theatre Museum** (Map pp86-7; ☎ 7955 4791; www.thegarret.org.uk; 9A St Thomas St SE1; admission £4; ☺ 10.30am-5pm; ❸ London Bridge). The primitive surgical tools of the 19th century are terrifying.

There's also an apothecary where medicinal herbs were stored; it now houses a medical museum hung with bunches of herbs.

Southwark Cathedral

Although the central tower dates from 1520 and the choir from the 13th century, **Southwark Cathedral** (Map pp86-7; ☎ 7367 6722; Montague Close SE1; admission by donation; ☺ 8am-6pm; ❸ London Bridge) is largely Victorian. It's been scrubbed up in recent years and has a new visitor centre. Inside are monuments and details galore and it's worth picking up one of the small guides. Catch Evensong at 5.30pm on Tuesday and Friday, 4pm on Saturday and 3pm on Sunday.

Shakespeare's Globe & Exhibition

The rebuilt **Globe Theatre** (Map pp86-7; ☎ 7401 9919; www.shakespeares-globe.org; 21 New Globe Walk SE1; adult/child £8/5.50; ☺ 10am-5pm; ❸ London Bridge) offers the opportunity to see Shakespeare as it was originally performed in this faithful replica of the original 'Wooden O' under a thatched roof and surrounded by standing and often unruly punters.

The original Globe was erected in 1599, burned down in 1613 and immediately rebuilt. The Puritans, who regarded theatres as dreadful dens of iniquity, eventually closed it down in 1642. Beneath it, an exhibition focuses on Elizabethan London and the struggle by American actor and director Sam Wanamaker to get the theatre rebuilt.

Visits include a guided tour of the theatre itself, although in summer there are usually matinee performances and tours take place in the morning only.

Tate Modern

This former power station is home to the wonderful **Tate Modern** (Map pp86-7; information ☎ 7887 8008; www.tate.org.uk; Queen's Walk SE1; admission free; ☺ 10am-6pm Sun-Thu, 10am-10pm Fri & Sat; ❸ Blackfriars or London Bridge), Europe's most successful contemporary art gallery and London's number-one attraction.

Enter through the vast and dramatic Turbine Hall and lick your lips. The collection is spread over five floors and encompasses art in all its forms from the beginning of the 20th century. The works are displayed thematically rather than chronologically and some of the early stuff gets a little lost compared to the bolder contemporary works. Although the displays change regularly, you're certain to clap eyes on pieces by Monet, Picasso, Dali, Pollock, Warhol and Rothko as well as various members of '90s brat pack (including Damien Hirst and Tracey Emin).

However, it's with its temporary exhibitions (for which there are always admission fees) that the Tate really shines (check listings for details). Another attraction is the view from the top-floor **restaurant** and **café**. The **audio guides** (£1) are worthwhile for their descriptions of selected works.

Millennium Bridge

Although it nowadays provides a smooth river crossing, the Millennium Bridge will long be known to Londoners as the 'wobbly bridge'. Designed by Norman Foster and Anthony Caro, its low-slung frame looks pretty spectacular, particularly when it's lit up at night with fibre-optics – the so-called 'blade of light' effect. But it's hard to forget this footbridge's abortive opening in June 2000. It was closed after just three days, when it began to sway alarmingly under the weight and movement of pedestrian traffic. A year and a half, plus £5 million worth of dampeners, later, it reopened and has since conveyed crowds, without incident, between Peter's Hill (in front of St Paul's) on the Thames' northern bank and Tate Modern and Bankside south of the river.

SOUTH BANK

Twentieth-century planners weren't too kind to the area south of Waterloo Bridge. Although presenting the South Bank with a wealth – and a labyrinth – of cultural and arts venues like the Royal National

Theatre and the National Film Theatre, the architecture in which they were housed is indescribably ugly. But they've gone a long way towards making amends. The South Bank is now home to the cherished London Eye, the Saatchi Gallery, extended Jubilee Gardens and the latest Norman Foster landmark, a futuristic glass egg designed to house the Greater London Authority (GLA) headquarters.

Saatchi Gallery

The greatest hits of the '90s Britart, or the Young British Art (YBA) movement – from Damien Hirst's sheep in formaldehyde to Tracy Emin's bed – are to be found here, in the rather incongruous Edwardian setting of the former County Hall. Now the **Saatchi Gallery** (☎ 0870 1160 278; www.saatchi-gallery.co.uk; County Hall, Westminster Bridge Rd SE1; admission £8.75; ⏰ 10am-8pm Sun-Thu, 10am-10pm Fri & Sat; ✈ Westminster or Waterloo), it's filled with works that became world famous in the twilight of the 20th century when Britannia's artists famously and controversially waived the rules.

Hayward Gallery

New foyer notwithstanding, the trick with the monolithic **Hayward Gallery** (Map pp84-6; ☎ 7928 3144; www.hayward-gallery.org.uk; Belvedere Rd SE1; admission prices vary; ✈ Waterloo) is to get inside quick – away from the ugly concrete exterior into the roomy, modernist interiors that provide a perfect backdrop to the leading international exhibitions of contemporary art held here.

London Eye

Right on the Thames, the British Airways' **London Eye** (Map pp84-6; ☎ 0870 500 0600; www.ba-londoneye.com; admission £11.50; ⏰ 9.30am-8pm Mon-Fri Oct-Apr, 9.30am-8pm daily May, 9.30am-9pm daily Jun & Sep, 9.30am-10pm daily Jul-Aug; ✈ Waterloo) is the world's largest sightseeing wheel. (For all sorts of technical reasons it can't be called a Ferris wheel.) It's certainly the most fondly regarded of all London's millennium projects.

It is a thrilling experience to be in one of the 32 enclosed glass gondolas, enjoying views of some 25 miles (on clear days) across the capital. The 135m-tall wheel takes 30 minutes to rotate completely and it's best experienced at dusk.

Such is the wheel's popularity that, even though the opening hours keep extending, if you turn up without a ticket you might not get on; phone ahead or book online. To rock up and ride, you either have to arrive before opening to nab one of the few same-day tickets or run the gauntlet of the touts.

London Aquarium

One of the largest in Europe, the **London Aquarium** (Map pp84-6; ☎ 7967 8000; www.london aquarium.co.uk; County Hall, Westminster Bridge Rd SE1; adult/child £8.75/5.25; ⏰ 10am-6pm; ✈ Westminster or Waterloo) has three levels of fish organised by geographical origin, none of which you'll see during school holidays when the place is stuffed to the gills with kiddies.

LAMBETH

Lambeth is the district just south of Westminster Bridge, home to a few interesting museums and Lambeth Palace, the official residence to successive archbishops of Canterbury since the 12th century.

Imperial War Museum

Even committed pacifists appreciate the **Imperial War Museum** (Map pp78-9; ☎ 7416 5000; www.iwm.org.uk; Lambeth Rd SE1; admission free; ⏰ 10am-6pm; ✈ Lambeth North) because, alongside its internationally famous collection of planes, tanks and other military hardware, it provides a telling lesson in modern history. Highlights included a recreated WWI trench, recreated WWII bomb shelter and a **Holocaust Exhibition**.

Florence Nightingale Museum

Attached to St Thomas's Hospital and celebrating the achievements of social campaigner and the world's most famous nurse is the **Florence Nightingale Museum** (Map pp84-6; ☎ 7620 0374; www.florence-nightingale.co.uk; 2 Lambeth Palace Rd SE1; adult/child £5.80/4.20; ⏰ 10am-5pm Mon-Fri, 11.30am-4.30pm Sat & Sun, last admission 1hr before closing; ✈ Westminster or Waterloo). The museum recounts the story of 'the lady with the lamp' who led a team of nurses tending to the injured during the Crimean War. Upon returning to London she established a training school for nurses at this hospital in 1859. The small and thoughtful museum contains displays of personal mementos and other belongings.

Chelsea, South Kensington & Earl's Court

Much of west London could be classed as uptown. The residents of Kensington and Chelsea have the highest incomes of any London borough (shops and restaurants will presume you do too) and the area, like the Chelsea football team, is thoroughly cosmopolitan chic. Thanks to the 1851 Great Exhibition, South Kensington is first and foremost museum land, boasting the Natural History, Science and Victoria & Albert Museums all on one road.

Further west, Earl's Court is lively and cosmopolitan, although less prosperous. It's particularly popular with travelling Antipodeans and was once known as Kangaroo Valley.

VICTORIA & ALBERT MUSEUM

A vast, rambling and wonderful museum of decorative art and design, the **Victoria & Albert (V&A) Museum** (Map pp82-3; ☎ 7942 2000; www .vam.ac.uk; Cromwell Rd SW7; admission free; ☿ 10am-5.45pm Thu-Tue, 6.30-9.30pm Wed; ✚ South Kensington) is part of Prince Albert's legacy to Londoners in the wake of the successful Great Exhibition of 1851.

It's a bit like the nation's attic, comprising four million objects collected over the years from Britain and around the globe. Spread over nearly 150 galleries, it houses the world's greatest collection of decorative arts including ancient Chinese ceramics, modernist architectural drawings, Korean bronze and Japanese swords, samples from William Morris' 19th-century Arts and Crafts movement, cartoons by Raphael, spellbinding Asian and Islamic art, Rodin sculptures, Elizabethan gowns and dresses straight from this year's Paris fashion shows, ancient jewellery, a 1930s' wireless set, an all-wooden Frank Lloyd Wright study, and a pair of Doc Martens. Yes, you'll need to plan. Alternatively, take one of the introductory hour-long **guided tours** (admission free; ☿ 10.30am-4.30pm).

NATURAL HISTORY MUSEUM

Kids – and most adults – will lose their minds at the **Natural History Museum** (Map pp82-3; ☎ 7938 9123; www.nhm.ac.uk; Cromwell Rd SW7; admission free; ☿ 10am-5.50pm Mon-Sat, 11am-5.50pm Sun; ✚ South Kensington), where the main collections are divided between adjoining Life and

CRYSTAL PALACE & THE GREAT EXHIBITION

In 1851 Queen Victoria's consort, a German-born prince, Albert, organised a huge celebration of global technology in Hyde Park. The so-called Great Exhibition was held in a 7.5-hectare revolutionary iron-and-glass hothouse, a 'Crystal Palace' designed by gardener and architect Joseph Paxton. So successful was the exhibition – more than two million people flocked to see its more than 100,000 exhibits – that Albert arranged for the profits to be ploughed into building two permanent exhibitions, which today house the Science Museum and the Victoria & Albert Museum. The Crystal Palace itself was moved to Sydenham, where it burned down in 1936.

Earth Galleries. Where once the former was full of dusty glass cases of butterflies and stick insects, there are now wonderful interactive displays on themes such as Human Biology and Creepy Crawlies. Plus there's the crowd-pulling exhibition on mammals and dinosaurs, which includes animatronic movers and shakers such as the 4m-high Tyrannosaurus Rex. The Earth Galleries are equally impressive. An escalator slithers up and into a hollowed-out globe where two main exhibits – Earthquake and the Restless Surface – explain how wind, water, ice, gravity and life itself impact on the earth.

The **Darwin Centre**, a vast new education centre, houses some 22 million zoological exhibits, which can be visited by tour.

SCIENCE MUSEUM

With seven floors of interactive and educational exhibits, the **Science Museum** (Map pp82-3; ☎ 7942 4455; www.sciencemuseum.org.uk; Exhibition Rd SW7; admission free; ☿ 10am-6pm; ✚ South Kensington) helps you discover everything from the history of the Industrial Revolution to the exploration of space. There is something for all ages from vintage cars, old trains and antique aeroplanes to labour-saving devices for the home, a wind tunnel and flight simulator. The even more hi-tech extension, the **Wellcome Wing**, focuses on contemporary science and makes presentations on recent breakthroughs. There's also a 450-seat **IMAX cinema**.

TOP FIVE MULTIETHNIC LONDON

- Dancing at the **Notting Hill Carnival** (p120)
- Eating in **Brick Lane** (p128)
- Hanging out in **Brixton** (p117)
- Gigging in **Hackney** (p137)
- Walking through **Chinatown** (p103)

CHELSEA PHYSIC GARDEN

Established in 1673 to provide a means for students to study medicinal plants and healing, this peaceful **garden** (Map pp88-9; ☎ 7352 5646; www.chelseaphysicgarden.co.uk; 66 Royal Hospital Rd SW3; admission £5; ☑ noon-5pm Wed Apr-Oct, noon-5pm Mon-Fri, 2-6pm Sun during Chelsea Flower Show in May; ⊖ Sloane Square) is one of the oldest botanical gardens in Europe and contains many rare trees and plants.

ROYAL HOSPITAL CHELSEA

Designed by Christopher Wren, the **Royal Hospital Chelsea** (Map p90; ☎ 7881 5204; Royal Hospital Rd SW3; admission free; ☑ 10am-noon & 2-4pm Mon-Sat, 2-4pm Sun; ⊖ Sloane Square) is a superb structure that was built in 1692 to provide shelter for exservicemen. Today it houses hundreds of war veterans known as Chelsea Pensioners, who are fondly regarded as a national treasure. As you wander around the grounds or inspect the elegant chapel you may see them in their winter blue coats or summer reds. The Chelsea Flower Show takes place in the hospital grounds in May.

Knightsbridge & Kensington

These are among London's poshest precincts and of particular interest to shoppers with black credit cards. Knightsbridge is where you'll find some of London's best-known department stores, including Harrods and Harvey Nichols, while Kensington High St has a lively mix of chains and boutiques.

KENSINGTON PALACE

Dating from 1605, **Kensington Palace** (Map pp82-3; ☎ 7937 9561; www.hrp.org.uk; Kensington Gardens W8; adult/child £10.80/7; ☑ 10am-5pm; ⊖ High Street Kensington) was the birthplace of Queen Victoria in 1819 but is best known today as the last home of Princess Diana. Hour-long tours take you around the surprisingly small **State-rooms**. A collection of Princess Di's dresses is on permanent display along with frocks and ceremonial gowns from HRH and her predecessors. There's an **audio tour**, included in the entry fee, if you want to explore on your own.

KENSINGTON GARDENS

These **royal gardens** (Map pp82-3; ☑ dawn till dusk) are part of Kensington Palace but blend in almost seamlessly with Hyde Park. There's a splendid, contemporary art space, the **Serpentine Gallery** (Map pp82-3; ☎ 7402 6075; www .serpentinegallery.org; admission free; ☑ 10am-6pm; ⊖ Knightsbridge or Lancaster Gate), beautifully located south of the lake. The **Sunken Garden**, near the palace, is at its prettiest in summer, while tea in the **Orangery** is a treat.

On the southern edge of the gardens, opposite the Royal Albert Hall, is the restored **Albert Memorial** (⊖ South Kensington or Gloucester Road), as over-the-top as the subject, Queen Victoria's German husband Albert (1819–61), was purportedly humble. It was designed by George Gilbert Scott in 1872.

On the far side of the gardens is **Diana, Princess of Wales Memorial Playground**, an elaborate amusement park your kids will love.

Notting Hill

The status of the Notting Hill Carnival (in late August) reflects the multicultural appeal of this part of West London, into which West Indian immigrants moved in the 1950s. After decades of exploitation and strife, the community took off in the 1980s and the area is now a thriving, vibrant corner of central London that is retaining its charm despite steady gentrification.

Bayswater, to the east, was neglected for centuries, but is now mainly a fairly well-to-do residential area with Queensway as its main thoroughfare.

Hyde Park

At 145 hectares, **Hyde Park** (Map pp82-3; ☑ 5.30am-midnight) is central London's largest open space. Henry VIII expropriated it from the Church in 1536, when it became a hunting ground and later a venue for duels, executions and horse-racing. The 1851 Great Exhibition was held here and during WWII it became an enormous potato field. These days, it serves as an occasional concert venue and a full-time green space for fun and frolics.

There's boating on the Serpentine for the physically energetic or, near Marble Arch, there's **Speaker's Corner** for oratorical acrobats. These days, it's largely nutters and religious fanatics who maintain the tradition begun in 1872 as a response to rioting.

A plaque on the traffic island at Marble Arch indicates the spot where the infamous Tyburn Tree, a three-legged gallows, once stood. It is estimated that up to 50,000 people were executed here between 1300 and 1783, many having been dragged from the Tower of London.

A more soothing structure, in memory of Princess Diana – a meandering stream that splits at the top, flows gently downhill and reassembles in a pool at the bottom – was unveiled here in mid-2004 with inevitable debate over matters of taste and gravitas.

MARBLE ARCH
London's grandest bedsit – with a one-room flat inside – **Marble Arch** (Map pp82-3; ⊖ Marble Arch) was designed by John Nash in 1827 as the entrance to Buckingham Palace. However, it was too small and unimposing for the job so was moved here in 1851.

Marylebone
Increasingly hip Marylebone is home to several attractions, from London's primo tourist trap Madame Tussaud's to the artistic treasure trove that is the oft overlooked Wallace Collection.

WALLACE COLLECTION
Arguably London's finest small gallery, the **Wallace Collection** (Map pp84-6; ☎ 7935 0687; www .the-wallace-collection.org.uk; Hertford House, Manchester Sq W1; admission free; ⊙ 10am-5pm Mon-Sat, 2-5pm Sun; ⊖ Bond Street) comprises a wealth of 17th- and 18th-century European artefacts and art including works by Rubens, Titian, Rembrandt and Gainsborough, all housed in a splendid and sumptuously restored Italianate mansion. Free guided tours take place daily; phone for the exact times.

MADAME TUSSAUD'S
This toweringly tedious **waxworks collection** (Map pp84-6; ☎ 0870 400 3000; www.madame-tussauds .com; Marylebone Rd NW1; prices vary according to time of year & entry, adult/child incl Planetarium £12-22/£7- 16; ⊙ 10am-5.30pm Mon-Fri, 9.30am-5.30pm Sat & Sun; ⊖ Baker Street) is still living off the name it made for itself in Victorian times and attracts almost three million punters every year. If you want to join them you'd better reserve your ticket and arrive early in the morning or late in the afternoon to avoid the long queues (particularly in summer).

LONDON PLANETARIUM
Attached to Madame Tussaud's (and included in the admission charge), the **London Planetarium** (Map pp80-6; www.madame-tussauds.com; admission £3; ⊙ 10am-5.30pm Mon-Fri, 9.30am-5.30pm Sat & Sun) presents a 15-minute star show projected onto the dome ceiling. It has galactic bits and bobs in the foyer to keep the kids occupied while you wait for the next screening.

Regent's Park
A former royal hunting ground, **Regent's Park** (Map pp80-1; ⊖ Baker Street or Regent's Park) was designed by John Nash early in the 19th century, although what was actually laid out is only a fraction of the celebrated architect's grand plan. Nevertheless, it's a lovely space in the middle of the city – at once lively and serene, cosmopolitan and local – with football pitches, tennis courts and a boating lake. **Queen Mary's Gardens**, towards the south of the park, are the prettiest part of the gardens with spectacular roses in summer when the **open-air theatre** (☎ 7486 7905) hosts performances of Shakespeare.

LONDON ZOO
Established in 1828 and one of the world's oldest, **London Zoo** (Map pp80-1; ☎ 7722 3333; www .londonzoo.co.uk; Regent's Park NW1; adult/child £13/9.75; ⊙ 10am-5.30pm Mar-Oct, 10am-4pm Nov-Feb; ⊖ Camden Town) got into hot water because its historical buildings weren't conducive to animal comforts. Smarting from the criticism, the zoo embarked on a 10-year, £21 million project focusing on conservation, education and breeding programmes. All the same, you'll find this zoo as thrilling or upsetting as any other. Feeding times, reptile handling and the petting zoo are always popular.

North London
The northern reaches of central London stretch in a broad arc from St John's Wood in the west to Islington in the east. Camden Market and Hampstead Heath are among North London's most popular attractions,

LONDON

while Islington is awash with lively pubs and eateries, and Upper St, in particular, is worth a wander.

EUSTON & KING'S CROSS

These aren't especially inviting areas and will be most familiar to users of the tube and anyone taking a train to the north of England. If you're due to pass through King's Cross St Pancras, rise to the surface and check out St Pancras station, the pinnacle of the Victorian Gothic revival architecture.

British Library

Colin St John's new **British Library** (Map pp80-1; ☎ 7412 7000; www.bl.uk; 96 Euston Rd NW1; admission free; 🕑 9.30am-6pm Mon & Wed-Fri, 9.30am-8pm Tue, 9.30am-5pm Sat, 11am-5pm Sun; ⊖ King's Cross St Pancras), which opened in 1998, has copped some flak for its red-brick façade, but the interior is superb. You need to be a 'reader' (ie member) to use the collection of every British publication in print, but historical documents, including the Magna Carta, are on public display.

ST JOHN'S WOOD

Posh St John's Wood is where you'll find Lord's, the home of world cricket. It will also be of interest to Beatles fans as 3 Abbey Rd is where the four recorded most of their albums, including *Abbey Road* (1969) itself, with its cover shot taken on the zebra crossing outside.

MCC Museum & Lord's Tour

The next best thing to watching a test at **Lord's Cricket Ground** (Map pp78-9; ☎ 7432 1033; www.lords.org; St John's Wood Rd NW8; adult/child £7.50/5.50; tours 10am, noon & 2pm Apr-Sep, noon & 2pm Oct-Mar when there's no play; ⊖ St John's Wood) is the absorbingly anecdotal 90-minute tour of the ground and facilities, which takes in the famous (members only) Long Room and a museum featuring evocative memorabilia.

CAMDEN

Camden's popularity has grown out of all proportion in recent years, largely propelled by **Camden Market** (see the boxed text p139), London's most popular 'unticketed' tourist attraction with an estimated 10 million visitors a year. This was a working-class Irish and Greek enclave just two

decades ago but has been largely gentrified since. There are a few outstanding pubs, restaurants and music venues, but it's the Camden vibe people swear by.

HAMPSTEAD & HIGHGATE

These quaint and well-heeled villages, perched on hills above central London, are home to an inordinate number of celebrities and intelligentsia. The villages are largely as they were laid out in the 18th century and boast close proximity to the vast Hampstead Heath, where it's as easy to forget you're in a big city as it is to get completely lost.

Hampstead Heath

With its rolling woodlands and meadows, **Hampstead Heath** (Map pp78-9; ⊖ Hampstead, Gospel Oak or Hampstead Heath mainline station) is a million miles away – well approximately four – from the city of London. A walk up Parliament Hill affords one of the most spectacular views of the city.

Kenwood House (Map pp78-9; ☎ 8348 1286; Hampstead Lane NW3; admission free, tour admission £3.50; 🕑 10am-6pm Apr-Sep, 10am-5pm Mar & Oct, 10am-4pm Nov-Feb; ⊖ Archway or Golders Green) is a magnificent neoclassical mansion on the northern side of the heath, and houses a small collection of paintings by European masters. From the station catch bus No 210.

The Heath also has several swimming ponds – for the strong and hardy – with separate ponds for single-sex and mixed bathing. Once you've worked up a thirst, that's *after* your swim, there are several good pubs in the vicinity (see p135).

Highgate Cemetery

Most famous as the final resting place of Karl Marx and other notable mortals, **Highgate Cemetery** (Map pp78-9; ☎ 8340 1834; Swain's Lane N6; admission £2; eastern section 🕑 10am-5pm Mon-Fri, 11am-5pm Sat & Sun Apr-Oct; 10am-4pm Mon-Fri, 11am-4pm Sat & Sun rest of yr; ⊖ Highgate) is set in 20 wonderfully wild and atmospheric hectares with absurdly overdecorated Victorian graves and sombre tombs.

The cemetery is divided into two parts. You can visit Marx on the maintained east side on your own, but to visit the vine-covered western section of this Victorian Valhalla you'll have to take a **tour** (adult/child £3/1; 🕑 noon Mon-Fri, on the hr 11am-4pm Sat & Sun Apr-Oct; on the hr 11am-3pm Sat & Sun Nov-Mar).

Keats House

The golden boy of the Romantic poets lived in this elegant Regency **house** (Map pp78-9; ☎ 7435 2062; Wentworth Pl, Keats Grove NW3; adult/child £3/free; ✆ noon-4pm Tue-Sun Nov-late Mar, noon-5pm Tue-Sun Mar-Oct; tours by appointment; ✆ Hampstead) from 1818 to 1820 – until doctors advised him to move to sunnier climes – and penned some of his most famous works here. He wrote *Ode to a Nightingale* under a tree in the secluded garden, although, unfortunately, the original tree has long since been replaced. Among the personal mementos are love letters and old manuscripts. Restorations are scheduled to take place, so ring ahead.

Freud Museum

After fleeing Nazi-occupied Vienna in 1938, Sigmund Freud came to this house where he lived the last 18 months of his life. The **Freud Museum** (Map pp78-9; ☎ 7435 2002; www.freud.org.uk; 20 Maresfield Gardens NW3; adult/child £4/free; ✆ noon-5pm Wed-Sun) contains the psychoanalyst's original couch, his books and his Greek and Asian artefacts.

East London

The eastern reaches of central London are taken up by the East End – the London of Christmas pantomimes and old Hollywood films – and the sprawl of the Docklands, where the brand new sits alongside the old and decaying.

EAST END

The East End districts of Shoreditch, Hoxton, Spitalfields and Whitechapel may lie within walking distance of the City, but the change of pace and style is extraordinary. Traditionally, this was working-class London, settled by different waves of immigrants all of whom have left their mark. Run down and neglected by the 1980s, it is now looking up and pockets of it, like Hoxton, have become centres of cool. There are no major attractions to drag you into the East End, but it's a good place to immerse yourself in modern, multicultural London. (See the boxed text p139.)

Geffrye Museum

With a sequence of recreated domestic interiors, running chronologically from Elizabethan times to the end of the 20th century along 14 interconnected 18th-century almshouses, the **Geffrye Museum** (Map pp78-9; ☎ 7739 9893; www.geffrye-museum.org.uk; 136 Kingsland Rd E2; admission free; ✆ 10am-5pm Tue-Sat, noon-5pm Sun; ✆ Old Street, then bus No 243) provides a delightfully engaging peek at British domestic style. There's a lovely walled herb garden, a design centre, shop and restaurant.

DOCKLANDS

The Port of London was once the world's greatest port, the hub of the British Empire and its enormous global trade. Since being pummelled by the Luftwaffe in WWII its fortunes have been topsy-turvy, but new development and infrastructure have seen people and tenants return in recent years.

The new **Museum in Docklands** (Map p94; ☎ 7515 1162; www.museumindocklands.org.uk; Hertsmere Rd, West India Quay E17; adult/child £5/free; ✆ 10am-5.30pm), housed in a heritage-listed warehouse, uses artefacts and multimedia to chart the history of the Docklands from Roman trading to its renewal in the twilight of the 20th century. It's a fascinating look through the Docklands window into Britain's past.

South London

Glamorous Greenwich is the main attraction south of London's centre but you will also have fun exploring Brixton's colourful market or visiting the excellent Horniman Museum in Forest Hill.

GREENWICH

Quaint and village-like, Greenwich (*gren-itch*) is a delightful place with a recharging sense of space, splendid architecture and strong connections with the sea, science, sovereigns and time. It has earned its place on Unesco's list of World Heritage Sites and you should allow a full day to do your visit justice. All the great architects of the Enlightenment made their mark here, largely due to royal patronage, and there's an extraordinary cluster of classical buildings to explore.

The **TIC** (Map p94; ☎ 0870 608 2000; fax 8853 4607; 2 Cutty Sark Gardens SE10; Docklands Light Rail (DLR) Cutty Sark; ✆ 10am-5pm) has all the information you need on the area and sells the **Greenwich Passport ticket** (adult/child £12/2.50) covering admission to the *Cutty Sark*, National Maritime Museum and Royal Observatory.

Cutty Sark

A famous Greenwich landmark, this **clipper** (Map p94; ☎ 8858 3445; www.cuttysark.org.uk; King

William Walk; adult/child £4/3; ⏰ 10am-5pm) was the fastest ship in the world when it was launched in 1869. You can stroll on its decks, admire the beautiful and ongoing restoration and descend into the hold to inspect maritime prints, paintings and the world's largest collection of ship figureheads.

Old Royal Naval College

Walk south along King William Walk and you'll see the **Old Royal Naval College** (Map p94; ☎ 8858 2154; www.greenwichfoundation.org.uk), designed by Wren and a magnificent example of monumental classical architecture. Now used by the University of Greenwich, you can still view the **chapel** and the fabulous **Painted Hall** (adult/child £5/free; ⏰ 10am-5pm Mon-Sat, 12.30-5pm Sun), which took artist Sir James Thornhill 19 years of hard graft to complete.

National Maritime Museum

Further south along King William Walk, you'll come to the **National Maritime Museum** (Map p94; ☎ 8312 6565; www.nmm.ac.uk; Romney Rd SE10; admission free; ⏰ 10am-5pm), a magnificent neoclassical building by Inigo Jones, which houses a massive collection of marine paraphernalia recounting Britain's seafaring history. Exhibits range from interactive displays to old-fashioned humdingers like Nelson's tunic complete with a hole from the bullet that killed him.

Queen's House

Attached to the National Maritime Museum on its eastern side, the **Palladian Queen's House** (Map p94; ☎ 8858 4422; admission free; ⏰ 10am-5pm) has been restored to something like Inigo Jones' intention when he designed this place in 1616. It is a stunning exhibition venue, focusing on illustrious seafarers and historic Greenwich.

Royal Observatory

Charles II had the **Royal Observatory** (Map p94; ☎ 8858 4422; www.rog.nmm.ac.uk; admission free; ⏰ 10am-5pm) built here in 1865 to help solve the riddle of longitude. Success was confirmed in 1884 when Greenwich was designated as the prime meridian of the world, and Greenwich Mean Time (GMT) became the universal measurement of standard time. On this spot you can stand with your feet straddling the western and eastern hemispheres.

If you arrive just before lunch time, you will see a bright red ball climb the observatory's northeast turret at 12.58pm and drop at 1pm – as it has every day since 1833, when it was introduced to allow the ships on the Thames to set their clocks. If you arrive just *after* lunch time, you can console yourself with superb views across London or a visit to the atmospheric preserved rooms containing the actual timepieces described in Dava Sobel's *Longitude*, the bestselling book about the fascinating quest to measure longitude.

Fan Museum

Greenwich also provides the engaging **Fan Museum** (Map p94; ☎ 8305 1441; www.fan-museum.org; 12 Croom's Hill SE10; DLR Greenwich; adult/child £3.50/2.50; ⏰ 11am-5pm Tue-Sat, noon-5pm Sun), housed in an 18th-century Georgian house and one of only two of its kind in the world. Only a fraction of the hand-held folding fans, collected from around the world and dating back to the 17th century, are on display at any one time, but there's always enough to stoke your enthusiasm and you'll find yourself eagerly exploring the history.

Getting There & Away

Greenwich is now most easily reached on the DLR; Cutty Sark is the station closest to the TIC and most of the sights. There are fast, cheap trains from Charing Cross to Greenwich station (preferably Maze Hill) about every 15 minutes.

Alternatively, to get yourself in the mood, come by boat. **Thames River Services** (☎ 7930 4097; www.westminsterpier.co.uk) departs hourly from both Westminster Pier (Map pp84-6) and Greenwich, and the trip takes approximately 50 minutes (return £8.25).

AROUND GREENWICH
Millennium Dome

The public never took to the **dome** (Map p94), the centrepiece of Britain's millennium celebrations. And it gobbled up millions of pounds as the government held on, waiting for a white knight to save its white elephant. Help eventually came from a multinational consortium, which took out a 999-year lease on the dome in 2002. It is being transformed into a 20,000-seater sports and entertainment arena, surrounded by shops, restaurants and affordable housing. It won't be completed before spring 2007.

BRIXTON

West Indian immigrants flocked to Brixton after WWII and infused the ramshackle area with the flavour of the Caribbean. A generation or so later, economic decline, Margaret Thatcher and hostility between the police and black residents (who accounted for less than a third of the local population at the time) sparked several serious riots, which earned Brixton world notoriety. The mood is decidedly more upbeat these days, and the streets are full of vitality and verve. Despite gradual gentrification, it retains its edge, and the partying is hardcore. (For a description of the Brixton Market, see p139.)

FOREST HILL
Horniman Museum

This extraordinary museum, specialising in African art and sculpture, would be a major draw if it weren't so far out of town. Set in an Art Nouveau building with a clock tower and mosaics, **Horniman Museum** (Map pp78-9; ☎ 8699 1872; www.horniman.ac.uk; 100 London Rd SE23; admission free; ⏰ 10.30am-5.30pm Mon-Sat, 2-5.30pm Sun; ➌ Forest Hill) has an assorted jumble of exhibits that were collected by the Victorian tea-merchant Frederick John Horniman. There's everything from Africa's largest masks to a superb collection of musical instruments. Turn left out of Forest Hill station along Devonshire Rd, then right along London Rd, and you'll see the Horniman on your right.

West London
KEW GARDENS

In 1759 botanists began rummaging around the world's gardens for specimens they could plant in the three-hectare plot known as the **Royal Botanic Gardens at Kew** (☎ 8332 5000, recorded message ☎ 8940 1171; www.rbgkew .org.uk; Kew Rd, Kew; admission £5; ⏰ 9.30am-6.30pm Mon-Fri, 9.30am-7.30pm Sat & Sun; ➌ Kew Gardens). They never stopped collecting, and the gardens, which have bloomed to 120 hectares, provide the most comprehensive botanical collection on earth as well as a delightful pleasure garden for the people of London.

Any time is a good time to visit although the gardens are at their most picturesque in spring and summer, when weekends are normally chock-a-block. First-time visitors should board the **Kew Explorer** (adult/child £3.50/1.50), a hop-on hop-off road train that leaves from Victoria Gate – where you will enter from if you get the tube – and takes you around the gardens' main sights.

Its wonderful plants and trees aside – including the world's largest collection of orchids – Kew has all sorts of charms within its borders. Highlights include the enormous **Palm House**, a hothouse of metal and curved sheets of glass; the stunning **Princess of Wales Conservatory**; the red-brick, 17th-century **Kew Palace** (1631); the celebrated **Great Pagoda** designed by William Chambers in 1762; and the **Temperate House**, which is the world's largest ornamental glasshouse and home to its biggest indoor plant, the 18m Chilean Wine Palmand.

The gardens are easily reached by tube but, during summer, you might prefer to cadge a lift on a riverboat from the **Westminster Passenger Services Association** (☎ 7930 2062; www.wpsa.co.uk; 1½hr), which runs boats several times daily departing from Westminster Pier from April to September (return £15).

HAMPTON COURT PALACE

Built by Cardinal Thomas Wolsey in 1514, but coaxed out of him by Henry VIII just before the chancellor fell from favour, **Hampton Court Palace** (☎ 8781 9500; www.hrp.org.uk; Hampton Court station; admission £11.80; ⏰ 9.30am-6pm Tue-Sun, 10.15am-6pm Mon mid-Mar–Oct; 9.30am-4.30pm Tue-Sun, 10.15am-4.30pm Mon Nov–mid-Mar) is the largest and grandest Tudor structure in England. It was already one of the most sophisticated palaces in Europe when, in the 17th century, Christopher Wren was commissioned to build an extension. The result is a beautiful blend of Tudor and 'restrained baroque' architecture.

Steeped in history, the palace makes for an enthralling visit and you should set aside the best part of a day to savour it. At the ticket office by the main Trophy Gate, pick up a leaflet listing themed guided tours led by historians bedecked in period clobber.

If you're in a rush, or have an aversion to guided tours, highlights include **Henry VIII's State Apartments**, including the Great Hall with its spectacular hammer-beamed roof; the **Tudor Kitchens**, staffed by 'servants'; and the **Renaissance Picture Gallery**. Spend some time in the superb gardens and get lost in the 300-year-old **maze**.

Hampton Court Palace is 13 miles southwest of central London and is easily reached by train from Waterloo station via Hampton Court station. Alternatively, you can take the 3½-hour riverboat journey from Westminster Pier (p117).

RICHMOND PARK
London's wildest park spans more than 1000 hectares and is home to all sorts of wildlife, most notably herds of red and fallow deer. It's a terrific place for bird-watching, rambling and cycling.

To get there from the Richmond tube station, turn left along George St, then left at the fork that leads up Richmond Hill until you come to the main entrance of Richmond Gate.

WHITEHALL WALKING TOUR
Lined with government buildings, statues, monuments and other historical sights, Whitehall (⊖ Charing Cross or Westminster), and its extension, Parliament St, is the wide avenue that links Trafalgar Sq with Parliament Sq. Whitehall was once the administrative heart of the British Empire and is still the focal point for British government.

The best way to take it all in is with the following short and leisurely stroll.

Start at the southern end of Trafalgar Sq as it leads into Whitehall. As you start walking south, on the right you'll see 1910 **Admiralty Arch** (1; p97) and the **Old Admiralty** (2). Further along on the left is the **Ministry of Defence** (3), on the far side of which you'll find the **Banqueting House** (4; p98).

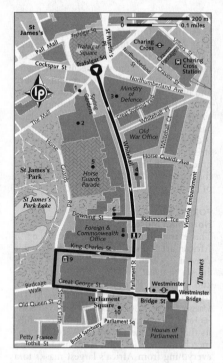

On the other side of Whitehall is **Horse Guards Parade** (5; ⊗ 11am Mon-Sat, 10am Sun), where the mounted troopers of the Household Cavalry are changed in a ceremony

---

LONDON'S OTHER CHURCHES
St Bartholomew-the-Great (Map pp86-7; West Smithfield; ⊖ Barbican) is one of London's oldest and most atmospheric churches. It featured in the film *Four Weddings and a Funeral* and has Norman arches encasing a dimly lit interior.

St Martin-in-the-Fields (Map pp91-3; Trafalgar Sq; brass-rubbing ☎ 7766 1199; ⊖ Charing Cross) is an early 18th-century masterpiece by James Gibbs that contributes to one of London's greatest vistas. The curious and ancient activity of 'brass-rubbing' is practised in the crypt, but perhaps the biggest draw at this acoustically gifted church, where Handel and Mozart once jammed, is the calendar of classical concerts throughout the year and the evensong at 5pm each Sunday.

St Mary-le-Bow (Map pp86-7; Cheapside EC2; ⊖ Bank or St Paul's) is another famous Wren (1673). Its bells dictate who is – and who isn't – a cockney; if you were born within the sound of their peal, you're the genuine article. The delicate steeple is particularly impressive.

Temple Church (Map pp84-6; King's Bench Walk, Inner Temple EC4; ⊖ Temple) is London's only church with a round interior in London, and was built by the secretive Knights Templar in 1185. Its frequently shifting opening times are just as mysterious as its founders, so ring ahead.

St Paul's Church (Map pp91-3; Bedford St WC2; ⊖ Covent Garden) is known as the 'actors' church' because of its long association with actors and thespians. Interior walls are lined with memorials to actors such as Charlie Chaplin and Vivien Leigh. The first recorded Punch and Judy show took place under the church's portico in 1662.

you'll find more accessible than the one outside Buckingham Palace.

The next intersection south of Horse Guards Parade brings you to **Downing St (6)**, site of the British prime minister's official residence since 1732, when George II presented No 10 to Robert Walpole. Tony Blair and his family actually now live in the larger apartments at No 11.

Whitehall becomes Parliament St and, on your left, you'll see the **Cenotaph (7)** – Greek for 'empty tomb' – a memorial to Commonwealth citizens killed during the two world wars.

On your right is the **Foreign & Commonwealth Office (8**; p98).

A right turn down King Charles St will bring you to the **Cabinet War Rooms (9**; p98).

Whitehall ends at **Parliament Square (10)**, watched over by statues of past prime ministers. Left along Bridge St is the ultramodern **New Parliament Building (11)**.

LONDON FOR CHILDREN

Getting around with little 'uns can be difficult here, but London offers a wealth of sights and museums that will get your kids excited about their trip. Apart from the obvious destinations like the London Dungeon, London Zoo, Madame Tussaud's, the Science Museum, Tower of London, the aquarium, *Cutty Sark* and the London Eye, there are many playground facilities throughout the centre and children are widely welcomed and catered for everywhere except pubs.

All top-range hotels offer in-house baby-sitting service. Prices vary enormously from hotel to hotel, so ask the concierge about hourly rates. You might also like to try www .babysitter.co.uk – membership costs £49 plus VAT, then sitters cost as little as £5.20 per hour.

TOURS

If you're short on time and big on company, the **Original London Sightseeing Tour** (☎ 8877 1722), the **Big Bus Company** (☎ 7233 9533) and **London Pride Sightseeing** (☎ 7520 2050) offer tours of the main sights on hop-on hop-off, double-decker buses, which you'll see trundling through town. They cost adult/child £15/10 for the day, but are only worth getting if you're in town for a short stopover. London Pride Sightseeing includes Docklands and Greenwich in one of its tours.

Citisights (☎ 8806 4325; www.chr.org.uk/cswalks .htm), **Historical Tours** (☎ 8668 4019), **London Walks** (☎ 7624 3978; www.walks.com) and **Mystery Tours** (☎ 8558 9446; mysterywalks@hotmail.com) offer a variety of themed walking tours.

More imaginative and rewarding tours include the following:

Black Taxi Tours of London (☎ 7935 9363; www .blacktaxitours.co.uk; 8am-6pm £75, 6pm-midnight £85) Takes you on a two-hour spin past the major sights with a chatty cabbie as your guide.

Cabair Helicopters (☎ 8953 4411; www.cabair.com; Elstree Aerodrome, Borehamwood, Herts; tours £129) Offers 30-minute helicopter 'flight-seeing' tours over London every Sunday.

City Cruises (☎ 7740 0400; www.citycruises.com; Westminster Pier SW1; cruises £8.70; ☾ 10am-4.30pm, later in Jun-Aug, fewer sailings Nov-Mar) Operates a year-round ferry service from Westminster Pier to Tower Pier and Tower Pier to Greenwich in a continuous loop that allows passengers to jump on and off at various stops. Boats depart every 20 to 40 minutes, with later departures in summer, fewer in winter.

London Bicycle Tour Company (☎ 7928 6838; www .londonbicycle.com; 1A Gabriel's Wharf, 56 Upper Ground SE1; £14.95 incl bike) Offers themed cycle tours of the 'East', 'Royal West' and 'Middle London'.

London Duck Tours (☎ 7928 3132; www.london ducktours.co.uk; departing from County Hall; adult/child £16.50/11; ☾ 10am-6pm) Uses the same sort of amphibious landing craft used on D-Day in WWII. You cruise the streets of central London before making a dramatic plunge into the Thames.

FESTIVALS & EVENTS

Although not renowned as a festival city, London has a few events that might influence your plans or give you advance warning of when and where it will be busy.

London Art Fair (www.londonartfair.co.uk; ☎ 0870 7399500 for tickets; Business Design Centre, Islington; admission £12 with unlimited access) Held in January, this fair sees over 100 major galleries participating in what is now one of the largest contemporary art fairs in Europe.

Chinese New Year (www.chinatown-online.co.uk; Chinatown) Late January or early February sees Chinatown snap, crackle and pop with a colourful street parade and eating aplenty.

Chelsea Flower Show (www.rhs.org.uk; Royal Hospital Chelsea) Held in May, this is the world's most renowned horticultural show and attracts green fingers from near and far.

Royal Academy Summer Exhibition (www.royal academy.org.uk; Royal Academy of Arts) Beginning in June and running through August, this is an annual showcase of works submitted by artists from all over Britain, gratefully distilled to a thousand or so pieces.

Wimbledon Lawn Tennis Championships Held at the end of June, the world's most splendid tennis event is as much about strawberries, cream and tradition as smashing balls.

Pride Parade In July, this is London's gay and lesbian community's opportunity to paint the town pink, with a parade and a huge party in Hyde Park.

Notting Hill Carnival (www.thecarnival.tv) Held in August, this is Europe's largest and London's most vibrant outdoor carnival, which celebrates its Caribbean community with music, dancing, costumes and a little street crime over the summer bank holiday weekend.

SLEEPING

Wherever you choose to lay your head, the cost may well put a serious dent in your travel budget. Weigh up your options very carefully and decide what order of centrality, comfort and affordability should be in your plans.

At the lower end of the market, it's worth booking at least a couple of nights' lodgings before you arrive, particularly in July and August. Anything below £55 for a double is pretty 'budget' in London.

Earl's Court is one of your safest bets for budget beds, while Bloomsbury and the area around the more upmarket South Kensington have lots of mid-range places to stay. You can forget about staying in or around the West End or the 'old money' London of Mayfair unless you've got money to burn. That said, there's a reasonable spread of accommodation options and you should try to park yourself close to where you intend spending most of your time.

West End – Soho to the Strand

You can't get more central than this so, naturally, accommodation here comes at a price. It specialises in deluxe hotels, many of which are tourist attractions in their own right.

BUDGET

Oxford St YHA (Map pp91–3; ☎ 0870 770 5984; oxford st@yha.org.uk; 14 Noel St W1; 3- or 4-bed dm £22, tw per person £22; ⊖ Oxford Circus) The most central of the hostels, it's basic, clean and welcoming. There's a large kitchen but no meals are served apart from a packed breakfast. Most of the 75 beds are twins.

MID-RANGE

Regent Palace Hotel (☎ 0870 400 8703; fax 7734 6435; Piccadilly Circus, cnr Glasshouse St W1; s with shared facilities/ en suite d from £50/80; ⊖ Piccadilly). In the middle of Picadilly Circus, this place is great for checking out the sights but a little too frenetic for anyone's idea of a holiday. Serving some 1000 rooms, the hotel lobby is just as busy and the whole place feels rather impersonal.

Harlingford Hotel (☎ 7387 1551; www.harlingford hotel.com; 61 Cartwright Gardens WC1; d from £75, f £110; ⊖ Russel Square) This jolly good hotel comprises three 19th-century townhouses and a bewitching chain of halls and stairways. The further up the stairs you go (there's no lift), the bigger and brighter the rooms generally get, although bathrooms are small whichever level you're on.

BOOKING SERVICES

It's possible to make same-day accommodation bookings for free at most of the TICs, and **Visit London** (☎ 08456 443 010; www.visitlondonoffers.com) also has good deals.

At Home in London (☎ 8748 1943; www.athomeinlondon.co.uk) Can arrange B&B accommodation and charges percentage booking fees.

British Hotel Reservation Centre (☎ 0800 282888; www.bhronline.com; Victoria train station; per reservation £3; ⊗ 24hr)

First Option (£5 per booking) There are kiosks at the Britain Visitor Centre, Euston (☎ 7388 7435); King's Cross (☎ 7837 5681), Victoria (☎ 7828 4646) and Gatwick Airport (☎ 01293-529372) train stations; and South Kensington tube station (☎ 7581 9766).

London Homestead Services (☎ 8949 4455; www.lhslondon.com; Coombe Wood Rd, Kingston-upon-Thames KT2 7JY) Takes bookings for a minimum of three days and charges £5 per person.

Youth Hostels Association (YHA; ☎ 0870 870 8808; lonres@yha.org.uk) Operates its own central reservations service provided you can give them at least two weeks' notice.

Fielding Hotel (Map pp91-3; ☎ 7836 8305; www
.the-fielding-hotel.co.uk; 4 Broad Ct, Bow St WC2; s/d from
£80/110; ✪ Covent Garden) On a pedestrianised
street a block away from the Royal Opera
House. Space is at a premium and the décor
is shop-bought but there's no better place
to be located if you want to take in a lot of
London in just a few days.

TOP END

Hazlitt's (Map pp91-3; ☎ 7434 1771; www.hazlittshotel
.com; 6 Frith St W1; d from £205, ste £300; ✪ Tottenham
Court Road) The former abode of author William Hazlitt is a charming Georgian house
and one of central London's finest hotels.
There are 23 individually decorated rooms,
each brimming with character.

St Martin's Lane (Map pp91-3; ☎ 7300 5500, 0800
634 5500; www.ianschragerhotels.com; 45 St Martin's Lane;
r from £195; ✪ Leicester Square) A joint effort between international hotelier Ian Schrager
and French designer Philippe Starck, and is
so cool that you would hardly notice it was
there. The rooms have floor-to-ceiling windows affording sweeping views of the West
End. The public rooms are bustling meeting points and everything – and everyone –
is beautiful.

DELUXE

Brown's Hotel (Map pp91-3; ☎ 7493 6020; www.browns
hotel.com; 30 Albemarle St W1; s/d from £320/370; ✪ Green
Park) A stunning hotel that opened in 1837
and the first in London to have a lift, telephone and electric lighting. Service is tip
top and the atmosphere quintessentially
English.

Covent Garden Hotel (Map pp91-3; ☎ 7806 1000;
www.firmdale.com; 10 Monmouth St WC2; d/ste £210/350;
✪ Covent Garden) Combines gorgeous fabrics
and a theatrical theme to stake out its in-
dividuality among the deluxe boutiques
(although it's really the location you pay
for).

One Aldwych (Map pp91-3; ☎ 7300 1000; www.one
aldwych.com; 1 Aldwych WC2; d/ste from £370/570;
✪ Covent Garden) Luxurious and trendy, with
(mostly) spacious rooms and lots of modern
art. The highly regarded **Axis Restaurant & Bar**
is the place to be seen and hosts food and live
jazz evening on Tuesday and Wednesday.

The Ritz (Map pp91-3; ☎ 7493 8181; www.theritzhotel
.co.uk; 150 Piccadilly W1; d/ste from £320/600; ✪ Green Park)
London's most celebrated hotel. After lend-
ing its name to the English lexicon, you might

> ## TOP FIVE ROMANTIC LONDON
>
> ■ Kissing in the back of a black cab
> ■ A squeeze on top of the **London Eye** (p109)
> ■ Jumping hand-in-hand across puddles
> ■ Walking back from the pub together just *before* closing time
> ■ Canoodling on, or by, a canal

expect this most ritzy of establishments to
rest on its laurels, don some slippers and fade
out. Not so. While it's still the royal family's
home away from home, such is the Ritz's
unyielding cred that even the new generation
of cultural elite are taking to it. The rooms
are expectedly opulent while the restaurant
is decked out like a rococo boudoir.

The Trafalgar (Map pp91-3; ☎ 7870 2900; www.the
trafalgar.hilton.com; 2 Spring Gardens SW1; d from £340;
✪ Charing Cross) Where the young, hip and
fashionable savour tasteful minimalism and
some spectacular views of the square.

Westminster & Victoria

Victoria isn't the most attractive part of
town although you'll be close to the action
and the budget accommodation is generally
better value than in Earl's Court. Pimlico is
more residential and is convenient for Tate
Britain at Millbank.

BUDGET

Luna & Simone Hotel (Map p90; ☎ 7834 5897; www.luna
simonehotel.com; 47-49 Belgrave Rd SW1; standard s/d from
£35/50; en suite d £80; ✪ Victoria) A central, spot-
lessly clean and comfortable place, the best
among many on this street. A full English
breakfast is included and there are free storage facilities if you want to leave bags while
travelling. If all of London's budget hotels
were like this, we'd probably stay longer.

MID-RANGE

Hamilton House Hotel (☎ 7821 7113; www.hamilton
househotel.com; 60 Warwick Way SW1; basic/en suite d
£65/90; ✪ Victoria) Friendly and close to Victoria's transport options. Although a little
small, the 40 rooms are bright and cheerful.

Morgan House (Map p90; ☎ 7730 2384; www.mor
ganhouse.co.uk; 120 Ebury St SW1; d from £90, ste £125;
✪ Victoria) Alongside the British Museum,

Morgan House is one of the best mid-priced hotels in London. The warmth and hospitality more than make up for the slightly cramped guest quarters.

Windermere Hotel (Map p90; ☎ 7834 5163; www .windermere-hotel.co.uk; 142-144 Warwick Way SW1; d from £84; ⊖ Victoria) An award-winning hotel with 22 small, distinctive rooms in a sparkling-white, mid-Victorian town house.

St James's and Mayfair
This is the top end of town, 'old money' London, and you shouldn't even read the listings unless money's no object.

TOP END
Chesterfield (Map pp84-6; ☎ 7491 2622; www.redcarn ationhotels.com; 35 Charles St W1; d from £100; ⊖ Green Park) Comprises five floors of refinement and lustre hidden behind a fairly plain Georgian town house. It has moulding ceilings, marble floors and period-style furnishing as you'd expect from a grande dame of London digs.

DELUXE
Claridges (Map pp84-6; ☎ 7629 8860; www.savoy -group.co.uk/claridges; Brook St W1; d from £370; ⊖ Bond Street) One of the greatest of London's five-star hotels, a leftover from a bygone era and *the* place to sip martinis whether you're a paying guest or not. Many of the Art Deco features of the public areas and suites were designed in the late 1920s.

The Lanesborough (Map pp84-6; ☎ 7259 5599; www.lanesborough.com; Hyde Park Corner; r from £320; ⊖ Hyde Park Corner) Where visiting divas doze and Regency opulence meets state-of-the-art technology.

Bloomsbury & Fitzrovia
Bloomsbury is very convenient, especially for the West End and the British Museum, and there are lots of places – of varying quality – on Gower and North Gower Sts. This one-time bohemian enclave of Fitzrovia is off the tourist map, yet within easy walking distance of Soho and lots of good restaurants. Tucked away in leafy Cartwright Gardens to the north of Russell Sq, you'll find some of London's best-value hotels.

BUDGET
The Generator (Map pp80-1; ☎ 7388 7666; www .the-generator.co.uk; Compton Pl, 37 Tavistock Pl WC1;

dm £12.50-17, s £37; ⊖ Russell Square) One of the liveliest budget options in central London. The futuristic décor looks like an updated set from Terry Gilliam's film *Brazil*. Along with 207 rooms (830 beds), it has flirtatious staff and a bar that stays open until 2am – but the two don't necessarily go together. There's also a pool, Internet access, safe-deposit boxes and a large eating area but no kitchen. All prices include breakfast.

MID-RANGE
Hotel Cavendish (Map pp80-1; ☎ 7636 9079; www.hotel cavendish.com; 75 Gower St WC1; basic s/d from £38/48; ⊖ Goodge Street) Spick, span and run by an amiable family, this hotel can be a budget option if you don't mind sharing bathroom facilities. Rates include breakfast, and the purple and burgundy rooms are simply furnished and comfy. If the Cavendish is full, you'll be referred to its sister hotel **Jesmond Hotel**, nearby, where rates and standards are similar.

Crescent Hotel (Map pp80-1; ☎ 7387 1515; www .crescenthoteloflondon.com, 49-50 Cartwright Gardens WC1; standard s from £46, en suite d from £89; ⊖ Russell Square) Built in 1810, it has a mix of rooms ranging from poky singles without facilities, to relatively spacious double en suites. The staff are hospitable either way.

Jenkins Hotel (Map pp80-1; ☎ 7387 2067; www .jenkinshotel.demon.co.uk; 45 Cartwright Gardens WC1; standard s £52, en suite s/d from £85; ⊖ Russell Square) A smoke-free zone and has pretty rooms with washbasin, TV, phone and fridge. The rooms are small but the welcome is huge.

Ridgemount Hotel (Map pp84-6; ☎ 7636 1141; www.ridgemounthotel.co.uk; 65-67 Gower St WC1; en suite d from £50/65; ⊖ Goodge Street) An old-fashioned place, this hotel offers a warmth and consideration you don't come across very often in the city.

St Margaret's Hotel (Map pp84-6; ☎ 7636 4277; www.stmargaretshotel.co.uk; 26 Bedford Pl WC1; basic/en suite d from £63/98; ⊖ Russell Square or Holborn) An exceedingly friendly Italian family-run hotel in a classic Georgian town house, with bright and comfy public and guest rooms and a lovely garden.

TOP END
Charlotte Street Hotel (Map pp91-3; ☎ 7806 2000; www.firmdale.com; 15 Charlotte St W1; d from £220; ⊖ Goodge Street) A favourite with media types, this place is where Laura Ashley goes post-modern and comes up smelling of roses.

Holborn & Clerkenwell

The availability of accommodation hasn't kept pace with Clerkenwell's revival although things are quickly changing, and this central area is becoming an increasingly good choice to lay your head.

MID-RANGE

Malmaison (Map pp84-6; ☎ 70123700; www.malmaison .com; Charterhouse Sq EC1; weekday/weekend d from £165/99; ⊖ Farringdon) One of a modern Scottish boutique chain providing value for money in trendy Clerkenwell. Suave, sophisticated and refreshingly understated.

The Zetter Hotel (Map pp80-1; ☎ 7324 4455; www .thezetter.com; 86-88 Clerkenwell Rd EC1; d from £145; ⊖ Farringdon) A stylish, 21st-century conversion of a 19th-century warehouse. The furnishings are an enticing blend of old and new, and the facilities cutting edge.

TOP END

The Rookery (Map pp80-1; ☎ 7336 0931; www.rookery hotel.com; Peter's Lane, Cowcross St EC1; s/d from £215/245; ⊖ Farringdon) Occupies a row of once-derelict 18th-century Georgian houses and provides a discreet, luxurious hideaway in fashionable Clerkenwell. Rooms have period furniture including Victorian baths, showers and toilets.

The City

Obviously very central, the City can offer good deals on weekends when the workers are back in the suburbs tending to their gardens. But be mindful – you'll be swamped with them during the week, and there's very little action at night.

BUDGET

City of London YHA (Map pp84-6; ☎ 0870 5764; city@ yha.org.uk; 36 Carter Lane EC4; dm £15-26; ⊖ St Paul's) An excellent facility (193 beds in three- to 15-bed dorms) that stands in the shadow of St Paul's Cathedral. There's a licensed cafe-teria but no kitchen. Although right in the centre of London, it's pretty quiet around here outside business hours.

TOP END

Great Eastern Hotel (Map pp86-7; ☎ 7618 5010; www .great-eastern-hotel.co.uk; Liverpool St EC2; s/d from £225/265; ⊖ Liverpool Street) Just the right mix of hip and classic, without any unnecessary attitude.

Borough & Southwark

Just south of the river is good if you want to immerse yourself in workaday London, still be central and get fairly modest, nondescript accommodation (that doesn't cost the earth) in the numerous chain hotels that have sprung up here in recent years.

BUDGET

St Christopher's Village (Map pp86-7; ☎ 7407 1856; www.st-christophers.co.uk; 163 Borough High St SE1; dm £15-19, tw £45; ⊖ Borough) The flagship of a chain of hostels that has gained a reputation for being cheap and reliable, fun and relaxed. The empire is expanding and it now has hostels in Camden, Shepherd's Bush and Greenwich, plus three along this street in Southbank. Facilities here include a sauna, solarium and hot tub.

MID-RANGE

County Hall Travel Inn Capital (Map pp84-6; ☎ 7902 1600; www.travelinn.co.uk; Belvedere Rd SE1; r £85; ⊖ Waterloo) Fairly bare bones, but the rooms are large and reasonable. If you can't get in here, there are about a dozen Travel Inns throughout London.

Chelsea, South Kensington & Knightsbridge

Classy Chelsea and 'South Ken' offer easy access to the museums and fashion retailers. The prices are reasonable for the neighbourhood and there's a relaxing villagey vibe.

BUDGET

Holland House (Map pp82-3; ☎ 0870 770 5866; holland house@yha.org.uk; Holland Walk W8; dm £22; ⊖ High Street Kensington) With 201 beds, it's built into the Jacobean wing of Holland House and overlooks Holland Park. Though large, very busy and rather institutional, the position can't be beaten. There's a café and kitchen, and breakfast is included.

MID-RANGE

Abbey House (Map pp82-3; ☎ 7727 2594; www.abbey housekensington.com; 11 Vicarage Gate W8; standard s/d from £45/74; ⊖ High Street Kensington) A humble but pleasant abode near Kensington Palace. The floral motif may not be to everybody's taste, but the rooms are undeniably cosy and the price is right. There's a rustic breakfast room and a kitchen where guests can make tea and coffee.

SERVICED APARTMENTS

Aston's Apartments (☎ 7590 6000; www
.astons-apartments.com; 39 Rosary Gardens SW7;
⊖ Gloucester Road)

Holiday Serviced Apartments (☎ 7373
4477; reservations@holiday apartments.co.uk; 273
Old Brompton Rd SW5; ⊖ Gloucester Road)

Vancouver Studios (☎ 7243 1270; www.vienna
-group.co.uk; 30 Princes Sq W2; ⊖ Bayswater)

Five Sumner Place (Map pp88-9; ☎ 7584 7586;
www.sumnerplace.com; 5 Sumner Pl SW7; s/d from £85/130;
⊖ South Kensington) On a quiet leafy road just
off Old Brompton Rd, this place is restful,
refined and elegant. It has 13 well-equipped
rooms (any room with a drinks cabinet is
'well equipped') and there's an attractive
conservatory and courtyard garden.

Swiss House Hotel (Map pp88-9; ☎ 7373 2769;
www.swiss-hh.demon.co.uk; 171 Old Brompton Rd SW5;
standard s £51, en suite s/d from £71/89; ⊖ Gloucester
Road) An outstanding place for the price.
It's set in a Victorian terrace house that's
festooned with flowers, the staff are gracious and welcoming, and the amply sized
rooms are cosily shabby chic. Rooms at the
rear look out over a pleasant garden and
don't get any noise from the street.

TOP END
Basil St Hotel (Map pp82-3; ☎ 581 3311; www.thebasil
.com; Basil St SW3; d from £145; ⊖ Knightsbridge) A
lovely, antique-stuffed hideaway in the heart
of Knightsbridge. It's decidedly low-tech –
baths instead of showers, no lifts etc –
but it's a delightful vision of little England
in big London.

The Gore (Map pp82-3; ☎ 7584 6601; www.gorehotel
.com; 189 Queen's Gate SW7; d from £190; ⊖ High Street
Kensington or Gloucester Rd) Features include lots of
polished mahogany, Turkish carpets, antique-
style bathrooms, aspidistras, thousands of
portraits and prints, and a great bar.

Number Sixteen Hotel (Map pp88-9; ☎ 7589 5232;
www.numbersixteenhotel.co.uk; 16 Sumner Pl SW7; d from
£165; ⊖ South Kensington) A gorgeous spot, with
bright and muted rooms, embroidered bedspreads, relaxing guest lounges and a tree-
filled garden and conservatory.

Earl's Court

Although not really within walking distance
of many places of interest, Earl's Court is

the centre of inexpensive digs and the tube
station is a busy tourist interchange with an
infectious holiday atmosphere.

BUDGET
Barmy Badger Backpackers (Map pp88-9; ☎ /fax
7370 5213; barmy_badger.b@virgin.net; 17 Longridge Rd
SW5; dm from £16; ⊖ Earl's Court) A basic hostel
with dorm beds; rates include breakfast.
There's a big kitchen and safe-deposit
boxes. (There's also a YHA hostel nearby.)

York House Hotel (Map pp88-9; ☎ 7373 7519;
yorkhh@aol.com; 27-28 Philbeach Gardens SW5; basic s/d
from £35/55, en suite r from £48/73; ⊖ Earl's Court) Situated on a pretty, unassuming Earl's Court
crescent, this small place has seen better
days, but is good value, particularly if you
are happy to share facilities.

MID-RANGE
Philbeach Hotel (Map pp88-9; ☎ 7373 1244; www.phil
beachhotel.freeserve.co.uk; 30-31 Philbeach Gardens; en suite
s/d £65/90; ⊖ Earl's Court) In a pleasant, quiet side
street, this is one of London's few gay hotels,
and its interiors are suitably stylish and
unique. The garden restaurant **Wilde about
Oscar** and **Jimmy's** bar on the ground floor are
both popular with the local gay crowd.

Notting Hill, Bayswater & Paddington

Bayswater is an extremely convenient location though some of the streets immediately to the west of Queensway, which has
a decent selection of restaurants, are pretty
grim. Scruffy Paddington has lots of cheap
hotels and is a handy transit point. Notting
Hill is expensive in comparison, but has lots
of good bars and restaurants.

BUDGET
Balmoral House Hotel (Map pp82-3; ☎ 7723 7445;
fax 7402 0118; 156-157 Sussex Gardens W2; basic/en suite
d £48/68; ⊖ Paddington) Immaculate and comfortable, although they've gone totally over
the top with the room décor (not for light
sleepers). There are two properties directly
opposite one another on a street lined with
small hotels and, sadly, lots of traffic.

Garden Court Hotel (Map pp82-3; ☎ 7229 2553; www
.gardencourthotel.co.uk; 30-31 Kensington Gardens Sq W2;
standard s/d £39/58, en suite s/d £58/88; ⊖ Bayswater) Although it barely squeezes into this category,
it's one of London's best budget options. It is
cobbled from two 19th-century town houses
and overlooks an attractive Victorian square.

The same friendly family has run it for aeons and all its 34 rooms have a phone and TV.

MID-RANGE

Pavilion Hotel (Map pp82-3; ☎ 7262 0905; www.msi .com.mt/pavilion; 34-36 Sussex Gardens W2; d from £100; ⊖ Paddington) Has 'Fashion, Glam & Rock 'n' Roll' as the motto and 30 singularly themed rooms which are fun and good value although definitely B-list.

TOP END

Portobello Hotel (Map pp82-3; ☎ 7727 2777; www.porto bello-hotel.co.uk; 22 Stanley Gardens W11; d from £160; ⊖ Notting Hill Gate) A firm favourite with rock and rollers and movie stars down the years. Rooms and furnishing are eccentric in a funky, haphazard way, and there's a 24-hour bar to fuel guests on their merry way. The most coveted room is number 16, featuring a round bed which has seen action from the likes of Johnny Depp and Kate Moss.

Marylebone

Increasingly hip and groovy Marylebone is central and with graceful Georgian squares and bustling High Sts. It's within walking distance of Hyde Park, staggering distance of West End nightlife and, for our money, one of the best neighbourhoods to stay.

BUDGET

Glynne Court Hotel (Map pp82-3; ☎ 7723 4613; fax 7724 2071; 41 Great Cumberland Pl W1; s/d from £50/60; ⊖ Marble Arch) Fairly typical for this price range and location, it has 15 rooms, all with TV and phone.

MID-RANGE

Bryanston Court Hotel (Map pp82-3; ☎ 7262 3141; www.bryanstonhotel.com; 56-60 Great Cumberland Pl W1; standard d from £120; ⊖ Marble Arch) Open fireplaces, leather armchairs, creaky floors and oil paintings give it a hushed and traditional English atmosphere. There are 60 pleasantly furnished rooms, although the ones at the back are quieter and brighter.

Edward Lear Hotel (Map pp82-3; ☎ 7402 5401; www .edlear.com; 28-30 Seymour St W1; basic/en suite d from £70/93; ⊖ Marble Arch) In a terrific location just a short walk from Hyde Park Corner. You can eat a full English breakfast, with meat provided by HRH's traditional butcher. Rooms and furnishings are a little threadbare and there are four floors and no lifts.

Outside Central London

Staying outside the centre and commuting can be a drag, but these places are handy for great attractions on the outskirts.

BUDGET

Hampstead Heath YHA (☎ 0870 770 5846; hampstead@ yha.org.uk; 4 Wellgarth Rd NW11; dm £22; ⊖ Golders Green) With 200 beds it's perfect if you want easy access to the centre of London but value fresh air at the same time. There's a well-kept garden, the dormitories are comfortable and each room has a washbasin. There's a licensed café and a kitchen.

Rotherhithe YHA (Map pp78-9; ☎ 0870 770 6010; rotherhithe@yha.org.uk; 20 Salter Rd SE16; dm £24, tw £55; ⊖ Rotherhithe) YHA's flagship London hostel is right by the River Thames and the perfect choice for anyone who's keen on spending time in historical Greenwich but doesn't mind being a little isolated. There are 320 rooms, most of which have four or six beds, though there are also 22 doubles (four of them adapted for disabled visitors); all have an en suite. There's a bar and restaurant, as well as kitchen facilities and a laundry. Rates include breakfast.

MID-RANGE

Hampstead Village Guesthouse (☎ 7439 8679; www .hampsteadguesthouse.com; 2 Kemplay Rd NW3; standard s/d £54/72, en suite s/d £66/84; ⊖ Hampstead) Only 20 minutes by tube to the centre of London, it has rustic, antique décor and furnishings, comfy beds and a delightful back garden in which you can enjoy a cooked breakfast (if you pay the extra £7). There's also a studio flat, which can accommodate up to five people.

AIRPORT HOTELS

Europa Hotel Gatwick (☎ 01293 886666; Balcombe Rd, Maidenbower, Crawley, West Sussex RH10 7ZR; d from £84) As good as any other mid-range airport hotel, and it has half-hourly transfers to the airport.

Hotel Ibis Heathrow Airport (☎ 8759 4888; fax 8564 7894; 112-114 Bath Rd, Hayes UB3 5AL; d from £65) It has clean, serviceable rooms and a restaurant.

Radisson SAS Hotel Stansted Airport (☎ 0127 966 1012; Stansted Airport; d from £105) A five-minute walk from the terminal.

EATING

There has been an astonishing growth in the number and type of restaurants in London over the last decade or so, and dining out has become so fashionable that you can hardly open a menu without banging into some celebrity chef or restaurateur. Unfortunately, this new status doesn't automatically guarantee quality. Food and restaurants can be hit and miss no matter how much you spend. In this section, we steer you towards restaurants and cafés distinguished by their location, value for money, unique features, original settings and, of course, good food.

Opening hours vary. Many restaurants in Soho close Sunday, those in the City for the whole weekend. We've tried to note where places stray from the standard 'open daily for lunch and dinner' (standard business hours are outlined on p735), but it's always safest to call and check.

'Gastro-pubs' are hugely popular here, so you should also check the pub section for options. Vegetarians needn't worry. London has a host of dedicated meat-free joints, while most other restaurants offer vegetarian options.

West End – Soho to the Strand

Soho is the gastronomic heart of London, with stacks of restaurants and cuisines to choose from. The liveliest streets tend to be Greek, Frith, Old Compton and Dean Sts. Gerrard and Lisle Sts are chock-a-block with Chinese eateries. Bear in mind, though, the phrase 'West End prices' is well known to Londoners.

BUDGET

Café in the Crypt (Map pp91-3; ☎ 7839 4342; St Martin-in-the-Fields, Duncannon St WC2; mains £5-7, 'quick meals' from £3.95; Ⓨ closed Sun; ⊖ Charing Cross) An atmospheric crypt in which to rest weary bones

---

MEAL COSTS

Our pricing categories for London are per person for a two-course dinner and a drink. You'll pay much less for lunch.

- Budget – under £15
- Mid-range – £15–£40
- Top end – over £40

---

and enjoy good food from soups to casseroles. Lunch time is frantic.

Food for Thought (Map pp91-3; ☎ 7836 0239; 31 Neal St WC2; mains under £5) A classic old vegetarian joint that's big on sociability and flavour but small on price and space. Food ranges from soups to traditional Indian *thalis* (all-you-can-eat mixed plates)

Wong Kei (Map pp91-3; ☎ 7437 3071; 41-43 Wardour St W1; mains £4.50-7.50, set menus from £6; ⊖ Leicester Square) Legendary for its rude waiters, although they're really not that bad (or good, depending on what you're after). The Cantonese food is a little stodgy but as good value as you'll find on a (plastic) plate.

MID-RANGE

Kettners (Map pp91-3; ☎ 7734 6112; 29 Romilly St W1; mains £9-16; ⊖ Leicester Square) A gem, serving mouth-watering pizzas and burgers, which you can wash down with champagne while soaking in the gently fading grandeur with a piano tinkling softly in the background.

Gay Hussar (Map pp91-3; ☎ 7437 0973; 2 Greek St W1; mains £12.50-20; ⊖ Tottenham Court Road) An old-style, Hungarian eatery and Soho institution that's hardly changed in more than half a century. The menu is rich, authentic and meaty, and the portions are colossal.

Tokyo Diner (Map pp91-3; ☎ 7287 8777; 2 Newport Pl WC2; mains £8-10; ⊖ Leicester Square) Does everyday Japanese food at everyday prices. It's great for a quick and hassle-free bowl of noodles or plate of sushi to launch you into the night, or a set bento box on the run.

Mildred's (Map pp91-3; ☎ 494 1634; 45 Lexington St W1; mains £5-7; ⊖ Piccadilly Circus) The best veggie restaurant in central London and a treat for carnivores and herbivores alike. Don't be shy about sharing a table or you'll miss out on excellent and hugely portioned wholesome veggie fare from stir-fries to beanburgers.

Neal's Yard Bakery & Tearoom (Map pp91-3; ☎ 7836 5199; 6 Neal's Yard WC2; snacks £2.50-4.50; Ⓨ lunch only) This great vegetarian café – relaxed upstairs, hectic below – has terrific filled rolls, burgers and soups. There is a cluster of veggie places nearby.

Ozer (Map pp91-3; ☎ 7323 0505; 5 Langham Pl W1; mains £7.50-13; Ⓨ closes 11.30pm Mon-Sat; ⊖ Oxford Circus) Does 'Ottoman cuisine' that is lighter and more refined than the Turkish norm, as local workers and shoppers fully appreciate. Its Ankara sibling is supposed to be one of the best restaurants in Turkey.

SOHO CAFÉS

Soho's cafés are great for whiling away the hours inside or, weather permitting, on underused street furniture. These are a few stand-outs.

Bar Italia (☎ 7437 4520; 22 Frith St W1; ✪ Leicester Square) A great favourite with slumming celebrities lapping up the reviving juices and hunky paninis amid cool 1950s décor. It's always packed and buzzing but you can normally get a seat – after 1am.

Maison Bertaux (☎ 7437 6007; 28 Greek St W1; ✪ Tottenham Court Road) Has exquisite confections, unhurried service, a French bohemian vibe and 130 years of history.

Monmouth Coffee House (☎ 7836 5272; 27 Monmouth St WC2; ✪ Covent Garden) Brews beans sourced from all over the coffee-growing world. It's essentially a shop but has a few seats upon which you can slowly savour the magnificent blends.

Old Compton Café (☎ 7439 3309; 34 Old Compton St; ⏰ 24hr) A friendly, often frantic place with cheap snacks, and the epicentre of gay Soho.

Pâtisserie Valerie (☎ 7437 3466; 44 Old Compton St W1; ✪ Tottenham Court Road or Leicester Square) A sweet Soho institution with delicate pastries, stylish sandwiches and strictly no phones *le mobile*.

Back to Basics (☎ 7436 2181; 2A Foley St W1; mains £14-16; ✪ Oxford Circus) There are other options on the menu but fish is the focus at this superb corner restaurant, which you'll find cosy or cramped, loud or just lively depending on your mood.

Rasa Samudra (Map pp91-3; ☎ 7637 0222; 5 Charlotte St W1; mains £9-12; ✪ Goodge Street) Just north of Oxford St, Rasa Samudra is one of many restaurants on this street, but its tantalising South Indian vegetarian cuisine and Keralan seafood set it apart.

Rock & Sole Plaice (Map pp91-3; ☎ 7836 3785; 47 Endell St WC2; fish & chips £8-13) A classic, central chippy with restaurant, outdoor tables and takeaway. It's a model for modern British cuisine (ie traditional foods, even mushy peas, cooked the right way).

Saigon (Map pp91-3; ☎ 7437 7109; 45 Frith St W1; mains around £11; ✪ Leicester Square) Saigon is required dining for anyone on a gastronomic tour of Asia, via Chinatown. While London isn't particularly well endowed with Vietnamese eateries, this one manages to satisfy body and soul with authentic tastes and furnishings.

Spiga (Map pp91-3; ☎ 7734 3444; 84-86 Wardour St W1; mains £9-14; ✪ Tottenham Court Road) One of a small, upmarket chain specialising in feisty pizzas, perky pastas and excellent vegetarian antipasto in sleek, casual surroundings.

Wagamama (Map pp91-3; ☎ 7292 0990; 10A Lexington St W1; mains £5-8; ✪ Leicester Square) This (or any of its dozen or so central London branches) is the place to throw back a bowl of Japanese noodles while sitting at a long communal table listening to anything but your own thoughts (which you won't be able to hear). Queuing seems *de rigueur*.

Woodlands (Map pp91-3; ☎ 7839 7258; 37 Panton St SW1; thalis £7-9; ✪ Leicester Square) One of an Indian chain that in India is only so-so but here…wow. Superb thalis are a highlight as is anything from the South Indian menu.

Zipangu (Map pp91-3; ☎ 7437 5042; 8 Little Newport St WC2; set menus £10-14; ✪ Leicester Square) Though not much to look at, it's got three storeys of outstandingly tasty, constantly fresh, exceedingly good food and graceful service.

TOP END

The Admiralty (Map pp91-3; ☎ 7845 4646; Somerset House, Strand WC2; set lunches £25; ✪ Embankment) The flagship restaurant of the restored Somerset House, it has a traditional interior and modern French food. There's a lovely terrace outside overlooking the Thames. The degustation menus – including vegetarian – are sublime.

J Sheekey (Map pp91-3; ☎ 7240 2565; 28-32 St Martin's Ct WC2; mains £10-25; ✪ Leicester Square) A jewel of the local scene. It is incredibly smart and has four discreet rooms in which to savour the riches of the sea, cooked simply and exquisitely. Waiters are tall and handsome while the menu is short and select.

Rules (Map pp91-3; ☎ 7836 5314; 35 Maiden Lane; mains £18-24) Established in 1798, this is London's oldest restaurant and specialises in classic game cookery, serving some 18,000 birds a year. Despite the history, it's not a museum piece and its sustained vitality attracts locals as well as the tourist masses.

Sketch (Map pp91-3; ☎ 0870 777 4488; 9 Conduit St W1; Lecture Room mains £50-75; Gallery mains from £10; ⊖ Oxford Circus) A design enthusiast's wildest dream, with shimmering white rooms, designer Tulip chairs and toilet cubicles shaped like eggs. And that's just the downstairs video art gallery, which becomes a buzzy restaurant at night, then a funky club after midnight. Upstairs in the Lecture Room is the most expensive eatery in London with starters going for £65.

The Wolseley (Map pp91-3; ☎ 7499 6996; 160 Piccadilly W1; afternoon tea £15; ⊖ Piccadilly) Occupies a grand 1920s building that once served as a showroom for Wolseley cars. These days, it's a classic Viennese café serving everything from emergency quick croissants to a slow trot around a global menu.

Westminster & Pimlico

There's very little action around these parts at night, although the following restaurants are worth a short detour in themselves.

BUDGET

Jenny Lo's Tea House (Map p90; ☎ 7259 0399; 14 Eccleston St SW1; mains £5-7; ⊖ Victoria) A simple, friendly Asian place that serves soups and rice dishes, but specialises in noodles and other wok-based specials.

TOP END

Cinnamon Club (Map pp84-6; ☎ 7222 2555; Old Westminster Library, 30 Great Smith St W1; mains £10-18; ⊖ St James's Park) Has domed skylights, high ceilings, parquet flooring and a book-lined mezzanine that evokes an atmosphere reminiscent of when this place was the Westminster Library. Hushed, eager-to-please waiters hover like anxious footmen although they really have no need to be concerned because the Indian food here is fit for a rajah.

Tamarind (Map pp84-6; ☎ 7629 3561; 20 Queen St W1; mains £10-30; ⊖ Green Park) One of those places where you're passed along a chain of assorted staff before sitting down – à la Bobby de Niro in *Goodfellas*. The slightly older crowd is fru fru, in keeping with the restaurant and neighbourhood, while the food – a cavalcade of Indian classics – is out of this world.

East End & the City

It can be difficult to find a decent, affordable restaurant that stays open after office hours in the City. Meanwhile, from the hit-and-miss Indian and Bangladeshi restaurants of Brick Lane to the trendy eateries of Hoxton and Shoreditch, the East End has finally made it onto London's culinary map.

BUDGET

Arkansas Café (Map pp86-7; ☎ 7377 6999, Unit 12, Spitalfields Market, 107B Commercial St E1; ⊙ noon-2.30pm Mon-Fri, noon-4pm Sun; mains £4-12.50; ⊖ Liverpool Street or Aldgate East) Serves good ole, down-home country cookin' on the unprepossessing edges of Spitalfield market (and reached via the inside of the market). Not for vegetarians.

Brick Lane Beigel Bake (Map pp78-9; ☎ 7729 0616; 159 Brick Lane E2; most bagels less than £1; ⊙ 24hr; ⊖ Shoreditch) A relic of London's Jewish East End, it's more of a delicatessen than a café and sells the cheapest bagels anywhere in London. You only get what you pay for, but they're a good snack on a bellyful of booze.

Crussh (Map pp86-7; ☎ 7626 2175; 48 Cornhill EC3; ⊖ Bank) The perfect place to pep up, with a range of juices and light, healthy snacks.

Dim Sum (Map pp84-6; ☎ 7236 1114; 5-6 Deans Ct EC4; mains £4-7; ⊙ Mon-Fri; ⊖ St Paul's) A budget traveller's delight and convenient for St Paul's and the City of London YHA hostel. It serves Peking and Sichuan dishes and has an all-you-can-eat buffet (minimum four people) in the evening from Monday to Friday.

Le Taj (Map pp86-7; ☎ 7247 4210; 134 Brick Lane E1; mains £4-8; ⊖ Liverpoool Street or Shoreditch) A modestly dressed Bengali favourite, it's one of the better restaurants on this strip.

The Place Below (Map pp86-7; ☎ 7329 0789; St Mary-le-Bow Church, Cheapside EC2; light meals £6-8; ⊙ lunch only, closed weekend; ⊖ St Paul's or Mansion House) A vegetarian café in a church crypt that's free of pinstripes and serves decent salads, pastas and quiches.

MID-RANGE

The Real Greek (Map pp78-9; ☎ 7739 8212; 15 Hoxton Market N1; meze £9, mains £14-17; ⊙ closed Sun; ⊖ Old Street) Set in Hoxton Market, London's trendy area du jour. This popular restaurant, in an old pub, specialises in innovative Greek cuisine, and if you think it looks familiar, you're thinking of the fight scene from the film *Bridget Jones's Diary*.

Sweeting's (Map pp86-7; ☎ 7248 3062; 39 Queen Victoria St EC4; mains £9-20; ⊖ Mansion House) An old-fashioned place with a mosaic floor and waiters in white aprons standing behind narrow counters serving up a cavalcade of fresh and seasonal seafood.

TOP END
Fifteen (☎ 7251 1515; 15 Westland Pl N1; ☺ booking line 9.30am-5.30pm Mon-Fri, restaurant noon-3pm & 7-10pm Mon-Fri, 7-10pm Sat; mains £11-26; ⊖ Old Street) Jamie Oliver's not-for-profit venture to train and employ young, disadvantaged kids. Reviews are mixed but people like to visit for a glimpse of the cheeky chappy himself, so you'll need to book ahead.

Southwark, Bermondsey & Lambeth
This part of south London is not immediately attractive as somewhere to eat out, although there are several good places and they are better value than the ones across the river.

BUDGET
Konditor & Cook (Map pp86-7; ☎ 7620 2700; 10 Stoney St SE1; most dishes under £3; ⊖ London Bridge) The original location of arguably the best bakery in London, it serves excellent hot and cold lunches. There's not much space but everything is yours to take away.

Manze's (Map pp86-7; ☎ 7407 2985; 87 Tower Bridge Rd SE1; pie & mash £2.50; ⊖ London Bridge) One of London's oldest and prettiest pie shops, it's been doling out the working-class staples of jellied eels and pie and mash for over a century.

MID-RANGE
Delfina (Map pp86-7; ☎ 7357 0244; 50 Bermondsey St SE1; ☺ noon-3pm Mon-Fri; mains £9.95-14; ⊖ London Bridge) A chic artists' cooperative canteen that serves mean and modern international cuisine.

Blue Print Café (Map pp78-9; ☎ 7378 7031; Design Museum, Butlers Wharf, Shad Thames SE1; starters £5-6.50, mains £11-16.50; ⊖ Tower Hill) A restaurant by Sir Terence Conran, the man who first put London on the gastronomic map, this place serves an everchanging cavalcade of modern international seasonal fare. There are spectacular views of the river from here and the Design Museum is next door.

Fish! (Map pp86-7; ☎ 7836 3236; Cathedral St SE1; mains £9-18; ⊖ London Bridge) Situated in an all-glass Victorian pavilion overlooking Borough Market and Southwark Cathedral, it's

part of a fast-breeding chain serving fresher-than-fresh fish and seafood that's prepared simply: steamed or grilled. Noisy!

Mesón Don Felipe (Map pp84-6; ☎ 7928 3237; 53 The Cut SE1; tapas £2.50-5; ⊖ Waterloo) Tops for tapas and authentic Spanish atmosphere, helped along by classical Spanish guitar in the evenings. There are about half a dozen vegetarian options, more than you get in Spain.

Tas (Map pp84-6; ☎ 7928 1444; 33 The Cut SE1; mains £5-15; ⊖ Southwark) An outstanding Turkish place with plush surroundings, fab kebabs and an unusually large range of vegetarian fare. There's also a café attached.

TOP END
Oxo Tower Restaurant & Brasserie (Map pp84-6; ☎ 7803 3888; Barge House St SE1; mains around £17; ⊖ Waterloo) Offers good grub – a bit Mediterranean, a bit French, some Pacific Rim – and is all about special-event dining. There are splendid views over the Thames and St Paul's Cathedral. This price guide is for the slightly cheaper brasserie.

Chelsea, South Kensington & Knightsbridge
These three areas boast an incredible array of eateries to suit all budgets, ranging from Michelin-starred indulgence to reliable caffs. There is such a concentration of French people in South Kensington that it's sometimes referred to as 'Little France'. You'll find a lot of French-operated businesses just southwest of South Kensington tube station.

BUDGET
New Cultural Revolution (Map pp88-9; ☎ 7352 9281; 305 King's Rd SW3; mains around £6; ⊖ Sloane Square) A trendy, good-value dumpling and noodle bar.

MID-RANGE
Francofill (Map pp88-9; ☎ 7584 0087; 1 Old Brompton Rd SW7; meals around £10) Around the corner from Bute St, it's a delightful café-restaurant.

Made in Italy (Map pp88-9; ☎ 7352 1880; 249 King's Rd SW3; mains £6-15; ⊖ Sloane Square) Family run and convivial, with the best pizzas for miles, it's as close as you'll get to southern Italy without packing a bag.

Boxwood Café (Map pp84-6; ☎ 7235 1010; Berkeley Hotel, Wilton Pl SW1; mains £13-16; ⊖ Knightsbridge) A New York–style café set up by super-chef

Gordon Ramsay in a valiant attempt to kick back with young folk and make fine dining in London 'a little bit more relaxed'. The décor is a little dreary but the food first rate.

Daquise (Map pp88-9; ☎ 7589 6117; 20 Thurloe St SW7; mains £5.50-12.50; ✆ South Kensington) An attractively dowdy Polish diner and as charming a place as you're likely to find this close to the centre. The menu has lots of vegetarian as well as meat options; and the borscht (beetroot and bean soup) is a stand-out.

Wódka (Map pp82-3; ☎ 7937 6513; 12 St Alban's Grove W8; mains £11-14; ✆ High Street Kensington) An authentic Polish joint providing Kraków-chic on a quiet residential strip not far from Kensington High St. Specialities include *blinis* (filled pancakes), fishcakes and eye-popping vodkas.

TOP END
Bibendum (Map pp88-9; ☎ 7581 5817; 81 Fulham Rd SW3; full meals with wine about £60; ✆ South Kensington) Another Sir Terence Conran establishment, it's in one of London's finest settings for a restaurant – the Art Nouveau Michelin House (1911). The popular **Bibendum Oyster Bar** (half-dozen oysters £3.60-10.20) is on the ground floor, where you really feel at the heart of the architectural finery. Upstairs is lighter and brighter.

Gordon Ramsay (Map pp88-9; ☎ 7352 4441; 68-69 Royal Hospital Rd SW3; set lunch/dinner £35/65; ✆ Sloane Square) One of Britain's finest restaurants and the only one in the capital with three Michelin stars. The food is, of course, blissful and perfect for a luxurious treat. The only quibble is that you don't get time to linger. Bookings are made in specific eat-it-and-beat-it time slots and, if you've seen the chef on TV, you won't argue.

Nahm (Map pp84-6; ☎ 7333 1234; Halkin Hotel, Halkin St SW1; mains £25-30; ✆ Hyde Park Corner) A hotel restaurant serving up scandalously good tucker prepared by Aussie chef David Thompson. It's the only Thai eatery outside the kingdom to have a Michelin star.

Nobu (Map pp84-6; ☎ 7447 4747; Metropolitan Hotel, 19 Old Park Lane W1; mains £5-28; ✆ Hyde Park Corner) Not so much a Japanese restaurant as a London designer's idea of a Japanese restaurant. It's nonetheless a strong contender for the best Asian food in town. Comfortably minimalist, anonymously efficient and out of this frikkin' world when it comes to

exquisitely prepared and presented sushi and sashimi.

Tom Aikens (Map pp88-9; ☎ 7584 2003; 43 Elystan St SW3; set lunch menu £25; average à la carte without drinks £75; ✆ South Kensington) Tom Aikens is the name of the notorious kitchen firebrand who runs this wonderful modern European restaurant where the setting is handsome and the food fab.

Notting Hill, Bayswater & Marylebone
Notting Hill teems with good places to eat, from cheap takeaways to atmospheric pubs (see p134) and restaurants worthy of the fine-dining tag.

BUDGET
Geales (Map pp82-3; ☎ 7727 7528; 2 Farmer St W8; fish & chips £10; ✆ Notting Hill Gate) A popular fish restaurant that's more expensive than your average chippy (prices vary according to weight and season), but worth every penny.

Jacob's (☎ 7581 9292; 20 Gloucester Rd SW7; meals around £10; ✆ Gloucester Road) A charismatic Armenian joint serving salads, falafel and kebabs that are a treat for your palate and a relief to your purse.

Raw Deal (Map pp82-3; ☎ 7262 4841; 65 York St W1; main & 2 salads £6.50; ✆ Baker Street) Occupies a glass corner of a Marylebone backstreet, and feels like the café on a Victorian railway platform where trains never come. Kooky and compelling, it's run by friendly South American smoothies who dish up robust and hearty salads along with pre-made hot dishes that never disappoint.

Sausage & Mash Café (Map pp82-3; ☎ 8968 8898; 268 Portobello Rd W10; mains £5-7; ✆ Ladbroke Grove) Takes the British favourite of bangers and mash to new levels. There is not just a choice of different sausages, as you'd expect, but also variations of creamy mounds of mash and even gravy in this S&M club that won't give your wallet a spanking.

MID-RANGE
La Fromagerie Café (Map pp84-6; ☎ 7935 0341; 2-4 Moxon St W1; mains £6.50-9.50; ✆ Baker Street or Bond Street) It's like food writer and owner Patricia Michelson's own kitchen, with bowls of delectable salads, antipasto, peppers and beans scattered about the long communal table. Huge slabs of bread just invite you to tuck in, and all the while the heavenly waft from

the cheese room beckons. Sensational food, smiley service, sensible prices.

Villandry (Map pp84-6; ☎ 7631 3131; 170 Great Portland St W1; mains £10-20; ⊖ Great Portland Street) Enter through a shop stocked with tempting goodies into this simple, stylish dining room where you can enjoy terrific modern European dishes like white bean stew with black truffle shavings.

Market Thai (Map pp82-3; ☎ 7460 8320; 240 Portobello Rd; mains £5-8; ⊖ Ladbroke Grove) is a delightful restaurant with dripping white candles, carved arches and wrought iron chairs. It occupies the 1st floor of the Market Bar but feels way, way, way beyond the market crowds. Hospitable staff and fresh, delicately spiced Thai cuisine make this place a little money very well spent.

Providores (Map pp84-6; ☎ 7935 6175; 109 Marylebone High St W1; tapas £2-10, mains £10-15; ⊖ Baker Street or Bond Street) A sassy, sociable and sexy restaurant that is split into two levels, with tapas tempting grazers on the ground floor and full meals along the same broadly Spanish lines in the elegant and understated dining room above.

TOP END

E&O (Map pp82-3; ☎ 7229 5454; 14 Blenheim Cres W11; mains £6-20; ⊖ Notting Hill Gate or Ladbrooke Grove) A Notting Hill hotspot and one of the best in a notable neighbourhood. E&O presents fusion fare, which usually starts with an Asian base and then pirouettes into something resembling Pacific Rim. The décor is stark and minimalist, but you're better off appreciating it at lunch because the evenings are mentally busy. You can dim sum at the bar.

Bloomsbury, Holborn & Clerkenwell

Holborn and Bloomsbury have relatively few good restaurants and nightspots to tempt you after dark while Clerkenwell has truly arrived on/as the scene.

BUDGET

The Greenery (Map pp84-6; ☎ 7490 4870; 5 Cowcross St EC1; light meals £2-7; ⊖ Farringdon) A salt-of-the-earth veggie café, surviving for the moment amid the gentrification of Clerkenwell.

St John (Map pp84-6; ☎ 7251 0848; 26 St John St EC1; ⊖ Farringdon) Next to Smithfield Market, it offers an intrepid romp through ye olde English staples such as pigs' trotters, smoked eel and an awful lot of offal.

MID-RANGE

Abeno (Map pp91-3; ☎ 7405 3211; 47 Museum St WC1; mains £5-25; ⊖ Tottenham Court Road) An understated little restaurant specialising in *okonomi-yaki*, a kind of Japanese savoury pancake combined with the ingredients of your choice (there are over 20 varieties with anything from sliced meat, vegetables, egg, noodles and cheese). It's all cooked in front of you on the hotplate that makes up most of your table.

The Eagle (Map pp80-1; ☎ 7837 1353; 159 Farringdon Rd EC1; mains £5-12.50; ⊖ Farringdon) Small and vivacious, it doesn't try to be too clever despite its trendy appeal and status as London's first gastro-pub. Menus are seasonal, creative and Mediterranean-influenced.

North Sea Fish Restaurant (Map pp80-1; ☎ 7387 5892; 7-8 Leigh St WC1; mains £8-17; ⊖ Russell Square) This place cooks fresh fish and potatoes – a simple ambition realised with aplomb. Look forward to jumbo plaice or halibut steaks, deep-fried or grilled, and a huge serving of chips. The setting is characterless, but the charismatic staff amply compensate.

TOP END

Club Gascon (Map pp84-6; ☎ 7796 0600; 57 West Smithfield EC1; mains from £30; ⊖ Farringdon) Right next to glorious St Bartholomew's-the-Great, it has a Michelin star and exquisite food from southwest France. Dishes are served tapas-style in multiple portions.

Hakkasan (Map pp91-3; ☎ 7907 1888; 8 Hanway Pl W1; meals £6-30; ⊖ Tottenham Court Road) Hidden down a lane like all the most fashionable haunts need to be, it combines celebrity status, a stunning design, persuasive cocktails and surprisingly sophisticated Chinese food. It was the first Chinese restaurant to get a Michelin star.

Camden & Islington

There are plenty of decent places to eat on and around Camden High St and Upper St in Islington. There are far fewer worthwhile stops in Euston and King's Cross in between.

BUDGET

Afghan Kitchen (Map pp80-1; ☎ 7359 8019; 35 Islington Green N1; mains around £5; ☾ closed Sun & Mon; ⊖ Angel) Small, laid-back and perpetually hip, it serves simple, tasty Afghan fare – half vegetarian, half with meat – and the prices are charitable.

Diwana (Map pp80-1; ☎ 7387 5556; 121 Drummond St; mains £3-6.50; ✚ King's Cross) The first of its kind on the street – and still the best according to many. It specialises in Bombay-style *bel poori* (a sweet and sour, soft and crunchy 'party mix' snack) and *dosas* (filled pancakes). There's an all-you-can-eat lunchtime buffet for £5.80.

MID-RANGE

Almeida (Map pp80-1; ☎ 7354 477730; Almeida St N1; mains £11-20; ✚ Angel) Has trolleys of pâtés and terrines for starters, classic French mains, and tarts for desserts. It's a Sir Terence Conran and it's a winner.

Café Delancey (Map pp80-1; ☎ 7387 1985; 3 Delancey St NW1; mains £7-15; ✚ Camden Town) The grandaddy of French-style brasseries in London, it offers the chance to get a decent cup of coffee with a snack or full meal in relaxed, European-style surroundings complete with newspapers. The bickering staff and Charles Aznavour soundtrack are suitably Parisian.

Le Mercury (Map pp80-1; ☎ 7354 4088; 140A Upper St N1; mains £5.95, specials £7-12; ✚ Highbury or Islington) A cosy Gaelic haunt ideal for a romantic tête-à-tête. Sunday lunch by the open fire upstairs is a treat although you'll have to book.

The Engineer (Map pp80-1; ☎ 7722 0950; 65 Gloucester Ave NW1; mains £10-15; ✚ Chalk Farm) One of London's original gastro-pubs serving up consistently good international cuisine to hip north Londoners. There's a good selection of wines and beers, and a splendid garden.

Fulham

Fulham Rd is a good place for a meal and a night out. The two restaurants listed here are London stand-outs.

The Gate (Map pp78-9; ☎ 8748 6932; 51 Queen Caroline St W6; mains £8-12; ✚ Hammersmith) This place alone is enough reason to include a Fulham section here. It's one of London's best restaurants. Taste, service and presentation are paramount but never get in the way of fun and friendliness. And it just happens to be vegetarian.

The River Café (Map pp78-9; ☎ 7386 4200; Thames Wharf, Rainville Rd W6; mains £20-30; ✚ Hammersmith) A see-and-be-seen Italian eatery that owes its fame as much to the cookbooks it has spawned as to the food actually served here,

which is based on the very best ingredients cooked simply.

Outside Central London

If you're visiting the sights in Brixton, Greenwich, Hampstead, Kew or Richmond consider a meal at any of the following restaurants and save yourself having to bolt back to the centre of town.

BRIXTON

Bug Bar Restaurant & Lounge (Map pp78-9; ☎ 7738 3366; St Matthew's Church, Brixton Hill SW2; ☉ 5-11pm Mon-Thu, 5-11.30pm Fri & Sat, 11am-11pm Sun; mains £7.50-10.50; ✚ Brixton) Situated in the crypt of St Matthew's Church. Arches, candles and gilt mirrors all create an ecclesiastical flavour, but it's Bug's organic, vegetarian or free-range meat cuisine that will be most memorable.

GREENWICH

Goddards Ye Olde Pie Shop (Map p94; ☎ 8293 9312; 45 Greenwich Church St SE10; meals under £3.50; ☉ Tue-Sun lunch only) Truly a step back into the past. A real London caff, with wooden benches and meals such as steak and kidney pie with liquor and mash, and shepherd's pie with beans and a rich brown gravy.

HAMPSTEAD

Jin Kichi (Map pp78-9; ☎ 7794 6158; 73 Heath St NW3; mains £5.50-13; ✚ Hampstead) One of the best Japanese restaurants in north London. It's small and slightly shabby but so popular with London's Japanese that you won't be able to enjoy its grilled meats and other Oriental flavours unless you book.

KEW

The Glasshouse (☎ 8940 6777; 14 Station Parade W9; set lunch/dinner £17.50/30; ✚ Kew Gardens) Virtually next to the tube station, it specialises in modern British cuisine and is a fabulous way to round off a visit to the gardens. The menus are set although the choice is large and the flavours will be etched on your palate all the way home.

Newens Maids of Honour (☎ 8940 2752; 288 Kew Rd; set teas £5.45; ☉ Tue-Sun; ✚ Kew Gardens) An old-fashioned tearoom famed for its 'maid of honour', a dessert supposedly concocted by Henry VIII's second wife, the ill-fated Anne Boleyn. You'll find it a short distance north of Victoria Gate, the main entrance to Kew Gardens.

RICHMOND

Chez Lindsay (☎ 8948 7473; 11 Hill Rise; 3-course set dinner £15; ⊖ Richmond) A gregarious Breton hideaway renowned for its seafood as well as sweet and savoury crêpes chased down with cider.

DRINKING

The pub is the social focus of London life and savouring pub life is one of the pleasures of any visit. From ancient atmospheric taverns to slick DJ bars, London has a lot to offer the discerning tippler no matter how hard the themed and chain bars try to take over.

West End – Soho to the Strand

Coach & Horses (Map pp91-3; 29 Greek St W1; ⊖ Leicester Square) A splendidly seedy Soho institution, made famous by writer and newspaper columnist Jeffrey Bernard who, more or less, drank himself to death here.

Freedom Brewing Company (Map pp91-3; 41 Earlham St WC2; ⊖ Covent Garden) London's primo microbrewery, although it might be a little expensive for the casual drinker.

Intrepid Fox (Map pp91-3; 99 Wardour St W1; ⊖ Leicester Square or Picadilly Circus) It's so not Soho. This loud, unaffected rock 'n' goth pub will be recognisable by the demented gargoyle above the door, the fake spiders and bats along the walls and the motley human assembly of Goths, punks and metal-heads with indoor complexions and impressive cleavages. The music is loud, the toilets grubby, the beer inexpensive and the bullshit barred.

Lamb & Flag (Map pp91-3; 33 Rose St WC2; ⊖ Covent Garden) A popular historic pub and everyone's Covent Garden 'find' so is often jammed. It was built in 1623 and was formerly called the 'Bucket of Blood'.

Punch & Judy (Map pp91-3; 40 The Market WC2; ⊖ Covent Garden) Inside Covent Garden's central market hall itself, it's a very busy and touristy two-level boozer. However, it has a balcony that lets you look down on St Paul's Church and the buskers, and is great on a sunny afternoon.

Scruffy Murphy's (Map pp91-3; 15 Denman St W1; ⊖ Piccadilly Circus) The most authentic of the Irish bars in Soho, short on ceremony and tall on tales.

Westminster & Pimlico

The Red Lion (Map pp84-6; 48 Parliament St SW1; ⊖ Westminster) A classic, late-19th-century pub with polished mahogany and etched glassware. The TV shows parliamentary broadcasts just in case a sitting kicks off in the house and the MPs have to rush back.

Westminster Arms (Map pp84-6; 9 Storey's Gate SW1; ⊖ Westminster) A pleasant, atmospheric place just around the corner from Big Ben so it gets its fair share of politicians. It's great for a swift half pint after a tour of Westminster Abbey (think of the convenience).

Bloomsbury, Holborn, Hoxton & Clerkenwell

Cantaloupe (Map pp78-9; 35-43 Charlotte Rd EC2; ⊖ Old Street or Shoreditch) Was one of the pioneers of the Shoreditch warehouse conversion scene and is still a popular gastro-pub, although not nearly as fashionable (thankfully).

Cock Tavern (Map pp84-6; East Poultry Ave EC1; ⊖ Farringdon) A legendary pub where you can top up between 6.30am and 10.30am when it feeds and waters the workers from Smithfield Market.

Dragon Bar (Map pp78-9; ☎ 7490 7110; 5 Leonard St N1; ⊖ Old Street) Super cool in that louche, moody (as opposed to overtly posey) Hoxton way. It's easy to miss as the name is only embossed on the entrance stairs, but once inside it's all exposed brick, Chinese lanterns, velvet curtains and no suits.

Museum Tavern (Map pp91-3; 49 Great Russell St WC1; ⊖ Tottenham Court Road) Where Karl Marx used to retire to for a sup after a hard day in the British Museum Reading Room. If it was good enough for him…

Princess Louise (Map pp91-3; ☎ 7405 8816; 208 High Holborn WC1; ⊖ Holborn) Ww-oW! We've used the word 'gem' before, but we take all of the other instances back. This late-19th-century Victorian boozer is spectacularly decorated with a riot of fine tiles, etched mirrors, plasterwork and a stunning central horseshoe bar. There are invariably more bums than seats until the after-workers split.

Sosho (Map pp78-9; 2 Tabernacle St EC2; ⊖ Moorgate) Sexy, glamorous and off limits if you're not feeling either of the above; although the cocktails could soon get you in the mood.

East End & the City

Captain Kidd (Map pp78-9; 108 Wapping High St E1; ⊖ Wapping) A great little pub on the Thames, it has large windows, a fine beer garden and a mock scaffold recalling the hanging of the eponymous pirate in 1701.

Jamaica Wine House (Map pp86-7; 12 St Michael's Alley EC3; ↔ Bank) It stands on the spot of London's first coffee house and is actually a traditional Victorian pub, not a wine bar.

Prospect of Whitby (Map pp78-9; 57 Wapping Wall E1; ↔ Wapping) Dating from 1520 – last remodelled in the 18th century – it's one of London's oldest boozers. It's firmly on the tourist trail but there's a terrace overlooking the Thames, a decent restaurant upstairs and open fires in winter.

Ye Olde Cheshire Cheese (Map pp84-6; Wine Office Ct EC4; ↔ Blackfriars) Rebuilt six years after the Great Fire, it was popular with Dr Johnson, Thackeray, Dickens and the visiting Mark Twain. Touristy but always atmospheric and enjoyable for a pub meal (mains around £7).

Ye Olde Mitre (Map pp84-6; 1 Ely Ct EC1; ↔ Chancery Lane) An 18th-century treasure hidden down an alley. Just finding it makes you feel like claiming it as your local.

Borough, Southwark & Bermondsey

The Anchor (Map pp86-7; 34 Park St SE1; ↔ London Bridge) An 18th-century boozer just east of the Globe Theatre, it has a terrace offering superb views over the Thames. Dr Johnson is said to have written some of his dictionary here.

George Inn (Map pp86-7; Talbot Yard, 77 Borough High St SE1; ↔ London Bridge or Borough) Tucked away in a cobbled courtyard not far from the Thames, is London's last surviving galleried coaching inn and dates from 1676. Charles Dickens used to frequent the Middle Bar.

The Market Porter (Map pp86-7; 9 Stoney St SE1; ↔ London Bridge) Across the road from Borough Market, this pub has a good range of beers and a diverse crowd.

Chelsea, South Kensington & Knightsbridge

Grenadier (Map pp84-6; 18 Wilton Row SW1; ↔ Hyde Park Corner) Down a quiet and rather exclusive mews, the Grenadier is as pretty as a picture from the outside and welcoming within (despite the sabres and bayonets on the walls).

King's Head & Eight Bells (Map pp88-9; 50 Cheyne Walk SW3; ↔ Sloane Square) An attractive corner pub pleasantly hung with flower baskets in summer. It was a favourite of the painter Whistler and the writer Carlyle.

Nag's Head (Map pp82-3; 53 Kinnerton St SW1; ↔ Knightsbridge) In a serene mews not far from bustling Knightsbridge, this terrific early-19th-century drinking den has eccentric décor, a sunken bar and no mobile phones.

Notting Hill, Bayswater & Marylebone

The Churchill Arms (Map pp82-3; 119 Kensington Church St W8; ↔ Notting Hill Gate) A lovely, traditional tavern stuffed with Winston memorabilia and bric-a-brac. There's an excellent Thai restaurant upstairs (mains around £7) and a pleasant conservatory out the back.

The Cow (Map pp82-3; ☎ 7221 5400; 89 Westbourne Park Rd W2; ↔ Westbourne Park or Royal Oak) A superb gastro-pub with outstanding food and a jovial pub-is-a-pub atmosphere. Seafood is a speciality and the staff are much friendlier than you'd expect from somewhere so perpetually hip.

Mash (Map pp91-3; ☎ 7637 5555; 19-21 Great Portland St W1; ☻ closes 2am Mon-Sat; ↔ Oxford Circus) Has a microbrewery and café so it's an all-day and all-week affair, although the main, huge and high-ceilinged bar requires a crowd to take off and is probably best kept for the weekend. It's a futuristic setting in an old car showroom, and the mechanics make mean mojitos.

Windsor Castle (Map pp82-3; 114 Campden Hill Rd W11; ↔ Notting Hill Gate) A memorable pub with oak partitions separating the original bars. The panels have tiny doors so big drinkers will have trouble getting past the front bar. It also has one of the loveliest walled gardens (with heaters in winter) of any pub in London.

Camden & Islington

Bar Vinyl (Map pp80-1; 6 Inverness St NW1; ↔ Camden Town) With loud music and groovy clientele, it's an earful of the Camden scene.

Crown & Goose (Map pp80-1; 100 Arlington Rd NW1; ↔ Camden Town) One of our favourite London pubs. The square room has a central wooden bar between British Racing Green Walls studded with gilt-framed mirrors and illuminated by big shuttered windows. More importantly, it combines a good-looking crowd, good beer, easy conviviality and top tucker.

Medicine Bar (Map pp80-1; 181 Upper St N1; ↔ Highbury or Islington) Coolly unpretentious, it plays good music from funk to disco and stays open until 2am at the weekend. This place is members only at weekends. It also has a sister bar in Shoreditch.

Pembroke Castle (Map pp80-1; 150 Gloucester Ave NW1; ⊖ Chalk Farm) A light, airy retro place where you can feel just as comfortable supping wine as ale.

Outside Central London

BRIXTON
Brixtonian Havana Club (Map pp78-9; 11 Beehive Pl SW9; ⊖ Brixton) As laid-back as you might expect a bar with hundreds of different kinds of rum to be. Cocktails are the speciality and DJs set the mood.

GREENWICH
Trafalgar Tavern (Map p94; Park Row SE10; DLR Cutty Sark) A Regency-style pub that was built in 1837 and stands above the site of the old Placentia Palace where Henry VIII was born. It is the former drinking den of Dickens, Gladstone and Disraeli.

HAMPSTEAD
The Hollybush (22 Holly Mount (above Heath St, reached via Holly Bush Steps) NW3; ⊖ Hampstead) A beautiful pub that makes you envy the privileged residents of Hampstead. It has an antique Victorian interior, a lovely secluded hill-top location, open fires in winter and a knack for making you stay longer than you had intended any time of the year.

Old Bull & Bush (North End Way NW3; ⊖ Hampstead) Has origins dating back to Charles I. One of London's most celebrated pubs, it was immortalised in the old music hall song *Down by the Old Bull and Bush.*

Spaniard's Inn (Spaniard's Rd NW3; ⊖ Hampstead, then bus No 21) A marvellous tavern that dates from 1585 and has more character than a West End musical. Dick Turpin, the dandy highwayman (or was that Adam Ant?) was born here and used it as a hangout in his later years, while more savoury sorts like Dickens, Shelley, Keats and Byron also availed themselves of its charms. There's a big, blissful garden and good food.

ENTERTAINMENT
Okay, now we're getting into holiday mode. Chances are you've come to the capital to be entertained; you won't be disappointed. Whatever you want – from cutting-edge clubs and international bands to Hollywood stars doing theatre turns and the world's best footballers strutting their stuff – you'd need a lifetime to exhaust the op-

portunities for fun. This list only scratches the surface; make sure to check the listings (see p95) for what's going on.

Theatre
London is a world capital for theatre and there's a lot more than mammoth musicals to tempt you into the West End. The term 'West End' – as with Broadway – generally refers to the big-money productions like musicals, but also includes such heavyweights as the **Royal Court** (Map pp88-9; ☎ 7565 5000; Sloane Sq SW1; ⊖ Sloane Square), the patron of new British writing; the **Royal National Theatre** (Map pp84-6; ☎ 7452 3000; South Bank; ⊖ Waterloo), which has three auditoriums and showcases classics and new plays from some of the world's best companies; and the **Royal Shakespeare Company** (RSC; ☎ 7638 8891), with productions of the Bard's classics and stuff he might have been interested in. Unfortunately, at the time of writing, the RSC is without a permanent home and is staging performances at various West End theatres.

On performance days you can buy half-price tickets for West End productions (cash only) from the **Leicester Square Half-Price Ticket Booth** (Map pp91-3; ◷ noon-6.30pm; Leicester Sq; ⊖ Leicester Square), on the south side of Leicester Sq. The booth is the one with the clock tower – beware of touts selling dodgy tickets. It charges £2 commission for each ticket.

Off West End – where you'll generally find the most original works – includes venues like the recently refurbished **Almeida** (Map pp80-1; ☎ 7359 4404; www.almeida.co.uk; Almeida St N1), **Battersea Arts Centre** (Map pp78-9; Lavender Hill SW1) and the **Young Vic** (Map pp84-6; 66 The Cut, Waterloo Rd SE1). The next rung down is known as the fringe and these shows take place anywhere there's a stage (and can be very good).

For a comprehensive look at what's being staged where, consult *Time Out,* pick up a copy of the free pamphlet *The Official London Theatre Guide* or visit www.official londontheatre.co.uk.

Clubs
This clubbers' capital has been propping up the vanguard of dance since the term 'recreational party drugs' was coined. From low-key DJ bars to warehouses and 'superclubs', the city has an astonishing range of venues offering everything from sexy R&B to thumping garage. Some venues have several different

rooms, while others change the tempo according to the night. Admission prices vary from £3 to £10 Sunday to Thursday, but on Friday and Saturday can be as much as £20.

Astoria (Map pp91-3; ☎ 7434 9592; www.g-a-y.co .uk; 157-165 Charing Cross Rd WC2) This dark, sweaty and atmospheric club has a G-A-Y night Saturday, a cheap Pink Pounder Monday and a disco-orientated Camp Attach Friday. There are good views of the stage and a huge dance floor.

Bar Rumba (Map pp91-3; ☎ 7287 2715; 36 Shaftesbury Ave W1; ❺ Piccadilly Circus) Along a Soho backstreet, it's a small club with a big reputation. There's a different style each night – from Latin and jazz to deep house and garage – but everyone's a winner.

Cargo (Map pp78-9; ☎ 7739 3440; 83 Rivington St EC2; admission £5-10; ❺ Old Street) A hugely popular club with local and international DJs and a courtyard where you can simultaneously enjoy big sounds and the great outdoors. The music policy is particularly innovative, but you can usually rely on Latin house, nu-jazz and rare grooves.

The Cross (Map pp80-1; ☎ 7837 0828; Goods Way Depot, York Way N1; ❺ King's Cross St Pancras) A little out of the way, in the King's Cross wastelands, but it's one of London's leading clubs serving up a Continental-style beat to a convivial crowd.

The End (Map pp91-3; ☎ 7419 9199; 16A West Central St WC1; admission £5-15; ❺ Holborn) Has industrial décor and a big sound. It's the best venue around the West End for serious clubbers who like their music hard.

Fabric (Map pp84-6; ☎ 7490 0444; 77A Charterhouse St EC1; admission £10-15; ❺ Farringdon) The latest feather in Clerkenwell's well-plumed cap and boasts three dance floors in a converted meat cold-store. Residences have included Sasha and Groove Armada. Expect to queue.

The Ghetto (Map pp91-3; ☎ 7287 3726; 5-6 Falconberg Ct W1; ❺ Tottenham Court Road) London's gay venue du jour and hosts not only the celebrity-attended, mixed-evening Nag, Nag, Nag on Wednesday, but also Friday's electro/pop the Cock, among others. It's popular with Muscle Marys, trannies, punks and polysexual fashionistas.

Heaven (Map pp91-3; ☎ 7930 2020; The Arches, Villiers St WC2; ❺ Charing Cross) One of the world's best-known gay clubs. It has three rooms; some nights are mixed but it positively fizzes with party boys on Saturday night, while there are cheap drinks and no pretension at Monday's Popcorn.

Madame Jo Jo's (Map pp91-3; ☎ 7734 3040; 8 Brewer St W1; ❺ Leicester Square or Piccadilly Circus) A renowned transvestite cabaret, which is sleazy, fun and kitsch. It gives way to a deep house/nu-jazz club night on Saturday and a 'Deep Funk' night on Friday.

Ministry of Sound (Map pp86-7; ☎ 7378 6528; www .ministryofsound.co.uk; 103 Gaunt St SE1; admission £12-15; ⏰ until 8am; ❺ Elephant & Castle) Where the global brand started. It lost a little of its edge over time, but sharpened up with a major refurbishment in late 2003. It's London's most famous club and still packs in a diverse crew with big local and international names.

Notting Hill Arts Club (Map pp82-3; ☎ 7460 4459, 21 Notting Hill Gate W11; ⏰ 6pm-1am Tue-Sat, 6pm-2am Fri & Sat, 4-11pm Sun; ❺ Notting Hill Gate) A laidback, funky basement club that attracts an eclectic crowd and has indie music celebrity residences.

333 (Map pp78-9; ☎ 7739 5949; 333 Old St EC1; ⏰ 10pm-5am Fri, 10pm-4am Sat & Sun) A Hoxton old-timer with three different shambling levels of breakbeats, techno to funk, and a determinedly down-to-earth vibe.

Live Music
ROCK
London's live music scene is fantastic, and any night of the week you can catch bands and performances that would be the envy of any other gig-goer around the world.

Barfly @ the Monarch (Map pp80-1; ☎ 7691 4244, 7691 4245; www.barflyclub.com; Monarch pub, 49 Chalk

Farm Rd NW1; ⊖ Chalk Farm or Camden Town) Pleasantly grungy, and the place to see the best upcoming bands.

Borderline (Map pp91-3; ☎ 7734 2095; www.borderline.co.uk; Orange Yard W1; ⊖ Tottenham Court Road) A small, relaxed venue, hosting bands on the verge of the mainstream. It's also your best bet to see big-name acts performing under pseudonyms.

Brixton Academy (Map pp78-9; ☎ 7771 2000; www.brixton-academy.co.uk; 211 Stockwell Rd SW9; ⊖ Brixton) An enormous, user-friendly place with a sloping floor that allows you to see the band no matter how far back you are. Great bands and always thrumming with bonhomie.

Garage (Map pp80-1; ☎ 7607 1818; www.meanfiddler.com; 20-22 Highbury Corner N5; ⊖ Highbury or Islington) A good, medium-sized venue that hosts local and visiting indie bands on their way up. It can be ridiculously hot and sweaty in summer.

The Forum (Map pp78-9; ☎ 7344 0044; 9-17 Highgate Road NW5; ⊖ Kentish Town) A grand old theatre and one of London's best large venues.

Hackney Ocean (Map pp78-9; ☎ 8986 5336; 270 Mare St E8; ⊖ Bethnal Green) Has sensational acoustics and hosts the usual headliners, but adds a strong line in world music, reflecting the multiculturalism of Hackney.

Jazz Café (Map pp80-1; ☎ 7344 0044; 5 Parkway NW1; ⊖ Camden Town) A rather swanky restaurant venue. While you don't have to eat, it's better to book a table for the big names.

Ronnie Scott's (Map pp91-3; ☎ 7439 0747; 47 Frith St W1; ⊖ Leicester Square) Familiar to aficionados as the best jazz club in London. The food, atmosphere and acts are always spot-on.

Shepherd's Bush Empire (☎ 7771 2000; www.shepherds-bush-empire.co.uk; Shepherd's Bush Green W12; ⊖ Shepherd's Bush) A slightly dishevelled, mid-size theatre that hosts some terrific bands watched by laid-back punters.

100 Club (Map pp91-3; ☎ 7636 0933; 100 Oxford St W1; ⊖ Oxford Circus) This legendary London venue once showcased the Stones and was at the centre of the punk revolution. It now divides its time between jazz, rock and even a little swing.

CLASSICAL
With four world-class symphony orchestras, two opera companies, various smaller ensembles, brilliant venues, reasonable prices and high standards of performance, London is a capital for classical.

TOP FIVE VIEWS OF LONDON
- Of Buckingham Palace from the footbridge over **St James's Park lake** (p101)
- From the **London Eye** (p109)
- From **Marble Arch viewing platform** (p113)
- From **Waterloo Bridge** (preferably at sunset)
- From the gardens of **Royal Hospital Chelsea** (p112) across the Thames to Battersea Power Station

South Bank Centre (Map pp84-6; ☎ 7960 4242; South Bank; ⊖ Embankment) has three premier venues in the **Royal Festival Hall** and the smaller **Queen Elizabeth Hall** and **Purcell Room**, which host classical, opera, jazz and choral music. It houses a range of cafés and restaurants, and there are free recitals in the foyer.

The **Barbican Centre** (Map pp86-7; ☎ 7638 8891; www.barbican.org.uk; Silk St EC2; ⊖ Barbican) may be aesthetically challenged, but its acoustics are sound and it is home to the London Symphony Orchestra, which plays some 80 concerts here every year.

The Royal Albert Hall (Map pp82-3; ☎ 7589 8212; www.royalalberthall.com; Kensington Gore SW7; ⊖ South Kensington) is a splendid Victorian arena that often hosts classical concerts, but is best known as the venue for the Proms.

Opera & Dance
The once starchy and now gleaming **Royal Opera House** (Map pp91-3; ☎ 7304 4000; www.royaloperahouse.org; Royal Opera House, Bow St WC2; tickets £6-150, midweek matinees £6.50-50; ⊖ Covent Garden) has been attracting a young, wealthy audience since its £213 million millennium redevelopment, which seems to have breathed new life into programming. The home of the progressive **English National Opera** is the **Coliseum** (Map pp91-3; ☎ 7632 8300; St Martin's Lane WC1; ⊖ Leicester Square).

The **Royal Ballet** (☎ 7304 4000; www.royalballet.com; Royal Opera House, Bow St WC2; tickets £4-80; ⊖ Covent Garden), the best classical-ballet company in the land, is also based at the Royal Opera House, while there are four other major dance companies and a host of small and experimental ones. **Sadler's Wells** (Map pp80-1;

☎ 7863 8000; www.sadlers-wells.com; Rosebery Ave EC1; tickets £10-40; ✆ Angel) is a glittering modern venue that was in fact first established in the 17th century. It has been given much credit in recent years for bringing modern dance to the mainstream.

Cinemas

Glitzy British premieres take place in Leicester Sq, usually at the mega, near-2000-seater Odeon. Blockbusters apart, London is a great place to catch a range of films that might not even make it to a cinema near you at home, although mainstream films are often released later here for some reason. *Time Out* is indispensable.

National Film Theatre (Map pp84-6; ☎ 7928 3232; South Bank Centre; ✆ Waterloo) A film-lover's dream, it screens some 2000 flicks a year, ranging from vintage classics to foreign art-house.

Sport

As the capital of a sports-mad nation, you can expect London to be brimming over with sporting spectacles throughout the year. As always, the entertainment weekly *Time Out* is the best source of information on fixtures, times, venues and ticket prices.

FOOTBALL

Tickets for Premier League football matches are ridiculously hard to come by for casual fans these days, and London's top-flight clubs play to full stadiums most weeks. But if you want to try your luck, the telephone numbers for the Premiership clubs are listed here:

Arsenal	☎ 7704 4040
Charlton	☎ 8333 4010
Chelsea	☎ 7386 7799
Fulham	☎ 7893 8383
Crystal Palace	☎ 8771 8841
Tottenham Hotspur	☎ 0870 112222

RUGBY

Twickenham (☎ 8892 2000; Rugby Rd, Twickenham; tickets around £30; ✆ Hounslow East, then bus No 281 or Twickenham mainline station) is the home of English rugby union, but as with football, tickets for internationals are difficult to get unless you have contacts. The ground also boasts the state-of-the-art **Museum of Rugby** (admission incl stadium tour £8; ⊗ 10am-5pm Tue-Sat, 2-5pm Sun).

CRICKET

Despite a so-so England team, cricket remains popular in the land of its origin. Test matches take place at two venerable grounds: **Lord's Cricket Ground** (Map pp78-9; ☎ 7432 1066; St John's Wood Rd NW8; ✆ St John's Wood) and the **AMP Oval Cricket Ground** (Map pp78-9; ☎ 7582 7764; Kennington Oval SE11; ✆ Oval). Tickets are from £15 to £50, but if you're a fan you'll know it's worth it.

SHOPPING

From world-famous department stores to quirky backstreet retail revelations, London is a mecca for shoppers with an eye for style and a card to exercise. If you're looking for something distinctly 'British', eschew the Union Jack–emblazoned kitsch of the tourist thoroughfares and fill your bags with Burberry accessories, Duffer layers, Tiffany sparkles, Ben Sherman shirts, Royal Doulton china and, perhaps, a Saville Row suit. Of course, everything will seem more prestigious if it's in a Harrods bag.

Fashion

If there's a label worth having, you'll find it in central London. Shopping options are well scattered, although some streets are renowned for their specialities. Oxford St is the place for High St fashion, while the chains of Regent St crank it up a notch. Kensington High St has a nice mix of chains and boutiques, while the streets around Covent Garden are crammed with groovy street labels and alternative boutiques. Mayfair's South Molton St is the strip for local and international urban chic, while Bond

---

WEST END BUYS

Some streets have particular specialities:

- **Bond St** – designer clothes and accessories
- **Cecil Court** – antiquarian bookshops
- **Charing Cross Rd** – new and second-hand books
- **Denmark St** – musical instruments, sheet music, books about music
- **Hanway St** – used records
- **Saville Row** – bespoke men's tailoring
- **Tottenham Court Rd** – electronics/computer equipment and homewares

---

TO MARKET, TO MARKET

London has more than 350 markets selling everything from antiques and curios to flowers and fish. Some, such as Camden and Portobello Rd, are well known to tourists, while others exist just for the locals and have everything from dinner to underwear for sale in the stalls. Here's a sample.

Bermondsey Market (Map pp86-7; ☎ 7351 5353; Bermondsey Sq SE1; ✹ 5am-1pm Fri; ✦ Borough) The place to come if you're after old opera glasses, bowling balls, hatpins, costume jewellery, porcelain or other curios. The main market is outdoors on the square, although adjacent ware-houses shelter the more vulnerable furnishings and bric-a-brac.

Borough Market (Map pp86-7; cnr Borough High & Stoney Sts SE1; ✹ 9am-6pm Fri, 9am-4pm Sat; ✦ London Bridge) A farmers market sometimes called London's Larder, it has been here in some form since the 13th century. It's a wonderfully atmospheric food market, where you'll find everything from organic falafel to a boar's head.

Brick Lane Market (Map pp78-9; Brick Lane E1; ✹ 8.30am-1pm Sat; ✦ Shoreditch or Aldgate East) This is an East End pearl, a sprawling bazaar featuring everything from fruit and veggies to paintings and bric-a-brac.

Brixton Market (Map pp78-9; Electric Ave & Granville Arcade; ✹ 8am-5.30pm Mon-Sat, 8am-1pm only Wed; ✦ Brixton) A cosmopolitan treat that mixes everything from the Body Shop and reggae to slick Muslim preachers, South American butcher shops and exotic fruits. On Electric Ave and in the covered Granville Arcade you can buy wigs, unusual foods and spices, and homeopathic root cures.

Camden Market (Map pp80-1; Camden High St NW1; ✹ 9am-5pm Thu-Sun; ✦ Camden Town) One of London's most popular tourist attractions although it stopped being cutting edge a long time ago. It's positively mobbed at the weekend.

Petticoat Lane Market (Map pp86-7; Middlesex St E1; ✹ 8am-2pm Sun; ✦ Aldgate, Aldgate East or Liverpool Street) A cherished East End institution overflowing with cheap consumer durables of little interest to tourists (although you'll see a hell of a lot of them).

Portobello Rd Market (Map pp82-3; Portobello Rd W10; ✦ Notting Hill Gate, Ladbroke Grove or West-bourne Park) One of London's most famous (and crowded) street markets, that has taken over from Camden in the hip stakes. New and vintage clothes are its main attraction.

Spitalfields Market (Map pp86-7; Commercial St E1; ✹ 9.30am-5.30pm Sun, organic market 9.30am-5pm Fri; ✦ Liverpool Street) In a Victorian warehouse, with a great mix of arts and crafts, clothes, books, food and *joie de vivre*.

St is the fat end of the high-fashion wedge. Knightsbridge draws the hordes with quint-essentially English department stores.

DEPARTMENT STORES

It's hard to resist the lure of London's famous department stores, even if you don't intend to spree.

Harrods (Map pp82-3; ☎ 7730 1234; 87 Brompton Rd SW1; ✦ Knightsbridge) Like a theme park for fans of the British establishment, Harrods is always crowded with slow tourists. There are more rules than at an army boot camp but even the toilets will impress.

Harvey Nichols (Map pp82-3; ☎ 7235 5000; 109-125 Knightsbridge SW1; ✦ Knightsbridge) London's temple of high fashion. The jewellery and perfume departments are worth a short prison sentence.

Fortnum & Mason (Map pp82-3; ☎ 7734 8040; 181 Piccadilly W1; ✦ Piccadilly Circus) The byword for quality and service from a bygone area, steeped as it is in 300 years of tradition. It is especially noted for its old-world ground-floor food hall where Britain's elite come for their cornflakes and bananas.

Selfridges (Map pp84-6; ☎ 7629 1234; 400 Oxford St W1; ✦ Bond Street) The funkiest and most vital of London's one-stop shops where fashion runs the gamut from street to formal. The food hall is unparalleled and the cosmetics hall the largest in Europe.

Liberty (Map pp91-3; ☎ 7734 1234; 214-220 Regent St W1; ✦ Oxford Circus) An irresistible blend of con-temporary styles in an old-fashioned atmos-phere. And you can't leave London without some 'Liberty Florals' (printed fabrics).

Antiques

Curios, baubles and period pieces abound along Camden Passage, Bermondsey Mar-ket, the Saturday market at Portobello and

LONDON

along Islington's Upper St from Angel towards Highbury Corner (see To Market, to Market p139 for market details).

Antiquarius Antiques Centre (Map pp88-9; ☎ 79 69 1500; 131 King's Rd SW3; ⊖ Sloane Square) Packed with 120 stalls and dealers selling everything from top hats and corkscrews to old luggage and jewellery.

London Silver Vaults (Map pp84-6; ☎ 7242 3844; 53-63 Chancery Lane WC2; ⊖ Chancery Lane) Has 72 subterranean shops forming the world's largest collection of silver under one roof.

Music

If it's been recorded, you can buy it in London. For the biggest general collections of CDs and tapes, take on the West End giants of **Tower Records** (Map pp91-3; ☎ 7439 2500; 1 Piccadilly Circus W1; ☒ until midnight Mon-Sat; ⊖ Piccadilly Circus), **HMV** (Map pp91-3; ☎ 7631 3423; 150 Oxford St W1; ☒ until 8pm Mon-Fri; ⊖ Oxford Circus) and **Virgin Megastore** (Map pp91-3; ☎ 7631 1234; 14-30 Oxford St W1; ☒ until 9pm Mon-Sat; ⊖ Tottenham Court Road).

For personality, visit the following:

Rough Trade Neal's Yard (Map pp91-3; ☎ 7240 0105; 16 Neal's Yard WC2; ⊖ Covent Garden); Talbot Rd (☎ 7229 8541; 130 Talbot Rd W11; ⊖ Ladbroke Grove) In the basement of Slam City Skates, it's the most central outlet of this famous store that was at the forefront of the punk explosion in the 1970s. This – and its original store in Notting Hill – is the best place to come for underground specials, vintage rarities and pretty much anything of an indie or alternative bent.

Ray's Jazz Shop (Map pp91-3; ☎ 7437 5660; Foyle's, 113-119 Charing Cross Rd WC2; ⊖ Tottenham Court Road) Where aficionados will find those elusive back catalogues from their favourite jazz and blues artists.

Black Market Records (Map pp91-3; ☎ 7437 0478; 25 D'Arblay St W1; ⊖ Oxford Circus) Your best bet for dance, and if they haven't got what you're after, they'll know who has.

GETTING THERE & AWAY

London is the major gateway to Britain, so further transport information can be found in the main Transport chapter.

Air

For information on flying to/from London via the main airports of Heathrow and Gatwick, see p747 in the Transport chapter. The following are London's smaller airports.

STANSTED

London's third-busiest airport, **Stansted** (STN; ☎ 0870 000 0303; www.baa.com/main/airports/stansted) is 35 miles northeast of the centre. It is Europe's fastest growing airport thanks to the success of no-frills carriers **Ryanair** (www.ryanair.com) and **Easyjet** (☎ 0870 600 0000; www.easyjet.com).

LONDON CITY

London City Airport (LCY; ☎ 7646 0000; www.london cityairport.com), 6 miles east of central London in the Docklands, is largely used for business travellers and serves 22 Continental European and eight national destinations.

LUTON

A small airport some 35 miles north of central London, **Luton** (LTN; ☎ 01582 405100; www .london-luton.co.uk) is the main base of low-cost airline EasyJet and smaller charter flights.

Bus

Most long-distance coaches leave London from **Victoria coach station** (Map p90; ☎ 7730 3466; 164 Buckingham Palace Rd SW1; ⊖ Victoria, then about a 10-min walk), a lovely 1930s-style building. The arrivals terminal is in a separate building across Elizabeth St from the main coach station.

Car

See p751 of the Transport chapter for reservation numbers of the main car-hire firms, all of which have airport and various city locations.

Train

London has 10 mainline terminals, all linked by the tube and each serving a different geographical area of the UK.

Charing Cross (Map pp91-3) Southeast England

Euston (Map pp80-1) Northern and northwest England, Scotland

King's Cross (Map pp80-1) North London, Hertfordshire, Cambridgeshire, northern and northeast England, Scotland

Liverpool Street (Map pp86-7) East and northeast London, Stansted airport, East Anglia

London Bridge (Map pp86-7) Southeast England

Marylebone (Map pp82-3) Northwest London, the Chilterns

Paddington (Map pp82-3) South Wales, western and southwest England, southern Midlands, Heathrow airport

St Pancras (Map pp80-1) East Midlands, southern Yorkshire

Victoria (Map pp84-6) Southern and southeast England, Gatwick airport, Channel ferry ports

Waterloo (Map pp84-6) Southwest London, southern and southwest England

Most stations now have left-luggage facilities (around £4) and lockers, toilets (a 20p coin) with showers (around £3), newsstands and bookshops, and a range of eating and drinking outlets. Victoria and Liverpool Street stations have shopping centres attached.

GETTING AROUND
To/From the Airports
HEATHROW

The airport is accessible by bus, the Underground (between 5am and 11pm), mainline train and taxi. The fastest way to and from central London is on the **Heathrow Express** (☎ 0845 600 1515; www.heathrowexpress.co.uk), an ultramodern train to and from Paddington station (adult/child one way £6/11.50, return £13/25, 15 minutes, every 15 minutes 5.10am to 11.30pm). You can purchase tickets on board (£2 extra), online or from self-service machines (cash and credit cards accepted) at both terminals. The cheapest way between Heathrow and central London is on London Underground's Piccadilly line (£3.80, one hour, departing every five to 10 minutes 5.30am to 11.45pm), accessed from all terminals. The **Airbus A2** (☎ 08705 747777) links King's Cross station and Heathrow (one way/return £8/15, 1½ hours, departing 5.30am to 10pm from Heathrow, every 30 minutes during peak times). A black cab to the centre of London will cost you around £50, a minicab around £30.

GATWICK

The **Gatwick Express train** (☎ 0870 530 1530; www.gatwickexpress.co.uk) runs nonstop between Victoria train station and the South Terminal (adult return £21.50, 30 minutes, departing every 15 minutes 5.50am to 1.35am, with an earlier train at 5.20am). The normal train service is slower but cheaper. **Airbus No 025** (☎ 08705 747777; www.nationalexpress.com) operates from Victoria coach station to Gatwick (one way/return £5/10, 18 daily 6am to 11pm to Gatwick, 4.15am to 9.15pm to London). A black cab to/from central London costs around £80 to £85.

STANSTED

The **Stansted Express** (☎ 0845 748 4950; www.stanstedexpress.com) connects with Liverpool Street station (one way/return £13.80/24, 45 minutes, departing every 15 minutes 8am to

5.30pm, otherwise every 30 minutes). The **Airbus A6** (☎ 08705 747777) links with Victoria coach station (one way/return £6/15, departing every 20 minutes 5.30am to midnight). A black cab to/from central London costs about £100 to £105.

LONDON CITY

The blue airport **Shuttlebus** (☎ 7646 0088; www.londoncityairport.com/shuttlebus) connects with Liverpool Street train station (one way/return £6/12, 25 minutes), departing every 10 minutes 6.50am (11am Sunday) to 10pm (1.15pm Saturday). From Liverpool Street station, the first bus leaves at 9pm weekdays (12.45pm Saturday); the last departs at 9.08pm weekdays (12.40pm Saturday and 8.50pm Sunday). The journey takes eight minutes from Canary Wharf. The green airport **Shuttlebus** (☎ 7646 0088; www.londoncityairport.com/shuttlebus) links London City and Canning Town station (adult/child £2/1, five minutes), departing every 10 minutes 6am (10.05am Sunday) to 10.20pm (1.15pm Saturday), which is on the Jubilee tube, the DLR and Silverlink lines. A black taxi costs around £20 to/from central London.

LUTON

Thameslink (☎ 0845 748 4950; www.thameslink.co.uk) runs trains from King's Cross and other central London stations to Luton Airport Parkway station (adult/child one way £9.50/4.75, 35 minutes, departing every five to 15 minutes 7am to 10pm), from where a shuttle bus will get you to the airport within eight minutes. A black taxi costs around £75 to/from central London.

Car

Driving in London is the perfect way to ruin a good holiday. Traffic is very heavy, parking is a nightmare and wheel-clampers are very busy. If you bring your car into central London from 7am to 6.30pm on a weekday, you'll need to pay a £5 per day **congestion charge** (☎ 0845 900 1234; www.cclondon.com to register) or face a fine.

Public Transport

Transport for London (TfL; www.transportforlondon.gov.uk/tfl) is an organisation that aims to integrate the entire London transport network. Its website is very handy for information on all modes of transport in the capital.

As you might imagine, servicing a city this large is a logistical nightmare for planners who get no end of criticism from locals. But amazingly, the system works pretty well, especially since Mayor Ken Livingstone has made it his cause célèbre. Trains, tube lines, day and night buses, cabs and even shuttle boats work in tandem to fill the gaps and make it possible to navigate the behemoth (unless you're trying to get out of Soho on a weekend night, of course).

A Travelcard (see opposite) can be used on all forms of public transport: the tube, suburban trains, the Docklands Light Rail (DLR), day and night buses, and for discounts on boats. The relatively new pre-pay **Oystercard** (www.oystercard.com) can also be used throughout the public transport network and is particularly handy if you're going to be in London for an extended period.

BOAT
There is a myriad of boat services on the Thames, with more being announced all the time. Travelling by boat allows you to avoid the traffic while enjoying great views. Travelcard holders get one-third off all fares.

City Cruises (☎ 7740 0400; www.citycruises.com) operates year-round from Westminster Pier (for more details see p119).

Westminster Passenger Services Association (☎ 7930 2062; www.wpsa.co.uk) is the only company that operates a schedule service up-river from Westminster. It takes in Kew Gardens and Hampton Park (for prices see Kew Gardens p117).

The London Waterbus Company (☎ 7482 2660) runs trips between Camden Lock and Little Venice, or try **Jason's Canal Trips** (☎ 7286 3428; www.jasons.co.uk) at Little Venice. London has some 40 miles of inner-city canals, mostly built in the 19th century and in the process of renewal.

BUS
Travelling round London by double-decker bus is an enjoyable way to explore the city and get a feel for its districts and size. For short journeys it's often more efficient to take a bus than the tube. The free *Central London Bus Guide Map* is an essential planning tool, and is available from most TICs and tube stations. Make sure to catch one of the open-backed Routemasters before they're phased out. A recommended 'scenic' route is No 24, which runs from Victoria to Hampstead Heath through the West End.

Buses run regularly between 7am and midnight. Single-journey bus tickets (valid for two hours) cost adult/child £1/40p, day passes are adult/child £2.50/1. In central London, at stops with yellow signs it's important to buy your ticket from the automatic machine *before* boarding. Otherwise, buy it as you board.

Less-frequent night buses (prefixed with the letter 'N') wheel into action when the tube stops. They stop on request, so clearly signal the driver with an outstretched arm. Trafalgar Sq, Tottenham Court Rd and Oxford Circus are the main terminals for them.

Stationlink buses (☎ 7941 4600) have a driver-operated ramp for wheelchair access and follow a similar route to the Underground Circle Line, joining up all the main-line stations. People with mobility problems and those with heavy luggage may find this easier to use than the tube, although it only operates once an hour. From Paddington there are services clockwise (the SL1) from 8.15am to 7.15pm, and anticlockwise (the SL2) from 8.40am to 6.40pm.

DLR & TRAIN
The independent, driverless **Docklands Light Railway** (DLR; ☎ 7363 9700; www.dlr.co.uk) links the City at Bank and Tower Gateway with

---

THE TUBE – FUN FACTS TO KNOW & TELL

The tube is the world's oldest (1863), most extensive (253 miles of track) and busiest (785 million journeys a year) underground transport system in the world. With breakdowns every 16 minutes on average, it is also the most unreliable, and for the journey between Covent Garden and Leicester Sq (£1.60 for 250m), the per-kilometre price makes taking the tube more expensive than it is to take a stretch limo.

The London Underground map, used by millions of people every day, is so familiar that it's often used as a symbol for the city itself. It was created in 1931 by Henry Beck, an engineering draughtsman, who received five guineas (£5.25) for his efforts.

SOME HAVE THE KNOWLEDGE – OTHERS HAVEN'T A CLUE

Once you've been around the block a few times with a hackney cab driver – during which the car's broken down, he's consulted the *London A–Z* twice and telephoned base for directions – you'll begin to appreciate the more expensive black cabs. To get an all-London licence, 'cabbies' must pass a rigorous test, which requires them to memorise up to 25,000 streets within a 6-mile radius of Charing Cross and know all the points of interest from hotels to churches. It's a feat that can sometimes take years to achieve, and ensures, according to the Public Carriage Office, that only the most committed join the noble trade.

Canary Wharf, Greenwich and Stratford. It provides good views of development at this end of town. The fares operate in the same way as those on the tube.

Several rail companies also operate suburban rail services in and around London. These are especially important south of the river where there are few tube lines. Once again, fares operate in the same way as those on the tube.

LONDON UNDERGROUND
The 12 lines of the 'tube' extend as far as Buckinghamshire, Essex and Heathrow. There are Underground travel information centres at all Heathrow terminals, a half-dozen major tube stations and at larger main-line train stations. Services run from 5.30am to roughly midnight (from 7am on Sunday).

The Underground is divided into six concentric zones. The basic fare for Zone 1 is adult/child £2/60p; to cross all six zones (eg, to/from Heathrow) costs £3.80/1.50. A carnet of 10 tickets for Zone 1 costs £15/5. Tickets can be bought from machines or counters at the entrance to each station.

If you're travelling through a couple of zones or several times in one day, consider a Travelcard. One-day Travelcards can be used after 9.30am weekdays (any time at weekends) on all transport – tubes, main-line trains, the DLR and buses (including night buses). Most visitors find a one-day Travelcard for Zones 1 and 2 (adult/child £4.30/2) is sufficient. Before 9.30am Monday to Fri-

day, you need a Peak Travelcard (£5.30/2.60 for Zones 1 and 2). A weekly for Zones 1 and 2, valid any time of day, costs £20.20/8.20. A Weekend Travelcard, valid Saturday and Sunday in Zones 1 and 2, costs £6.40/3. Family Travelcards are also available.

Taxi
Drivers of licensed black cabs have undergone extensive training to obtain 'the knowledge' of every central London street, so you're sure to arrive at your destination. Cabs are available for hire when the yellow light above the windscreen is lit. Fares are metered, with flag fall at £1.60 and each successive kilometre costing 90p. To order a black cab by phone, try **Dial-a-Cab** (☎ 7253 5000); you must pay by credit card and will be charged a premium.

Minicabs, some of which are now licensed, are cheaper competitors to cabs. However, they can only be hired by phone or from a minicab office; every neighbourhood and High St has one. Some minicab drivers also have a limited idea of how to get around efficiently – or safely. Minicabs can carry up to four people and don't have meters, so get a quote before you start. Bargaining is sometimes acceptable. Small companies are based in particular areas. Try a large **24-hour operator** (☎ 7387 8888, 7272 2222, 7272 3322 or 8888 4444).

Be aware that there have been many reports of assault by unlicensed minicab drivers. Solo female travellers should be very wary of jumping into a minicab alone.

The Home Counties

CONTENTS

Both blessed and cursed because of their proximity to London, the five counties immediately adjoining the city – Hertfordshire, Bedfordshire, Buckinghamshire, Berkshire and Surrey – are more than just commuter hubs and business satellites (though you'll find that too). Here there's a hidden wealth of natural beauty as well as some important historic sites and a much slower pace of life. The Home Counties are also home to some of the country's wealthiest and most important individuals, including the queen herself.

With the exception of Windsor and Eton and the great Windsor Castle, many of the towns in this part of the country won't make many people's top 10 lists. But that's to your advantage. Largely free of the big summer crowds you'll find elsewhere in the south, the Home Counties can offer a relaxing atmosphere with friendly locals happy to welcome you into their quaint cafés, country pubs and small B&Bs.

HIGHLIGHTS

- Enjoying a pint at **Ye Olde Fighting Cocks** (p149) in St Albans, one of England's oldest pubs
- Visiting the grand **Windsor Castle** (p154) for a peek at royal living
- Looking at **Roman Ruins and Verulamium Museum** (p148) in St Albans
- Touring the magnificent interior of **Hatfield House** (p149)
- Driving among the baboons at **Woburn Safari Park** (p151)

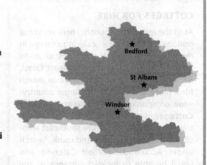

- POPULATION: 3.1 MILLION
- AREA: 3174 SQ MILES

Information

The slow pace of life and the lack of tourists in the Home Counties means there isn't an abundance of tourist offices. The ones that are here are found in the larger towns such as St Albans and Farnham and they can help with the surrounding sights. Because of the brisk business that's done in the areas immediately surrounding London, the hotels here tend to be higher priced than elsewhere. Conversely, in the more remote towns, the selection of hotels and hostels is slim but cheaper. Banks and ATMs are easy to find (after all, many of London's bankers live here). For more information, try the general websites for South and Southeast England: www.tourismsoutheast.com.

Activities

There aren't a lot of well-known outdoor destinations in the Home Counties, which doesn't mean they aren't there. It just means it might take a little bit more looking. The rugged Chiltern Hills in Buckinghamshire offer good hiking and mountain biking whereas the rolling hills of Surrey that make up the North Downs are good for walking and cycling.

Several longer walking pathways start in the Home Counties (or end, depending on which way you're headed) and end up much further afield. It is possible to do only a section of these trails as a day or two-day walk. **North Downs Way** (157 miles/253km) The path starts in Farnham and goes to Dorking before heading east to Ashford and Dover.

Thames Path (173 miles/279km) This one follows Britain's best-known river from its source in the Cotswolds

---

COTTAGES FOR HIRE

As in the rest of the country, there are some options for hiring a self-catering cottage in the Home Counties, though not as many as you might find on the Southeast Coast. Because of that, your best bet is to search for a place to stay with the larger country-wide companies like **Hoseasons Country Cottages** (www.hoseasons.co.uk). Also, try the tourism office for the entire southeast website, www.southeastengland.co.uk. Search under Accomodation/Self Catering and you'll be able to located cottages in any of the five Home Counties.

(p406) to London. Before it reaches the capital, it skirts Reading and Windsor in Berkshire.

The Ridgeway (90 miles/145km) This one starts near Avebury Stone Circle (p244) and runs to Ivinghoe Beacon near Aylesbury in Buckinghamshire.

For shorter walks, Box Hill and the Devils Punchbowl in the Surrey Hills offer excellent views, sloping grasslands and some wooded areas. This is also a good area to come for mountain biking as there are a number of bridleways. On top of the hill is a **visitor information centre** (☎ 01306-885502; ✆ 11am-dusk) where you'll find information on guided walks, self-guided walk leaflets, maps and an ice-cream kiosk.

Getting There & Around

All the places mentioned in this chapter are close enough to London to be done as a day trip, and are quite easy to reach by train or bus. The problem with some places in the Home Counties is that it's not always easy to go from one town to the next by train, as all tracks usually lead into London and then back out again. Renting a car is a great option, but watch out for the commuter traffic around the rush hours from 6am to 9.30am and from 4pm to 7pm. The **National Traveline** (☎ 0870 608 2608) provides information on all public transport throughout the region.

BUS

Explorer tickets (adult/child £5.50/4) provide day-long unlimited travel on most buses throughout the region; buy them at bus stations or on your first bus.

Country Rover tickets (£5/2.50) are valid after 9am weekdays and all day at weekends.

Diamond Rover tickets (£7/5) are good for Green Line services any time and day excluding service into London before 9am Monday to Friday.

Arriva (☎ 01279-426349) offers a variety of day, weekly and monthly passes and has good deals for families travelling in Buckinghamshire, Hertfordshire and Surrey.

All these tickets and passes can be purchased on the buses.

TRAIN

For general rail information call ☎ 08457 48 49 50.

BritRail SouthEast Pass (p753) allows unlimited rail travel for three or four days

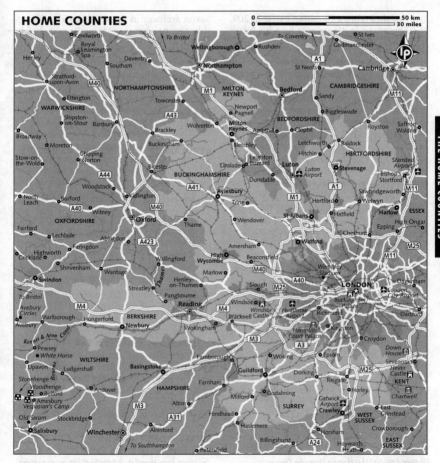

HOME COUNTIES

in eight, or seven days out of 15. Must be purchased outside the UK.

Network Railcard (☎ 08457 225 225; www.railcard.co.uk/network/network.htm; per yr £20) is a discount card available for visitors travelling in London, the Home Counties and southern England. It costs £20 and passengers get a 34% discount (children ride for £1), but they have to travel at off peak times.

HERTFORDSHIRE

Sleepy Hertfordshire is a small county of fast-disappearing though still pastoral farmland. Still, it's not all daisies and buttermilk here. Hertfordshire is also home to the

stunning St Albans, a predominantly Georgian town that dates back to Roman times, and Hatfield House, one of Britain's most important stately homes and the county's top attraction.

ST ALBANS
☎ 01727 / pop 82,429

The lovely town of St Albans is one of the best and most popular towns to visit in any of the Home Counties. Its short distance from London (25 minutes by train) makes it a perfect day trip.

Founded by the Romans as Verulamium after their invasion of AD 43, St Albans was renamed in the 3rd century after a Roman soldier, Alban, who had made the mortal error of sheltering a Christian priest in 209. His Samaritan instincts cost him his head, but he was England's first Christian martyr and the town soon became a major centre for pilgrimage.

Visitors with more earthly concerns will find St Albans worth a stop for its magnificent cathedral, outstanding Roman museum and the town's aesthetically pleasing mix of Tudor and Georgian architecture. They also take their beer seriously here and have the real-ale pubs and the festivals to prove it (see boxed text, opposite).

Orientation & Information

St Peter's St, 10 minutes' walk west of the train station on Stanhope Rd, is the focus of the town. East of St Peters, St George St turns into Fishpool St, a lovely neighbourhood lane that winds its way past country pubs to Verulamium Park.

The **TIC** (☎ 864511; tic@stalbans.gov.uk; Market Pl; ⊗ 9.30am-5.30pm Mon-Sat Easter-Oct & Mon-Sat 10am-4pm Nov-Easter) is in the grand town hall in the town's bustling marketplace. It sells the useful *Discover St Albans* town trail (£1). The *Official Visitors Guide* is free and features a detailed town walk that covers all the sights. There are free guided walks of the town at 11.15am and 3pm on Sunday, Easter to September – meet at the **Clocktower** (High St). On Wednesday and Saturday mornings the central marketplace really comes alive.

All the major banks and ATMs are on St Peter's St, near the TIC. The main **post office** (St Peter's St; ⊗ 9.30am-5pm Mon-Sat) is also in the town centre. Internet access is free in the **library** (☎ 737333; Malting Shopping Centre).

Paton Books (34 Holywell Hill) is a marvellous bookshop full of new titles and dusty old ones (including those hard-to-find ones) housed in an elegant 17th-century building.

There's a **laundrette** (13 Catherine St) off St Peter's St.

Sights

ST ALBANS CATHEDRAL

In the 8th century, King Offa of Mercia founded a Benedictine abbey on the site of Alban's martyrdom, but the actual **cathedral** (☎ 860780; ⊗ 8am-5.45pm) you see today dates from 1077, when the first Norman abbot, Paul, ordered the construction of a new one, albeit incorporating elements of the earlier Saxon building – you can see remnants of a

Saxon archway in the southern aisle alongside the presbytery. Many Roman bricks were also used and they sit conspicuously in the central tower. Considerable restoration took place in 1877.

There are guided **tours** (⊗ 11.30am & 2.30pm Mon-Fri, 11.30am & 2pm Sat, 2.30pm Sun) of the cathedral. In the southern aisle you can watch a free audiovisual account of the cathedral's history. Admission is by donation.

VERULAMIUM MUSEUM & ROMAN RUINS

Nowhere in England can you learn more about everyday life under the Romans than at this excellent **museum** (☎ 751810; St Michael's St; admission £3.30; ⊗ 10am-5pm Mon-Sat, 2-5pm Sun). There are interactive and audiovisual displays as well as recreations of how rooms would have looked in a Roman house. Most impressive is the Mosaic Room, where five outstanding floors uncovered between 1930 and 1955 are laid out.

Tickets allow you a return visit on the same day. You can take a free guided walk of the 'city' of Verulamium – essentially the grassed-over area where it once stood – from the museum at 3pm every Sunday.

In adjacent **Verulamium Park** you can inspect remains of a basilica, bathhouse and parts of the city wall. Across the busy A4147 are the remains of a **Roman theatre** (☎ 835035; adult/child £1.50/50p; ⊗ 10am-5pm Mar-Oct, 10am-4pm Nov-Feb) which appear to be just a collection of grassy ditches and mounds and a few ruins.

MUSEUM OF ST ALBANS

The **museum** (☎ 819340; Hatfield Rd; admission free; ⊗ 10am-5pm Mon-Sat, 2-5pm Sun) is a straightforward rundown of the city's history from Roman times to the present. Exhibits include tools used between 1700 and 1950 by English tradesmen and displays of Victorian memorabilia. It's not the Verulamium but it's still worth a quick look.

WORTH THE TRIP

If you like roses or even think you might like roses, then this is heaven. With about 30,000 specimens, the **Gardens of the Rose** (☎ 850461; adult/child £4.50/free; ⊗ 9am-5pm Mon-Sat mid-Jun–mid-Oct), 3 miles southwest of St Albans, contain the world's largest rose collection.

CLOCK TOWER

The medieval **clock tower** (High St; admission 30p; 🕑 10.30am-5pm Sat, Sun & bank holidays Apr-Oct) was built between 1403 and 1412. It's the only medieval belfry in England and the original bell (called 'Gabriel') is still there. The top proffers great views over the town.

Sleeping

Mrs Thomas' (☎ 858939; 8 Hall Place Gardens; s/d £20/40) This small but lovely spot has spacious rooms and garden views with shared bathrooms.

Wren Lodge (☎ 855540; 24 Beaconsfield Rd; s/d £35/60) An elegant Edwardian home where you'll be looked after with care, 10 minutes' walk from the town centre.

The White Hart (☎ 853624; fax 840237; 25 Holywell Hill; s/d from £40/55, family r £75; ✗) A charming half-timbered hotel with exposed beams and creaky floors just a couple of minutes' walk from the centre. A full English breakfast is £5.50 extra.

Eating

There are lots of eateries near the town centre and all the pubs in town serve good pub food.

The Waffle House (☎ 853502; St Michael's St; mains £3-6; 🕑 10am-6pm Mon-Sat, 11am-5pm Sun; ✗) While the specialty is Belgian waffles, this popular eatery inside the Saxon-era Kingsbury Water Mill serves dishes such as sweet potato coconut soup and lamb moussaka as well.

Claude's Creperie (☎ 846424; 15 Holywell Hill; mains £6-9.50; 🕑 10.30am-6pm Tue-Fri, 10.30am-11pm Sat & Sun; ✗) Long a local hangout, Claude's is so cozy it's almost communal dining. Serves French and Italian regional cooking.

Thai Rack (☎ 850055; 13 George St; mains £5-10; 🕑 lunch & dinner) This peaceful and small restaurant has a meditative outdoor patio and excellent curry.

Drinking

St Albans has one of the best collections of pubs in South England.

Ye Olde Fighting Cocks (☎ 865830; 16 Abbey Mill Lane) This charming spot is loaded with dark wood and cozy nooks and is supposedly one of the oldest pubs in England. Beer has been poured here since the 13th century.

The Rose & Crown (☎ 851903; 10 St Michael's St) This charming spot, with a beautiful beer garden, features live music Monday at 9pm and Irish music on Thursday at 8pm.

ST ALBANS BEER FESTIVAL

They don't mess about with beer in England, and just to prove it, the South Hertfordshire branch of Campaign for Real Ale (Camra) puts on a four-day festival at the tail end of every September to celebrate the sanctity of good beer and its key role in the national culture. There are many such beer festivals in England worth checking out, and this one is no exception. Close to 5000 people converge on the Civic Centre in St Peter's St to sample and talk about the 200 or so 'real' ales and ciders on display. (For more information on real ales see p69). Some of the beers are brewed locally just for the occasion, but most of them are available throughout the country. There's food available, and on Friday and Saturday evenings there's music to keep everyone entertained. Depending on the day you go, tickets range from £1 to £5. For more information contact local TICs.

The Goat (☎ 833934; 37 Sopwell Lane) Tucked away on a residential lane, this nice old pub in a Tudor-style building is popular with the locals.

Also recommended:

The Black Lion Inn (☎ 851786; 198 Fishpool St) Roman malting ovens were found here. Probably the least atmospheric of all St Albans pubs.

The Six Bells (☎ 856945; 16-18 St Michael's St) Next door to the Rose & Crown, this popular, low-ceilinged spot has a cozy fireplace and good pub food.

Lower Red Lion Freehouse (☎ 855669; 36 Fishpool St) Has regular beer festivals. A little rough around the edges, but there's a charming outdoor beer garden.

Getting There & Away

Rail is the most direct way to get to St Albans, although if you are coming from Heathrow you can catch Green Line bus No 724 which leaves hourly and takes an hour. St Albans station is on Stanhope Rd, a 10-minute walk east of St Peter's St. Thameslink trains depart every 15 minutes from London King's Cross to St Albans station (£7.40, 23 minutes).

AROUND ST ALBANS
Hatfield House

England's most magnificent Jacobean mansion, **Hatfield House** (☎ 01707-262823; admission £7.50 Sat-Thu, £10.50 Fri, park only £2; 🕑 noon-4pm, gardens

TOP FIVE SIGHTS

- **Windsor Castle** (Windsor & Eton; p154)
- **Verulamium Museum and Roman ruins** (St Albans; 148)
- **Hatfield House** (near St Albans; p149)
- **Farnham Museum** (Farnham; p158)
- **Waddesdon Manor** (Aylesbury; p151)

11am-4pm Easter-Sep) was built in 1607–1611 for Robert Cecil, first earl of Salisbury and secretary of state to both Elizabeth I and James I.

Inside, you'll find famous portraits, a grand marble hall and a magnificent oak staircase, decorated with carved figures, including one of John Tradescant, the 17th-century botanist responsible for the gardens.

Five-course Elizabethan banquets, complete with minstrels and court jesters, are held in the great hall on Tuesday, Friday and Saturday nights for around £40. Book on ☎ 01707-262055.

The house can only be visited by guided tour on weekdays; they depart as soon as a large enough group gathers. It's opposite Hatfield train station, and there are numerous trains from London King's Cross station (£7, 25 minutes). **Green Line** (☎ 02087 608 7261) runs bus No 797 from London to Hatfield hourly, and bus No 724 between St Albans and Hatfield every hour.

Shaw's Corner

This **Victorian villa** (☎ 01438 820307; Ayot St Lawrence; admission £3.80; ☽ 1-4.30pm Wed-Sun Apr-Oct) is where playwright George Bernard Shaw died in 1950. It has been preserved much as he left it. In the garden is a revolving summerhouse (revolving to catch the sun) where he wrote several works including *Pygmalion*, the play on which *My Fair Lady* was based.

Bus No 304 from St Albans drops you at Gustardwood, 1¼ miles from Ayot St Lawrence.

BEDFORDSHIRE

The largely rural county of Bedfordshire is one of the more low-key destinations located in the Home Counties, with one major town and a fine stately home

situated at Woburn. The River Great Ouse winds across the fields to the north and through Bedford, creating several pristine nature reserves and some good woodland walks. It's also very accessible to London with the M1 motorway running across its semi-industrial south. For information on buses around the county, phone the **Traveline** (☎ 0870 608 2608) or check the website of **Stagecoach** (www.stagecoachbus.com), the main regional bus company, for its local timetable.

BEDFORD

☎ 01234 / pop 82,488

For literature students or fans of John Bunyan (1628–88), the 17th-century nonconformist preacher and author of *The Pilgrim's Progress*, there are several good reasons to come to the sleepy town of Bedford. For others, this is little more than a bland, if pretty, riverside town.

Located in the town hall, the **TIC** (☎ 215226; touristinfo@bedford.gov.uk; 10 St Paul's Sq; ☽ 9.30am-5pm Mon-Sat, plus 11am-3pm Sun May-Aug) stocks the *Bedford What's On Guide* as well as a free guide to places with a Bunyan connection. Guided walks depart the TIC at 2.15pm on summer Sundays.

Sights

The **Bunyan Meeting Free Church** (☎ 213722; Mill St; ☽ 10am-4pm Tue-Sat Mar-Oct) was built in 1849 on the site of the barn where Bunyan preached between 1671 and 1678. The church's bronze doors, which were inspired by Ghiberti's doors for the Baptistry in Florence, show scenes from *The Pilgrim's Progress*.

The **John Bunyan Museum** (☎ 213722; admission free; ☽ 11am-3.45pm Tue-Sat Mar-Oct) next door has displays on the author's life as well as 169 editions of *The Pilgrim's Progress* from around the world.

Cecil Higgins Art Gallery (☎ 211222; Castle Lane; ☽ 11am-5pm Tue-Sat & 2-5pm Sun) houses a splendid collection of glass, porcelain and colourful Victorian furniture, and an enviable collection of watercolour paintings by artisits Blake, Turner, Rosetti and Millais. The **Bedford Museum** (☎ 353323; ☽ 11am-5pm Tue-Sat, 2-5pm Sun), with archaeological and historical exhibits, is next door. Admission to both is £2.30 for adults and free for children.

Information

Tourism South East (www.seetb.org.uk) is the official website for south and southeast England.

Activities

Among the numerous country lanes and tiny villages that make the Southeast Coast the most crowded corner of Britain, you'll be surprised to find there are lots of walking and cycling options. This section gives a quick rundown of the options. More information is given in the Outdoor Activities chapter, and suggestions for shorter walks and rides are given throughout this chapter. Regional tourism websites all contain walking and cycling information, and TICs all stock leaflets plus maps and guides covering walking, cycling and other activities.

CYCLING

Seeking out quiet roads for cycle touring can take persistence in southeast England, but some good routes definitely exist here.
Garden of England Cycle Route (170 miles/274km) London to Dover and then Hastings; part of the National Cycle Network (boxed text p62).
Downs & Weald Cycle Route (150 miles/242km) Hastings to London.
South Downs Way National Trail (100 miles/160km) Mountain bikes can legally ride it end to end. Hard nuts do it in two days. Four would be more enjoyable.

Another great off-road area in the region is the New Forest, which has a wonderfully vast network of tracks, ideal for gentle or beginner mountain biking, and also offers a week of organised cycling tours every July. Also, the country lanes on the Isle of Wight are less crowded than those on the mainland. There are a few off-road trails here too.

WALKING

The southeast coast has two long-distance trails running through its confines as well as a number of smaller walks that can make for great adventures, even if they're just for a few hours, a day or a weekend.
South Downs Way (100 miles/160km) roller-coaster walk between Winchester, the ancient capital of England, and Eastbourne.
North Downs Way (157 miles/253km) The far western end of this trail starts near Farnham (see p146) but one of the best sections of the trail can be found in Kent from Ashford to Dover.

COTTAGES FOR HIRE

There are excellent options for self-catering country cottages throughout the area. Here are a few resources to get you started in the southeast:
Best of Brighton & Sussex Cottages (☎ 01273 308779; www.bestofbrighton.co.uk)
Garden of England Cottages (☎ 0172 369168; www.gardenofenglandcottages.co.uk)
Kent Holiday Cottages (☎ 01233 820425; www.kentholidaycottages.co.uk)

Perhaps not surprisingly, the areas traversed by the long-distance routes are also ideal for shorter walks; the South Downs has extensive footpath networks and is a popular destination for walkers. Even more popular is the New Forest, England's newest national park. The Isle of Wight off the south coast has a good network of paths and some fine stretches of coastline.

Getting There & Around

All the places mentioned in this chapter are quite easy to reach by train or bus, and could be visited in a day trip from London. The **National Traveline** (☎ 0870 608 2608) provides information on all public transport throughout the region.

BUS

Explorer tickets (adult/child £5.50/4) provide day-long unlimited travel on most buses throughout the region; buy them at bus stations or on your first bus.

Country Rover tickets (£5/2.50) are valid after 9am Monday to Friday and all day on Saturdays and Sundays.

Diamond Rover tickets (£7/5) are good for Green Line services any time and day excluding service into London before 9am Monday to Friday.

Arriva (☎ 01279-426349) offers a variety of day, weekly and monthly passes and has good deals for families travelling in Buckinghamshire, Hertfordshire, Essex, Kent, Surrey and Sussex.

Stagecoach Coastline (www.stagecoachbus.com) serves the coastline, East Kent and East Sussex areas. Travellers can buy an unlimited day (£5) or week (£20) Solent Travel Card good on 10 bus lines along the Hampshire coast.

SOUTHEAST COAST

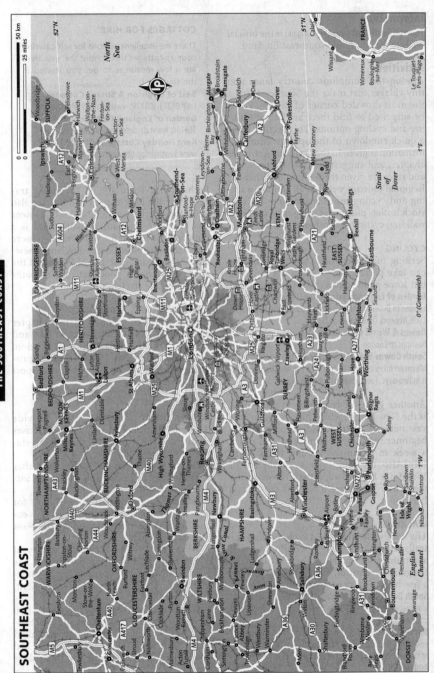

TRAIN

For general rail information call ☎ 08457 48 49 50. The BritRail SouthEast Pass allows unlimited rail travel for three or four days in eight, or seven days in fifteen and must be purchased outside the UK; see the Transport chapter.

The **Network Railcard** (☎ 08457 225 225; www .railcard.co.uk/network/network.htm; per yr £20) is a discount card available for visitors travelling in London, the Home Counties and South England. Passengers get a 34% discount (children ride for £1), but they have to travel at off-peak times.

ESSEX

No matter which country you go to there's always one region that has long been the butt of everyone's jokes. In England, that ignominious role goes to Essex. Locals are routinely pilloried for their white trainers, promiscuous attitudes and loud cars (see the boxed text p166), and Essex can't shake the notion that all it has to offer is Southend-on-Sea, a tacky seaside resort that is one of the country's most popular. But if you're ever inclined not to read a book by its cover, this is the time. Essex is home to Britain's oldest town as well as a number of exquisite medieval villages and some stunning countryside that inspired the painter Constable.

SOUTHEND-ON-SEA

☎ 01702 / pop 269,415

Southend is more pugnacious and brash than some of England's other fun-by-the-sea destinations and unless you're after tacky seaside arcades, flash amusement rides or sleazy nightspots, there's not much to do in Essex's largest town and most popular seaside resort. Still, if you're after a day trip fuelled by rock candy and fish-and-chips, look no further. Southend is less than 50 miles (80km) from London and was pegged as an out-of-town retreat at the turn of the 19th century when the Prince Regent brought his wife Princess Caroline here to enjoy healthier climes, while he disappeared off to Brighton to indulge himself.

Information

The **TIC** (☎ 215120; marketing@southend.gov.uk; Western Esplanade; ✆ 8am-6pm Mon-Fri & 8am-8pm Sat

& Sun May, 8am-10pm Mon-Fri & 8am-8pm Sat & Sun Jun-Sep, 8am-4pm Oct-Apr) is at the entrance to the pier. Banks and most of the shops run along the High St.

Sights & Activities

Southend action seems to pool along the coast to each side of its 1.3-mile-long **pier** (admission £2.20; ☎ 8am-10pm daily Apr-Oct, 8am-5pm Mon-Fri & 8am-7pm Sat & Sun Nov-Mar) which is supposedly the longest in the world.

The free trip on the old and cramped **Pier Railway** isn't all that great, especially considering that the walk to the end of the pier is mercifully quiet. Underneath the pier is a small **museum** (☎ 01702 215620; admission £1; ✆ 11am-5pm Sat-Wed May-Oct) with a collection that includes 19th-century pier train carriages and antique slot machines.

If you have kids, the **Sealife Adventure** (☎ 442200; Eastern Esplanade; adult/child £5.50/4; ✆ 10am-7pm), about half a mile east of the pier, has the usual aquatic suspects behind glass, including a couple of sharks. The same company also runs **Adventure Island** (☎ 443 400; Western Esplanade; ✆ daily Apr-Aug, Sat & Sun Sep-Mar), an amusement park near the pier. There are plenty of rides, all individually priced at about £2 each.

Sleeping & Eating

For those who can't get their fill of candy floss and bingo in one day, Southend has a number of B&Bs.

Mayflower Hotel (☎ 340489; www.themayflower hotel.co.uk; 6 Royal Tce; s/d/tr from £28.20/42.30/56.40; ✗) This charming Victorian row-house B&B has flower-lined wrought-iron balconies and pier and beach views.

Gleneagles Hotel (☎ 333635; www.thegleneagles hotel.co.uk; 5 Clifftown Pde; s/d £39.50/50; ✗) Close to the High St and pier, this crisp well-appointed B&B has lovely patio and frontal rooms overlooking a conservation garden and the sea.

Despite the tackiness of its seafront, Southend offers a surprising number of stylish restaurants.

Bailey's Fry Inn (☎ 467680; 20 Eastern Esplanade; mains £3-4; ✆ 11.45am-3pm & 5-10pm Mon-Fri, 11.45am-10pm Sat & Sun) Front and centre on the seafront, this is a fabulously greasy fish-and-chips dive with timeless, local charm.

For eats away from the glitter of the seaside, walk up the hill to **Singapore Sling**

(☎ 431313; 12 Clifftown Pde; mains £4-10; ✆ lunch & dinner Tue-Sun; ✗), an Asian bistro with Thai, Japanese and Vietnamese fare. Nearby is **Fleur de Provence** (☎ 532987; 54 Alexandra St; mains £16-18; ✆ noon-2pm & 7-10pm Mon-Fri, 7-10pm Sat; ✗), an elegant French restaurant with blonde-wood floors, lilac wallpaper and white tablecloths all set up for a special night out. A three-course prix fixe lunch is £15.

Getting There & Around

From London, **Green Line** (☎ 0870 608 7261) bus No X1 departs at 9am, noon and 4.30pm from London Victoria to Victoria Station in Southend (£5.50, 2½ hours).

There are several trains each hour from either London Liverpool St to Southend Victoria station or from London Fenchurch St to Southend Central station (£10, 55 minutes).

The seafront is a 15-minute walk from the train station and getting around town on foot is easy. The **First Thamesway** (☎ 01268 525 251) Southend Hopper £3 ticket gives you unlimited travel in and around Southend.

If you need a taxi try **Southend Six Seater** (☎ 304848) or **Southend Radio Cars** (☎ 345678).

COLCHESTER

☎ 01206 / pop 104,390

Most visitors to Essex tend to overlook Colchester but they shouldn't. This charming place is England's oldest city with a recorded settlement dating back to the 5th century BC, hundreds of years before the Romans arrived in AD 43 to make Colchester their Northern capital. Back then, the city was known as Camulodunum. Today, it's pos-

sible to see the evidence of Roman life at the town's main feature – the impressive Norman castle built by William the Conqueror atop the ruins of an old Roman fortress. Apart from the rich history, Colchester is an easy-going place perfect for a day trip from London.

Orientation & Information

There are two train stations, but most services stop at North station, about half a mile north of the town centre. The **bus and coach station** (☎ 282645) is in the centre of town, near the TIC and the castle. A **First Day ticket** (adult £2.20) allows unlimited bus service in the Colchester area.

The **TIC** (☎ 282920; www.visitcolchester.com; 1 Queen St; ✆ 9.30am-6pm Mon-Sat, 11am-4pm Sun) is opposite the castle.

There are a couple of **post offices** (North Hill and Longe Wyre St) in town. Banks and ATMs can be found on Culver St West and on the High St.

Sights & Activities

Situated at the edge of a beautiful park across from the TIC, **Colchester Castle** (☎ 282939; admission £4.50; ✆ 10am-5pm Mon-Sat, 11am-4.30pm Sun) is a great place to linger. The structure was built by William I on the foundations of a Roman fort, the walls of which are still visible just outside the front door. Construction began in 1076 and was completed in 1125. It boasts the largest castle keep in Europe – bigger than the Tower of London keep. The museum contains Roman mosaics and statues. For another £1.50 you can

---

THE ESSEX GIRL & BOY

She's a bottle blonde, loves Bacardi Breezers and has a wardrobe better suited to Ibiza in July than Colchester in January. His hair has enough styling gel to make him a fire risk, he wears jack-up trousers that show off his white socks and screeches around a flat urban wasteland in an XR3i with fluffy dice dangling from the rear-view mirror. They complement each other perfectly: her sexual morals are more a guide than a rule, and he thinks the cheesy chat-up is an undervalued art form (or he would if he knew what art was).

Who are they? They're Essex Girl and Boy, England's most enduring local stereotype. And it's getting more entrenched. Since WWII, Essex's inhabitants have been the butt of jokes questioning their intelligence, but in the last 10 years or so the stereotype has evolved so much that the 'typical' Essex Boy and Girl have been defined right down to their fingernails.

You won't need us to tell you that it's just a stupid myth, and that Essex is no different to most other counties, but still the jokes pour forth. Sadly, it does the county no favours, and the image is now so deep-rooted that it's in danger of scaring off potential new business and affecting the county's economy.

take a guided tour of the Roman vaults, the Norman chapel on the roof of the castle and the top of the castle walls.

In Tymperleys – a magnificent, restored 15th-century building about 100m east of the castle just off the High St – is the **Clock Museum** (☎ 282931; admission free; ⌚ 10am-1pm & 2-5pm Mon-Sat Apr-Oct), with one of the largest collections of clocks in Britain. The **Dutch Quarter**, just north of High St, is interesting; it was established in the 16th century by Protestant refugee weavers from Holland.

Opposite the castle, the **Natural History Museum** (☎ 282932; High St; ⌚ 10am-5pm Mon-Sat, 11am-5pm Sun) has exhibits devoted to the local area, with hands-on displays, live animals and a small nature reserve.

About 5 miles to the northeast is **Colchester Zoo** (☎ 331292; Maldon Rd, Stanway; admission £11.99; ⌚ 9.30am-6pm Easter-Jun, Sep & Oct, 9.30am-6.30pm Jul & Aug, 9.30am-dusk Oct-Mar), one of the best zoos in Europe, with a huge selection of animals. It's very modern and extremely well organised.

Eastern National bus No 75 to Tiptree stops at the zoo. It leaves on the hour from stand 17 at the bus station.

Tours

The TIC has a variety of themed, guided **walking tours** (£2.50; ⌚ Apr-Oct) of the town at 11.30am several days of the week. Call ahead to ask for details. The TIC also sells tickets for **open-top bus tours** (£5.75; ⌚ mid-Jul–Sep).

Sleeping

Most accommodation in Colchester is in the mid-range category though you can definitely splurge if you want to.

Peveril Hotel (☎ /fax 574001; 51 North Hill; s/d from £30/42; ✗) Conveniently located on the road to the train station, this 17-room hotel is a good value. Most rooms share bathrooms.

The Old Manse (☎ 545154; www.doveuk.com/old manse; 15 Roman Rd; s/d £34/53; ✗) This wonderful Victorian home is only a few minutes' walk from the centre and is a run by a lovely, engaging couple. It doesn't cater for children. Part of the Roman wall is at the bottom of the garden.

The Red Lion (☎ 577986; www.redlion@brook -hotels.co.uk; High St; s/d from £55/65; P ✗) This well-preserved Tudor hotel has comfortable rooms furnished with period-style antiques. The restaurant serves steak-and-kidney pie and other takes on traditional English fare.

Rose & Crown Hotel (☎ 866677; www.rose-and -crown.com; East St; s/d from £66/76; P ⌨ ✗) The Rose & Crown may be the oldest hotel in town, but it features a sharp, modern wing. All 30 rooms are en suite and loaded with amusing distractions.

The George (☎ 578494; www.londonandedinburgh inns.com/ColchesterGeorge/; 116 High St; s/d from £85/95; ✗) Don't let the charming sloped floors in this gorgeous 15th-century inn fool you. The rooms here are clean with modern amenities although smoking rooms can be a bit musty.

Eating

The Garden Café at the Minories Art Gallery (☎ 500169; 74 High St; mains £4-6; ⌚ 10am-4.30 Mon-Sat; ✗) This is an eclectic, artsy and airy café with an enormous garden. If they've run out of main dishes (they're cooked fresh daily and served until 3pm), go for the amaretto bombe. The café is housed in a gallery that shows local, national and international traveling exhibits of contemporary art.

Franco (☎ 549080; Balkerne Passage off North Hill; mains £5-15; ⌚ noon-2pm & 6-10pm Tue-Fri, 6-10pm Sat; ✗) Look no further for sophisticated but traditional Italian country dishes such as risotto, mussels, and melon with figs. The atmosphere is colourful and lively.

The Lemon Tree (☎ 767337; 48 St John's St; mains £9-13; ⌚ 10.30am-9.30pm Mon-Sat; ✗) This place seems a bit plain until you notice part of an original Roman wall and cavern in the corner. It's the only place to sit for good upscale French cuisine or even a simple pot of tea.

Getting There & Away

Colchester is 62 miles (100km) from London. There are daily National Express buses from London Victoria (£9) and rail services every half hour or so from London Liverpool St (£16.90, 45 minutes).

AROUND COLCHESTER
Dedham Vale

'I love every stile and stump and lane… these scenes made me a painter'
John Constable

Known to the locals as Constable country, Dedham Vale in the Stour Valley, near the border with Suffolk, was an oft-used subject for early–19th-century painter John Constable. His landscapes depicting country lanes, springtime fields and babbling creeks may have been romantic visions of times past but there's no doubt that the charm of the local countryside still exists. The Vale centres on the villages of Dedham, East Bergholt (in Suffolk, where the painter was born) and Flatford. The area is best explored in your own car but there are bus and train services.

Flatford Mill (not the original) was once owned by Constable's father and now houses arts courses. Public access comes only in the form of **tours** (☎ 01206-298283).

Bridge Cottage (☎ 01206-298260; admission free; ⏱ 10am-5.30pm daily May-Sep, 11am-4.30pm daily Oct, 11am-5pm Wed-Sun Mar-Apr & Nov-Dec, 11am-3.30pm Sat & Sun Jan-Feb) has Constable landscapes on display as well as a tea-garden, boat hire and access to National Trust land. When guided tours are not available audio tapes can be hired (tours/tapes £2).

Several bus companies operate services from Colchester to East Bergholt. It's better to come by train (get off at Manningtree), as you get a pleasant 1¾-mile walk along footpaths through Constable country. If you are in Manningtree, make a quick diversion and walk up the hill to the town of Mistly for a wonderful view over the estuary of the River Stour. The TIC in Colchester sells cycling maps of Dedham Vale.

SAFFRON WALDEN
☎ 01799 / pop 14,313

The curiously titled Saffron Walden gets its name from the saffron crocus cultivated in the surrounding fields, an activity that helped make this beautiful medieval town a bustling market centre from the 15th century to the first half of the 20th century. There is a small-but-interesting museum, and streets that are packed with antique shops.

The **TIC** (☎ 510444; www.uttlesford.gov.uk; 1 Market Pl; ⏱ 9.30am-5.30pm Mon-Fri, 9.30am-1pm & 1.30-5.30pm Sat, 10am-noon Sun) sells a useful town trail leaflet for 25p.

The **museum** (☎ 510333; admission £1; ⏱ 10am-5pm Mon-Sat, 2-5pm Sun) has a wealth of material and is well worth a visit. It includes a very interesting local-history exhibit and has an odd collection of objects from all over the world, including a mummy from Thebes. The ruins of **Walden Castle Keep**, built about 1125, are next to the museum.

The **Church of St Mary the Virgin**, off Museum St, dates mainly from 1450–1525,

when the town was at the height of its prosperity. It's one of the largest in the county and has some very impressive Gothic arches, decorative wooden ceilings and a 60m spire which was added in 1832. On the eastern side of the town is an ancient earthen **maze**; a path circles for almost a mile, taking you to the centre if you follow the right route.

Sleeping & Eating
Most of the B&Bs are in tiny houses and have only one or two rooms, but there aren't too many visitors and you shouldn't have any problems finding somewhere to stay.

YHA Hostel (☎ 0870 770 6014; cnr Myddylton Pl & Bridge St; dm £10.60) The hostel is in the best-preserved 15th-century building in town.

Archway Guesthouse (☎ 501500; 11 Church St; s/d £35/55) The rooms are lovely in this odd place, with an unusual mix of décor and a huge collection of 'stuff'.

The **Old Forge** (☎ 521494; 23 Fairycroft Rd; s/d £28/44) Old-world appeal and modern-day comforts make this B&B in the centre of town an appealing stopover.

Dorringtons (☎ 522093; 9 Cross St) This bakery has delicious, fresh pastries and sandwiches from 80p to £1.50.

There are some lovely old pubs around town including the 16th-century **Eight Bells** (☎ 522790; 18 Bridge St), about three minutes' walk from the centre.

Getting There & Away
On weekdays, trains leave from London Liverpool St every 20 minutes (£14.90, one hour) for Audley End station, 2½ miles west of town. On Saturday the train leaves every hour, and on Sunday there is one in the morning and three after 8pm.

Stansted Transit (☎ 01763-289798) bus No 301 will collect you from the station and take you into Saffron Walden at 9.40am, 10.40am, 12.40pm or 2.40pm (£2, six minutes). **Hedingham** (☎ 01206-769778) commuter bus No 59 leaves the station at 9.50am, 1.20pm and 5.02pm.

AROUND SAFFRON WALDEN
Audley End House
Built in the early 17th century, this Jacobean **mansion** (EH; ☎ 01799-522399; admission house & park £8.50, park £4; ⏱ noon-5pm Wed-Sun Apr-Sep, last admission 4pm) was used as a royal palace by Charles II, even though it had been

described by James I as 'too large for a king'. The 30 rooms on display house a fine collection of paintings, silverware and furniture. It's set in a magnificent landscaped **park** (☼ 11am-6pm Wed-Sun, last admission 5pm), the handiwork of Lancelot 'Capability' Brown.

Audley End House is one mile west of Saffron Walden on the B1383. Audley End train station is 1¼ miles from the house. Taxis leave from the town marketplace (£3).

KENT

Kent is not known as the 'Garden of England' for nothing. Inside its sea-lined borders you'll find rolling farmland pocked with farm stores, country estates, Scottish cattle and most important of all, the world-renowned Kent hops, the main ingredient in some of England's (and the world's) finest ales. In addition, the county is home to beautiful 19th-century beach resorts complete with Punch-and-Judy puppet shows, picturesque Canterbury and its marvellous cathedral, and the port of Dover where you can jump a ferry to France for the day.

Unfortunately, Kent is by no means a well-kept secret. Its popularity as a holiday destination began with the construction of the railway in the 19th century and the crowds haven't abated since. The county's close proximity to London also means that many of the small towns are within commuting distance, leading to rush-hour clogging of the main routes to and from the capital.

Even so, trails along the North and South Downs attract walkers from all over the world (see the Activities section, p163). Between the North and South Downs lies an area known as the Weald, much of it designated an Area of Outstanding Natural Beauty (AONB).

For general information about the county, contact the very well-organised **Kent Tourism Alliance** (☎ 01271-336020; www.kenttourism.co.uk; 3 The Precincts, Canterbury, Kent CT1 2EE).

CANTERBURY

☎ 01227 / pop 45,055

Canterbury should make the Top Ten of any English must-visit list, at the very least because of its cathedral, which is considered by many to be one of the finest in Europe. Yet even without the spires Canterbury is a great town to explore. It is vibrant and youthful

with some great pubs, excellent restaurants and an easy, laid-back atmosphere all set in a gorgeous medieval centre that has retained much of its original character. If you plan to visit the nearby coastal towns, Canterbury is a great place to base yourself. However, it's essential to book ahead for hotels and some of the nicer restaurants. The crowds of visitors that descend on the city year-round are not to be underestimated.

History

Canterbury's past is as rich as it comes. From AD 200 there was a Roman town called Durovernum Cantiacorum here, which later became the capital of the Saxon kingdom of Kent. When St Augustine arrived in England in 597 to carry the Christian message to the pagan hordes, he chose Canterbury as his *cathedra*, or primary see, and set about building an abbey on the outskirts of town. Following the martyrdom of Thomas Becket (see the boxed text p171), Canterbury became northern Europe's most important centre of pilgrimage, which in turn led to Geoffrey Chaucer's *The Canterbury Tales*, one of the most outstanding poetic works in English literature (see p49).

Blasphemous murders and rampant tourism aside, Canterbury remains the primary see for the Church of England.

Orientation

The old town of Canterbury is enclosed by a medieval city wall and a modern ring road. Most streets in the Old Town are closed to cars, but there is parking inside the wall, and meandering down the streets is an added attraction.

Information
BOOKSHOPS
Chaucer Bookshop (Beer Cart Lane) A wonderful, well-stocked used-book shop.
Waterstones (☎ 456343; 20-21 St Margaret's St)

INTERNET ACCESS
Main library (☎ 452747; High St; ☼ Mon-Sat) Free Internet access. Located inside the Royal Museum & Art Gallery.

MEDIA
Two free magazines, *What, Where & When* and *Great Days Out*, have details of what's on in Canterbury and Kent. They're both available from the TIC.

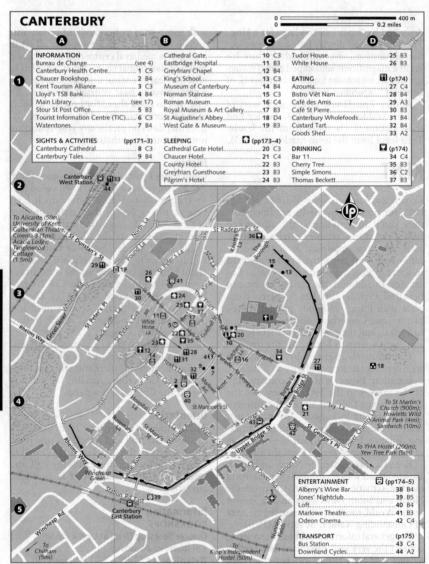

CANTERBURY

0   400 m
0   0.2 miles

INFORMATION	
Bureau de Change	(see 4)
Canterbury Health Centre	1 C5
Chaucer Bookshop	2 B4
Kent Tourism Alliance	3 C3
Lloyd's TSB Bank	4 B4
Main Library	(see 17)
Stour St Post Office	5 B3
Tourist Information Centre (TIC)	6 C3
Waterstones	7 B4

SIGHTS & ACTIVITIES	(pp171–3)
Canterbury Cathedral	8 C3
Canterbury Tales	9 B4

Cathedral Gate	10 C3
Eastbridge Hospital	11 B3
Greyfriars Chapel	12 B4
King's School	13 C3
Museum of Canterbury	14 B4
Norman Staircase	15 C3
Roman Museum	16 C4
Royal Museum & Art Gallery	17 B3
St Augustine's Abbey	18 D4
West Gate & Museum	19 B3

SLEEPING	(pp173–4)
Cathedral Gate Hotel	20 C3
Chaucer Hotel	21 C4
County Hotel	22 B3
Greyfriars Guesthouse	23 B3
Pilgrim's Hotel	24 B3

Tudor House	25 B3
White House	26 B3

EATING	(p174)
Azouma	27 C4
Bistro Viêt Nam	28 B4
Café des Amis	29 A3
Café St Pierre	30 B4
Canterbury Wholefoods	31 B4
Custard Tart	32 B4
Goods Shed	33 A2

DRINKING	(p174)
Bar 11	34 C4
Cherry Tree	35 B3
Simple Simons	36 C2
Thomas Beckett	37 B3

ENTERTAINMENT	(pp174–5)
Alberry's Wine Bar	38 B4
Jones' Nightclub	39 B5
Loft	40 B4
Marlowe Theatre	41 B3
Odeon Cinema	42 C4

TRANSPORT	(p175)
Bus Station	43 C4
Downland Cycles	44 A2

THE SOUTHEAST COAST

MEDICAL SERVICES

Canterbury Health Centre (☎ 452444; 26 Old Dover Rd) For general medical consultations.

Kent & Canterbury Hospital (☎ 766877; Etherbert Rd) Has an emergency room and is a mile from the centre.

MONEY

ATMs and other major banks are on High St, near the corner of St Margaret's St.

Lloyd's TSB (28 St Margaret's St) has a bureau de change.

POST

Stour St post office (cnr St Peter's & Stour Sts; ⏰ 9.30am-5.30pm Mon-Sat)

TOURIST OFFICES

TIC (☎ 378100; www.canterbury.co.uk; 12 Sun St;

KEEP YOUR ENEMIES CLOSE...

In 1162 King Henry II did what every good monarch should do. He appointed his good mate Thomas Becket to the highest clerical office in the land in the hope that a friendly archbishop could force the increasingly vocal religious lobby to toe the royal line. But Henry didn't count on Thomas taking his job as seriously as he did, and by 1170 Henry had become exasperated with his former favourite's penchant for disagreeing with virtually everything the king said or did. He sulked and raged for a while, then late in the year 'suggested' to four of his knights that Thomas was a little too much to bear. The dirty deed was done on December 29. Becket's martyrdom – and canonisation in double-quick time (1173) – catapulted the cathedral to the top spot in northern Europe's top 10 pilgrimage sites. Mindful of the growing opprobrium at his role in Becket's murder, Henry arrived here in 1174 for a dramatic *mea culpa*, and after allowing himself to be whipped and scolded was granted absolution.

9.30am-5.30pm Mon-Sat, 10am-4pm Sun) Across from the cathedral gate.

Sights

There are some great things to see in Canterbury, headed up of course by the great cathedral.

CANTERBURY CATHEDRAL

The Church of England could not have a more splendid and imposing mother church. This extraordinary **cathedral complex** (☎ 762862; adult/child £4.50/3.50; 9am-6.30pm Mon-Fri May-Aug, 9am-5pm Mon-Fri Sep-Apr, plus 9am-2.30pm & 4.30-5.30pm Sunday year-round) is undoubtedly worth the few hours you can spend visiting. The sheer wealth of detail, treasure and stories associated with the cathedral is worthwhile, so we recommend you join a **tour** (adult/child £3.50/£1.50; 10.30am, noon & 2.30pm Mon-Fri, 10.30am, noon & 1.30pm Sat), or you can take a 30-minute **self-guided audio tour** (adult/child £2.95/£1.95). At the very least, pick up a free leaflet that briefly points out the many sights. There is an additional charge (£4) to take photographs inside the cathedral during your visit.

The first church built here was badly damaged by fire in 1067. A replacement cathedral was begun in 1070, but only fragments of this remain today, as a second fire in 1174 destroyed most of the eastern half of the building. Thankfully, the magnificent crypt beneath the choir survived.

Following the martyrdom of Thomas Becket (see the boxed text above), the cathedral's fortunes increased dramatically. Pilgrims began appearing in droves, and a new cathedral, created by William of Sens, was constructed to reflect the town's growing importance. It is the first major Gothic construction in England, built in a style now known as 'Early English'. In 1988 Unesco declared the cathedral – along with St Augustine's Abbey and St Martin's Church – a World Heritage Site.

The spot where Becket was murdered is in the northwest transept, marked by a lit candle. The original **Altar of Sword's Point** – the final destination of millions of pilgrims over the last 1000 years – was replaced by a modern version of the same in 1982, when Pope John Paul II came here.

When you leave the cathedral, go round the eastern end and turn right into **Green Court**, surrounded on the eastern (right) side by the Deanery and the northern side (straight ahead) by the early–14th-century Brewhouse and Bakehouse, which now house part of the very exclusive prep school, **King's School**. In the northwestern corner (far left) is the famous **Norman Staircase** (1151).

MUSEUMS

The first three museums listed here can all be visited with one ticket costing £5/3 per adult/child. Individual admission costs are given below.

An excellent place to visit, the **Roman Museum** (☎ 785575; Butchery Lane; admission £2.80; 10am-5pm Mon-Sat year round, plus 1.30-5pm Sun Jun-Oct) is one of the few museums of this kind where you are allowed to actually touch old stuff. And not only can you handle original artefacts uncovered in the remains of a Roman town house lying below the museum, you can also walk around a reconstructed kitchen (smelling the odours) and check out the extensive remains of a mosaic floor.

Once the Poor Priests' Hospital, the **Museum of Canterbury** (☎ 452747; Stour St; adult/child £3.10/2.10; 10.30am-5pm Mon-Sat year-round, plus

THE SOUTHEAST COAST

1.30-5pm Sun Jun-Oct) has wonderful exhibitions and artefacts including a visual breakdown of the people and events leading up to the assassination of Becket. There's also a new Rupert Bear addition (Mary Tourtel, the creator of the children's character, was born in Canterbury) where the kids can join Rupert for a spot of tea or time travel.

The **West Gate & Museum** (☎ 452747; St Peter's St; admission £1.10; 🕙 11am-12.30pm & 1.30-3.30pm Mon-Sat) dates from the 14th century and is the only remaining city gate. It's now a small museum featuring arms and armour. Kids – and some adults – might enjoy trying on the replica armour.

The **Royal Museum & Art Gallery** (☎ 452747; High St; admission free; 🕙 10am-5pm Mon-Sat) houses contemporary and historical art as well as military memorabilia, but really the best thing about it is the front façade, a splendid study of high Victorian architecture. The city's central library is in this building as well.

THE CANTERBURY TALES
In a former church, the **Canterbury Tales** (☎ 479227; St Margaret's St; adult/child £6.95/5.25; 🕙 10am-5pm Mar-Jun, 9.30am-5pm Jul-Aug, 10am-5pm Sep-Oct, 10am-4.30pm Nov-Feb) is a three-dimensional take on Chaucer's classic story. It's entertaining enough but the jerky, hydraulic puppets don't do the historic stories justice. It's usually crammed with schoolchildren.

ST AUGUSTINE'S ABBEY
Founded in AD 597, this site is an important link to the city's Christian past. Unfortunately, all that remains of **St Augustine's Abbey** (☎ 767345; admission £3; 🕙 10am-6pm Apr-Sep,

10am-5pm Oct, 10am-4pm Nov-Mar) is the foundation. However, a small but interesting museum houses original artefacts dug up in and around the abbey. Admission includes a very worthwhile audio tour.

ST MARTIN'S CHURCH
England's oldest parish church in continuous use, **St Martin's** (☎ 768072; North Holmes Rd; admission free; 🕙 10am-3pm Tue & Thu, 10am-1pm Sat, or by appointment) is located about 900m east of the abbey. This is where Queen Bertha (wife of the Saxon King Ethelbert) welcomed Augustine upon his arrival in the 6th century. The original Saxon church has somewhat disappeared under a thorough medieval refurbishment, but it's still worth a quick visit.

EASTBRIDGE HOSPITAL & GREYFRIARS CHAPEL
Founded in 1180, the Hospital of St Thomas the Martyr **Eastbridge** (☎ 462395; 25 High St; admission £1; 🕙 10am-5pm Mon-Sat) was built as a hospice for poor pilgrims visiting Becket's shrine (the recessesions in which they slept can be found between the pillars in the Undercroft). Its almshouses (dating from 1584) are still in use today.

Behind the hospital in a surprisingly serene garden setting, you'll find the **Greyfriars Chapel** (☎ 471688; 25 High St; admission free; 🕙 2-4pm Mon-Sat mid-May–Sep). This was the first English monastery built by Franciscan monks in 1267 (they were known as Grey Friars due to the colour of their cassocks). The small upstairs chapel is a serene place where you can recharge your spirit away from the

---

THE CANTERBURY TALES

If English literature has a father figure, then it is certainly Geoffrey Chaucer (1342/3–1400). Chaucer was the first English writer to introduce characters – rather than 'types' – into fiction, and he did so to greatest effect in his most popular work, *The Canterbury Tales*.

Written between 1387 and his death, the *Tales* is an unfinished series of 24 stories supposedly told by a party of pilgrims on their journey from London to the shrine of Thomas Becket at Canterbury and back. Chaucer successfully created the illusion that the pilgrims, not Chaucer (though he appears in the tales as himself), are telling the stories, which allowed him unprecedented freedom as an author to explore the rich fictive possibilities of a number of genres.

Chaucer's achievement remains a high point of European literature, but it was also the first time that English came to match Latin (the language of the Church) and French (spoken by the Norman court) as a language of high literature. *The Canterbury Tales*, summed up by Dryden as 'God's Plenty', remains one of the pillars of the literary canon, even if contemporary modern readers would probably enjoy a modern transliteration more than the original Old English version.

crowds. The Eucharist is celebrated here every Wednesday at 12.30pm.

Tours

A variety of guided walks are offered by **Canterbury Walks** (☎ 459779; www.canterbury-walks .co.uk; £3.75; ☺ 11.30am daily Apr-Oct, Mon-Sat Jul & Aug). Call ahead to book.

Cross the footbridge at Canterbury Station East to walk atop the city's **medieval walls**.

Popular **ghost tours** (☎ 575831; www.greenbard .8m.com; adult/child £5/£4) of the Old Town depart from outside Alberrys wine bar in St Margaret's St at 8pm every Friday and Saturday all year in all weather. Bookings are only needed for groups.

Canterbury Historic River Tours (☎ 07790-534744; www.canterburyrivertours.co.uk; adult/child £5/4; ☺ 10am-5pm Mon-Sat & 11am-5pm Sun Apr-Sep) will take you on a rowing-boat tour including (prebooked) candlelit tours, from behind The Old Weaver's House on St Peter's St.

Festivals & Events

For two weeks in mid-October, the **Canterbury Festival** (www.canterburyfestival.co.uk) features arts, music and theatre from around the world. Contact the TIC for a detailed programme of events.

Sleeping

BUDGET

Kipp's Independent Hostel (☎ 786121; info@kipps -hostel.com; 40 Nunnery Fields; dm from £11; ✕) This bright and cheery, family-run place has clean facilities, Internet access (£1 per halfhour), and a lovable dog named Cuba.

YHA Hostel (☎ 0870 770 5744, www.yha.org.uk; 54 New Dover Rd; dm beds £16.40; ☺ Feb–late-Dec; P ✕ 🖳) Staying in a fine Victorian Gothic villa was never so affordable. Amenities include a bureau de change and a large garden. Located 1¼ miles southeast of the centre.

Yew Tree Park (☎ 700306; Stone St, Petham; camping per tent & 1/2 adults £5/8; ☺ Apr-Oct; 🐾) This camp site, located 5 miles south of Canterbury, is surrounded by trees and there's plenty of soft grass to pitch a tent on. Call for directions and transportation information.

MID-RANGE

White House (☎ 761836; www.canterburybreaks.co.uk; 6 St Peter's Lane; s/d from £35/55; 🖳 ✕) A gorgeous Regency townhouse that was owned by the Church of England until 1979 with spacious,

---

comfortable rooms and unparalleled service. Heaven for vegetarians in the land of the full English breakfast (also available).

Cathedral Gate Hotel (☎ 464381; cgate@cgate .demon.co.uk; 36 Burgate; s/d with shared bathroom from £35/50, with private bathroom from £60/90, cots extra £8.50; ✕) Although the floors slope, the walls are thin and it's above a – gasp! – Starbucks, the rooms at this spot next door to the Cathedral Gate are very comfortable and the views of the cathedral are stunning.

Pilgrim's Hotel (☎ 464531; pilgrimshotel@netscap online.co.uk; 18 The Friars; s/d £50/70; P ✕) Exit stage left from the Marlowe Theatre and find yourself on the doorstep of this fine Tudor hotel whose clean conservative rooms are appointed with country-style antiques.

Tudor House (☎ 765650; 6 Best Lane, s/d £22/46; ☺ Apr-Oct; ✕) This quaint, family-run spot is right on the river near the High St. Rooms are standard but clean.

Greyfriars Guesthouse (☎ 456255; www.greyfriars -house.co.uk; 6 Stour St; s/d from £25/50, family £65-90; P ✕) Greyfriars was once the dormitory for the Church of the Greyfriars. Now it has fairly standard, simple but spacious rooms.

Other options include:

Acacia Lodge & Tanglewood Cottage (☎ 769955; www.acacialodge.com; 39 London Rd; s/d from £30/38; P ✕)

Alicante (☎ /fax 766277; 4 Roper Rd; s/d £35/65; ✕)

SOMETHING SPECIAL

The Goods Shed (☎ 459153; www.producedinkent.co.uk; Station Rd West; lunch £8-12, dinner £10-16; ☺ farmer's market 10am-7pm Tue-Sat & 10am-4pm Sun, restaurant Tue-Sun; P ✗) This converted railway warehouse situated next door to Canterbury West Station and overlooking the rails is far and away the best restaurant in town. Come in for an elegantly plated sit-down breakfast, lunch or dinner with food made from the breads, veggies, fruits, fish and meats offered at the farmer's market that sets up shop on the warehouse floor. The country French menu changes daily based on what comes in for the market and it's always imaginative and extraordinarily fresh. The extensive wine list includes a collection of locally made vintages.

TOP END
County Hotel (☎ 766266; www.macdonaldhotels.co.uk; 30 High St; s/d £112/122; P ✗) Located just across from the striking Royal Museum & Art Gallery on the High St, the rooms in this wonderful building are laden with antiques. This hotel is pet friendly.

Chaucer Hotel (☎ 464427; www.swallowhotels .com; 63 Ivy Lane; s/d from £60/90; P ✗) Once a Georgian house, this top-class hotel has been substantially altered to create a comfortable and modern place to stay. Breakfast is additional.

Eating
There's a good range of eateries in Canterbury. Bookings are recommended for the pricier spots, especially at weekends.

Custard Tart (☎ 785178; 35a St Margaret's St; mains £3-4.50; ☺ lunch & dinner; ✗) Start your morning with a fresh and heavenly sugar-dusted chocolate donut (55p) from the takeaway counter. The lunchtime sandwiches in the upstairs café are very popular.

Bistro Việt Nam (☎ 760022; The Old Linen Store, White Horse Lane; mains £5-10; ☺ lunch & dinner; ✗) The modern southeast Asian menu features a range of well-presented dishes including a superb Vietnamese tapas menu. It is simply fabulous.

Café des Amis (☎ 464390; 93-95 St Dunstan's St; mains £7-13; ☺ lunch & dinner; ✗) The décor is rustic and colourful. Go for a casual bite and a frozen margarita to a Mexican rhythm.

Azouma (☎ 760076; www.azouma.co.uk; 4 Church St; mains £8-11; ☺ lunch & dinner) Follow the smell of roasted couscous, raisins and paprika for an inventive Middle Eastern experience in a beautifully lush and authentic setting.

Café St Pierre (☎ 456791; 41 St Peter's St; ☺ 8am-6pm Mon-Sat 9am-5.30pm Sun; breakfast £3; ✗) A good stop for French pastries, cakes, coffee and people-watching on the High St.

For self-catering, try **Canterbury Wholefoods** (☎ 464623; 1-2 Jewry Lane; ☺ 9am-6pm Mon-Sat, 11am-5pm Sun), a wholefood shop with postings for political events, yoga classes, gay and lesbian gatherings and the like.

Drinking
Canterbury has a lively student population, so there are plenty of nightlife options.

Thomas Beckett (☎ 464384; 21 Best Lane; mains £6-9) This is as good as it gets for English pubs. A cosy fireplace, copper pots and bushels of dried Kent hops hang from the ceiling. The cool jazz standards on the sound system give the place a timeless charm. Better-than-average pub fare.

Simple Simons (☎ 762355; 3-9 Church Lane) If you've come to England to sample the beer look no further. This wonderfully woody 14th-century building serves at least six different hand-pulled real ales and it has the expert drinkers to prove it.

Cherry Tree (☎ 451266; White Horse Ln) This back-alley pub is quiet and friendly with dark wood and smoky nooks and crannies.

Bar 11 (☎ 478707; 11 Burgate) This popular modern spot draws a hip, youthful and well-dressed crowd.

Entertainment
NIGHTCLUBS
Loft (☎ 456515; 516 St Margaret's St) Chill out to cool electronic beats in a modern setting with one extremely long couch, a black granite bar and DJs spinning from Thursday to Saturday. The crowd is sophisticated and international.

Alberry's Wine Bar (☎ 452378; www.alberrys.co.uk; St Margaret's St) Situated right across the street from the Loft, this hot after-hours jazz bar is the place to be for Canterbury's young professionals. DJs and live music on Monday and Thursday play smooth jazz and hip-hop.

Jones' Nightclub (☎ 462520; 15 Station Rd East) This long-time favourite is getting some stiff competition from Alberry's but it's still a jumping scene after 11pm. Look for a more edgy crowd with house beats.

CINEMAS
Showing the latest mainstream movies is **Odeon Cinema** (☎ 453577; cnr Upper Bridge St & St George's Pl).

Cinema 3 (☎ 769075; University of Kent) is part of the same complex as the Gulbenkian Theatre and usually shows off-beat, arty films and old classics.

THEATRE
Marlowe Theatre (☎ 787787; www.marlowetheatre .com; The Friars) This newly remodelled building brings in some truly wonderful events year round, including plays, dances, concerts and musicals.

Gulbenkian Theatre (☎ 769075; www.kent.ac.uk /gulbenkian; University of Kent) Located on the university campus, this long-time performance venue is larger than the Marlowe with fewer frills. They put on some serious contemporary plays, modern dance and great live music.

Getting There & Away
Canterbury is 58 miles (93km) from London and 15 miles from Margate and Dover.

BUS
The bus station is just within the city walls at the eastern end of High St.

There are frequent buses from London Victoria to Canterbury (bus No 20, £10.50, one hour 50 minutes, hourly). Buses from Canterbury go to Dover (No 5, 45 minutes, every 20 minutes). Bus Nos 8, 8A and 88 travel from Canterbury to Margate (45 minutes, half hourly), to Broadstairs (one hour) and to Ramsgate (one hour 20 minutes).

TRAIN
There are two train stations: Canterbury East (for the YHA hostel), accessible from London Victoria; and Canterbury West, accessible from London's Charing Cross, Victoria and Waterloo stations.

London to Canterbury trains leave frequently (£17.30, 1½ hours, every ½ hour), as do Canterbury East to Dover Priory trains (30 minutes, every ½ hour).

Getting Around
Cars are not permitted to enter the centre of town. There are car parks at various points along and just within the walls. Parking vouchers cost £3.60 for 24 hours or £1 from 6pm to 10am.

For a taxi, try **Laser Taxis** (☎ 464422) or **Cabwise** (☎ 712929).

Downland Cycles (☎ 479643) is based at Canterbury West station. Mountain bikes cost £10 per day or £50 per week with a £25 deposit.

AROUND CANTERBURY
Howlett's Wild Animal Park
The world's largest collection of Lowland gorillas can be observed at this 28-hectare **park** (☎ 1303 264647; www.howletts.net; Bekesbourne; admission £11.95; 🕙 10am-dusk). However, rather than simply keep them in captivity, the park funds a project in Congo to reintroduce these magnificent animals back to the wild. You'll also see elephants, monkeys, wolves, small wild cats and tigers. Save 20% with tickets purchased in advance.

The park is 4 miles east of Canterbury. By car, take the A257 and turn right at the sign for Bekesbourne, then follow the signs to the Animal Park. From the main bus station you can catch Stagecoach bus Nos 111/211 or 611–14 to Littlebourne, from where it's an eight-minute walk to the park.

WORTH THE TRIP

You wouldn't know Polish nobleman and auto enthusiast Count Louis Vorrow Zborowski (1895–1923), except by the name of his car. In 1921 Zborowski custom built his beloved Chitty Chitty Bang Bang out of a Mercedes and an aeroplane engine. It never flew, but the imaginations of children around the world did when Ian Fleming (of James Bond fame) wrote a book based on the car in 1964. It was later made into a movie, and the rest is history.

Zborowski built Chitty Chitty Bang Bang at **Higham Park** (☎ 01227-830830; admission garden £3, house tour only £2; 🕙 11am-6pm Sun-Thu Apr-Oct), a magnificent Palladian mansion with superb Italianate gardens about 3 miles south of Canterbury off the A2. From Canterbury, bus Nos 16 and 17 to Folkestone stop nearby (£1, 10 minutes).

THE SOUTHEAST COAST

TOP FIVE PUBS FOR A PINT OF REAL ALE

■ **Simple Simons** (Canterbury; p174)

■ **The Thomas Becket** (Canterbury; p174)

■ **The Thatched Bar** (Beachy Head near Eastbourne; p192)

■ **Giant's Fireplace Bar & Lounge** (Rye; p189)

■ **The Spy Glass Inn** (Ventnor, Isle of Wight; p223)

Chilham

Five miles southwest of Canterbury on the A252, Chilham is one of the best examples of a medieval village you'll see anywhere on your travels through England. Built in true feudal fashion around the small square at the front of a castle, the village consists of a 13th-century Norman church (added to in the 15th century) and a collection of Tudor and Jacobean timber-framed houses.

Chilham lies on the North Downs Way (see p163) and would make a pleasant day's walk from Canterbury. Alternatively, bus No 652 from Canterbury makes the trip in 24 minutes and departs hourly.

WHITSTABLE

☎ 01227 / pop 30,195

Compared with Margate, Broadstairs and Ramsgate, Whitstable has more of a remote, unspoilt charm, which may be why it's known as the 'Pearl of Kent'. A quiet fishing village with street names such as Squeeze Gut Alley and Skinner's Alley, the town is known for its superb seafood – particularly the oysters – as well as its somewhat odd multicoloured beach huts lining the Tankerton Slopes east of town. Higher up on the lawn-edged cliffs of the Slopes you can also get a perfect view of the Street, a narrow shingle ridge stretching half a mile out to sea (but only visible at low tide).

The **TIC** (☎ 275482; 7 Oxford St; ☼ 10am-5pm Mon-Sat Jul & Aug, 10am-4pm Mon-Sat Sep-Jun) runs a free accommodation booking service.

Sights & Activities

Whitstable isn't an overly touristy kind of place. People come here to stroll the seafront, eat some wonderful sea fare and generally just hang around.

If you need to see something, however, the **Whitstable Museum & Gallery** (☎ 276998; 8 Oxford St; admission free; ☼ 10am-4pm Mon-Sat year-round, plus 1-4pm Sun Jul & Aug) has good exhibits on Whitstable's fishing industry, with a special emphasis on oysters.

In recent years, Whitstable has developed a vibrant art scene, and there are plenty of art galleries that you can wander into for a look. Most of the best ones line Harbour St, on the seafront.

Festivals & Events

July hosts the **Whitstable Oyster Festival** (www .whitstableoysterfestival.co.uk), an arts and music extravaganza where you can wash down oysters with Guinness or champagne. The programme of events is interesting, featuring everything from how-to demonstrations of various crafts to jazz bands and classical quartets. The whole town lends a hand and it's the highlight of the summer. For info on upcoming events, contact the TIC.

Sleeping

As Whitstable is popular with weekenders and day-trippers from all over southeast England, there are plenty of B&Bs.

Hotel Continental (☎ 280280; www.hotelcontinen tal.co.uk; 29 Beach Walk; s/d/huts from £50/55/100; ☒) This Art Deco building on the seafront has elegantly appointed rooms as well as eight converted Fisherman's Huts on the beach that are just plain charming, if a little close together. Room rates increase at weekends, July and August.

Rooms at both **The Duke of Cumberland** (☎ 280617; www.thedukeinwhitstable.co.uk; High St; d from £60; ☒) and **The Marine** (☎ 272672; www .shepherd-neame.co.uk; 33 Marine Pde; s/d £55/75; ☒) are above bright, spacious and tastefully appointed pubs. Outdoor seating at the Marine comes with a sea view.

Eating

Fish is the speciality here. Oysters are the real treat, but all restaurants serve up a varied seafood menu.

Wheeler's Oyster Bar (☎ 273311; 8 High St; mains £13.50-18.75; ☼ 1-7.30pm Thu-Sat, Mon & Tue, 1-7pm Sun; ☒) Sit up front at the bar at this one-of-a-kind find, or duck into the tiny and rustic Oyster Parlour for an elegant meal surrounded by old photos and seafaring paraphernalia. The staff are wonderful.

THE SOUTHEAST COAST

More great seafood can be had at **Pearson's Crab & Oyster House** (☎ 272005; The Horsebridge; mains $12-16; ✹ lunch & dinner; ✗), another great atmospheric stop, and at the **Whitstable Oyster Fishery Co Restaurant** (☎ 276856; 17-20 Sea St; mains £12.50-25; ✹ lunch & dinner; ✗), where the whole roasted sea bass with garlic and rosemary is delectable.

Getting There & Away

Stagecoach bus Nos 4, 4A, 4B or 4C leave Canterbury every 15 minutes for the 30-minute trip to Whitstable.

AROUND WHITSTABLE
Herne Bay

The one reason to visit less-than-charming Herne Bay is to ride on the **Wildlife** (☎ 01227-366712; www.wildlifesailing.com; £16.50), a small boat that sails to an offshore sandbank that is packed with seals. Guide and captain Mike Turner is a local wildlife specialist, and his excellent tours also include visits to bird sanctuaries. Trips last five hours and discounts are given for parties of four.

Two miles east of Herne Bay is **Reculver Country Park** (☎ 01227-740676; admission free; ✹ 10am-5pm), where you can enjoy a pleasant stroll that will lead you to the remains of a Roman fort built in AD 280 and the 7th-century Saxon Church of St Mary, which collapsed in 1809 due to coastal erosion. The following year, the government bought the site and rebuilt the twin Reculver Towers, which had been added to the church in the 12th century. The adjacent **information centre** (✹ 11am-5pm Tue-Sun Apr-Aug, 11am-5pm Wed-Sun Sep, 11am-3pm Sun Oct-Mar) has excellent displays on the area's ecological significance as well as on the fort and church.

Buses from Whitstable to Herne Bay leave every 15 minutes. The trip takes 15 minutes. Local buses also go from Herne Bay train station to Reculver Park. The 2-mile walk is a great way to stretch your legs and see a bit of the coastline.

ISLE OF THANET

No, that's not a typo – nor is this peninsula at the far eastern tip of the country an island, at least not anymore. It lost that distinction sometime during the first millennium when the Watsun Channel, as it was known, started to dry up. When Thanet was surrounded by water, the Romans used it as a base in the first century AD. It was here that Augustine landed in AD 597 to kick off his Conversion of Pagan England Tour. Your reason for coming, however, is to visit a couple of pretty seaside towns. And if you fancy some exercise, try the **Thanet Coastal Path**, a 20-mile trail that hugs the far eastern shore from Margate to Pegwell Bay via Broadstairs and Ramsgate.

Margate
☎ 01843 / pop 58,465

Because of its proximity to London and its nice sandy beach, Margate was one of the first seaside resorts to be developed in England. It remains very popular and much of its Victorian glamour is still intact. Here you'll find painted striped beach huts, period architecture, Punch-and-Judy puppet shows and tasty fish and chips.

The **TIC** (☎ 583333; 12-13 The Parade; ✹ 9.15am-1pm & 1.45-4.45pm Mon-Fri, 10am-4pm Sat & Sun) will tell you all you need to know about the town.

Margate's most famous attraction is the **Shell Grotto** (☎ 220008; Grotto Hill; admission £2; ✹ 10am-5pm daily Easter-Oct, 11am-4pm Sat & Sun Nov-April), discovered in 1835 and lined with elaborate shell mosaics. It's truly a unique adventure and well worth the visit.

The Margate **caves** (☎ 220139; 1 Northdown Rd; admission £2; ✹ 10am-5pm May-Sep) are the town's other big draw, but you're better off just strolling around the Old Town with its antique shops and cafés.

SLEEPING & EATING

Walpole Bay Hotel (☎ 221703; 5th Ave, Cliftonville; s/d from £40/60; ✗) A couple of miles from the centre, in the suburb of Cliftonville, this superb hotel is a slice of Victorian heaven. Not only are the rooms furnished with period antiques but most of the hotel is an actual museum with glass-cased displays showing off the owner's collection of memorabilia from the 1800s. Wraparound porches overlook the sea and a stately bowling green.

Elonville Hotel B&B (☎ 298635; 70-72 Harold, Cliftonville; s/d £26/52; ✗) The hostess at this clean and cosy guesthouse goes out of her way to serve you. Dinner and breakfast costs an additional £31.

For budget accommodation, there's a good **YHA Hostel** (☎ 0870 770 5956; margate@yha .org.uk; The Beachcomber, 3-4 Royal Esplanade; dm £11.50; ✹ mid-Apr–Oct; ✗) on the water's edge by the

THE SOUTHEAST COAST

beach. Families welcome. You must book 48 hours in advance.

Eating in Margate leaves a lot to be desired. Nevertheless, for a simple but refined atmosphere with country French cuisine, try **Newbys Wine Bar & Brasserie** (☎ 292888; 1 Market St, Old Town; mains £8-12; ☺ dinner Thu, lunch & dinner Fri & Sat). Also, **La galleria** (☎ 229900; 2-14 High St; mains £5.25-16.95; ☺ lunch & dinner) is an Italian bistro with a chic pre-club downstairs that's open from 8pm to 1am.

GETTING THERE & AWAY
Buses to Margate leave from London Victoria (£10.50, 2¼ hours, five daily) and from Canterbury take bus No 8 or 88 (45 minutes, half hourly).

Trains run hourly to Margate from London Victoria or Charing Cross, costing £20.40 and taking an hour and 40 minutes.

Broadstairs
☎ 01843 / pop 22,712
While Margate and Ramsgate have embraced the casinos and seaside arcades that populate much of the English seaside, Broadstairs seems to have resisted. Because of that, this quaint and pretty village has retained a nostalgic Victorian atmosphere that will remind many of childhood summers filled with sandy beaches, buckets and spades and rock candy. Of course, Victorian nostalgia wouldn't be complete without Charles Dickens, who holidayed here regularly, as the TIC and several other establishments in town are proud to remind you. Behind the scenes is Broadstairs' long history of smuggling and shipbuilding.

The **TIC** (☎ 862242; fax 865650; 6b High St; ☺ 9.15am-4.45pm Mon-Fri, 10am-4pm Sat) has all the information you'll need, including details of the annual, week-long **Dickens Festival** in June which culminates in a ball in Victorian dress.

TOP FIVE BEACH TOWNS
- Brighton & Hove (p195)
- Broadstairs (above)
- Margate (p177)
- Whitstable (p176)
- Eastbourne (p191)

Dickens wrote parts of *Bleak House* and *David Copperfield* in the cliff-top house above the pier between 1837 and 1859. Now a museum, the appositely named **Bleak House** (☎ 862224; adult/child £3/2.80; ☺ 10am-6pm Mar-Dec, 10am-9pm Jul & Aug) has three rooms arranged pretty much as they were when Dickens rented it. They're quite interesting, but what makes this place worth visiting are the displays on local shipwrecks and a terrific room devoted to smuggling.

The **Dickens House Museum** (☎ 861232; 2 Victoria Pde; admission £2.30; ☺ 2-5pm Apr-Oct) wasn't actually his house but the home of Mary Pearson Strong, on whom he based Betsey Trotwood in *David Copperfield*. Dickensiana on display includes personal possessions and letters.

SLEEPING & EATING
There are a few lovely places to stay in Broadstairs, most of them only a stone's throw from the beach.

Royal Albion Hotel (☎ 868071; www.albionbroadstairs.co.uk; 6-12 Albion St; s/d from £60/78 Sep-Jun, £70/105 Jul-Aug) This is the town's top spot, but unless you're willing to shell out for one of the two Dickens suites, you'll have to make do with slightly small, albeit elegantly appointed rooms. Sea-facing rooms are more expensive.

YHA Hostel (☎ 0870 770 5730; fax 604121; broadstairs@yha.org.uk; Thistle Lodge, 3 Osborne Rd; dm £10.60; ☒) A great spot near the town centre with small rooms and a small garden and sun room.

Thai Four Two (☎ 862925; 42 York St; mains £4-6; ☺ 6-9pm Mon & Tue, 6-10pm Wed-Thu, 6-11pm Fri & Sat) Highly recommended, this small and cosy restaurant has the best home-cooked Thai food this side of the Hindu Kush.

Marchesi Brothers (☎ 862481; www.marchesi.co.uk; 18 Albion St; mains £10-14; ☺ lunch & dinner Tue-Sun) For well-constructed and elegant Italian fare, this spot near the beach is Broadstairs' fanciest restaurant.

GETTING THERE & AWAY
A bus timetable for the area is available from the TIC.

Stagecoach bus Nos 100, 101, 200 and 201 all run hourly from Broadstairs to Margate, Ramsgate, Sandwich, Deal and Dover. Bus Nos 100 and 200 also go to Canterbury. A National Express bus leaves from the top of the hill next to the war memorial for London Victoria via Hempstead Valley shopping centre at 10.30am, 2pm and 5pm daily. The trip takes 2½ hours and costs £10.50.

Trains from London Victoria, London Bridge or Charing Cross make the 2½-hour trip to Broadstairs every hour for £21.50. You may have to change at Ramsgate.

Ramsgate

☎ 01843 / pop 37,967

Ramsgate feels a bit larger than Margate, its sister city up the coast, though economically it certainly hasn't fared as well. Evidence of hard times can be seen with the surfeit 'For Let' and 'For Sale' signs posted all over town and the peeling paint on many of the buildings. And yet this adds to Ramsgate's charm as an out-of-the-way destination with an easygoing air. There is a charming harbour filled with yachts and fishing boats, a testament to the town's rich maritime history. There are also several good places to eat as well as some interesting Victorian architecture, a great car museum and a long sandy beach with some decent surf.

Located down a small alleyway just off Leopold St, the **TIC** (☎ 585353; www.tourism .thanet.gov.uk; 17 Albert Ct; ☉ 9.15am-4.45pm Mon-Fri, 10am-4pm Sat) is optimistically stocked with information. There is a self-guided walking map of the area smuggler's caves.

SIGHTS & ACTIVITIES

Ramsgate's main attraction, like most of Thanet, is the beach, and the city has just finished refurbishing the seafront and promenade, located to the east of the main harbour under an imposing cliff. Aside from the sea and surf there are a couple of good distractions here as well. The best is the cliff-top bunker-like **Motor Museum** (☎ 581948; Westcliff Hall; adult/child £3.50/1; ☉ 10.30am-5.30pm daily Apr-Sep, 10am-5pm Sun Oct-Mar) where you can see a superb collection of motorbikes and cars spanning the entire 20th century. Highlights include a 1953 Messerschmit, a 1915 Harley and a massive 1937 Packard convertible. After you're done gawking, spend some time talking to the charming host, who is a walking encyclopedia of cars (and the petrol industry).

The small but interesting **Ramsgate Maritime Museum** (☎ 587765; www.ekmt.fsnet.co.uk; The Clock House, Royal Harbour; admission £1.50; ☉ 10am-5pm Tue-Sun Easter-Sep, 11am-4.30pm Thu-Sun Oct-Easter), is a worthwhile stop to find out more about Ramsgate's seagoing history that dates back to Roman times. It's inside the town's 19th-century clocktower near the harbour.

SLEEPING

There are a few large chains in town, including a new, bland Ramada Hotel opposite the harbour, but you'll also find some friendly B&Bs in stately homes near the waterfront.

The Crescent (☎ 59141; thecrescent@onetel.net.uk; 19 Wellington Cres; s/d from £19/35) Located on the cliff over the promenade and main beach, this registered Georgian house offers 12 very clean comfortable rooms with views.

Sunnymeade Hotel (☎ 593974; sunnymead@tiny world.co.uk; 10 Truro Rd; s/d from £25/45) This family-run B&B is in a stately Victorian house near the Crescent. The three rooms are clean and large with views of the sea. Children under 12 stay for half price.

EATING

There's a surprising diversity to Ramsgate's restaurants and you'll find many up and down the beachfront.

Surin Restaurant (☎ 592001; www.surinrestaurant .co.uk; 30 Harbour St; mains £6-13; ☉ lunch & dinner; ✗) This may be the best spot in town. The owner/chef serves stunning northeastern Thai, Cambodian and Lao dishes as well as her own label micro-brewed beers.

Peter's Fish Factory (97 Harbour St; haddock & chips £2.50; ☉ 11.30am-11.30pm) This is a classic fish-and-chip shop with wonderfully greasy, crisp and cheap seaside delicacies.

Mariners Restaurant (42-44 Harbour St; mains £4-7; ☉ 9am-5pm Mon-Sat, 10am-5pm Sun) For breakfast, lunch and cappuccino, come to this French-influenced spot near the harbour. On nice days, the large windows overlooking the harbour are opened for lovely sea breezes.

DRINKING & ENTERTAINMENT

Ramsgate Brew House (☎ 594758; 98 Harbour Pde; ☉ lunch & dinner) This local favourite not only makes its own beer but its own fresh bread and pastries as well, which makes sense, kind of. The sawdusty interior is vast with rustic parquet wood floors, thrown-open doors and windows and two questionable larger-than–life-sized nude statues.

The Jazz Room (☎ 595459; 88 Harbour Pde; ☉ 1-11pm) This open-aired and modern upscale

THE SOUTHEAST COAST

spot seems a little out of place on Ramsgate's Victorian seafront, but after a few martinis who cares. Live jazz and funk can be heard from Monday to Saturday. Over-25s only.

GETTING THERE & AWAY
National Express bus No 22 runs from London Victoria to Margate and on to Broadstairs and Ramsgate (£9.50/15 one way/return or £11 day-return, 2¼ hours, five daily). Stagecoach East Kent has a service from Canterbury to Margate and on to Broadstairs and Ramsgate. Trains run hourly from London Victoria or Charing Cross (£21.70, two hours).

SANDWICH
☎ 01304 / pop 4398
Not as popular as Rye but equally as charming, sleepy Sandwich is one of the most complete medieval towns in all of southern England. Its twisting street plan and peg-tiled rooftops makes for good strolling and that's exactly what much of the retirement-age community does here. Historically, Sandwich was one of the Cinque Ports offering an important stop for ships travelling between England and the continent until the port silted up during the 17th century. Now it's home base for many of the 1500 employees of the nearby US-owned Pfizer pharmaceutical company. It's also the location of Royal St George, perhaps the finest golf links in England and a regular host of the British Open Championship.

Inside Guildhall, the **TIC** (☎ /fax 613565; New St; 🕙 10am-4pm Apr-Oct) has a good information pack detailing seven walks in the area. Guided tours of the town can be arranged by contacting **Frank Andrews** (☎ 613476; evenings only).

Sights & Activities
The most pleasant thing to do in town is enjoy the unspoiled charm of a destination as lovely as Rye minus the horde of tourists. A number of buildings have Dutch or Flemish influences (note the stepped gables in some buildings), the legacy of Protestant Flemish refugees who settled in the town in the 16th century. The impressive **Barbican** is a tollgate dating from this period. Also, the half-timbered houses on Strand St are particularly admirable.

The **Church of St Clement** has one of the finest surviving Norman towers in England. **St Peter's Church** (King St) is the earliest of Sandwich's churches though its tower was rebuilt in 1661.

The only museum of note in Sandwich is in the **Guildhall museum** (☎ 617197; admission £1), which has fairly dramatic and detailed exhibits on the town's rich history and a choice selection of Roman artefacts. Tours can be arranged with the town sergeant (call the Guildhall).

You can catch the **Sandwich River Bus** (☎ 07958 376183; adult/child from £4/3; 30 min Thu-Sun) beside the toll bridge for a river trip complete with cream tea or buffet by arrangement.

Sleeping & Eating
King's Arms Hotel (☎ 617330; s/d £40/75; mains £8-17; P ✕) Rumour has it that Elizabeth I stayed in this polished 1850s inn and it's confirmed that Hugh Grant and Boy George have. Rooms are big and clean. Fare in the pub is posh and includes vegetarian selections.

Fleur-de-Lis (☎ 611131; www.verinitaverns.co.uk; 6-8 Delf St; s/d £60/70; P ✕) This relatively new inn (it's only 200 years old) is suitable for families, and has original paintings throughout the bright pub and restaurant.

No Name Shop (☎ 612626; 1 No Name St; sandwiches £2.50-3; 🕙 10am-5.30pm Mon-Sat) Sit and watch the world go by while you munch on a baguette and speciality cheese from this takeaway-only French delicatessen with epicurean delights straight from the very nearby continent.

Fisherman's Wharf (☎ 613636; The Quay, near the toll bridge; mains £8.95-16.95; 🕙 lunch & dinner) The courtyard here is festooned with a mast and rope, appropriate to the family-friendly atmosphere of this fine seafood eatery.

Getting There & Away
National Express runs a bus from London Victoria to Deal (£10.50, three hours), from where a local bus takes you to Sandwich (37 minutes).

Trains run half-hourly from Dover Priory (£6, 25 minutes) or from London's Victoria or Charing Cross (£20.70, two hours) to Sandwich.

From Sandwich, buses go to Dover (45 minutes, hourly) and Canterbury (45 minutes, every half hour).

CINQUE PORTS

Due to their proximity to Europe, the coastal towns of southeast England were the frontline against Viking raids and invasions during Anglo-Saxon times. In the absence of a professional army and navy, these towns were frequently called upon to defend themselves, and the kingdom, at land and sea.

In 1278, King Edward I formalised this already ancient arrangement by legally defining the Confederation of Cinque (pronounced sink, meaning five) Ports. The five head ports – Sandwich, Dover, Hythe, Romney (now New Romney) and Hastings – were granted numerous privileges in exchange for providing the king with ships. The number of Cinque Ports gradually expanded to include about 30 coastal towns and villages.

By the end of the 15th century most of the Cinque Ports' harbours had become largely unusable thanks to the shifting coastline, and a professional navy was based at Portsmouth.

Although their real importance evaporated, the pomp and ceremony remains. The Lord Warden of the Cinque Ports is a prestigious post now given to faithful servants of the crown. The most recent warden was the Queen Mother, while previous incumbents included the Duke of Wellington, Sir Winston Churchill and Sir Robert Menzies, former prime minister of Australia.

AROUND SANDWICH

Standing amid the ruins of **Richborough Castle** (☎ 612013; admission £3.50; ☷ 10am-6pm Apr-Sep), 4 miles north of Sandwich, you'll have to really use your imagination to recreate the imposing Roman fort built in AD 275. The visible walls and defensive ditches offer some kind of clue, but the panorama has been seriously marred by the construction of the large Pfizer pharmaceutical plant on Pegwell Bay below. You'll be thrilled to know, however, that this is the spot from which the successful Roman invasion of Britain was launched in AD 43. Some of the relics found here are on display in Sandwich's Guildhall Museum (see p181).

The **Sandwich River Bus** (☎ 07958 376183; adult/child from £4/3; ☷ Thu-Sun) runs to Richborough by way of the Stour. The half-hour journey departs roughly every 45 minutes.

The nearby town of **Deal** was the place where Julius Caesar and his armies landed in 55 BC. It's a peaceful town with a great stretch of beach and an unusual circular castle – another link in Henry VIII's chain of defence on the south coast. Also here is **Walmer Castle**, the official residence of the warden of the Cinque Ports (see the boxed text above).

DOVER

☎ 01304 / pop 39,078

If you took away Dover Castle and the white cliffs, the only thing the bland town of Dover would have going for it would be its port. For it is here that you can catch ferries to Europe (Calais in France is a mere 20 miles over the English Channel). Still, history buffs should find plenty to hold their interest as Dover has been an important strategic location since Roman times. And anyone interested in castles should not miss Dover's. Built by the Normans and modified right up through WWII, this hilltop fortress is, with good reason, Dover's premier tourist attraction, along with the spectacular white cliffs. Otherwise, the town is a bit too run down and noisy to offer any charm, and a bit too small to offer very many restaurants that you haven't seen before.

Orientation

Dover Castle dominates the town from a high promontory to the east of town, above the white cliffs. The town itself runs back from the sea along a valley formed by the unimpressive River Dour. Ferry departures are from the Eastern Docks (accessible by bus) southeast of the castle, but the Hoverport is below the Western Heights. Dover Priory train station is a short walk to the west of the town centre. The bus station is closer to the centre of things on Pencester Rd.

Information

Banks and ATMs are located on Market Square.

Mangle laundrette (Worthington St; ☷ 9am-4pm Mon-Fri, 9am-1pm Sat & Sun) Around £3 a load.

Post office (Pencester Rd; ☷ 9am-5.30pm Mon-Sat)

White Cliffs Medical Centre (☎ 201705; 143 Folkestone Rd) Five minutes' walk from the centre of Dover.

THE SOUTHEAST COAST

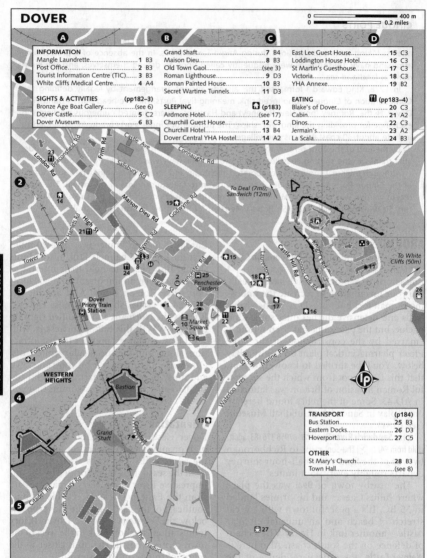

DOVER

0 — 400 m
0 — 0.2 miles

INFORMATION	
Mangle Launderette	1 B3
Post Office	2 B3
Tourist Information Centre (TIC)	3 B3
White Cliffs Medical Centre	4 A4

SIGHTS & ACTIVITIES	(pp182–3)
Bronze Age Boat Gallery	(see 6)
Dover Castle	5 C2
Dover Museum	6 B3

Grand Shaft	7 B4
Maison Dieu	8 B3
Old Town Gaol	(see 3)
Roman Lighthouse	9 D3
Roman Painted House	10 B3
Secret Wartime Tunnels	11 D3

SLEEPING	(p183)
Ardmore Hotel	(see 17)
Churchill Guest House	12 C3
Churchill Hotel	13 B4
Dover Central YHA Hostel	14 A2

East Lee Guest House	15 C3
Loddington House Hotel	16 C3
St Martin's Guesthouse	17 C3
Victoria	18 C3
YHA Annexe	19 B2

EATING	(pp183–4)
Blake's of Dover	20 C3
Cabin	21 A2
Dinos	22 C3
Jermain's	23 A2
La Scala	24 B3

TRANSPORT	(p184)
Bus Station	25 B3
Eastern Docks	26 D3
Hoverport	27 C5

OTHER	
St Mary's Church	28 B3
Town Hall	(see 8)

William Harvey Hospital (☎ 01233-633331; Kennington Rd, Wilesborough) Has an accident and Emergency Department. Located in Ashford, 20 miles west of Dover.

TIC (☎ 205108; www.whitecliffscountry.org.uk; Biggin St; ⌚ 9am-5.30pm Mon-Fri, 10am-4pm Sat & Sun) Located in the Old Town Gaol and has accommodation and ferry-booking services (both free).

Sights & Activities

DOVER CASTLE

The virtually impregnable **Dover Castle** (EH; ☎ 211067; admission £8.50; ⌚ daily Feb-Oct, Thu-Mon Nov-Jan) is one of the most impressive in Britain, a mighty fortress commanding a superb view of the English Channel and the town below. On the vast grounds are a restored

Saxon church and the remains of a **Roman lighthouse**, which dates from AD 50 and may be the oldest standing building in Britain.

Henry II's mighty **keep** is a striking sight (its walls are 7m thick in places) but it's the series of **secret wartime tunnels** under the castle that are the most interesting attraction here. The first tunnel was dug during the Napoleonic Wars and they were expanded in WWII to act as a command post. The highly entertaining 50-minute tour is included in the general admission price.

Bus Nos 90, 91 and 111 run from Dover Priory station to the castle.

ROMAN PAINTED HOUSE

The **Roman Painted House** (☎ 203279; New St; admission £2; ☼ 10am-5pm Tue-Sun Apr-Sep) may be the finest Roman house on show in Britain. It was built around AD 200 as a *mansio*, or official hotel, for travellers crossing the channel – Britain's first B&B? The house was largely destroyed by Roman troops in AD 270, but thankfully they inadvertently preserved more than 400 sq ft (37 sq metres) of painted plaster, the most extensive wall painting found north of the Alps.

OTHER SIGHTS AND ACTIVITIES

The small **Dover Museum** (☎ 201066; Market Sq; admission £2; ☼ 10am-5.30pm Mon-Sat Oct-Mar, 1-5.30pm Mon-Sat Apr-Sep) covers Dover's prehistoric past. The displays won't hold your interest for long. The best thing here is the second-floor, award-winning **Bronze Age Boat Gallery**, which features a 3600-year-old boat discovered off the Dover Coast in 1992. It is the world's oldest known seagoing vessel and measures a pretty impressive 9.5m by 2.4m.

Next door to the TIC is the **Maison Dieu** (admission free; ☼ 10am-6pm) which was built as a hospice for pilgrims and wounded soldiers in 1203. It now contains a collection of arms, armour and portraits of England's kings and dignitaries.

Beginning at Snargate St, the **Grand Shaft** (admission £1; ☼ 2-5pm Tue-Sun Jul & Aug) is worth a quick peek. This 43m triple staircase was cut into the white cliffs as a shortcut to town for troops stationed on the Western Heights during the Napoleonic Wars.

Tours

City Sightseeing Guide (☎ 01273-540893; child/adult £7/2.50) runs hourly hop-on, hop-off tours

of Dover and the surrounding area between 10am and 4pm daily. Tickets can be bought at the Market Sq stop, the TIC (at a discount) or on board the bus.

Sleeping

Most B&Bs are along Castle St and Maison Dieu Rd. If there are others along Folkestone Rd. If you want a sea view, be prepared to pay for it.

BUDGET

Dover Central YHA Hostel (☎ 0870 770 5798; fax 202236; 306 London Rd; dm £14.90; ✗ ☐) The old Georgian building is a little far from the town centre (though it is close to the train station) and its exterior is a little worse for wear. Still, it's friendly, clean and includes breakfast. The hostel annexe in Godwyne Rd is more convenient.

MID-RANGE

St Martin's Guesthouse/Ardmore Hotel (☎ 205938; www.stmartinsgh.co.uk; 17 Castle Hill Rd; s/d £24/48; ✗) This friendly spot (the two hotels are basically one) has good-sized, spotless and cosy rooms.

Victoria (☎ 205140; wham101496@aol.com; 1 Laureston Pl; s/d from £28/40; ✗) Run by an extremely friendly elderly couple, the Victoria is a highly attractive home with four large and comfortable rooms.

Churchill Guest House (☎ 204622; www.toastof dover.com/churchill.html; 6 Castle Hill Rd; s/d from £35/55, winter £25/45; ✗) In the same quiet neighbourhood as Victoria and St Martin, the Churchill has six very clean and comfy rooms. It does not cater to children.

Also recommended:

East Lee Guest House (☎ 210176; www.eastlee.co.uk; 108 Maison Dieu Rd; s/d £35/48; ✗) Good value with vegetarian breakfasts.

Loddington House Hotel (☎ 201947; sscupper@aol .com; 14 East Cliff, Marine Pde; s/d £40/54) Upmarket B&B overlooking the marina.

Eating

There are a few places where you can get a decent meal.

Cabin (☎ 206118; 91 High St; mains £9-12; ☼ dinner Tue-Sat; ✗) Aside from the shabby exterior and the busy street out front, this is a fine place to dine on wild rabbit and other English delicacies. Be sure to try one of the dozen puddings on the ever-changing menu.

Dino's (☎ 204678; 58 Castle Hill Rd; mains £6-13; ☙ dinner Tue-Sun) Join the locals for some good family Italian at this tucked-away spot.

Blake's of Dover (☎ 202194; www.blakesofdover .com; 52 Castle St; mains £9-16; ☙ noon-3pm & 6-11.30pm Mon-Fri, dinner only Sat; ☒) Surround yourself with dark wood and candlelight and sample one of 52 malt whiskeys in this upmarket English restaurant.

Also recommended:

La Scala (☎ 208044; 19 High St; mains £5-13; ☙ lunch & dinner Mon-Sat; ☒) Italian fare in the High St.

Jermain's (☎ 205956; Beaconsfield Rd; mains £4-7; ☙ lunch) No-frills lunch spot close to the hostel.

Getting There & Away

Dover is 75 miles (120km) from London and 15 miles from Canterbury.

BOAT

Ferries depart from the Eastern Docks (which are accessible by bus; see right above) below the castle. **P&O Stena** (☎ 0870 600 0600; www.poferries.com) ferries leave for Calais every 30 minutes. **Seafrance** (☎ 08705 711711; www .seafrance.com) ferries leave hourly. The **Hoverspeed** (☎ 0870 240 8070; www.hoverspeed.com) Hoverport is below the Western Heights; the Seacat (one hour) to Calais leaves hourly. Fares vary according to season and advance purchase. See the websites for specials.

BUS

Dover's **bus station** (☎ 240024; Pencester Rd) is in the heart of town. Stagecoach East Kent has a Canterbury to Dover service (45 minutes, every 20 minutes). National Express coaches leave half-hourly from London Victoria (£10.50, two hours 25 minutes).

Buses from Dover go to Brighton, Hastings (£5.50, three hours 20 minutes, every hour and a half), Canterbury (45 minutes, every 30 minutes), and Sandwich (one hour 10 minutes, hourly).

CHANNEL TUNNEL

The Channel Tunnel begins its descent into the English Channel 9 miles west of Dover, just off the M20 between London and Dover. The nearest station foot passengers can board the **Eurostar** (☎ 08705 186186) train is at Ashford. From Dover, it's easier if you have a car: take junction 11A for the Channel Tunnel (it's very well signposted). To cross the channel via the **Eurotunnel** (☎ 08705

35 35 35; www.eurotunnel.com) can cost anywhere from £50 to £200 depending on specials and how far ahead you book. The tunnel crossing is described on p749.

TRAIN

There are more than 40 trains daily from London Victoria and Charing Cross stations to Dover Priory via Ashford and Sevenoaks (£20.70, two hours).

Getting Around

The ferry companies run complimentary buses between the docks and the train station as they're a long walk apart. On local buses a trip from one side of town to the other costs about £1.70.

Heritage (☎ 204420) and **Central Taxis** (☎ 240 441) both have 24-hour services. You could also try **Star Taxis** (☎ 228822). A one-way trip to Deal costs about £11; to Sandwich it's about £17.

AROUND DOVER
The White Cliffs

The world-famous white cliffs extend for 10 miles on either side of Dover, but it is the 6-mile stretch east of town – properly known as the Langdon Cliffs – that has captivated visitors for centuries. Once you visit, you'll see why.

The chalk here is about 250m deep, and the cliffs themselves are about half a million years old, formed when the melting waters from the giant icecap that covered all of northern Europe forced a channel through the landmass that was then France and England, creating at once the English Channel and the cliffs.

You can appreciate their majesty – and get in some decent exercise – by walking along the path that snakes its way for 2 miles along the top from the car park (£1.60 per car). It's a pretty bracing walk so be sure to wear appropriate footwear. On the eastern side is the **South Foreland Lighthouse** (☎ 202756; admission £2; ☙ 1-5pm Thu-Mon), built in 1843. It was from here, on 24 December 1898, that Guglielmo Marconi made the world's first shore-to-ship and international radio transmission.

The Langdon Cliffs are managed by the National Trust, which has recently opened a **visitor centre** (☎ 01304-202756; admission free; ☙ 10am-5pm Mar-Oct, 11am-4pm Nov-Feb) on the western side of this section.

The cliffs are located at the end of Upper Rd, 2 miles east of Dover along Castle Hill Rd and the A258 road to Deal. Bus No 113 from Dover stops near the main entrance. City Sightseeing Guide includes the cliffs as part of their hop-on, hop-off town tours (see p183). The first departure is from Market Square in Dover at 10am; the last departure from the car park at the cliffs is at 4.40pm.

If you fancy seeing the cliffs from the sea, **White Cliffs Boat Tours** (☎ 01303-271388; www .whitecliffsboattours.co.uk; adult/child £5/3; ☀ 10am-5pm daily Jun-Aug, Sat & Sun Apr-May & Sep-Oct) run water tours aboard the 70-seater *Southern Queen*. Trips run hourly from De Bradelei Wharf at the Eastern Docks and children are welcome to take the helm.

Romney Marsh

The 40-sq-mile (104-sq-km) flat plain that is Romney Marsh was once submerged beneath the Channel, but the lowering of the water table during the Middle Ages, as well as subsequent reclamations, added new territory to the island in the form of a marsh. The area is now the location of the world's smallest-gauge public railway, the **Romney, Hythe & Dymchurch Railway** (☎ 01797-362353; www.rhdr.org.uk/rhdr/rhdr.html; adult £9.80; ☀ daily Apr-Sep, Sat & Sun Oct, Dec & Mar), opened in 1927. It runs 13½ miles from Hythe to Dungeness lighthouse and back.

Romney Marsh Countryside Project (☎ 01797-367934) arranges guided walks and bicycle rides around the area. Pick up a pamphlet from the Royal Society for the Protection of Birds (RSPB) Nature Reserve visitor centre in Dungeness.

Dungeness

On the western edge of Romney Marsh is a low shingle spit dominated by a nuclear power station and a lighthouse. Despite the apocalyptic bleakness, the area is home to the largest seabird colony in the southeast. The **Royal Society for the Protection of Birds (RSPB) Nature Reserve** (☎ 01797-320588; Dungeness Rd; adult/child £3/1; ☀ 9am-sunset) has displays on local bird life and information on nearby bird-watching hideouts (or you can bird-watch right from the centre). Explorer backpacks for children can be purchased at the **visitor centre** (☀ 10am-5pm Mar-Oct, 10am-4pm Nov-Feb).

THE KENT WEALD

The Weald, as it's known locally, is really an area covering part of Kent and some of East Sussex with the town of Royal Tunbridge Wells pretty much at its centre. Its name comes from the Old German world *wald*, meaning forest, though the only trees you'll find are the oft-pruned ones in the many well-manicured gardens in the area; most of the timber here was harvested long ago. Instead, you'll find pretty rolling hills, country lanes and well-to-do villages that house some of England's wealthiest citizens. It's also home to three extraordinary castles and two much-visited manor houses.

Sevenoaks

☎ 01732 / pop 26,99

Very near to the M25, and therefore very much the home of choice for many a London commuter, Sevenoaks has become somewhat homogenised over the years. Even the trees that gave the town its name are gone, knocked over in a freak storm in 1987. That said, the reason to visit is to see the country estate Knole House; you won't be disappointed.

At the southern end of High St, you'll find **Knole House** (☎ 450608; admission £6; ☀ 11am-4pm Wed-Sun Apr-Oct), which is one of the most treasured houses in England. The estate has existed since the 12th century, but in 1456 the Archbishop of Canterbury, Thomas Bouchier, bought the whole property for £266 and set about rebuilding the lot to make it 'fit for the Princes of the Church'. The result is impressive indeed; the house has been curiously designed to match the calendar, so there are seven courtyards, 52 staircases and 365 rooms. You can also visit the **garden** (admission £2; ☀ 1st Wed of month May-Sep).

The house is about 1½ miles from Sevenoaks train station and less than one mile from the bus station.

There are no direct bus services from London to Sevenoaks so you're better off catching the train. From nearby Tonbridge, however, there is a bus to Sevenoaks.

The station is on London Rd. Trains leave three times an hour from London Charing Cross station (£7, 35 minutes) and continue to Tunbridge Wells (£6, 20 minutes) and Hastings (£14, one hour 10 minutes).

THE SOUTHEAST COAST

OAST HOUSES

Oast houses were basically giant, housed kilns for drying hops, a key ingredient in the brewing of beer, introduced to the region in the early 15th century.

An oast house is made up of four rooms: the kiln (oven), the drying room (located above the kiln), the cooling room, and the storage room where hops were pressed and baled, ready to go to the local inn brewery. The cone-shaped roof was necessary to create a draught for the fire. The bits sticking out from the top of the cone are cowls. They could be moved to regulate the airflow to the fire.

Many oast houses have been converted into homes, and are increasingly sought after as prime real estate. Oast house B&Bs are becoming more and more common throughout the county; check with the various tourist information centres for information on local possibilities or call the **Kent Tourism Alliance** (☎ 01622-696165), which will locate a B&B in your area.

Chartwell

Six miles east of Sevenoaks is **Chartwell** (☎ 01732-868381; Westerham; admission £7, garden & studio only £3.50; 11am-5pm Wed-Sun Apr-Jun, 11am-5pm Tue-Sun Jul & Aug, 11am-5pm Wed-Sun Sep-Oct & part of Nov), Sir Winston Churchill's home from 1924 until his death in 1965. Architecturally unremarkable, this much-altered Tudor house is nevertheless a fascinating place, as well as being one of the most visited of all NT-owned properties.

The rooms and gardens are pretty much as Winnie left them, full of pictures, books, personal mementos and plenty of maps. Churchill was also an artist of considerable talent, and the interesting collection of sketches and watercolours in the garden studio display a softer side of the cigar-chomping bombast of popular perception.

The Chartwell Explorer bus runs six times daily between Sevenoaks train/bus stations and Chartwell on weekends and bank holidays mid-May to mid-September, and Wednesday to Friday in July and August. The trip takes 30 minutes and the ticket (adult/child £4.50/3) includes a pot of tea at Chartwell. A combined ticket, with return rail travel from London to Sevenoaks, bus transfer to Chartwell and admission costs £15/7.50; enquire at Charing Cross station.

Hever Castle

A few miles west of Tonbridge, idyllic **Hever Castle** (☎ 01732-865224; admission £8.80, gardens only £7; noon-5pm Mar-Oct, noon-4pm Nov) was the childhood home of Anne Boleyn, mistress to Henry VIII and then his doomed queen. Walking through the main gate into the courtyard of Hever is like stepping onto the set of a period film. It's beautiful.

The moated castle dates from 1270, with the Tudor house added in 1505 by the Bullen (Boleyn) family, who bought the castle in 1462. Although the castle was home to two queens – Anne Boleyn and, later, Anne of Cleves – it fell into disrepair until 1903, when it was bought by the American multimillionaire William Waldorf Astor, who poured obscene amounts of money into a massive refurbishment. The exterior is unchanged from Tudor times, but the interior now has superb Edwardian carved wooden panelling.

Hever is a great place to bring the kids. There are hedge and water mazes, playgrounds and other childhood delights that will keep kids of all ages occupied for hours.

From London Victoria trains go to Hever (change at Oxted), a 1-mile walk from the castle (£7, 50 minutes, hourly). Alternatively, you could take the train to Edenbridge, from where it's a 4-mile taxi ride. A nice idea is to hire a bicycle in Edenbridge and ride to Hever. From Edenbridge High St the route to Hever is signposted.

Penshurst

The attractive village of Penshurst, 10 miles east of Edenbridge on the B2176, is lined with timber-framed Tudor houses and features a gorgeous church with four spires.

What draws people here, though, is the wonderful medieval manor house that is **Penshurst Place** (☎ 870307; www.penshurstplace.com; adult/child £7/5; noon-5pm Sun-Fri, noon-4pm Sat Apr-Oct), the home of Philip Sidney, Viscount de L'Isle, whose family has owned the property since 1522. At its heart is the magnificent **Baron's Hall** where a number of English monarchs, including Henry VIII, enjoyed lavish feasts and spectacles beneath the stunning 18m-high chestnut roof.

Surrounding the house are the splendid 4.5-hectare **walled gardens** (10.30am-6pm Apr-Oct), which were originally designed in 1346 and have remained virtually unchanged since Elizabethan times. The remainder of the grounds are wonderful for a bit of walking. Taking in parkland and riverside, the walks vary from 2 to 4 miles in length and usually take one to two hours. The ticket office has details.

From Edenbridge, Metrobus bus Nos 231, 232 and 233 leave for Tunbridge Wells via Penshurst every hour. The manor is 15 minutes from Edenbridge.

Leeds Castle

Just to the east of Maidstone, **Leeds Castle** (EH; ☎ 01622-765400; adult/child Mar-Oct £12.50/9, Nov-Feb £10.50/7; 10am-5pm Apr-Oct, 10am-3pm Nov-Mar) is one of the most famous and most visited castles in the world. It stands on two small islands in a lake surrounded by a huge estate that contains woodlands, an aviary and a really weird grotto that can only be entered once you've successfully negotiated your way through a hedge maze.

The building dates from the 9th century. Henry VIII transformed it from a fortress into a palace, and it was privately owned until 1974 when Lady Billie, the castle's last owner, died. Furniture and other décor in the castle date from the last eight centuries.

A private trust now manages the property and, as part of a requirement that the castle serve as more than just a tourist attraction, some of the rooms are used for conferences and other events. This creates a problem for the visitor in that some of the rooms are closed to the public quite regularly. If you want to be sure you can see all the rooms and get your money's worth, ring ahead. Another problem is the sheer number of people to be negotiated – at weekends it's the families, during the week it's the school groups.

National Express runs one direct bus daily from London Victoria coach station, leaving at 9am and returning at 3.05pm (£11, 1½ hours). It must be pre-booked.

Sissinghurst Castle Garden

One of England's loveliest and most famous gardens, **Sissinghurst Castle Garden** (☎ 01580-710700; Sissinghurst, near Cranbrook; admission £7; 11am-5.30pm Fri-Tue Apr-Oct) is a spectacular example of English planned landscaping. The castle itself dates back to the 12th century, but the romantic gardens were crafted by Vita Sackville-West and her husband Harold Nicolson after they bought the estate in 1930. Highlights include the famous rose garden and the White Garden, where all the blooms are, yes, white. Sissinghurst is 2 miles northeast of Cranbrook and one mile east of Sissinghurst village off the A262.

EAST SUSSEX

East Sussex is home to gorgeous countryside, medieval villages and inspired nightlife, making this lovely part of England one of the most popular for tourists and weekending Londoners looking to wind down. Here you'll find the cobblestone streets of ancient Rye, the historically important Battle, where William the Conqueror first engaged the Saxons in 1066, and the breathtaking white cliffs of Beachy Head, near Eastbourne. For a taste of 'London by the sea' head to Brighton, without doubt one of the coolest cities in England.

RYE

☎ 01797 / pop 4195

If you've come to England to find a medieval village, look no further than Rye. Once a Cinque Port, this exquisitely picturesque town looks like it has been preserved in historical formaldehyde. Not even the most talented Hollywood set designers could have come up with a better representation of Ye Olde Englishe Village: the half-timbered Tudor buildings, winding cobbled streets, abundant flowerpots and strong literary associations should be enough to temper even the most hard-bitten cynic's weariness of the made-for-tourism look.

Inevitably, its beauty *has* made it a tourist magnet, but thankfully most wander about the town in almost muted appreciation, lest their gasps of surprise disturb the air of genuine tranquillity and perfection that pervades the place. If you do visit – and you absolutely should – avoid summer weekends.

Information

There is a crowded but helpful **TIC** (☎ 226696; ryetic@rother.gov.uk; Strand Quay; 9.30am-5pm Mar-Oct,

THE SOUTHEAST COAST

THE SOUTHEAST COAST

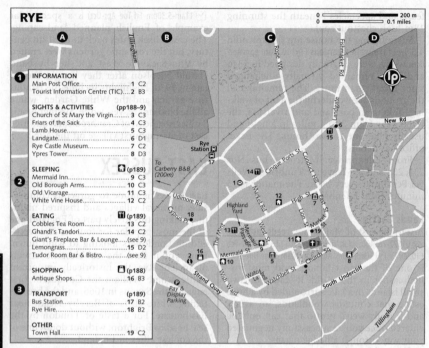

RYE

0 ━━━━ 200 m
0 ━━━━ 0.1 miles

INFORMATION
Main Post Office..................1 C2
Tourist Information Centre (TIC)....2 B3

SIGHTS & ACTIVITIES (pp188–9)
Church of St Mary the Virgin........3 C3
Friars of the Sack.................4 C3
Lamb House.......................5 C3
Landgate.........................6 D1
Rye Castle Museum................7 C2
Ypres Tower......................8 D3

SLEEPING (p189)
Mermaid Inn......................9 C3
Old Borough Arms.................10 C3
Old Vicarage.....................11 C3
White Vine House.................12 C2

EATING (p189)
Cobbles Tea Room.................13 C2
Ghandi's Tandori................14 C2
Giant's Fireplace Bar & Lounge....(see 9)
Lemongrass.......................15 D2
Tudor Room Bar & Bistro..........(see 9)

SHOPPING (p188)
Antique Shops....................16 B3

TRANSPORT (p189)
Bus Station......................17 B2
Rye Hire.........................18 B2

OTHER
Town Hall........................19 C2

10am-4pm Nov-Feb) where you can view the Rye Town Model Sound & Light Show, a visual history, for £2.50. The town is easily covered on foot and the TIC sells the *Rye Town Walk* map, which gives a detailed history of the town's buildings for £1. There's also a self-guided audio tour costing £2.50. For guided walks around town phone ☎ 01424-882343 or ☎ 01424-882466.

There are several pay-and-display parking lots around town. The one closest to the centre is across the river from the TIC.

Sights & Activities

Around the corner from the TIC, in Strand Quay, are a number of antique shops selling all kinds of wonderful junk. From here walk up cobbled **Mermaid St**, one of the most famous streets in England, with timber-framed houses dating from the 15th century.

Turn right at the T-junction for the Georgian **Lamb House** (☎ 224982; West St; admission £2.75; ⏰ 2-6pm Wed & Sat Apr-Oct), mostly dating from 1722. It was the home of American writer Henry James from 1898 to 1916; he wrote *The Wings of the Dove* here.

Continue around the dogleg until you come out at Church Sq. This gorgeous square is surrounded by a variety of attractive houses, including the **Friars of the Sack** on the southern side at No 40. Now a private residence, it was once part of a 13th-century Augustinian friary. The **Church of St Mary the Virgin** incorporates a mixture of ecclesiastical styles. The turret clock is the oldest in England (1561) and still works with its original pendulum mechanism. There are great views from the **church tower** (admission £2).

Turn right at the square's east corner for **Ypres Tower** (admission £1.90; ⏰ 10.30am-1pm & 2-5pm Mon &Thu-Sun Apr-Oct, 10.30am-3pm Sat & Sun Nov-Mar), pronounced 'wipers', part of a 13th-century fort with great views over Romney Marsh and Rye Bay. It now houses one part of the **Rye Castle Museum** (☎ 226728; 3 East St; admission £1.90; ⏰ 10.30am-1pm & 2-5pm Thu-Mon Apr-Oct, 10.30am-3.30pm Nov-Mar tower only), home to select loot from the city's past.

At the northeastern edge of the village is **Landgate**. Built in 1329 to fortify the town, it's the only remaining gate out of four.

If you're up for a longer historic walk, the 31-mile **1066 Country Walk** takes you through the East Sussex countryside from Rye to Battle and Pevensey where it joins the South Downs Way.

Festivals & Events

The town celebrates its medieval heritage with a two-day festival each August, and in September there is the two-week **Festival of Music and the Arts** (www.ryefestival.co.uk).

Sleeping

Accommodation is plentiful and of a very high standard.

Mermaid Inn (☎ 223065; www.mermaidinn.com; Mermaid St; s/d £80/160) This marvellously atmospheric hostelry has been around since 1420 but the site dates back to 1156 and comes complete with a resident ghost.

Old Borough Arms (☎ 222128; www.oldborough arms.co.uk; The Strand; s/d £40/70; ✕) A former smugglers inn, this truly lovely guesthouse has spacious and clean neo-rustic rooms complete with four-poster beds. The downstairs café serves sandwiches and cream teas.

White Vine House (☎ 224748; www.whitevine house.co.uk; 24 High St; s/d £60/90; ✕) This sumptuous Tudor building houses a stunning hotel with superb service. Enjoy afternoon tea and coffee in their fun, exquisitely painted dining rooms.

Old Vicarage (☎ 222119; www.oldvicaragerye.co.uk; 66 Church Sq; s/d £60/90; P ✕) Located down a cobble-stone lane with a lovely garden and views of St Mary's Church, this salmon-coloured former vicarage has exquisitely appointed rooms. Children over five only.

Carberry (☎ 223740; dave@rotherplus.com; 40 Udimore Rd; s/d £25/55; P ✕) The owners are very welcoming to this thoughtfully appointed B&B. Family rooms are available.

Eating & Drinking

Cobbles Tea Room (☎ 225962; 1 Highland Yard; mains £4-7; ⏰ 10am-5pm Wed-Mon; ✕) Ladies in white aprons serve the tea and cakes (breakfast too) at this home-style tearoom with lace curtains.

Ghandi's Tandoori (☎ 223091; Cinque Ports St; mains £4-8; ⏰ lunch & dinner) Eat here not only for the name but for inexpensive curries, biryanis and other south Indian specialities.

Lemongrass (☎ 222327; 1 Tower St; mains £6-9; ⏰ lunch & dinner) For Thai food in Rye (and

pretty good Thai at that) you'll need to appreciate the way curry looks on a pink tablecloth.

Tudor Room Bar & Bistro (☎ 223065; Mermaid St; mains £14.50-18, 3-/4-course lunch £19.50/35, 4-course dinner £36.50; ⏰ lunch & dinner) This fine restaurant at the Mermaid Inn is worthy of the ancient building that houses it. Try delights such as a smoked quail salad and a rump of English lamb.

Giant's Fireplace Bar & Lounge (☎ 223065; Mermaid St) One of the best pubs in town – though a decidedly upscale one – is also at the Mermaid Inn. It features low ceilings, half-timbered walls and, yes, a really big medieval fireplace.

Getting There & Away

Stagecoach Bus No 711 runs hourly between Dover and Hastings via Rye (two hours).

From London Charing Cross, trains run twice hourly to Rye (£19.20, two hours), but you must change either in Hastings or Ashford.

Getting Around

You can rent bikes from £10 per day (with a £25 deposit) from **Rye Hire** (☎ 223033; 1 Cyprus Pl; ⏰ 8am-5pm Mon-Fri). It's possible to arrange hires for Saturday and Sunday; just call ahead. A cycling map of East Sussex is available from the TIC.

BATTLE

☎ 01424 / pop 5190

The tiny village of Battle has a big reputation as the place where the French duke William of Normandy defeated the local ruler King Harold in 1066, thereby ushering in a monumental new phase of British history.

The lovely town grew up around the abbey that William, flush with the thrill of victory, ordered built to commemorate his success.

Orientation & Information

The train station is a short walk from High St, and is well signposted. The **TIC** (☎ 773721; fax 773436; 88 High St; ⏰ 9.30am-5.30pm Apr-Sep, 10am-5pm Oct, 10am-4pm Nov-Mar) is in the Battle Abbey Gatehouse along with a wonderful gift shop that can supply you with chain mail and Christian crusader outfits for kids back home. The post office, banks and ATMs are also on High St.

THE SOUTHEAST COAST

Sights

BATTLEFIELD & BATTLE ABBEY

Battle Abbey (☎ 773792; admission £4.50; ☼ 10am-dusk Apr-Oct, 10am-4pm Nov-Mar) is a pretty interesting place, but more for its unique location, built smack in the middle of the battlefield, so your visit should be steeped in historical significance. The guided walk – courtesy of a free audio unit – gives blow-by-blow descriptions of the battle.

Construction of the abbey began in 1070. It was occupied by Benedictines until the dissolution of the monasteries in 1536 (p35). Only the foundations of the church can now be seen and the altar's position is marked by a plaque, but quite a few monastic buildings survive and the scene is very painterly.

BODIAM CASTLE

If the traditional castle of childhood imagination – four towers, crenellated walls, a drawbridge and a moat – has an archetype, then **Bodiam** (☎ 01580-830436; admission £4.20; ☼ 10am-6pm daily Feb-Oct, 10am-4pm Sat & Sun Nov-Jan) is surely it.

After the French captured the Channel ports in 1372, Sir Edward Dalyngrigge built the castle in 1385 to guard the lower reaches of the River Rother from further French attack.

Following the Civil War, Parliamentarian forces ruined it and it fell into such disrepair that photographs from the 1890s show ivy-clad ruins and vegetables planted in the courtyard. In 1917 Lord Curzon, former Viceroy of India, bought it and restored the exterior to its impressive origins, but the interior is still little more than a collection of ruins. It's possible to climb to the top of the battlements for some excellent views of the surrounding countryside.

Arriva Bus No 254 stops at Bodiam from Hastings each hour during the day from Monday to Saturday. The **Kent & East Sussex steam railway** (☎ 01580-765155; www.kesr.org .uk) runs from Tenterden in Kent through 10½ miles of beautiful countryside to the village of Bodiam from where a bus takes you to the castle. It costs £10 and operates most days from May to September and at the weekend and school holidays in October, December and February. It's closed November, January and most of March.

Sleeping & Eating

The Abbey Hotel (☎ 772755; 84 High St; s/d from £28/56) The pub rooms, conveniently located opposite the abbey, come with easy access to a pint.

Brickwall Hotel (☎ 870253; www.brickwallhotel .com; The Green, Sedlescombe; s/d Apr-May £42/55, Jun-Oct £45/60; ☒) Approximately 5 miles away in Sedlescombe, you'll find this stately Tudor manor house situated on a quiet country road. The atmosphere and amenities are comfortable and refined.

Beauport Park Hotel (☎ 851222; www.beauport parkhotel.co.uk; Battle Rd, nr Battle; s/d £65/130; ☒) After spending your day practicing any number of pleasant diversions, sit back and enjoy a speciality flambé dish in the restaurant overlooking a formal Italian garden. This elegant country house has everything you could want from an upscale retreat.

Pilgrim's Restaurant (☎ 772314; 1 High St; mains £11-22; ☼ 10.30am-9.30pm; ☒) Modern beats play gently over the clink of wine glasses and fine silver in a 16th-century Tudor set up for a special night out. The inventive and expertly thought out collection of seafood and local meat dishes represent new English cuisine at its best. Open for lunch, afternoon tea, cocktails and dinner.

Getting There & Away

National Express bus Nos 023 and 024 from London to Hastings pass through Battle twice daily (£9.25, 2¼ hours), and Eastbourne Buses No 22 service runs from Eastbourne to Battle on weekdays (three daily). From Battle you can reach Pevensey (45 minutes) and Bodiam (20 minutes) on the irregular No 19 service. Local Rider bus No 4/5 runs hourly to Hastings.

Trains run to and from London Charing Cross every half-hour (£17, 1½ hours), via Hastings (£2.30, 20 minutes).

TOP FIVE CASTLES

- **Leeds Castle** (Kent Weald; p187)
- **Dover Castle** (Dover; p182)
- **Arundel Castle** (Arundel; p203)
- **Hever Castle** (Kent Weald; p186)
- **Bodiam Castle** (Battle; above)

THE SOUTHEAST COAST

THE LAST INVASION OF ENGLAND

The Battle of Hastings in 1066 was a fairly dramatic event. Harold's army arr[...]
on October 14th and created a three-ring defence consisting of archers, then cav[...]
massed infantry at the rear. William marched north from Hastings and took up a positi[...]
400m south of Harold and his troops. He tried repeatedly to break the English cordon,
Harold's men held fast. William's knights then feigned retreat, drawing some of Harold's troops
after them. It was a fatal mistake. Seeing the gap in the English wall, William ordered his remaining troops to charge through, and the battle was as good as won. Among the English casualties
was King Harold who, according to events depicted in the Bayeux Tapestry, was hit in or near the
eye by an arrow. While he tried to pull the arrow from his head he was struck down by Norman
knights. At the news of his death the last of the English resistance collapsed.

In their wonderfully irreverent *1066 And All That*, published in 1930, WC Sellar and RJ Yeatman suggest that 'the Norman conquest was a Good Thing, as from this time onward England stopped being conquered and thus was able to become top nation...' When you consider that England hasn't been successfully invaded since, it's hard to disagree.

AROUND BATTLE
Bateman's
About half a mile south of the town of Burwash along the A259 is **Bateman's** (☎ 01435-882302; admission £5.50; ⊙ 11am-5pm Sat-Wed Apr-Oct), the home of Rudyard Kipling from 1902 until his death in 1936. Inside this beautiful Jacobean home built in 1634, everything is pretty much just as the writer would have left it, down to the blotting paper on the desk of his cluttered study. The furnishings reflect Kipling's love of the East, and there are plenty of oriental rugs and Indian artefacts. This is a great side trip.

A small path leads down to the River Dudwell, where the writer converted a watermill to generate electricity. These days, the mill grinds corn every Saturday at 2pm. Also on display is the Rolls Royce Kipling kept to explore the Sussex countryside.

EASTBOURNE
☎ 01323 / pop 106,562
Long a favourite south-coast resort for octogenarians, Eastbourne is a lovely Victorian seaside town that your bold and artsy aunt might enjoy. Its pier is well kept and the seafront has manicured gardens rather than the tacky casinos that plague much of the southeast coast. If you're looking for nightlife, head to Brighton. But if you're looking for a relaxed time eating Mr Softy by the seashore, you've come to the right place.

The **TIC** (☎ 411400; eastbournetic@btclick.com; Cornfield Rd; ⊙ 9.30am-5.30pm Mon-Fri, 9.30am-5pm Sat Apr-Sep) has a number of helpful leaflets and will find you accommodation for £3.

Sights & Activities
Eastbourne's prettier-than-most pier has the usual selection of arcades, trinket shops and bars, though it's still a nice place to watch the sun set over the water.

The enjoyable **Eastbourne Heritage Centre** (☎ 411189; 2 Carlisle Rd; admission £1; ⊙ 2-5pm May-Sep), west of the centre, explores the development of the town from 1800 to the present day. There's a special exhibit devoted to the work of Donald McGill, the pioneer of the 'naughty postcard'!

The **Museum of Shops** (☎ 737143; 20 Cornfield Tce; adult/child £3.50/2.50; ⊙ 10am-5pm) has a collection of 100,000 dioramas of shops, rooms and displays devoted to nostalgic, how-we-lived memorabilia – antiques, books, toys, you name it.

Sleeping
Lindau Lodge (☎ 640792; 71 Royal Pde; per person from £18) This homey, clean B&B is five minutes' walk west of the centre along the seafront and is the best choice of places around here. A three-course evening meal costs £10.

Alexandra Hotel (☎ 720131; www.alexandrahotel .mistral.co.uk; King Edward's Pde; per person £28) In a grand, white Victorian on the seafront, this (small) dog-friendly hotel also has special terms for children. For a sea view rates increase by £4 per person.

Devonshire Park Hotel (☎ 728144; www.devonshire -park-hotel.co.uk; Carlisle Rd; r £60; ☒ ▣) A stunning hotel with wonderfully elegant and sophisticated rooms. Ask for a rear view overlooking the private Victorian lawn. Children over 14 only. Tariffs drop in the off season.

mains £5–0, ... pub fare in the Old Town, the .... place to go.

Getting There & Away

National Express runs one bus a day to Eastbourne from London Victoria, departing at 3pm (£10.50, 2¾ hours), plus an 8.45am bus from Eastbourne to Brighton (£3.25, 55 minutes). The slower No 712 runs every three times an hour (twice hourly on Sunday) to Brighton (one hour 20 minutes). Bus No 711 runs hourly (every two hours on Sunday) from Dover to Eastbourne (£5.20, 2¾ hours).

Trains from London Victoria leave every half-hour for Eastbourne (£18.50, 1½ hours), and there are half-hourly trains (20 minutes) between Eastbourne and Brighton.

AROUND EASTBOURNE
Pevensey Castle

The ruins of William the Conqueror's first stronghold, **Pevensey Castle** (☎ 01323-762604; admission £3.50; ☽ 10am-6pm daily Apr-Oct, 10am-4pm Wed-Sun Nov-Mar), lie 5 miles east of Eastbourne, off the A259. They sit within a Roman defensive wall and on the site of a Roman fort which was built between AD 280 and 340.

The Mint House (☎ 01323 762337; admission £1), just across the road from the castle, dates from 1342 and is absolutely bursting with one of the biggest and weirdest collections of antiques and bits and pieces you may ever see. The atmosphere is decidedly nutty.

Regular train services between London Victoria and Hastings via Eastbourne stop at Westham, half a mile from Pevensey. Otherwise, you'll have to drive.

Beachy Head

The chalk cliffs at Beachy Head are the highest point of the famous Seven Sisters Cliffs that mark this rugged stretch of coast at the southern end of the South Downs.

THE LONG MAN

If you're travelling along the A27 between Eastbourne and Lewes, be sure to look southwards out the window, just east of the town of Wilmington, to see the stick-figure-like **Long Man of Wilmington**. No-one really knows how this 70m-high man got here. The original markings in the grass have been replaced by white concrete blocks to preserve the image.

There is a turn-off for the Long Man at the town of Wilmington from where you can get a better view. Wilmington is 7 miles west of Eastbourne. If you're walking this section of the South Downs you will pass him and get a close-up view

---

The sheer, 175m-high coastal cliffs are awe-inspiring enough in themselves, but when they're chalk white and backed by emerald-green turf they're breathtaking.

A few miles further, past Beachy Head, is the tiny seaside village (it's more like a collection of houses) of Burling Gap. Stop at the **Thatched Bar** (☎ 01323-423197; ☽ 11am-11pm Mon-Sat, noon-11pm Sun) at the Burling Gap Hotel, a stupendous country pub with good food and ice cream. You can access the rocky beach below the pub by a set of metal stairs riveted to the side of the cliff and it's possible to make the several-mile walk all the way back to the lighthouse. Just watch the tide.

If you're coming by car, Beachy Head is off the B2103, from the A259 between Eastbourne and Newhaven. Follow the road along the cliffs until you reach Burling Gap.

Charleston Farmhouse

Five miles west of Eastbourne, **Charleston Farmhouse** (☎ 01323-811265; off A27; adult/child £6/4.50; ☽ 2-5pm Wed-Sun Apr-Oct) was the country retreat of the Bloomsbury Group and a superb example of the rich intellectual and aesthetic life that they came to represent.

In 1916 Virginia Woolf's sister, painter Vanessa Bell, moved here with her lover Duncan Grant and they set about painting and decorating the place in a style that owed much to the influence of Italian fresco painting and the Post-Impressionists. Every wall, door and piece of furniture was decorated thus, and in 1939 Vanessa's husband Clive brought his collection of exquisite furniture here, and the walls featured paintings by Picasso, Derain, Delacroix and others.

This intellectual and artistic hive survived well into the 1960s, by which time the group had more or less dissolved itself or simply blended into the London scene. Thankfully, the house has survived almost intact, and is well worth a stop. There's also a handsome garden and interesting outbuildings, including a medieval dovecote.

Visits are by guided tour only except on Sunday and bank holiday Mondays. The nearest train station is at Berwick, on the Brighton to Eastbourne line, a 2-mile walk from the farmhouse.

LEWES
☎ 01273 / pop 15,988
Lewes (locally pronounced like the name Lewis) is a lovely old town with a long skinny High St located just off a spur above the River Ouse. At first glance, it may seem a little staid and old-fashioned, but it's a charming place that's fast emerging as one of the most desirable places to live on the south coast, as well as one of the most expensive.

Surrounding William de Warenne's ruined castle, built shortly after the Norman invasion of 1066, Lewes today is mostly Georgian in appearance, but the medieval street plan – basically a bunch of narrow, winding streets called *twittens* off the main High St – gives it a really intimate feel.

The town's past is pretty turbulent, culminating in the burning of 17 Protestants in 1556 at the height of Mary Tudor's Catholic revival. Lewes has not forgotten, and every 5 November tens of thousands of people gather for the famous fireworks display, and an effigy of the pope is burnt in memory of the Protestant martyrs. Locals dress in medieval garb and bonfires are lit throughout the area. It all sounds a little ominous, but there's absolutely no sectarian fervour and in recent years it's become one of the most enjoyable nights on the southeastern calendar.

Orientation & Information
The town occupies a steep ridge between the river and the castle ruins, with High St climbing the spine and the *twittens* running off it.

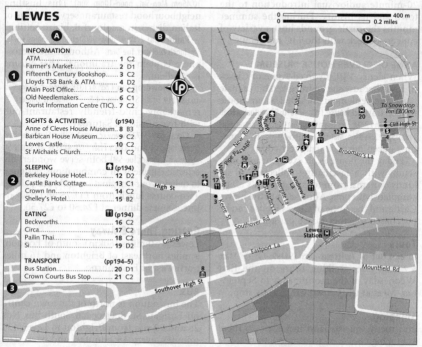

LEWES

INFORMATION		
ATM	1	C2
Farmer's Market	2	D1
Fifteenth Century Bookshop	3	C2
Lloyds TSB Bank & ATM	4	D2
Main Post Office	5	C2
Old Needlemakers	6	C1
Tourist Information Centre (TIC)	7	C2

SIGHTS & ACTIVITIES	(p194)	
Anne of Cleves House Museum	8	B3
Barbican House Museum	9	C2
Lewes Castle	10	C2
St Michaels Church	11	C2

SLEEPING	(p194)	
Berkeley House Hotel	12	D2
Castle Banks Cottage	13	C1
Crown Inn	14	C2
Shelley's Hotel	15	B2

EATING	(p194)	
Beckworths	16	C2
Circa	17	C2
Pailin Thai	18	C2
Si	19	D2

TRANSPORT	(pp194–5)	
Bus Station	20	D1
Crown Courts Bus Stop	21	C2

0   400 m
0   0.2 miles

To Snowdrop Inn (300m)

St John's St
Castle Banks
New Rd
Pipe Passage
Westgate St
High St
Keere St
Cliff High St
Brooman's La
St Andrews
Waterside La
St Martin's La
Southover Rd
Grange Rd
Eastport La
Southover High St
Mountfield Rd
Lewes Station

THE SOUTHEAST COAST

The **TIC** (☎ 483448; 187 High St; ☺ 9am-5pm Mon-Fri, 10am-5pm Sat & 10am-2pm Sun Apr-Sep) is located at the top of the hill.

The **main post office** (High St) is near the corner of Watergate Lane, **Lloyds TSB & ATM** (Cliff High St) is at the eastern end of the centre. There's an interesting collection of craft shops in the **Old Needlemakers** (West St); the **Lewes Farmers Market** takes place on the first Saturday of every month on Cliff High St at the bottom of Lewes High St; while the simply fabulous **Fifteenth Century Bookshop** (☎ 474160; 99 High St) is the place to go for second-hand books and new editions.

Sights
LEWES CASTLE & MUSEUM
Although little more than a set of impressive ruins, William de Warenne's **castle** (☎ 486290; 169 High St; admission £4; ☺ 10am-5.30pm Tue-Sat, 11am-5.30pm Sun-Mon) affords some excellent views over the town and the meadows of the surrounding countryside. The adjacent **Barbican House Museum** has a worthwhile collection of prehistoric, Roman, Saxon and medieval objects, as well as an excellent 20-minute audiovisual introduction to the town and its history. During the summer months the castle grounds host a variety of concerts; check with the TIC for details.

ANNE OF CLEVES HOUSE MUSEUM
When Henry VIII divorced Anne of Cleves in 1541 (because she hadn't given him a male heir), the settlement included a handsome timber-framed **house** (☎ 474610; 52 Southover High St; admission £2.90; ☺ 10am-5pm Tue-Sat year-round, plus 11am-5pm Sun-Mon Mar-Oct), although the one-time queen never actually moved in.

Today the house is an excellent folk museum, with a fascinating collection of all kinds of items, from toys to a witch's effigy complete with pins. Admission to the Lewes Castle and the Anne of Cleves House can be purchased together for £6 per adult.

Tours
In and Out of Twittens (☎ 894199; £3; ☺ 11am & 2.30pm) does walking tours on the first Wednesday of the month, May to September. Meet at the Crown Courts bus stop.

Sleeping
Not many tourists land in Lewes, so there isn't a big choice of accommodation.

Castle Banks Cottage (☎ 476291; www.smooth hound.co.uk/hotels/castlebanks.html; 4 Castle Banks; s/d £25/50; ✗) The owner of this two-room, period cottage with easy-going atmosphere, is also the author of a book on the history of Lewes.

Crown Inn (☎ 480670; www.crowninn-lewes.co.uk; 191 High St; s/d from £40/60) This highly recommended 17th-century inn serves superb breakfasts in a glass-ceilinged conservatory.

Berkeley House Hotel (☎ 476057; www.berkeley househotel.co.uk; 2 Albion St; s/d from £60/80) This bright and airy Georgian townhouse has tastefully appointed rooms. Children must be over eight years old.

Shelley's Hotel (☎ 472361; fax 483152; High St; s/d from £120/155; ✗) This is the poshest place in town, full of old-world atmosphere. It was originally built in the 1520s, but was converted to a manor house in the 1590s. Tariffs drop for stays of more than one night.

Eating
For some reason there seems to be an overabundance of Italian restaurants in town.

Si (☎ 487766; 197 High St; mains £5-10; ☺ 11.45am-10.45pm Mon-Sat, noon-10pm Sun) This bustling neighbourhood restaurant serves a range of Italian dishes in a colourful, bistro setting.

Pailin Thai (☎ 473906; 20 Station St; mains £6-10; ☺ lunch & dinner Tue-Sun) Although the atmosphere is plain the traditional Thai cuisine is excellent.

The Snowdrop Inn (☎ 471018; www.snowdropinn .co.uk; 119 South St; mains £4-8; ☺ lunch & dinner) A remarkably child-friendly restaurant-pub with live music on Saturday.

Circa (☎ 471777; www.cc.com; 145 High St; ☺ lunch & dinner Tue-Sat) and **Circa Fish** (☎ 471333; Westgate St; ☺ lunch & dinner Tue-Sat) both serve wonderfully eclectic cuisine with combinations designed to delight your imagination and your palette. Two-course lunch from £11.75 and two- or three-course dinner at £24.50 to £27.50.

Getting There & Away
Lewes is 50 miles (80km) south of London, 9 miles northeast of Brighton and 16 miles northwest of Eastbourne.

BUS
The bus station is north of the town centre off Eastgate St. Stagecoach South bus Nos 28 and 29 run from Brighton to Lewes (35 minutes, every 15 minutes) and back. The

WORTH THE TRIP

In 1934 John Christie, a science teacher at Eton, and his opera singer wife built a 1200-seat opera house in the middle of nowhere. It was a magnificent folly at the time. Now it is **Glyndebourne** (☎ 01273-812321; www.glyndebourne.com), one of England's best places to enjoy the lyric arts, with a season that runs from late May to the end of August. Tickets can be very difficult to obtain and range in price from £27 to £140. Standing-only tickets cost £12, but you need to be on the mailing list to buy them. And then there's the dress code: strictly black tie and evening dress. For all information, call the box office on ☎ 01273-813813. Glyndebourne is 4 miles east of Lewes off the B2192. Coaches can be arranged for pick up at Lewes station (☎ 01273-815000). See below for train services between Lewes and London. By car, the trip from the capital takes about 2½ hours.

No 29 runs half-hourly between Brighton and Royal Tunbridge Wells (one hour 50 minutes) via Lewes.

TRAIN
Lewes is well served by rail, being on the main line between London Victoria and Eastbourne and on the coastal link between Eastbourne and Brighton. Trains leave every 15 minutes from Brighton (£3, 15 minutes), three times an hour from Eastbourne (£5, 20 minutes) and every half-hour from London Victoria (£15.90, one hour).

BRIGHTON & HOVE
☎ 01273 / pop 206,648
If ambitious London has an artistic little sister then she is Brighton. Flush with retro boutique shops, cool bars, fabulous restaurants, art galleries and vibrant crowds, this coastal city is one of England's gems and should be a highlight of any visit to this part of the country. In December 2000, Brighton Town merged with its lesser-known neighbour Hove to become Brighton & Hove, though that distinction is lost on most Brightonians, many of whom still haven't managed to visit the 'new neighbourhood'.

The great thing about Brighton is its diversity. You'll find beef-eating urban jet-setters rubbing elbows with vegetarian dreadlocked hippies as well as transvestites in six-inch heels strolling past young mums and their prams. Throw this mix into a laid-back seaside atmosphere with a large (but rocky) beach front and crowds of sunbathing beauties and there's nowhere else you could be but Brighton. Whatever you're into, there's a spot for you here.

Brighton's wonderful eccentricity can be traced to the beginning of the 19th century when the Prince Regent came to town to party. For more formal good times George eventually built the Royal Pavilion, now a showpiece museum that's well worth a visit. These days, if it's nightlife you're after, Brighton is – relative to its size – easily a match for London and Manchester. It also has some of the best cafés and restaurants south of the M25, though you won't run into London prices. There's no doubt that England should be proud of London's little sister.

Orientation
Old Steine (pronounced steen) is the major road from the pier to the city centre. To the west is the warren of pedestrian-only streets known as The Lanes, full of good restaurants and boutiques. Immediately north is the North Laine, full of quirky shops and lovely cafés that generally define the city's more bohemian character. The train station is half a mile north of the beach. The tiny bus station is tucked away in Poole Valley. Hove lies to the west.

Brighton's vibrant gay scene thrives in Kemptown, east of Old Steine along St James' St.

Information
BOOKSHOPS
Borders Books (☎ 731122; Churchill Square Shopping Centre) Has CDs, a café and the occasional live event.
Brighton Books (☎ 693845; 18 Kensington Gardens) A second-hand and specialist bookshop.

INTERNET ACCESS
Curve Internet (☎ 603031; 44-47 Gardner St; ⏰ 10am-11pm; per hr £1.50) Next door to Komedia Theatre.

LAUNDRY
Bubbles Laundrette (75 Preston St)

THE SOUTHEAST COAST

BRIGHTON & HOVE

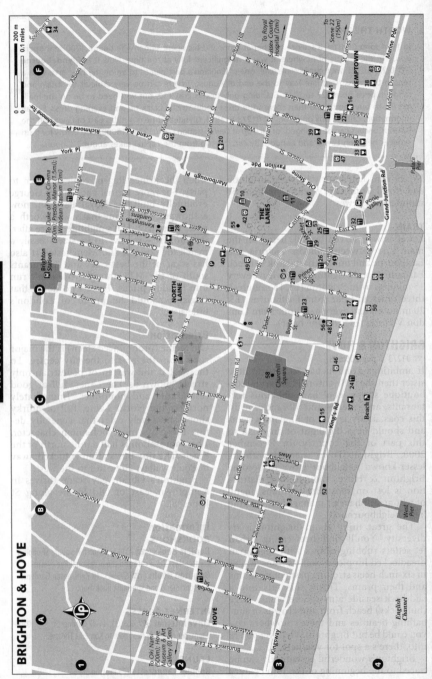

0   200 m
0   0.1 miles

To Oki Nami
(500m); Hove
Museum & Art
Gallery (0.5mi)

To Duke of York Cinema
(300m); Preston Manor (1.5mi);
Withdean Stadium (2mi)

To Royal
Sussex County
Hospital (2mi)

To
Scene 22
(150m)

KEMPTOWN

NORTH LAINE

THE LANES

Churchill Square

West Pier

Palace Pier

Poole Valley

English Channel

MEDICAL SERVICES

Royal Sussex County Hospital (☎ 696955; Eastern Rd) Has an accident and emergency department 2 miles east of the centre.

Wiston's Clinic (☎ 506263; 138 Dyke Rd) For general medical consultations; under a mile from the centre.

MONEY

American Express (☎ 712906; 82 North St) Has a bureau de change.

NatWest (Castle Sq) Has an ATM near the entrance to the Royal Pavilion.

Thomas Cook (☎ 329872; 153 North St)

POST

Main post office (Ship St; ☿ 9.30am-5.30pm Mon-Sat) There is a smaller branch on Western Rd.

TOURIST INFORMATION

TIC (☎ 292599; www.visitbrighton.co.uk; 10 Bartholomew Sq; ☿ 9am-5pm Mon-Fri, 10am-5pm Sat, 10am-4pm Sun Easter-Sep, 9am-5pm Mon-Sat Sep-Easter) Has a 24-hour accessible computer with resources for accommodations, restaurants and sights.

Sights

ROYAL PAVILION

The **Royal Pavilion** (☎ 290900; admission £5.95; ☿ 10am-4.30pm Oct-Mar, 9.30am-5pm Apr-Sep) is an absolute must and a highlight of any trip to southern England. This extraordinarily lavish fantasy is one of the most sumptuously hedonistic buildings you'll see anywhere in England and is a fitting symbol of Brighton's 'un-English' decadence. Unlike so many of the country's grand but slightly

dreary stately homes, the Pavilion does not disappoint. In fact, the stunning Moorish and Indian-styled exterior is merely a prelude to the flamboyant, no-expense-spared décor of the rooms inside. This is one hell of a holiday cottage (see the boxed text p198).

A free visitors' guide is available which takes you through the place, room by room, but we strongly recommend that you take one of the guided tours, which take place at 11.30am and 2.30pm daily.

BRIGHTON MUSEUM & ART GALLERY

Aside from its collection of 20th-century art and design (including a Salvador Dali sofa in the shape of Mae West's lips), **Brighton Museum & Art Gallery** (☎ 290 900; Royal Pavilion Gardens; admission free; ☿ 10am-7pm Tue, 10am-5pm Wed-Sat, 2-5pm Sun) has a fascinating exhibit on world art, including a genuine Hindu shrine created in collaboration with the local Gujerati community. Also worth checking out is the Images of Brighton exhibit, featuring a collection of interesting and revealing oral histories of the city.

PALACE PIER

With the Royal Pavilion, this **pier** (admission free) is Brighton's most distinctive landmark and the epitome of seaside tackiness. It's got the usual selection of fairground rides (including the Helter Skelter made famous by the Beatles' song), dingy amusement arcades, and food stalls, where you can buy a stick of the famous Brighton Rock. It's cheesy, but because it's the only part of

THE SOUTHEAST COAST

THE PRINCE, THE PALACE & THE PISS-UP

The young Prince George (1762–1830), eldest son of George III, was not your typical wayward kid. By the age of 17 he was drinking with abandon and enjoying the pleasures of women. But he was the king's heir, and daddy was none too impressed. The elder George's displeasure turned to contempt when his son began hanging out with his dissolute uncle the Duke of Cumberland, who was enjoying himself royally by the sea in Brighton.

George loved the town so much that in 1787 he commissioned Henry Holland (1745–1806) to design a neoclassical villa where he could party. The elegant result, known as the Marine Pavilion, was George's personal pleasure palace. In the years he waited to accede to the throne (when his father was declared officially insane in 1810 he was sworn in as Prince Regent), George spent the bulk of his time organising extravagant piss-ups for himself, his mistresses and his aristocratic mates, which included the day's most notorious dandy and arbiter of fashion, Beau Brummell.

Ever conscious of what was trendy and what was not, George decided in 1815 to convert the Marine Pavilion so as to reflect the current fascination with all things Eastern. He engaged the services of John Nash (1752–1835), who laboured for eight years to create a Mogul Indian–style palace, complete with the most lavish Chinese interior imaginable.

George finally had a palace suited to his outlandish tastes, and to boot he was now the king. He continued to throw parties, but the boundless energy of his youth was fast disappearing, and he last visited Brighton in 1827. Three years later, he died of respiratory problems.

His brother and successor, William IV (1765–1837), also used the pavilion as a royal residence, as did William's niece Victoria (1819-1901) when she became queen in 1837. But the conservative queen didn't quite take to the place in the manner of her uncles and in 1850 she sold it to the town, but not before stripping it of every piece of furniture – 143 wagons were needed to transport the contents. Thankfully, many of the original items were later returned by the queen and successive monarchs, and today the house has been almost fully restored to its former elegance.

Brighton to bear any resemblance to a typical British seaside resort, it's terrific fun.

On the far side of the beach you'll notice the skeletal remains of the **West Pier** whose middle collapsed into the sea late in 2002. Once a Victorian splendour, it now serves as a charred eyesore.

PRESTON MANOR

Filled to the brim with paintings, ornaments and antiques, **Preston Manor** (☎ 290900; Preston Drove; admission £3.80; ☼ 10am-5pm Tue-Sat, 2-5pm Sun, 1-5pm Mon) is a typical Edwardian upper-class home, 2½ miles north of the centre. It was originally built around 1600 but was rebuilt in 1738, which is why the exterior is so understated. The guided tour takes in about 20 rooms, but it is the section 'below stairs', comprising the kitchen and servants' quarters, that is particularly interesting. You can get there on bus No 5 or 5A from the centre or take a local train to Preston Park station, only 200m from the house.

BOOTH MUSEUM OF NATURAL HISTORY

This **museum** (☎ 292777; 194 Dyke Rd; admission free; ☼ 10am-5pm Mon-Sat, 2-5pm Sun) is a Victorian 'dead zoo' with more than 500,000 specimens. The bird room is particularly creepy, especially if you've seen the Hitchcock movie. The museum is about half a mile north of the train station. Buses 27 and 27A stop nearby on Dyke Rd.

HOVE MUSEUM & ART GALLERY

You may be surprised to know that Hove is the birthplace of British cinema, with the first short film shot in 1898. You can see it, along with other fantastic attractions, at this impressive Victorian villa, built in the 1870s, which houses the **museum and art gallery** (☎ 290200; 19 New Church Rd; ☼ 10am-5pm Tue-Sat, 2-5pm Sun). The wonderful children's room lights up with fairy lights when you enter and exhibits include old zoetropes, a magic lantern and a small cupboard with a periscope inside. Highlights also include the Toy Gallery and interactive Film Gallery. For public transport take bus Nos 1, 1A, 6, 6A or 49.

Tours

Guided tours covering a range of interests can be booked through the TIC. They cost around £4 and take about one hour.

Guide Friday (☎ 746205) open-top buses stop on either side of the Palace Pier and take you around the main sights of Brighton. You can hop on and off as much as you like. Tickets are available from the driver and cost £6.70/2.70 per adult/child.

Brighton Walks (☎ 888596; www.brightonwalks .com; £6) offers a range of standard and off-beat themes including the Quadrophenia Tour (£8), Gay's The Word and Ghost Walk. Show up for prescheduled walks or contact to book.

Festivals & Events

The three-week-long **Brighton Festival** (☎ 292 961 or 709709; www.brighton-festival.org.uk) is the largest arts festival in Britain after Edinburgh. Held in May, it features a packed and varied programme of theatre, dance and music that draws performers from all over the world. The free programme is available months in advance from the TIC.

Sleeping

There's plenty of choice for accommodation in Brighton though prices are generally higher than in some of the surrounding smaller towns. You should book ahead for weekends in summer and during the Brighton Festival in May.

BUDGET

Brighton's independent hostels are a genuinely relaxed bunch, although some might say a little too much so. What they lack in tidiness, however, they make up for in atmosphere.

Baggies Backpackers (☎ 733740; 33 Oriental Pl; dm/d £13/35) This is the best hostel in town. Close to the seafront, it has good facilities but what wins our vote is its general cleanliness and easygoing atmosphere. There's a £5 room-key deposit.

Brighton Backpackers Hostel (☎ 777717; www .brightonbackpackers.com; 75-76 Middle St; dm per night/week £13/70, in seafront annexe £15/80; ⌨) Colourful borders on psychedelic in this laid-back spot. It's rough around the edges but has a friendly staff.

University of Brighton (☎ 643167; Grand Pde; flats per person per week from £70; ⌚ Jul-Sep) It's only open for three months but during that time you can get great deals here when the students are gone. The flats sleep two to eight people.

MID-RANGE

There are a lot of good mid-range hotels in Brighton. Our favourites are among the more expensive of the lot. There are loads of moderately priced guest houses just off Regency Sq.

Neo Hotel (☎ 711104; 19 Oriental Pl; s/d £50/100; ✖) This highly recommended light and bright boutique hotel offers very sleek and modern décor including bamboo wallpaper and cutting-edge art. The hotel does not cater to kids.

Oriental Hotel (☎ 205050; www.orientalhotel.co.uk; 9 Oriental Pl; d with shared bathroom £35, with private bathroom Sun-Thu £55, Fri & Sat £80; ⌨ ✖) Stylishly decorated in mint and rouge with a cool modern atmosphere, its groovy interior is Brighton to a tee.

Brighton House Hotel (☎ 323282; www.brighton househotel.co.uk; 52 Regency Sq; s £35-85, d 50-120; ✖) The proprietor is lovely and helpful at this luxurious Regency hotel on Regency Sq. The rooms are immaculate and breakfast is refreshingly healthy. Children are not catered to here.

Genevieve Hotel (☎ 681653; www.genevievehotel .co.uk; 18 Madeira Pl; s/d from £65; ✖) There is a minimum two-night stay at weekends in this refurbished but standard lodging. Luxury rooms are more attractive and come with four-poster beds.

TOP END

De Vere Grand Hotel (☎ 224300; www.grandbrighton .co.uk; King's Rd; s/d from £170/250; Ⓟ) The IRA tried to kill Margaret Thatcher and her cabinet here in 1983 by exploding a huge bomb. Life is all leisure and comfort here now, with luxurious facilities.

Hotel du Vin (☎ 718588; www.hotelduvin.com; Ship St; rooms from £125; ✖) Housed in a collection of Gothic buildings near the seafront, this lovely hotel has bright and attentive staff and a wonderful bistro with an extensive wine list. Rooms are thoroughly modern and elegant.

Eating

Brighton has the best dining options on the south coast. Wander around the Lanes and North Laine or walk along Preston St, which runs back from the seafront near West Pier, and you'll uncover a wide selection of cafés, diners and restaurants of every hue and taste.

BUDGET

Food For Friends (☎ 202310; 17a Prince Albert St; mains £4-8; ☺ 11.30am-10pm) This very inventive vegetarian food is complimented by a bright interior and staff. With organic beer.

Nia Café (☎ 671371; 87-88 Trafalgar St; mains £9-14; ☺ 9am-11pm Mon-Sat, 9am-6pm Sun) Hang out over a mug of cappuccino at a rustic sidewalk table, or try one of the delicious ciabatta sandwiches.

Coach House (☎ 719000; www.coachhousebrighton .com; 59a Middle St; mains £8-11; ☺ noon-11pm) The eclectic menu at this bright and stylish former coach house includes Italian, Moroccan and Sunday roast. Sip a cappuccino or bar drink by the courtyard fountain.

Cherry Tree (☎ 698684; 107 St James' St; ☺ 9am-6pm Mon-Sat, 10am-5pm Sun; ☒) A wonderfully rustic Mediterranean food mini-grocery and deli where you can get cold sandwiches and salads.

Little Shop (☎ 325594; 48a Market St, The Lanes; mains £3-6; ☺ lunch) Here you'll find award-winning sandwiches – and indeed they *are* delicious.

For a Zen moment amid the bustle of Brighton meditate on the quality Japanese cuisine at **Oki Nami** (☎ 773777; www.okinami.com; 208 New Church Rd, Hove; mains £8.95-15.95; ☺ lunch Wed-Sun, dinner Mon-Sun), an intimate spot with minimalist design. Or snatch a Bento box (£2.50 to £4.40) and a Hello Kitty purse at the **Oki Nami Japanese Shop** (☎ 677702; 12 York Pl; ☺ 8.30am-6.30pm) across from St Peter's Church and head back into the fray.

Infinity Foods (25 North Rd; ☺ 9.30am-6pm Mon-Sat, 11am-4pm Sun) is a natural and organic grocery co-op on the North Laines.

MID-RANGE

The Saint (☎ 607835; 22 St James' St; mains £8-11; ☺ lunch & dinner Tue-Sun) The Italian and Spanish bistro cuisine such as Lamb Navarin with leek pomme puree (although the menu changes weekly) is popular so book ahead at weekends.

Casa Don Carlos (☎ 327177, 303274; 5 Union St, The Lanes; tapas £3-6; ☺ noon-3pm & 6-11pm Mon-Fri, noon-11pm Sat & Sun; ☒) Tables spill out onto a brick pedestrian lane in this fabulous tapas spot that captures the rustic, casual elegance of Spain.

Terre á Terre (☎ 729051; 71 East St; mains £10-15; ☺ noon-3pm Wed-Fri, 6-10pm Wed-Fri, noon-10.30pm Sat & Sun) Orange walls hold large oil paintings and a colourfield mural in this refined and well-known vegetarian restaurant. The staff are very professional.

Due South (☎ 821218; 139 Kings Rd arches; mains £11-14; ☺ noon-10pm) Only local and organic ingredients are used in the creative English and French fare. Look out the open arched windows of the upstairs dining room or sit near the promenade for refined beachfront dining.

De Vere Grand Hotel (☎ 224300; King's Rd; afternoon tea £13.50) This is *the* place to go for that most English of afternoon activities. Ask for a table in the conservatory and discover the delights of cucumber sandwiches washed town with pots of tea. Afternoon tea is served from 3pm to 6pm daily.

English's Oyster Bar (☎ 327980; 29-31 East St; mains £11-25; ☺ lunch & dinner) This crowded eatery serves enormous portions of steak and seafood and a variety of oysters on the half shell at outdoor tables on The Lanes.

Gingerman (☎ 326688; 21a Norfolk Sq, Hove; 2/3 courses £15.95/18.95) You could make a meal out of several of the inventive starters here, although the classic French dishes are also solid and savoury.

Drinking

The nightlife here is on par with London's so you won't have any trouble finding a cool places to wet your whistle in style.

The Bar With No Name (☎ 601419; 58 Southover St) The epitome of a Brighton bar, this traditional pub is popular with local artists, clubbers and those simply looking for a good pint and a chat.

Dorset (☎ 605423; 28 North Rd) The laid-back atmosphere is perfect for morning coffee or an evening pint, in the heart of North Laine district. In good weather the doors and windows are open wide.

Tin Drum (☎ 777575; 43 St James' St) This place is known for its East European theme and wide selection of vodka. It gets pretty full on weekend nights, but it's a nice and relaxing spot for Sunday brunch.

Riki Tik (☎ 683844; 18a Bond St) This is a favourite pre-club spot for young clubbers who kick off their night over cocktails and loud music.

Gemini Beach Bar (☎ 327888; 127 King's Rd Arches) On a nice summer's day, there's nowhere better to sit and watch the weird and wonderful parade down the promenade than at this perfect beach bar.

GAY & LESBIAN BRIGHTON

Perhaps it's Brighton's long-time association with the theatre, but for more than 100 years the city has been a gay haven. Gay icons Noel Coward and Ivor Novello were regular visitors, but in those days the scene was furtive and separate. From the 1960s onwards, the scene really began to open up, especially in the Kemptown area and around Old Steine. Today, with more than 25,000 gay men and 10,000-15,000 lesbians living in the city, it is the most vibrant queer community in the country outside London.

Kemptown (aka Camptown), on and off St James' St, is where it's all at. In recent years the old Brunswick Town area of Hove has emerged as a quieter alternative to the traditionally cruisy (and sometimes seedy) Kemptown, but the community here has responded by branching out from the usual pubs that served as nightly pick-up joints. Now you will find a rank of gay-owned businesses, from cafés and hotels to bookshops as well as the more obvious bars, clubs and saunas. There's even a Gay's The Word walking tour (see Brighton Walks, p199).

For up-to-date information on what's going on in Gay Brighton, check out the websites at www.gay.brighton.co.uk or www.REALBrighton.com.

For dining...

St James' St has plenty of cafés and restaurants to suit your every taste.

- **Scene 22** (129 St James' St; snacks £2-3) is where you should go to get the latest word on everything going on in town, make hotel bookings, collect tickets for shows and leave messages on the bulletin board. There is free wireless Internet use with refreshment purchase.

For drinking...

- Brighton's gay pubs are generally raucous, no-holds-barred kind of places, but there are a number of cooler, more reserved bars.
- **Amsterdam** (11-12 Marine Pde) is a European-style hotel, sauna and bar on the seafront that attracts a mixed crowd.
- **Charles St** (8-9 Marine Pde), a couple of doors down, is trendy, but fun nonetheless, though you may feel slightly out of place without designer clothing.
- **Legends** (31-32 Marine Pde) is modern cool, with live entertainment and karaoke throughout the week.
- **The Queen's Arms** (7 George St) has our favourite sign in town: 'A friendly welcome greets you in the Queen's Arms'. There is plenty of camp in the cabaret and karaoke acts, making it a definite stop on the Brighton Sunday trail.

For dancing...

Bars and pubs may be fun, but the real action takes place on and off the dance floor.

- **Club Envy** (8-9 Marine Pde) is upstairs from Charles St. Cool, sophisticated and trendy, it still gets down and dirty when it's full.
- **Storm** (5 Steine St) has a more relaxed and friendly feeling as well as the legendary Electro Homo Disco Freakshow on Sunday.

Entertainment

Brighton has the best choice of entertainment on the south coast, with a selection of clubs better than you'll find anywhere else outside of London or Manchester. As with anywhere, what's hot and what's not comes and goes with the tide, so keep an eye out for *This is Brighton*, *The Brighton Latest*, *The List* or *The Source* to keep on top.

NIGHTCLUBS

If Britain's top DJs aren't spending their summers playing to the crowds in Ibiza or Aya Napia, you'll most likely find them in

Brighton. All clubs open until at least 2am, some as late as 5am.

Sumo (☎ 749469; 9-11 Middle St; admission £2) DJs spin the latest in cool R&B and club tunes in this dim lounge with red lighting and hip art.

Honey Club (☎ 07000-446639; www.thehoneyclub .co.uk; 214 Kings Rd Arches; admission £5-12) The crowd is young and out to party at this trendy spot right on the beach promenade where cyber and flamboyant dress is encouraged.

Concorde 2 (☎ 320724; Marine Pde, Kemptown; admission £10-11) This spot is jam-packed every second Friday from June to September for Fatboy Slim's Big Beat Boutique. Other nights, though, are just as popular, with a choice of club sounds, from R&B to house.

Ocean Rooms (☎ 699069; 1 Morley St; admission £1-10) Sumptuously decorated in red – red sofas, red drapes and red cushioned walls – this spot is a favourite with the late-20s–early-30s crowd, who come here at weekends for the excellent soul, funk and disco.

Zap Club (☎ 202407; King's Rd Arches; admission £5-8) This slightly cheesy club hosts '70s nights (Chopper Choons) and funky soulful house on Saturday. It's a well-worked formula with phenomenal appeal, judging from the queues outside at weekends.

CINEMA
The multiscreen **Odeon Cinema** (☎ 244007; cnr King's Rd & West St) shows mainstream films. The **Duke of York** (☎ 602503; Preston Circus), about a mile north of North Rd, generally runs a programme of art-house films and old classics.

THEATRE
Brighton Dome (☎ 709709; www.brighton-dome.org .uk; 29 New Rd) Once the stables and exercise yard of King George IV, this Art Deco complex houses three theatre venues within the Royal Pavilion estate. The box office is on New Rd.

Theatre Royal (☎ 328488; Bond St) Built by decree of the Prince of Wales in 1806, this venue hosts plays, musicals and operas.

Komedia Theatre (☎ 467100; www.komedia.co.uk; Gardner St, North Laine) A former Tesco supermarket, now a stylish fringe theatre and cabaret space in the centre of Brighton.

SPORTS
The **Seagulls** (Brighton & Hove Albion FC; ☎ 778855; Withdean Stadium, Tongdean Lane) are probably your best chance of seeing good, competitive football in the area. In 2002 Norman Cook (aka Fatboy Slim) bought 11% of the club, which benefits from the passionate support of its fans. It's relatively easy to obtain tickets: contact the **ticket office** (☎ 776992; 5 Queen's Rd). The season runs from mid-August to late May.

Shopping
The Lanes is Brighton's most popular shopping district, a confusing maze of small streets and tiny alleyways that are chocka-block with shops and boutiques selling everything from 17th-century rifles to the latest foot fashions. There's less of a touristy, upmarket feel in **North Laine** – a series of streets northwest of The Lanes, including Bond, Gardner, Kensington and Sydney Sts which abound with retro-cool boutiques, record and CD stalls, Asian import shops and local craft outlets.

Getting There & Away
Brighton is 53 miles (85km) from London and bus and train services are fast and frequent.

BUS
National Express has an office at the bus station and tickets can also be bought at the TIC. Coaches leave hourly from London Victoria to Brighton (£9, two hours 10 minutes).

Stagecoach Buses leave Brighton for: Arundel (two hours, half-hourly); Chichester (2½ hours, half-hourly); Portsmouth (3¾ hours, half-hourly); Lewes (45 minutes, every 15 minutes) and Eastbourne (one hour 20 minutes, every 15 minutes).

Tickets for Stagecoach buses can be purchased from the drivers.

Airlinks (☎ 08705 757747) is a daily coach service to/from all London airports.

TRAIN
There are twice-hourly services to Brighton from London Victoria and King's Cross stations (£15.90, 50 minutes). For £1.50 on top of the rail fare you can have unlimited travel on Brighton & Hove buses for the day. There are hourly services to Portsmouth (£13.90, one hour 20 minutes) and frequent services to Eastbourne, Hastings, Canterbury and Dover.

Getting Around

Brighton is large and spread out though you'll be able to cover all the sights mentioned in this section on foot if you enjoy walking.

The local bus company is **Brighton & Hove** (☎ 886200). A day ticket costs £2.70 from the driver.

Parking in Brighton can be a nightmare. To park in any street space you will need a voucher. They can be purchased from garages and various shops around town and cost about £1 per half-hour but prices do vary.

If you need a cab, **Brighton Streamline Taxis** (☎ 747474), **Yellow Cab Company** (☎ 884488) or **Radio Cars** (☎ 414141) are all worth a try. There is a taxi rank on the junction of East and Market Sts.

WEST SUSSEX

West Sussex doesn't have the crowds that Brighton and other parts of East Sussex have and for that it's a welcome respite for many travellers. The countryside is dominated by the manicured rolling hills of the South Downs. Beautiful Arundel makes a good base for exploring the county, which also includes some excellent Roman ruins.

ARUNDEL

☎ 01903 / pop 3297

Arundel is one of West Sussex's prettiest towns, sitting comfortable atop a hill beneath the stunning 700-year-old castle that is the seat of the dukes of Norfolk. Here you'll find a surprising number of excellent restaurants, some great antique stores and plenty of personable locals. Despite its medieval appearance and long history, most of the town dates from Victorian times.

Information

The **TIC** (☎ 882268; fax 882419; 61 High St; 🕑 10am-6pm Mon-Sat, 10am-1pm & 1.30-4pm Sun Easter-Oct, 10am-3pm daily Nov-Easter) is where you can pick up *A Walk Around Arundel* (40p), although everything to see in the town is pretty well signposted.

Sights & Activities

Arundel Castle (☎ 882173; admission £9.50; 🕑 noon-5pm Sun-Fri Apr-Oct) is a great sight and well worth the entry fee. It was originally built in the 11th century, but it was thoroughly ruined during the Civil War. Most of what you see today is the result of enthusiastic reconstruction by the eighth, 11th and 15th dukes (the current duke still lives in part of the castle). The building's highlight is the massive Great Hall and the library, which has paintings by Gainsborough and Holbein among others.

The four-hectare **Waterfowl Park** (☎ 883 355; Mill Rd; adult/child £5.75/3.75; 🕑 9am-5.30pm Apr-Sep, 9.30am-4pm Oct-Mar), a mile east from the centre, is a nice place to visit for those keen on bird-watching.

The town's other architectural landmark is the 19th-century **cathedral** (☎ 882297; 🕑 9am-6pm summer, 9am-dusk winter), built in the French Gothic style by Henry, the 15th duke. Inside are the remains of the fourth duke's son, St Philip Howard, a Catholic martyr who made the grievous error of being caught praying for a Spanish victory against the English in 1588. He died in the Tower of London and was canonised in 1970.

You can hire a boat to Littlehampton (a small, out of the way fishing village on the coast) or cruise the river Arun with the swans while you dine on an **evening buffet** (☎ 07814 183824; 12 person min, per person £20). Trips depart from the Town Quay at the foot of the High St.

An excellent collection of antique stores lines the High St.

Sleeping

Arundel YHA (☎ 0870 7705676; www.yha.org.uk/hostel /hostelpages/154.html; Warning Camp; dm £13.40; ✉ 📖) Catering to South Downs walkers and travelling families, this large Georgian house isn't as warm a hostel as some, but its facilities are superb. It's located on a pleasant country lane about a 20-minute walk from the town centre off the A27 (call ahead for directions).

St Mary's Gate Inn (☎ 883145; www.stmarysgate .co.uk; London Rd; r £39; mains from £10) This lovely country-style inn next door to the cathedral has a wonderful local atmosphere and family-run feeling. The restaurant and pub are both worth a visit.

Town House (☎ 883847; www.thetownhouse.co.uk; 65 High St; s/d from £50/60; ✉) This elegant, beautifully furnished boutique hotel is simply marvellous, with a welcoming atmosphere and top-notch service. The restaurant downstairs is equally exquisite.

THE SOUTHEAST COAST

SOMETHING FOR THE WEEKEND

With one of the more fairytale castles in southern England and its relatively quiet but distinctly romantic European streets that wind down a hillside lined with charming shops and appealing restaurants, a weekend in Arundel is as fine an experience as England has to offer.

Getting into town in time to visit the antique shops and stroll the High St in the quiet of the early evening is a must before checking into the elegant **Town House hotel** (p203). Then fill your champagne glass at the downstairs bar before dining in the romantic **Papperdelle Ristorante** (below).

Spend Saturday in town shopping at the farmer's market before a leisurely picnic and a boat ride along the river. Make sure you've reserved a table at the **Town House restaurant** (below) in advance for the evening.

On Sunday visit the magnificent **Arundel Castle** (p203), a splendid reminder that your wealth is no match for the duke of Norfolk's, before hopping aboard a jaunty London-bound train.

The Swan Hotel (☎ 882314; www.swan-hotel.co.uk; 27-29 High St; s/d Mon-Thu £60/65, Fri-Sun £75/80; ✗) The clean and modern rooms sit above a pub serving a popular, family-owned ale (among others) in this Victorian hotel.

The Norfolk Arms (☎ 882101; www.forestdale.com; High St; s/d from £75/120; ✗) Built in 1800 by the 10th duke, this handsome coaching inn has beautifully appointed rooms and the largest sign in town. You can't miss it.

Eating

The Town House (☎ 883847; www.thetownhouse.co.uk; 65 High St; mains £14-18; ✗) The gold and walnut ceiling is as immaculate as the cuisine in this cosy, special-night-out spot. The jaunty proprietor adds to the bubbly champagne-like spirit. Book ahead.

Papperdelle Ristorante (☎ 882025; 41a High St; mains £7-12; ✆ noon-2.30pm Tue-Sat, 6.30-10.30pm Mon-Sat; ✗) Vines cling to the hand-painted walls of this romantic Italian restaurant. Fresh, authentic dishes are served by professional and knowledgeable staff. Ask for the bay window seat overlooking High St.

Pallant of Arundel (☎ 882288; 17 High St) Set yourself up for an English picnic with a selection of local cheese, fresh bread, pâté, wine and other delicatessen treats from this superb speciality shop. Spit-roasted chickens are available next door at the butcher.

Tudor Rose (☎ 883813; 49 High St; mains £5-7) This popular tearoom serves the usual selection of sandwiches and hot dishes.

Getting There & Away

Rail is the best way of getting to/from Arundel.

There are trains to Arundel from London Victoria (£17.40, 1½ hours, twice hourly),

to Brighton (£7, 57 minutes, twice hourly) and to Chichester (£3.80, 21 minutes, twice hourly).

AROUND ARUNDEL
Bignor Roman Villa

In 1811, farmer George Tupper was doing a little ploughing when he struck a large stone. After digging around a bit, Tupper realised that he had discovered something quite out of the ordinary.

Much excavation later, it was realised that the plough had struck the remains of a **Roman villa** (☎ 869259; admission £3.65; ✆ 10am-6pm daily Jun-Sep, 10am-5pm daily May & Oct, 10am-5pm Tue-Sun Mar-Apr) built around AD 190. Unfortunately, only the mosaic floors and hypocaust (the Roman version of duct heating) remain, but the mosaics are simply fantastic. New findings are still being made; the most recent was the complete skeleton of a child dating from the fourth century.

Bignor is 6 miles north of Arundel off the A29, but it's a devil of a place to get to unless you have your own car. A terribly slow bus (one hour) from Chichester stops 300m from the entrance, but it only runs twice daily.

CHICHESTER
☎ 01243 / pop 27,477

Situated on the flat meadows between the South Downs and the sea, Chichester is home to a great theatre and arts festival each July as well as some good Roman ruins. Otherwise, it's a fairly uninspiring, though bustling Georgian market town that serves as the administrative capital of West Sussex.

Founded as a port garrison by the Romans shortly after their invasion in AD 43,

Chichester later became an important Norman settlement. Besides the cruciform street plan that converges on Market Cross and the foundations of the enormous villa at Fishbourne, little else remains of the town's Roman origins. Its Norman heritage has fared a little better in the form of its elegant cathedral, even if the once-imposing castle has long since disappeared.

Orientation & Information

The Market Cross, built in 1501 to shelter marketgoers, is the centre of town. The streets around it are pedestrianised and everything you'd want to see is within walking distance. The town is surrounded by walls, around which is a ring road.

There is a **TIC** (☎ 775888; chitic@chichester.gov .uk; 29a South St; ☉ 9.15am-5.15pm Mon-Sat year-round, plus 11am-3.30pm Sun Apr-Sep) and a **post office** (cnr Chapel & West Sts) in town.

Sights
CHICHESTER CATHEDRAL

The elegant **cathedral** (☎ 782595; donation £3; ☉ 7.15am-7pm Jun-Aug, 7.15am-6.30pm Sep-May) is one of the few Romanesque churches not to have undergone a major restructuring. It was begun in 1075, burnt down and rebuilt in the 13th century, and only cosmetically altered since then. The only major changes were the construction of the freestanding church tower in the 15th century and the addition of a 19th-century spire. Inside is a

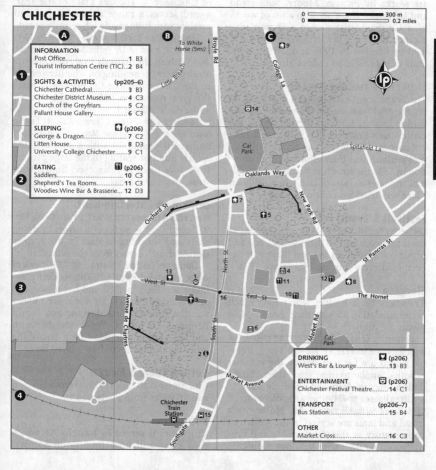

CHICHESTER

0 — 300 m
0 — 0.2 miles

INFORMATION
Post Office.............................1 B3
Tourist Information Centre (TIC)...2 B4

SIGHTS & ACTIVITIES (pp205–6)
Chichester Cathedral..................3 B3
Chichester District Museum........4 C3
Church of the Greyfriars.............5 C2
Pallant House Gallery.................6 C3

SLEEPING (p206)
George & Dragon.......................7 C2
Litten House............................8 D3
University College Chichester......9 C1

EATING (p206)
Saddlers.................................10 C3
Shepherd's Tea Rooms...............11 C3
Woodies Wine Bar & Brasserie...12 D3

DRINKING (p206)
West's Bar & Lounge.................13 B3

ENTERTAINMENT (p206)
Chichester Festival Theatre........14 C1

TRANSPORT (pp206–7)
Bus Station.............................15 B4

OTHER
Market Cross...........................16 C3

To White Horse (5mi)

Broyle Rd
Little Breach
College La
Spitalfield La
Car Park
Oaklands Way
New Park Rd
Orchard St
St Pancras St
North St
West St
East St
The Hornet
Avenue de Chartres
South St
Market Rd
Car Park
Market Avenue
Chichester Train Station
Southgate

THE SOUTHEAST COAST

marvellous stained-glass window by Marc Chagall.

Guided tours operate at 11am and 2.15pm Monday to Saturday, Easter to October and the cathedral choir sings daily at **evensong** (🕑 5.30pm Mon-Sat, 3.30pm Sun).

PALLANT HOUSE GALLERY

Of the many fine Georgian houses in town, **Pallant House** (🕿 774557; 9 North Pallant; adult/child £4/free; 🕑 10am-5pm Tue-Sat, 12.30-5pm Sun) is outstanding. It was built by a wealthy wine merchant who spared no expense. It has since been carefully restored and now houses an excellent collection of 20th-century, mainly British, art in the form of paintings, furniture, sculpture and porcelain. Among them are works by Picasso, Moore, Sutherland and Cézanne. There are also a lot of works by a German artist named Feibusch who escaped the Nazis in Germany in 1933. He died in London in 1998 and left the contents of his studio to Pallant House.

CHURCH OF THE GREYFRIARS

The Franciscans established a **church** (🕿 784 683; Priory Park; admission free; 🕑 noon-4pm Sat Jun–mid-Sep) here in 1269 on the old site of the castle – now Priory Park – in the northeastern corner of the town. The simple building that remains was their choir. After dissolution in 1536 the structure became the guildhall and later a court of law, where William Blake was tried for sedition in 1804.

Festivals & Events

Chichester Festivities (🕿 780192; www.chifest.org.uk) is a three-week festival that includes arts and music but specialises in great theatre. It has been held every June and July since 1974.

Sleeping

Travellers on a budget won't find much accommodation to suit their needs. Most places are mid-range.

University College Chichester (🕿 816070; College Lane; rooms from £25; 🕑 Jun-Aug) The 218 single rooms are for rent during the summer months. Similar to most student accommodation, they're clean and relatively basic.

Litten House (🕿 774503; www.littenho.demon.co.uk; 148 St Pancras St; double from £48; 🗵) Home-made bread and jams are served in the garden or conservatory at this comfortable and centrally located B&B with spacious rooms.

George & Dragon (🕿 775525; www.georgeanddragoninn.co.uk; 51 North St; s/d £50/85) Sleep in a converted barn at the back of this eponymous pub with worn wooden floors and quiet window seats. The 10 rooms are thoroughly modern and quite charming.

White Horse (🕿 535219; www.whitehorsechilgrove .co.uk; Chilgrove; s/d per person weekdays £65/47.50, weekends £95/60) Just outside Chichester in Chilgrove, this polished eight-room boutique coaching inn is well worth the drive. The restaurant is gorgeous and refined.

Eating

Shepherd's Tea Rooms (🕿 774761; 35 Little London; 🕑 9.15am-5pm Mon-Fri, 10am-4pm Sun) Down a small lane off East St, this three-time winner of Chichester's 'Top Tea Place of the Year' award serves a range of sandwiches and rarebits with homemade white-milk bread.

Woodies Wine Bar & Brasserie (🕿 779895; 10-13 St Pancras St; mains £8-12; 🕑 lunch & dinner Mon-Sat; 🗵) With an alternatively lively or romantic atmosphere (depending on whether you are in the darker front or the glassed-in rear) this great spot serves Italian, Mediterranean and a dash of French.

Saddlers (🕿 774765; 1 Sadler's Walk, 41 East St; mains £8-13; 🕑 11am-11pm Mon-Sat) This cool and rustic restaurant with a sophisticated air has outdoor seating in the large garden. It's a nice place to relax over dinner, with steak, pasta and tapas.

Drinking & Entertainment

West's Bar & Lounge (🕿 539637; St Peters Church, West St) Tempt God to strike you down by doing shots and watching football in this former Gothic church across from the cathedral.

Chichester Festival Theatre (🕿 781312; www.cft .org.uk; Oakland's Park; tickets £9-35) This modern playhouse was built in 1962 and has a long and distinguished history. Sir Laurence Olivier was the theatre's first director and Ingrid Bergman, Sir John Gielgud, Maggie Smith and Sir Anthony Hopkins are a few of the other famous names to have played here.

Getting There & Away

Chichester is 60 miles (97km) from London and 18 miles from Portsmouth.

BUS

Chichester is served by bus No 700 which runs every half hour (hourly on Sunday) between Brighton (2½ hours) and Portsmouth (one hour). National Express has a rather protracted daily service from London Victoria (£12.20, five hours 12 minutes).

TRAIN

Chichester can be reached easily from London Victoria (£17.40, 1½ hours, half-hourly) via Gatwick airport and Arundel. It's also on the coast line between Brighton (£8.20, 45 minutes) and Portsmouth (£5.10, 25 minutes). Trains run every half-hour.

AROUND CHICHESTER

South of town is the gorgeous **Chichester Harbour**, an Area of Outstanding Natural Beauty (AONB). A wide, sandy beach west of the harbour offers the only real distraction, but it's a top spot for a stroll. At West Itchenor, 1½-hour harbour cruises are run by **Chichester Harbour Water Tours** (☎ 670504; www .chwt.co.uk; adult/child £5.50/2.50), complete with refreshments. To get here, follow the signposted towpath from Chichester.

Fishbourne Roman Palace & Museum

Fishbourne Palace (☎ 01243-785859; Salthill Rd; admission £5.20; ☺ 10am-5pm daily Mar-Jul & Sep-Oct, 10am-6pm Aug, 10am-4pm Nov-Dec 15, 10am-4pm Sat & Sun Dec 16-Feb) is the largest known Roman residence in Britain. For decades, locals had been uncovering period artefacts in the area and were bemused as to their origin. Then, in 1960, a labourer's shovel hit upon the mother lode and excavations began in earnest.

It is thought that the luxury house was built around AD 75 for Cogidubnus, a Romanised local king. And although all that survives are foundations and some extraordinary mosaic floors and hypocausts, the ruins still convey a vision of 'modern' style and comfort.

The pavilion that shelters the site is an ugly creation, but there are some excellent reconstructions and the garden has been replanted as it would have been in the 1st century.

The palace is 1½ miles west of Chichester, just off the A259. Bus Nos 11 and 700 leave hourly from Monday to Saturday (No 56 on Sunday) from outside Chichester Cathedral and stop at the bottom of Salthill Rd (five minutes' walk away). The museum is 10 minutes' walk from Fishbourne train station, on the line between Chichester and Portsmouth.

Petworth

Twelve miles northeast of Chichester is the pleasant village of Petworth. On the outskirts is **Petworth House** (☎ 01798-342207; admission £7; ☺ 11am-5.30pm Sat-Wed Apr-Oct), a stately home built in 1688. The architecture is impressive (especially the western front), but the art collection is extraordinary. JMW Turner was a regular visitor and the house is still home to the largest collection (20) of his paintings outside the Tate Gallery. There are also many paintings by Van Dyck, Reynolds, Gainsborough, Titian and Blake.

Petworth is, however, most famous for **Petworth Park** (adult/child £1.50/free; ☺ 8am-sunset), which is regarded as the supreme achievement of Capability Brown's natural landscape theory. It's also home to herds of deer.

Petworth is 6 miles from the train station at Pulborough. There's a limited bus service (No 1/1A) from the station to Petworth Square (Monday to Saturday).

HAMPSHIRE

Once part of the great Kingdom of Wessex (along with parts of Wiltshire and Dorset), Hampshire is now largely an agricultural area with thatched-roof farmhouses and lovely country lanes. There are, however, several notable exceptions. The former capital city of Wessex – Winchester – is a must-see destination with its magnificent cathedral at the top of many a top-10 list. Also, anyone with an interest in maritime history will relish a trip to Portsmouth, the long-time home of the once-powerful Royal Navy.

The county is well served by bus. The *Public Transport Map of Hampshire* is very useful and stocked by TICs. For information on all public transport in the county phone ☎ 01962-846992.

WINCHESTER

☎ 01962 / pop 41,420

Easily reached from London, the beautiful cathedral city of Winchester makes for a superb weekend away. Nestled in a valley of the River Itchen, this ancient capital city for many a Saxon king has a rich history that is evident in the bronze statues of past heroes, the cobbled streets and the magnificent church that dominates the centre. The town is also home to a vibrant collection of bars and restaurants, reflecting the youthful tastes of Winchester's growing University College and its new £6 million Performing Arts and Conference Centre.

History

The Romans built the town of Venta Bulgarum, later giving way to a Saxon settlement, but Winchester really took off in AD 670 when the powerful West Saxon bishops moved their Episcopal see here. Thereafter, Winchester was the most important town in the powerful kingdom of Wessex. King Alfred the Great (r 871–99) made it his capital, and it remained so under Knut (r 1016–35) and the Danish kings. After the Norman invasion of 1066, William the Conqueror arrived here to claim the throne of England, and in 1086 he commissioned local monks to write the all-important *Domesday Book* (pronounced 'doomsday'), an administrative survey of the whole country that ranks as the most important clerical accomplishment of the Middle Ages. Winchester thrived until the 12th century, when a fire gutted most of the city, after which it was superseded in importance by London. A long slump lasted until the 18th century, when the town was largely rebuilt and found new life as a prosperous market town.

Orientation

The city centre is compact and easily managed on foot. Partly pedestrianised High St and Buttercross run from west to east through the town, and most of the sights are on or just off them. The bus and coach station is smack in the middle of town opposite the Guildhall and TIC, while the train station is five minutes' walk northwest. Jewry St borders the western side of the centre and was once part of the city's Jewish quarter – today it is where you'll find a chunk of the town's nightlife.

Information

The **TIC** (☎ 840500; fax 850348; www.winchester.gov .uk; ✆ 9.30am-5.30pm Mon-Sat & 11am-4pm Sun May-Sep, 10am-5pm Mon-Sat Oct-Apr) is in the Guildhall on Broadway.

There is a **post office** (✆ 9.30am-6pm Mon-Sat) on Middle Brook St. Internet access can be had at the **Byte Internet Café** (✆ 863235; Parchment St; ✆ 9am-5pm Mon-Fri). There are plenty of banks and ATMs on High St.

Sights

WINCHESTER CATHEDRAL

Winchester's main attraction is one of the world's great buildings, a magnificent testament to English architecture more than 900 years old and one of the finest examples of the Gothic Perpendicular style to be found anywhere.

The present-day **cathedral** (☎ 853137; admission donation £3.50; ✆ 8.30am-6pm) is just south of the town's original minster church built by King Cenwalh in 643. In 1070 the first Norman bishop, Walkelin, decided to replace the old church (even then the largest in the country) with a new one built in the Romanesque style. The new cathedral, completed in 1093, featured a nave that was 164m long and was 14m wider than the current building. On August 15th of that year, the monks officially blessed the new cathedral by depositing the remains of St Swithin (bishop of Winchester from 852 to 862) in a new, purpose-built chapel.

Soggy ground and poor workmanship did not augur well for the church, and the collapse of the central tower in 1107 was just one of several problems the authorities had to deal with. Major restructuring began around 1200 and continued until the mid 15th century; the nave was transformed from a Norman Romanesque to an English Gothic style between 1350 and 1450, thanks in large part to the efforts of William of Wykeham (1366–1404). Floors are still wavy due to settling of the gravel bed underneath in the last 800 years.

Near the entrance in the northern aisle is the grave of Jane Austen, who died a stone's throw from the cathedral in 1817 at **Jane Austen's House** (College St), where the writer lived for the last six weeks of her life; it's now a private residence. The transepts are the most original parts of the cathedral. Note the early Norman rounded arches and painted wooden ceiling.

Crypt tours are often suspended due to flooding but it can be seen from the entrance where the powerful sculpture by Anthony Gormley – of *Angel of the North* fame (see p705) – called *Sound 2* is on display.

Tours (recommended donation £3; ✆ every hr 10am-3pm Mon-Sat) of Winchester Cathedral are run by enthusiastic local volunteers. There are also **tower and roof tours** (£3; ✆ 2.15pm Wed, 11.30am & 2.15pm Sat Jan-May, 2.15pm Tue, Wed & Fri,

THE SOUTHEAST COAST

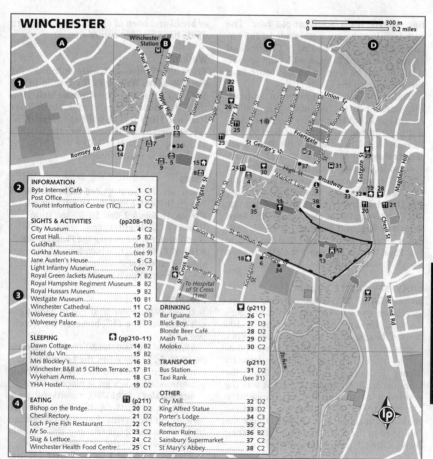

WINCHESTER

0 — 300 m
0 — 0.2 miles

INFORMATION
Byte Internet Café.................................1 C1
Post Office...2 C2
Tourist Information Centre (TIC).........3 C2

SIGHTS & ACTIVITIES (pp208–10)
City Museum.......................................4 C2
Great Hall...5 B2
Guildhall...(see 3)
Gurkha Museum...............................(see 9)
Jane Austen's House............................6 C3
Light Infantry Museum.....................(see 7)
Royal Green Jackets Museum...............7 B2
Royal Hampshire Regiment Museum...8 B2
Royal Hussars Museum.........................9 B2
Westgate Museum.............................10 B1
Winchester Cathedral........................11 C2
Wolvesey Castle................................12 D3
Wolvesey Palace................................13 D3

SLEEPING (pp210–11)
Dawn Cottage....................................14 B2
Hotel du Vin......................................15 B2
Mrs Blockley's....................................16 B3
Winchester B&B at 5 Clifton Terrace..17 B1
Wykeham Arms..................................18 C3
YHA Hostel...19 D2

EATING (p211)
Bishop on the Bridge..........................20 D2
Chesil Rectory....................................21 D2
Loch Fyne Fish Restaurant..................22 C1
Mr So...23 C2
Slug & Lettuce....................................24 C2
Winchester Health Food Centre..........25 C1

DRINKING (p211)
Bar Iguana...26 C1
Black Boy...27 D3
Blonde Beer Café...............................28 D2
Mash Tun...29 D2
Moloko..30 C2

TRANSPORT (p211)
Bus Station..31 D2
Taxi Rank......................................(see 31)

OTHER
City Mill..32 D2
King Alfred Statue..............................33 D2
Porter's Lodge....................................34 C3
Refectory...35 C2
Roman Ruins......................................36 B2
Sainsbury Supermarket......................37 C2
St Mary's Abbey.................................38 C2

11.30am or 2.15pm Sat Jun-Sep). Photography is permitted inside. Sunday services take place at 8am, 10am and 11.15am, with Evensong at 3.30pm. Evensong is also held at 5.30pm Monday to Saturday.

MUSEUMS

City Museum (☎ 863064; The Square; admission free; ☯ 10am-5pm Mon-Fri, 10am-1pm Sat & 2-5pm Sat & Sun Apr-Sep, 10am-5pm Tue-Fri, 10am-1pm Sat & 2-5pm Sat & Sun Oct-Mar) has interesting displays on Roman ruins, a collection of Winchester shop fronts and the story of Saxon and Norman Winchester.

Located in the old medieval gateway, **Westgate Museum** (☎ 848269; High St; admission free; ☯ 10am-5pm Mon-Sat, noon-5pm Sun Apr-Oct, 10am-

4pm Tue-Sat, noon-4pm Sun Feb & Mar) is a one-time debtors' prison with a macabre set of gibbeting irons last used to display the body of an executed criminal in 1777. You can also see graffiti carved into the walls by prisoners.

The **Great Hall** (☎ 846476; admission free; ☯ 10am-5pm) was the only part of Winchester Castle that Oliver Cromwell did not destroy. The castle was begun by William the Conqueror in 1067 and was added to and fortified by many successive kings of England. It was the site of a number of dramatic moments in English history, including the trial of Sir Walter Raleigh in 1603. It was last used as a court from 1938 to 1978.

The Great Hall long claimed to house King Arthur's Round Table, but don't get too excited: it's a 600-year-old fake. The wonderful steel gates were made in 1981 to commemorate the wedding of Charles and Diana. Part of the Roman wall, built around AD 200, can be seen in an enclosure near the entrance to the Great Hall.

There are also a number of military museums open to the public. All of these except the Royal Hampshire Regiment Museum are inside the Peninsula Barracks on Romsey Rd. They include the **Royal Green Jackets Museum** (☎ 828549; admission £2; ☼ 10am-5pm Mon-Sat, noon-4pm Sun), the **Gurkha Museum** (☎ 828536; www.thegurkhamuseum.co.uk; adult/child £1.50/free; ☼ 10am-5pm Mon-Sat, noon-4pm Sun), the **Light Infantry Museum** (☎ 828550; admission free; ☼ 10am-4pm Tue-Sat, noon-4pm Sun), the **Royal Hampshire Regiment Museum** (☎ 863658; Southgate St; admission free; ☼ 11am-3.30pm Mon-Fri) and the **Royal Hussars Museum** (☎ 828541; admission free; ☼ 10am-4pm Tue-Fri, noon-4pm Sat & Sun).

WOLVESEY CASTLE & PALACE

Wolvesey Castle (☎ 854766; admission free; ☼ 10am-5pm Apr-Sep) owes its name to a Saxon king's demand for an annual payment of 300 wolves' heads, or so the story goes. Work began on the castle in 1107, and was completed more than half a century later by Henry de Blois, grandson of William the Conqueror. In the medieval era it was the residence of the bishop of Winchester. Queen Mary I and Philip of Spain had their wedding breakfast here. It was largely demolished in the 1680s and today the bishop lives in the adjacent Wolvesey Palace.

HOSPITAL OF ST CROSS

Henry de Blois was a busy man, but he found time in his hectic schedule to found this **hospital** (☎ 851375; St Cross Rd; adult/child £2.50/50p; ☼ 9.30am-5pm Mon-Sat Apr-Oct, 10.30am-3.30pm Mon-Sat Nov-Mar) in 1132. Rather than simply treat the ill or house the poor, Henry's idea was that the hospital would also provide sustenance and a bed for pilgrims and crusaders before they set off to foreign lands to convert and kill the heathens. It's the oldest charitable institution in the country and is still home to 25 brothers who continue to provide alms. Within the complex is the church, the brethren hall, the kitchen and the master's garden. Take the 1-mile Water Meadows Walk to get here. The admission entitles you to the Wayfarer's Dole, a crust of bread and horn of ale (although the horn of ale is now a tiny cup of sherry).

Walking

From the Wolvesey Castle entrance, the **Water Meadows Walk** goes for a mile to the St Cross Hospital. The **Riverside Walk** runs from the castle along the bank of the River Itchen to High St. The walk up to **St Giles' Hill** is rewarded by great views over the city. It's at the top of East Hill, half a mile from the castle, and is signposted.

Tours

There are 1½-hour **guided walks** (£3, under-16 free; ☼ 11.30am & 2.30pm Mon-Sat & 11.30am only Sun May-Sep, 11.30am & 2.30pm Sat Oct-Apr) from the Wolvesy Castle entrance.

If you prefer you can take the **Phantasm Ghostwalk** (☎ 07990-876217), which leaves from outside the cathedral at sunset each day and lasts for one hour. You'll need to book ahead.

Sleeping

B&Bs in Winchester tend not to hang signs out the front. The TIC, however, has a complete list.

YHA Hostel (☎ 0870 770 6092; City Mill, 1 Water Lane; dm £10.60; ✗) Located in the beautiful 18th-century water mill on the river, this basic accommodation is a great place to stay.

Mrs Blockley's (☎ 852073; mcblockley@tcp.co.uk; 54 St Cross Rd; s/d £26/45; ✗ P) The rooms are well appointed in this charming Edwardian house. The service is friendly and it's only a short walk from the cathedral.

Winchester B&B at 5 Clifton Terrace (☎ 1962 890053; 5 Clifton Tce; s/d/family £50/60/80) On a proper terrace that could be in Bath, this elegant two-room B&B, in a balconied Georgian townhouse, has a charming and friendly proprietor who is a great cook.

Dawn Cottage (☎ 869956; dawncottage@hotmail .com; 99 Romsey Rd; s/d from £45/60) This is a truly elegant B&B with three beautiful rooms only a mile west of the city centre.

Wykeham Arms (☎ 853834; 75 Kingsgate St; s/d £80/90, r with shared bathroom from £55; ✗) This place has the best character in town so book ahead. The pub and restaurant are very welcoming and popular with the locals (see Eating, opposite).

Hotel du Vin (☎ 841414; admin@winchester.hotel duvin.co.uk; Southgate St; rooms £105-185) This luxurious, modern hotel is the most fashionable spot in town. Relax on Egyptian linen and use your minibar, VCR and CD player all at the same time.

Eating

Mr So (☎ 861234; 3 Jewry St; mains £6-9; 🍽 lunch & dinner Mon-Sat; ✕) The dark red walls and cosy atmosphere make this Winchester's best Chinese restaurant. Its menu offers Cantonese and Szechwan specialities as well as Peking Duck.

Slug & Lettuce (☎ 850666; 12-13 The Square; mains £6-11; 🍽 11am-11pm Mon-Sat, noon-10pm Sun) With gourmet sandwiches for lunch and char-grilled lamb or smoked haddock for dinner this chain spot has an upbeat atmosphere and good scene.

Bishop on the Bridge (☎ 855111; 1 High St; mains £7-10) The upscale bar food is as good as the beer and is best enjoyed on the secluded outdoor seating area overlooking the river.

Wykeham Arms (☎ 853834; 75 Kingsgate St; mains £9-13) This is an excellent place to eat (and drink), with a cheaper bar menu; although no food is served on Sunday. With school desks as tables and tankards hanging from the ceiling the look is very olde Englishe.

Loch Fyne Fish Restaurant (☎ 853566; www .lochfyne.com; 18 Jewry St; mains £9-15; 🍽 9am-10pm Mon-Thu, 9am-11pm Fri, 10am-11pm Sat, 10am-9.30pm Sun; ✕) There are fireplaces throughout this beautiful Tudor building. The atmosphere can be both lively and romantic.

Chesil Rectory (☎ 851555, 1 Chesil St; 2-/3-course lunch £30/35, 3-course dinner £45; 🍽 noon-2pm Sat, 7-10pm Tue-Sat; ✕) Here you'll find a romantic and refined setting inside Winchester's oldest house (1450). Dinner comes complete with white tablecloths and smiling, if sombre, wait staff.

For healthy self-catering there's the **Winchester Health Food Centre** (☎ 851113; 41 Jewry St; 🍽 9.30am-5.30pm Mon-Sat).

Drinking

Bar Iguana (18 Jewry St) This is one of the trendiest pubs in town, especially for students. On weekends DJs spin a pretty good mix of funk, both old and new.

Mash Tun (60 Eastgate St) Strictly for the young bohemian set, this is one of the nicest places in town to chill out and enjoy a drink in the riverside garden.

Moloko (31b The Square) The red modern interior is luscious and fun. It's popular with Winchester's more fashion-conscious crowd and known for the range of vodkas.

Blonde Beer Café (5 Bridge St) Suede bar stools, elegant chrome light fixtures and a beautiful fireplace make for a modern cool interior at this bar. The food here is an upscale version of pub grub.

On the other side of the river from The Wykeham Arms, the **Black Boy** (1 Wharf Hill) has the atmosphere of an art-house pub. Bookshelves line the walls and there is an outdoor terrace.

Getting There & Away

Winchester is 65 miles (105km) from London and 15 miles from Southampton.

BUS

National Express has several direct buses to Winchester from London Victoria Bus Station (£11, one hour 55 minutes).

Stagecoach Hampshire (☎ 01256-464501) has a good network of services linking Salisbury, Southampton, Portsmouth and Brighton. **Explorer tickets** (adult/child £5.70/4.10) are good on most Wilts & Dorset buses, which serve the region further to the west, including the New Forest.

TRAIN

There are fast links with London Waterloo, the Midlands and south coast. Trains leave about every 15 minutes from London (£20, one hour), Southampton (£5.50, 20 minutes) and Portsmouth (£9, one hour).

Getting Around

Your feet are the best form of transport. There's plenty of day parking within five minutes' walk of the centre or you can use the park-and-ride service which costs £1.50.

If you want a taxi try the rank outside Sainsbury's on Middle Brook St or phone **Wintax Taxis** (☎ 854838 or 866208) or **Wessex Cars** (☎ 853000).

PORTSMOUTH
☎ 023 / pop 442,252

Anyone interested in maritime history should flag this page. Not only is Portsmouth home to Lord Nelson's 18th-century warship, the HMS Victory, which led the charge at Trafalgar in 1805, but it is also the principal port of Britain's Royal Navy, whose ships once exported the empire to the

THE SOUTHEAST COAST

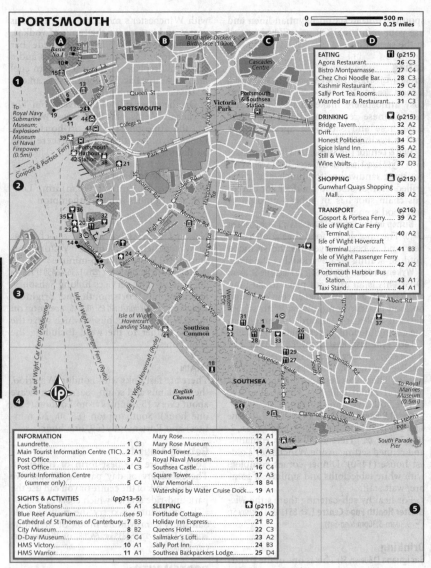

PORTSMOUTH

EATING 🍴 (p215)
Agora Restaurant...............26 C3
Bistro Montparnasse..........27 C4
Chez Choi Noodle Bar........28 C3
Kashmir Restaurant............29 C4
Sally Port Tea Rooms..........30 A2
Wanted Bar & Restaurant....31 C3

DRINKING 🍷 (p215)
Bridge Tavern....................32 A2
Drift................................33 C3
Honest Politician...............34 C3
Spice Island Inn.................35 A2
Still & West......................36 A2
Wine Vaults......................37 D3

SHOPPING 🛍 (p215)
Gunwharf Quays Shopping
Mall............................38 A2

TRANSPORT (p216)
Gosport & Portsea Ferry.....39 A2
Isle of Wight Car Ferry
Terminal......................40 A2
Isle of Wight Hovercraft
Terminal......................41 B3
Isle of Wight Passenger Ferry
Terminal......................42 A2
Portsmouth Harbour Bus
Station........................43 A1
Taxi Stand.......................44 A1

INFORMATION
Laundrette...........................1 C3
Main Tourist Information Centre (TIC)..2 A1
Post Office...........................3 A2
Post Office...........................4 C3
Tourist Information Centre
(summer only).....................5 C4

SIGHTS & ACTIVITIES   (pp213–5)
Action Stations!.....................6 A1
Blue Reef Aquarium............(see 5)
Cathedral of St Thomas of Canterbury..7 B3
City Museum.........................8 B2
D-Day Museum.....................9 C4
HMS Victory.........................10 A1
HMS Warrior........................11 A1

Mary Rose...........................12 A1
Mary Rose Museum...............13 A1
Round Tower........................14 A3
Royal Naval Museum..............15 A1
Southsea Castle....................16 C4
Square Tower........................17 A3
War Memorial.......................18 B4
Watersphips by Water Cruise Dock.. 19 A1

SLEEPING 🛌 (p215)
Fortitude Cottage..................20 A2
Holiday Inn Express...............21 B2
Queens Hotel.......................22 C3
Sailmaker's Loft...................23 A2
Sally Port Inn.......................24 B3
Southsea Backpackers Lodge....25 D4

far-flung corners of the world and now sit in ominous grey readiness. Though the city was heavily bombed during WWII, the areas around The Point and The Hard still manage to evoke an atmosphere of salty dogs and scurvy scallywags, especially if you can manage a visit during cold rainy weather, which shouldn't be too difficult. The rest of the city is fairly bland and boring with the exception of the edgy suburb of Southsea where you'll find some good beaches, bars, restaurants and places to sleep.

Orientation

Your first stop in town should be the quay known as The Hard, which is where you'll find the TIC, the entrance to the Naval Heritage Area, the Portsmouth Harbour train station and the passenger ferry terminal for the Isle of Wight. About a mile east along the water is Old Portsmouth and The Point, a cluster of sea-worn, atmospheric buildings around the old harbour, called The Camber.

Southsea, where the beaches are, as well as most of the accommodation and restaurants, is about 2 miles south of Portsmouth Harbour.

The rest of the city has a number of interesting museums, but most of your sightseeing and activities are likely to be concentrated along the water's edge.

Information

The **TIC** (☎ 9282 6722; tic@portsmouthcc.gov.uk; The Hard; 9.30am-5.45pm) provides guided tours and an accommodation service. Next to the Blue Reef Aquarium in Southsea is a **TIC branch** (☎ 9283 2464; fax 9282 7519; Clarence Esplanade; 9.30am-5.45pm May-Sep).

There's a **post office** (42 Broad St) in Old Portsmouth and another **post office** (Palmerston Rd) in Southsea. Both are open 9am to 5.30pm Monday to Saturday. There are ATMs on Osbourne Rd, Southsea, as well as a laundrette.

Internet access is available at **Southsea Backpackers Lodge** (☎ 239 28324954; Clarence Rd, Southsea; per ½-hr £2). You don't have to be a guest to use it.

Sights & Activities

FLAGSHIP PORTSMOUTH (NAVAL HERITAGE AREA)

The **Naval Heritage Area** (☎ 9286 1512; adult/child 3-for-2 ticket £13.75/11, all-inclusive attraction ticket £15.50/12.50, season ticket £28/23.50; 10am-5.30pm Apr-Oct, 10am-5pm Nov-Mar) is the city's main (some say only) draw, and it's a humdinger. Three classic ships and a handful of excellent museums form the core of England's tribute to the historical might of the Royal Navy, on the edge of the country's most important naval port. Even the most devoted landlubber should find this a good day out.

And it is indeed a full day out. There are individual admission costs for each ship or you can buy a three-for-two ticket that includes any three attractions for the price of two. It is valid for seven days. If you want to see more than one attraction, we recommend the all-inclusive ticket, which covers single admissions to all of the ships and museums. The season ticket offers unlimited entry to all the attractions for two years…and a subscription to the *Semaphore* newsletter.

The Ships

The main attraction is **HMS Victory** (adult/child £9.50/8), Lord Nelson's flagship at the Battle of Trafalgar in 1805. This remarkable ship carried up to 900 crew and had a top speed of 10mph when she led the British fleet at Trafalgar, which resulted in victory against the French but cost Nelson his life. The ship limped into harbour and out of active duty in 1922, where it was fully refurbished and converted into a museum, although incredibly it remains in commission and as such is subject to military regulations, which basically means no photography.

Which is a shame, because the pre-timed, 40-minute tours of the ship are one of the best you'll find anywhere. Conducted at breakneck speed but with liberal doses of great humour, the tours are as close as you'll get to a step back in time.

Nearby are the remains of the **Mary Rose** (adult/child £9.70/8). Built in 1509 under the orders of Henry VIII, the 700-tonne ship sank in shallow water off Portsmouth in 1545. There was much speculation about why she sank. At the time it was put down to 'human folly and bad luck'. The ship and her time-capsule contents were raised to the surface in 1982, after 437 years under water. Finds from the ship are displayed in the Mary Rose Museum (see p214).

Dating from 1860, and at the cutting edge of the technology of the time, **HMS Warrior** (adult/child £9.70/8) was a transition ship, as wood was forsaken for iron and sail for steam. The four decks of the ship illustrate life in the navy in the Victorian era. It's not nearly as impressive as the others though. You are free to wander around at your leisure.

Royal Naval Museum

Housed in five separate galleries, this huge **museum** (admission £3.75) has an extensive collection of ship models, dioramas of naval battles, and exhibits on the history of the Royal Navy, medals and paintings. Audiovisual displays recreate the Battle of Trafalgar and one even lets you take command of a battleship – see if you can cure the scurvy and avoid mutiny and execution. One gallery is entirely devoted to Lord Nelson and, among many other things, there are personal items from his private ship quarters – life at sea must have been pretty tough for the officers, who had their own wine coolers!

Mary Rose Museum

A massive salvage operation that began in 1965 resulted in the raising of the *Mary Rose*, and you discover all there is to know about the ship and its recovery at this fascinating **museum** (adult/child £9.70/8) through exhibits, audiovisuals and great sound effects. It also recounts the failed salvage attempt made in the late 16th century by two hopeful Venetians. A 15-minute film about the raising of the Mary Rose is shown every half-hour. The ticket also covers admission to the ship itself (see The Ships, p213).

Action Stations!

Opened in 2001, this **interactive experience** (adult/child £9.70/8) is not quite a museum but a showcase (some say recruitment drive) for the modern navy. Inside you'll find movies and interactive multimedia displays, and find out whether you have what it takes to make it in the navy. Apparently we don't.

GOSPORT

On the other side of Portsmouth Harbour is Gosport, which is easily reached by ferry from The Hard. Not surprisingly, the naval theme is continued here.

Royal Navy Submarine Museum

This **museum** (☎ 9252 9217; adult/child £4.50/3; ⏰ 10am-5.30pm Apr-Oct, 10am-4.30pm Nov-Mar) is the only place in Britain where you can climb aboard a submarine, in this case the HMS Alliance. It may be a massive and impressive bit of naval engineering, but conditions were awfully cramped for the sailors.

Explosion! Museum of Naval Firepower

If munitions and ordnance (and their effects) are of interest, then this new **museum** (☎ 9250 5600; Priddy's Hard; adult/child £5.50/3.50; ⏰ 10am-5.30pm Apr-Oct, 10am-4.30pm Nov-Mar) will tell, and show, you everything you need to know. The entire experience is a showcase for graphic designers and computer animators to display their skills in recreating the horror and fear of being under attack, and they do so quite convincingly.

OTHER SIGHTS & ACTIVITIES

One of the more pleasant spots in town is **The Point**, along the cobbled streets of Old Portsmouth, which has a few atmospheric old pubs that, on a sunny day, are ideal spots to sit and watch the ferries and navy ships go in and out of the harbour.

Nearby is the **Cathedral of St Thomas of Canterbury**, although only fragments of the original 12th-century church remain. The nave and tower were rebuilt around 1690 and more additions were made in 1703 and between 1938 and 1939. Immediately south of Old Portsmouth is the **Round Tower**, originally built by Henry V, a stretch of old fort walls and the **Square Tower** of 1494.

At the Southsea end of the waterfront there's a cluster of attractions on Clarence Esplanade. The **Blue Reef Aquarium** (☎ 9287 5222; admission £5.95; 9.30am-5pm Mar-Oct, 10am-3pm Nov-Feb) is more interesting than most other sea-life centres in that the attractions – including a huge walk-through aquarium filled with coloured corals and plenty of different fish – have a much more hands-on feel.

Portsmouth was a major departure point for the Allied D-Day forces in 1944 and the **D-Day Museum** (☎ 9282 7261; Clarence Esplanade; admission £5; ⏰ 10am-5.30pm Apr-Oct, 10am-5pm Nov-Mar) recounts the story of the Normandy landing with the 83m-long Overlord Embroidery (inspired by the Bayeux Tapestry) and other exhibits.

Southsea Castle (☎ 9282 7261; admission £2.50; ⏰ 10am-5.30pm Apr-Oct) was built by Henry VIII to protect the town against French invasion. It was altered in the early 19th century to accommodate more guns and soldiers, and a tunnel under the moat. It's said that Henry VIII watched the *Mary Rose* sink from the castle.

The **Royal Marines Museum** (☎ 9281 9385; Barracks Rd; admission £4.75; ⏰ 10am-4pm Jun-Aug, 10am-3.30pm Sep-May) tells the story of the navy's elite force, while an assault course outside puts the kids through the paces.

City Museum (☎ 9282 7261; Museum Rd; admission free; ⏰ 10am-5pm) tells the history of Portsmouth through audiovisual displays, reconstructions of various rooms in typical houses from the 17th century to the 1950s, and other exhibits.

Charles Dickens' Birthplace (☎ 9282 7261; 393 Old Commercial Rd; admission £2.50; ⏰ 10am-5.30pm Apr-Oct) is furnished in a style appropriate to 1812, the year of Dickens' birth, but the only genuine piece of Dickens' furniture is the couch on which he died in 1870!

Tours
To be able to see all the ships, old and new, from a different angle, you can take a **Waterships by Water** (per adult/child £3.50/2) 40-minute guided cruise around the harbour. If you have an all-inclusive attraction ticket the cruise is included.

Sleeping
The hotels and B&Bs in Portsmouth could use a thorough updating. That said, some of the better B&Bs are near The Point in Old Portsmouth, though you'll find a bed in Southsea as well. Rooms fill up quickly so you'll need to book in advance.

Southsea Backpackers Lodge (☎ 9283 2495; 4 Florence Rd, Southsea; dm/d £10/25) The friendly owners have made the place homely and comfortable.

Sailmaker's Loft (☎ 9282 3045; sailmakersloft@aol .com; 5 Bath Sq; s/d £25/54) This is so close to the sea you can hear the ferry boats coming in.

Fortitude Cottage (☎ 9282 3748; fortcott@aol .com; 51 Broad St; s/d from £35/58) With views of the ferry port but lacking the charm of Sailmaker's, this is a clean and comfortable back-up.

Queens Hotel (☎ 9282 2466; www.bw-queenshotel .co.uk; Clarence Pde, Southsea; s/d from £40/80; P) Join a somewhat elderly clientele in this stately mansion with views of the water. The lobby is packed with marble columns and ceiling murals. It may be the best place in town.

Sally Port Inn (☎ 9282 1860; fax 9282 1293; High St; s/d from £40/60, f £75) This 16th-century inn is a bit musty and old which is one way of saying it's historic. There are no en suite facilities but doubles have showers in the room.

Holiday Inn Express (☎ 0870 417 6161; The Plaza, Gunwharf Qays; rooms from £70; P ⊠) The rooms won't surprise you but they are sparkling new and it's inside the Gunwharf Quays shopping centre, making it a short trip to drag back your newly acquired loot.

Eating
Southsea offers a variety of dining options, many of which are quite tasty.

Sallyport Tea Rooms (☎ 9281 6265; 35 Broad St; breakfasts £3.75-5.25, lunch £3-5; 🕙 10am-5pm; ⊠)

As spry as she ever was, the 75-year-old proprietor serves up traditional tearoom delights such as a smoked mackerel and horseradish baguette while you enjoy the 1940s jazz.

Chez Choi Noodle Bar (☎ 9282 6900; 46 Osborne Rd; mains £3.95-30; 🕙 lunch & dinner Mon-Sat; ⊠) This small and cosy, newly remodelled spot serves Szechwan and Cantonese style cuisine.

Kashmir (☎ 9282 2013; 91 Palmerston Rd; mains £4-10; 🕙 lunch & dinner; ⊠) The lush colours of this Indian restaurant (that stays open as late as 1am Friday and Saturday) are as pleasing as the food.

Wanted Bar & Restaurant (☎ 9282 6858; 39 Osborne Rd; mains £4-10; 🕙 11am-11pm; ⊠) An eclectic and inventive menu accompanies soul jazz in this high style bar and restaurant, serving steak, mussels and gnocchi.

Agora Restaurant (☎ 9282 2617; 9 Clarendon Rd; mains £7-10; 🕙 9am-4pm & 5.30-11.30pm; ⊠) This Turkish hookah bar is tucked into an English Tudor building with exposed beams on the ceiling and tasty Greek and Turkish food on the plates. There's a children's menu.

Bistro Montparnasse (☎ 9281 6754; 103 Palmerstown Rd; 2-/3-course lunch £13/16, dinner £20/25; 🕙 lunch & dinner Tue-Sat; ⊠) This cosy but feisty bistro serves inventive French cuisine with an English flavour amid bright orange walls and old wood floors.

Drinking
A few pubs on The Point are good for a summer's evening drink, but the real action is to be found in Southsea.

Drift (78 Palmerston Rd) This is a very atmospheric and hip London-style bar and lounge with DJs on the weekends. Be sure to visit the unusual bathrooms.

The Honest Politician (47 Elm Grove) This wonderfully mellow bar is perfect for an afternoon's drink over the newspaper.

Wine Vaults (43-47 Albert Rd) This is another great bar that is very popular with the local intelligentsia.

Popular bars on The Point include **Bridge Tavern** (54 East St), whose fireplace makes for a cosy afternoon drinking companion on a rainy day, **Still & West** (2 Bath Sq), with an upscale sea-dog's look about it, and **Spice Island Inn** (65 Broad St), with nice wooden booths to sip a pint in.

Getting There & Away

Portsmouth is 75 miles (121km) southwest of London.

BOAT

There are a number of ways of getting to the Isle of Wight from Portsmouth. (For information see p221.) **Condor Ferries** (☎ 0105-761555) runs a car-and-passenger service from Portsmouth to Jersey and Guernsey (6½ hours) and costs from £55 one way. **P&O Ferries** (☎ 0870 242 4999) sails twice a week to Bilbao in Spain and daily to Cherbourg (five to six hours, two hours longer at night) and Le Havre in France. **Brittany Ferries** (☎ 0870 901 2400; www.brittanyferries.co.uk) has overnight services to St Malo, Caen (six hours) and Cherbourg in France. For more information, check the website. The continental Ferryport is north of Flagship Portsmouth.

BUS

There are National Express buses every hour or so from London (£12, 2¼ hours), some via Heathrow airport (£12, 2¾ hours) and Southhampton (£2.75, 50 minutes). Between Brighton and Portsmouth a bus leaves every half-hour (£3.20, 3½ hours).

Stagecoach Coastline bus No 700 also runs between Brighton and Portsmouth and on to Southampton via Chichester (half-hourly Monday to Saturday, hourly on Sunday). No 69 runs to Winchester (one hour 50 minutes, hourly).

TRAIN

There are trains every 10 minutes or so from London Victoria (£17.50, two hours 20 minutes) and Waterloo stations (£21, 1½ hours).

Trains from Portsmouth go to Brighton (£12.80, one hour 40 minutes, hourly), Winchester (£7.30, one hour, hourly) and Chichester (£4.90, 40 minutes, three hourly).

For the ships at Flagship Portsmouth get off at the final stop, Portsmouth Harbour.

Getting Around

Local bus No 6 operates between the Portsmouth Harbour bus station, right beside the train station, and South Parade Pier in Southsea. Bus Nos 17 or 6 will take you from the station to Old Portsmouth.

Ferries shuttle back and forth between The Hard and Gosport (£1.60 return, bicycles travel free) every few minutes Monday to Saturday (every 15 minutes on Sunday). For a taxi try **MPS Taxis** (☎ 8261 1111) in Southsea. There's also a taxi stand near the TIC in Flagship Portsmouth.

SOUTHAMPTON

☎ 023 / pop 304,400

Frankly, there isn't much to see or do in Southampton, but it wasn't always the case. Its strategic location on the Solent – an 8-mile inlet into which flow the Itchen and Test Rivers – made it one of England's most important medieval trading centres, doing roaring business with France and other continental countries. Even when trade declined, Southampton turned its efforts to large-scale shipbuilding, and made a good job of it too (the *Queen Mary* was built here). This is also where the *Titanic* set sail on its doomed voyage in 1912; 600 local residents (mostly crew members) were killed in the tragedy. In addition, the city ran a profitable sideline in aircraft manufacturing, but during WWII its industries were the targets of a concerted bombing effort: over two nights alone, more than 30,000 bombs rained down on factories and virtually everything else as well.

Therein lies Southampton's biggest problem. Apart from the impressive city walls, there is little left of the town's medieval past, and the modern city is hardly beautiful. Still, there are a few things to pique your interest while waiting for the Isle of Wight ferry, including a couple of museums and a large-scale waterfront shopping and entertainment complex, from where you may also catch a glimpse of the huge ocean liners that still dock here, including the *QEII*.

The **TIC** (☎ 8083 3333; 9 Civic Centre Rd; ☒ 8.30am-5.30pm Mon, Tue & Thu-Sat, 10am-5.30pm Wed) offers free **guided walks** (☒ 10.30am Sun & bank holidays year-round, 10.30am & 2.30pm daily late-Jun–mid-Sep) of the old town. Meet at the Bargate on High St.

Sights & Activities

Opposite the TIC is the massive Civic Centre, which houses the excellent **Southampton Art Gallery** (☎ 8083 2277; admission free; ☒ 10am-5pm Tue-Sat, 1-4pm Sun). The permanent collection features the best of 20th-century British art, including work by Sir Stanley Spencer, Matthew Smith and Philip Wilson Steer.

The tragic story of the Titanic, as well as the history of Southampton's port since 1838, is told in detail at the **Maritime Museum** (☎ 8022 3941; The Wool House, Town Quay; admission free; ⏰ 10am-5pm Tue-Sat & 2-5pm Sun Apr-Oct, 10am-4pm Tue-Sat & 1-4pm Sun Nov-Mar). The building was used as a prison, and as an aircraft factory. Ring to ensure the museum is open.

Of Southampton's medieval heritage, the timbered **Medieval Merchant's House** (☎ 8022 1503; 58 French St; adult/child £2/1.50; ⏰ 10am-5pm) is a faithfully restored property dating from 1290.

Getting There & Away

AIR
The ultra-modern **Southampton International Airport** (☎ 0870 040009) has flights to Brussels, Paris, Zurich, Amsterdam, Dublin and major holiday resorts in Spain. Bus 101 leaves regularly from the airport to the city centre. There are four trains hourly between the airport and the main train station (£2, seven minutes).

BOAT
Ferries run by **Red Funnel** (☎ 8033 4010; www.redfunnel.co.uk) go to the Isle of Wight and there is a ferry service to Hythe in the New Forest (p219). **Channel Hoppers** (☎ 01481-728 680, info@channelhoppers.com) has a ferry service between Southampton and the Channel Islands and France.

BUS
National Express coaches run to Southampton from London and Heathrow hourly (£12, 2½ hours). National Express also runs a 6.45pm bus to Lymington (40 minutes) via Lyndhurst (20 minutes) in the New Forest.

Stagecoach Bus No 700 runs between Portsmouth and Southampton. Nos 47 and 29 run between Southampton and Winchester (£2.40, 40 minutes) every half-hour with reduced services on Sunday. Wilts & Dorset bus No 56/56A goes to all the main towns in the New Forest hourly (every two hours on Sunday). Explorer tickets are valid on these routes.

TRAIN
Trains from Portsmouth run three times an hour (£6.45, 45 minutes). Trains for Winchester (£4, 17 minutes) leave about every 15 minutes.

NEW FOREST

As England's newest national park, the New Forest is a remarkable 150-sq-mile (388-sq-km) swathe of woodland and wild heaths that is the largest area of relatively natural vegetation in England. But it's not all wildlife and warblers down here (though there are some very rare species of birds). The Forest is home to a network of very prosperous villages with upper-crust prep schools and well-preserved traditions dating back 1000 years (for more details see the boxed text p219).

To really get a feel for this wildlife-filled landscape, it's best to rent a car. Better still is to get off the roads and onto some of the excellent cycling and walking tracks. The New Forest is a popular destination for campers, but make sure you pitch your tent in a proper campsite; the TIC in Lyndhurst has a brochure with all the details. For more general information click to www.thenewforest.co.uk.

Activities

CYCLING
The New Forest is a great place to cycle and there are several rental shops. You will need to pay a deposit (usually £20) and provide one or two forms of identification. You can pick up cycle route maps from TICs and bicycle shops.

AA Bike Hire (☎ 8028 3349; www.aabikehirenewforest.co.uk; Fern Glen, Gosport Lane, Lyndhurst; per ½/full day £6/10)

Cyclexperience (☎ 01590-624204; www.cyclex.co.uk; Brookley Rd, Brockenhurst)

Forest Leisure Cycling (☎ 01425-403584; www.forestleisurecycling.co.uk; The Cross, Village Centre, Burley; per day from £10)

HORSE RIDING
This is a great way to explore the New Forest but we're not talking about saddling up one of the wild ponies here. There are a couple of trail-riding set-ups where you can arrange a pleasant one- or two-hour ride. Both places welcome beginners.

Sandy Balls (☎ 01425-653042; www.sandy-balls.co.uk) (honestly!) is at Godshill in Fordingbridge

Burley-Villa School of Riding (☎ 01425-610278) is off the B3058, just south of New

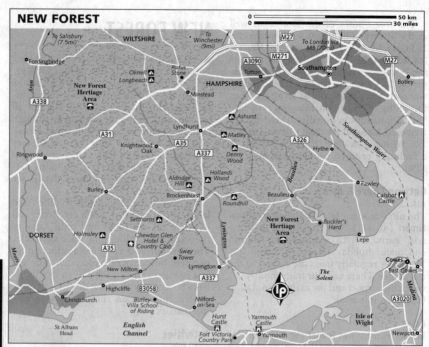

NEW FOREST

0 _____ 50 km
0 _____ 30 miles

Milton and has Western riding, English riding and Forest Hacking.

Getting There & Around
Southampton and Bournemouth bracket the New Forest and there are regular bus services from both.

Busabout tickets offer unlimited travel on main bus lines for seven days and cost £21/12 per adult/child. The Solent Blue line X1 service goes through New Forest taking the Bournemouth-Burley-Lyndhurst-Southampton route.

LYNDHURST
☎ 023 / pop 2281
The clean well-to-do town of Lyndhurst is a pleasant stopover on your way through the woodland. It's larger than many of the other small villages in the area (though not by much) and it has a couple of good local pubs and restaurants. Lyndhurst would make a good base for exploring the surrounding countryside.

The **TIC** (☎ 8028 2269; www.thenewforest.co.uk; High St; 10am-5pm), next to the library, sells

a wide variety of information on the New Forest including cycling maps (£2 to £3.50), a map showing walking tracks (£1.50), a more comprehensive Collins map (£5.99), and a free camping and caravanning guide. It also sells the Ordnance Survey (OS) map (No 22, £5.95) which covers the area in greatest detail.

Sleeping & Eating
South View (☎ 8028 2224; Gosport Lane; per person with shared bathroom £20, s/d with private bathroom £30/50; ✗) This eight-room B&B has a friendly atmosphere and a lovely dog.

Primrose Cottage (☎ 1300 341352; 29 The Street; r per person £23; ✗) This cob and thatched roof cottage has an Inglenook fireplace with a wood stove but modern amenities in the rooms.

Le Poussin at Parkhill (☎ 8028 2944; www.le poussinatparkhill.co.uk; Beaulieu Rd; r from £65; 2-course lunch £15, 4-course dinner from £35; ✗) One of Hampshire's finest hotels, Le Poussin has sumptuous rooms overlooking its own private park. The hotel is also home to an award-winning restaurant.

VERDERERS, AGISTERS & PONIES

The New Forest is the only area of England to remain relatively untouched since Norman times, thanks in large part to its unsuitability as agricultural land. If the presence of so much unfenced territory is remarkable enough, what is truly fascinating about the New Forest is that it still retains a code of law first handed down during the reign of William the Conqueror.

Although the presence of wild ponies was recorded by King Knut's Forest Law of 1016, William officially declared the whole area a royal hunting preserve in 1079, thereby protecting it from any form of development. The crown still owns 100 sq miles (260 sq km) of the New Forest, though it is the Forestry Commission that has been responsible for its maintenance since 1924.

The remaining 50 sq miles (130 sq km) are owned by verderers, or commoners, who in the pre-automobile age reared the ponies as work horses. Today they are either reared as riding ponies or left to graze the land at will. The verderers' status is protected by the Commoners' Charter, first laid down in 1077, which guaranteed them six basic rights, the most important of which is the 'common', or right, to pasture. Every year, the 300-odd verderers that still exercise their rights gather to elect five agisters, who are responsible for the daily management of the 3000 ponies, 1800 cattle and smaller numbers of donkeys, pigs and sheep in the New Forest, including ensuring that each pony bears the brand of the verderer who owns it.

Now that the New Forest has received official National Park status (the first new park in the country in 50 years), locals are worried that their rights as commoners will be infringed upon and they are actively campaigning to make sure that doesn't happen.

Outsiders are more than welcome to wander freely throughout the forest, but are strongly requested not to feed or touch the ponies. These are wild animals, and feeding them will attract them onto the roads; furthermore they have a nasty bite. To protect the ponies, as well as cyclists and walkers, there is a 40mph speed limit on unfenced roads. If you find an injured pony phone Lyndhurst Police on ☎ 023-8028 2813; try to stay with the animal (but don't touch it) to protect it from further injury.

The Crown Hotel (☎ 8028 2922; www.crownhotel -lyndhurst.co.uk; High St; s/d from £80/135; **P**)) Situated in an old English country house with mullioned windows and lots of character, this is one of the nicest places to stay. The rates rise £5 July to October and reduce by £10 for stays of more than one night.

Mad Hatter Tea Rooms (☎ 8028 2341; 10 High St; mains £4-6; ☺ 10am-5pm; ✗) You can get a delicious breakfast, ploughman's lunch and rarebits at this beautiful café. A children's menu is available.

La Pergola Ristorante & Wine Bar (☎ 8028 4184; Southampton Rd; mains £8-15; ☺ lunch & dinner Tue-Sun; ✗) It is decidedly lively, but there are some romantic corners in this old pub that serves pizza pasta, antipasta, steak, veal and other classic Italian fare.

Getting There & Away

Wilts & Dorset bus Nos 56 and 56a run twice hourly from Southampton to Lyndhurst (£2. /4.50 one-way/return) daily except Sunday.

Lyndhurst has no train station, and the nearest stop is Brockenhurst, 8 miles south.

Trains run every half-hour from London Waterloo station via Brockenhurst (£25.60, 1½ hours) to Bournemouth, Poole and Weymouth.

White Horse Ferries (☎ 8084 0722) operates a service from Southampton to Hythe, 13 miles southwest of Lyndhurst, every half-hour (£3.90 return, 12 minutes).

AROUND LYNDHURST
Beaulieu & National Motor Museum

The New Forest's most impressive and most visited (non-natural) attraction is a tourist complex, **Beaulieu** (☎ 01590-612345; admission £14; ☺ 10am-6pm May-Sep, 10am-5pm Oct-Apr), pronounced bewley. Once the site of England's most important Cistercian monastery, it was founded in 1204 by order of King John as an act of contrition after he ordered that a group of monks be trampled to death. The 3200-hectare abbey was dissolved following Henry VIII's monastic land-grab of 1536 and sold to the ancestors of the Montague family in 1538.

Lord Montague's **National Motor Museum** is the biggest attraction. There are 250 vehicles on show, including buses, cars and motorcycles spanning the whole history of motor transport. As well as some classics, you can run your hands along a £650,000 McLaren F1 and the jet-powered *Bluebird*, which broke the land-speed record (403mph, or 649km/h) in 1964 (see p668). There's also a ride-through display giving you the lowdown on car history. Rev-heads will love it, but you don't need to be one to enjoy it.

Beaulieu's **Palace House** (11am-6pm May-Sep, 11am-5pm Oct-Easter) was once the abbey gatehouse and is an odd combination of 14th-century Gothic and 19th-century Scottish Baronial architecture, as converted by Baron Montague in the 1860s. Unlike other manor homes you might visit, this place really feels like a home and exudes a certain warmth.

The 13th-century **abbey** has an excellent exhibit on everyday life in the monastery. If you're into ghosts, the abbey is supposed to be one of England's most haunted places.

Bus No 49 runs to Beaulieu from Brockenhurst Station at 11.05am, 12.35pm, 2.05pm and 3.35pm (45 minutes). You can also get here from Southampton by taking a ferry to Hythe and catching bus Nos 112 or X9. Solent Blue Line buses also run here from various towns in New Forest.

Trains from London Waterloo run to Brockenhurst (p218), from where it's a short taxi ride.

BUCKLER'S HARD
☎ 01590

A secluded hamlet of historic 18th-century cottages, this is one of the most beautiful destinations in the New Forest. It was the brainchild of John, a Duke of Montague, who in 1722 wanted to build a port to finance an expedition to the West Indies. Despite a number of attractive incentives (99-year lease at a nominal rent and timber to build a house), only six houses were built by 1740 and his expedition never got off the ground.

But then came war with France, and a number of Nelson's warships were built in the port, whose sheltered location and gravel-hard seafront made it the perfect spot to build in secrecy and in a hurry. By the middle of the 19th century the shipbuilding industry had died out, but in 1894 the Gosport Steam Launch Company began organising day trips here from Southampton, and a tourist destination was born.

Today, the whole place is a well-run **heritage centre** (614645; adult/child £4.50/3; 10.30am-5pm Easter-Nov, 11am-4pm Dec-Easter). You can wander around to your heart's content, but be sure to stop by the **Maritime Museum** and its excellent exhibits on the history of great ships. Also here is a labourer's cottage from the late 18th century, immaculately preserved for tourist curiosity.

The Master Builders House Hotel (616253; www.themasterbuilders.co.uk; s/d from £125/225) was exactly that before it was converted into a hotel with 25 luxuriously appointed rooms. Also on the premises is a fine restaurant (mains from £11) and the Yachtsman's Bar, which serves delicious pub grub for around £9 a dish.

Buckler's Hard is 2 miles downstream from Beaulieu along the river, which has a walking path the entire route.

LYMINGTON
☎ 01590 / pop 14,227

With a bustling High St full of book shops, old inns and restaurants, the quaint harbour and market town of Lymington is a great base for visits to both the New Forest and the Isle of Wight. Lymington was once a centre for salt manufacture and it has long been a yachting centre, still reflected in its two marinas and the occasional yacht race. It was also known as a smugglers port. The **St Barbe Museum** (676969; New St; admission £4; 10am-4pm Mon-Sat) has a detailed history of Lymington's past and its dependence on the nearby ocean.

The **TIC** (689000, www.thenewforest.co.uk; New St; 10am-5pm) is a block off the High St next to the St Barbe Museum and sells walking tours of town (25p) as well as a variety of information on the New Forest in general. They will also help you find accommodation. More information can be found on www.hants .gov.uk/localpages/south_west/lymington.

Free Internet can be had at the Lymington **library** (673050; North Close; 9.30am-5pm Mon-Sat), which is a few blocks from Lymington Town train station.

ATMs, banks and a variety of shops are on the Georgian and Victorian High St. The bus station is behind the optometrists on the High St and there's a post office at the end of the High St near St Thomas Church. There are also train links to Southhampton and destinations onward.

SOMETHING SPECIAL

A mile north of the pretty little village of New Milton, on the southern outskirts of the New Forest, you'll find **Chewton Glen Hotel & Country Club** (☎ 01425-275341; www.chewtonglen.com; r £250-720), a spot that Gourmet magazine calls 'the best country house hotel in the world'. The service at this resort is unsurpassed, and every comfort is provided for, including full spa treatments and a range of outdoor activities including golf and croquet clinics. For those looking to unwind in style look no further.

Sleeping & Eating

The Angel Inn (☎ 672050; angelinn.lymingont@eldridge -pope.co.uk; 108 High St; s/d from £35/70; ☒ ℗) This highly recommended eclectic boutique hotel is housed in a newly remodelled Georgian coach inn and features clean modern rooms and an imaginative bistro downstairs. All rooms are en suite and rates are £10 less during the week.

Café Uno (☎ 688689; 118 High St; mains £5-14; ☽ lunch & dinner; ☒) For a fun but elegant atmosphere with brick-oven pizza and Italian cooking, try this colourful spot. With rustic wood tables, yellow ceilings and orange walls, the casual cool restaurant promotes a lively chatter on the weekends. Children are welcome.

Getting There & Away

Lymington has two train stations: Lymington Town and Lymington Pier, which is where the Isle of Wight ferry drops off and picks up. Trains to Southampton leave roughly every half-hour, take 40 minutes and cost £7.20.

Wightlink Ferries (☎ 0990 827744; www.wight link.co.uk) connects Lymington to Yarmouth on the Isle of Wight every half-hour for about £9.

ISLE OF WIGHT

A holiday getaway for yachties, cyclists, ramblers and beachgoers alike, the Isle of Wight may be only a couple of miles off the Hampshire coast, but it's also a world away. Here you'll find grazing cattle and sheep on lush green hills that roll down to 25 miles of clean and unspoilt beaches. In fact, more than a third of the island is an Area of Outstanding Natural Beauty (AONB). Plus, the weather here is milder than anywhere else in Britain, which all adds up to a great place to come to enjoy the outdoors. Although most visitors are day trippers,

there's enough here to warrant staying at least a couple of days, particularly if you set about exploring the lovely coastal towns.

For good online information, check out www.islandbreaks.co.uk.

Activities

CYCLING

The island is a cyclist's paradise. There is a 62-mile (100km) cycleway, and in 2002 a Cycling Festival was inaugurated; check with the TICs for details. Enthusiasts should also check out the *Cyclist's Guide to the Isle of Wight* (£3.50) by Ron Crick and the two-volume *Cycling Wight* by John Goodwin and Ian Williams (£3 each), all sold at **Offshore Sports** (☎ 866269; www.offshore -sports.co.uk; 19 Orchardleigh Rd, Shanklin or ☎ 290514; 2-4 Birmingham Rd, Cowes).

Bike rentals are available in Cowes, Freshwater Bay, Ryde, Sandown, Shanklin, Ventnor and Yarmouth. **Wavells** (☎ 760738; The Square, Yarmouth; per half-day/day £7/12, deluxe £10/15 for deluxe) with free helmets and locks.

WALKING

There are 500 miles (800km) of well-marked walking paths and bridleways, which make the island one of the best places in southern England for less strenuous walks and gentle rambling. They are so serious about their walking here that there is an annual **Walking Festival** (☎ 813818), which takes place over two weeks in May. In 2004 the festival offered 160 different guided walks over more than 500 miles of trails. The event draws walkers from around the world.

Getting There & Away

Wightlink (☎ 0990 827744; www.wightlink.co.uk) operates a passenger ferry from The Hard in Portsmouth to Ryde pier (15 minutes) and a car-and-passenger ferry (35 minutes) to Fishbourne. They run about every half-hour (£9.90 day return). Car fares start at £49 for a day return.

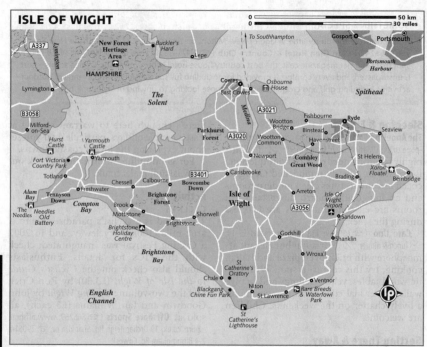

ISLE OF WIGHT

Hovertravel (☎ 01983-811000; www.hovertravel .co.uk) hovercrafts zoom back and forth between Southsea (near Portsmouth) and Ryde (£8.60 day return, 10 minutes).

Red Funnel (☎ 0870 444 8898; www.redfunnel.co.uk) operates car ferries between Southampton and East Cowes (£8.70 return, from £51 with car, 55 minutes) and high-speed passenger ferries between Southampton and West Cowes (£8/9.80 one-way/return, 10 minutes). The Wightlink car ferry between Lymington (in the New Forest) and Yarmouth costs £7.50 for passengers and £49.50 for cars. The trip takes half an hour and ferries run every half-hour. Children travel for half price.

Getting Around

Southern Vectis (☎ 827005; 32 High St, Cowes) operates a comprehensive bus service around the island. Buses circumnavigate the island hourly, and run between the towns on the eastern side of the island about every 30 minutes. Trains run twice hourly from Ryde to Shanklin and the Isle of Wight Steam Railway branches off from this line at Havenstreet and goes to Wootton.

Rover Tickets give you unlimited use of buses and trains for £6.50 for a day, £10.50 for two days and £27 for a week.

COWES
☎ 01983

Located at the northern tip of the island, Cowes is a hilly, Georgian harbour town. This is a major yachting centre and the late-July/early-August **Cowes Week** is an important international yachting event. Naturally, the town has a **maritime museum** (☎ 01983 293394; Beckford Rd; admission free; ☯ 9.30am-4.30pm Mon-Wed, Fri & Sat).

Since its appearance in the film *Mrs Brown*, **Osborne House** (EH; ☎ 200022; admission £8.50; ☯ 10am-6pm Apr-Sep) has become English Heritage's most visited attraction. The house was built between 1845 and 1851, and Queen Victoria died here in 1901. Osborne House has an antipodean connection: the Australian state of Victoria's Government House, near Melbourne's Botanic Gardens, is a copy, built in 1872. The house is in East Cowes, which is separated from the rest of the town by the River Medina, and linked by a chain ferry. From October to March, it opens from 10am to 4pm Sunday through Thursday for guided tours only (£5.50/3.50 per adult/child).

Sleeping & Eating

Doghouse (☎ 293677; Crossways Rd, East Cowes; s/d £25/35) This four-diamond rated guesthouse has two gorgeous rooms, impeccable service and is anything but punishment.

Fountain (☎ 292397; High St; mains around £7) Here you'll find a wonderful, traditional old pub that serves filling meals as well as a good pint.

RYDE

☎ 01983

Most visitors to the island land at Ryde, and then move on very quickly. It has a handful of elegant Victorian buildings, but it's the least pretty of the island's towns.

There is a **TIC** (☎ 813818; 81-83 Union St). At **St Cecilia's Abbey** (Appley Rise) you can hear Gregorian chants by Benedictine nuns during Mass at 9.15am daily (10am Sunday).

Seahaven Hotel (☎ 563069; seahaven@netguides.co.uk; St Thomas St; s/d £29/50) is a comfortable Victorian house with great views of the sea – provided you ask for a room at the front.

AROUND RYDE

Binstead

The main reason for stopping in this quiet little village is to visit the ruins of **Quarr Abbey**, built in 1132 and one of the island's oldest Christian relics. It was dissolved in 1536 and comprehensively plundered thereafter, leaving a set of stunted-but-evocative ruins. Just to the west is another **abbey** (🕑 9am-9pm), built in 1908 for the Benedictines. You can hear vespers daily at 5pm. Binstead is 2½ miles southwest of Ryde.

Brading

What is believed to be the island's oldest standing house is in the middle of this pretty village about 4 miles south of Ryde. Unfortunately, it now houses the **Isle of Wight Wax Works** (☎ 4584477; admission £5.25; 🕑 10am-5pm), which is pretty much what you thought it would be, including the not-so-scary Chamber of Horrors. Hours are extended during high season.

Just south of the village are the remains of a **Roman Villa** (☎ 406223; admission £3; 🕑 9.30am-5pm Apr-Oct), which *are* worth visiting for the exquisitely preserved mosaics. The villa's owners were – apparently – notoriously bacchanalian in their pursuit of pleasure, which perhaps explains the mosaic of a man with a cockerel's head.

Bembridge

The quiet town of Bembridge, about 3 miles southeast of Ryde, is a nice spot to chill out. If you're looking for something to do you should pop your head into the pretty interesting **Shipwreck Centre & Maritime Museum** (☎ 872223; Sherborne St; admission £2.70; 🕑 9.30am-5pm Apr-Oct), basically a collection of nautical bits and bobs salvaged from the sea by the museum's diver owner. The village's **Heritage Centre** (☎ 873100; admission 50p; 🕑 10am-4pm Mon-Fri, 10am-noon Sat Mar-Oct) is stacked with maritime curios and old photographs.

Xoron Floatel (☎ 874596; Embankment Rd; en suite rooms per person £24) is an actual houseboat that is very clean and surprisingly roomy.

Bus Nos 1 and 2 go from Ryde every 30 minutes. A scenic 5-mile coastal walk leads from Bembridge to Sandown.

VENTNOR

☎ 01983

Of the island's larger towns, Ventnor is easily the most pleasant, probably because it's chilled out and doesn't seem to notice whether visitors are around or not.

The **TIC** (☎ 813818; 34 High St) is near the bus stop in a beautiful stone building high on a bluff with coastal views, good displays on the island's geography, free town maps and cheery staff.

One mile south of the town, off the A3055, is the **Rare Breeds & Waterfowl Park** (☎ 852649; Undercliffe Dr; adult/child £3.90/3; 🕑 10am-5.30pm Apr-Sep, 11am-4pm Oct) which is home to a large array of rare and not-so-rare farm animals, including llamas, African cattle and Falabella miniature horses. Bus Nos 7, 7A and 31 will get you there from Ryde or Ventnor.

Ventnor Guided Walks (☎ 856647) organises a mixed bag of walks, including ghost walks, rock pool rambles and explorations of smugglers' caves. They run on Tuesday and Thursday from June to September and cost £3/1 per adult/child.

The Spy Glass Inn (☎ 855338; The Esplanade; 2-person flats £60) provides accommodation in self-contained flats (no kids, no dogs) situated above the beach with great views of the town. The atmosphere in the pub below is charged and friendly, and there's live music most nights.

Choose between Thai curries, Chinese noodles and Vietnamese spring rolls in a fun, bright and irreverent atmosphere at **Shanghi Lil's** (☎ 856825; 7 Belgrave Rd; mains £5-7; ⏰ dinner Mon-Sat).

AROUND VENTNOR

The southernmost point of the island is marked by **St Catherine's Lighthouse** which was built between 1837 and 1840. Looking like a stone rocket ship, **St Catherine's Oratory** is a lighthouse dating from 1314 and marks the highest point on the island. A couple of miles further west from here is the **Blackgang Chine Fun Park** (☎ 730330; www.black gangchine.com; 4 & up £7.50; ⏰ 10am-5pm) which opened in 1843 as a landscaped garden but slowly evolved into a theme park with water gardens, animated shows and a hedge maze. The fun park stays open until 10pm from mid-July to August.

WEST WIGHT

The road from Ventnor to Alum Bay offers a winding, bumpy scenic drive past sheep and cattle farms, ancient stone farmhouses with thatched roofs, beaches and some amazing views of the cliffs off the far western tip of the island.

Henry VIII's last great fortress was **Yarmouth Castle** (EH; ☎ 760678; Quay St; admission £2.30; ⏰ 10am-6pm Apr-Oct). Its façade, which is all that's left of it now, dates from 1547.

One mile west of Yarmouth off the A3054 is **Fort Victoria Country Park** (☎ 760860; admission per area £1.50), which is home to an aquarium, a marine museum, a planetarium and the Sunken History Exhibition. Only the exhibition warrants the admission fee.

The **Needles**, at the western tip of the island, are three towering rocks which rise out of the sea to form the postcard symbol of the island. At one time there was another rock, a 37m-high spire which really was needlelike, but it collapsed into the sea in 1764.

The **Needles Park at Alum Bay** (☎ 458 0022; admission free; ⏰ 10am-dusk Apr-Nov) has a range of attractions (about £2 each) including kiddie rides, crazy golf, a motion simulator, boat rides and a chairlift down to the beach. Our favourite is the sweet factory, where you can watch how those teeth-rotters are actually made.

A walking path leads a mile from Alum Bay to the **Needles Old Battery** (☎ 754772; admission £3.60; ⏰ 10.30am-5pm Sun-Thu Apr-Jun, Sep & Oct, 10.30am-5pm daily Jul & Aug), a fort established in 1862 and used as an observation post during WWII. There's a 60m tunnel leading down through the cliff to a searchlight lookout. Buses run between Alum Bay and the battery hourly (every half-hour in peak season).

Sleeping

Totland Bay Youth Hostel (☎ 0870 770 6070; Hirst Hill, Totland; dm £11.80) A marvellous Victorian house overlooking the water.

Brighstone Holiday Centre (☎ 740244; www.brigh stone-holidays.co.uk; tents 2/4 persons £7/12, caravans from £14, B&B adult/child £21/11, 2-person cabins per week from £160) This caravan park and B&B, perched high on the cliffs overlooking the island's most stunning stretch of coastline, is the most scenic place to stay and is also close to walking trails. There are self-catering cabins and B&B (continental breakfast). It's located on the A3055, 6 miles east of Freshwater.

Wessex

Wessex has always been historically important, and remarkable legacies of the region's glorious past litter the gentle hills of the area, now the modern-day counties of Somerset, Dorset and Wiltshire. The area drew the first wave of Iron Age settlers and their all-powerful druids to build mysterious stone circles in Stonehenge and Avebury and the impenetrable fort of Maiden Castle, just outside Dorchester.

The Romans swept over the area leaving an enduring mark with the establishment of the spa town of Bath. In medieval times religious fervour gripped the area, bestowing the magnificent cathedrals and abbeys of Glastonbury, Wells, Malmesbury and stunning Salisbury on the pagan masses, while in rural areas the picture-postcard villages of Lacock and Corfe Castle were taking shape.

The wealthy and noble flocked here in the 16th and 17th centuries to build their stately homes at Wilton, Montacute and Longleat, diversifying in the 18th century to invest their money in fashionable Bath – creating the elegant crescents and squares that grace the city today. Nearby Bristol was booming on trade with the New World and today is the hub of the region with a thriving modern scene from cutting edge music to kick-ass clubs, fine restaurants and buzzing bars.

Wessex really is a fine cross-section of all that is best in England, from charming little villages to massive chalk figures and mysterious crop circles. It can't fail to impress.

HIGHLIGHTS

- Exploring regal, Regency **Bath** (p273)
- Getting in touch with the ancestors at **Avebury** (p244) and **Stonehenge** (p235)
- Having it large on a wasted weekend in **Bristol** (p261)
- Walking the wilds of **Exmoor** (p291)
- Snapping stately **Salisbury's** cathedral and historic centre (p231)
- Exploring timeless villages like **Corfe Castle** (p252), **Lacock** (p241) and **Castle Combe** (p241)

Castle Combe ★
★ Bristol   ★ Avebury
Bath ★   ★ Lacock
Exmoor NP ★
Stonehenge ★
Salisbury ★
★ Corfe Castle

| POPULATION: 1.3 MILLION | AREA: 3570 SQ MILES |

History

Founded in the 6th century by the Saxon Cerdic, by the 9th century Wessex *was* England – the only sizable part of the Anglo-Saxon lands not overrun by the Danes. King Alfred (849–99) was its leader and, effectively, the first king of England. At its peak, Wessex stretched west to Cornwall and east to Kent and Essex.

Moving on a few centuries, Wessex features strongly in the novels of Thomas Hardy, Dorset's most famous son, who set most of his stories here.

Orientation & Information

The three counties of Wessex are roughly the same size. Dorset has the south coast, Somerset the north, and Wiltshire sits inland of them. Bristol, in the central north of the region, is the main transport and industrial hub, and the only big city.

Two websites, www.visitsouthwesteng land.com and www.westcountrynow.com, have general information on the area and links to more specific sites.

Activities

Wessex has numerous options for outdoor activity. This section provides a few ideas; there's more information in the Outdoor Activities chapter. Suggestions for shorter walks and rides are given throughout this chapter. Regional tourism websites and TICs all have information covering a range of activities.

CYCLING

Gentle gradients and a network of quiet country lanes make Wessex ideal cycling country. Wiltshire is particularly good and the 160-mile (258km) circular **Wiltshire Cycleway** makes a good basis for longer or shorter rides.

Of the long-distance cycle routes in this region, the **West Country Way** is one of the most popular – a fabulously contrasting 250-mile (400km) jaunt from Bristol to Padstow in Devon.

For off-road riding, good areas include the **North Wessex Downs** and **Exmoor** (p292).

WALKING

If you're a mile-eater, look no farther than the 610-mile (982km) **South West Coast Path**. The path starts at Minehead in Somerset, then loops round Devon and Cornwall, coming into Dorset at Lyme Regis and finishing at Poole.

In northeast Wiltshire, the **Ridgeway** national trail starts near Avebury and winds 44 miles (three days) through chalk hills to meet the River Thames at Goring. The trail then continues another 41 miles (another three days) through the Chiltern Hills.

Stretches of these two paths that are ideal for short or long walks include **Exmoor** (p292), the **Mendip Hills** (p285) and the **Quantock Hills** (p289).

OTHER ACTIVITIES

Apart from fine walking and cycling, active types can choose from horse riding on Exmoor, windsurfing and kite surfing at Poole or scuba diving in the sea off Weymouth.

Getting Around

BUS

Local bus services are fairly comprehensive, but services to out-of-the-way spots can be extremely sparse and it pays to have your own wheels. Route maps and timetables are available online and at TICs. See p277 for details of Bath-based bus tours of the region.

First Travel (www.firstgroup.com) The largest service provider in the region. The First Day Explorer ticket (adult/child £5/4.25) is valid for one day on all First buses in the area.

National Express (☎ 08705 808080; www.nationalex press.com) Provides reasonable connections between the main towns.

Wilts & Dorset (☎ 01202-673555; www.wdbus.co.uk) One-day Explorer tickets (£6) cover transport on Wilts & Dorset as well as other local service providers.

CAR

There are plenty of car-hire companies in the region. Rates start at around £35 per day, though single-day rentals can be much more (see p751).

TRAIN

The main railway hubs are Bristol and Salisbury. Bristol has connections to London and Birmingham, while Salisbury is a link between the capital and the southwest. Train services in the west are reasonably comprehensive. For more information contact **National Rail Enquiries** (☎ 0845 748 4950; www.nationalrail.co.uk).

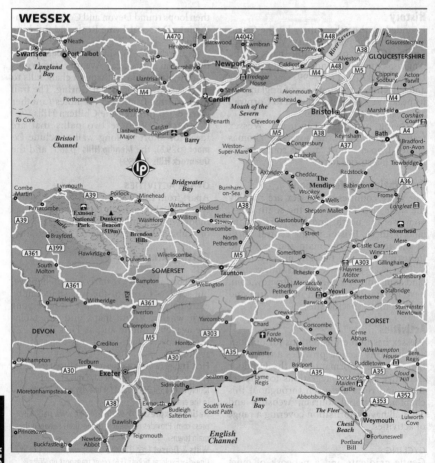

WESSEX

WILTSHIRE

Mystifying ancient monuments, stunning cathedrals, chocolate-box villages and elegant stately homes are strewn across the rolling chalk hills of the largely rural county of Wiltshire. Britain's most important prehistoric sites, Stonehenge and Avebury, are still drawing crowds and baffling archaeologists thousands of years after their completion; the spectacular cathedral at Salisbury boasts the country's highest spire; and the stunning villages of Lacock and Castle Combe are a magnet for photographers. It's a fantastic place to just roam the rural roads and lanes, soaking up the atmosphere.

Information

In addition to town and district TICs, **Visit Wiltshire** (☎ 0870 240 5599; www.visitwiltshire.co.uk) and **Wiltshire Tourism** (www.wiltshiretourism.co.uk) have general county-wide information.

Activities

Some walking and cycling ideas are suggested in the Activities section on p227. For a historical slant, **Foot Trails** (☎ 01747-861851; www.foottrails.co.uk; 2 Underdown Mead, White Rd, Mere) leads various walks around Stonehenge, Salisbury, Purbeck, Old Wardour Castle, Stourhead and Old Sarum.

Cyclists should pick up the *Wiltshire Cycleway* leaflet in TICs. It details the route and its various options, and lists cycle

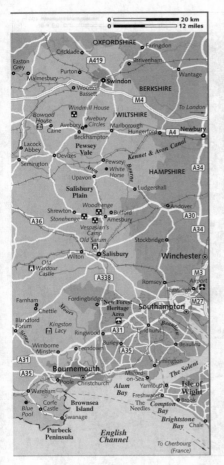

Getting Around

BUS

Unfortunately, there are gaping holes in bus coverage in northwest Wiltshire, so either use your own wheels or be prepared for long waits.

First Badgerline (☎ 01934-620122; www.firstbadgerline.co.uk) Services in the far west of the county.

Wilts & Dorset Buses (☎ 01722-336855; www.wdbus.co.uk) Covers most destinations.

Wiltshire Bus Line (☎ 0845 709 0899) The Wiltshire Day Rover (£6.50/4.50) is valid with most operators in the county, and can be bought from bus drivers.

TRAIN

Rail lines run from London to Salisbury and beyond to Exeter and Plymouth, branching off north to Bradford-on-Avon, Bath and Bristol. Trains from London Paddington to Bath stop at Chippenham, the northwest's largest town and transport hub, which is otherwise uninspiring. Chippenham is a useful jumping-off point for Lacock and Castle Combe.

Unless you're going to Salisbury or Bradford, train travel isn't really useful within the county.

SALISBURY

☎ 01722 / pop 43,335

Although dominated by its stunning cathedral and often deluged with visitors, Salisbury manages to maintain a distinctly authentic air to everyday proceedings with the bustling market square packing in the punters since medieval times. This gracious little city is a wonderful base for touring the area with several fine museums and numerous historic buildings covering every style since the Middle Ages including some beautiful, half-timbered, black-and-white Tudor creations.

Orientation

Salisbury's compact town centre revolves around Market Sq, which is dominated by its impressive guildhall. The train station is a 10-minute walk to the west, while the bus station is just 100 yards north up Endless St.

Information

Lloyds TSB (☎ 413443; 38 Blue Boar Row)

Main post office (cnr Castle St & Chipper Lane)

Nat West (☎ 0845 610 1234; 48 Blue Boar Row)

Starlight InterNetGate (☎ 349309; 1 Endless St; per 15 min £1; ☼ 9.30am-8pm Mon-Sat, 9.30am-4.30pm Sun)

shops and rental outlets. *Off-Road Cycling in Wiltshire* (£6) is a waterproof guide with maps for mountain-bikers.

If you fancy something more leisurely, the 87-mile-long (140km) **Kennet & Avon Canal**, which runs all the way from Bristol to Reading, has some fine stretches of towpath for walking and cycling. The stretch from Bath to Bradford-on-Avon is accessible and scenic, with notable aqueducts and a flight of 29 locks just outside Devizes. You can hire narrowboats at various points. Weekly rates start at around £620 for four people in winter, rising to about £1500 for a 10-berth boat in August. Try **Sally Boats** (☎ 01225-864923; www.sallyboats.ltd.uk) located in Bradford-on-Avon.

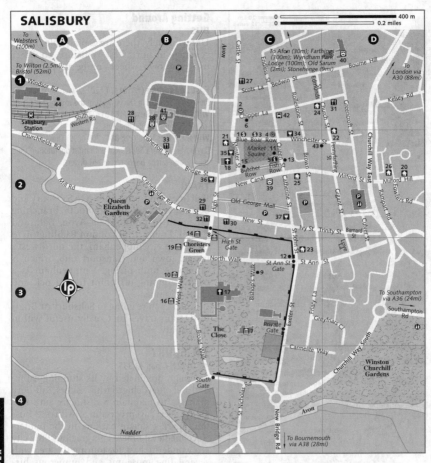

SALISBURY

TIC (☎ 334956; www.visitsalisbury.com; Fish Row;
🕓 9.30am-5pm Mon-Sat Oct-May, 9.30am-6pm Mon-Sat
Jun-Sep, plus 10.30am-4.30pm Sun May-Sep). Stocks the
useful *Walk Around Salisbury* guide (80p)
Washing Well Laundrette (☎ 421874; 28 Chipper
Lane; 🕓 7.30am-8.30pm)

Sights

SALISBURY CATHEDRAL

One of the most beautiful and cohesive
churches in Britain, the **Cathedral Church of
the Blessed Virgin Mary** (☎ 555100; www.salisbury
cathedral.org.uk; 🕓 7.15am-6.15pm Sep-mid-Jun, 7.15am-7.15pm mid-
Jun-Aug) owes much to the incredible speed
of its construction. Built between 1220 and
1258, the cathedral is a masterpiece of the

Early English Gothic style which first introduced pointed arches, flying buttresses
and a feeling of austerity. Little subsequent
work was done to interfere with the uniform style apart from the addition of the
magnificent spire later in the century. At
123m, it is the highest in Britain.

The main entrance is by the highly decorative **West Front**, which is graced by scores of
statues. A small door leads into the beautiful
cloister passage and on into the soaring
70m-long nave. Lined with handsome Purbeck marble piers, the nave is rather bare,
the interior elements having been 'tidied up'
by James Wyatt between 1789 and 1792.
Look out for a fascinating old **clock** from
1386 in the north aisle, probably the oldest

working clock in the world. In the south aisle a **model** shows the cathedral's elaborate construction.

Neatly lining the walls are monuments and tombs, including that of **William Longespée**, son of Henry II and half-brother of King John. When the tomb was excavated a well-preserved rat was found inside Longespée's skull. Rumours persist that the earl had been poisoned.

At the eastern end of the ambulatory the magnificent vivid blue **Prisoners of Conscience** stained-glass window (1980) lords over the grandiose tomb of Edward Seymour (1539–1621) and Lady Catherine Grey. Also at the eastern end is **Trinity Chapel**, the first part of the cathedral to be built. It was completed in 1225 and has fine Purbeck marble pillars.

The cathedral's most impressive feature though, is its soaring spire. It was added well after the completion of the main building, and the additional weight has visibly bent the four central piers of the nave. Flying buttresses were later added externally to support the four corners of the original tower, while buttresses and scissor arches at the openings to the eastern transepts reinforced the interior.

In 1668 Sir Christopher Wren, creator of St Paul's in London, surveyed the cathedral and calculated that the spire was leaning by 75cm. A **brass plate** in the floor of the nave is used to measure any shift, but no further lean was recorded in 1951 or 1970. Despite this, reinforcement work on the notoriously 'wonky spire' continues to this day.

If you'd like a closer view you can take a 1½-hour **tower tour** (adult/child £4/3; 11.15am & 2.15pm daily Mar & Oct, 11.15am, 2.15pm & 3.15pm daily Apr-Sep, plus 5pm Mon-Sat Jun-Aug).

Before leaving make sure you visit the beautiful Gothic **Chapter House** (9.30am-5.30pm Mon-Sat Sep-mid–Jun, 9.30am-7.15pm Mon-Sat mid-Jun–Aug, noon-5.30pm Sun year-round) which houses one of the four surviving original versions of the **Magna Carta**, the agreement made between King John and his barons in 1215. The delicate fan-vaulted ceiling is supported by a single central column while a medieval, carved frieze around the room recounts Old Testament tales.

CATHEDRAL CLOSE

Salisbury Cathedral has England's largest, and arguably most beautiful, cathedral close. Many of the buildings were built at the same time as the cathedral, although it owes most of its present appearance to Wyatt's late–18th-century clean-up. The close was actually walled in, physically separating it from the town, in 1333, using the cathedral at Old Sarum (p235) as a source of building material. To this day it remains an elite enclave, with the gates in the wall still locked every night.

The close has several museums and houses open for visits.

The **Salisbury & South Wiltshire Museum** (332151; www.salisburymuseum.org.uk; 65 The Close; admission £4; 10am-5pm Mon-Sat year-round, plus 2-5pm Sun Jul & Aug), in the listed King's House, contains a very impressive collection, including exhibits from Old Sarum, an interactive Stonehenge gallery and watercolours of the town by Turner.

In the magnificent, 13th-century **Medieval Hall** (412472; www.medieval-hall.co.uk; West Walk, The Close; admission £2.25; 11am-5pm), a 40-minute audiovisual presentation, *Discover Salisbury*, describes the city's history.

Home to the **Redcoats military museum**, the **Wardrobe** (☎ 414536; 58 The Close; www.thewardrobe .org.uk; adult/child £2.75/75p; ⏰ 10am-5pm daily Apr-Oct, Tue-Sun Feb-Nov) – another impressive 13th-century building – tells the story of a soldier's life over 250 years and displays paraphernalia associated with the Royal Gloucestershire, Berkshire and Wiltshire Regiment. It has a lovely garden reaching down to the River Avon.

Built in 1701, **Mompesson House** (NT; ☎ 335 659; The Close; admission £4; ⏰ 11am-5pm Sat-Wed Easter-Sep) is a fine Queen Anne house with magnificent plasterwork ceilings, exceptional period furnishings and a wonderful carved staircase. There's also a peaceful walled garden.

With a façade by Wren, **Malmesbury House** (☎ 327 027; The Close) was a canonry in the 13th century and later the residence of the earls of Malmesbury, visited by notables including Charles II and Handel. It can be seen on pre-booked group tours only (£5.50).

Just inside narrow High St Gate is the **College of Matrons**, founded in 1682 for widows and unmarried daughters of clergymen. South of the cathedral is the **Bishop's Palace**, now the Cathedral School, parts of which date back to 1220. The **Deanery**, on Bishop's Walk, mainly dates from the 13th century.

ST THOMAS'S CHURCH
Anywhere else, the splendid **St Thomas's Church** would attract a lot of attention, but overshadowed as it is by the cathedral, it is saved from the hoards of tourists. Originally built for cathedral workmen in 1219 and named, unusually, after St Thomas Becket (the archbishop murdered in Canterbury Cathedral), the light, airy edifice seen today dates mainly from the 15th century. It's renowned for the superb 'doom', or **judgement-day painting**, which spreads up and over the chancel arch. It was painted around 1470 and shows Christ sitting in judgement astride a rainbow surrounded by scenes of heaven and hell. On the hell side look out for a bishop and two kings (naked except for their mitre and crowns), for a miser with his money-bags and a female alehouse owner, the only person allowed to hang on to her clothes.

MARKET SQUARE
Markets were first held here in 1219, and since 1361 the hustle and bustle of cheer-ful trading has engulfed the square every Tuesday and Saturday. The narrow lanes that surround the square reveal their medieval specialities in names like Oatmeal Row, Fish Row or Silver St, but today the action is confined to the square where you can pick up anything from fresh fish to dodgy digital watches.

The square is dominated by the lovely late–18th-century guildhall and facing it, two **medieval houses**. Immediately behind Market Sq look out for **Fish Row**, with some fine old houses, and a 15th-century **Poultry Cross**.

Tours
Salisbury City Guides (☎ 320349; www.salisburycity guides.co.uk) lead excellent 1½-hour walking tours (adult/child £2.50/1) departing the TIC at 11am from April to October, Saturday and Sunday only November to March. At 8pm on Friday (May to September) there's a ghost walk (£3/1.50).

Festivals & Events
The **Salisbury Festival** (☎ 320333; www.salisbury festival.co.uk) is a prestigious, wide-ranging arts event encompassing classical, world and pop music, theatre, literature, art and puppetry. It runs over three weeks from late May to early June.

Sleeping
BUDGET
Salisbury YHA Hostel (☎ 0870 770 6018; salisbury@yha .org.uk; Milford Hill; dm £14.90; Ⓟ ☒) A lovely 200-year-old building in secluded grounds, this hostel has comfortable but basic rooms and is just a short walk from town. The dormitories are pretty big, but there are also smaller rooms available at a slightly higher price.

Matt & Tiggy's (☎ 327443; 51 Salt Lane; dm £11-16) Small, basic but comfortable, the rooms here are good value and the atmosphere is very laid back. It's convenient for the bus station and town centre and a good option if you want something more homely than the YHA.

MID-RANGE
Castle Rd has a wide choice of B&Bs between the ring road and Old Sarum.

Websters (☎ 339779; www.websters-bed-breakfast .com; 11 Hartington Rd; s/d £38/48; Ⓟ ☒ 🖳 wheelchair access) This quiet house in a colourful Victorian terrace is an excellent choice with fantastic service and attention to detail. The rooms are bright and cheerful with subtle floral décor. Both vegan and vegetarian breakfasts are available.

Griffin Cottage (☎ 328259; mark@brandonasoc.demon.co.uk; 10 St Edmunds Church St; d £45-49; ✗) This largely 17th-century cottage is an atmospheric place to stay with its mix of antique furniture, beamed rooms and modern comforts. Lavender-scented beds, a roaring fire and home-baked bread make it feel very cosy and welcoming.

Farthings (☎ 330749; www.farthingsbandb.co.uk; 9 Swaynes Close; s/d £25/46; P ✗) Tucked into a beautiful quiet close, Farthings is a distinctive Victorian house with a lovely garden and wonderful views of the cathedral. The spacious rooms have bright patchwork quilts and simple décor. The cheaper rooms have shared bathrooms.

Wyndham Park Lodge (☎ 416517; www.wyndhamparklodge.co.uk; 51 Wyndham Road; s/d £39/49; ✗ P) This classically elegant place has spacious rooms featuring coordinating wallpaper and fabrics and period antiques, but it's not too over the top. The house is set on a quiet road within easy walking distance of the centre and has a lovely garden.

Other options:

94 Milford Hill (☎ 322454; 94 Milford Hill; s/d £22/44; ✗) A quiet 17th-century town house with simple but comfortable rooms and pleasant décor.

Cormarket Inn (☎ 412925; cornmarket@intown.net; 32 Cheese Market; s/d £45/55; ✗ 🖳) An inn with surprisingly good rooms.

TOP END

Red Lion Hotel (☎ 323334; www.the-redlion.co.uk; Milford St; s/d £94/122; P ✗) Much nicer and more atmospheric than the tacky façade suggests, this 13th-century place was originally built to house cathedral draughtsmen. Pretty, traditional-style rooms with period features and antique furniture surround the charming creeper-clad courtyard.

King's Arms Hotel (☎ 327629; kingsarmshotelsalisbury@fsmail.net; 9-11 St John St; s/d £79/99; P ✗ 🖳) Creaky sloping floors, tilting ceilings, crooked beams and plenty of charm make this character-filled old place an excellent choice. The rooms are decorated in a very traditional style but don't go over the top on floral patterns or frills.

SOMETHING SPECIAL

Castleman Hotel and Restaurant (☎ 01258-830096; www.castlemanhotel.co.uk; Chettle; s/d £50/75; mains £11-14; P ✗) The secluded village of Chettle is genuinely unspoilt and is home to a charming hotel with incredibly priced rooms. The 16th-century Queen Anne manor house has Jacobean and Victorian panelling and a galleried hall. The rooms are huge but understated and the restaurant serves traditional and modern British cuisine (mains £10 to £15). Chettle is just off the A354, 16 miles southwest of Salisbury.

Eating
BUDGET

Prezzo (☎ 341333; 52-54 High St; mains £7-9; 🕑 lunch & dinner) A sleek, modern place with giant windows streaming light into the wood- and leather-bound interior, this Italian stands out from the pizza-pasta norm with some interesting specialities and a cool but unpretentious atmosphere.

Lemon Tree (☎ 333471; 92 Crane St; mains £7.50-9.50; 🕑 lunch & dinner) This small but light and airy place has a fresh look and a lovely garden and conservatory dining area. The excellent food spans the globe, there are plenty of veg choices and children are welcome.

Thai Café (☎ 414778; 58a Fisherton St; mains £7-8; 🕑 lunch & dinner, closed Sun) Tucked away above a laundrette, this tiny Thai place uses plenty of fresh ingredients, has a no-MSG policy and very good prices. The food is fantastic and unadulterated for Western palettes, so beware when you order that curry.

MID-RANGE

Afon (☎ 552366; Millstream Approach; lunch mains £5-9, 2/3-course dinner £15/18; 🕑 lunch & dinner) A modern brasserie-bar ideal for warm summer suppers, this stylish place with a relaxed and friendly attitude dishes up innovative international cuisine. The fantastic riverside location is a real plus, and on summer evenings there's an Aussie-style barbeque.

Café Med (☎ 328402; 68 Castle St; 2-course set menu £19; 🕑 lunch & dinner) A cosy, rustic-style place, this popular joint serves up an eclectic mix of English and continental cuisine, both modern and highly traditional, from its buzzing kitchen. There's good seafood and plenty of vegetarian options.

WESSEX

SOMETHING SPECIAL

Museum Inn (☎ 01725-516261; www.museum inn.co.uk; Farnham; s £60, d £75-95) This stylishly renovated 17th-century inn is a real gem. The rooms, either above the bar or in converted stables, have some antique furniture and traditional touches but are predominantly stylish and contemporary with big squashy beds and great bathrooms. The restaurant (mains £9 to £18) is equally swish and serves up some prime traditional British food given a modern makeover. There are lighter snacks at the traditional bar and a gourmet breakfast if you decide to stay.

Farnham is just off the A354, 16 miles southwest of Salisbury.

Mojito (☎ 417999; 2 Salt Lane; mains £6-16; ☺ lunch & dinner) This fun, ultra-modern bistro with a strong Latin theme has an open kitchen dishing up great modern Mediterranean dishes and interesting tapas (£2.20 to £5.95). If you really want to get into it they also sell a range of Cuban cigars.

Gallery (☎ 500200; 108 Fisherton St; 2-course evening menu £15; ☺ lunch Tue-Sat, dinner Thu-Sat) Set in a stylishly restored, 17th-century grain mill, this place has a wonderful outside seating area and a creative menu featuring global cuisine. Specials feature anything from chicken and noodle laksa with coconut and coriander to tomato, fennel and potato stew.

TOP END

LXIX (☎ 340000; 67-69 New St; mains £9-19; ☺ lunch & dinner Mon-Sat) Cool, trendy and exclusive, Salisbury's hottest restaurant serves up creative modern British cuisine in sleek and stylish surroundings. The Aprés LXIX (☎ 320000; mains £5-13) bistro next door is more relaxed and cheaper but equally good.

Drinking

Haunch of Venison (☎ 322024; 1-5 Minster St) An atmospheric medieval pub full of nooks and crannies, this wonderful bar serves more than 50 malt whiskies. It has an excellent choice of food in its top-floor restaurant (mains £5 to £14) ranging from wraps and salads to venison steak and aubergine caviar.

Escoba (☎ 329608; 5-7 Winchester St) A modern, funky Spanish bar with big comfy seats, giant windows and a good range of tasty tapas (priced from £3 to £6), Escoba serves a young bubbly crowd who throng the place at weekends.

Moloko (☎ 507050; 5 Bridge St) A hip and happening little joint with passionate red décor and wannabe-trendy clientele, Moloko is a late night haunt with DJs at weekends and an alarming array of flavoured vodkas.

Spirit (☎ 338387; 46 Catherine St) A hip bar-club with DJs, cocktails and a range of tunes from live music on Wednesday nights to Thursday's hip-hop, weekend house and Sunday night's mellow vibes. This place generally acts as a pre-club venue for sister act NN Bar next door.

Entertainment

Classical concerts take place regularly in many venues around town. Visit www.music insalisbury.org for up-to-date listings and information.

The lively **Salisbury Arts Centre** (☎ 321744; www.salisburyartscentre.co.uk; Bedwin St), set in a converted church and recently refurbished, is one of the best in the south. It has an interesting programme of contemporary music and theatre performances.

Highbrow classical dramas, musicals, comedy and new writing are the staple at the traditional **Salisbury Playhouse** (☎ 320333; www.salisburyplayhouse.com; Malthouse Lane), while you can catch mainstream touring shows next door at the **City Hall** (☎ 327676; www.city hallsalisbury.co.uk; Malthouse Lane).

The **Odeon Cinema** (☎ 0870 505 0007; New Canal) is probably the only cinema in the world with a medieval foyer.

Getting There & Away

BUS

Three National Express coaches run daily to London via Heathrow (£13, three hours). There is only one service to Bath (£7.75, 1½ hours) and Bristol (£7.75, two hours).

There's also the local bus X4 running hourly via Wilton (10 minutes) to Warminster (one hour), where there are immediate connections on buses X5 and X6 to Bath (two hours) via Bradford-on-Avon (1½ hours). Bus X3 runs to Bournemouth (1¼ hours) and Poole (1½ hours) hourly, every two hours on Sunday.

TRAIN

Trains run half-hourly from London Waterloo station (£24.20, 1½ hours) and hourly on to Exeter (£21, 1¾ hours). Another line runs from Portsmouth (£11.60, 1½ hours, hourly) or Brighton (£21.60, 2½ hours, hourly) via Southampton (£6.40, 30 minutes, half-hourly) to Bradford-on-Avon (£7.50, 45 minutes, hourly), Bath (£10.40, one hour, every 30 minutes) and Bristol (£12.60, 1¼ hours, half-hourly).

Getting Around

The ride to Stonehenge along the Woodford Valley is popular. Bikes can be hired from **Hayball Cycle Shop** (☎ 411378; 26-30 Winchester St; per day £10, £25 deposit).

AROUND SALISBURY
Old Sarum

The massive, Iron Age hill fort of **Old Sarum** (☎ 01722-335398; admission £2.50; ☻ 10am-6pm Apr-Sep, 10am-5pm Oct, 10am-4pm Nov-Mar) was home to successive generations, from the Romans right through to the Normans. The contents of the impressive 22-hectare earthworks are the legacy of William the Conqueror, with fine views of Salisbury from the Norman ramparts and ruins of a castle, cathedral and bishop's palace.

The first cathedral on the site was completed in 1092, and although Old Sarum flourished in medieval times, the pope granted permission in 1217 to move the cathedral to a better location. The action immediately shifted to Salisbury and Old Sarum was abandoned. By 1331 the cathedral had been demolished to provide building material for the walls of the new cathedral close. A scale model of 12th-century Old Sarum in Salisbury Cathedral gives a good impression of how the site once looked.

There are free guided tours at 2.30pm on Monday, Wednesday and Friday in July and August, and medieval tournaments, open-air plays and mock battles on selected days.

Old Sarum is 2 miles north of Salisbury; between them, bus Nos 3, 5, 6, 8 and 9 run every 15 minutes (10 minutes, hourly on Sunday).

Wilton House

One of the finest stately homes in the country, **Wilton House** (☎ 01722-746729; www .wiltonhouse.com; adult/child house £9.75/5.50, gardens only £4.50/3.50; ☻ 10.30am-5.30pm Tue-Sat Apr-Oct; wheelchair access) has been home to the Earls of Pembroke since 1542. The house has marvellous art and furniture collections and wonderful grounds with 17th-century landscaping and fantastic water features.

The house's majestic rooms have attracted plenty of filmmakers, with scenes from *Sense and Sensibility*, *The Madness of King George* and *Mrs Brown* all shot here. Magnificent painted ceilings, elaborate plaster work and paintings by Van Dyck can be seen in the Single and Double Cube Rooms designed by Inigo Jones. You'll also spot the famous Pembroke Palace dolls' house (1907) and works by Rembrandt, Brueghel and Reynolds. The Victorian laundry and Tudor kitchen are also worth a look.

Wilton House is 2½ miles west of Salisbury on the A30; bus Nos 60, 60A and 61 run from New Canal in Salisbury (10 minutes, every 15 minutes). Last admission is at 4.30pm.

STONEHENGE

Europe's most famous prehistoric site, the 5000-year-old ring of enormous standing stones at **Stonehenge** (EH/NT; ☎ 01980-624715; www.nationaltrust.org.uk/main/news/stonehenge.htm; admission £5.20; ☻ 9.30am-6pm mid-Mar–May & Sep–mid-Oct, 9am-7pm Jun-Aug, 9.30am-dusk mid-Oct–mid-Mar)

FUTURE OF STONEHENGE

For a relatively small site, Stonehenge has always received a daunting number of visitors – over 800,000 per year. Despite its World Heritage status, the site is hemmed in by busy roads and visitors are funnelled through a tunnel under the road and then stare at the stones from behind a wire barricade with a constant backdrop of roaring traffic.

Plans are now afoot to tunnel the roads and build a brand new visitor centre 2 miles from the site from where visitors will be bussed to the monument. This will return the site to relative silence and restore the portentous ambience. The visitor centre should be completed by 2006 and the road tunnels by 2008. In the meantime, be prepared for crowds and road noise.

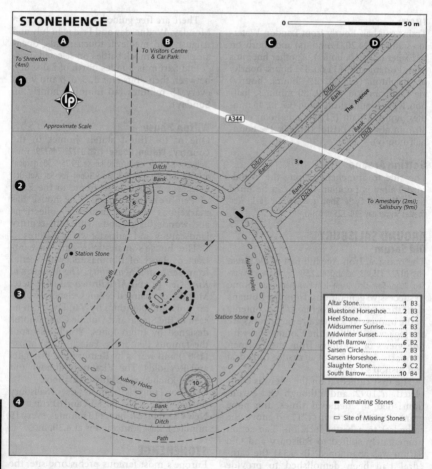

STONEHENGE

0 ————————— 50 m

Altar Stone	**1** B3
Bluestone Horseshoe	**2** B3
Heel Stone	**3** C2
Midsummer Sunrise	**4** B3
Midwinter Sunset	**5** B3
North Barrow	**6** B2
Sarsen Circle	**7** B3
Sarsen Horseshoe	**8** B3
Slaughter Stone	**9** C2
South Barrow	**10** B4

■ Remaining Stones

□ Site of Missing Stones

is a mystical and magical place and one of England's most popular attractions. Archaeologists are unsure about its original purpose, but it is likely to have been some sort of astronomical calendar or place of sun worship and ritual sacrifice. Whatever its purpose, it is clear from its size and construction that the site was of incredible significance to ancient peoples.

The Site

Construction at Stonehenge started around 3000 BC when the outer circular bank and ditch were erected. A thousand years later an inner circle of granite stones, known as bluestones from their original colouring, was added. Incredibly, these four-ton mammoths had been hauled 250 miles (403km) from the Preseli Mountains in South Wales.

Around 1500 BC, the huge stones that make Stonehenge instantly recognisable were dragged to the site, erected in a circle and topped by equally massive lintels to make the trilithons (two vertical stones topped by a horizontal one). The sarsen (a type of sandstone) stones were cut from an extremely hard rock found on the Marlborough Downs 20 miles from the site. It's estimated that dragging one of these 50-ton stones across the countryside to Stonehenge would require about 600 people.

Also around this time, the bluestones from 500 years earlier were rearranged as an **inner horseshoe** with an **altar stone** (a name given for no scientific reason) at the centre. Outside this a **second horseshoe** of five trilithons was erected. Three of these are intact, the other two have just a single upright. Then came the **major circle** of 30 massive vertical stones, of which 17 uprights and six lintels remain.

Much farther out was **another circle** delineated by the 58 Aubrey Holes, named after John Aubrey who discovered them in the 1600s. Inside are the **South and North Barrows**, each originally topped by a stone. Between them are two other stones, though not quite on the east–west axis. Surrounding all this is a bank and then a ditch.

The inner horseshoes are aligned along the sun's axis on rising in midsummer and setting in midwinter, but little is really known about the significance of this and Stonehenge's ultimate purpose. Leading out from the site is the **Avenue**, the entrance to the circle marked by the **Slaughter Stone** (another 18th-century name-tag) and further out the **Heel Stone** on one side. Excavations have revealed that another Heel Stone stood on the other.

Admission includes an audio tour but once in, you are kept at some distance from the stones. Private views can be arranged with **English Heritage** (☎ 01980-626267) if you apply well in advance.

Getting There & Away

Buses depart from Salisbury bus station for Stonehenge (40 minutes, nine times daily in summer), picking up at the train station, from 10am.

Several companies offer organised tours to the site:

City Sightseeing (☎ 01789-294466; £15; 3 daily Apr–Oct) Two-hour tours from Salisbury train station to Stonehenge via Old Sarum. Price includes admission to the site.

Foot Trails (☎ 01747-861851; www.foottrails.co.uk; £35) Six-mile walk to Stonehenge on the first and third Wednesday of the month (June to September). The price includes picnic lunch, entry to Stonehenge and guided tour of the stones.

AROUND STONEHENGE

A collection of much-less-visited prehistoric sites surrounds Stonehenge, adding to the mystery of the area. The *Stonehenge Estate Archaeological Walks* leaflet details walks round the sites within the NT boundaries. Others are on private property and not open to the public.

Just north of Amesbury and 1½ miles east of Stonehenge is **Woodhenge**, where concrete

---

SOLSTICE AT STONEHENGE

During the summer solstice in 1973 latter-day druids celebrated the first Stonehenge Peoples' Free Festival. By the mid-'80s it had grown into a massive event attracting New Age travellers and hard-core party animals. Chanting, banging drums, braiding hair and hanging out were the main events but as the party grew it also started to get out of hand; cars got burnt out, drugs were freely for sale and revellers often just forgot to leave, lingering around the site for weeks afterwards. A clampdown on solstice celebrations turned into an annual stand-off in the late '80s and the barbed-wire fencing surrounding the site is one legacy of the clashes. Peaceful solstice gatherings have returned over the past few years and controlled open access is now allowed.

---

posts mark the site of a concentric wooden structure that predates Stonehenge.

North of Stonehenge and running approximately east–west is the **Cursus**, an elongated embanked oval whose purpose is unknown. The **Lesser Cursus** looks like the end of a similar elongated oval. Other prehistoric sites around Stonehenge include a number of burial mounds, like the **New King Barrows**, and **Vespasian's Camp**, an Iron Age hill fort.

STOURHEAD

Inspired by classical images of Italy, **Stourhead** (NT; ☎ 01747-841152; Stourton; admission garden or house £5.40, house & garden £9.40; ☉ house 11am-5pm Fri-Tue mid-Mar–Oct, garden 9am-7pm or sunset year-round) is landscape gardening at its finest. The Palladian house has some fine Chippendale furniture and paintings by Claude and Gaspard Poussin, but for most visitors it's the sideshow to the magnificent gardens. The garden spreads across the valley and features stunning vistas, rare plants, magnificent trees and ornate temples. A lovely 2-mile circuit takes you past the most ornate follies, around the lake and to the **Temple of Apollo**. If you're feeling energetic, from near the **Pantheon**, a 3½-mile side trip can be made to **King Alfred's Tower** (admission £2; ☉ noon-5pm mid-Mar–Oct), a 50m-high folly with wonderful views.

Stourhead is off the B3092, 8 miles south of Frome in Somerset; public transport is virtually nonexistent.

WESSEX

WHITE LINES

The rolling fields of Wessex are a green cloak over a chalk substructure, and the practice of cutting pictures into the hillsides has a long history. Some of the chalk figures may date back to prehistoric times, though the history of the oldest is uncertain. Although Wiltshire has more chalk figures than any other county, the best are probably the 55m-tall Cerne Abbas Giant (with his even more notable 12m penis; p254) in Dorset and the 110m-long Uffington White Horse in Oxfordshire (which really requires a helicopter or hot-air balloon for proper inspection; p402).

Horses were particularly popular subjects for chalk figures in the 18th century. In more recent times, regimental badges and even a giant kiwi have been cut into the hillsides. Kate Bergamar's *Discovering Hill Figures* (Shire Publications) gives the complete lowdown on England's chalky personalities, or you can pick up the excellent *Wiltshire's White Horse Trail* booklet (£6.50) at TICs.

LONGLEAT

Stately-home-turned-circus-act, **Longleat** (☎ 01985-844400; www.longleat.co.uk; adult/child house £9/6, grounds £3/2, safari park £9/7, all-inclusive passport £16/13; ⊗ house 10am-5.30pm Easter-Sep, guided tours only 11am-3.30pm Oct-Easter, safari park 10am-4pm Apr-Oct, other attractions 11am-5.30pm Apr-Nov) is spectacular if you can see past the blatant commercialism.

The 16th-century house was extensively remodelled in the Victorian era when baroque décor was introduced. The rooms are sumptuously furnished and boast magnificent tapestries and ornate ceilings. The extensive grounds were landscaped by Lancelot 'Capability' Brown in the 18th century.

After WWII, taxation and skyrocketing maintenance costs forced the sixth Marquess of Bath to open Longleat to the public. A safari park was added to increase the appeal and today the estate also boasts mazes, a narrow-gauge railway, a Dr Who exhibit, a Postman Pat village, a pets' corner and a butterfly garden. Each of the attractions has an admission charge, so if you're planing to see more than one opt for the passport ticket.

Longleat is off the A362 between Frome and Warminster, about 3 miles from both and has no public transport.

BRADFORD-ON-AVON

☎ 01225 / pop 8800

The narrow winding streets of honey-coloured Bradford slither down a hillside to the banks of the Avon. Graceful buildings, elegant town houses and fine old churches line the streets of this lovely little town, while a huge tithe barn gives a clue to its importance in times past.

The **TIC** (☎ 865797; www.bradfordonavon.com; 50 St Margaret's St; ⊗ 10am-5pm Apr-Dec, 10am-4pm Jan-

Mar) sells numerous leaflets (30p) on attractions and themed walks.

At **Cottage Co-op** (see opposite), Internet access costs £1 for 15 minutes.

Sights & Activities

Bradford is a great town for rambling and admiring the architecture. A few Saxon buildings bear testament to its earlier history, but it was the growth of the weaving industry in the 17th and 18th centuries that brought wealth to Bradford. The magnificent factories and imposing houses were the showpieces of the town's clothing entrepreneurs.

Start at the TIC and nip into the **Bradford-on-Avon Museum** (☎ 863280; Bridge St; admission free; ⊗ 10.30am-12.30pm & 2-4pm Wed-Sat, 2-4pm Sun Easter-Oct, 2-4pm Nov-Easter) for some local history.

Around the corner is **Westbury House**, where a riot against the introduction of factory machinery in 1791 led to three deaths. The machinery in question was subsequently burned on **Town Bridge**. The unusual room jutting out from the bridge was originally a chapel but later became a lock-up.

Ramble up to the dainty **Shambles**, the original marketplace, and check out the lovely **Coppice Hill** before wandering up Market St and beyond to the attractive terrace houses of **Middle Rank** and **Tory**. The restored **St Mary's Tory** was built as a hermitage chapel in the late 15th century and was then used as a cloth factory in the 18th century.

Follow the hill down to the 12th-century **Holy Trinity Church**, now almost completely submerged beneath 14th-century extensions and 15th- and 19th-century rebuilding. Just opposite is one of Britain's finest Saxon churches, tiny **St Laurence**, which dates from around 1001.

WESSEX

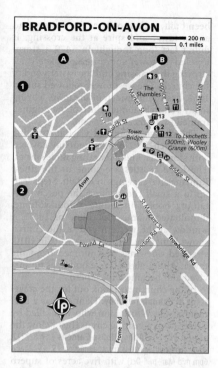

BRADFORD-ON-AVON

INFORMATION	
Post Office..1	B1
Tourist Information Centre..........................2	B1

SIGHTS & ACTIVITIES	(pp238–9)
Bradford-on-Avon Museum..........................3	B2
Church of St Laurence.................................4	A1
Holy Trinity Church......................................5	A2
St Mary's Tory...6	A1
Tithe Barn...7	A3
Westbury House...8	B2

SLEEPING	(p239)
Bradford Old Windmill..................................9	B1
Priory Steps...10	A1

EATING	(p239)
Bunch of Grapes...11	B1
Cottage Co-op..12	B1
Le Mangetout...13	B1

TRANSPORT	(pp239–40)
Lock Inn...14	B3

From here, cross the bridge and take the riverside path to the 14th-century **Tithe Barn** (EH; admission free; 10.30am-4pm) on the edge of the bank of the Kennet and Avon Canal. The imposing 51m-long barn was used to store tithes (taxes in kind) in the Middle Ages and was roofed with a whopping 100 tons of stone tiles.

If you're feeling energetic there's a pleasant 1½-mile walk or cycle ride along the canal to neighbouring Avoncliff, with its impressive Victorian aqueduct.

Sleeping & Eating

Lynchetts (866400; www.lynchetts.co.uk; 15 Woolley St; s/d £40/60; P) This 18th-century town house has a charming mix of beamed cottage rooms and high-ceilinged Georgian reception rooms. Brass beds and subtle rose-patterned wallpaper decorate the pretty bedrooms, most of which have great views.

Priory Steps (862230; www.priorysteps.co.uk; Newtown; s/d £65/85) Originally six 17th-century weavers' cottages, this luxurious B&B is a stunning place with charming old-style décor, an atmospheric library and beautiful rooms. The views from its hillside garden are wonderful and children are very welcome.

Woolley Grange (864705; www.luxuryfamilyhotels.com; Woolley Green; s £90-120, d £95-380; P) Exhausted parents in need of a break should look no further than this beautiful Jacobean manor house set in extensive grounds. The antique-filled bedrooms are stylish and full of character but child-friendly. The restaurant (mains £18.50) is a grand affair with gourmet, country-house cooking and an alternative menu for children.

Cottage Co-op (867444; 33 Silver St; mains £4-6; 10am-5.30pm Mon-Sat) This tiny, 17th-century cottage serves top-notch vegetarian and organic goodies made with fair-trade ingredients, so you can fuel up with a clear conscience. There's a retro lounge upstairs with patchwork cushions, wicker furniture and Internet access.

Le Mangetout (863111; Silver St; mains £6-17; lunch & dinner) The best place to eat in town, this bright brasserie-bar has few airs and graces but an excellent modern British and French menu served up in some style in the relaxed conservatory.

Other options:

Bradford Old Windmill (866842; www.bradford oldwindmill.co.uk; 4 Masons Lane; s £59-99 d £120-200; P) A sensational converted windmill with unique rooms.

Bunch of Grapes (863877; 14 Silver St; mains £6-9; lunch & dinner) An unashamedly traditional pub and restaurant.

Getting There & Away

Bath is only 8 miles away, making a day trip an easy option. Bus Nos X4, X5 and

WESSEX

SOMETHING SPECIAL

Full Moon (☎ 01373 830936; www.thefullmoon .co.uk; Rudge; s/d £45/69; P ✕ 🖳 📺 wheelchair access) A gorgeous 17th-century inn, the Full Moon is an incredible place with some fantastic rooms decorated in a classical but modern style. There are also some selfcatering cottages if you'd like to chill out for a few days. The restaurant has a loyal local following for its modern British and international food (mains £8 to £14) dictated by the availability of fresh local ingredients. There's a lovely large beer garden, plenty of real ales on tap and an endearingly friendly atmosphere to the whole place. It doesn't get much better than this.

Rudge is just off the A36, 6 miles south of Bradford-on-Avon.

X6 run from Bath (30 minutes, half-hourly, every two hours on Sunday), continuing to Warminster for an easy connection with bus No X4 to Salisbury (1¾ hours, hourly).

Trains go roughly hourly from Bath (15 minutes).

Getting Around
Bicycles can be hired for £10 a day from the **Lock Inn** (☎ 868068; 48 Frome Rd). They also hire only Canadian canoes for £14 for a half day.

MALMESBURY
☎ 01666 / pop 6094
The delightful hilltop town of Malmesbury is somewhat marred by its sprawling suburbs but persevere and you'll reach the ancient cottages, superb semi-ruined abbey church and late–15th-century market cross that mark the centre of town.

The **TIC** (☎ 823748; www.malmesbury.gov.uk; Market Lane; ⏰ 9am-4.50pm Mon-Thu, 9am-4.20pm Fri, 10am-4pm Sat) is in the town hall.

Malmesbury Abbey
A wonderful blend of ruin and living church, **Malmesbury Abbey** (☎ 826666; donation requested; ⏰ 10am-5pm Mon-Sat mid-Mar–Oct, 10am-4pm Mon-Sat Nov–mid-Mar) is an evocative place with an eventful history. The abbey started out as a 7th-century monastery, later replaced by a Norman church. By the 14th century a massive edifice 100m long had

been built, with a tower at the western end and a tower and spire at the crossing. It didn't last long though. In 1479 a storm toppled the tower and spire, completely destroying the crossing and the eastern end of the church. The west tower followed suit in 1662, destroying much of the nave, leaving today's church, about a third of the original, framed by ruins at either end.

The church is entered via the stunning south porch, its Norman doorway covered with stone carvings illustrating Bible stories. The huge **Apostles** are some of the finest Romanesque carvings in Britain. Steps lead up to a small room above the porch containing books, including a four-volume, illuminated-manuscript Bible of 1407. A window at the western end of the church shows Elmer the Flying Monk who, in 1010, strapped on wings and jumped from the tower. Although he broke both legs he survived and became a local hero.

In the churchyard look out for the **gravestone of Hannah Twynnoy**. Hannah was a barmaid at the White Lion who was killed by a tiger from a visiting circus. Just below the abbey are the **Abbey House Gardens** (☎ 822212; www.abbeyhousegardens.co.uk; admission £5; ⏰ 11am-6pm mid-Mar–mid-Oct) with five acres of superb colour, a herb garden, river and waterfall.

Sleeping & Eating
Kings Arms (☎ 823383; www.kingsarmshotel.info; High St; s/d £40/60; P ✕) A 14th-century coaching inn with plenty of character, this place is a good central option although the rooms are of the frilly, traditional school of décor. The restaurant (mains £7 to £11) does decent but uninspired food.

Old Bell Inn (☎ 822344; www.oldbellhotel.com; Abbey Row; s £85, d £110-170; P ✕) Reputed to be the oldest hotel in England (c 1220) this luxurious place is a mix of styles from medieval and Edwardian in the main building to a Japanese theme in the coach house. It's a family-friendly place with lots of character, restrained traditional rooms and an elegant restaurant (mains £9 to £15).

Whole Hog (☎ 825845; 8 Market Cross; mains £6-12; ⏰ lunch & dinner) This café-cum-winebar has a clutter of old enamel signs on the exposed stone walls and giant windows letting in a swathe of light. You can choose from a reasonable range of pasta, seafood and steaks or go for the house speciality: hogburgers.

Getting There & Away

Bus No 31 runs to Swindon (45 minutes, hourly Monday to Saturday), while No 92 heads to Chippenham (35 minutes, hourly Monday to Saturday). There are no buses after 7pm or on Sunday.

AROUND MALMESBURY
Watley Manor

If you're in need of some serious pampering, total seclusion or you just appreciate feeling like a star, head straight for **Whatley Manor** (☎ 01666-822888; www.whatleymanor.com; Easton Grey; d £275-605; P ☒ ☒), where the whiff of exclusivity will meet you at the automatic gates. Low-key luxury meets high-maintenance client at this beautiful manor house with unashamedly modern décor. Contemporary art and sculpture contrast with wood panelling, antiques and rich fabrics and sublime food springs from the two restaurants: a Swiss-chalet-style brasserie (three-course set menu £24) and the formal French restaurant (three-course menu £60) with lavish Chinese wallpaper and extravagant green crystal chandeliers.

Easton Grey is 3 miles west of Malmesbury on the B4040.

CASTLE COMBE
☎ 01249

An idyllic English village, Castle Combe claims to be the prettiest in the country, and frankly it's hard to dispute. With the medieval castle long gone, the charms of this town fall squarely in the hands of the flower-strewn stone cottages of the main street, the gorgeous weavers' cottages by the packhorse bridge and the 13th-century **market cross**.

The beautiful medieval **church of St Andrew** is central to the village and contains a remarkable 13th-century monument of Sir Walter de Dunstanville, lord of the manor, in chain mail. Bizarrely, there's also a motor-racing track nearby and the whine of engines punctures the peace on still days.

If you want to stay, the atmospheric 12th-century **Castle Inn** (☎ 783030; www.castle-inn.info; s/d £76/100; ☒) has traditional-style rooms complete with exposed beams and whirlpool baths in many rooms. The restaurant has a good reputation and dishes up a mix of traditional and modern British food (mains lunch £7 to £9, dinner £14 to £15).

The people's choice for food is the **White Hart** (☎ 782295; mains £6-12), a homely traditional inn with a friendly charm, good sambos (£4) and a healthy choice of traditional pub meals (£7 to £12).

Between them bus Nos 35, 635 and 75 go to Chippenham bus station (30 minutes) six times daily Monday to Friday and four times on Saturday. On Wednesdays bus No 76a makes one trip direct to and from Bath (one hour).

LACOCK
☎ 01249

There are no TV aerials, no yellow lines and no overhead cables in this gorgeous medieval village where few buildings date from after 1800 – it's almost a surprise to see electric light in the windows. It's a really lovely place, used as a set for the BBC's acclaimed production of *Pride and Prejudice* and, more recently, parts of the *Harry Potter* films, and well worth a detour if you're in the area. The NT produces a free *Lacock Abbey* leaflet plotting a route round the most interesting buildings.

Lacock Abbey

Established as a nunnery in 1232, **Lacock Abbey** (NT; ☎ 730227; admission abbey, museum, cloisters & grounds £7, abbey, cloisters & grounds only £5.60; ☒ abbey 1pm-5.30pm Wed-Mon Apr-Oct; wheelchair access) passed into the hands of Sir William Sharington in 1539. He converted the nunnery into a home,

SOMETHING SPECIAL

George and Dragon (☎ 01380-723053; Rowde; mains £9-16) It's food first, beer later at this renowned gastro-pub just outside Devizes. The 17th-century inn is a charming place with low ceilings and outside loos – and a passion for fresh fish. The cushions and benches are covered in them and the daily changing menu on the blackboard relies strongly on its frequent deliveries from Cornwall's shores. Skate with capers and black butter or roast hake with aioli and red peppers have the punters coming from miles around.

demolished the church, tacked a tower onto the corner of the abbey and added a brewery. The wonderful Gothic entrance hall is lined with many bizarre terracotta figures; spot the scapegoat with a lump of sugar on its nose. Some of the original 13th-century structure is evident in the cloisters and there are traces of medieval wall paintings. The recently restored botanic garden is also worth a visit.

In the early 19th century, William Henry Fox Talbot (1800–77), a prolific inventor, conducted crucial experiments in the development of photography here. Inside the entrance to the abbey the **Fox Talbot Museum of Photography** (☎ 730459; admission museum, cloisters & grounds only £4.40; ⌚ 11am-5.30pm Mar-Oct) details his pioneering work in the 1830s. Fox Talbot's contribution was the photographic negative, from which further positive images could be produced – before that a photograph was a one-time, one-image process. His grave can be seen in the village cemetery.

Sleeping & Eating

Staying overnight allows you to enjoy the charm of the ancient village once the coaches have left.

Old Rectory (☎ 730335; www.oldrectorylacock.co.uk; Cantax Hill; s/d £30/50; Ⓟ ✕) This gorgeous Victorian Gothic house, just two minutes stroll from the village, has mullioned windows, creeper-clad walls and great-value rooms. The décor is firmly traditional and there's a quintessentially English croquet lawn and tennis court in the grounds.

King John's Hunting Lodge (☎ 730313; king johns@amserve.com; 21 Church St; s/d £50/75; Ⓟ ✕) Dating partly from the 13th century, the

oldest house in the village is a friendly place with the prerequisite old beams, antique furniture and roaring fires. The rooms are traditional but not over the top and there's a lovely garden for kids to play in.

Sign of the Angel (☎ 730230; angel@lacock.co.uk; 6 Church St; s £75, d £100-150; Ⓟ) The oak panelling, log fires and creaky floorboards create a charming and authentic old-world feel in this 15th-century place. Choose from an ancient antique-filled bedroom in the main house or a rustic cottage across the stream. There's simple but stylish English food (mains £9 to £17) available in the beamed dining room and a variety of snacks at the bar.

Other options:

George Inn (☎ 730263; 4 West St; mains £8-14) An atmospheric old pub serving hearty steaks and fish.

Lacock Pottery (☎ 730266; www.lacockbedandbreak fast.com; 1 The Tanyard; s/d £40/65; Ⓟ ✕) A converted workhouse with restrained décor and plenty of antiques.

Getting There & Away

Bus No 234 operates roughly hourly from Chippenham (Monday to Saturday, 20 minutes) and on to Frome (one hour).

AROUND LACOCK
Corsham Court

An Elizabethan mansion dating from 1582, **Corsham Court** (☎ 01249-701610; www.corsham-court .co.uk; admission £5; ⌚ 2-5.30pm Tue-Thu, Sat & Sun Mar-Sep, 2-4.30pm Sat & Sun Oct–late-Mar, closed Dec) is in the small country town of Corsham. The mansion was enlarged and renovated in the 18th century by Capability Brown and John Nash to house a superb art collection including works by Reynolds, Caravaggio, Rubens and Van Dyck. Don't leave before taking a walk through the lovely gardens to the gorgeous Gothic bath house.

Corsham Court is 3 miles southwest of Chippenham, 2 miles northwest of Lacock.

DEVIZES
☎ 01380 / pop 14,379

Devizes is north Wiltshire's largest market town and boasts the biggest marketplace in England: a grandiose semicircular affair flanked by elegant Georgian houses and two ancient churches. The town also has some interesting medieval buildings, an excellent museum and its own brewery (shire horses are still used to deliver beer to local pubs on weekday mornings).

The **TIC** (☎ 729408; www.kennet.gov.uk; Cromwell House, Market Pl; ⏰ 9.30am-5pm Mon-Sat) provides the free *Medieval Town Trail* leaflet, and houses a small visitor centre with interactive displays.

Sights

Between St John's St and High St, **St John's Alley** has a wonderful collection of Elizabethan houses, their upper storeys cantilevered over the street. **St John's Church**, on Market Pl, displays elements of its original Norman construction, particularly in the solid crossing tower. Other interesting buildings include the **Corn Exchange**, topped by a figure of Ceres, goddess of agriculture, and the **Old Town Hall** of 1750–52.

There are outstanding prehistory sections with artefacts associated with Avebury and Stonehenge at the **Wiltshire Heritage Museum & Gallery** (☎ 727369; www.wiltshireheritage.org.uk; 41 Long St; adult/child £3/free, free Sun & Mon; ⏰ 10am-5pm Mon-Sat, noon-4pm Sun). The museum also has social-history displays and a sizable art collection relating to the county.

Just north of the town centre the **Kennet & Avon Canal Museum** (☎ 729489; The Wharf; adult/child £1.50/50p; ⏰ 10am-4.30pm Easter-Sep, 10am-4pm Oct-Dec & Feb-Easter) has displays detailing the conception, construction and everyday use of the canal and its restoration. The **Caen Hill** flight of 29 successive locks raises the water level 72m in 2½ miles on the western outskirts of Devizes.

Sleeping & Eating

Asta (☎ 722546; 66 Downlands Rd; B&B s/d £18/36; P ✗) A small, family-run B&B in a modern house on the outskirts of town, Asta has simple bright rooms and a friendly atmosphere. It's about a 15-minute walk from town.

Bear Hotel (☎ 722444; www.thebearhotel.net; Market Pl; s/d £50/75; P ✗) This historic place in the centre of town dates from the 16th century and combines old-world beams with elegant period furnishings. The spacious rooms are traditional in style but not too frilly.

Healthy Life (☎ 725558; 4 Little Britox; mains lunch £4-6, dinner 3-course set menu £19.95; ⏰ Mon-Sat) A sophisticated health-food shop and bistro, this place specialises in organic, fair-trade and vegetarian delicacies and the dishes really are sublime. If you just want a quick snack the shop serves some wonderful pasties.

> **GOING ROUND IN CIRCLES**
>
> As crop-circle capital of the world, Wiltshire attracts croppies, scientists, practical jokers and romantics in equal measure. Designs range from simple circles to highly complex fractals and usually occur in cereals such as barley and wheat. Some are convinced they represent an extra-terrestrial message from alien life forms, but sceptics argue they are a very terrestrial message from farmers, artists or practical jokers.
>
> Scientists have studied the circles in some detail, and although they alter the molecular structure of the plants and the chemical composition of the soil, the crops continue to grow. The best areas to spot the circles are the Marlborough Downs and Pewsey Vale. Visit the Barge Inn (see p244) or see www.cropcircles.co.uk for locations. Many of the circles are on private land so ask before you go stomping around.

Getting There & Away

Bus No 49 serves Avebury (25 minutes, hourly Monday to Saturday, five on Sunday), while bus No 2 runs from Salisbury (1¼ hours, eight Monday to Saturday).

AROUND DEVIZES
Bowood House

The stately **Bowood House** (☎ 01249-812102; www.bowood.org; adult/child £6.40/4.10; ⏰ 11am-5.30pm Apr-Oct) was first built around 1725 and has been home to the successive earls of Shelburne (now the Marquess of Lansdowne) since 1754. The house has an impressive picture gallery and a fine sculpture gallery, as well as the laboratory where Dr Joseph Priestly discovered oxygen in 1774. The gardens, designed by Capability Brown, are an attraction in themselves and include a terraced rose garden. There's also a large adventure playground and ball pool for younger visitors.

Bowood is 3 miles southeast of Chippenham and 6 miles northwest of Devizes.

PEWSEY VALE

Heading east along the Kennet and Avon Canal from Devizes, the Vale of Pewsey is a timeless blur of undulating hills, fields and thatched villages. There are several white chalk horses carved into the surrounding slopes, and the area is the epicentre of crop-circle action. To check out where the latest mystical designs have appeared, follow the ley lines to the **Barge Inn** (☎ 01672-851705; camping per person £4; mains £5.50-8.50) in tiny Honeystreet, 5 miles east of Devizes. The pool room is designated Crop Circle Central, with pictures and updates on the action. Even if alien visits aren't your thing, it's a gorgeous canalside spot for a cool drink.

Another good stop along this route is the **Seven Stars** (☎ 01672-851325; Bottlesford; mains £9-17; ♥ closed Sun eve & Mon) in Bottlesford. A traditional thatched inn, it is renowned for its sensational modern English and French food.

AVEBURY
☎ 01672

In many ways more dramatic than Stonehenge, Avebury is an awe-inspiring and much-less-visited prehistoric site. Its massive stone circle envelopes the pretty village of the same name and seeps across the surrounding fields into a complex of ceremonial sites, ancient avenues and burial chambers. Although the stones aren't as gargantuan as Stonehenge's trilithons, the site is bigger, older and quieter and there's none of the barbed wire and distant musing. Avebury is also the western end of the Ridgeway national trail.

Orientation & Information

Avebury village has narrow, dead-end streets with no parking. Take advantage of the car park on the A4361 – it's only a short stroll from the circle. The **TIC** (☎ 539425; allatic@kennet.gov.uk; Chapel Centre, Green St; ♥ 9.30am-5pm Wed-Sun) is right in the centre of the ring.

Sights
STONE CIRCLE

The massive stone circle dates from around 2500 to 2200 BC, between the first and second phase of construction at Stonehenge. With a diameter of about 348m, it's one of the largest stone circles in Britain. The site originally consisted of an outer circle of 98 standing stones from 3m to 6m in length, many weighing up to 20 tons. These had been selected for their size and shape, but had not been worked to shape like those at Stonehenge. The stones were surrounded by another circle formed by a 5½m-high earth bank and a 6m- to 9m-deep ditch.

Inside were smaller stone circles to the north (27 stones) and south (29 stones).

The circles remained largely intact through the Roman period. A Saxon settlement grew up inside the circle from around 600 but in medieval times, when the church's power was strong and fear of paganism even stronger, many of the stones were deliberately buried. As the village expanded in the late 17th and early 18th centuries, the stones were broken up for building material.

In 1934 Alexander Keiller supervised the re-erection of the buried stones and the placing of markers to indicate those that had disappeared. The wealthy Keiller eventually bought Avebury in order to restore 'the outstanding archaeological disgrace of Britain'.

Modern roads into Avebury neatly dissect the circle into four sectors. Start from High St, near the Henge Shop, and walk round the circle in an anticlockwise direction. There are 11 standing stones in the southwest sector, one of them known as the **Barber Surgeon Stone**, after the skeleton of a man found under it. The equipment buried with him suggested he was a medieval travelling barber-surgeon, killed when a stone accidentally fell on him.

The southeast sector starts with the huge **portal stones** marking the entry to the circle from West Kennet Ave. The **southern inner circle** stood in this sector and within this circle was the **Obelisk** and a group of stones known as the **Z Feature**. Just outside this smaller circle, only the base of the **Ring Stone** remains. Few stones, standing or fallen, are to be seen around the rest of the southeast or northeast sectors. Most of the northern inner circle was in the northeast sector. The **Cove**, made up of three of the largest stones, marked the centre of this smaller circle.

The northwest sector has the most complete collection of standing stones, including the massive 65-ton **Swindon Stone**, the first stone encountered and one of the few never to have been toppled.

MUSEUMS

Two **museums** (NT; ☎ 539250; combined admission £4.20; ♥ 10am-6pm Apr-Oct, 10am-4pm Nov-Mar) tell the tale of the stone circle and the man who did the most to solve the enigmas.

Housed in the vast, 17th-century thatched Great Barn is the exhibition **Avebury: 6000 Years of Mystery**. Despite the rather over-ripe

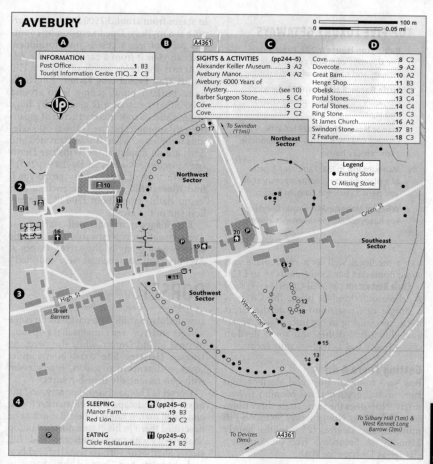

AVEBURY

0 — 100 m
0 — 0.05 mi

INFORMATION
Post Office.................................1 B3
Tourist Information Centre (TIC)..2 C3

SIGHTS & ACTIVITIES (pp244–5)
Alexander Keiller Museum........3 A2
Avebury Manor.........................4 A2
Avebury: 6000 Years of
Mystery.............................(see 10)
Barber Surgeon Stone...............5 C4
Cove...6 C2
Cove...7 C2
Cove...8 C2
Dovecote..................................9 A2
Great Barn..............................10 A2
Henge Shop.............................11 B3
Obelisk....................................12 C3
Portal Stones...........................13 C4
Portal Stones...........................14 C4
Ring Stone...............................15 C3
St James Church......................16 A2
Swindon Stone.........................17 B1
Z Feature.................................18 C3

Legend
● Existing Stone
○ Missing Stone

SLEEPING (pp245–6)
Manor Farm.............................19 B3
Red Lion.................................20 C2

EATING (pp245–6)
Circle Restaurant.....................21 B2

title, it's a series of well-presented, inter-active displays detailing the construction of the site and the relevance of various finds.

The **Alexander Keiller Museum**, in the former stables of Avebury Manor, explains the history of the Avebury Circle and houses finds from here and nearby Neolithic sites, as well as describing Keiller's work.

THE VILLAGE
St James Church (10am–dusk) contains round Saxon windows, a carved Norman font and a rare surviving 15th-century rood (cross) loft. There's a lovely 16th-century circular **dovecote** close by.

Graceful **Avebury Manor** (NT; ☎ 539250; admission manor £3.80, garden only £2.90; manor 2–4.30pm Sun-Tue, gardens 11am–5.30pm Fri-Tue) dates back to the 16th century but has Queen Anne and Edwardian alterations; visits are by timed tour only. The garden features fine topiary and medieval walls.

Sleeping & Eating
Manor Farm (☎ 539294; High St; s/d £40/60; P ☒) The only real B&B in the village, this comfortable 18th-century farmhouse has spacious en suite rooms with pretty traditional décor and warm, friendly service.

Red Lion (☎ 539266; redlion.avebury@whitbread .com; s/d £40/60; P ☒) A creaky, well-worn, thatched pub with exposed beams and resident ghost. It has fairly standard new rooms in an addition at the back. The dining room

WESSEX

TOP FIVE LUXURY GETAWAYS

■ **Babington House** (p288; Babington) The doyenne of stylish countryside retreats and hang-out of media darlings.

■ **Little Barwick House** (p260; Barwick) Elegantly informal yet oozing charm and style.

■ **Manor House Hotel** (p241; Castle Combe) Old-style luxury in an elaborate 14th-century house.

■ **Museum Inn** (p234; Farnham) A gem of a place blending contemporary style and period charm at bargain prices.

■ **Whatley Manor** (p241; Easton Grey) Low-key luxury for high-maintenance clients.

has a medieval well as a centrepiece and some upmarket bar food (mains £6 to £12).

Circle Restaurant (☎ 539514; mains £5-6; ⌚ lunch) A wholesome kind of place, the Circle is a simple café/restaurant beside the Great Barn, specialising in organic, veggie, vegan and gluten-free dishes and some devilish cakes. It also has a child-friendly menu.

Getting There & Away

Bus No 5 from Salisbury and Marlborough runs to Avebury five times Monday to Saturday. No 6 does the same route three times on Sunday. Bus No 49 serves Swindon (40 minutes) and Devizes (25 minutes, hourly Monday to Saturday, five on Sunday); change at Devizes for Bath.

AROUND AVEBURY

Several excellent walks link the important sites around Avebury.

Lined by 100 pairs of stones, the 1½-mile **West Kennet Ave** links the Avebury circle with the **Sanctuary**. The stones along the avenue alternate between column-like shapes and triangular ones. Keiller thought they might have been intended to signify male and female. Post and stone holes indicate that a wooden building surrounded by a stone circle once stood at the Sanctuary.

West of here, massive **Silbury Hill** rises abruptly from the surrounding fields. It is one of the largest artificial hills in Europe, its 40m-high summit ending in a flat top measuring 30m across. It was constructed

in stages from around 2500 BC, but its purpose is a mystery. Due to erosion by countless pairs of feet access is now forbidden; you can view it from a car park on the A4.

Across the fields south of Silbury Hill stands **West Kennet Long Barrow**, England's finest burial mound, dating from around 3500 BC. Its entrance is guarded by huge sarsens and its roof is constructed of gigantic overlapping capstones. About 50 skeletons were found when it was excavated and finds are on display at the Wiltshire Heritage Museum & Gallery in Devizes (p243).

North west of the Avebury circle you'll find **Windmill Hill**, a Neolithic enclosure or 'camp' dating from about 3700 BC, the earliest site in the area.

The **Ridgeway national trail** starts near Avebury and runs westwards across **Fyfield Down**, where many of the sarsen stones at Avebury (and Stonehenge) were collected.

DORSET

Low undulating hills dotted with picturesque villages and Iron Age remains make up most of rural inland Dorset, while the sweeping Unesco Heritage Site coast boasts quiet coves and renowned fossils, interspersed with quintessentially British resorts.

Dorset is Thomas Hardy country, and the unspoiled landscape, bustling market towns and small manor houses are still much as he described them in his classic novels. Hilltop Shaftesbury with the magnificent Gold Hill, sleepy Sherborne with its wonderful abbey, and chocolate-box Cerne Abbas, home to one of England's best-known chalk figures, are all worthy ports of call.

Coastal Dorset is quite a contrast with the ruddy-cheeked resorts and beautiful beaches of Bournemouth and Weymouth and the more genteel refinement of literary Lyme Regis. Linking them all is the fantastic Dorset Coast Path.

Orientation & Information

Dorset stretches along the south coast from Lyme Regis on the western (Devon) border to Christchurch abutting Hampshire on the east. Dorchester, the county town, sits in between and is the most central base for exploring, but Lyme Regis or Weymouth will suit those who prefer the coast.

WESSEX

Dorset has a good web presence. For more information try the following websites:

Dorset County Council (www.dorset-cc.gov.uk)
Rural Dorset (www.ruraldorset.com)
West Dorset (www.westdorset.com)
Visit East Dorset (www.visiteastdorset.com)

Getting Around

One of the reasons for Dorset's backwater status is that few major transport routes cross it. There are two slow railway lines, running from Bristol and Bath through Dorchester West to Weymouth, and from London and Southampton to Bournemouth and Poole.

For buses your best bet is to pick up a free copy of *Dorset & South West Hampshire Bus Times* from TICs or bus stations. It has comprehensive listings of routes and timetables across the county. Otherwise call **Traveline** (☎ 0870 608 2608; www.traveline.org.uk).

The main operator in east and central Dorset is **Wilts and Dorset** (☎ 01202-673555; www.wdbus.co.uk). For western Dorset and on to Devon and southern Somerset, **First Southern National** (☎ 01305-783645; www.firstsouthernnational.co.uk) is the main operator.

BOURNEMOUTH

☎ 01202 / pop 167,527

Seven miles of golden beach sweep along the Bournemouth seafront firmly sealing its fortune as a seaside resort forevermore. The town has seen waves of prosperity and neglect roll by and clings to the traditional guesthouses, seafront promenades and variety shows of the blue-rinse brigade while positively encouraging the wild antics of beery stag nights and Ibiza-style clubbing at the same time. Plans for an artificial reef to improve surfing conditions are well under way and Bournemouth is hoping to turn its somewhat schizophrenic image into something young, hip and happening.

Orientation & Information

Bournemouth is a sprawling town that spreads along the coast towards Poole to the west and Christchurch to the east. The pier marks the central seafront area, and northeast from there is the town centre and train station.

Cyber Place (☎ 290099; 25 St Peter's Rd; per hr £2; 9.30am–midnight) There's a second branch at 132 Charminster Rd.

TIC (☎ 451700; www.bournemouth.co.uk; Westover Rd; 9.30am-5.30pm Mon-Sat year-round, plus 10.30am-5pm Sun May-Sep) Beside the Winter Gardens.

Sights & Activities

Bournemouth is noted for its beautiful *chines* (sharp-sided valleys running down to the sea), most of which are lined with villas.

An interesting mix of Italianate and Scottish baronial pile, the **Russell-Cotes Art Gallery & Museum** (☎ 451800; www.russell-cotes.bournemouth.gov.uk; Russell-Cotes Rd; admission free; 10am-5pm Tue-Sun) is a fascinating place looking out to sea near Bournemouth Pier. It hosts changing exhibitions as well as Victorian paintings by the likes of Rossetti, and an exquisite Japanese collection.

Right next to Bournemouth Pier, **Oceanarium** (☎ 311933; www.oceanarium.co.uk; admission £6.50; 10am-6pm) is a glitzy aquarium with themed areas housing sea and river life from around the world. There are flesh-eating piranhas to scare the kids and an underwater tunnel for close-ups of sharks, turtles and stingrays.

On a clear day it's worth considering a trip on the **Bournemouth Eye** (☎ 314539; www.bournemouthbaloon.com; Lower Gardens; wheelchair access), a tethered helium balloon. Flights last about 15 minutes and go up 500ft, giving great views over the city, the sea and surrounding countryside.

Free **guided walks** (10.30am Mon-Fri, 2.30pm Sun Jun-Sep) depart from the TIC. **City Sightseeing** (☎ 01789-294466; www.citysightseeing.co.uk; adult/child £6/2.50; 10am-4.30pm May-Sep) operates one-hour open-top bus tours leaving every 30 minutes from opposite Bournemouth Pier.

Sleeping

Bournemouth is plastered in B&Bs and hotels, many of them with one foot firmly in the past, but they fill up quickly in the summer. The TIC makes free bookings (accommodation line only ☎ 451700).

Bournemouth Backpackers (☎ 299491; www.bournemouthbackpackers.co.uk; 3 Frances Rd; dm/d £15/36) This friendly hostel near the bus and train stations has small dorms with basic but comfortable facilities and a few private rooms. Reception hours are limited so call ahead or be prepared to wait.

Ventura Hotel (☎ 761265; www.venturahotel.co.uk; 1 Herbert Rd; s/d £29/48; P) You'll get spacious high-ceilinged rooms with big windows at this relatively classy B&B in pleasant Alum Chine, west of the centre. There's plenty of strong colour and floral patterns in the décor but it's not too over the top.

Tudor Grange (☎ 291472; www.tudorgrangehotel .co.uk; 31 Gervis Rd; s/d £45/60; **P**) This lovely old half-timbered house is set in pleasant gardens and has loads of character. The public rooms are all oak-panelled and a fantastic staircase brings you up to the pretty, traditional-style rooms with subtle floral patterns and antique furniture.

Langtry Manor (☎ 553887; www.langtrymanor .com; Derby Rd, East Cliff; s/d £70/140; **P** 🏋) This gorgeous house was given to socialite and actress Lillie Langtry by her lover, the future King Edward VII. Nowadays, it endeavours to create an air of romance with four-posters, stylish period décor and a six-course Edwardian banquet (£34.75) on Saturday nights.

Eating

Coriander (☎ 552202; 22 Richmond Hill; mains £6.50-11; 🕙 lunch & dinner) Cacti, sombreros and colourful stripy blankets set the scene at this fun Mexican restaurant. The menu serves excellent combos of all the reliables and there are high chairs and children's menus so you can enjoy the jugs of Margaritas without a mutiny on your hands.

Retro (☎ 315865; 79-81 Charminster Rd; mains £6-10; 🕙 lunch & dinner) This excellent Lebanese restaurant is a bright and lively place serving up a range of classic dishes and a huge selection of meze and grilled meats. There's plenty of choice for vegetarians, and sticky deserts if you can fit them in.

CH2 (☎ 296296; 37 Exeter Rd; mains £6-18; 🕙 lunch & dinner) There's a young trendy crowd at this modern minimalist place with a strange mix of bright artwork, light woods and formica tables. The creative menu features plenty of fish and steaks – the swordfish with spinach and tomato, coriander and pine-nut salsa is excellent.

Westbeach (☎ 587785; Pier Approach; 2/3-course set lunch £14.95/16.95, 2/3-course set dinner £21.95/24.95) This swanky place is bathed in light from the giant windows overlooking the beach. The modern British menu features simple but sophisticated dishes focusing strongly on fish, and on Thursday nights it packs in the crowds for its live jazz sessions.

Entertainment

Finding a pub (as opposed to a chain boozer or café-bar) in the centre is nigh on impossible and long queues are the norm for most clubs on weekends. Try Firvale Rd, St Peter's Rd or Old Christchurch Rd for action.

Elements (☎ 311178; Firvale Rd) This is Bournemouth's biggest club with four floors of fairly middle-of-the-road music so you're bound to find something to your taste.

K-bar/K1 (☎ 317818; 4 Terrace Rd) In a long-abandoned casino, this bar and club mixes Miami vice with 1930s Art Deco styling and hosts everything from comedy and cabaret to serious garage club sounds. K-bar acts as a pre-club venue with live music and top local DJs in the evenings while the club plays a mix of garage, hip-hop and R&B.

Opera House (☎ 399922; 570 Christchurch Rd) An incredible converted theatre, this is Bournemouth's answer to the superclub. The omnipresent Slinky franchise has sunk its teeth in here, playing crowd-pleasing choons from Monday's Bak to Skool night through to Saturday cheese.

Getting There & Away

National Express runs from London (£16, 2½ hours, hourly) and Oxford (£16.50, three hours, three daily). Bus No X3 runs hourly from Salisbury (1¼ hours) and on to Poole (20 minutes), while the No X33 comes from Southampton (one hour, 10 Monday to Saturday). There's a multitude of buses between Bournemouth and Poole (15 minutes).

Trains run every half-hour from London Waterloo (£22.50, two hours); half of these continue on to Poole (£2.50, 10 minutes), Dorchester South (£7.70, 40 minutes) and Weymouth (£9.70, one hour).

POOLE

☎ 01202 / pop 144,800

Marketed as the 'Palm Beach of Britain', Europe's largest natural harbour plays host to B-list celebs and supposedly has the fourth-highest property prices in the world! The town itself is pretty unassuming, with a lovely old harbour surrounded by narrow winding streets, but the up-and-coming Sandbanks area has a blue-flag beach, lots of watersports and a clutch of upmarket eateries.

The **TIC** (☎ 253253; www.pooletourism.com; Poole Quay; 🕙 10am-5pm Mon-Sat, noon-5pm Sunday, noon-3pm Sat & Sun Nov-Mar) is on the quay.

Sights & Activities

Poole Old Town has attractive 18th-century buildings, including a wonderful **Customs House** and **Guildhall**.

The well-presented **Waterfront Museum** (☎ 262600; Old High St; admission free; ☒ 10am-5pm Mon-Sat, noon-5pm Sun Apr-Oct, noon-3pm Nov-Mar) recounts the town's history, with a reconstructed Victorian High St and displays of paintings, pottery, archaeology and artefacts from the fishing trade.

A medieval merchant's house, **Scaplen's Court Museum** (☎ 633558; Old High St; 10am-5pm Mon-Sat, noon-5pm Sun Aug only) is open to the public in August for local interest exhibitions (call the TIC for details).

Deep-sea fishing and mackerel fishing are popular in Poole; half-day trips with **Sea Fishing** (☎ 679666; www.seafishingpoole.co.uk; The Quay) start at around £15. You can hire your own boat from **Yellow Penguin** (☎ 710448; www.yellowpenguin.co.uk; Turks Lane) for £160 per day.

Out at Sandbanks, windsurfing lessons start at £79 per day, with hire from £10 per hour. **Poole Harbour Boardsailing** (☎ 700503; www.poolehar bour.co.uk; 284 Sandbanks Rd) offers one-/two-day kite-surfing courses for £95/165. **Cool Cats** (☎ 701100; www.coolcatswatersports.com) hires kayaks (£10 per hour) and bikes (£10 to £19 per day), and offers windsurfing and sailing lessons (from £149 for two days).

For something more cultural, **Poole Lighthouse** (☎ 685222; www.lighthousepoole.co.uk; 21 Kingland Rd) which is one of the largest arts centres outside London and hosts a lively events calendar including live music, theatre, film and exhibitions.

Sleeping & Eating

Laurel Cottages (☎ 730894; laurel.cottages@btopenworld.com; 41 Foxholes Rd; s/d £30/50; ☒ ☒) Slightly out of town but good value, this Victorian cottage has a country feel, with a beautiful garden and tastefully traditional rooms. It's a very relaxed place with an outdoor heated pool and a warm welcome for children.

Mansion House (☎ 685666; www.themansionhouse.co.uk; Thames St; s/d £75/130; P ☒) This gorgeous, creeper-clad Georgian house has a grand, sweeping staircase leading up to the beautiful, themed rooms – choose from country cottage, Indian summer or oriental. The excellent restaurant (a two-/three-course set menu costs £21/27) focuses on fish, seafood and game.

Storm (☎ 674970; 16 High St; mains £12.50-16; ☒ dinner) Cool, relaxed and a hit from the start, this place serves some of the best seafood in Poole. Although the interior is all rustic charm with rough stone walls and wooden floors, the menu is more refined with delicate flavours and tender fish in some daring combinations.

Jazz Café (☎ 670851; Poole Quay; mains £6-11; ☒ lunch & dinner) For more informal dining hit this bright-and-breezy café bar with great snacks, and a decent, if predictable, menu. Bag a seat outside on sunny afternoons for maximum exposure and retire inside for the sultry jazz on Friday and Sunday nights.

Getting There & Away

Countless buses cover the 20-minute trip to Bournemouth. National Express runs hourly to London (£16, three hours). Train connections are as for Bournemouth, just 13 minutes closer to London Waterloo (£25.30).

Sandbanks Ferry (☎ 01929-450203; www.sandbanksferry.co.uk; pedestrian/car 90p/£2.60) shuttles across to Studland every 20 minutes. This is a short cut from Poole to Swanage, Wareham and the west Dorset coast, but summer queues can be horrendous.

Bus No 152 goes from Poole to Sandbanks (15 minutes, hourly).

WIMBORNE

☎ 01202 / pop 14,844

Dominated by its impressive old minster, sleepy Wimborne is a dignified old town with a cluster of picturesque buildings, narrow rambling streets and several local sites worth a visit. It makes a good day trip from Bournemouth or a relaxed base away from the dazzle of the seaside resorts.

The helpful **TIC** (☎ 886116; wimbornetic@eastdorset.gov.uk; 29 High St; ☒ 9.30am-5.30pm Mon-Sat Apr-Sep, 9.30am-4.30pm Oct-Mar) is situated near the minster.

Next to the TIC is the 16th-century **Priest's House Museum** (☎ 882533; 23-27 High St; adult/child £3/1; ☒ 10am-4.30pm Mon-Sat Apr-Oct), an interesting local-history museum with a reconstructed Victorian kitchen, Georgian parlour and village school room.

Wimborne Model Town (☎ 881924; www.wimborne-modeltown.com; adult/child £3/2; ☒ 10am-5pm Easter-Sep) is an oddity, a 1:10 scale model of the town as it was in the 1950s.

Wimborne Minster

Founded around 1050, the **Wimborne Minster** (☎ 884753; ⏱ 9.30am-5.30pm) was considerably enlarged in Decorated style in the 14th century and became the parish church in 1537 when Henry VIII dissolved the monasteries. Aside from the impressive 15th-century perpendicular tower, highlights include the remarkable 14th-century astronomical clock, a Saxon chest hewn from a single tree, and tessellated Roman mosaic tiles that can be seen in the nave. The nave columns, the piers of the central tower and the north and south transepts are the main Norman survivors. Traces of 13th- to 15th-century painted murals can be seen in a Norman altar recess in the north transept.

In **Holy Trinity Chapel** is the tomb of Ettricke, the 'man in the wall', a local eccentric who refused to be buried in the church or village and was interred in the church wall.

Above the choir vestry is a wonderful **chained library** (⏱ 10.30am-12.30pm & 2-4pm Mon-Thu, 10.30am-12.30pm Fri Easter-Oct), established in 1686 and containing books and manuscripts from well before then.

Kingston Lacy

One of the country's finest 17th-century houses, **Kingston Lacy** (NT; ☎ 01202-883402; admission house £7.20, grounds only £3.60; ⏱ house 11am-5pm Wed-Sun Easter-Oct, grounds 10.30am-6pm Easter-Oct) is much as it was when the last occupant left in 1981 without selling a thing. The house

is dense with furniture and art, much of it collected by William Bankes, who was responsible for major renovations in the 1830s. The extensive 18th-century landscaped gardens and estate encompass the Iron Age hill fort of **Badbury Rings**. Kingston Lacy is 2 miles west of Wimborne down a wonderful leafy road.

Sleeping & Eating

Beechleas (☎ 841684; www.beechleas.com; 17 Poole Rd; s/d £69/79; Ⓟ ⌧ wheelchair access) This delightful B&B is set in a beautifully restored Georgian house with a lovely walled garden. The restored coach house has cosy rooms with beamed ceilings, while rooms in the main house retain their period character.

King's Head (☎ 880101; www.thekingsheadhotel.com; The Square; s/d £75/95) This traditional Georgian coaching inn has been recently refurbished, but the large rooms are a little soulless with corporate-style features and little character. The bar and restaurant retain more period features and do decent but predictable food (mains £6 to £13).

Shapwick House Hotel (☎ 01458-210321; Monks Dr, Shapwick; s £85, d £100-160; 2-/3-course dinner £20/24.50; Ⓟ) This wonderful Tudor country house has huge rooms with eclectic décor and a great restaurant serving traditional English classics and more imaginative modern fare. Shapwick is 4 miles northwest of Wimborne off the A350.

Getting There & Away

Bus Nos 132 and 133 run between Bournemouth (45 minutes) and Poole (40 minutes) via Wimborne every half-hour Monday to Saturday (every two hours on Sunday). Bus Nos 182 and 183 run to Bournemouth and, more frequently, to Shaftesbury (1¼ hours, hourly, Monday to Saturday).

SOUTHEAST DORSET

The Purbeck peninsula in the southeastern corner of Dorset is strewn with pretty thatched villages and crumbling ruins, while the spectacular Dorset Coast Path, part of the South West Coast Path, runs along secluded coves and towering cliffs.

Wareham & Around

☎ 01929 / pop 2568

The charming town of Wareham on the River Frome has a lovely quay, remarkable

---

TOP FIVE PUBS FOR SUNDAY LUNCH

■ **Acorn Inn** (p255; Evershot) Trendy metropolitan style at a 16th-century coaching inn.

■ **Fox Inn** (p260; Corscombe) Rustic favourites at this idyllic rose-clad pub.

■ **Full Moon** (p240; Rudge) Modern British and international food in a gorgeous 17th-century inn.

■ **George** (p285; Norton St Philip) Stunningly atmospheric dining in England's oldest continually licensed inn.

■ **George and Dragon** (p242; Rowde) Food first, beer later at this renowned gastro-pub.

SOMETHING FOR THE WEEKEND

Start off your weekend by checking in to **Mortons House Hotel** (p252) in Corfe Castle and taking a stroll around the gorgeous village and magnificent castle. Wander back to the hotel for an intimate dinner and settle in for the night. On Saturday, make your way to the **Blue Pool** (p252) and across the moors to the spectacular coastline around **Lulworth Cove and Durdle Door** (p252). Fuel up on something fishy at **Lulworth Beach Hotel** (p252) and if you're feeling energetic take a walk along the coast path. Drive on to the market town of Dorchester and check in to the **Old Manor** (p254) before strolling around the town and dining at **Sienna** (p254) or nearby **Yarlbury Cottage** (p254). Head north on Sunday morning to the delightful village of **Cerne Abbas** (p254) and hike up the hill to the rather well-hung **Cerne Giant** (p254). Tumble back down the hill and pop in to the atmospheric **Royal Oak** (p255) to toast the weekend with a glorious lunch.

---

remains of Saxon town walls and an impressive church dating from the same period. It also has a string of Lawrence of Arabia connections and sturdy earth banks surrounding the town.

Purbeck TIC (☎ 552740; www.purbeck-dc.gov.uk; Holy Trinity Church, South St; ☿ 9.30am-5pm Mon-Sat & 10am-1pm & 1.45-4pm Sun Apr-Sep, 10am-3pm Mon-Sat Oct-Mar) stocks an excellent free guide and walking-tour map.

SIGHTS

The bijou **Wareham Museum** (☎ 553448; East St; admission free; ☿ 10am-4pm Easter-Oct) has a Lawrence of Arabia collection supplementing the usual local items with relics of early settlers from the Iron Age and Roman occupation.

Standing on the wall beside North St is the tiny but delightful Saxon **St Martin's Church**, which dates from about 1020. Although the porch and bell tower are later additions, and larger windows have been added over the centuries, the basic structure is unchanged. Inside there's a 12th-century fresco on the northern wall and a marble effigy of Lawrence of Arabia.

You'll find more Lawrence memorabilia at his tiny, austere former home, **Clouds Hill** (NT; ☎ 405616; admission £3.10; ☿ noon-5pm Thu-Sun Apr-Oct), still much as he would have left it after his death in 1935. Lawrence was an enigmatic figure renowned for his heroic achievements in WWI and his immense book *Seven Pillars of Wisdom*. His life was immortalised in David Lean's epic film *Lawrence of Arabia*.

Lawrence was stationed at Bovington Camp, now an interesting **Tank Museum** (☎ 405 096; www.tankmuseum.org; adult/child £8/6; ☿ 10am-5pm; wheelchair access) 6 miles from Wareham.

He died at Bovington Military Hospital six days after a motorcycle accident nearby. The museum has a collection of over 300 armoured vehicles, from the earliest WWI prototypes to remnants from the first Gulf War.

Close by is a fascinating sanctuary for abused chimpanzees. **Monkey World** (☎ 462537; www.monkeyworld.co.uk; Longthorns; adult/child £8/6; ☿ 10am-5pm Sep-Jun, 10am-6pm Jul & Aug; wheelchair access) houses the largest group of chimpanzees outside Africa as well as a collection of orang-utans, lemurs and macaques.

SLEEPING & EATING

Gold Court House (☎ 553320; St John's Hill; s/d £37.50/55; ☒) In the centre of town but with great views, this charming B&B is a real find. There's an air of restrained luxury throughout the 18th-century house. The bright, uncluttered rooms feature cream walls, exposed beams and mahogany furniture.

Old Granary (☎ 552010; The Quay; d £60-95) Right on the river banks, this charming old place has a hidden door in the oak panelling taking you up a winding staircase to the little rooms with low ceilings, exposed beams and a clutter of period furniture. The restaurant serves a mix of decent baguettes (£3.50) and more substantial and sophisticated bistro-style food (mains £6.50 to £15).

Harry's Café Bar (☎ 551818; 20 South St; mains £4-6; ☿ lunch & dinner) This place is about as trendy as Wareham gets, with modern design and a minimalist attitude, but the whole effect is spoiled by the fruit machines in the corner. There's free Internet access for customers and a range of fairly standard sambos, wraps and hot panini. By night it's a wine bar with a mixed clientele.

WESSEX

GETTING THERE & AWAY

Bus Nos 142, 143 and 144 run between Poole (35 minutes) and Wareham hourly (every two hours on Sunday). Bus Nos 101, 102, 103 and 104 run between Wareham (15 minutes) and Dorchester (one hour, hourly Monday to Saturday), but stop at Monkey World only from June to September. Clouds Hill is a 1-mile walk from the nearest stop.

Corfe Castle

☎ 01929

The magnificent ruins of **Corfe Castle** (NT; ☎ 01929-481294; admission £4.70; ◷ 10am-6pm Apr-Oct, 10am-5pm Mar, 10am-4pm Nov-Feb) tower above the gorgeous stone village of the same name, offering wonderful views of the countryside. Even by English standards, the 1000-year-old castle has a dramatic history, with royal poisonings, treacherous stabbings and Civil War sieges. Elements of early Norman brickwork are still evident, but it's the fractured grandeur of the scene that draws the crowds.

The **Castle View visitor centre** at the bottom of the hill houses an exhibition on the castle's construction while the **Model Village** (☎ 481234; The Square; admission £2.50) has a reconstruction of the castle and ancient village in 1646.

The village has several pubs and B&Bs, and there are camp sites nearby. The castle ruins loom large above the **Greyhound** (☎ 01929-480205; mjml@greyhound-inn.fsnet.co.uk; The Square; d £60), reputedly the most photographed pub in Britain. Parts of the inn date from 1580 and the low ceilings and exposed beams give it an old-world charm. It has a pleasant garden overlooking the castle, and provides comfortable B&B and traditional pub food (mains £9 to £16).

If you fancy something grander, **Mortons House Hotel** (☎ 01929-480988; www.mortonshouse .co.uk; s £75, d £124-168; ℗ ✗ wheelchair access) is a 400-year-old manor built in the shape of an 'E' to commemorate Elizabeth I. The rooms are luxurious but simple and stylish, with four-posters, sleigh beds and period features. The restaurant (mains £15 to £25) serves impeccable traditional English food with local meat, fish and game featuring strongly on the menu.

Bus Nos 142, 143 and 144 run hourly from Poole (50 minutes) through Wareham (15 minutes) to Swanage (20 minutes) via Corfe Castle.

The Blue Pool

Designated a Site of Special Scientific Interest (SSSI), the **Blue Pool** (☎ 01929-551408; www .bluepooluk.com; Furzebrook; admission £3.80; ◷ from 9.30am Mar-Nov) has water with a chameleon-like tendency to change colour. The grounds are home to rare wildlife including green sand lizards and Dartford warblers. The pool is signposted from the A351; hourly bus Nos 142, 143 and 144 from Wareham (10 minutes) stop nearby.

Lulworth Cove & the Coast

☎ 01929

The coastline between Swanage and Weymouth is simply stunning, with a fantastic drive across the moors from Corfe Castle to Lulworth and spectacular clifftop walks. There are some excellent beaches around **Durdle Door** where a natural arch is formed by folding rock. At Lulworth Cove, a mile to the east, towering cliffs enclose an almost perfectly circular bay.

Stumpy **Lulworth Castle** (☎ 400352; www .lulworth.com; East Lulworth; admission £7; ◷ 10.30am-6pm Apr-Oct, 10.30am-4pm Nov-Mar) is in a picturesque village about 3 miles inland. The castle is 'modern' compared with many in England and was built as a hunting lodge in 1608. It contains exhibits about its history and has a children's adventure playground outside. You can see jousting shows here throughout August.

There are lots of places to stay around Lulworth. Campers should head for **Durdle Door Holiday Park** (☎ 400200; durdle.door@lulworth .com; tent £11-16; ◷ Mar-Oct), spectacularly situated on fields above the cliffs. In the lovely village of West Lulworth you'll find a small **YHA Hostel** (☎ 0870 770 5940; www.yha.org.uk; School Lane; dm £11.80; ◷ Mar-Oct) and the Victorian **Graybank** (☎ 400256; West Lulworth; s/d £20/36; ℗ ✗), an excellent-value B&B set in a Purbeck stone house with modest, traditional-style rooms.

For greater comfort and a wonderful location try **Lulworth Beach Hotel** (☎ 400404; www .lulworthbeachhotel.com; Lulworth Cove; s/d £45/80), just steps from the beach. It has been recently refurbished and modernised and is now bright and airy with colourful artworks on the walls. It has two restaurants (mains £8 to £14) specialising in seafood and game.

Bus No 103 runs from Dorchester (40 minutes, five Monday to Saturday) to Lulworth Cove.

DORCHESTER

☎ 01305 / pop 16,171

Thomas Hardy hub and bustling market town (on Wednesday at least), Dorchester is a pleasant place with a core of pretty 17th-century and Georgian buildings. Not content to let the town's charms speak for themselves though, it is now also home to Prince Charles' lesson in ideal town planning and a string of bizarre museums shamelessly pandering to the tourist market.

Orientation & Information

Most of Dorchester's action takes place along South St, which runs north into pedestrianised Cornhill and then emerges in High St.

The **TIC** (☎ 267992; dorchester.tic@westdorset-dc .gov.uk; Antelope Walk; ☉ 9am-5pm Mon-Sat & 10am-3pm Sun Apr-Oct, 9am-4pm Mon-Sat Nov-Mar) stocks the guide *All About Dorchester* (£1), with interesting walks around town. There's also lots of Hardy literature, including a set of leaflets (50p each) tracing the scenes of individual novels.

Sights

The foundations of a 1st-century **Roman town house** are behind the town hall on Northern Hay. The layout of the house is clearly visible and the remains of the main building, housed within a glass structure, boast remarkable mosaic floors. Just across the road is the pretty **Hangman's Cottage**, another reminder of Judge Jeffrey's pleasant interlude in the area (see boxed text above right).

To the northern end of town is **Poundbury Village**, HRH Prince Charles' vision of a model development for 21st-century communities.

The Hardy memorabilia at **Dorset County Museum** (☎ 262735; High West St; admission £3.50; ☉ 10am-5pm daily May-Oct, Mon-Sat Nov-Apr), featuring the novelist's study, is only part of a wide-ranging collection, which includes relics from the archaeological excavations at Maiden Castle, fossil finds from Lyme Regis and artefacts from the Roman town house.

The **Tutankhamun Exhibition** (☎ 269571; www .tutankhamun-exhibition.co.uk; High West St; adult/child £6/4.50; ☉ 9.30am-5.30pm) may seem out of place in Dorset but it's nevertheless an intriguing place to visit. The discovery of the tomb and its contents has been recreated in montages complete with sounds and smells.

THE BLOODY ASSIZES

In 1685 the Duke of Monmouth, illegitimate son of Charles II, landed at Lyme Regis intending to overthrow James II and become king. His rebellion ended in defeat at the Somerset Battle of Sedgemoor; the duke was beheaded in the Tower of London – it took four swings of the axe to sever his head. Judge Jeffreys, the chief justice, tried the rebels in Dorchester in a barbaric trial known as the Bloody Assizes.

Over 300 rebels were hanged and their gruesome drawn-and-quartered remains were displayed in towns and villages all over the region. Nearly 1000 more rebels were transported to Barbados and many others were imprisoned, fined or flogged.

You can see more exotic displays at the **Terracotta Warriors Museum** (☎ 266040; www.terra cottawarriors.co.uk; East High St; admission £5; ☉ 10am-5.30pm) where eight full-size reconstructions of the 2m-high clay warriors found in Xi'an are on show.

Other museums include the **Keep Military Museum** (☎ 264066; www.keepmilitarymuseum.org; Bridport Rd; adult/child £3/2; ☉ 9.30am-5pm Mon-Sat Apr-Sep, Tue-Sat Oct-Mar, plus 10am-4pm Sun Jul & Aug) which traces Dorset and Devon military valour overseas, and the **Dinosaur Museum** (☎ 269880; www.dinosaur-museum.org.uk; Icen Way; adult/child £6/4.50; ☉ 9.30am-5.30pm) featuring fossils and life-size reconstructed beasts.

THOMAS HARDY SITES

The TIC has a free leaflet *The Hardy Trail* with information on Hardy connections around the town and surrounding area.

Designed by Thomas Hardy, **Max Gate** (NT; ☎ 262538; Alington Ave; admission £2.60; ☉ 2-5pm Mon, Wed & Sun Apr-Sep) was his home from 1885 until his death in 1928. It contains pieces of his furniture, but otherwise there's not exactly a wealth of memorabilia. Here he wrote several of his most famous works including *Tess of the D'Urbervilles* and *Jude the Obscure*. It's a mile east of the town centre on the A352.

Similarly, the small cob-and-thatch **Hardy's Cottage** (NT; ☎ 01305-262366; admission £3; ☉ 11am-5pm Thu-Mon Apr-Oct) where Hardy was born, is furnished in appropriately simple style, but is unremarkable. It's located at Higher

WESSEX

Bockhampton, about 3 miles northeast of Dorchester and reached by a 10-minute walk from the car park.

Sleeping & Eating

Dorchester is blessed with some beautiful hotels and excellent restaurants and makes a great base for the surrounding area.

Casterbridge Hotel (☎ 264043; www.casterbridge hotel.co.uk; 49 High East St; s £48-64, d £80-98; wheelchair access) This lovely upmarket Georgian guesthouse has a choice of period rooms with traditional flowers and frills or contemporary rooms with bright, neutral colours. It has a lovely courtyard garden and despite the refined air children are very welcome.

Yalbury Cottage (☎ 262382; www.yalburycottage .com; Lower Brockhampton; s/d £59/94; 3-course dinner £30; P ⊠) A gorgeous, 17th-century thatched cottage near Hardy's birthplace, this charming place has rooms with exposed beams and rustic, period furnishings. The restaurant serves excellent contemporary food.

Old Manor (☎ 01305-261110; www.kingston-maur ward.co.uk; Kingston Maurward; s/d £65/96; P ⊠) Just on the outskirts of town, this Elizabethan manor has a wonderfully luxurious but completely relaxed feel. The stately rooms have mullioned windows, huge four-poster beds, flagged or wooden floors and beautiful rugs.

Potters Bistro & Café (☎ 260312; 19 Durngate St; mains lunch £4-6, dinner £7-14; ⊙ 9am-4pm) This beautifully renovated property blends traditional features with clean modern design. The daytime menu has gourmet sandwiches, stunning homemade soups, and interesting salads and pastas. In the evening it steps up a level with tempting dishes such as marinated Balmoral venison or pan-fried fillet of wild sea bass.

Sienna (☎ 250022; 36 High West St; 2-course set lunch/dinner £13/24; ⊙ Tue-Sat) This tiny modern restaurant offers top-notch cuisine. Go for lemon sole fillets with tiger prawn tortellini or pot-roasted quail with wild mushrooms and a puy lentil sauce and follow it up with the wicked bitter chocolate mousse.

Other options:

Sunrise Guest House (☎ 262425; 34 London Rd; s/d £25/40; P) A modern house with comfortable, good-value rooms.

6 North Square (☎ 267679; 6 North Sq; mains £8-14; ⊙ closed Sun) A small modern brasserie serving excellent but homely cooking including plenty of veg choices.

Getting There & Around

National Express coaches run from London (£17.50, four hours, once daily). Bus No 31 runs from Weymouth (25 minutes) and on to Lyme Regis (1¼ hours) hourly (every two hours on Sunday); No 10 also serves Weymouth every 20 minutes (every two hours on Sunday). Bus No 184 goes to Salisbury (1¾ hours, six Monday to Saturday, three on Sunday).

There are two train stations, Dorchester South and Dorchester West, both southwest of the town centre. Trains run hourly from Weymouth (£2.70, 11 minutes) to London (saver return £31, 2½ hours) via Dorchester South, Bournemouth (£7.70, 45 minutes) and Southampton (£15, 1¼ hours). Dorchester West has connections with Bath (£10.50, 1¾ hours) and Bristol (£11.40, two hours).

Dorchester Cycles (☎ 268787; 31 Great Western Rd; per day £10) hires bikes.

AROUND DORCHESTER
Maiden Castle

The massive earthwork ramparts of Maiden Castle, Europe's largest and finest Iron Age hill fort, stretch for 3 miles and enclose nearly 20 hectares. The site has been inhabited since Neolithic times but the first fort was built here around 800 BC. It was abandoned and rebuilt. Later the earth walls were extended and enlarged. Despite the addition of more defences, the Romans still captured it in AD 43, finally abandoning it in the 4th century. The sheer size of the walls and ditches and the area they enclose is stunning, and there are wonderful views. Finds from the site are displayed at Dorset County Museum (p253). Maiden Castle is 1½ miles southwest of Dorchester.

Cerne Abbas & the Cerne Giant

The gorgeous village of Cerne Abbas, with its fine 16th-century houses, is an idyllic place to stroll and admire the wonderful buildings and quiet lanes – and the chalk man with a huge weapon.

The much rebuilt **abbey house** is now a private residence, although the **ruins** (adult/ child £1/20p) behind the house can be explored when the gate is open. The Abbot's Porch (1509) was once the entrance to the whole complex. Fourteenth-century **St Mary's Church** is also worth a gander to see the rare medieval frescoes and impish gargoyles.

SOMETHING SPECIAL

Acorn Inn (☎ 01935-83228; www.acorn-inn.co.uk; 28 Fore St, Evershot; s/d £75/90; P ✗ 💻) This lovely 16th-century coaching inn, nestled in a picturesque village, was the inspiration for the 'Sow & Acorn' in Thomas Hardy's *Tess of the d'Urbervilles*. Each of the pretty rooms is named after characters and locations from the novel. Individually decorated with great elegance and character, the bedrooms are country chic with a mix of rustic tradition and modern design. Downstairs there's a traditional bar and slick restaurant (mains £12 to £16) serving interesting modern combinations of local produce, including fish and game.

Evershot is 10 miles north of Dorchester on the A37.

Just north of the village is the **Cerne Giant**, one of Britain's best-known chalk figures. The giant stands 55m tall, wields a 37m-long club and is estimated to be anything between a few hundred and a couple of thousand years old. One thing is obvious – this old man has no need of Viagra! The poor fellow only regained his manhood last century; the prudish Victorians had allowed grass to grow over his vital parts.

Cerne Abbas is a peaceful, atmospheric place to stay. **Cerne River Cottage** (☎ 01300-341355; www.cernerivercottage.co.uk; 8 The Folly; d £55; P ✗) is a beautiful 18th-century house set in a lovely walled garden by the River Cerne. The rooms are bright and fresh with modest, country décor.

For refreshment visit the thatched **Royal Oak** (☎ 01300-341797; Long St; mains £5-8; ☒ lunch & dinner), a gorgeous pub just dripping with character and good cheer. It serves some excellent pub-grub in its low, beamed bar hung with hundreds of cups and mugs and there's a lovely courtyard garden outside. There's plenty of real ale on tap and a varied menu featuring old favourites and more sophisticated modern classics.

Dorchester, 8 miles to the south, is reached on bus No 216 (20 minutes, six times Monday to Saturday).

WEYMOUTH

☎ 01305 / pop 48,279

A traditional family resort by summer and a rather soulless place in winter, Weymouth has the anaesthetised charm of the archetypal English seaside resort. Stripy deckchairs, donkey rides and Punch-and-Judy shows line the beach, while traditional boarding houses and hotels flank the gracious Georgian esplanade. George III clinched Weymouth's fortunes when he took an experimental dip in the waters here in 1789.

Orientation & Information

Central Weymouth is only a few blocks wide with the Esplanade following the sea front. To the west is the charming old harbour with coloured terraced cottages lining the narrow winding streets.

The **TIC** (☎ 785747; tic@weymouth.gov.uk; The Esplanade; ☒ 9.30am-5pm Apr-Oct, 10am-4pm Nov-Mar) is opposite the vivid statue of King George III, patron saint of Weymouth tourism. If you're planning to visit any of the attractions in Weymouth or Abbotsbury you can buy your tickets at the TIC at a substantial discount.

You can check your email at **Cobwebs** (☎ 779688; 28 St Thomas St; per 20 min £1; ☒ 9.45am-9.30pm Mon-Fri, 10am-6pm Sat, noon-6pm Sun).

Sights & Activities

Over in the old part of town, Brewer's Quay has a shopping centre and plentiful attractions, including the excellent **Timewalk** (☎ 777622; Hope Sq; adult/child £4.50/3.25; ☒ 10am-5.30pm), a series of historic tableaux depicting the town's early history as a trading port, the disaster of the Black Death, the drama of the Spanish Armada and Weymouth's development as a resort.

Also in Brewer's Quay is the fascinating **Weymouth Museum** (admission free; ☒ 10am-5pm), uncovering the town's maritime heritage with displays on smuggling, paddle steamers and shipwrecks.

Nearby, there's the wonderful **Tudor House** (☎ 812341; 3 Trinity St; adult/child £2.50/50p; ☒ 11am-3.45pm Tue-Fri Jun-Sep, 2-4pm 1st Sun of the month Oct-May) dating from around 1600. It's furnished in Tudor style and admission includes a guided tour delving into everyday life in those days.

Don't be put off by the 'family fun' tag and gift-shop entrance at **Deep Sea Adventure** (☎ 0871 222 5760; www.deepsea-adventure.co.uk;

WESSEX

9 Custom House Quay; adult/child £4/3; ☉ 9.30am-7pm Sep-Jun, 9.30am-8pm Jul & Aug) – it's actually an absorbing examination of the history of diving, with exhibits on local shipwrecks and the *Titanic*. Last entry is 1½ hours before closing time.

A largely outdoor branch of the aquarium chain, **Sea Life** (☎ 788255; www.sealife.co.uk; Lodmoor Country Park; adult/child £8.95/6.25; ☉ 10am-5pm; wheelchair access) is one of the more extensive and enjoyable of its kind, featuring seal and otter sanctuaries, a penguin enclosure and a shark nursery.

Perched on the end of the promontory, 19th-century **Nothe Fort** (☎ 766465; Barrack Rd; adult/child £3.75/free; ☉ 10.30am-5.30pm daily May-Sep, 2.30pm-4.30pm Sun Oct-Apr) houses a museum concentrating on life in the fort for soldiers over the years. It's a substantial affair, with extensive collections of weapons and fine views of the harbour and coast.

For windsurfing lessons (from £50 for three hours) and hire (£10 to £25 per hour), contact **Windtek** (☎ 787900; www.windtek.co.uk; 109 Portland Rd). They also do a beginners kitesurfing course for £95. For Portland-based operators offering diving and sailing around Weymouth see opposite.

Sleeping

The TIC keeps a daily vacancy list (50p) and makes accommodation bookings free of charge. Weymouth has a colossal number of guesthouses and hotels; most are pretty standard affairs with little character. If you're camping there are plenty of sites near Chesil Beach and Weymouth Bay.

Victoria Hotel (☎ 761438; www.victoriaweymouth .com; 56-57 The Esplanade; s/d £26.50/45; ℗ ⊠) This really friendly place on the waterfront has great-value rooms. Although the bathrooms are a bit of a squeeze, the rooms are spacious and tastefully decorated. Children are very welcome.

Chatsworth (☎ 785012; www.thechatsworth.co.uk; 14 The Esplanade; s/d £33/70; ℗) There's quite a range of rooms on offer at this smart guesthouse with views of the Old Harbour and the bay so take a look at a few before deciding. The rooms are classically stylish but not overly fussy.

Oaklands (☎ 767081; www.oaklands-guesthouse .co.uk; 1 Glendinning Ave; s/d £40/50; ℗ ⊠ wheelchair access) This lovely Edwardian house is in a quiet area but within an easy stroll of the beach. The ground floor is elaborately restored with bright plaster mouldings and stained glass, but the bedrooms are modern with simple, light décor.

Acropolis Hotel (☎ 784282; www.acropolishotel .co.uk; 53 Dorchester Rd; s/d £45/70; ℗ ⊠ 🐾) Another good-value option is this large bright hotel with a lovely garden terrace and spacious modern rooms with unassuming décor. There's a good pool and a children's playroom to keep the nippers happy.

Eating

Yako (☎ 780888; 97 St Mary St; mains £4.80; ☉ lunch & dinner) This excellent Japanese noodle bar has a great selection of traditional dishes ranging from sushi to soba and bento boxes. The portions are generous, making it excellent value.

Isobar (☎ 750666; 19 Trinity Rd; mains £12.95-15.50; ☉ dinner) A lush, baroque bar-restaurant, this funky place offers modern British and world cuisine with plenty of seafood, game and local meats. It's got welcoming velvet sofas and is a tempting spot to loll for the evening with a long drink.

Chatsworth Brasserie (☎ 785012; 14 The Esplanade; mains £8-14; ☉ lunch & dinner) This modern Mediterranean-style brasserie is strong on locally caught fish, but also does a good range of meat dishes. The food is interesting and there's also a great terrace overlooking the waterfront.

Perry's (☎ 785799; 4 Trinity Rd; mains £12.95-15.95; ☉ dinner daily, lunch Tue-Fri & Sun) This classical but unstuffy place on the old harbour front has a simple menu featuring a good selection of excellently prepared fish and a handful of meat and pasta dishes.

Getting There & Away

BOAT

High-speed catamaran car-ferries operated by **Condor** (☎ 761551; www.condorferries.com) whiz across to St Malo, France (4½ hours) and the Channel Islands. Day trips start at £15 return.

BUS

National Express coaches run to London (£17.50, 4¾ hours, six daily). Bus Nos 10, 31, 101, 102, 103, and 104 between them serve Dorchester (30 minutes) at least every 20 minutes. Bus No 31 goes on to Lyme Regis (1¾ hours, hourly), as does No X53 (four Mon-

COTTAGES FOR HIRE

Need a home away from home? Visit some of these sites for ideas on self-catering options in Wessex:

Cottages Direct (www.cottagesdirect.com)
Cottage Guide (www.cottageguide.co.uk)
CottageNet UK (www.cottagenet.co.uk)
Dorset Coastal Cottages (www.dorsetcoastal cottages.com)
Somerset Cottages (www.somersetcottages .com)

day to Saturday), which continues to Exeter (three hours). Bus No 184 runs to Salisbury (1¾ hours, six Monday to Saturday, three on Sunday). First Explorer all-day travel tickets cost £2.50 and cover Weymouth, Portland and Dorchester.

TRAIN

Trains run hourly to London (£36.30, 2¾ hours) via Dorchester South (£2.70, 11 minutes), Bournemouth (£9.70, one hour) and Southampton (£15.90, 1¾ hours), and every two hours to Dorchester West, Bath (£10.80, two hours) and Bristol (£12, 2¼ hours).

AROUND WEYMOUTH
Portland

Renowned as the source of the eponymous hard limestone, quarried here for centuries, Portland is essentially an island joined to the mainland by the long sweep of Chesil Beach. There are incredible views from the top of the craggy outcrop and it's a popular place for climbing and bird-watching. The clear waters surrounding it are also good for windsurfing and diving.

For superb views across the channel make for the **lighthouse** (☎ 01305-861233; ☼ 11am-5pm Apr-Sep), which houses the summer-only **TIC** (☎ 01305-861233), at the end of Portland Bill. It costs £2.50/1.50 to climb the 41m-high tower.

Sturdy **Portland Castle** (EH; ☎ 820539; admission £3.50; ☼ 10am-6pm Apr-Sep, to 5pm Oct, to 4pm Fri-Sun Nov-Mar) is one of the finest examples of the defensive castles constructed during Henry VIII's castle-building spree, spurred by fear of an attack from France. You can try on period armour and get great views over Portland harbour.

Portland Museum (☎ 01305-821804; 217 Wakeham St; adult/child £2.30/free; ☼ 10.30am-5pm Fri-Tue Easter-Oct) has varied displays on local history, smuggling and literary connections, as well as some huge ammonites (fossils).

There are excellent wreck and drift dives around Portland and Weymouth. **Old Harbour Dive School** (☎ 861000; www.oldharbour diveschool.co.uk; 2 Coastguard Cottages, North Point) organises trips to the best sites from £40 per day, plus £45 to hire equipment.

Weymouth & Portland Sailing Academy (☎ 860 101; www.wpsa.org.uk; Osprey Quay) runs two-day sailing courses for £150.

Bus No 1 runs to Portland from Weymouth every 10 minutes, while No 501 goes every 30 minutes.

Chesil Beach

A massive expanse of pebbles stretches along the coast for 10 miles between Portland and Abbotsbury, at times reaching up to 15m high. It's an incredible sight and encloses Fleet Lagoon, a haven for water birds.

The stones vary from pebble size at Abbotsbury in the west to around 15cm in diameter at Portland. Local fishers can supposedly tell their position along the bank by gauging the size of the stones.

Chesil Beach Centre (☎ 01305-760579; Ferrybridge; ☼ 11am-6pm Apr-Sep, 11am-4pm Oct-Mar) provides information, and organises talks and guided walks.

Abbotsbury
☎ 01305

This gorgeous little village was once the site of a medieval abbey, but only scant remains of its devout past remain. However, the village in itself is worth a ramble and with three popular attractions it well merits a detour.

SIGHTS

The huge, 83m-long tithe barn, at one time a communal storage site for farm produce, now houses **Smuggler's Barn** (☎ 871817; adult/child £5.20/3.80; ☼ 10am-6pm Easter-Oct), a children's farm and play area with a smidgen of smuggling lore. Traces of Abbotsbury's Benedictine monastery remain by the barn.

On the coast is **Abbotsbury Swannery** (☎ 871858; New Barn Rd; admission £6.50; ☼ 10am-6pm mid-Mar-Oct), founded by the monks of Abbotsbury's monastery, about 600 years ago. The colony can number up to 600-plus

WESSEX

cygnets, and the walk through will tell you all you ever wanted to know about swans. Come in May for the nests, or in late May and June for the cygnets.

The energetic can walk up to 14th-century **St Catherine's Chapel** for superb views of the swannery, the village and Chesil Beach.

Laid out in 1765 as a kitchen garden, **Abbotsbury Subtropical Gardens** (☎ 871387; admission £6.50; ☺ 9am-5pm 10am-3pm Sun Apr-Oct, 10am-4pm Nov-Mar) are now lush with camellias, hydrangeas and rhododendrons. Last admission is one hour before closing.

Joint tickets to Smuggler's Barn and either the Swannery or the Subtropical Gardens costs £10/6 per adult/child; see www.abbotsbury-tourism.com.

SLEEPING & EATING

Abbotsbury has several comfortable B&Bs and places to eat.

Linton Cottage (☎ 871339; www.lintoncottage.co.uk; s/d £45/54; P ✗) An attractive place owned by the local beekeeper, this B&B has traditional country-style rooms with subtle floral patterns, swags and frills. The rooms have lovely views over the village and garden.

Ilchester Arms (☎ 871243; www.ilchesterarms.co .uk; 9 Market St; s/d £60/75; ✗ wheelchair access) The rooms at this old stone inn are very comfortable and traditionally styled though not truly atmospheric. The public areas have more character and are full of rustic knick-knacks and old furniture. They do a decent, if predictable, menu (mains £9 to £15) of meat, game and fish.

GETTING THERE & AWAY

Bus No X53 runs from Weymouth (30 minutes) to Lyme Regis (one hour) via Abbotsbury six times Monday to Saturday (four on Sunday).

LYME REGIS

☎ 01297/ pop 4406

Nestled around an old fishing village, the charming narrow streets of genteel Lyme Regis maintain a graceful, dignified air, but still attract the bucket-and-spade crowd throughout the summer months. Jane Austen succumbed to the town's charms and wrote parts of *Persuasion* while staying here, featuring the town prominently in her classic novel. More recently its fame grew with the filming of *The French*

Lieutenant's Woman, penned by local writer John Fowles.

Lyme's other claim to fame is prehistoric. The limestone cliffs on either side of town are some of Britain's richest sources of fossils, and some of the first dinosaur skeletons in the world were discovered here.

Information

Lyme Regis' **TIC** (☎ 442138; lyme.tic@westdorset-dc .gov.uk; Guildhall Cottage, Church St; ☺ 10am-5pm Mon-Sat & 10am-4pm Sun Apr-Oct, 10am-3pm Mon-Sat Nov-Mar) is on the corner of Church and Bridge Streets.

Sights

The excellent **Lyme Regis Philpot Museum** (☎ 443 370; www.lymeregismuseum.co.uk; Bridge St; adult/child £2/free; ☺ 10am-5pm Mon-Sat, 11am-5pm Sun Apr-Oct, Sat & Sun Nov-Mar) is in a quirky building with displays of paintings and other artefacts relating to local history and literary connections. It contains a good fossil collection and displays on the life and finds of Mary Anning, world-famous Lyme Regis palaeontologist.

If your own fossil-hunting happens to be unsuccessful, head to **Dinosaurland** (☎ 443541; www.dinosaurland.co.uk; Coombe St; adult/child £4/3; ☺ 10am-5pm), where you'll see extensive fossil displays and reconstructed dinosaurs – and you can pick up an ammonite in the shop.

The **Cobb** is a 183m-long stone jetty-cum-breakwater, first constructed in the 13th century. The pleasantly low-tech **Marine Aquarium** (☎ 443678; admission £2.50; ☺ 10am-5pm Apr-Oct, extended hr peak season) has tanks housing local underwater life – find out what a furry sea mouse is here.

Sleeping & Eating

Armada House (☎ 445785; penny@lymeregis.com; 8 Coombe St; s/d £30/48; P ✗) This pretty little courtyard cottage tucked away in old Lyme has spacious rooms, king-size beds, subtle décor and large bathrooms with power showers. It's a charming place with a warm welcome and just a short stroll from the sea.

Cobb Arms (☎ 443242; Marine Pde; s/d £40/60; P ✗) This waterfront pub has a few excellent rooms with bright modern décor and simple colour schemes. The friendly bar does a good range of snacks as well as decent pub grub (mains £5 to £10).

Mariners Hotel (☎ 442753; www.hotellymeregis.co .uk; Silver St; s/d £60/90; P ✗) This 17th-century place has bright, spacious rooms with subtle modern features and an excellent restaurant serving three-course dinners (£20.50) featuring fresh local fish. If it's warm you can eat out in the lovely garden.

Café Clemence (☎ 445757; Mill Lane; mains £10-13; ☽ lunch & dinner) You'll find this snug little bistro in the atmospheric old mill complex. It serves a good range of modern Mediterranean cuisine with a healthy dose of fish and seafood dishes, and has a pleasant courtyard area for alfresco dining.

Jurassic Seafood (☎ 444345; 47 Silver St; mains £9-15; ☽ lunch & dinner) This bright and cheerful restaurant and wine bar dishes up some excellent seafood from its busy open kitchen. There's plenty of vegetarian choice and a children's menu. Other options:

Old Lyme Guest House (☎ 442929; www.oldlyme guesthouse.co.uk; 29 Coombe St; s/d £30/52; **P** ☒) Award-winning B&B with cosy country-style rooms.

Millside (☎ 445999; Mill Lane; mains £8-13; ☽ lunch Tue-Sun, dinner Tue-Sat) Wine bar-cum-bistro with a range of Mediterranean-style meat and pasta dishes.

Getting There & Away
Bus No 31 runs to Dorchester (1¼ hours) and Weymouth (1¾ hours) hourly (every two hours on Sunday). Bus No X53 goes west to Exeter (1¾ hours) and east to Weymouth (1½ hours) seven times Monday to Saturday, four times on Sunday.

AROUND LYME REGIS
Forde Abbey
Originally a Cistercian monastery constructed in the 12th century, **Forde Abbey** (☎ 01460-221290; www.fordeabbey.co.uk; adult/child abbey £7.50/free, gardens £5.50/free; ☽ abbey noon-4pm Tue-Fri & Sun Apr-Oct, gardens 10am-4.30pm) was updated in the 17th century and has been a private home since 1649. The building boasts magnificent plasterwork ceilings and fine tapestries but it's the outstanding gardens that are the main attraction: 12 hectares of lawns, ponds, shrubberies and flower beds with many rare and beautiful species. It's about 10 miles north of Lyme Regis; public transport is a non-starter.

SHERBORNE
☎ 01935 / pop 9350

The mellow stone village of Sherborne is today a peaceful country town, but its marvellous abbey and two magnificent castles,

defiantly placed at either side of Sherborne Lake, give clues to its former importance and glory as capital of Wessex.

Sherborne's **TIC** (☎ 815341; sherborne.tic@west dorset-dc.ov.uk; Digby Rd; ☽ 9am-5pm Mon-Sat Apr-Oct, 10am-3pm Mon-Sat Nov-Mar) stocks the free *All About Sherborne* leaflet with a map and town trail. **Walking tours** (£2.75; ☽ 11am Fri May-Sep) depart from the TIC and last 1½ hours.

Sherborne Museum (☎ 812252; Church Lane; adult/child £1/free; ☽ 10.30am-4.30pm Tue-Sat, 2.30pm-4.30pm Sun Apr-Oct) features local history and prehistory, a scale model of the Old Castle and an excellent antique dolls' house.

Sights
SHERBORNE ABBEY
Established early in the 8th century, the **Abbey Church of St Mary the Virgin** (☎ 812452; suggested donation £2; ☽ 8.30am-6pm late-Mar–late Oct, 8.30am-4pm Nov–mid-Mar) became a Benedictine abbey in 998 and functioned as a cathedral until 1075. The church boasts the oldest fan vaulting in the country and the monks' choir stalls feature interesting misericords.

Elsewhere the church's earlier architectural features are on show. Solid Saxon-Norman piers support the abbey's soaring central tower and the main entrance has a sturdy Norman porch built in 1180. On the edge of the abbey close are the cloistered 1437 **St Johns' Almshouses** (admission £1.50; ☽ 2-4pm Tue & Thu-Sat May-Sep), containing a medieval chapel.

OLD CASTLE
East of the town centre stand the ruins of the **Old Castle** (EH; ☎ 812730; admission £2.30; ☽ 10am-6pm Apr-Sep, 10am-5pm Oct), originally constructed from 1107 by Roger, Bishop of Salisbury. Sir Walter Raleigh acquired it (with the help of Elizabeth I) in the late 16th century, and spent large sums of money modernising the castle before deciding it wasn't worth the effort and moving across the River Yeo to start work on his new castle. Cromwell destroyed the 'malicious and mischievous castle' after a 16-day siege in 1645, leaving behind the evocative ruins you see today.

SHERBORNE CASTLE
Sir Walter Raleigh commenced building his **New Castle** (☎ 813182; www.sherbornecastle.com; house adult/child £7/free, gardens only £3.50/free; ☽ 11am-4.30pm Tue-Thu & Sun, 2.30-4.30pm Sat Easter-Sep) – really a splendid manor house – in 1594. However,

by 1608 he was back in prison, this time at the hands of James I, who eventually sold the castle to Sir John Digby, the Earl of Bristol, in 1617. It's been the Digby family residence ever since, and contains fine collections of art, furniture and porcelain, as well as grounds landscaped by Capability Brown.

Sleeping & Eating

Eastbury Hotel (☎ 813131; www.theeastburyhotel .co.uk; Long St; s/d £44/80; P ✗) This charming Georgian hotel set in walled gardens has traditionally decorated spacious rooms, with subtle floral patterns and neutral colours. The conservatory restaurant has a good selection of seafood, meat and vegetarian dishes (mains £9 to £14).

Little Barwick House (☎ 01935-423902; www.little barwickhouse.co.uk; Barwick; s/d £65/120; P ✗) This stunning place oozes true charm and style. The rooms are luxurious, and decorated in an elegant but informal contemporary style with big beds, beautiful light-coloured fabrics and fresh flowers. The restaurant (lunch £15.50, dinner £28.50) is equally stylish and serves excellent modern British fare. Barwick is 5 miles southwest of Sherborne off the A37.

Green (☎ 813821; 3 The Green; mains lunch £8.95-13.50, dinner £17; ✆ Tue-Sat) This chic little bistro, with antique wooden tables and chairs, starched linen and contemporary décor, serves an excellent range of tempting dishes prepared with local fish, meat and game.

SOMETHING SPECIAL

Fox Inn (☎ 01935-891330; www.fox-inn.co.uk; Corscombe; s/d £50/70; mains £8-18) This idyllic, rose-clad 17th-century pub is pretty much unspoilt with beamed ceilings, flagstone floors, slate-topped counters and hunting prints on the walls. Blue gingham cloths cover the rustic tables tucked away in nooks and crannies, and the menu features imaginative pub food such as rabbit braised in cider and more exotic dishes such as lamb tagine with couscous, or monkfish with red pepper salsa. Wash it all down with ale tapped from the cask or the pub's own sloe gin and you'll be retiring to one of the charming cottage bedrooms, tucked beneath the thatch, to sleep it all off.

Corscombe is 13 miles north of Dorchester on the A356.

Other options:

Britannia Inn (☎ 813300; Westbury; s/d £25/45) A 300-year-old pub with simple rooms and decent pub grub (£4 to £8).

Pear Tree Deli (☎ 812828; Half Moon St; mains £3.50-5.50; ✆ lunch) Stock up here for gourmet picnics or stop off for an excellent lunch in the café.

Getting There & Away

Nearby Yeovil is a handy transport hub. Bus No 57 runs hourly from Yeovil (30 minutes, Monday to Saturday), as does the quicker No 58 (12 minutes, every two hours Monday to Saturday), which sometimes continues to Shaftesbury (1½ hours). Bus No 216 runs to Dorchester (one hour; six Monday to Saturday) via Cerne Abbas (30 minutes).

Trains run from Exeter (£12.20, 1¼ hours) to London (£32.30, 2¼ hours) via Salisbury (£8.50, 45 minutes) roughly hourly.

SHAFTESBURY & AROUND
☎ 01747 / pop 6665

Old-fashioned, old-world Shaftesbury sits on top of a sandstone outcrop and commands excellent views of the surrounding countryside. The town is also home to the remains of an ancient abbey and charming Gold Hill – made famous by the Hovis bread ad.

The **TIC** (☎ 853514; www.shaftesburydorset.com; 8 Bell St; ✆ 10am-5pm Apr-Sep, 10am-3pm Mon-Sat Oct-Mar) is by the Bleke St car park.

Sights

Situated on top of the 240m-high ridge, **Shaftesbury Abbey** (☎ 852910; www.shaftesburyabbey .co.uk; Park Walk; admission £2; ✆ 10am-5pm Apr-Oct) was founded in 888 by Alfred the Great and was at one time England's richest nunnery. Henry VIII's gentle attentions finished it off in 1539. Today, you can wander around the foundations with a well-devised audio guide, and visit the museum, which tells the abbey's history. St Edward was said to have been buried here, and King Knut died at the abbey in 1035.

The picturesquely steep, cobbled **Gold Hill** tumbles down the ridge from beside the abbey ruins, offering great views of the surrounding plains. Its photogenic qualities have been exploited by postcard-makers and advertising companies alike.

The small **Shaftesbury Museum** (☎ 852157; Sun & Moon Cottage, Gold Hill; adult/child £1.50/free; ✆ 10.30am-4.30pm Thu-Tue) is worth visiting to see the Shaftesbury Hoard of coins, some dating from 871, including many Saxon pieces. The museum also has a collection of local buttons for which the town was once famous, and the decorative Byzant, traditionally carried round town to symbolise the town's need for water.

Old Wardour Castle

The unique six-sided **Old Wardour Castle** (EH; ☎ 01747-870487; admission £2.60; ⏰ 10am-6pm Apr-Sep, 10am-5pm Oct, 10am-4pm Wed-Sun Nov-Mar) was built around 1393 and suffered severe damage during the Civil War, leaving the magnificent remains you see today. It's an ideal spot for a picnic and there are fantastic views from the upper levels. Although it's actually in Wiltshire, Old Wardour is more easily reached from Dorset; bus No 26 runs from Shaftesbury (four Monday to Friday), 4 miles west.

Sleeping & Eating

Cobwebbs (☎ 853505; www.cobwebbs.me.uk; 14 Gold Hill; s/d £30/50; ✗) This white thatched cottage right on picturesque Gold Hill has beautiful bright and airy rustic rooms, an oak-beamed sitting room and lovely garden terrace with great views over the surrounding countryside.

La Fleur de Lys (☎ 853717; www.lafleurdelys.co .uk; Bleke St; s/d £50/75; Ⓟ ✗ ▣ wheelchair access) You'll find old-world luxury mixed with modern comforts at this restaurant with accommodation. The charming place has lovely rooms and an excellent choice of ambitious food (mains £16.50 to £20) at its intimate restaurant. Traditional ingredients such as roe venison and veal sweetbreads feature strongly but in an innovative modern way.

Ship Inn (☎ 853219; Bleke St; mains £6.50-9) For an excellent lunch or something more informal try this lovely old stone pub with a good selection of traditional pub grub, renowned pie and mash and a varied choice of real ales.

Getting There & Away

Bus Nos 182 and 183 run to Blandford (40 minutes, eight Monday to Saturday); some go on to Bournemouth (two hours) though most require a change. Bus Nos 26/27 run from Salisbury (1¼ hours, four Monday to Saturday).

BRISTOL

☎ 0117 / pop 551,066

Hip and happening, Bristol has emerged as *the* hottest spot in southwest England with high-tech industries and a vibrant youth culture combining to give it the financial clout and all-important street-cred to take on the world. Bristol has, in the last decade, turned its fortunes and rescued its crumbling docks and warehouses, converting them into excellent museums, galleries and interactive attractions, while the air of urban cool has been indelibly stamped on the city by musical trendsetters such as Massive Attack, Portishead, Tricky and Roni Size.

Bristol is also a major port and home to the biggest housing development in Europe. It's a real city, alternatively choked with traffic and pride, passion and poverty. The genteel suburb of Clifton echoes the elegance of nearby Bath, while the city's streets are lined with trendy shops and an endless choice of excellent restaurants, bars and clubs. The buzz is palpable.

HISTORY

A small Saxon village at the confluence of the Rivers Frome and Avon became the thriving medieval Brigstow (later Bristol) as the city began to develop its trade in cloth and wine with mainland Europe. Religious houses were established on high ground (now Temple) above the marshes and it

BRISTOL IN TWO DAYS

Kick-start your tour with a visit to **@tBristol** (p263) before strolling along the waterfront and across to the **Industrial Museum** (p263) for the lowdown on Bristol's history. Grab some lunch at **riverstation** (p269) and then hop onto the **Bristol Harbour Railway** (p263) or the **ferry** (p272) and cruise down to the **SS Great Britain** (p265). Return to town and check in to the slick **Hotel du Vin** (p268) before heading up the Whiteladies Rd for some top nosh and buzzing nightlife. In the morning head up to the **British Empire & Commonwealth Museum** (opposite) or stroll down to the beautiful **St Mary Redcliffe Church** (p266). Hop onto bus No 8 or 9 to genteel Clifton for brunch at the **Primrose Café** (p269) or **Clifton Sausage** (p269) and stroll around the leafy streets of Regency grandeur before watching the sun set from the incredible **suspension bridge** (p265).

was from here that celebrated 'local hero' John Cabot (actually a Genoese sailor called Giovanni Caboto) sailed to discover Newfoundland in 1497. Soon Bristol's wealth was dependent on the triangular trade in slaves, cocoa, sugar and tobacco with Africa and the New World.

By the 18th century the city was suffering from competition, from Liverpool in particular, and with large ships having difficulty reaching the city-centre docks, trade moved to new ports at Avonmouth and Portishead instead. Bristol was losing ground fast. To compensate, the city developed a range of manufacturing industries, making it a target for WWII bombing which devastated the centre. Typically, much reconstruction was unfortunate and it is only in the last decade that Bristol has regained its prosperity thanks mainly to the aerospace industry, communications and design.

ORIENTATION

The city centre, north of the river, is easy to get around on foot but very hilly. The central area revolves around the narrow streets by the markets and Corn Exchange and around the newly developed docklands. Park St is lined with trendy shops and cafés while a strip of Whiteladies Rd is the hub of bar and restaurant life. The genteel suburb of Clifton, with its Georgian terraces and boutique shops, is a short bus ride west of the centre.

The suburb of St Paul's, just northeast of the centre, remains a run-down part of town with a heavy drug scene, best not visited alone at night.

The main train station is Bristol Temple Meads, a mile southeast of the centre. Some trains use Bristol Parkway, 5 miles to the

north. The bus station is on Marlborough St, northeast of the city centre.

INFORMATION
Bookshops
Blackwell's/George's (☎ 927 6602; 89 Park St) Vast new, used and academic store; if you want it, it's here.
Waterstones (☎ 925 2274; The Galleries, Broadmead) Good general bookshop in the shopping centre.

Emergency
Police (☎ 927 7777; Nelson St)

Internet Access
BristolLife.co.uk (☎ 945 9926; 27-29 Baldwin St; per hr £2-4; ⏰ 10am-8pm Mon-Fri, 11am-8pm Sat)
Internet Café (☎ 973 6323; 140 Whiteladies Rd; per first half hr £3, per subsequent half hr £1.50; ⏰ 10.30am-7pm Mon-Fri, 11am-6pm Sat, 11am-4pm Sun)

Internet Resources
This is Bristol (www.thisisbristol.com) News, information and what's on at the online version of the *Bristol Evening Post*.
Venue (www.venue.co.uk) Comprehensive details of what's on in Bristol with reviews of restaurants, bars and pubs.
Visit Bristol (www.visitbristol.co.uk) Official tourism website with attractions, events, accommodation and restaurant listings.

Laundry
Alma Laundrette (☎ 973 4121; 78 Alma Rd; ⏰ 7am-9pm)
Redland (☎ 9706537; Chandos Rd; ⏰ 8am-8pm)

Medical Services
Bristol Royal Infirmary (☎ 923 0000; 2 Marlborough St)

Money
You'll find all the main banks along Corn St including Barclays at No 40, Lloyds at No 55, and NatWest at No 32.

WESSEX

Post
Post office (Upr Maudlin St & The Galleries, Broadmead)

Tourist Information
i-plus points Free touch-screen kiosks scattered around the city providing tourist information.

TIC (☎ 0906 711 2191; www.visitbristol.co.uk; The Annexe, Wildscreen Walk, Harbourside; ☾ 10am-6pm Mar-Oct, 10am-5pm Mon-Sat, 11am-4pm Sun Nov-Feb) Stocks the *Slave Trade Trail* leaflet (£1.60), as well as mini-leaflets on literary and maritime walks.

Travel Agencies
STA Travel (☎ 929 4399; 43 Queen's Rd)
Trailfinders (☎ 929 9000; 48 Corn St; ☾ 9am-6pm)

SIGHTS
@tBristol
Next to the TIC in Millennium Sq is an award-winning complex of attractions, **@tBristol** (☎ 0845 345 1235; www.at-bristol.org.uk; Harbourside; combined tickets: Explore & Wildwalk or Explore & IMAX adult/child £12/8.20, Wildwalk & IMAX £11/7.75, all three £16.50/11.45; ☾ 10am-6pm).

Explore (adult/child £7.50/4.95) is Bristol's impressive, interactive science museum, with four themed zones covering brainpower, the history of technology, global communication and the Curiosity Zone – basically fascinating bits and pieces about the planet that aren't covered in the other three sections. There are loads of hands-on exhibits and lots of action for children.

The emphasis at **Wildwalk** (adult/child £6.50/4.50) is the natural world, spanning the breadth of biology from DNA to dinosaurs, with a healthy dollop of enviro-info and a walk-through rainforest.

IMAX (adult/child £6.50/4.50) is another 3D, monster-screen cinema; the eye-popping films tend to relate to the other @tBristol attractions.

Look out for **Cary Grant** (born Archibald Leach in Bristol in 1904) among the many statues in Millennium Sq.

Museums
The city's municipal **museums** (www.bristol-city .gov.uk/museums) are free and, unless otherwise stated, open 10am to 5pm Saturday to Wednesday April to October.

The **City Museum & Art Gallery** (☎ 922 3571; Queen's Rd) is a rambling old place with interesting local ceramics and archaeological relics as well as collections of British and French painting, and good touring exhibitions. The building itself is beautiful and there's plenty to keep children occupied with toddler steps and quiz sheets.

The gritty **Industrial Museum** (☎ 925 1470; Princes Wharf, Wapping Rd; ☾ 10am-5pm Sat-Wed Apr-Oct, 10am-5pm Sat & Sun Nov-Mar), illustrating the city's maritime, rail and aeronautical heritage, has a fine collection of model trains and a mock-up of Concorde's cockpit (the supersonic airliner was developed in Bristol). There are also examples of Bristol-built cars, buses and bikes. The steam-driven **Bristol Harbour Railway** (single/return £1/60p) runs along the wharf from outside the museum to SS *Great Britain* (p265); the service operates several times on fortnightly weekends from March to October.

The 18th-century **Georgian House** (☎ 921 1362; 7 Great George St) is immaculately presented, complete with period fixtures and fittings; the breakfast room and kitchen are particularly interesting. The house shows life above and below stairs and has some horrific mementoes of the slave trade.

The Elizabethan **Red Lodge** (☎ 921 1360; Park Row) was built in 1590 but was much remodelled in 1730; it's now furnished in keeping with both periods. It houses 17th-century French engravings and boasts an attractive Tudor-style knot garden, but the highlight is the Oak Room, with superb carved panels, doorframes and fireplace.

In the northern suburb of Henbury lies **Blaise Castle House Museum** (☎ 950 6789; Henbury Rd), a late–18th-century house and social history museum. Displays include an array of vintage toys, costumes, wonderful paintings and general Victoriana. Across the road is **Blaise Hamlet**, a cluster of picturesque thatched cottages designed for estate servants by John Nash in 1811.

Bus No 43 (45 minutes, every 15 minutes) passes the castle from Colston Ave; bus No 1 (20 minutes, every 10 minutes) from St Augustine's Pde doesn't stop quite as close, but is quicker and more frequent.

British Empire & Commonwealth Museum
Brunel's marvellous old train station at Temple Meads houses the **British Empire & Commonwealth Museum** (☎ 925 9480; www.empire museum.co.uk; Clock Tower Yard; adult/child £6.50/3.95; ☾ 10am-5pm; wheelchair access), which tells the

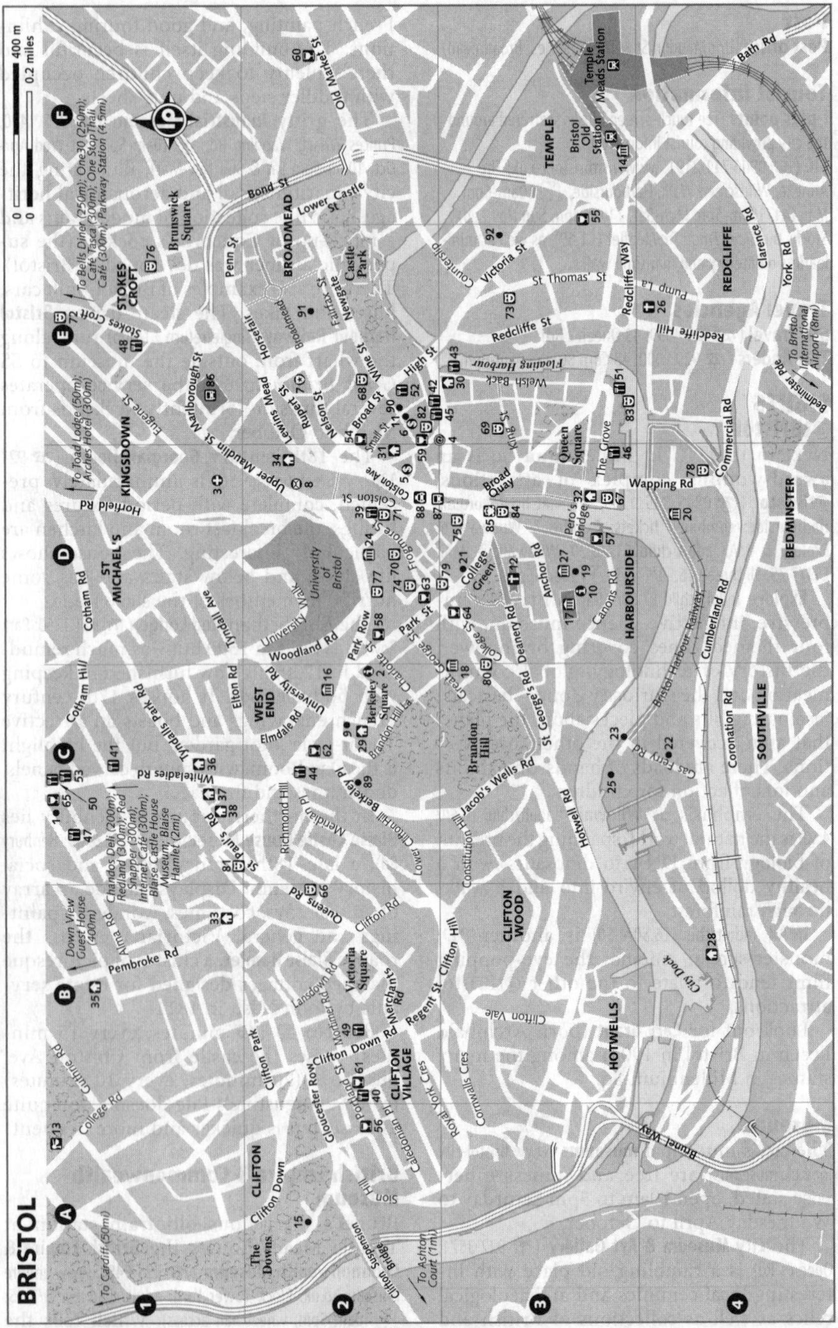

BRISTOL
0 400 m
0 0.2 miles
To Cardiff (50m)
To Ashton Court (1mi)
To Bells Diner (250m); One30 (250m); Café Tasca (300m); One StopThali Café (300m); Parkway Station (4.5mi)
To Toad Lodge (50m); Arches Hotel (300m)
Down View Guest House (400m)
Chandos Deli (200m); Redland (300m); Red Snapper (300m); Internet Café (300m); Blaise Castle House Museum; Blaise Hamlet (2mi)
To Bristol International Airport (8mi)
The Downs
CLIFTON
Clifton Down
Clifton Suspension Bridge
CLIFTON VILLAGE
Victoria Square
CLIFTON WOOD
HOTWELLS
City Dock
Brandon Hill
WEST END
ST MICHAEL'S
KINGSDOWN
STOKES CROFT
Brunswick Square
BROADMEAD
Castle Park
Floating Harbour
College Green
Queen Square
Broad Quay
HARBOURSIDE
Pero's Bridge
TEMPLE
Bristol Old Station
Temple Meads Station
REDCLIFFE
BEDMINSTER
SOUTHVILLE
University of Bristol
Bristol Harbour Railway
College Rd
Guthrie Rd
Clifton Park
Pembroke Rd
Alma Rd
Queens Rd
Clifton Rd
Whiteladies Rd
Tyndalls Park Rd
Cotham Hill
Cotham Rd
Elton Rd
Tyndall Ave
Woodland Rd
University Rd
Elmdale Rd
Richmond Hill
Park Row
Park St
Berkeley Square
Great George St
Jacob's Wells Rd
St George's Rd
Deanery Rd
Anchor Rd
Canons Rd
Hotwell Rd
Clifton Vale
Cornwalls Cres
Royal York Cres
Sion Hill
Regent St
Clifton Down Rd
Gloucester Row
Portland St
Merchants Rd
Lansdown Rd
Mortimer Rd
Constitution Hill
Horfield Rd
Upper Maudlin St
Marlborough St
Lewins Mead
Rupert St
Nelson St
Broad St
Wine St
High St
Colston Ave
Colston St
Small St
Horsefair
Broadmead
Fairfax St
Newgate
Penn St
Bond St
Lower Castle St
Old Market St
Stokes Croft
Eugene St
Counterslip
Victoria St
St Thomas' St
Redcliffe St
Redcliffe Way
Redcliffe Hill
Pump La
Welsh Back
King St
The Grove
Wapping Rd
Cumberland Rd
Coronation Rd
Commercial Rd
Clarence Rd
York Rd
Bath Rd
Bedminster Pde
Gas Ferry Rd
Brunel Way
A B C D E F
1 2 3 4

story of 500 years of British exploration, trade and conquest. There's everything here from flickering old films to Inuit whalebone sunglasses and a Hawaiian feather cape. The museum confronts all the gruesome facts including slavery, exploitation and disrespect for indigenous culture. A series of fascinating oral histories from across the globe and from Bristol's own multiracial population helps puts everything in context.

SS Great Britain

In 1843 Brunel designed the mighty oceangoing **SS Great Britain** (☎ 929 1843; www.ss-great -britain.com), the first large iron ship to be driven by a screw propeller. For 43 years the ship served as a cargo vessel and a liner, carrying passengers as far as Australia before being damaged in 1886 near the Falkland Islands. The owners sold it for storage and the ship remained in the Falklands for decades, forgotten and rusted, before it was towed to Bristol in 1970. Since then it has been undergoing restoration in the dry dock where it was originally built. Works should be complete by mid-2005.

Moored nearby is a replica of John Cabot's ship *Matthew*, which undertook the journey from Bristol to Newfoundland in 1497.

Entrance is via the informative **Maritime Heritage Centre** (☎ 927 9856; Great Western Dockyard, Gas Ferry Rd; admission £6.25; ⊗ 10am-5.30pm Apr-Oct, 10am-4.30pm Nov-Mar), which celebrates Bristol's shipbuilding past.

Clifton & the Suspension Bridge

The genteel suburb of Clifton is often compared with Bath. It too boasts some splendid Georgian architecture, including **Cornwallis Cres** and **Royal York Cres**. The area effectively stretches from Whiteladies Rd to Clifton Village and the river; the farther west you go, the posher the houses become. Clifton village is full of boutiques from wonderful delis and traditional barbers to interior designers and upmarket shoe shops.

The much-photographed, 75m-high **Clifton Suspension Bridge** (www.clifton-suspension-bridge .org.uk), designed by Brunel, spans a dramatic stretch of the Avon Gorge and is both elegant and intriguing, with elements seemingly inspired by ancient Egyptian structures. Work on the bridge began in 1836 but wasn't completed until 1864, after Brunel's death. The bridge is an inevitable magnet for stunt artists and, more poignantly, suicides. In 1885 Sarah Ann Hedley jumped from the bridge after a lovers' tiff,

WESSEX

THE KINGDOM, THE (STEAM) POWER & THE GLORY

Bristol was home to the Victorian engineering genius Isambard Kingdom Brunel (1806–59), known for, among many other things, the Clifton Suspension Bridge. Brunel was seriously injured while resident engineer on the Thames Tunnel in London: the tunnel breached in 1827 and 1828 and he made daring rescue descents in a diving bell to free trapped workers. While recovering, he entered a competition to design a bridge over the Avon at Clifton. Although his first submission by rejected, his second was chosen as the best option, though he didn't live to see it completed.

Brunel's subsequent achievements were numerous and lauded: he built more than 1000 miles of railway lines; designed the first great transatlantic steamship, the *Great Western*; constructed the first iron-hulled, screw-propeller vessel, *Great Britain* (p265); and the world's largest passenger vessel *Great Eastern*.

By any standards he was a workaholic but Brunel had a lighter side too and was almost killed when a coin lodged in his throat while he was entertaining children with conjuring tricks.

---

but her voluminous petticoats parachuted her safely to earth and she lived to be 85.

A new Clifton Suspension Bridge visitor centre will open in late summer 2005. In the meantime **guided tours** (☎ 9744665; visitinfo@ clifton-suspension-bridge.org.uk) are available by arrangement.

On Durdham Downs, overlooking the bridge, a rather tatty observatory houses a fascinating **camera obscura** (☎ 974 1242; admission £1; ✆ from 12.30pm Mon-Fri, 10.30am Sat & Sun), which offers some incredible views of the suspension bridge. Opening hours vary depending on the weather.

Nearby is **Bristol Zoo Gardens** (☎ 973 8951; www.bristolzoo.org.uk; Clifton; adult/child £9.50/6; ✆ 9am-5.30pm summer, 9am-4.30pm winter), a facility that aims to promote conservation as well as entertain. Attractions include a group of West African gorillas, underwater walkways for viewing seals and penguins, and a Brazilian rainforest section where you can get up close and personal with agouti, capybara and golden lion tamarins.

Bus Nos 8 and 9 (10 minutes, eight hourly) run to Clifton and the zoo from St Augustine's Pde; add another 10 minutes from Temple Meads.

Bristol Cathedral

Originally founded as the church of an Augustinian monastery in 1140, **Bristol Cathedral** (☎ 926 4879; www.bristol-cathedral.co.uk; College Green; ✆ 8am-6pm) has a remarkably fine Norman chapter house and gate, while the attractive lady chapels have eccentric carvings and fine heraldic glass. Although much of the nave and the west towers date from the 19th century, the 14th-century choir

has fascinating misericords depicting apes in hell, quarrelling couples and dancing bears. The south transept shelters a rare Saxon carving of the 'Harrowing of Hell', discovered under the chapter-house floor after a 19th-century fire.

St Mary Redcliffe

Described as 'the fairest, goodliest and most famous parish church in England' by Queen Elizabeth I, **St Mary Redcliffe** (☎ 929 1487; www .stmaryredcliffe.co.uk; Redcliffe Way; ✆ 8.30am-5pm Mon-Sat) is a stunning piece of perpendicular architecture with a soaring, 89m-high spire and a grand hexagonal porch that easily outdoes the cathedral in splendour. The extraordinary, 14th-century south porch is carved with intricate birds and animals while inside the wonderful vaulted ceiling has fine gilt bosses. At the entrance to the America Chapel there is a the whale rib presented to the church by John Cabot as a souvenir of his pioneering trip to Nova Scotia and Newfoundland in 1497.

Lord Mayor's Chapel

Once the chapel of St Mark's Hospital, the **Lord Mayor's Chapel** (☎ 929 4350; Park St; ✆ 10am-noon & 1-4pm Tue-Sun) is a medieval gem squeezed in between shops opposite the cathedral and packed with 16th-century, stained-glass windows, medieval monuments and ancient tiles. The church-loving poet John Betjeman dubbed it 'for its size one of the very best churches in England'.

BRISTOL FOR CHILDREN

Bristol is an excellent city for entertaining children, with loads of hands-on activities and interesting events. On the whole, cafés and all but the most exclusive restaurants are quite tolerant of little people and most have highchairs. Most hotels and some B&Bs can rustle up a baby cot or heat up a bottle; confirm that when you book. Baby-changing facilities are available in most supermarkets, department stores, shopping centres and at major attractions.

The city doesn't have a huge variety of playgrounds, but most green areas will at least have some swings and a slide. More formal attractions are numerous though: @Bristol (p263) has loads to keep children enthralled, you can become a deck detective on the **SS Great Britain** (p265); **Bristol Zoo Gardens** (p265) has an excellent programme of children's events as well as a good play area; and the **British Empire & Commonwealth Museum** (p263) and **City Museum & Art Gallery** (p263) worked hard to make their collections relevant to youngsters. A trip on the **Harbour Railway** (p263) is also a good bet, as is the **Pirate Walk** (☎ 07950 566483; adult/child £3.50/2.50; 6.15pm Tue, Thu & Sat Apr-Sep), a two-hour trail of piracy geared towards kids. In July look out for information on the **Bristol Children's Festival**, a full-day event with jugglers, story-tellers, puppeteers and more.

Most hotels will help to organise a baby-sitter, if not try the following agencies:

Park Lane Nannies (☎ 373 0003; www.parklane nannies.com)

Tinies (☎ 3005630; bristol@tinieschildcare.co.uk)

TOURS

Bristol Tour Guides (☎ 968 4638; studytours@aol.com; £3; ☾ 11am & 2pm Apr-Sep) run themed walks including Bristol Highlights, Maritime Bristol, Brunel Tours, Bristol Merchants and the Slave Trade, and High Society Clifton. Tours start from the TIC.

City Sightseeing (☎ 926 0767; www.citysightseeing .co.uk; adult/child £7.50/6.50; ☾ 10am-4pm Easter-Sep) has a hop-on, hop-off open-top bus visiting all the major attractions. Buses leave St Augustine's Pde hourly (every 30 minutes July to September).

Bristol Packet Boat Trips (☎ 926 8157; www .bristolpacket.co.uk; adult/child £4/2.50; Mar-Oct) is one of a number of companies running boat trips (with commentary) around the historic harbour. Cruises last about 45 minutes and depart from the harbour next to the Watershed seven times daily. It also runs several other cruises including a day trip to Bath (adult/child £17.50/13).

FESTIVALS & EVENTS

Bristol has a lively annual programme of events. For full details ask at the TIC or try www.visitbristol.co.uk. In April the

---

GAY & LESBIAN BRISTOL

Bristol has a fairly vibrant gay scene, with venues clustered behind the Hippodrome. There's no specific gay publication in the city but *Venue* magazine (www.venue.co.uk; £1.20) is a good source for up-to-date listings. Another good bet for information is www.pridebristol.co.uk/bristol.

For local advice or information try **Bristol Gay & Lesbian Switchboard** (☎ 942 0842; ☾ 8pm-10pm). Following are some of the best-loved spots for a night on the town:

- **Queen's Shilling** (Q/-; ☎ 926 4342; 9 Frogmore St) A popular gay bar, this trendy place with wall-to-wall mirrors lures a young attractive crowd. It has a late licence and dancing DJs weekends.

- **Fusion** (☎ 925 6969; 7-9 St Nicholas St) You'll find a mixed but mostly gay crowd at this kicking club with the usual bingo and karaoke nights, live music on Thursday, funk on Saturday and house and tribal sounds on a Sunday.

- **Justwins** (☎ 955 9269; 23-25 West St; free-£5) There's a strict dress code at this renowned place, but if you're into a wild night out with the guys dressed in leather and uniforms this is the only place to go.

- **Pineapple** (☎ 907 1162; 37 St George's Rd) This place has a gay-only door policy and the clientele is mostly male. There's plenty of in-house entertainment with karaoke on Monday, quiz night on Tuesday, bingo on Wednesday, student night on Thursday and disco inferno weekends.

- **Vibes** (☎ 934 9076; 3 Frog Lane; free-£4) A popular gay club with a friendly atmosphere, plenty of cheesy retro disco and party pop sounds as well as pretty people dancing their socks off.

bristolive (www.bristolive.co.uk) international festival for amateur ensembles attracts the crowds, but the real action takes place in July. It starts with the street spectacle **St Paul's Carnival** (☎ 944 4176) on the first Saturday and follows up with the **Ashton Court Festival** (www.ashtoncourtfestival.co.uk) featuring the best music, theatre and arts from the Bristol area. Also in July is the **Bristol Harbour Festival** (☎ 922 3148), the city's biggest waterside event. In August there's the **International Balloon Fiesta** (☎ 953 5884; www.bristolfiesta.co.uk), when hundreds of hot-air balloons take to the skies, followed by the **International Kite Festival** (☎ 977 2002; www.kite-festival.org) in September.

SLEEPING

Accommodation in Bristol tends to be far from inspiring in the mid-range bracket. Expect old-fashioned style and service as a given. Pick up a copy of the free *Visit Bristol* for accommodation listings and a handy map.

Budget

Bristol YHA Hostel (☎ 0870 770 5726; bristol@yha.org .uk; Hayman House, 14 Narrow Quay; dm/d £16.40/30; ✕) This sympathetically restored warehouse makes an ideal base if you're on a budget and is a much better bet than most of the reasonably priced B&Bs. It has all the usual facilities and is at the heart of the Waterfront nightlife area.

Bristol Backpackers (☎ 925 7900; www.bristolback packers.co.uk; 17 St Stephen's St; dm/d £14/35; ✕ 🖵) Another good choice in the centre of town, but slightly more grungy, this lively eco-friendly hostel has standard dorm rooms and fairly decent private accommodation. There's cheap Internet access, a bar and discounts on many attractions.

Baltic Wharf Caravan Club Site (☎ 926 8030; Cumberland Rd; tent £4-7) A lovely riverside spot just 1½ miles southwest of the centre, this caravan site has only a few tent spots so get there early. To get there take the Baltic Wharf Loop Bus (see p272) or the ferry (see p272).

Mid-Range

Sunderland Guest House (☎ 973 7249; sunderland .gh@blueyonder.co.uk; 4 Sunderland Pl; s/d £30/40; 🅿 ✕) A great-value choice in posh Clifton, this place is tucked away off Whiteladies Rd and offers simple tidy rooms with restrained décor and vegetarian breakfasts.

Toad Lodge (☎ 924 7080; www.toadlodge.com; 12 Cotham Park; s/d £25/35; 🅿) This elegant Georgian house is an excellent-value option, with bright simple rooms, a lovely garden and a friendly atmosphere. It's a little out of the city centre but has regular bus connections.

Park Hotel (☎ 973 5407; www.tyndallsparkhotel .co.uk; 4 Tyndalls Park Rd; s/d £48/58; ✕) An elegant Victorian house with period style and grace, this is one of the best places in the Whiteladies Rd enclave. The rooms are traditional in style but are a good size and have understated décor.

Channings Hotel (☎ 973 3970; 20 Pembroke Rd; s/d £50/60) A Tyndalls gentleman's residence, this grand, ivy-clad pub is rather old-fashioned in its manner but elegant all the same. It has decent rooms, good service and the traditional bar food (mains £4 to £9) won't break the bank.

Washington Hotel (☎ 973 3980; washington@clif tonhotels.co.uk; St Paul's Rd; s £35-49, d £59-64; 🅿 ✕) The simplest and most reasonable of the row on St Paul's Rd, the cheaper rooms share bathrooms but are otherwise great value. The rooms are recently refurbished and have bright simple décor and period furnishings.

Naseby House Hotel (☎ 973 7859; www.naseby househotel.co.uk; 105 Pembroke Rd; s/d £45/65; 🅿) Many original Victorian architectural features have been retained at this plush B&B in Clifton. The charming rooms are bathed in light and decorated with bright colours and classical style.

Other options:

Arches Hotel (☎ 924 7398; www.arches-hotel.co.uk; 132 Cotham Brow; s/d £25/44; 🅿 ✕) Great-value rooms with one foot set firmly in the past.

Downs View Guest House (☎ 973 7046; www .downsviewguesthouse.co.uk; 38 Upper Belgrave Rd; s/d £40/60; 🅿 ✕) Classic-style rooms with period features and fantastic views.

Top End

Hotel du Vin (☎ 925 5577; www.hotelduvin.com; Narrow Lewins Mead; s £125-160; 🅿 ✕) Six listed warehouses have been superbly converted into this designer emporium. The bright sleek rooms make the most of the simple elegance of their industrial past and feature wonderful beds, walk-through showers and oversized baths. The New York–style lofts are fantastic.

Berkeley Square Hotel (☎ 925 4000; berkeley@ cliftonhotels.com; 15 Berkeley Sq; s £54-106, d £90-127; P ⊠ ⌨) Set on an elegant square, this lovely hotel has a mix of classical features (think swag curtains and antiques) in the public rooms and sleek contemporary style in the restaurant and bedrooms. The rooms are bright and comfortable with widescreen TVs and a complimentary decanter of sherry.

Brigstow Hotel (☎ 929 1030; www.brigstowhotel .com; Welsh Back; d £89-186; P ⊠ ⌨ ⌨) Another designer joint, the Brigstow is all clean modern lines and low lighting. The rooms are stylish but fairly compact and feature plasma-screen TVs in the bathrooms. It's a fantastic waterside location and ideal if you plan some late-night revelling.

EATING

Eating out in Bristol is a real pleasure with excellent options in every price category.

Budget
RESTAURANTS

Budokan (☎ 914 1488; 31 Colston St; mains £7-10; ☺ lunch & dinner Mon-Sat) Contemporary, pan-Asian food is served up at communal tables at this trendy joint with floor-to-ceiling windows. The flexible menu means you can fuel up on a selection of snacks, plunge for one main course or go for the bargain rapid-refuel menus (£5 to £6.50).

One Stop Thali Café (☎ 942 6687; 12a York Rd; set meal £6.50; ☺ lunch) This Bristol institution serves good honest Asian street food in slightly kitsch surroundings. There's a jumble of furniture, silk cushions and some rather strange mannequins. There's no menu, just the daily set 'thali', a combination of six vegetarian dishes served with rice and salad.

Primrose Café (☎ 946 6577; 1 Boyces Ave; mains £4-6; ☺ lunch) Soups, sandwiches, hot snacks and home-made ice cream pull in shoppers and families to this funky little café in the wonderful Clifton Arcade. From Thursday to Saturday evenings it also doubles as a BYO bistro (three-course menu £17.95) specialising in fish dishes.

Other options:

Double Dutch (☎ 929 0433; 45-47 Baldwin St; mains £4-6; ☺ lunch & dinner) Classic Dutch dishes and fabulous pancakes at this unique vaulted place with a rustic atmosphere.

Café Tasca (☎ 942 6799; 12 York Rd; mains £4-7; ☺ lunch & dinner) Tiny place serving baguettes, tortillas and traditional Portuguese cuisine.

QUICK EATS

Mr Wolf (☎ 927 3221; 33 St Stephen's St; mains £4-6; ☺ closed Sun) A real gem, this funky noodle bar has colourful décor, a chilled atmosphere and a great selection of Asian classics. It also serves beer and opens late (to 2am) on Friday and Saturday nights.

Pie Minster (☎ 942 9500; 24 Stokes Croft; ☺ lunch) Pie fanatics look no further, this funky little place to the north of the centre does a mean line in interesting pies. Choose anything from humble pie (steak, kidney, herbs and ale) to Matador pie (chorizo, olives and sherry).

St Nicholas Market (Corn St; ☺ 9.30am-5pm Mon-Sat) Classics such as bangers and beans, jacket spuds and toasties can be found in this warren of stalls, as well as deli bread and cheeses, imaginative sambos at **Royce Rolls** and sublime goat's cheese and walnut crêpes (£1.50 to £2.50) at **Crêperie**.

Mid-Range

Clifton Sausage (☎ 973 11192; 7-9 Portland St; mains £8.50-14; ☺ lunch & dinner) Church candles, oak furniture and flagstone floors set the atmosphere at this rustic gastro-pub. It's sausage central here, with eight varieties of bangers to choose from and plenty of classic comfort foods from potato cakes and black pudding to steak and mussels.

riverstation (☎ 914 4434; The Grove; mains £14; ☺ lunch & dinner) Sleek and chic, riverstation plays host to the city's uber-cool with its adventurous menu and buzzy atmosphere. There's a bright and airy deli and espresso bar on the ground floor and innovative cooking served on the waterside balconies above.

One30 (☎ 944 2442; 130 Cheltenham Rd; mains £11-16; ☺ lunch & dinner) New kid on the block, One30 has striped floors, brick walls, leather sofas and a modern bar. Tapas are available during the day but by night it's the delicate flavours of Catalan seafood stew and spider crab on bruschetta that draw the crowds.

Touareg (☎ 904 4488; 77 Whiteladies Rd; mains £15.50-17; ☺ lunch & dinner) Sultry North African surrounds with carved woodwork, twinkling lanterns and secluded alcoves make this atmospheric restaurant an excellent choice for

WESSEX

an intimate dinner. Tagine, couscous and lamb dominate the menu, though there's also a good choice of meze.

Bells Diner (☎ 924 0357; 1-3 York Rd; mains £10-18; ☽ lunch & dinner) This converted '50s grocery shop turned bistro dishes up smart contemporary cooking from an array of tempting local organic produce. The creative cooking blends classic flavours with wild ingredients and boasts a loyal following among those in the know.

Other good options:
Mud Dock (☎ 934 9734; 40 The Grove; mains £8.95-14.95; ☽ lunch & dinner) A loud and lively waterside warehouse with a massive bike shop and happening bistro.
Le Monde (☎ 934 0999; Triangle West; mains £8-16; ☽ closed Sun dinner) A huge bunker of a place with icy modern design and slick cuisine.

Top End

Quartier Vert (☎ 973 4482; 84 Whiteladies Rd; mains £10.50-18.50; ☽ lunch & dinner) Deceptively simple cooking rules at this impeccable modern restaurant serving up fantastic rustic Mediterranean food. You can stay in the bar with some tapas (£5 to £7) and a jug of sangria or go the whole hog and book well in advance for a table in the restaurant.

Deason's (☎ 973 6230; 43 Whiteladies Rd; mains £13-20; ☽ closed Sun dinner) Stylish minimalist décor, modern artwork and epic flower arrangements set the scene at this ultra-smart restaurant frequented by the rich and the beautiful. The food is largely modern British though some Continental and Asian influences manage to sneak in.

Other classy options:
Glassboat (☎ 929 0704; Welsh Back; lunch mains £7-8, dinner mains £12-19; ☽ closed Sun) A beautifully converted barge serving world cuisine and some excellent lunch deals.
Red Snapper (☎ 973 7999; 1 Chandos Rd; mains £11-19.50; ☽ closed lunch Mon, dinner Sun) Smart but informal restaurant with a reputation for fantastic modern European food.

Self-Catering

Papadeli (☎ 973 6569; 84 Alma Rd) Tapas-style takeaways draw the crowds to this haven of edible goodies stocking all sorts of delicacies from artichokes soaked in garlic to a fantastic selection of fresh hummus and other dips.

Chandos Deli (☎ 9706565; 121 Whiteladies Rd & 6 Princess Victoria St) Queues filter out the door at lunch time at this popular deli with an incredible sandwich bar and shelves of fresh sushi, tapas, handmade tapenade and artisan chocolate.

DRINKING

The fortnightly listings magazine **Venue** (www.venue.co.uk; £1.20) gives the lowdown on what's on in Bristol and Bath with details of theatre, music, exhibitions, bars, clubs and almost anything else in the entertainment field. The more upmarket and style-oriented freebie mag *Folio* is published monthly.

Mall (☎ 974 5318; 66 The Mall, Clifton) Deep leather sofas, giant floor-to-ceiling windows and a classical style make this relaxed but stylish bar an excellent spot for a quiet drink or lazy afternoon. A good range of snacks (£3 to £5) is available including flat breads, pizzas and mussels.

Arc (☎ 922 6456; 27 Broad St) This dark, slightly kitschy little disco bar pulls in the crowds at weekends for a mix of funk, hip-hop soul and disco. The dance floor is tiny though so don't plan any big moves.

Cornubia (☎ 925 4415; 142 Temple St) If you're looking for old-world charm then come straight to this secluded bar with a fine selection of real ales. It's a great place to meet the local beer lovers and debate the merits of genuine brews.

Elbow Room (☎ 930 0242; 64 Park St) With big windows opening out onto the street this bar/club/pool-hall is a great place for cool, edgy types to hang out on a fine day. There's a contemporary lounge upstairs with jazz, funk and R&B at weekends.

Park (☎ 940 6101; 37 Triangle West) Pre-club bar and bohemian hang-out, this stylish place mixes funky beats with classic boogie on Wednesday and Thursday and hosts monthly residencies with some of Bristol's finest DJs on Friday and Saturday nights.

Coronation Tap (☎ 973 9617; Sion Pl) Up near the suspension bridge, this legendary traditional bar will appeal to cider-lovers. It usually has five varieties of the adult apple juice available including some so strong they're sold by the half glass only.

Other options:
Z Bar (☎ 973 7225; 96 Whiteladies Rd) Killer cocktails fuel a young and beautiful crowd.
E-shed (☎ 907 4287; Canons Rd) Funky red hang-out playing hip-hop, house, R&B and drum'n'bass.

ENTERTAINMENT
Nightclubs

Trendy nightspots come and go with alarming frequency, but there's always something going down along Canon's Rd and at Stokes Croft, though the latter isn't the best place to go wandering after dark.

Lakota (☎ 942 6208; 6 Upper York St; free-£15) Long-time Bristol favourite attracting big-name DJs, live acts and elaborate theme nights. Entertainment can feature anything from circus acts and giant projections to hard trance, hardcore, techo and nu-skool.

Thekla (☎ 929 3301; The Grove; £5-7) The finest funky house music vies with heavy drum'n'bass for the attentions of the young clubbers and vodka-heads on a serious night out on this moored trawler.

Nocturne (☎ 929 2555; 1 Unity St) Cooler than cool, this members club is part owned by Massive Attack and if you want in you've got to dress smart, act cool and get there really early.

Hatchet (☎ 941 1808; Frogmore St; £3) A 1st-floor youth hang-out with serious attitude and music ranging from garage rock, punk and new wave to electronic '80s and industrial sounds.

Level (☎ 902 2001; 24 Park Row; £4) Cool student hangout in a space designed to resemble a '70s airport lounge. Funk, disco, alternative, commercial hip-hop and plenty of booze promotions keep the young ones happy.

Carling Academy (☎ 0870 711 2000; Frogmore St; £6-10) A Bristol institution and happening venue featuring big-name acts and serious DJs.

Theatre

Arnolfini Arts Centre (☎ 929 9191; www.arnolfini.org.uk; 16 Narrow Quay) About to reopen (summer 2005) after a major overhaul, this avant-garde arts centre stages performance art and contemporary dance, as well as housing an exhibition space and one of the city's art-house cinemas.

Bristol Old Vic (☎ 987 7877; www.bristol-old-vic.co.uk; King St) This well-respected theatre sticks with classic and contemporary drama, with occasional forays into comedy and dance.

Hippodrome (☎ 0870 607 7500; St Augustine's Pde) Bristol's giant auditorium, featuring blockbuster musicals, large touring shows and a smattering of opera, ballet and concerts.

Colston Hall (☎ 922 3686; www.colstonhall.org; Colston St) An eclectic mix of opera, comedy, world music and pop.

BRISTOL'S LIVE-MUSIC SCENE

There's a fundamental key to understanding the current Bristol music scene: it probably doesn't sound like you think it does. Yes, the shadow of Portishead, Massive Attack et al was a large one – and for too long straightforward rock bands with DJs bolted onto the side hoped to mirror that sound – but Bristol has moved on.

Today, it's ambition – as opposed to coat-tail-hanging – that's driving the scene. Not ambition in the sense of minting a major label deal, but of playing whatever seems right for any given act and to hell with whether anyone else 'gets' it. And, almost despite itself, the resultant, wholly divergent music is increasingly beginning to make waves on a national level. The wonderfully dark, claustrophobic and extraordinarily sung anti-folk of Gravenhurst, for example, has been snapped up by Warp, while the poppy glitch-rock of Chikinki now resides at Island, and War Against Sleep's twisted torch songs have found a home at Fire. Such successes have clearly stirred capital-based A&R bods into action, with increasing numbers heading down the M4 to inquire about – and witness firsthand – the gloriously melodic, harmony-heavy sounds of Valley Forge, the inspired inventiveness of Termites, the brutal onslaught of Ivory Springer, and many more besides.

The other crucial change is bands' increasing willingness to stage their own shows, and, consequently, a host of venues – including the **Croft** (p272), **Bar Unlimited** (☎ 904 8523; 209 Gloucester Rd), **Polish Club** (☎ 973 6244; 50 St Paul's Rd) and **Seymour's** (☎ 929 0093; 47-49 Barton Vale, St Phillips) – have joined the longstanding **Fleece & Firkin** (p272) and **Louisiana** (☎ 926 5978; Wapping Rd, Bathurst Tce) as staples of the live scene, with larger touring acts still ably housed in the **Carling Academy** (272), **Colston Hall** (above) and the **Anson Rooms** (☎ 954 5810; Students' Union, Queens Rd).

Confidence, in short, is high. And getting higher.

Julian Owen
Music editor, Venue magazine

WESSEX

Watershed (☎ 927 5100; www.watershed.co.uk; 1 Canon's Rd) This art-house cinema has a steady diet of foreign and left-of-centre films.

Live Music

Big names tend to play in the **Carling Academy** (see p272), while a host of smaller venues feature the wave of up-and-coming Bristol bands and smaller tours.

Fleece & Firkin (☎ 945 0996; St Thomas St) Regular live-music slots from cover bands to aspiring punk rockers.

Croft (☎ 987 4144; 117-119 Stokes Croft) Chilled club-bar and live-music venue with a policy of supporting new music of every style, especially local talent.

Tantric Jazz (☎ 940 2304; 39 St Nicholas St) Live jazz and world music every night of the week at this shabby-chic retro joint with a loyal local following and a laid-back air.

Bierkeller (☎ 926 8514; All Saints St) A legendary place that has played host to plenty of rock stars. It still hosts some hot newcomers and older legends and gets packed out at weekends.

GETTING THERE & AWAY
Air

Bristol International Airport (☎ 0870 121 2747; www.bristolairport.co.uk) is 8 miles southwest of town. Most flights are holiday charters but there's also a limited number of scheduled flights to European destinations. **Easy Jet** (☎ 0870 600 0000; www.easyjet.com) and **British Airways** (☎ 0845 773 3377; www.ba.com) fly domestic routes to Glasgow and Edinburgh. Easyjet also flies to Newcastle, and **Air Southwest** (☎ 0870 241 6830; www.airsouthwest.com) flies to Plymouth.

Bus

National Express coaches go to Birmingham (£15.50, two hours, nine daily), London (£14.50, 2½ hours, at least hourly), Cardiff (£6, 1¼ hours, four daily) and Exeter (£10.75, two hours, five daily). There's also one bus a day each to Nottingham (£23, 4¾ hours), Oxford (£14.50, three hours) and Stratford-upon-Avon (£15, 2½ hours).

Bus Nos X39 and 337/8/9 run to Bath (50 minutes) several times an hour. Bus No 376/377 goes to Wells (one hour, hourly), and No 673 runs to Cheddar (£3.75, 1½ hours, roughly hourly). You'll need to change in Wells or Bath for most destinations in Somerset and Wiltshire.

Train

Bristol is an important rail hub, with regular connections to London (£34, 1¾ hours, half-hourly). Bath makes an easy day trip (single £4.80, 11 minutes, four an hour). There are also frequent links to Cardiff (£7.20, 45 minutes, hourly), Oxford (£12.40, 70 minutes, hourly) and Birmingham (£26, 1½ hours, half hourly).

GETTING AROUND
To/from the Airport

Bristol International Flyer runs buses (single/ return £5/7, 30 minutes, half-hourly 5am to 11pm) to the airport from Marlborough St bus station and Temple Meads train station. A taxi to the airport costs around £20.

Bicycle

Hilly as Bristol is, masochists might want to hire bikes at **Blackboy Hill Cycles** (☎ 973 1420; 180 Whiteladies Rd; per day £9; ☺ 9am-5.30pm Mon-Sat).

Boat

The nicest way to get around is to use **Bristol Ferry Boat Co** (☎ 927 3416; www.bristolferryboat .co.uk) boats that ply the Floating Harbour every 20 minutes from April to September (weekends only in winter), stopping at the SS *Great Britain*, Hotwells, Baltic Wharf, the centre (by Watershed), Bristol Bridge, Castle Park and Temple Meads. A short hop is £1.20, or you can pay £5 for a day's unlimited travel.

Bus

Buses run from Parkway Station to the centre every 15 minutes (30 minutes). Bus Nos 8 and 9 run every 15 minutes to Clifton (10 minutes) from St Augustine's Pde; add another 10 minutes from Temple Meads. The Baltic Wharf Loop Bus (No 500; 10 minutes, half-hourly Monday to Saturday) runs from Temple Meads and St Augustine's Pde.

FirstDay tickets (adult/child/family £3.20/2.30/5.50) are valid on all buses for one day in the Greater Bristol area. Most bus numbers are prefaced by 50 outside peak hours; hence, bus No 8 becomes No 508.

Car & Motorcycle

Bristol's one-way systems seem designed to confuse, and parking can be a problem. **Park-and-ride** (☎ 922 2910; return £2.50, every 10mins

THE MARSHFIELD MUMMERS

Every Boxing Day at 11am crowds descend on the south Cotswolds town of Marshfield to see seven characters, or mummers, dressed in costumes made from strips of newsprint and coloured paper perform a traditional morality play. Some say the tradition of these Old Time Paper Boys dates back to the time of the Crusades. It's all done in rhyme and is repeated as the mummers follow the town crier down the street. The final performance is outside one of the town pubs where the landlord finishes proceedings with whisky for the 'boys'.

Marshfield is 11 miles east of Bristol on the A420. There is no public transport on Boxing Day.

Mon-Sat) services operate at Portway, Bath Rd, Tollgate and Long Ashton. They're well signed on routes into the city.

Taxi

The taxi rank on St Augustine's Pde is a central but rowdy place on weekend nights. There are plenty of companies; try **Bristol Hackney Cabs** (☎ 953 8638).

BATH

☎ 01225 / pop 90,144

Undeniably beautiful and oozing an air of gentility and sophistication, Bath is an architectural gem with over 5000 listed buildings and a grandeur unmatched elsewhere in Britain. The city's fortune was built on the presence of the only hot springs in the country; it was first a Roman city and then in the 18th century a fashionable haunt of English society. Aristocrats flocked here to gossip, gamble and flirt, building in the process the glorious honey-coloured Georgian terraces that have won the city Unesco World Heritage status.

A definite air of languid exclusivity still pervades the city with its chi-chi boutiques and galleries, and specialist shops, but Bath is also home to a series of excellent museums and a fine selection of hotels and restaurants. Although Bath can be overrun by tourists with camcorders instead of faces, it's not difficult to escape the crowds and find your own patch of undiscovered Palladian splendour.

HISTORY

Prehistoric peoples probably knew about the hot springs, and legend has it that King Bladud, a Trojan refugee and father of King Lear, founded the town some 2800 years ago. He was supposedly cured of leprosy by a bath in the muddy swamps. The Romans established the town of Aquae Sulis in AD 44 and built the extensive baths complex and a temple to the goddess Sulis-Minerva.

Long after the Romans had departed, the Anglo-Saxons arrived and in 944 a monastery was founded on the site of the present abbey. Throughout the Middle Ages, Bath was an ecclesiastical centre and a wool-trading town and it wasn't until the early 18th century that Allen and Richard 'Beau' Nash (see the boxed text, p276) made Bath the centre of fashionable society. Ralph Allen developed the quarries at Coombe Down and employed the two John Woods (father and son) to create the glorious buildings you see today.

As the 18th century wore on, Beau Nash lost his influence and sea bathing started to draw visitors away from Bath; by the mid-19th century the city was thoroughly out of fashion. Fortunately, most of Bath's grand architecture has been preserved.

ORIENTATION

Like Rome, Bath is famed for its seven hills, and although the city centre is compact it will test your legs. Most street signs are carved into the golden stone of the buildings.

The train and bus stations are both south of the TIC at the end of Manvers St. The most obvious landmark is the abbey, across from the Roman Baths and Pump Room.

INFORMATION

Bath Quarterly (www.bathquarterly.com) Guide to sights, accommodation, restaurants and events in the city.
Click (☎ 481008; 13a Manvers St; ⏰ 10am-10pm; Internet per 20 min £1)
i-plus points Free touch-screen kiosks providing tourist information, scattered around the city.
Laundrette (4 St Margaret's Bldgs; per load £2; ⏰ 6am-9pm)
Main post office (☎ 0845 722 3344; Old Bond St)
Retailer Internet Manvers St (☎ 443181; 12 Manvers St; ⏰ 9am-9pm Mon-Sat, 3-9pm Sun; per 30 min £1.50);

BATH

400 m
0.2 miles

A **B** **C** **D** **E** **F**

1
2
3
4

To Royal United Hospital (700m)
To Royal Crescent Hotel

To Bath Spa University (2mi); Newton Mill Camping Park (3mi)

Royal Ave

Royal Victoria Park

Marlborough La

Upper Bristol Rd

Gt Stanhope St

Charlotte St

Queen Sq

Monmouth Pl

New King St

James St West

Julian Rd

Circus Mews

Brock St

Bennett St

Alfred St

Bartlett St

Russel St

Lansdown Rd

The Paragon

Walcot St

Broad St

Milsom St

George St

Gay St

Queen Sq

Princes St

Monmouth St

Charles St

John St

Quiet St

Green St

New Bond St

Union St

High St

Cheap St

Corridor

York St

Stall St

Bath St

Westgate St

Trim St

Upper Borough Walls

Parsonage La

Lower Borough Walls

Westgate Buildings

James St

Beau St

Barton St

St James Pde

Corn St

Avon St

Milk St

Kingsmead

Green Park Rd

Green Park

Midland Bridge Rd

Upper Oldfield Park

Avon

To Dorian House (5mi)

To Andelle House (500m)

Henrietta Rd

Henrietta Gdns

Henrietta Park

Henrietta St

Henrietta Mews

Grove St

Laura Place

Pulteney Mews

Great Pulteney St

Edward St

Daniel St

Sydney Pl

Darlington St

Sydney Rd

To Bathampton (2mi)

To Bath Boating Station (200m); Bathampton (2mi)

Sydney Gardens

Bathwick Hill

Bathwick Rd

Pulteney Rd

Recreation Ground

Avon

Pulteney Gdns

Pulteney Ave

Lime Gve

Broadway

Rossiter Rd

Cricket Ground

North Pde Rd

North Pde

South Pde

Duke St

Pierrepont St

Grand Pde

Bridge St

Abbey Green

Manvers St

Newark St

Railway Pl

Southgate

Broad Quay

Dorchester St

Claverton St

Bath Spa Station

New Orchard St

Henry St

Ambury

To Bath YHA Hostel (400m)

To Ring O'Bells (200m); Prior Park (1.2mi)

To Rondo Theatre (300m)

To Bath Spa Station

10
25
26
24
66
48
46
19
40
16
35
37
22
51
49
68
69
70
17
11
8
62
55
56
59
33
44
64
50
12
41
63
34
47
39
45
29
58
38
30
57
7
31
61
54
13
52
14
27
32
36
2
15
21
9
20
28
23
42
1
4
5
60
67
53
3

Walcot St (☎ 445999; 128 Walcot St; ☑ 10.30am–7.30pm Mon-Sat; per 30 min £1.50)

Royal United Hospital (☎ 428331; Combe Park)

TIC (☎ 0906 711 2000 (50p per min); www.visitbath .co.uk; Abbey Churchyard; ☑ 9.30am-6pm Mon-Sat, 10am-4pm Sun) Has a range of leaflets, including the free *Jane Austen Bath Walk* and can help with accommodation bookings for a £5 fee.

What's On (www.whatsonbath.co.uk) Up-to-date listing on the city's events and nightlife.

SIGHTS
Baths

The city's steaming soul is the bath-and-temple complex built by the Romans over one of Bath's three natural hot springs from the 1st century AD. The buildings were left to decay after the Romans departed and, apart from a few leprous souls who came looking for a cure in the Middle Ages, it wasn't until the end of the 17th century that the numbers of those coming to 'take the cure' in Bath began to rise again. In 1702 the visit of Queen Anne set the seal on the trend, and a few years later Ralph Allen started his town expansion programme.

The **Roman Baths Museum** (☎ 477785; www .romanbaths.co.uk; Abbey Church Yard; adult/child £9/5, incl Museum of Costume £12/7; ☑ 9am-5pm Mar-Jun, Sep & Oct, 9am-9pm Jul & Aug, 9.30am-4.30pm Nov-Feb) is one of England's most popular attractions and can be overrun in summer. Ideally, visit early on a midweek morning and allow at least an hour to fully appreciate it.

The monumental remains are some of the best preserved in Britain and your first sight is that of the **Great Bath** from the Victorian gallery terrace. Head down to water level and along the raised walkway to see the Roman paving and lead base. A series of excavated passages and chambers beneath street level lead off in several directions and let you inspect the remains of other smaller baths and hypocaust (heating) systems, while an audio guide explains the details. One of the most picturesque corners of the complex is the 12th-century **King's Bath**, built around the original sacred spring; 1.5 million litres of hot water still pour into the pool every day. You can see the ruins of the vast 2000-year-old **Temple of Sulis-Minerva** under the Pump Room, and recent excavations of the **East Baths** give an insight into its 4th-century form.

Head outside to Bath St and note the convenient arcading constructed so bathers could walk between the town's three sets of baths without getting wet. At the end of Bath St stands the **Cross Bath** where Mary of Modena, wife of James II, erected a cross in gratitude for her pregnancy in 1688. Opposite is the **Hot Bath**, the third bath built over Bath's hot springs. These two historic sites have been restored and, together with the Hetling Pump Room, are now part of the **Thermae Bath Spa** (☎ 331234; www.thermaebathspa.com; Hot Bath St). Massively over budget and beset by legal problems, Bath's privately run and superbly

WESSEX

BEAU NASH: PRINCE REGENCY

If Ralph Allen, John Wood the Elder and John Wood the Younger were responsible for the physical construction of Georgian Bath, Richard 'Beau' Nash was the force that shaped high society in its heyday. A contradictory character, Nash was a dandy, gambler and womaniser, yet he was also purportedly charming, friendly, witty, influential and (at least to some degree) philanthropic.

Born in Wales in 1674, Richard Nash was an Oxford scholar and ex-soldier who was appointed Master of Ceremonies in Bath in 1705. By revitalising spa culture and providing entertainment for the rich, Nash effectively created a prestigious social milieu over which he would rule, imposing strict regulations on behaviour and dress, for almost 50 years.

Quite how he wielded such power is something of a mystery. He wasn't a public leader or employee, and he derived his income from a proportion of gambling-house profits. In any case, by the 1750s his influence was waning and he died in poverty in 1761. However, there's no doubt that Bath was changed irrevocably by his presence and simply wouldn't be what it is without his legacy.

designed complex was due to open in 2002 but has yet to actually let any bathers in the door. Promises of top-class treatments and a stunning rooftop pool have customers eagerly awaiting the final go-ahead.

Bath Abbey

Edgar, the first king of united England, was crowned in a church in Abbey Courtyard in 973, but the present **Bath Abbey** (☎ 422462; requested donation £2.50; ☉ 9am-6pm Mon-Sat Easter-Oct, 9am-4.30pm Nov-Easter, afternoons only Sun), more glass than stone, was built between 1499 and 1616, making it the last great medieval church raised in England. The nave's wonderful fan vaulting was erected in the 19th century.

The most striking feature of the abbey's exterior is the west façade, where angels climb up and down stone ladders, commemorating a dream of the founder, Bishop Oliver King. The abbey boasts the second-largest collection of wall monuments after Westminster Abbey. Among those buried here are Sir Isaac Pitman, who devised the Pitman method of shorthand, and Beau Nash. Also worth a look are the choir stalls, carved with mythical beasts.

On the abbey's southern side, steps lead down to a vault in which the small **Heritage Vaults Museum** (admission £2.50; ☉ 10am-4pm Mon-Sat; wheelchair access) describes the abbey's history and its links with the baths and fashionable Georgian society. It also contains fine stone bosses, robes and other artefacts.

Royal Crescent & The Circus

The crowning glory of Georgian Bath and the city's most prestigious address, Royal Crescent, is a semicircular terrace of mag-nificent houses decorated with a continuous façade of Ionic columns. Designed by John Wood the Younger (1728–82) and built between 1767 and 1775, the houses would have originally been rented by the season by wealthy socialites.

Superbly restored to the minutest detail of its 1770 magnificence, the grand Palladian town house **No 1 Royal Crescent** (☎ 428126; www.bath-preservation-trust.org.uk; adult/child £4/3.50; ☉ 10.30am-5pm Tue-Sun mid-Feb–Oct, 10.30am-4pm Nov) is well worth visiting to see how people lived during Bath's glory days; staff dressed in period costume complete the effect.

A walk along Brock St leads to **The Circus**, a magnificent circle of 30 houses. Plaques on the houses commemorate famous residents such as Thomas Gainsborough, Clive of India and David Livingstone. To the south is the restored 18th-century **Georgian Garden**, with gravel taking the place of grass to protect women's long dresses from staining.

Assembly Rooms & Museum of Costume

In the 18th century, fashionable Bath visitors gathered to play cards, dance and listen to music in the **Assembly Rooms** (☎ 477785; www.museumofcostume.co.uk; Bennett St; ☉ 11am-5pm Mar-Oct, 11am-4pm Nov-Feb). You can wander round the rooms free, taking in the grand décor and engravings, but most people head for the basement **Museum of Costume** (adult/child £6/4, incl Roman Baths Museum £12/7), displaying costumes worn from the 16th to late 20th centuries, including alarming crinolines that would have forced women to approach doorways side on. There's an audio guide to talk you through the fickle vagaries of fashion.

Jane Austen Centre

For devotees, a visit to the **Jane Austen Centre** (☎ 443000; www.janeaustin.co.uk; 40 Gay St; admission £4.45; ⊙ 10am-5.30pm Mon-Sat, 10.30am-5.30pm Sun; wheelchair access), dedicated to one of Bath's most eminent residents, is a must. Displays include period costume, contemporary prints of the city and exhibits relating to the author's personal life, family and homes. It's a mecca for fans and insightful for the rest of us.

Also of interest to Austen fans is a **plaque** at No 4 Sydney Pl, opposite the Holburne Museum, commemorating the author who lived here for three (not particularly happy) years. She wrote parts of *Persuasion* and *Northanger Abbey* here; both vividly describe fashionable life in the city around 1800.

Other Museums

The fine 18th-century **Holburne Museum** (☎ 466669; Great Pulteney St; admission £4; ⊙ 10am-5pm Tue-Sat mid-Feb–mid-Dec) houses the booty of Sir William Holburne, a 19th-century Bath resident who brought together an outstanding collection of porcelain, antiques, and paintings by great 18th-century artists such as Gainsborough, Turner and Guardi.

Housed in the 18th-century Gothic chapel, the **Building of Bath Museum** (☎ 333895; www.bath-preservation-trust.org.uk; The Vineyards; admission £4; ⊙ 10.30am-5pm Tue-Sun mid-Feb–Nov) details how Bath's Georgian splendour came into being.

In 1781 William Herschel discovered the planet Uranus from the garden of his home, which now houses the **William Herschel Museum** (☎ 311342; 19 New King St; admission £3.50; ⊙ 2-5pm Mon, Tue, Thu & Fri, 11am-5pm Sat & Sun, Feb-Nov). The house is decorated as it would have been in the 18th century.

The municipal **Victoria Art Gallery** (☎ 477233; www.victoriagal.org.uk; Pulteney Bridge; admission free; ⊙ 10am-5.30pm Tue-Fri, 10am-5pm Sat, 2-5pm Sun) has changing exhibitions of mostly modern art, and permanent collections of fine ceramics, Flemish masters and English paintings by Gainsborough and Turner.

The **Museum of East Asian Art** (☎ 464640; www.meaa.org.uk; 12 Bennett St; admission £3.50; ⊙ 10am-5pm Tue-Sat, noon-5pm Sun) contains more than 500 jade, bamboo, porcelain and bronze objects from Cambodia, Korea and Thailand, and substantial Chinese and Japanese carvings, ceramics and lacquerware.

FESTIVALS & EVENTS

The annual **Bath Literature Festival** (☎ 463362; www.bathlitfest.org.uk) takes place in early March and attracts the world of words.

From mid-May to early June the **Bath International Music Festival** (www.bathmusicfest .org.uk) is in full swing with events in all the town's venues. This festival focuses on classical music and opera, although there are also world music and jazz weekends.

Running concurrently is the **Bath Fringe Festival** (www.bathfringe.co.uk), the biggest fringe festival in England, involving a blend of comedy, drama, performance art and world music.

BITE (Bath International Taste Extravaganza) is the city's July food festival, featuring specialist markets, restaurant deals and events.

Bookings for all events are handled by the **Bath Festivals box office** (☎ 463362; www.bath festivals.org.uk; 2 Church St; ⊙ 9.30am-5.30pm Mon-Sat).

TOURS

Free two-hour **walking tours** (☎ 477411; www .thecityofbath.co.uk) of the city leave from outside the Pump Room at 10.30am and 2pm Sunday to Friday, 10.30am on Saturday. From May to September there are additional tours at 7pm on Tuesday, Friday and Saturday.

Guides proudly declare their lack of cultural and historical knowledge on **Bizarre Bath Comedy Walks** (☎ 335124; www.bizarrebath.co.uk; adult/child £5/4.50; ⊙ 8pm Mar-Sep), a hilarious and irreverent look at the city. They leave from outside the Huntsman Inn on North Parade Passage and last about 1½ hours.

Jane Austen's Bath (☎ 443000; adult/child £3.50/2.50) traces the footsteps of the author on tours leaving the KC Change in Abbey Church Yard at 1.30pm in July and August, Saturday and Sunday only September to June. Tours last 1½ hours.

Tuk-tuk Tours (☎ 425866; www.tuktuktours.co.uk; for 4 people £30) offers one-hour tours of Bath by tuk-tuk, visiting many places the tour buses can't get to. Pick up and drop off available.

Several companies including **Classic Citytour** (☎ 07721 559686; adult/child £6.50/2) and **City Sightseeing** (☎ 330444; www.city-sightseeing.co.uk; £8; ⊙ Mar-Nov, Sat & Sun only Dec-Feb) offer hop-on, hop-off bus tours around the city operating from about 9am to 6pm every 20 minutes and can be picked up at numerous points around the city centre.

WESSEX

The following Bath-based tours go to Wessex's top attractions. A one-day tour costs about £18.

Danwood Tours (☎ 465965) One-day City Safari taking in the Cotswolds, Avebury, Stonehenge, Salisbury and Longleat.

Mad Max Tours (☎ 325900; www.madmaxtours.com) One-day tours visiting Stonehenge, Avebury, Lacock and Castle Combe; and full-day tours of the Cotswolds.

SLEEPING

Finding somewhere to stay during busy periods can be tough. The TIC will book rooms for a £5 booking fee plus a deposit of 10% of the first night's accommodation. It also sells a brochure, *Bath & Beyond* (£1), with comprehensive listings.

BUDGET

YMCA (☎ 325900; reservations@ymcabath.co.uk; International House, Broad St Pl; dm £14, s/d £20/32) An excellent option right in the centre of town, the rooms here are bright and modern but lacking in character. There's a great health suite and a cheap restaurant, and reduced rates for stays of a week or more.

Bath YHA Hostel (☎ 465674; bath@yha.org.uk; dm £11.80, s/d £24/38; [P] [X]) If you're looking for some cheap crumbling grandeur, this hostel is set in a wonderful old Italianate mansion. It's a steep climb uphill (or a short hop on bus No 18) from the city centre, but the views are magnificent.

Bath Backpackers' Hostel (☎ 446787; bath@ hostels.co.uk; 13 Pierrepont St; dm £12; [💻]) An effortlessly easy attitude and a lively atmosphere make this grungy hostel a popular choice. There are plenty of bright street-style murals on the walls, large dorms and a party 'dungeon' for late nights in.

Other budget options:

St Christopher's Inn (☎ 481444; www.st-christophers .co.uk; 9 Green St; dm/d £12/25 per person; [💻]) Basic but comfortable rooms in the heart of the city.

Newton Mill Camping Park (☎ 333909; www.camp inginbath.co.uk; Newton Rd; tent £4-13, caravan £11-17) About 3 miles west of Bath on the B3310. Bus No 5 (15 minutes, every 10 minutes) from the bus station.

MID-RANGE

Central B&Bs in the guise of 'hotels' tend to be overpriced and nothing special. It's worth moving slightly out of the centre for a much better deal.

Roban House (☎ 445390; www.bathholidayrooms .co.uk; 26 Lr Oldfield Pk; s £25, d £40-62; [X] [💻]) A cross

between university rooms and a hotel, this modern place has simple contemporary-style rooms. Although there isn't much character, it's an excellent deal and you get a fridge and DVD player in your room and free broadband access.

Koryu (☎ 337642; japanesekoryu@aol.com; 7 Pulteney Gardens; s/d £40/50; [P] [X]) Newly refurbished and extolling the values of simple living, this Anglo-Japanese guesthouse is a real treat. The great-value rooms are bright, modern and minimalist and the service is very friendly.

Dorian House (☎ 426336; www.dorianhouse.co.uk; 1 Upper Oldfield Park; s £42-78, d £55-150; [P] [X]) Pick of the crop in this price bracket, this excellent-value choice has luxurious rooms that blend Victorian elegance and contemporary Italian style. Rooms are furnished with Asian antiques and fine art from around the world. The Stradivari and Elgar rooms have terrific views.

Beckford's (☎ 334959; www.beckford-house.com; 59 Upper Oldfield Park; s/d £48/65; [P] [X]) The lovely large rooms here are bright and beautiful with kingsize beds, oversized showers and lots of books and magazines. Victorian features blend wonderfully with contemporary design and rooms have a pair of binoculars for you to admire the view.

Athole House (☎ 320009; www.atholehouse.co.uk; 33 Upper Oldfield Park; s/d £48/78; [P] [X]) Bright, modern and without a hint of chintz, this large Victorian home is set in lovely gardens and has sleek and stylish rooms with good bathrooms. The owners are happy to pick you up or drop you off at the station.

Other options:

Albany Guest House (☎ 313339; www.albanybath .co.uk; 24 Crescent Gardens; s £32-45, d £40-60; [P] [X]) Good-value, cosy, country-style rooms.

Pulteney Hotel (☎ 460991; www.pulteneyhotel.co.uk; 14 Pulteney Rd; s/d £40/65; [P] [X]) Elegant Victorian house with period-style rooms.

TOP END

Bath has some classy hotels and if you're planning to splash out this is the place to do it.

Royal Crescent Hotel (☎ 823333; www.royalcrescent .co.uk; 16 Royal Cres; d £207-837; [P] [X] [💻]) Oozing charm and style, Bath's top place to stay, is on the grandest of grand crescents, but has the understated air of true refinement. There's a gorgeous secret garden and the period rooms are simply stunning. Pampering comes extra in the striking hotel spa with its numerous holistic treatments and therapies.

Queensberry Hotel (☎ 447928; enquiries@bath queensberry.com; Russell St; s £100-140, d £100-285; P ⊠) Four marvellous Georgian town-houses make up this wonderful hotel with secluded terraced gardens and chic décor. The bedrooms blend period character with contemporary style, gorgeous colours and sumptuous fabrics.

Dukes (☎ 787960; www.dukesbath.co.uk; Great Pulteney St; s £75-115, d £95-155; P) This magnificent Palladian mansion takes its inspiration from the fashionable travel destinations of the Georgian era with a series of magnificent suites featuring oriental Chinoiserie, classical English botanica, and French and Italian themes. Rich, heavy fabrics, moody lighting and sultry colour schemes complete the boudoir effect.

EATING
Budget
RESTAURANTS

Pastiche Bistro (☎ 442323; 16 Argyle St; 2 courses £10; ⏰ lunch & dinner) This trendy joint just over Pulteney Bridge has a great choice of world dishes including moussaka meatballs and swordfish on sagaloo with mint dressing. The service is as slick as the décor and the food really should cost a lot more.

Walrus & the Carpenter (☎ 314864; 28 Barton St; mains £5-8; ⏰ lunch & dinner) There's a warren of rooms at this fun and funky place dishing up top-notch homemade global cuisine with a heavy vegetarian bias. It does brilliant burgers and some killer Walrus cocktails.

Las Iguanas (☎ 36666; 12 Seven Dials, Sawclose; mains £5-8) Salsa music, bright colours and funky lighting set the mood at this lively Latino place with a good choice of tapas in the bar and everything from xinxim (chicken in peanut, crayfish and lemon sauce) to sizzling fajitas in the restaurant. The early-bird menus are brilliant value at £7 for three courses.

Other options:

Demuth's (☎ 446059; 2 North Parade Passage; mains £5-7; ⏰ lunch) A hip Bath institution, serving an innovative range of vegan and vegetarian food.

Sally Lunn's (☎ 461634; 4 North Parade Passage; mains lunch £5-7, dinner £7.50-9.50) A quintessential English tea house serving up hearty traditional food.

CAFÉS

Café Retro (☎ 339347; 18 York St; mains £5-11) This hip, boho hangout is a bit of a cult classic with café-style dining downstairs and a rush for the window seats upstairs. There's a good choice of paninis, burgers and salads as well more substantial fare to go with the super-chilled atmosphere.

Octagon Café (☎ 447991; 43 Milsom St; mains £3-6) Photos line the walls of this café-cum-brasserie with a creative menu of delicacies such as warm puy lentil salad with grilled goat's cheese and almond profiteroles with praline cream. When you're done, scoot upstairs to see the exhibits at the Royal Photographic Society Gallery.

Adventure Café (☎ 462038; 5 Princes Bldgs; mains £3-6) Packed to the gunwales by day and night, this place serves gourmet sandwiches and soups to a young crowd people-watching from the full-length windows. The surroundings are smart, but it's a very relaxed vibe with moody jazz, funk or soul as a soundtrack.

QUICK EATS

Boston Tea Party (☎ 313901; 19 Kingsmead Sq; ⏰ Mon-Sat) Gourmet sambos, soups and smoothies attract the crowds to this trendy joint. Just try making it out the door without giving in to those brownies too.

F-east (☎ 333500; 27 High St; mains £6-8) For a quick but substantial bite head for this oriental emporium serving a selection of modern pan-Asian food in swish contemporary surroundings.

Café Fromage (☎ 313525; 1 John St; ploughman's £4.95; ⏰ Mon-Sat) You'll find the best ploughman's in town at this tiny little place above a cheesemongers. Choose from six varieties dripping with home-made chutney.

SELF-CATERING

Self-caterers should head for the covered **Guildhall Market**, where you'll also find crêpes and other takeaway food. The major supermarket chains are all represented in the city.

Fine Cheese Co (☎ 483407; 29-31 Walcot St) is a gourmet deli that does a fine line in cheeses as well as fantastic sandwiches and pastas.

Mid-Range

Moon & Sixpence (☎ 460962; 6a Broad St; mains £10-15) Tucked away in a courtyard, this classy but relaxed diner serves fusion food in a stylish, understated space. You can sit outside in summer but otherwise opt for the ground floor as it's more atmospheric than upstairs.

Bistro Papillon (☎ 310064; 2 Margaret's Bldgs; 2-course lunch £7.50, mains £10-13.50; ☾ Tue-Sat) Bright and modern, this French place has an informal rustic charm with its check tablecloths, heavily accented staff, Edith Piaf soundtrack and relaxed atmosphere. The food is understated yet sublime and the set lunch menu is a snip.

Ring O'Bells (☎ 448870; 10 Widcombe Pde; mains £8-12) This unassuming little place is actually an excellent gastro-pub with a simple but sophisticated menu featuring jazzed-up old favourites. The interior is bright and airy with modern design and old-world character mixing seamlessly.

No 5 (☎ 444499; 5 Argyle St; mains £14.50-15.80) Classic French bistro-style food with a hint of the Mediterranean draws the crowds to this informal but stylish place. The food is expertly prepared with subtle flavours and beautiful presentation. Go for the veal kidneys if you can handle the guilt.

Wife of Bath (☎ 461745; 12 Pierrepont St; mains £10-15) Be prepared for giant portions at this warren of Georgian cellar rooms filled with alcoves with booth-style seating. The food spans the globe, featuring dishes from as far apart as Australia and the Caribbean with a classic European touch thrown in.

Hop Pole (☎ 446327; 7 Albion Bldgs; mains £8-16) This unassuming country-style pub with exposed beams and bright and airy rooms isn't quite what you'd expect in this city, but the juicy Sunday roasts and steaming steak and ale pies are famous round town.

Other good options:

Circus (☎ 318918; 34 Brock St; mains £15-18; ☾ Tue-Sun) Compact and bijou place serving fine modern British cuisine.

Woods (☎ 314812; 9-13 Alfred St; mains £9-16; ☾ Mon-Sat) A temple of gourmet Anglo-French cuisine with lots of veg choices.

Top End

Olive Tree Restaurant (☎ 447928; Russell St; 2-/3-course lunch £13.50/15.50, 3-course dinner £26) Chic and sleek, and one of the finest restaurants in town, this understated place with oak floors and dark leather furniture serves up a top-notch menu of simple modern British and French cuisine.

Moody Goose (☎ 466688; 7a Kingsmead Sq; 3-course dinner £25; ☾ Mon-Sat) There's often a Gallic

twist to the superb modern English food at this stylish restaurant with simple bright décor. Seasonal ingredients dictate the menu but the set meals are better value.

Hole in the Wall (☎ 425242; 16 George St; mains £13-17) A top-notch joint serving modern British cooking rich with organic ingredients and a healthy dose of fish and vegetarian choices. The interior is wonderful with natural stone floors, a giant hearth and dazzling white linen.

DRINKING

Old Green Tree (☎ 329314; 12 Green St) More a broom cupboard than a pub, this tiny place has only three rooms but is worth the squash for the convivial atmosphere, friendly crowd and real ales. They have occasional blues and jazz nights too.

Pulp (☎ 466411; 38 Monmouth St) A hip café-bar with streetside tables and good cocktails, this retro-chic place is ultra-cool but still manages to be really friendly. It has a vast cocktail list and trendy clientele and is a great place to just people watch.

Bath Tap (☎ 404344; 19-20 St James Pde; £2.50) One of Bath's top gay bars with a lively programme of cabaret, dance and karaoke, this place is also a good pre-club venue with plenty of cheesy tracks, a wicked wild side and a good mixed crowd.

DYMK? (☎ 330470; 11-12 Westgate Bldg; £1.50) Bath's hottest new gay venue, Does Your Mother Know? packs 'em in for the usual mix of drag, cabaret, karaoke and bingo but it's bigger and brassier than most and is a really friendly place for punters of any persuasion.

Common Room (☎ 425550; 2 Saville Row) An intimate late-night drinking den, this place is all natural wood, leather and clean stylish lines. Dress smart and act cool at the door and they won't ask if you're a member.

Other worthy haunts:

Fez (☎ 444162; 7a Bladud Bldgs, The Paragon; £3-5) Laid-back souk-bar with groovy DJs playing funky sounds.

Delfter Krug (☎ 443352; Sawclose) Trendy bar-club with '60s-throwback décor and plenty of attitude.

ENTERTAINMENT

Venue magazine (www.venue.co.uk; £1.20) has comprehensive listings with details of theatre, music, gigs – the works, basically – for Bristol and Bath. Pick up a copy at any newsagent.

Nightclubs

Cadillacs (☎ 464241; 90b Walcot St; £4-6) A popular late-night haunt, this place hosts the city's most popular salsa night on Monday, student booze fest on Tuesday and a mix of chart, dance, R&B and soul into the weekend.

Moles (☎ 404445; 14 George St; £4-5) The best alternative club and live-music venue in town. It's a good place to see Bath's up-and-coming bands playing everything from reggae and ska to hard rock. Club nights feature a variety of sounds but lots of hip-hop.

Babylon (☎ 465002; Kingston Rd; £3-5) Bath's best late night out, Babylon is a glitzy dance spot featuring anything from Wednesday's boozy students' night with major drinks promotions and serious cheese, to Thursday's alternative rock, indie and punk and the weekend's R&B, drum'n'bass and '70s and '80s funk.

Theatre & Cinema

Theatre Royal (☎ 448844; www.theatreroyal.org.uk; Sawclose) This sumptuous venue features comedy drama, opera, ballet, and world music on its eclectic programme at the main theatre, and more experimental and student productions at its smaller Ustinov Studio.

Rondo Theatre (☎ 463362; www.rondotheatre.co.uk; St Saviours Rd, Larkhall) This small but adventurous rep theatre mixes professional, amateur and community work in a varied programme of comedy, panto, music and drama.

Little Theatre (☎ 466822; St Michael's Pl) Bath's art-house cinema, screening mostly fringe and foreign-language films.

Classical Music

At **Bath Abbey** (☎ 422462) there's a regular programme of lunchtime recitals while the **Bath Spa University Concert Series** (☎ 463362; Michael Tippett Centre) has a mix of classical, world music and sonic art.

GETTING THERE & AWAY
Bus

National Express coaches run to London (£14.50, 3½ hours, 11 daily) via Heathrow (£14.50, 2½ hours), and to Manchester (£29, 6½ to 10½ hours, eight daily) and Oxford (£29.50, 2¼ hours, one daily).

Bus Nos X39 and 337/8/9 run to Bristol (50 minutes) several times an hour. Other useful services include bus Nos X5 and X6 to Bradford-on-Avon (30 minutes, half-hourly), Nos X71 and X72 to Devizes (one

hour, hourly) and Nos 173/773 to Wells (1¼ hours, hourly).

Map-timetables for individual routes are available from the **bus station office** (☎ 464446; Manvers St; ◷ 8am-5.30pm Mon-Sat).

Train

There are half-hourly trains to London Paddington (£28.50, 1½ hours) and Cardiff (£11.90, 1¼ hours), and several each hour to Bristol (£4.80, 11 minutes). Trains go to Oxford roughly hourly (£9.80, 1¼ hours); Weymouth (£10.80, 2¼ hours) every two hours via Bradford-on-Avon (£2.80, 15 minutes) and Dorchester West (£10.50, two hours); and Portsmouth (£13, 2½ hours) hourly via Salisbury (£10.40, 50 minutes).

GETTING AROUND
Bicycle

Bikes can be hired from **Avon Valley Cycles** (☎ 461880; www.bikeshop.uk.com; Arch 37; half/full day £10/15). Cyclists can use the 12-mile Bristol and Bath Railway Path that follows a disused railway line.

Boat

Companies run half-hourly passenger boats from Pulteney Bridge to Bathampton (£5, 50 minutes). Alternatively, you can hire canoes, punts or rowing boats to propel yourself along the Avon from £6 per hour; try **Bath Boating Station** (☎ 312900; Forester Rd; ◷ Mar-Oct).

Bus

Bus No 18 runs from the bus station, High St and Great Pulteney St up Bathwick Hill past the YHA to the university every 10 minutes. Bus No 4 runs every 20 minutes to Bathampton from the same places. A First Day Pass for unlimited bus travel in the city costs adult/child £3/2.50.

Car

Bath has a bad traffic problem and an infuriating one-way system. **Park-and-ride services** (☎ 464446; return £1.60, 10 min to centre, every 10-15 min 7.15am-7.30pm) operate at Lansdown to the north, Newbridge to the west and Odd Down to the south.

AROUND BATH
Prior Park

The beautiful 18th-century **Prior Park** (NT; ☎ 833 422; admission £4.10; Ralph Allen Dr; ◷ 11am-5.30pm

Wed-Mon Feb-Nov, Fri-Sun Dec & Jan; wheelchair access) is a landscaping glory created by Capability Brown. The gardens are set in a small sweeping valley and have spectacular views of Bath, a famous Palladian bridge and cascading lakes. Prior Park is 1 mile south of the centre but it's only accessible by bus (No 2 or 4, every 10 minutes) or on foot. There's a £1 refund if you show your bus ticket.

SOMERSET

Heavily laden tractors, fat bumblebees and cider-swilling ruddy-cheeked yokels populate the slow-moving agricultural county of Somerset – or so the stereotype goes. Outside the tourist honey pot of Bath, the bohemian swing of Glastonbury and the magnificent gorge in Cheddar, Somerset *is* a sleepy kind of place, but its drowsy pace cloaks picturesque villages, a wonderful cathedral city and excellent walking and cycling territory, all relatively free from tourist hordes.

Orientation & Information

Somerset nestles around the crook in the elbow of the Bristol Channel. The Mendip Hills follow a line below Bristol, just north of Wells and Cheddar, while the Quantocks sit just east of Exmoor. Most places of interest are in northern Somerset. Bath or Wells make good bases to the east, as do Lynton and Lynmouth to the west.

Most towns have TICs and there's a central **Somerset Visitor Centre** (☎ 01934-750833; somersetvisitorcentre@somerset.gov.uk; Sedgemoor Services M5 South, Axbridge, Somerset BS26 2UF) for general information. Online you'll find information at www.somerset.gov.uk/celebrating somerset.

Getting Around

Bus services in Somerset are roughly split between **First Badgerline** (☎ 0117-955 8211; www .firstbadgerline.co.uk) north of Bridgwater, including Bath and Bristol, and **First Southern National** (☎ 01823-366100; www.firstsouthernnational .co.uk) to the south, with other local operators chipping in.

The county council produces area-specific timetables available at bus stations and most TICs.

WELLS
☎ 01749 / pop 10,406

England's smallest city is a charmingly dignified place with a magnificent hidden cathedral and the imposing Bishop's Palace. Medieval buildings are scattered around town and the water from the three natural springs that give Wells its name gurgles down the High St. There's also a good choice of hotels and restaurants, making Wells an excellent base for touring the Mendips, Cheddar Gorge and unruly cousin Glastonbury 6 miles to the south.

Information

The **TIC** (☎ 672552; www.wells.gov.uk; Market Pl; ⏰ 9.30am-5.30pm Apr-Oct, 10am-4pm Nov-Mar) stocks the *Wells City Trail* leaflet (30p) and has information on nearby walking and cycling routes. Wednesday and Saturday are market days.

Wells Laundrette (☎ 01458-830409; 39 St Cuthbert St; ⏰ 8am-8pm) is opposite St Cuthbert's Church.

Sights
WELLS CATHEDRAL

Set in a marvellous close and hidden from view until the last moment, the **Cathedral Church of St Andrew** (☎ 674483; Chain Gate, Cathedral Green; requested donation adult/child £4.50/1.50; ⏰ 7am-7pm Sep-Jun, 7am-8.30pm Jul & Aug) is a magnificent place built in stages between 1180 and 1508. The building incorporates several Gothic styles, but its most famous asset is the wonderful **west front**, an immense sculpture gallery with over 300 figures, built in the 13th century and restored to its original splendour in 1986. Apart from the figure of Christ, installed in 1985 in the uppermost niche, all the figures are original.

Inside, the most striking feature is the pair of **scissor arches** separating the nave from the choir, a brilliant solution to the problem posed by the subsidence of the central tower; they were added in the mid-14th century, shortly after the tower's completion. High up in the north transept is a wonderful **mechanical clock** dating from 1392 – the second-oldest surviving in England after the one in Salisbury Cathedral (p230). The clock shows the position of the planets and the phases of the moon.

Other highlights are the elegant **lady chapel** (1326) at the eastern end and the seven **effigies** of Anglo-Saxon bishops ringing the choir. The 15th-century **chained library** houses books and manuscripts dating back to 1472. Access is from the **reading room** (admission 50p; ☺ 2.30-4.30pm Fri & Sat Apr-Oct) upstairs from the south transept.

From the north transept follow the worn steps to the glorious **Chapter House** (1306), with its delicate ceiling ribs sprouting like a palm from a central column. Externally, look out for the **Chain Bridge** built from the northern side of the cathedral to Vicars' Close to enable clerics to reach the cathedral without getting their robes wet. The **cloisters** on the southern side surround a pretty courtyard.

Guided tours (☺ 10am, 11am, 1pm, 2pm & 3pm Mon-Sat) of the cathedral are free. Regular **concerts** (☎ 832201) and cathedral choir **recitals** (☎ 674483) are held in the cathedral throughout the year.

CATHEDRAL CLOSE

Wells Cathedral is the focal point of a cluster of buildings whose history is inextricably linked to its own. Facing the west front, on the left are the 15th-century **Old Deanery** and a salmon-coloured building housing **Wells Museum** (☎ 673477; 8 Cathedral Green; wellsmuseum@ukonline.co.uk; admission £3; ☺ 10am-5.30pm Easter-Oct, 10am-8pm Aug, 11am-4pm Wed-Mon Nov-Easter), with exhibits on local life, cathedral architecture and the infamous Witch of Wookey Hole.

Farther along on the left, **Vicars' Close** is a stunning cobbled street of uniform houses dating back to the 14th century with a chapel at the end; members of the cathedral choir still live here. It is thought to be the oldest complete medieval street in Europe. Passing under the Chain Bridge, inspect the outside of the lady chapel and a lovely medieval house called The Rib, before emerging at a main road called The Liberty.

Penniless Porch, a corner gate leading onto Market Sq and built by Bishop Bekynton around 1450, is so-called because beggars asked for alms here.

BISHOP'S PALACE

Beyond the cathedral is the moated 13th-century **Bishop's Palace** (☎ 678691; www.bishopspalacewells.co.uk; adult/child £4/3; ☺ 10.30am-5pm Tue-Fri, 1-5pm Sun Apr-Oct), purportedly the oldest inhabited building in England. Set in a quad and surrounded by a huge wall, it is an incredible place with fine Italian Gothic state rooms, an imposing Great Hall and beautiful gardens. The springs that give the town its name bubble and babble here, feeding the moat. The swans in the moat have been trained to ring a bell outside one of the windows when they want to be fed.

Sleeping

Infield House (☎ 670989; www.infieldhouse.co.uk; 36 Portway; s/d £36/52; ℗ ✗) This beautifully restored Victorian townhouse has classical rooms with period furnishings and portraits, original fireplaces, bay windows and small bathrooms. Single rooms are £10 cheaper in low season.

Old Farmhouse (☎ 675058; www.plus44.com/oldfarmhouse; 62 Chamberlain St; s/d £40/60; ✗) Set right in the city in a beautiful walled garden, this 17th-century former farmhouse has lovely bright cottage-style rooms with large beds, subtle floral patterns and period charm.

Beryl (☎ 678738; www.beryl-wells.co.uk; Hawkers Lane; s/d £55/75; ℗ ✗ ☎) If you fancy a bit of grand Victoriana you'll find this small but stunning Victorian Gothic mansion set in extensive parklands just a mile outside town. The luxurious rooms are full of character with period furnishings, antiques and family portraits on the walls.

Ancient Gate House Hotel (☎ 672029; www.ancientgatehouse.co.uk; Browne's Gate; s/d £63/78; ✗) Actually part of the Great West Gate of Cathedral Close, this charming old place has little passages running to the warren of atmospheric rooms with period character, four-poster or half-tester beds and rich fabrics.

Other options:

Bay Tree House (☎ 677933; www.baytree-house.co.uk; 85 Portway; s/d £28/42; ℗ ✗) A stylish 1930s house with bright, pleasant rooms and rural décor.

Swan Hotel (☎ 836300; swan@bhere.co.uk; Sadler St; s/d £89/125; ℗ ✗) Elegant, 15th-century coaching inn with swanky rooms.

Eating

Le Café Bleu (☎ 677772; 9 Heritage Courtyard; mains £4-6; ☺ lunch & dinner) This hip and happening place, tucked off Sadler St, has a good range of sambos, salads and hot bakes, a chilled atmosphere and mellow soundtrack. There's lots of outdoor seating for fine weather and live music every other Friday night.

Fountain Inn & Boxers (☎ 672317; 1 St Thomas St; mains £8-14; ☺ lunch & dinner) This fine gastro-pub and restaurant is the local favourite for its relaxed atmosphere and wonderful food. Fish and game feature heavily but there's also a good choice of vegetarian dishes and a children's menu.

Rugantino (☎ 672029; Brown's Gate; 3-course dinner £16.90; ☽ dinner) Part of the atmospheric Ancient Gate House, this rustic Italian restaurant serves a fine selection of traditional regional fare. The excellent-value set menu features a good range of interesting pastas and classic meat dishes.

Ritchers (☎ 679085; 5 Sadler St; 2/3-course meals £19.50/23; ☽ lunch & dinner) This smart little restaurant knocks up the city's finest modern French and British cuisine. There's bistro dining downstairs and a more refined restaurant atmosphere upstairs. Expect the likes of steamed lamb pudding with a prune and Armagnac jus or char-grilled sea bass with coriander, ginger and plum sauce.

Getting There & Around

National Express runs to London once a day (£16.50, 4½ hours) but connecting services run from Bristol (Bus Nos 376 and 377; one hour, hourly) and Bath (Nos 173 and 403; 1¼ hours). Bus No 163 runs hourly to Glastonbury (15 minutes). Bus Nos 126 and 826 travel hourly (every two hours on Sunday) to Cheddar (20 minutes). There's no train station in Wells.

Bike City (☎ 671711; 31 Broad St; ☽ 9am-5.30pm Mon-Sat) charges £12 per day for bike hire.

WOOKEY HOLE

On the southern edge of the Mendips, the River Axe has carved out a whole series of caves known as **Wookey Hole** (☎ 01749-672243; www.wookey.co.uk; adult/child £8.80/5.50; ☽ 10am-5pm Apr-Oct, 10.30am-4.30pm Nov-Mar). The caves contain a spectacular lake and some fascinating stalagmites (one of which gave rise to the legend of the Witch of Wookey Hole). Various Iron Age finds are displayed in the small museum, but essentially the caves are now run as a 'family attraction', with an ancient handmade-paper mill, an Edwardian fairground, a maze of mirrors and an arcade of vintage amusement machines.

Camping is available at **Homestead Park** (☎ 01749-673022; homesteadpark@onetel.net.uk; tent £6-9; ☽ Easter-Sep) just steps from the caves. Children under 14 are not accepted.

Alternatively you can go for something far grander and funkier at the **Wookey Hole Inn** (☎ 01749-676677; www.wookeyholeinn.com; s £50, d £75-90). The rooms here are really homely with plenty of knick-knacks strewn around, a cult video library, Japanese-style king-sized beds, widescreen TVs and lots of CDs. The inn also does a great menu of classic food (£6 to £15) and draught Belgian beers.

Bus No 171 runs hourly from Wells (10 minutes). A 3-mile walk to Wookey Hole is signposted from New St in Wells. Note that the village of Wookey just west of Wells is not the same as Wookey Hole.

CHEDDAR GORGE
☎ 01934

Dramatic Cheddar Gorge with its steep stone cliffs cuts a mile-long swathe through the southern side of the Mendip Hills. At some points the cliff walls tower 138m above the winding narrow road that lies at its base. A signposted 3-mile round walk follows the cliffs along the most spectacular parts of the gorge.

The attractions of the gorge, more or less natural, are now part of **Cheddar Caves & Gorge** (☎ 742343; www.cheddarcaves.co.uk; Explorer Ticket adult/child £9.50/6.50; ☽ 10am-5.30pm Jul & Aug, 10am-5pm Sep-Jun), a 'family' day out – expect tearooms, fish-and-chip and gift shops, and big crowds in summer.

THE BEE'S KNEES CHEESE

The country's most famous cheese only began to become widely known when people started visiting Cheddar Gorge and taking it home, although Cheddar was just one of many Somerset villages that produced this type. Cheddar has become a generic name for many bland mass-produced cheeses but mature, traditional farmhouse Cheddar can be crumbly, tangy and delicious.

If you are interested in the process of making genuine Cheddar cheese, visit the **Cheddar Gorge Cheese Company** (☎ 01934-742810; www.cheddargorgecheeseco.co.uk) to watch cheese-makers at work. It's part of the **Rural Village** (adult/child £2/1.50; ☽ 10am-6pm May-Sep, 10am-4pm Apr & Oct), just off the B3135, that also has demonstrations of lace-making, fudge-making and spinning.

The stalactite- and stalagmite-filled Cox's and Gough's caves are indisputably very impressive; a 40,000-year-old skeleton (imaginatively named Cheddar Man) was discovered in the latter. Add-on features include an open-top bus tour (Easter to September only), lookout tower and Crystal Quest theme cave for kids.

There's a TIC (☎ 744071; cheddar.tic@sedgemoor .gov.uk; ⏰ 10am-5pm Easter-Sep, 10.30am-4.30pm Oct, 11am-4pm Sun Nov-Easter) in the gorge.

Cheddar village, southwest of the gorge, has an elegant church and an ancient market cross but is otherwise disappointing. A mile southwest of the caves on the western side of the village is the **Cheddar YHA Hostel** (☎ 0870 770 5760; cheddar@yha.org.uk; Hillfield; dm £11.80).

Bus Nos 126 and 826 run to Wells (25 minutes) hourly Monday to Saturday and every two hours on Sunday. Bus Nos 672/3/4 run from Bristol to Cheddar (1½ hours, six times Monday to Friday, five on Saturday, four on Sunday).

MENDIP HILLS

The Mendip Hills are a ridge of limestone hills stretching from the coast near Weston-Super-Mare to Frome in eastern Somerset. Their highest point is Black Down (326m) to the northwest – but because they rise sharply, there are panoramic views towards Exmoor and across northwest Wiltshire.

Historically, the area has seen its share of action, and Neolithic earthworks, Bronze Age barrows and Iron Age forts can be found scattered over the hills. More recently lead and coal mining have left their mark with remains of mines dotting the area around Radstock and Midsomer Norton. Quarrying for stone is an important (and controversial) industry to this day.

Until the Middle Ages, large tracts of land lay beneath swampy meadows, and the remaining wetlands provide an important habitat for wildlife and flora. The marshland hid relics too, including a Lake Village excavated at the turn of the 20th century (see p286).

The landscape is dotted with pretty villages and isolated pubs that once served the thirsty miners. The villages are home to some delightful timbered houses, and several have fine perpendicular church towers. The one at **Chewton Mendip** (off the A37 between Bristol and Wells) is especially impressive

---

SOMETHING SPECIAL

The George (☎ 01373-834224; www.thegeorge inn-nsp.co.uk; High St, Norton St Philip; s/d £80/90; P ⊠) One of the oldest continuously licensed houses in England, the George is a stunningly atmospheric place with charming beamed rooms with hand-carved beds, beautiful antiques and loads of character. They're all different, so look at a few before deciding which should be your own little hideaway for the night. The two dining rooms are even more impressive with their high-beamed ceilings and cosy atmosphere. The menu (mains £10 to £16) features a good selection of modern fish and meat dishes as well as some vegetarian choices.

Norton St Philip is 6 miles southwest of Bradford-on-Avon on the A36.

---

and has a nice medieval churchyard cross. Farther west, the village of **Priddy**, the highest in the Mendips, has a massive sheep fair on the green in mid-August, while the village of **Compton Martin** has a Norman church with a 15th-century tower. A mile to the east, **West Harptree** is prettier, with two 17th-century former manor houses. Near **East Harptree** are the remains of Norman Richmont Castle. Local TICs stock leaflets with information on walking and cycling in the area.

The A371 skirts the southern side of the Mendip Hills, and any of the towns along it make good touring bases, though Wells has the best range of facilities.

Getting There & Away

Bus Nos 126 and 826 run between Wells and Cheddar (hourly, every two hours on Sunday). Bus No 173 runs from Bath to Radstock (30 minutes), Midsomer Norton (40 minutes) and Wells (1¼ hours, hourly, four on Sunday).

GLASTONBURY

☎ 01458 / pop 8429

Ley lines converge, mystics convene and bongo-playing hippies hang out in this bohemian small town that is now a centre of New Age culture. Glastonbury claims to be both the birthplace of English Christianity and the burial place of King Arthur and Queen Guinevere, and for years has attracted those in search of spiritual enlightenment of one

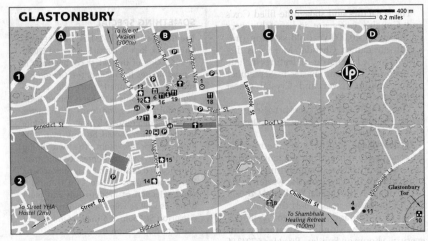

GLASTONBURY

kind or another. The town is now a mass of New World shops selling crystals and wind chimes, incense and salvation, and its strange mix of messiahs, massages and meat-free meals makes it an interesting stop for the sceptic or the shaman.

Information

Glastonbury's **TIC** (☎ 832954; www.glastonburytic .co.uk; The Tribunal, 9 High St; ☉ 10am-5pm Apr-Sep, 10am-4pm Oct-Mar) stocks free maps and accommodation lists, and sells leaflets describing local walks and the *Glastonbury Millennium Trail* (60p).

There is Internet access at Café Galatea (see p288).

Sights

GLASTONBURY ABBEY

Legend suggests that Joseph of Arimathea, great-uncle of Jesus, owned mines in this area and returned here with the Holy Grail (the chalice from the Last Supper) after the death of Christ and founded the first church here. However, the earliest evidence of Christianity is from the 7th century when King Ine

gave a charter to a monastery. In 1184 the church was destroyed by fire and reconstruction began in the reign of Henry II.

In 1191 monks claimed to have had visions confirming hints in old manuscripts that the 6th-century warrior-king Arthur and his wife Guinevere were buried in the grounds. Excavations uncovered a tomb and the couple was reinterred in front of the high altar of the new church in 1278. The tomb survived until 1539 when Henry VIII dissolved the monasteries and had the last abbot hung, drawn and quartered on the tor. After that, the abbey complex gradually collapsed, its component parts scavenged to provide building materials.

The ruins you see at Glastonbury today are mainly of the church built after the 1184 fire. They include: some nave walls; parts of the crossing arches, which may have been scissor-shaped like those in Wells Cathedral (p282); some medieval tiles; remains of the choir; and the St Mary's or lady chapel with an elaborately carved doorway. The site of the supposed tomb of Arthur and Guinevere is marked in the grass.

An award-winning **museum** explores the site's history and has a model showing what the abbey would have looked like in its hey-day. Entrance to the abbey is through the **Abbey Gatehouse** (☎ 832267; www.glastonburyabbey .com; Magdalene St; admission £3.50; site ☙ 9.30am-6pm Mar-May & Sep-Nov, 9am-6pm Jun-Aug, 10am-dusk Dec-Feb).

GLASTONBURY TOR

Considered a sacred site by many and thought to be home of Gwyn ap Nudd, King of the Underworld, Glastonbury Tor is an exhilarating place with fantastic views over the surrounding countryside. *Tor* is a Celtic word used to describe a hill, and this 160m-high summit was a place of pilgrim-age for many years. All that remains of the medieval church of St Michael is the tower, silhouetted by sunrise and sunset and visible for miles around.

It takes 45 minutes to walk up and down the tor. Parking is not permitted nearby so take the Tor Bus (£1) from Dunstan's car park near the abbey. It runs to the tor and back every 30 minutes from 9.30am to 5pm April to September and also stops at Chalice Well and the Rural Life Museum.

CHALICE WELL & GARDENS

Mysticism and mythology have long sur-rounded the **Chalice Well & Gardens** (☎ 831154; www.chalicewell.org.uk; admission £2.70; ☙ 10am-6pm Apr-Oct, 11am-5pm Feb, Mar & Nov, noon-4pm Dec & Jan), supposedly the hiding place of the Holy Grail. The iron-red water may have begun the myth: the Holy Grail was supposed to have been used to catch blood from Christ's wounds while he was on the cross. How-ever, the spring was probably used by Celts long before Christ or the 800-year-old well. Its water has traditions of healing. You can drink as it pours out through a lion's-head spout, or rest your feet in basins surrounded by flowers. Mysticism aside, the gardens and meadows are beautiful spots to relax.

The Chalice Well is also known as the Red or Blood Spring; its sister **White Spring** sur-faces across Wellhouse Lane. Spigots from both springs empty into the street, where there's often a queue to fill containers.

RURAL LIFE MUSEUM

Artefacts associated with farming, cider-making, cheese-making and other aspects of Somerset country life are displayed at the interesting **Rural Life Museum** (☎ 831197; Abbey Farm, Chilkwell St; admission free; ☙ 10am-5pm Tue-Fri, 2-6pm Sat & Sun Easter-Oct, 10am-5pm Tue-Sat Nov-Easter). A key exhibition follows the life of a Vic-torian farm worker through birth, school and marriage. Don't miss the three-seater toilet, with holes for Mum, Dad and Junior. The late–14th-century tithe barn has fine carvings on the gables and porch, and an impressive timber roof; it now houses a col-lection of vintage agricultural machinery.

GLASTONBURY STORY

This brand new exhibition tells the **Glastonbury Story** (☎ 831666; www.glastonburystory.org.uk; St John's Sq; admission £2.95; ☙ 11am-5pm late-Mar–Oct) from the discovery of King Arthur's grave in the abbey grounds to the present time. It does a good job of explaining why Glastonbury has been a place of pilgrimage for thousands of years, fascinating artists, travellers and poets as well as mystics and New Agers.

LAKE VILLAGE MUSEUM

Upstairs from Glastonbury's TIC, in the medieval courthouse, the **Lake Village Mu-seum** (EH; admission £2) displays finds from a prehistoric bog village discovered nearby.

Tours

Many companies offer tours of the main Glastonbury sights guided by modern-day druids. They cost about £50 per carload and last three hours. The TIC has listings; try **Merlin Tours** (☎ 01963-240613) or **Goddess Tours** (☎ 275084).

Glastonbury Festival

This massive music festival is a renowned, three-day summer extravaganza held each year in late June. **Glastonbury Festival** (www .glastonburyfestivals.co.uk) is *the* summer music event in England, revered by musicians and punters alike for its unique atmosphere and wild carnival fringe. The 2004 line-up included Garbage, Air and Coldplay and a myriad of smaller bands gigging their hearts out on numerous stages scattered in the fields. Around the main stages a huge alternative carnival involving world music, theatre, circus acts and natural healing takes place. The whole event is based at Worthy Farm in Pilton, 8 miles east of Glastonbury. Admission is by advance ticket only (about £112 for the whole festival).

Sleeping

Many Glastonbury B&Bs offer aromatherapy, muesli breakfasts, vegetarian meals and so on. The TIC has a complete list.

Glastonbury Backpackers (☎ 833353; www.glastonburybackpackers.com; 4 Market Pl; dm/d £10/35; P) A bright, lively hostel with excellent-value private rooms, this popular place also has a good bar with live bands, a courtyard area and a funky café which serves noodles, salads and burritos (£5 to £6.50).

No 1 (☎ 835845; www.no1parkterrace.co.uk; Park Tce; s/d £25/40; P ⬜) This spacious Victorian house has good-value rooms decorated in period style with heritage colours, antique furniture and pretty but subtle florals. It's central and very friendly.

Shambhala Healing Retreat (☎ 831797; www.shambhala.co.uk; Coursing Batch, s/d £36/72) For rest, healing or spiritual regeneration head for this meditation sanctuary on the slopes of the tor providing detox programmes, healing massage and DNA activation (£44 to £80). Accommodation (two nights minimum) is in a choice of beautiful rooms with Egyptian, Chinese-and Tibetan themes, surrounded by water gardens and meditation spaces.

No 3 (☎ 832129; www.numberthree.co.uk; 3 Magdalene St; s/d £75/100; P ✗) A grand Georgian house with a quaint garden annex, this luxury B&B has really spacious bright rooms with classical but stylish décor and lovely views over the stunning garden and abbey.

Other possibilities:

Isle of Avalon (☎ 833618; Godney Rd; tent/person £8/3) A pleasant camp site with good facilities half a mile northwest of town, off the B3151 (Meare Rd).

Street YHA Hostel (☎ 0870 770 6056; www.yha.org.uk; The Chalet, Ivython Hill; dm £10.60; P ✗) A simple chalet hostel about 4 miles south of town. Take hourly bus No 376 (15 minutes).

Eating

Glastonbury is perfect for vegetarians, one of the few places in England where nut roasts are more common than pot roasts.

Café Galatea (☎ 834284; 5a High St; mains £7.50; ☺ 11am-4pm Mon, 11am-9pm Wed-Sun; ✗) This lovely gallery café has a globally inspired and predominantly vegetarian menu with everything from enchiladas to cannelloni and stir-fries. You can check your email here (£5 per hour), wander the sculpture gallery or catch some live music on the weekend.

Mocha Berry (☎ 832149; 14 Market Pl; mains £5-8; ☺ Sun-Wed) This small and welcoming bistro is a great place to fuel up on comfort food and frothy milkshakes. It does a wonderful choice of fish specials and excellent home-made cakes and pies.

Rainbow's End (☎ 833896; 17a High St; mains £4-6; ☺ 10am-4pm) Hearty vegan and vegetarian food is on offer at Glastonbury's legendary café. Great hot bakes, casseroles and salads supplement the huge chunks of chocolate cake and excellent coffee.

Olly's Café (☎ 834521; 52 High St; mains £5-8; ☺ Mon-Sat) This lively new café has a good choice of Mediterranean meat dishes as well as local vegetarian favourites. It has a lovely enclosed courtyard and hosts live music in the evenings.

Getting There & Away

There's one early morning National Express service to Bath and on to London (£17.50, 4¼ hours) but more services connect through Wells (bus Nos 376/377, hourly, 15 minutes) and Bristol (bus Nos 376/377, hourly, 1½ hours). Bus Nos 29 and 929 go to Taunton (one hour) every two hours. There is no train station.

SOMETHING SPECIAL

Babington House (☎ 01373-812266; www.babingtonhouse.co.uk; Babington; d £215-395; P ✗ ⬜ ⬜)
The doyenne of stylish countryside retreats, Babington has been the country hangout of London media darlings since its opening. The ornamental lake and fake cows hint at the eclectic style of the place with designer '60s and '70s furniture mixed with junk-shop bargains, solid-oak floors, bare stone walls and extravagant Italian touches.

The distinctly contemporary rooms are individually designed, with large bathrooms and loads of gadgets – just in case the stress of being away from the city with nothing to do is too much to bear. The restaurant (dinner £35) serves a choice of simple or swish dishes from oven-baked pizzas to Iranian caviar with vodka. For more indulgence you can try the funky Cowshed beauty parlour with tipis and Mongolian yurts for treatments, an indoor/outdoor infinity pool, and a host of sports facilities.

QUANTOCK HILLS

A ridge of red sandstone hills, the Quantocks (from a Celtic word meaning rim) run for 12 miles down to the sea at Quantoxhead in western Somerset. They're about 3 miles wide, and at their highest only 385m, but they can be wild and bleak at times and make enjoyable walking country.

Some of the most attractive country is owned by the National Trust, including the Beacon and Bicknoller Hills which offer views of the Bristol Channel and Exmoor to the northwest. In 1861 red deer were introduced to these hills from Exmoor and there's a local tradition of stag hunting.

The Quantock Hills have been designated an Area of Outstanding Natural Beauty (AONB) – not quite a national park, but protected and managed by legislation and rangers. The **AONB Service** (☎ 01278-732845; www.quantockhills.com; Castle St, Nether Stowey), in the library at Nether Stowey, organises guided walks.

Nether Stowey & Holford

The attractive village of **Nether Stowey** has plenty of old-world charm and the remains of an 11th-century castle topping a nearby hill. Poet Samuel Taylor Coleridge wrote *The Rime of the Ancient Mariner* while living in **Coleridge Cottage** (NT; ☎ 01278-732662; admission £3.20; ⏱ 2-5pm Thu-Sun Apr-Sep) in the village from 1797 to 1800.

Coleridge's friend William Wordsworth, and Wordsworth's sister Dorothy, also spent 1797 at nearby Alfoxden House in **Holford**, a pretty village near a wooded valley. *Lyrical Ballads* (1798) was the joint product of Coleridge's and Wordsworth's sojourns.

If you'd like to stay, the **Manse** (☎ 01278-732917; Lime St, Nether Stowey; d £40; ⏱ Easter-Sep; ℗) is a well-furnished B&B in an early-19th-century house opposite Coleridge Cottage. Alternatively, the **Old Cider House** (☎ 01278-732228; www.oldciderhouse.co.uk; 25 Castle St, Nether Stowey; s/d £35/50; ℗ ✕) is an elegant Edwardian house with simple bright rooms with country-house styling, rustic pine furniture and pastel floral patterns. It also serves classic home cooking (three-course dinner £16.50) with vegetables from their organic garden.

Set in a wooded area 1½ miles west of Holford is the **Quantock Hills YHA Hostel** (☎ 0870 770 6006; www.yha.org.uk; Sevenacres; dm £10.60; ℗ ✕). It's often booked out so call ahead. Bus Nos 15 and 615 from Bridgwater gets you to Holford or Kilve (50 minutes, six daily), and No 23 from Taunton (one hour, five daily) will drop you at Kilve; in either case it's then a 1½-mile walk.

Also in Holford you'll find luxurious **Combe House** (☎ 01278-741382; www.combehouse .co.uk; s/d £65/90; ℗ ✕ ☏) set in tranquil gardens. You can choose from bright contemporary rooms or more traditional ones with patterned wallpaper and floral bedspreads. The beamed restaurant serves traditional British food (three-course dinner £25) and there's an indoor pool and sauna.

Crowcombe

One of the prettiest Quantock villages, Crowcombe still has cottages made of stone and cob (a mixture of mud and straw), many with thatched roofs. The ancient **Church of the Holy Ghost** has wonderful carved 16th-century bench ends with surprisingly pagan themes (the Green Man is common). Part of its spire still stands in the churchyard where it fell when lightning struck in 1725.

There aren't many accommodation or eating options in Crowcombe – Nether Stowey has more facilities.

Quantock Orchard Caravan Park (☎ 01984-618618; www.quantock-orchard.co.uk; Flaxpool; tent or caravan £7.95-10.95) is an excellent camp site with superb facilities, including a heated swimming pool. It's off the A358, just southeast of Crowcombe. It offers a couple of simple, bright rooms at £18 per person.

A large country house, the **Crowcombe YHA Hostel** (☎ 0870 770 5782; www.yha.org.uk; Heathfield; dm £10.60; ⏱ Mon-Sat Easter-Jun, Jul & Aug; ℗ ✕) is 2 miles southeast of the village and half a mile from Crowcombe station. It's a 7-mile hike over the Quantocks from the hostel in Holford.

In nearby Triscombe you'll find the **Blue Ball Inn** (☎ 01984-618242; mains £8-14), an unspoilt 18th-century thatched pub offering imaginative pub food and a friendly atmosphere. It's a popular choice for hikers as well as locals and has a daily-changing blackboard menu featuring delicacies such as lamb loin stuffed with apricots and pistachio nuts or pheasant with Calvados and caramelised apples.

Getting There & Away

The Quantocks' lanes and villages are best enjoyed by avoiding crowded day-tripper weekends. Hourly trains from Bristol call at Taunton (£7.90, 45 minutes); from there, you really need your own wheels as buses are limited. Half-hourly bus No 28 runs from Taunton to Minehead but only stops at Crowcombe (30 minutes) once daily. Bus No 302 runs between Crowcombe and Taunton once on Tuesday and four times on Saturday. Bus No 23 runs between Taunton and Nether Stowey (30 minutes, three times daily Monday to Friday).

TAUNTON

☎ 01823 / pop 58,241

There's little in Somerset's administrative capital to detain you but it's a good transport hub and gateway to the Quantocks. The most famous landmark is the **Church of St Mary Magdalene** (🕑 10am-4pm Mon-Fri, 10am-1pm Sat), with its 50m-high tower carved from red Quantock rock.

Battered **Taunton Castle**, sections of which date from the 12th century, hosts the **Somerset County & Military Museum** (☎ 320201; www .somerset.gov.uk/museums; Castle Green; admission free; 🕑 10am-5pm Tue-Sat Apr-Oct, 10am-3pm Tue-Sat Nov-Mar), displaying prehistoric and Roman artefacts, fossils and collections of silver, ceramics and toys. The museum is housed in the Great Hall where Judge Jeffreys held one of his bloodiest assizes in 1685 (see the boxed text p253).

The **TIC** (☎ 336344; tautic@somerset.gov.uk; Paul St; 🕑 9.30am-5.30pm Mon-Fri, 9.30am-5pm Sat) is in the library.

B&Bs are concentrated along Wellington Rd and Staplegrove. Try **Brookfield** (☎ 272786; www.brookfieldguesthouse.uk.com; 16 Wellington Rd; s/d from £30/50; P 🗶), a pleasant Georgian house near the centre with simple but stylish traditional rooms, dark-wood furniture and subtle florals.

There are plenty of cafés around High and East Sts. Sleek, chic **Brazz** (☎ 252000; Castle Bow; mains £9-12) is a brasserie with a good, high-speed lunch deal (£5.95), a grazing menu if you fancy lingering over a drink and some munchies, or a full menu with Mediterranean meat, pasta and fish dishes.

National Express coaches run to London (£14.50, four hours, six daily), Bristol (£5.75, 1½ hours, four daily) and Exeter (£5.25, 45 minutes, six daily). Hourly bus Nos 28 (Monday to Saturday) and 928 (Sunday, every two hours) cross the Quantocks to Minehead (1¼ hours). Bus Nos 29 (Monday to Saturday) and 929 (Sunday) run to Glastonbury (50 minutes) and Wells (one hour) every two hours.

Trains run to London (£35, two hours, every two hours), to Exeter (£7.60, 30 minutes, half-hourly) and to Plymouth (£20, 1½ hours, half-hourly).

AROUND TAUNTON
Montacute

The ancient village of Montacute, named after the pointed hill originally called Mons Acutus, is home to one of England's finest Elizabethan mansions, **Montacute House** (NT; ☎ 01935-823289; montacute@ntrust.org.uk; admission house £6.90, garden only £3.70; 🕑 house 11am-5pm Wed-Mon Apr-Oct, garden 11am-4pm Wed-Sun Nov-Mar). The house boasts remarkable interior plasterwork, fine chimneypieces, magnificent tapestries and carved parapets. Montacute House was built in the 1590s for Sir Edward Phelips, a Speaker of the House of Commons, and its state rooms display Tudor and Jacobean portraits on loan from London's National Portrait Gallery (p97). Formal gardens and a landscaped park surround the house.

Bus No 681 from Yeovil (20 minutes, hourly Monday to Saturday) to South Petherton passes close by.

Haynes Motor Museum

This 300-strong car collection at **Haynes Motor Museum** (☎ 01963-440804; www.haynesmotor museum.com; Sparkford; admission £6.50; 🕑 10am-4.30pm Nov-Feb, 9.30am-5.30pm Mar-Oct, 9.30am-6.30pm summer school holidays; wheelchair access) includes a fabulous array of the outstanding, the old and the merely odd – Aston Martins and Ferraris rub shoulders with Austins and, well, the Sinclair C5. And yes, it's *that* Haynes, of the ubiquitous repair manuals that you'll find in charity shops throughout the country. The museum is on the A359 off the A303 near Yeovil.

YEOVIL TO TAUNTON

The countryside between Yeovil and Taunton hides a clutch of gorgeous little villages of old stone houses and winding lanes where traditional Somerset crafts such as cider-making and willow-weaving are still strong to this day. **Barrington** is one of the prettiest with an unusual parish church, which has an octagonal central crossing tower dating from the 13th century. Surrounding the church and green are a string of lovely thatched hamstone cottages lining the village street to the Tudor manor house **Barrington Court** (NT; ☎ 01460-241938; Barrington; admission £5.50; ☯ 11am-5.30pm Thu-Tue Apr-Sep, 11am-4.30pm Thu-Sun Oct-Mar; wheelchair access), the first property to be acquired by the National Trust. The house is now used as a reproduction-furniture showroom, but the working kitchen garden and landscaped parkland are well worth a visit.

Further west is the village of **Hatch Beauchamp**, surrounded by green fields and traditional cider orchards. The St John the Baptist Church, the burial place of Colonel Chard, the hero of the Zulu wars at Rorke's drift, is central to the town and next to the magnificent Palladian mansion and deer park at Hatch Court. The house if one of the finest in Britain but is no longer open to the public.

Just north of here is **Curry Mallet**, a small, quiet village almost entirely owned by the Duchy of Cornwall. Traditions are strong in this place and every January the 15th-century church holds a plough-blessing ceremony when local farmers and tradespeople bring their tools to the church for a blessing. Nearby, in **North Curry**, traditional buildings spread out from Queen Sq. The fine church of St Peter and Paul dominates the village and the surrounding Levels and is known as 'The Cathedral of the Moors'.

West Somerset Railway

For those who enjoy extended train trips through pretty countryside, trains on the **West Somerset Railway** (24-hr talking timetable ☎ 01643-707650, other information ☎ 01643-704996; www.west-somerset-railway.co.uk), Britain's longest privately run railway, steam between Bishops Lydeard and Minehead, 20 miles away (£11 return, 1¼ hours). Trains run daily from mid-March to October, otherwise occasional days only.

Bus Nos 28 and 28A run from Taunton (15 minutes, half-hourly Monday to Saturday); No 928 runs every 1½ hours on Sunday.

EXMOOR NATIONAL PARK

Wooded valleys, bleak windswept moorland, idyllic villages and rocky coastal cliffs tumbling into the sea make up this small national park (265 sq miles; 687 sq km) that stretches from western Somerset into North Devon. It's a breathtakingly beautiful place with excellent walking.

Rising to 366m, the dramatic sea cliffs give way to an undulating inland plateau home to England's largest herd of wild red deer along with an ancient stock of Exmoor ponies and horned sheep. The hills are cut by fast-flowing streams, hidden valleys and wooded dells, a magical landscape which inspired Blackmore's swashbuckling romance, *Lorna Doone.*

More than 600 miles (966km) of public paths and bridleways criss-cross the park and there are some wonderful villages in the area to use as a base. Picture-postcard Dunster with its partly medieval castle and gorgeous streetscape is one, while coastal Lynton and Lynmouth, joined by a water-operated railway, are endowed with a more genteel charm.

Orientation

The park is only about 21 miles wide from west to east and just 12 miles from north to south. Waymarked paths criss-cross the park and a dramatic section of the South West Coast Path runs from Minehead, just outside the northeastern boundary of the park, to Padstow in Cornwall.

Information

For the best maps, books and advice, contact one of the following five National Park Authority (NPA) visitor centres (all open 10am to 5pm Easter to October, with limited hours November to Easter):

Combe Martin (☎ 01271-883319; Cross St)
County Gate (☎ 01598-741321; A39 Countisbury)
Dulverton (☎ 01398-323841; dulvertonvc@exmoor-nationalpark.gov.uk; 7-9 Fore St)
Dunster (☎ 01643-821835; Dunster Steep)
Exmoor NPA Administrative Offices (☎ 01398-323665; info@exmoor-nationalpark.gov.uk; Exmoor House, Dulverton)
Lynmouth (☎ 01598-752509; The Esplanade)

WESSEX

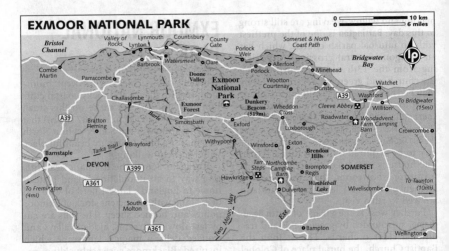

EXMOOR NATIONAL PARK

The *Exmoor Visitor* is a free annual newspaper listing useful addresses, accommodation and a programme of guided walks and bike rides. Most of the villages on Exmoor are tiny so ATMs are few and far between – get cash in Dulverton, Lynton or Minehead, or bring plenty.

There are three comprehensive websites covering Exmoor:

Exmoor National Park (www.exmoor-nationalpark.gov.uk) The official NPA site.

Exmoor Tourist Association (www.exmoor.com) The Exmoor Tourist Association site listing details on accommodation and activities.

What's On Exmoor (www.whatsonexmoor.com) Local listings and information.

Activities
ADVENTURE SPORTS

You can sail, surf and kayak at **Wimbleball Lake Watersports Centre** (☎ 01398-371460; 2hr session £26) while **Exmoor Adventure** (☎ 01271-830628; www.exmooradventure.co.uk; half/full day £74/152) can arrange rock climbing and abseiling.

CYCLING

Official areas for cyclists include a coastal route, along the old Barnstaple railway line, parts of the Tarka Trail, the Brendon Hills and Crown Estate woodland. The West Country Way runs through Exmoor from Padstow to Bristol.

NPA visitor centres sell leaflets (75p each) describing routes through areas where cycling is permitted.

MOORLAND SAFARIS

Several companies offer 4WD safari trips, some tracking wild red deer, costing around £18 for three hours.

Barle Valley Safaris (☎ 01643-851386; www.exmoor-barlevalley-safaris.co.uk; Dulverton & Minehead)

Discovery Safaris (☎ 01643-863080; www.discoverysafaris.com; Porlock)

Exmoor Safari (☎ 01643-831229; www.exmoor-hospitality-inns.co.uk; Exford)

PONY TREKKING & HORSE RIDING

Exmoor is popular riding country and stables scattered around the park offer trips of a few hours to a full day; *Exmoor Visitor* has contact information for many. Charges start at about £12 per hour. Wet weather gear is recommended – it can turn cold and wet very quickly.

Some recommended operators:

Burrowhayes Farm (☎ 01643-862 463; www.burrowhayes.co.uk; Porlock)

Outovercott Stables (☎ 01598-753341; www.outovercott.co.uk; Lynton)

West Anstey Farm (☎ 01398-341354; Dulverton)

WALKING

There are numerous waymarked paths in Exmoor. The park is prone to sudden blankets of sea mist shrouding the heather-clad hills though, so be prepared for sudden changes in conditions.

The best-known routes are the **Somerset and North Devon Coast Path** (part of the South West Coast Path) and the Exmoor section of the **Two Moors Way**, which starts in Lyn-mouth and follows the River Barle through Withypool and on to Dartmoor.

Part of the 180-mile (290km) **Tarka Trail** (based on the countryside that inspired Henry Williamson's *Tarka the Otter*) is in the park. Join it in Combe Martin and walk to Lynton/Lynmouth, then inland to Bray-ford and Barnstaple.

Exmoor's main walking centres are Lyn-ton, Porlock, County Gate, Oare, Horner, Exford, Simonsbath, Withypool and Dul-verton. Walks led by the NPA or other or-ganisations go most days in the summer; they cost £3/5 under/over four hours. Details are in *Exmoor Visitor*, or the *Guided Walks & Events* leaflet from NPA visitor centres, which also stock a variety of leaflets (75p each) describing walks in specific areas.

Sleeping & Eating

There are YHA hostels in Minehead and Il-fracombe (outside the park), and Lynton and Exford in the park. Camping is allowed with the landowner's permission and there are regular camping grounds along the coast.

There are also **camping barns** (☎ 01200-420102 for bookings; per person about £4.50) at Woodadvent Farm near Roadwater and Northcombe, a mile from Dulverton. Bring your own sleeping bag.

There's no shortage of B&Bs and hotels in the park and plenty of places to eat. If you'd like to hire a cottage **Exmoor Holiday Group** (www.exmoor-holidays.co.uk) is a good bet.

Getting There & Around

Bus services are limited, and virtually non-existent in the west of the park. On the other hand, the narrow streets of Exmoor villages quickly clog up in peak season and the tiny narrow roads can be an adventure in themselves.

BICYCLE

Several places around the park hire moun-tain bikes.

Fremington Quay (☎ 01271-372586; www.biketrail .co.uk; Fremington; per day £6.50-14.50)

Tarka Trail (☎ 01271-324202; Train Station, Barnstaple; per day £6-9.50)

BUS

National Express runs from London to Barnstaple (£25, 5½ hours, three daily) and

Ilfracombe (£25, 6½ hours, once daily), and from Bristol to Barnstaple (£16.50, three hours, one daily).

The *Exmoor & West Somerset Public Transport Guide*, free from TICs, is invalu-able. From Ilfracombe, bus No 300 runs to Lynton (one hour) and Porlock (1¾ hours) three times daily from Easter to October (weekends only November to Easter).

From Minehead bus No 38 runs to Porlock (20 minutes, nine daily Monday to Saturday) and Porlock Weir (25 min-utes, seven daily Monday to Saturday) via Selworthy. Nos 28 and 39 run to Dunster (15 minutes, every 30 minutes Monday to Saturday), while No 928 runs on Sunday (every two hours).

From Tiverton, No 398 runs to Dulverton (30 minutes) and Dunster (1½ hours) six times daily Monday to Saturday, occasion-ally diverting to Exford.

From Barnstaple, No 307 goes to Dul-verton (1¼ hours, every two hours Monday to Saturday) and on to Taunton (1¼ hours from Dulverton), while Nos 309 and 310 run to Lynton (one hour, hourly).

TRAIN

Trains from London stop at Taunton (£35, two hours, every two hours), Tiverton Parkway (£36, 2½ hours, hourly) and Ex-eter (£37, 2½ hours, at least hourly). From Exeter, the scenic Tarka Line runs to Barn-staple (£10.10, one hour, every two hours Monday to Saturday, four on Sunday).

DULVERTON
☎ 01398

The sleepy village of Dulverton is the local 'capital' and a good spot to start your tour of Exmoor. The main NPA visitor centre is here, there are loads of boutiquey shops lining the streets and plenty of upmarket country folk in wellies and Barbour jackets chatting in the streets.

The **NPA Visitor Centre** (☎ 01398-323841; dulver tonvc@exmoor-nationalpark.gov.uk; 7-9 Fore St; ☉ 10am-5pm Easter-Oct) is in the same building as the library.

For more information visit the commu-nity website www.dulverton.com.

Walking

There's a stunning 12-mile circular walk along the river from Dulverton to Tarr

Steps – an ancient stone clapper bridge haphazardly placed across the River Barle and shaded by gnarled old trees. The bridge was supposedly built by the devil for sunbathing. It's a four- to five-hour trek for the average walker. You can add another three or four hours to the walk by continuing from Tarr Steps up Winsford Hill for distant views over Devon.

By Tarr Steps, **Tarr Farm** (☎ 01643-851507; www.tarrfarm.co.uk; s/d £70/110; P ✂) has a few gorgeous rooms decorated in contemporary style. The bar serves a good range of pub grub (mains £6 to £10) such as wild boar sausages with bubble and squeak and in the evening the restaurant has an imaginative fine-dining menu (mains £13 to £18).

Sleeping & Eating

Town Mills (☎ 323124; www.townmillsdulverton.co .uk; High St; s/d £35/56; ✂) This Georgian mill house has charming rooms with crackling open fires, rustic antique furniture and plenty of brightly coloured florals. It's the only really central B&B and offers breakfast in bed as the norm.

Winsbere House (☎ 323278; www.winsbere.co.uk; 64 Battleton; s/d £20/40; P ✂) Just a mile outside town, this bright, traditionally decorated farmhouse set in large gardens has pretty rooms with a floral frieze and bedspreads, and country furniture.

Archiamma (☎ 323397; 26 High St; mains lunch £6.50-10.50, dinner £9.50-17; ⏱ lunch Wed-Sat, dinner Tue-Sat) This smart, modern bistro has an

---

SOMETHING SPECIAL

Royal Oak Inn (☎ 01643 851455; www.royal oak-somerset.co.uk; Winsford; s/d £80/125; P)
Idyllically situated by a babbling brook and opposite the village green, this former farmhouse sits beneath its crown of thatch just begging to be photographed. The cosy rooms are in keeping with the period of the house with exposed beams, antique furniture, warm colours and old-fashioned floral patterns. You can eat at the relaxed traditional bar (mains £4 to £6) or go for the more formal traditional dining in the restaurant (mains £9 to £14) with its Wedgwood table settings and cut glass.

Winsford is 5 miles north of Dulverton just off the A396.

---

attractive vine-decked garden for summer days and a cosy but stylish interior. The British/Mediterranean menu is strong on local produce including Exmoor beef and fish.

Woods (☎ 324007; 4 Bank Sq; mains £9-14; ⏱ lunch & dinner) Dulverton's newest asset is this rustic restaurant and bar with big old benches and a good choice of cask ale. Choose from the imaginative tapas menu in the bar or the more formal, modern international cuisine in the dining area.

Other options:
Northcombe Camping Barn (☎ 01200-420102; per person £5.50) A converted watermill about 1 mile from town.
Highercombe Farm (☎ 323616; www.highercombe .demon.co.uk; s/d £30/48; P ✂) An excellent farmhouse B&B with cottage rooms 3 miles north of Dulverton.

EXFORD
☎ 01643
Straddling the River Exe, the photogenic hamlet of Exford is one of the area's most picturesque villages. It has a good choice of accommodation and makes a popular base for hiking, especially to Dunkery Beacon (519m), the highest point on Exmoor, 4 miles northeast.

Sleeping & Eating
Exford YHA Hostel (☎ 0870 770 5828; www.yha.org .uk; Exe Mead; dm £11.80; ⏱ Jul & Aug, Mon-Sat Feb-Jun, Sep & Oct; P ✂) This lovely Victorian house is set right on the banks of the River Exe in the centre of the village and is just steps from the pub. Dorms are fairly basic but atmospheric.

Exford Bridge (☎ 831304; www.exfordbridge.co.uk; Chapel St; s/d £40/60; ✂) If you fancy a break from the chintz and the florals this lovely B&B offers bright, stylishly contemporary rooms with deep-coloured walls, white bedspreads, power showers and DVD players. The restaurant (mains £9.50 to £13) offers a good selection of traditional British and modern international cuisine.

Crown Hotel (☎ 831554; www.crownhotelexmoor .co.uk; s/d £55/95; Chapel St; P ✂) This wonderful old coaching inn has been completely overhauled and has a selection of luxurious rooms with tasteful traditional décor complete with swags and florals. There's a great bar serving pub grub and a good selection of fine-dining choices in the restaurant (mains £10 to £15).

Royal Oak (☎ 01643-831506; www.royaloak withypool.co.uk; Withypool; s/d £60/90; P) One of the best places to stay in Exmoor, the Royal Oak has luxurious rooms with exposed beams, antique furniture, deep warm colours or subtle neutrals – and no swirly carpets or queasy florals. There are also two lovely old self-catering cottages decorated in a contemporary style (£600 to £700 per week). The two old-world bars have roaring fires, hunting prints and stag heads on the walls, and a selection of wonderful food (mains £8 to £13) with a strong emphasis on local meat and game and a good selection of fish.

Withypool is 7 miles northwest of Dulverton off the B3223.

Getting There & Away

Over the moor, it's a 7-mile walk to Exford from Porlock, 10 miles from Minehead YHA Hostel, 12 miles from Dunster and 15 miles from Lynton.

See p293 for bus details.

SIMONSBATH

A little oasis in the middle of the park, Simonsbath is a tiny settlement with good walks along the Barle towards Withypool, Tarr Steps and Hawkridge.

The nicest place to stay in the area is **Emmett's Grange** (☎ 01643-831138; www.emmetts grange.co.uk; s/d £40/60; P ✗), a charming Georgian house tucked away off the road just west of the village. The rooms are beautifully decorated with heritage papers and prints and antique furniture.

LYNTON & LYNMOUTH

☎ 01598

Tucked away in a steeply wooded gorge where the West Lyn River meets the sea, the picture-postcard smuggler's harbour of Lynmouth is looking a little forlorn these days but still manages to charm its visitors with its stunning location and collection of fudge shops and cheap souvenirs.

A quick ride away on an incredible water-operated cliff railway is the refined Victorian resort of Lynton with its host of guesthouses and eateries. There's good walking along the spectacular coast around the towns and close by in the northern part of the park.

The **TIC** (☎ 0845 660 3232; info@lyntourism.co.uk; Lynton Town Hall, Lee Rd; ☯ 9.30am-5pm Apr-Oct, 10am-4pm Nov-Mar) provides the **Lynton & Lynmouth Scene** (www.lyntonandlynmouthscene.co.uk), which is a free newspaper with accommodation, eating and activities listings.

By Lynmouth harbour there's an **NPA visitor centre** (☎ 752509; The Esplanade; ☯ 10am-5pm Apr-Oct, 10am-9pm Jul & Aug).

Sights

In 1952 storms caused the East and West Lyn rivers to flood, sending a cascading mudslide down the cliffs destroying 98 houses and claiming the lives of 34 people. The disaster is recorded at the **Lyn & Exmoor Museum** (☎ 752317; St Vincent's Cottage, Market St, Lynton; adult/child £1/20p; ☯ 10am-12.30pm & 2-5pm Mon-Fri & 2-5pm Sun late-Mar–late Oct), along with varied collections of tools, paintings and local curios.

The **Cliff Railway** (☎ 753486; www.cliffrailway lynton.co.uk; adult/child one way £1.50/1; ☯ 8.45am-7pm Easter-Nov) is a simple piece of environmentally friendly Victorian engineering. Two cars linked by a steel cable descend or ascend the slope according to the amount of water in their tanks. It's the best way to get between the two villages and the views across to the Exmoor cliffs are incredible.

From the Lynmouth crossroads follow signs 200m to **Glen Lyn Gorge** (☎ 753207; adult/child £3.50/2; ☯ Easter-Oct). There are pleasant riverside walks and a small **exhibition centre** housing a collection of steam engines and exhibits on hydroelectric power.

Walking

Lynton TIC and the NPA visitor centre have information about the many local walks. The South West Coast Path and the Tarka Trail pass through the villages, and the Two Moors Way, linking Exmoor with Dartmoor, starts in Lynmouth.

The **Valley of the Rocks**, which is believed to be where the River Lyn originally flowed, was described by the poet Robert Southey as 'rock reeling upon rock, stone piled upon stone, a huge terrifying reeling mass'. It's just over a mile west of Lynton; the walk along the coastal footpath is rewarded with fantastic views. The lighthouse at **Foreland Point** east of Lynmouth is a good focus for a walk.

There is also popular hike to the confluence of two rivers at **Watersmeet**, 2 miles along the river from Lynmouth.

Sleeping & Eating

There are loads of accommodation options with a whole bank of B&Bs along Lee Rd in Lynton.

Lynton YHA Hostel (☎ 0870 770 5942; www.yha .org.uk; Lynbridge; dm £10.60; ☯ Tue-Sun Mar-Jun, Jul & Aug, Tue-Sat Sep & Oct; P ✗) This large Victorian house set right in the gorge has standard dorms but a welcoming atmosphere. It's a steep 500m walk south of town.

Sinai House (☎ 753227; www.sinaihouse.co.uk; Lynway, Lynton; s/d £25/50; P ✗) You'll get fantastic views of the stunning coastline from the beautiful, period rooms at this Victorian gentlemen's residence. There's also a deepred breakfast room and a lively residents' lounge and bar.

Sea View Villa (☎ 753460; www.seaviewvilla.co.uk; 6 Summer House Path; s £40, d £50-90; ✗) This gorgeous Georgian house is one of the best places to stay in town with its luxuriously elegant rooms, stylish but restrained classical décor and effortless charm. It's a world away from the standard B&Bs and is well worth a visit.

Rising Sun (☎ 753223; www.risingsunlynmouth .co.uk; Harbourside; s/d £49/79) This atmospheric, 14th-century thatched smugglers' inn sits on Lynmouth harbour. It has a good choice of simple, contemporary standard rooms or old-world ones with frills and four-posters. The oak-panelled restaurant (mains cost £18 to £24) serves up ambitious meat and game dishes.

Mad Hatters Bistro (☎ 753614; Church Steps, Lynton; mains £7.50-13; ☯ dinner Mon-Sat) This relaxed, cosy eatery serves up hearty portions of traditional local fare including a good range of tasty fish and vegetarian dishes as well as venison and local free-range duck.

Getting There & Away

Driving between Lynton and Porlock, note that Countisbury Hill and Porlock Hill are notoriously steep; there are two alternative toll roads (£2) avoiding Porlock Hill, both scenic and less drastic.

For bus information, see p293.

PORLOCK & AROUND

☎ 01643

Thatched cottages wind along the narrow twisting main street of this lovely village. The town gets choked with tourists on summer weekends, but is a great place to visit outside

busy times. The charming little harbour of Porlock Weir is 2 miles farther west.

The picturesque NT-owned village of **Selworthy** is 2½ miles east of Porlock. Its cream-painted cob-and-thatch cottages make it a popular movie location; Thomas Hardy's *The Return of the Native* was filmed here.

Porlock's helpful **visitor centre** (☎ 863150; www.porlock.co.uk; West End, High St; ☯ 10am-1pm & 2-5pm Mon-Sat & 10am-1pm Sun Apr-Oct, 10.15am-1pm Mon-Fri & 10am-2pm Sat Nov-Mar) offers a free accommodation booking service and has a small exhibition on Exmoor and Porlock life.

The tiny **Dovery Manor Museum** (High St; admission free; ☯ 10am-1pm & 2-5pm Mon-Fri, 10am-noon & 2.30-4.30pm Sat May-Oct) is housed in a pretty, 15th-century building, and exhibits artefacts and interesting photos of the village.

Sleeping & Eating

Myrtle Cottage (☎ 862978; www.smoothhound .co.uk/hotels/myrtle.html; High St; s/d £30/50; P ✗) This delightful, 16th-century thatched cottage has beautiful, cosy rooms with subtle modern décor and pretty fabrics. It's ideally located in the heart of the village and has a lovely small garden.

Porlock Vale House (☎ 862338; www.porlockvale .co.uk; West Porlock; s/d £65/100; P ✗) An old hunting lodge, this stunning property is an informal place with all the traditional trappings such as chintz sofas, Persian rugs, shelves of books and sporting prints. The beautiful rooms are furnished with period pieces, while the bar has oak panelling and mullioned windows looking out over the glorious garden.

Andrew's on the Weir (☎ 863300; Porlock Weir; d £75; mains £18; ☯ lunch & dinner) This elegant Georgian restaurant with rooms overlooking the weir is renowned for its exquisite traditional fish dishes and a smattering of local beef and lamb. The luxurious but chintzy rooms have antiques galore and fine views of the waterfront.

Other options:

Ship Inn (☎ 862507; www.shipinnporlock.co.uk; High St; s/d £32/54; P) A wonderful 13th-century thatched hostelry with spacious modern rooms and a good selection of pub food (mains £4.50 to £9).

Piggy in the Middle (☎ 862647; 2 High St; mains £10-14; ☯ dinner) A relaxed, rustic restaurant specialising in local seafood and game.

DUNSTER
☎ 01643

The gorgeous and well-trodden village of Dunster is a charming place, its snakelike main street flanked by wonderful old buildings, a 16th-century stone dovecote and an unusual 17th-century octagonal yarn market. There's also a wonderful old packhorse bridge, and the side streets are well worth a ramble for their beautiful cottages and views of the town's crowning glory, the dramatic clifftop castle lording over the scene below.

Central to the village is the beautiful **St George's Church**, which dates mostly from the 15th century and boasts a wonderfully carved fan-vaulted rood screen. Further down the road is the **watermill** (☎ 821759; Mill Lane; admission £2.40; ☽ 11am-5pm Apr-Oct), a working 18th-century mill with a pleasant tea room.

The **NPA visitor centre** (☎ 821835; Dunster Steep; ☽ 10am-5pm Easter-Oct) is in the main car park.

Dunster Castle

Heavily restored to the Victorian ideal of how castles should look – turrets, crenulations and all – **Dunster Castle** (NT; ☎ 821314; admission castle £6.80, garden & park only £3.70; ☽ 11am-5pm Sat-Wed late-Mar–late-Oct) dates back to Norman times, although only the 13th-century gateway of the original structure survives. Inside are Tudor furnishings, stunning 17th-century plasterwork and portraits of the Luttrell family, including a bizarre 16th-century portrait of Sir John skinny-dipping. The surrounding terraced gardens and park are open most of the year.

Sleeping & Eating

Old Priory (☎ 821540; Priory Green; s/d £35/65) A huge stone fireplace and uneven floors give this amazing 12th-century house a wonderful uncontrived charm. It's set in walled gardens opposite the dovecote and has pretty rooms oozing grace and character.

Higher Orchard (☎ 821915; 30 St Georges St; s/d £25/40; ☒) This charming Victorian house is set in lovely gardens on a hill behind the church. The cottage-style rooms are bright and simple, if a little compact, the welcome is warm and it's handy for the village.

Luttrell Arms (☎ 851555; 32-36 High St; www .bhere.co.uk; s £65-105, d £95-140; ☒) The top spot in town is this medieval guesthouse replete with 15th-century ambience. The rooms vary enormously from stunning high-ceilinged affairs to garish rooms with gaudy fabrics, so look before you book. The restaurant serves classic British cuisine (mains £11 to £17) while the bar has more modest fare (£4 to £6).

Hathaways Restaurant (☎ 821725; 5-8 West St; mains £9-11) This quaint 16th-century building with low ceilings and rustic décor houses another good eating option with an emphasis on pasta, poultry and steaks. The dishes are predominantly traditional, but there are a few modern twists thrown in.

Other options:

Minehead YHA Hostel (☎ 0870 770 5968; minehead@yha.org.uk; dm £10.60; ☽ Mon-Sat Easter-Jun, Jul & Aug; ℗ ☒) In Alcombe Combe, within walking distance of Dunster.

Restaurant in the High Street (☎ 821304; 3 High St; lunch £5-8, dinner mains £8-11.50) Simple modern restaurant focusing on local game and seafood.

Getting There & Away

See p293 for bus details and p290 for the West Somerset Railway.

298

Devon & Cornwall

CONTENTS

Flung out on the far-western edge of England, the neighbouring counties of Devon and Cornwall may share a border, but they couldn't be more different in terms of landscape and character. From the green pastures and neat market towns of rural Devon to the stern granite settlements and wild cliff tops of Cornwall, the southwest is one of Britain's most varied and fascinating areas. But it's what the counties have in common that keeps the summertime visitors returning year after year: beautiful rural countryside, unspoiled villages and, of course, some of the most breathtaking coastline anywhere in Britain.

Of the two counties, Devon is more immediately accessible; it's a largely rural region with a long maritime heritage and lots of small villages and pretty coastal towns. But venture inland towards the Dartmoor National Park and you'll find a very different side of Devon, a wild landscape of rocky tors and windswept heath, perfect for backcountry hiking and biking. Cornwall is best known for its dramatic cliffs and beaches, but dig a little deeper and you'll also discover the county's rich legends, ancient history and industrial heritage. One thing's for sure – whether it's coastal walks, Celtic culture or cream teas you're after, this is one region of Britain that can't possibly disappoint.

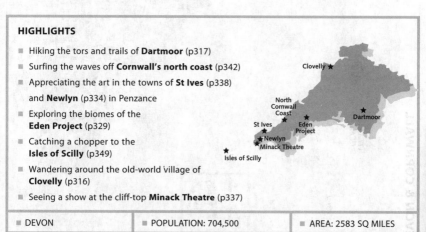

HIGHLIGHTS

- Hiking the tors and trails of **Dartmoor** (p317)
- Surfing the waves off **Cornwall's north coast** (p342)
- Appreciating the art in the towns of **St Ives** (p338) and **Newlyn** (p334) in Penzance
- Exploring the biomes of the **Eden Project** (p329)
- Catching a chopper to the **Isles of Scilly** (p349)
- Wandering around the old-world village of **Clovelly** (p316)
- Seeing a show at the cliff-top **Minack Theatre** (p337)

DEVON	POPULATION: 704,500	AREA: 2583 SQ MILES
CORNWALL	POPULATION: 501,300	AREA: 1364 SQ MILES

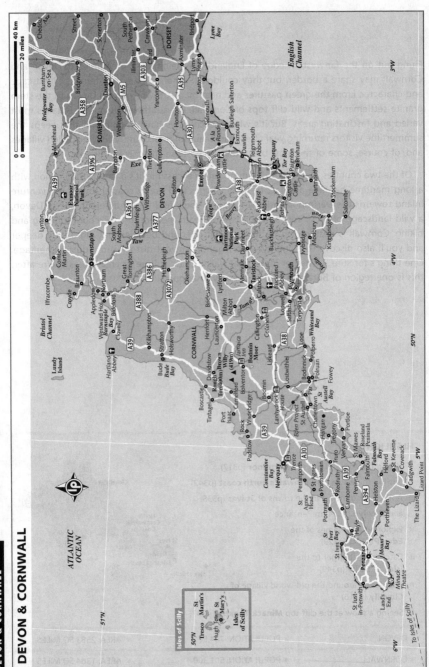

DEVON & CORNWALL

Orientation & Information

Imagine this region as the leg of England. Devon is the thigh, Cornwall the calf and foot; Plymouth sits at the back of the knee, while the Isles of Scilly hover above the toe of Land's End. With the notable exception of Dartmoor, most of the region's attractions line the coast.

The **South West Tourist Board** (www.visitsouth westengland.com) covers a huge area from Gloucester and Dorset down to the Isles of Scilly. Its website has snippets such as weather trends, plus links to localised sites such as www.cornwall-devon.com, with accommodation listed by town. For specific accommodation information go to www.westcountry now.com.

You can pick up the free monthly magazine **twenty4-seven** (www.twenty4-seven.co.uk) from Tourist Information Centres (TICs), bars and restaurants for listings and previews of events, bars, gigs and clubs.

Activities

With such wonderful countryside, it's no surprise that Devon and Cornwall are havens for outdoor activities. Regional tourism websites contain walking and cycling information, and TICs stock leaflets (free) plus maps and guides (usually £1 to £5) covering walking, cycling and other activities.

CYCLING

Devon and Cornwall make for spectacular cycling, but you'll need legs and lungs of steel. Some areas such as Dartmoor and Exmoor are surprisingly hilly, and the coastal routes can be very tiring.

Of the long-distance cycle routes in this region, the **West Country Way** is one of the most popular – a 250-mile (402.5km) jaunt from Bristol to Padstow via Glastonbury, Taunton and Barnstaple. The shorter **Devon Coast to Coast Cycle Route** travels for 100 miles (161km) through Exmoor and Dartmoor.

For off-road riding, the best areas are Dartmoor and Exmoor, which have many tracks and bridlepaths, plus some old railways that have been converted for two-wheel use. Other scenic former railways include the **Camel Trail** from Padstow (named after a river – not your form of transport) and the **Tarka Trail** around Barnstaple (named after a fictitious but famous otter). Bikes can be hired in most major

regional centres, including Plymouth, Penzance, Exeter and Padstow.

SURFING

The capital of English surfing is Newquay in west Cornwall, and surfable coast runs from Porthleven (near Helston) in Cornwall, west around Land's End and north to Ilfracombe. Popular spots include Perranporth, St Agnes and Bude in Cornwall, and Croyde in north Devon. Check **Surfcall** (☎ 0906 836 0360) for up-to-date surf conditions in the southwest; calls cost 60p per minute.

WALKING

At 610 miles (982km) the **South West Coast Path** is Britain's longest national trail. Only the hardiest hikers do it all in one go but following a small section is very popular – the 14-day loop from Padstow to Falmouth is the most scenic stretch and gets the most visitors.

Other walking areas include Dartmoor National Park. Larger and wilder than neighbouring Exmoor, Dartmoor has some of the highest hills in southern England and is crossed by several specific routes, including the popular Two Moors Way, which also crosses Exmoor.

OTHER ACTIVITIES

Other activities include horse and pony riding, especially in Exmoor and Dartmoor; rock climbing on the tors (rocky outcrops) of Dartmoor or on the cliffs of Cornwall; windsurfing and kitesurfing on the region's beaches; and scuba diving around Lundy Island, the Isles of Scilly and the many wrecks around Cornwall's coastline.

Getting Around

Look out for the *Car-Free Days Out* leaflet in TICs, which has comprehensive public-transport listings. Alternatively, visit www .carfreedaysout.com.

Public transport (particularly the bus network) is sketchy in rural areas; to get to the more remote areas, you'll need your own transport. Most larger towns have car-hire outlets.

BUS

National Express provides frequent connections to the main towns and cities. Transport around Dartmoor is skimpy in summer, and virtually nonexistent at other times; the same is true for much of west Cornwall. For regional timetables, call ☎ 01392-382800 in Devon or ☎ 01872-322142 in Cornwall, or contact the **National Traveline** (☎ 0870 608 2608).

The **First group** (☎ 0845 600 1420 for general inquiries, ☎ 01752 402060 for fares & timetables; www .firstgroup.com) provides the majority of the region's bus services. The **First Bus & Rail Card** (adult £10) allows unlimited travel for one day on First Great Western trains and most First buses in Cornwall and Devon west of Totnes. The pass can be bought from bus drivers and train conductors, or at Totnes or Plymouth railway stations. The **Firstday Southwest** (adult £7) is valid on most First buses in Devon and Cornwall as well as Dorset and Somerset.

TRAIN

Train services are mostly limited to the south coast. Beyond Exeter, a single line follows the coast as far as Penzance, with spurs to Barnstaple, Paignton, Gunnislake, Looe, Falmouth, St Ives and Newquay. The line from Exeter to Penzance is one of England's most scenic routes.

Several regional rail passes are available from train stations, including the **Freedom of the SouthWest Rover pass** (adult £61), which allows eight days' unlimited travel over 15 days in an area west of (and including) Salisbury, Bath, Bristol and Weymouth.

DEVON

To many people, Devon is the classic English county: a green and pleasant corner of a green and pleasant land, dotted with rolling meadows, secluded coves and sleepy market towns. As a result, Devon remains one of the most popular holiday spots in Britain for foreign and domestic tourists alike, but needless to say, the holiday-brochure image only tells half the story. There are certainly plenty of picturesque places to choose from – but there are also big, busy cities (Exeter and Plymouth) and vibrant small towns (Dartmouth and Totnes) as well as classic seaside resorts such as Torquay, Paignton and Ilfracombe. Perhaps the most impressive natural scenery can be found right in the heart of the county on the wild hills of

Dartmoor – the destination of choice for hikers. History buffs can visit the county's houses, churches and castles, while surfers and beach bums should head for the north-coast around Braunton and Croyde.

Orientation

Devon is bounded to the east by Somerset and Dorset, the border skirting the southern edge of Exmoor and hitting the coast west of Lyme Regis. The border with Cornwall follows the River Tamar from its source near the north Devon coast to the estuary at Plymouth. Dartmoor claims much of the inland area between Plymouth and Exeter in the east.

Getting Around

Contact the **Devon County Public Transport Help Line** (☎ 01392-382800; www.devon.gov.uk/devon bus; ☽ 9am-5pm Mon-Fri) for information and timetables. It also provides the invaluable *Devon Public Transport Map* and the *Discovery Guide to Dartmoor*.

First Western National (☎ 01271-376524; www .firstgroup.com) serves most of north Devon and much of the south and east, including most Dartmoor services.

Stagecoach Devon (☎ 01392-427711; www.stage coachbus.com) operates mostly local services and buses from Plymouth to Exeter or Totnes. Timetables are available to download from the website. The **Explorer Day pass** (adult £6) allows one day of unlimited travel on Stagecoach Devon buses; for longer periods the **Goldrider pass** (one week £16) offers the best value.

Devon's rail network skirts along the south coast through Exeter and Plymouth to Cornwall. There are picturesque stretches where the line hugs the seashore. Two branch lines run north: the 39-mile Tarka Line from Exeter to Barnstaple and the 15-mile Tamar Valley Line from Plymouth to Gunnislake. The **Devon Rover** allows three days' travel in a week (adult £24) or eight days' travel in 15 days (adult £39.50).

EXETER

☎ 01392 / pop 106,780

Thanks to its size, location and large student population, Exeter has more in common with Britain's big cities than the rest of Devon. The city has the buzziest nightlife and culture in the southwest, and it's also home to one of the finest medieval cathedrals in the region. Many of the older buildings were destroyed in the devastating air raids of WWII and, outside the cathedral close, much of the city is modern, although its long-disused quayside is being restored into a shopping and nightlife precinct.

History

Exeter was founded by the Romans around AD 50 as the administrative capital for the Dumnonii of Devon and Cornwall, although an earlier settlement existed on the banks of the River Exe. By the 3rd century the city, which became an important Saxon settlement, was surrounded by a thick wall, parts of which can still be seen. Its fortifications were battered by Danish invaders and then by the Normans: in 1068 William the Conqueror took 18 days to break through the walls. He appointed a Norman *seigneur* (feudal lord) to construct a castle, the ruins of which can still be seen in Rougemont and Northernhay Gardens.

Exeter was a major trading port until a weir was built across the river in 1290, halting river traffic. It wasn't until 1563, when the first ship canal in Britain was dug to bypass the weir, that the city began to re-establish itself, especially through the wool and cloth trades.

Orientation

South of the ruined castle, the city centre radiates out from the leafy square around the cathedral; the redeveloped Quay is 500m south. There are two main train stations, Central and St David's; most long-distance trains use St David's, a mile northwest of the centre.

Information

BOOKSHOPS
Waterstone's (☎ 218392; 48-49 High Street; ⊗ 9am-5.30pm Mon-Fri, 9am-6pm Sat, 10am-4.30pm Sun) Main branch of this large chain bookshop.

EMERGENCY
Police station (☎ 08452 777444; Heavitree Rd; ⊗ 24hr)
Royal Devon & Exeter Hospital (☎ 411611; Barrack Rd)

INTERNET ACCESS
BHTS Training (☎ 678940; 8 Coombe St; per ½hr £1.25; ⊗ 8.30am-6pm Mon-Sat)

Exeter Library (☎ 384201; Castle Street; per hr £3; ⊗ 9.30am-7pm Mon, Tue, Thu & Fri, 10am-5pm Wed, 9.30am-4pm Sat, 11am-2.30pm Sun)

LAUNDRY
Silverspin (12 Blackboy Rd; ⊗ 8am-10pm)
Soaps (Isambard Pde; ⊗ 8.15am-7.45pm Mon-Sat, 9.15am-5.45pm Sun) Beside St David's train station.

MEDIA
The List is a free magazine detailing events, listings and bars and restaurants in the Exeter area.

POST
Main branch (☎ 223344; Bedford Rd; ⊗ 9am-5.30pm Mon-Sat)

TOURIST INFORMATION
Quay House Interpretation & Visitor Centre (☎ 265213; The Quay; ⊗ 10am-5pm Easter-Oct, weekends only Nov-Easter) Offers tourist information and displays on the Quay's history.
TIC (☎ 265700; tic@exeter.gov.uk; Paris St; ⊗ 9am-5pm Mon-Sat)

Sights

EXETER CATHEDRAL
The magnificent **Cathedral Church of St Peter** (☎ 255573; www.exeter-cathedral.org.uk; The Close; suggested donation £3; ⊗ 7.30am-6.30pm Mon-Fri, 11.30am-5pm Sat, 8am-7.30pm Sun) has stood largely unchanged for the last 600 years, despite some WWII bomb damage. Built within a fairly short time span, it's one of the most graceful of England's cathedrals, with celebrated features including the 14th-century stained glass of the East Window, the West Window and the Gothic rib-vaulting (the world's longest) above the central nave.

There's been a church on this spot since 932; in 1050 the Saxon church was granted cathedral status, and between 1112 and 1133 a Norman cathedral replaced the original building. In 1270 Bishop Bronescombe instigated the remodelling of the whole building, a process that took about 90 years and resulted in a mix of Early English and Decorated Gothic styles.

You enter through the impressive Great West Front, which boasts the largest collection of 14th-century sculpture in England. The niches around the three doorways

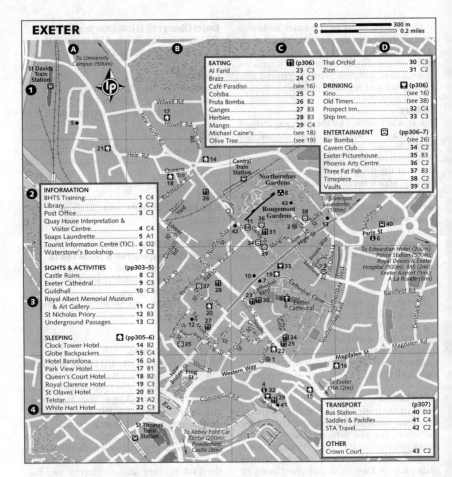

EXETER

EATING	**(p306)**
Al Farid	23 C3
Brazz	24 C3
Café Paradiso	(see 16)
Cohiba	25 C3
Fruta Bomba	26 B2
Ganges	27 B3
Herbies	28 B3
Mango	29 C4
Michael Caine's	(see 18)
Olive Tree	(see 19)

Thai Orchid	30 C3
Zizzi	31 C2
DRINKING	**(p306)**
Kino	(see 16)
Old Timers	(see 38)
Prospect Inn	32 C4
Ship Inn	33 C3
ENTERTAINMENT	**(pp306-7)**
Bar Bomba	(see 26)
Cavern Club	34 C2
Exeter Picturehouse	35 B3
Phoenix Arts Centre	36 C2
Three Fat Fish	37 B3
Timepiece	38 C3
Vaults	39 C3

INFORMATION	
BHTS Training	1 C4
Library	2 C2
Post Office	3 C3
Quay House Interpretation & Visitor Centre	4 C4
Soaps Laundrette	5 A1
Tourist Information Centre (TIC)	6 D2
Waterstone's Bookshop	7 C3

SIGHTS & ACTIVITIES	**(pp303-5)**
Castle Ruins	8 C2
Exeter Cathedral	9 C3
Guildhall	10 C3
Royal Albert Memorial Museum & Art Gallery	11 C2
St Nicholas Priory	12 B3
Underground Passages	13 C2

SLEEPING	**(pp305-6)**
Clock Tower Hotel	14 B2
Globe Backpackers	15 C4
Hotel Barcelona	16 D4
Park View Hotel	17 B1
Queen's Court Hotel	18 B2
Royal Clarence Hotel	19 C3
St Olaves Hotel	20 B3
Telstar	21 A2
White Hart Hotel	22 C3

TRANSPORT	**(p307)**
Bus Station	40 D2
Saddles & Paddles	41 C4
STA Travel	42 C2
OTHER	
Crown Court	43 C2

---

are decorated with weatherworn statues of Christ and the Apostles surrounded by saints, angels, and kings (including King Knut and King Alfred).

Inside, the carved **Pulpitum Screen**, completed in 1325, features some marvellous 17th-century ecclesiastical paintings. Behind is the choir, decorated with fine 13th- and 14th-century misericords, including one of an elephant given to King Henry III by Louis IX of France. Nearby, the huge oak canopy over the **Bishop's Throne** was carved in 1312, and the **minstrels' gallery** (1350) is decorated with 12 angels playing musical instruments. Cathedral staff will point out the famous sculpture of the **lady with two left feet**.

Excellent 45-minute free guided tours run at 11am and 2.30pm Monday to Friday, 11am on Saturday and 4pm on Sunday, April to October. Extra tours are available in summer. It's also worth attending a service: evensong is at 5.30pm Monday to Friday and 3pm on Sunday.

UNDERGROUND PASSAGES

The medieval maintenance passages for the subterranean 14th-century lead water pipes still survive. They're dark, dank and definitely not for claustrophobics, but the **guided tours** (☎ 665887; admission £3.75; ⏰ 2-5pm Tue-Fri & 10am-5pm Sat Oct-Jun, 10am-5.30pm Mon-Sat Jul-Sep) are surprisingly interesting. The entrance is in the alleyway beside Boots on High St.

ROYAL ALBERT MEMORIAL MUSEUM & ART GALLERY

This multipurpose **museum** (☎ 665858; Queen St; admission free; ⌚ 10am-5pm Mon-Sat) ranges from prehistory to the present; highlights include some Roman artefacts and a reconstructed town house from the late 16th century. There are also good ethnography collections with costumes from around the globe. The gallery has a programme of changing exhibitions, emphasising local artists.

GUILDHALL

Parts of the **Guildhall** (☎ 665500; High St; admission free) date from 1160, making it the oldest municipal building in the country still in use. It was mainly built in the 14th century and the impressive portico that extends over the pavement was added at the end of the 16th century. Inside, the city's silver and regalia are on display. Opening hours vary, depending on civic functions, so call ahead for times.

ST NICHOLAS PRIORY

Built as accommodation for overnight visitors, the guest wing of the 900-year-old Benedictine **St Nicholas Priory** (☎ 665858; The Mint; admission 50p; ⌚ 2-4.30pm Apr-Oct) became the house of a wealthy Elizabethan cloth merchant. It looks just as it might have done when inhabited by the merchant and his family, with period furniture, wood-panelled rooms and plaster ceilings.

Tours

Free guided tours led by volunteer Exeter 'Redcoats' last 1½ to two hours and cover a range of subjects, from medieval-themed tours to ghost walks and visits to the catacomb. Tours leave from the Royal Clarence Hotel or Quay House several times a day in summer. Ask at the TIC or contact ☎ 265203 or guidedtours@exeter.gov.uk for details.

Sleeping

BUDGET

Exeter YHA Hostel (☎ 0870 770 5826; exeter@yha.org.uk; 47 Countess Wear Rd; dm £13.40) Occupying a large house overlooking the River Exe, this hostel is 2 miles southeast of the city towards Topsham. Catch bus K or T from High St, or No 57 or 85 from the bus station to Countess Wear post office, from where it's half a mile.

Globe Backpackers (☎ 215521; caroline@globebackpackers.freeserve.co.uk; 71 Holloway St; dm £10, 7th night free; 💻) Near the Quay, this busy, reader-recommended hostel is a short walk from the city centre. Facilities include Internet access, bike hire and a large kitchen and dining area.

Telstar (☎ 272466; www.telstar-hotel.co.uk; 75-77 St David's Hill; s £25-35, d £45-60; ⊠) One of a string of B&Bs along the hill towards St David's station, with a small private garden and comfortable, unremarkable rooms.

MID-RANGE

Clock Tower Hotel (☎ 424545; www.clocktowerhotel.co.uk; 16 New North Rd; s £40, d £45-65; P ⊠) A good, central city hotel, decorated with plain colours and modern furnishings. Parking permits are available for the street outside, or there's an off-site covered car park.

Queen's Court (☎ 272709; www.queenscourt-hotel.co.uk; 6-8 Bystock Tce; s/d £59/64) This refurbished hotel, occupying a grand gabled building near New North Rd, offers 18 deluxe rooms decorated in muted shades of beige and magnolia; downstairs, the **Olive Tree** restaurant serves Mediterranean-influenced cuisine.

White Hart Hotel (☎ 279897; 66 South St; s £49-59, d £69-99; P ⊠) Horse-drawn coaches once clattered through the cobbled courtyard of this 15th-century inn. Though the hotel retains much of its old-fashioned character (wood-panelled walls, faded carpets and rambling public bars), the bedrooms have been thoroughly modernised, with warm colours, contemporary furnishings and en suite bathrooms.

Also recommended:

Park View Hotel (☎ 271772; www.parkviewhotel.freeserve.co.uk; 8 Howell Rd; s £24-40, d £45-60; P ⊠) End of terrace town house 10 minutes from the centre.

The Edwardian (☎ 276102; www.edwardianexeter.co.uk; 30/32 Heavitree Rd; s £40, d £56-64; P ⊠) Fine Edwardian house with period-styled rooms.

TOP END

St Olaves Hotel (☎ 217736; www.olaves.co.uk; Mary Arches St; d £105-155; P ⊠) This lavish period hotel, housed in a listed Georgian mansion, could be a country hotel in the heart of rural Devon. Set around a quiet courtyard and private gardens, all the bedrooms are decorated with country prints and traditional furniture.

SOMETHING SPECIAL

Hotel Barcelona (☎ 281000; www.hotelbar celona-uk.com; Magdalen St; s £85, d £95-115; P ⊠) Quite simply one of the hippest hotels in England. Housed in the old Eye In-firmary, the Barcelona has been converted with wit, style and enormous imagina-tion. Sixties furniture and abstract art sits alongside marble fireplaces, and the hotel is dotted with medical paraphernalia, from the original gurney lift to wheelchairs on the stairway. The bedrooms are just as styl-ish, with colourful bedspreads, anglepoise lamps and retro furniture – you can even sleep in the old operating theatre. And if that's not enough, there's also an Italian-style marquee-cum-bistro, **Café Paradiso**, and a baroque-noir cellar bar, **Kino**. Drop-dead cool.

Royal Clarence Hotel (☎ 319955; www.royalclarence hotel.co.uk; Cathedral Yard; s £105, d £130-155) Exeter's oldest top-end hotel dates back to the 14th century and overlooks the cathedral square; former guests include Lord Nelson and Tsar Nicholas I. The handsome whitewashed façade and chic rooms are set to undergo a complete refurbishment in 2005.

Eating

Mango (☎ 438538; The Quay; lunch £2.50-6; ☽ 10am-6pm Sep-Jun, 10am-10pm Jul & Aug) A funky water-side café serving wraps, salads and paninis on the outside terrace or in the barrel-ceilinged interior.

Herbies (☎ 258473; 15 North St; mains £5-8; ☽ lunch Mon-Sat, dinner Tue-Sat) A homely, popular veg-gie restaurant that draws a devoted local crowd; tuck into nutburgers, homity pie and vegetarian chilli, or plump for the best carrot cake in town.

Thai Orchid (☎ 214215; Cathedral Yard; mains £7-10) A top-notch Thai restaurant with possibly the largest menu you'll ever see (the owners compare it to *War & Peace*). The dining room is decorated with gilt Buddhas and musical instruments, and the cuisine is as authentic as it gets this side of Bangkok.

Brazz (☎ 252525; 10-12 Palace Gate; mains £5.50-15; ☽ lunch & dinner) Look no further for brasserie food in Exeter – Brazz has got the market cornered. Choose your aperitif at the bar, and head into the split-level dining room

for pan-fried sea bream, classic Niçoise salad and Tuscan chicken – and don't forget to check out the fibreoptic ceiling and cylindrical fish tanks.

Michael Caine's (☎ 310031; www.michaelcaines .com; Cathedral Yard; mains from £16.95) This restau-rant at the Royal Clarence Hotel has noth-ing to do with everyone's favourite Cockney actor. In fact, it's the flagship restaurant of Exeter's most renowned chef – serving modern European and British cuisine based around local produce.

Also recommended:

Al Farid (☎ 494444; 3 Cathedral Yard; mains £8-13; ☽ dinner Mon-Sat) Moroccan tapas downstairs and more substantial Middle Eastern fare up top.

Cohiba (☎ 678445; South St; tapas £3-7, mains £8-13; ☽ lunch & dinner) Hispanic dishes and modern tapas in a sleek, neutral space.

Fruta Bomba (☎ 412233; 44-45 Queen St; mains £8-11; ☽ lunch & dinner) Upstairs there's Mexican, Latin American and Cuban cooking; downstairs, **Bar Bomba** offers cocktails, DJs and Latin rhythms.

Ganges (☎ 272630; 156 Fore St; mains £5-12; ☽ din-ner) Great Indian specialising in regional dishes.

Zizzi (☎ 274737; 21/22 Gandy St; mains £6-8; ☽ lunch & dinner) Pizza and pasta served in an open-plan dining room.

Drinking

Ship Inn (☎ 272040; Martin's Lane) In the alley be-tween High St and the cathedral, this old tav-ern is said to have been Sir Francis Drake's favourite local; expect wood beams, crazy ceilings, and nooks and crannies aplenty.

Prospect Inn (☎ 273152; The Quay) A cosy 17th-century pub down on the redeveloped Quay. There's live jazz, and it's a great place to sit outside on a summer evening.

Old Timers (☎ 477704) Next door to Time-piece (see Entertainment, following), this great drinking hole is covered in battered signs, stickers, placards and plaster statues, and makes an atmospheric place for an evening pint and pub grub.

Kino (Magdalen St; members & guests only after 10pm) A fabulous, film-noir style bar in the cellar of the Hotel Barcelona, decked out with Chi-nese screens and moody lighting – there's live funk, blues, jazz or comedy most nights, and a late-night club on weekends.

Entertainment
NIGHTCLUBS

Three Fat Fish (☎ 424628; www.threefatfish.co.uk; 1 Mary Arches St) Exeter's newest bar and live-music venue, with regular nights devoted to DJs, bands, comedy and retro-music extravaganzas.

Cavern Club (☎ 495370; www.cavernclub.co.uk; 83-84 Queen St) Another excellent subterranean venue with live music or DJs each night; luminaries such as Coldplay and Groove Armada have gigged here, and the Cavern has a reputation for breaking new bands.

Timepiece (☎ 493096; www.timepiecenightclub .co.uk; Lt Castle St) Arguably the best club in town – Latin night (Tuesday) and indie night (Friday) are always jam-packed.

Other clubs include **The Vaults** (☎ 203939; 8 Gandy St), a friendly basement bar along Gandy Street, and **Casbar** (☎ 275623; 53 Bartholomew St West), a popular gay club with top nights on Friday and Saturday.

THEATRES & CINEMAS

Phoenix Arts Centre (☎ 667080; www.exeterphoenix .org.uk; Gandy St) An excellent arts complex hosting dance, theatre, films, DJs and live music. The café-bar's pretty hip, too.

Exeter Picturehouse (☎ 435522; Bartholomew St West) Screens a mix of mainstream and arthouse flicks.

Getting There & Away

AIR

Scheduled services connect **Exeter International Airport** (☎ 367433; www.exeter-airport.co.uk) and Dublin, the Channel Islands and the Isles of Scilly; chartered services go as far afield as the Algarve and Canada.

BUS

Bus No X38 runs to Plymouth (1¼ hours, every 90 minutes Monday to Saturday, every two hours Sunday); bus Nos 39 and X39 are slower (1¾ hours, at least every two hours) but stop at Buckfastleigh on the edge of Dartmoor. Bus No X46 runs to Torquay (one hour, hourly Monday to Saturday, every 90 minutes Sunday).

National Express runs regular coaches to Bath (£12.85, three hours, four daily), Birmingham (£30.50, four hours, four daily), Bristol (£10.75, two hours, four daily), London (£20, 4½ hours, eight daily) and Penzance (£20.50, 4½ hours, two daily).

TRAIN

The fastest trains between London and Exeter St David's use Paddington station and

take around 2½ hours (£42, hourly). There are also hourly connections with Bristol (£16.20, one hour) and Penzance (£19.90, three hours).

The 39-mile Tarka Line between Exeter Central and Barnstaple (£10.10, 1¼ hours, every two hours Monday to Friday, four on Sunday) follows the valleys of the Rivers Yeo and Taw and gives good views of the countryside with its characteristic, deepsunken lanes.

Getting Around

TO/FROM THE AIRPORT

The airport is 5 miles east of the centre, off the A30. Bus No 56 runs to the airport from the bus station (20 minutes, hourly Monday to Saturday).

BICYCLES & CANOES

Saddles & Paddles (☎ 424241; www.sadpad.com; 4 Kings Wharf, The Quay) rents out bikes (adult per day £13) and canoes (single kayaks per hour/day £5/15). It also organises 'paddling parties' to a nearby pub, plus canoeing weekends and cycle tours.

BUS

Exeter is well served by public transport. The one-day **Dayrider pass** (£3) gives unlimited transport on Stagecoach's Exeter buses. Bus N links St David's and Central train stations and passes near the bus station.

CAR

The TIC provides a list of car-hire offices; try **Abbey Ford Car Rental** (☎ 254037; www.abbey fordcarhire.co.uk; 30 Edwin Rd) for cheap rates.

Parking in the centre can be troublesome. Useful Park & Ride services run between Sowton and Matford via the centre (bus No PR1, at least every 10 minutes), and from Honiton Rd to the city (bus N, every 30 minutes).

TAXI

There are taxi ranks outside the train stations. Alternatively, try **Capital Taxis** (☎ 433433).

AROUND EXETER
Powderham Castle

Built in 1391 and later modified, **Powderham** (☎ 01626-890243; www.powderham.co.uk; admission £7.20; ☼ 10am-5.30pm Apr-Oct) was the former home of the 18th Earl of Devon. Guided tours explore the state rooms, the wood-panelled great hall, and the castle's collections of French china and Stuart and Regency furniture. Powderham is on the River Exe in Kenton, 8 miles south of Exeter. Bus No 85A runs from Exeter (20 minutes, every 15 minutes Monday to Saturday, every 30 minutes Sunday).

À la Ronde

Having returned from their European Grand Tour, sisters Jane and Mary Parminter planned to combine the magnificence of the Church of San Vitale, which they'd visited in Ravenna, with the homeliness of a country cottage to create the perfect home. The result, completed around 1796, is an intriguing 16-sided **house** (NT; ☎ 01395-265514; Summer Lane, Exmouth; admission £4.20; ☿ Sun-Thu Mar-Oct) with bizarre interior décor that includes a shell-encrusted room, a frieze of feathers, and sand and seaweed collages.

It's 2 miles north of Exmouth on the A376; Stagecoach Devon bus No 57 runs close by en route to Exeter (30 minutes, at least every 30 minutes).

SOUTH DEVON COAST
Torquay & Paignton
☎ 01803 / pop 110,370

The three Torbay towns (Torquay, Paignton and Brixham) collectively make up the area known (rather optimistically) as the English Riviera. Torquay is the classic South Devon seaside resort, a curious mix of old-world Victorian elegance and mass-market tourism. From the grand seafront promenade, the town climbs into a grid of streets lined with traditional tearooms, giftshops and endless hotels (one of which was run by the deranged hotelier, Basil Fawlty, in the classic British TV comedy *Fawlty Towers*). Around the bay to the south, Paignton is effectively the 'family fun' suburb of Torquay, big on coloured lights and candyfloss, less so on sophistication.

The **TIC** (☎ 0906-680126; torbay.tic@torbay.gov .uk; Vaughan Pde; ☿ 10am-6pm Sun & 9.30am-6pm Mon-Sat Jun-Sep, 9.30am-5pm Mon-Sat Oct-May) sells discounted tickets to local attractions.

SIGHTS & ACTIVITIES

Agatha Christie was born in Torquay, and the **Torquay Museum** (☎ 293975; 529 Babbacombe Rd; admission £3; ☿ 10am-5pm Mon-Sat & 1.30-5pm Sun summer, 10am-5pm Mon-Fri & 1.30-4pm Sun winter) and **Torre Abbey** (☎ 293593; Torre Abbey Meadows; admission £3.50; ☿ 9.30am-6pm Apr-Nov), an 18th-century house in the grounds of a ruined abbey, display Agatha memorabilia.

Pretty **Babbacombe Beach** is about 2 miles north of the centre; it's a delightful three-hour walk around the coast from the eastern end of the Esplanade, away from the lights and arcades.

SLEEPING

There are literally hundreds of B&Bs and hotels in Torquay, with a dense cluster around the Avenue Rd and Bridge Rd area. Most offer similar standards of accommodation and décor.

Torquay International Backpackers (☎ 299924; jane@torquaybackpackers.co.uk; 119 Abbey Rd; dm £12) The friendly owner of this hostel sometimes organises beach barbecues, trips onto Dartmoor and, more often, hops to the pub.

Norwood Hotel (☎ 294236; www.norwoodhotel torquay.co.uk; 60 Belgrave Rd; d £44-50; ☒) A classy B&B on Avenue Rd, with some very spacious and surprisingly chic bedrooms; the luxury rooms are worth the higher price.

Cranbourne Hotel (☎ 292766; 58 Belgrave Rd; s £30-60, d £60-70; ☒) Right next door, the Cranbourne is another superior choice; decorated in pale cream and lemon yellow, most of the bedrooms have large windows and tasteful furnishings.

Palace Hotel (☎ 200200; www.palacetorquay.co.uk; Babbacombe Rd; d £71-140; ⓟ ☒ ▢ ♨ ☒) The class act, a huge hotel set in 25 acres of grounds, boasting tennis courts, saunas, snooker rooms and a private golf course.

Also recommended:
Everglades Hotel (☎ 295389; www.evergladeshotel .co.uk; 32 St Marychurch Rd; d £50-56; ⓟ ☒) Detached hotel with an elevated sundeck and modern sea-view rooms.
Jesmond Dene (☎ 293062; 85 Abbey Rd; s £17-20, d £34-40) Old-school basic B&B, but it's friendly, cheap and central.

EATING & DRINKING

Mojo (☎ 294881; The Seafront, Torbay Rd; mains £6.50-10) Looks like a typically brash seaside bar but it's surprisingly mellow, with DJs Friday and Saturday, and decent fish and pasta.

Steps Bistro (☎ 201774; 1a Fleet St; mains £11-14) A tiny gem tucked away up some steps from Fleet St, worth seeking out for exceptional fresh fish and seafood.

The Hole in the Wall (☎ 298020; 6 Park Lane; mains £4-10) Allegedly the oldest pub in Torquay, with good local beer and top-notch pub grub in a largely grockle- (tourist) free zone.

GETTING THERE & AWAY
The No X46 express bus service runs hourly from Exeter to Torquay and Paignton (£4.50, one hour). Bus No 120 runs from Torquay and Paignton to Kingswear for the Dartmouth ferry (£5.30 return, 45 minutes, six daily Monday to Friday).

A branch railway line runs from Exeter via Torquay (45 minutes) to Paignton (50 minutes). The **Paignton & Dartmouth Steam Railway** (☎ 555872; www.paignton-steamrailway.co.uk) runs from Paignton on the scenic 7-mile trip to Kingswear on the River Dart, linked by ferry (six minutes) to Dartmouth; a combined ticket costs £8.50 return per adult. You can add on a river cruise (£13) or a Round Robin boat trip to Totnes and back to Paignton by bus (£13.50).

Brixham
☎ 01803 / pop 17,460
In the mid-19th century Brixham was the country's busiest fishing port and it's still the place to come for a fishing expedition; with its attractive harbour, it's also the most appealing (if quietest) of the Torbay resorts.

The **TIC** (☎ 0906-680126; brixham.tic@torbay.org .uk; Old Market House, The Quay; ☯ 9.30am-6pm Mon-Sat Jun-Sep, 9.30am-5pm Mon-Fri Oct-May) is right on the harbour.

Brixham Heritage Museum (☎ 856267; www .brixhamheritage.org.uk; Bolton Cross; admission £1.50; ☯ 10am-5pm Mon-Fri, 10am-1pm Sat) explores the town's history and its connection to the sea, and contains reconstructions of Victorian rooms and shops.

Anchored in the harbour is a replica of the **Golden Hind** (☎ 856223; admission £2; ☯ 9am-5.30pm Mar-Sep), Drake's surprisingly small globe-circling ship.

It costs around £20 for a half-day trip to fish for conger, ling and coalfish around the wrecks in the bay. Head for the kiosks lining the quay – try **Boy Richard** (☎ 529147) for mackerel or **Our Jenny** (☎ 854444) for wreck fishing.

Bus No 12 runs at least every 20 minutes along the coast from Torquay (30 minutes) to Paignton (15 minutes) and Brixham.

Dartmouth
☎ 01803 / pop 5520
Dartmouth, an appealing town dotted with Georgian houses, medieval buildings and attractive streets winding down to the Dart estuary, has been an important port since Norman times. The Pilgrim Fathers sheltered here in 1620 on their way to Plymouth and D-Day landing craft sailed for France in 1944, and one of the oldest naval colleges in Britain is here. Today, the harbour is mostly filled with yachts and pleasure boats, and the historic town draws sizable crowds.

The **TIC** (☎ 834224; www.discoverdartmouth.com; Mayor's Ave; ☯ 9.30am-5pm Mon-Sat year-round, plus 10am-4pm Sun Apr-Oct) offers free accommodation booking and houses the Newcomen Engine, an early (1712) steam engine.

DARTMOUTH CASTLE
The hands-on exhibits at **Dartmouth Castle** (EH; ☎ 833588; admission £3.50; ☯ 10am-6pm Jul & Aug, 10am-5pm Apr-Jun & Sep, 10am-4pm Oct, 10am-4pm Sat & Sun Nov-Mar) bring its 600-year history to life. With its companion castle at Kingswear, the fortress was designed so that a chain could be drawn across the estuary, blocking sea-vessels from entering the harbour. There's a ferry along the estuary to the castle, three-quarters of a mile outside the town, from South Embankment every 15 minutes from 10am to 4.45pm (adult £1.20 one way).

OTHER SIGHTS
In the centre, the **Butterwalk** is a row of 17th-century timber-framed houses, reconstructed following bomb damage sustained during WWII. Inside, the **Dartmouth Museum** (☎ 832923; Duke St; admission £1.50; ☯ 10am-4.30pm Mon-Sat Apr-Oct, noon-3pm Mon-Sat Nov-Mar) features exhibits on local and maritime history; check out the fine collection of ships in bottles.

SLEEPING
Little Admiral Hotel (☎ 832572; www.little-admiral .co.uk; 29 Victoria Rd; s £60-75, d £105-140; P X) This designer hotel is gaining a reputation as one of the best places to stay in South Devon. The individual rooms range from contemporary (magnolia walls and terracotta-tiled bathrooms) to old-fashioned (four-poster beds, goosedown pillows and Regency-style furniture); there's a funky mauve-walled foyer and guest lounge; and a great restaurant serving tapas and Mediterranean cuisine.

Hill View House (☎ 839372; www.hillviewdart
mouth.co.uk; 76 Victoria Rd; d £55-82; ✗) A stylish,
modern B&B near the town centre, with
rooms decorated with pale furnishings,
pine furniture and anglepoise lamps. Fruit
smoothies and fresh orange juice are included with the organic breakfasts.

Captain's House (☎ 832133; www.thecaptains
house.co.uk; 18 Clarence St; d £53-68; ✗) A listed
whitewashed Georgian town house with
character-filled rooms.

EATING & DRINKING

Café Alf Resco (☎ 835880; Lower St; mains £5; ☾ lunch
& dinner Wed-Sun) This excellent Mediterranean
brasserie would be at home on the streets
of Milan; shuttered windows, distressed
paintwork and a great terrace all add to the
effect. Look out for the flaming torch above
the gateway.

The New Angel (☎ 839425; 2 South Embankment;
mains £10-20) Run by a celebrity TV chef, this
super-modern bistro is a new addition to
Dartmouth's quay, serving bold modern
British cuisine in a muted interior, with an
open-plan kitchen and plate-glass windows
overlooking the harbour.

Strutt's Bistro (☎ 832491; 10 Fairfax Pl; mains £8-
14; ☾ lunch & dinner Wed-Sat, lunch only Sun) Global
seafood served in a bright, pastel-shaded
dining room.

RB's Diner (☎ 832882; 33 Lower St; mains £9-22;
☾ dinner) Another urban-styled diner, serving chargrilled tuna, baked Whitby cod and
steak measured by the inch.

Cherub Inn (☎ 832571; 13 Higher St) Allegedly
the oldest pub in the town.

GETTING THERE & AWAY

The best way to approach Dartmouth is by
boat, either on the ferry from Kingswear
(car/pedestrian £3/1, every six minutes) or
downstream from Totnes (adult £8 return,
1¼ hours). **River Link** (☎ 834488; www.riverlink
.co.uk) is one operator. From Exeter, take a
train to Totnes and a boat or bus No 111
(40 minutes, at least five daily) from there.

For details of the popular Paignton &
Dartmouth Steam Railway, see p308.

Totnes

☎ 01803 / pop 7930
Medieval legend has it that Totnes was
where Trojan prince Brutus founded Britain in 1170 BC. Whatever the truth of the

story, Totnes became rich trading Dartmoor tin in Tudor times, and a walk up
the High St reveals fine Elizabethan houses
and museums; Totnes has a higher percentage of listed buildings than any other town
in Britain. It's now a busy market town
with a thriving arts scene (thanks to the
nearby arts college) and a large new-age
community.

The **TIC** (☎ 863168; www.totnesinformation.co.uk;
Coronation Rd; ☾ 9.30am-5pm Mon-Sat) is in the
town's old mill.

SIGHTS

Totnes Elizabethan Museum (☎ 863821; 70 Fore St;
admission £1.75; ☾ 10.30am-5pm Mon-Fri Apr-Oct) is in
a house dating from 1575 and still retains
many Tudor and Elizabethan features. Its
displays explore the history of Totnes, and
there's a room dedicated to the mathemati-
cian Charles Babbage, father of the modern
computer.

The **Guildhall** (☎ 862147; Ramparts Walk; admission 75p; ☾ 10am-4pm Mon-Fri Apr-Oct) was once
the refectory of a Benedictine priory, and
was later used as the town's council chamber, courtroom and jailhouse.

The **Devonshire Collection of Period Costume**
(High St; admission £2; ☾ 11am-5pm Mon-Fri May-Sep)
features annually changing selections from
the extensive costume collection, one of the
finest in Britain.

Totnes Castle (EH; ☎ 864406; admission £2;
☾ 10am-6pm Jul & Aug, 10am-5pm Apr-Sep, 10am-4pm
Oct) occupies a commanding position on a
grassy hill top above town. Little remains
of the original Norman motte-and-bailey
fortress, but the outer keep is still standing, and the views from the hill top are
fantastic.

SLEEPING

Dartington YHA Hostel (☎ 0870 770 5788; dm
£10.60; ☾ mid-Apr–Aug) Two miles northwest
of Totnes off the A385 near Week. Bus No
X80 from Plymouth to Totnes stops nearby
at Shinners Bridge hourly.

The Old Forge (☎ 862174; www.oldforgetotnes.com;
Seymour Pl; s/d from £46/56; Ⓟ ✗) This 600-year
old forge has been impeccably converted to
provide the best bedrooms in Totnes, complete with fluffy pillows, huge beds and en
suite baths. There's a private garden, large
dining room and you can even see the old
jailhouse.

WORTH THE TRIP

Buckfast Abbey (☎ 01364-645500; www.buckfast.org.uk; admission free) Two miles north of Buckfastleigh, the abbey was founded in 1016 and flourished on wool money in the Middle Ages, but was abandoned after the dissolution of the monasteries in 1539. In 1806 the ruins were levelled and a mock-Gothic mansion erected; the house was purchased in 1882 by exiled French Benedictine monks, who rebuilt the abbey church to its original design between 1906 and 1938.

The abbey is now a popular tourist attraction, and the attached shop sells various gifts and souvenirs, including the famous Buckfast Tonic Wine.

The abbey is just outside Buckfastleigh on the A38 between Exeter and Plymouth. Bus X38 runs regularly through Buckfastleigh on its way from Exeter to Plymouth.

EATING

Willow Vegetarian Restaurant (☎ 862605; 87 High St; mains £4-5.50; ⏰ lunch Mon-Sat, dinner Wed, Fri & Sat) This rustic vegetarian restaurant is a great spot for organic meals, fresh-baked bread, hearty soups and chillis and live music at weekends.

Rumours (☎ 864682; 30 Fore St; mains £8.50-14.50; ⏰ 10am-11pm Mon-Sat, 6-10.30pm Sun) The most popular restaurant in Totnes has stripped wood floors and local art on the walls; the daily changing menu includes pasta, pizza and lots of blackboard specials.

Bistro 57 (☎ 862604; 67 Fore St; mains £6.50-9; ⏰ Mon-Sat) Another good choice for global cuisine, this sunny restaurant has a menu ranging through pinenut fritters, fajitas, Moroccan meatballs and chilli beef nachos.

GETTING THERE & AWAY

Bus No X64 runs to Exeter (£4.70 return, one hour, eight daily Monday to Saturday, two Sunday) and bus No X80 goes to Plymouth (1¼ hours, hourly). National Express coaches also run to Exeter (£6.50 economy return, 1½ hours, twice daily) and Plymouth (£3.25, 40 minutes, daily).

Frequent trains run to Exeter (£12.30 saver return, 45 minutes, several daily) and Plymouth (£10.40, 25 minutes, hourly). The train station is located half a mile from the centre.

A short walk from Totnes main-line train station, steam trains of the private **South Devon Railway** (☎ 0845 345 1420; www.southdevonrailway.org) run to Buckfastleigh (adult return £8, at least four daily Easter to October) on the edge of Dartmoor.

There are cruises on the river with frequent departures to Dartmouth in summer (p309).

PLYMOUTH

☎ 01752 / pop 243,800

There's no ignoring Plymouth's long maritime history, enlivened by characters such as the bowls-playing Sir Francis Drake and the Pilgrim Fathers, although you'd be forgiven for not finding much evidence of old Plymouth; the city was levelled during the air raids of WWII, and just a few vestiges of the old town remain. Consequently, Devon's largest city is mainly composed of modern suburbs and a bland commercial centre, but the well-preserved Barbican area, the largely Tudor quarter by the harbour, is steadily reinventing itself as one of the best eating and drinking spots in the city.

History

Plymouth really expanded in the 15th century with the development of larger vessels; Plymouth Sound provided a perfect anchorage for warships. Local hero Sir Francis Drake, who achieved his knighthood through an epic voyage around the world, set out from Plymouth in 1577 in the *Golden Hind*, returning three years later.

In 1588 Drake played a major part in the defeat of the Spanish Armada, the fleet sent to invade England by Philip II, who wanted to restore Catholicism to the country. Whether Drake really was playing bowls on the Hoe at the time of the Spanish attack is debatable, but the English fleet certainly did set sail from Plymouth. Drake led the chase to Calais; the English then attacked the fleet with fire ships. Many of the Spanish vessels escaped but were wrecked off the Scottish coast. Total losses: England nil, Spain 51.

The royal dockyard was established at Devonport beside the River Tamar in 1690 and is still a large naval base.

PLYMOUTH

0 _____ 300 m
0 _____ 0.2 miles

INFORMATION
Hoegate Laundromat...............1 C3
Plymouth Internet Café...........2 A2
Police Station.........................3 C2
Post Office..............................4 C3
Tourist Information Centre...(see 17)
University Bookseller.................5 C2
West Hoe Laundrette.................6 A4

SIGHTS & ACTIVITIES   (pp312–3)
Citadel Main Gate (Tours)........7 C4
City Museum & Art Gallery......8 C2
Drake Statue............................9 B4
Elizabethan House...................10 C3
Mayflower Steps.....................11 C4
Merchant's House...................12 C3
National Marine Aquarium......13 D3

Plymouth Boat Cruises...........14 C4
Plymouth Dome.....................15 B4
Plymouth Dry Gin Distillery....16 C3
Plymouth Mayflower..............17 C4
Royal Citadel..........................18 C4
Smeaton's Tower....................19 B4

SLEEPING   (pp313–4)
Adelphi Hotel.........................20 A3
Astor Hotel............................21 B4
Berkeleys of St James.............22 A3
Bowling Green Hotel...............23 B4
Cranbourne Hotel...................24 B3
Duke of Cornwall Hotel..........25 A3
Jewell's Hotel.........................26 B3
Plymouth Backpackers
    Hotel.................................27 A3

EATING   (p314)
Bar ZeegCo............................28 A2
Cuisine Spontaneé..................29 C3
Dutton's Café Continental.......30 C4
Harbour Seafood & Pasta........31 C3
Tanners Restaurant.................32 B3
Trading House.........................33 C3

DRINKING   (p314)
Bar Rakuda..........................(see 31)
Minerva Inn...........................34 C3
Ship......................................35 C3

ENTERTAINMENT   (pp314–5)
B-Bar...................................(see 37)
Barbican Jazz Café.................36 C3
Barbican Theatre....................37 C4
Cooperage.............................38 C3
Cuba.....................................39 C2
Drum Theatre.......................(see 42)
Plymouth Arts Centre.............40 C3
Plymouth Pavilions................41 A3
Ride....................................(see 39)
Theatre Royal........................42 B3

TRANSPORT   (p315)
Bus Station...........................43 C3

Orientation
Plymouth has three main sections. The pedestrianised centre is south of the train station, and contains the city's main shopping streets. Further south is the headland Hoe area, packed with guesthouses and B&Bs, and east of the Hoe is the regenerated Barbican, with some fine harbourfront cafés, bars and restaurants.

Information
Hoegate Laundromat (☎ 223031; 55 Notte St; ☺ 8am-6pm Mon-Fri, 9-5pm Sat)
Plymouth Internet Café (☎ 221777; 32 Frankfort Gate; per hr £5; ☺ 9am-5pm Mon-Sat)
Police station (Charles Cross; ☺ 24hr)
TIC (☎ 304849; www.visitplymouth.co.uk; 3-5 The Barbican; ☺ 9am-5pm Mon-Sat, 10am-4pm Sun May-Sep,

10am-4pm Mon-Sat Oct-Apr) Housed inside the Plymouth Mayflower building.
University Bookseller (☎ 660428; 42 Drake Circus; ☺ 9am-5.30pm Mon-Sat)
West Hoe Laundrette (☎ 667373; 1 Pier St; ☺ 9.15am-8pm Mon-Fri, 9am-6pm Sat, 10am-5pm Sun)

Sights & Activities
PLYMOUTH HOE
This famous promenade gives wonderful, breezy views over Plymouth Sound. In one corner there's a bowling green; the one on which Drake supposedly finished his game was probably where his statue now stands.

Red-and-white-striped **Smeaton's Tower** (The Hoe; admission £2; ☺ 10am-4pm daily Apr-Oct, Tue-Sat Nov-Mar) was built on the Eddystone Rocks in 1759, then rebuilt here in 1882 when it was replaced by a larger lighthouse. You can climb the 93 steps for great views and an insight into the history of the Eddystone lighthouses.

The take on history in **Plymouth Dome** (☎ 603300; The Hoe; admission £4.50; ☻ 10am-5pm Easter-Oct, 10am-4pm Oct-Easter) is both hi-tech and theatrical, with audiovisual shows and a Tudor street, complete with rowdy locals. A harbour observation deck with interactive computers brings it up to the minute.

East of the Hoe is the **Royal Citadel**, built by Charles II in 1670 and still in military use. There are guided **tours** (☎ 0117-975 0700; admission £3; ☻ 2.30pm Tue May-Sep).

BARBICAN
To get an idea of what old Plymouth was like before the Luftwaffe redesigned it, head for the Barbican, with its many Tudor and Jacobean buildings (now converted into galleries, craft shops and restaurants).

The Pilgrim Fathers' famous vessel *Mayflower* set sail for America from the Barbican on 16 September 1620. At the **Mayflower Steps** a sign lists the passengers and marks the point of departure. Another famous voyage was led by Captain James Cook, who set out from the Barbican in 1768 in search of a southern continent.

Plymouth Mayflower (☎ 306330; www.plymouth -mayflower.co.uk; 3-5 The Barbican; admission £4; ☻ 10am-6pm Apr-Oct, 10am-5pm Nov-Mar) is another hi-tech rundown on Plymouth's nautical heritage, providing the background to the Pilgrim Fathers' trip with plenty of interactive gizmos and multisensory displays.

The **Elizabethan House** (☎ 304774; 32 New St; admission £1.25; ☻ 10am-5pm Tue-Sat Apr-Nov) is the former residence of an Elizabethan sea captain, housing 16th-century furniture and other period artefacts.

Tours of the **Plymouth Dry Gin distillery** (☎ 665292; www.plymouthgin.com; 60 Southside St; admission £5), the oldest in England and working since 1793, run between 10.30am and 4.30pm daily in summer; phone ahead at other times.

The renowned marine **National Marine Aquarium** (☎ 220084; The Barbican; www.national -aquarium.co.uk; admission £8.75; ☻ 10am-6pm Apr-Oct, 10am-5pm Nov-Mar) is housed in an impressive building on Sutton Harbour. Following a route along ramps winding through the building, visitors can explore a range

of cleverly reproduced habitats: moorland stream, river estuary, shallow sea and deep reef – look out for the aquarium's four enormous sand tiger sharks.

MERCHANT'S HOUSE
Between the Barbican and the centre is the 17th-century **Merchant's House** (☎ 304774; 33 St Andrews St; admission £1.25; ☻ 10am-5.30pm Tue-Fri & 10am-5pm Sat year-round, closed 1-2pm Apr-Oct), a Jacobean building featuring models, pictures, local curiosities (including manacles and truncheons) and replicas of a Victorian schoolroom and apothecary's shop.

CITY MUSEUM & ART GALLERY
Near the University is the **City Museum & Art Gallery** (☎ 304774; Drake Circus; admission free; ☻ 10am-5.30pm Mon-Fri, 10am-5pm Sat) hosting collections of local history, porcelain and naval art. The Cottonian Collection includes some significant paintings, prints and etchings by artists including Joshua Reynolds.

BOAT TRIPS
Plymouth Boat Cruises (☎ 822797; Phoenix Wharf) offers boat trips to the dockyards and warships (adult return £4.50), and four-hour cruises up the River Tamar (adult return £8) to Calstock. Boats leave from Phoenix Wharf, near the Barbican.

Sleeping
BUDGET
Plymouth Backpackers Hotel (☎ 225158; plymback@ hotmail.com; 172 Citadel Rd; dm/d £11/28) A large hostel in an old town house on the Hoe, with a games room, large lounge, and comfortable dorms and double rooms.

MID-RANGE
The northwest corner of the Hoe around Citadel Rd is packed with B&Bs and hotels.

Jewell's Hotel (☎ 254760; 220 Citadel Rd; s £25, d £35-45; ✗) This excellent B&B, one of many along Citadel Rd, has been decorated to an extremely high standard, with immaculate bedrooms and sparkling bathrooms.

Bowling Green Hotel (☎ 209090; www.bowling greenhotel.co.uk; 9-10 Osborne Pl; d £58; P ✗) Another good-value B&B on the Hoe, opposite Francis Drake's famous bowling green. The 12 pleasant, simple bedrooms are decorated with tasteful pictures and floral bedspreads, and all have en suite bathrooms.

Berkeleys of St James (☎ 221654; 4 St James Pl East; s £25, d £40-50; ✕) A small, quality guest-house in a quiet side street, distinguished by its friendly owners and organic breakfasts.

Astor Hotel (☎ 225511; www.astorhotel.co.uk; Elliot Street; s £50-65, d £80-120; Ⓟ ✕) A refurbished Georgian hotel just steps from the Hoe promenade. The smart, white-walled bed-rooms are a little over-priced, but if you're looking for simplicity and quiet, away from the bustle of the town centre, the Astor is a good choice.

Also recommended:

Adelphi Hotel (☎ 225520; 59 Citadel Rd; s/d £35/48; Ⓟ ✕) Former naval officer's town house with large lounge, pleasant rooms and a small rear terrace.

Cranbourne Hotel (☎ 263858; cran.hotel@virgin .net; 278-282 Citadel Rd; s £20-30, d £40-49; Ⓟ ✕) Georgian hotel with plain rooms, old-fashioned service and a minimum of fuss.

TOP END

The Duke of Cornwall Hotel (☎ 275850; Millbay Rd; s £94, d £104-160) This striking Victorian Gothic hotel is one of the oldest in Plymouth, built in 1863. The dramatic frontage, decorated with balconies, gables and an elegant cir-cular turret, should give you some idea of what to expect from the rest of the hotel; think fruit baskets, champagne and four-poster beds for the top rooms.

Eating

CAFÉS

Dutton's Café Continental (☎ 255245; Madeira Rd; mains £7-8.50; ⏱ 9.30am-5.30pm) Housed in an 1847 cannon room below the citadel (the gunholes are now windows), this café does good lunch-time snacks and afternoon cakes, as well as more substantial meals.

Harbour Seafood & Pasta (☎ 260717; 10 Quay Rd; ⏱ lunch & dinner) Bustling brasserie next door to Bar Rakuda, with outside seating and an intimate dining room inside. Fresh scallops, huge seafood salads and generous pasta dishes all come highly recommended.

Bar ZeegCo (☎ 664754; Frankfort Gate; mains £4.25-15) Bright, modern café, serving good Medi-terranean and Middle Eastern food near the shopping centre.

RESTAURANTS

Cuisine Spontanée (☎ 673757; Century Quay; mains £13.95-16.95; ⏱ lunch & dinner Mon-Sat) This excit-ing glass-fronted bistro serves global food

with a twist – pick your ingredients (meat, fish or vegetables) and the chefs will cook them at your table in the flavour of your choosing (French, Thai, Chinese, Mexican, Italian etc).

The Trading House (☎ 257345; 8 The Parade; mains £10-17; ⏱ dinner) Sophisticated seafood served in a refined atmosphere is available on the top floor of this respected restaurant; downstairs, there's a relaxed bar and out-side terrace for tapas and cold beer.

Tanners Restaurant (☎ 252001; www.tannersrestau rant.com; Finewell St; 2-/3-course dinner £23/29; ⏱ lunch & dinner Tue-Sat) The city's finest French and British cuisine can be found in Plymouth's oldest house (1498) – head for one of the stone-walled dining rooms or the medieval courtyard for alfresco eating in summer.

Drinking

Plymouth has a buzzing nightlife, but the main club strip, Union St, has a reputation for trouble at kicking-out time. The area around the Barbican is wall-to-wall pubs and bars.

Bar Rakuda (☎ 221155; 11 Quay Rd; ⏱ 9am-11pm) This funky, modern café-bar is right on the waterfront and has a great selection of cof-fees, beers and cocktails.

The Ship (☎ 667604; Quay Rd) Just along the quay, this historical tavern is another popu-lar boozer in the Barbican.

Minerva Inn (☎ 223047; 31 Looe St) Reputedly the oldest pub in Plymouth, and once home of the naval press gangs; these days it's a low-ceilinged, smoky local, with live music at weekends.

Entertainment

BARS & NIGHTCLUBS

Barbican Jazz Café (☎ 672127; 11 The Parade; admis-sion Fri & Sat £2; ⏱ noon-2am Mon-Sat, noon-midnight Sun) This cavernous, barrel-ceilinged club has nightly jazz and a livelier vibe than you might expect.

B-Bar (☎ 242021; Castle St) The in-house café-bar of the Barbican Theatre, B-Bar hosts live music, DJs, cabaret and comedy.

The Cooperage (☎ 229275; www.thecooperage .co .uk; 134 Vauxhall St) This is the live-music venue of choice for new bands.

Ride (☎ 226655; 2 Sherwell Arcade) and **Cuba** (☎ 201520; 1 Sherwell Arcade) are popular stu-dent hang-outs aiming for the shooters-and-mixers crowd.

THEATRES & CINEMAS

Theatre Royal (☎ 267222; www.theatreroyal.com; Royal Pde) Plymouth's main theatre puts on West End musicals and dance productions, while its **Drum Theatre** stages the fringe plays.

Plymouth Pavilions (☎ 229922; www.plymouth pavilions.com; Millbay Rd) This large entertainment complex stages everything from Tom Jones to the Bolshoi Ballet.

Barbican Theatre (☎ 267131; www.barbicantheatre .co.uk; Castle St) This is Plymouth's foremost arts venue; it stages small-scale theatre, dance and exhibitions.

Plymouth Arts Centre (☎ 206114; www.plymouth ac.org.uk; 38 Looe St) An excellent art-house cinema and gallery; there's also a good vegetarian restaurant.

Getting There & Away

BUS

Express bus No X38 runs to Exeter (1¼ hours, every 90 minutes Monday to Saturday, every two hours Sunday). Another useful service is bus No 86 (roughly hourly Monday to Saturday, two on Sunday), which runs to Okehampton (1¾ hours) via Tavistock (55 minutes) and Lydford (1½ hours), sometimes going on to Barnstaple (£5.50 return, three hours).

National Express has direct connections to numerous cities, including London (£25, five hours, eight daily), Bristol (£23, three to four hours, five daily) and Birmingham (£38, five hours, five daily).

TRAIN

Services run to London (£63.20, 3½ hours, hourly), Bristol (£37, two hours, at least hourly), Exeter (£10.70, one hour, hourly) and Penzance (£10.70, two hours, hourly).

AROUND PLYMOUTH
Buckland Abbey

Originally a Cistercian monastery and 13th-century abbey church, **Buckland Abbey** (NT; ☎ 01822-853607; Yelverton; admission £5.30; ☉ 10.30am-5.30pm Fri-Wed mid-Mar–Oct, 2-5pm Sat & Sun Nov–mid-Mar) was transformed into a family residence by Sir Richard Grenville and bought in 1581 by his cousin and nautical rival Sir Francis Drake. Exhibitions on its history feature Drake's Drum, said to beat by itself when Britain is in danger of being invaded. There's also a fine Elizabethan garden.

Buckland is 11 miles north of Plymouth. Take bus No 83, 84 or 86 (40 minutes, every 30 minutes) to Yelverton, then bus No 55 (10 minutes, hourly) to Buckland Abbey.

NORTH DEVON

The stretch of coastline found between Exmoor and the Cornish border has it all: fine beaches, rugged cliffs and some of the top surfing spots in the country, as well as the obligatory pretty villages and fishing harbours.

Braunton & Croyde
☎ 01271 / pop 8420

Croyde Bay and the nearby beach at Saunton Sands are Devon's most popular surfing spots; Croyde is also a pleasant seaside village, with good campsites, B&Bs and pubs. Check the north Devon **Surfcall** (☎ 0906 800 7007) for surfing conditions; calls cost 60p per minute.

Braunton is the centre for surf shops and board hire. The **TIC** (☎ 816400; brauntontic@visit .org.uk; The Bakehouse Centre; ☉ 10am-4pm Mon-Sat) provides information and also houses a small local museum.

Croyde has numerous surf-hire shops, charging around £10 per day for board and wetsuit: try **Le Sport** (☎ 890147; Hobbs Hill; ☉ 9am-9pm Apr-Sep) or, for lessons, **Surf South West** (☎ 890400; www.surfsouthwest.com; per half/full day £20/40).

Bus No 308 runs from Barnstaple (40 minutes, hourly Monday to Saturday, five on Sunday).

SLEEPING & EATING

Campsites are plentiful but you should still book ahead. **Mitchum's Campsites** (☎ 890233; guy@croydebay.co.uk) has several locations; call for details and prices. **Bay View Farm** (☎ 890501; www.bayviewfarm.co.uk; sites £14), on the road from Braunton, is another good spot.

Chapel Farm (☎ 890429; www.chapelfarmcroyde .co.uk; Hobbs Hill; s £25-60, d £50-60; P ✗) A lovely old thatched farmhouse with beamed rooms, rustic furniture and an inglenook fireplace; there's also self-catering in the old smithy behind the house.

The Thatch (☎ 890349; www.thethatch.com; 14 Hobbs Hill; d £50-60) Legendary among surfers for its great pub atmosphere and hearty food; the upstairs rooms are fine, but the nightlife can get a little rowdy.

Billy Budd's (☎ 890606; Hobbs Hill; mains £4-10) Another popular surfer's hang-out, serving jacket potatoes, chilli, nachos and huge sandwiches, as well as more substantial main meals and local ales.

Ilfracombe
☎ 01271 / pop 10,510

Ilfracombe is north Devon's largest seaside resort. Steep hills frame its attractive little harbour, although the best beaches are 5 miles west at Woolacombe. With its grand promenade, faded Victorian buildings and classic seashore character, it makes an atmospheric place to stay in summer – though it can feel like the end of the earth on a wet winter's afternoon.

The **TIC** (☎ 863001; www.ilfracombe-tourism.co.uk; The Landmark, The Seafront; ☺ 10am-5pm Jun-Sep, 10am-5pm Mon-Fri, 10am-4pm Sat & Sun Oct-May) is in the striking twin-towered **Landmark Theatre**.

SLEEPING
Ilfracombe YHA Hostel (☎ 0870 770 5878; ilfracombe@yha.org.uk; 1 Hillsborough Tce; dm £10.25, tw £23.50; ☺ Easter-Nov) Decent hostel reached via a steep hike from the harbour.

Ocean Backpackers (☎ 867835; www.oceanbackpackers.co.uk; 29 St James Pl; dm £11) An excellent, lively hostel opposite the bus station.

Wellington's Retreat (☎ 864178; www.wellingtonsretreat.co.uk; 28 Fore St; d £56-70; ✗) A charming B&B in a listed Georgian building, right in the centre of old Ilfracombe. The priciest room is positively regal, with a huge canopied bed and views across the harbour, but the others are very pleasant too, decorated with gingham bedcovers and neutral colours.

Also recommended:
Beechwood Hotel (☎ 863800; Torrs Park; r £55-60; P ✗) A handsome detached house in Torrs Park, with elegant bedrooms and an antique-filled drawing room.

Darnley Hotel (☎ 863955; www.darnleyhotel.co.uk; 3 Belmont Rd; d £48-57; P ✗) Character-filled B&B with lovely, large rooms in a quiet corner of Ilfracombe.

Norbury House Hotel (☎ 863888; Torrs Park; s £20-25, d £45-60; P ✗) Fine Victorian gentleman's residence on the west side of town.

EATING
Atlantis Restaurant (☎ 867835; mains £5-12; ☺ dinner Wed-Sat) A simple, reliable restaurant with world music, quirky décor and global dishes (ranging from Thai red duck to Louisiana chicken).

The Terrace (☎ 863482; Fore St; tapas £4-6, mains from £8; ☺ dinner) Authentic Spanish tapas is served at this popular brasserie, including griddled king prawns, chargrilled skewers and *jamon serrano* (mountain ham).

Pier Tavern (☎ 866225; The Quay; mains £4-10) A seafront pub with fresh seafood, a chatty crowd and live music on Sunday.

GETTING THERE & AWAY
National Express coaches run from London (£25, six hours, two daily). Bus Nos 3 and 30 (40 minutes, every half-hour Monday to Friday, hourly Sunday) run to Barnstaple. Bus No 300 heads to Lynton (one hour) and Minehead (two hours) three times daily.

Knightshayes Court
This Victorian fantasy **manor house** (NT; ☎ 018 84-254665; Bolham; admission £6.20; ☺ 11am-5.30pm Sat-Thu Apr-Sep, to 4pm Oct) is remarkable for the evident clash in imagination and taste between the owner, Tiverton MP John Heathcoat Mallory, and the architect, William Burges. Burges was obsessed with the Middle Ages, and the stone curlicues and minstrels' gallery reflect his love of knightly lore; Mallory preferred straightforward grandeur, evident in the library and billiard room. The extensive gardens feature a waterlily pool and wonderful topiary.

Bus No 398 runs from Tiverton to Bolham (10 minutes, six daily Monday to Saturday), three-quarters of a mile away.

Clovelly
☎ 01237

The ancient village of Clovelly is one of the best-preserved fishing harbours in North Devon. Perched precariously on the edge of a sheer cliff, the village dates back to before the 11th century, and is even mentioned in the Domesday Book. For centuries life revolved around the tides and the daily catch, which was transported up from the harbour on donkey-drawn sledges. During the day, the impossibly picturesque (but cruelly steep) main cobbled street, lined with the cutest cottages, is always thronged with tourists looking to take the perfect picture of the quaint harbour. Stick around for the evening, however, and most of the tourists vanish, leaving you to explore the village in peace.

To some extent, Clovelly has turned itself into a living museum. During the day,

WORTH THE TRIP

Ten miles out in the Bristol Channel, **Lundy Island** is just 3 miles long and half a mile wide. There's a resident population of 18 people, one pub, one church and no roads. Visitors come to climb the cliffs, watch the birds, explore the marine nature reserve (one of the top dive sites in Britain) or just escape from the outside world for a few days.

Interesting properties that can be rented include the lighthouse, the castle and a converted pigsty, but they need to be reserved months in advance. You can also camp for £4 to £8 per person. The **Lundy Shore Office** (☎ 01271-863636; www.lundyisland.co.uk) handles ferry bookings, camping and short stays. The **Landmark Trust** (☎ 01628-825925), which looks after the island on behalf of the National Trust, handles property bookings.

You can take a day trip from Ilfracombe on the **MS Oldenburg** (adult day return £28; 2 hr; 2-5 sailings per wk Mar-Dec). You can also make day trips from Clovelly: the **Jessica Hettie** (☎ 431042; www .clovelly-charters.ukf.net; adult return £25) departs Wednesday or Thursday from April to October.

it costs £4 to park your car and enter via the **visitor centre** (☎ 431781), where there's a video presentation (and the obligatory gift shops); this also includes entry to the Kingsley Museum. From Easter to October, Land Rovers regularly ferry visitors up and down the slope for £2 between 10am and 5.45pm.

At the **Kingsley Museum** (Providence House; admission free; 9.15am-5pm summer, 10.30am-3.30pm winter) you can see Charles Kingsley's study (he wrote *Westward Ho!* here), then squeeze your way around the tiny old **Fisherman's Cottage** behind.

SLEEPING & EATING
There are only a few privately run B&Bs in the village; the visitor centre plugs the two hotels but has a list of other options.

Donkey Shoe Cottage (☎ 431601; 21 High St; d from £40) A friendly, flower-covered B&B halfway up the hill; bathrooms are shared.

New Inn (☎ 431303; newinn@clovelly.co.uk; High St; d £76.50-94; ✗) A classic old cob-walled pub with beautiful bedrooms refurbished in the style of William Morris, including embroidered tapestries, period furniture and *objets d'art*. Most rooms have balconies overlooking the cobbled street, and the downstairs pub is a great spot for pub grub and a pint.

Red Lion Hotel (☎ 431237; redlion@clovelly.co .uk; Harbour; d £93.50-115; ✗) If possible, this beautiful old-world inn is even more picturesque than the New Inn. The nautical-themed rooms look out onto the sea or the ancient harbour, and the downstairs restaurant serves hearty meals in one of the prettiest settings you could wish for.

GETTING THERE & AWAY
Bus No 319 runs five times daily to Bideford (40 minutes) and Barnstaple (one hour).

Hartland Abbey

This 12th-century **monastery-turned-stately-home** (☎ 01237-441264; www.hartlandabbey.com; admission £4.50; 2-5.30pm Wed, Thu & Sun Apr-Oct, plus Tue Jul & Aug) was another post-dissolution handout, given to the sergeant of Henry VIII's wine cellar in 1539. It boasts some fascinating murals, ancient documents, paintings by English Masters, and Victorian photos, as well as marvellous gardens.

Hartland Abbey is 15 miles west of Bideford, off the A39 between Hartland and Hartland Quay. Bus No 319 runs five times daily (twice Sunday) from Barnstaple (1½ hours) and Bideford (one hour).

DARTMOOR NATIONAL PARK

Some 280 million years ago, large volumes of molten rock formed a granite mass stretching from the Isles of Scilly to eastern Devon, and it's at Dartmoor that the largest area (about 365 square miles; 945 sq km) has been exposed. Why the geology lesson? To illustrate why Dartmoor is so remarkably rugged: it's essentially a huge granite plateau covered by a thin layer of peaty soil. Vegetation is sparse; purple heather and gorse cover most of the high ground, with green, marshy mire in lowland areas and a few oak woods remaining in the sheltered valleys or coombs. Sheep, cattle and

DEVON & CORNWALL

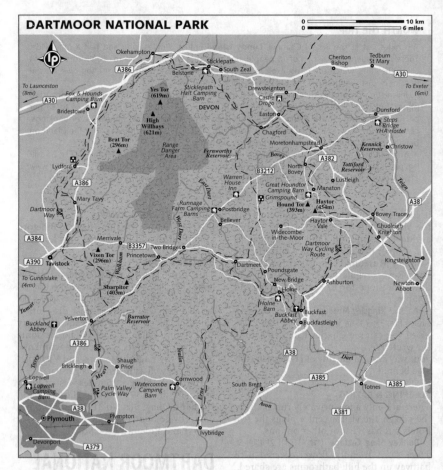

DARTMOOR NATIONAL PARK

semiwild Dartmoor ponies graze the land, interrupted by weirdly shaped tors – rock pillars or hills sculpted into strange forms by the wind and weather.

Dartmoor is named after the River Dart, which has its source here; the West and East Dart merge at Dartmeet. Most of the park is around 600m high – the highest spot is High Willhays (621m) near Okehampton. About 40% of Dartmoor is common land but 15% (the northwestern section, including High Willhays and Yes Tor) is leased to the Ministry of Defence and is closed for firing practice for part of the year.

Dartmoor encloses some of the wildest, bleakest country in England: suitable terrain for the Hound of the Baskervilles (one of Sherlock Holmes' more notorious foes). The landscape and weather can make this an extremely eerie place; try not to think of *An American Werewolf in London* on a dark, foggy night. With its wild, open landscape and scattered prehistoric remains, it's magnificent walking country, but bring a good map: it's easy to get lost, particularly when the mist rolls in.

Orientation

Dartmoor is 6 miles from Exeter and 7 miles from Plymouth. It's ringed by a number of small market towns and villages, including Ashburton, Buckfastleigh, Tavistock and Okehampton. Buses link these towns with Princetown, Postbridge and Moretonhampstead on the moor itself. The two main roads across the moor meet near Princetown, the only village of any size on Dartmoor.

Postbridge, with its medieval clapper bridge, is the focal point for car and coach visitors, and can be crowded in summer. Most sights are on the eastern side; the western part is mainly for serious walkers.

Information

There's information about Dartmoor at the TICs in Exeter (p303) and Plymouth (p312), and visitor centres at Okehampton, Tavistock, Ivybridge, Ashburton, Buckfastleigh and Bovey Tracey; alternatively, head for the website of the **Dartmoor Tourist Association** (www.dartmoor-guide.co.uk). The **National Park Authority** (NPA; www.dartmoor-npa.gov.uk) runs the High Moorland Visitors Centre in Princetown (p321), which is the best place to gather information.

The other national park visitor centres are at **Haytor** (☎ 01364-661520), **Postbridge** (☎ 01822-880272) and **Newbridge** (☎ 01364-631303). They're generally open from 10am to 5pm daily, from April to October.

These centres provide lots of useful literature, including the free *Dartmoor Visitor*, an annual newspaper that covers most aspects of getting out and about on the moor. The centres also stock walking and cycling guides, Ordnance Survey (OS) maps, and leaflets on hiking, care of the moor and letterboxing (see p321).

Don't feed the Dartmoor ponies as this encourages them to move dangerously near to the roads.

Activities

CLIMBING

Popular climbing areas are at Haytor, owned by the NPA, and the Dewerstone near Shaugh Prior, owned by the National Trust. Groups need to book in advance. Ask at a national park visitor centre or TIC for details.

CYCLING

Cycling is only allowed on public roads, byways, public bridlepaths and Forestry Commission roads.

The **Plym Valley Cycle Way** follows the disused Great Western Railway between Plymouth and Yelverton, on the edge of the

---

WARNING

Access to the Ministry of Defence (MOD) training area is restricted when firing is in progress. The areas are marked by red-and-white posts and notice boards at the main approaches. When there's live firing, there are red flags (red lights at night) in position. Always check the firing schedules with the **MOD** (☎ 0800 458 4868), the National Park Authority or a TIC.

---

moor. **The Dartmoor Way** (see the boxed text p320) is also the name of a 90-mile (140km) circular cycling route through Okehampton, Chagford, Buckfastleigh, Princetown and Tavistock. Cyclists can also follow the **Tarka Trail**.

Bikes can be hired in Exeter (p307) and from **Tavistock Cycles** (☎ 01822-617630; Brook St, Tavistock; per day £12). **Dartmoor Cycle Hire** (☎ 01822-618189; 6 Atlas House, West Devon Business Park), also in Tavistock, charges £12/6 for a full/half day; staff will deliver bikes to a number of hotels and guesthouses in Dartmoor.

FISHING

You can fish on certain stretches of the East and West Dart with a **Duchy of Cornwall permit** (☎ 01822-890205). Fishing is also permitted on seven reservoirs in the park; contact **South West Lakes Trust** (☎ 01837-871565). For fishing on the Rivers Tavy, Walkham, Plym, Meavy and Teign, a permit is usually needed; contact the **Environment Agency** (☎ 01925-653999).

PONY TREKKING & HORSE RIDING

There are riding stables located all over the park, including **Shilstone Rocks Riding Centre** (☎ 01364-621281; www.dartmoor-riding.com; Widecombe-in-the-Moor). *Dartmoor Visitor* has full details.

WALKING

Dartmoor is excellent walking country. Postbridge, Princetown and Chagford are all good centres, and south of Okehampton there is a high, wild area around Yes Tor and High Willhays (inside the MOD firing range). Haytor is also a popular hiking destination.

Guided walks focusing on wildlife, birdwatching, archaeology or folklore are arranged from April to October; they start from various points around the park. Some must be booked in advance by calling the **High Moorland Visitors Centre** (☎ 01822-890414). Prices range from £3 for two hours to £5 for six hours; bus travellers can join the walk free of charge. Details appear in the *Dartmoor Visitor*.

There are several waymarked walking routes on Dartmoor. The **Abbot's Way** runs along an ancient 14-mile route from Buckfast to Princetown. The **West Devon Way** is a 14-mile walk between Tavistock and Okehampton along old tracks and through pretty villages on the western edge of Dartmoor. YHA hostels are conveniently placed a day's walk apart across the moor, so a five-day circuit from either Exeter or Plymouth is possible.

Sleeping & Eating

If you're backpacking, the authorities and owners of unenclosed moorland don't usually object to campers who keep to a simple code: don't camp on moorland enclosed by walls or within sight of roads or houses; don't stay on one site for more than two nights; don't light fires; and leave the site as you found it. Bear in mind that there are specific areas that are also out of bounds; check with the NPA. With large tents, you can only camp in designated campsites. There are several camping and caravan parks around the area, many on farms.

There are YHA hostels at Postbridge (Bellever) and Steps Bridge, as well as at Okehampton, Exeter and Dartington. There are six YHA camping barns in the park, plus some independent barns and bunkhouses.

Cooking and shower facilities and a wood burner are provided. You sleep on the floor or a bunk bed; bring your own bedding. Charges are from £3.75 per person. For bookings, phone ☎ 01200-420102, or visit www.yha.org.uk.

The larger towns on the edge of the park (such as Okehampton and Tavistock) have plentiful B&Bs and hotels. There are several country-house hotels within the park itself, but you'll need to book ahead in summer.

Based above the High Moor Visitors Centre in Princetown, the **Dartmoor Tourist Association** (☎ 01822-890567; www.discoverdartmoor .com) produces an annual *Dartmoor Guide*, with accommodation listings. There's a charge of £2.75 if you book rooms through any of the visitor centres.

Getting There & Around

The best starting points for the park are Exeter and Plymouth. National Express has coach services between London and Exeter, Newton Abbot, Okehampton and Plymouth.

Before you start planning, get a copy of the *Discovery Guide to Dartmoor*, free from most Devon TICs and the NPA offices. It has details of bus and train services around the park.

The **Dartmoor Sunday Rover ticket** (adult £5; Jun-Sep) entitles you to unlimited travel on most bus routes, and to rail travel on the Tamar Valley Line from Plymouth to Gunnislake. Buy your ticket from bus drivers or at Plymouth train station.

The most useful bus across Dartmoor is No 82, the Transmoor Link, running between Exeter and Plymouth via Moreton-

---

DARTMOOR HIKES

The **Templer Way** is an 18-mile hike from Teignmouth to Haytor, following the route originally used to transport Dartmoor granite down to the docks.

The **Two Moors Way** is a longer option, running from Ivybridge, on the southern edge of Dartmoor, 103 miles (166km) across Dartmoor and Exmoor to Lynmouth on the north Devon coast.

The **Dartmoor Way** is a 90-mile (140km) circular route, stretching from Buckfastleigh in the south, through Moretonhampstead, northwest to Okehampton and south through Lydford to Tavistock. The *Dartmoor Way* pack (£7.95) includes a book and 1:25,000 scale map, and is available from TICs and NPA centres. For further information, call ☎ 0870 241 1817 or check www.dartmoorway.org.uk.

The **Tarka Trail** circles north Devon and links with Dartmoor, south of Okehampton; *The Tarka Trail: A Walkers' Guide* can be purchased for £6.45.

It's always wise to carry a map, compass and rain gear since the weather can change very quickly and not all walks are waymarked. OS OL Explorer Map No 28 (1:50,000; £6.99) is the most comprehensive map, showing the park boundaries and MOD firing-range areas.

LETTERBOXING

If you see a walker acting furtively and slipping an old Tupperware box into a tree stump or under a rock, you may be witnessing someone in the act of letterboxing. This wacky pastime has more than 10,000 addicts and involves a never-ending treasure hunt for several thousand 'letterboxes' hidden all over Dartmoor.

In 1844 the railway line reached Exeter, and Dartmoor started to receive visitors, who imagined themselves to be great explorers here. One guide for these intrepid Victorian gentlefolk was James Perrott of Chagford. In 1854 he had the idea of getting them to leave their calling cards in a glass jar at Cranmere Pool, the most remote part of the moor accessible at that time. In 1938 a second 'box' was established, and the idea really took off after WWII. Originally, people left their card with a stamped addressed envelope and if someone found it they would send it back.

There are now about 4000 boxes, each with a visitors' book for you to sign and a stamp and ink pad (if they haven't been stolen) to stamp your record book. Although it's technically illegal to leave a 'letterbox' (because in effect you're leaving rubbish on the moor), as long as the boxes are unobtrusive, most landowners tolerate them. Now there are even German, French, Belgian and American boxers, not to mention 'mobile boxers', odd characters who wander the moors waiting for a fellow letterboxer to approach them with the words 'Are you a travelling stamp?'!

Once you've collected 100 stamps, you can apply to join the '100 Club', whereupon you'll be sent a clue book with map references for other boxes. Contact **Godfrey Swinscow** (☎ 015488-21325; Cross Farm, Diptford, Totnes, Devon TQ9 7NU) for more information.

Inevitably, as more people go letterboxing, problems arise. A code of conduct now prohibits letterboxers from disturbing rocks, vegetation or archaeological sites in their zeal. Even so, there have been mutterings about the disturbance caused to nesting golden plovers and ring ouzels.

hampstead, Warren House Inn, Postbridge, Princetown and Yelverton (three daily Monday to Saturday, five Sunday, weekends only in winter).

There are four trains between Okehampton and Exeter on Sunday (£5.50 Day Rover, 40 minutes). The only other train stations near the park are at Ivybridge and South Brent on the Exeter–Plymouth line. Ivybridge (from Exeter: £12.90 saver return, 50 minutes, every two hours) is handy for the Two Moors Way.

PRINCETOWN
☎ 01822

Perched on a bleak rise of moorland 8 miles east of Tavistock, Princetown is England's highest town, but it's best known as the location of one of Britain's most infamous high-security prisons. The gloomy granite form of **Dartmoor Prison**, built in 1809 to house French and American prisoners of war, looms ominously over the northern edge of town. It's far from the most beautiful spot on Dartmoor, but Princetown's central location makes it a good base for walking.

The **Dartmoor Prison Museum** (☎ 890305; admission £2; ⏱ 9.30am-4.30pm Tue-Sat), on the Tavis-

tock road, gives an insight into the jail's early days, and sells crafts (mainly benches and garden gnomes) made by current prisoners.

The **High Moorland Visitors Centre** (☎ 890414; hmvc@dartmoor-npa.gov.uk; Old Duchy Hotel; ⏱ 10am-5pm) has displays on Dartmoor and an information centre that stocks maps, guides and books.

Sleeping & Eating

There's no great reason to stay in Princetown, but if you're desperate, both of the village pubs have basic B&B rooms.

Plume of Feathers Inn (☎ 890240; The Square; camping from £3, bunkhouse from £5.50, d £55), Princetown's oldest building, this country pub has plenty of rooms; it's popular so book well in advance.

Railway Inn (☎ 890232; railwayinnpl20@aol.com; Two Bridges Rd; d £40-50; 🅿) Another small pub-cum-B&B with some en suite doubles.

Both places dish up warming pub grub (fish and chips, cottage pie) for around a fiver.

Getting There & Away

Bus No 82 (the Transmoor Link) runs to Princetown from Exeter (one hour 40 minutes) and Plymouth (50 minutes).

DEVON & CORNWALL

THE DOGS OF DARTMOOR

In the parish church graveyard in Postbridge, in a heavy tomb built to ensure he couldn't rise, lies Sir Richard Cabell, the most hated man in Dartmoor. When this evil landowner died in the 17th century, it's said that black phantom hounds sped across the moor to howl beside his grave.

The legend of Sir Richard Cabell was also one of the main inspirations for Arthur Conan Doyle's classic Sherlock Holmes story, *The Hound of the Baskervilles*.

POSTBRIDGE
☎ 01822

A tiny village in the middle of the park, Postbridge is a popular walking centre. Little more than a few houses strung along the road, it's known for its granite clapper bridge across the East Dart, dating from the 13th century and made of large granite slabs supported by stone pillars.

Local legend tells of an 18th-century temperance-house landlady who began serving alcohol, much to the horror of her husband, who poured it in the river. A dog that paused to quench its thirst was driven mad by the potent mixture and died. Its tormented spirit is still said to haunt Dartmoor – one version of the story gave Conan Doyle the idea for *The Hound of the Baskervilles*.

From April to October, there's an **NPA centre** (☎ 01822-880272) in the car park. There's also a **post office** and **shop** in the village.

Sleeping & Eating

Bellever YHA Hostel (☎ 0870 770 5692; bellever@yha .org.uk; dm £11.80; Mar-Oct) Housed in former farm buildings, this rural hiking hostel is a mile south of Postbridge. Bus No 98 runs from Tavistock (40 minutes, daily Monday to Saturday) and Princetown (20 minutes).

SOMEWHERE SPECIAL

Lydgate House Hotel (☎ 880209; www.lyd gatehouse.co.uk; s £50-55; d £90-130; P) This lovely country hotel overlooks a sheltered river valley and rolling moorland. The rooms are all named after Dartmoor birds, and are decorated in a homely, rustic style – choose from rooms with private lounges, Victorian bathrooms or a granite fireplace.

The hotel is located just outside Postbridge along the B3212. Look out for the turning into the private drive near the bridge over the East Dart river.

Runnage Farm (☎ 880222; www.runnagecamping .barns.com; camping from £4, bunk-beds £4) This farm has two YHA camping barns. Take the small road off the B3212 towards Moretonhampstead just after Postbridge.

East Dart Hotel (☎ 880213; www.eastdart.force9 .co.uk; mains £5-12; s/d £26/48; P) Run by friendly folk, this old coaching inn is 100m north of the clapper bridge. The Huntsman's Bar is a popular spot with locals and hikers alike.

Warren House Inn (☎ 880208; mains £6-12) Two miles northeast of Postbridge, along the B3212 towards Moretonhampstead, this terrific country pub stands in an isolated spot surrounded by windswept moorland. There's real ale, pub food (from ploughman's lunches to home-made rabbit pie), and you can warm yourself by a fire which has allegedly been burning nonstop since 1845.

Getting There & Away

Bus No 82 runs through Postbridge between Plymouth (one hour) and Exeter (1½ hours). Bus No 98 runs to Tavistock daily (40 minutes).

WIDECOMBE-IN-THE-MOOR
☎ 01364

With its village green, quaint cottages, teashops and its 14th-century granite church (which is known as the Cathedral in the Moor), Widecombe is one of the prettiest of Dartmoor's villages. The village is commemorated in the traditional English folksong of Widdicombe Fair; the fair still takes place here on the second Tuesday of September.

There's a **visitor information point** at Sexton's Cottage, adjacent to the Church House. Built in 1537 as a brewhouse, the Church House is now the village hall.

Eating & Sleeping

Manor Cottage (☎ 621218; d from £40; P) Beside the post office, this snug little cottage is ideally situated near pubs and shops.

The Old Rectory (☎ 621231; d from £40; ☯ Apr–Oct; Ⓟ ☒) Once the home of the village vicar, this gorgeous little slate-roofed house makes a fine spot for a night's stay, with sweet, simple rooms and a lovely private garden.

The Old Inn (☎ 621207; mains £5-10) One of the most renowned pubs in Dartmoor, a fine old country inn with hearty meals, great beer and a pond garden.

The Rugglestone Inn (☎ 621327; mains from £4) Just outside the village, this stone-walled pub is covered in geraniums and hanging baskets in summer, and pulls a fine pint of ale.

Also recommended:

Cockingford Farm Campsite (☎ 621258; sites £3-8; ☯ mid-Mar–Nov) 1½ miles south of Widecombe.

Dartmoor Expedition Centre (☎ 621249; earle@ clara.co.uk; Rowden; camping from £3, bunkhouse £7.50, d £18) 1½ miles outside Widecombe. Private rooms, bunkhouses, and a range of organised activities.

Getting There & Away

Many buses only stop at Widecombe on Sunday during the summer, including the No 170 between Exeter and Plymouth and the No 174 between Totnes and Okehampton. The No 172 (two daily Monday to Saturday July to August, four daily Sunday May to September) runs via Tavistock, Princetown, Newton Abbot and Totnes.

Bus No 672 runs from Newton Abbot and Buckfastleigh via Widecombe once daily on Wednesday and Friday.

MORETONHAMPSTEAD
☎ 01647

With its unusual two-storey almshouses, traditional shops and gabled Georgian houses, the sleepy market town of Moretonhampstead is another place in Dartmoor where time seems to have stood still. It's mainly of interest as an accommodation centre and gateway to the eastern moor.

Bus No 82 runs from Moretonhampstead to Princetown (40 minutes), Plymouth (1½ hours) and Exeter (50 minutes). Bus No 359 also goes to Exeter (six daily Monday to Saturday).

Eating & Sleeping

Steps Bridge YHA Hostel (☎ 0870 770 6048; dm adult/ child £7.20/4.95; ☯ Apr–Sep) About 4½ miles east of Moretonhampstead along the B3212. Bus Nos 82 and 359 run to Moretonhampstead (15 minutes) and Exeter (40 minutes).

Sparrowhawk Backpackers (☎ 440318; www .sparrowhawkbackpackers.co.uk; 45 Ford St; dm £11, r £30) This excellent family-run, eco-friendly hostel has a nicely converted barn dorm, solar-powered showers and a pleasant outside courtyard.

Cookshayes (☎ 440374; cookshayes@eurobell.co.uk; 33 Court St; s £19, d £38-44; Ⓟ ☒) Near the village centre, this whitewashed Victorian house boasts en suite rooms; most have views over the large private garden.

The White Hart Hotel (☎ 441340; The Square; mains £10-13; d £90; Ⓟ ☒) This newly refurbished pub has a great restaurant serving local dishes including Brixham cod, king scallops and corn-fed chicken; the upstairs rooms are comfortable and contemporary.

CHAGFORD
☎ 01647

Sitting peacefully above the River Teign, Chagford has an interesting pepper-pot market house on its main square and is a handy base for the northeastern moor. In the 14th century it was a Stannary town, where locally mined tin was weighed and checked, and taxes paid.

Bus No 173 goes to Moretonhampstead (15 minutes) and Exeter (one hour) five times daily, Monday to Saturday. Bus No 179 provides a daily service to Okehampton (£2 return, 40 minutes).

Eating & Sleeping

Three Crowns Hotel (☎ 433444; threecrowns@msn .com; High St; d £74) This venerable thatched-roof inn dates back to the 13th century, and is said to be haunted by the ghost of Sydney Godolphin, a young poet-cavalier who died here during the English Civil War. The upstairs rooms are full of character, with four-poster beds and hefty oak furniture, and you can find dinner in the attached Godolphin Restaurant (mains from £8).

22 Mill St (☎ 432244; 2-/3-course dinner £29.50/34; ☯ lunch Wed-Sat, dinner Mon-Sat) The place for fine-dining fanatics: refined Mediterranean and French cuisine based on local game and fish, served in an award-winning restaurant.

The Courtyard (☎ 432571; 76 The Square; mains £4-8) This organic café has great cakes, sandwiches and wholefood snacks.

Ring O'Bells (☎ 432466; 44 The Square; mains £9-12) A wood-panelled pub with wholesome food and a beer garden.

WORTH THE TRIP

Castle Drogo (NT; ☎ 01647-433306; admission £5.70; ⌚ 11am-5.30pm Sat-Thu Apr-Oct) It may look like a medieval fortress, but the castle was actually constructed between 1910 and 1930 for self-made millionaire Julius Drewe. Clearly, if you're going to build a castle, it should be comfortable and elegant – and the elaborate design by the renowned architect **Sir Edward Lutyens** certainly doesn't skimp on style (or expense).

Castle Drogo is 2 miles northeast of Chagford. Bus 173 goes to Moretonhampstead (30 minutes) and Exeter (50 minutes) five times daily, Monday to Saturday.

OKEHAMPTON
☎ 01837 / pop 5850

Off the A30 just north of the national park, busy little Okehampton was once a prosperous wool-trading town, and now makes a good base for walks in the northern part of the moor. This region is within the MOD's firing area; phone ahead to check it's open.

The TIC (☎ 53020; oketic@visit.org.uk; Museum Courtyard, 3 West St; ⌚ 10am-5pm Mon-Sat Easter-Oct, hrs vary in low season) can help with local accommodation and walks.

Sights & Activities
A Norman motte and ruined keep is all that remains of Devon's largest **castle** (EH; ☎ 52844; admission £2.80; ⌚ 10am-5pm Apr-Jun & Sep, 10am-6pm Jul & Aug); a free audio guide fills in the missing parts.

It's a pleasant three- to four-hour walk along the Tarka Trail from Okehampton to Sticklepath, where the **Finch Foundry** (NT; ☎ 840046; admission £3; ⌚ 11am-5.30pm Wed-Mon Apr-Oct) has three working water wheels. Bus Nos X9 and X10 link Sticklepath with Okehampton (10 minutes).

Sleeping & Eating
Okehampton YHA Hostel (☎ 0870 770 5978; okehampton@yha.org.uk; Klondyke Rd; dm £13.40; ⌚ Feb-Nov; P ✗) One of the YHA's flagship Dartmoor hostels, housed in a converted goods shed beside the train station. It's also an activity centre with its own climbing wall.

Heathfield House (☎ 54211; Klondyke Rd; d £40-50; P ✗ ☕) This smart Victorian house offers lovely rooms, a guest conservatory and an outside swimming pool in summer.

Fountain Hotel (☎ 53900; www.thefountainhotel.co.uk; s/d £45/60; P ✗) A refurbished 15th-century coaching inn with stylish rooms and an in-house restaurant.

Meadowlea (☎ 53200; 65 Station Rd; d from £45; ✗) A simple B&B on the hill towards the train station.

Yertiz Caravan & Camping Park (☎ 52281; yertiz@dial.pipex.com; Exeter Rd; sites £4-8) This site is three-quarters of a mile east of Okehampton on the B3260.

Getting There & Away
National Express coaches run from London (£25, five hours, daily).

Bus No X9 runs to Bude (one hour), while No X10 goes to Boscastle (45 minutes); both also run to Exeter (one hour). Buses are roughly hourly Monday to Saturday; on Sunday No X9 runs four times each way. Bus No 86 runs to Plymouth (1¾ hours, hourly Monday to Saturday) and Barnstaple (1½ hours, every two hours Monday to Saturday, two on Sunday).

Four trains run from Exeter Central to Okehampton on Sunday (£5.50 Day Rover, 45 minutes). More interesting is the steam **Dartmoor Railway** (☎ 55637; www.dartmoorrailway.co.uk) that runs between Meldon (£2.50 single; five daily Saturday and Sunday, four daily Tuesday mid-September to mid-July, five daily school summer holidays) and Sampford Courtenay (£4 single; three daily Saturday and Sunday mid-September to mid-July, four to five daily school summer holidays) via Okehampton. Return tickets from Melton to Sampford Courtenay cost £6, or a day pass costs £10. Timetables change regularly; phone for details or check the website.

LYDFORD
☎ 01822

A secluded village on the western edge of the moor, Lydford has evidence of both Celtic and Saxon settlements and the remains of a square Norman **castle keep** (EH; admission free), which later acted as the Stannary courthouse and jail. Courts trying recalcitrant tin workers were particularly harsh; it was said that perpetrators would be hanged in the morning and tried in the afternoon.

Lydford is best known for the 1½-mile **Lydford Gorge** (NT; ☎ 820320; admission £4; ⌚ 10am-

5.30pm Apr-Sep, 10am-4pm Oct, 10.30am-3pm Nov-Mar). An attractive but strenuous riverside walk leads to the 28m-high White Lady waterfall past a series of bubbling whirlpools, including the Devil's Cauldron. Alternatively, you can drive to the car park at the other end of the track, near the waterfall itself.

A 5-mile walk leads to one of Dartmoor's best-known monuments, the **Widgery Cross** on Brat Tor, erected for Queen Victoria's golden jubilee in 1887. The scenery along the way is classic Dartmoor, rugged and windswept.

Sleeping & Eating

Lydford Camping & Caravanning Club Site (☎ 820 275; sites £3-8; ☺ Mar-Oct) Just outside the village itself; turn off at the war memorial.

Castle Inn (☎ 820241; www.castleinnlydford.co.uk; s/d £25/79) Right beside the castle, this pink-fronted 16th-century pub has rustic-style rooms, great traditional food, and a fantastic low-slung bar filled with comfy armchairs and country knick-knacks.

Getting There & Away

Bus No 86 runs to Okehampton (20 minutes), Barnstaple (1½ hours) and Plymouth (1½ hours), at least every two hours Monday to Saturday (only twice Sunday). Bus Nos 118 and 187 go to Tavistock (25 minutes) and Okehampton (30 minutes) six times a day on Sunday in the summer; No 118 is usually a vintage 1960s double-decker with conductor.

CORNWALL

Jutting out into the cold grey Atlantic like an exploratory toe, surrounded on three sides by the unforgiving sea, Britain's most westerly county has always seen itself as a nation apart from the rest of England. Throughout the centuries, artists, poets, pilgrims and pirates alike have been drawn to the county, seduced by its rugged beauty, its isolation, and most of all, by its wild, windswept shores.

With over 250 miles (402.5km) of coastline, Cornwall has one of the most dramatic seashores in Britain, from the rocky, sea-pounded cliffs and wide sandy bays of the north coast, to the gentle inlets and wooded creeks on the county's southern side. The same coastline that inspired John Betjeman and DH Lawrence to write, Terry Frost and Stanhope Forbes to paint, and Henry VIII to build countless castles continues to attract thousands of visitors each year.

Tourism is now by far Cornwall's biggest business, having almost entirely supplanted the traditional industries of mining and fishing, and in the summer months the county's beaches, villages and fishing towns are swamped by a tide of visitors that arrives in May and only ebbs in September. Visit outside the summer months, however, and you'll see Cornwall as it should be seen; in spring, when the headlands and hedgerows are covered with wildflowers, in late autumn, when the village pubs light up their wood-fires, or most dramatic of all, in the long, dark Cornish winter, with its brooding storms, bitter winds, and sudden spells of cold, brilliant sunshine.

Orientation & Information

Cornwall is a little over 50 miles (80km) wide at its broadest, near the Devon border, and it's only 77 miles (123km) from Penzance to Plymouth, just across the Tamar from Cornwall, so you're never far from the coast and the main attractions.

In addition to TICs, tourism is coordinated by districts, most of which publish handy brochures with accommodation listings. The website of the **Cornwall Tourist Board** (www .cornwalltouristboard.co.uk) has accommodation information and themed guides (beaches, festivals, gardens, heritage and so on). **The Guide** (www.cata.co.uk) lists details of the county's visitor attractions, divided into categories such as industrial heritage and maritime attractions. **Cornwall Online** (www.cornwall-online.co.uk) is another good planning resource.

Getting Around

For information about buses, you can make inquiries using the efficient **helpline** (☎ 01872-322142). The main bus operator is **First Western National** (☎ 01209-719988).

If you're taking the train, phone **rail information** (☎ 0845 748 4950). The main route from London ends in Penzance but there are branch lines to St Ives, Falmouth, Newquay and Looe. The **Cornish Rail Rover pass** (3-day pass £25.50 mid-May–mid-Sep, £18 mid-Sep–mid-May; 8-day pass £40.50 mid-May–mid-Sep, £33 mid-Sep–mid-May) allows three days' travel in a week or eight

---

SOMETHING FOR THE WEEKEND

Start your weekend by checking into the gorgeous **Abbey Hotel** (p335) in Penzance, before heading out for sumptuous seafood at the **Abbey Restaurant** (p336) or the more traditional **Harris's** (p336). On Saturday, you could choose to venture over to **St Michael's Mount** (p334) before a day exploring the dramatic coastline north around **The Lizard** (p332). Alternatively, head for the wild coastline around **St Just-in-Penwith** (p338) and **Zennor** (p338), where you'll discover some fabulous coast walks and a hearty pub lunch at **The Tinner's Arms** (p338). Book into the luxurious **Garrack Hotel** (p341) in St Ives for the night, and take your pick of the town's excellent restaurants, including the award-winning **Alba** (p341) or the **Pickled Fish** (p341). Sunday is left for exploring St Ives, with its many art galleries and craft shops, and of course the impressive collection at the **Tate St Ives** (p339). Grab a quick bite to eat in the sea-view restaurant on the top floor, and finish off the day with a visit to the **Barbara Hepworth Museum** (p339).

---

days' travel in 15 days; there's a 34% discount for children and railcard holders.

TICs stock the free annual *Public Transport Timetable* (with a map), listing all the air, bus, rail and ferry options in Cornwall.

TRURO

☎ 01872 / pop 20, 920

Truro is Cornwall's administrative and commercial centre, a busy provincial city filled with modern shops, pubs, bars and cafés. The present-day town grew up around a hilltop castle (no longer standing) built by Richard Lucy, a minister of Henry II. From the 14th century onwards, Truro was an important port, but the shipping trade was lost to the deep-water harbour at Falmouth, and the town's docks at Lemon Quay (in front of the Hall for Cornwall) were covered over. Truro instead became wealthy from the distribution of Cornish tin and copper, and the town is littered with reminders of its prosperous past, including a collection of fine Georgian town houses along Lemon St and Walsingham Pl. The city's most obvious landmark is its three-spired cathedral; built in the late 19th century, it was the first cathedral to be built in England since St Paul's.

Information

Library (☎ 279205; Union Pl; Net access per hr £3;
🕑 9am-6pm Mon-Fri, 9am-4pm Sat)
Post office (High Cross; 9am-5.30pm Mon-Sat)
TIC (☎ 274555; tic@truro.gov.uk; Boscawen St;
🕑 9am-5.30pm Mon-Fri, 9am-5pm Sat)

Sights

The **Royal Cornwall Museum** (☎ 272205; www .royalcornwallmuseum.org.uk; River St; admission free; 🕑 10am-5pm Mon-Sat) is the county's main

museum, and has some excellent exhibits on Cornish history and archaeology, as well as displays of ceramics, minerals and local art. Its fine-art collection includes pieces by Constable, Caravaggio and Blake.

The foundations of **Truro Cathedral** (☎ 276 782; www.trurocathedral.org.uk; High Cross; suggested donation £4) were laid in 1880 on the site of a 16th-century parish church, but the building wasn't completed until 1903. Built in soaring Gothic Revival style by the architect John Loughborough Pearson, Cornwall's only cathedral contains an impressive high-vaulted nave, some fine examples of Victorian stained glass and the world-famous Father Willis Organ.

The recently refurbished **Lemon Street Market** (Lemon St) houses craft shops, cafés, delicatessens and an upstairs art gallery.

Guided tours (☎ 271257; £3) of the town depart from the TIC at 11am Wednesdays.

Sleeping

Carlton Hotel (☎ 223938; www.carltonhotel.co.uk; 49 Falmouth Rd; s £40-47.50, d £57.50-65; P ⊠) An old Victorian merchant's house uphill from town, fronted with wrought-iron balconies and window boxes in summer. The interior has been converted to provide light, simply furnished rooms, some with skylights and garden views.

Royal Hotel (☎ 270345; www.royalhotelcornwall.co .uk; Lemon St; s £59, d £80-99; P ⊠ ⌨) Despite the grand Georgian front, the interior of this centrally positioned hotel is chic and contemporary, with individually styled rooms all with big beds, power-showers and CD players. The hotel also offers a range of award-winning 'aparthotels' (£110 to £150).

The Alverton Manor (☎ 276633; www.alverton manor.co.uk; Tregolls Rd; d £109-189; P ✗) An upmarket hotel in a converted convent surrounded by landscaped gardens, just outside the city centre. Large, elegant bedrooms, a good restaurant and the luxurious location make this the pick of the places to stay in the city.

Other B&Bs include:

The Fieldings (☎ 262783; averil@fieldingsintruro.com; 35 Treyew Rd; s/d £18/32) Pleasant Edwardian house with good views over town.

The Townhouse (☎ 277374; www.trurohotels.com; 20 Falmouth Rd; s £25, d £55-65; P ✗) Efficient city-style B&B with a communal kitchen/breakfast room, complete with fridge and microwave.

Eating

Mannings Restaurant (☎ 247900; www.trurorestaurants.co.uk; mains £7-18; ☽ lunch & dinner) This popular restaurant, attached to the Manning's Hotel, offers an eclectic menu ranging from local seafood to rib-eye steaks, with coffee and technicolour cocktails on offer in the foyer bar.

Café Citron (☎ 274145; www.cafécitron.co.uk; mains £6-12; ☽ lunch & dinner) A buzzy brasserie that does great morning coffee (cappuccinos, mochas), light lunches (ciabattas, smoked chicken salad) and evening meals (roast sea bass, oven-baked monkfish), all served in an informal Mediterranean-tinted dining room.

Indaba (☎ 274700; Tabernacle St; mains £5-12) A contemporary café-bar with sleek tables, industrial piping and plate-glass windows, serving sandwiches and salads for lunch and fusion food in the evening. Daily specials include local seafood and a 'Cornish plate'.

Saffron (☎ 263771; Quay St; mains £7-12.50; ☽ dinner Tue-Sat) Tiny backstreet bistro offering intriguing seafood dishes such as shark and spider-crab chowder.

Drinking

MI Bar (☎ 277214; Lemon Quay) A voguish café-bar with stark walls, stripped-wood floors, a large cocktail menu and terrace seating in summertime. Local DJs sometimes play guest spots.

Kasbah (☎ 272276; 3 Quay St) An eastern-themed wine-bar with cream bench seats and plush cushions, packed with a 30-something crowd at weekends.

WORTH THE TRIP

At the head of the Fal estuary, 4 miles south of Truro, **Trelissick Garden** (NT; ☎ 01872-862090; Feock; admission £4.80; ☽ 10.30am-5.30pm Feb-Oct, 11am-4pm Nov-Dec) has superb landscaped gardens, particularly renowned for their rhododendrons and hydrangeas. There are also panoramic views from here.

Trelissick Gardens are 4 miles from Truro on the B3289 minor road, signposted to the King Harry Ferry. The Truronian T16 bus runs from Truro (20 minutes, six daily) from Monday to Saturday.

Old Ale House (☎ 271122; Quay St) The best traditional pub in town serves a range of real ales in a suitably smoky atmosphere.

The Heron (☎ 272773; Malpas; ☽ 11am-3pm & 6-11pm Mon-Sat, 7-10.30pm Sun) Two miles from the city along the river estuary, in the tiny village of Malpas, this pastel-coloured pub serves excellent food and good beer in a gorgeous creekside setting.

Entertainment

Hall for Cornwall (☎ 262466; www.hallforcornwall.co.uk; Lemon Quay) The county's main venue for touring theatre and music, housed in Truro's former town hall on Lemon Quay.

Plaza Cinema (☎ 272894; www.wtwcinemas.co.uk; Lemon St) A four-screen cinema showing mainly mainstream releases.

Getting There & Away
BUS
Many National Express services change at Plymouth. There are direct coaches to London (£33, seven hours, four daily), Penzance (£4.25, 80 minutes, five daily) and St Ives (£3.50, one hour, two daily).

TRAIN
Truro is on the main rail line between London Paddington (£79, five hours, hourly) and Penzance (£6.60, 45 minutes, hourly). There's a branch line to Falmouth (£2.70, 20 minutes, hourly Monday to Saturday).

SOUTHEAST CORNWALL
With its mild climate, traditional fishing villages and gentle fields, southeast Cornwall has a mellower atmosphere than the north and west coasts, although the coastal

villages get packed in summer. Naturally verdant and with wonderful flowers in spring, the area is home to several stunning gardens and many plants that thrive nowhere else in England. TICs stock the free *Gardens of Cornwall* map and guide with full details.

The district has its own website at www .southeastcornwall.co.uk.

East & West Looe
☎ 01503 / pop 5280

Like so many of Cornwall's coastal communities, the twin villages of Looe are inextricably bound up with the sea. Looe has long been one of the county's busiest fishing and ship-building centres, but the town became a popular Victorian holiday spot during the 19th century, and tourism has been an important part of the local economy ever since. Linked by a seven-arched Victorian bridge, the two villages occupy opposite sides of the river estuary, and the narrow streets are dotted with tourist shops, fishermen's cottages, gabled buildings and quaint pubs – all of which attract visitors in their droves in summer. There are **boat trips** from the quay to Looe Island, an offshore nature reserve, and to Fowey and Polperro.

The **TIC** (☎ 262072; www.southeastcornwall.co.uk; Fore St; ☺ 10am-5pm Easter-Oct, noon-5pm Mon-Fri & 10am-5pm Sat & Sun Oct-Easter) is located in the Guildhall.

The **South East Cornwall Discovery Centre** (☎ 262777; West Looe; admission free; ☺ 10am-6pm Jul-Sep, 10am-4pm Oct-Jun) houses the Oceana exhibition, an interactive insight into the Cornish coastline.

Monkey Sanctuary (☎ 262532; www.monkeysanc tuary.org; St Martins; admission £5; ☺ 11am-4.30pm Sun-Thu Easter-Sep), a popular attraction half a mile west of Looe, is home to a colony of unfeasibly cute woolly monkeys and a colony of rare horseshoe bats.

An excellent 5-mile walk (part of the South West Coast Path) links Looe to Polperro via beaches, cliffs and the old smuggling village of Talland; allow around two hours, and take a picnic.

SLEEPING
Trehaven Manor Hotel (☎ 262028; www.trehaven hotel.co.uk; Station Rd; d £60-90; P ☒) This traditional 19th-century manor house is a short walk from town. The country-style rooms

are all beautifully decorated, and most have period features including original fireplaces and bay windows (some overlooking the river).

The Beach House (☎ 262598; www.thebeachhouse looe.com; Hannafore Point; d £56-80; P ☒) A stunning, modern B&B out on Hannafore Point. All the rooms are named after Cornish beaches – the best is Fistral, which offers picture windows and a private balcony with gorgeous sea views.

Tidal Court (☎ 263695; 3 Church St; d from £36; P ☒) An old-fashioned B&B in a slate-roofed gabled house in West Looe.

St Aubyn's (☎ 264351; www.staubyns.co.uk; Hannafore Point, West Looe; s £30-32, d £56-78; P ☒) An imposing pebble-dash Victorian house overlooking Hannafore Point.

GETTING THERE & AWAY
Trains travel the scenic Looe Valley Line from Liskeard (£2.40, 30 minutes, eight daily Monday to Saturday), on the London–Penzance line.

Polperro
Polperro is another ancient fishing village, a picturesque jumble of narrow lanes and fishing cottages set around a tiny harbour, best approached along the coastal path from Looe or Talland. It's always jammed with day-trippers and coach tours in summer, so arrive in the evening or out of season if possible.

Polperro was once heavily involved in pilchard fishing by day and smuggling by night; the small **Heritage Museum** (☎ 01503-272423; The Warren; admission £1; ☺ 10am-6pm Easter-Oct) features some fascinating smuggling memorabilia and tells some interesting tales.

Fowey
☎ 01726 / pop 2070

With its graceful pastel-coloured terraces and tiny alleyways teetering over a broad, tree-lined river estuary, Fowey (pronounced foy) is one of the prettiest towns in south Cornwall. It has a long maritime history, and in the 14th century raids on French and Spanish coastal towns were conducted from here. This led to a Spanish attack on Fowey in 1380; for defence, Henry VIII constructed **St Catherine's Castle** (EH; admission free), the remains of which overlook Readymoney

Beach, south of town. The town later prospered by shipping Cornish china clay, although its harbour is mainly filled by yachts these days. Stop to check out the fine Norman front of **St Fimbarrus Church**, founded in the 6th century but upgraded in 1336 and 1460.

The **TIC** (☎ 833616; www.fowey.co.uk; 5 South St; ☯ 9am-5.30pm Mon-Sat, 10am-5pm Sun) shares a building, phone and opening hours with the **Daphne du Maurier Literary Centre**.

Fowey is at the southern end of the Saints' Way, a 26-mile waymarked trail running to Padstow on the northern coast. **Ferries** (car/pedestrian £2/80p; ☯ in summer last ferry 8.50pm) cross the river to Bodinnick every few minutes to access the 4-mile Hall Walk to Polruan, from where ferries sail back to Fowey.

SLEEPING & EATING
Golant YHA Hostel (☎ 0870 770 5832; golant@yha .org.uk; Penquite House; dm £13.40; ☯ Feb-Nov) A substantial Georgian house overlooking the estuary 4 miles north of Fowey. Organised activities including walking on Bodmin Moor and night-time badger-watching.

The Globe Posting House Hotel (☎ 833322; 19 Fore St; s £22.50, d £40-75; ✗) This tiny little B&B is tucked away on the main street, and offers a rabbit warren of snug rooms, all with low ceilings and solid stone walls. The downstairs café is a good spot for tapas or a lunch-time salad.

Marina Hotel (☎ 833315; www.themarinahotel.co .uk; The Esplanade; d £100-188) A gorgeous boutique hotel in a converted town house, right above the river. The neutral-toned rooms are decorated with grace and style; the priciest have private balconies, patio tables and views to die for. The attached **Waterside Restaurant** (mains £18-23) is the best place for fish and seafood in town.

Also recommended:

The King of Prussia (☎ 627208; www.smalland friendly.co.uk; Town Quay; d £55-65) Atmospheric pub on Town Quay, named after a notorious local smuggler.

The Ship Inn (☎ 839431; www.westcountryhotel rooms.co.uk; Trafalgar Square; d £50-60) Another notorious local drinking hole, built in 1570 by John Rashleigh, cousin to Francis Drake and Walter Raleigh.

GETTING THERE & AWAY
Bus No 24 from St Austell (45 minutes, every 30 minutes) runs to Fowey via Par, the closest train station.

IN SEARCH OF MANDERLEY

Fowey's most famous resident was the British thriller writer **Daphne du Maurier** (1907–1989), who lived most of her life in a house at nearby Polridmouth Cove (used as the model for Manderley in *Rebecca*). Many of her books were inspired by Cornish landscapes and locations – the real **Frenchman's Creek** (p333) can be found along the Helford estuary, and the original **Jamaica Inn** (p348) stands in a wild, desolate spot on Bodmin Moor. Every May, Fowey hosts the **Daphne du Maurier Literary Festival** in her honour; find out more at www.dumaurier.org.

Lanhydrock House
Set in 900 acres of private grounds above the River Fowey, **Lanhydrock** (NT; ☎ 01208-73320; house & gardens £7.50, gardens only £4.20; ☯ house 11am-5.30pm Tue-Sun late-Mar–Sep, 11am-5pm Tue-Sun Oct, gardens 10am-6pm year-round) was a substantial 16th-century manor devastated by fire in 1881, but was later rebuilt in lavish style.

A magnificent plaster ceiling depicts Old Testament scenes in the 17th-century Long Gallery, which survived the fire, but the house is principally of interest for its insight into *Upstairs Downstairs* life in Victorian England. The kitchens are particularly fascinating, complete with gadgets that were mod-cons 100 years ago. Outside, the beautiful gardens are particularly renowned for their magnolias, rhododendrons and camellias.

Lanhydrock is located 2½ miles southeast of Bodmin. Bus No 55 runs from Bodmin Parkway train station, 1¾ miles from Lanhydrock.

Restormel Castle
Perched on a hill top overlooking the River Fowey, 1½ miles north of Lostwithiel, the circular Norman keep of this ruined 13th-century **castle** (☎ 01208-872687; admission £2.20; ☯ 10am-6pm Jul & Aug, 10am-5pm Apr-Jun & Sep, 10am-4pm Oct) gives spectacular views over the countryside; you can see why Edward, the Black Prince, chose it as his home.

The Eden Project
Cornwall's *cause célèbre*, and the proof that not all domes are doomed to failure. The three biomes of the **Eden Project**

THE EDEN SESSIONS

Since 2002, the Eden Project has hosted summer gigs in the shadow of the biomes, which are transformed into a spectacular illuminated backdrop by night. Previous artists include Pulp, Moby, The Doves, PJ Harvey, Supergrass, Air and Brian Wilson (of the Beach Boys) and the **WOMAD** (www.womad .org) World Music Festival. Check www.eden project.com for details.

(☎ 01726-811911; www.edenproject.com; Bodelva; admission £12; ☺ 10am-6pm Apr-Oct, 10am-4.30pm Nov-Mar) – the largest greenhouses in the world – were raised from the dust of an abandoned china clay pit near St Austell in 2000, and have become one of Britain's great success stories. Tropical, temperate and desert environments have been recreated inside the biomes with flora and fauna from around the globe.

It's impressive and immensely popular: crowds (and queues) can be large, so avoid peak times if possible, especially during summer. Eden is about 3 miles northeast of St Austell. Shuttle buses run from St Austell, Newquay, Helston, Falmouth and Truro; you can buy a combined bus and admission ticket on the bus. Contact Truronian on 01872-273453 for details.

The Lost Gardens of Heligan

Rediscovered back in 1991 by Tim Smit, the entrepreneur behind the Eden Project, **Heligan** (☎ 01726-845100; www.heligan.com; Pentewan; admission £7.50; ☺ 10am-6pm summer, 10am-5pm winter) was once numbered among Britain's finest Victorian landscaped gardens. It fell into disrepair during WWI, when most of its staff were killed. The lost gardens are only now regaining something of their former glory thanks to a dedicated team of gardeners and volunteers. Formal terraces, flower gardens, a working kitchen garden and a

spectacular jungle walk through the 'Lost Valley' are just some of Heligan's secrets.

The Lost Gardens of Heligan are 1½ miles from Mevagissey and 7 miles from St Austell. Bus No 526 goes from St Austell Station (30 minutes, nine daily Monday to Saturday, five on Sunday). Bus Nos X1 and X3 also run via St Austell and the Eden Project on certain days in summer.

Cotehele

One of Britain's finest Tudor manor houses, **Cotehele** (NT; ☎ 01579-351346; St Dominick; admission £7, garden & mill only £4; ☺ 11am-5pm Sat-Thu Apr-Oct) was built between 1485 and 1627 and was the Edgcumbe family home for centuries. The main hall is particularly impressive, and many rooms are hung with fine tapestries. Look out for some medieval suits of armour, and keep an eye open for the ghostly figures said to wander through the house, accompanied by music and a peculiar herbal smell.

Outside, the lovely terraced gardens include both a Victorian summerhouse and a medieval dovecote. **Cotehele Quay** is part of the National Maritime Museum and has a small museum with displays on local boat-building and river trade, while the restored **Cotehele Mill** is a 15-minute walk away.

Cotehele is 7 miles southwest of Tavistock on the western bank of the Tamar. You can get to Calstock, 1 mile from Cotehele, from Tavistock on bus No 79.

Roseland Peninsula

South of Truro, this beautiful rural peninsula gets its name not from flowers (although there are plenty) but from the Cornish word *ros*, meaning promontory. Highlights include the coastal villages of **Portloe**, a wreckers' hang-out on the South West Coast Path, and **Veryan**, awash with daffodils in spring and entered between two thatched roundhouses. Nearby are the beaches of **Carne** and **Pendower**, which join at

SOMETHING SPECIAL

The Tresanton Hotel (☎ 01326-270055; www.tresanton.com; 27 Lower Castle Rd, St Mawes; d £165-225; Ⓟ ✗) One of Cornwall's most quietly desirable destinations, and a hotel which brings a distinctly Mediterranean chic to the pretty seafront of St Mawes. Created as a yachtsman's club in the 1940s, and later a swish 60s hotel, the Tresanton has been completely redesigned with glamorous bedrooms, private sea-view terraces, antique furniture and even a private cinema.

low tide to form one of the best stretches of sand on Cornwall's south coast.

St Mawes has an unusual clover-leaf-plan **castle** (EH; ☎ 01326-270526; admission £3.20; ☻ 10am-6pm Jul & Aug, 10am-5pm Apr-Jun & Sep, 10am-4pm Oct, 10am-4pm Fri-Mon Nov-Mar), the best preserved of Henry VIII's coastal fortresses. Across the Fal estuary is Pendennis Castle (below); together the two fortresses were designed to protect the crucial waterway from Spanish and French invasion.

St-Just-in-Roseland boasts one of the most beautiful churchyards in the country, full of flowers and tumbling down to a creek with boats and wading birds.

SOUTHWEST CORNWALL

Cornwall's southwest coastline, dotted with inlets, estuaries and wooded creeks, has long been one of the county's main maritime areas. The deepwater port at Falmouth – the third-largest natural harbour in the world – is still a busy seafaring town, and the remote area further to the west around the Lizard was once notorious as a haven for smugglers and wreckers. These days, history and natural scenery are the main attractions, with long stretches of protected coastline, fine beaches and some of Cornwall's most impressive subtropical gardens all within easy reach of Falmouth.

Falmouth

☎ 01326 / pop 28,800

Falmouth is a seaside resort, a working dock and a student town, and these three elements combine well: there's plenty to see and do but it's not merely a tourist ghetto and it has a lively atmosphere. The port came to prominence in the 17th century as the terminal for the Post Office Packet boats taking mail to America, and the dockyard is still important for repairs and shipbuilding.

The **TIC** (☎ 312300; falmouthtic@yahoo.co.uk; 28 Killigrew St; ☻ 9.30am-5.15pm Mon-Sat Apr-Sep, Mon-Fri Oct-Mar, plus 10am-2pm Sun Jul & Aug) is opposite the bus terminal.

SIGHTS

On the end of the promontory is Cornwall's largest castle, **Pendennis Castle** (EH; ☎ 316594; admission £4.50; ☻ 10am-6pm Jul & Aug, 10am-5pm Apr-Sep, 10am-4pm Oct-Mar), built by Henry VIII as the sister fortress to St Mawes (p330),

on the opposite side of the estuary. The hands-on Discovery Centre explores the castle's 450-year history, while the sights and sounds of battle are recreated in the gun tower, with cannons firing and gunsmoke billowing.

The **National Maritime Museum** (☎ 313388; www.nmmc.co.uk; Discovery Quay; admission £6.50; ☻ 10am-5pm), housed in an award-winning building by Falmouth Docks, contains vessels and exhibitions exploring Britain's seafaring heritage through the ages. The Flotilla Gallery houses more than 40 boats from the national collection.

ACTIVITIES

In summer, **boat trips** set out from the Prince of Wales pier to the Helford River and Frenchman's Creek (£8 return), a 500-year-old smuggler's cottage upriver (£6.50 return), and Truro (£8 return, one hour). The pier is lined with boat companies' booths; try **Enterprise Boats** (☎ 374241) or **Cornish Belle** (☎ 01872-580309).

Passenger ferries cross to St Mawes and Flushing from the pier every hour during summer.

The nearest beach to town is the busy **Gyllyngvase**, just a short walk from the town centre. Further along the headland, Swanpool and Maenporth are usually quieter.

SLEEPING

B&Bs and small hotels line Melvill Rd and Avenue Rd near the train station.

Dolvean Hotel (☎ 313658; www.dolvean.co.uk; 50 Melvill Rd; s £35, d £70-80; P ☒) An impeccably updated Victorian gentleman's residence decorated with lashings of lace and luxurious drapes, this is the best (and frilliest) B&B in Falmouth. Enjoy the little touches such as complimentary umbrellas, and chocolates by your bedside.

Chellowdene (☎ 314950; Gyllyngvase Hill; d from £42) An unusually shaped gabled house within easy reach of Falmouth Bay and Gyllyngvase Beach, offering prim, plain rooms.

Green Lawns Hotel (☎ 312734; www.greenlawns hotel.com; Western Tce; s £60-110, d £110-120; P ☒ ☻ ☐) This ivy-covered château-style hotel is one of the best in Falmouth. Upstairs from the grand Georgian lobby and the fine-dining restaurant you'll discover a selection of top-notch rooms, the best

SOMETHING SPECIAL

The Pandora Inn (☎ 01326-372678; Restrong uet Creek; mains £4-12) One of Cornwall's oldest pubs, in a beautiful riverside setting on the Fal estuary – expect great pub food, rustic character and weekend sailors in abundance. Hardy souls can sample some of the Pandora's fabled smuggler's rum: at 80% proof, though, you might need to arrange for a taxi home.

of which boast antique furniture, sunken Jacuzzis and four-poster beds.

Other options include:

Rosemary Hotel (☎ 314669; www.rosemaryhotel .co.uk; 22 Gyllyngvase Tce; s/d from £28/56; P ☒) Small sea-view hotel near Gyllyngvase Beach.

Rosemullion Hotel (☎ 314690; gail@rosemullionhotel .demon.co.uk; Gyllyngvase Hill; d £45-55; P ☒) Impressive Tudor-style hotel split over three floors.

EATING & DRINKING

De Wynn's (☎ 219259; Church St; ☿ 10am-5pm Mon-Sat, plus 11am-4pm Sun in summer) A traditional teashop on the main street: the house speciality is the 'thunder and lightning' cream tea, which comes with treacle instead of jam.

Pipeline (☎ 312774; 21 Church St; mains £4-10; ☿ lunch & dinner Wed-Sat, lunch Sun) Mexican, Cajun and Italian cooking served in a colourful, surf-styled interior.

No 33 (☎ 211914; 33 High St; mains £11-15; ☿ dinner only Mon-Sat) The best place for seafood in Falmouth, a relaxed and rustic restaurant offering huge plates of local mussels, whole-roasted flounder and Provençal fish soup. Highly recommended.

Hunky Dory (☎ 212997; 46 Arwenack St; mains £12-25; ☿ dinner) A smart restaurant with low timber ceilings, simple wooden tables and local art on the walls, serving fresh fusion dishes including sushi, giant Mozambique prawns, baked Newlyn cod and five-spice roast duck.

Falmouth's best pubs are the **Quayside** (☎ 312113; Arwenack St), with outside seating on the harbour, and the nautical-themed **Chain Locker** (☎ 311685; Quay St) for that genuine fishing-town feel.

ENTERTAINMENT

Falmouth Arts Centre (☎ 314566; www.falmoutharts .org; Church St) A good arts venue, the Falmouth has programmes of theatre, music and cinema and also hosts the **Cornwall Film Festival** (www.cornwall-film-festival.co.uk) in November.

GETTING THERE & AWAY

National Express coaches run to London (£41 economy return, eight hours, daily) and Penzance (£4.75, one hour, daily).

Bus No 2 runs to Penzance (every 30 minutes). Bus No T8 runs to Truro (1¼ hours, five daily Monday to Saturday).

Falmouth is at the end of the branch railway line from Truro (£2.30 single, 20 minutes, every two hours from Monday to Saturday).

The Lizard
☎ 01326

England's most southerly point stands in marked contrast to the commercial excesses of Land's End. A wonderful section of the South West Coast Path winds its way around the coastline, much of which is owned by the NT, protecting the area from unsightly development. Rare plant species flourish and there are stretches of unusual red-green serpentine rock; keep an eye out for seals, sharks and dolphins. For more information on this unique area, visit www .lizard-peninsula.co.uk.

HELSTON

The gateway to the Lizard, Helston is most famous for the **Furry Dance**, which takes place every year on May 8. The whole town takes to the streets in period costume to perform a stately dance – the last remnant of an old pagan festival commemorating the coming of spring and the passing of winter.

Helston Folk Museum (☎ 564027; Church St; adult/ child £2/50p; ☿ 10am-1pm Mon-Sat, 10am-4pm summer hols), housed in the old butter market, explores the history of the Furry Dance and displays a mishmash of heritage artefacts, including a 5½-ton cider press from 1750.

The **TIC** (☎ 565431; info@helstontic.demon.co.uk; 79 Meneage St; ☿ 10am-1pm & 2-4.30pm Mon-Fri, 10am-1pm Sat, until 4pm Sat Aug) has visitor information.

GOONHILLY EARTH STATION

In 1901 Marconi transmitted the first transatlantic radio signals from Poldhu. The Lizard is still associated with telecommunications – somewhat surprisingly, the huge satellite dishes of the **Goonhilly Earth**

Station (☎ 0800-679593; www.goonhilly.bt.com; admission £5; ☺ varying – check website or call) make up the largest satellite station on earth. The multimedia visitor centre explores the history of international communications.

HELFORD RIVER

Across the north of the Lizard flows the **Helford River**, lined with overhanging oaks and hidden inlets: the perfect smugglers' hideaway. **Frenchman's Creek**, the inspiration for Daphne du Maurier's novel of the same name, can be reached on foot from the car park in **Helford** village.

On the northern bank of the river is **Trebah** (☎ 250448; www.trebahgarden.co.uk; admission £5 Mar-Oct, £2.50 Nov-Feb; ☺ 10.30am-5pm), touted as Cornwall's 'Garden of Dreams'. First planted in 1840, it's one of Cornwall's finest subtropical gardens, dramatically situated in a steep ravine filled with giant rhododendrons, huge Brazilian rhubarb plants and jungle ferns.

Located just to the east are the gardens of **Glendurgan** (☎ 250906; glendurgan@ntrust.org.uk; admission £4.20; ☺ 10.30am-5.30pm Tue-Sat Feb-Oct), established in the 18th century by the Fox family, who made their fortune importing exotic plants from the New World. There are stunning views of the Helford River from the lush valley, and there's also a 19th-century maze and a secluded beach near Durgan village.

Near Gweek, 6 miles from Helston at the western end of the river, is the **National Seal Sanctuary** (☎ 221361; www.sealsanctuary.co.uk/corn1 .html; adult/child £7.50/5.50; ☺ 10am-5pm May-Sep, 9am-4pm Oct-Apr), which cares for sick, injured and orphaned seals before returning them to the wild. The centre also cares for otters and sea lions.

LIZARD POINT & AROUND

Three miles west of Helston is **Porthleven**, another quaint fishing port with excellent beaches nearby. **Cadgwith** is the quintessential Cornish fishing village, with thatched, whitewashed cottages and a small harbour. **Lizard Point** is a 3½-mile walk along the South West Coast Path.

At the peninsula's tip is the **Lizard Lighthouse** (☎ 290065), built in 1751 and now entirely automated. Lizard Point is one of the most treacherous coastal areas in Cornwall; hundreds of ships have foundered on the peninsula's rocky shores and cliffs over the years. Below the lighthouse, a rough track leads down to the disused lifeboat station and a shingle cove. The views from the surrounding cliff tops are some of the most dramatic in all of Cornwall.

A mile west is the beautiful National Trust beach of **Kynance Cove**, overlooked by towering cliffs and flower-covered headland. Much of the red-green serpentine rock fashionable during the Victorian era was mined here.

SLEEPING

Lizard YHA Hostel (☎ 0870 770 5780; lizard@yha .uk; dm £13.40; ☺ Apr-Oct) A wonderful hostel housed in a former Victorian hotel beside the Lizard Lighthouse – the views have to be seen to be believed.

Coverack YHA Hostel (☎ 0870 770 5780; coverack@ yha.org.uk; Coverack; dm £11.80; ☺ Mar-Oct) A period country house above the pretty harbour of Coverack.

Housel Bay Hotel (☎ 01326 290417; www.housel bay.com; The Lizard; d £56-150; P ✗) This historic hotel commands a stunning position overlooking secluded Housel Bay, a short walk from Lizard Point. Constructed by a group of Victorian entrepreneurs at the end of the 19th century, the gabled building boasts a smart table d'hôte restaurant, endearingly old-world furnishings and a range of elegant rooms, many with sea views to die for. George Bernard Shaw, King George V and GK Chesterton are just some of the famous names to be found in the hotel's guestbook.

Polurrian Hotel (☎ 01326 240421; www.polurrian hotel.com; Polurrian Road, Mullion; d £128-260; P ✗ ☎) There are hundreds of holiday cottages dotted throughout the Lizard peninsula (some villages, like the tiny fishing port of Cadgwith, have literally nothing else), but the Polurrian Hotel is one of the smartest places to stay, with an unrivalled cliff-top position, grand Edwardian-style rooms, and easy access to the beach at Polurrian Cove below.

GETTING THERE & AWAY

The Lizard's transportation hub is Helston, served by **Truronian buses** (☎ 01872-273453; www .truronian.co.uk). Bus No T1 runs from Truro via Helston (45 minutes) to Lizard village (1½ hours, 14 daily, four Sunday).

TOP FIVE GARDENS

- **Glendurgan** (p333; Helford River)
- **Heligan** (p330; near Mevagissey)
- **Lanhydrock** (p329; near Bodmin)
- **Trebah** (p333; Helford River)
- **Trelissick** (p327; near Truro)

Bus No T2 runs from Helston to Goon-hilly (20 minutes), Coverack (25 minutes) and St Keverne (40 minutes, around 10 daily Monday to Saturday).

Bus No T4 runs from Helston to Falmouth (70 minutes) via Gweek (25 minutes) and Trebah (45 minutes, every two hours Monday to Saturday, four Sunday).

A Day Rover ticket valid on all Truronian buses costs £5.

St Michael's Mount

Perched on a rocky island and cut off from the mainland at high tide, **St Michael's Mount** (NT; ☎ 01736-710507; admission £5.20; ⏰ 10.30am-5.30pm daily Jun-Sep, 10.30am-5.30pm Sun-Fri Mar-Jun & Oct; last admission 4.45pm) is one of Cornwall's most famous landmarks. Named after a fisherman's vision of the archangel Michael, in 1070 the mount was bequeathed to the monks who built Mont St Michel off the Normandy coast, and became an important place of medieval pilgrimage. Since 1659 the mount has been the home of the St Aubyn family. The dramatic 12th-century castle rises up from the crags and steep cliffs of the island, and the lavish interior features a ro-coco Gothic drawing room, an armoury and a 14th-century priory church. There are also subtropical **hanging gardens** (admission £2.50).

At low tide, you can walk across from Marazion but at high tide in summer there's a **ferry** (☎ 01736-710265; per adult £1). Bus No 2 passes Marazion as it travels from Penzance to Falmouth.

PENZANCE

☎ 01736 / pop 20,260
The far-westerly town of Penzance has al-ways had a peculiar end-of-the-line feel: last stop on the railway from London, it's the last decent-sized town between mainland Britain and the great grey expanse of the Atlantic Ocean. Once a busy shipping port and an

important railway terminus, the town now has a mix of characters; it's part hippy hang-out, part artistic haven, and part commercial centre. Dotted with craftshops, galleries, restaurants and B&Bs, as well as plenty of mainstream shops, it makes a great base for exploring the rest of west Cornwall, includ-ing St Ives, Zennor, St Just and Land's End.

Orientation

The harbour spreads along Mount's Bay, with the ferry terminal to the east, the train and bus stations to the north and the main beach to the south. **Newlyn**, out on the west-ern edge of Penzance, was the centre of a community of artists in the late 19th cen-tury; these days it's still a busy fishing port and has some good restaurants and B&Bs.

Information

Library (☎ 363954; Net access per hr £3; Morrab Rd)
Polyclean Laundrette (☎ 364815; 4 East Tce; ⏰ 7.30am-7.30pm; Net access per min 5p)
TIC (☎ 362207; pztic@penwith.gov.uk; Station Approach; ⏰ 9am-6pm Mon-Sat & 10am-1pm Sun May-Sep, 9am-6pm Mon-Fri & 10am-1pm Sat Oct-Apr) In the car park by the bus station.

Sights & Activities

Penzance has some attractive Georgian and Regency houses in the older part of town around Chapel St, where you'll also find the exuberant early–19th-century **Egyptian House** with its bizarre, florid front.

The **Trinity House National Lighthouse Centre** (☎ 360077; Wharf Rd; admission £3; ⏰ 10.30am-4.30pm Apr-Oct) relates the history of the lighthouses that have helped keep ships from harm along the treacherous Cornish coastline.

Penlee House Gallery & Museum (☎ 363625; www .penleehouseorg.uk; Morrab Rd; admission £2, free on Sat; ⏰ 10am-5pm Mon-Sat May-Sep, 10.30am-4.30pm Mon-Sat Oct-Apr) displays a fine range of paintings by artists of the Newlyn school, including Stanhope Forbes, while the museum de-votes itself to local archaeology.

WALKING

The 25-mile section of the South West Coast Path around Land's End between Penzance and St Ives is one of the most scenic parts of the whole route. The walk can be broken at the Land's End YHA hostel at St Just-in-Penwith, and there are plenty of farm B&Bs along the way.

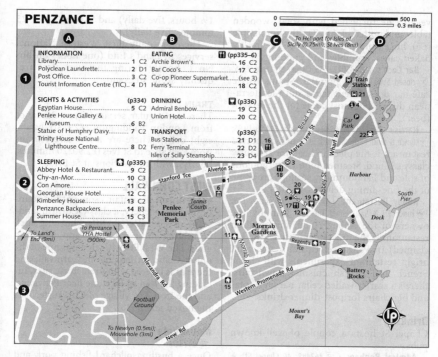

PENZANCE

Sleeping

BUDGET

Penzance YHA Hostel (☎ 0870 770 5992; penzance@
yha.org.uk; Castle Horneck, Alverton; dm £11.60) An
18th-century Georgian mansion on the outskirts of town, with fantastic bay views. Bus
Nos 5B, 6B and 10B run from the train station; it's a 500m walk from the bus stop.

Penzance Backpackers (☎ 363836; pzbackpack@
ndirect.co.uk; Alexandra Rd; dm/d £10/24) A cheery,
comfortable hostel in a converted town
house. Bus Nos 1, 1A, 5A and 6A travel
from the bus station.

Penzance's budget B&Bs are concentrated
along the Western Promenade, Alexandra
Rd and Morrab Rd. They include:

Con Amore (☎ 363423; www.con-amore.co.uk;
38 Morrab Rd; d £28-38; ✗) Popular B&B with country-
style rooms, near the town centre.

Kimberley House (☎ 362727; 10 Morrab Rd; s/d £
25/40) Family-run B&B in a smart Cornish-stone house.

MID-RANGE & TOP END

The Summer House (☎ 363744; www.summerhouse
-cornwall.com; Cornwall Tce; s £70, d £75-95; ☾ closed
Nov-Mar; ℗ ✗) This grand Regency house

was once an artist's studio, but it's been
transformed into one of Penzance's best
places to stay. The bedrooms have been
converted with lashings of style: huge beds,
sunny colours, wood floors, original cornicing and cast-iron fireplaces. There's also an
in-house Mediterranean restaurant.

Abbey Hotel (☎ 366906; www.theabbeyonline.com;
Abbey St; d £120-190) The best hotel in Penzance.
An extravagant 17th-century town house
which still retains its period character, from
an oak-panelled dining room to the stately
drawing room and walled garden. Most of
the sumptuous bedrooms have bay views,
and the bathrooms are huge.

Chy-an-Mor (☎ 363441; www.chyanmor.co.uk; 15
Regent Tce; d £56-68; ℗ ✗) A highly recommended B&B, with a range of individually
styled rooms near the seafront.

Georgian House Hotel (☎ 365664; 20 Chapel St;
s/d £28/52; ✗) A comfortable, old-world B&B
in the former mayor's residence.

Eating

Archie Brown's (☎ 362828; Bread St; mains £3-6;
☾ 9.30am-5pm Mon-Sat) A colourful veggie/

vegan café furnished with sofas, wooden tables and potted plants. Try the homity pie (£5), huge sandwiches (£3 to £6) or freshly baked cakes, crumbles and puddings.

Bar Coco's (☎ 350222; 13 Chapel St; tapas £2-5; ☺ closed Sun) This popular Spanish-style café-bar does decent tapas and Mediterranean dishes, but most come for the *cerveza* (beer).

Harris's (☎ 364408; 46 New St; mains £14.95-19.95; ☺ lunch & dinner Tue-Sat) This much-respected restaurant is the place to head for seriously classy seafood. Steamed John Dory, goujons of sole and Falmouth bay scallops are some of the fine-dining delights on offer.

Abbey Restaurant (☎ 330680; 3 courses £19; ☺ lunch Fri & Sat, dinner Tue-Sat) Run by the owners of the Abbey Hotel, this modern restaurant is the most imaginative (and acclaimed) in Penzance. Upstairs, the light, bright restaurant experiments with classic French and British cuisine; downstairs, there's a scarlet-walled cellar bar with sofas and big chairs for post-dinner drinks.

Drinking

Chapel St hosts a couple of well-known pubs.

Admiral Benbow (☎ 363448; 46 Chapel St) A super-kitsch pub covered with ship's wheels, tankers, and plaster statues, all with a salty sea-dog theme.

Union Hotel (☎ 362951; Chapel St) Once the centre of Georgian Penzance (housing both the assembly rooms and town theatre), this venerable old inn has a couple of snug bars to choose from – ask at the bar about why there's a figure of Nelson in the doorway.

Getting There & Away

BUS

National Express coaches run direct to London (£33, nine hours, six daily), Bristol (£34.50, 6½ hours, two daily), Exeter (£20.50, five hours, two daily), Plymouth (£6, 3½ hours, seven daily), Truro (£4.25,

1½ hours, five daily) and St Ives (£2.75, 25 minutes, five daily).

There are daily First Western National services to Land's End (one hour) on bus No 1, hourly during the week, less frequently at the weekend.

TRAIN

There are regular services from Penzance from London Paddington (£79, six hours, eight daily). There are a few direct trains from Penzance to St Ives (£2.90, 20 minutes, hourly), with connections at St Erth.

WEST CORNWALL

West Cornwall contains some of the county's wildest scenery, a classic Cornish landscape of sea-battered cliffs, churning surf, crumbling mine-workings and wheeling gulls. The West Penwith area was one of the oldest Celtic settlements in Cornwall, and the area is littered with prehistoric sites, including the **Mên-an-Tol** stone near Penzance, and the Iron Age village of Chysauster (see the boxed text p338).

Mousehole

☎ 01736
Once a bustling pilchard-fishing port, and now a popular spot for second-homers, the village of Mousehole (pronounced mowsel) is centred on the cluster of stone cottages around the old harbour. Described by Dylan Thomas as 'the loveliest village in England', it's certainly beautiful, but it's always packed in summer and in December, when the town switches on its famous Christmas lights.

The Old Coastguard (☎ 731222; www.oldcoast guardhotel.co.uk; s £35-48, d £75-110) is a smart, modernised hotel, with a pleasant bar-diner overlooking the sea.

The cosy **Ship Inn** (☎ 731234; South Cliff; s/d £32.50/55), nestled down by the harbour, does good seafood and fresh fish.

Bus Nos 5A/5B and 6A/6B run the 20-minute journey to Penzance half-hourly.

THE LOST LANDS OF LYONESSE

Legend tells that Land's End was once joined to the Isles of Scilly by the land of Lyonesse, which was engulfed by the sea around 900 years ago. The sole survivor was a man named Trevilian, who foresaw the disaster and outrode the advancing waves on a swift white horse, taking refuge in a cave near Marazion. The older fisherman around Mount's Bay still say that submerged buildings can sometimes be seen around the Seven Stones Lighthouse.

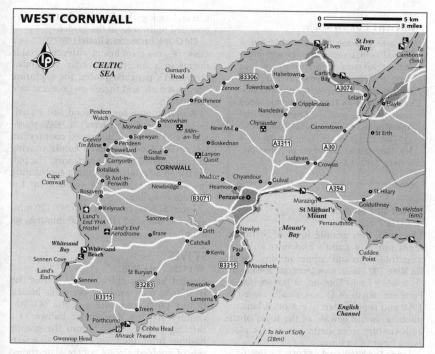

WEST CORNWALL

0   5 km
0   3 miles

CELTIC SEA

St Ives Bay

St Ives

To Camborne (5mi)

B3306 Halsetown Carbis Bay

Gurnard's Head

Zennor Towednack

Lelant

Porthmeor

A3074

Nancledra Cripplesease

Hayle

Pendeen Watch

Trevowhan

Chysauster

Canonstown

Morvah Bojewyan

Mên-an-Tol New Mill

St Erth

Geevor Tin Mine

Pendeen Boskednan

A3311

Trewellard

Great Bosullow

Lanyon Quoit

Ludgvan

A30

Carnyorth

CORNWALL

Crowlas

Botallack

Madron Chyandour

St Just-in-Penwith

Cape Cornwall

Heamoor Gulval

A394

St Hilary

Bosavern

Newbridge

B3071 Penzance

Marazion

Goldsithney

Kelynack

St Michael's Mount

To Helston (6mi)

Land's End YHA Hostel

Sancreed

Perranuthnoe

Land's End Aerodrome

Brane Drift Newlyn

Mount's Bay

Whitesand Bay

Catchall

Cudden Point

Whitesand Beach

Kerris Paul

Sennen Cove

B3315 Mousehole

Land's End

St Buryan

Sennen

B3283

Trewoofe

Treen

Lamorna

English Channel

Porthcurno

Cribba Head

Gwennap Head

Minack Theatre

To Isle of Scilly (28mi)

Minack Theatre

Surely the world's most spectacularly located theatre, the **Minack** (☎ 01736-810181; www.minack .com; tickets from £7.50) is carved into the cliffs overlooking Porthcurno Bay. The **visitor centre** (admission £3; ⏰ 9.30am-5.30pm Apr-Sep, 10am-4pm Oct-Mar) recounts the story of Rowena Cade, the indomitable local woman who conceived and oversaw the theatre until her death in 1983. From the original production in 1929, the Minack has now grown into a full-blown theatrical venue, with a 17-week season running from mid-May to mid-September – though aficionados always bring umbrellas and blankets in case the British weather should take centre stage. The centre is closed when there's a matinee.

The Minack is above the beautiful beach of Porthcurno, 3 miles from Land's End and 9 miles from Penzance. Bus No 1 from Penzance to Land's End stops at Porthcurno, Monday to Saturday.

Land's End

The coast on either side of Land's End is spectacular. Standing at the last promontory of the English mainland, gazing out over the vast expanse of the Atlantic Ocean, is quite a magical experience.

At least, it was until the **Legendary Land's End** (☎ 0870 458 0099; www.landsend-landmark.co.uk; admission £10; ⏰ 10am-5pm summer, 10am-3pm winter) theme park began drawing in the hordes. The 'attractions' include a sweet factory, restored farm and several half-hearted multimedia shows, but you'll do better skipping the complex entirely, and taking to the coast path instead. A short walk along the headland, the last rocky outcrops of Britain crumble into the pounding waves, and on a clear day, it's possible to see all the way to the Scilly Isles, 28 miles out to sea.

Land's End is 9 miles from Penzance and 886 miles (1418km) from John o'Groats. Bus No 15, usually open-top in summer, runs along the coast to St Ives (1½ hours, four daily), and bus Nos 1, 1A and 1C (one hour) run hourly from Penzance.

Westward Airways (☎ 788771) offers sightseeing flights over Land's End from the airfield at St Just; a seven-minute hop costs from £18.

ANCIENT CORNWALL

The area between St Just and St Ives is littered with standing stones and other ancient remains. If prehistory is your thing, track down **Lanyon Quoit** (a table-shaped dolmen between Madron and Morvah), the **Mên-an-Tol stone** (a ring-shaped stone near Madron) and **Chysauster Iron Age Village** (☎ 07831-757934; admission £2; ☯ 10am-6pm Jul & Aug, 10am-5pm Apr-Jun & Sep, 10am-4pm Oct), the most complete prehistoric settlement in Cornwall.

St Just-in-Penwith
☎ 01736 / pop 1890

The stern, grey-granite town of St Just, 6 miles north of Land's End, was formerly a centre for tin and copper mining. **Geevor Tin Mine** (☎ 788662; www.geevor.com; admission £6; ☯ 9am-5pm Sun-Fri Easter-Oct, to 4pm Nov-Mar) at Pendeen, north of St Just, finally closed in 1990 and is now open to visitors. Claustrophobics should beware of the tours of the 18th-century mineshafts, which take place every hour in summer.

Land's End YHA Hostel (☎ 0870 770 5906; Letcha Vean; dm £11.80; ☯ May-Sep, Mon-Fri Feb-Apr & Oct-Nov) is a remote hostel about half a mile south of the village; it's tricky to find (call for directions) but wonderfully isolated, near the coast path.

Bus No 15 runs regularly from St Ives (one hour, four daily), while bus Nos 10, 10A, 10B and 11A go from Penzance (30 minutes, every 30 minutes).

Zennor
☎ 01736

A stunning 6-mile stretch of the South West Coast Path runs from St Ives to the windswept village of Zennor, where DH Lawrence wrote much of *Women in Love*. **St Senara's Church** dates from at least 1150. Look for the carved Mermaid Chair; legend tells of a beautiful, mysterious woman who lured a chorister into the sea at Mermaid's Cove, where you can still hear them singing.

The Wayside Folk Museum (☎ 796945; admission £2.75; ☯ 10.30am-5.30pm Easter-Oct) is the oldest private museum in Britain, and houses an eclectic mix of local-interest exhibits, including displays on tin mining, fishing, farming and archaeology. Look out for the two water-powered millwheels in the garden.

Old Chapel Backpackers Hostel (☎ 798307; dm/d £12/40; P) is a great hostel with comfortable dorms in a smartly converted Methodist chapel. It's perfectly placed for exploring the coast path, and there's an excellent café downstairs.

A perfect stop for pub food and a fortifying pint, the **Tinner's Arms** (☎ 792697; ploughman's lunch £5.50) is a slate-roofed country inn where DH Lawrence lived before moving into an isolated farmhouse nearby. The pub remained a favoured drinking spot during his year-and-a-half-long sojourn on the Zennor coastline.

From St Ives, catch Bus No 300 (20 minutes, five daily) or No 343 (20 minutes, six daily).

ST IVES
☎ 01736 / pop 9870

Nestled into the cliffs west of Carbis Bay is St Ives, once one of Cornwall's busiest fishing ports, and later a centre of 20th-century art, but now better known as a thriving holiday town. From the granite harbour front, the town climbs into a warren of cobbled streets, where slate-roofed cottages, old pubs and tumbledown chapels jostle for space with tourist shops, trendy restaurants, galleries and holiday homes. It's an intriguing blend of old and new worlds, where heritage and commerce collide head-on. Every year thousands of visitors are attracted to its vibrant art scene, atmospheric architecture and bustling cafés and bars, not to mention its beautiful seaside setting.

Orientation

St Ives lies on the west side of St Ives Bay. The main road is lined with B&Bs and hotels, and passes the bus and train stations above Porthminster Beach, before joining the main shopping streets of Tregenna Pl, the High St and Fore St. The best restaurants and cafés are along the harbour, while most of the art galleries are west of Fore St.

Information

Library (☎ 795377; 1 Gabriel St; Net access per hr £3)
Post office (☎ 795004; Tregenna Pl; ☯ 9am-5.30pm Mon-Fri, 9am-12.30pm Sat)
stives-cornwall.co.uk Official town website with accommodation and activity guides.

WHEN DID CORNISH DIE?

A Celtic language akin to Welsh, Cornish was spoken west of the Tamar until the 19th century. Written evidence indicates that it was still widely spoken at the time of the Reformation, but suppressed after a Cornish uprising in 1548. By the 17th century only a few people in the far west of Cornwall still claimed it as their mother tongue.

Towards the end of the 18th century linguistic scholars foresaw the death of Cornish and scoured the peninsula for people who still spoke it. One such scholar, Daines Barrington, visited Mousehole in 1768 and recorded an elderly woman called Dolly Pentreath abusing him in Cornish for presuming she couldn't speak her own language.

Dolly died in 1769 and has gone down in history as the last native speaker of Cornish. However, Barrington knew of other people who continued to speak it into the 1790s, and an 1891 tombstone in Zennor commemorates John Davey as 'the last man to possess any considerable knowledge of the Cornish language'.

Recently efforts have been made to revive the language – unfortunately there are now three conflicting varieties of 'Cornish' (Unified, Phonemic and Traditional), so reintroduction could prove tricky. You can find out more on www.cornish-language.org.

TIC (☎ 796297; ivtic@penwith.gov.uk; Street-an-Pol; ◷ 9am-6pm Mon-Sat Easter-Sep, 10am-1pm Sun Easter-Jun & Sep, 10am-4pm Sun Jul & Aug, 9am-5pm Mon-Fri, 10am-1pm Sat Oct-Easter) Inside the Guildhall.

Sights & Activities

TATE ST IVES

The streets of St Ives are dotted with art galleries, but the most impressive collection is held at the **Tate St Ives** (☎ 796226; www.tate.org.uk/stives; Porthmeor Beach; admission £5.50, joint ticket with Barbara Hepworth museum £8.50; ◷ 10am-5.30pm Mar-Oct, 10am-4.30pm Tue-Sun Nov-Feb). Built in 1993 above Porthmeor Beach, and designed to echo its surroundings in glass, stone and white concrete, the building is almost a work of art in itself. The gallery contains work by celebrated local artists, including Terry Frost, Patrick Heron and Barbara Hepworth, along with commissioned pieces and special exhibitions. On the top floor there is a stylish café-bar with the best sea views in town.

BARBARA HEPWORTH MUSEUM & SCULPTURE GARDEN

The Tate also oversees this **museum** (☎ 796226; www.tate.org.uk/stives; Barnoon Hill; admission £4.50, joint ticket with Tate St Ives £8.50; ◷ 10am-5.30pm Mar-Oct, 10am-4.30pm Tue-Sun Nov-Feb), in Barbara Hepworth's house and studio on Barnoon Hill. Hepworth was one of the leading abstract sculptors of the 20th century, and a key figure in the St Ives art scene. The museum and gallery contains an archive of her letters and belongings, while the adjoining garden contains some of her most famous sculptures.

The studio has remained untouched since her death in a fire in 1975. Hepworth's work is scattered throughout St Ives; look for her sculptures outside the Guildhall and inside the 15th-century parish church of St Ia.

ST IVES MUSEUM

Housed in a pier-side building variously used as a pilchard-packing factory, laundry, cinema, sailor's mission, and copper mine, the **heritage museum** (☎ 796005; admission £1.50; ◷ 10am-5pm Mon-Fri & 10am-4pm Sat Mar-Oct) contains local artefacts relating to blacksmithery, fishing and shipwrecks.

BEACHES

The largest town beaches are **Porthmeor** and **Porthminster**, but the tiny cove of **Porthgwidden** is also popular, thanks to the beachside café and its sheltered position beside the grassy headland known as **The Island**. Nearby, the pre–14th-century **Chapel of St Nicholas**, patron saint of children and sailors, is the oldest church in St Ives, and with only one room, certainly the smallest. **Carbis Bay**, to the southeast, is also worth seeking out.

Several places on Porthmeor Beach and Fore St rent wetsuits and surfboards; try **Windansea** (☎ 794830; 25 Fore St).

BOAT TRIPS

Unsurprisingly given St Ives' maritime heritage, fishing and sailing are popular pastimes. **The St Ives Pleasure Boat Association** (☎ 01736 796080/07712 386162) runs deep-sea fishing trips from the harbour: expect to

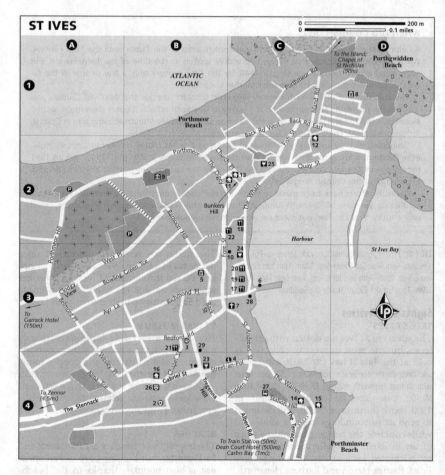

ST IVES

ATLANTIC OCEAN

Porthmeor Beach

To the Island; Chapel of St Nicholas (50m)

Porthgwidden Beach

St Ives Bay

Porthminster Beach

To Train Station (50m); Dean Court Hotel (500m); Carbis Bay (1mi)

To Zennor (4.5mi)

To Garrack Hotel (150m)

---

pay £30 to £50 a day. It also offers coastal cruises, including a 90-minute trip to the grey-seal colony on Seal Island (£8).

Sleeping

St Ives has no shortage of places to stay, ranging from budget B&Bs to boutique hotels, but the cheaper rooms get booked up quickly, so plan ahead.

BUDGET

St Ives International Backpackers (☎ 799444; www.backpackers.co.uk/st-ives; The Stennack; dm £10-16, d £30-35; 🖳) Housed inside an old Wesleyan chapel school, this sprawling hostel has grungy character (mismatched décor, colourful wall murals), but the rooms are cramped and very basic. You have to stay for at least a week in July and August.

The Anchorage (☎ 797135; 5 Bunkers Hill; s £27-30 d £55-60; ✗) One of the best B&Bs in old St Ives. The 18th-century cob-walled house has bags of rustic charm with original oak beams, granite fireplace and exposed stonework. The rooms are small, but some have harbour views.

The Grey Mullet (☎ 796635; greymulletguesthouse@ lineone.net; 2 Bunkers Hill; s £25, d £48-52; ✗) Housed in a flower-covered building dating from 1776, this traditional B&B is full of old-world appeal, with photographs, sketches and period prints on the walls, and snug rooms overlooking the cobbled street or the harbour.

MID-RANGE

Cornerways (☎ 796706; www.cornerwaysstives@aol .com; Bethesda Pl; d from £65) In the quiet Downalong quarter of St Ives, this attractive house hosted Daphne du Maurier during the 1940s; it's been updated since then but still has an air of elegance and understated style.

Kynance Guest House (☎ 796636; www.kynance .com; 24 The Warren; d £50-58; ☼ Mar-Oct; P ☒) An attractive B&B in an old tin-miners' cottage, along a quiet backstreet near Porthminster Beach. The wood-beamed dining room and lounge are decorated with local art, and there's a patio garden reached from the second floor.

Dean Court Hotel (☎ 796023; www.deancourt hotel.com; Trelyon Ave; d £70-102; P) A smart midrange hotel in a double-fronted Victorian town house on the main avenue into St Ives. The rooms are impeccably furnished in neutral tones, and the best have bay windows overlooking St Ives.

TOP END

Pedn-Olva Hotel (☎ 796222; pednolva@smalland friendly.co.uk; Porthminster Beach; d £110-140; P ☎) A completely refurbished hotel overlooking Porthminster Beach, with bright Mediterranean colours, private sun terraces, an excellent seafood restaurant, and fabulous views from the panoramic windows.

Garrack Hotel (☎ 796199; www.garrack.com; Burthallen Lane; s/d from £68/114; P ☒ ☎) One of several upmarket establishments in St Ives, this ivy-covered hotel feels like an exclusive country club, with landscaped grounds, an indoor swimming pool and huge, smartly decorated rooms, some with four-poster beds and antique furniture.

Eating

Alba (☎ 797222; Old Lifeboat House; mains £12-17; ☼ lunch & dinner) This renowned split-level restaurant offers superb seafood in a sleek, contemporary setting, with starched white tablecloths, modern furniture and picture windows overlooking the harbour.

Onshore (☎ 796000; The Wharf; ☼ lunch & dinner) Further along the wharf, this chrome-styled restaurant serves pasta and award-winning pizzas cooked in a roaring wood-fired oven.

Alfresco (☎ 793737; The Wharf; mains £10-14; ☼ lunch & dinner) Stylish fish and seafood with a Mediterranean flavour served in a beautiful location on the waterfront, with sliding doors that open onto the wharfside terrace in summer.

The Pickled Fish (☎ 795100; 3 Chapel St; mains £13-18; ☼ dinner Mon-Sat) The owner-chef of this tiny restaurant started out at the Dorchester Hotel, and now serves up some of St Ives' best food, based on local produce and top-quality ingredients.

Seafood Café (☎ 794004; 45 Fore St; mains £8.95-15.95; ☼ lunch & dinner) Buzzy, informal bistro offering gourmet burgers, bouillabaisse, huge ciabattas, and mussels for under £10.

The Hub (☎ 799099; The Wharf; mains £6-10; ☼ 10am-11pm) This Metropolitan-style café-bar has good coffee, lunch-time sandwiches and lively night-time drinking.

Drinking

Isobar (☎ 796042; Tregenna Pl; ☼ to 2am) St Ives' most popular nightspot. There's a buzzy cocktail and café-bar on the ground floor, and a club with regular house/techno nights upstairs.

DEVON & CORNWALL

ST IVES & THE ARTS

Ever since JMW Turner sketched the town in 1811, St Ives has been a focal point for British art. During the 19th century, St Ives was linked with the Newlyn School, a group of figurative painters headed by Stanhope Forbes, who found ideal subjects among the rustic characters and landscapes of Cornwall. James Whistler and Walter Sickert made regular visits, and by the beginning of the 20th century there were scores of artists working in and around St Ives. In the 1930s and '40s, the work of abstract painters like Peter Lanyon, Henry Moore and Ben Nicholson, and his wife, the sculptor Barbara Hepworth, led to the formation of the Penwith Society of Artists in 1949. Their avant-garde techniques inspired a third wave of St Ives artists in the 1960s and '70s, including Terry Frost, Patrick Heron and Roger Hilton. Today, St Ives continues to hold an enduring fascination – the Penwith area supports more working artists than almost anywhere else in Britain.

Sloop Inn (☎ 796584; The Wharf) The walls of this 14th-century inn are hung with paintings by local artists, but on summer evenings most people ignore them and drink out by the harbour.

The Lifeboat Inn (☎ 794123; The Wharf) On the other side of the harbour, this place has a warm, welcoming atmosphere and a good selection of Cornish ales.

Entertainment

The Royal Cinema (☎ 796843; www.merlincinemas .co.uk; The Stennack) Shows new films and often has cheap matinées.

The Guildhall (☎ 796888; 1 Street-An-Pol) Regular programmes of music and theatre, especially during September, when it becomes the focus for the St Ives Folk Festival.

Getting There & Away

National Express operates coaches to London (£33, 8½ hours, three daily), Plymouth (£6, three hours, four daily), Exeter (£20.50, five hours, one daily) and most local towns.

Local First buses No 16/16B, 17A and 17B regularly connect St Ives with Penzance; Bus No 300 travels to Land's End en route. Most bus services stop at Zennor, Sennen and St Just. There are also direct services to Truro and Newquay.

St Ives is on a scenic branch railway line from St Erth (£1.70, 20 minutes, hourly), on the main London–Penzance line.

A Park & Ride train service operates from the Lelant Saltings Rail Halt 2 miles south of town.

NORTH CORNWALL COAST

Overlooking the vast expanse of the Atlantic Ocean, the north coast is for many people the quintessential Cornish landscape, a wild mix of granite rocks, craggy cliff tops and booming surf, beloved by surfers, cyclists, hikers and beach-bums alike. Seen in winter, lashed by wind and sheeting rain and blanketed in sea-fog, it can be a bleak and forbidding place; but in spring, the cliff tops are covered with wildflowers and gorse, the sunshine (when it appears) is warm and gentle, and the views can't be bettered anywhere else in Britain.

The coastline is dotted with sandy bays and secluded coves, but the best beaches are near Hayle at **Gwithian** and **Godrevy**. At low tide, 3 miles of sand are revealed by the receding tide; strong winds make this a popular spot for kite-boarders and surfers, though the swell can be powerful and unpredictable, so take care.

Further north, beyond the little harbour of **Portreath**, the beaches around **Porthtowan** and **St Agnes** are popular with both surfers and holiday-makers, especially the tiny National Trust cove of **Chapel Porth**, from where the coast path leads up to the abandoned mine workings of **Wheal Coates**. North of St Agnes is the busy seaside town of **Perranporth**, where there's another excellent beach and plenty of accommodation and summer nightlife.

Northwards along the coast towards Newquay are several more stunning beaches, including **Crantock** and **Holywell Bay**. Most dramatic of all are the stately rock towers of **Bedruthan Steps**, 7 miles north of Newquay.

Sleeping

Rose-in-Vale Hotel (☎ 01872-552202; www.rose-in-vale -hotel.co.uk; Mithian; d from £120; P ⊠ ⊑) A gorgeous hotel inside an ivy-covered Georgian manor house, 2 miles from St Agnes, with landscaped grounds, renovated rooms, and a sauna, outdoor pool and summerhouse.

The Driftwood Spars (☎ 01872-552428; www.drift woodspars.com; Trevaunance Cove; d £74-84; P ✕) A popular spot with Cornwall's surfing community, moments from the beach at Trevaunance Cove near St Agnes. Nautical-themed B&B rooms with sea views can be found above the 17th-century pub.

Penkerris (☎ 01872-552262; www.penkerris.co.uk; St Agnes; d £30-70; P ✕) A creeper-covered house on the edge of St Agnes village.

The Seiners Arms (☎ 01872-573118; www.seiners arms.com; Perranporth; d £54-72; P ✕) Modern pub and hotel overlooking Perranporth Beach.

Eating & Drinking

The Watering Hole (☎ 01872-572888; Perranporth Beach) One of the liveliest nightspots on the north coast, a relaxed bar-restaurant on Perranporth Beach with outside decking and a buzzy surf-shack vibe. Regular bands play at weekends and throughout the summer.

The Blue Bar (☎ 01209-890329; www.blue-bar.co.uk; Porthtowan; ☽ lunch & dinner Thu-Sun) A great café-brasserie overlooking Porthtowan beach, with a bright surf-style interior and a gorgeous sea-view patio. Burgers, sandwiches and salads are on the menu, and there is live music, parties and DJs at weekends.

Getting There & Away

Bus No 301 travels up and down the North Coast from Newquay four times daily in July and August, stopping at Perranporth (40 minutes), St Agnes (50 minutes), Hayle (80 minutes) and Penzance (two hours).

NEWQUAY

☎ 01637 / pop 19,570

Newquay is the kind of place you either love or loathe. Scattered across the cliff tops above the broad beaches of Fistral and Towan, it's indisputably one of the most famous surfing spots in England, and has an attitude to match. More recently, Newquay has also gained a reputation as Cornwall's biggest party town, with countless nightspots ranging from the ultra-tacky to the pseudo-chic, and throughout the summer the evening streets are jammed with clubbers, surfers and late-night drinkers.

Much of Newquay is relentlessly modern, but on the cliff north of Towan Beach stands the 14th-century **Huer's House**, a lookout for approaching pilchard shoals (until they were fished out early in the 20th century, these shoals were enormous: one catch of 1868 netted a record 16.5 million fish). Cornish fishing villages all once had a watchtower.

Information

Cyber Surf (☎ 875497; 2 Broad St; per min 7p; ☽ 10am-late)

Laundrette (☎ 875901; 1 Beach Pde, Beach Rd)

Tad & Nick's Talk'n'Surf (☎ 874868; 72 Fore St; Net access per hr £3; ☽ 10am-6pm daily)

TIC (☎ 854020; www.newquay.co.uk; Marcus Hill; ☽ 9.30am-5.30pm Mon-Sat & 9am-3.30pm Sun Jun-Sep, 9.30am-4.30pm Mon-Fri & 9.30am-12.30pm Sat Oct-May)

Sights & Activities

Blue Reef Aquarium (☎ 878134; www.bluereefaquar ium.co.uk; Towan Promenade; admission £5.95; ☽ 10am-5pm), right on Towan beach, has a good selection of weird and wonderful underwater characters, including local species, a great tropical tank and a predator's gallery.

Newquay Zoo (☎ 873342; www.newquayzoo.co.uk; admission £6.95; ☽ 9.30am-6pm Apr-Nov) is big on cute beasties (meerkats, penguins, tamarins) and has some big cats and macaques, too.

BEACHES

Fistral Beach, west of town round Towan Head, is England's most famous surfing beach. There are fast hollow waves, particularly at low tide, and good tubing sections when there's a southeasterly wind.

Watergate Bay is a 2-mile-long sandy beach on the eastern side of Newquay Bay. At low tide it's a good place to learn to surf. A mile (or 3 miles by car) southwest of Newquay, **Crantock** is a small northwest-facing sheltered beach, where the waves are best at mid to high tide.

SURFING

Lots of surf shops hire out equipment, including boards (£10/25/45 for one/three/ seven days) and wetsuits (£5/12/25 for one/ three/seven days). Try **Fistral Surf Co** (☎ 850808; 19 Cliff Rd; ☽ 9am-6pm) or **Fistral Beach Surf Hire** (☎ 850584; Fistral Beach).

Surf schools abound; all-inclusive, half-day beginner's lessons cost £20 to £25. Try **British Surfing Association** (Fistral Beach ☎ 850737 Tolcarne Beach ☎ 851487; www.nationalsurfingcentre .com) or **Offshore Extreme** (☎ 877083; www.offshore -extreme.co.uk). If you choose another school, make sure the instructors are certified by the BSA.

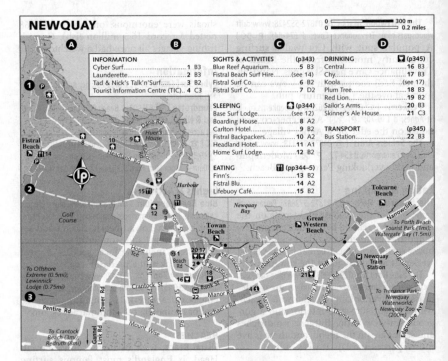

NEWQUAY

INFORMATION	
Cyber Surf	1 B3
Launderette	2 B3
Tad & Nick's Talk'n'Surf	3 B2
Tourist Information Centre (TIC)	4 C3

SIGHTS & ACTIVITIES	(p343)
Blue Reef Aquarium	5 B3
Fistral Beach Surf Hire	(see 14)
Fistral Surf Co	6 B2
Fistral Surf Co	7 D2

SLEEPING	(p344)
Base Surf Lodge	(see 12)
Boarding House	8 A2
Carlton Hotel	9 B2
Fistral Backpackers	10 A2
Headland Hotel	11 A1
Home Surf Lodge	12 A1

EATING	(pp344–5)
Finn's	13 B2
Fistral Blu	14 A2
Lifebuoy Café	15 B2

DRINKING	(p345)
Central	16 B3
Chy	17 B3
Koola	(see 17)
Plum Tree	18 B3
Red Lion	19 B2
Sailor's Arms	20 B3
Skinner's Ale House	21 C3

TRANSPORT	(p345)
Bus Station	22 B3

Sleeping
BUDGET

There are plenty of surf lodges in Newquay, but choose carefully; some are real dives catering mainly for beer-boys and stag parties. The best lodges have secure board storage and links with local surf schools.

The Boarding House (☎ 873258; www.theboardinghouse.co.uk; 32 Headland Rd; dm £17.50-20; P 🖳) By far the best surf lodge in town, in a fantastic position 50m from Fistral Beach. Wood floors, tropical plants and a funky downstairs café-bar with an outside sundeck make this feel more like a boutique hotel than a hostel; upstairs, there are dorms and en suite rooms with TVs and board lockers.

Home Surf Lodge (☎ 873387; www.homesurflodge.co.uk; 18 Tower Rd; dm £15-20; 🖳) A lively, friendly spot, with free Internet access and a bar, though the dorms are pretty cramped.

Base Surf Lodge (☎ 874852; www.basesurflodge.com; 20 Tower Rd; dm £10-20) Right next door, a spotless hostel with a licensed bar and reasonably spacious dorms (but no kitchen).

Fistral Backpackers (☎ 873146; www.fistralbackpackers.co.uk; 18 Headland Rd; dm £7-15.50) Chaotic and large, but well positioned right on Fistral Beach; facilities include a pool room, movie lounge, kitchen, dorms and doubles.

MID-RANGE & TOP END

Carlton Hotel (☎ 872658; www.carltonhotelnewquay.co.uk; 6 Dane Rd; d £52-60; P ✗) One of the smartest B&Bs in Newquay, with a selection of rooms decorated in neutral tones, all with huge beds, fluffy pillows and DVD players. The rear patio is a lovely spot for a summer evening tipple.

Headland Hotel (☎ 872211; www.headlandhotel.co.uk; Fistral Beach; d £77-270; P ✗ ✗ 🖳 🐾) Newquay's grandest hotel, a fabulous brick Victorian edifice perched above Fistral Beach. The impeccably decorated rooms range from budget singles to ornate sea-view suites with balconies and luxury bathrooms, and there are tennis courts, two pools, and a nine-hole golf course. The hotel was used in the film version of Roald Dahl's *The Witches*.

Eating

Finn's (☎ 874062; South Quay Hill; mains £15-30; 🌙 lunch & dinner) If you're after local seafood, look no further than this beachside bistro beside the harbour. The sophisticated menu includes sashimi tuna steak and pad Thai noodles – but you can't go wrong with a good old Cornish crab sandwich.

Fistral Blu (☎ 879444; www.fistral-blu.co.uk; Fistral Beach; mains £12-20; ☽ lunch & dinner) Newquay's newest, trendiest restaurant, housed in the recently opened shopping complex on Fistral Beach. Fusion flavours are served in the glass-fronted restaurant; downstairs, there's an informal café for sandwiches and lunchtime salads.

Lifebuoy Café (☎ 878076; Lower Tower Rd; mains £4.50-12) This colourful café is an ideal spot for lunch, offering jacket potatoes, huge burgers, baguettes and Cajun dishes.

Lewinnick Lodge (☎ 878117; Pentire Headland; mains £11-17; ☽ lunch & dinner) Out on Pentire Head, this contemporary restaurant serves European-influenced seafood dishes in a light, airy dining room with amazing cliff-top views.

Drinking

Newquay is crammed with pubs, bars and (mostly dodgy) clubs.

Chy (☎ 873415; www.the-chy.co.uk; 12 Beach Rd) This stylish, loft-style café-bar makes a welcome change from most of Newquay's drinking spots, with a huge chrome-fronted bar, designer seats, stainless-steel fittings and a fabulous terrace above the beach.

Koola (☎ 873415; www.thekoola.com; 12 Beach Rd) Underneath the Chy, the Koola is still the hippest venue in town, with a reputation for breaking new acts and underground tunes.

The Central (☎ 878310; 11 Central Sq) One of the most popular pubs in the town centre, with a rowdy outdoor terrace that's always jammed at weekends.

Red Lion (☎ 872195; North Quay Hill) This rambling pub is the traditional surfers' hang-out. Stick around for live bands on Friday and Saturday.

Skinner's Ale House (☎ 876391; 58 East St) A spit-and-sawdust pub tailor-made for downing real Cornish ales; there's live music from Thursday to Sunday.

Plum Tree (☎ 872814; 19 Bank St) The latest pre-club option, with DJs, tangerine walls and a lethal cocktail menu.

Sailor's Arms (☎ 872838; Fore St) Shamelessly downmarket pub-club playing cheesy house and chunky choons.

> ## TOP FIVE BEACHES
>
> - **Perranporth** (p342)
> - **Carne** (p330; Roseland Peninsula)
> - **Gwithian** (p342; near St Ives)
> - **Fistral** (p343; Newquay)
> - **Holywell Bay** (p342; near Newquay)

Getting There & Away

National Express has direct buses to London (£41 economy return, seven hours, three daily), Exeter (£16.50, 3½ hours, two daily), Plymouth (£6, 1½ hours, four daily), Penzance (£5.50, 1¾ hours, three daily) and St Ives (£5.50, 1¼ hours, three daily).

There are four trains daily between Newquay and Par (£4.30 single, 45 minutes), on the main London–Penzance line.

AROUND NEWQUAY
Trerice

Escape the cultural void of Newquay at **Trerice** (NT; ☎ 01637-875404; admission £4.70; ☽ 11am-5.30pm Sun-Fri Jul-Sep; Sun, Mon, Wed-Fri Mar-Jun & Oct), a charming Elizabethan manor. Built in 1571, much of the structure and elaborate plasterwork is original, including the elaborate barrel-vaulted ceiling of the great chamber, and there is some fine oak and walnut furniture from the 17th and 18th centuries. An oddity is the lawnmower museum in the barn, with over 100 grass-cutters going back over a century.

Trerice is 3 miles southeast of Newquay. During summer, bus No 50 runs directly here several times a day.

PADSTOW
☎ 01841 / pop 2450

Gourmet capital of Cornwall, Padstow is a popular fishing village on the Camel estuary, famous for its **May Day Festival** (see the boxed text p346). There are some wonderful stone cottages, a pretty harbour and some excellent accommodation, although these days TV chef Rick Stein has the place pretty much sewn up – the town is often known these days by its alternative name of 'Pad-stein'.

The **TIC** (☎ 533449; www.padstowlive.com; North Quay; ☽ 9.30am-5pm Mon-Sat & 9.30am-4pm Sun Easter-Oct, 9am-4pm Mon-Fri & 9am-noon Sat Nov-Easter) charges £3 to book accommodation.

MY KINGDOM FOR AN OSS

Padstow's raucous May Day fertility rite, featuring the fabled Obby Oss (hobby horse), may be the oldest such event in the country. The ritual begins just before midnight on 30 April, as villagers sing to the innkeeper at the Golden Lion with the news that summer is 'a-come'. Then, at 10am the next morning the Blue Ribbon Oss – a man garbed in a huge hooped sailcloth dress and wild-looking horse headdress – dances around the town, grabbing any woman close enough and daubing her with coal (or, often, pinching her – it's believed to aid childbearing!). He's followed at 11am by the Old Original (or Red) Oss and the madness continues until late.

Above the village is **Prideaux Place** (☎ 532 411; admission £6; ☼ 12.30-4pm Sun-Thu Easter Sun–mid-Apr & mid-May–Oct), a lavish manor house built in 1592 by the Prideaux-Brune family (who still reside here), purportedly descendants of William the Conqueror. Its grand plasterwork ceilings and stately grandeur have been used as the setting for numerous period dramas.

The **Camel Trail** is a disused railway line, and now makes one of Cornwall's most popular cycling tracks. The trail starts in Padstow and runs east through Wadebridge (5¾ miles), Bodmin (11 miles) and beyond. Bicycles can be hired from **Padstow Cycle Hire** (☎ 533533; South Quay; ☼ 9am-5pm) for around £8 per day and **Brinhams** (☎ 532594; South Quay; ☼ 9am-5pm) for a similar price.

Sleeping

Treyarnon Bay YHA Hostel (☎ 0870 770 6076; Tregonnan; dm £11.80; P ☒) A refurbished hostel and café in a fantastic headland position above Treyarnon Bay, 4½ miles west of Padstow. Bus No 55 from Padstow stops at nearby Constantine.

Althea Library (☎ 532717; www.althealibrary.co.uk; 27 High St; d £64-72; P ☒) A delightful, listed cottage offering vegan and vegetarian breakfasts. Choose from three colour-themed rooms (green, yellow or ivory), all with large beds and pine furniture, and relax in the gorgeous A-framed lounge.

St Petroc's Hotel & Bistro (☎ 532700; www.rickstein .com; 4 New St; mains £13.50-14.50; d £110-180; P ☒)

Boutique chic hits Padstow at this beautifully converted town house, part of the Rick Stein stable. Behind the neatly clipped hedges and clematis-covered front of the whitewashed house, you'll find a range of smart, contemporary rooms, complete with designer bedding and wrought-iron bedsteads.

Tregea Hotel (☎ 532455; www.tregea.co.uk; 16-18 High St; d £82-98; P ☒) This ivy-clad hotel is another excellent choice, with warm-toned bedrooms and a designer lounge and dining room.

Dennis Cove Camping (☎ 532349; sites £10-14; ☼ May-Sep) A small, well-appointed site overlooking the estuary.

Eating

The Seafood Restaurant (☎ 532700; www.rickstein .com; Riverside; mains £16.50-28; ☼ lunch & dinner) There's no denying the calibre of the cuisine at Rick Stein's sleek flagship restaurant – undoubtedly among the best in Britain – but his fame ensures you'll need to book months in advance.

Rick Stein's Café (☎ 532700; Middle St; mains £8-14; ☼ closed Sun) A stripped-down version of the Seafood's menu is available at this bistro – various concoctions of fish, steak, chicken and salads are all on the daily-changing menu.

Stein's Fish & Chips (South Quay; mains £4-8; ☼ noon-2.30pm & 5-9pm Mon-Tue & Thu-Sat, noon-6pm Sun) If all else fails, you can always try the latest addition to the Stein menu – an upmarket fish-and-chip shop down by the quay.

Also recommended:

London Inn (☎ 532554; 6/8 Lanadwell St; mains £6-13) Cosy local with good Cornish beers and daily fish specials.

Rojano's (☎ 532796; 9 Mill Sq; mains £5-10; ☼ lunch & dinner Tue-Sun) Bright, buzzy pizza and pasta joint with outside tables.

Getting There & Away

Bus No 55 runs to Bodmin Parkway (50 minutes) and the Eden Project (1½ hours) hourly till 6pm. Bus No 555 goes to Truro (1¾ hours, four daily Monday to Saturday), while bus No 556 serves Newquay (1¼ hours, five daily Monday to Saturday, four Sunday).

PORT ISAAC

A steep-sided cove and natural harbour gives Port Isaac picture-postcard looks. The old village has several welcoming pubs and

DEVON & CORNWALL

galleries, but it's far from overrun by tourists so well worth a stop.

The Old School Hotel & Restaurant (☎ 01208-880721; oldsch.hotel@eclipse.co.uk; Fore St; s £35-45, d £70-90; **P** **⊠**) A beautifully converted schoolhouse overlooking the harbour, with fine sea-view rooms decorated using bold primary colours; the cheery restaurant has local art on the walls and serves excellent seafood, as well as vegetarian and meat dishes.

TINTAGEL
☎ 01840

The mostly modern village of Tintagel sprawls inland from the cliff tops and has little to offer beyond chintzy tearooms, souvenir shops and day-trippers. The real attraction lies closer to the coast. The ruins of **Tintagel Castle** (EH; ☎ 770328; admission £3.70; ⓨ 10am-6pm Apr-Sep, 10am-5pm Oct, 10am-4pm Nov-Mar) are scattered across the rocky cliffs around Tintagel Head, reached down a steep track from the village. The present-day ruins mostly date from the 13th century, but were built on the site of a much earlier fortress – local legend has it that this was the birthplace of King Arthur. Whatever the truth of the legend, the views from the castle and cliff tops are stunning so don't miss them. Part of the stronghold stands on a rock tower cut off from the mainland, accessed via a bridge and steep steps; bring a head for heights.

Back in the village, the **Old Post Office** (NT; ☎ 770024; Fore St; admission £2.40; ⓨ 11am-5.30pm Apr-Sep, 11am-4pm Oct) is a fascinating 14th-century manor house that served as a post office in the 19th century.

The **TIC** (☎ 779084; tintagelvc@btconnect.com; Bossiney Rd; ⓨ 10am-5pm Mar-Oct, 10.30am-4pm Nov-Feb) has small exhibits exploring local history and the Arthur legend.

Sleeping & Eating
Tintagel YHA Hostel (☎ 0870 770 6068; tintagel@yha .org.uk; Dunderhole Point; dm £10.60; ⓨ Mar-Oct) A tiny whitewashed cottage in a spectacular cliff-top setting on the South West Coast Path, three-quarters of a mile south of the village.

The Old Borough House (☎ 770475; www.tintagel hotel.co.uk; Bossiney Rd; d £70-78; **P** **⊠**) A beautiful ivy-clad 16th-century Cornish mansion, once owned by JB Priestley, with wonderfully converted rooms making use of the original ceiling beams and exposed stone-

work. The more expensive rooms have fine views and private sitting rooms.

Ye Olde Malthouse Inn (☎ 770461; d £46-50; **P** **⊠**) A 14th-century slate-roofed pub with good Cornish beer and bar food.

The Old Millfloor (☎ 770234; Trebarwith Strand; d £50; **P** **⊠**) Delightful 17th-century mill cottage in a brookside dell, 3 miles west of Tintagel.

Getting There & Away
Bus No 122/124 runs from Wadebridge (1¼ hours, eight daily Monday to Friday) and No X10 comes from Exeter (2¼ hours, four daily Monday to Saturday); both go on to Boscastle (10 minutes).

BOSCASTLE
☎ 01840

The natural harbour that made Boscastle a suitable fishing port and a thriving smuggling centre now attracts visitors in droves. The **harbour wall** dates from 1584 and was built on the orders of Sir Richard Grenville, captain of Elizabeth I's ship *The Revenge*. It's worth hunting out **Minster Church**, in a wonderful wooded valley about a mile southeast of the visitor centre.

In August 2004, just after this guide was researched, Boscastle was hit by the worst floods in living memory, and sustained millions of pounds worth of damage. As a result, many of the places listed here may be closed or have limited hours until at least summer 2005, so phone ahead.

The **visitor centre** (☎ 250010; visitorcentre@bos castle.demon.co.uk; Cobweb Inn Car Park; ⓨ 10am-5pm Mar-Oct) houses a small local history exhibition.

The **Museum of Witchcraft** (☎ 250111; The Harbour; admission £2; ⓨ 10.30am-5.30pm Mon-Sat, noon-5.30pm Sun) is a fascinating and informative glimpse into the world of Wicca and associated beliefs. Its bizarre collection of artefacts includes witches' costumes, altars and cauldrons and a brass 'Hand of Fatima' to ward off the evil eye.

Boscastle Harbour YHA Hostel (☎ 0870 770 5710; boscastle@yha.org.uk; dm £10.60; ⓨ Apr-Sep) is a beautiful hostel housed in the old harbour stables, and its perfect portside location means it's got some of the best views in town

Affectionately known as The Welly, the grand turreted **Wellington Hotel** (☎ 250202; www.boscastle-wellington.com; The Harbour; d £70-110; **P** **⊠**) is one of the oldest establishments

SOMETHING SPECIAL

The Old Rectory (☎ 250225; www.stjuliot .com; St Juliot; d from £52; P ✗ ; ☿ Mar-Nov) This charming detached house once belonged to the local vicar of St Juliot; it was also the house where Thomas Hardy stayed as a young architect and fell in love with his future wife, Emma Lavinia Gifford. Beautifully refurbished with Victorian antiques and period furnishings, and set in three acres of private gardens, B&Bs just don't get much more romantic.

From Boscastle, take the B3263 road towards Bude and follow the signposts towards St Juliot. You'll need your own car as there is no public transport.

in Boscastle. The fine country rooms and homely public bars have entertained a number of guests down the years, including Thomas Hardy and Guy Gibson (of the Dambusters).

If you want B&Bs, the snug **Old Coach House** (☎ 250398; www.old-coach.co.uk; Tintagel Rd; s £30, d £40-48; P ✗) occupies a network of old coach-houses at the top of the village, while in the centre of Boscastle is the large **Riverside Hotel** (☎ 250216; d from £40; P ✗), with extra accommodation in Bridge House across the street.

BODMIN MOOR

Cornwall's 'roof' is a high heath pockmarked with bogs and high tors, including Brown Willy (419m) and Rough Tor (400m). It's a desolate place that works on the imagination; the Beast of Bodmin, a large black catlike creature, has been seen regularly for many years. The murder of Charlotte Dymond in 1844 is another story that's still discussed; you can participate in a recreation of the trial of her alleged killer, Matthew Weeks, at **Bodmin Shire Hall** (☎ 01208-76616; Mount Folly; admission £3; ☿ 11am-3pm Mon-Sat).

Bodmin TIC (☎ 01208-76616; www.bodminlive .com; Mount Folly; ☿ 10am-5pm Mon-Sat) has leaflets on exploring the moor; the small **Town Museum** (☎ 01208-77067; Mount Folly; admission free; ☿ 10.30am-4.30pm Mon-Sat Apr-Sep) is opposite. The bizarre **Bodmin Jail** (☎ 01208-76292; Berrycombe Rd; admission £4; ☿ 10am-6pm Mon-Fri & Sun, 11am-6pm Sat) exhibition is in the 18th-century

county prison; its tales of true crimes of old are amateurish but strangely enthralling.

The A30 cuts across the centre of the moor from **Launceston**, which has a ruined 11th-century **castle** (EH; ☎ 01566-772365; admission £2; ☿ 10am-6pm Jul & Aug, 10am-5pm Apr-Jun & Sep, 10am-4pm Oct), and a granite **church** with extensive carvings.

Jamaica Inn (☎ 01566-86250; www.jamaicainn .co.uk; s/d £40/60; P ✗), out on the desolate Bodmin Moor near Bolventor, was made famous by Daphne du Maurier's novel. On a misty winter's night the place still feels hugely atmospheric; the inn also contains a small smuggling museum and a room devoted to du Maurier.

About a mile south is **Dozmary Pool**, said to have been where Arthur's sword, Excalibur, was thrown after his death. It's a 4-mile walk northwest of Jamaica Inn to Brown Willy.

Bodmin has bus connections with St Austell (No 29, one hour, hourly Monday to Saturday), as well as Bodmin Parkway (No 56, 15 minutes, hourly Monday to Saturday), a station on the London to Penzance line. Bus No 76/X76 runs from Launceston to Plymouth (1½ hours, hourly Monday to Saturday).

BUDE
☎ 01288 / pop 5980

Just this side of the Cornwall–Devon border, Bude is a popular bucket-and-spade resort with great surf. Crooklets Beach is the main surfing area, just north of town. Nearby Sandymouth is good for beginners, and Duckpool is also popular. Summerleaze, in the centre of Bude, is a family beach.

Bude Visitor Centre (☎ 354240; www.visitbude .info; The Crescent; ☿ 10am-5pm Mon-Sat, plus 10am-4pm Sun in summer) is a little way south of the town centre.

There are plenty of surf schools; try **Outdoor Adventure** (☎ 361312; www.outdooradventure .co.uk; Atlantic Court; per half/full day lesson £16/30).

Fairway House (☎ 355059; www.fairwayguest house.co.uk; 8 Downs View; d £40-50; P ✗) One of the best B&Bs in Bude, a Victorian terraced house near the town centre, with comfortable rooms (all named after famous golf courses) and quilted bedspreads.

Life's a Beach (☎ 355222; Summerleaze Beach; mains £5-16; ☿ Mon-Sat) is a beachside café which transforms from a snack stop to a snazzy seafood bistro at night, while **JJ's Bar** (☎ 352555; The Headland) is a popular pub on the headland behind Summerleaze Beach.

National Express coaches run from Exeter (£7.80 economy return, 1¾ hours, five daily), as does local bus No X9 (two hours, six daily).

ISLES OF SCILLY
☎ 01720

Legend has it that the Isles of Scilly, 28 miles southwest of mainland Cornwall, are the last remains of the fabled lost lands of Lyonesse. Whatever the truth of the legend, there's no doubt that the islands seem rooted in another age. Of the 140 islands, only five are inhabited: St Mary's is by far the largest and busiest island, closely followed by Tresco, while Bryher, St Martin's and St Agnes are home to tiny resident populations. Traditional crafts such as fishing, farming and flower growing are still important local industries, though tourism has become the islands' main source of income, and it's not hard to see what keeps drawing the holiday-makers back year after

year: broad, sandy beaches, sparkling bays and hidden inlets, rugged coastal scenery, world-class gardens, excellent diving, and a unique community atmosphere. With few roads, few residents and even fewer cars, the Scilly Islands is a place where it's truly possible to escape from the hustle and bustle of the outside world.

Information

The **Isles of Scilly Tourist Board** (☎ 422536; tic@scilly.gov.uk; Hugh Town, St Mary's; ⏰ 8.30am-5.30pm Mon-Thu, 8.30am-5pm Fri & Sat Easter-Oct, plus 10am-noon Sun Jun-Sep; closes noon Sat Nov-Dec, closed all day Sat & Sun Jan-Easter) is on St Mary's. The *Standard Guidebook, Isles of Scilly* (£3) is a good fold-out map with explanatory text.

You can find background information at www.scillyonline.co.uk, while the TIC website (www.simplyscilly.co.uk) helps with accommodation listings.

Accommodation should be booked well in advance. Many places close between November and May. All the islands, except Tresco, have a simple, reasonable campsite. There are plenty of self-catering options; the

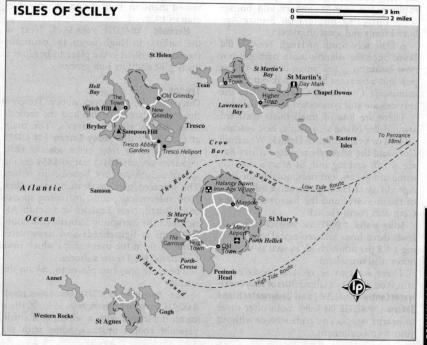

biggest operator is **Island Properties** (☎ 422211; www .isles-ofscilly.co.uk/island-properties.html), whose flats start at around £200 per week. Every Friday evening you can watch gig racing, with traditional six-oar boats (some over 100 years old) originally used to race out to wrecked ships.

St Mary's

The largest island in the chain, and the most populated, St Mary's is the first port of call for most visitors, as it's the point of arrival for the *Scillonian* ferry and flights from the mainland. With miles of breathtaking coastline, secluded beaches and bays, and many fine walking trails, it's little wonder that St Mary's gets crowded in summer; like the rest of the Scillys, the best time to visit is in spring or autumn, when the high season holiday-makers have left for home.

About a mile south of the airport is the main settlement of **Hugh Town**, where you'll find most of the island's hotels and guesthouses, and the **Isles of Scilly Museum** (☎ 422337; Church St; adult/child £2/50p; ◐ 10am-noon & 1.30-4.30pm Mon-Sat, plus 7.30-9pm Mon, Tue & Thu-Sat May-Sep, 2-4pm Wed Oct-Apr, or by arrangement) which explores the islands' history and houses some intriguing displays on Bronze Age burial finds and local shipwrecks.

A little way south of Hugh Town is **Old Town**, once the island's main harbour, but now home to a few small cafés, a village pub and a pleasant beach. Look out for the minuscule Old Town Church, where the services are still conducted by candlelight.

There are lots of small inlets scattered around the island's coastline, best reached on foot or by bike: Porth Hellick, Watermill Cove and the relatively remote Pelistry Bay are worth seeking out. St Mary's also has some unique ancient sites, notably the Iron Age village at Halangy Down, a mile north of Hugh Town, and the barrows at Bant's Carn and Porth Hellick.

Scilly Walks (☎ 423326; www.scillywalks.co.uk) leads three-hour archaeological tours, costing £4/2 per adult/child, as well as visits to other offshore islands.

There are two accredited diving operations on St Mary's island: **Isles of Scilly Underwater Centre** (☎ 422595) and **Underwater Island Safaris** (☎ 422732; Old Town). Both offer dives to nearby wrecks and reefs with or without your own equipment.

SLEEPING & EATING

Campsite (☎ 422670; tedmoulson@cs.com; Tower Cottage, Garrison Farm; tent sites £4.50-8) West of Hugh Town.

Evergreen Cottage (☎ 422711; The Parade; d £45-60) A charming 300-year-old sea captain's cottage, complete with whitewashed cob walls, slate roof and small, cosy rooms.

The Wheelhouse (☎ 422719; Porthcressa; s £33.50-39.50, d £77-79; ✗) This smart B&B is an excellent base from which to explore the rest of the island. The spacious rooms and brilliant location near Porthcressa Beach make it very popular, so you'll need to book ahead.

Star Castle Hotel (☎ 422317; www.star-castle .co.uk; The Garrison; d £98-260; ✗ ⊠) Built as part of a fort in 1593, this is now St Mary's top hotel, boasting quirky rooms, solid granite walls and elegant furnishings, as well as two award-winning restaurants, tennis courts and a heated swimming pool.

Wingletang (☎ 422381; The Parade; s/d £37/74; ◐ May-Oct; ✗) A pretty, traditional granite house in the centre of Hugh Town.

St Mary's Hall Hotel (☎ 422316; www.stmarys hallhotel.co.uk; d £128-188; ✗) A stunningly refurbished mansion, built for an Italian nobleman in 1938.

Mermaid (☎ 422701; mains £6-10) Next to the harbour in Hugh Town, the nautically themed Mermaid is the place to head for a lively pint and fine pub grub.

Tresco

Once owned by Tavistock Abbey, Tresco is the second largest island, and the second-most visited after St Mary's. The main attraction is the **Abbey Garden** (☎ 424105; www.tresco.co.uk/the_abbey_garden; admission £8.50; ◐ 9.30am-4pm), first laid out in 1834 on the site of a 10th-century Benedictine abbey. The terraced gardens feature more than 5000 subtropical plants, including species from Brazil, New Zealand and South Africa, and the intriguing Valhalla collection, made up of figureheads and nameplates salvaged from the many ships which have foundered off Tresco's shores.

There are only two places to stay on the island.

The **New Inn** (☎ 422844; newinn@tresco.co.uk; d £82-115 depending on season; mains £6-16; ✗) is a comfortable pub with a selection of small, pleasant rooms upstairs, some with sea views over the Tresco channel and the nearby island of Bryher.

The swish **Island Hotel** (☎ 422883; island hotel@tresco.co.uk; half-board £117-283; 🛇 ✕ 🕿) occupies a stunning position overlooking Old Grimsby Sound. The bedrooms are spread across several wings, and most have sweeping views and luxurious interiors; the best have private balconies and access to the gardens and private beach.

Bryher & Samson

Home to approximately 70 people, Bryher is the smallest and wildest inhabited island in the Scillys. Much of the landscape is covered by rough bracken and heather, and the coast often takes the full force of the Atlantic weather; Hell Bay in a winter gale is a powerful sight. There are good views over the islands from the top of Watch Hill, and Rushy Bay is one of the finest beaches in the Scillys. From the quay, occasional boats visit local seal and bird colonies and deserted Samson Island, where abandoned settlers' cottages tell a story of hard subsistence living.

The **campsite** (☎ 422886; sites £4.50-8) is near the quay.

Hell Bay Hotel (☎ 422947; hellbay@aol.com; d £180-400; ✕ 🕿) is a beautiful hotel that consists entirely of upmarket, impeccably finished suites, most of which boast sleek, contemporary décor, en suite sitting rooms and private balconies.

St Martin's

The most northerly of the main islands, St Martin's is renowned for its beautiful beaches. The largest settlement is **Higher Town**, where you'll find a small village shop and the **Isles of Scilly Dive School** (☎ 422848; www .scillydiving.com; Higher Tow-n; dives from £36). A short way to the west is **Lower Town**, home to a cluster of tightly huddled cottages and the island's only hotel.

There are several small art galleries scattered across the island, as well as a tiny vineyard and a flower farm.

On the island's southern shore is Lawrence's Bay, which reveals a broad sweep of sandy flats at low tide. Along the northern side is Great Bay, arguably the finest beach in the Scillys; from the western end, you can cross to White Island at low tide. If you walk east along the windswept northern cliffs you'll find the Day Mark, a red-and-white candy-striped landmark which was built back in 1687, and the secluded cove of Perpitch.

The **campsite** (☎ 422888; chris@stmartinscampsite freeserve.co.uk; Middle Town; tent sites £4-8) is near Lawrence's Bay at the western end of the island.

Polreath (☎ 422046; Higher Town; s £40-50, d £70-90; ✕) is a traditional cottage and one of the few B&Bs on the island. Rooms are snug and cosy, and it's handy for the island bakery and post office.

St Martin's on the Isle (☎ 422090; www.stmartins hotel.co.uk; d £115-215; ✕ 🕿) is the only hotel on St Martin's, and arguably one of the best in the Scillys, with landscaped grounds, an indoor swimming pool and a private quay. The 30 bedrooms have a choice of sea or garden views, and there are several upmarket suites with private sitting rooms. The in-house restaurant is renowned throughout the islands.

St Agnes

England's most southerly community somehow transcends even the tranquillity of the other islands in the Isles of Scilly; it's an ideal spot to stroll, unwind and reflect, with lots of cloistered coves, coastal walks and even a scattering of prehistoric sites. Visitors disembark at **Porth Conger**, near the decommissioned **Old Lighthouse**, which is indeed one of the oldest lighthouses in the country. Other points of interest include the tiny **Troy Town Maze**, and the historic inlets of Periglis Cove and St Warna's Cove (dedicated to the patron saint of shipwrecks). At low tide you can cross over to the island of **Gugh**, where you'll find some intriguing Bronze Age remains as well as standing stones.

The **campsite** (☎ 422360; Troy Town Farm; tent sites £4-8) is at the southwestern corner of the island.

The little stone-walled **Covean Cottage** (☎ 422620; d £23.50-30.50) is the perfect location for getting away from the crowds; it offers four pleasant, good-value rooms and serves excellent cream teas, light meals and sticky treats during the day.

The most southwesterly pub in all of Britain, the **Turk's Head** (☎ 422434; mains £6-10) is a real treat, with fine views, excellent beers, good pub grub and a hearty island atmosphere.

DEVON & CORNWALL

Getting There & Away

There's no transport to or from the islands on a Sunday.

AIR

The **Isles of Scilly Skybus** (☎ 0845 710 5555; www.ios-travel.co.uk) flies between St Mary's and Land's End (£108.50, 15 minutes) and Newquay (£125, 30 minutes) up to five times daily, Monday to Saturday year-round. Cheaper saver fares are available for travel from Monday to Friday after 3pm or before 11am. Flights also connect with Exeter (£119, 50 minutes) and Bristol (£245, 70 minutes).

British International (☎ 01736-363871; www.isleofscillyhelicopter.com) helicopters fly to St Mary's (20 minutes, 17 daily Monday to Saturday April to October, five daily Monday to Saturday November to March) and Tresco (20 minutes, six daily Monday to Saturday April to October, four daily November to March) from Penzance heliport. Adult/child return fares are £117/58.50. Cheaper short-break and day -return fares are also available. Parking costs £5 per day, and a minibus from Penzance train station connects with flights (£1.25 single, 10 minutes).

BOAT

The **Isles of Scilly Steamship** (☎ 0845 710 5555; www.ios-travel.co.uk) *Scillonian* sails between Penzance and St Mary's (£78 return, two hours 40 minutes, daily Monday to Saturday). Children under 12 are charged half the adult price.

Getting Around

Boats sail from St Mary's harbour daily in summer, several times daily to Tresco. A return trip to most offshore islands costs around £6.40, while a triangular return (eg St Mary's–Tresco–Bryher–St Mary's) costs around £8. Fares to the uninhabited islands vary but are usually between £6 and £8.

The **airport bus service** (£2.50) departs from The Strand in Hugh Town 40 minutes before each flight. A circular bus service runs around St Mary's several times daily in summer (£1 to all destinations). There are tours of St Mary's by vintage 1948 **bus** (☎ 422387; £5) or 1929 Riley open-top **car** (☎ 422479; per 2/3/4 people £15/20/22).

Bikes are available at **Buccabu Hire** (☎ 422 289; Porthcressa, Hugh Town; per day £6) and **Tresco Bicycle Hire** (☎ 422807; per day £8).

The Marches

Largely untouched by time or mass tourism, this beautiful strip of the country oozes an understated charm and a wonderful blend of Welsh and English character. The area has been shaped by centuries of ferocious fighting; life on the edge of England was punctuated by battles for control and autonomy, and its undulating hills are now littered with castles and ruins, testimony to the tension of times past.

Today the Marches is all rustic charm, and the unhurried pace of life offers a rewarding alternative to the beaten track. It's a region where the locals are genuinely glad to see you, and the rolling hills, lush farmland and simple pleasures of English country life make it excellent walking and cycling territory. To the south the meandering River Wye is ideal for canoeing.

On top of all this, the region is blessed with a wealth of absorbing attractions: Shropshire, the jewel in the Marches' crown, with its handsome Tudor capital, Shrewsbury; a fascinating industrial-heritage site at Ironbridge Gorge; a gourmet hub in historic Ludlow; and the pretty villages and placid peaks of the south Shropshire Hills. Further south, sleepy Herefordshire is home to some stunning scenery along the winding River Wye, plenty of water-based activities, a string of magnificent black-and-white villages and the marvellous medieval Mappa Mundi. Bordering onto the Cotswolds, serene Worcestershire is home to an impressive cathedral in its capital, the genteel Victorian resort of Great Malvern and the celebrated Malvern hills: an excellent spot to muddy your hiking boots.

HIGHLIGHTS

- Strolling around the atmospheric streetscapes of **Shrewsbury** (p371), England's most picturesque Tudor town

- Stepping back through time at **Ironbridge Gorge** (p375), the cradle of the Industrial Revolution

- Rambling through the gentle hills and tranquil valleys of Shropshire's **Long Mynd** (p380)

- Navigating the extraordinary 13th-century **Mappa Mundi** (p363) in Hereford

- Taking in the stunning views and water adventures on the River Wye at **Symonds Yat** (p369)

- Dining in style in the Marches' gourmet capital, **Ludlow** (p382)

★ Shrewsbury
Long Mynd ★ ★ Ironbridge Gorge

★ Ludlow

★ Hereford

★ Symonds Yat

■ POPULATION: 1 MILLION	■ AREA: 2541 SQ MILES

History

This region has seen territorial scuffles and all-out battles rage for centuries. These conflicts took place between feuding kingdoms along what is today the border separating England and Wales. In the 8th century the Anglo-Saxon king, Offa of Mercia, built an earthwork barricade along the border to try to quell the ongoing tension. It became known as Offa's Dyke, and much of it is still traceable as a popular walking route today.

In an effort to subdue the Welsh and secure his new kingdom, William the Conqueror set up powerful, feudal barons – called Lords Marcher after the Anglo-Saxon word *mearc,* meaning boundary – along the border, from where they repeatedly raided Wales, taking as much territory as possible under their control. Ten centuries have past since the Lords Marcher were instated – the counties of Shropshire, Herefordshire and Worcestershire are still known as the Marches.

Activities

The Marches region has areas perfect for gentle walking, cycling and other outdoor activities.There are hundreds of miles of paths and tracks here, snaking through pastoral idylls, wooded valleys and gentle hills.

This section provides a few ideas; see the Outdoor Activities chapter for more information.

CYCLING

Many parts of the Marches make good cycling country. Shropshire in particular is ideal for touring, and you can rent bikes in Shrewsbury, Church Stretton, Ludlow and Ledbury.

Areas that are suitable for off-road bike riding include the woods of Hopton near Ludlow, as well as Eastridge near Shrewsbury. High-level riding on the Long Mynd above Church Stretton can also be very rewarding.

In Herefordshire, you'll find the **Ledbury Loop** – a 17-mile rural circuit based which is around the town of Ledbury.

Cycling for Pleasure in the Marches, which is available from TIC tourist information offices, has comprehensive route maps and notes.

WALKING

The best-known long-distance walk in this region is **Offa's Dyke**, which is a 177-mile (285km) national trail that follows the ancient border defence. Running south–north from Chepstow to Prestatyn, it passes through some of the most spectacular scenery in Britain, but it's not for the inexperienced or unfit.

A more gentle option is the 107-mile (172km) **Wye Valley Walk**, which also starts in Chepstow and follows the course of the River Wye upstream to Rhayader in Wales. Yet another favourite is the 106-mile (170km) **Three Choirs Way** linking the cathedral cities of Hereford, Worcester and Gloucester.

Areas that are ideal for shorter walks include the Shropshire Hills, with the well-known ridges of Wenlock Edge (p379) and the lovely Long Mynd (p380). These are all taken in by the 136-mile (218km) **Shropshire Way**, which loops from Shrewsbury south to Ludlow.

The region's other main walking area is the **Malvern Hills** (see p361), which straddle the boundary between Worcestershire and Herefordshire, offering easy paths and breathtaking views.

OTHER ACTIVITIES

Symonds Yat on the River Wye makes a perfect base for canoeing (either easy-grade whitewater, or longer river trips), while rocky buttresses above the river mean rock climbing is also popular. Farther north the Long Mynd is a renowned area for gliding and paragliding.

Getting Around

Without your own transport, getting around the Marches can be infuriating. Exploring rural attractions needs time, planning and patience. TICs stock timetables for most rural routes or call **Traveline** (☎ 0870 608 2608; www.traveline.org.uk).

Railway lines radiate from the Shrewsbury, Hereford and Worcester, but they only serve the largest towns.

The main bus operators are:

Arriva (☎ 08701 201088) An Arriva day ticket (£3.75) gives one day of unlimited travel.

First Travel (☎ 01905-359393) A First Tourist ticket (adult/child £4.60/3.10) offers the same deal on the First network.

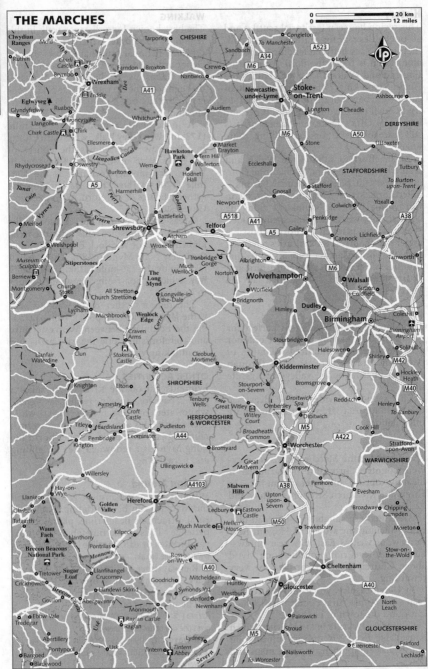

THE MARCHES

WALKING

| 0 | | 20 km |
| 0 | | 12 miles |

Clwydian Ranges · Buckley · Tarporley · CHESHIRE · Congleton · To Manchester · A523 · To Manchester
Mold · Sandbach · Leek
Ruthin · Chirk Castle · Llay · Farndon · Broxton · Crewe · M6 · A34
Brymbo · Wrexham · Nantwich · Newcastle-under-Lyme · Stoke-on-Trent · Ashbourne
Eglwyseg · Ruabon · Erddig · Whitchurch · Audlem · Longton · Cheadle · DERBYSHIRE
Glyndyfrdwy · Pontcysyllte · Dee · Market Drayton · Eccleshall · Stone · A50 · Uttoxeter
Llangollen · Chirk Castle · Chirk · Ellesmere · Llangollen Canal · Wem · Hawkstone Park · Tern Hill · Wollerton · Hodnet Hall · STAFFORDSHIRE · Tutbury · A38
Rhydycroesau · Oswestry · Burlton · Harmerhill · Roden · Newport · Gnosall · Stafford · Penkridge · Colwich · Yoxall · To Burton-upon-Trent
Tanat · Cain · A5 · Perry · Battlefield · Severn · A518 · Telford · A41 · A5 · Gailey · Cannock · Lichfield
Welshpool · Shrewsbury · Atcham · Wroxeter · Ironbridge Gorge · Albrighton · Wolverhampton · M6 · Walsall · Tamworth
Museum of Sculpture · Stiperstones · The Long Mynd · Much Wenlock · Norton · Worfield · Himley · Dudley · Sutton Coldfield · Coleshill
Berriew · Montgomery · Church Stoke · All Stretton · Church Stretton · Longville-in-the-Dale · Bridgnorth · Birmingham · Birmingham Airport
Lydham · Marshbrook · Wenlock Edge · Stourbridge · Halesowen · Shirley · Solihull · M42
Llanfair Waterdine · Clun · Craven Arms · Corve · Cleobury Mortimer · Bewdley · Kidderminster · Hockley Heath · M40
Knighton · Elton · Stokesay Castle · Ludlow · SHROPSHIRE · Stourport-on-Severn · Bromsgrove · Redditch · Henley · To Banbury
Aymestry · Croft Castle · Tenbury Wells · Great Witley · Droitwich Spa · Cook Hill
Titley · Eardisland · Pudleston · HEREFORDSHIRE & WORCESTER · Witley Court · Ombersley · Droitwich · A422 · Stratford-upon-Avon
Pembridge · Leominster · A44 · Broadheath Common · M5 · WARWICKSHIRE
Kington · Bromyard · Worcester
Willersley · Ullingswick · Great Malvern · Kempsey · Pershore · Evesham
Hay-on-Wye · Dorstone · A4103 · Malvern Hills · Upton-upon-Severn · A38 · Broadway · Chipping Campden
Llanigon · Golden Valley · Hereford · Ledbury · Eastnor Castle · M50 · Moreton
Clasbury · Talgarth · Kilpeck · Much Marcle · Hellen's House · Tewkesbury · Stow-on-the-Wold
Waun Fach · Llanthony · Pontrilas · Monnow · Ross-on-Wye · Wye · Cheltenham · A40
Brecon Beacons National Park · Tretower · Sugar Loaf · Llanfihangel Crucorney · Goodrich · Mitcheldean · Huntley · Gloucester · A40 · North Leach
Crickhowell · Govilon · Llandewi Skirrid · Symonds Yat · Cinderford · Westbury · Newnham · GLOUCESTERSHIRE
Abergavenny · Monmouth · Painswick
Ebbw Vale · Brecon Canal · Usk · Raglan Castle · Raglan · Fairford
Tredegar · Lydney · M5 · Stroud · Cirencester · Lechlade
Abertillery · Pontypool · Tintern · Tintern Abbey · Severn · Nailsworth
Bargoed · Blackwood · Usk · To Worcester

WORCESTERSHIRE

Lush, rolling hills with serious walking potential embrace the rural idyll of little England in south and west Worcestershire. Fringed by the Cotswolds and Malvern Hills, the area is riddled with waterways and attractive riverside market towns. Plonked right in the centre is the regional capital, Worcester, with a magnificent cathedral and some beautiful Elizabethan and Tudor architecture. The flat plains of the north and east of the county blend seamlessly into the industrial Midlands and offer little in the way of attractions.

Information

For online county-wide information try www.worcestershire-tourism.co.uk.

Activities

The **Severn Way** walking route winds its way through Worcestershire, passing through Worcester and Upton-upon-Severn, while the **Three Choirs Way** links Worcester to Hereford and Gloucester.

Cyclists should pick up the handy leaflet *Elgar Ride Variations* (35p) from TICs. It has a choice of routes around the Malverns.

Getting Around

Regular rail links are thin on the ground. Kidderminster is the southern railhead of the popular Severn Valley Railway.

The **Wye Valley Wanderer** (☎ 01432-260948) links Pershore and Worcester with Ledbury, Ross-on-Wye and Hereford on summer Sundays and bank-holiday Mondays.

WORCESTER

☎ 01905 / pop 94,050

On first glance Worcester (*woos*-ter) is a disappointment, with modern architectural blunders overshadowing the city's finer buildings and its disjointed structure creating a soulless city centre. However, if you scratch under the surface you'll find some gorgeous Tudor and Georgian architecture, a magnificent cathedral and the factory works of the world-renowned Royal Worcester Porcelain.

Information

The **TIC** (☎ 726311; www.cityofworcester.gov.uk; Guildhall, High St; ☻ 9.30am-5pm Mon-Sat) will organise

walking tours (adult £3; 1½ hrs; ☻ 11am Mon-Fri, 2.30pm Wed, May-Sep).

Sights

WORCESTER CATHEDRAL

Dominating the centre of the city, **Worcester Cathedral** (☎ 28854; www.worcestercathedral.org.uk; requested donation £3; ☻ 7.30am-6pm) encapsulates a medley of different styles displaying renovators' skills down through the ages. Begun in 1084 by Bishop – later Saint – Wulfstan, the cathedral boasts the largest Norman crypt in the country and a beautiful choir and lady chapel in 13th-century Early English style. Other highlights include an impressive 12th-century circular chapterhouse, one of the first of its kind, and some splendid Victorian stained glass.

King John of Magna Carta fame, whose treachery towards his brother Richard left the country in turmoil at his death, is buried in the choir (apart from his thumb, which was nicked as a souvenir). Knowing he stood only the flimsiest chance of making it through the Pearly Gates, the dying king asked to be buried disguised as a monk.

If you're fit and fond of a view, there are tours up the 249 steps (60m) of the tower for £1.50. To really appreciate the splendour of the cathedral come for evensong; it's held at 5.30pm Monday to Wednesday, Friday and Saturday, and at 4pm Sunday.

COMMANDERY CIVIL WAR CENTRE

Not far from the cathedral, the **Commandery** (☎ 361821; www.worcestercitymuseums.org.uk; admission adult/child £3.95/2.95; ☻ 10am-5pm Mon-Sat, 1.30-5pm Sun) is a splendid Tudor building currently undergoing a major overhaul. Improvements to the building, new exhibits and restoration of the painted chamber which contains important frescoes from the 15th century should be complete by 2006. Meanwhile, the exhibits detailing the ins and outs of the Civil War and battles in 17th-century England are still on view.

ROYAL WORCESTER PORCELAIN WORKS

In 1751 Dr John Warne and his buddies began making ornate bone china as a hobby; the result is the longest continuous production of any porcelain company in England. The firm was granted a royal warrant in 1789 and still supplies HRH with some of her preferred crockery.

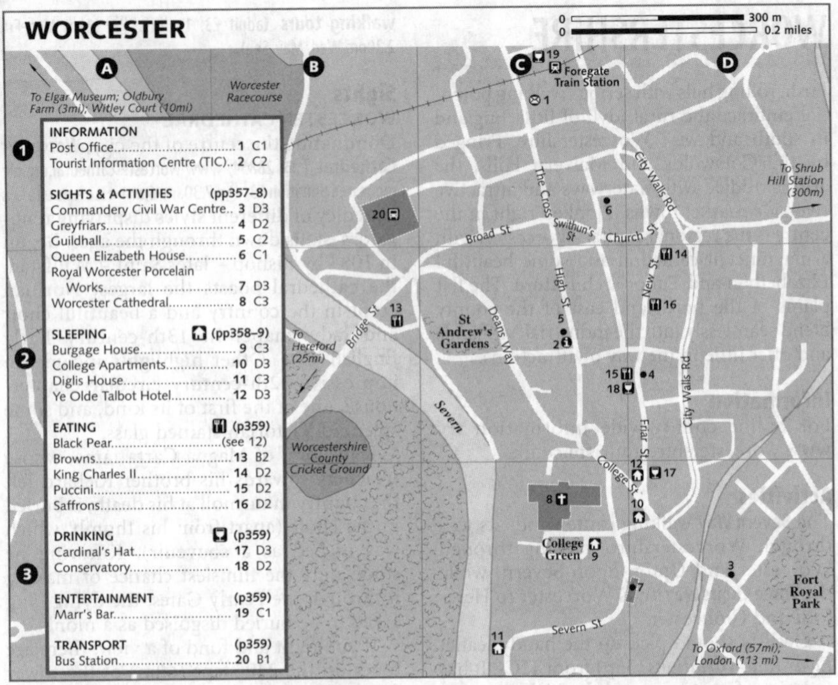
WORCESTER
0 300 m
0 0.2 miles
A
B
C
D
1
2
3
To Elgar Museum; Oldbury Farm (3mi); Witley Court (10mi)
Worcester Racecourse
Foregate Train Station
To Shrub Hill Station (300m)
The Cross
City Walls Rd
Broad St
Swithun's St
Church St
New St
High St
St Andrew's Gardens
Deans Way
Bridge St
To Hereford (25mi)
Severn
Worcestershire County Cricket Ground
Friar St
College St
College Green
Fort Royal Park
Severn St
To Oxford (57mi); London (113 mi)
INFORMATION
Post Office 1 C1
Tourist Information Centre (TIC) 2 C2
SIGHTS & ACTIVITIES (pp357–8)
Commandery Civil War Centre 3 D3
Greyfriars 4 D2
Guildhall 5 C2
Queen Elizabeth House 6 C1
Royal Worcester Porcelain Works 7 D3
Worcester Cathedral 8 C3
SLEEPING (pp358–9)
Burgage House 9 C3
College Apartments 10 D3
Diglis House 11 C3
Ye Olde Talbot Hotel 12 D3
EATING (p359)
Black Pear (see 12)
Browns 13 B2
King Charles II 14 D2
Puccini 15 D2
Saffrons 16 D2
DRINKING (p359)
Cardinal's Hat 17 D3
Conservatory 18 D2
ENTERTAINMENT (p359)
Marr's Bar 19 C1
TRANSPORT (p359)
Bus Station 20 B1

The **Royal Worcester Porcelain Works** (☎ 746 000; www.royal-worcester.co.uk; Severn St; factory tours £5; 9am-5.30pm Mon-Sat, 11am-5pm Sun) has an entire visitor complex, with tours, shops, a restaurant and a museum.

The **visitor centre** (admission adult/child £2.25/1.75) gives you an impression of a 19th-century potter's life and details the history of the company, while the **museum** (admission adult/child £3/2.25; 9.30am-5pm Mon-Fri, 10am-5pm Sat) tells the factory's story through an intricate and extravagant collection of works, from the company's very first pieces to its most recent creations. A ticket for everything costs £8/6.75 per adult/child, a significant saving if you're a real fan.

HISTORICAL PROPERTIES

For an impression of what Worcester looked like before modern planners got their filthy paws on it, stroll down New St and Friar St, both flanked by fine Tudor and Elizabethan buildings.

Built in 1480, **Greyfriars** (NT; ☎ 23571; Friar St; admission £3.20; 1-5pm Wed-Sat Apr-Oct) is an attractively restored, timber-framed Tudor merchant house, full of textiles and furnishings, with a pretty walled garden.

The splendid **Guildhall** (High St) is a Queen Anne building of 1722, designed by Thomas White, a pupil of Sir Christopher Wren, who died in poverty after the city dragged its heels on paying him his dues. The period decoration inside is exceptional.

Originally a hospital almshouse, **Queen Elizabeth House** (The Trinity) is a beautiful 15th-century galleried timber-framed building. Local legend claims that Queen Elizabeth I addressed the people of Worcester from the balcony in 1575.

Sleeping

Lodgings in Worcester can be hard to come by midweek – there's a fairly grim bunch of B&Bs on Barbourne Rd if you're stuck.

Burgage House (☎ 25396; 4 College Precincts; s/d £30/50; ☒) Far and away the best B&B in town, this lovely place on a quiet cobbled street has huge and comfortable rooms with bath or shower. The front rooms have great views of the cathedral and children are very welcome.

Oldbury Farm (☎ 421357; Lower Broadheath; s/d £30/50) An elegant Georgian farmhouse with fishing rights and stables, this quiet option has beautiful country-style rooms with light colours and rustic furnishings. There are lovely views of the surrounding hills and easy access to local walking routes. Oldbury Farm is next to Elgar's birthplace (see p360), about 3 miles out of town.

Ye Olde Talbot Hotel (☎ 23573 www.yeoldetalbot hotel.tablesir.com; Friar St; s/d £70/86; 🖳) One of the best-value options in town, the cosy rooms at this central hotel are tastefully decked out in warm colours, rich fabrics and a mix of antique and modern furniture. Each room features plenty of little gadgets including CD players and DVDs.

Other options:

Diglis House (☎ 353518; www.diglishousehotel.co.uk; Severn St; s/d £65/90; Ⓟ wheelchair access) A comfortable but old-fashioned place perched on the riverbank.

College Apartments (☎ 01886-822114; info@prima properties.co.uk; 26 College St; apt £75; ✖) Georgian townhouse apartments (sleeping four) with stylish modern décor in the heart of town.

Eating

Most of Worcester's best options for food are on Friar and New Sts.

Browns (☎ 26263; 24 Quay St; set lunch £20.50, set dinner £38.50; ⓨ closed Mon) Undoubtedly *the* best food in Worcester. The modern British delicacies are best eaten at a window table overlooking the river at this elegant converted cornmill.

Black Pear (☎ 23573; Friar St; mains £7-13; ⓨ lunch & dinner) Good-quality bistro-style pub grub ranging from steaks and salads to some more adventurous Mediterranean and Asian fare is served at this low-ceilinged place with modern furniture and deep leather chairs.

Saffrons (☎ 610505; 15 New St; meals £14-16; ⓨ lunch & dinner) Scarlet walls and wooden tables give this bright colourful bistro a cheerful and relaxed atmosphere. The modern British food is confidently put together and beautifully presented but gloriously free from airs and graces.

Other possibilities:

King Charles II (☎ 22449; 29 New St; mains £9.50-14; ⓨ lunch & dinner) An atmospheric olde worlde place with good continental cuisine.

Puccini (☎ 27770; 12 Friar St; mains £6-7; ⓨ lunch & dinner) Rustic Italian with red gingham cloths and decent pizza and pasta.

Drinking

Cardinal's Hat (☎ 22066; 31 Friar St) A Worcester institution, this atmospheric old half-timbered place has been round almost as long as the cathedral. It's pretty snug inside and serves a selection of Austrian beers in traditional steins and flutes and a choice of Austrian food at lunchtime.

Conservatory (☎ 26929; Friar St) A modern minimalist café bar with a relaxed atmosphere and down-to-earth crowd, the Conservatory is equally good for a mid-afternoon coffee or a civilised night on the town.

Entertainment

Marr's Bar (☎ 613336; 12 Pierpoint St) A former dance studio turned live-music venue, this popular place has sprung floors and gigs almost every night making it a perfect spot to dance your socks off. Bands range from hard rock to world music; check in advance.

If sport is more your thing you can catch spring and summer racing festivals at the **Worcester Racecourse** (☎ 0870 220 2772), while the central **Worcestershire County Cricket Ground** (☎ 748474) is a lovely spot to cheer on the chaps.

Getting There & Around

Worcester has two train stations but most services run to Worcester Foregate (the other station is Worcester Shrub Hill). Trains from here run roughly hourly to London Paddington (£25.80, 2¼ hours) and Hereford (£5.80, 40 minutes).

National Express has two coaches to London (£16.50, 3½ hours). Bus No 44 runs hourly to Great Malvern (35 minutes), bus No 372 goes to Gloucester (1½ hours) via Upton (40 minutes) every two hours, and bus No 417 goes to Ledbury (45 minutes, four daily Monday to Saturday).

Bikes can be hired from **Peddlers** (☎ 24238; 46 Barbourne Rd; per day/week £10/35).

A COTTAGE OF YOUR OWN

If you'd like to tour the countryside from your own base try these websites for self-catering properties:

Come Stay with Us (www.comestaywithus.com)
Cottage Breaks (www.cottage-breaks.co.uk)
Cottageguide (www.cottageguide.co.uk)
Vivat Trust (www.vivat.org.uk)

AROUND WORCESTER

Elgar Birthplace Museum

In 1857 a humble cottage 3 miles west of Worcester was the birthplace of England's greatest composer, and it now houses the **Elgar Museum** (☎ 01905-333224; www.elgarmuseum .org; Lower Broadheath; admission adult £4.50; ⌚ 11am-4.15pm). Elgar's gramophone, writing desk, musical manuscripts and various personal mementos are kept inside, while next door the **Elgar Centre** contains stacks more Elgar memorabilia and, more importantly, a place to listen to his music and appreciate what all the fuss is about.

Bus Nos 311 and 317 go from Worcester to Broadheath Common, a short walk away from the museum (15 minutes, three times Monday to Saturday).

Witley Court

Arguably the most venerable and romantic ruin in England, **Witley Court** (EH; ☎ 01299-896636; Great Witley; admission adult £4.90; ⌚ 10am-5pm Mar-Oct, 10am-4pm Thu-Mon Nov-Feb) was one of Britain's most extravagant private homes when it was built in the mid-19th century. It was sadly neglected over the years, but even derelict the house is stunning and the gardens are well on their way back to their former Victorian glory. The fountains, in particular, are spectacular.

The adjacent **Great Witley Church** is widely considered to be one of the finest baroque churches in England, its rather simple exterior belying a sumptuous interior featuring exquisite paintings by the likes of Antonio Bellucci and some exceptionally ornate carving and glasswork.

Bus No 758 from Worcester or Kidderminster to Tenbury Wells pass this way infrequently.

Droitwich Spa & Around

The centre of England's salt industry since Norman times, Droitwich opened brine baths to the public when the industry began to decline in the 19th century and transformed itself into a spa town. Many fine medieval buildings still survive, along with some extravagant merchant houses.

The **Heritage Centre** (☎ 10905-774312; Victoria Sq; ⌚ 10am-4pm Mon-Sat) tells the story of the town's salty past and also houses the **TIC**.

The town's biggest attraction is the early-18th-century **Hanbury Hall** (NT; ☎ 01527-821214;

School Rd; admission £5.40; ⌚ 11am-5pm Sat-Wed Mar-Oct), a country house with stunning grounds. The house is famed for its painted ceilings and elaborate staircase and also features an orangery, ice house and Victorian dairy.

Nearby, the picturesque black-and-white village of **Ombersley** is worth a visit for its numerous and excellent pubs and restaurants. Pick of the bunch is the **Venture Inn** (☎ 01905-620552; Main Rd; set lunch £16.95, set dinner £30.50), a wonderful place serving stunning modern British cuisine in massive portions. Just down the road is the **Kings Arms** (☎ 061905-620552; Main Rd), an atmospheric 15th-century inn serving modern pub food (mains £9 to £16).

Bus No 144 runs to Worcester (25 minutes) every half hour.

Redditch

Suffering from its proximity to big city Birmingham, Redditch is rooted in the commuter belt but still retains some interesting attractions.

The **Forge Mill Needle Museum** (☎ 01527-62509; Needle Mill Lane; admission adult/child £3.50/50p; ⌚ 11am-4.30pm Mon-Fri & 2-5pm Sat & Sun Easter-Sep) tells the fascinating and sometimes gruesome story of needle making in Victorian times. Much of the original Victorian water-powered machinery remains and is working most weekends.

The museum is set in the tranquil grounds of the now-ruined 12th-century **Bordesley Abbey**. A museum in a reconstructed medieval barn tells the story of the Cistercian abbey and the exhaustive excavations that have taken place here.

Buses run to Worcester (1¼ hours) roughly every half hour with a change in Bromsgrove (15 minutes).

GREAT MALVERN

☎ 01684 / pop 35,600

This genteel Victorian resort is now a well-heeled but sleepy place, centre of a cluster of towns and villages along the slopes of the Malvern Hills, which rise dramatically from the flat plains of Worcestershire. The town tumbles gracefully down the steep hillside with lofty gas lamps and elegant houses flanking the main street. Today the medicinal water that brought the town fame has been harnessed for a thriving bottled-water business.

The **TIC** (☎ 892289; www.malvernhills.gov.uk; 21 Church St; 🕙 10am-5pm, 10am-4pm Sun) has all you need to know. Guided tours of Victorian Great Malvern leave here at 10.30am on Saturday (£2, 1½ hours).

In early June the town hosts the bi-annual **Elgar Festival** (☎ 892277; www.elgar-festival.com) celebrating the life and works of the composer who lived nearby at Malvern Link.

Sights & Activities
MALVERN PRIORY
Packed with remarkable features, the **priory church** (☎ 561020; www.greatmalvernpriory.org.uk; Church St; admission free; 🕙 9am-6.30pm Apr-Oct, 9am-4.30pm Nov-Mar) was founded in 1085 and has original Norman pillars lining the nave as well as a wonderful collection of 15th-century stained glass and medieval tiles. You can also see many fine misericords under the tip-up seats of the monks' stalls. They depict mythology and various domestic scenes from the 14th century and feature an almost complete set of the labours of the months from the 15th century.

A shop inside the priory has a handy pamphlet pointing out the features of interest.

MALVERN MUSEUM OF LOCAL HISTORY
For the story of the town, visit the fascinating **Malvern Museum of Local History** (☎ 567811; admission adult £1.50; 🕙 10.30am-5pm Easter-Oct, except Wed during school term), housed in the impressive Priory Gatehouse (1470) of the town's former Benedictine abbey. As you enter there are two large embroidered murals depicting all of the things for which Great Malvern is renowned. The museum tells the story of everything from the geology of the Malvern Hills to Victorian water cures and modern enterprise in the area.

MALVERN THEATRES
One of Britain's leading provincial theatres, **Malvern Theatre** (☎ 892277; www.malvern-theatres .co.uk; Grange Rd) hosts a lively programme of classical concerts, dance comedy, drama, opera and cinema.

Set in a converted Victorian men's lavatory, the **Theatre of Small Convenience** (☎ 568933; www.wctheatre.co.uk; Edith Walk) is recognised by the Guinness statisticians as the world's smallest theatre. It seats 12 and hosts varied (mainly amateur) arts from puppetry to poetry.

WALKING
The Malvern Hills are 18 named peaks straddling the boundary between Worcestershire and Herefordshire. The highest point is Worcestershire Beacon (419m). The hills are crisscrossed by more than 100 miles of paths; trail guides (£1.75) and maps are available at the TIC. More than 70 springs and fountains pouring out the famous medicinal waters are dotted around the hills. The TIC has a guide (£3.95) that will lead you to them.

Sleeping
There's lots of excellent accommodation in Great Malvern but it tends to be pricey. Head to the smaller villages for cheaper options.

Como House (☎ 561486; kevin@como-house.free serve.co.uk; Como Rd; s/d £25/45; **P** **X** wheelchair access) This beautiful 19th-century Malvern stone house is a good-value option for its bright, subtle and comfortable rooms and quiet location. There's a large garden and the owner will gladly pick you up from the station or drop you off at walking points.

Cowleigh Park Farm (☎ 01684-566750; www .cowleigh parkfarm.co.uk; Cowleigh Rd; s/d £40/60; **P** **X**) A 13th-century farmhouse, this black-and-white timber-framed place is an atmospheric option with smart rooms and a tranquil setting. The rooms are tasteful, with period furnishings and restrained traditional style.

Bredon House Hotel (☎ 566990; suereeves@bredon househotel.co.uk; 34 Worcester Rd; s/d £45/70; **P** **🖳**) Nestled high on a hill, this lovely 19th-century house has fantastic views over the area. Its elegant rooms are excellent value and are decorated in a subtle modern style with brass beds and rustic furniture.

Other possibilities:
Malvern Hills YHA Hostel (☎ 0870 770 5948; malvern@yha.org.uk; 18 Peachfield Rd, Malvern Wells; dm £10.60; 🕙 mid-Feb–Oct) An elegant Edwardian house 1½ miles south of Great Malvern.
Cottage in the Wood Hotel (☎ 575859; www .cottageinthewood.co.uk; Holywell Rd; s/d £85/170; **P** **🖳**) A bastion of tradition with rather frumpy rooms but spectacular views.

Eating
Malvern's restaurants seem to come and go at an alarming rate but one perennial option is the doily and tea-cosy brigade: the town's many teashops.

St Ann's Well Cafe (☎ 560285; St Ann's Well; 🕙 lunch) The pick of the Malvern bunch, this vegetarian place is in Victorian premises at the top of a steep climb where you can wash down your wholesome salads or delicious cake with a glass of fresh spring water bubbling into a basin by the door.

Anupam (☎ 573814; 85 Church St; mains £8-9.50; ☺ lunch & dinner) Probably the best place in town is this modern Indian restaurant just off the main drag. The décor is stylish and contemporary and the menu features some outstanding specials such as *masala ma murg ka salan*, a subtle but flavoursome chicken dish with lime, fenugreek and coconut.

Rendezvous (☎ 290357; 78 Church St; mains £11-16; ☺ lunch & dinner) Another popular option, this refined place dishes up excellent modern English cuisine in its lovely atmospheric restaurant, cellar and walled garden. Although meat and fish feature strongly on the menu there are always some vegetarian options.

Benedicto's (☎ 578288; 5 Church Walk; mains £7-11; ☺ lunch & dinner Mon-Sat) This reliable Italian joint is a family-friendly place dishing up large portions of pasta classics and some interesting pizzas.

Getting There & Away
There are trains roughly hourly to Worcester (15 minutes) and Hereford (30 minutes).

National Express runs one bus daily to London (£17, 4½ hours) via Worcester – ask at the post office for details. Bus No 44 connects Worcester (35 minutes) with Great Malvern hourly, while bus No 675 runs every two hours to Ledbury (20 minutes, Monday to Saturday).

UPTON-UPON-SEVERN
☎ 01684 / pop 1800

A gorgeous little town with narrow winding streets flanked by a jumble of Tudor and Georgian architecture, Upton is well worth a stopover or a visit for the Oliver Cromwell jazz festival at the end of June.

The **TIC** (☎ 594200; upton.tic@malvernhills.gov.uk; ☺ 10am-5pm Mon-Sat, 10am-4pm Sun) is on High St. Map enthusiasts should head for the **Map Shop** (☎ 593146; www.themapshop.co.uk; 15 High St), which has one of the best selections outside London.

The town's oldest building, the Pepperpot, now houses the **Heritage Centre** (☎ 92679; Church St; free; ☺ 1.30-4.30pm May-Sep), where displays detail the development of the town. Also worth a visit is **Tudor House** (☎ 592447; 16 Church St; admission adult £1; ☺ 2-5pm Apr-Oct), now a museum of local life and history.

Sleeping & Eating
Star Inn (☎ 592300; www.starinnupton.co.uk; s/d £40/55; **P**) This 17th-century hotel near the waterfront is one of the best options in town, with bright simple rooms and the odd exposed beam for character. The bar downstairs does good but traditional pub grub (mains £6 to £13) and often has live music.

White Lion (☎ 592551; www.whitelionhotel.biz; 21 High St; s/d £55/80; **P** ✗) This 16th-century coaching inn has some charming old-style rooms with plenty of frills and newer, more modern and functional rooms. The lovely, oak-beamed **Pepperpot Brasserie** (mains £12-14) downstairs serves little portions at big prices.

Getting There & Away
Bus No 372 runs between Upton and Worcester (25 minutes) every two hours from Monday to Saturday (fewer on Sunday).

HEREFORDSHIRE

A sleepy county, virtually untouched by tourism but bearing evocative remnants of old England, Herefordshire is a patchwork of lush fields, bucolic orchards and pretty villages. The gorgeous black-and-white trail meanders through a region of half-timbered villages and the scenic River Wye ambles through the county, providing ample opportunity for water sports. County capital Hereford has a small cathedral, home to the medieval Mappa Mundi, and perched on the border with Wales is the kingdom of books, Hay-on-Wye.

Information

For online county-wide information on attractions, accommodation and events:

Herefordshire Council (www.herefordshire.gov.uk)

Herefordshire Tourism (www.herefordshire-tourism .org.uk)

Visit Heart of England (www.visitheartofengland.com)

Activities

Several long-distance walking paths pass through this area (see p355). **Offa's Dyke Path** runs along the western border with Wales, while the 107-mile (172km) **Wye Valley Walk** begins in Chepstow (Wales) and follows the river's course upstream into Herefordshire. The **Three Choirs Way** is a 100-mile (160km) route connecting the cathedrals of Hereford, Worcester and Gloucester, where the music festival of the same name has been celebrated for more than three centuries.

Getting Around

There are railway stations at Hereford, Leominster and Ledbury with good links to the major English cities.

Numerous local and national bus companies provide services around the county but you can pick up a free *Public Transport Map & Guide* from TICs and bus stations. Alternatively, try the **National Traveline** (☎ 0870 608 2608).

HEREFORD

☎ 01432 / pop 56,400

An agricultural capital, Hereford is famous for cattle and cider. Despite being the county capital, the town has the feel of a rural backwater with a sluggish pace of life and an old-fashioned attitude. Its prized possession is the magnificent medieval map, Mappa Mundi, housed at the town's odd cathedral.

Orientation & Information

The triangular, pedestrianised High Town is the heart of the city, just north of the River Wye. The cathedral is close to the river while the bus and train stations lie to the northeast, on Commercial Rd.

The **TIC** (☎ 268430; www.visitherefordshire.co.uk; 1 King St; ☼ 9am-5pm Mon-Sat) is opposite the cathedral. You can access the Internet for free at the **library** (Broad St; ☼ 9.30am-6pm Tue-Thu, 9.30am-8pm Fri, 9.30am-4pm Sat).

Hereford Cathedral

After the Welsh torched the town's original cathedral, the new **Hereford Cathedral** (☎ 374200; www.herefordcathedral.co.uk; 5 College Cloisters; ☼ 7.30am-8pm) was begun on the same site in the 11th century. The building has evolved into a well-packaged lesson on the entire history of English architecture: the sturdy south transept is Norman but holds a 16th-century triptych; the exquisite north transept with its soaring windows dates from the 13th century; the choir and the tower date from the 14th; while the Victorian influence is visible almost everywhere.

The cathedral, however, is best known for two ancient treasures, the most famous being the magnificent **Mappa Mundi** (☎ 374 209; adult/child £4.50/3.50; ☼ 10am-4.15pm Mon-Sat & 11am-3.15pm Sun May-Sep, 10am-3.15pm Mon-Sat Oct-Apr), a vellum map from the late 13th century recording how scholars of the time saw the world in spiritual and geographical terms. It is the largest and best-preserved example of this type of cartography and a fascinating pictorial encyclopaedia of the times.

On the same ticket you can visit the largest surviving **chained library** in the world, containing a unique collection of rare books and manuscripts. The oldest book in the collection – and the oldest artefact in the cathedral – is the *Hereford Gospels*, created in the 8th century.

SOMETHING SPECIAL

Three Crowns Inn (☎ 01432-820279; www .threecrownsinn.com; Ullingswick; 3-course set lunch £12, dinner £20) Hidden away deep in the countryside, this 300-year-old half-timbered gastro-pub is one of Herefordshire's best-kept secrets and well worth seeking out for its simple but sophisticated food at incredible prices. The daily changing menu revolves around the availability of locally sourced organic food, rare-breed meats and homemade cheese. A list of suppliers is pinned to the wall so you know exactly where everything comes from.

Ullingswick is about 5 miles northeast of Hereford.

THE MARCHES

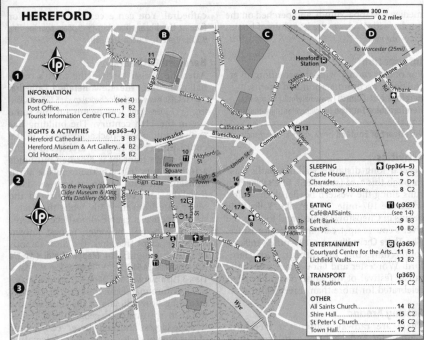

HEREFORD

INFORMATION
Library...(see 4)
Post Office...**1** B2
Tourist Information Centre (TIC)..**2** B3

SIGHTS & ACTIVITIES (pp363–4)
Hereford Cathedral..............................**3** B3
Hereford Museum & Art Gallery......**4** B2
Old House...**5** B2

SLEEPING (pp364–5)
Castle House...**6** C3
Charades...**7** D1
Montgomery House...............................**8** C2

EATING (p365)
Café@AllSaints..................................(see 14)
Left Bank..**9** B3
Saxtys...**10** B2

ENTERTAINMENT (p365)
Courtyard Centre for the Arts......**11** B1
Lichfield Vaults...................................**12** B2

TRANSPORT (p365)
Bus Station...**13** C2

OTHER
All Saints Church................................**14** B2
Shire Hall...**15** B2
St Peter's Church................................**16** C2
Town Hall...**17** B2

The **Three Choirs Festival** (www.3choirs.org), an event shared with Gloucester and Worcester Cathedrals, is held here every three years. You can catch evensong at 5.30pm Monday to Saturday and 2.30pm on Sunday.

Other Sights

Marooned in the middle of High Town, the **Old House** (☎ 260694; admission free; ☻ 10am-5pm Tue-Sat year round, plus 10am-4pm Sun Apr-Sep) is a marvellous black-and-white, three-storey wooden house, built in 1621 and fitted with 17th-century wooden furnishings showing the typical domestic arrangements of the time.

The **Cider Museum & King Offa Distillery** (☎ 354207; www.cidermuseum.co.uk; Pomona Pl; admission adult/child £2.70/2.20; ☻ 10am-5pm Apr-Oct, 11am-3pm Tue-Sun Nov-Mar) explores cider-making history, with a reconstructed farm cider house and 19th-century bottling machinery. The place is just off the A438 to Brecon, or a dreary 10-minute walk from the centre of town.

The lively **Hereford Museum & Art Gallery** (☎ 260692; Broad St; admission free; ☻ 10am-5pm Tue-Sat year round, plus 10am-4pm Sun Apr-Sep) displays a diverse range of exhibits from Roman antiquities and English watercolours to Saxon combs and a hive of bees. There's also a wonderful dressing-up box to keep younger visitors amused.

Sleeping

Charades (☎ 269444; 34 Southbank Rd; s/d £30/50; P ✗) Built as a gentleman's residence around 1890, this lovely Georgian house has bright, comfortable rooms with plenty of character but reassuringly subtle décor. It's handy for the bus station but a 10-minute walk from the town centre.

Montgomery House (☎ 351454; lizforbes@lineone .net; 12 St Owen's St; s/d £45/60; P ✗) A lovely Georgian townhouse with a touch of finesse, this classical place has elegant but restrained rooms with big comfy beds, Egyptian cotton sheets and blankets, and plenty of little extras.

Castle House (☎ 356321; www.castlehse.co.uk; Castle St; s/d £95/165-215; P wheelchair access) Once the bishop's residence, this elegant hotel is Hereford's most elegant option. The luxurious rooms have stylish but classical décor and the seriously sophisticated **La Rive** restaurant (mains £12 to £19) offers fine dining of the rich, classical sort.

Eating

Hereford isn't exactly blessed when it comes to eating out and you may well be best off with some of the ubiquitous chain restaurants.

Café @ All Saints (☎ 370415; High St; mains £5-6; ⏰ lunch) *The* most atmospheric place to eat in town, you can sit within spitting distance of the altar at this working church. The design is sleek and stylish and the menu features wholesome and mostly vegetarian fare. Look out for the medieval carving of a gentleman mooning.

Other options:

Saxtys (☎ 357872; 33 Widemarsh St; mains £8-12; ⏰ lunch & dinner Mon-Sat) Laid-back, 30-something café bar with mellow modern vibes, European beers and an excellent evening menu.

Left Bank (☎ 340200; Bridge St; ⏰ lunch & dinner) Slick but soulless home to **Floodgates Brasserie** (mains £12-16) and **Charles Cocktail Bar** (small/large tapas £3.45/6.25).

Drinking & Entertainment

Plough (☎ 273868; 86 White Cross Rd) The best place in town to catch up on live music, this well-run venue plays host to the county's finest bands from folk to rock as well as some bigger touring names.

Lichfield Vaults (☎ 267994; 11 Church St) A real-ale-drinker's pub with a revolving selection of local brews, this place attracts a mixed group of people, which is unusual for Hereford's pubs. There's a small patio at the back for fine weather, and a cheerful atmosphere.

Courtyard Centre for the Arts (☎ 359252; www .courtyard.org.uk; Edgar St) This lively arts centre has two venues staging a busy and varied schedule of events, from comedy to theatre, film and poetry.

Getting There & Away

There are hourly trains to London (£30, three hours) via Worcester (£5.80, 45 minutes); and to Birmingham (£8.50, 1½ hours). National Express goes to London (£14.50, four hours, three daily) via Heathrow, Gloucester and Ross-on-Wye or Ledbury.

From St Peter's Sq bus Nos 419/420 run hourly to Worcester (45 minutes, three on Sunday). No 38 runs hourly to Gloucester (50 minutes) via Ross-on-Wye (20 minutes,

---

SOMETHING SPECIAL

Ford Abbey (☎ 01568-760700; www.fordabbey .co.uk; Pudleston; s/d £75-135/120-190; P ⊠ ♿ wheelchair access) This fantastic medieval abbey has been sympathetically converted into a luxury retreat with all the trimmings. The spacious rooms have the prerequisite beams, antique furniture and four-poster beds, but period features blend with modern styling: some even have unusual bathroom pods in the centre of the room. The public areas mix fine antiques with junk-shop bargains and the restaurant serves up fantastic food (three-course set menu £35), with much of the produce from the hotel's own farm. The abbey is surrounded by extensive gardens, and children are very welcome.

Pudleston is about 10 miles north of Hereford.

---

six on Sunday), and No 476 goes hourly to Ledbury (20 minutes, five on Sunday) both from the bus station on Commercial Rd.

AROUND HEREFORD
Golden Valley

The Golden Valley, at the foot of the Black Mountains, was made famous by the author CS Lewis and the film *Shadowlands*. It follows the course of the meandering River Dore and boasts beautiful unspoilt rural vistas, studded by historical ruins evoking the border valley's tumultuous past. *This* is why you brought the car.

Riverside Inn

A 16th-century half-timbered inn on the River Lugg, **Riverside Inn** (☎ 01568-708440; www .theriversideinn.org; Aymestry; s/d £40/65; P) is dripping with character and has some lovely rooms with low ceilings, oak beams and thick uneven walls. As beautiful as the accommodation is, though, it's the food that really draws the crowds; you can choose from simple bar food to fine dining in the cosy restaurant with hop-strewn beams and red lamps. The ambitious menu (mains £11 to £16) is mainly modern British with an emphasis on local ingredients. If you're a walker this place is mid-point on the Mortimer Trail and makes a wonderful stopover.

Aymestry is on the A4110, 15 miles north of Hereford.

BLACK-&-WHITE VILLAGES

A triangle of Tudor England survives almost untouched in northwest Herefordshire, where higgledy-piggledy black-and-white villages cluster round idyllic greens, seemingly oblivious to the modern world. The area makes for a wonderful drive and a 40-mile circular route, the **Black & White Village Trail**, meanders through the most popular spots taking in handsome timber-framed buildings, old churches, convivial pubs and tranquil villages. The route starts at Leominster and climaxes at **Eardisland**, the most picturesque village of all. You can pick up a guide from any TIC for £1 (or £4.99 for the cassette or CD version).

Pembridge is another gem, with a huddle of classic houses and its useful **Black & White Villages Centre** (☎ 01544-388761; ☺ 9am-6pm) with TIC, tearooms, gift shop and cycle hire. The village makes a good base for touring the area, with lots of circular walks radiating from town and the Mortimer Trail just north of the village. Visit www.mediaeval-pembridge.com or ask at the TIC or very helpful Old Forge Picture Gallery for information on accommodation options.

For stunning food head for the **Stagg Inn** (☎ 01544-230221; www.thestagg.co.uk; Titley; mains £11-16; ☺ closed Sun evening & Mon), set in yet another picturesque village. The Stagg was the first pub to be awarded a Michelin star, and its reputation proceeds it so book in advance. It's a traditional country inn with roaring fires and antiques, combining the best of culinary expertise with a down-to-earth attitude. Suppliers' lists cover the blackboards and the modern British menu rarely disappoints. The pub also has a few very comfortable rooms (s/d £50/70).

The three-mile Titley Loop Walk begins here and winds through gorgeous countryside, making it a good way to work up an appetite.

Kilpeck Church

Deep within lush Herefordshire countryside is the tiny hamlet of Kilpeck, where you'll find an astonishing church that remains practically unchanged since the 12th century. Inside, remarkable corbels and original carvings ring the building. They range from the profound to the comical and include a famous sheila-na-gig (a Celtic fertility figure) on the south side.

Just 9 miles from Hereford, Kilpeck is less than 2 miles off the A465 and well worth a detour.

HAY-ON-WYE
☎ 01497 / pop 1400

A bookworm's paradise, Hay-on-Wye is *the* place for idle browsers, serious hunters, burrowing academics and anyone who enjoys a rummage through dusty tomes, trashy novels and out-of-print titles in search of that rare book find. The tiny town has sold its soul to the second-hand book trade and is now host to a whopping 39 bookshops stocking hundreds of thousands of volumes covering every subject ever committed to paper.

Physically, the town straddles the England–Wales border and famously declared itself independent from Britain on 1 April 1977, ensuring a furious rebuff from the local council and a media storm (see boxed text p368). Today it is famous worldwide and becomes the centre of the literary universe for a week in May/June when the world of words descends for the **Hay Festival of Literature**. Don't bet on a bed *anywhere* in the vicinity at this time of year.

The **TIC** (☎ 820144; www.hay-on-wye.co.uk; Oxford Rd; ☺ 10am-1pm & 2-5pm Easter-Oct, 11am-1pm & 2-4pm Nov-Easter) is at the top of town by the main car park.

Activities

Hay is on the northeastern corner of Brecon Beacons National Park and makes an excellent base for exploring western Herefordshire and the Black Mountains of Wales. The **Offa's Dyke** walking route (see p355) passes nearby.

For fun on the River Wye, you can hire kayaks and Canadian canoes from **Paddles & Pedals** (☎ 820604; www.canoehire.co.uk; 15 Castle St), which, despite the name, doesn't do bikes. Canoe hire is £18/28 for a half/full day and kayak hire £12/18. Rental prices include free return transport to points along the Wye, depending on which route you're taking.

Shopping

The TIC and most shops stock the indispensable pamphlet guide to the town's 39 general and specialist bookshops, where

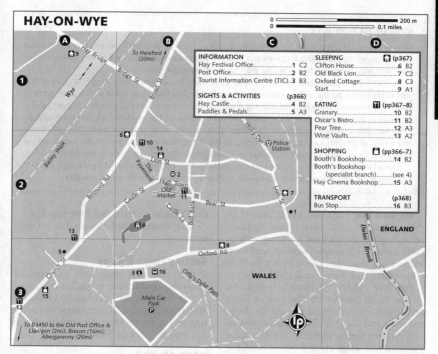

HAY-ON-WYE

0 ——————— 200 m
0 ——————— 0.1 miles

INFORMATION
Hay Festival Office.....................1 C2
Post Office.................................2 B2
Tourist Information Centre (TIC)..3 B3

SIGHTS & ACTIVITIES (p366)
Hay Castle.................................4 B2
Paddles & Pedals........................5 A3

SLEEPING (p367)
Clifton House.............................6 B2
Old Black Lion...........................7 C2
Oxford Cottage..........................8 C3
Start.......................................9 A1

EATING (pp367–8)
Granary.....................................10 B2
Oscar's Bistro............................11 B2
Pear Tree..................................12 A3
Wine Vaults...............................13 A2

SHOPPING (pp366–7)
Booth's Bookshop.......................14 B2
Booth's Bookshop
(specialist branch)................(see 4)
Hay Cinema Bookshop................15 A3

TRANSPORT (p368)
Bus Stop...................................16 B3

quantity generally rules over quality. The most famous and largest shop is **Booth's Bookshop** (☎ 820322; 44 Lion St), a smaller specialist arm of which is housed in a Jacobean mansion built into the walls of the battered 13th-century town castle. Another good bet is the excellent **Hay Cinema Bookshop** (☎ 820071; Castle St) in the old picture house.

Sleeping

Outside the festival, accommodation options are generally plentiful and very good value.

Start (☎ 821391; www.the-start.net; Hay Bridge; s/d £30/50; Ⓟ ✕) This beautiful 18th-century stone building perches right on the river and has compact but lovely, bright rooms with antique country-style furniture, light colours and patchwork quilts. Hikers and bikers are welcome and there's lock-up and drying facilities.

Old Post Office (☎ 820008; www.theoldpostoffice .co.uk; Llanigon; s/d £25/36-56; Ⓟ ✕) If you've got your own wheels this 17th-century house just outside town is a wonderful option. The rooms feature polished oak floors, sumptuous king-size beds, exposed beams and restored rural Welsh furniture. Each has fantastic views of the Black Mountains. The B&B is 2 miles from Hay on the B4350 to Brecon.

Old Black Lion (☎ 820841; www.oldblacklion.co.uk; Lion St; s/d £42.50/80; Ⓟ ✕) An atmospheric 17th-century inn with medieval beams and low lighting, the spacious bedrooms here have recently been overhauled and feature warm colours, floral bedspreads, sturdy country-style furniture – and teddy bears.

Other options include:

Clifton House (☎ 821618; www.cliftonhousehay.co.uk; 1 Belmont Rd; s/d £35/50; ✕) Spacious bright rooms with a lovely mix of modern styling and antique furniture.

Oxford Cottage (☎ 820008; Oxford Rd; s/d £20/40) Rustic rooms in a central location.

Eating

Granary (☎ 820790; Broad St; mains £5-10; ◷ lunch & dinner) Housed in a former granary, this wonderful licensed café and restaurant serves up wholesome and hearty food and features plenty of original vegan and vegetarian choices. There's a great choice of salads, local cheeses, smoked fish and variety of local meat and game dishes on offer.

KING OF HAY-ON-WYE

King of the world's first book town, Richard Booth opened his first bookshop in Hay in 1961 but was dismayed by the falling fortunes and declining populations of rural areas. Not content to sit back and watch, he hatched a wacky plan to regenerate the town.

By 1977 he had persuaded a clutch of other booksellers to join him and on April Fools Day of that year declared the border town independent from Britain. The town celebrated with a giant party as Booth was crowned in royal robes, orb and a sceptre made from an old ball-cock and copper piping. As weird as the idea was, it had the desired effect and Hay hit the headlines all over the country.

Almost 30 years on, Hay has more bookshops than even the most dedicated bibliophile can handle and a host of thriving local business catering to the five million visitors a year. It has also been the inspiration for roughly 20 other international book towns, often in rural areas facing similar decline.

If you fancy a piece of the action you can apply for Hay Peerage, awarded by the king himself. Aspiring lords and ladies should visit www.haypeerage.freeserve.co.uk for information.

Old Black Lion (☎ 820841; Lion St; mains £8-16; ☽ lunch & dinner) This cosy candle-lit place serves top-notch pub food featuring memorable dishes such as spicy venison and local lamb. It's a charming place with a friendly atmosphere and some wonderful local ales.

Pear Tree (☎ 820777; 6 Church St; mains £11-15; ☽ lunch Thu-Sat, dinner Tue-Sat) The pick of Hay's restaurants, this informal place with deep-red walls and old-style décor has an innovative modern menu featuring the best local produce and inspiration from around the globe. Everything is home cooked, down to the chutneys and truffles, and tastes divine.

Other places to consider:

Wine Vaults (☎ 820409; 10 Castle St; mains £5-6; ☽ lunch & dinner) Small modern café-bar with a good range of simple dishes.

SOMETHING SPECIAL

Penrhos Court (☎ 01544 230720; www.penrhos .co.uk; Kington; s/d £80/105-165; Ⓟ ✗) This half-timbered hotel is a real gem, with luxurious traditional-style rooms looking out onto bucolic countryside. The hotel is passionate about its food, and the hub of activity is the great cruck-beamed dining room with its sturdy wooden tables, stone flags and vast inglenook fireplace. The limited but wholly organic menu (four-course dinner £32.50) is largely vegetarian with the odd fish or chicken dish sneaking in. Every dish is a masterpiece, from courgette and chive-blossom soup to nettle ravioli and sea trout with marsh samphire. It's enough to convert any carnivore.

Kington is about 12 miles north of Hay-on-Wye.

Oscar's Bistro (☎ 821193; High Town; mains £7-8; ☽ lunch) Organic meat and vegetarian dishes in a simple bistro.

Getting There & Away

If you're driving, allow time to cruise because the countryside is spellbinding.

Bus No 39 from Hereford (55 minutes) and from Brecon (45 minutes) runs five times Monday to Saturday, and bus No 40 has four services on Sunday.

ROSS-ON-WYE

☎ 01989 / pop 10,100

Perched on a bluff above a bend in the river, picturesque Ross-on-Wye is a sleepy backwater but a pleasant base for exploring the lovely surrounding countryside. The town comes alive in mid-August when the International Festival brings on fireworks, live music and street theatre.

The 17th-century Market House has a **Heritage Centre** (☎ 260675; Market Pl; 10am-4pm Mon-Sat) and local history museum. The **TIC** (☎ 562768; Edde Cross St; ☽ 9.30am-4.30pm Mon-Sat) has information on activities and walks.

Sleeping & Eating

Accommodation is plentiful and there are a couple of good eateries. The nearest hostel is 6 miles south of Ross at Welsh Bicknor (see opposite).

Linden House (☎ 565373; www.lindenhousewyenet .co.uk; 14 Church St; s/d £30/50; Ⓟ ✗) This lovely brick house right in the centre of town has bright comfortable rooms with exposed beams and brass beds. The décor is cheerful with warm hues and simple modern furnishings.

Glewstone Court (☎ 770367; www.glewstonecourt .com; Glewstone; s £50-80, d £80-110; P) This lovingly restored Georgian house has plenty of charm and is chock-full of antiques, comfy sofas, period memorabilia and crackling open fires. The rooms have polished wooden floors, Eastern rugs and very traditional décor. The restaurant (three-course set menu £26) is popular for Sunday lunch.

Pheasant at Ross (☎ 565751; 52 Edde Cross St; mains £15; ☺ lunch & dinner Thu-Sat) Famed for its extensive wine list and excellent food, the Pheasant is an intimate wood-beamed place with an unpretentious attitude. The fine English cuisine features many rare-breed meats and succulent local game but makes few concessions to vegetarians.

Other options include the following:

Riverside Inn(☎ 564688; www.wyenot.com/riverside; Wye St; s/d £25/45; P) A lively pub with great-value rooms and a popular restaurant (mains £5-8).

Meaders (☎ 562803; 1 Copse Cross St; mains £7.50-10; ☺ lunch & dinner Tue-Sat) Hearty eastern European fare featuring lots of meat and creamy sauces.

Getting There & Around

Bus Nos 38 and 33 run hourly Monday to Saturday (five on Sunday) to and from Hereford and Gloucester respectively (30 minutes each way).

You can hire bikes from **Revolutions** (☎ 562 639; 48 Broad St) from £12 per day.

AROUND ROSS-ON-WYE
Goodrich

From the roof of the keep at **Goodrich Castle** (EH; ☎ 01600-890538; admission £4; ☺ 10am-5pm Mar-Oct, 10am-4pm Thu-Mon Nov-Feb) are spectacular views of the Wye Valley. You can appreciate how important – and impenetrable – this fortress would have been when it was built as a border stronghold in the 12th century. Even after a four-month siege by Cromwell's troops during the Civil War it is still one of the most complete medieval castles in Britain.

From the village, it's a steep 1½-mile hill-hugging climb up to **Welsh Bicknor YHA Hostel** (☎ 0870 770 6086; welshbicknor@yha.org.uk; dm £11.80; ☺ Apr-Oct, Fri & Sat only rest of year; P ✗), a Victorian rectory standing in 10 hectares of gorgeous riverside grounds.

Goodrich is 5 miles south of Ross off the A40. Bus No 34 stops here every couple of hours on its way between Ross and Monmouth.

TOP FIVE PUBS FOR SUNDAY LUNCH

■ **Riverside Inn** (p365; Aymestry) Charming 16th-century inn just dripping with character

■ **Stagg Inn** (p366; Titley) Michelin-starred food with a down-to-earth attitude

■ **Sun Inn** (p375; Marton) Where the locals come to play darts and the discerning come to dine

■ **Three Crowns Inn** (p363; Ullingswick) Simple but sophisticated food at incredible prices

■ **Waterdine Inn** (p382; Llanfair Waterdine) Organic meats and wild game in a gorgeous riverside setting

Symonds Yat
☎ 01600

A gorgeous spot on the River Wye, Symonds Yat gets crammed with visitors on sunny Sundays and bank holidays, but is well worth a visit at quieter times. An ancient hand ferry (60p) joins the two pretty villages on either bank. Above Symonds Yat West you'll find a big, tacky fairground with kiss-me-quick hats and an entirely different vibe.

The village is a centre for watersports but as flat as it may look, the river has a strong current and is not suitable for swimming.

ACTIVITIES

This area is renowned for canoeing and rock climbing and there's good hiking in the nearby Forest of Dean. The **Wyedean Canoe Centre** (☎ 01594-833238; www.wyedean.co.uk) hires out canoes and kayaks for £17 for a half day and also organises multiday kayaking trips, whitewater trips, caving and climbing.

From Symonds Yat East, it's a steep but easy walk – at least on a dry day – up 504m to the crown of the region, **Symonds Yat Rock**, which provides tremendous views of the river and valley. Two pairs of rare peregrine falcons nest in the cliffs opposite but there's a 90m-drop over the harmless looking low wall, so keep children and dogs under a watchful eye.

SLEEPING & EATING

There is a string of accommodation and feeding options on the east side of the river.

Old Court Hotel (☎ 890367; www.oldcourthotel .com; s/d £50/90; P ☎) This 15th-century manor house set in great gardens has excellent-value rooms with exposed beams, uneven floorboards and traditional but not-too-frilly décor. The Tudor restaurant serves up good food (mains £8 to £14) and cheaper bar snacks to feed the children.

Walnut Tree Cottage (☎ 5890828; www.walnut treehotel.co.uk; Symonds Yat West; s/d £45/70; P ✗) Set high above the river, this good-value option has simple, bright rooms with fantastic views, rustic furniture and light floral patterns. You can also have dinner here (set menu £20) but the food doesn't hold any surprises.

Saracen's Head (☎ 890435; www.saracensheadinn .co.uk; s/d £45/64) A traditional inn by the river, this popular joint has some standard rooms and two new luxury suites in the boathouse that only cost a few pounds extra. You can dig into some decent bar food (£5 to £8) or choose from the more refined restaurant menu (£8 to £14).

GETTING THERE & AWAY

Bus No 53 goes to Symonds Yat West from Ross-on-Wye (25 minutes) on Friday only. Bus No 34 can drop you on the main road 1½ miles from the village on other days.

LEDBURY

☎ 01531 / pop 8500

A lovely little town with a wealth of historical architecture and plenty of antique shops, Ledbury makes a good day trip or an enjoyable stopover. The best way to enjoy the town is just to ramble the narrow lanes of crooked black-and-white buildings radiating from the main street.

The helpful **TIC** (☎ 636147; tic-ledbury@hereford shire.gov.uk; 3 The Homend; ☑ 10am-5pm Mon-Sat) has maps of the Ledbury Loop, a lovely 17-mile circular ride along secondary roads through rural Herefordshire.

Sights

Ledbury's centrepiece is the delightfully dainty **Market House** (☑ 11am-1pm & 2-4pm Mon-Fri, 2-5pm Sun), a 17th-century, black-and-white timber-framed structure on oak columns. From here, you can wander up the creaky and cobbled **Church Lane**, chock-a-block

with notable architecture, including the **Painted Room** (☑ 11am-3pm Mon-Fri), with 16th-century floral frescoes.

Still in Church Lane, **Butcher's Row House** (☎ 632942; Church Lane; admission free; ☑ 11am-5pm Easter-Sep) is an engaging folk museum with displays ranging from 19th-century school clothing to a remarkable 18th-century communal 'boot' bath that used to be carted from door to door for the poor to scrub in.

At the lane's end is the 12th-century parish church of **St Michael and All Angels**, with its splendid 60m spire and tower, which are separate from the church. The spire was a 1733 addition to the Norman core.

Sleeping & Eating

Talbot Hotel (☎ 632963; www.talbotledbury.co.uk; New St; s/d £32.50/60; P) The best-value option in town, this historic place has compact but comfortable rooms in period style and an amazing dining room with incredible oak panelling and rich traditional food (mains £8 to £15). Breakfast (£8.50) is not included in the room price.

Verzons Country Inn (☎ 670381; Trumpet; s/d £70/100; P ✗ ▱) Originally a Georgian farmhouse, this country inn has stylish accommodation that blends modern comforts with old style décor. The bar area is decorated with farming scenes but its modern menu (mains £8 to £11) has a heavy European bias with some Asian influences. Verzons is two miles west of Ledbury on the A438.

Feathers Hotel (☎ 635266; www.feathers-ledbury .co.uk; High St; s/d £74.50/95.50; P ☎) Charming rooms with rich colours and modern styling are the order of the day at this homey Tudor establishment where there's also a small gym and pool. The **Fuggles** restaurant downstairs (named after a locally grown hop; mains £8 to £14) serves modern British brasserie-style food.

Ceci Paolo (☎ 632976; www.cecipaolo.com; 21 High St; mains £6-7; ☑ lunch) This food emporium combines city chic with country portions and has become a Ledbury institution. The top-notch cuisine features wholesome delicacies such as the Italian platter of tasty morsels. Downstairs there's a superb deli, wine and kitchen shop.

Other eating and sleeping options include the following:

Grove House (☎ 650584; www.thegrovehouse .co.uk; Bromesberrow Heath; d £73; P ✗) A gorgeous

15th-century house with beautiful rooms, well worth the three-mile drive from town.

Prince of Wales (☎ 632250; Church Lane; meals £4-7; ⏰ lunch & dinner) Cheap pub grub and a wonderfully atmospheric pint.

Getting There & Around

There are hourly trains to Hereford (15 minutes), Great Malvern (10 minutes), Worcester (20 minutes) and Birmingham (£7.40, one hour).

Bus No 476 runs to Hereford hourly (30 minutes, every two hours on Sunday); bus No 132 runs to Gloucester (45 minutes, six daily Monday to Saturday); and No 675 to Great Malvern (20 minutes, every two hours Monday to Saturday).

You can hire bikes at **Saddle Bound Cycles** (☎ 633433; 3 The Southend; per day £8).

AROUND LEDBURY
Eastnor Castle

Straight out of the pages of a fairy tale, **Eastnor Castle** (☎ 01531-633160; www.eastnorcastle .com; admission adult/child £6.50/4, grounds only £4.50/3; ⏰ 11am-5pm Sun-Fri July & Aug, plus Sun & bank holidays Apr-early Oct) is an immaculate romantic Gothic folly. The interior is sumptuously designed with richly decorative Gothic and Italianate features, heavy tapestries and oodles of antiques. Even when the castle is closed, the extensive grounds, which include a deer park, maze, adventure playground and arboretum of rare trees, are worth a look.

The castle is just over 2 miles east of Ledbury on the A438.

Much Marcle

The village of Much Marcle is a tiny and remarkable place, home to two of the most impressive tourist attractions in the Marches.

First up is the enthralling historical house of **Hellens** (☎ 01531-660504; www.hellens manor.com; admission adult £5; ⏰ tours 2pm, 3pm & 4pm Wed, Sat & Sun Apr-Sep), one of the oldest houses in Britain and still occasionally inhabited by descendants of the family who built it in the 13th century. The largely 17th-century interior has been almost perfectly preserved through benign neglect. Admission is by tour only but is a mesmerising journey through the house and its history. You can also walk through the lovely garden to the charming brick dovecote.

You're deep in cider country here and can celebrate the fact with a visit to **Westons Cider Mills** (☎ 01531-660233; www.westons-cider.co.uk; The Bounds). Henry Weston started making cider for friends and family on this site in the 1870s and soon the local MP had persuaded him to go commercial and got Westons cider put on tap in the parliament bar. Tours of the mill (£3.50, 1½ hours) are at 2.30pm Monday to Friday. Admission to the Edwardian-style garden and museum is free.

Bus No 45 passes through Much Marcle four times daily Monday to Saturday on its run between Ross-on-Wye and Ledbury.

SHROPSHIRE

Sparsely populated and seriously beautiful, Shropshire ripples across the country and over the Severn from Birmingham to the Welsh border. The attractive Tudor town of Shrewsbury is the county capital, and close by you'll find the county's most remarkable attraction, the World Heritage–listed Ironbridge Gorge. The north of the county is rather flat and unexceptional but the Shropshire Hills to the south – the 'blue remembered hills' of local scribe AE Housman – are stunningly beautiful and littered with lovely villages. In the far south you'll find historic Ludlow, with its fine castle and passion for good food.

Information

For online county-wide information:

Shropshire Tourism (www.shropshiretourism.info)
South Shropshire (www.southshropshire.org.uk)
Virtual Shropshire (www.virtual-shropshire.co.uk)

Getting Around

There are useful rail services from Shrewsbury to Church Stretton, Craven Arms and Ludlow. The invaluable *Shropshire Bus & Train Map,* available free from TICs, shows all bus routes.

SHREWSBURY

☎ 01743 / pop 67,150

The higgledy-piggledy charms of England's finest Tudor town more than make up for its scarcity of specific attractions. Ancient passageways wind between crooked black-and-white half-timbered houses, several

THE MARCHES

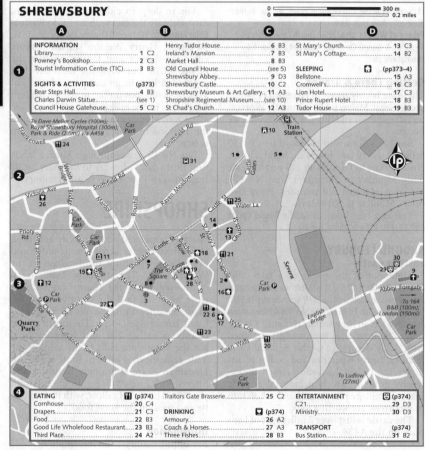

SHREWSBURY

0 — 300 m
0 — 0.2 miles

INFORMATION		
Library............................	1	C2
Powney's Bookshop..........	2	C3
Tourist Information Centre (TIC)....	3	B3

SIGHTS & ACTIVITIES		(p373)
Bear Steps Hall................	4	B3
Charles Darwin Statue.......	(see 1)	
Council House Gatehouse...	5	C2

Henry Tudor House............	6	B3
Ireland's Mansion..............	7	B3
Market Hall.....................	8	B3
Old Council House............	(see 5)	
Shrewsbury Abbey.............	9	D3
Shrewsbury Castle.............	10	C2
Shrewsbury Museum & Art Gallery..	11	A3
Shropshire Regimental Museum....	(see 10)	
St Chad's Church..............	12	A3

St Mary's Church..............	13	C3
St Mary's Cottage.............	14	B2

SLEEPING		(pp373–4)
Bellstone........................	15	A3
Cromwell's.....................	16	C3
Lion Hotel......................	17	C3
Prince Rupert Hotel...........	18	B3
Tudor House....................	19	B3

To Dave Mellor Cycles (100m);
Royal Shrewsbury Hospital (300m);
Park & Ride (2.5mi) via A458

24

Car Park

10

Train Station

31

1

5

Castle Gates

25 Water La

Smithfield Rd

Victoria Ave

26

Car Park

14

13

Priory Rd

Car Park

11

18

21

15

12

Car Park

The Square

19

4

28

8

2

16

Car Park P

Severn

30

29

9

Abbey Foregate

To 164
B&B (100m);
London (150mi)

27

3

22 6

17

23

Quarry Park

St Chad's

Swan Hill

20

Town Walls

English Bridge

Car Park

To Ludlow
(27mi)

EATING	🍴	(p374)
Cornhouse.......................	20	C4
Drapers..........................	21	C3
Food..............................	22	B3
Good Life Wholefood Restaurant....	23	B3
Third Place......................	24	A2

Traitors Gate Brasserie.......	25	C2

DRINKING	🍷	(p374)
Armoury.........................	26	A2
Coach & Horses................	27	A3
Three Fishes....................	28	B3

ENTERTAINMENT	🎭	(p374)
C21...............................	29	D3
Ministry..........................	30	D3

TRANSPORT		(p374)
Bus Station......................	31	B2

fine churches grace the town, and the impressive castle provides wonderful views over the meandering River Severn.

Set within a horseshoe loop of the river, the town's defensive potential was first exploited by the Saxons and for centuries was pivotal in keeping the Welsh in line. Later the town prospered from the wool trade. It is also the birthplace of Charles Darwin (1809–82), who rocked the world with his theory of evolution.

Orientation

Shrewsbury's near-island status helps preserve the Tudor and Jacobean streetscapes of its centre and protects it from unattractive urban sprawl. The train station

is a five-minute walk northeast of the centre and is as far as you'll need to venture.

Information

Powney's Bookshop (☎ 369165; www.powneysbook shop.demon.co.uk; 4-5 Alkmund's Pl) A good source for walking maps.

Royal Shrewsbury Hospital (☎ 261000; Mytton Oak Rd)

Shrewsbury Library (☎ 255300; Castle Gates; 🕙 9.30am-5pm Mon, Wed, Fri & Sat, 9.30am-8pm Tue & Thu) Free Internet access.

TIC (☎ 281200; www.shrewsburytourism.co.uk; Music Hall, The Square; 🕙 9.30am-5.30pm Mon-Sat & 10am-4pm Sun May-Sep, 9.30am-5pm Mon-Sat Oct-Apr) Guided walking tours (adult £3, 1½ hours) leave the TIC at 2.30pm from May to September and at 2.30pm Saturday only from November to April.

Shrewsbury Abbey

The large red-sandstone **abbey** (☎ 232723; www.shrewsburyabbey.com; Abbey Foregate; admission £2 donation; ☯ 10am-4.45pm Easter-Oct, 10.30am-3pm Nov-Easter) is what's left of a Benedictine monastery founded in 1083. The architecture is in three different styles – Norman, Early English and Victorian – but its finest feature is the huge 14th-century west window of heraldic glass. You can also see the controversial sculpture of a crucified and decomposing Jesus: *The Naked Christ* by local artist Michelle Coxon. The abbey is renowned for its acoustics and a noticeboard inside provides information on recitals.

Shrewsbury Museum & Art Gallery

Housed in beautifully restored 16th- and 17th-century buildings, the **Shrewsbury Museum** (☎ 361196; www.shrewsburymuseums.com; Barker St; admission free; ☯ 10am-4pm Tue-Sat year round, 10am-5pm Tue-Sat & 10am-4pm Sun Jun-Sep) exhibits many Roman finds from Wroxeter (see p375) and displays on local life. The **art gallery** has a mixed bag of contemporary art.

Walking Tour

Starting from the TIC, the 16th-century **Market Hall** (☎ 351067), the centre of the historic wool trade, is in front of you. Look out for the holes on the insides of the pillars, which were used to record the number of fleeces sold.

The most impressive of Shrewsbury's timber-framed buildings, **Ireland's Mansion** is on your right at the junction with High St. Cross over into narrow **Grope Lane** with its overhanging buildings and you'll end up in lovely Fish St before going up the steps to the restored 14th-century **Bear Steps Hall** (☯ 10am-4pm). There are several more atmospheric black-and-white houses along Butcher Row.

From here head for medieval **St Mary's Church** (St Mary's St) with its magnificent spire – one of the highest in England. Inside the great Jesse window is made from rare mid-14th-century English glass.

Pass the 17th-century **St Mary's Cottage** into Water Lane and head back down into Castle St. At the northern end is **Shrewsbury Castle**, which houses the **Shropshire Regimental Museum** (☎ 358516; admission adult £2; ☯ 10am-5pm Tue-Sat & 10am-4pm Sun-Mon May-Sep, 10am-4pm Wed-Sat Feb-Apr), although the view is more worthwhile than the collection.

Down the alley near the entrance is the Jacobean-style **Council House Gatehouse**, dating from 1620, and the **Old Council House**, where the Council of the Welsh Marches used to meet.

Across the road from the castle is the elaborate **library** with a **statue of Charles Darwin**. Returning to St Mary's St, follow it into Dogpole and turn right into Wyle Cop, Welsh for 'hilltop'. Henry VII is said to have stayed in the **Henry Tudor House** before the Battle of Bosworth.

Head down Wyle Cop and then left and you'll reach the graceful 18th-century **English Bridge** offering magnificent views of the town's skyline. **Shrewsbury Abbey** is ahead of you.

Double back over the bridge and stroll left along the riverside to the manicured gardens of **Quarry Park**. Finally, wander up to the impressive **St Chad's Church**, built in 1792.

Sleeping

Shrewsbury has a plenty of hotels in the centre and B&Bs clustering around Abbey Foregate.

164 (☎ 367750; www.164bedandbreakfast.co.uk; 164 Abbey Foregate; s/d £35/50; P ⊗) An escape from the chintz brigade, this contemporary B&B has bright, modern rooms in a lovely 16th-century property. There are colourful pictures on the walls, good bathrooms and as an extra treat breakfast is served in bed.

Tudor House (☎ 351735; www.tudorhousehrews bury.com; 2 Fish St; s/d from £35/74; ⊗) If nostalgia is your thing, this medieval masterpiece has buckets of character with pretty oak-beamed rooms decorated in light neutral colours. It's slap bang in the centre of town but on a really quiet street, and provides organic cooked breakfasts.

Cromwell's (☎ 361440; www.cromwellsinn.com; 11 Dogpole; s/d £55/60; ⊗) Tudor chic combines with modern styling at this frill-free modern guesthouse. The rooms have period features but contemporary furnishings, and the oak-panelled restaurant downstairs does a wonderful modern British menu (mains from £11 to £17).

Lion Hotel (☎ 0870 609 6167; www.corushotels.com /thelion; Wyle Cop; s/d from £76/82; P) A classic 17th-century coaching inn, the Lion has played host to many a passing luminary. If you can, bump up to the more expensive rooms as the standard rooms have an unexceptional corporate style and lack any real character. The suites, however, are the real McCoy and are furnished with stunning period antiques.

Other options include the following:

Bellstone (☎ 242100; www.bellstone-hotel.co.uk; Bellstone; s/d £40/45; ✗) Simple modern rooms with a touch of character.

Prince Rupert Hotel (☎ 499955; www.prince-rupert-hotel.co.uk; Butcher Row; s/d £69/99; **P** ✗) Décor your granny would just love complete with oak panelling, suits of armour and heraldic crests.

Eating

Traitors Gate Brasserie (☎ 249152; www.traitorsgate.co.uk; Castle St; mains £9-15; ✗ lunch & dinner) A warren of little cellars and intimate alcoves; the warm stone walls, and rustic décor are a perfect setting for the ambitious Continental cuisine at Traitors Gate. Try the pan-fried venison with crushed juniper berries or the baked breast of chicken with blue cheese.

Cornhouse (☎ 231991; 59a Wyle Cop; mains £8-13; ✗ lunch & dinner) Excellent seasonal British food is served up in this cosy retreat with an eclectic range of artwork and interesting décor. The restaurant is dominated by a superb cast-iron spiral staircase, live piano music tinkers in the background and there's blues on Sunday just in time for brunch.

Good Life Wholefood Restaurant (☎ 350455; Barracks Passage; mains £4-6.50; ✗ lunch) Good honest meals and a pious glow emanate from this cosy little wholefood nook off Wyle Cop. It's a fantastic place for healthy, hearty and delicious fare, from sturdy salads to hot bakes and gorgeous desserts.

Drapers (☎ 344679; Drapers Hall, St Mary's Pl; mains £9.50-15.50; ✗ lunch & dinner) Expertly prepared classic French and English dishes are served up at this 16th-century hall with an elegant Elizabethan façade. The restaurant has a giant open fireplace, oak-panelled walls and simply stunning food. For more relaxed dining try the Yellow Room (mains £6.50 to £9).

Other options include the following:

Third Place (☎ 272401; 135 Frankenwell; mains £6-12; ✗ lunch) Café-bistro specialising in gargantuan meat pies.

Food (☎ 340560; 82 Wyle Cop; mains £10-14; ✗ lunch & dinner) A modern minimalist joint with a globe-trotting menu.

Drinking

Three Fishes (☎ 344793; 4 Fish St) Smoke free and gloriously creaky, this fine Tudor alehouse has a reputation for good bar food

(£8 to £12) and a mellow clientele. There are plenty of real ales on tap at surprisingly good prices.

Coach & Horses (☎ 365661; Swan Hill) This wonderful old inn is one of the best in town with a lively atmosphere and friendly punters. It does a brilliant game roast and other hearty fare (£9 to £13) under the ageing beams and low lighting.

Armoury (☎ 340525; Welsh Bridge) Housed in a converted warehouse overlooking the river, this huge open shell of a pub features considerate lighting and a successful mix of old pictures and antiques lining the walls. It also serves a range of modern British food (£7 to £10).

Entertainment

For late night action:

C21 (☎ 355055; 21 Abbey Foregate) A sleek cosmopolitan club with mainstream choons.

Ministry (Abbey Foregate; cover charge £5) Themed nights from disco to garage, as well as occasional live music.

Getting There & Around
BIKE

You can hire bikes at **Dave Mellor Cycles** (☎ 366 662; 9 New St) from £10 a day.

BUS

National Express has two direct buses to London (£15.50, 4½ hours) and two more via Birmingham (5½ hours). Bus No 96 serves Ironbridge (30 minutes) every second hour Monday to Saturday. Bus No 435 travels to Ludlow (1¼ hours) via Church Stretton (45 minutes) six times daily and bus No 553 heads to Bishop's Castle (one hour) six times daily.

TRAIN

There are no direct trains connecting Shrewsbury and London – you must change at Wolverhampton, and journey times vary from three to 6½ hours (£34.10). There are hourly trains to Ludlow (30 minutes, £7.10).

Shrewsbury is a popular starting point for two scenic routes into Wales: one loop takes in Shrewsbury, northern Wales and Chester; the other, **Heart of Wales Line** (☎ 01597-822053; www.heart-of-wales.co.uk), runs southwest to Swansea (£15.80, 3¾ hours, six daily) and connects with the Cardiff to Fishguard main line.

AROUND SHREWSBURY
Attingham Park
The grandest of Shropshire's stately homes, the late-18th-century mansion **Attingham Park** (NT; ☎ 01743-708123; admission to house & grounds adult £5.50; ☒ noon-5pm Fri-Tue mid-Mar–Oct; grounds 10am-dusk Mar-Oct) combines elegance and ostentation in equal measures. Behind its imposing neoclassical façade, you'll find a picture gallery by John Nash and magnificent Regency interiors containing impressive collections of silver and lavish Italian furniture. The landscaped grounds shelter a herd of deer and a sculpture trail, and provide pleasant walks along the River Tern.

Attingham Park is 4 miles southeast of Shrewsbury at Atcham. Bus No 81 runs five times Monday to Friday, less on weekends.

Wroxeter Roman City
The scant remains of Roman Britain's fourth-largest city, Viroconium, can be seen at **Wroxeter** (EH; ☎ 01743-761330; admission adult £4; ☒ 10am-5pm Mar-Oct, 10am-4pm Nov-Feb). Remote-sensing techniques show a city as large as Pompeii lying under the lush farmland, but the costs of excavation are prohibitive. For the time being at least, you'll need a strong imagination and have to make do with the extensive remains of the public baths and a few archaeological finds in the small **museum**.

Wroxeter is 6 miles southeast of Shrewsbury, off the B4380. Bus Nos 81 & 96 stop nearby, and run five times Monday to Friday, less on weekends.

SOMETHING SPECIAL

Sun Inn (☎ 01938-561211; Marton; mains £11.50-13.50; wheelchair access) This unpretentious country pub does a very rare thing by providing a top-notch menu in a proper traditional bar. It's the kind of place where the locals come to play darts and the discerning come to dine. The simple menu focuses on fresh ingredients from local farms and can feature anything from roast monkfish teamed with baby squid to plump beef cooked to perfection. Each dish is lovingly prepared and immaculately presented and will leave you sighing in contentment. Marton is 12 miles southwest of Shrewsbury on the B4386.

IRONBRIDGE GORGE
☎ 01952
The cluster of picturesque villages that wind up this wooded gorge were the birthplace of the Industrial Revolution. Three generations of the Darby family transformed industrial processes here and changed the face of the world, ensuring the area a place in history and status as a World Heritage site.

It all started in 1709 when Abraham Darby pioneered the technique of smelting iron ore with coke, paving the way for local factories to mass-produce the first iron wheels, rails and steam locomotives. Abraham Darby II invented the forging process that enabled single beams of iron to be produced, allowing Abraham Darby III to blaze a trail with the world's first iron bridge, constructed here in 1779. The bridge itself is the centrepiece of the main village and is surrounded by quaint houses slithering down the sides of the gorge. Ten fascinating museums explain the history of the area and ensure an engaging visit for even the most reluctant history student.

Orientation & Information
The museums are scattered along the gorge and driving makes life a lot easier. See p378 for public-transport options.

The **TIC** (☎ 884391; www.ironbridge.org.uk, www .visitironbridge.co.uk; Tollhouse; ☒ 9am-5pm Mon-Fri, 10am-5pm Sat & Sun) is by the bridge. You can buy a **passport ticket** (adult £13.25) that will admit you to all the sites here.

Sights & Activities
The museums open from 10am to 5pm unless stated otherwise.

MUSEUM OF THE GORGE
A good way to begin your tour of the area is a visit to the **Museum of the Gorge** (The Wharfage; admission adult £2.20), housed in a Gothic warehouse by the river. A small exhibition covers the history of the gorge, with an absorbing video setting the museum in its historical context. The displays provide an overview of the Industrial Revolution and look at the environmental consequences of industrialisation. Allow about 45 minutes for a visit.

COALBROOKDALE MUSEUM OF IRON & DARBY HOUSES
The early industrial settlement of Coalbrookdale has survived almost intact with

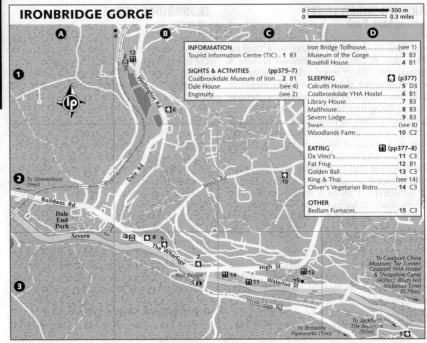

IRONBRIDGE GORGE

INFORMATION
Tourist Information Centre (TIC).. **1** B3

SIGHTS & ACTIVITIES (pp375–7)
Coalbrookdale Museum of Iron....**2** B1
Dale House.............................(see 4)
Enginuity.............................(see 2)

Iron Bridge Tollhouse................(see 1)
Museum of the Gorge................**3** B3
Rosehill House.........................**4** B1

SLEEPING (p377)
Calcutts House........................**5** D3
Coalbrookdale YHA Hostel.........**6** B1
Library House..........................**7** B3
Malthouse.............................**8** B3
Severn Lodge..........................**9** B3
Swan.................................(see 8)
Woodlands Farm.....................**10** C2

EATING (pp377–8)
Da Vinci's.............................**11** C3
Fat Frog..............................**12** B1
Golden Ball...........................**13** C3
King & Thai...........................(see 14)
Oliver's Vegetarian Bistro..........**14** C3

OTHER
Bedlam Furnaces.....................**15** C3

workers cottages, chapels and a church all undisturbed. A small army of local men and boys worked at the iron foundry, now converted into the **Museum of Iron** (admission adult £4.50). In its heyday in the 19th century, the foundry churned out heavy-duty iron equipment and delicate castings and it was here that Abraham Darby first succeeded in smelting iron ore with coke. The museum charts the history of the company and houses some extraordinary products of iron making. Allow about an hour to visit.

Just up the hill from the museum you can visit the beautifully restored 18th-century **Rosehill House** (☎ 433522; admission adult £3.10; ☙ closed Nov-Mar). Next door is **Dale House** and the office where the third Darby pored over his designs for the bridge. Combined admission to the museum and houses is £5.30.

IRON BRIDGE & TOLLHOUSE
The graceful arching bridge that gives the area its name was a symbol of the success of the iron industry and the pioneering achievements of this Shropshire town. As well as providing a crossing over the river,

Abraham Darby III's world-first iron bridge promoted the area and his technological prowess, ensuring the village's place in history as well as employment for all. The **tollhouse** (admission free) now houses an exhibition about the bridge's history.

BLISTS HILL VICTORIAN TOWN
A vast open-air Victorian theme park, **Blists Hill** (☎ 433522; Legges Way, Madeley; admission adult £8.50) is a complete reconstructed village with everything from a working foundry to sweet shops, a bank, grocer and chemist. Costumed staff explain the displays, craftspeople demonstrate skills, and special events such as Victorian weddings thrill the coach tours. If it all gets too much exchange some cash for shillings and grab yourself a stiff drink at the Victorian pub. Allow three to four hours and a healthy dose of patience to get round all the exhibits. Call ahead for winter opening hours.

COALPORT CHINA MUSEUM & TAR TUNNEL
When iron making moved elsewhere, Coalport china slowed the region's decline and

the beautifully restored buildings of the old china works now house an absorbing **China Museum** (admission adult £4.50) tracing the region's glory days as a manufacturer of elaborate pottery and crockery. Craftspeople demonstrate techniques used in making bone china and the children's workshops help keep younger visitors interested. Allow about 1½ hours for a visit.

A short stroll along the Shropshire Canal brings you to an amazing source of natural bitumen. The remarkable underground **Tar Tunnel** (admission adult £1.20; ☻ closed Oct-Apr) was discovered 200 years ago and the black stuff just keeps oozing from the walls.

JACKFIELD TILE MUSEUM

Newly reopened, the **Jackfield Tile Museum** (admission adult £4.50) has a wonderful display of thousands of decorative tiles and ceramics, mainly from Victorian times, in a series of gas-lit galleries in period style. Displays show the tiles in use in suburban villas, country churches, shops and tube stations. You can drop in to the workshops of student designers and manufacturers and see the 'Great Rock Sandwich' geological exhibition in the museum. Allow about an hour for a visit.

BROSELEY PIPEWORKS

A wonderfully preserved time capsule, the **Broseley Pipeworks** (admission adult £3.10; ☻ 1-5pm May-Sep) charts the history of smoking in what was once Britain's most prolific pipe manufacturer. Production of the famous clay pipes came to a halt in 1957 and the factory's doors were closed, sealing 350 years of tradition. The building is largely as it was when the last worker turned out the lights. It's a captivating place and well worth an hour's visit.

ENGINUITY

Interactive design and technology centre **Enginuity** (admission adult £5.30) champions Ironbridge's pioneering spirit and celebrates the area's engineering and technological achievements. The hands-on, feet-on, full-on exploration of design and engineering in modern life allows visitors to become apprentice engineers for a day and experiment with gadgets and gear used to design and make the things we see and use every day. Allow about two hours for your visit.

Sleeping

There are YHA hostels at either end of Ironbridge Gorge.

Coalport YHA Hostel (☎ 0870 770 5882; ironbridge@ yha.org.uk; High St, Coalport; dm £13.40; P ✗) Housed in the old china factory, this hostel has a stunning setting by the canal but the rooms are more functional than historic.

Coalbrookdale YHA Hostel (Paradise Rd, Coalbrookdale; dm £11.50; P ✗) is in the 19th-century Literary and Scientific Institute near the Museum of Iron and offers comfortable rooms within walking distance of town.

Woodlands Farm (☎ 432741; www.woodlandsfarm guesthouse.co.uk; Beech Rd; s/d £22.50/48; P ✗) One of the best-value places in town, Woodlands has bright, simple rooms with light neutral and pastel furnishings. Most rooms have views over the garden and digital TV.

Calcutts House (☎ 882631; www.calcuttshouse .co.uk; Calcutts Rd; s/d £30/50; P ✗) Tucked away from the relative hubbub, this 18th-century pad has opulent rooms named after celebrated ironmasters who lived here over the years. The styling is very traditional but tastefully done. The Alexander Brodie room is particularly pretty.

Malthouse & Swan (☎ 433712; The Wharfage; s/d £59/69; P) Sister establishments in the centre of town, these two places offer beautiful bright, beamed rooms with contemporary style and modern furnishings. Each room is different so it's worth looking at a few.

Other options:

Severn Lodge (☎ 432147; www.severnlodge.com; New Rd; s/d £52/66; P ✗) Elegant rooms with large beds, antique wardrobes and country-house styling.

Library House (☎ 432299; www.libraryhouse.com; 11 Severn Bank; s/d £55/65; P ✗) A lovely Georgian house overwhelmed by frills.

Eating

Oliver's Vegetarian Bistro (☎ 433086; 33 High St; mains £8.95; ☻ lunch & dinner) Small and stylish, this place has contemporary artwork and music, top-notch dishes at great prices and a vast menu. Delicacies include cashew-nut and carrot roast, and wild-mushroom and sundried-tomato sausage.

King & Thai (☎ 433913; 33a High St; mains £8-11; ☻ dinner) Above Oliver's, this split-level Thai emporium serves up generous portions of spicy Thai food untamed for the English market. It's an unpretentious and friendly place with some seriously good food.

Malthouse (☎ 433712; The Wharfage; mains £9-15; ☺ lunch & dinner) Try fasting before dining out here: the portions are enormous and the food is so good you won't want to leave any behind. The vibrant restaurant dishes up traditional favourites with a modern twist and there's live music in the bar from Wednesday to Saturday.

Fat Frog (☎ 433269; Coalbrookdale; mains £13-19; ☺ lunch & dinner) This French restaurant has whitewashed walls, red gingham tablecloths and battered wooden chairs, giving it the rustic charm of backstreet Provence. The food is excellent, there's a choice of traditional ales at the bar and frogs everywhere.

Other options for a bite:

Da Vinci's (☎ 432250; 26 High St; mains £11-17; ☺ dinner) A swish Italian place with a wood-panelled dining room.

Golden Ball (☎ 432179; Newbridge Rd; mains £9.50; ☺ lunch & dinner) Eighteenth-century pub with lots of character and excellent fusion food.

Getting There & Away

The nearest train station is 5 miles away at Telford. Bus No 96 runs every two hours (Monday to Saturday) between Shrewsbury (30 minutes) and Telford (10 minutes).

SOMETHING FOR THE WEEKEND

Start your weekend off by checking in to the wacky **Hundred House Hotel** (p380) and ensconce yourself for a night of romance and fine dining. In the morning nip over to the industrial-heritage site of **Ironbridge Gorge** (p375) and check out a museum or two. Trundle south for lunch among the patchwork of historic buildings in **Much Wenlock** (right). Breeze through the fantastic Shropshire countryside en route to **Ludlow** (p382), the gourmet capital, and check in to the **Feathers Hotel** (p383) or **Dinham Hall** (p383). Take a quick tour of impressive **Ludlow Castle** (p382) or stroll the lovely winding streets and lanes to work up an appetite. You'll be spoiled for choice for good food, but **Merchant House** (p383) and **Mr Underhill's** (p383) never fail to impress. On Sunday morning head south for the picture-postcard **black-and-white villages** (p366) of Pembridge and Eardisland. Toast the weekend with a rip-roaring Sunday lunch at the **Stagg Inn** (p366) and promise yourself you'll go straight to the gym on Monday.

Getting Around

Bus WH1 connects the museums roughly every half hour on weekends and bank holidays only. The WH2 and WH3 run to Much Wenlock four times on Saturday and once on Sunday. Midweek your only options are to walk or hire a bike from **Cycle Adventures** (☎ 07947-131349; www.cycleadventures.co.uk; half/full day £9/14), who will deliver bikes to you.

MUCH WENLOCK
☎ 01952 / pop 2650

Narrow winding streets, a patchwork of historical buildings from Tudor to Georgian times, a beautiful timbered guildhall and the evocative ruins of a 12th-century priory make this little town a real treasure. It also has strong claims to being the birthplace of the modern Olympics (see the boxed text opposite).

The **TIC** (☎ 727679; The Square; ☺ 10.30am-1pm & 2-5pm Mon-Sat Apr-Oct, plus Sun Jun-Aug) shares a 19th-century building with the local museum.

Sights & Activities

The TIC provides a free map to the town's sights of historical interest, as well as copies of *The Olympian Trail*, a pleasant 1½-mile walking tour of the town exploring the link between the village and the modern Olympics.

The main sight of interest is the enchanting ruins of the 12th-century **Much Wenlock Priory** (EH; ☎ 727466; adult £3; ☺ 10am-6pm daily Jun-Aug, 10am-5pm Thu-Mon Mar-May & Sep-Oct, 10am-4pm Fri-Sun Nov-Feb), set in beautiful grounds studded with pine and cherry trees. An audio tour (included in the admission price) gives a monk's impression of life at the priory. There's also a display of kooky Victorian topiary including squirrels and teddy bears. In July and August the ruins make a stunning backdrop to performances of Shakespeare's plays.

Sleeping & Eating

Stokes Bunkhouse Barn (☎ 727293; www.stokesbarn .co.uk; Newton House Farm; dm £7; P ☒) This beautifully converted 19th-century threshing barn has comfortable, character-filled dorms and a magnificent dining area. The barn is in a lovely rural location signposted off the A458.

Talbot Inn (☎ 727077; www.the-talbot-inn.com; 13 High St; s/d £38/75; P ☒) A wonderfully atmospheric old place with colossal beams and

---

GRANDDADDY OF THE MODERN OLYMPICS

Local doctor and sports enthusiast William Penny Brookes fused his knowledge of the ancient Olympics and rural British pastimes to launch the Much Wenlock Olympic Games in 1850. Begun as a distraction for the beer-swilling local youth, the games soon became an annual event and pricked the interest of Baron Pierre Coubertin, who came to Much Wenlock in 1890 to see them for himself.

He and Brookes became firm friends, with the shared dream of reviving the ancient Olympics. Coubertin went on to launch the modern Olympics in Athens in 1896; the games featured many of the events he had seen in Much Wenlock (although chasing a greased pig around town never really caught on). Brookes was invited to the event but he died, aged 86, before the games opened.

The good doctor never really got his share of the Olympic limelight until almost a century later, when International Olympic Committee President JA Samaranch visited his grave to 'pay tribute and homage to Dr Brookes, who really was the founder of the Modern Olympic Games'. The Much Wenlock Olympics are still held every July.

---

cavernous fireplaces, the rooms here have retained some period features and rustic furniture but the décor is generally bright and contemporary. The restaurant (mains £10 to £15) serves a fine French menu.

Raven Hotel (☎ 727251; www.ravenhotel.com; Barrow St; s/d £65/95-130; 3-course meals £20; P ⊠) The top spot in town, these gorgeous converted stables have country-chic styling with real attention paid to the little details. The excellent restaurant (mains £11 to £15) serves up traditional European classics with a hint of modern style.

Edge (☎ 727977; 14a High St; mains £9-13; ☻ lunch & dinner Tue-Sat) Rustic charm, Cajun music and some unusual modern artworks set the scene for the interesting modern creations at this café and restaurant. Simple lunches (£4 to £6) give way to stylish evening fare with plenty of local and organic ingredients.

Getting There & Away

Bus No 436 runs from Shrewsbury (40 minutes) to Bridgnorth (20 minutes) approximately every two hours (five on Sunday).

AROUND MUCH WENLOCK
Wenlock Edge

This steep limestone escarpment stretches 15 miles from Much Wenlock to Craven Arms and provides terrific walking with superb views. The National Trust owns much of the ridge, and there are many waymarked trails starting from car parks dotted along the B4371. The Wenlock Wanderer runs from Church Stretton to Much Wenlock via Wenlock Edge five times on Saturday and Sunday, but you'll need your own transport midweek.

For sustenance try the **Wenlock Edge Inn** (☎ 01746-785678; Hilltop; s/d £50/70), an award-winning pub with a loyal local following. It's quite an ordinary place with a relaxed atmosphere and unassuming décor serving up hearty homemade comfort food (mains £7 to £8). The pub is about 4½ miles southwest of Much Wenlock on the B4371.

Rooms at the Wenlock Edge are pretty hick and you'd be much better off at the **Wilderhope Manor YHA Hostel** (☎ 0870 770 6090; wilderhope@yha.org.uk; Longville-in-the-Dale; dm £11.80; ☻ Feb-Oct; P ⊠), a grand, gabled Elizabethan manor house, set deep in lush countryside. The 16th-century pile has oak spiral staircases and a grand dining hall, making it a really atmospheric place to stay.

You can catch buses from Ludlow and Bridgnorth to Shipton, a half-mile walk from Wilderhope. At weekends the **Wenlock Wanderer** stops here en route to Church Stretton.

BRIDGNORTH & AROUND
☎ 01746 / pop 11,900

Tumbling down a sandstone bluff, Bridgnorth has a dramatic location above the River Severn and has an interesting 17th-century Town Hall and a domed church by Thomas Telford. The **Bridgnorth Cliff Railway** (☎ 762052; www.bridgnorthcliffrailway.co.uk; 70p; ☻ 8am-8pm Mon-Sat & noon-8pm Sun May-Sep, to dusk Oct-Apr) joins High Town, at the top of the bluff, and Low Town below.

Bridgnorth is also the northern terminus of the **Severn Valley Railway** (☎ 01299-403816; www.svr.co.uk; adult/child £10.80/5.40; ☻ May-Sep, Sat & Sun Oct-Apr), whose trains chug down the picturesque valley to Kidderminster.

If you fancy staying in the area the pleasingly potty **Hundred House Hotel** (☎ 730353; www.hundredhouse.co.uk; Norton; s/d £85/99; P X), 6 miles north of town, has antique beds, lavender-scented sheets and flamboyant décor. Some rooms even have suggestive velvet-covered swings hanging from the ceiling. The place is passionate about food and the excellent international menu (mains £13 to £19) focuses on local produce and has an interesting choice of veggie options.

Another good option for food is the award-winning **Dog** (☎ 01746 716020; Main St, Worfield; mains £10-15; wheelchair access) in the picture-postcard village of Worfield. It's a real foodie pub but totally unpretentious, and has a fine menu serving up simple but divine food in generous portions.

Getting There & Away

Bus No 436 runs from Shrewsbury to Bridgnorth eight times daily (one hour, five times on Sunday), and you can catch the steam train from any of the stations in the Severn Valley.

CHURCH STRETTON & AROUND

☎ 01694 / pop 3850

Church Stretton is a picturesque settlement in a deep valley formed by the Long Mynd and the Caradoc Hills. Apart from the lack of a decent boozer, it makes a terrific base for exploring the surrounding hills and has quite a few interesting old buildings, including an early-12th-century Norman church with a rare sheila-na-gig (Celtic fertility symbol) over the north doorway.

The **TIC** (☎ 723133; Church St; ☺ 10am-1pm & 2-5pm Mon-Sat Apr-Sep) has lots of useful walking information.

Walking

The splendidly rolling **Long Mynd** is the most famous of Shropshire's hills and one of the best walking areas in the Marches. The Victorians called the area Little Switzerland, promoting it as a health resort and bottling the local spring water. The entire area is webbed with walking trails with memorable views.

You could start with the **Carding Mill Valley Trail**, which starts just outside Church Stretton and leads up to the 517m (1695ft) summit of the Long Mynd. This trail can get very busy at weekends and in summer, so you might prefer to pick your own peak or

cross the A49 and climb towards the 459m (1506ft) summit of Caer Caradoc.

You can drive part of the way up the Carding Mill Valley, although the NT would rather you took the **Long Mynd Shuttle bus** (return trip £2; weekends only Apr-Oct) from Beaumont Rd or the station.

Sleeping

Staying on or near the hills is a good option if you're here to ramble.

Bridges Long Mynd YHA Hostel (☎ 01588-650656; www.yha.org.uk; Ratlinghope; dm £9.30; P X) Hidden away in the Shropshire hills, this old village school now houses basic but comfortable big dorms. The Shropshire Way passes close by and paths lead to Long Mynd and Stiperstones. Boulton's bus No 551 comes here from Shrewsbury on Tuesday only. At weekends from April to October the Long Mynd shuttle runs hourly to Church Stretton.

Sayang House (☎ 723981; www.sayanghouse.com; Hope Bowdler; s/d £30/55; P X) A modern house built in a traditional style, this lovely B&B has oak-beamed rooms and an inglenook fireplace in its antique-filled lounge. The rooms are bright and spacious and tastefully decorated in muted colours. The house is one mile east of Church Stretton but you can arrange to be picked up at the station.

Jinlye Guest House (☎ 723243; www.jinlye.co.uk; Castle Hill, All Stretton; s/d £45/60; P X) Perched on the Long Mynd, this 16th-century property is an excellent choice with lots of character and beautifully furnished rooms. Old beams, log fires and leaded windows feature in the public rooms while the bedrooms are bright and beautiful, and furnished with a combination of antiques and delicate floral fabrics.

Other options include the following:

Willowfield (☎ 751471; www.willowfieldguesthouse .co.uk; Lower Wood; s/d £35/70; P X) Country-style rooms at a 17th-century farmhouse.

Longmynd Hotel (☎ 722244; www.longmynd.co.uk; Cunnery Rd; s/d £60/110; P X) Bright, airy rooms, breathtaking views and excellent modern European food (mains £13-19).

Eating

Berry's Coffee House (☎ 724452; 17 High St; meals £5-7; ☺ lunch) Organic free-range products rule the roost at this wonderful café off the main street. There's lots of hearty and wholesome dishes to choose from, and the desserts will make your knees wobble. You can also check your email while you wait.

Studio (☎ 722672; 59 High St; meals £13-15; dinner only Tue-Sat, lunch Sun) This former artist's studio has been converted into an intimate restaurant serving modern British and traditional French food. Local meats and game feature strongly on the menu, as do the fish specials.

Station Inn (☎ 781208; Marshbrook; mains £8-9; lunch & dinner; wheelchair access) The best place for pub grub in the area, this homely place by the train tracks has railway memorabilia and large portions of traditional favourites such as steak-and-mushroom pie and some more unusual choices such as swordfish.

For delicious snacks to take on the trail make a beeline for **Van Doesburg's Deli** (High St).

Getting There & Around

There are about a dozen trains to Shrewsbury (20 minutes) and bus No 435, which runs between Shrewsbury and Ludlow six times daily, stops here.

You can hire mountain bikes and tandems from **Shropshire Hills Bike Hire** (☎ 723302; 6 Castle Hill, All Stretton; mountain bikes/tandems per day £12/24), and bikes can be delivered and collected for an extra charge.

BISHOP'S CASTLE

☎ 01588 / pop 1630

This pretty little border town has an appealing collection of crooked half-timbered houses, second-hand bookshops and eclectic boutiques. At the centre of town is the tiny Georgian **Town Hall** and nearby the picturesque 16th-century **House on Crutches** (☎ 630007; admission 50p; noon-4pm Sat & Sun), housing the town's museum. The eponymous castle no longer exists but the town is famed for its pub breweries.

Tourist information is available from the beguilingly batty **Old Time** (☎ 638467; www .bishopscastle.co.uk; 29 High St; 10am-10pm Mon-Sat, 10am-2pm Sun).

Breweries

Six Bells Inn (☎ 630144; Church St; mains £6-12) The locals' choice, this historic 17th-century coaching inn still produces its own ales in the adjoining brewery and serves them on tap at the bar. The pub also has a reputation for good traditional food like Shropshire fidget pie and Cloud Nine (a local ale) cobbler.

Three Tuns (☎ 638797; Salop St) A traditional alehouse and former brewery, this is one of Shropshire's most famous, if quite ordinary, pubs. Unfortunately brewing has moved elsewhere, but you can still sample the house brews at the bar.

Walking

After becoming acquainted with the breweries, you can walk off your indulgences along the **Shropshire Way**, which runs through the town and joins up with **Offa's Dyke Path** to the south; the **Kerry Ridgeway** to the south; or head north and risk the forbidding ridges of the **Stiperstones**, where Satan is said to hold court.

Sleeping & Eating

Poppy House (☎ 638443; www.poppyhouse.co.uk; 20 Market Sq; s/d £40/70;) This lovely old place with timber-framed walls and oak floors has some wonderful rooms with deep red bedspreads and lots of little extras. The restaurant downstairs features an interesting menu (£5 to £8) with good vegetarian options and some traditional favourites.

Castle Hotel (☎ 638403; www.bishops-castle .co.uk/castlehotel; The Square; s/d £37.50/65; P) A lovely 18th-century coaching inn, this unfussy place has traditional beamed rooms with antique furniture and subtle floral patterns – if you're really looking for atmosphere try the lovely No 8. The oak-panelled restaurant (mains £6 to £9) serves traditional British food.

Capricho Café (☎ 638181; 39 High St; mains £4-6; lunch Mon, Tue & Thu-Sat) The best bet for a light meal, this modern café and deli serves wonderful homemade soups, great sambos, Mediterranean deli snacks and delicious cakes. There's an emphasis on organic and fair-trade products and a wide selection of Spanish and Italian olives, cheeses, biscuits and antipasti.

Other possibilities:

Old Brick (☎ 638467; www.oldbrick.co.uk; 7 Church St; s/d £35/60; P) A rambling 18th-century house with lovely terraced gardens.

Old Time (☎ 638467; www.oldtime.co.uk; 29 High St; s/d £30/56) Simple, comfy rooms in a 15th-century cottage.

Getting There & Away

Bus No 553 runs to and from Shrewsbury (one hour) six times daily.

SOMETHING SPECIAL

Waterdine Inn (☎ 01547-528214; www.the-water dine.co.uk; Llanfair Waterdine; s/d £55/80; P 🗶) Hidden away in the borderlands, this lovely 16th-century longhouse is a bit of a gem. The pretty cottage-style rooms have low ceilings, modern pine or antique furniture and big squashy beds. The food, however, is the real reason people come here. The stylish modern British and French menu (mains £11 to £16) focuses on organic meats and wild game as well as a few more exotic choices. There are plenty of real ales to choose from, and the view from the riverside garden is stunning.

Llanfair Waterdine is about 12 miles west of Ludlow.

LUDLOW

☎ 01584 / pop 9550

A temple of gastronomy and bastion of historical architecture, this wonderful town has the twin temptations of culinary excellence and cultural allure. It's the kind of place where you can just sit back, relax and pile on the pounds.

Set around the rambling ruins of a Norman castle, the half-timbered Jacobean buildings and elegant Georgian streets are made for wandering and are surprisingly free from tourists, making Ludlow a glorious base for discovering the nearby Shropshire hills. The town is also a real foodie heaven with a cluster of Michelin-starred restaurants, independent butchers, bakers, grocers and cheesemongers lining the narrow winding streets.

Ludlow's **TIC** (☎ 875053; ludlow.tourism@shrop shire-cc.gov.uk; Castle St; 🕑 10am-5pm) is in the 19th-century **assembly rooms** (☎ 878141; www.ludlow assemblyrooms.co.uk), now a lively arts and community centre with plenty of exhibitions and a good programme of live shows. There's also a small museum here.

Sights & Activities

Ludlow is best enjoyed by just rambling the lovely streets and exploring the winding lanes lined with antique dealers and specialist food shops.

The town's biggest sight is the impressive **Ludlow Castle** (☎ 873355; www.ludlowcastle .com; Castle Sq; admission adult £3.50; 🕑 10am-5pm Apr-Sep, 10am-4pm Oct-Mar, Sat & Sun only Jan), one of a line of fortifications built along the Marches to

ward off the marauding Welsh. Built around 1090, the sturdy Norman keep has wonderful views over the surrounding hills and the rivers below. The castle was transformed into a palace by Roger Mortimer in the 14th century but its chequered history is reflected in its different architectural styles. The round chapel in the inner bailey was built in 1120 and is one of few surviving. There is a wonderfully evocative audio tour (free) and the castle grounds provide an attractive setting for productions during the Ludlow Festival.

The waymarked 30-mile **Mortimer Trail** to Kington starts just outside the castle entrance. The TIC can provide information on the trail.

The **Church of St Laurence** (King St), one of the largest parish churches in Britain, was extensively rebuilt in the 15th century but has some original Early English features, along with a lofty tower, fine stained glass and some extraordinary, ornate medieval misericords ranging from the pious to the seemingly profane.

Guided walks run from April to October leaving the Cannon in Castle Sq at 2.30pm on Saturday and Sunday (£1.50). You can also take the **ghost walk** (adult £3.50; 🕑 8pm Fri) from the Buttercross.

Festivals & Events

There is a busy calendar of festivals throughout the year, the biggest being the **Ludlow Festival** (☎ 872150; www.ludlowfestival.co.uk), a fortnight of theatre and music that takes place in June and July. The **Ludlow Marches Food & Drink Festival** (www.foodfestival.co.uk) is promoted as Britain's foremost, and takes place over a long weekend in September. Accommodation can be nigh on impossible to find during these festivals.

Sleeping

Accommodation in Ludlow tends to be expensive.

Mount (☎ 874084; rooms@themountludlow.co.uk; 61 Gravel Hill; s/d £30/50; P 🗶) A good bet, this large Georgian house has bright, spacious rooms with simple, modern décor and a lovely garden. It's perched high on a hill and has great views of the town and countryside.

Number Twenty Eight (☎ 876996; info@ludlow no28.com; 28 Lower Broad St; d £75-120; 🗶 wheelchair access) Right in the centre of town, this refined group of small period houses has charming

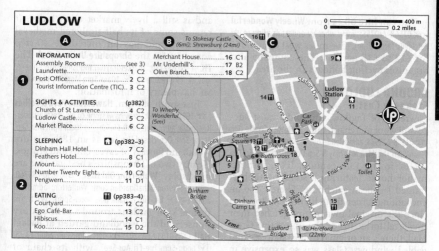

LUDLOW

INFORMATION
Assembly Rooms..................(see 3)
Laundrette..........................1 C2
Post Office..........................2 C2
Tourist Information Centre (TIC)..3 C2

SIGHTS & ACTIVITIES (p382)
Church of St Lawrence..........4 C2
Ludlow Castle.......................5 C2
Market Place........................6 C2

SLEEPING (pp382–3)
Dinham Hall Hotel.................7 C2
Feathers Hotel......................8 C1
Mount..................................9 D1
Number Twenty Eight...........10 C2
Pengwern............................11 D1

EATING (pp383–4)
Courtyard............................12 C2
Ego Café-Bar........................13 C2
Hibiscus..............................14 C1
Koo......................................15 D2

Merchant House....................16 C1
Mr Underhill's.......................17 B2
Olive Branch........................18 C2

rooms and several self-contained apartments. The mixture of period features and modern luxury makes it a very popular choice.

Feathers Hotel (☎ 875261; www.feathersatludlow .co.uk; Bull Ring; s/d £70/90) This stunningly picturesque timber-framed Jacobean property is the most atmospheric place to stay in town. It has magnificent public rooms and luxurious guest quarters, but ask for one in the original building, as the newer bedrooms are more frilly than fascinating.

Other options include the following:

Pengwern (☎ 874635; www.pengwern.org.uk; 5 St Julian's Ave; s/d £35/55; ✗) A large Edwardian house with bright modern rooms.

Dinham Hall Hotel (☎ 876464; www.dinhamhall.co.uk; s £75-180, d £150-200; P ✗) Sumptuous rooms, period design and a world-class restaurant (three-course dinner £35).

Eating

Courtyard (☎ 878080; Quality Sq; mains £5-7; ☽ lunch) Baked crab with lime and ginger or pheasant in red wine are some of the delicacies on offer at this wonderful lunch spot. Tucked away in a pretty courtyard, it has a loyal local following for its excellent-value food and simple snacks.

Koo (☎ 878462; 127 Old St; 4-course set menu £22.50; ☽ lunch & dinner Tue-Sat) This tiny Japanese place makes dinner a cultural experience, with a Japanese language lesson and tips on table etiquette thrown into the bargain. The minimalist décor reflects the traditional style of the food, which really is exquisite. A full option of vegetarian choices is also available.

Merchant House (☎ 875438; 62 Lower Corve St; set menu £33; ☽ lunch & dinner) Legendary in food terms yet totally unpretentious, this small and unassuming place has an international reputation. Creaky floors, low beams and rather old-style décor compliment the classic European dishes done to absolute perfection. Plan ahead though – this place is often booked up weeks in advance.

Mr Underhill's (☎ 874431; Dinham Weir; set menu £32; ☽ lunch & dinner) A wonderful riverside setting makes this a fantastic place on a summer evening. Bag a table by the window overlooking the weir and tuck in to the incredible modern British food. The restaurant also has some luxurious modern **rooms** (s/d £80/90-140) upstairs.

Some other options:

Olive Branch (☎ 874314; 2-4 Old St; mains £5-8) A wholesome lunch stop with simple, mainly vegetarian, food.

Ego Café-Bar (☎ 878000; Quality Sq; mains £7-14; ☽ lunch & dinner) Modern but cosy place with a rambling modern menu and Sunday-afternoon jazz.

Hibiscus (☎ 872325; 17 Corve St; set dinner menu £35; ☽ lunch & dinner) Contemporary Michelin-starred cuisine with a strong French accent and a fling with fusion.

Getting There & Around

Trains go almost hourly to Shrewsbury (£7.10, 30 minutes), Church Stretton (£3.90, 15 minutes) and Hereford (£5.50, 25 minutes). Bus routes radiate to Hereford (No 492, one hour, six daily), Birmingham (No 192, 2¼ hours, nine daily, five on Sunday) and Shrewsbury (No 435, 1¼ hours, six daily).

You can hire bikes from **Wheely Wonderful** (☎ 01568-770755; www.wheelywonderfulcycling.co.uk; Petchfield Farm, Elton), five miles west of Ludlow, for £12 to £15 per day. The company also organises cycling holidays in the area.

AROUND LUDLOW
Stokesay Castle
Lawrence of Ludlow, England's most successful wool merchant, built **Stokesay Castle** (EH; ☎ 01588-672544; admission £4.50; ⏰ 10am-6pm Jun-Aug, 10am-5pm Thu-Mon Mar-May & Sep-Oct, 10am-4pm Fri-Sun Nov-Feb) in the 13th century. It's a fortified manor house featuring a stunning timber-framed Jacobean gatehouse. There's also an enchanting garden that's hardly been touched since the original owners first pitched their medieval forks. Inside the impressive Great Hall, there's an original timber staircase and gabled windows. Glass was so expensive in the 17th century that the family carried the panes with them whenever they moved.

Stokesay Castle is 7 miles northwest of Ludlow, just off the A49. Bus No 435 runs five times daily between Shrewsbury and Ludlow. Alternatively, catch the train to Craven Arms, just over a mile away.

Croft Castle
The sturdy exterior of the Croft family residence **Croft Castle** (NT; ☎ 01568-780246; admission £4.40; ⏰ 1-5pm Wed-Sun Apr-Sep, Sat & Sun Mar & Oct) dates from the 14th century, although most of its flamboyant and decorative interior is 18th and 19th century and includes fine plaster-work ceilings, a splendid Georgian staircase and rare furniture. The castle has a lovely avenue of 350-year-old Spanish chestnuts, a walled garden and an interpretive centre.

The castle is 9 miles south of Ludlow off the B4362. Bus No 492 from Hereford (one hour) or Ludlow (15 minutes) runs seven times daily and stops at Gorbett Bank, 2 miles away.

NORTH SHROPSHIRE
Market Drayton to Ellesmere
Originally a Saxon town, **Market Drayton** was famed for its damson fairs and gingerbread, and is still a lively market town today. It retains some of its half-timbered medieval buildings and has an incredible 40-step aqueduct for the **Shropshire Union Canal**. The **TIC** (☎ 652139; marketdrayton.tourism@shropshire-cc .gov.uk; 49 Cheshire St; ⏰ 10am-5pm Mon-Fri, 10am-4pm Sat) has plenty of information.

Just south of town, **Hawkstone Park & Follies** (☎ 10939-200300; www.hawkstone.co.uk; Weston-under-Redcastle; admission adult £5.50; ⏰ 10am-4pm Mar-Sep, 10am-3pm Oct, closed Nov-Feb) is an 18th-century woodland fantasy of caves, cliffs and grottos. Nearby two of Shropshire's best gardens are on display: **Wollerton Old Hall** (☎ 01630-685760; www.wollertonoldhallgarden.com; Wollerton; admission adult £4; ⏰ Fri, Sun & bank hols noon-5pm), with its formal knot gardens around a 16th-century house, and the woodland garden at **Hodnet Hall** (☎ 01630-685202; Hodnet; admission adult £3.75; ⏰ noon-5pm Tue-Fri Apr-Sep), with its chain of ornamental ponds and magnolia walk.

Further west the six glacial lakes of **Ellesmere** are ideal for gentle walking, with many circular routes leading through woodland and gardens. You can pick up information on routes at the **Mere's Interpretive Centre** (☎ 10691-622981; Mereside, Ellesmere; ⏰ 11am-4pm), which also has displays about the local landscape and wildlife. Ellesmere itself has a mix of Tudor, Georgian and Victorian buildings and a choice of accommodation.

One of the best places to stay in North Shropshire is the **Pen-y-Dyffryn Hotel** (☎ 01691-653700; www.peny.co.uk; Rhydycroesau, Oswestry; s/d £78/98-140; P ✗), tucked away in a valley with gorgeous views of the Welsh mountains. This gem of a hotel is based in a former Georgian rectory and has lovely terraced riverside gardens, restrained traditional style rooms and an organic restaurant (three-course set menu £21.50).

Another good option is the **Burlton Inn** (☎ 01939-270284; www.burltoninn.co.uk; Burlton; s/d £50/80; P ✗ wheelchair access), a quaint 18th-century, family-run inn with bright cottage-style rooms with contemporary furniture and rich fabrics. In-the-know locals flock here for the excellent traditional British and classic European dishes (mains £9 to £14).

Oxfordshire, the Cotswolds & Gloucestershire

CONTENTS

Soaked in history and riddled with implausibly picturesque towns and villages, this area comes very close to the misty-eyed romantic ideal that most visitors have of England. The lush, rolling hills and mellow, honey-stone cottages attract as many locals as tourists though, and monstrous 4WDs hurtle down the narrow country roads while tourist coaches clog up the village lanes.

Legendary Oxford, cloaked in centuries of academic achievement, makes an ideal base, wooing its visitors with its incredible buildings, stunning museums and lively student haunts. To the west, Regency Cheltenham oozes a genteel air and elegant refinement while nearby Gloucester has the gracious lines of a magnificent Gothic cathedral. Dotted in between are the chocolate-box villages that give the Cotswolds their undeniable charm, the distorted houses of Tudor Tewksbury and the extraordinary Churchill pile of Blenheim Palace in Woodstock.

Although the area can get swamped with visitors in summer, it's easy to get off the beaten track. Take to the hills on foot or by bike to explore the real heart of the region and get an idea of how life once was when the wool trade ruled supreme. The really best bits aren't mentioned on any tourist itinerary or in any guidebook – you just happen upon them by accident. Throw away your map and follow your nose down winding country lanes to the most idyllic of tiny villages with an impossibly charming pub plucked out of a medieval Monday and serving the most perfect of pints.

HIGHLIGHTS

- Admiring the overwhelming beauty of **Oxford University** (p392)
- Visiting **Blenheim Palace** (p400) and its superb gardens
- Appreciating the muted elegance of **Regency Cheltenham** (p423)
- Exploring **Gloucester Cathedral** (p418) and its magnificent cloisters
- Seeing the honey-stone villages of the **Cotswolds** (p405), particularly **Stow-on-the-Wold** (p414)
- Checking out the **National Hunt Festival** (p421) in Cheltenham in March, a highlight of the social and racing calendar

- POPULATION: 1.2 MILLION
- AREA: 2222 SQ MILES

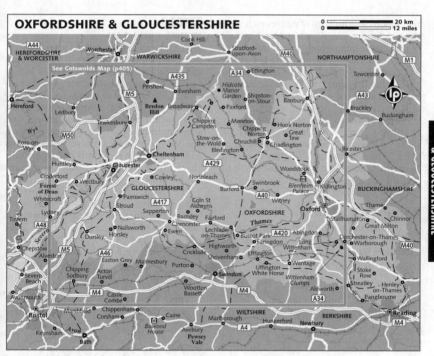

OXFORDSHIRE & GLOUCESTERSHIRE

Activities

The Cotswold counties are inundated with visitors in peak season, but an ideal way to get away from the hordes and really appreciate the area is to do some walking or cycling. For more information, see the Outdoor Activities chapter or specific suggestions for walks and rides throughout this chapter.

CYCLING

Dedicated cycle ways, quiet country lanes, gated roads and gentle gradients make the Cotswold counties ideal for cycling. The Cotswold Hills themselves are especially scenic, but the steep western escarpment can be a bit of a shock for the unprepared.

Waymarked, long-distance routes in the region include the **Thames Valley Cycle Way**, part of the National Cycle Network (see the boxed text p62), which starts in Oxford and leads eventually to London.

The **Cotswolds** and **Chilterns** both have many bridleways open to mountain bikers, and in the west of the region, the **Forest of Dean** has many dirt-track options, and some dedicated mountain-bike trails.

WALKING

The most popular long-distance route in this region is the **Cotswold Way** (www.cotswold-way .co.uk), an absolute classic covering 102 miles (164km) from Bath to Chipping Campden. The full trail takes about a week to walk. Alternatively, choose a section of it and meander along at your own pace. The **Cotswold Hills** also offer endless opportunities for shorter walks.

Another popular choice is the **Thames Path** (www.thames-path.co.uk) national trail following the river downstream from its source near Cirencester all the way to London. Plan on about two weeks to tackle the whole 173 miles, or try the very enjoyable five-day section from near Cirencester to Oxford.

OXFORDSHIRE

Increasingly urbane yet stubbornly rural, Oxfordshire is home to both a world-famous university and the muddied wellies of its Barbour-clad country folk. Oxford's incredible architecture and international reputation draw millions of visitors each year, the weight of academic achievement and air of gentility seeping from its very walls.

To many visitors, Oxfordshire *is* Oxford, but past the ivy-clad quads and gowned cyclists lies the gentle charm of bucolic England – an area steeped in history and culture and increasingly popular with money-ed commuters. To the south of the county is affluent Henley-on-Thames, famous for its Royal Regatta. Near here, the mysterious giant White Horse of Uffington is carved from the limestone hills, and just north of Oxford is the spectacular birthplace of Sir Winston Churchill, Blenheim Palace.

Activities

As well as the national trails, other long walking routes in this county include the **Oxfordshire Way** – a 65-mile waymarked trail running from Bourton-on-the-Water to Henley-on-Thames. Leaflets available from local TICs divide the route into 16 walks of between 2 and 8 miles in length.

Oxfordshire is also good cycling country, with many quiet roads and few extreme gradients. If you don't have your own wheels Oxford is the best bet for bike rental (p399). Cycling routes through the county include the **Oxfordshire Cycleway**, which takes in Woodstock, Burford and Henley.

Getting Around

TICs stock bus and train timetables showing routes and giving contact numbers for each operator. Oxford and Banbury are the main train stations, with services to London Paddington and Euston, Hereford, Birmingham, Bristol and Scotland.

The main bus operators offer day and weeklong bus passes that can be a good deal if you plan on doing a lot of bus travelling. See p751 for details.

Cotswold Roaming (☎ 308300; tours@cotswold -roaming.co.uk) Runs guided bus tours from Oxford between April and October. Half-day tours run to Blenheim Palace (adult/child £16/10), full-day tours go to Bath and Castle Combe (£30/18), and the Cotswolds (£32.50/20).
National Rail Enquiries (☎ 08457 484 950)
Oxford Bus Company (☎ 01865-785 400; www .oxfordbus.co.uk)
Stagecoach (☎ 01865-772250; www.stagecoach -oxford.co.uk)
Traveline (☎ 0870 608 2608; www.traveline.org.uk) For all public transport information.

OXFORD

☎ 01865 / pop 143,016

Internationally renowned yet incredibly insular, Oxford is a city of remarkable beauty and stunning contrast. Birthplace of Mensa and the Morris motor car, home to the academic elite and the working-class majority, Oxford is, at its best, an open-air museum, its beautiful buildings oozing charm and a distinguished past. At its worst, it is a divided town where university students and townspeople rarely mix and where tour buses threaten to mow down pedestrians on the street.

The whole city is steeped in history, its colleges jealously guarding some of Britain's best architecture, its student population a heady mix of hormones, intellectual ideas and old money. And although the streets may be thronged with camera-wielding tourists, inside the college walls a studious calm descends on the ivy-clad quads and ornate doorways.

There is much more to Oxford than the colleges, though, and you shouldn't leave without capsizing a punt, peering at a case full of shrunken heads and sampling the buzzing nightlife. For maximum effect just lose yourself in the winding lanes and alleys that crisscross the city, many of them unchanged since the time of Auden, Wilde and Tolkien.

History

Strategically placed at the confluence of the River Cherwell and the Thames (called the Isis here, from the Latin name *Tamesis*), Oxford was a key Saxon town heavily fortified by Alfred the Great in the war against the Danes.

Oxford's importance grew dramatically after 1167, when all Anglo-Norman students were expelled from the Sorbonne in Paris. Oxford's Augustinian abbey attracted students in droves but they managed to create a lasting enmity between themselves and the local townspeople, culminating in the St Scholastica's Day Massacre in 1355 (see opposite). Thereafter, the king ordered that the university be broken up into colleges, each of which then developed its own traditions.

The first colleges were built in the 13th century, with at least three more being added in each of the following three centuries. The newer colleges, such as Keble, were added in the 19th and 20th centuries to cater for an ever-expanding student population. Today, there are about 16,500 students spread among 39 separate colleges. So many brains in the one place didn't necessarily bring enlightenment, though: lecturers were not allowed to marry until 1877 and women were not admitted to the university until a year later. Even then, it took another 42 years before women would be granted a degree for their four years of hard labour. Today St Hilda's clings on doggedly as the last remaining all-female college.

Meanwhile the arrival of the canal system in 1790 created a link with the Midlands' industrial centres and the town began to expand outside its academic core. However, the city's real industrial boom came when William Morris began producing cars here in 1912. The Bullnose Morris and the Morris Minor were both produced in the Cowley factories to the east of the city where BMW's new Mini runs off the production line today.

Orientation

The city centre can easily be covered on foot. Carfax Tower makes a good central landmark and there are frequent buses from the train station to the west. Alternatively, it's a 15-minute walk. The bus station is nearer the city centre, off Gloucester Green.

University buildings are scattered throughout the city, with the most important and architecturally interesting in the centre. Jericho, in the northwest, is upmarket but bohemian with trendy bars and restaurants, while Cowley Rd, southeast of Carfax, is the edgy student and immigrant area packed with cheap places to eat and drink and late-night shops.

Information

BOOKSHOPS

Blackwell's (☎ 792792; 48-51 Broad St) Stocks any book you could ever need and has a vast basement worth a visit in itself.

Little Bookshop (☎ 559176; Covered Market) Tiny shop bursting with first editions and rare books.

EMERGENCY

Police (☎ 266000; St Aldate's)

INTERNET ACCESS

Mices (☎ 726364; 118 High St; per 30min £1; 9am-11pm Mon-Sat, 10am-11pm Sun) There's another branch on Gloucester Green.

Virgin (☎ 723906; 18 Cornmarket St; per 30min before noon £1, after noon £3; 9am-7pm Mon-Sat, 11am-5pm Sun)

INTERNET RESOURCES

Daily Info (www.dailyinfo.co.uk) Everything you needed to know about gig, cinema, theatre and exhibition listings.

Oxford City (www.oxfordcity.co.uk) Extensive accommodation and restaurant listings as well as entertainment and shopping.

ST SCHOLASTICA'S DAY MASSACRE

Ever since the arrival of the first students in Oxford there has been friction with the locals. Name-calling often erupted into full-scale violence and in 1209 and 1330 battered scholars abandoned Oxford and established universities in Cambridge and Stamford respectively. What happened on February 10 and 11 1355, however, made previous riots seem like an innocent pillow fight.

Celebrations for St Scholastica's Day grew nasty when two drunken students started a fist fight with a tavern landlord. The fight spilled out into the street where students and townspeople soon took to each other's throats. The chancellor ordered the pealing of the bells and every student who heard it rushed to join the brawl. By the end of the day the students had claimed victory and an uneasy truce was established. The next morning, however, the furious townspeople returned with the help of local villagers armed with pickaxes, shovels and pikes. By the end of the day 63 students and 30 townspeople were dead. King Edward III ordered troops to quell the riot, and after reviewing the situation decided to bring the town under the control of the university.

On the anniversary of the riot each year the mayor and burgesses (citizens) were ordered to attend a service and pay the vice chancellor a penny for every student killed. The practice continued until 1825 when the mayor flatly refused to pay the fine, as did his successors until 1955 when the university eventually extended the olive branch and awarded a Doctorate of Civil Law to Mayor William Richard Gowers, MA, Oriel.

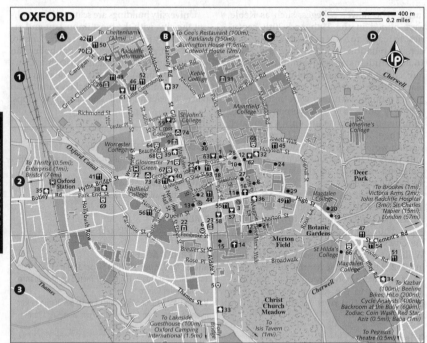

Oxford Online (www.visitoxford.org) Tourism Oxford's site with information on everything from accommodation to activities.

LAUNDRY

Coin Wash (127 Cowley Rd; per load £2.60; 9.15am-1pm & 3.15-7pm Mon-Sat)

MEDICAL SERVICES

John Radcliffe Hospital (☎ 741166; Headley Way, Headington) Three miles east of the city centre.

MONEY

Every major bank and ATM is represented on or near Cornmarket St.

POST

Post office (☎ 223344; 102 St Aldate's; 9am-6pm Mon-Sat)

TOURIST INFORMATION

Oxford Information Centre (☎ 726871; www .visitoxford.org; 15-16 Broad St; 9.30am-5pm Mon-Sat, 10am-3.30pm Sun Easter-Oct) The TIC stocks a *Welcome to Oxford* (£1) brochure, which has a walking tour with college opening times, as well as the *University of Oxford* leaflet

and *Oxford Accessible Guide* for travellers with disabilities. Also look out for two free publications: *In Oxford,* which lists events, museums, restaurants and accommodation options and the less-useful *WOW (What's on Where).* The centre can book accommodation for a £3 fee plus a 10% deposit.

UNIVERSITIES

Oxford Brookes (☎ 741111; www.brookes.ac.uk) Oxford's lesser-known university.
Oxford University (☎ 270000; www.ox.ac.uk)

Sights

UNIVERSITY & PITT RIVERS MUSEUMS

Many would say there are plenty of dinosaurs lurking around Oxford, but you can see the real thing at the **University Museum** (☎ 272950; www.oum.ox.ac.uk; Parks Rd; admission free; noon-5pm) housed in a superb Victorian Gothic structure worth a visit for its architecture alone. Inside, a glorious fantasy space of slender, cast-iron columns and ornate capitals lead to a soaring glass roof. The museum is devoted to natural science and has a whopping collection of over five million exhibits ranging from exotic insects and fossils to a towering T-Rex skeleton.

At the back of the museum a door leads into the half light of an Aladdin's cave of treasures: the **Pitt Rivers Museum** (☎ 270927; www.prm.ox.ac.uk; admission free, audio tour £1; ☺ noon-4.30pm Mon-Sat, 2-4.30pm Sun). Feathered cloaks, necklaces of teeth, blowpipes, magic charms, mummies and head-hunters' trophies including scalps and shrunken heads bulge out of cabinets and glass cases and should be enough to satisfy every armchair adventurer's wildest dreams. The museum also runs an excellent series of workshops for children (usually the first Saturday of the month).

ASHMOLEAN MUSEUM
England's oldest museum, the mammoth **Ashmolean** (☎ 278000; www.ashmol.ox.ac.uk; Beaumont St; admission free; ☺ 10am-5pm Tue-Sat, 2-5pm Sun) occupies one of Britain's best examples of neo-Grecian architecture. It houses a vast collection of treasures based on the stash squirrelled away by John Tradescant, Charles I's gardener, and Dr Elias Ashmole.

The collection is so vast that it's difficult to take it all in. It's bursting with Egyptian, Islamic and Chinese art; rare porcelain, tapestries and silverware; priceless musical instruments; and extensive displays of European art (including works by Raphael and Michelangelo). You'd be well advised to study the floor plan and choose a manageable route through the sumptuous rooms and hallways.

MODERN ART OXFORD
An antidote to the musty hallways of history, **Modern Art Oxford** (☎ 722733; www.modernartoxford .org.uk; 30 Pembroke St; admission free; ☺ 10am-5pm Tue-Sat, noon-5pm Sun) is one of the best contemporary art museums to be found outside London. It has a wonderful gallery space, excellent touring exhibitions and plenty of activities for children. The focus is on 20th-century painting, sculpture and photography.

MUSEUM OF OXFORD
For an excellent introduction to the history behind the city and university visit the **Museum of Oxford** (☎ 252761; St Aldate's; adult/child £2/50p; ☺ 10am-4pm Tue-Fri, 10am-5pm Sat, noon-4pm Sun). Exhibits range from a mammoth's tooth and an Elizabethan pavement of cattle bones, to a series of rooms from different eras and a Morris Minor used to illustrate car production's huge part in the city's manufacturing boom.

OXFORD STORY
More fanfare and less information is on offer at the **Oxford Story** (☎ 728822; www.oxford story.co.uk; 6 Broad St; adult/child £6.95/5.25; ☺ 9.30am-5pm Jul-Aug, 10am-4.30pm Mon-Sat & 11am-4.30pm Sun Sep-Jun), which is incredibly popular with tourists, but derided by locals and students. Basically, it's a 25-minute ride through the 900 years of university history in carriages designed to look like college desks.

THE BRAINS BEHIND THE OED

In what was to become one of the greatest legacies of the Victorian era, the Oxford University Press agreed to fund the century's biggest literary project: the compilation of what was then called *The New English Dictionary of Historical Principles*. Recognising the mammoth task ahead, editor James Murray issued a circular in 1878 recruiting an army of bookworms to read every book ever published and make precise notes on word usage.

Of the thousands of volunteers who signed up, the most prolific of all was Dr WC Minor, a US Civil War surgeon. Over the next 20 years, he contributed tens of thousands of illustrative quotations and notes on word origins and usage. Dr Minor submitted all his contributions by post from Broadmoor, a hospital for the criminally insane. Murray considered him his most valued contributor and in 1891 made a point of travelling to meet the venerable doctor.

Murray soon discovered, however, that Dr Minor was the asylum's longest-serving inmate, a schizophrenic committed in 1872 for the motiveless murder of a man in London. Despite this, Murray was deeply taken by Minor's complete devotion to his dictionary project and continued to work with him. Neither lived to see the publication of the Oxford English Dictionary – a 12-volumed masterpiece – in 1928. It was the most comprehensive lexicographical project ever undertaken and a full second edition did not appear until 1989.

For a full version of the darkly compelling story visit the **Oxford University Press Museum** (☎ 267527; Great Clarendon St; admission free; ☙ by appointment only), which also tells the history of printing, or look out for Simon Winchester's *The Surgeon of Crowthorne*.

CARFAX TOWER

The sole reminder of medieval St Martin's Church, **Carfax Tower** (☎ 792653; admission £1.40; ☙ 10am-5.30pm Mon-Sat & 11am-5pm Sun May-Oct, 10am-3.30pm Nov-Apr), stands at the junction of four streets and derived its name from the Latin *quadri furcus*, meaning 'four forks'. The tower is adorned by a pair of quarter-boys (figures who hammer out the quarter hours on bells) and there's a good view over the city centre from the top.

UNIVERSITY BUILDINGS & COLLEGES
Christ Church College

The largest and most spectacular of all of Oxford's colleges, **Christ Church** (☎ 286573; www.visitchristchurch.net; St Aldate's; adult/child £4/3; ☙ 9am-5.30pm Mon-Sat, noon-5.30pm Sun) is also its most popular. The college was founded in 1525 by Cardinal Thomas Wolsey – who suppressed 22 monasteries to acquire the funds.

Thirteen British prime ministers were educated here as well as Albert Einstein, philosopher John Locke, poet WH Auden and Charles Dodgson (the real name of storyteller Lewis Carroll). More recently it was used as a location for the Harry Potter films.

The main entrance is below **Tom Tower**, the upper part of which was designed by former student Sir Christopher Wren. The 7-ton tower bell chimes 101 times each evening at 9.05pm (Oxford is five minutes west of Greenwich), the time when the original 101 students were called in.

Visitors, however, must enter through the smaller gate further down St Aldate's. Immediately to the left is the 15th-century cloister, a relic of the ancient Priory of St Frideswide whose shrine was a focus of pilgrimage. From here you go up to the magnificent **Great Hall**, the college's dining room on the south side of **Tom Quad**, the largest quadrangle in Oxford.

From the quad you enter **Christ Church Cathedral**, the smallest cathedral in the country, with brawny Norman columns topped by elegant vaulting and some beautiful, stained-glass windows including a rare depiction of the murder of Thomas Becket.

You can also explore another two quads and the **Picture Gallery**, with its modest collection of Renaissance art. Leave the college by the south entrance to stroll the leafy lanes of **Christchurch Meadow**.

Merton College

Small, smart and rich, **Merton College** (☎ 276 310; www.merton.ox.ac.uk; Merton St; admission free; ☙ 2-4pm Mon-Fri, 10am-4pm Sat & Sun) was one of the original three colleges founded in 1264 and represents the earliest form of collegiate planning.

The charming 14th-century **Mob Quad** was the first of the college quads. The **Old Library** leading off it is the oldest medieval library in use, with some books still chained up, an ancient antitheft device. JRR Tolkien (who taught here) undoubtedly spent many a day leafing through the dusty tomes in search of arcane runes and old Saxon words that helped shape *The Lord of the Rings*. Another literary giant associated with the college is TS Eliot.

If you're visiting in summer don't miss the wonderful candlelit concerts in the chapel in the evening.

Magdalen College

Oxford's wealthiest and probably most beautiful college, **Magdalen** (mawd-len; ☎ 276000; www.magd.ox.ac.uk; High St; adult/child £3/2; ☺ noon-6pm Jul-Sep, 1pm-dusk Oct-Jun) even has its own herd of deer.

The medieval chapel, with its 43m-high bell tower, is well worth a visit as is the stunning cloister with its strange gargoyles and carved figures, said to have inspired CS Lewis' stone statues in *The Chronicles of Narnia*. Oscar Wilde, poet laureate Sir John Betjeman and actor Dudley Moore were also students.

The college also boasts a fine choir that sings every May Day from the top of Magdalen Tower at 6am. The event now marks the culmination of a solid night of drinking for most students before they gather in their glad rags on Magdalen Bridge to listen to the madrigals.

Opposite Magdalen are the beautiful **Botanic Gardens** (☎ 286690; www.botanic-garden.ox .ac.uk; adult/child £2.50/free; ☺ 9am-6pm May-Sep, 9am-4.30pm Oct-Apr) that sweep along the banks of the River Cherwell. The gardens are the oldest in Britain and were founded in 1621 for the study of medicinal plants.

All Souls College

Founded in 1438 as a centre of prayer and learning, **All Souls College** (☎ 279379; www.all -souls.ox.ac.uk; High St; admission free; ☺ 2-4pm Mon-Fri) is reputed to be one of the oddest colleges in Oxford.

Traditionally a postgraduate college, legend has it that only undergraduates of exceptional intelligence and impeccable table manners have been admitted, following a bizarre examination including questions on the correct disposal of a stone from a cherry tart.

The college is dominated by two mock-Gothic towers, which were lambasted for ruining the Oxford skyline when erected in 1710. It also has a beautiful sundial by Wren and a lovely chapel.

Radcliffe Camera

The quintessential Oxford landmark and one of the city's most photographed buildings, the **Radcliffe Camera** (Radcliffe Sq; ☺ closed to the public) is a spectacular circular library built in 1748 in the Palladian style.

For excellent views of the Radcliffe Camera climb the 14th-century tower in the beautiful **Church of Saint Mary the Virgin** (☎ 279111; cnr High & Catte Sts; tower admission £2/1; ☺ 9am-7pm Jul-Aug, 9am-5pm Mon-Sat, noon-5pm Sun Sep-Jun).

Brasenose College

More enchanting than the larger colleges, 16th-century **Brasenose College** (☎ 277830; admission £1; ☺ 2-4.30pm) has a charm and elegance somewhat lacking in its more famous neighbours. The college takes its name from an 11th-century snout-like door knocker that was stolen in 1334 by students from Stamford College, Lincolnshire. In 1890 Brasenose bought the whole of Stamford College so as to reacquire the door knocker. It now hangs above the high table in the dining hall. Next to it is a portrait of Alexander Nowell, a college principal, whose claim to fame is the 'invention' of bottled beer.

New College

Stroll under the **Bridge of Sighs**, a 1914 copy of the famous bridge in Venice, to **New College** (☎ 279 555; cnr Holywell St & New College Lane; admission £2 Easter-Sep, free Oct-Easter; ☺ 11am-5pm Easter-Sep, 2-4pm Oct-Easter) founded in 1379. The college is a fine example of the perpendicular style and has a chapel full of treasures. Superb stained glass, much of it from the 14th century, adorns the windows, and Sir Jacob Epstein's disturbing statue of Lazarus is also here. If you're visiting during term time it is well worth stopping in for Evensong at 6pm.

A former college warden named William Spooner gave rise to the term 'spoonerism' after his habit of transposing the first consonants of words. It's claimed that he once reprimanded a student by saying, 'You have deliberately tasted two worms and can leave Oxford by the town drain'.

Sheldonian Theatre

The university's main public building, the **Sheldonian Theatre** (☎ 277299; www.sheldon.ox.ac .uk; Broad St; adult/child £1.50/1; ☒ 10am-12.30pm & 2-4.30pm Mon-Sat) was the first major work of Christopher Wren, at that time Professor of Astronomy. It is used for college ceremonies and public concerts and the ceiling of the main hall has a fine 17th-century painting of the triumph of truth over ignorance. There are good views of the surrounding buildings from the cupola.

Bodleian Library

One of England's three copyright libraries, the **Bodleian Library** (☎ 277224; www.bodley.ox.ac .uk; cnr Broad St & Parks Rd; ☒ 9am-4.45pm Mon-Fri, 9am-12.30pm Sat; tours £4; no children under 14) is one of the oldest public libraries in the world. The building is accessed via the stunning Jacobean-period **Old Schools Quadrangle.** Tours take place at 10.30am, 11.30am, 2pm and 3pm, and show off the mysterious Duke Humfrey's library (1488).

Also not to be missed is the **Divinity School** (admission free), which is the oldest teaching room in the university. It is renowned as a masterpiece of 15th-century English Gothic architecture and has a superb fan-vaulted ceiling.

Other Colleges

Sandwiched between Christ Church and Merton you'll find the small and beautiful **Corpus Christi College** (☎ 276700; Merton St; admission free; ☒ 1.30-4.30pm). Look out for the pelican sundial in the middle of the front quad.

Nearby medieval **St Edmund Hall** (☎ 279000; Queen's Lane; admission free; ☒ sunrise-sunset) is the sole survivor of the original halls – the teaching institutions that preceded colleges in Oxford. Its small chapel was decorated by William Morris and Edward Burne-Jones.

Set back off Broad St, **Trinity College** (☎ 279900; Broad St; admission £1.50; ☒ 10am-noon & 2-4pm Mon-Fri, 2-4pm Sat & Sun) is worth a visit for the exquisite carvings in its chapel and Wren's beautiful Garden Quad.

Exeter College (☎ 279600; Turl St; admission free; ☒ 2-5pm) is known for its elaborate 17th-century dining hall and ornate chapel that houses *The Adoration of the Magi*, a William Morris tapestry.

Activities
PUNTING

A trip to Oxford wouldn't be quite complete without an attempt to retain composure and look elegant while punting down the river through a tangle of reeds and low branches. It's one of the best ways of soaking up the local atmosphere, and the secret to controlling these flat-bottomed boats is to push *gently* on the pole to get the punt moving and then use it as a rudder to keep on course.

You can punt on both the Cherwell and the Isis, but the latter is popular with training rowers and far less atmospheric. Punts are available from Easter to September and hold five people including the punter, and cost £12 per hour.

The most central location to rent punts is on the Isis at Magdalen Bridge from **Howard C & Sons** (☎ 202643; www.oxfordpunting.com; High St; deposit £30). Far better, though, is the **Cherwell Boat House** (☎ 515978; www.cherwellboathouse.co.uk; Bardwell Rd; deposit £60) for a countryside amble where the destination of choice is the busy boozer the **Victoria Arms** (☎ 241382; Mill Lane). To get to the boathouse take bus No 2 or 7 from Magdalen St to Bardwell Rd and walk five minutes.

Tours

Blackwell's (☎ 333606; oxford@blackwell.co.uk; 53 Broad St) Runs tours from April to October. Literary tours (adult/child £6/5.50) run at 2pm Tuesday, 11am Thursday and noon on Saturday. Inklings tours (£7/6.50) are at 11.45am on Wednesdays and Alice in Wonderland tours (£7/6) run on Fridays at 2pm. Cost includes admission to Christchurch.

City Sightseeing (☎ 790522; www.citysightseeing oxford.com; adult/child £9/3) and **Full Circle Tours** (☎ 01789-720 002; www.fullcircletours.co.uk; adult/child £8/3) run hop-on, hop-off city bus tours every 15 to 20 minutes from 9.30am to 6pm between April and October, less often in winter. Both leave from the train station.

Oxford Information Centre (see p390) Runs a guided 'Oxford Past and Present' walking tour (adult/child £6.50/3) at 11am and 2pm. Inspector Morse tours (£7/3.50) follow the trail of the fictional Oxford sleuth every Saturday at 1.30pm. Ghost tours (£5/3) depart at 7.45pm on Friday and Saturday, June to September.

Sleeping

Accommodation in Oxford in general favours floral patterns over cutting-edge design. Between May and September beds fill up very quickly, so book in advance or join the queue at the TIC and pay £3 for help.

Oxford is best appreciated by staying in the centre, but good bus services to areas just outside the centre mean you can save on accommodation costs without missing any action.

BUDGET

New Oxford YHA Hostel (☎ 727275; oxford@yha.org.uk; 2a Botley Rd; dm/d £19.50/46; P ✗ 🖥 wheelchair access) This friendly hostel has the best budget beds in town and is well worth considering for a double room over some of the city's grotty B&Bs. Rooms are bright and airy, if a little functional, and facilities include bike storage, luggage lockers and a laundry room.

Oxford Backpackers (☎ 721761; 9 Hythe Bridge St; dm £13; ✗ 🖥) Convenient for town, this grungy hostel has bright murals, ancient armchairs and its own bar, which can mean things get a bit loud at weekends. It's a little dingy and dorms can have as many as 18 beds but plenty of visitors stay long-term and take advantage of the £60 weekly rate.

Oxford Camping International (☎ 244088; 426 Abingdon Rd; camping per person £8.85) This large, well-serviced campsite is 1½ miles south of the city centre. It's a very popular spot and gets booked out well in advance.

MID-RANGE

Burlington House (☎ 513513; www.burlington-house .co.uk; 374 Banbury Rd; s/d from £58/80; P ✗) A top-notch option, this lovingly maintained, Victorian merchant house is simply but elegantly decorated. Rooms are bright and cheerful and the generous breakfast will keep you going for most for the day.

Lakeside Guesthouse (☎ 244725; www.lakeside -guesthouse.co.uk; 118 Abingdon Rd; s/d without bathroom £38/50; P ✗) This family-run Victorian guesthouse has smart, good-value rooms and lots of outdoor space. Situated by a park and near the river it's a pleasant place with easy access to the centre.

Parklands (☎ 554374; stay@parklandsoxford.co.uk; 100 Banbury Rd; s/d £59/89; P ✗) Bright modern rooms with understated décor and neutral tones make this Victorian town house worth a visit. Just a mile from town, it is a good compromise option and children are very welcome.

Head of the River (☎ 721600; headoftheriver@ fullers.co.uk; Folly Bridge; s/d £75/85) Go punting in your pyjamas from this surprisingly good hotel above a pub. The comfortable, taste-fully decorated rooms are good value and in a beautiful location overlooking the Isis.

St Michael's Guesthouse (☎ 242101; 26 St Michael's St; s/d £35/50; ✗) Ideally located on a quiet street in the heart of the city, this friendly B&B has modest but comfortable rooms and is often booked out well ahead.

Cotswold House (☎ 310558; www.cotswoldhouse .co.uk; 363 Banbury Rd; s/d £50/75; P ✗) Bright, comfortable rooms with traditional décor, a warm welcome and a great breakfast make this excellent B&B, about 2 miles north of the city centre, well worth the effort.

Two other options:

Isis Guest House (☎ 248894; fax 243 492; 45-53 Iffley Rd; s/d £35/60; ☼ Jul-Sep; P ✗) Decent rooms close to town.

Old Mitre Rooms (☎ 279821; mitre@lincoln.ox.ac.uk; 4b Turl St; s/d £30/55; ☼ Jul-Aug; ✗) Student rooms varying considerably so ask to see more than one.

TOP END

Old Parsonage Hotel (☎ 310210; www.oldparsonage -hotel.co.uk; 1 Banbury Rd; s £125, d £135-195; P ✗) Once home to Oscar Wilde and now Oxford's best hotel, this place oozes charm and character from its 17th-century walls and individually furnished rooms. The antique furniture and floral patterns won't suit everyone, but the newer rooms at the back are more contemporary and just as luxurious.

Old Bank Hotel (☎ 799599; www.oldbank-hotel .co.uk; 92 High St; s/d from £140/160; P ✗ ✗ 🖥) A haven of slick modern design in a city of tradition, this hotel combines clean lines and urban chic in its stylishly sleek rooms in muted natural tones. Most rooms have stunning views of Oxford's roofline and all have large screen TVs and CD players.

Other top-end options:

Bath Place Hotel (☎ 791812; www.bathplace.co.uk; 4-5 Bath Pl; s/d from £110/130; P ✗) A luxurious 17th-century retreat with creaky floors and tiny winding stairs.

Randolph Hotel (☎ 0870 400 8200; randolph@ macdonaldhotels.co.uk; Beaumont St; s/d from £120/140; ✗) Oxford's most famous and overrated hotel with old-world style. A favourite of old-school businessmen.

Eating

Oxford has loads of eating options but there are plenty of joints serving up mediocre meals and willing to relieve gormless tourists and wealthy parents of their cash, so beware. For cheap-and-cheerful meals head for the student strip on Cowley Rd.

OXFORDSHIRE, THE COTSWOLDS & GLOUCESTERSHIRE

BUDGET

Cafés

Joe's (☎ 201120; 21 Cowley Rd; mains £6-9; ☺ lunch & dinner) Serving what are possibly the best breakfasts in town, with or without a cocktail on the side, tiny Joe's dishes up a simple but delicious menu to everyone from those looking for a hangover cure to the hip brunch crew. Lunch and dinner specials make it worth a visit later on too.

Grand Café (☎ 204463; 84 High St; high tea £13.50; ☺ lunch) This is Oxford's most elegant coffee house, where you can dine on cucumber sandwiches, scones, strawberries and truffles in opulent surroundings. The service is charming.

Jericho Café (☎ 310840; Walton St; mains £5-7; ☺ lunch & dinner) This cool, laid-back café is a great spot to refuel on healthy goodies, from tasty bruschettas and interesting salads to imaginative pizzas. Linger over a latte in mid afternoon, or drop in for a bite before a late show at the Phoenix Picturehouse.

Restaurants

Edamame (☎ 246916; 15 Holywell St; mains £6-7.50; ☺ lunch & dinner) Look out for the queue halfway down Holywell St and you've found tiny Edamame where simple but delicious Japanese home cooking gets dished up to the lucky ones who made it inside. They don't take bookings but it's well worth the wait. Thursday night is sushi (£2 to £3.50) night.

La Plaza Tapas (☎ 516688; 11 Little Clarendon St; mains £8-11, tapas £3.20-4.50; ☺ lunch & dinner) Set in a beautiful narrow building with warm walls and a lovely bar. It's easy to pass a few hours here nibbling on the great tapas

> ### SOMETHING SPECIAL
>
> **HiLo** (☎ 725984; 68-70 Cowley Rd; mains around £8) A little enclave of Jamaica on the Cowley Rd, this ramshackle place has no fixed menu, no qualms about standards of service, no fixed opening hours and only a price 'guide'. Customers get charged whatever the management feels they can afford. Red snapper and curried goat get washed down with Jamaican beer and rum while drunken students dance to the heavy reggae music. The grungy atmosphere is a far cry from Oxford sophistication, but it's certainly an experience; you'll either love it or hate it.

or settling in for the long haul with a traditional Spanish meal of salt cod or paella.

SoJo (☎ 202 888; 6-9 Hythe Bridge St; mains £6-9; ☺ lunch & dinner) This chic, sultry new place offers incredible-value meals and an extensive menu ranging from dim sum and hot pots to a Mongolian buffet (one visit £4.50) where you can see your food cooked in front of you. Wash it all down with a SoJo MoJo and you'll be set for the night.

Other good options:

Red Star (☎ 251248; 187 Cowley Rd; mains £5.50-7; ☺ lunch & dinner) Tiny but popular Asian place with daily changing specials and giant bento boxes.

Aziz (☎ 794 945; 228 Cowley Rd; mains £7-10; ☺ lunch & dinner) Popular Bangladeshi restaurant serving incredible food with lots of vegetarian options.

Quick Eats

If you're doing a whirlwind tour of the city and just can't stop for lunch, try some of these options for a quick but hearty sandwich (£2 to £4):

Mortons (☎ 200867; 103 Covered Market & 22 Broad St) An Oxford institution and perennially popular for its great sandwiches.

Felson's Baguette Bar (☎ 316631; 32 Little Clarendon St) Tiny place dishing up great takeaway treats.

Gluttons Deli (☎ 553748; 110 Walton St) Does some of the best sandwiches and pies in town.

Self-Catering

As soon as you walk into the **Covered Market** (Market St) you're hit with the smell of food wafting through the air – from the freshly baked cookies at one end to the traditional pies and fresh fruit at the other. You can pick up anything from Sicilian sausage to a pork and apricot pie, freshly made sandwiches, luscious fruit and excellent olives.

Apart from the food you'll also find old-style barbers and cobblers, funky clothes stalls and traditional butchers. If you're in Oxford at Christmas the displays of freshly hung deer, wild boar, ostrich and turkey are quite amazing.

MID-RANGE

Branca (☎ 556111; 111 Walton St; mains £9-15; ☺ lunch & dinner) Dine with the smart set at this trendy Italian joint with its swish bar, balcony kitchen and strangely industrial design features. Rustic pizza and pasta and killer cocktails mean the place is buzzing most nights, so you'll need to book in advance.

Chutneys (☎ 724241; 36 St Michael's St; mains £7.50-10.50; 🕐 lunch & dinner) Great food and chilled surroundings lure the crowds to this fantastic bright and airy Indian. The extensive menu always delivers something delicious, just don't go wild on the poppadums or you'll have no room for the succulent main courses.

Moya (☎ 200111; 97 St Clements; mains £9-11; 🕐 lunch & dinner) Crisp, contemporary and minimalist, Moya serves up some weird but wonderful Slovak dishes like the incredible devil's toast (sausage, chilli and goat's cheese). The service is faultless and the cocktails (£4.50) are worth a visit in themselves.

Bangkok House (☎ 200705; 42a Hythe Bridge St; mains £9-12; 🕐 lunch & dinner) Sink into an enormous carved chair for what is simply the best Thai food in town. Delicious, coconut-based curries, sublime mushroom-and-galangal soup, faultless service and moderate prices make this place an excellent choice for a special night out.

Sip (☎ 311322; 102 Walton St; dishes £3-6.50; 🕐 lunch & dinner) Seriously stylish and packed with trend-conscious cocktail drinkers, this minimalist restaurant serves up a tapas-style menu of Asian and fusion foods. The nosh is excellent, but by the time you've filled your belly your Prada purse will be quite a bit lighter.

Fishers (☎ 243003; St Clements; mains £9-15; 🕐 lunch & dinner) Subtle seafaring décor plays backdrop to a wonderful fish and seafood restaurant serving up a mixture of traditional dishes and modern innovations. If you're a fish lover just go the whole hog and try a seafood platter.

TOP END

Quod (☎ 202505; 92 High St; mains £9-17; 🕐 lunch & dinner) Popular with a trendy young crowd and the merely moneyed, Quod dishes up thoroughly good Mediterranean brasserie-style food. The place is buzzing every night and in summer the cool terrace with trickling water features is a real draw. Bright modern art adorns the walls inside and the stylish bar is a good place to sip cocktails.

Gee's Restaurant (☎ 553540; 61 Banbury Rd; mains £11-20; 🕐 lunch & dinner) Set in a Victorian conservatory that was once a flower shop, this swanky restaurant dishes up an innovative feast of modern European food. It's a great place for a special evening out, but a bit stuffy for a night on the town.

SOMETHING SPECIAL

Sir Charles Napier (☎ 01494-483011; Sprigg's Alley, Chinnor; mains £11.50-17.50, 2-course menu £16.50) A veritable legend in food terms, the Sir Charles Napier is renowned for its excellent food, lavish gardens, stunning views and eclectic artwork. The unmatched chairs and bold sculptures all add to the charm. The menu is Anglo-Mediterranean with wild local game in winter and Cornish lobster drawing the crowds in summer. The wine list is well chosen, and the food – nothing short of divine.

Chinnor is about 15 miles east of Oxford.

Drinking

Oxford is overrun with watering holes, from the faithfully traditional where famous writers, politicians and scholars have debated their ideas for centuries, to the slick, modern bars for the urbane cool. Some of the best are listed below.

PUBS

Turf Tavern (☎ 243235; 4 Bath Pl) One of the best-loved pubs in town, the Turf is hidden down a tiny alley near the Bridge of Sighs. It does a stunning array of ales and is filled with a mix of locals, students and tourists, spilling out of the snug low-ceilinged bar into the three courtyards outside.

Eagle & Child (☎ 310154; 49 St Giles') The cosy cubby holes of this 17th-century place were once the favourite haunt of JRR Tolkien, CS Lewis and their literary friends. The wonderful atmosphere can get spoiled by the hordes of tourists, but if you're lucky it'll just be a few dusty academics you'll have to contend with.

White Horse (☎ 721860; 52 Broad St) More a large cupboard than an actual pub, this tiny place plays host to an eclectic mix of dons and bookish students. It was a favourite retreat for TV detective Inspector Morse and gets crowded easily so come early if not mid-afternoon.

Bear (☎ 721783; Alfred St) Sloping floors, low ceilings and a wooden interior have survived intact through the centuries at what is thought to be Oxford's oldest pub. The walls are adorned with a significant collection of old ties and on Tuesday nights the University Challenge pub quiz teams go head to head.

Isis Tavern (☎ 247006; Iffley Lock, Iffley Village) Nestled in a picturesque spot on the banks of the river, the Isis is a great place to lose a few hours on a sunny afternoon. To get there, stroll downriver from Folly Bridge for just over a mile and reward yourself with a cool drink in the garden while you watch the rowers go by. If you can pull yourself away, nip across the lock to Iffley village with its beautiful old stone cottages and 12th-century church.

BARS

Kazbar (☎ 202920; 25-27 Cowley Rd) A cavernous place with a Moroccan theme, it's easy to lose yourself for a few hours under the low lighting and the influence of several cocktails. The clientele is cool but laid-back and the Spanish and North African tapas (£2.50 to £4.50) are excellent.

Raoul's (☎ 553732; 32 Walton St) This sleek bar has a trendy retro look and is usually packed with fun-loving young people who come for the extensive cocktail menu (from £5) and funky jazz music. It gets very busy so you may have to queue.

Baby Love (☎ 200011; 3 King Edwards St) This place is packed most nights with hip young things sipping cocktails and you'll have to vie for space on the dance floor downstairs – unless you volunteer for some pole dancing in the corner. Watch out for the glass floor as you walk in the door, and don't bother apologising for entering the wrong loo – they're unisex.

Baba (☎ 203011; 240 Cowley Rd) This groovy low-lit Moroccan bar is pretty slick and well worth the hike up Cowley Rd. It's small so you need to get there early but the minty drinks are great and there are plenty of North African options for nibbles.

Frevd (☎ 311 171; 119 Walton St) Entombed in a converted neoclassical church complete with stained-glass windows, this crumbling café-bar is one of the best-loved spots in town. It's popular with a young style-conscious clientele nibbling on pizzas (£5 to £7) at lunch and throbbing with cocktail-sipping luvvies by night.

Entertainment

NIGHTCLUBS

Considering the number of students and Oxford's legacy as the birthplace of Radiohead, Ride and Supergrass, the city isn't blessed with the best choice of clubs. However, there are a few real gems among the dross.

Po Na Na (☎ 249171; 13-15 Magdalen St; admission up to £6) The best club in town, this is one of the originals of the Po Na Na Moroccan-style chain. Cavelike and very hip, the playlist features soulful Latin jazz, funk, hip-hop and the very best boogie choons in town.

Zodiac (☎ 420042; 190 Cowley Rd; admission up to £5) An Oxford institution and the city's best live-music venue, the Zodiac oozes a flirty indie vibe and is generally packed with an eclectic and seriously unpretentious crowd intent on having a good time. Live gigs range from guitar-thrashing bands kicking off their England tours to jazz instrumentalists, while club nights feature anything from drum 'n' bass to trashy disco.

Backroom at the Bully (☎ 244516; 162 Cowley Rd; admission up to £5) A regular student favourite, the Bullingdon Arms hosts everything from jazz and acoustic gigs to cheesy '70s disco, trance and occasional techno nights. Check the listings to see what the latest offerings are.

Park End (☎ 250181; 37 Park End St; admission up to £6) Oxford's largest mainstream nightclub comes complete with six bars and three floors of shirt-drenching dance, chart, garage and soul music that rarely moves out of the safe, commercial genre – much like its punters. In summer, it gets some top-name DJs.

THEATRE

The **Oxford Playhouse** (☎ 305305; www.oxford playhouse.com; Beaumont St; wheelchair access) is the city's main stage for drama, and hosts an impressive selection of touring productions of theatre, music and dance. Just around the corner the **Burton Taylor Theatre** (☎ 798600; Gloucester St) goes for more offbeat student productions. The **Pegasus Theatre** (☎ 722851; www.pegasustheatre.org.uk; Magdalen Rd; wheelchair access) is popular for its low-budget, independent productions while the **New Theatre** (☎ 0870 606 3500; George St) has large-scale touring shows and ageing pop stars.

CLASSICAL MUSIC

Oxford hosts plenty of classical concerts in beautiful venues such as the Sheldonian Theatre, Christchurch Cathedral and Jacqueline du Pré Music Building. Keep an eye out for posters around town or visit www.musicatoxford.com. There is also a series of Sunday-morning coffee concerts held at the Holywell Music Room try www .coffeeconcerts.com for details.

Getting There & Away
BUS
Competition on the route to London is fierce with three companies serving the route.

London Espress (☎ 785400; www.oxfordbus.co.uk; return £11; 1½hr) Runs the same route as the Oxford Tube, at similar times.

Megabus (www.megabus.com; one way from £1; 1¾ hr) Coaches run from Oxpens Coach Park to Gloucester Pl in London six times a day.

Oxford Tube (☎ 772250; www.oxfordtube.com; return £11; 1½hr) Runs to London's Victoria coach station every 12 to 20 minutes 24 hours a day.

The Heathrow Express (three-month return £17, 70 minutes) runs half-hourly 7am to 11pm, hourly 11pm to 7am, while the Gatwick Express (three-month return £24, two hours) runs hourly 7am to 10pm and every two hours 10pm to 6am.

National Express has five buses to Birmingham (£9.25, two hours), one service to Bath (£10.50, two hours) and Bristol (£14, 2¼ hours), and two to Gloucester (£8.50, 1½ hours).

Stagecoach serves most of the small towns in Oxfordshire. If you're planning a lot of bus journeys it's worth buying a Megarider Plus Pass allowing unlimited bus travel in Oxfordshire for seven days. It costs £9.

Multi-operator passes known as the Plus Pass cost £5/14/40 for one day/week/month.

CAR & MOTORCYCLE
Oxford has a serious traffic problem and parking is a nightmare. Five Park & Ride car parks surround the town. Parking costs 60p and a return bus journey to town (10 to 15 minutes, every 10 minutes) costs £1.80.

TRAIN
There are half-hourly services to London Paddington (one way £14.90, one hour); and hourly trains to Coventry (£15, one hour), Birmingham (£18, 1½ hours), Worcester (£11.50, 80 minutes) and Hereford (£14.70, two hours).

To connect with trains to the southwest you have to change at Didcot Parkway (one way £3.80, 15 minutes). There are many connections to Bath (one way £9.80, 1½ hours).

Getting Around
BICYCLE
The *Cycle into Oxford* map, available from the TIC, shows all local cycle routes. The following companies rent bikes:

Beeline Bikes (☎ 246 615; 61-63 Cowley Rd; per day/week £12/20; deposit £50) Hybrid and mountain bikes available.

Cycle Analysts (☎ 424444; 150 Cowley Rd; per day/week £10/18; deposit £100) Hybrid bikes, locks and lights supplied.

BOAT
Salter Bros (☎ 243421; www.salterbros.co.uk) offers several interesting jaunts from Folly Bridge from May to September.

BUS
You can walk almost everywhere in Oxford's centre, but if you're feeling less than energetic there are buses serving the area. Bus Nos 1 and 5 serve Cowley Rd from Carfax, Nos 2 and 7 go along Banbury Rd from Magdalen St and Nos 31 and 35 along Abingdon Rd from St Aldates.

TAXI
There are taxis outside the train station and near the bus station, as well as on St Giles' and at Carfax. Be prepared to join a long queue after closing time. A taxi to Blenheim Palace costs around £20.

SOMETHING SPECIAL

Old Trout (☎ 01844 212146; 29-30 Lower High St, Thame; s/d £65/90; **P**) As charming as it is idiosyncratic, the Old Trout is an excellent retreat for a quiet meal or a memorable night. The 500-year-old building is riddled with narrow passages and nooks and crannies and you may even have trouble finding your room. The bedrooms are traditional in character with bulging walls, and beds made specially to compensate for the sloping floors. You'll have to crawl into Room 1: the door is just over 3ft high. Downstairs the restaurant serves up excellent seasonally inspired local food with an international twist (mains £9.50 to £17.50).

Thame is about 12 miles east of Oxford.

SOMETHING SPECIAL

Crazy Bear (☎ 01865-890714; www.crazybear group.co.uk; Bear Lane, Stadhampton; s £65-120, d £110-290; Ⓟ ✕) Secluded in a quiet village, this 16th-century country inn is a gleefully eccentric haven of urban chic mixed with a touch of glam rock. Pink leather upholstery, a stuffed black bear and Grecian busts somehow manage to coexist in near-perfect harmony. The slick, themed rooms combine Art Deco with novelties such as tiger heads and double baths. Two equally idiosyncratic restaurants serve up fine food. Choose either the superb Thai brasserie (mains £8.50 to £16) or the excellent modern British cuisine (mains £16 to £18) in the main restaurant. Sip some draught champagne while you wade through the cigar menu, lap up the decadent surroundings and just pile on the pounds.

Stadhampton is about 7 miles southeast of Oxford.

WOODSTOCK

☎ 01993 / pop 2389

Steeped in history and oozing charm, the lovely village of Woodstock is home to a fine collection of 17th- and 18th-century buildings and the glorious country pile of the Churchill family, Blenheim Palace. Also worth a look are the town hall, built at the Duke of Marlborough's expense in 1766, and the church, which has an 18th-century tower tacked onto a medieval interior.

Opposite the church, Fletcher's House accommodates the **Oxfordshire Museum** (☎ 811456; Park St; admission free; ☽ 10am-5pm Tue-Sat, 2-5pm Sun), which has displays and dioramas on local history, art, archaeology and the environment. The **TIC** (☎ 813276; Park St; ☽ 9.30am-5.30pm Mon-Sat, 1-5pm Sun) is attached to the museum.

Blenheim Palace

Queen Anne's relief was so great after the defeat of the French at the Battle of Blenheim (*blen*-num) that she decided on a cash award as a thankyou to John Churchill, Duke of Marlborough, for his role in the victory. The end result was the extravagant **Blenheim Palace** (☎ 08700 60 20 80; www .blenheimpalace.com; admission £11; park & garden only £6; ☽ 10.30am-5.30pm mid-Feb–Oct, park open year-round) and its lavish gardens, now a Unesco World Heritage Site. The palace is one of Europe's

largest and was designed by Sir John Vanbrugh and Nicholas Hawksmoor between 1705 and 1722. Today, it is home of the 11th duke and duchess.

The interior of this remarkable baroque fantasy palace is stuffed with a variety of paintings, antiques, carvings and tapestries but the crowds and the heady pace of the free guided tour make it hard to appreciate. First up is the **Great Hall**, which has 20m-high ceilings adorned with images of the first duke at the battle that earned him the house.

You proceed to the **Churchill Exhibition**, four rooms devoted to the life, work and writings of Sir Winston, who was born at Blenheim in 1874. According to a notice on the wall he was born prematurely, but historians have long since discounted this as a necessary lie – it seems Winnie's folks got a little ahead of themselves and couldn't wait until the wedding day. Churchill and his wife, Lady Clementine Spencer-Churchill, are buried in nearby Bladon Church, whose spire is visible from the Great Hall.

On your way to the drawing rooms you'll pass the **China Cabinet**, which has entire collections of Meissen (Dresden) and Sèvres porcelain. Though the other rooms in the house are all magnificent, the most impressive of all is the 55m **Long Library**, with books collected by the 9th duke.

The extensive grounds are large enough that you can lose most of the crowds if you're willing to walk a little. Parts were landscaped by Lancelot 'Capability' Brown and are simply stunning. Just north of the house a dramatic artificial lake boasts a beautiful bridge by Vanbrugh.

Sleeping & Eating

It's top-notch hotels only in Woodstock so plan a day trip if you're travelling on a budget.

Kings Arms Hotel (☎ 813636; www.kings-hotel -woodstock.co.uk; 19 Market St; s/d £70/130; ✕) Sleek, simple rooms with contemporary furnishings allow you to flee the chintz in style at this Georgian hotel. The bright brasserie (mains £8 to £14) serves up surprisingly good modern British fare in the large atrium area and the clutter-free bar.

Feathers Hotel (☎ 812291; www.feathers.co.uk; Market St; s £99, d £135-225; Ⓟ ✕ ▯) Seven 17th-century town houses have been knocked together to form this labyrinthine hotel with winding staircases and hidden rooms. The whole place drips with character and the luxurious rooms are tastefully decorated with rich fabrics, antiques and beds to wallow in. The restaurant serves up fine French food (mains £19 to £23), which it takes *very* seriously, announcing every dish as it arrives.

Brotherton's Brasserie (☎ 811114; 1 High St; mains £8-13; ☾ lunch & dinner) This gas-lit brasserie lures you in with warm orange walls and rustic wooden furniture, and keeps you there with a range of competent Mediterranean favourites and a healthy wine list.

Zaki's Deli (☎ 811535; 31 Oxford St; ☾ lunch) If you need a quick snack or supplies for a palatial picnic on Blenheim lawn, Zaki's will stock you up with everything from fine cheeses and olives to choice meats and local Cotswold smoked salmon. Alternatively, you can eat in and refuel on delicious sambos (£3 to £4), coffee and cake.

Getting There & Away

Stagecoach bus No 20 runs every half hour (hourly on Sunday) from Oxford bus station (20 minutes). **Cotswold Roaming** (☎ 308300; www.cotswold-roaming.co.uk) offers organised excursions to Blenheim from Oxford, departing at 10am and returning at 1.50pm. The cost is £16/10 per adult/child, and includes admission to Blenheim.

DORCHESTER & THE WITTENHAMS

A street of old coaching inns and a magnificent medieval church are more or less all there is of **Dorchester-on-Thames**, although in Saxon times there was a cathedral here. In the 12th century an abbey was founded on the site and it later became the parish church of **SS Peter & Paul**. It's worth stepping inside to see the rare Norman lead font, a wonderful Jesse window tracing Christ's ancestry, and a 13th-century monument of a knight. There's a small museum in the **Abbey Guest House,** which also dates back to the Middle Ages.

From the village you can take a pleasant 3-mile walk to **Wittenham Clumps**, two ancient tree-topped hills by a curve in the river. For centuries the hills held an important defensive position overlooking the Thames and there are wonderful views from the top.

At the bottom of the hills lies the village of **Little Wittenham**, well known in the area for its beautiful cottages, and **St Peter's**

SOMETHING SPECIAL

Le Manoir aux Quat' Saisons (☎ 01844-278881; www.manoir.co.uk; Church Rd, Great Milton; d £265-465; P X 🖳) Chef Raymond Blanc has created a haven of indulgence at his 15th-century manor house just outside Oxford. The gastro-hotel is gloriously unstuffy, but the rooms and food are pure decadence. The Mermaid Rose suite has a spiral staircase leading to a bathroom with two canopied tubs, while the Opium Suite has its own secluded Zen garden. The restaurant (mains £36 to £38, three-course set lunch £45) is top of the heap in food terms and is renowned for its seven-course menu gourmand (£95). For those aspiring to bring a little bit of Le Manoir home, the hotel also offers cookery courses (a one-day non-residential costs £185).

Church, a gorgeous stone building. At the end of March each year the **Pooh Sticks World Championships** are held in Little Wittenham. Competitors drop sticks in the river and watch them 'race' to the finish line.

Two miles by road from Little Wittenham you'll come to the beautiful village of **Long Wittenham** where incredible thatched cottages line the road. The 12th-century St Mary's Church contains a 900-year-old lead font and what is thought to be the smallest sculpted monument in England: a three-foot effigy of a crusader.

Stop by the 15th-century **Barley Mow Inn** (☎ 01865-407847) where Jerome K Jerome wrote most of his timeless classic *Three Men in a Boat* and described it as '…without exception the quaintest most old-fashioned inn up the river'. The pub draws large crowds at the weekends for its real ales and fine food (mains £8 to £14).

Bus No 107 connects Long Wittenham to Didcot (15 minutes) and Oxford (25 minutes) hourly Monday to Saturday. Bus No 139 connects Dorchester with Abingdon (15 minutes) hourly Monday to Saturday (five on Sunday).

WARBOROUGH

If you're looking for the kind of rural village that Thomas Hardy might have set one of his novels in, Warborough is as close as you'll get. There are no museums to visit or

OXFORDSHIRE, THE COTSWOLDS & GLOUCESTERSHIRE

TOP FIVE PUBS FOR SUNDAY LUNCH

- **Churchill Arms** (p415; Paxford) Honest gourmet fare in a seriously unpretentious setting.

- **Crooked Billet** (p404; Stoke Row) Temple of gastronomy in the one-time hangout of highwayman Dick Turpin.

- **Falkland Arms** (p412; Great Tew) Authentic, old-world charm in a stunning Cotswold village.

- **Kings Head** (p414; Bledington) Timeless, 16th-century inn with fine menu featuring local produce.

- **Sir Charles Napier** (p397; Chinnor) A culinary Oxford institution renowned for its food and eclectic artwork.

churches of note to admire, just a gorgeous village that seems oblivious to the passing of time. At the centre of everything is the village green, which doubles up as the cricket pitch, and around it a host of attractive buildings including the gorgeous thatched **Six Bells on the Green** (☎ 01865-858265), an old-world pub with low ceilings, open fires, real ales and hearty home-cooked food (mains £6 to £8.50). There's a lovely garden at the back and a pair of muddy boots as a counterweight on the door.

The only public transport to Warborough is the shopper's bus to Wallingford (nine minutes), once on a Friday. Bus Nos X39 (25 minutes) and 105 (one hour) run between Oxford and Wallingford hourly.

WANTAGE
☎ 01235 / pop 17,913

A medieval market town, Wantage is a handsome place providing easy access to the Ridgeway less than 3 miles to the south. Alfred the Great was born here in 849 and his statue dominates the main square (for more on King Alfred see p32).

The **TIC** (☎ 760176; www.wantage.com; 10am-4.30pm Mon-Sat, 2.30-5pm Sun) is in the **Vale & Downland Museum Centre** (☎ 771447; www.wantage.com/museum; Church St; adult/child £2.50/1; 10am-4.30pm Mon-Sat, 2.30-5pm Sun), a converted 16th-century cloth merchant's house. The museum has information on everything from the geological past of the valley to

King Alfred and 21st-century industry – as well as an excellent café.

Sleeping & Eating
Ridgeway YHA Hostel (☎ 0870 770 6064; www.yharidgeway.org.uk; Court Hill; dm per adult/child £13.40/9.30; May-early Sep;) Set in a series of converted barns clustered around a courtyard, this hostel boasts an oak-beamed dining room and excellent views over the Vale. It's just 500m from the Ridgeway trail and an ideal base for walkers. The hostel is about 2 miles south of Wantage off A338.

Manor Farm (☎ 763188; www.manorfarm.uk.net; Silver Lane, West Challow; s/d £40/60; P) This beautiful 15th-century manor house, just outside Wantage, is a charming place and excellent value for money. The spacious rooms are traditional with high ceilings, cast-iron fireplaces, exposed beams and antique furniture.

Thyme & Plaice (☎ 760568; 8 Newbury St; lunch mains £5.80-7.95, dinner £14.20-14.80; Tue-Sat) Set in an 18th-century town house, the newbie on the Wantage scene has been setting high standards. The simple interior with its light walls and deep-red chairs is the perfect setting for the excellent modern British fare, which has strong hints of Asia and the Mediterranean. The three-course set dinner is good value at £18.50, but you'll find few vegetarian options on this or the à la carte menu.

Getting There & Away
Bus Nos 31, 32 and X31 serve Wantage about five times an hour from Oxford (25 minutes) and Abingdon (15 minutes).

AROUND WANTAGE
Uffington White Horse
The stylised image of a white horse cut into the side of a hill is, along with Stonehenge, one of the most remarkable and mysterious of England's ancient sites, but incredibly gets nowhere near the same amount of visitors.

This extraordinary chalk figure, which measures 114m long and 49m wide, was carved into the turf about 3000 years ago, and the lines of perspective are such that the horse is best viewed from a distance. What exactly it is supposed to represent remains anyone's guess. The most accepted legend claims that King Alfred cut the figure to celebrate his victory over the Danes

SOMETHING SPECIAL

Bell (☎ 01635-578272; Bell Lane, Aldworth) Completely unspoiled, the rustic 13th-century Bell is well worth a visit and a handy spot to warm up after a hard day on the Ridgeway path. The pub has been in the same family for 200 years and is honest to the core. The only food is hot filled rolls and soup. Gentlemen wishing to answer the call of nature will have to visit 'the Planetarium', a three-walled, roofless outdoor toilet. Aldworth is on the B4009 near Goring.

at the nearby Battle of Ashdown in 871. A number of burial sites have also been uncovered in the area.

Just below the figure is **Dragon Hill**, so-called because it is believed that St George slew the dragon here. Above the chalk figure are the grass-covered earthworks of **Uffington Castle**. From the youth hostel, near Wantage, a wonderful 5-mile walk leads along the Ridgeway to the White Horse.

Thomas Hughes, author of *Tom Brown's Schooldays*, was born in Uffington village. His house is now **Uffington Museum** (☎ 01376-820259; www.uffington.net/museum; Broad St; admission 60p; ⏱ 2-5pm Sat & Sun Easter-Oct).

You can stay at the 17th-century thatched farmhouse, the **Craven** (☎ 01367-820449; www.thecraven.co.uk; Fernham Rd; s from £28, d £55-85), which is smothered in roses and clematis in summer. Collections of old mugs, milk jugs and lids line the walls of the house, and the pretty rooms have hand-embroidered bed linen.

HENLEY-ON-THAMES
☎ 01491 / pop 10,513

Studded with chichi shops, pretty stone houses and a few elegant Tudor buildings, affluent Henley lies firmly on the commuter belt and is a sleepy but pleasant place for most of the year. During the first week of July, however, the world-famous regatta transforms the town into a jolly good show of boaters, blazers and the upwardly mobile.

The **TIC** (☎ 578034; The Barn, King's Rd; ⏱ 9.30am-5pm Mon-Sat & 11am-4pm Sun May-Sep, 10am-4pm Oct-Apr) is next to the handsome town hall.

Sights
Henley's impressive **River & Rowing Museum** (☎ 415600; www.rrm.co.uk; Mill Meadows; adult/child £6/4; ⏱ 10am-6pm Mon-Sat, 10.30am-6pm Sun; wheelchair access) tells the story of the town's obsession with boating and the people, wildlife and culture of the River Thames. Interesting multimedia displays liven up

the proceedings for younger visitors and a walk-through *Wind in the Willows* exhibition brings Kenneth Grahame's stories of Ratty, Mole, Badger and Toad to life.

St Mary's Church, which dates back to the 13th century, dominates the main drag, Hart St. On the graceful Georgian bridge across the river you'll find **sculptures** of Isis and Father Thames. Two fine **coaching inns**, the Red Lion and the Angel, stand sentinel at the Hart St end of the bridge.

Festivals & Events
HENLEY ROYAL REGATTA
In 1839 the cream of English society descended on Henley to watch the first Oxford and Cambridge boat race. Within a few years the one-day event became a five-day spectacle and Henley's place in boating history was secured.

Today, corporate entertainment reaches its pinnacle at this weeklong pompous picnic where hanging out on the lawn swilling champagne and looking rich and beautiful is the main event. Although rowers of the highest calibre compete, most spectators appear to take little interest in what's happening on the water.

The regatta is held in the first week of July each year, but you'll need contacts in the rowing or corporate worlds to get tickets to the stewards' enclosure. Access to the public enclosure is £8 on Wednesday and Thursday, £12 on Friday and Saturday and £10 for the Sunday final.

For more information visit www.hrr .co.uk.

HENLEY FESTIVAL
Surprisingly, for such a conservative town, **Henley Festival** (☎ 843404) features a vibrant and diverse programme, ranging from opera to avant-garde French percussionists, including jazz, rock, poetry and theatre. It's held at a variety of venues all over town in the week following the regatta, though the

OXFORDSHIRE, THE COTSWOLDS & GLOUCESTERSHIRE

SOMETHING SPECIAL

Crooked Billet (☎ 01491-681048; www.thecrookedbillet.co.uk; Stoke Row; mains £12-19) Drawing the crowds from miles around, the Crooked Billet, one-time hideout of highwayman Dick Turpin, is a 17th-century inn turned gastro-pub. The place is full of romance with an inglenook fireplace, hop bine–adorned windows, low beams and a charming atmosphere. The seasonal menus have a strong emphasis on carefully prepared local produce and include delicacies such as roast loin of Oxfordshire pork with crackling, apple sauce and roast potatoes. The set Sunday lunch (£16.95 for three courses) is very popular, so arrive early.

---

main events take place on a floating stage on the Thames. Tickets range from £7 for the car park to £87 for the front row of the grandstand by the riverside – although the latter tend to be block-booked by corporate sharks long before the event.

Sleeping

During regatta and festival weeks, rooms here are impossible to find, so book well in advance.

Alftrudis (☎ 573099; www.alftrudis.co.uk; 8 Norman Ave; s/d £45/55; P ✕) Close to the centre of town, yet extremely quiet, this beautiful Victorian house offers elegant accommodation at a great price. The pretty, traditional-style rooms have floral curtains and cosy beds but steer clear of being too fussy.

Falaise House (☎ 573388; www.falaisehouse.com; 37 Market Pl; s/d £50/65; ▣) This Georgian town house in the centre of town offers trad-itional luxury B&B. The rooms are bright and airy and have a balanced mix of coun-try cottage chintz and modern restraint.

Apple Ash (☎ 574198; aidan@mills-thomas.freeserve .co.uk; Woodlands Rd, Harpsden Woods; d £65-90; P ✕) Two miles from town but worth the drive is this gorgeous Edwardian country house with huge rooms and top-notch service. The rooms are extremely comfortable and there's a large garden for children to play in.

Thamesmeade House Hotel (☎ 574745; www .thamesmeadhousehotel.co.uk; Remenham Lane; s/d £105/125; P ✕ ▣) Overlooking the town's cricket green, this splendidly posh boutique hotel is an exercise in restraint. The rooms feature uncluttered Scandinavian design merged with classic style, rich fabrics and hand-painted furniture. Children are very welcome.

Other possibilities:

Red Lion Hotel (☎ 572161; www.redlionhenley.co.uk; Hart St; s/d £99/145; P ▣) The top dog in town offer-ing unadulterated luxury and period features.

Hotel du Vin (www.hotelduvin.com; d £105-250; P) In the former Brakspears Brewery, the newest kid on the block should be open by the time you read this. It promises to be as stylish and luxurious as its sister ships.

Eating

Good food is surprisingly hard to come by in Henley. There are a few good pubs, but most eateries are predictable chain restaurants.

Victoria (☎ 575628; 48 Market Pl; mains £4.50-8.50; ◔ lunch & dinner) This stylish café bar offers a decent assortment of baguettes, panini and ciabattas and some wood-fired pizzas. The décor mixes exposed beams with deep leather sofas. There's a decked garden at the back and live acoustic music on Friday and Saturdays nights.

Magoos (☎ 574595; 22 Hart St; mains £7.50-12.50; ◔ lunch & dinner) Bright, colourful and cheerful, this wine and coffee bar has good intentions, but the bathroom murals are a bit much. The food is good, though, and ranges from steaks and salads to devilish deserts. You can eat in the garden at the back in summer.

Loch Fyne (☎ 845780; Market Pl; mains £7.95-13.95; ◔ lunch & dinner) Part of the successful Loch Fyne fish brigade, this wonderful light-filled restaurant has plenty of good choices for fish lovers. There's a paved garden outside and the two-course set lunch is an excellent deal at £9.95.

Kathmando (☎ 574422; 34 Reading Rd; mains £6.95-11.95; ◔ lunch & dinner) All clean lines and streaming light, the minimalist chic of this trendy Nepalese restaurant stands in glorious contrast to the hearty portions of contemporary Nepalese curries and Asian classics served up by the friendly staff.

Getting There & Around

Bus No 139 links Henley and Abingdon (30 minutes, hourly) from where frequent buses run to Oxford. Trains to London Paddington take about one hour (£10.50, hourly).

Henley is the perfect place to indulge in a bit of messing about on the river. On summer Sundays, **Hobbs & Son** (☎ 572035; www .hobbs-of-henley.com) organise jazz cruises (£17) and short river trips (adult/child £5/4). You can also hire five-seater rowing boats (£10 per hour) or a four-seater motorboat (£20 per hour).

THE COTSWOLDS

Peppered with beautiful old mansions, mellow, honey-coloured villages and picturesque churches, the rolling, green hills of the Cotswolds are a haven for tourists in search of quintessential English charm. The medieval wool trade made the area prosperous, but today tourism is the main money-spinner. The region's enduring beauty means that it is now riddled with affluent residents, and its main centres are besieged by tourists and traffic.

Luckily, most tourists are about as adventurous as the sheep that brought the area its wealth and stick to the most stunning villages (Stow-on-the-Wold, the Slaughters and Bourton-on-the-Water). So it's easy to escape the camera-clicking crowds and chaotic coach parking – especially in the less-frenzied south.

For the best sightseeing just throw away your map and wander the narrow winding roads to the gloriously sleepy villages lurking in the hills.

Orientation & Information

The Cotswolds extend across a narrow band of land east of the M5, stretching almost as far as Oxford at their widest point. The region can be separated into two distinct areas: the southern and northern Cotswolds roughly divided by the sweep of the A40.

For online information on attractions, accommodation and events in the area try:
Cotswolds Calling (www.cotswolds-calling.com)
Cotswolds Tourism (www.cotswolds.gov.uk/tourism)
Oxfordshire Cotswolds (www.oxfordshirecotswolds.org)

Activities

The gentle hills of the Cotswolds are perfect for walking and the 102-mile (164km)

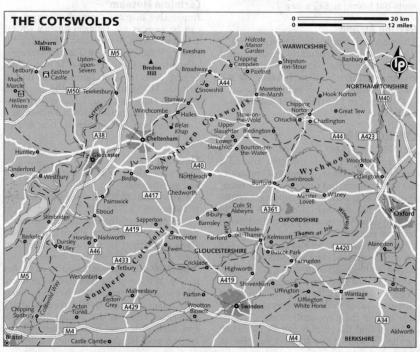

THE COTSWOLDS

A COTTAGE OF YOUR OWN

If you fancy renting your own Cotswold cottage, try the websites below for properties throughout the region:

Country Cottages Online (www.country cottagesonline.com)

CottageNet UK (www.cottagenet.co.uk)

Discover the Cotswolds (www.discoverthe cotswolds.net)

English Country Cottages (www.english -country-cottages.co.uk)

Manor Cottages & Cotswold Retreats (www.manorcottages.co.uk)

Cotswold Way makes a wonderful starting point. The route meanders gently from Chipping Campden to Bath, with no major climbs or difficult stretches. Several companies offer guided or unguided walking tours: try **Cotswold Walking Holidays** (☎ 01242-254353; www.cotswoldwalks.com; Cheltenham).

Cycling is equally popular in the Cotswolds. **Cotswold Country Cycles** (☎ 01386-438706; www.cotswoldcountrycycles.com; Chipping Campden) rents out bikes for £12 a day.

Getting Around

There are only limited bus services through the Cotswolds (particularly in the north) and the rail network only skims the northern and southern borders. **Traveline** (☎ 0870 608 2608) has details of all public transport.

Car hire can be arranged in most major centres (see p751).

CIRENCESTER

☎ 01285 / pop 15,861

A sleepy market town clustered around a fine perpendicular-style church, Cirencester is a fairly affluent but refreshingly unpretentious place. It's the most important settlement in the southern Cotswolds and in Roman times was second only to London in terms of size and importance. Little remains of its glory days under the Roman Empire except the grassed-over ruins of one of the largest amphitheatres in the country. During the Middle Ages the town regained some of its prosperity as a thriving wool town and rich merchants built the impressive buildings seen in the town centre today.

You'll find the church and **TIC** (☎ 654180; Corn Hall; 🕑 9.30am-5.30pm Apr-Dec, 9.30am-5pm Jan-Mar) on Market Sq where lively markets still take place every Monday and Friday. You can walk through the magnificent grounds of Cirencester House (closed to the public) from the entrance on Cecily Hill. The amphitheatre is on Cotswold Ave.

Church of St John the Baptist

One of England's largest churches, St John's seems more like a cathedral with its soaring arches, magnificent fan vaulting and wild flying buttresses. The interior is bathed in light and plays host to a 15th-century painted stone pulpit and memorial brasses recording the matrimonial histories of important wool merchants. The east window contains fine medieval stained glass, while a wall safe displays the **Boleyn Cup**, made for Anne Boleyn, second wife of Henry VIII, in 1535.

The superb perpendicular-style tower dominates the exterior, but it is the majestic three-storey south porch, which faces the square, that is the real highlight. Built as an office by late-15th-century abbots, it subsequently became the medieval town hall.

Corinium Museum

Impressive displays from the Roman era can be seen at the **Corinium Museum** (☎ 655 611; www.cotswolds.gov.uk/museum; Park St; adult/child £3.50/2; 🕑 10am-5pm Mon-Sat, 2-5pm Sun) recently renovated to show off what is one of the largest collections of Roman artefacts in Britain. Highlights include the beautiful Hunting Dogs and Four Seasons floor mosaics, a reconstructed Roman kitchen and butcher's shop, and a dramatic new Anglo-Saxon gallery.

Sleeping

On Victoria Rd you'll find a string of B&Bs and guesthouses.

Corner House (☎ 641958; www.thecornerhouse.info; 101a Victoria Rd; s/d £32/40; P ⊠) Large, bright rooms and tastefully restrained décor make this good value and a cut above many others along this strip. Children are welcome and there's a garden for outdoor games.

No 12 (☎ 640232; www.no12cirencester.co.uk; 12 Park St; d £70; ⊠) One of the best choices in town, this elegant Georgian town house successfully mixes antiques with a contemporary ambience. The spacious rooms are simple and sleek with great beds, feather pillows, merino wool blankets and fine bed linen.

Wild Duck Inn (☎ 770310; www.thewildduckinn
.co.uk; Ewen; s £60, d £80-100; P X) Three miles
south of town but well worth the trip, the
Wild Duck is a 16th-century inn. Its traditional rooms have rich fabrics, chunky
furniture and exposed beams. The rustic
restaurant has a good choice of comfort
foods (lunch mains cost £6 to £10, dinner
mains £12 to £17) and a range of real ales.

Eating

1651 (☎ 658507; Market Pl; mains £9.95-11.95; ☺ lunch
& dinner) A cross between a wine bar and
a brasserie this stylish place at the Fleece
Hotel has deep-red walls and stripped
floors and serves an excellent selection of
modern British and international cuisine.
There are plenty of vegetarian options and
very sensible prices.

Mackenzies Café Bar (☎ 656567; 34 Castle St;
mains £5.75-8.95; ☺ lunch & dinner) Trendy young
things flock here by night but by day the
bright, modern surroundings and the quiet
atmosphere make it a good choice for
lunch. The surprisingly good menu offers
up everything from reliable old favourites
such as wraps and nachos to more interesting pasta, meat and fish dishes.

Bell at Sapperton (☎ 01285-760298; www.food
atthebell.co.uk; Sapperton; mains £9.50-16; ☺ lunch &
dinner) Worth the trip 4 miles out of town,
the 300-year-old Bell serves up a delicious
seasonally changing menu of imaginative
country foods. Organic and rare-breed
meats feature strongly, as do fish and wonderful homemade bread.

Getting There & Away

National Express buses run roughly hourly
from Cirencester to London (£14.50, 2½
hours), Cheltenham Spa (40 minutes) and
Gloucester (one hour). Stagecoach bus No
51 also runs to Cheltenham hourly (40
minutes).

AROUND CIRENCESTER
Barnsley
☎ 01285
The picturesque village of Barnsley has become a hideout for the rich and famous in
recent years thanks mainly to the presence of
two top-notch establishments that make the
village worth a detour on anyone's itinerary.

Barnsley Village Pub (☎ 740421; www.thevillage
pub.co.uk; Barnsley; s £65, d £80-125; P) This

unpretentious-looking place has a series
of beautifully refurbished rooms with oak
four-posters or Victorian iron bedsteads
and beautiful bathrooms with antique
freestanding baths. The pub itself is wonderfully informal with a jumble of mixed
furniture, oriental rugs and mahogany
bookcases. Even if you don't stay it's well
worth tucking into some of the deceptively
simple dishes (mains £9.50 to £15.50) from
the modern British menu.

Barnsley House (☎ 740000; www.barnsleyhouse
.com; d £250-450; P X ⊡) Acclaimed as one
of the world's finest hotels, Barnsley House
is all about indulgence and sensuous sophistication. The design is funky chic.
Lime-and-mauve Room No 2 features a
disco mirrorball, while Room No 1 is all
subtle browns and beiges and boasts a vast
bathroom with his-and-hers freestanding
tubs and plasma-screen TV. The restaurant, with its excellent but limited Italian
menu, looks out over the fabulous gardens
designed by former owner Rosemary Verey,
Prince Charles' favourite gardener.

Bibury
☎ 01285
The impossibly quaint riverside village of
Bibury suffers from too much exposure
and is overrun with tourists in the summer
months. Plan to arrive early in the morning
or late in the evening to avoid the worst of
the crowds and experience what William
Morris aptly described as 'the most beautiful village in England'.

There are some lovely houses, most notably on **Arlington Row**, which is perhaps the
most photographed street in Britain with its
line of NT-owned weavers' cottages, spawn-
ing countless calendars and postcards.

Opposite, is the 17th-century **Arlington Mill**
(☎ 740368; admission £2; ☺ 10am-5.30pm), which
was converted in 1913 to aid the wartime
effort, and now houses a folk museum.

If you'd like to stay, the **Swan** (☎ 740695;
www.swanhotel.co.uk; s £140-190, d £140-220; X) is
an imposing 17th-century place on the
banks of the river. The superior rooms are
traditional chintz and floral, but the more
contemporary standard rooms are somewhat easier on the eye.

For food, head up the road to the **New
Inn** (☎ 750651, www.new-inn.co.uk; Coln-St-Aldwyns; s/d
£90/120; mains £8-12) a jasmine-clad, 16th-century

SOMETHING FOR THE WEEKEND

Start your weekend by checking in to the magnificent **Lygon Arms** (p416 in Broadway); enjoy a peaceful stroll around the village and head back to the majestic Great Dining Hall for the excellent cuisine. In the morning get your boots on and hike up to **Broadway Tower** (p416) with breathtaking views of 12 counties. Take a leisurely drive to Winchcombe and dig in to some sumptuous food at either **Wesley House** (p417) or **5 North St** (p417). After lunch, take a stroll around the Tudor pile **Sudeley Castle** (p417) and then head east to Bourton-on-the-Water and check in to the incredible **Dial House** (p413). Dine here or wander up to beautiful Upper Slaughter for an exquisite dinner at **Lords of the Manor** (p414). On Sunday morning head south towards the picture-perfect village of **Bibury** (p407) and take a stroll along the river to Arlington Row. Finish off the weekend with lunch at the uber-trendy but totally unpretentious **Barnsley Village Pub** (p407).

---

place with plenty of character, beamed ceilings and antique weapons on the walls. The imaginative menu features fresh, local produce and stylish, rustic dishes. The bedrooms are very comfortable but frilly.

Bus Nos 863, 865 and 866 pass through Bibury en route to Cirencester seven times daily from Monday to Friday (20 minutes). There are no weekend services.

PAINSWICK
☎ 01452 / pop 1666

The 'Queen of the Cotswolds', Painswick is a rare delight: a gorgeous, unspoiled village seldom overrun by tourists. The tiny narrow streets lined with picture-perfect cottages and medieval inns seem genuinely lost in time.

St Mary's Church dominates the village and its 99 yew trees are its main claim to fame. Legend has it that, should the hundredth be allowed to grow, the devil would appear and shrivel it. They planted it anyway, to celebrate the millennium – so far, no sign of the Wicked One.

The streets behind the church are lined with handsome merchants' houses. Bisley St, with several 14th-century houses, was the original thoroughfare, while New St is a medieval addition. Rare iron stocks stand in the street just south of the church.

In early July the town celebrates a Victorian market day. Ask at the **TIC** (☎ 813552; library, Stroud St; 🕙 10am-4.30pm Tue-Fri, 10am-1pm Sat & Sun Easter-Oct) for details. The **Cotswold Way** runs through the village and is an excellent starting point for walks in the surrounding area.

Painswick Rococo Garden
The flamboyant pleasure gardens of **Painswick House** (☎ 813204; www.rococogarden.co.uk; admission £4; 🕙 11am-5pm Jan-Oct), half a mile north of town, are a restored version of original gardens designed in the 1740s by Benjamin Hyett. They're laid out with geometrical precision allowing stunning vistas of the many architectural features, while winding paths and a children's nature trail and maze break up the formality.

Sleeping & Eating

Hambutts Mynd (☎ 812352; ewarland@aol.com; Edge Rd; s/d £27/50; **P** ✗) This converted, early-18th-century corn mill has retained most of its original characteristics with old beams and crackling fires giving a warm welcome to weary hikers. The rooms are simple but tasteful.

Cardynham House (☎ 814006; www.cardynham .co.uk; The Cross; s/d from £47/65; ✗) Four-poster beds and heavy, patterned fabrics are the order of the day at this 15th-century place. The themed rooms have plenty of space, great views and fine linens. 'Palm Beach' is particularly light and airy. Despite the sumptuous surroundings, children are welcome.

Painswick Hotel (☎ 812160; www.painswickhotel .com; Kemps Lane; s/d from £75/125; **P**) The top spot in town, this former Georgian rectory has luxurious rooms decorated with beautiful antiques and rich fabrics. The restaurant (mains £12 to £19) serves delicacies such as wild venison, and is a good venue for a special night out.

March Hare (☎ 813452; Tibbiwell St; set dinner £23.50) Two tiny rooms with stone walls and wooden floors get packed out with happy diners digging in to the terrific Thai food at this cosy place. The set, six-course dinner is excellent value and guaranteed to have you rolling out the door.

Getting There & Around
Bus No 46 connects Cheltenham (30 minutes) and Stroud (10 minutes) with Painswick hourly (four on Sunday).

STROUD
☎ 01453 / pop 32,052

Hidden away in a steep-sided river valley, Stroud was once a thriving centre for the wool industry and the beautiful mill buildings surrounding the town give an idea of its importance. Today, of the old mills, only a handful is still in use and the town is slightly worse for wear but it is fast becoming an ecocentre with an influx of New Agers, fair-trade shops and wholefood traders.

The Tudor **town hall** is worth a look as are the **Subscription Rooms,** home to the **TIC** (☎ 760960; George St; ☷ 10am-5pm Mon-Sat).

If you stop for lunch try **Woodruffs Organic Café** (☎ 759195; 24 High St; mains £5-8), a bright and cheerful place with murals on the walls and a serious line in wholesome foods. Hearty snacks, salads and hot mains cater for almost all diets, and there's even a special service for children.

Bus No 46 runs hourly to Painswick (10 minutes) and Cheltenham (40 minutes). Bus Nos 92 and 93 operate half-hourly to Gloucester (25 minutes).

ULEY
☎ 01453

This tiny, picturesque village nestles beneath the overgrown remains of the largest Iron Age hill fort in England, **Uley Bury.** To get there on foot, follow the steep path that runs from the village church. If you have your own wheels, you can drive right up to the car park by the fort entrance. The site is closed off, but the 2-mile perimeter walk affords some breathtaking views.

One mile east of the village is **Owlpen Manor** (☎ 860261; www.owlpen.com; adult/child £4.80/2; ☷ 2-5pm Tue-Sun Apr-Sep), a glorious Tudor mansion built between 1450 and 1616. It lay derelict until 1926 when it was partially refurbished by architect Norman Jewson, a follower of William Morris. The highlight of the house is the magnificent **Grand Hall,** fully restored to its original best. You can also see some interesting painted textiles, family portraits, and a good collection of Arts and Crafts (see p433) furniture and fittings. The house is surrounded by fabulous formal gardens.

A mile north of Uley a massive Victorian house lies unfinished, doors leading nowhere, fireplaces stuck halfway up a wall and corridors ending at ledges with views of the ground below. **Woodchester Mansion** (☎ 750455; www.themansion.co.uk; adult/child £5/free; ☷ 11am-4pm Sat & Sun Easter-Oct) also features an impressive set of gruesome gargoyles and is home to one of England's largest colonies of greater horseshoe bats.

If you'd like to stay in the area the **Priory** (☎ 834282; www.theprioryhorsley.com; Horsely; s/d £50/80; ℗ ☒ wheelchair access) is a former medieval monastery and prison oozing character and a warm welcome. It gleefully mixes fine antiques, junk-shop finds and modern luxuries. The bedrooms and dining room are quite amazing and it makes an ideal base for exploring the area. Horsley is 3 miles east of Uley on the B4058.

Bus No 20 runs hourly between Uley and Stroud (Monday to Saturday, 40 minutes).

BERKELEY
☎ 01453 / pop 1865

Perched in terraced Elizabethan gardens, **Berkeley Castle** (☎ 810332; www.berkeley-castle.com; adult/child £7/4, grounds only £4/2; ☷ 11am-4pm Tue-Sat, 2-5pm Sun Apr-Sep, Sun only Oct) is a beautiful medieval fortress where Edward II was imprisoned and then murdered by order of his wife Queen Isabella and her lover in 1327. It is a gruesome story of tortuous imprisonment before a final impalement by a red-hot poker.

From the castle follow the path through **St Mary's** churchyard, with its unusual detached bell tower, to the **Jenner Museum** (☎ 810631; www.jennermuseum.com; adult/child £3.50/2; ☷ 12.30-5.30pm Tue-Sat, 1-5.30pm Sun Apr-Oct), in the house where Edward Jenner performed the first smallpox vaccination in 1796.

Beaumont's bus No B7 runs between Gloucester and Berkeley five times a day (35 minutes) Monday to Saturday.

TETBURY
☎ 01666 / pop 5250

Once a prosperous wool-trading centre, the charming town of Tetbury features a feast of timeless, old buildings and almost as many antique shops. The market square has a lovely, 17th-century **Market House**, and close by you'll find the Georgian Gothic **Church of St Mary the Virgin** with its graceful towering spire and wonderful interior.

The friendly **TIC** (☎ 503552; www.tetbury.com; 33 Church St; ⏲ 9.30am-4.30pm Mon-Sat Mar-Oct, 10am-1pm Mon-Sat Nov-Feb) has plenty of information on the town and its history.

The village of Westonbirt is 2½ miles southwest of Tetbury, and the nearby **Westonbirt Arboretum** (☎ 880220; www.forestry.gov.uk /westonbirt; adult/child £6/1; ⏲ 10am-dusk) boasts a magnificent selection of temperate trees and is famed for its autumn colour. It's a wonderful place for walking – ask at the TIC for a trail guide.

Sleeping & Eating

No 65 (☎ 503346; www.number65.co.uk; 65 Long St; s/d £25/45; ✗) This excellent-value place in the centre of town has a couple of bright, comfortable rooms with simple, country décor. It also has a very good restaurant serving classic and modern English food (a set three-course menu costs £24).

Calcot Manor (☎ 890391; www.calcotmanor.co.uk; A4135; s £140, d £165-205; P ✗ � 🏊) Clustered round a 14th-century courtyard, this collection of Cotswold-stone buildings is a haven for families attempting to please both adults and children. The rooms are sleek and stylish, there are spa treatments and adventurous cuisine (mains £15 to £21) for the adults and a wonderful children's play area and early meals for the nippers. The hotel is 2 miles west of Tetbury off the A4135.

Blue Zucchini (☎ 505852; Church St; mains £5-8; ⏲ lunch & dinner) This modern bistro-bar is one of the best lunch places in town. The design is sleek with wooden floors, plenty of chrome and trendy furniture. The menu is mostly Mediterranean with the focus on pizza and pasta, and a mean seafood pie.

Trouble House (☎ 502206; Cirencester Rd; mains £12-15; ⏲ lunch & dinner) Polished wood floors, dark beams, warm walls and a jumble of tables and chairs give this place a wonderfully informal, lived-in feel. So when the food arrives you really aren't expecting it to be quite so exceptional. The menu features plenty of comforting classics as well as more-adventurous modern British fare.

Getting There & Away

Bus No 92 serves Tetbury every two hours from Stroud (30 minutes) before transforming itself into No 620 and proceeding toward Bath (1¼ hours), making a stop at the Westonbirt Arboretum en route.

LECHLADE-ON-THAMES

☎ 01367 / pop 2415

A lovely Cotswold town, Lechlade is dominated by the graceful spire of **St Lawrence's Church**. Originally a wool church, it was rededicated to the Spanish saint by Catherine of Aragon.

Well worth a side trip is the gorgeous Tudor pile **Kelmscott Manor** (☎ 252486; www .kelmscottmanor.co.uk; admission £8.50; ⏲ 11am-5pm Wed Apr-Sep & selected summer Sats) once home to William Morris, the poet, artist and founder of the Arts and Crafts movement (p433). The house displays fabrics and furniture designed by Morris as well as exotic, lacquered work introduced by Rossetti. The village of Kelmscott is 3 miles east of Lechlade off the Faringdon road.

Another worthwhile side trip from Lechlade is **Buscot Park** (NT; ☎ 240786; www.buscot-park .com; admission £6.50, grounds only £4.50; ⏲ 2-6pm Wed-Fri, grounds only Mon & Tue Apr-Sep & selected weekends), a Palladian mansion that is home to the Faringdon art collection, which includes paintings by Rembrandt, Reynolds, Rubens, Van Dyck and Murillo, as well as a comprehensive series of pre-Raphaelite British works. The house is 2½ miles southeast of Lechlade on the Faringdon road.

There are four buses, Monday to Saturday, from Lechlade to Cirencester (40 minutes).

BURFORD

☎ 01993

Slithering downhill to the medieval bridge over the River Windrush, Burford's High St is a picturesque medley of fine Cotswold stone houses, specialist boutiques and antique shops peddling flowery china and nostalgia. The town attracts visitors in their droves and can be frustratingly busy in mid-summer. However, the lovely side streets are quieter and the gorgeous **Church of St John** is a peaceful oasis at any time.

You'll find the **TIC** (☎ 823558; Sheep St; ⏲ 9.30am-5.30pm Mon-Sat Mar-Oct, 10am-4.30pm Mon-Sat Nov-Feb) by the Lamb Inn. Nearby, the 16th-century **Tolsey Museum** (Toll House; High St; admission by donation; ⏲ 2-5pm Tue-Fri & Sun Apr-Oct) perches on pillars and houses a small museum on Burford's history.

For younger visitors the excellent **Cotswold Wildlife Park** (☎ 823006; www.cotswoldwild lifepark.co.uk; adult/child £8/5.50; ⏲ 10am-4.30pm

Mar-Sep, 10am-3.30pm Oct-Feb) is home to everything from ants to white rhinos and giant cats as well as an adventure playground.

If you have the time it's worth the effort to walk east along the river to the untouched and rarely visited village of **Swinbrook** (3 miles) where the beautiful church has some remarkable tombs including the Fettiplace family's with its comical carvings.

Sleeping & Eating

Priory (☎ 823249; 35 High St; s/d £15/40) The cheapest option in town, this basic place has small functional rooms around a little courtyard. Newer and better rooms (with private bathroom) at the back cost £50, although they're far from spacious. The café out front serves a decent selection of baguettes, salads and roasts (£4.95 to £7.95).

Burford House Hotel (☎ 823151; www.burford house.co.uk; 99 High St; s £80, d £105-140; ✕) This traditional but relaxed hotel offers luxury B&B with plenty of personal touches. The rooms are individually styled with dark woods, tasteful décor, antique furniture and wonderful bathrooms. It's a thoroughly charming place and serves up a fantastic breakfast.

Lamb Inn (☎ 823155; www.lambinn-burford.co.uk; Sheep St; s £80-120, d £130-200; P) Dating from the 15th century, Burford's oldest pub is now a gorgeous place to stay with beamed ceilings, flagged floors, creaking stairs and a charming, laid-back atmosphere. The bright, period rooms are a tasteful mix of antique and chintz.

Jonathan's at the Angel (☎ 822714; www.the angel-uk.com; s/d £70/90; mains £14-19; lunch & dinner) This informal, country brasserie occupies a 16th-century coaching inn and serves up an excellent selection of modern British and European food. Three themed bedrooms offer luxury B&B in classic style.

For something lighter, the character-filled **Mermaid** (High St; mains £5.45-9.45) and the **Golden Pheasant** (High St; mains £6-11) do bar snacks and full meals.

Getting There & Away

From Oxford, Swanbrook runs four buses a day (two on Sun) to Burford (45 minutes) via Witney. Stagecoach bus Nos 233 and X3 run between Witney and Burford nine times a day, Monday to Saturday only (20 minutes).

WITNEY

☎ 01993 / pop 22,765

An attractive market town, Witney built its fortunes on the production of blankets and the baroque, 18th-century Blanket Hall dominates genteel High St. A cluster of beautiful, old buildings surrounds the central green, while the 17th-century Buttercross, originally a covered market, stands in Market Sq.

The **TIC** (☎ 775802; witney.tic@westoxon.gov.uk; 26a Market Sq; 9.30am-5.30pm Mon-Sat Mar-Sep, 10am-4.30pm Mon-Sat Oct-Feb) provides information on local attractions though the only real one of note is **Cogges Manor Farm Museum** (☎ 772602; www.cogges.org; adult/child £4.40/2.30; 10.30am-5.30pm Tue-Fri, noon-5.30pm Sat & Sun late Mar-Nov), a 13th-century manor house reconstructed as a working farm. The real draw for children, however, is the domestic farm animals roaming the grounds.

Sleeping & Eating

Witney Hotel (☎ 702137; fax 705337; 7 Church Green; s/d £38/56) This family-run B&B is in a lovely listed building overlooking the village green. The refined, rustic rooms are bright and tasteful, and the service is excellent.

Fleece (☎ 892270; thefleece@peachpubs.com; 11 Church Green; s/d £75/85; P ✕ wheelchair access) Sleek, stylish rooms with modern furnishings and muted colours make this hotel a joy for anyone seeking a little designer style in the land of floral patterns. The spacious brasserie downstairs offers a good choice of pizza, pasta and modern meat dishes (mains £7 to £13.50).

Suwanna (☎ 770771; 44 Church Green; mains £6.20-8.90; lunch & dinner) This modern Thai restaurant serves up a good choice of Asian classics and prides itself on fresh ingredients and imported spices. The décor is modern with heavy, carved wooden chairs providing some Oriental style.

Getting There & Away

Swanbrook runs four buses Monday to Saturday (two on Sunday) between Cheltenham (one hour) and Oxford (30 minutes) via Witney. This service also goes to Gloucester (£6.20, 1½ hours) and serves a number of Cotswold towns along the way, including Northleach, Minster Lovell and Burford.

Stagecoach bus No 11 runs from Oxford to Witney roughly every half hour Monday to Saturday (one hour).

SOMETHING SPECIAL

Falkland Arms (☎ 01608-683653; www.falklandarms.org.uk; Great Tew; s £65, d £70-80) Time has stood still in the village of Great Tew where a cluster of stunning thatched buildings gathers round the green. The village's 16th-century tavern has low ceilings rippled with oak beams hung with an assortment of mugs and jugs. The floor is original flagstone, the toilet is down the road and there's an atmospheric inglenook fireplace whose smoke masks the smell of wet dogs and wellies. Real ales and whiskies are on offer as well as such essentials as clay pipes and snuff. Food ranges from baguettes (£4.25) to full Sunday roasts (£8.50). Upstairs the comfortable rooms are set out in period style with exposed beams and iron-frame beds. It doesn't get much more genuine than this.

Great Tew is about 4 miles east of of Chipping Norton.

MINSTER LOVELL
☎ 01993

Skirting a bend in the meandering River Windrush, this gorgeous village was one of William Morris's favourite spots in the Cotswolds, and it's easy to see why. An idyllic spot, it's a wonderful place to start a valley walk.

On the village outskirts are the ruins of **Minster Lovell Hall**, the family home of Viscount Francis Lovell who fought with King Richard III at the Battle of Bosworth in 1485. After Richard's defeat and death, Lovell organised a rebellion against the new king but was soundly beaten. He disappeared from the battlefield and was never seen again. In 1708 a skeleton seated at a table was discovered inside a secret vault in the house; it is thought that Lovell died here while in hiding.

If you fancy staying overnight, **The Mill & Old Swan** (☎ 774441; www.millandoldswan-isc.co.uk; s/d £40/60; P ⬜) is a beautiful place on the banks of the river. The Old Swan has creaking old stairs and narrow corridors leading up to charming rooms, while the adjacent Mill is a vast modern conversion decked out in Scandinavian design. You can get decent pub food (£6 to £9) at the Old Swan.

Swanbrook coaches stop here on the Oxford to Cheltenham run (see p411). Stagecoach bus Nos 233 and X3 between Witney and Burford stop here nine times a day, Monday to Saturday (10 minutes each way).

CHIPPING NORTON & AROUND
☻ 01608 / pop 5688

A once-prosperous wool town, Chipping Norton is a sleepy but attractive place with a beautiful market square surrounded by handsome stone houses and half-timbered inns. The secluded **Church of St Mary** has a wonderful setting just past a row of beautiful almshouses on Church St. The church itself is a classic example of Cotswold wool churches and has a wonderful 15th-century perpendicular nave. On the outskirts of town on the road to Moreton-in-Marsh, the **Bliss Tweed Mill** is a striking monument to the industrial architecture of the 19th century.

A small, local-history **museum** (☎ 643779; 4 High St; admission £1.25; ☻ 2-4pm Tue-Sun Easter-Oct) has displays on the town's wool-manufacturing traditions.

Five miles north of town you'll find the **Hook Norton Brewery** (☎ 737210; www.hooky.co.uk; admission £2; ☻ 9am-5pm Mon-Fri) an independent family-run Victorian tower brewery still churning out old-fashioned ale with a fascinating 25-horsepower steam engine.

There's plenty of accommodation in the area including the **Forge** (☎ 658173; theforge@ rushbrooke.co.uk; B4450, Churchill; s/d £45/55; P ✗), a lovely, 200-year-old country house offering top-notch B&B. Log fires, oak beams and four-poster beds add to the character and one room has its own Jacuzzi.

For good food head for the **Tite Inn** (☎ 6764 75; Mill End, Chadlington; mains £9-14), a beautiful, 17th-century village pub serving an inspired menu and real ale. The informal restaurant has a garden room covered with the pub's own vine and serves up classic British food using the freshest local ingredients.

Worth's (☎ 677322; www.worthscoaches.co.uk) bus Nos 70 and 71 run from Oxford to Chipping Norton (one hour) six times a day. Stagecoach No 20 runs every hour Monday to Saturday (80 minutes); on Sunday the X50 does the same route four times (45 minutes).

NORTHLEACH
☎ 01451 / pop 1923

A stunning market town, Northleach is a wonderful mixture of architectural styles with a series of late-medieval cottages clustered around the gorgeous market square. The town is also home to perhaps the finest of the wool churches, a masterpiece of the Cotswold perpendicular style, with an unrivalled collection of medieval memorial brasses.

The **TIC** (☎ 860715; Fosse Way), on the A249, is in the old Northleach House of Correction, once a model 19th-century prison. Also here is the **Cotswold Heritage Centre** (admission £2.50; ⌚ 10.30am-5pm Mon-Sat, noon-5pm Sun Apr-Oct), fronted by a superb collection of old carts and shepherds' vans. Inside, you can watch some wonderful local films from the 1930s.

Near the square is Oak House, a 17th-century wool house that contains **Keith Harding's World of Mechanical Music** (☎ 860181; www .mechanicalmusic.co.uk; admission £5; ⌚ 10am-6pm), where you can hear Rachmaninoff played on a piano roll.

About 4 miles southwest of Northleach is **Chedworth Roman Villa** (NT; ☎ 01242-890256; Yanworth; adult/child £4.10/2; ⌚ 10am-5pm Tue-Sun Apr-Oct, 11am-4pm Feb-Mar & Nov), one of the best exposed Roman villas in England. Built around 120 for a wealthy landowner, it contains some wonderful mosaics illustrating the seasons.

If you fancy staying overnight, the 17th-century **Prospect Cottage** (☎ 860875; www.prospect cottage.co.uk; West End; s/d £45/60; ✗) has bright, airy rooms with exposed beams, pine furniture and light linens. Alternatively, try **Cotteswold House** (☎ 860493; Market Sq; d £55-70; ✗), a former wool merchant's cottage with beamed ceilings and 16th-century wood panelling. The bedrooms are full of character but a little twee.

The best bets for sustenance, solid or liquid, are the **Sherborne Arms**, the charming **Red Lion** and the **Wheatsheaf**, all around Market Sq.

Getting There & Away
Swanbrook runs four buses Monday to Saturday (two on Sunday) between Cheltenham (30 minutes) and Oxford (one hour) via Northleach.

BOURTON-ON-THE-WATER
☎ 01451 / pop 3093

Exceptionally beautiful and thoroughly over-exposed, Bourton is a major tourist trap best seen in the evening when the coachloads of octogenarians have gone, or in winter when there are far fewer of them.

On a quiet day it's a gorgeous little place with the River Windrush passing beneath a series of low bridges in the village centre and an array of handsome houses in Cotswold stone lining the narrow lanes.

Not content with the lure of the village alone, a series of 'attractions' – including a model railway and village, perfume exhibition, maze and motor museum – has opened in town. The most interesting of the lot is **Birdland** (☎ 820480; admission £4.85; ⌚ 10am-5pm Apr-Oct, 10am-3pm Nov-Mar), a serious bird-conservation project.

If you don't mind battling with the crowds an annual **water football match** is held in the River Windrush on the August Bank Holiday Monday. The tradition dates back to the 1800s.

There's no shortage of places to stay, and considering that most coach tours leave town before dark, you should have few problems finding somewhere to bunk down. **Trevone** (☎ 805250; www.the-mad-hatter-tearoom.co.uk; Moore Rd; s/d £20/40; P) is a Cotswold-stone house just a short hop from the village centre and has beautiful, bright simple rooms. It is one of the best-value options in town.

For something much more classy head for **Dial House** (☎ 822244; www.dialhousehotel.com; High St; s/d £55/88; ✗), which offers pure luxury at incredible rates. It's one of the best places to stay in the Cotswolds. The rooms are bright and modern and subtly mix traditional, hand-painted wallpaper with contemporary design features, big comfy beds and luxurious linens. The restaurant (lunch mains £8 to £10, dinner mains £16 to £19) should be your first port of call for food and serves up excellent-value modern British cuisine.

Bus Nos 1 & 55 run to Moreton-In-Marsh roughly every 90 minutes between them (Monday to Saturday, 20 minutes).

THE SLAUGHTERS
☎ 01451

Despite the gruesome names these two villages are amongst the most famously picturesque in the Cotswolds. Every building is worth a photo and unfortunately they have become a real honeypot for tourists and their cameras. If you can, stay the night and experience the area as it should be after the hordes have moved on. The village names derive from the old English 'sloughre' meaning slough.

The Slaughters are best reached on foot from Bourton, just over a mile away. The walk takes roughly an hour following part of the Warden's Way, across the Fosse Way, over a meadow and along a path into Lower Slaughter. Continue on past the **Victorian flour mill** (admission £2; 10am-6pm Mar-Oct) for another mile (about three quarters of an hour's walk) into Upper Slaughter.

Accommodation in the Slaughters is exclusive. The 17th-century **Lower Slaughter Manor** (820456; www.lowerslaughter.co.uk; s £95, d £220-400; P) is the kind of place where a decanter of sherry lies waiting for you in your room. Bursting with antique furniture, gilded frames, rich fabrics, log fires and stucco ceilings, it is unashamedly traditional in a frilly kind of way.

In Upper Slaughter the **Lords of the Manor** (820243; www.lordsofthemanor.com; s £100, d £160-200; P) is a 17th-century rectory with secluded gardens (complete with croquet lawn), individual bedrooms and wonderful views. Antique beds, oil paintings, chess sets, antiquarian books, freestanding cast-iron baths and roaring fires make the rooms snug and inviting, while the restaurant overlooking the wonderful grounds serves up more contemporary cuisine (mains £12 to £26).

STOW-ON-THE-WOLD

01451 / pop 2074

A genuinely elegant town, Stow-on-the-Wold is home to a plethora of antique shops lining the steep-walled alleyways that once funnelled sheep into the handsome market square. Craft shops, teashops and galleries take up any remaining space and sell beautiful and expensive trinkets to the crowds of visitors. A medieval cross at the south of the square was built to remind traders to be honest when brokering deals.

The **TIC** (831082; Hollis House; 10-5pm Mon-Sat) is on Market Sq.

Sleeping & Eating

Stow-on-the-Wold YHA Hostel (0870 770 6050; www.yha.org.uk; The Square; dm £13.40; Apr-Sep, Fri & Sat only Nov-Feb; P) Ideally located right in the centre of town, this beautiful 16th-century town house has top-class hostel accommodation in four- to eight-bed dorms. Children are very welcome and there's a play area in the garden.

Fox Inn (870555; www.foxinn.net; Lower Oddington; rooms £68-95; P) This creeper-clad inn about 3 miles east of Stow on the A436 has simply stunning rooms. Each is carefully decorated with period furniture, and features antique wooden beds. The pub itself is well known for its fine food (mains £8 to £11) and good local beers.

King's Arms (830364; www.kingsarms-stowonthewold.co.uk; Market St; d £90; P) A former coaching inn, this 500-year-old hotel is a charming place with exposed stone walls and beams offsetting the contemporary furnishings, CD players and widescreen TVs. The bistro-style restaurant is usually buzzing with punters who come for the imaginative modern dishes (£6 to £12).

Hamiltons Brasserie (831700; Park St; mains £12-15; lunch & dinner) Cool urban chic has made it to Stow in the shape of this modern British brasserie with an enviable local reputation. The deep-blue seats, modern art and light tiles give the place sharp, clean lines while the chef turns out excellent specials such as blue-fin tuna with sautéed radicchio and roast artichoke with saffron sauce.

Eagle & Child (830670; Digbeth St; mains £9.95-12.75; lunch & dinner) Supposedly the oldest inn in the country, the Eagle and Child and adjoining 947 restaurant are all exposed beams, polished floors, real ales and old-world charm. The service is wonderful, and the deceptively simple menu, featuring lots of local meat and game, comes up trumps again and again.

SOMETHING SPECIAL

Nestled into a crook in a river, the **Kings Head** (01608-658365; www.kingsheadinn.net; Bledington; d £ 70-100; P) is a gorgeous and timeless 16th-century English inn. The sumptuous rooms are tastefully decorated with light colours, big comfortable beds and period features. The real draw, however, is the food in the traditional bar. Meat and game are sourced locally, and fish arrives daily from Cornwall. The menu (mains £9 to £15) features a fine collection of modern British dishes, good vegetarian options and a serious selection of local and foreign cheeses.

Bledington is on the B4450 5 miles southeast of Stow-on-the-Wold.

Getting There & Away

Pulhams Coaches and Beaumont Travel link Stow with Moreton-in-Marsh (15 minutes, every 90 minutes) Monday to Saturday.

The nearest train stations are 4 miles away at Kingham and Moreton-in-Marsh.

MORETON-IN-MARSH

☎ 01608 / pop 3198

A less assuming and more worklike Cotswold town, Moreton has the best transport connections of the area. On Tuesdays the weekly **market** overtakes the town in a lively flurry of trading from the 200 or so stalls selling everything from fresh organic produce to fascinating junk.

About 1½ miles west of Moreton is the spectacular, Mogul-style **Sezincote House** (house £6.50, garden adult/child £4.25/1.25; ☺ house 2.30-6pm Thu & Fri May-Jul & Sep, garden 2-6pm Thu-Fri Jan-Nov), built in 1810 by Charles Cockerell of the East India Company and thought to have inspired Brighton Pavilion. There are tours of the house on Thursday and Friday afternoons in May, June, July and September. Children are not admitted to the house.

If you get stuck overnight the cosy **Acacia** (☎ 650130; 2 New Rd; s/d £25/40; ✗) is good value, offering homely B&B in a charming Cotswold-stone house. It has simple but comfortable rooms, most with shared bathroom, overlooking a quiet garden.

Getting There & Away

Pulhams Coaches run between Moreton and Cheltenham (12 Monday to Saturday, two on Sunday May to September only, one hour) via Stow-on-the-Wold (15 minutes) and Bourton-on-the-Water (20 minutes).

There are trains roughly every hour to Moreton from London Paddington (£21.20, 1¾ hours) via Oxford (£8.20, 30 minutes) and on to Worcester (£8.90, 40 minutes) and Hereford (£12, 1¼ hours).

CHIPPING CAMPDEN

☎ 01386 / pop 1943

Relatively unspoiled by the tourist hordes, the gently curving main street of Chipping Campden is a real delight. Flanked by a succession of golden-hued terraced houses, each subtly different from the next, it stands in contrast to the equally stunning thatched roofs, clipped hedges and gorgeous gardens of the cottages off the main drag.

SOMETHING SPECIAL

Churchill Arms (☎ 01386-594000; www.the churchillarms.com; Paxford; s/d £40/70; P) Honest to the core, the Churchill is a seriously unpretentious place with a few very pretty rooms and a passion for good food. There's a motley collection of chairs and tables in the main dining room, menus scrawled on blackboards and a roaring fire in the hearth. The pasta is made in-house, and many dishes successfully team meat or fish with fruit, such as the crispy duck leg confit with roast pears and artichoke purée. Get there early as there is a no-bookings policy.

Paxford is on the B4479 5 miles northwest of Moreton-in-Marsh.

The **TIC** (☎ 841206; www.chippingcampden.co.uk; Noel Arms Courtyard; ☺ 10am-5pm Mon-Fri) is off High St. Across the road, the gabled **Market Hall** dates from 1627. At the western end is **St James**, a very fine Cotswold wool church with some splendid 17th-century monuments. Nearby are the Jacobean lodges and gateways of the vanished manor house, and a remarkable row of **almshouses**.

About 4 miles northeast of Chipping Campden, **Hidcote Manor Garden** (NT; ☎ 438333; Hidcote Bartrim; admission £6.20; ☺ 10.30am-6pm Sat-Wed Mar-Oct) is one of the finest examples of Arts and Crafts (see p433) landscaping in Britain.

Sleeping & Eating

Eight Bells (☎ 840371; www.eightbellsinn.co.uk; Church St; s/d £45/70; ✗) This friendly, 14th-century inn has lovely bright rooms with simple but tasteful décor. Downstairs the excellent restaurant serves a British and Continental menu (mains £8) in rustic settings with diners spilling out into the sunny courtyard and garden in warm weather.

Kings Arms (☎ 840256; www.thekingsarmshotel .com; The Square; s/d £70/85; P) The good-value rooms at this 300-year-old hotel are bright and spacious, blending the contemporary with period touches. Mood lighting and antique furniture mix with the decidedly modern British fare (mains £9) at the stylish brasserie downstairs.

Cotswold House Hotel (☎ 840330; www.cots woldhouse.com; The Square; s/d from £110/125; P ✗) Contemporary style reigns at this Regency town house. The classic-chic bedrooms are luxuriously kitted out with cashmere throws, aromatic sleep sprays and massive bathrooms. The indulgence overflows into Hick's Brasserie downstairs where the slick décor complements the ambitious and highly successful menu (mains £11 to £15).

Getting There & Around

Bus Nos 21, 22 and 522 run hourly to Stratford or Moreton. If you're feeling energetic you can hire a bike from **Cotswold Country Cycles** (☎ 438706; Longlands Farm Cottage; per day/week £12/60).

BROADWAY

☎ 01386 / pop 2496

Villages just don't get much more picturesque than this. Broadway has inspired writers, artists and composers with its gorgeous buildings and graceful air. Tourists descend upon the place in droves and the village facilitates their cravings for old England with plenty of boutiques, antique shops and overpriced galleries.

The **TIC** (☎ 852937; 1 Cotswold Ct; ☺ 11am-1pm & 2-5pm Mon-Sat) is in a shopping arcade off the northern end of High St.

The lovely, medieval **Church of St Eadburgha** is a signposted 30-minute walk from town. For a longer walk (an uphill two miles), take the footpath opposite the church that leads up to **Broadway Tower** (☎ 852390; adult/child £3/2; ☺ 10.30am-5.30pm Apr-Oct, 11am-3pm Sat & Sun Nov-Mar), a crenulated, 18th-century Gothic folly

---

SOMETHING SPECIAL

Lygon Arms (☎ 852255; www.thelygonarms .com; High St, Broadway; s £119-159, d £179-495; P ☐ ☐ wheelchair access) Not just the top hotel in town, but probably the best in all of the Cotswolds, this elegant old place is all period charm and impeccable service. The bedrooms each have a distinctive character and boast plenty of antiques to match their rustic appearance. A huge open fireplace and barrel-vaulted ceiling dominate the oak-panelled Great Hall dining room, which also has a 17th-century minstrels gallery. The terrific food is British with a heavy French influence. If you're in need of some more pampering you can opt for hot stone therapy at the hotel's elegant spa.

---

on the crest of an escarpment. It has a small William Morris exhibition on one floor and stunning views from the top.

There's plenty of accommodation in Broadway, though all of it tends to be on the frilly side. The **Olive Branch Guest House** (☎ 853 440; www.theolivebranch-broadway.com; 78 High St; s/d £36/55) is a listed, 16th-century guesthouse with heaps of floral patterns and chintzy cushions. The rooms are comfortable and elegant enough if you like that kind of thing.

Its bright, airy rooms make **Milestone House** (☎ 853432; www.milestone-broadway.co.uk; High St; s/d £45/80; P ☒) another good option. The rooms in this 17th-century coaching inn have giant beds, exposed beams and subtle floral décor. Breakfast is particularly generous and children are very welcome.

There are plenty of teashops serving light snacks around town and most of the pubs serve up innocuous meals. For something slightly better, **Garford's** (☎ 858522; High St; mains £6.50) is a popular option for filling pies and bakes.

Getting There & Away

Bus Nos 21, 21A and 22 go to Moreton-in-Marsh (four daily Monday to Saturday, 20 mins) and bus No 606 goes to Cheltenham (six Monday to Saturday, 1½ hours).

AROUND BROADWAY

There are several sights of interest clustered around Broadway.

Beautiful gardens surround **Snowshill Manor** (NT; ☎ 01386-852410; admission £6.50, garden only £3.80; ☺ 11am-5.30pm Wed-Sun mid-Mar–Oct) once home to the marvellously eccentric Charles Paget Wade, who stocked his house with everything from Japanese armour to Victorian perambulators. It's an uphill walk to get here from Broadway, about 3 miles south.

Other sights include the baroque water gardens of **Stanway House** (☎ 01386-584469; adult/child £6/1.50; ☺ 2-5pm Tue & Thu Jul-Sep, garden only 2-5pm Sat) and the evocative ruins of **Hailes Abbey** (NT; ☎ 01242-602398; admission £3.20; ☺ 10am-6pm Easter-Oct, 10am-4pm Wed- Sun Nov-Easter).

WINCHCOMBE

☎ 01242

The most important town in the Cotswolds until the Middle Ages, Winchcombe was

---

THE COTSWOLDS OLIMPICKS

Founded in 1612, the Cotswolds Olimpicks is one of the most entertaining and bizarre sporting competitions in England. Events originally included welly wanging (throwing), shin-kicking, the sack race and climbing a slippery pole.

The competition was reinstated in 1951 and – incredibly – has earned the official sanction and support of the British Olympic Association. Most of the old disciplines are included, except for shin-kicking, which somehow isn't deemed a worthwhile event. Held at the beginning of June and running over the Spring Bank Holiday, they take place on Dover's Hill, on the edge of town.

---

also the capital of the Saxon kingdom of Mercia. The town has gorgeous old houses, most notably those on Dents Tce and Vineyard St, and the evocative remains of a Benedictine abbey, once one of the country's main pilgrimage centres. Also look out for the fine gargoyles on the lovely St Peter's Church.

TIC (☎ 602925; www.winchcombe.co.uk; ⏰ 10am-5pm Mon-Sat, 10am-4pm Sun Apr-Oct) is located on High St.

The town's main attraction, however, is **Sudeley Castle** (☎ 604357; www.sudeleycastle.co.uk; adult/child £6.85/3.85; ⏰ 10.30am-5.30pm Easter-Oct), once a favoured retreat of Tudor and Stuart monarchs. Henry VIII's last wife, Catherine Parr, came to live here after she married the Lord of Sudeley following the king's death. Her tomb is in the chapel and one of her teeth is displayed inside the house, along with paintings by Constable and Turner. The house also has an interesting exhibition on Antarctic explorer Ernest Shackleton and outside, the truly beautiful Queen's Garden.

Sleeping & Eating

Old White Lion (☎ 603300; www.theoldwhitelion .com; 37 North St; s/d £38/58) This delightful, 15th-century coaching inn in the heart of town offers good-value, country-style rooms with patterned wallpaper and floral bedspreads.

A HIKE TO BELAS KNAP

One of the most scenic short walks in the Cotswolds is the 2½-mile hike along the Cotswold Way from Winchcombe to **Belas Knap**, the best-preserved Neolithic burial chamber in the country. Visitors are not allowed inside this extraordinary 5000-year old construction, but the views of Sudeley Castle and the surrounding countryside are simply breathtaking.

The Oyster Restaurant downstairs serves classic British food (mains £8 to £12.)

White Hart Inn (☎ 602359; www.the-white-hart -inn.com; d £65-125; ✗) Sleek, stylish rooms at this old inn vary in style from warm Moroccan to rustic French Provencal and cool New England. To top off the international theme the restaurant dishes up traditional Swedish food (mains £14 to £17), while the basement pizzeria serves more humble classics for around £8.

Wesley House (☎ 602366; www.wesleyhouse .co.uk; High St; s/d £90/150) This half-timbered Tudor building has sympathetic rooms with a mix of antique furniture and contemporary furnishings. The restaurant has fantastic mullioned windows with views of Sudeley Castle and serves an excellent three-course French dinner for £35.

5 North St (☎ 604566; 5 North St; 2-course lunch £15.50, 2-course dinner £23.50) This small Michelin-starred place has deep red walls, fine table settings and an unpretentious air. The chef serves up an ambitious selection of classic French and modern British cuisine such as braised pig cheek with parsley mash and sage onion confit.

Getting There & Away

Buses run hourly Monday to Saturday (two on Sunday), from Winchcombe to Cheltenham (25 minutes) or Broadway (40 minutes).

GLOUCESTERSHIRE

A bucolic idyll, Gloucestershire is the heart of pastoral England and home to some incredibly picturesque stone villages. Less trampled than many parts of the Cotswolds, it's a wonderful area for cycling and walking and just oozes a mellow, unhurried charm.

The county is bisected by the River Severn. To the east of the river is the county capital,

Gloucester, with its magnificent cathedral, and the elegant Regency town of Cheltenham. To the west, and geographically part of Wales, are the Forest of Dean and the beautiful Wye Valley (see Herefordshire p362).

Information

For online information on attractions, accommodation and events see www.visit -glos.org.uk.

Activities

Gloucestershire is perfect for walking and cycling, with plenty of footpaths and quiet roads, gentle gradients and fine pubs for refreshment. TICs stock walking guides and a useful pack called *Cycle Touring Routes in Gloucestershire*.

Compass Holidays (☎ 250642; www.compass-holidays .com) has bicycles for hire for £34 for two days and £64 for a week from Cheltenham train station and also offers a bag drop service (£6) and guided cycling tours of the area.

Getting Around

Most TICs stock local bus timetables, or you can phone **Traveline** (☎ 0870 608 2608).

GLOUCESTER

☎ 01452 / pop 123,205

Waves of success and popularity have rolled through Gloucester (*glos*-ter) since its foundation under the Roman Empire. An important Saxon and then Norman town, it became a place of pilgrimage after Edward II was buried here, and in modern times it prospered on the back of heavy industry.

Today it is a rather dowdy town with only a glimmer of its medieval character. The main reason for visiting is to see the magnificent Norman cathedral and exquisite cloister, one of the most stunningly beautiful you'll see anywhere in England.

Orientation & Information

The city centre is based on a medieval cruciform pattern with Northgate, Southgate, Eastgate and Westgate Sts, converging on The Cross. The **TIC** (☎ 396572; 28 Southgate St; ☺ 10am-5pm Mon-Sat year-round, 11am-3pm Sun Jul-Aug) runs 1½-hour **guided walks** (£2.50; ☺ 2.30pm mid-Jun–mid-Sep) of the historic centre.

Gloucester Library (☎ 426973; Brunswick Rd; ☺ 9.30am-7.30pm Mon, Tue & Thu, 9.30am-5pm Wed & Fri, 9.30am-4pm Sat) has free Internet access.

Sights

GLOUCESTER CATHEDRAL

The city's crowning glory is the magnificent Gothic **Gloucester Cathedral** (☎ 528095; www.gloucestercathedral.org.uk; College Green; admission £3 donation; ☺ 7.30am-6pm, 7.30am-5pm Sat & Sun), an outstanding example of the English perpendicular style. Originally the site of a Saxon abbey, a church was added by a group of Benedictine monks in the 12th century.

Edward II was buried here after his murder in 1327 and his tomb proved so popular that Gloucester became a centre of pilgrimage. Income generated as a result financed its conversion into the magnificent building visible today.

Inside, the cathedral skilfully combines the best of Norman and Gothic design. The nave has retained much of its original character, from the thick, sturdy columns that lend it an air of gracious solidity, to the wonderful Norman arcading, draped with beautiful mouldings. From the elaborate 14th-century wooden choir stalls you'll get a good view of the imposing eastern window, the largest in England. The window commemorates local participation in the Battle of Crecy.

You can take a closer look from the tribune gallery, where there is an **exhibition** (admission £2; ☺ 10.30am-4pm Mon-Fri, 10.30am-3pm Sat) on the cathedral's history and the making of the window. Here you'll also hear the won-

---

THE TAILOR OF GLOUCESTER

One of Beatrix Potter's most famous stories, *The Tailor of Gloucester*, was inspired by a real-life tailor, John Prichard of Gloucester. As in her tale, the waistcoat he was making for the city's mayor was only at the cutting stage on the Saturday before the Monday when the garment was due. When he returned to the shop on Monday, he found the waistcoat complete, bar a single buttonhole. A note pinned to it read, 'No more twist'.

Mystified (but commercially minded), he placed a note in his window encouraging people to come in and see where 'waistcoats are made at night by the fairies'. In fact, the tailor's assistants had finished the work after kipping in the shop because they'd stayed out too late to get home.

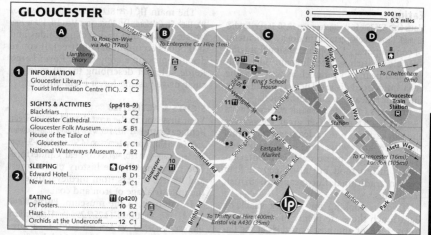

derful effects of the whispering gallery: you can pick up even the quietest of murmurs across the wonderfully elaborate lierne vaulting that spiders across the ceiling. Beneath the window in the northern ambulatory is Edward II's magnificent tomb. Nearby the late-15th-century **lady chapel** is a glorious patchwork of stained glass.

The **Great Cloister**, completed in 1367, is the first example of fan vaulting in England and is only matched in beauty by Henry VI-II's Chapel at Westminster Abbey. You (or your children) might recognise the cloister from the Harry Potter films: it was used in the corridor scenes at Hogwart's School.

You can get fabulous views of Gloucester from the 225ft **tower** (tours adult/child £2.50/1; 2.30pm Wed-Fri, 1.30pm & 2.30pm Sat & bank holidays). There are free guided **tours** (10.30am-4pm Mon-Sat, noon-2.30pm Sun) of the cathedral.

OTHER SIGHTS & ACTIVITIES

Once Britain's largest inland port, **Gloucester Docks** (www.glosdocks.co.uk) lay derelict for years, but now many of the beautiful Victorian warehouses have been restored.

The most interesting of these is Llanthony, the largest warehouse. It houses the excellent **National Waterways Museum** (318054; www.nwm .org.uk; adult/child £5/4; 10am-5pm), which charts the history of the local waterways and has a varied collection of historic vessels.

Another good bet is the **Gloucester Folk Museum** (396467; 99 Westgate St; admission £2; 10am-5pm Tue-Sat), housed in a set of won-

derful Tudor and Jacobean timber-framed buildings dating from the 16th and 17th centuries. The museum features local history, domestic life, crafts and industries from 1500 to the present.

Also worth a look is **Blackfriars** (Ladybellgate St; admission free; tours 3pm Sun Jul & Aug), Britain's finest surviving example of a 13th-century Dominican priory.

Fans of Beatrix Potter will love the **House of the Tailor of Gloucester** (422856; www.hop -skip-jump.com; admission £1; 10am-5pm Mon-Sat Apr-Oct, 10am-4pm Nov-Mar), off Westgate St, established in the shop that inspired the story of the same name.

Sleeping

Gloucester has a dismal choice of hotels and you may want to consider staying in Cheltenham instead.

Edward Hotel (525865; www.edwardhotel -gloucester.co.uk; 88-92 London Rd; s/d £40/60; P ✕) This Victorian town house near the train station is one of the best options in town, with bright, newly renovated rooms. The décor mixes the old with the new and manages to avoid being too fussy. Children are very welcome.

New Inn (522177; www.newinnglos.com; 16 Northgate St; s/d £45/80; ✕) One of the most atmospheric places in town, this medieval galleried inn has been welcoming guests since 1455. The rooms have dark-wood panelling and traditional styling, but go a little over the top on the floral patterns and stripy wallpaper.

Eating

Haus (☎ 525359; 56 Westgate; mains £8.50-16; ♥ lunch & dinner) This sleek restaurant does a fine menu of contemporary European cuisine featuring specialities such as Gressingham duck with poached pear and caramel, as well as some Asia-influenced dishes. The décor is all clean lines, sultry leathers and dark wood.

Dr Fosters (☎ 300990; Kimberly Warehouse; mains £9-15; ♥ lunch & dinner) Get great views over the docks from a deep leather sofa at this brasserie and wine bar in a renovated warehouse. The menu dabbles in international fusion food but also keeps a firm eye on traditional European and British favourites.

If you're looking for a quick snack or light lunch there are plenty of cafés round town. One of the best is **Orchids at the Undercroft** (☎ 308920; Gloucester Cathedral; mains £5-6; ♥ lunch), part of the former monastery hall. It does a standard menu of sandwiches, pies, soups and bakes all served up in generous quantities.

Getting There & Away

National Express has buses every two hours to London (£14.50, 3½ hours). Bus No 94 runs to Cheltenham every 10 minutes (30 minutes), but the quickest way to get there is by train (every 20 minutes, 10 minutes).

AROUND GLOUCESTER
Forest of Dean
☎ 01594

An undisturbed backwater, the lovely Forest of Dean was the first National Forest Park in England. Formerly a royal hunting ground and centre of iron and coal mining, this tract of forest covers a 42-sq-mile swathe between Gloucester, Ross-on-Wye and Chepstow. JRR Tolkien was a regular visitor and the forest is said to have inspired the setting for *The Lord of the Rings*. A web of well-maintained trails now covers the area and makes it an excellent place for walking and cycling.

Coleford is the Forest of Dean's main town with good bus connections to Gloucester making it a convenient base for touring the area. In the south the magnificent youth hostel near Lydney makes a fantastic base with regular trains back to the city from nearby Lydney Junction.

The main **TIC** (☎ 812388; www.forestofdean.gov .uk; High St, Coleford; ♥ 10am-4pm Mon-Fri, 10am-2pm Sat) stocks walking and cycling guides and also books accommodation (free). If you're driving, pick up a copy of the *Royal Forest Route*, a leaflet describing the 20-mile circular drive passing forest highlights.

SIGHTS & ACTIVITIES

Your first stop in the area should be the **Dean Heritage Centre** (☎ 822170; www.deanheritagemuseum .com; Camp Mill, Soudley; admission £4.50; ♥ 10am-5.30pm Apr-Sep, 10am-4pm Feb, Mar & Oct) near Cinderford. The museum tells the history of the forest and its free miners from medieval times to the industrial age of iron and coal.

In contrast to the museum, **Puzzle Wood** (☎ 833187; adult/child £3.25/2.25; ♥ 11am-5.30pm Tue-Sun Mar-Sep, 11am-4pm Feb & Oct) is a pre-Roman, open-cast ore mine which has been allowed to grow over. It is an extraordinary area with a maze of paths, eerie passageways through moss-covered rocks, hidden dead ends, weird rock formations, tangled vines and gorgeous untamed scenery. It's a brilliant place for children. Puzzle Wood is 1 mile south of Coleford on the B4228.

Mined since the Iron Age, **Clearwell Caves** (☎ 832535; www.clearwellcaves.com; adult/child £4/2.50; ♥ 10am-5pm Mar-Oct) is a warren of dank, spooky caves littered with vestiges of the mining era as well as shimmering pools and wonderful rock formations. Special events take place at major holiday periods with an underground rave at Halloween followed by a magical grotto in time for Christmas. The caves are signposted off the B4228 a mile south of Coleford.

The pretty village of Newland is worth a visit to see the 13th-century **All Saints,** the so-called 'Cathedral of the Forest'. It was restored and partially rebuilt in the 19th century and houses some fine stained-glass windows as well as a unique brass depicting a miner with a *nelly* (tallow candle) in his mouth, a pick in his hand and a *billy* (backpack) on his back.

SLEEPING & EATING

St Briavels Castle YHA Hostel (☎ 0870 770 6040; www.yha.org.uk; Lydney; beds £11.80; (P) (✕)) Probably the most impressive youth hostel in the country, this imposing, moated place was once a hunting lodge used by King John. The dorms have four to eight beds and are

SOMETHING SPECIAL

Cowley Manor (☎ 01242-870900; www.cowleymanor.com; Cowley; d £220-445; P X ▣ ☒) A cool, minimalist getaway for jaded urbanites, Cowley Manor offers luxury in a chintz-free zone. The rooms are simple yet elegant and feature oak and leather, funky furniture and loads of gadgets. Elsewhere, the hotel is more playful, with a polka-dot, leather-walled pool room and sunken swimming pools in the lawn outside. The restaurant is pretty laid-back, with wood-panelled walls and a menu that features both comfort food and sophisticated fare. There's also a children's playroom, wonderful gardens and a spa offering a range of treatments.

Cowley is just off the A435 5 miles south of Cheltenham.

pretty unique. If you're around in August it's well worth staying for a medieval banquet (Wednesdays and Saturdays).

Forest House Hotel (☎ 832424; www.forest-house -hotel.co.uk; Cinder Hill, Coleford; s/d £40/70; P X) Beautiful, bright, modern rooms and excellent food (mains £8 to £12) make this restored 18th-century house a good option. The rooms are spacious and chintz-free, with colourful furnishings and good bathrooms.

Tudor Farmhouse (☎ 0800 7835935; www.tudor farmhouse.co.uk; High St, Clearwell; s/d £60/80; X) This charming 13th-century hotel sits in extensive grounds and has rooms with plenty of period features, oak beams and chunky wooden furniture. The hotel also has a cosy restaurant (mains £12 to £18) serving modern British dishes in beautiful surroundings.

Cider Press (☎ 54472; The Cross, Drybrook; mains £ 9-17; ☟ lunch Fri-Sun, dinner Wed-Sat) A gourmet oasis, this popular restaurant is an elegant, intimate place just north of Cinderford. The chef serves up delicious seafood, game and organic meats from a classic French menu with some contemporary twists. You need to book ahead if you want a table.

GETTING THERE & AROUND

From Gloucester, bus No 31 runs to Coleford every 15 minutes (one hour) and trains run to Lydney Junction (20 minutes) eight times daily. The **Dean Forest Railway** (☎ 843423; www.deanforestrailway.co.uk) runs steam trains from Lydney to Whitecroft (adult/child return £6.50/4.50) from March to October. Call or check the website for days of service.

You can hire bikes (£12 a day), buy maps and get advice on cycling routes at **Pedalabikeaway** (☎ 860065; www.pedalabikeaway.com; Cannop Valley, nr Coleford).

CHELTENHAM
☎ 01242 / pop 98,875

Once Britain's most popular spa town, Cheltenham retains much of its period charm in its graceful streets lined with elegant architecture, beautifully proportioned terraces, wrought-iron balconies, leafy crescents and expensive boutiques. It's a well-heeled kind of town, with a fine choice of hotels, great restaurants and a plethora of festivals, making it an excellent base for exploring the area.

In March, hordes of racegoers descend upon the town for the National Hunt Festival, but there's also a jazz festival in late April and early May; and the Literature Festival in October.

History

Just another Cotswolds town until 1716, when pecking pigeons were discovered to be eating salt crystals from a spring, Cheltenham quickly developed into the definitive spa, a rival to its more illustrious sibling Bath. The town began attracting the sick and hypochondriac in ever-increasing numbers but a visit by George III in 1788 sealed the spa's future and new wells were built, as well as houses to accommodate the many visitors, among them Handel and Jane Austen.

Orientation

Cheltenham train station is out on a limb to the west; bus D or E will run you to the town centre for 90p. The bus station is behind The Promenade in the town centre.

Central Cheltenham is easily walkable. The High St runs roughly east–west; south from it is The Promenade, a more elegant shopping area, which extends into Montpellier, the most exclusive area of town. Pittville Park and the old Pump Room are about a mile north of High St.

OXFORDSHIRE, THE COTSWOLDS & GLOUCESTERSHIRE

CHELTENHAM

0   300 m
0   0.2 miles

INFORMATION
Cheltenham Main Library............ 1 B2
Equals..................................... 2 B2
Main Post Office..................... 3 B2
Tourist Information Centre (TIC).. 4 B3

SIGHTS & ACTIVITIES   (pp422-3)
Art Gallery & Museum.............. 5 B2

SLEEPING   (p423)
Cheltenham Townhouse........... 6 C1
Hannaford's............................ 7 C1
Hotel Kandinsky..................... 8 A3
Hotel on the Park................... 9 C1
Lonsdale House...................... 10 B4
University of Gloucestershire.... 11 C1
University of Gloucestershire.... 12 B1
University of Gloucestershire.... 13 A4
YMCA.................................... 14 B3

EATING   (pp423-4)
Daffodil................................. 15 B4
Le Champignon Sauvage.......... 16 B4
Le Sacré Fleur........................ 17 A3
Murasaki................................ 18 A3
Orange Tree........................... 19 B2
Storyteller............................. 20 C2

DRINKING   (p424)
Beehive.................................. 21 B4
Fish & Fiddle.......................... 22 B3
Montpellier Wine Bar.............. 23 A3
Retreat.................................. 24 B4

ENTERTAINMENT   (p424)
Axiom Centre for the Arts....... 25 C2
Everyman Theatre................... 26 B2
Town Hall.............................. 27 B2

TRANSPORT   (p424)
Bus Station............................ 28 B2
Bus Stop for Pittville Park....... 29 C2
Enterprise Car Rental.............. 30 B2

OTHER
Cheltenham General Hospital.. 31 C4
Cheltenham Ladies' College..... 32 A3
Cotswold Walking Holidays..... 33 A3
Edward Wilson Statue............. 34 B3
St Luke's Church..................... 35 C4

Information

All the major banks and the main post office can be found on High St. Other useful services in town:

Cheltenham Main Library (☎ 532688; Clarence St; ☒ 9.30am-7pm Mon, Wed & Fri, 9.30am-5.30pm Tue & Thu, 9.30am-4pm Sat) Free Internet access.

Cheltenham Spa (www.visitcheltenham.info) The city's tourism site with information on everything from accommodation to attractions.

Equals (☎ 237292; 287 High St; Internet access per 30 min £2)

TIC (☎ 522878; 77 Promenade; ☒ 9.30am-5.15pm Mon-Sat) Stocks Cotswold walking and cycling guides, as well as *The Romantic Road*, a guide to a 30-mile circular driving tour of the Southern Cotswolds. It also runs a free accommodation service.

Sights
THE PROMENADE

The Promenade is the heart of Cheltenham and is at its best in summer, when its hanging baskets are full of flowers. The **Municipal Offices**, built as private residences in 1825, are among the best features of one of Britain's most beautiful thoroughfares. Following The Promenade towards Montpellier, you come to the **Imperial Gardens**, built to service the Imperial Spa.

PITTVILLE PUMP ROOM

Set in a delightful area of villas and parkland a mile from the town centre, the **Pittville Pump Room** (☎ 523852; Pittville Park; admission free; ☒ 11am-4pm Wed-Mon) is the town's finest Regency building. Built between 1825 and 1830, it was constructed as a spa and social centre for Joseph Pitt's new estate. Upstairs, there are occasional art exhibitions and downstairs (where you can still taste the spa water if you wish) the former ballroom is now used for concerts. The park itself is also used for Sunday concerts throughout the summer.

ART GALLERY & MUSEUM
Cheltenham's history is imaginatively displayed at the **Art Gallery & Museum** (☎ 237431; www.cheltenham.artgallery.museum; Clarence St; admission free; ☒ 10am-5.20pm Mon-Sat), which has excellent sections covering Edward Wilson, William Morris and the Arts and Crafts movement (p433), as well as Dutch and British art. There's a temporary exhibition gallery on the ground floor.

CHELTENHAM RACECOURSE
On Cheltenham's northern outskirts is one of the country's top courses which attracts 40,000 punters a day for an event known simply as The Festival, the highlight of the National Hunt racing calendar. For five days in March half of Ireland decamps to Cheltenham and thousands of race enthusiasts turn out for England's premier steeplechase event. Even if you're not prone to a flutter on the gee gees, it's well worth experiencing the passion and atmosphere of a big day at The Festival. Tickets (about £25) can be booked by calling ☎ 226226. At other times it's worth a trip for the **Hall of Fame museum** (☎ 513014; admission free; ☒ 8.30am-5.30pm Mon-Fri), which charts the history of steeplechasing since 1819.

Tours
Walking tours (£2.50; 1¼ hr; ☒ 11am Jun-Sep) of Regency Cheltenham depart from the TIC.

Sleeping
Cheltenham has a good choice of hotels but book early if you're coming for any of the festivals. The Montpellier area, just southwest of the town centre, is the best spot for good B&Bs.

YMCA (☎ 524024; www.cheltenhamymca.org; 6 Victoria Walk; dm £18) This elegant but run-down place near the centre has standard dorms and good facilities. Rates include breakfast and access to the attached fitness centre.

University of Gloucestershire (☎ 532774; www.glos.ac.uk/conferences; s £22; P ☒ ☐) The uni-

versity lets its single-bed study rooms at three sites from July to late September. The rooms are modern and comfortable, and although the décor is pretty standard they're excellent value.

Cheltenham Townhouse (☎ 221922; www.cheltenhamtownhouse.co.uk; 12 Pittville Lawn; s £30-55, d £55-95; P ☐ wheelchair access) Slightly out of the town centre on a quiet leafy street, this excellent-value B&B is well worth the trip. The sleek, spacious rooms are bright and stylish with contemporary décor, great bathrooms and comfy beds.

Hannaford's (☎ 515181; sue@hannafords.icom43.net; 20 Evesham Rd; s/d £40/45; P ☒) If you want true Regency elegance at an affordable rate, this hotel is a wonderful choice. It has retained its ornate ceilings, marble fireplaces and period features throughout.

Hotel Kandinsky (☎ 527788; www.hotelkandinsky.com; Bayshill Rd; s/d £75/90; P ☒ ☒) Eclectic art and ethnic furniture, warm colours, smart furnishings and a chic air of junk shop mixed with the stylishly new make this *the* place to stay in Cheltenham. Hints of long-lost colonial grandeur surface throughout and downstairs there's a popular 1950s-style club and a stylish modern restaurant (mains £9 to £10).

Other options:

Lonsdale House (☎ 232379; lonsdalehouse@hotmail.com; Montpellier Dr; s/d £25/49; P ☒) Bright comfortable rooms in a charming Regency town house.
Hotel on the Park (☎ 518898; www.hotelonthepark.co.uk; 38 Evesham Rd; s/d £97/134; P ☒) Luxurious Regency hotel with wonderfully potent themed rooms featuring extravagant décor.

Eating
Cheltenham has an excellent range of places to eat and something to suit everyone's taste and budget.

Storyteller (☎ 250343; 11 North Pl; mains £6-15; ☒ lunch & dinner) This buzzing eatery has a small restaurant area and a large heated conservatory and serves up an extensive menu of hearty meals to the masses. The food spans the globe, from Californian kitchen to Mexican, Mediterranean and Asian dishes including seafood, pastas and game.

Daffodil (☎ 700055; 18-20 Suffolk Pde; mains £12-20, 2-course lunch £10; ☒ lunch & dinner; wheelchair access) This former cinema now houses a dramatic, Art Deco restaurant with two elegant staircases winding up to the upper level. The open kitchen is a frenzy of activity as chefs cook up excellent English, French and Mediterranean-brasserie food. There's live jazz on Monday nights.

Orange Tree (☎ 234232; 317 High St; mains £8-15; ☺ lunch & dinner) A vegetarian's heaven, this place has plenty of choice for vegans and allergy sufferers as well. The extensive menu features interesting, innovative dishes. There's a toy box for children, organic wines and beers and plenty of newspapers for lingering meals.

Le Champignon Sauvage (☎ 573449; 24-26 Suffolk Rd; set menu 2-/3-course £19/23; ☺ lunch & dinner; wheelchair access) A Cheltenham institution, this unassuming-looking restaurant has two Michelin stars, some pretty naff décor and probably the best food in town. The ambitious French menu has some unusual combinations of flavours: try the rose geranium cream with damson for some surprise ingredients.

Other good options:
Le Sacré Fleur (☎ 525230; 15 Rotunda Tce; mains £11-14; ☺ lunch & dinner) A small, slick French restaurant.
Murasaki (☎ 227757; 8 The Courtyard; mains £8-12; ☺ lunch & dinner) A Japanese restaurant with excellent sushi.

Drinking
Beehive (☎ 579443; 1-3 Montpellier Villas) The gleefully haphazard interior and jumble of furniture in this traditional boozer make it one of the best and most popular pubs in town. There's a pretty little courtyard and a top-notch restaurant upstairs (mains £8 to £12) serving a wonderful collection of modern fusion food.

Retreat (☎ 235436; 10-11 Suffolk Pde) This trendy little place has deep-red walls, dark furniture and mellow music. It also serves up some interesting sambos like goat's cheese and Italian sausage (£6) and has a lovely beer garden at the back.

Fish & Fiddle (☎ 238001; 1 Imperial Lane) A funky little place just off The Promenade, this music pub pumps out the choons to happy crowds who pour in at weekends. Friday night is a strange mix of drum 'n' bass and hip-hop, and on Saturday night it's funk, soul and jazz.

Montpellier Wine Bar (☎ 527774; Bayshill Lodge, Montpellier St) Full of fashion-conscious locals watching the world go by, this slick urbane hangout is a good place to meet

Cheltenham's well-to-do young things or have some better than average modern food (mains £11 to £14).

Entertainment
THEATRE & MUSIC
The **Everyman Theatre** (☎ 572573; Regent St) stages anything from comedy and panto to Shakespeare. The **Pittville Pump Room** often hosts classical music concerts, while the **Town Hall** (☎ 227979; Imperial Sq) offers the more popular stuff. The **Axiom Centre for the Arts** (☎ 690243; 57 Winchcombe St) has a regular programme of less-mainstream theatrical events and music.

Getting There & Away
BUS
National Express runs buses to London roughly hourly (£14.50, 3 hours). Swanbrook Coaches has three buses to Oxford Monday to Saturday (one on Sunday, £6.20, 1½ hours).

Bus No 94 runs to Gloucester every 10 minutes (30 minutes), Monday to Saturday, every 20 minutes on Sunday. Bus No 51 goes to Cirencester hourly (30 minutes).

Pulhams P1 bus runs to Moreton (one hour) via Bourton and Stow six times daily Monday to Saturday. Castleways Coaches run regularly to Broadway (45 minutes) via Winchcombe (20 minutes), Monday to Saturday. Stagecoach bus No 164 does the same journey four times on Sunday.

TRAIN
Cheltenham has hourly trains to London (£32, 2½ hours), Bristol (£7.50, 45 minutes), Bath (£11.50, one hour), and regular departures for Gloucester (£2.60, 10 minutes).

Getting Around
Compass Holidays (☎ 250642; www.compass-holidays .com; per day £17) has bicycles for hire at the train station.

TEWKESBURY
☎ 01684 / pop 9978
Buckled, timber-framed buildings line the main street and wonderful alleys of Tudor-heavy Tewkesbury, an attractive but depressed town that can get choked with traffic. Church St, Mill St and Mill Bank are particularly worth exploring. The town also has a lovely riverside area but its most

glorious building is the magnificent medieval abbey church.

The **TIC** (☎ 295027; www.tewkesburybc.gov.uk; Barton St; ⊙ 9.30am-5pm Mon-Sat, 9.30-4pm Sun) has lots of information and a small museum upstairs. If you're visiting at the end of May ask about the Coopers Hill cheese-rolling competition, a 200-year-old tradition that sees locals chase seven-pound blocks of Double Gloucester cheese down the hill for some unknown reason.

Tewkesbury Abbey

The town's focal point is the magnificent **Tewkesbury Abbey** (☎ 850959; www.tewkesbury abbey.org.uk; admission £2 donation; ⊙ 7.30am-6pm), one of Britain's largest churches and the last of the monasteries to be dissolved by Henry VIII. The building survived after being bought by the townspeople.

Stone to build the abbey was brought by sea and river from Normandy in the 12th century. It has a massive 40m-high tower, some spectacular Norman pillars lining the nave, 14th-century stained glass above the choir and an organ dating from 1631. The magnificent tombs of the wealthy wool traders are also worth a look, as is that of John Wakeman, the last abbot, who is shown as a vermin-ridden skeleton.

A **visitor centre** (⊙ 10am-4pm Mon-Sat), by the gate, houses an exhibition on the abbey's history.

Sleeping & Eating

Carrant Brook House (☎ 290355; www.carrantbrook house.co.uk; 3 Rope walk; s/d £30/50; **P** **✗**) Off the busy main street this quiet guesthouse has good-value, simple, bright rooms and a lovely patio area. Children are very welcome and the four-course breakfast should keep you refuelled for the day.

Royal Hop Pole (☎ 293236; www.corushotels.com; Church St; s/d £75/100; **P** **✗**) One of the oldest hotels in town, this half-timbered inn offers elegant period rooms and a delightful garden that leads down to the river. The restaurant (mains £11 to £15) serves up a decent array of traditional and modern British food.

Aubergine (☎ 292703; 73 Church St; mains £7.95-10.95; ⊙ lunch & dinner) This elegant café-bar serves up imaginative food – a welcome respite from the Tewkesbury norm. The menu features new world-fusion cuisine, ranging from subtle salmon-and-dill fish cakes to Moroccan lamb tagine.

Getting There & Away

Bus No X94 from Gloucester goes to Tewkesbury hourly (30 minutes). The nearest train station is at Ashchurch, 3 miles away.

Around Tewkesbury

If you're feeling energetic, majestic **Bredon Hill**, 6 miles northeast of Tewkesbury, makes an excellent spot for walking. The isolated hill is 961ft high and views from the top are simply amazing. It's the site of an Iron Age fort and the impressive ramparts can still be seen, now enclosing the strange 18th-century Parson's Folly. If you're driving you can climb the hill in about an hour from the village of Overbury. Otherwise, bus No 540 runs from Tewkesbury to Bredon every two hours (10 minutes), from where it takes about an hour and a half to get to the top.

The Midlands

CONTENTS

Tell any English person you're visiting the Midlands on holiday and with that something-smells-awful expression they'll demand *'Why?'*. But those who've spent time here can fire back plenty of good reasons: the wild countryside of the Peak District National Park; the russet ruins of Kenilworth Castle; the triple spires of Lichfield's cathedral; Nottingham's nightlife; Birmingham's balti; the lovely, untouristed market towns of England's industrial heartland...

On top of all that, the Midlands are home to two of the country's best-known attractions: Warwick Castle, one of the finest medieval buildings in England, and Stratford-upon-Avon, a pilgrimage site for Shakespeare lovers from around the world.

Of course, as England's manufacturing powerhouse, the region does contain some pretty dreary industrial settlements. The Industrial Revolution didn't have much use for aesthetics. In many cases, what the growth of industry didn't destroy, WWII bombing demolished.

But ten miles outside Nottingham you can be dodging pheasants on winding roads through charming villages. In Birmingham you can hop on a canal narrow boat and wend your way west along the peaceful arteries that once fed the industrial heart. Birmingham, Nottingham and Leicester also offer some of the best restaurants and nightlife in the country.

There's a wide gap in living standards between the northern cities and those south of Birmingham. The divide runs east–west, too: talk football and you'll hear forlorn tales of the former dominance of Leicester City and Nottingham Forest (east Midlands), while Birmingham and West Bromwich Albion (west) are joyfully back in the top flight.

A trip to the Midlands isn't about a castle, a museum or a mountain; it's a window onto the unique, proud and enduring character of each town or region you visit.

THE MIDLANDS

HIGHLIGHTS

- Wandering hill and dale from pub to pub in the **Peak District National Park** (p478)

- Following in the footsteps of the Virgin Queen on a visit to the red ruins of **Kenilworth Castle** (p445)

- Checking out one of England's gloomiest – and loveliest – cathedrals in the pretty market town of **Lichfield** (p452)

- Peeking into the bedroom of Lord Byron, where all sorts of decadence went down, at **Newstead Abbey** (p470)

- Launching yourself into the stratosphere at Leicester's **National Space Centre** (p461)

- Trying out torture devices and dodging rats in the dungeons of **Warwick Castle** (p441)

■ EAST MIDLANDS	■ POPULATION: 4,2 MILLION	■ AREA:11,551 SQ MILES
■ WEST MIDLANDS	■ POPULATION: 5,3 MILLION	

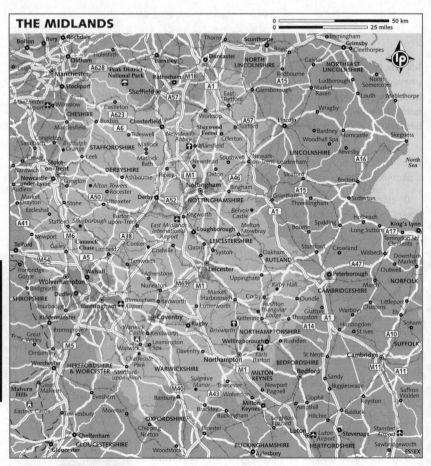

THE MIDLANDS

Orientation

It's perhaps appropriate that it's easiest to orientate yourself here by motorways. The M1 winds north from London, demarking the eastern third of the region (which is bounded to the east by the A1) and running parallel with a line of the east Midlands' major towns: Bedford, Northampton, Leicester, Derby and Nottingham, in that order. The M40 does the same for the south and west Midlands, passing Stratford-upon-Avon and Warwick on its way to the M42 and Birmingham, in the middle of the region. Routes spider out from Birmingham, the M6 running east towards Coventry and the M1, and northwest up towards Wolverhampton, Stafford and Stoke-on-Trent; the M54 splits off at Wolverhampton to head over to Telford and Shrewsbury. The Peak District is midway between the M1 and the M6.

Information

The **Heart of England Tourist Board** (☎ 01905 761100; www.visitheartofengland.com) has centralised tourist information for the region and is a good place to start your planning.

Activities

Many parts of the Midlands are predominantly urban, and the opportunities for outdoor activities among the factories and streets are limited. But out in those hinterlands, conditions are good for walking, cycling and water sports.

The Peak District National Park is one of the finest areas in England for walking and cycling – more details are given in the introduction to the Peak District section (p478). It's also home to the start of the Pennine Way national trail, which leads keen walkers for 256 miles (412km) through Yorkshire and Northumberland into Scotland. Under development, but with new sections opening all the time, the Pennine Bridleway runs roughly parallel to the walking route and is designed for horse-riding and off-road cycling.

But these long-distance epics are the tip of the iceberg; the Peak District is criss-crossed with a vast network of paths for walkers, country lanes for touring cyclists, and tracks and bridleways for mountain-bikers – with something for every level of ability, from mile-eating rides to gentle strolls. Ideal bases include the villages and small towns of Matlock Bath, Edale and Castleton, or the national park centre at Fairholmes on the Derwent Reservoirs. Bikes can be hired at Fairholmes and various other points around the Peak District, especially in the areas where old railway lines have been converted into delightful walking and cycling tracks.

In the south of the Midlands region, other good places for gentle walking and cycling include Cannock Chase and the National Forest, an ongoing project to plant 30 million trees across this part of central England. The main centre (called Conkers) is near Ashby-de-la-Zouch in Leicestershire.

Rutland Water, a large lake surrounded by cycling and walking trails, is also a great place for water sports such as sailing and windsurfing.

More information is given in the Outdoor Activities chapter.

Getting There & Around

National Express (☎ 08705 808080; www.national express.com) provides extensive coach services in the Midlands. Birmingham is a major hub. For regional bus timetables, consult **SCB East Midlands Travel & Leisure** (www.scbeastmidstravel .co.uk). Regional bus services are provided by **Stagecoach** (☎ 01788 535555; Explorer tickets £5.99). A comprehensive network of bus services around the west Midlands is provided by **Travel West Midlands** (www.travelwm.co.uk).

BIRMINGHAM

☎ 0121 / pop 970,892

If you haven't been to Birmingham in a while, or you know it only by reputation, its once-facetious designation as 'the Venice of the north' (because of its many canals) may inspire little more than laughter. England's second-largest city has never been known as a romantic getaway, much less an architectural wonder. But times have changed – and how. A visit to the new, improved Birmingham should be mandatory for anyone who clings to an outdated impression of the place.

The city's reputation as an aesthetically challenged pit of crime and grime, though once justified, has been reversed by several cutting-edge developments in former industrial wastelands; at the same time, the city and its surroundings still boast several older cultural and architectural joys. The manufacturing industry is still going strong here, and these days the locals play as hard as they work. What that means for the visitor is great shopping, excellent restaurants and some of the country's best bars and clubs. Colloquially, the city is known as Brum, its inhabitants as Brummies and their dialect as Brummie. Just about the only thing left to scoff at in Birmingham is the accent – it's consistently rated England's least attractive.

HISTORY

One of the great centres of the Industrial Revolution, Birmingham has been the birthplace of several inventions; it was home to steam pioneers James Watt (1736–1819) and Matthew Boulton (1728–1809) and chemist Joseph Priestley (1733–1804), to name a few. By the mid–19th century, though, the 'workshop of the world' exemplified everything that was bad about industrial development. It wasn't until the mid-1800s, under enlightened mayors such as Joseph Chamberlain (1836–1914), that the city first became a trendsetter in civic regeneration. But WWII air raids undid such leaders' good work, and postwar town planners completed the vandalism by designing ring roads and motorways that virtually obliterated the old city centre, bar a few gems.

Fortunately, in recent days the city's leadership has once again devoted itself to groundbreaking civic revitalisation, creating

THE MIDLANDS

BIRMINGHAM

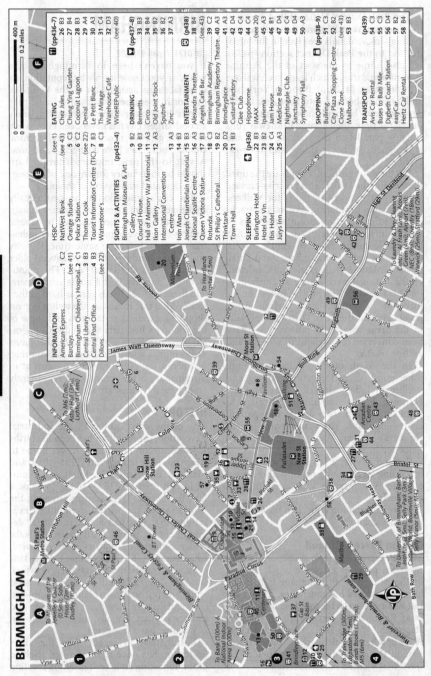

INFORMATION
American Express................1 C2
Barclays.............................(see 41)
Birmingham Children's Hospital..2 C1
Central Library....................3 B3
Central Post Office.............4 B3
Dillons..............................(see 22)

HSBC................................(see 1)
NatWest Bank...................5 C3
Orange Studio....................6 C3
Police Station....................6 C1
Thomas Cook....................(see 22)
Tourist Information Centre (TIC)..7 B3
Waterstone's.....................8 C3

SIGHTS & ACTIVITIES (pp432-4)
Birmingham Museum & Art
  Gallery..........................9 B2
Council House...................10 B3
Hall of Memory War Memorial..11 A3
Ikon Gallery......................12 A3
International Convention
  Centre............................13 A3
Iron Man..........................14 B3
Joseph Chamberlain Memorial..15 B3
National Sealife Centre........16 A3
Queen Victoria Statue.........17 B3
Rotunda...........................18 C3
St Philip's Cathedral...........19 B2
Thinktank.........................20 D2
Town Hall.........................21 B3

SLEEPING   (p436)
Burlington Hotel................22 B3
Hotel du Vin.....................23 B2
Ibis Hotel.........................24 C4
Jurys Inn.........................25 A3

EATING   (pp436-7)
Chez Jules.......................26 B3
Chung Ying Garden...........27 B4
Coconut Lagoon...............28 B3
Denial............................29 A4
Le Petit Blanc...................30 A3
Thai Mirage......................31 C4
Warehouse Café...............32 D3
WineREPublic...................(see 40)

DRINKING   (pp437-8)
Bennetts..........................33 B3
Circo.............................34 B4
Old Joint Stock.................35 B2
Sputnik..........................36 B2
Zinc..............................37 A3

ENTERTAINMENT   (pp438)
Alexandra Theatre.............38 B3
Angels Cafe Bar................(see 43)
Birmingham Academy.........39 C2
Birmingham Repertory Theatre..40 A3
Brindleyplace....................41 A3
Custard Factory.................42 D4
Glee Club.........................43 C4
Hippodrome......................44 C4
IMAX...............................(see 20)
Ipanema..........................45 A3
Jam House........................46 B1
Medicine Bar.....................47 D4
Nightingale Club................48 C4
Sanctuary.........................49 D4
Symphony Hall..................50 A3

SHOPPING   (pp438-9)
Bullring...........................51 C3
City Plaza Shopping Centre..52 B2
Clone Zone.......................(see 43)
Mailbox...........................53 B3

TRANSPORT   (p439)
Avis Car Rental..................54 C3
Buses to Balti Mile..............55 C3
Digbeth Coach Station........56 D4
easyCar...........................57 B2
Hertz Car Rental................58 B4

the award-winning Brindleyplace, the Mailbox, Millennium Point and, most recently, the Bullring in formerly grim and often dangerous urban wastelands.

ORIENTATION

The one aspect of Birmingham that's still indisputably a nightmare is driving in it. The endless ring roads, roundabouts and underpasses make it particularly confusing for motorists to navigate. It's wise to park somewhere and explore the city on foot until you get your bearings.

The city centre is the pedestrian precinct in front of the huge Council House. Head west from here to Centenary Sq, the International Convention Centre and Symphony Hall, and the development at Gas St Basin and Brindleyplace.

Southeast of Council House, most of Birmingham's shops can be found along pedestrianised New St and in the modern City Plaza, Pallasades and Pavilions shopping centres; the latter is overlooked by the landmark Rotunda office block. Between New St station and Digbeth coach station is a much-ballyhooed new development called the Bullring, once a potentially scary eyesore and now a sleek, architecturally inventive shopping complex (see www.bullring .co.uk). See Tourist Information (right) for information about maps.

INFORMATION

Bookshops
Bonds Books (☎ 427 9343; 97a High Street, Harborne)
Dillons (☎ 631 4333; 128 New St)
Waterstone's (☎ 633 4353; 24 High St)

Emergency
Police station (☎ 626 6000; Steelhouse Lane)
West Midlands Police (☎ 0845 113 5000)

Internet Access
Central Library (☎ 303 4511; Chamberlain Sq; ☼ 9am-8pm Mon-Fri, 9am-5pm Sat) Internet access is free by reservation.
Orange Studio (☎ 0800 790 0909; www.orangestudio .co.uk; 7 Cannon St; Internet access per hr £3; ☼ 8.30am-6.30pm Mon-Fri, 10am-6.30pm Sat) This hip 'chat café' off New St has DJs and a nightclub feel in the upstairs restaurant.

Internet Resources
BBC Birmingham home page (www.bbc.co.uk /birmingham)

Birmingham Museums & Art Gallery (www.bmag .org.uk) Information on most of the city's museums and galleries, including opening hours, admission costs and forthcoming exhibitions.
Birmingham UK (www.birminghamuk.com)
icBirmingham (http://icbirmingham.icnetwork.co.uk)
Itchy Birmingham (www.itchybirmingham.co.uk) An irreverent web guide to arts and culture.
Travel Birmingham (www.travelbirmingham.co.uk)

Laundry
Laundry & Dry Cleaning Centre (☎ 771 3659; 236 Warwick Rd, Sparkhill)

Left Luggage
New Street Station (Station St; ☼ 6.45am-9.45pm Mon-Sat, 11.15am-6.45pm Sun)

Media
Various free magazines litter hotel lobbies, bars and restaurants, providing handy updates on current exhibitions, the best eateries, and the hippest bars and clubs. Pick of the bunch is the fortnightly *What's On* – free at some bars and the TIC, elsewhere 80p.

Medical Services
Birmingham Children's Hospital (☎ 333 9999; Steelhouse Lane)
Heartlands Hospital (☎ 766 6611; Bordesley Green E) Catch bus Nos 15, 17, 96, 97 or 99.

Money
American Express (☎ 644 5555; Bank House, Cherry St)
Barclays (Brindleyplace)
HSBC Bank & Thomas Cook Exchange (☎ 643 5057; 130 New St)
NatWest Bank (Arcadian Centre)

Post
Central post office (1 Pinfold St, Victoria Sq; ☼ 9am-5.30pm Mon-Fri, 9am-6pm Sat)

Tourist Information
TIC (www.birmingham.org.uk) Main branch (☎ 643 2514; 2 City Arcade; ☼ 9.30am-5.30pm Mon-Sat); National Exhibition Centre office (near Birmingham airport; ☎ 780 4321; piazza@bmp.org.uk; ☼ 9am-5.15pm Mon-Fri) The main branch has a wide range of maps, including themed leaflets; many are available for free download from the website.

DANGERS & ANNOYANCES
What once were the scariest parts of Birmingham – the area around the Bullring, for example – have been transformed by

THE MIDLANDS

BIRMINGHAM IN...

Two Days

Spend your first day in Birmingham exploring the core of the city centre; wander through the pedestrian areas around Victoria, Chamberlain and Centenary Squares, where the best of the city's historic buildings are preserved. Then delve into the **Birmingham Museum & Art Gallery** (below). That evening, hit the Mailbox and Brindleyplace for dinner and nightlife. On day two, head for the **Jewellery Quarter** (opposite) for good souvenir shopping and, at the museum, a fascinating lesson in the history of British industry.

Four Days

Follow the two-day itinerary, adding a meal at a balti joint to sample Birmingham's contribution to British cuisine. Next morning, make a pilgrimage to the **Barber Institute** (p434) and **Aston Hall** (p434) to see the region's most outstanding art collections. Spend day four on a narrow-boat **cruise** (p435) of Birmingham's vast network of canals and waterways, then take the kids to **Cadbury World** (p439) for a sweet finale to your trip.

One Week

Follow the four-day schedule, then use the extra days to visit outlying areas. **Lichfield** (p452), with its marvellous three-spired cathedral, is only 14 miles to the northeast along the A38. The **Black Country Museum** (p440) in Dudley is also within easy reach for a day or half-day trip. Twenty miles east of Birmingham is Coventry, with Sir Basil Spence's fantastic postwar **St Michael's Cathedral** (p451), which towers alongside the still-standing walls of the bombed-out old cathedral. Or, for a longer jaunt, dash up to the **Peak District** (p478) for three days of long walks and cosy pubs.

the city's dramatic refurbishments. And the city's vibrant nightlife means there's as much activity on the busier streets at 2am as there is at 2pm. Still, as in most large cities, it's wise to avoid walking alone late at night in unlit areas, particularly for women.

SIGHTS & ACTIVITIES
Town Centre

The central pedestrian precinct of Victoria and Chamberlain Squares features a **statue of Queen Victoria**, a fountain, a **memorial to Joseph Chamberlain** and some of Birmingham's most eye-catching architecture. The imposing **Council House** forms the northeastern face of the precinct. Its northwestern corner is formed by the modernist **Central Library**, reminiscent of an inverted ziggurat, with the Paradise Forum shop and café complex next to it.

To the south stands the **Town Hall**, designed by Joseph Hansom (creator of the hansom cab, forerunner to London's black taxis) in 1834 to look like the Temple of Castor and Pollux in Rome. For those who won't make it to Gateshead to see Antony Gormley's *Angel of the North* statue (p705), his wingless *Iron Man* (1993), on Victoria Sq, is a step in the same direction.

West of the precinct, Centenary Sq is another pedestrian square closed off at the western end by the **International Convention Centre** and the Symphony Hall, and overlooked by the Repertory Theatre. Inside Centenary Sq is the Hall of Memory War Memorial.

The impressive **Birmingham Museum & Art Gallery** (☎ 303 2834; Chamberlain Sq; admission free; ☑ 10am-5pm Mon-Thu & Sat, 10.30am-5pm Fri, 12.30-5pm Sun) houses displays of local and natural history, fine archaeology and ethnography exhibits, and a renowned collection of Pre-Raphaelite paintings (see boxed text opposite). Other highlights include works by Degas, Braque, Renoir and Canaletto. The charming Edwardian tearoom provides cake and coffee, too.

England's smallest cathedral, **St Philip's** (☎ 236 4333; Colmore Row; donations requested; ☑ 7am-7pm Mon-Fri, 9am-5pm Sat & Sun), was constructed in neoclassical style between 1709 and 1715. The Pre-Raphaelite artist Edward Burne-Jones was responsible for the magnificent stained-glass windows: the *Last Judgement*, which can be seen at the western end, and *Nativity*, *Crucifixion* and *Ascension* at the eastern end.

Gas St, Brindleyplace & the Mailbox

Birmingham sits on the hub of England's canal network (the city actually has more canals than Venice), and visiting narrow boats can moor in the Gas St Basin right in the heart of the city. Nearby Brindleyplace, a waterfront development of trendy shops, restaurants and bars created during the 1990s, has transformed the area west of Centenary Sq into a buzzing nightlife scene. A similar development to the southeast, the Mailbox, is even more style-conscious, bristling with designer boutiques and sleek eateries.

The stylish **Ikon Gallery** (☎ 248 0708; www .ikon-gallery.co.uk; 1 Oozells Sq, Brindleyplace; admission free; �) 11am-6pm Tue-Sun & national holidays) is an airy, white space divided into several tiny rooms that feature changing exhibitions of modern art, ranging from the sublime to the ridiculous depending on one's taste. The attached café and coffee shop offers excellent food and even better trend-watching.

The **National Sealife Centre** (☎ 633 4700; www .sealife.co.uk; 3a Brindleyplace; admission £9.95; ☉ 10am-4pm Mon-Fri, 10am-5pm Sat & Sun), a state-of-the-art facility designed by Sir Norman Foster, is the largest inland aquarium in England; it swarms with exotic marine life. A seahorse breeding facility has recently been added; if you're lucky you might get a rare glimpse of a male seahorse delivering his thousand babies. The otter sanctuary is also a favourite with kids.

Jewellery Quarter

Birmingham has long been a major jewellery production centre, and the Jewellery Quarter is packed with manufacturers and showrooms. The TIC provides a free guide to the area, which includes background information about the industry and details of two walking trails around the district.

In the **Museum of the Jewellery Quarter** (☎ 554 3598; 75-79 Vyse St; admission free; ☉ 11.30am-4pm Tue-Sun Apr-Oct), the Smith & Pepper jewellery factory is preserved as it was on the day it closed in 1981 after 80 years of operation. You can explore the history of jewellery-making in Birmingham since the Middle Ages and watch demonstrations of the art.

The Jewellery Quarter is about three quarters of a mile northwest of the centre; catch one of a host of buses (No 101 is the easiest), or take the metro from Snow Hill or the train from Moor St to Jewellery Quarter station.

Within walking distance of the Jewellery Quarter is **Soho House** (☎ 554 9122; Soho Ave, Handsworth; admission free; ☉ 11.30am-4pm Tue-Sun Apr-Oct), where the industrialist Matthew Boulton lived from 1766 to 1809. It has been painstakingly restored to reflect the styles of Boulton's era, and features displays on the great man's life and associates, including James Watt. Bus Nos 74, 78 and 79 pass nearby, or take the metro to Benson Rd station from Snow Hill.

THE MIDLANDS

THE PRE-RAPHAELITES & THE ARTS AND CRAFTS MOVEMENT

The three young Brits who formed the Pre-Raphaelite Brotherhood, in a classic case of artists romanticising the 'good old days' they never experienced, shunned the art of their time in favour of the directness of art prior to the High Renaissance, especially the work preceding that of Raphael. Dante Gabriel Rossetti, William Holman Hunt and John Everett Millais led the movement in 1848; four others soon joined them. Their work was characterised by almost photographic attention to detail, a combination of hyper-realism and brilliant colours. The themes and methods attracted criticism at the time but ensured the movement's popularity to this day.

Birmingham Museum & Art Gallery (opposite) has one of the best collections of works by the Pre-Raphaelites. If you get the bug, there are more fine paintings in the **Lady Lever Art Gallery** (p642) at Port Sunlight near Liverpool.

The Arts and Crafts movement followed Pre-Raphaelitism in yearning for a pure, idealised mode. The socialist William Morris, the movement's leading light, was a close friend of Pre-Raphaelite Edward Burne-Jones and projected the same ideals into tapestries, jewellery, stained glass and textile prints, following the principles of medieval guilds, in which the same artists designed and produced the work.

Arlington Mill (p407) in Bibury, Gloucestershire has a fine display of Arts and Crafts furniture. Those passing through Birmingham should stop at **Wightwick Manor** (p440), an Arts and Crafts masterpiece complete with original William Morris wallpaper and fabrics.

Outlying Areas

East of the centre, the Millennium Point development was conceived as a way to bring technology to the people on a practical level. The focal point is **Thinktank** (☎ 202 2222; www.thinktank.ac; Curzon St; adult/child £6.95/4.95; ☯ 10am-5pm), a substantial and ambitious attempt to make science accessible (primarily to kids). Interactive displays cover topics such as the body and medicine, science in everyday life, nature, future technology, and industrial history. There's also Birmingham's first **Imax** cinema (☎ 202 2222; www.imax.ac; adult/child £4.50/2.50), with a five-storey screen.

A visit to the **Barber Institute** (☎ 414 7333; admission free; ☯ 10am-5pm Mon-Sat, 2-5pm Sun) is, for art lovers, the highlight of a visit to Birmingham. The collection takes in Renaissance masterpieces, paintings by old masters such as Rubens and Van Dyck, British greats including Gainsborough, Reynolds and Turner, an array of impressionist pieces and modern classics by the likes of Picasso and Schiele.

The Barber Institute is at the University of Birmingham, 2½ miles south of the city centre. Take bus No 61, 62 or 63, or the train from New St to University station.

Aston Hall (☎ 327 0062; Trinity Rd, Aston; admission free; ☯ 11.30am-4pm Tue-Sun Easter-Oct), a Jacobean mansion built between 1618 and 1635, boasts some impressive friezes and ceilings, and houses a good portion of the furniture, paintings and textiles from the Birmingham Museum's collections. It's about 3 miles north of the city centre. Get there on bus No 65 or 104, or take a train to Aston station from New St Station.

BRUM NIGHTLIFE WALKING TOUR

Birmingham's nickname 'the Venice of the north' feels a lot more apt at night, when the lights from the city's lively bars and clubs glimmer across the water of the canals. This tour meanders 1.5 miles through some of the city's best nightlife quarters, stopping in at a few clubs and pubs along the way. It'll take you between two and four hours, depending on the number of stops you make. Of course, you can do the tour in broad daylight as well, but these areas really shine at night.

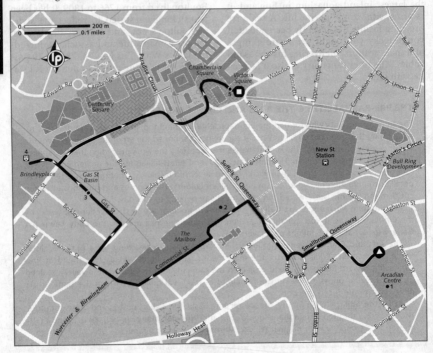

The tour begins at the **Arcadian Centre (1)**, where there's a convenient underground car park, an ATM, and a small collection of techno-pumping clubs and bars that feature mood lighting and cocktails in vivid primary colours. You can stand in the central courtyard and pick one at random, but we like **Angels Café Bar** (p438).

Refreshed, continue north along Queensway until you reach the **Mailbox (2)**, a former mail-sorting factory and the latest of Birmingham's desiccated industrial skeletons to be turned into a trendy, attractive shopping-eating-clubbing complex. You can walk right through the building; go up the steps and inside, then take escalators to the balcony at the top, where you can stand and gaze out over one small vision of Birmingham's future. There are multiple opportunities for snacks and drinks up here.

From this vantage point, take the pedestrian bridge down to **Gas St (3)**, and follow the route of the narrow canal boats. Cross Broad St to explore **Brindleyplace (4)**, a mecca of cool modern architecture blended with industrial scraps and dotted with restaurants, bars and galleries. Don't miss **Ipanema** (p438), the **Ikon Gallery** (p433) or **Le Petit Blanc** (p437).

Wander up and down Broad St to look at the sparkly people in sparkly clubs, and hope you pass muster with at least one or two of the bouncers. When you're tired of that, follow Broad St back up past Centenary Sq (stopping in at **wineREPublic**, p437, if you're still thirsty), through Paradise Circus and the spooky-at-night Chamberlain Sq, and into the centrally located **Victoria Sq (5)**, near the TIC, where our tour ends.

BIRMINGHAM FOR CHILDREN

Birmingham and the surrounding areas offer a few key attractions that'll keep the kids entertained. Most obvious is the **National Sealife Centre** (p433), where the playful otters entrance everyone, but especially the little ones. There's plenty to explore at the **Thinktank** (opposite), a gigantic attraction whose goal is to make science exciting and accessible, particularly at child level. Just outside of town, there's **Cadbury World** (p439), which is probably as much a guilty pleasure for parents as it is fun for their offspring. Finally, now that everyone's got a sugar high, try a family-friendly **cruise** down one of Birmingham's many narrow canals (below).

QUIRKY BIRMINGHAM

There's always something unusual going on at the **Custard Factory** (p438). The old industrial complex – built by Sir Alfred Bird, the inventor of custard – has been inventively converted into a hive of smaller galleries, bars, exhibition rooms, studios and performance spaces. Though slightly more upscale in feel, **Ikon Gallery** (p433) also regularly hosts some unconventional exhibits, such as David Cunningham's sonic manipulations and Joe Scanlan's miniature dirt-factory installation. And for those whose fetishes go beyond the realm of stiletto-heel shoes, there's the adults-only **Birmingham Bizarre Bazaar**, held the third Sunday of every month at the **Nightingale Club** (p438); for details, check out www.brumbazaar.co.uk or call ☎ 602-1316. It's bound to be one of the oddest Sunday brunches you'll have in a while.

TOURS

Second City Canal Cruises (☎ 236 9811; www.2ndcity boats.co.uk; adult/child £3/2) Tours leave by arrangement from the Canalside Souvenir Shop in Gas St Basin.

Sherborne Wharf (☎ 455 6163; www.sherbornewharf .co.uk; Sherborne St; ☼ trips at 11.30am, 1pm, 2.30pm & 4pm daily mid-Apr–Oct, Sat & Sun all year; adult/child £4.25/3.25) Canal cruises leave from the International Convention Centre quayside.

TIC (☎ 643 2514; www.birmingham.org.uk; 2 City Arcade; ☼ 9.30am-5.30pm Mon-Sat) The TIC provides two helpful leaflets on the city's canals for those wishing to explore in more depth, and leads themed walks year-round.

FESTIVALS & EVENTS

Birmingham is a substantial and diverse enough city to support a number of interesting cultural festivals throughout the year, many focusing on its ever-growing arts scene. Following are some of the highlights; for a detailed and updated list, visit www .bbc.co.uk/birmingham.

Artsfest (Sep; www.artsfest.org.uk) The UK's largest free arts festival features visual arts, dance and musical performances in various venues across the city.

Collide (May-Jun; ☎ 303 2434) Birmingham City Council runs this ambitious, groundbreaking arts festival dedicated to showcasing the work of local up-and-coming black and Asian artists.

Crufts Dog Show (Mar; www.the-kennel-club.org.uk) The world's largest dog show, with 20,000 canines on parade.

Heritage Open Days (Sep; ☎ 870 240 5251; www .heritageopendays.org) This unique event allows visitors

THE MIDLANDS

GAY & LESBIAN BIRMINGHAM

A comparatively strong appreciation for queer culture goes hand-in-hand with Birmingham's shiny new urban-chic image, thriving underground arts scene and party-all-night dance-club action. For dancing, the **Nightingale Club** (p438) is the biggest and best gay club; **Angels Café Bar** (p438) is a more casual gay-and-lesbian, straight-friendly hangout in the heart of the gay club scene based at the Arcadian Centre. **Clone Zone** (p439) sells all kinds of fun sex toys, accessories and clothing aimed at a gay audience.

Resources include **B-Glad** (☎ 622 6589), a support group for gays and lesbians suffering from depression; **Healthy Gay Life** (☎ 446 1085), an all-around information resource for gay and bisexual men; and the **Lesbian & Gay Switchboard** (☎ 622 6589; www.gaymidlands.org; ☻ operators 7pm-10pm, recorded info at other times), a help and crisis line.

free access to historic properties that are not usually open or normally charge an entrance fee, including 18 properties in and around Birmingham.

Horse of the Year Show (Oct; www.equine-world .co.uk) Top show-jumping equestrian event.

Latin American Festival (Jul; www.abslatin.co.uk) This annual festival celebrates the Latin-American community and culture in Birmingham.

SLEEPING

Central hotels court business visitors and can be at the higher end of the price spectrum, but they usually reduce their rates at the weekend. Check online or ask about specials at the TIC, which also makes accommodation bookings. Few B&Bs are central, but many lie within a 3-mile radius of the centre. Acocks Green (to the southeast) and the area stretching from Edgbaston to Selly Oak are popular areas.

Budget

Ashdale House Hotel (☎ 706 3598; www.ashdale house.co.uk; 39 Broad Rd, Acocks Green; s/d £25/46; P) This large, family-run place in a Victorian house overlooking a park is noted for its excellent vegetarian and organic breakfasts.

Cook House (☎ 429 1916; 425 Hagley Rd; s/d from £20/36; P) This B&B in the peaceful, mostly residential area of Edgbaston is known for being child- and pet-friendly.

Mid-Range

Most of the mid-range options in the city centre are basic, rather unexciting chain hotels, but they do tend to offer parking and a great location from which to explore the Brindleyplace nightlife.

Ibis Hotel (☎ 622 6010; fax 622 6020; Arcadian Centre, Ladywell Walk; r Mon-Thu/Fri-Sun £65/55; P per night £10) There's nothing particularly remarkable about this chain hotel except that it's sparklingly modern (with all the fixin's) and in a great location: inside the Arcadian Centre next to bars, cafés and Chinatown eateries aplenty.

Awentsbury Hotel (☎ 472 1258; www.awentsbury .com; 21 Serpentine Rd, Selly Park; s/d from £40/63; P) In a cool Victorian house in Selly Park, close to the university, this friendly, cosy B&B boasts a private vintage car collection which, if you're nice, the owners might show you.

Travelodge (☎ 191 4564; 230 Broad St; r Mon-Thu/Fri-Sun £52.95/49.95; P) A Travelodge is a Travelodge, but this one is ideally positioned for exploring Brindleyplace's nightlife. It fills up fast, so be sure to book ahead.

Top End

Burlington Hotel (☎ 643 9191; www.burlingtonhotel .com; Burlington Arcade, 126 New St; s/d Sun-Thu £130/160, Fri & Sat £88/108; P) The Burlington is grand and classy, one of the best of the central options; its 112 rooms have all the mod cons but are painstakingly designed to create the feel of a much smaller boutique hotel. There's also a noted restaurant.

Hotel du Vin (☎ 236 0559; info@birmingham.hotel duvin.com; Church St; d from £110) This place, part of a highly reputable chain, is a former Victorian eye hospital converted into the sleekest boutique hotel in town, with a fine bistro, a health spa, a humidor and an amazing *cave du vin* (wine cellar).

Jurys Inn (☎ 606 9000; www.jurysdoyle.com; 245 Broad St; s/d from £59/99; P) Also right in among the pulsating throngs mobbing Brindleyplace, Jurys has plush rooms and top-notch service, with a lobby that looks like a glowing shopping-mall entrance; weekend and online discounts are usually available.

EATING

Birmingham's contribution to cuisine is the balti, a Pakistani dish that has been adopted by curry houses across the country. The heartland is the Birmingham Balti Triangle in Sparkbrook, 2 miles south of the centre. Pick up a complete listings leaflet in the TIC (or see the website www.thebaltiguide.com) and head out on bus No 4, 5 or 6 from Corporation St.

Al Frash (☎ 753 3120; www.alfrash.com; 186 Ladypool Rd, Sparkbrook; mains £3-8; ⏲ 5pm-midnight Sun-Thu, 5pm-1am Fri & Sat; **P**) If you only get to try one balti joint, this is it – it's one of the best, consistently winning awards for its baltis and scoring points for having more tasteful décor than the average.

Bank (☎ 633 4466; 4 Brindleyplace; 3-course meal £12.50, mains £9.50-20; ⏲ breakfast, lunch & dinner Mon-Fri, lunch & dinner Sat & Sun; **P**) Bank – as in where all your money goes? – is a classy restaurant that serves complicated mod-Brit dishes fit for the pre-theatre crowd in a sophisticated atmosphere.

Chez Jules (☎ 633 4664; 5a Ethel St; mains £8.50-13, 2-course lunch £6.50; ⏲ lunch & dinner, closes 6pm Sun) It may be French, but this is a refreshingly unpretentious, faux-rustic place where bistro standards like steamed mussels are served on long, communal tables. Good prices on house wine seal the deal.

Chung Ying Garden (☎ 666 6622; 17 Thorp St; mains £7.50-13; ⏲ lunch & dinner) If you're anywhere near the Arcadian Centre, you'd be crazy to overlook this flagship of Birmingham's Chinatown, known for cooking up excellent Cantonese cuisine and turning out 70 varieties of dim sum.

Coconut Lagoon (☎ 643 3045; www.coconutlagoon.com; 12 Bennetts Hill; mains £10-14; ⏲ lunch & dinner) The inventive South Indian cuisine served at this branch of the small, award-winning regional chain have earned it the title of 'Best Indian Restaurant in the Midlands' in the Good Curry Guide for 2003–4.

Denial (☎ 643 3080; 120-122 Wharfside St; mains lunch/dinner £8.50/14.95, set 2-/3-course menu £12/13; ⏲ lunch & dinner Mon-Sat, breakfast & lunch Sun) Follow your ears to this canalside eatery in the Malibox – the sleek restaurant/bar is notorious for pumping out the loud beats all day, but what draws the evening crowds is its highly rated modern British cuisine with a Mediterranean slant.

Le Petit Blanc (☎ 633 7333; 9 Brindleyplace; 2-/3-course set menu £12.50/15.50, mains £8.50-15.75; ⏲ lunch & dinner; **P**) Serious foodies will enjoy a pilgrimage here to sample chef Raymond Blanc's cuisine, with traditional Francophile favourites such as duck cooked in armagnac,

and a substantial wine list. Reservations are recommended.

Thai Mirage (☎ 622 2287; 41-43 Hurst St; mains £5-20; ⏲ lunch & dinner) Another option in the Arcadian Centre area, the Thai Mirage has an extensive menu of regional classics and a refined interior.

wineREPublic (☎ 644 6464; Centenary Sq; bar menu £4-7, mains £8-14; ⏲ lunch & dinner Mon-Sat; **P**) The Rep theatre's restaurant is bright, sharp and airy, and the food comes in for plenty of praise. Everything on the extensive wine list can be bought by the glass or the bottle, so oenophiles can sample to their heart's content. Reservations are recommended.

Warehouse Café (☎ 633 0261; 54-57 Allison St, Digbeth; mains £3-6; ⏲ Tue-Fri noon-12.30am, lunch & dinner Sat) This is a great choice for a vegan or vegetarian lunch, with speciality Irish and jazz nights.

DRINKING

As with the dining scene in Birmingham, the world of drinking and dancing is constantly changing. Keep an eye on the magazines and flyers in bars for the latest news. Chain bars are the norm here; finding an honest-to-god 'pub' in the centre is tricky, but there are many places worth checking out, including two impressive banks-turned-boozers.

Bennetts (☎ 643 9293; 8 Bennetts Hill) A plush bar in a former bank, Bennetts is a massive space, like the interior of a regency hall; there's a mellow 'library' area if the grand surroundings get too much.

Circo (☎ 643 1400; 6 Holloway Circus) An alternative to the pub scene, this modern bar is a student hang-out midweek and a pre-club scene at the weekend, boasting some excellent guest DJs and stomach-lining tapas if required.

Old Joint Stock (☎ 200 1892; 4 Temple Row West) A vast, high-ceilinged cathedral of beer, this awesome venue in a former bank glitters with gilt mouldings and a glass dome and serves fine Fuller's ales to a cheerful crowd.

Sputnik (☎ 643 7510; Upper Temple St) If hygiene isn't your first priority, this is the place: it has that grungy feel licked, with a basement bar displaying B-movie posters and surprisingly varied tunes (reggae, drum'n'bass, funk and house), plus good beers and a friendly vibe.

THE MIDLANDS

Zinc (☎ 200 0620; Regency Wharf, Gas St Basin) It's probably obvious from the name…this is a Conran bar-diner; there's an enticing menu, and the cool, relaxed space lends itself to chilling to the jazz and funk soundtrack.

ENTERTAINMENT

There's no lack of things to do for fun in Birmingham. Tickets for most events can be purchased through the national **TicketWeb** (☎ 0870 771 2000; www.ticketweb.co.uk).

There's a range of entertainment options at the **Custard Factory** (☎ 604 7777; www.custard factory.com; Gibb St, Digbeth). So named because the building was constructed a century ago by custard magnate Sir Alfred Bird, this cool venue is a good place to start if you're looking for the motherlode of underground culture in Birmingham. Once a sprawling industrial site, the remarkable and ever-expanding arts and media centre has taken the city by storm; it houses a gallery, arts and recording studios, dance and theatre spaces, bars, cafés, you name it.

Nightclubs

Medicine Bar (☎ 693 6001; Custard Factory) The night-time hotspot within the Custard Factory, this is where the hip and the curious drink till late to the sounds of the region's up-and-coming DJs.

Ipanema (☎ 643 5577; 9 Brindleyplace) In an airy space reminiscent of a tremendously chic lighting store, this restaurant/dance club doles out tapas, a mellow vibe, guest DJs and the chance to brush up on your salsa skills.

Nightingale Club (☎ 622 1718; Essex House, Kent St) Birmingham's oldest and largest gay night-club, the Nightingale rocks on three levels (including a restaurant); it's an always-hopping, see-and-be-seen kind of place.

Angels Café Bar (☎ 244 2626; 127-131 Hurst St) A great place for a pre-club drink and snack, this Arcadian Centre club has a varied, gay-and lesbian-friendly crowd and is more casual than many of the other way-chic bars in the area.

Sanctuary (☎ 246 1010; 78 Digbeth High St) With the closure of the legendary Que club, this large electronica venue has absorbed a fair share of the techno-loving crowd, with drum'n'bass a speciality.

Glee Club (☎ 0870 241 5093; www.glee.co.uk; Arcadian Centre) The region's primary comedy club hosts comedians several nights a week.

Theatre

Hippodrome (☎ 0870 730 1234; www.birmingham -hippodrome.co.uk; Hurst St) This place, Brum's primary venue for major theatrical events, hosts the Birmingham Royal Ballet as well as touring musicals of the *Jesus Christ Superstar* calibre.

Alexandra Theatre (☎ 0870 607 7544; Suffolk St) This venue, near the train station, offers everything from *Aida* to *Annie* and seems particularly fond of talks by TV personalities.

Birmingham Repertory Theatre (☎ 236 4455; www.birmingham-rep.co.uk; Centenary Sq, Broad St) In two venues, the Main House and the more experimental Door, the Rep presents serious drama from around the UK and new plays straight from London's best theatres.

Live Music

National Exhibition Centre (☎ 909 4133; near Birmingham International Airport) This giant venue hosts major rock and pop acts, as does its sister venue, the **National Indoor Arena** (☎ 909 4144; King Edwards Rd) behind Brindleyplace.

Jam House (☎ 200 3030; www.thejamhouse.com; 1 St Paul's Sq) This well-known and very classy music bar features live swing, jazz, R&B and rock'n'roll. The top-floor restaurant is noted for serving global cuisine that far surpasses what you'd expect from a music club.

The best rock and pop venue in town is the **Birmingham Academy** (☎ 262 3000; www.birmingham -academy.co.uk; 52-54 Dale End). Acts that don't come through Birmingham usually play the **Civic & Wulfrun Halls** in Wolverhampton (p440). For classical music, including performances by the City of Birmingham Symphony Orchestra, seek out the ultramodern **Symphony Hall** (☎ 780 3333; Broad St; tickets from £7.50).

Sport

Villa Park (☎ 327 5353; www.avfc.co.uk; tickets adult/child from £5/15) Aston Villa football club play in this arena north of the city centre.

Warwickshire County Cricket Club (☎ 446 5506; www.wccc.co.uk; County Ground, Edgbaston; tickets from £12) Tickets for international test matches sell out early, but local matches are usually available.

SHOPPING

The **Jewellery Quarter** (www.the-quarter.com) is the obvious place for unique local shopping in Birmingham. In this region, where most of the jewellery manufactured in England comes from, more than a hundred shops sell traditionally handcrafted gold and silver jewellery, watches and more. The Museum of the Jewellery Quarter (p433) has leaflets detailing notable retail outlets and artisans.

Other options for serious retail therapy:

Bullring (☎ 632 1500) This latest hellhole-turned-gleaming-mall boasts '26 football pitches worth of shops, boutiques and restaurants'.

Clone Zone (☎ 666 6640; 84 Hurst St; ☺ 11am-9pm Mon-Sat, noon-7pm Sun) A gay-friendly shop selling sex toys, clothes, accessories and adult novelties.

Mailbox (☎ 632 1000; www.mailboxlife.com; Wharfside St) Chic designer boutiques – Armani etc – and cool restaurants in a converted mail-sorting factory.

GETTING THERE & AWAY
Air
Birmingham has an increasingly busy **international airport** (☎ 767 5511; www.bhx.co.uk) with flights to numerous European destinations and New York. It's on the outskirts of Birmingham, about 7 miles east of the centre.

Bus
National Express (☎ 0990 808080) runs coaches between Digbeth coach station and destinations around England including London (£13 single, 2¾ hours, hourly), Oxford (£14.65 single, 1½ hours, five daily) and Manchester (£10.25 single, 2½ hours, 11 daily). Bus X20 runs to Stratford-upon-Avon hourly on weekdays (1¼ hours).

Train
Most national trains run from New St Station, beneath the Pallasades shopping centre, including those to and from London (£24.90 cheap day single, 1¾ hours, every 30 minutes) and Manchester (£22 single, 1¾ hours, every 30 minutes). Other services, such as those to Stratford-upon-Avon (£4.95 single, 50 minutes, hourly), run from Snow Hill and Moor St stations.

In July and August, the **Shakespeare Express steam train** (☎ 707 4696; www.vintagetrains.co.uk; standard return £15) operates between Birmingham Snow Hill and Stratford-upon-Avon twice each Sunday. Journeys take one hour.

GETTING AROUND
To/From the Airport
Bus No 900 runs to the airport (45 minutes, every 20 minutes). Trains for the airport run between New St and Birmingham International station (45 minutes, every 10 minutes). A **taxi** (☎ 782 3744) from the airport to the centre costs about £18.

Bus
Centro (☎ 200 2700) The agency that runs public transport in Birmingham; for timetables, route information and ticket purchasing.
National Express (☎ 0870 580 8080; Ensign Court, 4 Vicarage Rd, Edgbaston)

Car
Avis (☎ 0121 782 6183; 7-9 Park St)
easyCar (☎ 0906 333 3333; www.easycar.co.uk; Horse Fair Car Park, Bristol St, Birmingham)
Hertz (☎ 0121 782 5158; Suffolk St)

Public Transport
Centro (☎ 200 2700; www.centro.org.uk), the transport authority for the Birmingham and Coventry area, provides general travel advice and a comprehensive guide to getting around the west Midlands for those with mobility difficulties. The **Daytripper ticket** (adult/child £4.10/2.60) gives all-day travel on buses and trains after 9.30am; if you need to start earlier, buy a **Centrocard** (£5.20). Tickets are available from the **Central Travel Information Centre** (New St Station).

Local trains operate from Moor St station, which is only a few minutes' walk from New St – follow the red line on the pavement.

Birmingham's tram system, the **Metro** (www.travelmetro.co.uk), runs from Snow Hill to Wolverhampton via the Jewellery Quarter, West Bromwich and Dudley. Fares start at 60p and rise to £2.20 for the full length. A day pass costs £3.50.

Black cabs (☎ 0121 782 3744) ideally should be reserved in advance.

AROUND BIRMINGHAM

CADBURY WORLD & BOURNVILLE VILLAGE
If you've ever fantasized about being in the centre of a giant Cadbury Creme Egg, you're officially a chocoholic and should go directly to **Cadbury World** (☎ 0121-451 4159; www.cadburyworld.co.uk; Linden Rd; adult/child £9/6.80), a lip-smacking exploration into the production, marketing and (naturally) consumption of chocolate, with interactive gizmos and plenty to keep kids entertained. Ride a beanmobile or take a wander down Cocoa Rd,

paved with 'talking chocolate splodges'. Not surprisingly, you must book ahead by phone. Opening hours are complicated; it's closed for much of December and January and open from 10am to 3pm or 10am to 4pm for most of the rest of the year (phone or check the website for details).

Cadbury World is part of pretty Bournville village, designed for early–20th-century factory workers by the Cadbury family; large houses, each unique, are set around a green. **Selly Manor** (☎ 0121-472 0199; Maple Rd; adult/child £2/50p; ☺ 10am-5pm Tue-Fri year-round, plus 2-5pm Sat & Sun Apr-Sep), dating from 1327 or earlier, was carefully taken apart and reconstructed by George Cadbury – who looks distressingly like Sigmund Freud – in order to save it from destruction. It now houses 18th-century furnishings and has a Tudor garden.

To get to Bournville take a train from Birmingham New St, or catch bus No 83, 84 or 85.

THE BLACK COUNTRY

The industrial region west of Birmingham is known as the Black Country, a 19th-century epithet bestowed because of the smoke from its foundries and factories. Though it's been cleaned up, it's still not a tourist hotspot, but anyone interested in how industry shapes a country should make a stop. Another reason to visit is the **New Art Gallery** (☎ 01922-654400; Gallery Sq; admission free; ☺ 10am-5pm Tue-Sat, noon-5pm Sun) in Walsall, home to the eclectic Gar-man Ryan collection, which includes works by Picasso, Rembrandt, Modigliani and Van Gogh. Trains to Walsall go to and from Birmingham New Street station (25 minutes, about hourly).

The extensive, lively **Black Country Living Museum** (☎ 0121-557 9643; www.bclm.co.uk; Tipton Rd, Dudley; adult/child £9.95/5.75; ☺ 10am-5pm daily Mar-Oct, 10am-4pm Wed-Sun Nov-Feb) features a coal mine, village and fairground, recreated as they would have been in the industrial heyday of the 19th century. It's a great place for a day out, with a full programme of mine trips, Charlie Chaplin films, and opportunities to watch glass-cutters and sweet-makers in action.

To get to the museum from Birmingham's city centre, take the No 126 bus from Corporation St and ask to be let off at Tipton Rd. It's a 10-minute walk along Tipton Rd to the museum, or you can catch bus No 311 or 313. Alternatively, take the train from Birmingham New St to Tipton, 1 mile from the museum. A Daytripper ticket will cover the entire bus or train journey.

Wolverhampton

If you thought Brummies sounded funny, wait'll you get to Wolverhampton. Situated just west of Birmingham, with a population of 251,000, this town has an accent unique even in the west Midlands.

For information on the area, visit the **TIC** (☎ 01902-556110; www.wolverhampton.tic.dial.pipex.com;

RUNNING FROM THE REPUBLICANS

Charles II (1630–85), England's merry monarch who 'never said a foolish thing, nor ever did a wise one', was almost captured by parliamentarians following his defeat at the Battle of Worcester in 1651. His father, Charles I, had already lost his head to the House of Commons, and Charles II, had he been captured, would likely have lost his, too. However, he escaped to the Continent with help from supporters along the way, and two of the houses that harboured him, Boscobel House, run by English Heritage (EH), and Moseley Old Hall, run by the National Trust (NT), are open to visitors.

Boscobel House (☎ 01902-850244; Brewood; admission £4.40; ☺ 10am-6pm daily Mar-Sep, 10am-5pm daily Oct, 10am-4pm Wed-Sun Nov), a modest 17th-century timber-framed house, is home to the so-called Royal Oak, the tree up which Charles hid when parliamentarians searched the house. It is 8 miles northwest of Wolverhampton, over the border in Shropshire.

Moseley Old Hall (☎ 01902-782808; Fordhouses; admission £4.20; ☺ 1-5pm Sat, Sun & Wed Apr-Oct) was a second house that saved the king and has a small priest-hole where Charles was able to hide. It is 4 miles north of Wolverhampton; take bus Nos 613 or 870/1/2.

After his escape, Charles II wandered Europe in exile for many years, scheming and plotting his return, with help from Catholic monarchs. A settlement was eventually negotiated returning him as king in 1660. He ruled until 1685, a volatile monarch with a combative attitude towards parliament. During the last four years of his rule, parliament was dissolved.

18 Queen Sq; 9.30am-5pm Mon-Sat Apr-Sep, 9.30am-4pm Mon-Sat Oct-Mar).

As well as **Wolverhampton Art Gallery** (019 02-552055; Lichfield St; admission free; 10am-5pm Mon-Sat), boasting fine collections of pop art and 18th- and 19th-century landscape paintings, Wolverhampton is home to **Wightwick Manor** (01902 761400; Wightwick Bank; admission £6; 1.30-5pm Thu, Sat & bank hols Mar-Dec). Run by the National Trust (NT), it is an Arts-and-Crafts masterpiece, complete with original William Morris wallpaper and fabrics, Kempe glass and de Morgan tiling.

The **Civic & Wulfrun Halls** (01902-552121; www.wolvescivic.co.uk; North St) draw fans from all across the west Midlands for rock, pop and alternative music concerts. Check the website for upcoming gigs.

WARWICKSHIRE

Warwickshire got lucky: it could have been just another picturesque English county full of green river valleys and well-preserved market towns, but a melding of marketing and history has given it a couple of essential sites. Not only is the county home to two of England's biggest tourist attractions – Shakespeare's birthplace at Stratford-upon-Avon and Warwick's superb castle – but also it boasts a number of less obvious pleasures. For starters, there are the gorgeously ruined and much-storied Kenilworth Castle and the stunning modern cathedral lurking over the bombed-out shell of its sister at Coventry. In between, historic houses and fascinating museums dot the county's inviting rural areas.

Orientation & Information
Warwickshire is roughly kidney shaped, with Coventry sitting between the lobes. Kenilworth, Leamington Spa and Warwick lie in the line running south from Coventry; Stratford-upon-Avon sits on the other side of the M40 motorway bisecting the southern lobe.

The Shakespeare Country tourism website (www.shakespeare-country.co.uk) has information on the whole region.

Getting Around
The Warwickshire transport site (www.warwickshire.gov.uk/transport) has details of local bus and train services, as well as news

on roads. Coventry is a major transport hub, with rail connections to London Euston, Birmingham New St and Leicester.

A good ticket option is the **Shakespeare Country Explorer** (adult one day £25, three days £30), which allows return train travel from London Marylebone or Paddington to Stratford, Warwick or Leamington Spa, plus unlimited travel between these towns for the duration of the ticket and discounted admission to attractions.

WARWICK
01926 / pop 23,350

The obvious reason to visit Warwick is its outstanding castle, an all-day event that'll impress parents and entrance kids. But don't rush off afterwards; despite a devastating fire in 1694, the quiet county town has several well-preserved historic buildings, many of which house interesting small museums, and it has a welcoming feel that invites casual strolling.

Orientation & Information
Warwick is simple to navigate; the A429 runs right through the centre with Westgate at one end and Eastgate at the other. The old town centre lies just north of this axis, the castle just south.

The **TIC** (492212; www.warwick-uk.co.uk; Court House, Jury St; 9.30am-4.30pm), near the junction with Castle St, sells the informative *Warwick Town Trail* leaflet (50p).

Sights
WARWICK CASTLE
Even without its sis-boom-bah presentation and eerily lifelike wax inhabitants, **Warwick Castle** (0870 442 2000; www.warwick-castle.co.uk; adult/child £13.50/8.25, peak dates £14.50/8.75; 10am-6pm Apr-Sep, 10am-5pm Oct-Mar, 10am-7pm Aug Sat & Sun; P) would be a stunner. For starters, it's incredibly well preserved: the walls decaying just enough to be picturesque and the rest of it solid enough to climb around. Warwick, with its strategic position, has been the site of fortifications since the 10th century. William the Conqueror ordered the construction of a wooden motte-and-bailey fort here in 1068, but the magnificent medieval castle is largely the 14th-century work of Thomas de Beauchamp, with 17th- to 19th-century interior embellishments. Lancelot 'Capability' Brown landscaped the splendid grounds

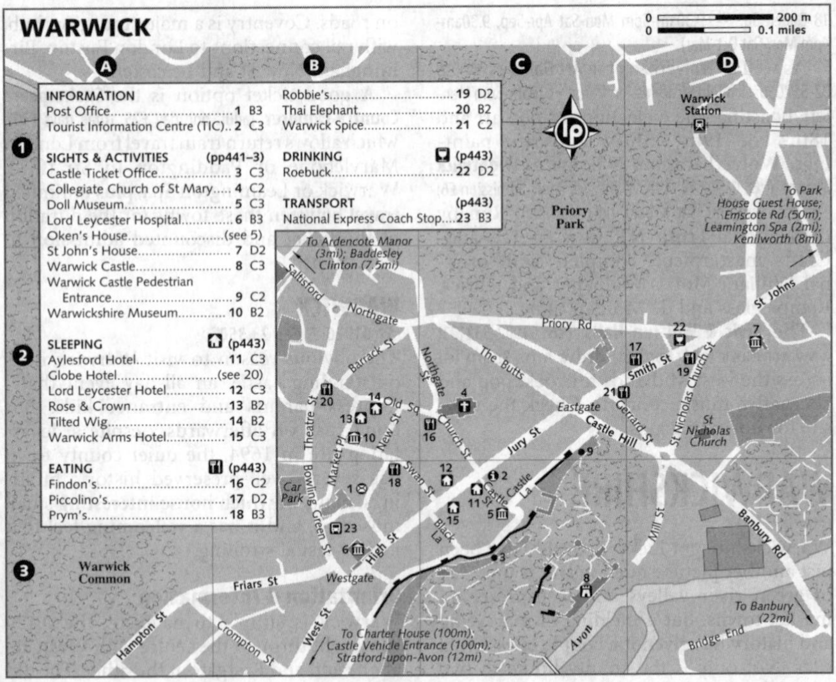

in 1753. The result is one of the most substantial and impressive castles in England: be prepared to spend hours wandering and wondering (and, in summer, queuing; it's very popular, though the crowds are well shepherded).

The castle is owned by Tussauds, and that influence is evident in the waxwork figures that populate the private apartments, arrayed as for a late 19th-century weekend party. The packaging and sheen don't mask the highlights, though: the superb furnishings and sheer splendour of the interior are fascinating, and a walk around the ramparts rewards with panoramic views. Kids love the arrays of weighty armour, the dungeons (with torture chamber) and the 'ghost tower', while the 19th-century mill house offers an insight into early power generation.

COLLEGIATE CHURCH OF ST MARY

Originally built in 1123, this fine **church** (☎ 403940; Old Sq; requested donation £1; 🕒 10am-6pm Apr-Oct, 10am-4.30pm Nov-Mar) was badly damaged by the Great Fire of Warwick in 1694 and rebuilt in a mishmash of styles. The remarkable perpendicular Beauchamp Chapel (built 1442–60 at a cost of £2400, a huge sum for the time) survived the fire, and the magnificent bronze effigy of Richard Beauchamp, 13th earl of Warwick, graces the centre of the chapel. The sinister-looking figure on the corner of the tomb is Richard 'Kingmaker' Neville, who also figures prominently in the displays at Warwick Castle. Don't miss the 12th-century crypt with remnants of a medieval dunking stool, used to drench scolding wives.

LORD LEYCESTER HOSPITAL

At the Westgate end of the town, the road cuts through a sandstone cliff, above which perches the impressive **Lord Leycester Hospital** (☎ 491422; High St; admission £3.20, garden only £1.50; hospital 🕒 10am-5pm Tue-Sun Apr-Sep, 10am-4pm Tue-Sun Oct-Mar), turned into an almshouse in 1571 by Robert Dudley, earl of Leicester and favourite of Queen Elizabeth I. Housed in a group of 14th-century timber-framed buildings, it has a beautiful courtyard, a fine chapel and a guildhall built by Kingmaker Neville.

OTHER SIGHTS

Other interesting sights include the **Warwickshire Museum** (☎ 412500; Market Pl; admission free; ⏱ 10am-5pm Tue-Sat year-round, plus 11.30am-5pm Sun Apr-Sep), in the 17th-century market building, with displays on the natural history and archaeology of the region. The **Doll Museum** (☎ 495546; Castle St; adult/child £1/75p; ⏱ 10am-5pm Tue-Sat, 11.30am-5pm Sun Apr-Sep, 10am-4pm Sat Oct-Mar), in the half-timbered medieval **Oken's House** – a worthy spectacle in its own right – contains a fine collection of early dolls and toys. **St John's House** (☎ 412132; St John's; admission free; ⏱ 10am-5pm Tue-Sat year-round, plus 2.30-5pm Sun Apr-Sep), a charming Jacobean mansion, features reconstructed Victorian rooms and a regimental museum.

Sleeping

The nearest hostel is in Stratford-upon-Avon (see p448). Mid-range B&Bs line Emscote Rd, the eastern end of the main road through Warwick heading for Leamington Spa.

Warwick Arms Hotel (☎ 492759; fax 410587; 17 High St; s/d £55/65; **P**) This plush hotel in an early–18th-century coaching inn has history and comfort galore.

Rose & Crown (☎ 411117; www.peachpubs.com; 30 Market Pl; r £65) Most of the rooms in this lively pub overlook the market square and are equipped with business-friendly technology.

Aylesford Hotel (☎ 492799; www.aylesfordhotel .co.uk; 1 High St; s/d £55/65) This first-class establishment opposite the TIC has great rooms (some with four-poster beds), a casual bistro and a medieval-styled cellar restaurant.

Tilted Wig (☎ 410466; tiltedwig@tiscali.co.uk; 11 Market Pl; s/d from £30/60) This pleasant old pub in the centre, with views onto the market square, has four nonsmoking rooms, good pub food and an outdoor area for summer dining.

Lord Leycester Hotel (☎ 491481; www.lord-leycester.co.uk; 17 Jury St; s/d from £57.50/65; **P**) This manor house, built in 1726, has smallish but comfortable modern rooms (some with four-poster beds). Downstairs is the well-respected Knights restaurant, with a menu of traditional English fare, and a lovely oak-panelled bar.

Also recommended are **Charter House** (☎ 496965; penon@charterhouse8.freeserve.co.uk; 87-91 West St; s/d from £57/90; **P**), with six rooms

decorated in period styles, and **Park House Guest House** (☎ 494359; 17 Emscote Rd; s/d £25/40), an affordable option in a Gothic-looking town house.

Eating & Drinking

Piccolino's (☎ 491020; 31 Smith St; pizza & pasta £5-7.50; ⏱ lunch & dinner) This family-run Italian hangout is deservedly popular, with a real trattoria atmosphere and an especially delicious seafood pasta.

Prym's (☎ 439504; 48 Brook St; mains £10-16; ⏱ lunch & dinner, lunch only Sun) Though it looks like a simple café, this local favourite serves up fine, game-heavy specialities such as guinea fowl and venison.

Warwick Spice (☎ 491736; 24 Smith St; mains £4.50-10; ⏱ dinner) Whether you're on a budget or willing to splurge, you'll find something to suit your taste at this relaxed place serving up Indian and Bangladeshi dishes.

Roebuck (☎ 494900; Smith St; ⏱ lunch & dinner) Justifiably plugging itself as an 'ale shrine', this is a friendly, snug pub with a selection of good cask beers and photos of old Warwick.

Other good choices include **Thai Elephant** (☎ 410688; fax 407170; 8 Theatre St; mains £7-10; ⏱ lunch & dinner), in the Globe Hotel, with exuberant décor and northeastern Thai specialities. Mellow, jazzy **Robbie's** (☎ 400470; 74 Smith St; mains £13-15.50; ⏱ dinner Tue-Sat) serves Med-influenced cuisine. And smart, sophisticated **Findon's** (☎ 411755; 7 Old Sq; lunch dishes £4.95, 2-course dinner £15.95; ⏱ lunch & dinner) has top-notch fine dining.

Getting There & Away

National Express coaches operate from Puckerings Lane on Old Square. Local bus Nos X16 and X18 run to Coventry (55 minutes), Stratford-upon-Avon (20 minutes) and Leamington Spa (15 minutes) from Market Square (hourly Monday to Saturday, every two hours Sunday).

Trains run to Birmingham (30 minutes, every half-hour), Stratford-upon-Avon (20 minutes, hourly) and London (1½ hours, hourly).

AROUND WARWICK

Baddesley Clinton (☎ 01564-783294; admission £6.20, grounds only £3.10; ⏱ 1.30-5pm Wed-Sun Mar, Apr, Oct & Nov, 1.30pm-5.30pm Wed-Sun May-Sep), an enchanting 13th-century moated house, boasts

WORTH THE TRIP

One wonders what the Bard, with his keen eye for the absurd, would have written about the seaweed baths and aromatherapy facials on offer these days in Shakespeare Country. Fortunately, patrons of **Ardencote Manor** (☎ 1926 843111; www.ardencote.com; Lye Green Rd, Claverdon; d/ste from £95/105), just outside of Warwick, are much too relaxed to care. In a converted coach house set among 40 acres of countryside, all manner of luxury spa treatments are available – reflexology, hydrotherapy, aromatherapy, Indian head massage, body wraps – as well as tennis, squash and swimming. The attached hotel has 75 plush rooms and an acclaimed restaurant.

Ardencote Manor is about 1 mile east of the village of Claverdon, which is 3 miles off the A46 along the A4189; the hotel is well signposted.

fine Elizabethan interiors that have hardly changed since the death of Squire Henry Ferrers in 1633. It served as a refuge for persecuted Catholics in the 16th century, as evidenced by three priest-holes.

Baddesley Clinton is 7½ miles northwest of Warwick, just off the A4141. Bus No 60 passes nearby, travelling between Warwick and Solihull.

LEAMINGTON SPA
☎ 01926 / pop 61,595

There's not a lot to do in Leamington, but its pleasant gardens, wide shopping streets and attractive Regency architecture make it a relaxing base from which to explore Stratford, Warwick and the surrounding areas.

The **TIC** (☎ 742762; leamington@shakespeare-country.co.uk; Royal Pump Rooms, the Parade; ⊙ 9.30am-5pm Mon-Sat year-round, 11am-4pm Sun Apr-Oct, 11am-3pm Sun Oct-Mar) carries a handy *Walk Around Leamington Spa* guide (50p).

The Pump Rooms also house a **Museum & Art Gallery** (☎ 742700; www.royal-pump-rooms.co.uk; admission free; ⊙ 10.30am-5pm Tue, Wed, Fri & Sat, 1.30-8pm Thu, 11am-4pm Sun), featuring a varied programme of exhibitions and a restored Victorian Turkish baths room.

Jephson Gardens, across from the Pump Rooms, have undergone several recent im-

provements and are in the process of being upgraded further; several of the gardens' historic buildings have been restored, with more in the works. Most notably, there's a new public greenhouse with the chic Restaurant in the Park (see below).

Sleeping & Eating
Dell Guest House (☎ 422784; www.dellguesthouse.co.uk; 8 Warwick Pl; s without/with private bathroom £22/28) Situated in a sprawling brick Victorian, this antique-furnished B&B near the munching and shopping district has a lot of character and a great breakfast; vegetarian alternatives are available.

Adams Hotel (☎ 450742; www.adams-hotel.co.uk; 22 Avenue Rd; s/d from £58/70) An impressive hotel in one of Leamington's prettiest Regency villas, the Adams has a variety of plush rooms in odd shapes and sizes, each individually decorated, plus a gorgeous bar and lounge.

Charnwood Guest House (☎ 831074; 47 Avenue Rd; s/d from £20/40; P) This friendly place is a good option in a handy spot, one of several B&Bs on Avenue Rd near the station.

Solo (☎ 422422; 23 Dormer Pl; 2-/3-course lunch £15/18, 3-course dinner £25-28) Foodies and critics alike love this place, hands down Leamington's best restaurant. Expect sophisticated, mostly French-influenced fare geared toward gourmets.

Other recommended options include **Casa Valle** (☎ 741128; www.casavalle.co.uk; 42 Regent St; mains £6-14; ⊙ Mon-Sat), a deli and restaurant whose simple menu steers clear of formulaic pasta and pizza; **Moo** (☎ 337763; Russell St), a retro-chic bar with a mellow vibe and tasty snacks; and the new **Restaurant in the Park** (☎ 311178; Jephson Gardens; Sunday lunch £12.95; ⊙ 10am-4pm), a large glassed-in garden eatery where diners can enjoy fine meals with a greenhouse effect.

Getting There & Away
National Express coaches run three times daily to London (2¾ hours). Bus No X12 runs to Coventry every 20 minutes; X14, X16 and X18 go there hourly (Nos X16 and X18 also serve Stratford-upon-Avon and Warwick). Trains run to Birmingham New St (40 minutes, every 20 minutes), London Marylebone or Paddington (1¾ hours, every 30 minutes), and Stratford-upon-Avon (30 minutes, roughly hourly).

KENILWORTH

☎ 01926 / pop 22,218

Famed for its ruined medieval castle, villagey old Kenilworth is away from (but walking distance to) the new town, which has accommodation and eateries but not much else; that said, it's not unpleasant, despite effectively existing as a dormitory town for nearby Coventry.

Information

Contact the **TIC** (☎ 852595; Library, 11 Smalley Pl; ⏲ 9am-7pm Mon, Tue, Thu & Fri, 9.30am-4pm Sat) for local tourist information.

Sights & Activities

Dramatic, red-sandstone **Kenilworth Castle** (EH; ☎ 852078; admission £4.80; ⏲ 10am-5pm Mar-May & Sep-Oct, 10am-6pm Jun-Aug, 10am-4pm Nov-Feb) was founded around 1120 and enlarged in the 14th and 16th centuries; it's been owned and inhabited by an array of powerful men, including John of Gaunt, Simon de Montfort and Robert Dudley, favourite of Elizabeth I, whose visits here were accompanied by gossip, intrigue and tremendous fanfare. The castle was partly dismantled and its vast lake drained in 1644 after the Civil War, but the huge 12th-century keep and extensive Norman walls remain. Don't skip the audio tour, which brings history to life as you wander around the atmospheric ruins. Various events and performances take place here throughout the year; call for details.

The impressive Georgian abbey-mansion **Stoneleigh Abbey** (☎ 858535; www.stoneleighabbey.org; admission £6; ⏲ tours 11am, 2pm & 3pm Tue-Thu & Sun Easter-Oct), founded in 1154, was undergoing restoration at the time of research, but a large chunk is open to the public. The splendid Palladian West Wing, completed in 1726, contains richly detailed plasterwork ceilings and panelled rooms; the medieval gatehouse, dating from 1346, is also interesting, as are the grounds, landscaped by Repton and Nessfield. Stoneleigh is about 2 miles east of Kenilworth town centre, off the B4115.

Sleeping & Eating

Castle Laurels Hotel (☎ 856179; www.castlelaurels hotel.co.uk; Castle Rd; s/d £40/60) This superior B&B near the castle is more like a small, exclusive hotel.

Ferndale Guest House (☎ 853214; 45 Priory Rd; s/d £28/40) One of several B&Bs on Priory Rd, the Ferndale has very comfortable en suite rooms.

Virgins & Castle (☎ 853737; 7 High St; pub food £4-6, Filipino meals £8-9, spring rolls £4.50) This comfortably worn old pub is a homey, sprawling place full of nooks and crannies, with a room for every mood (there's even a balcony) and a menu of Filipino specialities.

Clarendon Arms (☎ 852017; 44 Castle Hill; pub food £4-8, dinners £8-13) This pub, opposite the castle, is renowned for its food and has a garden and courtyard for summer supping. For local flavour try the Godiva burger (served 'with nothing on').

Getting There & Away

To get to Stratford-upon-Avon (50 minutes), Warwick (20 minutes), Coventry (25 minutes) or Leamington Spa (15 minutes), take bus No X16 or X18 (bus Nos X12 and X14 also run to Leamington Spa and Coventry); each runs hourly.

STRATFORD-UPON-AVON

☎ 01789 / pop 22,187

Don't let complaints about tourists and commercialism keep you away from this well-preserved market town. Certainly, its fame as the birthplace of renowned Elizabethan playwright William Shakespeare means that there are always crowds, and the unrelenting Bard-flogging can get a little out of hand. But Stratford has enough historic buildings, timber-framed houses and general aesthetic appeal that it's worth abandoning your cynicism for a brief stop. It can also be a handy base for exploring the surrounding areas: it's in a convenient spot near Coventry, and Warwick and Kenilworth Castles; the pretty Cotswolds are within striking distance; and there are lots of good accommodation and eating options.

Orientation

Arriving by coach or train, you'll find yourself within walking distance of the town centre, which is easy to explore on foot. Transport is only really essential for visiting Mary Arden's House.

Information

Two-hour **guided walks** (☎ 412602; ⏲ 10.30am Sat year-round, plus Sun Jul-Sep) are free and depart from outside the TIC at 10.30am.

STRATFORD-UPON-AVON

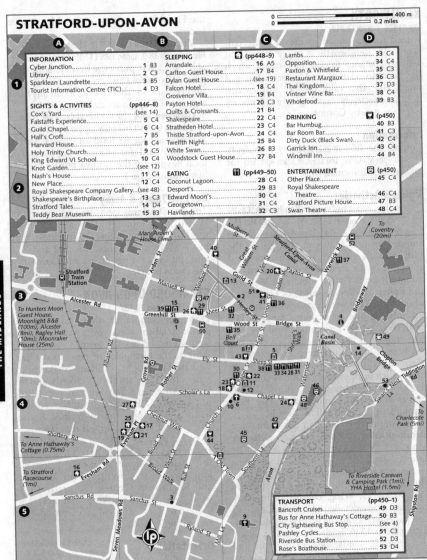

INFORMATION	
Cyber Junction	1 B3
Library	2 C3
Sparklean Laundrette	3 B5
Tourist Information Centre (TIC)	4 D3

SIGHTS & ACTIVITIES	(pp446–8)
Cox's Yard	(see 14)
Falstaffs Experience	5 C4
Guild Chapel	6 C4
Hall's Croft	7 B5
Harvard House	8 C4
Holy Trinity Church	9 C5
King Edward VI School	10 C4
Knot Garden	(see 12)
Nash's House	11 C4
New Place	12 C4
Royal Shakespeare Company Gallery	(see 48)
Shakespeare's Birthplace	13 C4
Stratford Tales	14 D4
Teddy Bear Museum	15 B3

SLEEPING	(pp448–9)
Arrandale	16 A5
Carlton Guest House	17 B4
Dylan Guest House	(see 19)
Falcon Hotel	18 C4
Grosvenor Villa	19 B4
Payton Hotel	20 C3
Quilts & Croissants	21 B4
Shakespeare	22 C4
Stratheden Hotel	23 C4
Thistle Stratford-upon-Avon	24 C4
Twelfth Night	25 B4
White Swan	26 B3
Woodstock Guest House	27 B4

EATING	(pp449–50)
Coconut Lagoon	28 C4
Desport's	29 B3
Edward Moon's	30 C4
Georgetown	31 C3
Havilands	32 C3

Lambs	33 C4
Opposition	34 C4
Paxton & Whitfield	35 C3
Restaurant Margaux	36 C3
Thai Kingdom	37 D3
Vintner Wine Bar	38 C4
Wholefood	39 B3

DRINKING	(p450)
Bar Humbug	40 B3
Bar Room Bar	41 C3
Dirty Duck (Black Swan)	42 C4
Garrick Inn	43 C4
Windmill Inn	44 B4

ENTERTAINMENT	(p450)
Other Place	45 C4
Royal Shakespeare Theatre	46 C4
Stratford Picture House	47 B3
Swan Theatre	48 C4

TRANSPORT	(pp450–1)
Bancroft Cruises	49 D3
Bus for Anne Hathaway's Cottage	50 B3
City Sightseeing Bus Stop	(see 4)
Pashley Cycles	51 C3
Riverside Bus Station	52 D3
Rose's Boathouse	53 D4

Cyber Junction (☎ 263400; 28 Greenhill St; ⏰ 10am-5.30pm Mon-Thu & Sat, 10am-6pm Fri, 10am-5pm Sun; £5/3 per one/half-hour) Internet access and game play.

Sparklean Laundrette (☎ 269075; 74 Bull St; ⏰ 8am-9pm)

TIC (☎ 293127; stratfordtic@shakespeare-country.co.uk; ⏰ 9am-6pm Mon-Sat, 10.30am-4.30pm Sun Apr-Oct,

9am-5pm Mon-Sat, 10am-3pm Sun Nov-Mar) Helpful, but frantically busy in summer.

Sights & Activities
THE SHAKESPEARE HOUSES
The **Shakespeare Birthplace Trust** (☎ 204016; www .shakespeare.org.uk; all 5 properties £13, three in-town houses £10; ⏰ generally 9am-5pm Mon-Sat, 10am-5pm Sun

Jun-Aug, variable at other times) manages five buildings associated with Shakespeare. Three of the houses are central, one is a short bus ride away, and the fifth a drive or bike ride out; a combination ticket costs about half as much as the individual admission fees combined. Opening times are complicated and vary during the off season (check the website for details). In summer, enormous crowds pack the small Tudor houses; a visit out of season is much more enjoyable. Note that wheelchair access to the properties is restricted.

The number-one Shakespeare attraction, **Shakespeare's Birthplace** (Henley St), has a modern exterior, but inside it's very much 'olde'. It's been a tourist hotspot for three centuries (though there's scant evidence Will was born here); famous 19th-century visitor-vandals have scratched their names on a window, and the guest book bears the signatures of some big-time literati. Family rooms have been re-created in the style of Shakespeare's time, and there's a 'virtual reality' display downstairs for visitors unable to gain access to the upper areas. A ticket includes admission to the adjacent **Shakespeare Exhibition**, where well-devised interpretive displays give the lowdown on Stratford's famous son.

The wealthy, retired Shakespeare bought a fine home at New Pl on the corner of Chapel St and Chapel Lane; the house was demolished in 1759, and an attractive Elizabethan **knot garden** now occupies part of the grounds. Displays in the adjacent **Nash's House**, where Shakespeare's granddaughter Elizabeth lived, describe the town's history and contain a collection of 17th-century oak furniture and tapestries.

Shakespeare's daughter Susanna married the eminent doctor John Hall, and their fine Elizabethan town house, **Hall's Croft** (Old Town), stands near Holy Trinity Church. The main exhibition is a fascinating insight into medical practice in Shakespeare's time.

Before their marriage, Shakespeare's wife lived in Shottery, a mile west of the centre, in a pretty thatched farmhouse now known as **Anne Hathaway's Cottage**. As well as contemporary furniture there's an orchard and **Shakespeare Tree Garden**, with examples of all the trees mentioned in Shakespeare's plays. A footpath (no bikes allowed) leads to Shottery from Evesham Pl, or catch a **bus** (☎ 404984) from outside the NatWest bank on Wood St to the end of Cottage Lane.

Mary Arden was Shakespeare's mother, and a **house** at Wilmcote, 3 miles west of Stratford, was her childhood home. If you cycle there via Anne Hathaway's Cottage, follow the Stratford-upon-Avon Canal towpath to Wilmcote rather than retracing your route or riding back along the busy A3400. The easiest way to get there otherwise is on a bus tour (see Getting Around, p451).

The home of William's mother is now used to house the **Shakespeare Countryside Museum**, with exhibits tracing local country life over the past four centuries. Plan to spend more time here than at the other properties to appreciate its unique collection of rare farm animals and a turn-of-the-20th-century farmhouse.

OTHER SIGHTS

Holy Trinity Church (☎ 266316; Old Town; suggested donation for chancel £1; ☽ 8.30am-6pm Mon-Sat & 12.30-5pm Sun Apr-Oct, 9am-4pm Mon-Sat & 12.30-5pm Sun Nov-Mar) has transepts from the mid–13th century and many later additions (the spire dates from 1763), but it's the Bard connections that draw crowds. In the chancel are photocopies of Shakespeare's baptism and burial records, the graves of Will and his wife, and a bust created seven years after Shakespeare's death but before his wife's and thus assumed to be a good likeness.

The exuberantly carved **Harvard House** (☎ 204016; High St; admission £2.50, free with Shakespeare Houses ticket; ☽ noon-5pm Wed-Sun Jul-Sep, Wed, Sat & Sun May, Jun & Sep-Nov) was home to the mother of John Harvard, after whom Harvard University in the USA was named in the 17th century. It now houses a **Museum of British Pewter**.

The **Royal Shakespeare Company Gallery** (☎ 412617; admission £2; ☽ 1.30pm-6.30pm Mon-Fri, 10.30am-6.30pm Sat, 10.30-4.30pm Sun), inside the Swan Theatre, features changing displays of the RSC's collection of props, costumes and theatrical paraphernalia. **Theatre tours** (☎ 403405; adult/child incl admission to RSC Gallery £5/4; ☽ 1.30pm & 5.30pm Mon-Sat, 11am & 5.30pm matinee days, noon, 1pm, 2pm & 3pm Sun) offer a fascinating glimpse behind the scenes of a working theatre.

Falstaff's Experience (☎ 298070; www.falstaffsexperience.co.uk; 40 Sheep St; admission £4.25; ☽ 10am-5.30pm), an old timbered building housing recreations of a witches' glade and a plague cottage, is like an extended, stationary ghost

THE MIDLANDS

ABOUT A BARD

William Shakespeare was born in Stratford-upon-Avon in 1564, the son of a local glovemaker. At 18 he married Anne Hathaway, eight years his senior, and their first daughter, Susanna, was born about six months later. Boy and girl twins, Hamnet and Judith, followed two years later.

Did the sheen of domestic bliss wear thin then? Around this time Shakespeare moved to London and began to write for the Lord Chamberlain's Company. This successful ensemble boasted the finest theatre (the Globe) and the best actors. It wasn't until the 1590s that Shakespeare's name appeared on his plays; before that, the company's name was regarded as more important than the dramatist's.

Shakespeare's 37 plays made novel and inventive use of the English language, often to ribald comic effect (although generations of schoolchildren would doubtless disagree), and boasted superb plot structures and deep insights into human nature – characteristics that have ensured not only their survival over the centuries but also their popularity in other languages. Early writings included comedies such as *The Comedy of Errors*, historical accounts such as *Henry VI* and *Richard III,* and tragedies including *Romeo and Juliet*. The new century saw the appearance of his great tragedies: *Hamlet, Othello, King Lear* and *Macbeth*.

Around 1610 Shakespeare retired and moved back to Stratford. He lived in comfortable circumstances until his death in 1616, whereupon his body (and a legacy of mass tourism) was conferred on the parish church. His wife outlived him by seven years.

Despite Shakespeare's prodigious output of plays, no letters or other personal writing have survived, and the little that is known about him and his family has been pieced together from birth, death and marriage files and other official records (including the will in which he left his wife his 'second-best bed'!). This paucity of information has bred theories that Shakespeare didn't actually write the plays. Since none have survived in manuscript form, there's no handwriting evidence to prove they're his. Some nonbelievers speculate that Shakespeare's origins and education were too humble to have provided the background, experience and knowledge to write the plays. Their favourites for the 'real' Shakespeare include the earl of Derby, the earl of Oxford and Will's fellow playwright Christopher Marlowe.

train with some history thrown in; mordant kids (and grown-ups) will love it.

Stratford Tales (☎ 404600; Cox's Yard, Bridgefoot; admission £4; ☿ 10am-5pm) features dioramas of scenes from the town's past with recorded commentaries. The surrounding development, Cox's Yard, is a small cluster of shops, cafés and a pub with its own microbrewery, with frequent live-music performances.

Meet the first Paddington Bear to appear on TV at the **Teddy Bear Museum** (☎ 293160; 19 Greenhill St; adult/child £2.50/1.50; ☿ 9.30am-5.30pm daily), a strangely unsettling place founded by former politician and broadcaster Gyles Brandreth. Smokey Bear and Fozzie Bear are also in residence. All those button eyes can seem a little creepy, but it's a popular spot with youngsters.

The **Guild Chapel** (cnr Chapel Lane & Church St) dates from 1269, though it was rebuilt in the 15th century; it's not open to the public except for services (10am Wednesday and noon Saturday April to September). Next door is **King Edward VI School**, which Shakespeare probably attended; it was originally the Guildhall.

Sleeping

Stratford's big hotels tend to be geared toward group travel, so they're often out of the price range of many independent travellers, and they fill up fast. B&Bs are plentiful, though, and generally offer good-quality accommodation in attractive Victorian houses. Prime hunting grounds are Evesham Pl, Grove Rd, Broad Walk and Alcester Rd. Accommodation can be hard to find during summer; if you're stuck, the TIC charges £3 plus 10% deposit to find something.

BUDGET

Stratford-upon-Avon YHA Hostel (☎ 0870 770 6052; stratford@yha.org.uk; Hemmingford House, Alveston; dm £12-17; Ⓟ) The youth hostel is in a large, 200-year-old mansion 1½ miles east of the town centre along Tiddington Rd. Bus Nos X18 and 77 run to Alveston from Bridge St.

Quilts & Croissants (☎ 267629; rooms@quilt-crois sants.demon.co.uk; 33 Evesham Pl; s/d £18/40; Ⓟ) The owners of this cute B&B have travelled widely themselves; they're extremely amiable and go far to make you comfortable.

Other good budget options:

Arrandale (☎ 267112; 208 Evesham Rd; d £17-20; (P))
A 10-minute walk from the centre.

Carlton Guest House (☎ 293548; 22 Evesham Pl;
s/d from £20/40; (P)) Light, airy rooms.

Dylan Guest House (☎ 204819; www.thedylan.co.uk;
10 Evesham Pl; s/d from £23/46; (P))

Grosvenor Villa (☎ 266192; marion@grosvenorvilla
.com; 9 Evesham Pl; s/d from £20/40; (P)) Spotless, friendly
and less flowery than some.

Moonlight (☎ 298213; 144 Alcester Rd; s/d £16/32; (P))

Riverside Caravan & Camping Park (☎ 292312; fax
415330; Tiddington Rd; pitches £5-9; (P)) A campsite, a
mile east of town.

Stratford Racecourse (☎ 267949; fax 415850; Lud-
dington Rd; 2-person pitches £10; ☼ Easter-Sep; (P))
Campsite just off Evesham Rd a mile west of town.

MID-RANGE

Moonraker House (☎ 267115; www.moonrakerhouse
.com; 40 Alcester Rd; s/d from £40/55; (P)) B&Bs don't
come much classier than this pristine yet
luxuriously comfortable home, done up like
an outsize doll's house, with canopied beds
and flowers everywhere, just five minutes'
walk from the train station. The owners
make you feel like you're at the Ritz, and
the gorgeous breakfast includes organic,
vegetarian and heart-healthy options.

Stratheden Hotel (☎ 297119; richard@stratheden
.fsnet.co.uk; 5 Chapel St; r from £35) An old building
(parts c 1673) in the thick of the Shakespeare
action, this hotel is tastefully furnished, very
friendly and good value for the location.

Twelfth Night (☎ 414595; reservations@twelfth
night.co.uk; 13 Evesham Pl; s/d from £35/42) An elegant
confection of flowers and lace, this sweetly
feminine B&B scores points with classy details, such as breakfast served on Wedgwood
china.

Other recommended mid-range options:

Hunters Moon Guest House (☎ 292888; www
.huntersmoonguesthouse.com; 150 Alcester Rd; s/d £25/46;
(P) ✗) Completely nonsmoking, with good vegetarian
breakfasts.

Payton Hotel (☎ 266442; www.payton.co.uk; 6 John
St; s/d from £45/60; (P)) A Georgian town house in a
quiet area.

Woodstock Guest House (☎ 299881; woodstockhouse@
compuserve.com; 30 Grove Rd; s/d from £22/45; (P))

TOP END

White Swan (☎ 297022; whiteswan@work.gb.com;
Rother St; s/d from £60/80; (P)) Stratford's most
character-drenched hotel has oak panelling
and heavy wooden beams in its pub-style
lobby and restaurant, and a choice between
modern rooms and old-fashioned ones,
some with brick fireplaces and four-poster
beds. It's just a few steps from the Birthplace.

Shakespeare (☎ 0870 400 8182; shakespeare@
macdonald-hotels.co.uk; Chapel St; r from £120; (P)) A
conglomeration of beautiful historic buildings, this place is a four-star establishment;
its labyrinthine warren of rooms and suites
are named for Shakespearean characters.
By necessity, they're a mishmash of different shapes and sizes, but all are beautifully
antique-furnished and updated with fancy
new bathrooms. Some even have four-
poster beds.

Falcon Hotel (☎ 279953; www.corushotels.com/the
falcon; Chapel St; s/d £105/125; breakfast £7-10 extra; (P))
You can choose between antique luxury and
ultra-modern luxury at this charming place,
with beautifully timeworn rooms in an old
timber-framed building and hip designer
rooms in a newer wing. Special deals are
sometimes available.

Thistle Stratford-upon-Avon (☎ 294949; stratford
.uponavon@thistle.co.uk; Waterside; s/d from £138/160;
(P)) One of Stratford's finest, the Thistle is
immediately across the road from the Swan
Theatre, overlooking the river and parkland.
Rooms have rich, velvety decorations and
four-poster beds. There's a terrace for summer dining. Discounts of 50% or more are
sometimes available in the low season.

Eating

Shakespearean tourism clearly makes you
hungry: there's no shortage of eateries in
town. Sheep St is just chock-a-block with
restaurants, most with a refined but relaxed
ambience ideal for a pre-theatre meal. Mains
typically cost between £8 (for vegetarian options) and £16 (for steak or seafood).

Desport's (☎ 269304; booking@desports.co.uk; 13-
14 Meer St; ☼ Tue-Sat) Named one of the best
restaurants outside London, chef Paul Desport's small restaurant in a 16th-century
building creates international cuisine with
Asian and Mediterranean influences, and
there's a well-thought-out wine list to boot.
The deli downstairs is a good option for
lunch or picnic treats.

Lambs (☎ 292554; www.lambsrestaurant.co.uk; 12
Sheep St; ☼ lunch daily, dinner Wed-Sat) Where the
locals take their in-laws to impress, this

highly regarded restaurant has an eclectic menu of interesting takes on classic dishes and an extensive wine list.

Vintner Wine Bar (☎ 297259; 5 Sheep St; 🕑 lunch & dinner from 10am) A great spot for tapas, wine and pre-theatre street theatre, thanks to its picture windows. The menu includes several inventive vegetarian options.

Edward Moon's (☎ 267069; 9 Chapel St; 🕑 lunch & dinner) This long-standing favourite has the feel of a classy, upmarket pub, with a tasty menu from around the globe and sinful desserts, including a tempting sticky-toffee pudding.

Coconut Lagoon (☎ 293546; 21 Sheep St; 🕑 lunch & dinner) At this outpost of a highly acclaimed chain, delicious South Indian regional specialities are served in a bright, modern space.

Georgetown (☎ 204445; 23 Sheep St; 🕑 lunch & dinner) Situated next door to the Coconut Lagoon, this sleek, upmarket Malaysian restaurant serves a good selection of vegetarian options.

Other recommendations:

Haviland's (☎ 415477; 5 Meer St; cream tea £3.95; 🕑 9am-5pm Mon-Sat) Lunch, coffee and homemade cake.

Opposition (☎ 269980; 13 Sheep St; 🕑 lunch & dinner) A popular Italian place, trendy but not snobby.

Restaurant Margaux (☎ 269106; 6 Union St; mains £8-18; 🕑 Mon-Sat) French-influenced food in fine surroundings.

Thai Kingdom (☎ 261103; 11 Warwick Rd; mains £6-11; 🕑 lunch & dinner Mon-Sat) Quality Thai classics.

SELF-CATERING

If you fancy making your own meal, there's **Wholefood** (☎ 292353; Greenhill St), a health-food shop that sells delicious vegetarian pastries, sandwiches and the like. **Paxton & Whitfield** (☎ 415544; 13 Wood St) has been selling cheeses to discerning palates (including the royals) since 1797; for cheese lovers, entering the shop is like reaching a very strong-smelling nirvana.

Drinking

Dirty Duck (☎ 297312; Waterside) Officially called the Black Swan, this pretty, riverside cubbyhole of a pub is an essential Stratford experience for thespians and theatre-goers alike. From its small terrace you can watch school groups harass each other in rented boats along the canal.

Windmill Inn (☎ 297687; Church St) Despite its 'historic' tag – it's supposedly the oldest pub in town – this place attracts a lively crowd and serves fine ales.

Garrick Inn (☎ 292186; 25 High St) Steeped in history and stooping with age, the Garrick is worth visiting just to marvel at the low ceilings, dark wood beams and leaded windows. It's also one of the few nonsmoking pubs around.

For something a little more (or less?) anachronistic, try the modern DJ hangout **bar room bar** (☎ 295009; 38 Guild St), or **Bar Humbug** (☎ 292109; 1 Guild St), which has school desks and a beer garden, and avoids both the 'olde' and 'too-hip' clichés.

Entertainment

Royal Shakespeare Company (☎ 0870 609 1110; www .rsc.org.uk; box office inside Royal Shakespeare Theatre; tickets £6-42; 🕑 9.30am-8pm Mon-Sat) Seeing a RSC production is a must; some major stars have graced the stage here, and your chances of seeing truly high-calibre theatre are good. Performances include the Bard's classics as well as contemporary offerings and take place in the main Royal Shakespeare Theatre, the adjacent Swan Theatre or the nearby Other Place. Ticket prices depend on the performance and venue, but there's a bewildering array of offers for under-25s, students, seniors and other selected groups, plus discounts for previews; it's best to call or check the website for details. For good seats, you'll want to book ahead, but there are always a few tickets sold on the day of performance and available only to personal callers.

Stratford Picture House (☎ 415500; www.picture house-cinemas.co.uk; Windsor St; tickets £5) This cinema, tucked away just off the main drag, shows Hollywood blockbusters as well as art-house films.

Getting There & Away

National Express destinations from Stratford's Riverside Bus Station include Birmingham (one hour, daily), Oxford (one hour, daily) and London Victoria (£16.50, 3½ hours, three daily).

The train station is a few minutes' walk west of the centre. There are only a few direct services from London Paddington (two hours), but some services from Marylebone that require a change at Banbury or Leamington Spa are almost as quick.

In July and August, the **Shakespeare Express steam train** (☎ 0121-707 4696; www.vintagetrains.co .uk; single adult/child £10/3, return £15/5, 1 hr, twice each Sunday) operates between Birmingham Snow Hill and Stratford station.

Getting Around
BUS
Open-top buses of **City Sightseeing** (☎ 299123; www.city-sightseeing.com; adult/child £8/3.50; ☺ every 15 min Apr-Sep, fewer in winter) circuit past the TIC and the five Shakespeare properties. They operate on a jump-on-jump-off basis, so you can spend as long as you like at each attraction, and are a convenient way of getting to the out-of-town houses.

BICYCLE
Stratford is small enough to explore on foot, but a bicycle is good for getting out to the surrounding countryside or the rural Shakespeare properties. The canal towpath offers a fine route to Wilmcote. **Warwickshire County Council** (☎ 01827-872660; Shire Hall, Warwick; ☺ 9am-5.30pm Mon-Thu, 9am-4.30pm Fri) produces leaflets detailing cycling routes.

Pashley Cycles (☎ 205057; Guild St; per half/full day from £5/10) hires bikes.

BOAT
Punts, canoes and rowing boats are available from **Rose's Boathouse** (☎ 267073; row boats/ punts per hr £3/2) by Clopton Bridge. **Bancroft Cruises** (☎ 269669; www.bancroftcruises.co.uk) runs 45-minute trips (£4, daily April to October) leaving from the Moat House Hotel pier.

AROUND STRATFORD-UPON-AVON
If you're tired of looking at historic landmarks and greenery from the ground, **Heart of England Balloons** (☎ 01789-488219; www.ukballoons .com; Cross Lanes Farm, Walcote; 1hr flight per person £140), based near Alcester, offers the chance to soar above it all in a hot-air balloon. Alcester is about 8 miles west of Stratford-upon-Avon along the A46.

Charlecote Park
Sir Thomas Lucy is said to have caught the young Shakespeare poaching deer in the grounds of **Charlecote Park** (☎ 01789-470277; charlecote@smtp.ntrust.co.uk; admission £6.40; ☺ noon-5pm Fri-Tue Mar-Sep, noon-4.30pm Fri-Tue Oct); deer still roam the park, which was landscaped by Capability Brown. The house, built around 1551, has an interior redesigned in Elizabethan style in the early

---

WORTH THE TRIP
Though Coventry itself isn't terribly alluring, its spectacular pair of **cathedrals**, one new and one ruined, make it a worthwhile day trip from Stratford, Warwick or Birmingham. Founded in the 12th century and rebuilt from 1373, **St Michael's** was one of England's largest parish churches when it became a cathedral in 1918, its spire topped only by those of Salisbury and Norwich cathedrals. Then, in 1940, a Luftwaffe raid gutted the cathedral, leaving only the outer walls and the spire standing amid the ruins.

After the war the ruins were left as a reminder. Immediately next to them, a **new St Michael's Cathedral** (☎ 7622 7597; www.coventrycathedral.org; requested donation £3) was built between 1955 and 1962. Designed by Sir Basil Spence, it's one of the few examples of postwar British architecture to inspire popular affection. It's noted for the soaring etched glass screen wall at the western end, for the Graham Sutherland tapestry above the altar, for Piper's lovely stained glass and for Epstein's sculpture of St Michael subduing the devil beside the entrance steps.

The **old cathedral spire** (☎ 7626 7070; admission £1.50) still looks down over the ruins; its 180 steps lead up to magnificent views. Opening hours are irregular, so call to check. The **Priory Visitor Centre** (☎ 7655 2242; Priory Row; admission free; ☺ 10am-5.30pm Mon-Sat, noon-4pm Sun) highlights the history of the original cathedral and priory, founded by the omnipresent Leofric 1000 years ago, with artefacts and computer-generated reconstructions.

National Express coaches go to London (2½ hours, nine daily) and Oxford (1¾ hours, two daily). Bus services are run by **Centro** (☎ 7655 9559). Bus Nos 157 (every 30 minutes) and X67 (hourly) run to Leicester (one hour), while bus Nos X16 and X18 run to Kenilworth (25 minutes), Leamington (40 minutes), Warwick (55 minutes) and Stratford (1¼ hours) from Trinity St hourly. The train station is just across the ring road, south of the centre. Birmingham (every 10 minutes) is less than 30 minutes away.

19th century; the Victorian kitchen and Tudor gatehouse are particularly interesting. Charlecote is in Wellesbourne, around 5 miles east of Stratford-upon-Avon. Bus X18 runs from Stratford, Warwick and Coventry hourly.

Ragley Hall

The **family home** (☎ 01789 762090; www.ragleyhall .com; adult/child £7.50/4.50; ☼ noon-5.30pm Thu-Sun Apr-Sep) of the Marquess and Marchioness of Hertford is a grand Palladian mansion built between 1679 and 1683, with a later baroque plasterwork ceiling and some good modern paintings. The intriguing South Staircase Hall with its murals and ceiling painting was restored between 1968 and 1982. Youngsters weary of behaving themselves indoors can be turned loose in Ragley Adventure Wood, a forest playground. Ragley is 2 miles southwest of Alcester off the A435/A46.

STAFFORDSHIRE

Staffordshire, in the words of Stoke-born novelist Arnold Bennett, has long been 'unsung by searchers after the extreme' – but if you took that to mean 'boring' you'd be mistaken. Though it's tucked between the urban sprawls of Birmingham and Manchester, the county has a surprising abundance of natural beauty – from rolling Cannock Chase to the prickly spine of the Peak District known as the Roaches. There are also a path-linked network of villages and quiet little market towns, the gorgeous gloom of Lichfield's wonderful cathedral, the wild rides at Alton Towers, and the neo-classical mansion of Shugborough.

Orientation

Staffordshire's attractions are spread fairly evenly around the county: Stoke to the northwest; the Peak District and Leek northeast, with Alton Towers just south; Lichfield to the southeast; and Stafford just southwest of the centre.

Information

Staffordshire Tourism (☎ 0870 500 4444; www.staf fordshire.gov.uk/tourism) distributes the *Canal County* leaflet on boating, cycling or walking along the county's waterways.

Getting There & Around

Busline (☎ 01782-206608)
Moorlands Traveller 21 (☎ 01538-386888) A flexible bus service linking the northeastern moorland villages with Leek.
Virgin Trains (☎ 0845 722 2333; www.virgin.com /trains)

LICHFIELD

☎ 01543 / pop 28,435
This pretty town, all cobblestones and courtyard gardens, is home to one of England's most beautiful cathedrals, its three spires visible from miles away. It's also been something of a thinktank in its time: famed wit and lexicographer Samuel Johnson was born here, and Erasmus Darwin (Charles' grandfather) lived and studied here for years.

Information

Contact the **TIC** (☎ 308209; www.lichfield-tourist .co.uk; Donegal House, Bore St; ☼ 9am-5pm Mon-Fri & 9am-4.30pm Sat Apr-Sep, 9am-4.45pm Mon-Fri & 9am-2pm Sat Oct-Mar) for local tourist information.

Sights & Activities
LICHFIELD CATHEDRAL

The fine **cathedral** (☎ 306100; requested donation £4; ☼ 7.30am-6.15pm) is instantly recognisable by its three spires. It boasts a fine Gothic west front adorned with exquisitely carved statues of the kings of England from Edgar to Henry I, and the major saints. Its blackened façade is stunning, especially as you approach from the Minster Pond. Most of what you see dates from the various rebuildings of the Norman cathedral between 1200 and 1350. The gold-leafed skull of St Chad, the first bishop of Lichfield, was once kept in St Chad's Head Chapel, just to the west of the south transept.

A superb illuminated manuscript from AD 730, the *Lichfield Gospels*, is displayed in the beautifully vaulted mid–13th-century chapterhouse. Don't miss the effigy of George Augustus Selwyn, first Bishop of New Zealand in 1841, in the lady chapel (which boasts 16th-century Flemish stained glass), or Sir Francis Chantrey's *Sleeping Children* at the eastern end of the south aisle, a poignant memorial to two young girls who died in tragic circumstances.

A stroll round **Cathedral Close**, which is ringed with imposing 17th- and 18th-century houses, is also rewarding.

OTHER SIGHTS & ACTIVITIES

The **Samuel Johnson Birthplace Museum** (☎ 264 972; www.lichfield.gov.uk/sjmuseum; Breadmarket St; admission £2.20; ☒ 10.30am-4.30pm Apr-Sep, noon-4.30pm Oct-Mar) is in the house where the pioneering lexicographer was born in 1709. His dictionary, together with the biography written by his close friend James Boswell (*The Life of Samuel Johnson*), established him as one of the great scholars, critics and wits of the English language. You can inspect the famous dictionary using the computer in the bookshop in the lobby, and learn about his life and his work through the museum's exhibits and videos.

Grandfather of the more famous Charles, Erasmus Darwin was himself a remarkable autodidact, doctor, inventor, philosopher and poet, influencing the Romantics. The **Erasmus Darwin Centre** (☎ 306260; Beacon St; admission £2.50; ☒ 10am-4.30pm Thu-Sat, noon-4.30pm Sun), in the house where he lived from 1756 to 1781, commemorates his life with a video, pictures and personal items. Exhibits and displays illustrate his varied work and association with luminaries such as Wedgwood, Boulton and Watt.

The **Heritage Centre & Treasury** (☎ 256 611; St Mary's Centre; adult/child £3.50/1; ☒ 10am-5pm), on Market Sq, houses an audiovisual presentation covering 1300 years of Lichfield history; the treasury exhibits a small but attractive display of civic, ecclesiastical and regimental silverware. Climb the tower (admission £2) for fine views of the city.

Festivals & Events

The **Lichfield Festival** (☎ 306543; www.lichfieldfestival.org), held in the first half of July, features classical and world music, cinema and theatre in a variety of venues around town.

Sleeping

No 8 (☎ 418483; www.ldb.co.uk/accommodation.htm; s/d from £28/48) Smack in front of the cathedral, No 8 The Close is a listed town house with three rooms, some with a great view of the cathedral face; its owners pride themselves on it being a home, not a hotel, so there's no sign; call in advance to make arrangements.

George Hotel (☎ 414822; www.thegeorgelichfield.co.uk; s/d Mon-Thu from £95/106, Fri-Sun £60/80) An 18th-century coaching inn right in the heart of the city, the George (now part of the Best Western chain) achieves an effortless blend of old-fashioned atmosphere and modern luxury. Rooms with four-poster beds and business-traveller accommodation are available.

There are several B&Bs on Beacon St, round the corner from Cathedral Close, including **32 Beacon St** (☎ 262378; s/d from £25/40), a cosy town house with two en suite rooms. The **Angel Croft Hotel** (☎ 258737; Beacon St; s/d from £55/69) is an imposing Georgian house opposite Cathedral Close.

Eating & Drinking

Cathedral Coffee Shop (☎ 306125; 19 The Close; sandwiches £1.70-3; ☒ 9.30am-4.45pm Mon-Sat, noon-4.45pm Sun) Set in a charming 18th-century house, this café beloved by local pensioners is a good place for a snack or a full Sunday lunch (1-/2-/3-course meals for £6.75/9/11).

Eastern Eye (☎ 415047; 19 Bird St; mains £5.50-11, veg thali £9.50; ☒ 5pm-midnight) This popular Indian restaurant has an award-winning chef who earned a place in the *Guinness Book of World Records* in 2000 for producing the biggest curry ever made (so far). Most of the dishes are normal-sized, however.

Chandlers Grande Brasserie (☎ 416688; 2-/3-course dinner £11.75/15) With a great location in the old Corn Exchange, Chandlers is locally renowned for continental cuisine and a fine ambience.

Samuel Johnson described Lichfield folk as 'the most sober, decent people in England' – but that was 250 years ago, and there are pubs aplenty these days. The **King's Head** (☎ 256822; 21 Bird St) is a good traditional one, with a conservatory area and a courtyard for sunbathing while supping. **Joott** (☎ 410022; 13 Bird St; ☒ noon-2am Mon-Sat, noon-12.30am Sun) is the place to head for late-night frolics, a comfortable café-bar with leather sofas and a balcony terrace.

Getting There & Away

Bus No 112 runs to Birmingham, while No 825 serves Stafford (both £2.50 single, 1¼ hours, hourly). There are two train stations: central Lichfield City and Lichfield Trent Valley. Trains run to both from Birmingham New St station (30 minutes, every 15 minutes). Journeys to London Euston involve changing at either Birmingham or Nuneaton.

THE MIDLANDS

THE MIDLANDS

STOKE-ON-TRENT

☎ 01782 / pop 259,252

Staffordshire's industrial heart, though historically important in pottery production, holds limited appeal to the visitor, except in one department: porcelain. You could visit on a day trip from any of six or seven nearby towns, though you'd want a whole day to really explore the potteries. For a preview, check out Arnold Bennett's memorable descriptions of the area in its industrial heyday in his novels *Clayhangar* and *Anna of the Five Towns* (something of a misnomer, as Stoke actually consists of six towns).

Orientation

Stoke-on-Trent is made up of Tunstall, Burslem, Hanley, Stoke, Fenton and Longton, together often called the Potteries. Hanley is the official 'city centre'. Stoke-on-Trent train station is south of Hanley, but buses from outside the main entrance run there in minutes. The bus station is in the centre of Hanley.

Information

Ask at the **TIC** (☎ 236000; stoke.tic@virgin.net; Quadrant Rd, Potteries shopping centre, Hanley; ⏱ 9.15am-5.15pm Mon-Sat) for a map with the locations of the various showrooms, factory shops and visitor centres.

Sights & Activities

It may sound unlikely, but one of the most exciting attractions in this part of the country is a bone china factory. The **Wedgwood Story Visitor Centre** (☎ 204218; www.thewedgwoodstory.com; Barlaston; Mon-Fri/Sat & Sun £8.25/7.50, with coalport tour £9.25; ⏱ 9am-5pm Mon-Fri, 10am-5pm Sat & Sun) offers a fascinating insight into the production process, with an extensive collection of historic pieces to gawp at, artisans who calmly paint freehand designs onto china while you watch, and best of all, a troupe of Star Wars-esque anthropomorphic robots dutifully churning out perfect plates and mugs with the Wedgwood stamp. Equally interesting are the film and displays on the life of founder Josiah Wedgwood (1730–95). An innovative potter whose consuming passion makes the quest for the perfect vase seem as exciting as the World Cup, he was also a driving force behind the construction of England's canal system and the abolition of slavery – altogether a remarkable man.

The **Potteries Museum & Art Gallery** (☎ 232323; Bethesda St, Hanley; admission free; ⏱ 10am-5pm Mon-Sat & 2-5pm Sun Mar-Oct, 10am-4pm Mon-Sat & 1-4pm Sun Nov-Feb) covers the history of the Potteries and houses an extensive ceramics display as well as a surprisingly impressive collection of fine art (Picasso, Degas) and high-profile touring exhibitions.

Constructed around Stoke's last remaining bottle kiln and its yard, the wonderful **Gladstone Pottery Museum** (☎ 319232; Uttoxeter Rd, Longton; adult/child £4.95/3.50; ⏱ 10am-5pm) is an evocative reconstruction of a typical small pottery in the early 20th century. A highlight for those of scatological bent is the Flushed With Pride exhibition, charting the story of the toilet from chamber pots and shared privy holes (with smell effects!) to modern hi-tech conveniences. Bus Nos 6, 7 and 8 serve Longton from Hanley.

Sleeping & Eating

Leek Rd, just off Station Rd, is convenient for the train station and has a few B&Bs. **North Stafford Hotel** (☎ 744477; fax 744580; Winton Sq; s/d £100/115, B&B per person Fri-Sun £40), opposite the station, offers all the trimmings expected of a three-star place.

The museums and visitor centres all have tearoom-style restaurants; the **Sir Henry Doulton Gallery Restaurant** (☎ 292451; Nile St, Burslem), **Ivy House** and **Josiah's Bistro** (the last two at the Wedgwood Story) are the best. Near the Art Gallery is **Churrasco** (☎ 206201; 39 Albion St, Hanley; baguettes £2-3.50, mains £5-10.50), a bar with good lunchtime snacks, better-than-average dinners with plenty of fish, and a relaxed atmosphere for a drink later.

Getting There & Away

National Express coaches run to/from London (four hours, five daily) and Manchester (1½ hours, eight daily). Bus No 101 runs to Stafford (1¼ hours) every 30 minutes. Trains run hourly to London (1¾ hours).

AROUND STOKE-ON-TRENT
Biddulph Grange Gardens

These gorgeous Victorian **gardens** (☎ 01782-517999; admission £4.80; ⏱ noon-6pm Wed-Fri, 11am-6pm Sat & Sun late-Mar-Oct & 11am-3pm Sat & Sun Nov-Dec) boast Chinese, Egyptian and Italian corners: it's a botanical world tour. A highpoint is the Rainbow, a huge bank of rhododendrons that flower simultaneously in spring. The gardens are 7 miles north of Stoke; take bus No 66 from Stoke train station (40 minutes, every 20 minutes).

Little Moreton Hall

England's most spectacular black-and-white **timber-framed house** (☎ 01260-272018; admission £5; ⏱ 11.30am-5pm Wed-Sun late-Mar–Oct, 11.30am-4pm Sat & Sun Nov–late-Dec) dates back to the 16th century; within its over-the-top exterior there are a series of important wall paintings and an indefinable sense of romance. Little Moreton is off the A34 south of Congleton.

Alton Towers

It's big and brash, but if you can look past the incredible commercialism, **Alton Towers** (☎ 0870-500 1100; www.altontowers.com; adult/child standard ticket £27/21; ⏱ 9.30am-5pm Oct–mid-Mar, longer hrs mid-Mar–Sep) is an absolute must for white-knuckle fiends and is deservedly England's most popular theme park. There are more than 100 rides, including vertical drops, flying roller coasters, log flumes and more; trying to pinpoint the biggest buzz is all part of the fun – new thrills are introduced frequently. Prices vary depending on arcane 'seasons', and are highest during school holidays.

There's a hotel within the park, but most visitors opt to stay in nearby villages; helpfully, the park's website features a list of accommodation options. Alton itself is an attractive village with several B&Bs. **Old School House** (☎ 01538-702151; old_school_house@talk21.com; Castle Hill Rd, Alton; d £56) is an exceptional B&B in an 1845 listed school building. **Dimmingsdale YHA Hostel** (☎ 01538-702304; Oakamoor; dm £10.60) is 2 miles northwest of the park.

Alton Towers is east of Cheadle off the B5032. Public transport is sketchy, but various train companies periodically offer all-in-one packages from London and other cities; check the website for current details.

Drayton Manor Park

Southern Staffordshire's answer to Alton Towers, **Drayton Manor** (☎ 01827-287979; www.draytonmanor.co.uk; weekday/weekend adult £16/18, child £12/14; ⏱ 10.30am-5pm Easter-Oct, longer hrs May-Sep) is another massive theme park with huge rides. They include the Apocalypse, a 54m 'stand up' drop from a tower, and the new Pandemonium, in which two 64-passenger gondolas swing around 360 degrees, producing a G-force of 3.8 and a lot of shriek-

ing. The park is near junctions 9 and 10 of the M42 on the A4091. Bus No X76 runs from Birmingham daily.

LEEK
☎ 01538 / pop 18,768

Gateway to the Staffordshire moorlands, especially the spectacular and climb-hungry Roaches, Leek is an attractive market town that makes a convenient base for visiting the Potteries and the Peak District.

The **TIC** (☎ 483741; tourism.smdc@staffordshire.gov.uk; 1 Market Pl; ⏱ 9.30am-5pm Mon-Fri, 10am-4pm Sat) provides information on attractions and accommodation and will book rooms for a £3 fee.

St Edward's Church (Church St; ⏱ 10am-4pm Wed, 10am-noon Fri & Sat), completed in 1306, has a beautiful rose window by William Morris.

Described by John Betjeman as 'one of the finest churches in Britain', **All Saints Church** (☎ 370786; Compton; ⏱ 11am-4pm Wed & Sat) features Morris & Co stained glass windows at the eastern end from designs by Edward Burne-Jones, and ornate Arts and Crafts wallpainting.

Brindley Mill (☎ 381446; Mill St; admission £2; ⏱ 2-5pm Mon-Wed mid-Jul-Aug, 2-5pm Sat & Sun Easter-Sep) was built in 1752 by canal pioneer James Brindley. It's been beautifully restored and once again mills corn; inside is a small museum dedicated to Brindley and the art of millwrighting.

The **Peak Weavers Hotel** (☎ 383729; www.peakweavershotel.com; 21 King St; s/d from £30/60) has plush doll's house-style rooms and a fine restaurant that's turned out like a very upscale old-fashioned ice-cream parlour.

For liquid refreshment, try the **Roebuck** (☎ 372179; 18 Derby St), a traditional smoky pub that dates back to 1626, although some say it was originally built in Shrewsbury and moved to Leek later.

Bus Nos 16 and 18 run to Leek from Hanley (Stoke-on-Trent).

STAFFORD
☎ 01785 / pop 63,681

The county town of Staffordshire was once a crossroads for travellers. Today it's a pleasant though fairly anonymous place, with a couple of attractions worth a look on your way through.

The **TIC** (☎ 619619; Market St; ⏱ 9.30am-5pm Mon-Fri, 10am-5pm Sat) is behind the town hall.

LEADING A MERRY DANCE

On Wakes Monday (the first Monday after 4 September), Abbots Bromley, 10 miles east of Stafford, is the venue for the Horn Dance, one of the most overtly pagan of all bizarre British ceremonies. Six men attired in faux-medieval costumes carry huge reindeer horns in a ritualised dance around the village, accompanied by a hobby horse, a bowman (or Robin Hood), a fool and Maid Marion. The fun begins at 7.45am outside St Nicholas Church, and the 'horn men' dance and prance for the rest of the day. First recorded in 1226, it's one of the oldest dances in England and resembles rites depicted in Stone-Age cave paintings in France and Derbyshire. The horns themselves are over 1000 years old. And in case you're thinking that watching grown adults spending a day prancing around a 12-mile circuit might get tedious (or embarrassing), be reassured that a great deal of the prancing occurs in or outside the many good pubs...

The **Ancient High House** (☎ 619619; Greengate St; admission free; ⏲ 10am-5pm Mon-Sat) is the largest timber-framed town house in the country and has period rooms containing displays on the history of the house since its construction in 1595.

There are only ruins left of **Stafford Castle** (☎ 257698; Newport Rd; admission free; visitor centre ⏲ 10am-5pm Tue-Sun Apr-Oct, 10am-4pm Nov-Mar), built by William the Conqueror, but it's in a gorgeous setting atop a hill that affords sweeping views. The castle hosts various special events throughout the summer. There's a small visitor centre (closed Mondays, but you can still wander the grounds) and a 'medieval herb garden,' as well as a small network of forested trails ideal for a post-picnic wander.

Bus No 101 runs between Stafford and Stoke-on-Trent (1¼ hours, every 30 minutes).

AROUND STAFFORD

Shugborough

The regal, neoclassical mansion of **Shugborough** (☎ 01889-881 388; admission £6; ⏲ 11am-5pm Tue-Sun Mar-Sep) is the ancestral home of renowned photographer Lord Lichfield (there's an exhibition of his work here). Started in 1693 and considerably extended during the 18th and 19th centuries, Shugborough has marvellous state rooms and a fine collection of Louis XV and XVI furniture. The estate is famous for the monuments within its grounds, including a Chinese House, a Doric temple and the Triumphal Arch. It includes the **Staffordshire County Museum**, exploring life 'below stairs' for servants, and a farm.

Shugborough is 6 miles east of Stafford on the A513; bus No 825 runs nearby.

NORTHAMPTONSHIRE

Beyond its obvious appeal as a batch of pretty villages and winding country lanes, Northamptonshire has special relevance for fans of George Washington, Princess Diana, Alan Moore, Doc Martens and religious eccentrics. Its far-flung attractions also include some historic Saxon churches, a wealth of honey-coloured historic towns and stately homes. It's a great region for driving – attractions are interspersed throughout lovely countryside – and as there's no single tourism blockbuster, you don't have to fight the masses to take in its charms.

Orientation & Information

Northamptonshire is roughly 50 miles long and 20 miles wide, running southwest to northeast. The M1 cuts diagonally across the county just below Northampton, which lies in the middle; attractions are scattered.

For general information about the county, check the website www.visitnorthamptonshire.co.uk. Northampton's TIC stocks plenty of information about the whole county.

Getting Around

Driving is the way to see the most of the county; turning a corner on a winding country lane and coming across a sleepy village is one of the joys of the region. All the major car-hire companies have branches in Northampton.

Buses run to most places of interest from Northampton and other nearby towns; some services run only a few times daily, so it's best to check times with the operator.

Stagecoach (www.stagecoachbus.com)
Traveline (☎ 0870 608 2608)

NORTHAMPTON

☎ 01604 / pop 197,199

Though it seems an unassuming place, there's a lot of behind-the-scenes significance to Northampton. In Saxon days it was perhaps the most important city in England, and Mary, Queen of Scots, was executed in nearby Fotheringhay. These days it's the home of comic-book genius Alan Moore, whose *Voice of the Fire* offers an unusual look at the place. A modern town with pockets of history, it's a fun place to shop or just wander around unencumbered by hordes of fellow visitors. Numerous factory shops – vestiges of the Industrial Revolution, when the town became a shoe-manufacturing centre – knock out cheap Doc Martens around town. There's enough here to keep you occupied for a day, and it's a good base for trips around the county.

Orientation

The town is centred on Market Sq, with the main pedestrianised shopping route, Abington St, running east from it, where it becomes the Kettering Rd, with its hotels and bars. To the south of Market Sq is the Guildhall and TIC, and the bus station is to the north.

Information

The **TIC** (☎ 622677; www.northampton.gov.uk/tourism; Guildhall Rd; ☼ 10am-5pm Mon-Sat, 2-5pm Sun, 10am-2pm bank hols) is inside the Central Museum; the free *Historic Town Trail* leaflet describes a walking tour of the town's hidden treasures.

Sights & Activities

Foot fetishists won't be the only ones fascinated by the **Central Museum & Art Gallery** (☎ 639415; Guildhall Rd; admission free; ☼ 10am-5pm Mon-Sat, 2-5pm Sun). Alongside its huge, well-presented collection of shoes from the 14th century to the present, there are some fine paintings and changing special exhibitions.

St Peter's Church (Mayfair) is a marvellous Norman edifice built in 1150 and restored in the 19th century by Gilbert Scott. The detail on the original capitals is outstanding. For rock nuts: William Smith, known as the father of modern geology, is buried here. Get the key from the Black Lion pub next door.

The **Church of the Holy Sepulchre** (☎ 754782; ☼ vary, call for details) has curiosity value as one of only four round churches in the country;

founded after the first earl of Northampton returned from the Crusades in 1100, it's a near facsimile of its namesake in Jerusalem.

Sleeping & Eating

Lime Trees Hotel (☎ 632188; info@limetreeshotel .co.uk; 8 Langham Pl; s/d from £50/75; ℗) This is a fine option, an attractive Georgian house about half a mile north of the centre with a pretty courtyard at the back.

Coach House Hotel (☎ 250981; fax 234248; 10 East Park Pde; s/d from £55/65; ℗) This hotel in a row of converted Victorian houses just off the Kettering Rd has modern, comfortable rooms.

Malt Shovel (☎ 234212; 121 Bridge St; ℗) A Campaign for Real Ale (Camra) favourite, this place at the edge of the town centre has good solid pub food and offers a taste of local spirit with its chalkboard advertising 'up to 13 real ales!' There are always guest beers as well as a huge international selection of bottled beers.

Joe's Diner (☎ 620022; 104a Abington St; mains £6.75-16.95; ☼ Mon-Sat) Breaking the mould of the American theme eatery, Joe's gets it right with a huge range of quality burgers, friendly staff and a healthy dearth of tacky 'memorabilia'.

A few coffee houses line St Giles St, including small and flowery **Young's** (at No 59) and **J Lawrence** (at No 37), with a vast array of gorgeous pastries. Other dining options include **Miraj** (☎ 637659; 28-34 Wellington St; mains £4.95-11.95), an upmarket Indian place, and the **Vineyard** (☎ 633978; 7 Derngate; mains £12.95-16.95; ☼ lunch Mon-Thu & Sat, dinner Mon-Sat), a smart place popular with businesspeople, serving fresh fish and French-influenced dishes.

Entertainment

Picturedrome (☎ 230777; www.thepicturedrome.com; 222 Kettering Rd) This stylish, buzzing bar hosts fortnightly comedy nights, live music and other events.

Roadmender (☎ 604222; www.roadmender.org; 1 Lady's Lane) This local landmark, is a uniquely versatile venue that features up-and-coming bands, theatre, comedy and club nights.

Derngate and the **Royal Theatre** (☎ 624811; www.northamptontheatres.com; Guildhall Rd) are managed cooperatively. Derngate is Northampton's arts centre and hosts anything from Tom Jones to Tom Thumb; the Royal is an impressive Victorian structure staging local theatre and quality West End productions.

Getting There & Away

National Express coaches run to London (£10.50 economy single, two hours, five daily), Nottingham (£9.50, 2½ hours, daily) and Birmingham (£5, 1½ hours, two daily). Greyfriars bus station is on Lady's Lane, just north of the Grosvenor shopping centre.

Northampton has excellent rail links with Birmingham (one hour, hourly) and London Euston (one hour, at least every 30 minutes). The train station is about half a mile west of town along Gold St.

AROUND NORTHAMPTON
Althorp

The late Diana, Princess of Wales, is commemorated in a memorial and museum in the grounds of her ancestral home, **Althorp Park** (bookings ☎ 0870 167 9000; www.althorp.com; admission £11.50, plus £2.50 access to upstairs of house; ☒ 11am-5pm Jul-Sep). The 16th-century mansion houses works by Rubens, Gainsborough and Van Dyck. Profits from ticket sales go to the Princess Diana Memorial Fund. The limited number of tickets must be booked by phone or on the website. Incidentally, Althorp should be pronounced *altrup*.

Althorp is off the A428 northwest of Northampton. There are four buses daily linking Althorp with Northampton train station.

Stoke Bruerne

The **Canal Museum** (☎ 01604-862229; www.thewater waystrust.co.uk; adult/child £3/2.50; ☒ 10am-5pm daily Apr-Oct, 10am-4pm Tue-Sun Nov-Mar), on a pretty stretch of the Grand Union Canal at Stoke Bruerne, 8 miles south of Northampton, is an informative centre that explores the development of English canals from the 17th century with the aid of models, photos, costumes, and pieces of vintage equipment.

If the displays catch your eye, take a cruise on the **Indian Chief** (☎ 01604-862428), run by the Boat Inn (see following); trips range from 25 minutes (£2) to six hours (£12).

The **Boat Inn** (☎ 01604-862428; www.boatinn.co .uk; mains £3-12) is a charming thatched canal-side pub, one of several in the village. **Waterways Cottage** (☎ 01604-863865; wendycox@waterways .junglelink.com; Bridge Rd; d from £45) is a comfortable B&B behind the Boat Inn.

Bus No 37 from Northampton to Milton Keynes calls at Stoke Bruerne (30 minutes, four daily Monday to Saturday).

Sulgrave Manor

Built by Lawrence Washington after Henry VIII sold him the property in 1539, **Sulgrave Manor** (☎ 01295-760205; www.stratford.co.uk/sulgrave; admission £5.75; ☒ 2pm-5.30pm Tue-Thu, Sat & Sun Apr-Oct) is a well-preserved Tudor mansion; unsurprisingly, the fact that 250 years later a certain family descendant named George Washington became the first president of the USA bolsters the interest of overseas visitors. That the family lived here for 120 years before Colonel John Washington moved to Virginia in 1656 doesn't seem to decrease the appeal.

Sulgrave Manor is located just off the B4525, 7 miles northeast of Banbury.

Brixworth

The main sight here is **All Saints** (☎ 01604 880286; ☒ usually 10am-6pm Apr-Sep, 10am-4pm Oct-Mar), England's largest relatively intact Saxon church (which doesn't mean it's huge!). Although the church itself is fascinating, it's almost more evocative viewed from the sheep-inhabited churchyard. Built on a basilica plan around AD 680, it incorporates Roman tiles from an earlier building. The tower and stair turret were added after 9th-century Viking raids, and the spire was built around 1350.

Brixworth is 6 miles north of Northampton off the A508. Bus X7 runs from Northampton (10 minutes, hourly Monday to Saturday, five on Sunday).

Earls Barton

Earls Barton's wonderful (and still very active) place of worship, **All Saints** (☎ 01604-810045; ☒ 10.30am-12.30pm & 2-4pm Mon-Sat Apr-Sep, by apt Oct-Mar), is notable for its solid Saxon tower with patterns that seem to imitate earlier wooden models. Probably built during the reign of Edgar the Peaceful (r. 959–75), it has a first-floor door that may have offered access to the tower during Viking raids. Around 1100 the Norman nave was added to the original tower; other features were added in subsequent centuries.

Earls Barton is 8 miles east of Northampton. Bus Nos 45 to 47 run from Northampton (10 minutes, every 20 minutes, seven on Sunday).

Rushton Triangular Lodge

To call the **lodge** (☎ 01536-710761; admission £2; ☒ 10am-5pm Thu-Mon Apr-Sep) a folly is to underestimate the power of faith on the mind of Sir Thomas Tresham. He designed a number of buildings in the area (and was imprisoned more than once for expressing his Catholic beliefs). With three of everything, from sides to floors to gables, the lodge is Tresham's enduring symbol of the trinity, built at the end of the 16th century. Mysterious, esoteric inscriptions and a magical setting among rapeseed fields give the place a surprising impact.

The lodge is 4 miles northwest of Kettering. Bus No 19 from Kettering stops in Desborough, 2 miles away (20 minutes, every 30 minutes Monday to Saturday, every two hours on Sunday). Kettering is 15 miles northeast of Northampton along the A43.

Kirby Hall

Once one of the finest Elizabethan mansions, the 'Jewel of the English Renaissance', **Kirby Hall** (☎ 01604-735400; admission £4; ☼ 10am-5pm Thu-Mon Apr-Jun, 10am-6pm daily Jul-Aug, 10am-5pm Thu-Mon Sep-Oct, 10am-4pm Thu-Mon Nov-Mar) was begun in 1570, and additions were made up to the 19th century. Abandoned and fallen into disrepair, it's still a remarkable, atmospheric site – it was used as the location for the 1999 film of Jane Austen's *Mansfield Park* – with fine filigree stonework, ravens cawing in the empty halls and peacocks roaming its restored formal parterre gardens.

Kirby Hall is 4 miles northeast of Corby; Corby is 9 miles north of Kettering along the A43.

Oundle & Fotheringhay

Its streets and squares graced with the honey-coloured Jurassic limestone and Colleyweston slate roofs of 16th- and 17th-century buildings, the village of Oundle is the photogenic face of Northamptonshire. It's also a good base for visiting nearby **Fotheringhay**, birthplace of Richard III (demonised by the Tudors and Shakespeare) and execution place of Mary, Queen of Scots, in 1587. The castle in which these events took place is now merely a hillock, but Fotheringhay is a charming village with thatched cottages and a pub famous for its excellent food, the **Falcon** (☎ 01832-226254).

Oundle's **TIC** (☎ 01832-274333; oundletic@east -northamptonshire.gov.uk; 14 West St; ☼ 9am-5pm Mon-Sat, also 1-4pm Sun Easter-Aug) sells a *Walking Trail* leaflet (£1) for exploring the quaint streets.

Haunted **Talbot Inn** (☎ 01832-273621; fax 274545; New St; s/d £75/95; bar food £3.85-6.35 served 11am-6pm), built in 1626, allegedly incorporates the staircase from nearby Fotheringhay Castle, which Mary descended on the way to her execution; her executioner reputedly stayed here before he gave her the chop. Its pleasantly refurbished rooms retain the atmosphere of the old inn, and there's an upmarket restaurant.

Bus X4 runs hourly from Northampton (1½ hours, four on Sunday) and from Peterborough (30 minutes).

LEICESTERSHIRE & RUTLAND

In typical Midlands fashion, Leicestershire self-deprecatingly plays down its own attractions, yet it boasts several picturesque villages, a rich industrial heritage and a few key historic sites – not to mention magnificent Belvoir Castle. The county town is one of the more interesting urban areas in the region, with its rich multi-ethnic culture and hopping nightlife.

Tiny Rutland was merged with Leicestershire in 1974, but in April 1997 regained its 'independence' as a county. With magnificent Rutland Water and charming settlements, it's a hit with lovers of water sports and quaint villages.

Orientation & Information

Leicestershire and Rutland together look like an upside-down map of Australia. Leicester is virtually bang in the centre of its county, with the M1 motorway running north–south just to the west, dividing the largely industrial towns and National Forest of the west from the more rural east, including Belvoir Castle. Rutland's little solar system, east of Leicester and tucked away between four counties, revolves around central Rutland Water.

For general county-wide information, contact **Leicestershire Tourism** (☎ 0116-265 7302; tourism@leics.gov.uk).

Getting There & Around

Arriva Fox County (☎ 0116-264 400) Operates Leicestershire bus services.
Traveline (☎ 0870 608 2608)

THE MIDLANDS

LEICESTER

☎ 0116 / pop 441,213

Filled with the sense of excitement that comes from a mix of cultures and ethnicities, Leicester (*les*-ter) may not be beautiful but it certainly has a lot going on. The Luftwaffe gave it an unwelcome facelift, industrial decline hollowed it out and a lack of urban planning capped off the aesthetic crimes against the city. But Leicester has reinvented itself as a socially and environmentally progressive melting pot that could teach other, bigger cities a thing or two about diversity. More than most cities its size, modern Leicester has a large and vibrant Asian community, with Hindu, Muslim, Jain and Sikh temples aplenty.

Many of the city's most interesting events are staged around festivals such as Holi, Diwali and Eid-ul-Fitr. And the nightlife options give neighbouring Nottingham a run for its money.

Orientation

Leicester is initially difficult to navigate as there are few landmarks, but the pedestrianised central area around the market and clock tower makes things a little simpler. For drivers, it's plagued by the usual maze of one-way streets and forbidden turns. Although there isn't a ring road as such, the A594 does almost a whole circuit and most attractions flank it or are contained within it.

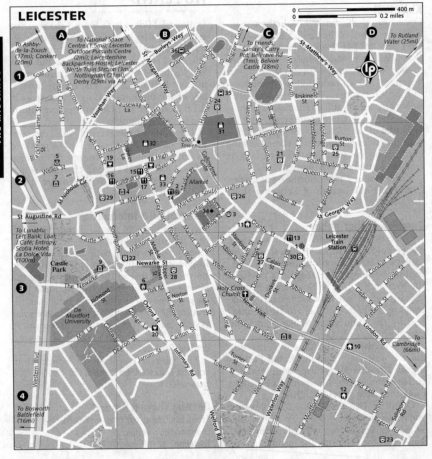

The centre of the Asian community, Belgrave Rd (the 'Golden Mile') is about a mile northeast of the centre. Castle Park, with many of the historic attractions, lies immediately west of the centre.

Information

CyberCuts (☎ 285 6661; 122 Granby St; ⏰ 7am-9pm Mon-Sat, 10am-9pm Sun; Internet access per hr £1) A barber's shop where you surf while you await your trim.

Ice Mango (☎ 262 6255; www.icemango.co.uk; 4 Market Pl; ⏰ 9am-7pm Mon-Sat, 11am-5.30pm Sun; Internet access per hr £2)

J:Café (☎ 254 9927; 49 Braunstone Gate; ⏰ 11am-7.30pm Mon-Sat, noon-6pm Sun; Internet access per hr £2) In the hip bar district west of Castle Park.

TIC (☎ 299 8888; www.discoverleicester.com; 7-9 Every St; ⏰ 9am-5.30pm Mon-Wed & Fri, 10am-5.30pm Thu, 10am-5pm Sat)

Sights
JEWRY WALL & MUSEUMS

All Leicester's **museums** (www.leicestermuseums.ac.uk; ⏰ 10am-5pm Mon-Sat & 1-5pm Sun Apr-Sep, 10am-4pm daily Oct-Mar) are free and have the same opening hours.

Despite its name, **Jewry Wall** is one of England's largest Roman civil structures and has nothing to do with Judaism. You can walk among excavated remains of the Roman public baths (around AD 150), of which the wall was part. Notwithstanding its grim external appearance, the **Jewry Wall Museum** (☎ 247 3021; St Nicholas Circle) contains wonderful Roman mosaics and frescoes, as well as an interactive exhibition, 'The Making of Leicester', with lots of artefacts and models.

New Walk Museum & Art Gallery (☎ 255 4100; New Walk) houses a collection of fine Victorian, German and decorative art as well as Egyptian mummies, natural history displays and changing exhibitions.

Newarke Houses Museum (☎ 247 3222; The Newarke) contains a surprisingly varied collection in two 16th-century buildings. There are some reconstructed period shops, displays of various oddities (an extensive selection of truncheons covers 1796–1886) and exhibitions on two of Leicester's best-known citizens: the mammoth Daniel Lambert (see Leicester's Weightiest Citizen, p538) and Thomas Cook, the package-holiday pioneer.

In the late–14th-century **Guildhall** (☎ 253 2569; Guildhall Lane), reputedly the most haunted building in Leicester, you can peer into old police cells and inspect a copy of the last gibbet used to expose the body of an executed murderer. There are also small temporary exhibitions.

NATIONAL SPACE CENTRE

This **centre** (☎ 0870 607 7223; www.spacecentre.co.uk; Exploration Dr; adult/child £8.95/6.95; ⏰ 9.30am-6pm Tue-Sun, plus Mon during Leicester school holidays, last entry 4.30pm) is a spectacular and successful attempt to bring space science to us ordinary mortals. Interactive displays cover cosmic myths, the history of astronomy and the development of space travel; in the Space Now! area you can check on the status of all current space missions. Films in the domed Space Theatre (included in the admission price) launch you to the far reaches

THE MIDLANDS

of the galaxy, and you can come back to earth with a coffee in Boosters café, sitting beneath huge booster rockets. Don't miss the displays on zero-gravity toilets and the amazing germ-devouring underpants.

The centre is off the A6 about 1½ miles north of the city centre. Take bus No 54 from Charles St or No 61 from Haymarket bus station.

TEMPLES

Materials were shipped in from India to convert a disused church into a **Jain Centre** (☎ 254 3091; www.jaincentre.com; 32 Oxford St; ⏲ 8.30am-8.30pm Mon-Sat, 8.30am-6.30pm Sun). The building is faced with marble, and the temple – the first outside the subcontinent and the only one in Europe – boasts a forest of beautifully carved pillars inside. Jainism evolved in India at around the same time as Buddhism.

Close to the Jewry Wall is the Sikh **Guru Nanak Gurdwara** (☎ 262 8606; 9 Holy Bones; ⏲ 1-4pm Thu or by arrangement). There is a small museum, which contains an impressive model of the Golden Temple in Amritsar.

Activities

Leicester Outdoor Pursuits Centre (☎ 268 1426; www.lopc.homestead.com; Loughborough Rd; adult/child 8-16 per 2hrs from £65/90), northwest of the city centre, offers canoeing, abseiling, archery and all manner of pastimes for the energetic.

Festivals & Events

Leicester hosts numerous cultural and religious festivals throughout the year; contact the TIC for details. The Asian community celebrates **Diwali** during autumn, and the celebration, the largest of its kind outside India, draws visitors from around the world. In August the city hosts the biggest **Caribbean carnival** (☎ 225 7770; www.lccarnival.org.uk) outside London's Notting Hill Carnival. The **comedy festival** (☎ 291 5511; www.comedy-festival.co.uk) in February is now the largest in the country, drawing big names and new talent.

Sleeping

Leicestershire Backpackers Hostel (☎ 267 3107; 157 Wanlip Lane, Birstall; tents £5, dm per night/week £10/48; Ⓟ) This odd little place 3 miles north of the centre takes under-26 travellers only; cooking is communal, and rates include a basic breakfast. Bus services are variable; phone the hostel for details.

Ramada Jarvis Hotel (☎ 255 5599; sales.leicester@ramadajarvis.com; Granby St; s/d Sun-Thu from £110/124, B&B Fri-Sun £49/78; Ⓟ) At the opposite end of the spectrum is this central, listed establishment, the city's top option.

Belmont House Hotel (☎ 254 4773; info@belmonthotel.co.uk; De Montfort St; s/d Sun-Thu £95/105, Fri & Sat £55/80; Ⓟ) This hotel, in a Georgian-style building, features modern rooms.

Scotia Hotel (☎ 254 9200; scotiahotel@amserve.com; 10 Westcotes Dr; s/d £30/45; Ⓟ) West of Castle Park, this is a friendly, old-school B&B.

Spindle Lodge (☎ 233 8801; spindlelodgeleicester@orange.net; 2 West Walk; s/d from £40/65; Ⓟ) This charming Victorian town house has a restaurant and bar.

Eating

The Golden Mile on Belgrave Rd is located a mile to the north of the centre (take bus No 22 or 37 from Haymarket bus station), and is noted for its fine Indian and vegetarian restaurants.

Friends (☎ 266 8809; 41-43 Belgrave Rd; mains £5-12; ⏲ dinner daily, lunch Mon-Sat) This award-winning tandoori eatery in the Golden Mile serves excellent North Indian food, with a range of fish and vegetarian dishes.

Sanjay's Curry Pot (☎ 253 8256; mail@thecurrypot.co.uk; 78-80 Belgrave Rd; mains £5-13; ⏲ Mon-Sat) Outside of Goa it's find a place that specialises in both Indian and Portuguese cuisines, but that's exactly what's on the menu in this bright, funky place.

Case (☎ 251 7675; 4-6 Hotel St; mains £7-16; ⏲ Mon-Sat) This standby epitomises stylish contemporary dining, in a bright, airy 1st-floor space. Food is fashionable (pan-fried calf liver, wild boar sausages, scallops) and competent; the basement Champagne Bar serves cheaper snacks.

Leicester sports countless other interesting eateries, including:

Bossa (☎ 233 4544; 110 Granby St; toasties £1) A cheerful, almost European atmosphere; at night it draws a gay crowd.

Dino's (☎ 262 8308; 13 Garrick Walk; 3-course lunch £9, mains £8.50-15; ⏲ Mon-Sat) Mediterranean and Pacific Rim cuisine in a modern, sleek environment.

La Dolce Vita (☎ 254 0006; 36 Narborough Rd; pasta £6-8; ⏲ 7-11pm Tue-Sat) Small, local Italian joint west of Castle Park.

Liquid (☎ 261 9086; 5 Guildhall Lane; toasted baguettes £2; ⏲ 8.30am-6pm Mon-Sat, plus Sun Dec) A cool juice bar for mid-shop munching.

Noodle Bar (☎ 262 9029; 1 St Nicholas Pl; noodles £4; ✟ dinner daily, lunch Mon-Sat) Tasty, filling Chinese food.

Opera House (☎ 223 6666; 10 Guildhall Lane; 2-/3-course lunch £11.75/13.50, dinner mains £15-19) Modern British cuisine with a hint of French; one of the swankier places in town.

Drinking

Leicester has a thriving nightlife, due partly to the huge student population at Leicester and De Montfort Universities. Places come and go by the month; check www.leicesterguide.co.uk/bars for up-to-the-minute tips. The centre has some good boozers and a few hip bars, as well as the inevitable rash of chain pubs. The left bank of the canal has been buzzing more recently; Braunstone Gate, Narborough Rd and Hinckley Rd are chock-a-block with bars and eateries.

Globe (☎ 262 9819; 43 Silver St) At last, here's that rare beast, a traditional old pub (built in 1720) situated in a city centre with fine draught ales, a warm atmosphere and decent bar snacks.

Loaf (☎ 299 9424; 58-64 Braunstone Gate) Newspapers, bottled beers and the immortal motto 'it is better to have loafed and lost, than never to have loafed at all' – what more could you want in a bar? It's west of Castle Park.

Other options worth exploring:

Entropy (☎ 225 9650; 42 Hinckley Rd; all-day breakfast £7) Cool, minimal décor, subtle lighting and smooth tunes; look for the H North sign, west of Castle Park.

Left Bank (☎ 255 2422; 26 Braunstone Gate) Good Eurocentric food, west of Castle Park.

Lunablu (☎ 255 1911; 54 Braunstone Gate) The pre-club bar of choice, west of Castle Park.

Orange Tree (☎ 223 5256; 99 High St; sandwiches £2-4, meals £4-7) Skylights and sofas.

Swan & Rushes (☎ 233 9167; 19 Infirmary Sq) Five ales on tap, 100-plus bottles.

Entertainment

NIGHTCLUBS

Charlotte (☎ 255 3956; www.thecharlotte.co.uk; 8 Oxford St) Leicester's legendary venue has played host to the biggies, including Oasis and Blur, before they became megastars. It's a small place with a late licence and regular club nights.

Po Na Na Souk Bar (☎ 253 8190; 24 Careys Close) Along with sister lounge bar Bam Bu Da, this outlet of the red-hot regional chain of clubs packs them in with danceable funk and house.

At **J21** (☎ 251 9333; 13 Midland St), one of Leicester's biggest clubs, big-name DJs play loud house. **Attic** (☎ 222 3800; Free Lane), a smallish venue off Halford Lane, drops hip-hop, breakbeat, Latin electronica and the occasional bit of indie rock. Bigger bands usually play at **De Montfort Hall** (☎ 233 3111; www.demontforthall.co.uk; Granville Rd), southeast of the centre, which also stages classical concerts.

THEATRE & COMEDY

Phoenix Arts Centre (☎ 255 4854; www.phoenix.org.uk; Newarke St) This is the main venue for art-house films, fringe plays, comedy and dance events.

Jongleurs Comedy Club (☎ 0870 787 0707; www.jongleurs.com; 30-32 Granby St) The primary local comedy stage and part of a well-known chain, Jongleurs sometimes hosts big-name acts.

Other venues for plays include the **Little Theatre** (☎ 255 1302; www.thelittletheatre.net; Dover St); **Haymarket Theatre** (☎ 253 9797; www.lhtheatre.co.uk; 1 Belgrave Gate), with more mainstream fare; and the **Y** (☎ 255 6507; 7 East St), a multipurpose theatre and bar attached to the YMCA, hosting concerts, poetry, plays and more.

Getting There & Away

National Express operates from St Margaret's bus station on Gravel St, north of the centre. The express bus No 777 runs to Nottingham (one hour, eight daily Monday to Saturday), while Nos X67 (one hour, hourly) and 157 (every 30 minutes) run to Coventry.

Trains run to London St Pancras (1½ hours, every 30 minutes) and Birmingham (one hour, every 30 minutes).

More a tourist jaunt than a serious transport option, the **Great Central Railway** (☎ 01509-230726; www.gcrailway.co.uk; tickets £10 return) operates steam locomotives between Leicester North station on Redhill Circle and Loughborough Central, the 8-mile route along which Thomas Cook ran his original package tour in 1841. The trains run daily from May to August and every weekend the rest of the year. Take bus No 37, 61 or 61A from Haymarket bus station.

THE MIDLANDS

Getting Around

Central Leicester is fairly flat and easy to get around on foot. As an alternative to local buses, **Discover Leicester** (☎ 299 8888; adult/child under 15 £5/3; ☿ 10am-4pm Jun-Sep on the hour) runs a jump-on-jump-off bus around the city and up to Belgrave Rd, the Great Central Railway and the National Space Centre. The main stop is at the bus station.

The **Bike Park** (☎ 299 1234; Town Hall Sq; ☿ 8am-6.30pm Mon-Fri, 8.30am-6pm Sat; bike hire per day £8, bike parking per hr/day 50p/£1, showers 65p) offers great services, including bike hire, parking, information and cycle maps.

AROUND LEICESTER
Bosworth Battlefield

The **Battlefield Visitor Centre** (☎ 01455-290429; admission £3.25; ☿ 11am-5pm daily Apr-Oct, Sun Nov & Dec, Sat & Sun March) features an exhibition about the Battle of Bosworth Field, where Richard III was defeated by the future Henry VII in 1485, ending the Wars of the Roses; 'a horse, a horse, my kingdom for a horse' was his famous death cry (at least according to the William Shakespeare). Richard III may be known as a villain for his supposed role in the murder of the 'princes in the tower', but Leicester has adopted him as something of a folk hero, not the hunchback of Shakespearean spin. The battle is re-enacted annually.

The battlefield is 16 miles southwest of Leicester at Sutton Cheny. Bus No 153 runs hourly from Leicester to Market Bosworth, 2 miles to the north.

Ashby-de-la-Zouch
☎ 01530 / pop 11,409

The excitingly named Ashby-de-la-Zouch is a likable market town, but its real draw is the **castle** (☎ 413343; admission £3.20; ☿ 10am-6pm Apr-Sep, 10am-5pm Oct, 10am-4pm Wed-Sun Nov-Mar). Built in Norman times and owned by the Zouch family until 1399, it was extended in the 14th and 15th centuries and then reduced to its present picturesquely ruined state in 1648 after the Civil War; a lively audio guide introduces the characters and details the history. Bring a torch to explore the underground passageway connecting the tower with the kitchen.

For accommodation, contact the **TIC** (☎ 411767; North St; ☿ 10am-5pm Mon-Fri, 10am-3pm Sat). Ashby is on the A511 about 15 miles

northwest of Leicester. Bus No 118 (No 218 Sunday) runs hourly from St Margaret's bus station in Leicester.

Conkers & the National Forest

The National Forest is an ongoing project to plant 30 million trees in a swath from Leicester through Derbyshire into Staffordshire. Central to the scheme is **Conkers** (☎ 01283-216633; www.visitconkers.com; Rawdon Rd, Moira; adult/child £5.95/3.95; ☿ 10am-5pm), a purpose-built visitor centre with a range of interactive displays on woodland life, biology and environmental issues. There's lots of touching, smelling and hearing: it's a multisensory experience designed to captivate children but fascinating for all.

Conkers is northwest of Leicester off the A444.

Belvoir Castle

In the wilds of the county is **Belvoir** (*bee*-ver) **Castle** (☎ 01476-870262; www.belvoircastle.com; adult/child £8/6; ☿ 11am-5pm Tue-Thu, Sat & Sun May-Sep, Sun Apr & Oct), a magnificent baroque and Gothic fantasy rebuilt in the 19th century after suffering serious damage during the Civil War, and home to the duke of Rutland. A hefty portion of the sumptuous interior is open to the public, and collections of weaponry, medals and art (including masterpieces by Reynolds, Gainsborough, Holbein and Rubens) are highlights. There are marvellous views across the countryside, and peacocks roam the delightful gardens.

Belvoir is 6 miles west of Grantham, off the A1; Grantham is about 25 miles east of Nottingham along the A52.

RUTLAND

Rutland's motto is 'Multum in Parvo' ('so much in so little') and it sure lives up to the name. Though it's England's smallest county, a huge proportion of it is given over to recreational activity, in the form of Rutland Water – a vast and attractive reservoir offering ample opportunity for water sports and outdoor pursuits of all kinds, including climbing, bird-watching and sailing.

Information

Oakham TIC (☎ 01572-724329; 34 High St; ☿ 10am-4pm Tue-Sat)
Rutland Water TIC (☎ 01572-653026; Sykes Lane, Empingham; ☿ 10am-4pm Tue-Sat)

Sights & Activities

In Rutland Water, the **Rutland Belle** (☎ 01572-787630; www.rutlandwatercruises.com; the Harbour, Whitwell Park; adult/child £5/4) offers pleasure cruises every afternoon, May to September.

The **Watersports Centre** (☎ 01780-460154; Whitwell) organises windsurfing, canoeing and sailing. **Rutland Sailing School** (☎ 01780-721999; www.rutlandsailingschool.co.uk; Edith Weston) offers tuition to sailors of all abilities.

For bike hire contact **Rutland Water Cycling** (☎ 01780-460705; www.rutlandcycling.co.uk; Whitwell Car Park).

The sleepy county town of **Oakham** has a famous school and **Oakham Castle** (admission free; ☺ 10am-1pm & 1.30-5pm Mon-Sat, 1-5pm Sun, shorter hours Nov-Feb), really the Great Hall and sole standing remnant of a Norman structure.

South of Oakham is the village of Lyddington, home to the **Bede House** (☎ 01572-822438; admission £3.20; ☺ 10am-6pm Apr-Sep, 10am-5pm Oct). Originally a wing of the medieval rural palace of the bishops of Lincoln, in 1600 it was converted into almshouses. Although the interior is sparsely furnished now, fine interpretative displays and an excellent free audio guide fill in the gaps.

Getting There & Away

Bus No 2 runs from Nottingham to Oakham in Rutland (1¼ hours, hourly); trains run roughly hourly from Leicester and Peterborough.

NOTTINGHAMSHIRE

Nottinghamshire seems to breed good stories: this is the land of the legendary Robin Hood and his merry men, and the home of provocative writer DH Lawrence and decadent bad-boy poet Lord Byron. Even its castles and pubs are draped in myth and mystery. The city of Nottingham itself draws movers and shakers from all over the region, in business as well as in clubbing.

Listen out for the peculiar Brum-cum-Yorkshire accent, and don't be alarmed if you're greeted with a hearty 'eyupmeduck'.

Orientation & Information

Nottinghamshire is tall and thin, spreading a surprising distance north of Nottingham to finish level with Sheffield, though most of the county's attractions are in the southern half, with Newstead and Eastwood just north of Nottingham, Sherwood Forest in the county's centre and Newark-on-Trent and Southwell to the east.

Find county-wide information at www.nottinghamshiretourism.co.uk.

Getting Around

Useful journey planners with details of bus transport around the county can be found at www.ukbus.co.uk and www.itsnottingham.info. **Sherwood Forester buses** (☎ 0115-977 4268; ☺ Sun & bank hols Jun-Aug; Ranger ticket £5) operate to tourist attractions all over Nottinghamshire, with tickets giving discounted admission to some attractions.

NOTTINGHAM

☎ 0115 / pop 666,358

Charmingly known as Snotingham in Saxon days, modern Nottingham had its primary moment of glory in the 19th century when the lace industry transformed the city centre. The Lace Market section of town remains an intriguing warren of shops and clubs. Lace-making declined during the 1890s and was virtually killed off by WWI, although the tourist industry supports some small-scale production.

These days, the old manufacturing base of Nottingham – long a centre of industry known for Raleigh bikes, the Boots pharmacy empire and cigarette production – is diminished. The buzz has a more cultural bent now: fashion designer Paul Smith is a leading light, the clubs and bars are some of the liveliest in the country, and Trent Bridge remains a major draw for cricket fans. Nottingham is also a mecca for shop-aholics from miles around, and a remarkably appealing town as shopping meccas go.

The city's famed Goose Fair dates back to the Middle Ages; these days it's an outsized funfair that takes place in the Forest Recreation Ground, a mile north of the city centre.

Orientation

Like other Midlands cities, Nottingham is chopped into pieces by an inner ring road enclosing most of the attractions, eateries and bars. The train station is south of the canal on the southern edge of the centre. There are two bus stations: Victoria bus station is hidden away behind the Victoria shopping centre, just north of the centre,

NOTTINGHAM

0 ——————— 200 m
0 ——————— 0.1 miles

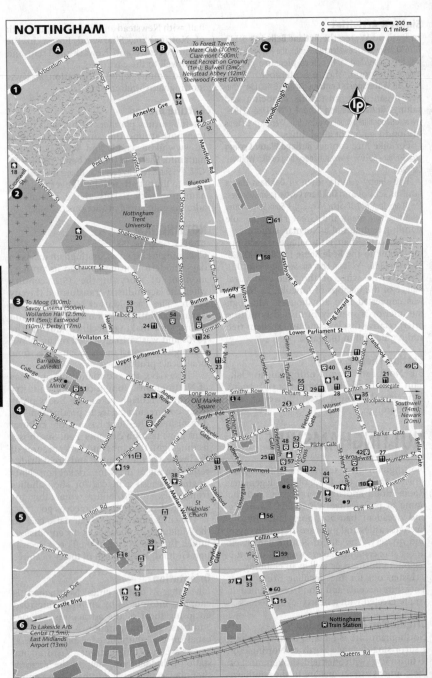

THE MIDLANDS

To Forest Tavern;
Maze Club (100m);
Claremont (500m);
Forest Recreation Ground
(1mi); Bulwell (3mi);
Newstead Abbey (12mi);
Sherwood Forest (20mi)

To Moog (300m);
Savoy Cinema (500m);
Wollaton Hall (2.5mi);
M1 (5mi); Eastwood
(10mi); Derby (17mi)

To
Southwell
(14mi);
Newark
(20mi)

To Lakeside Arts
Centre (1.5mi);
East Midlands
Airport (13mi)

Nottingham
Train Station

while Broadmarsh bus station is behind Broadmarsh shopping centre to the south.

Information

Alphanet Café (☎ 956 6988; 4 Queen St; 🕑 10am-6pm; Internet access per 30 min £2)

TIC (☎ 915 5330; www.visitnottingham.com; 1-4 Smithy Row; 🕑 9am-5.30pm Mon-Fri, 9am-5pm Sat, 11am-3pm Sun May-Sep) Ask about discount combination tickets for major attractions.

Sights & Activities

NOTTINGHAM CASTLE MUSEUM & ART GALLERY

Nottingham Castle was demolished after the Civil War and replaced with a mansion in 1674. The **museum** (☎ 915 3700; admission £2 Sat & Sun, free Mon-Fri; 🕑 8am-5pm Mar-Oct, 10am-4pm Sat-Thu Nov-Feb) opened inside the castle shell in 1875. It vividly describes Nottingham's history and displays some of the medieval alabaster carvings for which Nottingham was noted. Upstairs there's an art gallery with changing exhibitions and some fine permanent pieces (Lowry, Delacroix and Rossetti). There's a stylish café and an excellent shop.

An underground passageway, **Mortimer's Hole** (tours £2; 🕑 2pm & 3pm Mon-Fri), leads from the castle to Brewhouse Yard. Roger Mortimer, who arranged Edward II's murder, is said to have been captured by supporters of Edward III who entered via this passage.

CAVES OF NOTTINGHAM

Nottingham stands on a plug of Sherwood sandstone riddled with man-made caves

dating back to medieval times. Rather surprisingly, the entrance to the most fascinating, readily accessible **caves** (☎ 924 1424; admission £3.75; 🕑 10am-5pm Mon-Sat, 11am-5pm Sun) is inside Broadmarsh shopping centre. These contain an air-raid shelter, a medieval underground tannery, several pub cellars and a mock-up of a Victorian slum dwelling.

THE TALES OF ROBIN HOOD

The **tales** (☎ 948 3284; www.robinhood.uk.com; 30-38 Maid Marian Way; adult/child £6.95/4.95; 🕑 10am-6pm May-Sep, 10am-5.30pm Oct-Apr) is a silly but fun ride through models of Nottingham Castle and Sherwood Forest in the days when Robin was battling it out with the sheriff. After the dramatized version, you can find out more about the reality behind the legend. Look out for events like falconry days and jester workshops.

WOLLATON HALL

Built in 1588 by Sir Francis Willoughby, land and coal-mine owner, **Wollaton Hall** (☎ 915 3900; Wollaton Park, Derby Rd; admission free weekdays, £1.50 Sat & Sun; 🕑 11am-5pm Apr-Oct, 11am-4pm Nov-Mar) is a fine example of Tudor architecture at its most extravagant. Architect Robert Smythson was also responsible for the equally avant-garde Longleat in Wessex (p238). The hall now houses a decent natural history museum.

The **Industrial Museum** (admission free weekdays, £1.50, or £2 for combined ticket Sat & Sun; 🕑 10am-5pm Apr-Oct), in the 18th-century stable block,

THE MIDLANDS

THE LEGEND OF ROBIN HOOD

In the Middle Ages most of Nottinghamshire was covered in forest, the stomping ground (legend has it) of Robin Hood and his merry men, who were trying to stymie the wicked Sheriff of Nottingham in the name of absentee 'good' King Richard I.

Sites associated with Robin abound. Nottingham Castle obviously played a key role, as did St Mary's Church in the Lace Market. Robin is said to have married Maid Marian in Edwinstowe church, while Fountaindale, near Blidworth, is the supposed site of his battle with Friar Tuck.

But did Robin ever really exist? As long ago as 1377 William Langland made fleeting reference to him in his poem *Piers Plowman*, but it was only in the early 16th century that the story began to be fleshed out, most notably in the ballad *A Geste of Robyn Hoode*. In 1795 Joseph Ritson collected all the known accounts of Robin into one volume, and since then innumerable authors (including Scott and Tennyson) have produced torrid novels and poems, while heart-throbs such as Errol Flynn, Kevin Costner and, um, Jason Connery have portrayed the robber-of-the-rich on silver and square screens.

Disappointingly, researchers have failed to turn up any hard evidence that the outlaw actually existed. He is, for example, said to have been born in Lockesley in Yorkshire or Nottinghamshire, but no such place appears on any map. Optimists point to a Loxley in Staffordshire where Hood's father supposedly owned land, and even the suburb of Loxley in Sheffield – a fragile link that means the new regional airport (Sheffield Doncaster Robin Hood) is named after the 'local' lad. But it's more likely that 'Robin' is no more than a jumbled memory of ancient ideas about forest fairies, or a character made up to give voice to medieval resentments.

displays lace-making equipment, Raleigh bicycles, a gigantic 1858 beam engine and oddities such as a locally invented, 1963 video recorder that never got off the ground.

Wollaton Hall is on the western edge of the city, 2½ miles from the centre; get there on bus No 35, 36 or 37. Wollaton Park, surrounding the hall, is a popular picnic spot.

BREWHOUSE YARD MUSEUM

Housed in five 17th-century cottages virtually below the castle, this **museum** (☎ 915 3600; Castle Blvd; admission free Mon-Fri, £1.50 Sat & Sun; ☼ 10am-4.30pm) recreates everyday life in Nottingham over the past 300 years with particularly fine reconstructions of traditional shops, and hosts good temporary exhibitions.

MUSEUM OF COSTUME & TEXTILES

Arranged in period rooms, this intriguing **museum** (☎ 915 3500; Castle Gate; admission free; ☼ 10am-4pm Wed-Sun & bank hols) displays costumes from 1790 to the mid–20th century, as well as tapestries and lace. Again, it's housed in a row of 17th- and 18th-century houses and is worth a look even if needlework isn't your bag.

GALLERIES OF JUSTICE

In the impressive Shire Hall building on High Pavement, the **Galleries of Justice** (☎ 952 0555; www.galleriesofjustice.org.uk; High Pavement; adult/child £6.95/5.25, £1 discount if booked at TIC; ☼ 10am-5pm Tue-Sun Apr-Oct, 10am-4pm Tue-Sun Nov-Mar) takes you through the history of the judicial system from medieval ordeals by water or hot iron to modern crime detection. You're guided through much of the action by 'jailers' and 'prisoners', and it's highly interactive: careful, you may find yourself sentenced to death in a Victorian courtroom!

Tours

The knowledgeable guides of the **Nottingham Experience** (☎ 911 5005; www.visitnottingham.com /tours.asp; 30 mins; tickets £4) whisk visitors from the castle gatehouse on a rapid tour of the city, recounting the stories behind the sights. Longer themed group tours are also available.

The **Original Nottingham Ghost Walk** (☎ 01773-769300; www.ghost-walks.co.uk; tickets £4; 7pm Sat Jan-Nov) departs from Ye Olde Salutation Inn (see Drinking, opposite) to explore the spooky underbelly of the city's past.

Festivals & Events

Events including a Shakespeare Festival and Robin Hood Pageant are held at the Nottingham Castle Museum & Art Gallery (p467); call for details.

Sleeping

Rutland Square Hotel (☎ 941 1114; rutlandsquare@zoff anyhotels.co.uk; St James St; s/d from £95/110) This central business-class hotel has style, good service and serious discounts at the weekend.

Lace Market Hotel (☎ 852 3232; reservations@ lacemarkethotel.co.uk; 29-31 High Pavement; s/d £89/99) A gorgeous old hotel in an atmospheric part of town, this exclusive boutique hotel sometimes offers reduced weekend rates.

Igloo Backpackers Hostel (☎ 947 5250; www .igloohostel.co.uk; 110 Mansfield Rd; dm £12, breakfast extra) A favourite of backpackers, this 36-bed independent hostel is a short walk north of Victoria bus station. The entrance is on Fulforth St.

Other good options:

Adams Castle View Guest House (☎ 950 0022; 85 Castle Blvd; s/d £25/45)

Castle Rock Guest House (☎ 948 2116; 79 Castle Blvd; d from £39) This and the Adams are small, basic places just below the castle.

Claremont (☎ 960 8587; 2 Hamilton Rd; s £32-38, d 45-55) North of the city.

Eating

The area around Carlton St to the east of the centre is the epicentre of eating (and drinking). Good news for vegetarians: choices now range from burgers to haute cuisine.

V1 (☎ 941 5121; www.v-1.co.uk; Hounds Gate; meals £3.90-4.90; ☽ breakfast, lunch & dinner Mon-Sat, noon-4pm Sun) This could be the future of fast food. It's just like any burger chain – fast, cheap and delicious – but without the meat.

Skinny Sumo (☎ 952 0188; 11-13 Carlton St; sushi platters from £8, rolls £1.50-3.50; ☽ lunch & dinner Tue-Sun) This inventively named restaurant has a sushi-bar conveyor belt and a variety of authentic Japanese dishes; look out for speciality nights (curry, noodles) during the week.

Punchinello (☎ 941 1965; 35 Forman St; mains £7.50-13; ☽ lunch & dinner) Allegedly Nottingham's oldest restaurant, this charming place has been pleasing diners with Med-influenced fare for decades.

Fresh (☎ 924 3336; 15 Goose Gate; dinner mains £9-12; ☽ 8am-5.30pm Mon & Tue, 8am-9pm Wed-Fri, 9am-9pm Sat) Bright and confident, Fresh serves world cuisine all day and good snacks at lunch, with tasty vegetarian and fish selections.

Other recommended eateries:

Broadway Cinema Cafébar (☎ 952 1551; 14-18 Broad St; specials £5.25; ☽ lunch & dinner) Soup and baguettes at lunch, drinks with hip sounds later.

La Tasca (☎ 959 9456; 9 Weekday Cross; tapas £2-4, paella £7.50-9.50; ☽ dinner) Grab a sangria and head to the upstairs cushions overlooking the Weekday Cross.

Mogal-e-Azam (☎ 947 3820; 7-9 Goldsmith St; mains £6-15; ☽ dinner) An acclaimed Indian restaurant.

Sonny's (☎ 947 3041; 3 Carlton St; mains £10-15.50; ☽ dinner) Has modern British dishes, and large windows to see and be seen.

Squeek (☎ 955 5560; 23-25 Heathcote St; mains £8.95; ☽ dinner Mon-Sat) Fabulous vegetarian and vegan cuisine.

Drinking

Ye Olde Trip to Jerusalem (☎ 947 3171; Brewhouse Yard, Castle Rd) Tucked into the cliff below the castle, this is one of England's best (and oldest) pubs; it supposedly slaked the thirst of Crusaders pre-departure. Inevitably, a fair number of tourists pop their heads in for a look, but there are enough nooks and crannies cut into the rock in the upstairs bar that the crowds generally don't interfere with the atmosphere.

Bell Inn (☎ 947 5241; 18 Angel Row) A favourite with locals, the ever-popular Bell is one of the few places right in the centre where you can get a decent beer and relax on a weekend night. Neither trendy nor quaint, it's just a great pub.

Ye Olde Salutation Inn (☎ 988 1948; Maid Marian Way) Near the Trip to Jerusalem in location, atmosphere and era, this is another comfortable, unpretentious oldie (c 1240).

Other good drinkeries include:

Fellows, Morton & Clayton (☎ 950 6795; 54 Canal St) An excellent brewpub overlooking the re-emergent canalside area of town.

Forest Tavern (☎ 947 5650; 257 Mansfield Rd) Good selection of Belgian beers, north of the city.

Lincolnshire Poacher (☎ 941 1584; 161-163 Mansfield Rd) A brilliant pub with well-kept beer.

Maze Club (270 North Sherwood St) Part of the Forest Tavern; a happening little place north of the city.

Old Angel Inn (☎ 950 2303; Woolpack Lane) A popular student pub.

Pitcher & Piano (☎ 958 6081; the Unitarian Church, High Pavement) It converts the faithful daily (and nightly).

Via Fossa (☎ 947 3904; Castle Wharf, 44 Canal St) Huge interior with off-the-wall furnishings and plenty of space outside.

Entertainment

NIGHTCLUBS

Sometimes it seems as if the whole of the Lace Market area is one huge, hyper-hip café-bar. They come and go, some are

THE MIDLANDS

cooler than others, but they tend to follow the same pattern: brown leather sofas for lounging, subdued lighting for smooching and smooth-talking, sleek food for feeding, an unspoken dress code and DJs for added cred.

Social (☎ 950 5078; 23 Pelham St) Sibling of the equally cool London joint, this standout place has DJs and live guests and is one of *the* places to be seen.

Cookie Club (☎ 950 5892; 22 St James St; ☽ Wed-Sat 11pm-2am) Just west of Market Sq, this is a friendly little club with alternative nights and fair prices. It's a nice reprieve from the prevailing brown-couch scene.

Rock City (☎ 941 2544; www.rock-city.co.uk; 8 Talbot St) The major live venue for bands, Rock City has popular indie, rock and student club nights.

Picking the best nightclubs is always risky, but the current cream are probably **Brass Monkey** (☎ 840 4101; 11 High Pavement) for cocktails till 1am, **Dogma** (☎ 988 6830; 9 Byard Lane) for its big basement space, and **Bluu** (☎ 950 5359; 5 Broadway; ☽ until midnight Sun-Tue, 1am Wed-Sat) for live bands, great food and a friendly vibe. Others worth checking out include:

Beatroot (☎ 924 0852; 6-8 Broadway) An old-timer that still packs 'em in with a mellow vibe.

Bomb (☎ 950 6667; 45 Bridlesmith Gate) Blink and you'll miss it.

Edge (☎ 910 6880; 1265 Lower Parliament St) Gets the gay crowd going with dirty house.

Loft (☎ 924 0213; 217 Mansfield Rd) Further from the scene.

Moog (☎ 841 3830; Newdigate St) Retro-chic styling and cutting-edge DJs, west of the city.

Old Vic (☎ 910 0009; www.justthetonic.com; Fletcher Gate; ☽ Sat & Sun) Hosts some of the best comedy nights in the Midlands.

THEATRE, CINEMA & CLASSICAL MUSIC

Cornerhouse (Forman St) Opposite the Theatre Royal, this is a spanking modern development that has everything you might (or might not) want: glitzy clubs, chain restaurants (including Wagamama, TGI Fridays and a host of themed eateries), bars and a 15-screen **Warner Village cinema** (☎ 0870 240 6020; www.warnervillage.co.uk).

Broadway Cinema (☎ 952 6611; www.broadway .org.uk; 14-18 Broad St) The Broadway is the city's art-house film centre.

Savoy (☎ 947 5812; 233 Derby Rd) This kid-friendly vintage cinema west of the city has double seats and allows an interval for ice-cream consumption.

Lakeside Arts Centre (☎ 846 7777; www.lakeside arts.org.uk; DH Lawrence Pavilion, University Park) A multi-purpose venue southwest of the city, this centre hosts films, classical music, comedy and dance.

Dedicated theatres include the **Arts Theatre** (☎ 947 6096; www.artstheatre.org.uk; George St) and the **Nottingham Playhouse** (☎ 941 9419; www.nottinghamplayhouse.co.uk; Wellington Circus), a respected venue outside of which sits *Sky Mirror*, a superb Anish Kapoor sculpture. For musicals, try the Royal Concert Hall and the Theatre Royal, which share a **booking office** (☎ 989 5555; www.royalcentre-nottingham .co.uk; Theatre Sq) and an imposing building close to the centre.

Getting There & Away

East Midlands Airport (☎ 01332-852852; www .eastmidlandsairport.com)

Dunn Line Buses (☎ 08700 121212)

Trent Buses (☎ 01773-712265; www.trentbuses.co.uk) Buses depart from Broadmarsh and Victoria bus stations.

Getting Around

For information on buses within Nottingham, call **Nottingham City Buses** (☎ 950 3665; www.nctx.co.uk). A Day Rider ticket gives you unlimited travel for £2.20.

A new tram system (www.thetram.net; single/all-day from 80p/£2) runs from Bulwell through the centre and Hockley to the train station.

Bunney's Bikes (☎ 947 2713; 97 Carrington St; bike hire per day from £8) is near the train station.

AROUND NOTTINGHAM
Newstead Abbey

With its attractive gardens, romantic lakeside ruins and notable connections with scoundrel poet Lord Byron (1788–1824), whose country pile it was, **Newstead Abbey** (☎ 01623-455900; www.newsteadabbey.org.uk; admission £5, gardens only £2.50; ☽ house noon-5pm Apr-Sep, garden 9am-dusk year-round) is a popular weekend destination for tourists and local families alike. Founded as an Augustinian priory around 1170, it was converted into a home after the dissolution of the monasteries in 1539. Beside the still-imposing façade of the priory church are the remains of the manor. It now houses some interesting Byron memorabilia – you can peek into his bedroom and toilet, which might have amused him – and Victorian paintings and furnishings in the extant chambers.

The house is 12 miles north of Nottingham, off the A60. The Sherwood Forester bus runs right there on summer Sundays. Bus Nos 737, 747 and 757 run from Nottingham (25 minutes, every 20 minutes, hourly on Sunday) to the abbey gates.

DH Lawrence Sites

The **DH Lawrence Birthplace Museum** (☎ 01773-717353; 8a Victoria St, Eastwood; admission free Mon-Fri, £2 Sat & Sun; ☒ 10am-5pm Apr-Oct, 10am-4pm Nov-Mar), former home of Nottingham's controversial author (1885–1930), has been reconstructed as it would have been in Lawrence's childhood, with period furnishings. Down the road, the **Durban House Heritage Centre** (☎ 01773-717353; Mansfield Rd; admission £2, or £3.50 for both; ☒ 10am-5pm Apr-Oct, 10am-4pm Nov-Mar) sheds light on the background to Lawrence's books by recreating the life of the mining community at the turn of the 20th century.

Eastwood is about 10 miles northwest of the city; take Trent Buses service No 1.

Sherwood Forest Country Park

Don't expect to lose yourself like an outlaw: there are more tourists than trees in today's Sherwood Forest, although there are still peaceful spots to be found. The **Sherwood Forest Visitor Centre** (☎ 01623-823 202; www.sherwood-forest.org.uk; admission free; ☒ 10.30am-5pm Apr-Oct, 10am-4.30pm Nov-Mar) houses 'Robyn Hode's Sherwode', a cute but corny exhibition describing the lifestyles of bandits, kings, peasants and friars in radical Rob's day. One of the major attractions is the Major Oak, which is supposed to have been a hiding place for Mr Hood; these days it's more likely he'd have to hold it up, not hide in it. The Robin Hood Festival is a massive medieval re-enactment that takes place every August.

Sherwood Forest YHA Hostel (☎ 0870 770 6026; sherwood@yha.org.uk; Forest Corner, Edwinstowe; dm £12.75) is a modern hostel with comfortable dorms just a short distance from the visitor centre.

Sherwood Forester buses run the 20 miles to the park from Nottingham on Sunday; catch bus No 33 from Nottingham Monday to Saturday.

SOUTHWELL
☎ 01636 / pop 6285

An archetypal sleepy market town bursting with tearooms and antique shops, Southwell is a key stop for another reason: **Southwell Minster** (☎ 812649; suggested donation £2; ☒ 8am-7pm May-Sep, 8am-dusk Oct-Apr) is a Gothic cathedral unlike any other in England, its two heavy, square front towers belying the treats within. The nave dates from the 12th century, although there is evidence of an earlier Saxon church floor, itself made with mosaics from a Roman villa. A highlight of the building is the chapterhouse, filled with incredible naturalistic 13th-century carvings of leaves, pigs, dogs and rabbits. The library is also a fascinating place, housing illuminated manuscripts and heavy tomes from the 16th century and earlier.

A visit to **Southwell Workhouse** (☎ 817250; Upton Rd; admission £4.40; ☒ noon-5pm Thu-Mon Mar-Oct, 11am-5pm Thu-Mon Aug) is a sobering but fascinating experience. An audio guide, narrated by 'inmates' and 'officials', describes the life of paupers in the mid–19th century to good (if grim) effect, despite the fact that most of the rooms are empty.

Bus Nos 101 and 201 run from Nottingham (40 minutes, every 20 minutes, hourly on Sunday) and on to Newark-on-Trent (25 minutes, hourly, every two hours on Sunday).

NEWARK-ON-TRENT
☎ 01636 / pop 35,454

Another market town with a pedigree rich in history, Newark-on-Trent was once an important place. Key evidence of that is the ruined **Newark Castle** (admission to gate £2, grounds free; ☒ until dusk), one of the few to hold out against Cromwell's men during the Civil War – only for Charles I to order surrender, condemning the building to rapid destruction. An impressive Norman gate remains, part of the structure in which King John died in 1216. Entry to the gate itself is by guided tour only; contact the TIC for details.

The town has a large, cobbled square overlooked by the fine, timber-framed 14th-century **Olde White Hart Inn** (now a building society) and the **Clinton Arms Hotel** (now a shopping mall), from where former prime minister Gladstone made his first political speech and where Lord Byron stayed while his first book of poems was published.

The **TIC** (☎ 655765; gilstrap@newark-sherwooddc
.gov.uk; Gilstrap Centre, Castlegate; ☺ 9am-6pm Apr-Sep,
9am-5pm Oct-Mar) houses a small display on the
town's history. Pick up the *Walkabout Tour*
leaflet and explore.

Gannets Daycafé (☎ 702066; 35 Castlegate; snacks
£2-5) scoops the lunchtime trade with good
coffee and cream teas. The modern cuisine
at **Café Bleu** (☎ 610141; 14 Castlegate; mains £9.50-14;
☺ lunch daily, dinner Mon-Sat) is not noticeably
French, but has an accomplished menu with
good seafood and fish options.

Bus Nos 91, 101 and 201 run to Nottingham (1¼ hours, hourly, every two hours
Sunday); No 91 also runs via Southwell (25
minutes).

DERBYSHIRE

Without doubt one of the prettiest parts
of England, Derbyshire consists of an instantly winning combination of rolling
green hills dotted with lambs and lined with
stone fences, beautiful wild moors, remote
windswept farms, and attractively greying
villages.

Part of the county is within the Peak District National Park, and for many visitors
the two areas are synonymous – although
the park overlaps several other counties,
and there are parts of Derbyshire beyond
the national park boundary that contain
many other attractions. There's the mis-
placed seaside resort of Matlock Bath, the
twisted spire of Chesterfield cathedral, and
some wonderful stately homes – including
dishevelled Calke Abbey and unforgettable
Chatsworth.

Derbyshire is one of the most visited
counties in England, and justifiably so.

Activities

Outdoor activities in Derbyshire include
walking, cycling, rock climbing, caving
and paragliding, to name but a few. Many
take place inside the Peak District National
Park, and are covered under the Activities
heading in that section (p478).

Getting There & Around

Derbyshire Wayfarer (☎ 0870 608 2608, Traveline;
www.derbysbus.net; day pass adult/family £7.50/12) Covers
buses and trains throughout the county and beyond (eg to
Manchester and Sheffield)

Trent Buses (☎ 01773-712265; www.trentbuses.co.uk;
day ticket £3.50) Award-winning operator of the TransPeak
bus service.

DERBY

☎ 01332 / pop 236,738

The Industrial Revolution made a major
manufacturing centre out of this once sedate market town. Its fortunes were made
first by silk, then china, then railways, and
finally Rolls-Royce aircraft engines. It may
not invite several days' worth of lingering,
but it's a good place to visit for insight into
the historical side of English engineering,
and fans of bone china will enjoy a tour of
the Royal Crown Derby factory.

Orientation & Information

Central Derby has a fairly standard pedestrianised shopping core and an attractive old-town district. A partly cobbled
thorough-fare called Irongate, with a few
good pubs and cafés, leads to the cathedral.
Off Irongate branch a couple of narrow old
streets with several good options for eating and drinking (caffeine or something
stronger), and some of Derby's more interesting shops selling books, CDs, surf gear,
jewellery and designer clothes.

There's little in Derby to warrant an overnight stay, but the **TIC** (☎ 255802; Market Pl) can
help with accommodation.

Sights

Derby's grand 18th-century **cathedral** (Queen
St) boasts a 64m-high tower and magnificent
wrought-iron screens. A recent construction (for an English cathedral), it has an
unusual interior of creamy white plasterwork and large windows that give it a light,
airy feel. Among the many memorials, you
can't miss the huge tomb of Bess of Hardwick – one of Derbyshire's most formidable residents in days gone by; for more
about her, see Hardwick Hall (p477).

From the cathedral, stroll down the wonderfully named Amen Alley, and cross the
road to see the statue of **Bonnie Prince Charlie**;
he got this far from Scotland in the Jacobite
Rebellion of 1745. A cannon left by his troops
can still be seen at Kedleston Hall (opposite).

Next to the River Derwent, in a former
Silk Mill, **Derby Industrial Museum** (☎ 255308; Silk
Mill Lane; admission free; ☺ 11am-5pm Mon, 10am-5pm
Tue-Sat, 2-5pm Sun & bank hols) tells the city's manu-

THE MIDLANDS

facturing history; if you're into trains or, even better, aero-engines, this is heaven.

The factory of **Royal Crown Derby** (☎ 712841; Osmaston Rd; ⏱ 9am-5pm Mon-Sat, 10am-4pm Sun; tours £4.95, four daily Mon-Fri) turns out some of the finest bone china in England. There's no charge to visit the demonstration area to see workers skilfully make delicate china flowers, using little more than a hat-pin, spoon handle and – naturally – a head-lice comb. There's also a shop, piled high with teapots, collectable paperweights and various bargains (watch your elbows!), and a café. For the full inside view, the factory tour is fascinating even if china isn't your cup of tea; you'll see the entire process, from vats of raw powder and bone-mix through to the final touches of liquid gold decoration.

Eating & Drinking

Near the cathedral there's the traditional and intimate (OK, cramped) **Ye Olde Dolphin Inne** (Queen St; snacks & meals £2-5), with four little bars and good pub grub. Nearby, the **Silk Mill** (Full St; meals £3-8) is a roomier pub, while **Vida** (Queen St; mains £4-6) is a small café-bar with a good view of the cathedral.

Derby's best pubs are near the train station. The justifiably award-winning **Brunswick Inn** (Railway Tce) is worth a journey, with first-class beer (some brewed on site), and good, no-nonsense food; it's simultaneously crisply modern and appealingly old-fashioned, with blonde wood in one room and finely carved wooden wall panels in another.

Nearby, the **Alexandria Hotel** (Siddals Rd) is similarly excellent but with more energy and buzz, and continues the railway theme, with numerous loco-photos and a tongue-in-cheek 'no train spotters' sign at the door. The **Victoria Inn** (Midland Pl), directly across from the station, has all-ages live punk shows several nights a week.

Getting There & Away

TransPeak buses run every two hours between Nottingham and Manchester, via Derby, Matlock, Bakewell and Buxton (Derby to Nottingham 30 minutes, Derby to Bakewell one hour). The train station is southwest of the centre. From London, there are trains to Derby (two hours, about hourly), continuing to Chesterfield, Sheffield and Leeds.

AROUND DERBY
Kedleston Hall

Sitting proudly in vast landscaped parkland, the superb neoclassical mansion of **Kedleston Hall** (☎ 01332-842191; admission £5.80; ⏱ noon-4pm Sat-Wed Easter-Oct) is a must for fans of stately homes. The Curzon family has lived here since the 12th century; Sir Nathaniel Curzon tore down an earlier house in 1758 so this stunning masterpiece could be built. Meanwhile, the poor old peasants in Kedleston village had their humble dwellings moved a mile down the road, as they interfered with the view! Ah, the good old days…

Entering the house through a grand portico you reach the breathtaking Marble Hall, with its massive alabaster columns and statues of Greek deities. Curved corridors on either side offer splendid views of the park – don't miss the arc of floorboards, specially cut from bending oak boughs. Other highlights include richly decorated bedrooms and a circular saloon with a domed roof, modelled on the Pantheon in Rome. Things came full circle when another great building, Government House in Calcutta (now Raj Bhavan), was modelled on Kedleston Hall, as a later Lord Curzon was viceroy of India around 1900. His collection of oriental artefacts is on show, as is his wife's 'peacock' dress – made of gold and silver thread and weighing 5kg.

Kedleston Hall is 5 miles northwest of Derby. By bus, service No 109 between Derby and Ashbourne goes within about 1½ miles of Kedleston Hall (20 minutes, seven daily Monday to Saturday, five on Sunday), and on sunny days walking the rest is no hardship. On Sundays and bank holidays the bus loops right up to the house.

Calke Abbey

Looking like an enormous, long-neglected cabinet of wonders, **Calke Abbey** (☎ 01332-863822; admission £5.90; ⏱ 1-5.30pm Sat-Wed Apr-Oct) is not your usual glitzy, wealth-encrusted stately home. Built around 1703, it's been passed down among a dynasty of eccentric and reclusive baronets, so very little has changed – especially since about 1880. The result is a ramshackle maze of rooms crammed with ancient furniture, heaps of mounted animal heads, random stacks of dusty books, thousands of stuffed birds and

THE MIDLANDS

endless piles of bric-a-brac from the last three centuries. Some rooms are in fabulous condition, while others are deliberately untouched, complete with crumbling plaster and mouldy wallpaper. (You exit the house via a long, dark tunnel – a bit more thrilling than one might like, given the state of the buildings.) A stroll round the gardens is a similar time-warp experience – in the potting sheds nothing has changed since about 1930, but it looks like the gardener left only yesterday.

Admission to Calke Abbey house is by timed ticket. On summer weekends it's wise to phone ahead and check there'll be space. You can enter the gardens and grounds at any time. Calke is 10 miles south of Derby. Visitors coming by car must enter via the village of Ticknall. Bus Nos 68 and 69 from Derby to Swadlincote stop at Ticknall (40 minutes, hourly) and from there it's a 2-mile walk through the park.

Ashbourne

The thriving little market town of Ashbourne is about 15 miles northwest of Derby, on the road towards Buxton, at the very southern tip of the Peak District National Park. Fine old buildings from ages past line the marketplace and the precariously slanted main street; a great many are now antique and art shops drawing crowds of eager browsers at weekends. (Things get even busier once a year when the game of Shrovetide Football is rigorously pursued – see the boxed text below.)

The **TIC** (☎ 01335-343666; Market Pl; ☼ 9.30am-5pm Mon-Sat, 10am-4pm Sun) can provide leaflets or advice on B&Bs in the area. Of Ashbourne's many central pubs and teashops, our favourites include the **Gingerbread Shop** (St John's St), a bakery and tearoom in a half-timbered building (Ashbourne is famous for its gingerbread); **Smith's Tavern** (St John's St), a popular pub with traditional ambience, and good food and beer; and the **Horns** (Victoria Sq), another fine old pub, with outdoor seating on the square for when the sun shines.

Of particular interest to walkers and cyclists, Ashbourne is the southern terminus of the **Tissington Trail**, a former railway line and now a wonderful easy-gradient path cutting through fine west Derbyshire countryside. The Tissington Trail takes you north towards Buxton and connects with the High Peak Trail running south towards Matlock Bath – for more details on circular route possibilities see Activities in the Peak District National Park section (p478). About a mile outside town along Mapleton Lane, **Ashbourne Cycle Hire** (☎ 01335-343156) is

---

ANCIENT CUSTOMS

Shrove Tuesday comes before Ash Wednesday, the first day of Lent – the Christian time of fasting – so Shrove Tuesday is the day to use up all your rich and fattening food. This led to the quaint tradition of Pancake Day in England and the rather less staid Mardi Gras festival elsewhere in the world.

On Shrove Tuesday, various English towns celebrate with pancake races, but in Ashbourne they go for something much more energetic. Here they play Shrovetide Football – but it's nothing like the football most people are used to. For a start, the goals are 3 miles apart, the 'pitch' is a huge patch of countryside, and the game lasts all afternoon and evening (then starts again the day after). There are two teams, but hundreds of participants, and very few rules indeed. A large leather ball is fought over voraciously as players maul their way through fields and gardens, along the river, and up the main street – where shop windows are specially boarded over for the occasion. Visitors come from far and wide to watch, but only the brave should take part!

About 8 miles up the road from Ashbourne, in the Staffordshire village of Wetton, another 'traditional' event takes place on an early weekend each June – the World Toe Wrestling Championship. It started in 1976, when talk at Ye Olde Royal Oak Inn turned to sport. Depressed at England's inability to dominate in any global event, regulars decided to invent a sport that the home country would always win (because nobody else knew about it). One year later a random Canadian strolled in and beat the local champion. Game over. Resurrected in 1990, the annual event now pulls in hefty crowds (and serious money for charity), with men and women sitting on a 'toedium' attempting to force their opponent's toe onto the side of the 'toesrack'.

on the Tissington Trail, with a huge stock of bikes and trailers for all ages, and free leaflets showing the route with pubs and teashops along the way.

To get to Ashbourne by bus, there are numerous services from Derby; the trip takes about 30 to 45 minutes. Direct buses include No 107 (hourly Monday to Saturday), No 111 (three per day on Sunday and bank holidays), and No X1 (five daily Monday to Friday, four daily Saturday and Sunday), which continues to Manchester.

Dovedale

About 3 miles northwest of Ashbourne the River Dove winds through the steep-sided valley of Dovedale. It's one of the most accessible ways to sample the beauty of Derbyshire, so it can get crowded on summer weekends – especially near the famous Stepping Stones that cross the river – but the crowds thin out as you go further up, and midweek it's a lovely place for a walk.

The quaint *Dovedale Guide* (£1.25), available from Ashbourne's TIC, has more background and a map showing footpaths. Romantic Victorian travellers went on outings to Dovedale, bestowing fanciful names on the natural features, so today we can admire hills and rocky buttresses called Thorpe Cloud, Dovedale Castle, Lovers' Leap, the Twelve Apostles, Tissington Spires, Reynard's Kitchen and Lion Head Rock. Another early visitor was Izaak Walton, the 17th-century fisherman and author of *The Compleat Angler*. The **Izaak Walton Hotel** at the southern end of Dovedale is named in his honour, and the public bar and pretty garden here make it well worth a stop for after-walk refreshment.

MATLOCK BATH

☎ 01629 / pop 2202

An unashamedly brash and delightfully tacky little place, Matlock Bath is like a lost seaside resort, complete with a promenade of amusement arcades, an aquarium, cafés, pubs and souvenir shops – some with stock that seems left over since Victorian times. Roughly in the centre of Derbyshire, on the southeastern edge of the Peak District National Park, it sits next to the pleasant town of Matlock, which has little in the way of sights but is a handy gateway to the scenic dales on this side of the park.

Every weekend – and through the summer months – diverse groups come here from miles around, and there's a totally no-frills buzz about the place. At weekends, Matlock Bath is also especially popular with motorcyclists (the A6 is an irresistibly smooth, twisty road), so the buzz is sometimes a roar, but the throb of engines and parading leather-clad enthusiasts only adds to the general good-time atmosphere.

Orientation & Information

Matlock Bath is 2 miles south of Matlock. Everything revolves around North Pde and South Pde, a line of seaside-style shops, attractions and eateries along one side of the main road through town (the A6), with the River Derwent on the other side, standing in for the sea.

Matlock Bath's **TIC** (☎ 01629-55082; www.derbyshire.gov.uk; the Pavilion; ◷ 9.30am-5pm daily Mar-Oct, Sat & Sun Nov-Feb) has friendly staff and plenty of leaflets and local guidebooks.

Sights & Activities

Item one on the agenda: buy some chips or candyfloss and just stroll around. Then cross the river to stroll some more in the park on the other side, where some steep paths lead to great cliff-top viewpoints.

At the **Mining Museum** (☎ 583834; the Pavilion; admission £3; ◷ 10am-5pm), part of which, oddly enough, is a former dancehall, you can clamber through shafts and tunnels, and for £1.50 extra go down **Temple Mine** and try panning for 'gold'.

For a different view, go to the **Heights of Abraham** (☎ 582365; adult/child £8.50/5.50; ◷ 10am-5pm daily Mar-Oct, Sat & Sun Feb-Mar), a wholesome family attraction with underground caverns, an adventure playground, woodland nature trails and an audiovisual show. The price includes a spectacular cable-car ride up from the valley floor.

Near the cable-car base, **Whistlestop Centre** (admission free; ◷ 10am-5pm daily Apr-Oct, Sat & Sun Nov-Mar), at the old train station, has wildlife and natural garden exhibits, and children's activities in the summer.

From the cable-car base, walking trails lead up to airy viewpoints on top of **High Tor**; you can see down to Matlock Bath and over to **Riber Castle**, a Victorian folly.

Gulliver's Kingdom (☎ 01925-444888; admission £8.30; ◷ 10am-5pm late May–early Sep, weekends & hols

Oct-Apr) is a junior theme park. Kids aged four to 10 will like it, while mum and dad can grimace at the junk food they consume and the detritus others leave behind.

A mile south of Matlock Bath is **Masson Mill** (☎ 581001; admission £2.50; ☿ 10am-4pm Mon-Sat, 11am-4pm Sun), built in 1783 for pioneering industrialist Sir Richard Arkwright and acknowledged as a masterpiece of the era. Today it's a working museum, with renovated looms and weaving machines, and the world's largest collection of bobbins. If that's not draw enough, the attached 'shopping village' (three floors of High Street textile and clothing names) might pull you in.

From late August to October, don't miss the **Matlock Illuminations** (Pavilion Gardens; evenings from dusk Fri-Sun), with endless streams of pretty lights and outrageously decorated boats on the river, and occasional firework displays.

Sleeping

Matlock Bath has several B&Bs in the heart of things on North Pde and South Pde, and a few places just out of the centre. There are also more choices in nearby Matlock.

Hodgkinson's Hotel & Restaurant (☎ 582170; www.hodgkinsons-hotel.co.uk; 150 South Pde; s £38, d £68-88; P) More of a wonder cabinet than an ordinary hotel, this towering place has bizarrely shaped rooms, showers tucked into cupboards and stuffed animals glowering out from under antique chairs. The warmly Victorian décor and welcoming staff make it instantly cosy.

Temple Hotel (☎ 583911; Temple Rd; s/d £47/80; P) With its slightly dated seaside guest-

house feel – perfect for Matlock Bath – this hillside hotel makes a nice perch from which to gaze at the surroundings. The downstairs bar does good beer and pub food.

Sunnybank Guesthouse (☎ 584621; Clifton Rd; per person from £23; P) is a friendly little B&B on a quiet road just outside Matlock Bath. **Matlock YHA Hostel** (☎ 0870 770 5960; matlock@yha.org .uk; 40 Bank Rd; dm £11, r from £39) is a big, efficient housing block 2 miles from Matlock Bath.

Eating & Drinking

North Pde and South Pde are lined end-to-end with cafés, teashops and takeaways, all serving standards like chocolate cake, fish and chips, fried chicken, pies, and burgers – hear those arteries scream!

Of the pubs, the **Princess Victoria** (South Pde) is lively, the **County & Station** (Dale Rd) is relatively quiet, and the **Fishpond** (South Pde) has great live music and a patio showcasing the biker parade. On the hillside, the bar at the Temple Hotel (see Sleeping) does good pub food, and the terrace outside is a great place to watch the firework displays that tie in with the Matlock Illuminations (late August to October).

Getting There & Away

The Peak District is extremely well-served by public transport, and Matlock is a hub. Bus Nos 210, 213 or 214 go to and from Sheffield several times a day. There are hourly buses to and from Derby (1¼ hours) and Chesterfield (35 minutes). Several trains a day serve Derby (30 minutes). For detailed travel planning information, go to www.derbysbus.net.

THE DERWENT NATIONAL HERITAGE CORRIDOR

Flowing through the heart of Derbyshire, the River Derwent is not the best known of England's rivers, but it has a vitally important place in English history. Textile mills established here to exploit water power in the 18th century were a pivotal kick-start for the Industrial Revolution, which eventually made England a world power in Victorian times. Do you remember learning about Hargreave's 'spinning jenny' and Arkwright's 'water frame' in school history lessons? These machines transformed manufacturing processes across the world, but the humble Derwent Valley is where they came from.

Many mills are preserved as fascinating museums and visitor centres, and the Derwent Valley is home to numerous historical villages, wildlife sites and tourist attractions – from the high hills of the Pennines to the industrial city of Derby. The whole lot has been rolled into a bundle called the National Heritage Corridor, and in 2001 the section from Matlock Bath to Derby was declared a World Heritage Site by Unesco. Whatever your interest, a day or two here is bound to be rewarding.

A small selection of things to see includes the **Derwent Reservoirs** (p487), **Chatsworth** (p491), **Matlock** (p475), **Matlock Bath** (p475) and **Derby** (p472). For more information, you can get leaflets from local TICs.

AROUND MATLOCK BATH

From just outside Matlock town centre, about 2½ miles from Matlock Bath, steam trains and scenic railcars trundle along **Peak Rail** (☎ 01629-580381; www.peakrail.co.uk; adult/child return £6/4; 9 services daily Sat & Sun, Sun only Nov-Mar, extra weekday services Jun-Sep) via stops at Darley Dale to the northern terminus near the village of Rowsley. For train buffs and families it's a great ride.

From Rowsley train station a riverside path leads to **Caudwell's Mill** (adult/child £3/1; 10am-6pm Mar-Oct, Sat & Sun Nov-Feb), a huge and fascinating flour mill, full of working belts, shafts and other machinery – some almost a century old. There's a tearoom here, several craft-workers, and a shop selling gifts and...flour. You can also reach Rowsley direct from Matlock by bus, as it's on the road to Bakewell.

CHESTERFIELD

☎ 01246 / pop 100,879

The 'capital' of northeast Derbyshire, Chesterfield is best known for the remarkable crooked spire of **St Mary & All Saints Church** that overlooks the town. Dating from 1360, the spire twists and leans like something dreamed up by goth filmmaker Tim Burton. It's a giant corkscrew 68m high and 3m out of true – and no-one is really sure why.

The church can be visited at any time, but if you want to go inside the spire, **tours** (£2.50) are available most days; just ask the verger if he's got time to show you around.

Next to the church you'll find Chesterfield's **Museum & Art Gallery** (St Mary's Gate; admission free; 10am-4pm Mon-Tue & Thu-Sat). Pride of place goes to a huge medieval winding wheel that was used to build the famous spire long before the days of tower-cranes, while a builder's mug that sat forgotten on a beam for 250 years is a reminder of the human touch.

It's worth linking a visit to the large and lively **market** (High St) held every Monday, Friday and Saturday (as it has been since the 12th century). Thursday sees a huge flea market of antiques and oddities. The **TIC** (☎ 345777; Low Pavement) is nearby.

The easiest way to get here is by train; Chesterfield is between Nottingham/Derby (20 minutes) and Sheffield (10 minutes), with services about hourly.

CHESTERFIELD'S CROOKED SPIRE

Why is the church spire at Chesterfield twisted and bent? Reasons given for this ecclesiastical anomaly include the following: it's because the devil once flew by and got his tail caught; it's because a virgin once got married here and the spire was so surprised it bent down to have a look; it's because many craftsmen were killed off by the Black Death, and cowboy builders did the job; it's because heavy lead tiles were fixed over a poorly seasoned timber frame. Whatever the real reason, the people of Chesterfield prefer version two, and say that when another virgin gets married here, the spire will straighten up again.

AROUND CHESTERFIELD
Hardwick

If you're weighing up which stately homes to see, **Hardwick Hall** (☎ 01246-850430; admission £6.80; noon-4.30pm Wed-Thu & Sat & Sun Apr-Oct) should be high on your list. It was home to the 16th century's second most famous woman, Elizabeth, countess of Shrewsbury – known to all as Bess of Hardwick. Unashamedly modelling herself on the era's *most* famous woman – Queen Elizabeth I – Bess gained power and wealth by marrying four times, upwards each time.

When her fourth husband died in 1590, Bess had a huge fortune to play with, and built Hardwick Hall with the very best designs of the time. Glass was a status symbol, so she went all-out on the windows, and a contemporary ditty quipped 'Hardwick Hall – more glass than wall.' Also astounding are the magnificent High Great Chamber and Long Gallery; these and many other rooms and broad stairways are decorated with fabulous large and detailed tapestries.

This place is special because after Bess died her descendants rarely used Hardwick Hall, and over the centuries it escaped the modernisation that befell many other grand houses. The interior may not be as immediately sparkling as in some other stately homes, but what you see is truly Elizabethan.

Next door is **Hardwick Old Hall** (admission £3, joint ticket £9.20; 11am-6pm Mon, Wed, Thu, Sat & Sun Apr-Sep, 11am-5pm Mon, Wed, Thu, Sat & Sun Oct), Bess's first house, now a romantic ruin.

THE MIDLANDS

Also fascinating are the formal gardens, again virtually unchanged for centuries, and around the hall spreads the great expanse of **Hardwick Park** with short and long walking trails leading across fields and through woods. Pick up a (free) map at the ticket office. A point to aim for is the **Hardwick Inn**, which has a great sunny patio and does good pub food. You can also bring a picnic. All in all it's a great day out.

Hardwick Hall is 10 miles southeast of Chesterfield, just off the M1. A special historic coach runs from Chesterfield (Sunday only June to August, tickets £5, with half-price entry at Hardwick), out in the morning, back in the afternoon, giving about three hours at Hardwick. The bus also passes **Stainsby Mill** – a quaint working flour-mill dating from 1245 – and ends at **Bolsover Castle**, yet another stately home. For details, contact the Chesterfield TIC, or see www.cosycoach.co.uk.

PEAK DISTRICT

The Peak District National Park features some of England's wildest, most beautiful scenery – pretty villages, historic sites, grand houses, fascinating limestone caves and the southernmost hills of the Pennines. Called the Peak not because of the hills, which are quite rounded, but because early British tribe the Picts once lived here, this is one of the country's best-loved national parks. (It's the busiest in Europe, and the second busiest in the world after Mount Fuji.) But don't be put off by its popularity: escaping the crowds is no problem if you avoid summer weekends, and even then, with a bit of imagination, it's easy to enjoy this wonderful area in relative peace and solitude.

Orientation & Information

The Peak District is principally in Derbyshire but spills into five adjoining counties (including Yorkshire, Staffordshire and Cheshire) and is one of the largest national parks in England. This 555-sq-mile protected area is divided into two distinct zones: the harsher, higher, wilder Dark Peak to the north, characterised by peaty moors and dramatic gritstone cliffs called 'edges'; and the lower, prettier, more pastoral White Peak to the south, with green fields marked by dry-stone walls, and divided by deep dales.

There are TICs (those run by the national park are called visitor centres) in Buxton, Bakewell, Castleton, Edale and other locations, all overflowing with maps, guidebooks and leaflets detailing walks, cycle rides and other ideas to keep you occupied. For general information, the free *Peak District* newspaper and the official park website at www.peakdistrict.org cover transport, activities, local events, guided walks and so on.

Activities
CAVING & CLIMBING

The Peak District limestone is riddled with caves and caverns – including 'showcaves' open to the public in Castleton, Buxton and Matlock Bath (described in each of those sections). For serious caving (or pot-holing) trips, TICs can provide a list of accredited outdoor centres, and if you know what you're doing, Castleton makes a great base.

For guidebooks, gear (to buy or hire) and a mine of local information, contact **Hitch n Hike** (☎ 01433-651013; www.hitchnhike.co.uk; Mytham Bridge, North Bamford, Hope Valley, Derbyshire), a specialist caving and outdoor activity shop in Bamford, near Castleton. The website also has more info about caving in the area.

WELL-DRESSED DERBYSHIRE

The tradition of 'dressing' (decorating) wells or springs in thanksgiving for a good supply of water is unique to the county of Derbyshire and probably dates from Celtic times. Each year between May and September about 60 village wells are dressed with large and intricate mosaics of flower petals and leaves depicting scenes from the Bible, local history or events, or more modern issues such as rainforest protection. The event often includes a church service, or a village carnival with displays such as country dancing. Over the centuries many Derbyshire villages have become mining towns or even city suburbs, but the festival still takes place. June and July are the main months, and each village's well (or wells) is dressed for a week only. Pick up a *Well Dressing* leaflet in any TIC in Derbyshire for dates and locations.

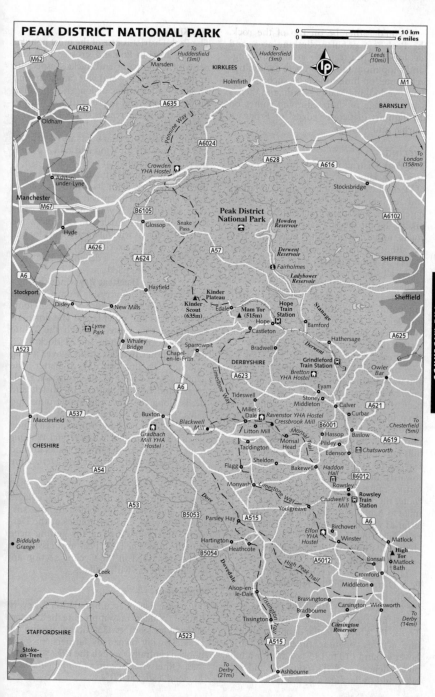

PEAK DISTRICT NATIONAL PARK

If you'd rather be on top of the rock, the Peak is a popular climbing area, and has long been a training ground for England's top mountaineers. There are multipitch routes on limestone faces such as High Tor, overlooking Matlock Bath, and there's a great range of short climbing routes on the famous gritstone 'edges' of Froggatt, Curbar and Stanage.

CYCLING

The Peak District is a very popular cycling area, especially the White Peak and the parts of Derbyshire south of here around Matlock and Ashbourne, which have a network of quiet lanes, and many tracks for mountainbikers. In the Dark Peak there are fewer roads, and they are quite busy with traffic, although there are some good off-road routes. A good place to start any ride is a TIC – all stock maps, books and leaflets for cyclists and mountain-bikers.

In the Dark Peak, Edale is a popular starting point for mountain bikers, and near the Derwent Reservoirs is also good. In the White Peak, all the villages mentioned in this section make good bases for cycle tours.

For easy traffic-free riding, head for the 17½-mile **High Peak Trail**, a route for cyclists and walkers on the mostly flat track of an old railway. You can join the trail at Cromford, near Matlock Bath, but it starts with a very steep incline, so if you seek easy gradients a better start is Middleton Top, a mile or so north. The trail winds beautifully through hills and farmland to a village called Parsley Hay, and continues on for a few more miles towards Buxton. At Parsley Hay another former-railway-turned-walking-and-cycling-route, the **Tissington Trail**, heads south for 13 miles to Ashbourne. You can go out and back as far as you like, or make it a triangular circuit, following the busy B5053 or (a better choice) the quiet lanes through Bradbourne and Brassington.

There are several cycle hire centres in the Peak District, including **Fairholmes** (☎ 01433-651261), for the Derwent area, and **Parsley Hay** (☎ 01298-84493) and **Middleton Top** (☎ 01629-823204) for the Tissington and High Peak Trails. TICs have a leaflet detailing all other hire centres, opening times etc. Charges hover around £10 to £15 per day for adults' bikes (deposit and ID required), and kids' bikes and trailers are also available.

WALKING

The Peak District is one of the most popular walking areas in England, crossed by a vast network of footpaths and tracks – especially in the White Peak – and you can easily find a walk of a few miles or longer, depending on your energy and interests. If you want to explore the higher realms of the Dark Peak, which often involves the local art of 'bog trotting', make sure your boots are waterproof and be prepared for wind and rain – even if the sun is shining when you set off.

The Peak's most famous walking trail is the **Pennine Way**, with its southern end at Edale and its northern end over 250 miles away in Scotland. If you don't have a spare three weeks, from Edale you can follow the trail north across wild hills and moors for just a day or two. An excellent three-day option is to Hebden Bridge – a delightful little town in Yorkshire (see p560).

The 46-mile **Limestone Way** winds through the Derbyshire countryside from Castleton to Rocester in Staffordshire on a mix of footpaths, tracks and quiet lanes. The northern section of this route, through the White Peak between Castleton and Matlock, is 26 miles, and hardy folk can do it over a long summer day, but two days is better. The route goes via Miller's Dale, Monyash, Youlgreave and Bonsall, with YHA hostels and B&Bs along the way, and ample pubs and cafés. TICs have a detailed leaflet.

The YHA in Derbyshire produces a handy set of leaflets entitled *Youth Hostel Walking Routes* (20p each) describing walks around and between Peak District and Derbyshire hostels.

Various shorter walks are described throughout this section. All the villages make good bases for exploring the surrounding area, and Fairholmes at the Derwent Reservoirs is great for getting deep into the hills. The High Peak and Tissington Trails described in the Cycling section are equally popular with walkers.

Sleeping

TICs have lists of accommodation for every budget. Walkers may appreciate the 13 **camping barns** (per person from £3.50) dotted around the Peak. Usually owned by farmers, they are booked centrally through the **YHA** (☎ 0870 870 8808). Otherwise, pick up a *Camping Barns in England* leaflet at TICs.

SOMETHING SPECIAL

One doesn't expect to find a posh gourmet restaurant out in the middle of nowhere, but that's exactly what you get at the **Druid Inn** (☎ 01629-650302; www.druidinnbirchover .co.uk; Main St, Birchover; mains £8-14; ☻ lunch & dinner Tue-Sun). Built in 1846 and renovated in 2004, the restaurant is worth a trip for its setting alone, perched on a wooded Peak District hill along a tiny, secluded road in the scattering of stone buildings that is Birchover. And then there's the food: halibut steak with lemon-lime gooseberry sauce, beef and venison casserole with orange and sherry, roast whole pheasant with port and redcurrant sauce…it keeps going like that. The wine list is impressive, and the atmosphere overall is remarkably sophisticated.

The village of Birchover is about 5 miles south of Bakewell along the B5056.

Getting There & Around

The Peak District authorities are trying hard to wean visitors off their cars, and TICs stock the excellent *Peak District Timetable* (60p) covering local buses and trains. For more details, see p472.

BUXTON
☎ 01298 / pop 20,836

With its grand Georgian architecture, leafy parks and busy tourist ambience, Buxton is frequently compared to Bath, and just like Bath, Buxton also has a natural warm-water spring discovered by the Romans. The town's heyday was in the 18th century when 'taking the waters' was highly fashionable. It may not be as pristine as its sister city, but in the past couple of years a batch of restoration projects have brought the gleam back to Buxton. Away from the historical sights, it's just like many other north-country market towns, although none the worse for that.

Every Tuesday and Saturday, Market Pl is full of colourful stalls and has a great atmosphere. Around town, there's also a vast selection of shops selling crafts, books and antiques, perfect for a day of idle browsing.

Situated just outside the border of the Peak District National Park, Buxton makes a handy gateway for the northern and western areas.

Orientation & Information

Buxton has two centres: the historical area, with the Crescent, Opera House and Pavilion; and Market Pl, surrounded by pubs and restaurants. There are several banks with ATMs on the Quadrant.

Northwest Computers (11 Bridge St; ☻ 9am-5pm Mon-Sat; Internet access per hr 50p)

Post office (Spring Gardens; ☻ 9am-6pm Mon-Fri, 9am-3pm Sat)

TIC (☎ 25106; www.peakdistrict-tourism.gov.uk; the Crescent) Sells useful leaflets on walks in the area.

Sights & Activities

There's scarcely a more inviting place in the land for puttin' on the ritz than Buxton's gorgeously restored **Opera House** (☎ 0845-127 2190; www.buxton-opera.co.uk; tours £2). This jewel of a building is the centre for Buxton's famous Opera Festival (held every July, and the largest of its kind in England), but for the rest of the year it enjoys a full programme of drama, dance, concerts and comedy. Tours of the auditorium and backstage areas are available at 11am most Saturday mornings.

Next to the Opera House is the **Pavilion**, a giant palace of glass built in 1871, which overlooks **Pavilion Gardens** – a pleasant park with lawns, ponds and a miniature train. **Broad Walk** is a traffic-free road alongside the edge of the gardens, ideal for an evening perambulation.

Perhaps Buxton's grandest construction is the **Crescent**, a graceful curve of houses modelled on the Royal Crescent in Bath. Just east of here is **Cavendish Arcade**, formerly a thermal bathhouse (you can still see the chair used for lowering the infirm into the restorative waters) with several craft and book shops, and a striking coloured-glass ceiling.

On the other side of the Crescent, the TIC is in the old **Natural Mineral Baths**, where you can still see the source of the mineral water – now Buxton's most famous export. A small display tells the full story.

Across from the TIC, the **Pump Room**, which dispensed Buxton's spring water for nearly a century, now hosts temporary art exhibitions. Just outside is **St Ann's Well**, a fountain where you can fill up on free mineral water.

Opposite the Crescent, a small park called the **Slopes** rises steeply in a series of grassy terraces. From the top there are views over the centre and across to the grand old **Palace Hotel** and the **Devonshire Hospital**, Buxton's

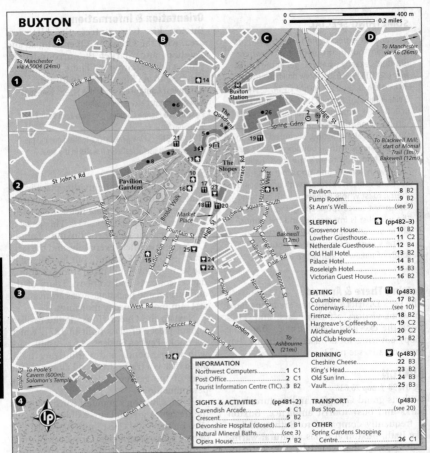

BUXTON

To Manchester via A5004 (24mi)

To Manchester via A6 (26mi)

Devonshire Rd

Park Rd

The Quadrant

Buxton Station

Bridge St

Spring Gdns

To Blackwell Mill, start of Monsal Trail (3mi); Bakewell (12mi)

St John's Rd

Pavilion Gardens

The Slopes

Terrace Rd

Market Place

Broad Walk

Fountain St

High St

Hardwick Square West

Hardwick St

Hardwick Square South

South Ave

To Bakewell (12mi)

St James's Rd

Dale Rd

Clough St

New Market St

Bennet St

West Rd

Spencer Rd

Compton Rd

London Rd

To Ashbourne (21mi)

Temple Rd

To Poole's Cavern (600m); Solomon's Temple

College Rd

Green Ln

Pavilion	8 B2
Pump Room	9 B2
St Ann's Well	(see 9)

SLEEPING 🛏 (pp482–3)	
Grosvenor House	10 B2
Lowther Guesthouse	11 C2
Netherdale Guesthouse	12 B4
Old Hall Hotel	13 B2
Palace Hotel	14 B1
Roseleigh Hotel	15 B3
Victorian Guest House	16 B2

EATING 🍴 (p483)	
Columbine Restaurant	17 B2
Cornerways	(see 10)
Firenze	18 B2
Hargreave's Coffeeshop	19 C2
Michaelangelo's	20 B2
Old Club House	21 B2

DRINKING 🍷 (p483)	
Cheshire Cheese	22 B3
King's Head	23 B3
Old Sun Inn	24 B3
Vault	25 B3

INFORMATION	
Northwest Computers	1 C1
Post Office	2 C1
Tourist Information Centre (TIC)	3 B2

SIGHTS & ACTIVITIES (pp481–2)	
Cavendish Arcade	4 C1
Crescent	5 B2
Devonshire Hospital (closed)	6 B1
Natural Mineral Baths	(see 3)
Opera House	7 B2

TRANSPORT (p483)	
Bus Stop	(see 20)

OTHER	
Spring Gardens Shopping Centre	26 C1

most eye-catching edifice, complete with towers and a massive dome that Jerusalem might envy. The hospital is in the process of becoming a new campus for the University of Derby.

Poole's Cavern (☎ 26978; www.poolescavern.co.uk; admission £5.50; ☾ 10am-5pm Mar-Oct) is a splendid showcave about a mile from the centre. Amiable and enthusiastic guides will take you deep underground to see an impressive selection of stalactites (including the longest in England) and stalagmites (including unique 'poached egg' formations). In spring and autumn, running water makes the cave even more dramatic.

From near the cave entrance, a 20-minute walk leads up through Grin Low Wood to **Solomon's Temple**, a small tower with fine views over the town and surrounding Peak District.

A longer walk is the **Monsal Trail**, beginning 3 miles east of the town, which leads all the way to Bakewell (p489) – see that section for details.

Sleeping

There are hundreds of hotels in Buxton, many dating from the Georgian and Victorian heydays. Around Pavilion Gardens and along Broad Walk are several particularly fine atmospheric places.

Old Hall Hotel (☎ 22841; the Square; s/d £65/96) Walking through the heavy doors and down the wood-panelled hallway of this grand establishment, which claims to be the oldest hotel in England, is as close as one gets to genuine time travel. Former guests include Mary, Queen of Scots, and Daniel Defoe.

Roseleigh Hotel (☎ 24904; www.roseleighhotel .co.uk; 19 Broad Walk; s/d from £25/55; **P**) This charming B&B, with a comfortable lounge full of travel books and deep leather armchairs, is run by a couple who are themselves seasoned travellers and adventure-tour guides.

Grosvenor House (☎ 72439; grosvenor.buxton@ btopenworld.com; 1 Broad Walk; s/d from £25/50; **P** 🖳) A friendly family-run hotel with a budget café downstairs.

Other options include **Lowther Guesthouse** (☎ 71479; 7 Hardwick Sq West; s from £21), **Netherdale Guesthouse** (☎ 23896; 16 Green Lane; d from £60), a comfortable place on a leafy street, and the **Victorian Guest House** (☎ 78759; www.buxton victorian.co.uk; 3a Broad Walk; s from £40; **P**), with amazing breakfasts and attic-room views over the park.

Eating & Drinking

The Market Pl and High St area has a good choice of cafés, pubs, restaurants and takeaways, and is definitely the place to be in the evening.

Columbine Restaurant (☎ 78752; Hall Bank; ☽ lunch Thu-Sat, dinner Mon-Sat; lunches around £5, dinner mains £10-12) A local favourite, the Columbine serves fine food, including a full vegetarian menu, in calm and intimate surroundings.

Firenze (☎ 72203; Market Pl; pastas £5-6, mains £8-10) Another popular spot, this casual Italian eatery serves Mediterranean-style pizzas, pastas and dishes in intimate surrounds (read: slightly cramped). **Michaelangelo's** (☎ 26640; Market Pl) is similar and also offers good-value early-evening special deals.

Spring Gardens, an otherwise uninspiring pedestrianised shopping street, has several cheap cafés. At **Hargreaves Coffeeshop** good cakes and straightforward meals are served in a room lined with glass cabinets, which are full of historic china and porcelain. For a break while sightseeing, there are also cafés at **Cavendish Arcade** and the **Pavilion**. The **Old Club House** (Water St) is a large pub with inside and outside seats, and food all day. **Cornerways** at Grosvenor House (see Sleeping) is a nice, quiet teashop with pavement tables.

Of the many watering holes, those worth a stop include the **King's Head** (Market Pl), favoured by a young crowd and also serving pub grub; the **Vault** (High St), a modern bar serving food until 6pm; and the **Cheshire Cheese** (High St), a traditional place with a pool table. Our favourite is the **Old Sun Inn** (High St), which could just be the perfect pub, with a friendly atmosphere, a warren of cosy bars, a good menu of very fine food and a range of well-kept beer to go with it.

Getting There & Away

Buxton is well served by public transport. Buses serve Derby (twice hourly, 1½ hours), Chesterfield (several daily, 1¼ hours) and Sheffield (twice hourly, 65 minutes). Trains run hourly to and from Manchester (50 minutes).

AROUND BUXTON
Tideswell

About 8 miles east of Buxton, deep in lovely White Peak countryside, the village of Tideswell makes a good base for walking, with delightful footpaths leading in every direction; all you need are good shoes and a map. The Buxton TIC also has booklets detailing local walks.

Tideswell's centrepiece is the massive parish church – known as the **Cathedral of the Peak** – which has stood here virtually unchanged for 600 years. The old box pews, ship-like oak ceiling and huge panels inscribed with the Ten Commandments are a firm reminder of the days when coveting your neighbour's maid just wasn't on.

For accommodation, **Poppies** (☎ 01298-871083; poptidza@dialstart.net; Bank Sq; B&B from £18) is frequently recommended by walkers, and can provide excellent evening meals. Tideswell also has **Hills & Dales Café** (☽ 10am-5pm Fri-Sun), several shops, a pharmacy and a self-service laundrette.

Bus No 65 runs about six times per day between Buxton and Calver, via Tideswell, and with connections to Sheffield and Chesterfield.

EDALE
☎ 01433

Tiny Edale, nestled in the Edale Valley dividing the White and Dark Peak areas, is as much a point of departure as a village. Most famous as the southern terminus of the Pennine Way, it's a good place to start walks of varying difficulty in just about any direction.

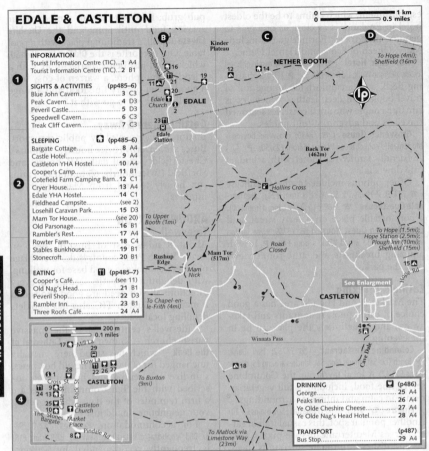

EDALE & CASTLETON

INFORMATION
Tourist Information Centre (TIC)....**1** A4
Tourist Information Centre (TIC)...**2** B1

SIGHTS & ACTIVITIES (pp485–6)
Blue John Cavern.......................**3** C3
Peak Cavern............................**4** D3
Peveril Castle..........................**5** D3
Speedwell Cavern......................**6** C3
Treak Cliff Cavern......................**7** C3

SLEEPING (pp485–6)
Bargate Cottage........................**8** A4
Castle Hotel............................**9** A4
Castleton YHA Hostel.................**10** A4
Cooper's Camp.........................**11** B1
Cotefield Farm Camping Barn..**12** C1
Cryer House...........................**13** A4
Edale YHA Hostel.....................**14** C1
Fieldhead Campsite..................(see 2)
Losehill Caravan Park................**15** D3
Mam Tor House....................(see 20)
Old Parsonage.........................**16** B1
Rambler's Rest........................**17** A4
Rowter Farm...........................**18** C4
Stables Bunkhouse....................**19** B1
Stonecroft.............................**20** B1

EATING (pp485–7)
Cooper's Café.......................(see 11)
Old Nag's Head.......................**21** B1
Peveril Shop..........................**22** D3
Rambler Inn...........................**23** B1
Three Roofs Café.....................**24** A4

DRINKING (p486)
George.................................**25** A4
Peaks Inn..............................**26** A4
Ye Olde Cheshire Cheese.............**27** A4
Ye Olde Nag's Head Hotel............**28** A4

TRANSPORT (p487)
Bus Stop...............................**29** A4

Heading south, a great walk from Edale takes you up to **Hollins Cross**, a point on the ridge that runs south of the valley. From here, you can aim west to the top of spectacular **Mam Tor** and watch the hang-gliders swoop around above. Or go east along the ridge, with great views on both sides, past the cliffs of **Back Tor** to reach Lose Hill (which, naturally, faces Win Hill). Or you can continue south, down to the village of Castleton (described on p485).

From Edale you can also walk north onto the **Kinder Plateau** – dark and brooding in the mist, gloriously high and open when the sun's out. Weather permitting, a fine circular walk starts by following the Pennine Way through fields to **Upper Booth**, then up

a path called Jacobs Ladder and along the southern edge of Kinder, before dropping down to Edale via the steep rocky valley of Grindsbrook Clough, or the ridge of Ringing Roger.

A small exhibition about the park, and all the leaflets, maps and guides you'll need can be found at the **TIC** (☎ 670207; www.edale-valley .co.uk; ⏰ 10am-5pm).

Sleeping

The TIC can provide details on the many accommodation options in farms and remote cottages in the surrounding area.

Edale YHA Hostel (☎ 0870 770 5808; edale@yha.org .uk; dm £11; **P**) This hostel is in a large old country house 1½ miles east of the village centre. It's also an activity centre and is very popular with youth groups.

Old Parsonage (☎ 670232; Grindsbrook; B&B per person from £16; P) This long-time favourite with walkers is straightforward, but clean and tidy.

Mam Tor House (☎ 670253; Grindsbrook; B&B per person around £18; P) A good mid-range place, this is right next to the church. If it's full, the owners can direct you to other B&Bs.

Stonecroft (☎ 670262; Grindsbrook; B&B per person from £26-30; P) The food and accommodation here are of excellent quality, and the service is very friendly.

Options abound for campers. **Fieldhead Campsite** (☎ 670386; per person £3.50; P) is neat and compact, with good facilities, and is near the TIC (visitor centre) and train station. **Cooper's Camp** (☎ 670372; per person £3; P) is a larger place at the upper end of the village; facilities are good, and there's a shop and café attached. **Cotefield Farm Camping Barn** (☎ 0870 870 8808; per person £4; P) is bookable through the YHA, while **Stables Bunkhouse** (☎ 670235; Ollerbrook Farm; per person £8; P) is another good cheap option. Both places are less than a mile east of the village centre.

Eating

For filling no-frills food, head for **Cooper's Café** (near Cooper's Camp), or the café at the train station; both are open from breakfast-time to 5pm.

Edale has two pubs, the **Old Nag's Head**, which is cosy and inviting, and actively courts walkers, and the **Rambler Inn**, which also does B&B; both serve passable pub grub (£4.95 to £6.95). But if you've got wheels, the **Cheshire Cheese**, about 2½ miles east of Edale towards the neighbouring village of Hope, is a much more appealing place to while away the evening over a pint.

Getting There & Away

Edale is on the train line between Sheffield and Manchester (about eight per day Monday to Friday, five at weekends). Trains also stop at several other Peak villages.

CASTLETON

☎ 01433

Nestled in the shadow of 517m-high Mam Tor and crowned by the ruins of Peveril Castle, the neat little settlement of Castleton has a central square (more of a triangle, actually), a couple of narrow lanes with sturdy gritstone houses and colourful gardens, and a good collection of cosy country pubs. Oh yes – and about a million tourists on summer weekends. But don't let that put you off. Come here at a quieter time to enjoy good walks in the surrounding area, and marvel at the famous 'showcaves', where a semiprecious stone called Blue John has been mined for centuries.

Orientation & Information

Castleton stands at the western end of the Hope Valley. The main route through the village (Cross St, the A6187) used to switchback up the side of notoriously unstable Mam Tor, but frequent landslips destroyed the road, and traffic now goes up the narrow, spectacular (and much older) Winnats Pass. On or just off Cross St are pubs, shops, cafés, B&Bs, the YHA hostel, and the sleek, modern **TIC** (☎ 620679; 🕙 10am-5.30pm daily Easter-Oct, Sat & Sun Oct-Apr).

Sights

Crowning the hill above Castleton is ruined **Peveril Castle** (☎ 620613; admission £2.70; 🕙 10am-6pm daily May-Jul, 10am-7pm Aug, 10am-5pm Sep-Oct, 10am-4pm Thu-Mon Nov-Mar, 10am-5pm daily Apr), well worth the steep walk up from the village. William Peveril, son of William the Conqueror, built it originally, and Henry II added the central keep in 1176. The ruins are interesting, but the real draw is the setting, with its stunning view over the Hope Valley, straight down to Castleton's medieval street grid and north to Mam Tor with the Dark Peak beyond.

The area around Castleton is riddled with caves, and four are open to the public. Although mostly natural, they have been extensively mined for Blue John, lead and silver, and so have been enlarged over the centuries. The most convenient of these, **Peak Cavern** (☎ 620285; admission £5; 🕙 10am-4pm daily April-Oct, Sat & Sun Nov-Mar), is easily reached by a pretty streamside walk from the village centre. The cave entrance is the largest in England, known (not so prettily) as the Devil's Arse. Visits are by hourly guided tour only.

The claustrophobic should avoid **Speedwell Cavern** (☎ 620512; 🕙 10am-4.30pm May-Sep, 10am-3pm Oct-Apr), but everyone else will get a thrill out of this former mineshaft near Winnats Pass. It's a unique flooded tunnel you travel along by boat to reach an underground lake called the 'bottomless pit'. The excellent guides have clearly practiced their routines, but not to the point of boredom.

Treak Cliff Cavern (☎ 620571; ☼ 10am-5.30pm Mar-Oct, 10am-3pm Nov-Feb) is a short walk from Castleton, with exposed veins of Blue John and great stalactites, including the much-photographed 'stork' (which actually looks more like a dinosaur with a stomachache).

Blue John Cavern (☎ 620638; ☼ 9.30am-5pm) is an impressive set of multicoloured chambers and passageways – a main source of Blue John. You can get here on foot up the closed section of the Mam Tor road.

Walking

Castleton is the northern terminus of the Limestone Way (see p480), which includes narrow, rocky Cave Dale, far below the east wall of the castle.

If you feel like a shorter walk, you can follow the Limestone Way up Cave Dale for a few miles, then loop round on paths and tracks to the west of Rowter Farm (see Sleeping, following) to meet the Buxton Rd. Go straight (north) on a path crossing fields and another road to eventually reach Mam Nick, where the road to Edale passes through a gap in the ridge. Go up steps here to reach the summit of Mam Tor, for spectacular views along the Hope Valley. (You can also see the fractured remains of the old main road.) The path then aims northwest along the ridge to another gap called Hollins Cross, from where paths and tracks lead back down to Castleton. This 6-mile circuit takes three to four hours; maps are available at the TIC.

A shorter option from Castleton is to take the path direct to Hollins Cross, then go to Mam Tor, and return by the same route (about 4 miles, two to three hours). From Hollins Cross, you can extend any walk by dropping down to Edale, or you can walk direct from Castleton to Edale via Hollins Cross.

Sleeping

Rambler's Rest (☎ 620125; Mill Bridge; s/d from £20/35; P) As the name implies, this attractive stone cottage offers a special welcome to walkers. It also has a large en suite room with three or four beds (£22 per person), ideal for small groups or people with kids. Some rooms have shared bathrooms.

Cryer House (☎ 620244; Castle St; r from £25; P) A long-standing favourite with affable hosts, this comfortable little B&B has a popular garden tearoom out the front.

Castleton YHA Hostel (☎ 0870 770 5758; castleton@yha.org.uk; Castle St; dm £11.80, r from £40) Large and often full of school groups, this hostel is a great source of information even if you're not staying there, with knowledgeable staff who also conduct guided walks.

Also recommended are **Bargate Cottage** (☎ 620201; Market Pl; d from £45), dating from the 1600s and full of character, and the supposedly haunted **Castle Hotel** (☎ 620578; Castle St; r Mon-Thu £59, Fri-Sun £69), with plush rooms in an annex and comfortable doubles upstairs from a restaurant/pub.

For campers, the nearest place is well-organised **Losehill Caravan Park** (☎ 620636; Hope Rd; per site £5-6, plus per adult £4-5). **Rowter Farm** (☎ 620271; per person £3) is a simple campsite up on the hills about 1 mile west of Castleton. Drivers should approach via Winnats Pass; if you're on foot you can follow paths from Castleton village centre, as described in the Walking section earlier.

Eating & Drinking

Ye Olde Nag's Head Hotel (☎ 620451; How Lane; bar meals £7-9, mains £17.95, B&B per person £30; ☼ breakfast, lunch & dinner) The Nag's has both sass and class – the dining room serves romantic candlelit suppers and Sunday lunches, while the bar is a late-night hotspot, the place where everybody in town winds up eventually (and they do get pretty wound up). There are comfy B&B rooms upstairs, though they're not ideal for people who sleep lightly.

George (☎ 620238; Castle St; mains around £7) Having grown out of a recent awkward phase, the George is thriving again under new proprietor Richard Symonds, whose outsized personality has made the place a mandatory stop on the village's busy pub circuit. An impressive menu and flagstone floor (to match the original) give the place a sophisticated air, but only until about 9pm, after which things get weird and rowdy in the way only a great small-town pub can.

Other walker-friendly pubs to try include **Ye Olde Cheshire Cheese** (How Lane), an excellent traditional pub of character, and the classy **Peaks Inn** (How Lane), which has a good trivia night and upscale B&B rooms.

For hot drinks, snacks and lunches, tea-shops abound in Castleton. Try the **Three Roofs Café** (Cross St). Near the bus stop, the **Peveril Shop** (How Lane) sells food and groceries, and does sandwiches to take away – ideal for a day on the hills or a long bus ride.

Getting There & Away
You can get to Castleton from Bakewell on bus No 173 (45 minutes, five per day Monday to Friday, three per day at weekends), via Hope and Tideswell.

The nearest train station is Hope, about 1 mile east of Hope village (a total of 3 miles east of Castleton) on the line between Sheffield and Manchester. At summer weekends a bus runs between Hope station and Castleton tying in with the trains, although it's not a bad walk in good weather.

DERWENT RESERVOIRS
In the centre of the Peak, three huge artificial lakes – Ladybower, Derwent and Howden, known as the Derwent Reservoirs – collect water for the cities of Derbyshire and the Midlands. They are also focal points for walking and mountain-biking.

The place to aim for is **Fairholmes**, a national park centre which has a **TIC** (☎ 01433-650953), a car park, a snack bar and cycle hire. Numerous walks start here, from gentle strolls along the lakeside to more serious outings on the moors above the valley. For cycling, a lane leads up the west

side of Derwent and Howden reservoirs (it's closed to car traffic at weekends), and a dirt track comes down the east side, making a good 12-mile circuit, while challenging off-road routes lead deeper into the hills. The TIC stocks a very good range of route leaflets, maps and guidebooks.

Fairholmes is 2 miles north of the A57, the main road between Sheffield and Manchester. Bus No 257 runs from Sheffield to Fairholmes (every 30 minutes Saturday and Sunday April to October) and continues up to the end of the road on the west side of Howden Reservoir – an excellent way to reach the high hills and one of the wildest parts of the Peak District.

EYAM
☎ 01433 / pop 900
The village of Eyam (pronounced ee-em, or eem) is a quaint little spot with a morbidly touching history. In 1665, a consignment of cloth from London delivered to a local tailor carried with it the dreaded disease known simply as the plague. What could have been a widespread disaster remained a localized tragedy: as the plague spread through Eyam, the rector convinced its inhabitants to quarantine themselves rather than transmit it further. Selflessly, they did so; by the time the plague ended in late 1666, around 250 of the village's 800 inhabitants had died, while people in surrounding villages remained relatively unscathed.

THE MIDLANDS

Even independently of this poignant story, Eyam is well worth a visit; its sloping streets of old cottages backed by rolling green hills form a classic postcard view of the Peak District.

Sights

The **church** dates from Saxon times and has many reminders of the plague, including a cupboard said to be made from the box that carried the infected cloth to Eyam. More sobering is the plague register, recording those who died, name by name, day by day. Many plague victims were buried in the churchyard, but only two headstones from the time exist – one for Catherine Mompesson, the rector's wife.

Also in the churchyard, but from a much earlier era, the 8th-century **Celtic cross** is one of the finest in England. Before leaving, check your watch against the **sundial** on the church wall.

In the church you can buy the *Eyam Map* (£2.50), and smaller leaflets (20p) which describe the village's history and all the sites associated with the plague. You can also find a leaflet describing some of the monuments and headstones in the churchyard.

Around the village, many buildings have information plaques attached; these include the **plague cottages**, where the tailor lived, next to the church.

Eyam Hall (☎ 631976; admission £4.25; ☼ 11am-4pm Wed, Thu & Sun Jun-Aug) is a fine old 17th-century manor house, and the courtyard contains a tearoom and numerous craft workshops.

Eyam Museum (www.eyammuseum.demon.co.uk; adult/child £1.75/1.25; ☼ 10am-4.30pm Tue-Sun Easter-Oct) digs into the stories behind Eyam's plague experience, but there are also neat exhibits on geology, Saxon history and the village's time as a lead-mining and silk-weaving centre.

Look out too for the **stocks** on the village green – somewhere handy to leave the kids, perhaps, while you look at the church.

Walking

Eyam makes a great base for walking and cycling in the surrounding White Peak area. A short walk for starters leads up Water Lane from the village square, then up through fields and a patch of woodland to meet another lane running between Eyam and Grindleford; turn right here and keep going uphill, past another junction to **Mompesson's Well**, where food and other supplies were left during the plague time for Eyam folk by friends from other villages. The Eyam people paid for the goods using coins sterilised in vinegar. You can retrace your steps back down the lane, then take a path which leads directly to the church. This 2-mile circuit takes about 1½ hours.

Sleeping & Eating

Eyam YHA Hostel (☎ 0870 770 5830; eyam@yha.org .uk; Hawkhill Rd; dm £11.80, r from £45) is in a fine old Victorian house on the village edge. If it's full, **Bretton YHA Hostel** (☎ 0870 7705720; Hope Valley) is only 1½ miles away. **Crown Cottage** (☎ 630858; Church St; d £50) is also known as the Old Rose & Crown. The very friendly people here welcome walkers and cyclists and can advise on routes in the area.

Miner's Arms (☎ 630853; Water Lane; r £30-40) is a fine old pub, with amiable management, good beer, decent food and very comfortable rooms. **Peak Pantry**, on the village square, has good cakes and coffee; **Eyam Tearooms**, just up the road, is slightly frillier, but the cakes are just as good (and B&B is also available).

Getting There & Away

Eyam is 7 miles north of Bakewell and 12 miles east of Buxton. Regular buses from

---

PLAGUE SURVIVOR MYSTERY

A mysterious aspect of the plague (and similar epidemics) that has long interested scientists is – to put it bluntly – why it didn't kill everyone, given its notoriously contagious nature. A possible answer came to light in 2001 when a fascinating study conducted by American scientists found that many local Eyam people descended from plague survivors carry a distinctive rare gene.

The same research then located a gay man in California who expected to contract AIDS yet remained immune, also carrying this same rare gene (possibly inherited from a Derbyshire forebear). The next challenge for the scientists is to isolate the 'Eyam gene' and use it in the ongoing quest for a cure for AIDS.

Bakewell towards Sheffield or Chesterfield go to Calver, from where you can walk along the main road to Stoney Middleton, then take a path up the steep valley side to Eyam (2 miles). From Buxton, bus No 65 runs about six times per day to and from Calver, via Eyam.

BAKEWELL

☎ 01629 / pop 3676

After Buxton, this is the largest town in the Peak District (though it's hardly a metropolis) and a good base for walking, cycling or touring. It's also a notorious traffic bottleneck on summer weekends, but at quieter times it's worth a stop to see some interesting sights. And everyone should do their part to help settle the debate over which of the Bakewell pudding shops in town actually invented the famous dessert (see boxed text, right).

Orientation & Information

The centre of town is Rutland Sq, from where roads radiate to Matlock, Buxton and Sheffield. The **TIC** (☎ 813227; Bridge St; ⏰ 10am-5pm), in the old Market Hall, has racks of leaflets and books about Bakewell and the national park.

Sights & Activities

Bakewell's weekly market is on Monday, when the square behind the TIC is very lively. Up on the hill above Rutland Sq, **All Saints Church** has some ancient Norman features, and even older Saxon stonework remains, including a tall cross in the churchyard, which sadly has suffered at the hands of time.

Near the church, **Old House Museum** (Cunningham Pl; admission £2.50; ⏰ 1.30-4pm Easter-Jun & Oct, 11am-4pm Jul-Sep) displays local miscellany, including a Tudor loo.

A stroll from Rutland Sq down Bridge St brings you – not surprisingly – to the pretty **medieval bridge** over the River Wye, from where riverside walks lead in both directions. Go upstream through the water meadows, and then along Holme Lane to reach **Holme Bridge**, an ancient stone structure used by Peak District packhorses for centuries.

On the northern edge of Bakewell, a former railway line has been converted to a walking and cycling track called the **Monsal Trail**. From Bakewell you can cycle

WHICH BAKEWELL PUDDING?

Bakewell blundered into the recipe books around 1860 when a cook at the Rutland Arms Hotel made strawberry tart, but mistakenly (some stories say drunkenly) spread the egg mixture on top of the jam instead of stirring it into the pastry, thus creating the Bakewell pudding (pudding, mark you, not tart). It now features regularly on local dessert menus and is certainly worth sampling.

Two of Bakewell's many pudding-selling establishments are locked in battle over whose is the original recipe, and both have records dating back to 1889. **Bloomers Original Bakewell Pudding Shop** (Water St) insists it's 'the first and only', while the **Old Original Bakewell Pudding Shop** (Bridge St) is adamant that its recipe is older. The latter certainly pulls in more trade, thanks to its position on the main thoroughfare.

History dictates that you should visit them both and do a comparison. It's good for fair play, if not for your waistline.

about 3 miles north and 1 mile south on the old railway itself – and there are numerous other tracks and country lanes nearby. **Bakewell Cycle Hire** (☎ 814004) at the old station has mountain bikes for about £10 per day; opening times depend on the weather, so phone ahead if possible.

Walkers on the Monsal Trail follow alternate sections of the old railway and pretty footpaths through fields and beside rivers. From Bakewell, an excellent out-and-back walk (3 miles each way) goes to the dramatic viewpoint at Monsal Head – where there's a good pub and a friendly café. Allow three hours for the round trip.

If you're out for the day, from Monsal Head you can keep following the Monsal Trail northwest towards Buxton. A good point to aim for is Miller's Dale, where impressive viaducts cross the steep-sided valley (and there's another good café), or you can go all the way to Blackwell Mill (3 miles east of Buxton) – a total distance of about 9 miles – and get a bus back. Alternatively, get a bus to Buxton, and walk back to Bakewell. The TICs at Bakewell and Buxton have a *Monsal Trail* leaflet with all the details.

Other walking routes go to the stately homes of Haddon Hall and Chatsworth

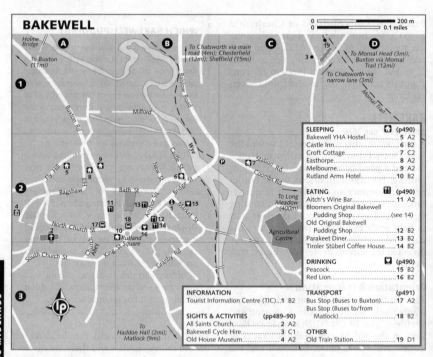

BAKEWELL

SLEEPING	⬆ (p490)
Bakewell YHA Hostel	5 A2
Castle Inn	6 B2
Croft Cottage	7 C2
Easthorpe	8 A2
Melbourne	9 A2
Rutland Arms Hotel	10 B2

EATING	🍴 (p490)
Aitch's Wine Bar	11 A2
Bloomers Original Bakewell	
Pudding Shop	(see 14)
Old Original Bakewell	
Pudding Shop	12 B2
Parakeet Diner	13 B2
Tiroler Stüberl Coffee House	14 B2

DRINKING	🍷 (p490)
Peacock	15 B2
Red Lion	16 B2

INFORMATION	
Tourist Information Centre (TIC)	1 B2

SIGHTS & ACTIVITIES	(pp489–90)
All Saints Church	2 A2
Bakewell Cycle Hire	3 C1
Old House Museum	4 A2

TRANSPORT	(p491)
Bus Stop (Buses to Buxton)	17 A2
Bus Stop (Buses to/from	
Matlock)	18 B2

OTHER	
Old Train Station	19 D1

House (opposite). You could take a bus or taxi there and walk back, so you don't put mud on the duke's carpet.

Sleeping

Bakewell YHA Hostel (☎ 0870 770 5682; Fly Hill; dm £10) A modern building just out of the centre at the top of a very steep hill. It's in a quiet residential area; curfew is 11pm, and there are no laundry facilities or Internet access, but it's a very comfortable, friendly place and a great base for walking in the area.

Rutland Arms Hotel (☎ 812812; rutland@bakewell .demon.co.uk; Rutland Sq; r from £45; ℗) This venerable establishment, cashing in fully on its history (see Which Bakewell Pudding?, p489) is especially popular with coach tour groups. Front rooms overlook the square but can be noisy.

Easthorpe and **Melbourne** (☎ 815357; Buxton Rd; r from £23; ℗) are run as one unit on either side of a busy road, with plenty of rooms and friendly service.

Also recommended are **Croft Cottage** (☎ 814 101; croftco@btInternet.com; Coombs Rd; r from £25), a

quaint old building near the bridge; **Long Meadow** (☎ 812500; Coombs Rd; r from £50; ℗), in one wing of a renovated old house; and the **Castle Inn** (☎ 812103; Bridge St; r £45), one of the better pubs in Bakewell.

Eating & Drinking

Bakewell's streets are lined with cute teashops and bakeries, most with 'pudding' in the name, selling the town's eponymous cake. There are several fish-and-chip shops too.

Parakeet Diner (Anchor Sq; ✆ breakfast, lunch & dinner) is a straightforward café, popular with walkers and cyclists, offering snacks, meals and fry-up breakfasts. **Tiroler Stüberl Coffee House** (Water St; ✆ breakfast, lunch & dinner) dares to be different, offering Austrian sausage and apple strudel alongside coffee, scones and snacks. **Aitch's Wine Bar** (☎ 813895; Buxton Rd; lunches £5-7, evening mains £11-15; ✆ lunch & dinner) is a long-standing place with a highly rated and imaginative menu: 'around the world in eighty plates'.

Of the pubs, the **Red Lion** (Bridge St) is cheap and cheerful, and the **Peacock** has a good atmosphere, with beer and food to match.

Getting There & Away

Buses serve Bakewell from Derby (twice hourly, most 90 minutes but there are some faster buses) and Chesterfield (hourly, 45 minutes).

AROUND BAKEWELL
Haddon Hall

Described as a medieval masterpiece, **Haddon Hall** (☎ 01629-812855; www.haddonhall.co.uk; admission £7.25; ☾ 10.30am-4.30pm Apr-Sep, 10.30am-4pm Thu-Sun Oct) was originally owned by William Peveril, son of William the Conqueror, and what you see today dates mainly from the 14th to 16th centuries. Haddon Hall was abandoned right through the 18th and 19th centuries, so it escaped the 'modernisation' experienced by so many other country houses. Highlights include the Chapel; the Long Gallery, stunningly bathed by natural light; and the vast Banqueting Hall, virtually unchanged since the days of Henry VIII. The popular film about Henry's daughter *Elizabeth* was shot here, and, not surprisingly, Haddon Hall made a perfect backdrop. Outside are beautiful gardens and courtyards.

The house is 2 miles south of Bakewell on the A6. You can get there on any bus heading for Matlock (about hourly) or walk along the footpath through the fields mostly on the east side of the river.

Chatsworth

The great stately home, manicured gardens and perfectly landscaped park of Chatsworth together form a major highlight for many visitors to England. The main draw is sumptuous **Chatsworth House** (☎ 01246-582204; www.chatsworth-house.co.uk; adult/child £9/3.50, Christmas season from 6 Nov additional £1/50p; ☾ 11am-4.30pm Easter-Oct, shorter hrs & days Nov & Dec). Known as the 'Palace of the Peak', this vast edifice has been occupied by the dukes of Devonshire for centuries. The original house was started in 1551 by the inimitable Bess of Hardwick; a little later came Chatsworth's most famous guest, Mary, Queen of Scots. She was imprisoned here between 1570 and 1581 at the behest of Elizabeth I, under the guard of Bess's fourth husband, the earl of Shrewsbury. The **Scots bedrooms** (adult/child £10.50/4, including admission to the house), nine Regency rooms named after the imprisoned queen, are sometimes open to the public.

The house was extensively altered between 1686 and 1707, and again enlarged and improved in the 1820s – much of what you see dates from these periods. Among the prime attractions are the painted and decorated ceilings, although the 30 or so rooms are all treasure-troves of splendid furniture and magnificent artworks.

The house is surrounded by 40 sq km of **gardens** (admission £4.50), complete with a fountain so high it can be seen when you're miles away in the hills of the Dark Peak. For the kids an **adventure playground** (admission £3.50) provides hours of fun. Beyond that is another 400 hectares of parkland, originally landscaped by Capability Brown, open to the public for walking and picnicking.

Chatsworth is 3 miles northeast of Bakewell. If you're driving, it's £1 to park. Bus No 179 runs twice daily (Monday to Saturday) and No 211 four times daily (Sunday). Virgin Trains runs a bus between Macclesfield, Buxton and Bakewell (two per day) that extends to Chatsworth June through September.

Another option is to walk or cycle from Bakewell. Start out on the quiet lane that leads uphill from the old train station; walkers can take footpaths through Chatsworth park via the mock-Venetian village of Edensor (pronounced en-sor), and cyclists can pedal via Pilsley.

THE MIDLANDS

Eastern England

CONTENTS

It's difficult to generalise about Eastern England. The cities and landscapes within its four counties – Cambridgeshire, Lincolnshire, Suffolk and Norfolk – are so varied and distinct that any statement that applies to one place is bound to be disproved just a few miles down the road. From the lovely and dignified brains trust that is Cambridge to arms-in-the-air beach resorts like Skegness, from the lonely beauty of the Norfolk Broads to the bustling modern shopping meccas at Peterborough and Norwich, and everywhere in between, this region offers a surprisingly wide selection of delights. Best of all, for the most part eastern England has the advantage of being mercifully free of mass tourism – though parts of the region are becoming favourites among weekend-breakers, thanks to an influx of luxury boutique hotels and ambitious new restaurants and a relatively recent interest in catering to the tourist trade.

The part of the region called East Anglia includes Norfolk, Suffolk and east Cambridgeshire and is separated (at least conceptually) from the rest of England by the Fens and the now-decimated Essex forests. Its rural areas present a pastoral idyll, but these stretches of countryside are also rich in historical significance and relics of medieval times. Many of this region's settlements possess the kind of stately air that comes from being a one-time economic powerhouse that has since settled into quiet anonymity. Centuries ago, this area created masses of wealth in the wool trade, and the evidence of those glory days can still be seen in the huge, elaborate monuments to economic health such as the cathedrals at Lincoln and Ely, as well as in the well-preserved half-timbered buildings and gorgeous parish churches of the smaller medieval market towns. Evidence of commercial success similarly graces the landscapes of Lincolnshire, mainly in the form of elaborate parish churches and film-friendly villages.

HIGHLIGHTS

- Walking and bird-watching in delightful **Burnham Deepdale** (p529)
- Strolling the regal streets of beautifully preserved **Stamford** (p538)
- Pondering the masses of brainpower that have passed through **Cambridge** (p496)
- Wondering at the gorgeous façades of **Lincoln Cathedral** (p535)
- Taking a cruise through the wilds of the **Norfolk Broads** (p526)
- Cooing over little pink thatch-roofed houses in **Lavenham** (p513)

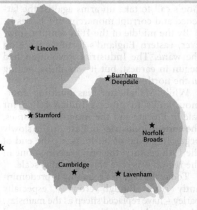

- POPULATION: 5.4 MILLION
- AREA: 19,000 SQ MILES

HISTORY

East Anglia was a major Saxon kingdom, consisting of the northern people (Norfolk) and the southern ones (Suffolk). Raedwald, who died sometime between AD 616 and 628, was the first East Anglian king of whom anything is known, but the discovery of the Sutton Hoo ship (see p511) and all its treasures in 1939 suggested that he and his ilk knew something of the good life.

From the early Middle Ages, East Anglia became a major centre for wool and the manufacture of woollen products. Then, in the 14th century, Edward III invited Flemish weavers to settle in the area, and for the next four centuries Norwich was England's most important weaving town. Evidence of the region's links with the Netherlands and Belgium is visible throughout eastern England; long drainage canals, windmills and the architecture (particularly in King's Lynn) have more than a hint of Dutch influence about them. The wealth this connection brought built scores of churches and helped subsidise the development of Cambridge.

By the 17th century the emergence of a work-happy urban bourgeoisie growing ever richer on successful trade with continental Europe, coupled with a fairly strong sense of religious duty, resulted in the twin principles of parliamentarianism and Puritanism that would climax in the Civil War. Oliver Cromwell, the uncrowned king of the parliamentarians, was a small-time merchant residing in Ely when he answered God's call to take up arms against the fattened and corrupt monarchy of Charles I.

By the middle of the 18th century, however, eastern England's fortunes were on the wane. The Industrial Revolution had begun in earnest, but it was all happening in the northwest.

While Manchester was building enormous mills to process Indian calico for sale in Europe and the American colonies, the cottage industries of East Anglia slowly began to go out of business. By the end of the 19th century, the only weaving done in the region was on a tiny, specialist scale.

Today the region's economy is predominantly rural, though crops – especially barley – have replaced sheep as the mainstay. Market gardening is also a major earner, and most of the towns have developed some form of light industry.

INFORMATION

Consult the **East of England Tourist Board** (☎ 01473-822922; www.visiteastofengland.com) for regional tourist information.

ACTIVITIES

Regional tourism websites all contain walking, cycling and sailing information, and TICs all stock leaflets, maps and guides that cover walking, cycling and other outdoor activities.

Walking

Eastern England is not classic walking country. To put it bluntly, there aren't enough hills. But if that's not a worry, then the area is perfect for easy rambles through gentle farmland, or alongside rivers and small lakes in the Norfolk Broads. For more saltwatery flavours, the coasts of Norfolk and Suffolk are both followed by footpaths.

The region's best-known long-distance walk is the **Peddars Way and Norfolk Coast Path**, a six-day, 88-mile (142km) national trail linking Cromer on the coast with Knettishall Heath near Thetford. It follows an ancient Roman road for its first half, then meanders along the beaches, sea walls, salt marshes and fishing villages of the coast for the second half. Any part of the route can be done just as a day or weekend option; this is much easier on the coast section, and especially rewarding if you're into bird-watching as there are some top-quality nature reserves along this stretch.

Farther south, the 50-mile **Suffolk Coast and Heaths Path** runs between Felixstowe and Lowestoft, via Snape Maltings, Aldeburgh, Dunwich and Southwold. As with all long routes, even if you don't want to go the whole way, it makes the perfect focus for shorter walks and rambles.

Cycling

With a long history of human settlement but little in the way of urbanisation, Norfolk, Suffolk, Lincolnshire and Cambridgeshire all have networks of quiet country lanes. Eastern England is also famous for being flat, and thus makes perfect country for gentle cycletouring – as long as the wind is minimal or behind you. If you head east into cold winds you'll realise there are no hills to deflect them between here and the Urals. But with an eye on the weather, and judicious use of

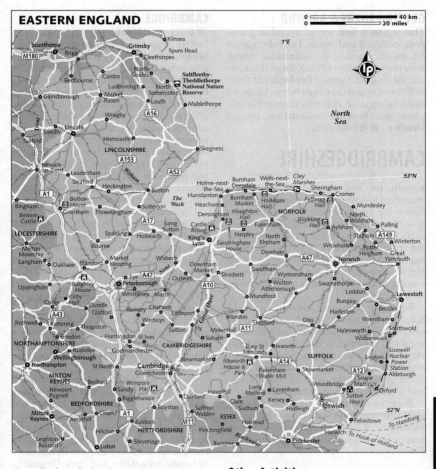

EASTERN ENGLAND

0 — 40 km
0 — 20 miles

the cycle-friendly local train service, you can have a great time on two wheels.

There's gorgeous riding along the Suffolk and Norfolk coastlines, and in the Fens. In the northern part of the region, King's Lynn and Hunstanton make good bases, and bike hire is available. In the south of the region, Cambridge is an excellent base for cycle tours, and bikes can be hired here, too.

For mountain bikers, Thetford Forest, near Thetford, is an ideal place to start, and much of Peddars Way (mentioned in the Walking section) consists of lanes and bridlepaths that are also open to cyclists, and makes a mixed on- and off-road route. (The contiguous Norfolk Coast Path is strictly for walkers only.)

Other Activities

On the coast and Norfolk Broads **sailing** is popular; there are several sailing centres from where you can hire boats or arrange lessons. Alternatively, many people tour the Broads in **motorboats** these days. At towns like Wroxham you can hire boats – anything from large cabin cruisers for a week, to little craft with phut-phut outboards for a couple of hours' gentle messing about on the river. More watery fun is available in Cambridge, where a visit is incomplete without a spot of **punting**. If you want to keep your feet dry, **landyachting** takes place on some of the long, wide and frequently empty beaches of the Norfolk coast.

GETTING THERE & AROUND

This region is well served by public transport, both rail and coach. For information on specific locales, see individual tourist information centres (TICs), listed throughout the chapter. Contact **One Anglia** (☎ 08457-484950; www.oneanglia.com; Anglia Plus pass 1/3 days in 7 £9/20) for regional rail information. For national bus timetable information, contact **Traveline** (☎ 0870 608 2608).

CAMBRIDGESHIRE

Known for and defined by its world-renowned university, Cambridgeshire nevertheless has plenty to offer beyond the realm of academia. A once-submerged area known as the Fens, this is conspicuously fertile land; the sense of abundance you feel when crossing its rich agricultural fields is overwhelming. It's also extremely flat, which means it's wonderful country for leisurely exploration on a bicycle.

From Cambridge, a towpath winds 15 miles to Ely, whose superb cathedral, on ground slightly higher than the surrounding plain, is known as the 'ship of the fens'. Peterborough, also known as England's shopping capital, has another fine cathedral in the north of the county. And of course Cambridge itself has few rivals for sheer beauty.

Short strolls and city ambles are suggested throughout this section. For longer walks, the TIC in Cambridge stocks a number of guides, including *Walks in South Cambridgeshire*.

Getting Around

Public transport centres on Cambridge, which is only 55 minutes by rail from London. This line continues north through Ely to terminate at King's Lynn in Norfolk. From Ely, branch lines run east through Norwich, southeast into Suffolk, and northwest to Peterborough and into Lincolnshire. The useful *Cambridgeshire and Peterborough Passenger Transport Map* is available at all TICs.

The primary services:

Cambridge Coach Services (☎ 01223-423900) Cambridge to Norwich.

Stagecoach Cambus (☎ 01223-423554) Links Cambridge, Bury St Edmunds and Ely.

Stagecoach United Counties (☎ 01604-620077) Cambridge to Huntingdon and Peterborough.

CAMBRIDGE

☎ 01223 / pop 131,465

Just try stepping off the bus or train in Cambridge and not being awed. Not only is there a palpable sense of erudition and tradition, it's also a simply beautiful city. Dominated by its famous institute of higher learning, Cambridge is a true university town – but, given the stature of this particular university, even its student population seems to radiate more solemnity than youthful mania. Which isn't to say it's no fun. There are endless opportunities here for relaxing at a quayside pub beside the peaceful River Cam, walking, cycling, punting, shopping, or just wandering through the cobblestoned streets.

Cambridge is smaller than 'the other place' (as Oxford is referred to here) and, partly because of the university's strong influence, it's more architecturally unified and is generally considered more aesthetically pleasing. The choir and chapel of King's College would be hard to beat in any city – they're indisputably among the highlights of any trip to England. The rest of the city is a breathtaking blend of medieval buildings, curving alleyways, elegant courtyards and expansive parks, particularly the Backs, where the gentle River Cam meanders along behind the various colleges.

Though it's hardly a centre of industry, Cambridge is certainly not rural. A busy market town brimming with history and antiquity, it boasts shopping streets lined with exclusive designer outlets and fancy boutiques, a few happening nightclubs, many more historic pubs, and its fair share of trendy restaurants and cafés. Despite its modern amenities, though, the impression Cambridge leaves is one of tranquillity, timelessness, and an unforgettable, ageless beauty unmatched in all of England.

History

At first a Roman fort and later a small Saxon settlement, Cambridge was just a tiny rural backwater until 1209, when the university town of Oxford exploded in a riot between scholars and townspeople, forcing a group of students to quit while their heads were still intact and move up to Cambridge to found a new university. The facts surrounding the foundation are a little hazy, undoubtedly due to another riot in 1261 between 'town and gown', when the university records were burnt. At the rioters' trial the judges ruled in favour of the students, setting a precedent that would last for centuries. The new university had found favour with the law and began to establish a firm footing within the town.

The collegiate system, unique to Oxford and Cambridge, came into being gradually. The first Cambridge college, Peterhouse, was founded in 1284 by Hugo de Balsham (later Bishop of Ely). The plan was for tutors and students to live together in a community, much as they would in a monastery.

From the 14th century on, a number of colleges were founded by royalty, nobility, leading church figures, statesmen, academics and trade guilds – all for men only. In 1869 and 1871, however, women were finally accorded the right to study here with the founding of women-only Girton and Newnham colleges – although they had to wait until 1948 before they were allowed to graduate.

The honour roll of famous graduates reads like an international who's who of high achievers, and a list of their accomplishments in a wide variety of fields could fill a couple of thick volumes. So far, the university has produced 78 Nobel Prize winners (29 from Trinity College alone), 13 British prime ministers, nine archbishops of Canterbury, an immense number of scientists, and a healthy host of poets and other scribblers…and this is but a limited selection. Today the university remains at the top of the research league in British universities. It owns a prestigious publishing firm and a world-renowned examination syndicate; it is the leading centre for astronomy in Britain; its Fitzwilliam Museum contains an outstanding art collection; and its library is used by scholars from around the world.

Orientation

The colleges and university buildings comprise the centre of the city. The central area, lying in a wide bend of the River Cam, is easy to get around on foot or by bike. The best-known section of the Cam is the Backs, which combines lush river scenery with superb views of six colleges, and King's College Chapel. The other 25 colleges are scattered throughout the city.

The bus station is central on Drummer St, but the train station is a 20-minute walk to the south. Sidney St becomes St Andrew's St to the south and Bridge St then Magdalene St to the north, and is the main shopping street.

Information

BOOKSHOPS

Dillons (☎ 351688; 22 Sidney St)
Galloway & Porter (☎ 367876; 30 Sidney St) Mostly remaindered and damaged stock.
Heffers (☎ 568582; 20 Trinity St) Best for academic books.
Heffers Children's Bookshop (☎ 568551; 29-30 Trinity St)
Heffers Music (☎ 568562; 19 Trinity St) Excellent selection of classical CDs.
WH Smith (☎ 311313; 26 Lion Yard)

EMERGENCY

Police station (☎ 358966; Parkside)

INTERNET ACCESS

CB1 (☎ 576306; 32 Mill Rd; ⏰ 10am-8pm; per hr £3.25)
International Telecom Centre (☎ 357358; 2 Wheeler St; ⏰ 9am-10pm; per hr 99p)

LAUNDRY

Cleanomat Dry Cleaners (☎ 464719; 10 Victoria Ave)

MEDICAL SERVICES

Addenbrooke's Hospital (☎ 245151)
Boots (☎ 350213; 28 Petty Cury)
Vantage Pharmacy (☎ 353002; 66 Bridge St)

MONEY

Abbey National (☎ 350495; 60 St Andrew's St)
American Express (☎ 345203; 25 Sidney St)
HSBC (☎ 314822; 75 Regent St)
Thomas Cook (☎ 543100; 8 St Andrew's St)

POST

Main post office (☎ 323325; 9-11 St Andrew's St; ⏰ 9am-5.30pm Mon-Sat)

TOURIST INFORMATION

TIC (☎ 322640; www.cambridge.gov.uk; Wheeler St; ⏰ 10am-6pm Mon-Fri, 10am-5pm Sat, 11am-4pm Sun Apr-Oct, 10am-5.30pm Mon-Sat Nov-Mar)

Cambridge University

Five of the colleges within the **university** – King's, Queen's, Clare, Trinity and St John's – charge admission to tourists (£1.50 to £4). You may also find that tourists are now

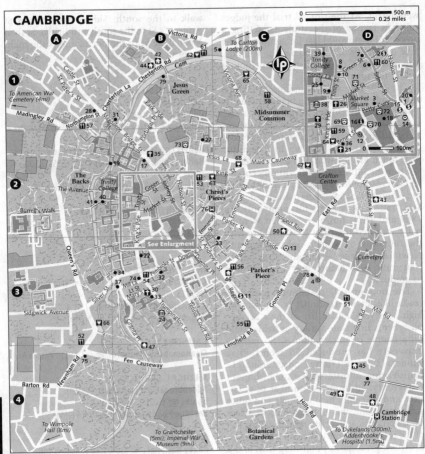

CAMBRIDGE

denied admission at some of the colleges described in this section; each year more colleges decide that the tourist bandwagon is just too disruptive. Most colleges are closed to visitors for the Easter term and all are closed for exams from mid-May to mid-June. Precise details of opening hours vary from college to college and year to year, so contact the TIC or the university's **central information service** (☎ 337733) for updates.

KING'S COLLEGE CHAPEL

All the college chapels are individually remarkable but **King's College Chapel** (☎ 331100) is supreme in its grandeur. It's one of the finest examples of Gothic architecture in England, comparable with Chartres cathedral in

France. The chapel was conceived as an act of piety by Henry VI, who laid its foundation stone in 1446, and is dedicated to the Virgin Mary. Building was completed around 1516. Henry VI's successors, notably Henry VIII, glorified the interior (and themselves in doing so). Services are led by its choir, originally choristers from Eton College, another of Henry VI's foundations. The choir's Festival of the Nine Lessons and Carols on Christmas Eve are heard all over the world.

Cromwell's soldiers destroyed many church windows in East Anglia but it is believed that, having been a Cambridge student, their leader spared King's.

Despite the original stained-glass windows, the atmosphere inside is light. The

INFORMATION		
Abbey National (Bank)	1	D1
American Express	2	D1
Boots	3	D1
CB1	4	C3
Cleanomat Dry Cleaners	5	C1
Dillons	6	D1
Galloway & Porter	7	D1
Heffers	8	D1
Heffers Children's Bookshop	9	D1
Heffers Music	10	D1
HSBC (Bank)	11	C3
International Telecom Centre	12	D2
Police Station	13	C3
Post Office	14	D1
Thomas Cook	15	D1
Tourist Information Centre (TIC)	16	D1
Vantage Pharmacy	17	B2
WH Smith	18	D1

SIGHTS & ACTIVITIES	(pp497–504)	
Bridge of Sighs	19	B2
Christ's College	20	D1
Church of St Bene't	21	D2
Corpus Christi College	22	B3
Emmanuel College	23	C3
Fitzwilliam Museum	24	B3
Gonville & Caius College	25	D1
Great St Mary's Church	26	D1
Jesus College	27	B2
Kettle's Yard	28	A1
King's College Chapel	29	D1

Little St Mary's	30	B3
Magdalene College	31	B1
Pembroke College	32	B3
Peterhouse College	33	B3
Queen's College	34	B3
Round Church	35	B2
Saxon Tower	36	D2
Scudamore's	37	B3
Senate House	38	D1
Trinity College	39	D1
Trinity Hall College	40	A2
Trinity Punts	41	A2

SLEEPING	(p504)	
Aaron House	42	B1
Ark	43	D2
Arundel House Hotel	44	B1
Cambridge YHA Hostel	45	D4
De Vere University Arms Hotel	46	C3
Garden House (Moat House)	47	B4
Sleeperz	48	D4
Tenison Towers Guest House	49	D4
Warkworth House	50	C2

EATING	(pp504–5)	
Al Casbah	51	D3
Choices Café	52	A3
Clowns	53	B2
Fitzbillies	54	B3
Gulshan	55	C3

Hobb's Pavilion	56	C3
Michel's Brasserie	57	A1
Midsummer House	58	C1
Rainbow	59	D2
Tatties	60	D1
Twenty-Two	61	B1

DRINKING	(p505)	
Boathouse	62	B1
Champion of the Thames	63	B2
Eagle	64	D2
Fort St George	65	C1
Granta (and Punt Hire)	66	A3
Sophbeck Sessions	67	C2
St Radegund	68	C2

ENTERTAINMENT	(pp505–6)	
Arts Theatre	69	D1
Corn Exchange	70	D1
Fez	71	D1
Fifth Avenue	72	D1
Po Na Na Souk Bar	73	B2

TRANSPORT	(p506)	
Ben Hayward Cycles	74	B3
Cambridge Recycles	75	A4
Drummer St Bus Station	76	B2
Geoff's Bike Hire	77	D4
Mike's Bikes	78	C3

OTHER		
Riverboat Georgina	79	B1

stunning interior of 12 bays is about 11m wide, 22m high and 80m long. This vast expanse is the largest in the world canopied by fan vaulting. It's the work of John Wastell, and is a miracle of beauty and skill. Upon seeing it, Christopher Wren reputedly said that he could have built it, but only if someone had shown him where to set the first stone.

The elaborate carvings, both in wood and stone, include royal coats of arms, intertwined initials, the royal beasts of heraldry, and flowers that were the emblems of Tudor monarchs and related families. Among the Yorkist roses on the western wall is one containing the figure of a woman; some claim she is Elizabeth of York but it's more likely that she's the Virgin Mary.

The antechapel and the choir are divided by the superbly carved **wooden screen**, another gift from Henry VIII. Designed and executed by the king's master carver, Peter Stockton, the screen bears Henry's initials entwined with those of Anne Boleyn, who supposedly inspired Henry's act of generosity. Almost concealed by the mythical beasts and symbolic flowers is one angry human face. Perhaps it is Stockton's jest for posterity?

Originally constructed between 1686 and 1688, the magnificent organ has been rebuilt and developed over the years, and its pipes now top the screen on which they

rest. The **choir stalls** were made by the same craftsman who worked on the screen, but the canopies are Carolingian. Despite the dark wood, the impression is still of lightness as one approaches the **high altar**, which is framed by Rubens' *Adoration of the Magi* and the magnificent east window.

The excellent **Chapel Exhibition** (adult £4) is in the northern side chapels, to the left of the altar. Here you can see the stages and methods of building the chapel set against the historical panorama from inception to completion. On display are costumes, paintings, illuminated manuscripts and books, plans, tools, and scale models, including a full-size model showing how the fan vaulting was constructed.

The vergers are helpful with information and there are occasional guided tours on the weekend. Weekday tours can be arranged at the TIC. The chapel comes alive when the choir sings; even the most pagan heavy-metal fan will find **Choral Evensong** (5.30pm Tue-Sat, 10.30am & 3.30pm Sun mid-Jan–mid-Mar, mid-Apr–mid-Jun, mid-late Jul, Oct–early Dec, & Dec 24 & 25) an extraordinary experience.

TRINITY COLLEGE

Henry VIII founded **Trinity College** (☎ 338400; Trinity St; admission £1.75) in 1546, but it was left to Dr Nevile, Master of Trinity (1593–1615) in Elizabeth's reign, to fulfil his wishes, as Henry died six weeks after founding the college.

EASTERN ENGLAND

As you walk through the impressive brick gateway (1535), have a look at the statue of Henry that adorns it. His left hand holds a golden orb, while his right grips a table leg, put there by students who removed the golden sceptre years ago. As you enter the **Great Court**, scholastic humour gives way to a gaping sense of awe, for it is the largest of its kind in the world. The place is dripping with history: to the right of the entrance is a small tree, planted in the 1950s and reputed to be a descendant of the apple tree made famous by Trinity alumnus Sir Isaac Newton.

The square is also the scene of the run made famous by the film *Chariots of Fire* – 350m in 43 seconds (the time it takes the clock to strike 12). Although plenty of students have a go, Harold Abrahams (the hero of the film) never actually attempted it, and his fictional run wasn't even filmed here. If you fancy your chances remember that you'll need Olympian speed to even come close to making it in time.

The Gothic antechapel to the right of the gate is full of huge statues of famous Trinity men, such as Tennyson and Newton. The vast hall has a hammer-beam roof and lantern. Beyond the hall are the cloisters of Nevile's Court and the dignified **Wren Library** (noon-2pm Mon-Fri all year, 10am-6pm Mon-Fri & 10.30am-12.30pm Sat during term). It contains 55,000 books printed before 1820 and more than 2500 manuscripts, including AA Milne's original *Winnie the Pooh*. Both he and his son, Christopher Robin, were graduates.

THE BACKS

Two notable bridges cross the canal in the parklike area behind the colleges known as the **Backs**: the **Bridge of Sighs** (built in 1831, a replica of the original in Venice) and the bridge at **Clare College**. The latter is ornamented with decorative balls and is the oldest (1639), most interesting bridge on the Backs. Its architect was paid a grand total of 15p for his design so, feeling aggrieved at such a measly fee, he cut a slice out of one of the balls adorning the balustrade (the next to last one on the left), thus ensuring that the bridge would never be complete. Or so the story goes.

GREAT ST MARY'S CHURCH

This university **church** (741716; Senate House Hill), built between 1478 and 1519 in the late-Gothic perpendicular style, has a feel-ing of space and light inside, thanks to its clerestory, wide arch and woodcarving. The traditional termly university sermons are preached here. To get your bearings, climb the 123 steps of the **tower** (admission £2) for a good view of the city. The building across King's Pde, on the right-hand side of the square, is the **Senate House**, designed in 1730 by James Gibbs. It's the most beautiful example of pure classical architecture in the city; graduations are held here.

GONVILLE & CAIUS

This fascinating old **college** (332400; Trinity St) was founded twice, first by a priest called Gonville, in 1348, and then again by Dr Caius (pronounced keys), a brilliant physician and scholar, in 1557. Of special interest here are the three gates: Virtue, Humility and Honour. They symbolise the progress of the good student, since the third gate (the *Porta Honoris,* a fascinating confection with a quirky dome and sundials) leads to the Senate House and thus graduation.

TRINITY HALL COLLEGE

This is a delightfully small **college** (332500; Trinity Lane), wedged among the great and the famous. Despite the name, it has nothing to do with Trinity College. It was founded in 1350 as a refuge for lawyers and clerics escaping the ravages of the Black Death, thus earning it the nickname of the 'Lawyers' College'. You enter through the newest court, which overlooks the river on one side and has a lovely fellows' garden on another. Walking into the next court, you pass the 16th-century library, which has original Jacobean reading desks, and books chained to the shelves to prevent their permanent removal – the 16th century's equivalent of electronic bar codes.

Just outside the first court is a tall, historic gate, which gets little attention. It's the entry to Old Schools, the administrative centre of the university. The lower part dates back to 1441 and the upper part was added in the 1860s.

CHRIST'S COLLEGE

Christ's (334900; St Andrew's St) was founded in 1505 by the pious and generous benefactress Lady Margaret Beaufort, who also founded St John's. It has an impressive entrance gate emblazoned with heraldic carving.

The figure of the founder stands in a niche, hovering over all like a guiding spirit. Note the stout oak door leading into First Court, which has an unusual circular lawn, magnolias and wisteria creepers. The court is a mixture of original buildings and 18th-century facings and windows. The hall was rebuilt in neogothic style in the 19th century, and the chapel's early sections include an oriel window that enabled the founder to join in services from her 1st-floor room.

Second Court has an interesting fellows' building, dating back to 1643. Its gate leads into a fellows' garden, which contains a mulberry tree under which Milton (who came up to the college in 1628) reputedly wrote *Lycidas*. Continuing through Iris Court you're confronted by the stark, grey, modern students' block, which seems totally out of place.

JESUS COLLEGE

The approach to **Jesus** (☎ 339339; Jesus Lane), founded 1496, via the long 'chimney' is impressive, as is the main gate, which is under a rebus of the founder, Bishop Alcock. A rebus is a heraldic device suggesting the name of its owner: the bishop's consists of several cockerels. The spacious First Court, with its redbrick ranges, is open on the western side – an unusual feature.

Be sure to look at the tiny, intimate cloister court to your right, and the chapel, which dates back to the St Radegund nunnery. The bishop closed the nunnery, expelled the nuns for misbehaving and founded the new college in its place. The inspiring chapel reflects the college's development over the centuries. It has a Norman arched gallery from the nunnery building, a 13th-century chancel and beautiful restoration work, and Art Nouveau features by Pugin, Morris (ceilings), Burne-Jones (stained glass) and Madox Brown.

MAGDALENE COLLEGE

Originally a Benedictine hostel, the **college** (☎ 332100; Magdalene St) was refounded in 1542 by Lord Audley. It has the dubious honour of being the last college to allow women students; when they were finally admitted in 1988, male students wore black armbands and flew the college flag at half-mast.

Its river setting gives it a certain appeal, but its greatest asset is the Pepys Library,

housing the magnificent collection of books the famous diarist bequeathed to his old college – he was a student here between 1650 and 1653.

CORPUS CHRISTI COLLEGE

Next door, at **Corpus Christi** (☎ 338000; Trumpington St), an entrance leads into Old Court, which has been retained in its medieval form and still exudes a monastic atmosphere. The door to the chapel is flanked by two statues; on the right is Matthew Parker, who was college master in 1544 and Archbishop of Canterbury for much of the reign of Elizabeth I. A pretty bright lad, Mr Parker was known for his curiosity; his endless questioning gave us the term 'nosy parker'. Playwright Christopher Marlowe (1564–93), author of *Dr Faustus* and *Tamburlaine*, was a Corpus man – as a plaque, next to a fascinating sundial, bears out. New Court, beyond, is a 19th-century creation.

The college library has the finest collection of Anglo-Saxon manuscripts in the world. With other valuable books, they were preserved from destruction at the time of Henry VIII's dissolution of the monasteries.

QUEENS' COLLEGE

One of the Backs' colleges, **Queens'** (☎ 335511; admission £1.20; Silver St) was the first Cambridge college to charge admission. This was initiated to pay for soundproofing its vulnerable site on this busy street. It takes its name from the two queens who founded it – Margaret of Anjou (wife of Henry VI) and Elizabeth of Woodville (wife of Edward IV), in 1448 and 1465 respectively – yet a conscientious rector of St Botolph's Church was its real creator.

The college's main entrance is off Queens' Lane. The redbrick gate tower and Old Court, which immediately capture your attention, are part of the medieval college. So is Cloister Court, the next court, with its impressive cloister and picturesque, half-timbered President's Lodge ('president' is the name for the master). The famous Dutch scholar and reformer Erasmus lodged in the tower from 1510 to 1514. He wasn't particularly enamoured of Cambridge: he thought that the wine tasted like vinegar, that the beer was slop and that the place was too expensive, but he did write that the local women were good kissers.

PETERHOUSE COLLEGE

Founded in 1284 by Hugo de Balsham, later Bishop of Ely, **Peterhouse** (☎ 338200; Trumpington St) is the oldest and smallest of the colleges. It stands to the west of Trumpington St, just south of the Church of St Mary the Less (more tactfully known as **Little St Mary's**). The church's original odd-sounding name was St Peter's-without-Trumpington-Gate (because it stood outside, or 'without', the old gate) and it gave the college its name. Inside is a memorial to Godfrey Washington, an alumnus of the college and a great-uncle of George Washington. His family coat of arms was the stars and stripes, the inspiration for the US flag. A walk through Peterhouse gives you a clear picture of the 'community' structure of a Cambridge college though, unusually, the master's house is opposite the college, not within it. The college's list of notable alumni includes the poet Thomas Gray, who came up in 1742, and Henry Cavendish, the first person to measure the density of water. He also calculated the weight of the planet: if you must know, Earth weighs six thousand million million tonnes.

First Court, the oldest, is small, neat and bright, with hanging baskets and window boxes. The 17th-century chapel is on the right, built in a mixture of styles that blend well. Inside, the luminous 19th-century stained-glass windows contrast with the older eastern window. The Burrough range, on the right, is 18th century and the hall, on the left, a restored, late-13th-century gem. Beyond the hall are sweeping grounds extending to the Fitzwilliam Museum.

PEMBROKE COLLEGE

Lovely gardens and lawns link the several courts of **Pembroke** (☎ 338100; Trumpington St). It was founded in 1347 by Marie de St Pol de Valence, the widowed countess of Pembroke. At 17 she'd married the 50-year-old earl, but he was killed in a joust on their wedding day, making her 'maid, wife and widow all in one day'. As usual, the oldest court is at the entrance. It still retains some medieval corner sections. The chapel, on the extreme right, is an early Wren creation (1665): his uncle Mathew Wren, bishop of Ely, had spent 18 years imprisoned in the Tower of London, courtesy of Oliver Cromwell, and had promised that if released he would build a chapel in his old college.

EMMANUEL COLLEGE

Founded in 1584, this medium-sized **college** (☎ 334200; St Andrew's St) comprises some 600 people. If you stand in Front Court, one of the architectural gems of Cambridge faces you – the Wren chapel, cloister and gallery, completed in 1677. To the left is the hall; inside, the refectory-type tables are set at right angles to the high table. The next court, New Court, is round the corner. It has a quaint herb garden reminiscent of the old Dominican priory that preceded the college.

There are a few remnants of the priory in the *clunch* (chalk) core of the walls of the Old Library. Turn right to re-enter Front Court and go into the chapel. It has interesting windows, a high ceiling and a painting by Jacopo Amigoni. Near the side door is a plaque to a famous scholar, John Harvard (BA 1632), who was among 30 Emmanuel men who settled in New England. He left money to found the university that bears his name in the Massachusetts town of Cambridge. His portrait also features in one of the stained-glass windows – but, as the artist had no likeness of Harvard from which to work, he used the face of John Milton, a contemporary of Harvard's at the college.

Round Church

The amazing **Round Church** (Church of the Holy Sepulchre; Bridge St; ☎ 518219) was built by the mysterious Knights Templar in 1130 to commemorate its namesake in Jerusalem and is one of only four in England. It's strikingly unusual, with chunky, round Norman pillars that encircle the small nave. The rest of the church was added later in a different style; the conical roof dates from just the 19th century. No longer a parish church, it's now a **brass-rubbing centre** (☎ 871621; ◷ 10am-6pm in summer, 1-4pm in winter; costs £5 to £24 depending on size of brass).

Church of St Bene't

The **Saxon tower** of this Franciscan **church** (☎ 353903; Bene't St), built in 1025, is the oldest structure in Cambridgeshire. The rest of the church is newer but full of interesting features. The round holes above the belfry windows were designed to offer owls nesting privileges; they were valued as mouse killers. It was here in 1670 that parish clerk Fabian Stedman invented change-ringing (the ringing of bells with different peals in

---

HOW TO PUNT

Punting looks pretty straightforward but, believe us, it's not. As soon as we dried off and hung our clothes on the line, we thought it was a good idea to offer a couple of tips on how to move the boat and stay dry.

1. Standing at the end of the punt, lift the pole out of the water at the side of the punt.
2. Let the pole slide through your hands to touch the bottom of the river.
3. Tilt the pole forward (that is, in the direction of travel of the punt) and push down to propel the punt forward.
4. Twist the pole to free the end from the mud at the bottom of the river, and let it float up and trail behind the punt. You can then use it as a rudder to steer with.
5. If you've not yet fallen in, raise the pole out of the water and into the vertical position to begin the cycle again.

---

a sequential order). The church also has a Bible that belonged to Thomas Hobson, owner of a nearby livery stable, who told customers they could hire any horse they liked as long as it was the one nearest the door – hence the term 'Hobson's choice', meaning no choice at all.

Fitzwilliam Museum

This massive **neoclassical edifice** (☎ 332900; Trumpington St; admission free; ⏰ 10am-5pm Tue-Sat, 2.15-5pm Sun; tours 2.30pm Sun) takes its name from the seventh Viscount Fitzwilliam, who bequeathed his fabulous art treasures to his old university in 1816. The building in which they are stored was begun by George Basevi in 1837, but he did not live to see its completion in 1848: while working on Ely Cathedral he stepped back to admire his handiwork, slipped and fell to his death. The Fitzwilliam was one of the first public art museums in Britain.

In the lower galleries are ancient Egyptian sarcophagi, Greek and Roman art, Chinese ceramics, English glass, and illuminated manuscripts. The upper galleries contain a wide range of paintings, including works by Titian, Rubens, the French Impressionists, Gainsborough, Stubbs and Constable, right up to Cézanne and Picasso. It also has fine antique furniture.

Kettle's Yard

This **house** (cnr Northampton & Castle Sts; admission free; ⏰ 11.30am-5pm Tue-Sun) was the home of HS 'Jim' Ede, a former assistant keeper at the Tate Gallery in London, and his wife, Helen. In 1957 they opened their home to young artists with a view to creating 'a home and a welcome, a refuge of peace

and order, of the visual arts and of music'. Their efforts resulted in a beautiful collection of 20th-century art, furniture, ceramics and glass by such artists as Henry Moore, Henri Gaudier-Brzeska and a host of other Britons. In 1966 they donated their home and collection to the university, which opened it as a **museum** (☎ 352124; admission free; ⏰ 2-4pm Tue-Sun) but didn't touch the arrangement of the pieces. In the adjoining exhibition gallery (opened 1970) there are temporary exhibits of contemporary art.

Activities
PUNTING

Taking a punt along the Backs is sublime, though it can also be a wet and hectic experience, especially on a busy weekend. If you wimp out, you can opt for a chauffeured punt, and if the water doesn't attract you at all, the Backs are also perfect for a walk or a picnic.

Granta (Newnham Rd; per hr £10) A pub that hires punts on the side.

Scudamore's (☎ 359750; Silver St; per hr £12, chauffeured £40)

Trinity Punts (☎ 338483; behind Trinity College; per hr £8)

WALKING & CYCLING

One of the prettiest walks in the whole region is the 3-mile walk to Grantchester from Cambridge along the River Cam. More of a gentle stroll than a serious walk, the route simply follows the meandering river as it winds its way southwest. In fine weather the river is full of punts.

For tooting around town by bike, the flat topography makes things easy, although beyond the city the scenery can get a bit monotonous. The Cambridge TIC stocks several useful guides including *Cycle Routes and the Cambridge Green Belt Area*, and the *Cambridge Cycle Route Map*.

Tours

Guide Friday/City Sightseeing (☎ 362444; adult/child £7.50/3) Hop-on hop-off tour buses, starting from the railway station but you can get on or off at points along the route, including Fitzwilliam Museum and the Round Church.

Riverboat Georgina (☎ 500111; day/evening £7/8.50) Two-hour cruises from the river at Jesus Lock.

Walking tours (☒ 1.30pm daily, with extra tours at 10.30am, 11.30am and 2.30pm May-Sep; tickets £7.25) The TIC arranges these, as well as other theme tours; book in advance.

Sleeping

BUDGET

Cambridge YHA Hostel (☎ 0870-770 5742; fax 312780; 97 Tenison Rd; dm £12.75; ℗) This popular hostel near the train station has small dormitories, all the basic facilities (lockers, laundry) and a restaurant.

Carlton Lodge (☎ 367792; info@carltonlodge.co.uk; 245 Chesterton Rd; s/d from £20/40; ℗) Northwest of the centre, the Carlton has comparatively large and well-appointed rooms, and is run by widely travelled, friendly people.

Also recommended are **Tenison Towers Guest House** (☎ 363924; 148 Tenison Rd; r £22-30), an excellent B&B with clean, comfortable rooms and attentive service, and the **Ark** (☎ 311130; 30 St Matthew's St; s/d from £28/38), with prettily appointed rooms painted in bright, airy colours.

MID-RANGE

Warkworth House (☎ 363682; Warkworth Tce; s/d from £40/58) This beautiful Victorian terraced house just off Parkside has comfortable rooms, a delicious breakfast and extremely friendly owners; it's popular with students from overseas.

Dykelands (☎ 244300; dykelands@fsbdial.co.uk; 157 Mowbray Rd; s/d from £30/38; ℗) An excellent choice, albeit a little far from the action, just south of the train station. The rooms, all furnished in pine, are extremely comfortable. Its location will be no problem to cyclists.

Sleeperz (☎ 304050; info@sleeperz.com; Station Rd; s/d from £30/45) Right outside the train station, this is an attractively converted railway warehouse that almost always has vacancies

for desperate late arrivals. Rooms are spartan and spotless with comfortable futon-style beds; those with double beds are larger – all others have cabin-style bunk beds.

Aaron House (☎ 314723; 71 Chesterton Rd; s/d from £30/48; ℗ ☒) This B&B in a Victorian home was the birthplace of a former archbishop of Canterbury, Arthur Ramsey. A 10-minute stroll north of the city centre, this quiet place in a residential neighbourhood has rooms overlooking Jesus Green and the River Cam. An outdoor pool and tennis courts are available for guests' use. Not all rooms are en suite.

TOP END

De Vere University Arms Hotel (☎ 351241; devere .uniarms@airtime.co.uk; Regent St; s/d from £80/130, specials often available; ℗) The top choice in Cambridge, this huge Victorian mansion overlooking Parker's Piece has elegant rooms, even the smallest of which have carefully chosen design flourishes. First-class service, conveniences for business travellers and a great breakfast buffet served in a gorgeous annexe overlooking the park sweeten the deal. Look out for the enormous, creaky cage lift from 1927.

Arundel House Hotel (☎ 367701; info@arundel househotels.co.uk; 53 Chesterton Rd; s/d from £68/85) A large Victorian terrace overlooking the Cam, this is an elegant place with beautiful rooms, many with views of the water.

Garden House (Moat House; ☎ 259988; Granta Pl, Mill Lane; s/d £169/200; ℗) More like something you'd find on an exclusive golf course, this posh, resorty hotel is right on the Cam and has its own private garden. It's an imposing, modern building with 117 luxurious bedrooms. Rates exclude breakfast. Look out for serious discounts on weekend rates.

Eating

Midsummer House (☎ 369299; set menu lunch £30, dinner £46; ☒ lunch Tue-Fri & Sun, dinner Tue-Sat) Overlooking the river on Midsummer Common is this smart, sophisticated place with a superb menu, said to have one of the most comprehensive wine lists outside Paris. It's a good idea to book several weeks in advance.

Twenty-Two (☎ 351880; 22 Chesterton Rd; set menu dinner £29.95) Cleverly disguised among a row of B&Bs is probably the best restaurant in town, with an outstanding gourmet menu (mostly French) that sends serious foodies straight to heaven; the service is top-notch.

Fitzbillies (☎ 352500; 52 Trumpington St) An institution in town, this is a brilliant bakery-café by day – the Chelsea buns (85p) are an outrageous experience and so is the chocolate cake, beloved by generations of students – and an elegant, classy restaurant by night. It's a good place to stock up on supplies before punting. Cakes and buns are also available by mail order.

Al Casbah (☎ 579500; 62 Mill Rd; mains £6-9) This tasty Algerian restaurant has a really good couscous for £8.95; the food is cooked on an indoor barbecue.

Gulshan (☎ 302330; 106 Regent St; mains from £5.95) This place has Indian food you'll dream about for months afterwards, especially the curry.

Tatties (☎ 323399; 11 Sussex St; £1-4) A longtime budget favourite, Tatties specialises not only in baked potatoes stuffed with a variety of tempting fillings but also in breakfasts, filled baguettes, salads and cakes.

Clowns (☎ 355711; 54 King St; sandwiches around £2.50) A great spot for reading the newspaper, this café is full of well-dressed old men, dark wood and a pleasantly weighty sense of time. Gelato is available.

Other recommendations:

Choices Café (☎ 360211; 38 Newnham Rd) Picnic hampers to go, £5 per person.

Hobb's Pavilion (☎ 367480; Park Tce; mains around £8; ☙ Tue-Sat) Great summer dining in the old cricket pavilion.

Michel's Brasserie (☎ 353110; 21 Northampton St; set lunches £8.95) An excellent French menu.

Rainbow (☎ 321551; 9a King's Pde; mains around £7) Funky, cheerfully painted vegetarian restaurant.

Drinking

Punting is a big deal in Cambridge, at least with a certain section of the university population, and even though members of that segment have earned themselves something of a reputation for being rowdy in the pub after a day's rowing, the punting pubs – where rowers hang out and tourists can rent punts – are definitely worth checking out. Away from the Cam, Cambridge has plenty of atmospheric pubs and trendy bars.

Fort St George (Midsummer Common) Said to be the oldest pub on the Cam, this one dates from the 16th century. The location is perfect – on the river at the north end of

Midsummer Common – which means it's a popular spot, particularly in summer. You can rent punts from here.

Eagle (Bene't St) Nobel Prize–winning scientists Crick and Watson spent equal time in the laboratory and here, so perhaps Greene King, the Suffolk brewers, played a part in the discovery of the structure of DNA. This 16th-century pub was also popular with American airmen in WWII; they left their signatures on the ceiling.

St Radegund (127 King St) This ancient, priceless little pub in what looks like a fortress has burlap curtains, sagging walls and endless character; it's understandably popular with locals.

Champion of the Thames (68 King St) Despite the name, this place is not remotely connected with punting. It's just an old-style traditional pub, with live music on Tuesday, and a wonderful spot for a pint of ale.

Granta (Newnham Rd) Serving double duty as a place for punt hire, the Granta is a popular riverside rower's pub.

Boathouse (14 Chesterton Rd) Taking the punt-to-the-pub idea even further, the Boathouse even has its own mooring place.

Sophbeck Sessions (14 Tredgold La) A Cajun-style bar in the northeast of town, this is a popular place with students and visitors alike for a drink and some live jazz and soul.

Entertainment

NIGHTCLUBS

Fez (☎ 519224; 15 Market Passage; admission £2-7, free before 9pm Mon & Wed; ☙ 8pm-2am Mon-Sat) The place to go if clubbing is your thing, with queues most nights and the music loud and thumping. Admission prices vary depending on the night.

Po Na Na Souk Bar (☎ 323880; 7b Jesus Lane; admission £1.50; ☙ to 2am) Part of a classy, well-designed regional chain, this is a terrific bar and club in the basement of a neoclassical building. The style is Moroccan kasbah, and the DJs spin a mix of Latin, house and other funky rhythms.

Fifth Avenue (☎ 364222; Heidelburg Gardens, Lion Yard; admission £5-7) This popular place is a bit of a meat market, but shopping can be good fun. It's a slice of Ibiza in Cambridge.

THEATRE

Corn Exchange (☎ 357851) Near the TIC, this interesting building is the city's main centre

CAMBRIDGE, AKA...

It seems ironic that, in a city renowned for its academic excellence and the superior quality of its scholarly research, there is still doubt over how exactly Cambridge got its name. One thing, however, is certain: at the heart of the matter are two rivers, the Cam and its tributary the Granta. Until at least AD 1000 it was the latter that was deemed more important. Britain's first historian, the Venerable Bede, made reference to the settlement of *Grantacaestir* in around AD 730, while 15 years later Felix of Crowland wrote of *Grontricc*. In 875 the *Anglo-Saxon Chronicle* mentioned *Grantebrycge*, but from 1107 the town was known variously as *Caumbrigge, Caumbregge, Caumberage* and *Cantabrigia*. The first line of Chaucer's *Reeve's Tale*, written at the end of the 14th century, reads: 'At Trumpington, not fer fro Cantebrigge'. But still the town's name continued to change. In 1478 it was Camebrygge, finally becoming Cambridge during Elizabethan times.

for arts and entertainment, attracting the top names in pop and rock as well as more classical artists, such as the English National Ballet.

Arts Theatre (☎ 503333; 6 St Edward's Passage) Cambridge's only real theatre puts on everything from pantomime to serious dramatic works.

Getting There & Away

Cambridge can easily be visited as a day trip from London (although it's worth staying at least a night) or en route north. It's well served by trains, though not so well by bus.

Trains run every 30 minutes from London's King's Cross and Liverpool St stations (55 minutes). There are also hourly connections to Bury St Edmunds (45 minutes), Ely (15 minutes) and King's Lynn (50 minutes).

Airlink/Jetlink (☎ 0870 575 7747) runs an Inter-Varsity Link via Stansted airport, and buses to Heathrow and Gatwick airports, from Drummer St bus station.

Getting Around

BICYCLE

It's easy enough to get around Cambridge on foot but, if you're staying out of the centre or plan to explore the Fens, a bicycle can be useful. You don't need a flash mountain bike, because there are few hills; most places rent three-speeds.

Ben Hayward Cycles (☎ 355229; www.benhaywardcycles.com; 69 Trumpington St; per day £12)

Cambridge Recycles (☎ 506035; 61 Newnham Rd; per day £8-10)

Geoff's Bike Hire (☎ 365629; 65 Devonshire Rd; per day/week £8/16)

Mike's Bikes (☎ 312591; 28 Mill Rd; per day £8)

BUS

A free gas-powered shuttle stops at Emmanuel St in the centre. Four bus lines (85p to £1.50) run around town from Drummer St bus station, including bus No 3 from the train station to the town centre. Dayrider passes (£3) offer unlimited travel on all buses within Cambridge for one day; Megarider passes (£7) are valid for one week.

CAR

Most vehicles are now banned from the centre of Cambridge. It's best to use the well-signposted Park & Ride car parks (£1.25) on the outskirts of town. Shuttle buses run between the centre and the car parks between 7am and 7pm daily.

TAXI

Contact **Cabco** (☎ 312444) for a taxi.

AROUND CAMBRIDGE

Grantchester

The poet Rupert Brooke, who was a student at King's before WWI, captured Grantchester's quintessential Englishness in the immortal lines: '...oh! yet/Stands the Church clock at 10 to three?/ And is there honey still for tea?' Three miles southeast of Cambridge, Grantchester is a delightful village of thatched cottages and flower-filled meadows beside the River Granta. The novelist Jeffrey Archer purchased the Old Vicarage here shortly before being jailed for perjury (he's out now and presumably back to keeping Grantchester literary).

There are teashops, some attractive pubs and the **Orchard tea garden**, where cream teas are served in comfortable lawn chairs under apple trees. The best of the pubs is the **Red Lion**, near the river, which has a very pleasant garden and a lot of nooks and crannies in which to squirrel yourself away with a post-punt pint.

Walking here via the signposted towpath makes a wonderful afternoon stroll from Cambridge (see Walking & Cycling, p503).

American War Cemetery

Four miles west of Cambridge, at Madingley, is a very moving **cemetery** (☎ 01954-210350; 🕑 8am-5.30pm mid-Apr–Sep, 8am-5pm Oct–mid-Apr) with neat rows of white-marble crosses stretching down the sloping site to commemorate 3811 Americans killed in battle while based in Britain. You can visit the cemetery as part of a City Sightseeing tour (see Tours, p504).

Imperial War Museum

Military hardware enthusiasts should head for this **war museum** (☎ 835000; admission £10; 🕑 10am-6pm mid-Mar–Sep, 10am-4pm Oct–mid-Mar) in Duxford, 9 miles south of Cambridge right by the motorway. The museum is housed in an airfield that played a significant role in WWII, especially during the Battle of Britain. It was the home of the famous Dambuster squadron of Lancasters, and today is home to the Royal Air Force's Red Arrows squadron, which performs all kinds of celestial trickery at air shows throughout the world. You'll find Europe's biggest collection of historic aircraft, ranging from WWI biplanes to jets, including the Concorde. The **American Air Museum**, designed by Norman Foster, is also on the site. It has the largest collection of American civil and military aircraft outside the United States. Air shows are frequently held here, and battlefield scenes are displayed in the land warfare hall, where you can check out WWII tanks and artillery. Kids will enjoy the adventure playground and the flight simulator.

The museum runs courtesy buses – the journey is included in the admission price – from Cambridge train station every 40 to 50 minutes between 9.40am and 3.40pm (until 2.20pm October to mid-March); they also stop outside the Crowne Plaza Hotel by the Lionyard.

Wimpole Hall

A large, gracious 18th-century mansion set in 140 hectares of beautiful parkland, **Wimpole Hall** (☎ 207257; admission £6.60, with Home Farm £9.80; 🕑 farm 10.30am-4pm Tue-Thu, Sat & Sun Mar-Nov, 10.30am-5pm Jul & Aug, hall 1-5pm Tue-Thu, Sat & Sun) was the home of Rudyard Kipling's daughter until her death in 1976. Wimpole Home Farm, next to it, was established in 1794 as a model farm; today it preserves and shows rare breeds.

Wimpole Hall is 8 miles south of Cambridge on the A603. There's no charge to just walk in the park, which is open dawn till dusk year round.

ELY

☎ 01353 / pop13,954

Until recently a quiet little market town, Ely (ee-lee) is becoming ever more popular as a retreat for locals looking to get away from the big city. Its neat Georgian houses, river port and great cathedrals make it eminently worthy of a visit. The town also has a bizarrely interesting history: today it stands in the centre of the Fens, but at one time it was an island, and derived its name from the eels that swam in the surrounding waters.

Information

TIC (☎ 662062; fax 668518; 29 St Mary's St; 🕑 10am-5.30pm Apr-Sep, 10am-5pm Mon-Sat, 11.15am-4pm Sun Oct-Mar), inside Oliver Cromwell's house, has details about the 'passport to Ely', a combined ticket (£11) for the main sights – Ely Cathedral, the Stained Glass Museum, Ely Museum and Oliver Cromwell's House. It also books accommodation and has information about the busy farmer's market, held in Market Pl from 8.30am to 3.30pm on Saturday twice a month.

The police station is at the corner of Egremont St and Lynn Rd, and there's a branch of Lloyd's TSB bank, with ATM, on High St.

Sights

ELY CATHEDRAL

The origins of **Ely Cathedral** (☎ 667735; admission £4.80; 🕑 7am-7pm Easter-Aug, 7.30am-6pm Mon-Sat, 7.30am-5pm Sun Sep-Easter), whose imposing silhouette dominates the town, lie with a remarkable queen of Northumbria, Etheldreda. She had married twice but was determined to pursue her vocation to become a nun. She founded an abbey in 673 and, for her good works, was canonised after her death. The abbey soon became a pilgrimage centre.

EASTERN ENGLAND

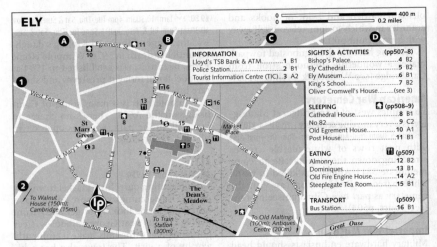

ELY

0 — 400 m
0 — 0.2 miles

INFORMATION	
Lloyd's TSB Bank & ATM...........1	B1
Police Station.............................2	B1
Tourist Information Centre (TIC)...3	A2

SIGHTS & ACTIVITIES	(pp507–8)
Bishop's Palace..........................4	B2
Ely Cathedral.............................5	B2
Ely Museum...............................6	B1
King's School.............................7	B2
Oliver Cromwell's House..........(see 3)	

SLEEPING	(pp508–9)
Cathedral House........................8	B1
No 82......................................9	C2
Old Egrement House................10	A1
Post House..............................11	B1

EATING	(p509)
Almonry..................................12	B2
Dominiques.............................13	B1
Old Fire Engine House.............14	A2
Steeplegate Tea Room.............15	B1

TRANSPORT	(p509)
Bus Station.............................16	B1

A Norman bishop, Simeon, first began the task of building the cathedral. It was completed in 1189 and remains a splendid example of the Norman Romanesque style. In 1322 – after the collapse of the central tower – the octagon and lantern, for which the cathedral is famous, were built. Other features of special interest include the gorgeous lady chapel, the largest of its kind in England, which was added in the 14th century. The niches were rifled by iconoclasts, but the delicate tracery and carving remain intact. There's an amazing view from just inside the western door – right down the nave, through the choir stalls and on to the glorious eastern window. There is no clutter, just a sublime sense of space, light and spirituality.

Ely was the first cathedral in the country to charge admission and, with funds gathered since 1986, it has managed to restore the octagon and lantern tower. There are free guided tours of the cathedral, and an octagon and roof tour (£4). There's a **stained glass museum** (adult/child £3.50/2.50) in the south triforium. Choral Sunday service is at 10.30am and evensong is at 5.30pm Monday to Saturday, 3.45pm on Sunday.

OTHER SIGHTS & ACTIVITIES

The area around the cathedral is historically and architecturally interesting. There's the former **Bishop's Palace**, now used as a nursing home, and **King's School**, which supplies the cathedral with choristers.

Oliver Cromwell's House (☎ 662062; admission £3.75) stands to the west, across St Mary's Green. Cromwell lived with his family in this attractive half-timbered 14th-century house from 1636 to 1646, when he was the tithe collector of Ely. The TIC, occupying the front room of the house, offers an audiovisual presentation and an interesting tour of the rooms.

The history of the town is further described in **Ely Museum** (☎ 666655; admission £2; 10.30am-5.30pm Sun-Fri, 1-5pm Sun May-Oct, 10.30am-4pm Wed-Mon Nov-Apr), in the Old Gaol House.

Signs lead down to the river on a nice stroll to an interesting **antiques centre**. The **Old Maltings** (☎ 662633; Ship Lane), which stages exhibitions and has a café, is nearby.

River Great Ouse is a busy thoroughfare – swans and ducks compete with boats for river space. The towpath winds up- and downstream: for a quiet walk, turn left; turn right for the pub and tea garden. If you continue along this path you'll see the Fens stretching to the horizon.

Sleeping

Post House (☎ 667184; 12a Egremont St; s/d from £20/40; P) Unmissable with the Union flag raised outside, this elegant building has plain but comfortable rooms and an ideal location.

Walnut House (☎ 661793; walnuthouse1@aol.com; 1 Houghton Gardens; s/d £25/50; P) Large and gorgeous with beautifully appointed rooms, this is another top choice for accommodation, southwest of the centre.

Other sleeping options:

Cathedral House (☎ 662124; farndale@cathedral house.co.uk; 17 St Mary's St; s/d £35/50)

No 82 (☎ 667609; 82 Broad St; s/d from £20/40) A pleasant Georgian house with four neat rooms.

Old Egremont House (☎ 663118; fax 666968; 31 Egremont St; s/d £45/55) An attractive house with a large garden.

Eating

Not too surprisingly, eels are a local delicacy served in several of the restaurants in Ely.

Old Fire Engine House (☎ 662582; St Mary's St; mains about £12; ☙ lunch & dinner Mon-Sat) Ely's best restaurant, this is a good place to sample eels. It's more like the comfortable house of a friend than a restaurant, with excellent food.

Dominiques (☎ 665011; St Mary's St; mains around £5; ☙ lunch & dinner; ✗) This restaurant, famed for its variety of vegetarian choices, serves cream teas, lunches and set dinners.

Steeplegate Tea Room (☎ 664731; 16 High St; snacks from £2.50) Right beside the cathedral, upstairs from a craft shop, the tearoom does light lunches and filling snacks such as baked potatoes.

Almonry (☎ 666360) To the left of the lady chapel, virtually within the cathedral grounds, this attractive garden restaurant has a wide range of teas and coffees.

Getting There & Away

Ely is on the A10, 15 miles northeast of Cambridge and an easy day trip from it. Following the Fen Rivers Way (map available from TICs), it's a 17-mile walk.

Bus Nos X11 and X12 run every half-hour from Cambridge's Drummer St bus station (one hour). The X8, which runs hourly to King's Lynn from Cambridge, is quicker, taking only 45 minutes to reach Ely.

There are hourly trains from Cambridge (15 minutes). From Ely, there are hourly trains to Peterborough (35 minutes), and half-hourly trains to King's Lynn (1½ hours) and Norwich (55 minutes).

PETERBOROUGH

☎ 01733 / pop 136,292

There are two big reasons to visit Peterborough: shopping and church. It's a classic example of a retail mecca, which might not be too exciting to those already familiar with British shopping centres and high-street chain stores. But Peterborough is also home to a wonderful cathedral, and it's an easy day trip from Cambridge.

The cathedral precinct is an extension of the busy Cowgate, Bridge St and Queensgate. The **TIC** (☎ 452336; tic@peterborough.gov.uk; 45 Bridge St; ☙ 8.45am-5pm Mon-Wed & Fri, 10am-5pm Thu, 10am-4pm Sat) is nearby. The bus and train stations are within walking distance of the TIC, just west of the city centre.

Peterborough Cathedral

In Anglo-Saxon times, when the region was part of the kingdom of Mercia, King Peada, a recent convert to Christianity, founded a monastic church here in 655. This was sacked and gutted by the Danes in 870. In 1118 the Benedictine abbot John de Sais founded the present **cathedral** (☎ 343342; requested donation £3; ☙ 9am-6.15pm) as the monastic church of the Benedictine abbey. It was finally consecrated in 1237.

As you enter the precinct from Cathedral Sq you get a breathtaking view of the early–13th-century western front, one of the most impressive of any cathedral in Britain. On entering the building, you're struck by the height of the nave and the lightness, which derives not only from the mellow Barnack stone (quarried close by and transported via the River Nene) but also from the clerestory windows. The nave, with its three storeys, is an impressive example of Norman architecture. Its unique timber ceiling is one of the earliest of its kind in England (possibly in Europe), and its original painted decoration has been preserved. The Gothic tower replaced the original Norman one but had to be taken down and carefully reconstructed after it began to crack in the late 19th century.

In the northern choir aisle is the tombstone of Henry VIII's first wife, the tragic Catherine of Aragon, buried here in 1536. Her divorce, engineered by the king because she could not produce a male heir, led to the Reformation in England. Her only child (a daughter) was not even allowed to attend her funeral. Every 29 January there is a procession in the cathedral to commemorate her death.

In the southern aisle, two standards mark what was the grave of Mary, Queen of Scots. On the accession of her son, James, to the throne, her body was moved to Westminster Abbey.

The eastern end of the cathedral, known as the New Building, was added in the 15th

EASTERN ENGLAND

century. It has superb fan vaulting, probably the work of master mason John Wastell, who worked on King's College Chapel in Cambridge.

Sleeping & Eating

Anchor Lodge (☎ 312724; 28 Percival St; s/d £44/54) is a gorgeous B&B with large, well-appointed rooms close to the city centre. The **Bull Hotel** (☎ 561364; fax 557304; Westgate; s/d £100/120), about 200m from the train station, is a good spot for business travellers, with very comfortable, functional rooms. Breakfast is extra.

For a pleasant atmospheric café in the town centre, try the newly opened **Fratelli's** (2-3 Rivergate Centre; pizzas from £6), which combines a shop selling Italian groceries and a café-restaurant serving coffees, snacks and meals.

Getting There & Away

Stagecoach United Counties (☎ 01604-620077) runs buses from Cambridge.

SUFFOLK

Until the 16th century, Suffolk was a wool-trading centre; the wealth produced in the region can be seen in the magnificent 'wool churches' (as in paid for by, not made of) that dot the landscape. The region's economic glory days are long gone, however, and it now revels in being a charmingly rural backwater. Careful observers who visit the well-preserved villages can still see the *pargeting* (decorative stucco plasterwork) for which Suffolk buildings are famous.

Like the rest of East Anglia, the county is pretty flat, but the landscape has a serene beauty, making it ideal for exploration by bicycle. As described by the painter Constable, the county is beloved for its 'gentle declivities, its woods and rivers, its luxuriant meadow flats sprinkled with flocks and herds, and its well-cultivated uplands, with numerous scattered villages and churches, farms and picturesque cottages'. Today's visitors will find that, for the most part, the description still holds true.

Getting Around

Contact **Suffolk County Tourism** (☎ 0845 958 3358) for local transport information.

IPSWICH

☎ 01473 / pop 141,658

Once a principal player in the Saxon world and a major trading centre during the Middle Ages, modern Ipswich barely registers on the list of England's most important towns. Yet the county capital is still an important commercial and shopping centre, as well as the county's transport hub. The town centre is a compact and relatively pleasant warren of small streets where you'll find a couple of beautiful examples of the Tudor style (Ancient House and Christchurch Mansion). Also worth checking out is the Wet Dock quayside, which is a thoughtful modern development.

The **TIC** (☎ 258070; tourist@ipswich.gov.uk; ⏰ 9am-5pm Mon-Sat) is in St Stephen's Church, off St Stephen's Lane, near the bus station and Ancient House. It organises 90-minute guided **tours** (☎ 462721 for reservations; adult/child £2/1.50) of the town at 2.15pm Tuesday and Thursday, and guided ghost tours at 8pm on the first Thursday of every month.

The train station is a 15-minute walk southwest of the TIC along Princes St and across the roundabout.

Sights

In the 17th-century **Ancient House** (☎ 214144; 40 Buttermarket; ⏰ 9am-5.30pm Mon-Sat), now oddly enough a branch of Lakeland kitchen outfitters, you can take a look at the exquisite hammer-beam roof on the first floor. The external décor, completed around 1670, is an extravagant example of the Restoration style, with plenty of stucco and some of the finest examples of pargeting in the country. The house is about 50m north of the TIC, just off St Stephen's Lane.

The **Unitarian Meeting House** (☎ 218217; Friars St; admission free; ⏰ noon-4pm Tue-Thu, 10am-4pm Sat, May-Sep) is a Grade I–listed building, erected in 1699 and known as one of the finest Dissenting Meeting Houses in the country.

The **Ipswich Museum** (☎ 433550; High St; admission free; ⏰ 10am-5pm Tue-Sat) has exhibits on natural history, geology and archaeology, and a particularly good collection of British birds.

Set in a 26-hectare park about 300m north of town, **Christchurch Mansion** (☎ 433554; Soane St; admission free; mansion & gallery ⏰ 10am-5pm Tue-Sat, 2.30-4.30pm Sun Mar-Sep, 10am-4pm Tue-Sat, 2.30-4.30pm Sun Oct-Feb) is a fine Tudor mansion built between 1548 and 1550. The exterior is festooned with Dutch-style gables, while the enormous interior is decorated with period furniture and the walls are adorned with an extensive collection of works by Constable and Gainsborough. The Wolsey Art Gallery hosts contemporary art exhibitions at the mansion. To get there, walk north from the TIC along St Stephen's Lane, which becomes Tower St. Turn right onto St Margaret's St and then take a left at the fork onto Soane St.

Ipswich's attractions for the visitor don't necessarily merit an overnight stay, but if you do need accommodation, contact the TIC.

Getting There & Away

There are half-hourly trains to London's Liverpool St station (£25, 1¼ hours) and Norwich (£15, 50 minutes), and 12 trains daily to Bury St Edmunds (£5, 30 minutes). Bus Services:

Beestons (☎ 823243) Buses every half-hour to Sudbury.
Chambers (☎ 01787-227233) Sunday bus service to Sudbury.

AROUND IPSWICH
Sutton Hoo

In 1939, archaeologists digging in and around a group of burial mounds close to the River Deben, 2 miles east of Woodbridge and 6 miles northeast of Ipswich, uncovered the hull of an Anglo-Saxon ship and a haul of other Saxon artefacts that together rank as one of the most important discoveries in British history. In March 2002 a new **exhibition hall** (NT; ☎ 01394-389700; www.suttonhoo.org; Woodbridge; admission £4, discounts for those arriving on foot or bicycle; ☻ 10am-5pm daily Jun-Sep, 10am-5pm Wed-Sun Easter-May & Oct, Sat only rest of year) opened to display these extraordinary finds, which include a full-scale reconstruction of King Raedwald's burial chamber and the Sutton Hoo ship. Other treasures recovered at the site, including a warrior's helmet and shield, gold ornaments and Byzantine silver, are on display in London's British Museum (p104).

There's a video introduction and a guided tour of the burial site. First Eastern Counties runs 12 buses to Woodbridge, Monday to Saturday (10 minutes, 50p); ask the driver to stop at Sutton Hoo.

Located in Woodbridge itself is **Seckford Hall** (☎ 01394-385678; reception@seckford.co.uk; s/d from £80/120), a lavish Tudor country house

set in 14 hectares of woodland. The rooms are luxurious, and it has an indoor pool and an adjacent 18-hole golf course.

STOUR VALLEY

Running along the border between Suffolk and Essex, the River Stour flows through a soft, pastoral landscape that has inspired numerous painters, the most famous being Constable and Gainsborough. The beautiful houses and elegant churches of some of the sedate villages along the Stour are reminders of a time when these places thrived as part of the medieval weaving trade. By the end of the 15th century the Stour Valley was producing more cloth than anywhere else in England.

Within 100 years, production had shifted to the bigger towns like Colchester, Ipswich and Norwich, and the villages receded into industrial obscurity. By the end of the 19th century the Stour Valley was a rural backwater, ignored by the Industrial Revolution and virtually everyone else – not so great for locals, but a godsend for today's visitors looking for a genuine experience of the gentle English countryside. While the more famously picturesque towns, notably Lavenham and Sudbury, attract significant numbers of visitors, the area is still quiet enough to ensure that you'll be able to explore it in peace.

Long Melford
☎ 01787 / pop 2734

Known for its 2-mile-long High St (the longest in England, locals say) and the lovely timber-framed buildings that line it, Long Melford has a magnificent church with some fine stained-glass windows, two stately homes and the obligatory antique shops.

Built in 1578, **Melford Hall** (☎ 880286; admission £4.50; ☻ 2-5.30pm Wed-Sun May-Sep, 2-5.30pm Sat & Sun Apr & Oct, phone for other times) is a turreted Tudor mansion in the centre of the village. There's an 18th-century drawing room, a Regency library, a Victorian bedroom and a display of paintings by Beatrix Potter, who was a relative of the Parker family, owners of the house from 1786 to 1960, when it passed into the hands of the Treasury as part payment of death duties.

On the edge of the village, at the end of a tree-lined avenue, lies **Kentwell Hall** (☎ 310207; www.kentwell.co.uk; admission £6.95;

(✹ noon-5pm Apr-Oct), another redbrick Tudor mansion, but one that's privately owned and makes much more of its origins. Once described in *Country Life* magazine as 'the epitome of many people's image of an Elizabethan house', this is not a museum but a house where the furnishings and décor have been meticulously restored over the past 30 years. It has received the Heritage Building of the Year award, given by the *Good Britain Guide*. The house is surrounded by a moat, and there's a brick-paved Tudor rose maze and a rare-breeds farm.

Although the house is a delight to visit at any time of year, the real treat occurs between mid-June and mid-July, when more than 200 Tudor enthusiasts abandon their contemporary cynicism and don their traditional hose and velvet jackets to recreate and live out a certain year in the Tudor calendar. Admission is more expensive during the historical re-enactment period.

The **Great Church of the Holy Trinity** (☎ 281 836) has lunchtime recitals starting at 1.10pm every Wednesday from mid-May until mid-September.

EATING & SLEEPING
High Street Farm House (☎ 375765; anroy@lineone .net; s/d from £38/60) Large and salmon-coloured, this 16th-century building dominates the northern end of town. The rooms are large and comfortable, and an excellent breakfast is served in the oak-beamed dining room.

Black Lion Hotel & Restaurant (☎ 312356; fax 374557; the Green; s/d from £75/95) Right on the village green, the Black Lion has simply gorgeous rooms and an excellent restaurant (mains around £8).

Scutcher's Bistro (☎ 310200; Westgate St; mains £12.90-15) Not just the top dining spot in town, but one of the most renowned restaurants in the Stour Valley. The exquisite menu features classic British cuisine with Continental touches. It's just west of the green, near the Black Lion.

Crown Hotel (☎ 377666; fax 379005; Hall St; s/d from £35/65) Another good choice for a bed and a bite, this place has well-appointed rooms and an atmospheric bar serving excellent ales.

There's also **Melford Valley Indian Cuisine** (☎ 310079; Hall St; mains around £8); or traditional Elizabethan fare at the **Bull** (☎ 378494; Hall St; mains around £8).

SHOPPING
Long Melford is littered with antique shops, including **Country Antiques** (☎ 310617; Westgate St), with plenty of 18th- and 19th-century bric-a-brac, and **Patrick Marney** (☎ 880533; Gate House, Melford Hall), an exclusive shop that specialises in barometers. Viewing appointments are required.

GETTING THERE & AWAY
Chambers Buses runs 12 buses from Monday to Saturday between Long Melford and Bury St Edmunds (one hour) calling at Sudbury (£1, five minutes). It also runs a circular bus route between Long Melford and Sudbury (10 minutes) at 10 and 40 minutes past the hour from Monday to Saturday.

Sudbury
☎ 01787 / pop 20,188
Recreated by Charles Dickens as Eatanswill in *The Pickwick Papers* (1836-7), Sudbury is the largest town in the western half of the Stour Valley. The groundwork for its success was laid in the Middle Ages, when the town went from strength to strength on the back of the roaring trade in wool. As in the rest of East Anglia, sheep have given way to crops, but Sudbury maintains a key link with the manufacture of cloth, especially silk weaving. Most visitors also drop in to visit the birthplace of the town's most famous son, portrait and landscape painter Thomas Gainsborough (1727-88), although Sudbury is a nice place to while away an afternoon even if you're not particularly interested in Gainsborough's work.

In the town hall is the **TIC** (☎ 881320; sud burytic@babergh.gov.uk; ✹ 9am-5pm Mon-Fri year-round, plus 10am-4.45pm Sat Apr-Sep, 10am-2.45pm Sat Oct-Mar).

The birthplace of one of England's most celebrated artists, **Gainsborough's House** (☎ 372958; 46 Gainsborough St; www.gainsborough.org; admission £3.50; ✹ 10am-5pm Tue-Sat, 2-5pm Sun) has been preserved as a shrine and is now a museum with the largest collection of his work in the country. The house features a Georgian façade built by Gainsborough's father, while the mulberry tree in the garden features in some of the son's paintings. Inside, the extensive collection features his earliest known work, *A Boy and a Girl in a Landscape*, now in two separate parts (the author of the separation is unknown), a portrait of *Reverend Tobias Rustat* and the

CELEBRITY DUEL: THOMAS GAINSBOROUGH VS SIR JOSHUA REYNOLDS

Although Thomas Gainsborough (1727–88) was undoubtedly one of the major English painters, his professional life was marked by a fairly intense but mutually respectful rivalry with the pre-eminent portrait artist of the 18th century, Sir Joshua Reynolds (1723–92).

For starters, while they may both have been accomplished painters, Gainsborough was in most ways the antithesis of Reynolds. Whereas Reynolds was sober-minded and a complete professional, Gainsborough (even though his output was prodigious) was much more easy-going and often overdue with his commissions, writing that 'painting and punctuality mix like oil and vinegar'. Although eager to advance his career, Gainsborough was lazier than Reynolds, who was an expert at currying favour with the rich and powerful. He always ensured that the dignity (and looks) of his sitters was enhanced, by basing their poses along classical lines, whereas Gainsborough preferred looser poses, often setting his subjects against a rich landscape, which sometimes took the focus away from the subject. Furthermore, Gainsborough was never exclusively a portraitist (the best path towards advancement in the vainglorious 18th century), saying that while he painted portraits by profession, he painted landscapes by choice.

Ever mindful of the successes of the other, the two painters' careers took similar strides. In 1768 both were founding members of the Royal Academy, and while Reynolds went on to be its president and George III's Principal Painter, Gainsborough's skill with the brush ensured that he soon became a favourite at the Royal Court. One story has it that at a Royal Academy dinner, Reynolds proposed a toast to 'Gainsborough, the best landscape painter in Britain', to which a fellow academician replied, 'and the best portrait artist too!' Reynolds, whose speciality was portraiture, was suitably incensed.

The two rivals were united, however, at Gainsborough's deathbed. The dying man asked for Reynolds to come and see him, and after his death Reynolds paid tribute to his rival in his 14th *Discourse*. Recognising the fluid brilliance of his brushwork, Reynolds praised 'his manner of forming all the parts of a picture together' and wrote of 'all those odd scratches and marks' that 'by a kind of magic, at a certain distance…seem to drop into their proper places'. Gainsborough, who disdained literature and preferred music, would have been grudgingly impressed.

---

exquisite *Lady Tracy*. This last work is particularly beautiful in its delicate portrayal of drapery. Gainsborough's studio features original furniture as well as his walking stick and pocket watch. In the parlour is a statue of a horse, the only known sculpture the artist ever produced.

The Gallery and the Weaving Room are home to constantly changing exhibits of modern art, while in summer the garden hosts sculpture exhibitions.

The **Old Bull Hotel** (☎ 374120; fax 379044; Church St; s/d from £45/55) is a family-run hotel in a 16th-century building with nine rooms, all decorated differently. **Boathouse Hotel** (☎ /fax 379090; Ballingdon Bridge; s/d from £40/50) is on the water, and the hotel rents out rowing boats.

GETTING THERE & AWAY

Bus travel in and out of Sudbury can be tricky. Beestons runs eight buses daily, Monday to Friday (seven on Saturday), to Ipswich (£3, one hour). To get just about anywhere else involves a few changes.

Sudbury also has a train station with an hourly service to London (£24.80, 1¼ hours).

Lavenham

☎ 01787

Lavenham is the prettiest village in Suffolk, at least the parts of it you can see peeking out from behind the tour buses. It's a beautifully preserved example of a medieval wool town, with more than 300 listed buildings. Some are timber-framed, others decorated with pargeting. There are cosy, pink thatched cottages, crooked houses, antique shops, art galleries, quaint tearooms and ancient inns. When the wool industry moved to the west and north of England in the late 17th century, none of Lavenham's inhabitants could afford to build anything more modern – too bad for them; lucky for modern-day visitors.

The **TIC** (☎ 248207; lavenham@babergh.gov.uk; Lady St; ⏲ 10am-4.45pm Apr-Oct, 11am-3pm Sat & Sun Mar & Nov) offers guided walks (£3) around the village departing at 2.30pm Saturday and 11am and 2.30pm Sunday.

SIGHTS

Market Pl, off High St, is dominated by the handsome **guildhall** (☎ 247646; admission £3.25; ⏲ 11am-5pm Apr-Oct, 11am-4pm Sat & Sun Mar-Nov), a superb example of a close-studded, timber-framed building, dating back to the early 16th century. It's now a local history museum, with displays on the wool trade.

Little Hall (High St; admission £2; ⏲ 2-5.30pm Wed, Thu, Sat & Sun Apr-Oct), which has soft ochre plastering and grey timber, is a private house – once belonging to a successful wool merchant – that is open to the public.

At the southern end of the village, opposite the car park, is the **Church of St Peter & St Paul**. Its soaring steeple is visible for miles around. The church bears witness to Lavenham's past prosperity as a centre of the local wool trade.

SLEEPING & EATING

Lavenham Priory (☎ 247404; www.lavenhampriory .co.uk; Water St; s/d from £70/90) Once the home of Benedictine monks, then medieval cloth merchants, it's now an upmarket B&B and is easily the most attractive sleeping option in town.

Swan Hotel (☎ 247477; fax 248286; High St; s/d from £80/160) One of the county's best-known hotels, the Swan is housed in a late medieval building that has been exquisitely restored and updated with modern amenities.

Angel (☎ 247388; Market Pl; mains around £14) Lavenham's top restaurant serves excellent modern British cuisine, with smoked fish the speciality of the house.

GETTING THERE & AWAY

Chambers Buses connects Lavenham with Bury St Edmunds (£1.70, 30 minutes) and Sudbury (£1.50, 20 minutes), with an hourly bus (until 6pm Monday to Saturday, no service on Sunday) from Bury St Edmunds to Colchester via Sudbury and Lavenham. There are no direct buses from Cambridge; you must go via Sudbury, also the location of the nearest train station.

Kersey

☎ 01473

If Lavenham has a rival for the title of most photogenic village in Suffolk, then Kersey is

it, although 'village' is an exaggeration; it's little more than a one-street hamlet. Many of the handsome Tudor-style, timber-framed houses have been bought up by city folk looking for a weekend getaway in Merrie Olde Englande, who have paid handsomely for the privilege. Kersey is genuinely charming, but there is little to do here save admire the architecture and marvel at the fact that the village's only street (appositely named the Street) dips and disappears into a shallow ford (known as the Water Splash) before reappearing on the other side.

Kersey Pottery (☎ 822092; the Street; ⏲ 10am-5.30pm Tue-Sat & 11am-5pm Sun) is a well-respected potter's studio and shop where you can browse and buy handmade stoneware.

The 14th-century, oak-timbered **Bell Inn** (☎ 823229) and the **White Horse** (☎ 824418) are good spots for a pint or a bit of pub grub.

Kersey is 8 miles southeast of Lavenham off the A1141. There are three buses daily between Kersey and Ipswich (one hour) from Monday to Saturday. The twice-daily Sunday service also serves Sudbury (£1.50, 20 minutes). From Lavenham, the only way to get here is by car or taxi; **Granger's Cars** (☎ 01787-247456, 0589 409237) charges around £8. The trip takes about 20 minutes.

Hadleigh

☎ 01473 / pop 7124

During the Middle Ages, Hadleigh was one of the largest wool and market towns in eastern England, outranked only by Ipswich and Bury St Edmunds. Today, the town remains relatively prosperous, but its heyday is long gone and it has to content itself with being an attractive, largish town with a rich architectural heritage.

At the centre of it all is the wonderful 15th-century **guildhall** (☎ 827752; admission £1.50; ⏲ 2-5pm Thu & Sun Jun-Sep), topped by a splendid crown-post roof. The building has been managed by the Hadleigh Market Feoffment (elected management committee) continuously since 1432. Admission includes a guided tour. In good weather, tea and scones are served in the guildhall garden.

Next door, the soaring **St Mary's Church** (Church St) is one of the largest parish churches in East Anglia, and its features date from the late-12th-century tower to the nave altar, which was completed in 1971.

To the west of the church is the **Deanery Tower** (not open to the public), built in 1495 by Archdeacon William Pykenham as a gatehouse for a projected mansion nearer the river (he died before it could be built). The battlements and machicolation over the oriel window are purely ornamental, but they're a little incongruous, considering this was basically a clergyman's house. The building is also where the Oxford Movement, which sought to reassert Catholic teaching within the Church of England, was launched in 1833.

Hadleigh is also the headquarters of the **East of England Tourist Board** (☎ 822922; eastofenglandtouristboard@compuserve.com; Toppesfield Hall), just off the High St. It is not a walk-in office, so all inquiries should be by phone or email. It provides comprehensive lists of what to see and do in the region, as well as where to stay and eat.

There are a couple of decent pubs in town. The **Cock Inn** (☎ 822879; 89 George St; mains around £5) is a typical country pub that serves a limited menu of bar food.

Hadleigh is 2 miles southeast of Kersey. There are hourly buses from Ipswich (£1.80, 30 minutes) and Sudbury (£1.50, 35 minutes).

BURY ST EDMUNDS

☎ 01284 / pop 36,218

Straddling the Rivers Lark and Linnet amid gently rolling farmland, Bury St Edmunds has a mysterious appeal – maybe it's the architecture, maybe it's the beer (Greene King, the famous Suffolk brewer, is based here). Bury's distinct Georgian flavour, with street upon street of handsome, 18th-century façades that hark back to a period of great prosperity, make it Suffolk's most attractive large town. It's now a busy agricultural centre, and cattle, vegetable and fruit markets are held at Angel Hill every Wednesday and Saturday.

Centrally placed, Bury is a convenient point from which to explore western Suffolk. Don't miss the ruined abbey, set in a beautiful garden. There's also a fascinating clock museum and guided tours of the brewery.

History

Bury's motto 'Shrine of a King, Cradle of the Law' recalls the two most memorable events in its history. The Danes decapitated Edmund, a Christian prince from Saxony who was destined to be the last king of East Anglia, in 855, and his body was brought here for reburial in 903. The shrine to this king (who later became a saint) was to be the focal point of a new Benedictine monastery called St Edmundsbury, around which the town grew. The abbey, now ruined, became one of the most famous pilgrimage centres in the country and, until the dissolution of the monasteries in 1536, was the wealthiest in the country.

The second memorable episode in Bury's early history took place at the abbey. In 1214, at St Edmund's Altar, the English barons drew up the petition that formed the basis of the Magna Carta.

Orientation & Information

Bury is an easy place to find your way around because it has preserved Abbot Baldwin's 11th-century grid layout. The train station is a quarter of a mile north of the town centre; there are regular bus connections to the centre (50p). The **bus station** (St Andrew's St N) is right in the heart of town.

The **TIC** (☎ 764667; tic@stedsbc.gov.uk; 6 Angel Hill; ⏲ 9am-5.30pm Easter-Oct, 9am-5.30pm Mon-Sat Nov-Easter) has plenty of information on the town and is also the starting point for guided walking tours (£3) that depart at 2.30pm Monday to Saturday, Easter to September. Tours of the Greene King Brewery (see p517) are popular, so you'll want to book ahead.

Sights

ABBEY & PARK

Although the **abbey** (admission free; ⏲ sunrise to sunset) is very much a ruin, it's a spectacular one, set in a beautiful **garden**. After the dissolution of the monasteries, the townspeople made off with much of the stone – even St Edmund's grave and bones have disappeared.

You can enter the abbey grounds through the main **Great Gate**, built sometime between 1327 and 1346, or farther up along Angel Hill via the older **Norman Tower**, built between 1120 and 1148 and designed to serve as the belfry for the adjacent church of St James (now St Edmundsbury Cathedral). These are the best-preserved buildings of the whole complex and give an impression of how imposing the whole pile must have been.

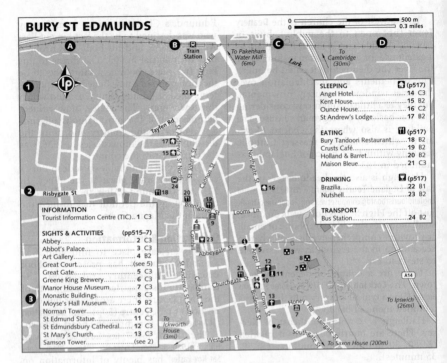

BURY ST EDMUNDS

0 — 500 m
0 — 0.3 miles

To Pakenham
Water Mill
(6mi)

To
Cambridge
(30mi)

Lark

Train
Station

SLEEPING (p517)
Angel Hotel...........................14 C3
Kent House............................15 B2
Ounce House.........................16 C2
St Andrew's Lodge.................17 B2

EATING (p517)
Bury Tandoori Restaurant.......18 B2
Crusts Café............................19 B2
Holland & Barret....................20 B2
Maison Bleue.........................21 C3

DRINKING (p517)
Brazilia..................................22 B1
Nutshell.................................23 B2

TRANSPORT
Bus Station.............................24 B2

Tayfen Rd

Risbygate St

Brentgovel St

Looms Ln

Abbeygate St

Churchgate St

Cornhill

Honey
Hill

Westgate St

To Saxon House (200m)

To Ipswich
(26mi)

A14

To
Ickworth
House
(3mi)

INFORMATION
Tourist Information Centre (TIC).. 1 C3

SIGHTS & ACTIVITIES (pp515–7)
Abbey...................................... 2 C3
Abbot's Palace........................ 3 C3
Art Gallery.............................. 4 B2
Great Court.......................(see 5)
Great Gate.............................. 5 C3
Greene King Brewery............... 6 C3
Manor House Museum............. 7 C3
Monastic Buildings................... 8 C3
Moyse's Hall Museum.............. 9 B2
Norman Tower........................ 10 C3
St Edmund Statue.................... 11 C3
St Edmundsbury Cathedral....... 12 C3
St Mary's Church..................... 13 C3
Samson Tower....................(see 2)

Just inside the Great Gate is the **Great Court**, which was once completely surrounded by buildings where the practical affairs of the abbey were conducted. Today it is an elegant formal garden. Just beyond the court is a dovecote that marks the only remains of the **Abbot's Palace**; his gardens have been transformed into a bowling green.

The most solid remains of the once-powerful and mighty abbey church are part of the western front and **Samson Tower**, which since the dissolution have had houses built into them. In the small garden in front of Samson Tower is a beautiful **statue of St Edmund** by Elizabeth Frink (1976). The rest of the abbey church spreads eastward like a fallen skeleton, with bits of stonework and the odd pillar giving a clue to its immense size. You can guide yourself around the ruins using the information boards, which help to show what a large community this must have been; just north of the church lie the ruined remains of a cluster of **monastic buildings** that at one time served as a dormitory, a lavatory, the prior's house and an infirmary.

ST EDMUNDSBURY CATHEDRAL

Also known as St James', the **St Edmundsbury Cathedral** (8.30am-8pm Apr-Oct, 8.30am-7pm Nov-Mar) dates from the 16th century, but the eastern end was added between 1945 and 1960, and the northern side was not completed until 1990. It was made a cathedral in 1914.

The architecture of the entrance porch has a strong Spanish influence, a latter-day tribute to the devotion of Abbot Anselm (1121–48), who instead of making a pilgrimage to Santiago de Compostela in Galicia chose to stay and build a church dedicated to St James (Santiago in Spanish) on the abbey grounds.

The interior is light and lofty, featuring a gorgeous painted hammer-beam roof. The Spanish theme continues in the lady chapel, located in the south transept. The north transept is home to a particularly beautiful sculpture by Elizabeth Frink, entitled *Christ Crucified*. The cathedral has recently undergone massive restoration, thanks to an award of £8 million from the Millennium Commission.

ST MARY'S CHURCH

Built around 1430, **St Mary's** contains the tomb of Mary Tudor (Henry VIII's sister and a one-time queen of France). A bell is still rung to mark curfew, as it was in the Middle Ages.

MANOR HOUSE MUSEUM & BREWERY

Near St Mary's is **Manor House** (☎ 757072; 5 Honey Hill; admission £2.50; ☻ 10am-5pm Tue-Sun), a magnificent museum of horology, art and costume housed in a Georgian building. It is worth being here around noon, when all the clocks strike. The nearby **Greene King Brewery** (☎ 763222; Crown St; day/evening £6/7; ☻ 2.30pm Mon-Thu) is worth visiting while you're in this part of the town.

ART GALLERY & MOYSE'S HALL MUSEUM

Bury's **art gallery** (☎ 762081; Cornhill; admission £1; ☻ 10.30am-5pm Tue-Sat) is in a Grade I–listed building designed in 1774 by Robert Adam, originally as a theatre. Inside there are rotating exhibitions of contemporary art.

Nearby is **Moyse's Hall Museum** (☎ 706183; Cornhill; admission free; ☻ 9am-5.30pm Mon-Sat), with an exhibit dedicated to the Suffolk Regiment – its history, feats of bravery, and uniforms. The rest of the museum is devoted to local archaeology, complete with interactive displays. At least as interesting, if not more so, is the building itself, which dates from the 12th century and is probably East Anglia's oldest domestic building.

Sleeping

Saxon House (☎ 755547; 37 Southgate St; s/d from £40/60) This fully restored, 15th-century timber-frame building, once an almshouse, has two gorgeously appointed bedrooms, one with exposed beams and candlelight, the other overlooking a courtyard and herb garden.

Angel Hotel (☎ 753926; sales@theangel.co.uk; 3 Angel Hill; s/d from £69/89) This crown jewel in the centre of Bury once lodged Charles Dickens and is where Mr Pickwick enjoyed an 'excellent roast dinner'.

Ounce House (☎ 761779; pott@globalnet.co.uk; Northgate St; s/d from £60/85) Ask for a room with a garden view at this elegant guesthouse.

Two decent budget B&Bs near the bus station are **St Andrew's Lodge** (☎ 756733; 30 St Andrew's St North; s/d £35/50), with motel-style rooms that are comfortable but characterless; and **Kent House** (☎ 769661; lizkent@supanet .com; 20 St Andrew's St North; s/d from £25/45), a small town house.

Eating

Maison Bleue (☎ 760623; 31 Churchgate St; mains £9-17.50, set menu £19.95; ☻ lunch & dinner Mon-Sat) This local fave is a highly recommended seafood restaurant, with creative preparations of brill, sea bass and monkfish.

Crusts Café (☎ 763293; 13 Brentgovel St; mains around £4; ☻ breakfast, lunch & dinner) This lovely café serves a wide range of dishes, from lasagne to steak and kidney pie.

Bury Tandoori Restaurant (☎ 724222; 108 Risbygate St; mains around £8.50; lunch & dinner) is the best Indian in town, with the usual menu of subcontinental dishes. **Holland & Barrett** (☎ 706677; 6 Brentgovel St; dishes around £3; ☻ 9am-5.30pm Mon-Sat) is a vegetarian restaurant and café.

Drinking

Nutshell (the Traverse) The best-known pub in Bury – because it claims to be Britain's smallest – is indeed tiny, with cheerful yellow walls and big windows ideal for people-watching.

Brazilia (☎ 769655; Station Hill; admission £4-7; ☻ Thu-Sat) At weekends the kids flock to this place, which features a popular mix of '70s disco and commercial house and trance. Dress up, as jeans and trainers will leave you in the cold.

Getting There & Away

There's a daily National Express bus to London (£12, two hours and 20 minutes). From Cambridge, Stagecoach Cambus runs buses to Bury (35 minutes) hourly from Monday to Saturday; the last bus back to Cambridge leaves at 5.05pm. First Eastern Counties runs buses every 30 minutes to Ipswich (1¼ hours).

Bury is on the Ipswich (20 minutes) to Ely (30 minutes) railway line, so trains to London (1¾ hours) go via these towns virtually every hour. From Cambridge, there are trains every two hours to Bury (45 minutes).

AROUND BURY ST EDMUNDS
Ickworth House & Park

Three miles southwest of Bury on the A143, **Ickworth House** (☎ 735270; house & park £6.40, park only £3; ☻ house 1-5pm mid-Mar–Oct, park 7am-7pm year round) is the eccentric creation of fourth Earl

THE ECCENTRIC EARL

The Hervey family had such a reputation for eccentricity that it was said of them that when 'God created the human race he made men, women and Herveys'. Perhaps the biggest weirdo of them all was the creator of Ickworth House, Frederick, the third son of the third Earl of Bristol. As Bishop of Derry (Ireland) he was renowned not for his piety but for his agnosticism, vanity and oddity: he would force his clergymen to race each other through peat bogs in the middle of the night, sprinkle flour on the floor of his house to catch night-time adulterers, champion the cause of Catholic emancipation (he was, after all, a Protestant bishop) and earn himself the sobriquet of 'wicked prelate' from George III.

Not content with his life in Ireland, in later years Frederick took to travelling around Europe, where he indulged each and every one of his passions: women, wine, art and intrigue. He tried to pass himself off as a spy in France, and for his trouble he was rewarded with a nine-month prison sentence in a Napoleonic jail. While in Italy, he horrified visiting English aristocrats with his dress sense and manners; he often dressed in military garb and once chucked a bowl of pasta onto a religious procession because he hated the sound of tinkling bells.

of Bristol and Bishop of Derry Frederick Hervey (1730–1803; see the boxed text above). It's an amazing structure, with an immense oval rotunda dating back to 1795. It contains a fine collection of furniture, silver and paintings (by Titian, Gainsborough and Velasquez). Outside, there's an unusual Italian garden and a park designed by Lancelot 'Capability' Brown, with waymarked trails, a deer enclosure and a hide.

First Eastern Counties runs a bus service (£1.50) at 12.35pm and 4.10pm daily, bound for Garboldisham (No 304), leaving from outside Bury train station.

Pakenham Water Mill

England's only remaining parish water mill and **windmill** (☎ 01359-230275; admission £2; ☼ 2pm to 5.30pm Wed, Sat & Sun Good Friday–Sep) still in operation is in the small village of Pakenham, 6 miles northeast of Bury St Edmunds along the A143. Corn has been ground here for over 900 years, and the mill makes an appearance in the Domesday Book. The mill ceased production in 1974, but it was taken over four years later by the Suffolk Preservation Society, who sponsored a painstaking restoration. During the restoration a Tudor mill was uncovered on the site of the present building, which dates from the late 18th century. Visitors get a guided tour of the building and can observe the grinding process from start to finish; you can also buy ground corn produced on the premises.

There are four buses daily from the Bury St Edmunds bus station from 1.05pm (No

337 to Thetford), Monday to Friday, and three on Saturday (20 minutes). The bus stops in front of the Fox pub; the mill is just up the street.

ALDEBURGH

☎ 01728 / pop 2654

So cute it has to be seen to be believed, diminutive Aldeburgh has a pretty shingle beach and a picturesque town centre. The sea is closing in on the village; the beach is now only yards away. Moot Hall, a 16th-century building, was once in the centre of town; now it's on the seashore. It's a shame to imagine the pretty little seaside town being gradually overtaken by saltwater, as it's one of the nicest in the country. Poet George Crabbe and composer Benjamin Britten both lived here; Britten founded the widely popular annual **Aldeburgh Festival** (☎ 453543; www.aldeburgh.co.uk), East Anglia's primary arts and music festival, which takes place in June.

The **TIC** (☎ 453637; atic@suffolkcoastal.gov.uk; High St; ☼ 9am-5.15pm Easter-Oct, 10am-4pm Mon-Sat Nov-Easter) can help with information.

Walking

The Suffolk Coast and Heaths Path passes through Aldeburgh, and you can follow it north beside the sea for a few miles and enjoy the salt air. Alternatively, from Aldeburgh follow the path inland for a lovely 3-mile walk towards the village of Snape, through some pleasant wooded areas and fields. Just south of Snape, where a road crosses the River Alde, are the large buildings of the Maltings.

Sleeping

White Lion Hotel (☎ 452720; Market Cross Pl; s/d from £75/115) Aldeburgh's oldest hotel overlooks the shingle beach and has recently received a 21st-century facelift. Sea-facing rooms are the best; they cost £10 extra.

Ocean House (☎ 452094; fax 453909; 25 Crag Path; s/d from £40/65, sea-facing r extra £5) This delightful guesthouse overlooking the sea in the middle of town has rooms all outfitted in period style.

Blaxhall Youth Hostel (☎ 688206; dm £12) Six miles from Aldeburgh, and west of Snape Maltings.

Eating

Café 152 (☎ 454152; 152 High St; mains £10-14; ⊗ closed Mon & Tue Nov-Mar) Seafood is the order of the day here, be it char-grilled squid on a bed of salad leaves or a less exotic (but equally delicious) grilled sole.

Captain's Cabin (☎ 452520; 170-172 High St; mains around £7) This cosy waterfront restaurant serves a mix of dishes from breaded plaice fillet to sausages and mash. Again, seafood is the obvious choice.

Lighthouse (☎ 453377; 77 High St; mains £8-10) One of Aldeburgh's most celebrated eateries, this is a big favourite with visiting Londoners. The imaginative menu features a range of eclectic dishes, with a particular emphasis on – what else? – fish.

AROUND ALDEBURGH

The coast on either side of Aldeburgh is one of great contrasts, with traditional seaside resorts such as Lowestoft to the north, the busy cargo port of Felixstowe to the south and some of the least-visited sec-

tions of coastline in England in between, but it is certainly worth taking the time to explore. It's a heritage coastline that's being gradually whittled away by the sea: the old section of the village of **Dunwich** – including all of its 12 churches – now lies completely underwater.

About 4 miles north of Aldeburgh is **Sizewell**, a nuclear-power plant topped by what is most kindly described as a giant golf ball. Its anomalous presence along this stretch of coast has been a major cause of concern for environmentalists and a host of other nuclear opponents, but the plant's two reactors won't be ceasing their atom-bashing activities any time soon.

With public transport virtually nonexistent in places it can be tough to get around if you don't have your own wheels, but this is excellent walking and cycling (and birdwatching) country, and the quiet serenity of some of the seaside villages makes this a good spot to idle away a few lazy days.

Orford

Few visitors get to this little village, 6 miles south of Snape Maltings, but there are several worthwhile attractions. The ruins of **Orford Castle** (EH; ☎ 01394-450472; admission £4; ⊗ 10am-5pm Apr-Oct, 10am-4pm Nov-Mar) date from the 12th century; only the keep has survived.

The spit of land outside the village (and only accessible by ferry from Orford Quay) is **Orford Ness** (☎ 01394-450900; admission incl ferry crossing £5.80 ; ⊗ 10am-5pm Tue-Sat Jul-Sep, Sat only Mar-Jun & Oct), a national nature reserve that between 1913 and the mid-1980s was a secret military testing ground. It is the largest

---

SOMETHING FOR THE WEEKEND

Start your weekend with a beachfront room at the **White Lion Hotel** (above) in adorable Aldeburgh; once you've checked in, take a stroll along the ever-diminishing coastline, then settle in for a seafood feast at **Café 152** (above). On Saturday, walk a section of the **Suffolk Coast and Heaths Path** (opposite) that passes through the village, or head inland on a three-mile walk to the industrial buildings of **Snape Maltings** (above). For lunch, head to the picture-perfect market town of **Kersey** (p514), where you'll find good pints and pub grub at either the Bell Inn or the White Horse. Don't use up all your film here, though, because the next stop may be even more gorgeous – medieval **Lavenham** (p513), arguably the prettiest village in the region. Here, you can shop 'til you drop or just stroll along the time-transcending streets. Check in to the **Lavenham Priory** (p514) for accommodation far more plush than monastic. Keeping with the theme, try the smoked fish for dinner at **Angel** (p514). Next morning, plan a trip to **Hadleigh** (p514) for a peek at the guildhall and the soaring 12th-century tower of St Mary's Church.

vegetated shingle spit in Europe, home to a variety of rare birds, animals and plants, including avocets, oystercatchers and migratory waders. There's a 3-mile path lined with information boards and military installations. The last ferry departs from Orford Quay at 2pm and from the reserve at 5pm.

Also from Orford Quay, **MV Lady Florence** (☎ 0831 698298) takes diners on all-inclusive, 2½-hour brunch cruises (9am to 11.30am) or four-hour lunch or dinner cruises, year round. The brunch cruise costs £20 all-inclusive (the menu is fixed), while the lunch and dinner cruises cost £12 per person for the boat plus the price of whatever you choose from the menu.

SOUTHWOLD

☎ 01502 / pop 3858

Southwold may have seen better days as a trading centre, but it's among the prettiest resort towns on this stretch of coastline. It has also triumphed by being perched safely atop a cliff, where it prospered as a fishing town in the middle of the 16th century while many of its neighbours began to disappear into the ocean. Its gorgeous sandy beach is a perennial Blue Flag (ie clean beach) award winner.

The **TIC** (☎ 724729; 69 High St; ☽ 10am-5.30pm Mon-Sat, 11am-4pm Sun Apr-Sep, 10.30am-5pm Mon-Fri, to 5.30pm Sat Oct-Mar) is in the heart of town.

The town's most interesting architectural landmark is the **Church of St Edmund** (Church St; admission free; ☽ 9am-6pm Jun-Aug, to 4pm rest of year), a 15th-century building with a superbly proportioned nave.

The **Southwold Museum** (☎ 07890-300532; Victoria St; admission free; ☽ 10.30am-noon Aug & 2-4pm Apr-Oct) has a good display on the town's history, with a particular emphasis on the Battle of Solebay (1672), fought between the English, French and Dutch fleets just off the coast. There were 132 ships and 50,000 troops involved, so it must've been one hell of a fight.

And of course there is the **pier**, originally built in 1899. It hasn't had the luckiest of histories: it was badly damaged by storms in 1934, 1955 and 1979 before eventually closing in 1998 for safety reasons. It has since reopened after a complete renovation and now boasts the requisite selection of bars, fast-food outlets and amusement arcades.

Sleeping & Eating

Saxon House (☎ 723651; 86 Pier Ave; s/d from £45/60) This mock-Tudor house has bright, airy rooms that are clean and comfortable. It is about 100m from the pier.

Amber House (☎ 723303; North Pde; s/d from £28/42) is a spacious Victorian terraced house with cosy, comfortable rooms. **Victoria House** (☎ 722317; 9 Dunwich Rd; s/d £25/50) is equally good, and the rooms are just that little bit bigger.

The **Dutch House** (☎ 723172; Ferry Rd; mains around £7; ☽ closed Mon) is a good spot for a bite of lunch or dinner.

Southwold is also home to the Adnams Brewery, although it's a little out of town. You should try some of its creamy ales in one of the town's pubs – we recommend the **Red Lion** (South Green).

Getting There & Away

First Eastern Counties buses stop here on the Ipswich to Great Yarmouth run.

AROUND SOUTHWOLD
Walberswick

☎ 01502

It's hard to believe, but the pretty village of Walberswick was a busy port from the 13th century right up to WWI. Cheese, bacon, corn, timber and fish were traded here in abundance. You can still buy fresh fish, but that's about it: today the village is a sleepy little getaway where well-to-do holiday-makers come to chill out. The English Impressionist Philip Wilson Steer (1860–1942) set the trend in the late 19th century, moving here to paint some of the finest landscapes of the day.

The primary source of excitement occurs in July or August, when the village hosts the **British Open Crabbing Championships** (☎ 722359; www.walberswick.ws/crabbing), in which contestants have 90 minutes to land the heaviest crab with only a single line and bait. Anyone can enter, but the competition is pretty fierce, with baits being a closely guarded secret.

The 600-year-old **Bell Inn** (☎ 723109; fax 722 728; s/d from £50/80) is the best option if you're looking to stay over. The rooms here are large and comfortable. The inn also houses a good seafood restaurant (mains £8 to £10) with flagged floors, low beams and open fires.

Walberswick is about a mile south of Southwold. From Southwold, there are two ways to get here. Pick up the path at the southern end of High St to reach a bailey bridge (for pedestrians and cyclists only) that spans the River Blythe. Alternatively, a summer **ferry** (50p; ⏰ 10am-12.30pm & 2-4.30pm Jun-Aug, weekends only Easter-May) crosses the Blythe at half-hourly intervals.

NORFOLK

From birds and broads to castles and cathedrals, Norfolk is a haven for tranquil pursuits. Much quieter and less populated than it was 500 years ago, when it prospered as an economic centre, the region these days is best for outdoor activities. Bird-watchers flock to its several large nature reserves. Its long coastlines are largely unspoilt, offering a peaceful alternative to the wild carnivalesque holiday seaside resorts in the rest of the country. The Norfolk Broads, a network of inland waterways that have long been popular for boating holidays, stretch diagonally across the county. If that sounds like a bit too much peace and quiet, head for the county town, Norwich; it has the lively feel of a university town, with the best nightlife in the region, and it's a great place to find funky diners, restaurants and casual hangouts that are friendlier to a student budget. The whole area is easily accessible from Cambridge.

Norfolk's inhabitants have a reputation for bloody-mindedness. A story illustrating this tells of the appointment of a new bishop to the diocese, who was told by his predecessor that if he wanted to lead someone in this part of the world, he should first find out where they were going and then walk in front of them. It is this doggedness that undoubtedly helped make the region such a commercial success in the Middle Ages.

Information

For a comprehensive online guide to what's on in Norfolk, consult www.visitnorfolk .co.uk. See the website www.norfolkcoast .co.uk for information about visiting the coast. **Independent Traveller's Norfolk** (www.it norfolk.co.uk) produces a free leaflet covering activities, hostels and campsites as well as local transport.

Activities

Several waymarked walking trails cross the county. The best known is the Peddars Way and Norfolk Coast Path national trail, mentioned in the Activities section at the start of this chapter. Other long routes include Weavers Way, a 57-mile (92km) walk from Cromer to Great Yarmouth via Blickling and Stalham, and the Angles Way, which follows the valleys of the Rivers Waveney and Little Ouse for 70 miles (113km).

The Around Norfolk Walk is a 220-mile (354km) circuit that combines the Peddars Way and Norfolk Coast Path, the Weavers Way and the Angles Way. Any of these routes can be followed for just an hour or two or a day or two, and TICs have leaflets, route maps and other inspirational literature for walkers – and even more material for cyclists.

Getting Around

County public transport phone line (☎ 08453-006116)
Norfolk Bus Information Centre (NORBIC; ☎ 01603-285007)

NORWICH

☎ 01603 / pop 194,839
For a time during the Middle Ages, this was England's largest city besides London. Norfolk's county town (pronounced nor-ritch) was a major player in the medieval world. Its historical importance is evident throughout the town, juxtaposed nicely with modern urban developments like the impressive Forum, a community centre that houses the TIC, restaurants and a display of the city's history. Altogether it's one of the most attractive cities in eastern England, with its angled streets zigzagging up and down steep hills, its large permanent market and its vibrant youth culture centered on the University of East Anglia. It may no longer be an economic powerhouse, as in the days when it prospered through trade with the Low Countries, but it's among the most entertaining cities in the region, and it makes an excellent base for exploring Norfolk's wild outlying areas.

History

The East Angles built the village of Northwic on a gravel terrace above the River Wensum, and by the time a bunch of marauding

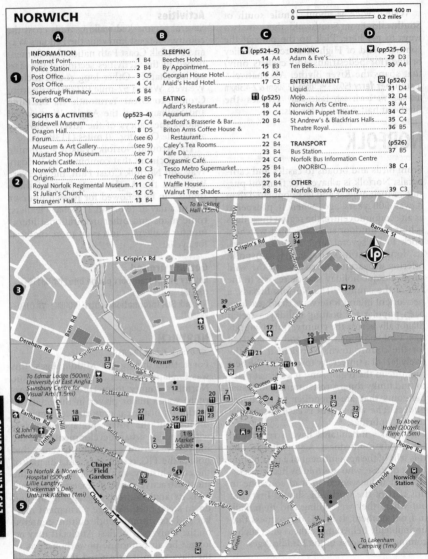

NORWICH

0 — 400 m
0 — 0.2 miles

INFORMATION	
Internet Point	1 B4
Police Station	2 B4
Post Office	3 C5
Post Office	4 C4
Superdrug Pharmacy	5 B4
Tourist Office	6 B5

SIGHTS & ACTIVITIES	(pp523–4)
Bridewell Museum	7 C4
Dragon Hall	8 D5
Forum	(see 6)
Museum & Art Gallery	(see 9)
Mustard Shop Museum	(see 7)
Norwich Castle	9 C4
Norwich Cathedral	10 C3
Origins	(see 6)
Royal Norfolk Regimental Museum	11 C4
St Julian's Church	12 C5
Strangers' Hall	13 B4

SLEEPING	▢ (pp524–5)
Beeches Hotel	14 A4
By Appointment	15 B3
Georgian House Hotel	16 A4
Maid's Head Hotel	17 C3

EATING	▢ (p525)
Adlard's Restaurant	18 A4
Aquarium	19 C4
Bedford's Brasserie & Bar	20 B4
Briton Arms Coffee House & Restaurant	21 C4
Caley's Tea Rooms	22 B4
Kafe Da	23 B4
Orgasmic Café	24 C4
Tesco Metro Supermarket	25 B4
Treehouse	26 B4
Waffle House	27 B4
Walnut Tree Shades	28 B4

DRINKING	▢ (pp525–6)
Adam & Eve's	29 D3
Ten Bells	30 A4

ENTERTAINMENT	▢ (p526)
Liquid	31 D4
Mojo	32 D4
Norwich Arts Centre	33 A4
Norwich Puppet Theatre	34 C2
St Andrew's & Blackfriars Halls	35 C4
Theatre Royal	36 B5

TRANSPORT	(p526)
Bus Station	37 B5
Norfolk Bus Information Centre (NORBIC)	38 C4

OTHER	
Norfolk Broads Authority	39 C3

Danes sacked the new-and-improved town of Norwich in 1004, it was already an important market centre. Shortly after their invasion in 1066, the Normans built the splendid castle keep, now the best-preserved example in the country. In 1336 Edward III encouraged Flemish weavers to settle here; their arrival helped establish the wool industry that would ensure Norwich's provincial importance until the end of the 18th century, when it was overtaken by the growing industrial cities of the north.

Norwich's links with the Low Countries were further strengthened in the 16th century, when mass immigration flooded the town with more weavers and textile workers.

In 1579 more than a third of the town's 16,000 citizens were foreigners (of a staunch Protestant stock, which proved beneficial during the Civil War, as the town's close ties with the parliamentary cause ensured that Norwich saw virtually no strife).

Modern Norwich remains one of England's most important centres of footwear manufacturing, and one of the country's largest agricultural and livestock markets.

Orientation

The castle is in the centre of Norwich. Below the castle lies what has been described as the most complete medieval English city still remaining. Clustered around the castle and the Anglican cathedral, within the circle of river and city walls, are more than 30 parish churches. The Roman Catholic cathedral lies to the west of the centre.

At the heart of the city is the **market** (Market Sq; ☺ roughly 8am-4.30pm), a patchwork of stall awnings known as tilts. This is one of the biggest and longest-running markets in the country. It was moved here 900 years ago from its original site in Tombland by what is now the Anglican cathedral.

Information

Internet point (☎ 760808; Row B of the market; per 15 min £1)
Norfolk & Norwich Hospital (☎ 286286; Wessex St)
Police station (☎ 768769; Bethel St)
Post office Central (☎ 220228; 13-17 Bank Plain); City South (☎ 761635; 84-85 Castle Mall)
Superdrug Pharmacy (☎ 619179; 25 Gentleman's Walk; ☺ 8.30am-6pm Mon-Sat)
TIC (☎ 727927; www.norwich.gov.uk; ☺ 10am-6pm Mon-Sat & 10.30am-4pm Sun Apr-Oct, 10am-5.30pm Mon-Sat Nov-Mar) Just inside the Forum on Millennium Plain.

Sights

NORWICH CASTLE MUSEUM & ART GALLERY

The massive Norman castle keep was built in about 1160 and measures 28m square by 21m high – a solid sentinel on the hill overlooking the medieval and modern cities. It's the best surviving example of Norman military architecture after the Tower of London and has worn pretty well, although it was refaced in 1834.

Bizarrely, **Norwich castle** (☎ 493636; castle & museum £3.50, art gallery & natural history exhibit £3, castle, museum & art gallery £5.25; ☺ 10.30am-6.30pm

Mon-Sat Jun-Sep, to 4.30pm Oct-May) has had a gigantic shopping centre grafted onto it, an embodiment of Norwich's quirky blend of modern and historic. A major refurbishment to the historic side of things did wonders for the castle's **museum** and **art gallery**.

You have a choice of what to see: you can buy one ticket that grants you access to the castle keep and the museum – which has well-presented and documented exhibits of natural history and Norfolk archaeology – or you can opt for the art gallery and the bit of the museum devoted to natural history. We recommend the latter, partly because the gallery houses the paintings of the Norwich School. Founded by John Crome in the early 19th century, this group painted local landscapes and won acclaim throughout Europe.

Also on the premises, in the Shirehall (entrance opposite the Anglia TV station), is the **Royal Norfolk Regimental Museum** (☎ 493649; admission £2; ☺ 10am-5pm Mon-Sat, 2-5pm Sun), detailing the history of the local regiment since 1830.

THE FORUM & ORIGINS

Built with funds obtained from the National Lottery, the extraordinary all-glass, horseshoe-shaped **Forum** is the most impressive building to hit Norwich's skyline in many decades. It is three storeys high and is home to Norfolk's largest library, a number of cafés, the TIC and a couple of shops.

Origins (☎ 727920; admission £5; ☺ 10am-6pm Mon-Sat, 10.30am-4.30pm Sun), in the same building as the Forum, is an interactive museum devoted to 2000 years of Norfolk and Norwich history, where kids get to try their hand at speaking the original Norfolk dialect (not easy) and flooding the Norfolk Fens. A 40m-long, two-storey-high screen shows 180-degree images of the area's past, a particularly enthralling experience for kids. It's not an in-depth look at the area's history, but it's a lot of fun and sure to impress.

ELM HILL

Thanks to imaginative restoration, this **street** has retained its medieval charm and atmosphere and is, appropriately enough, the centre of the local antique business. It's one of the most attractive parts of the city. From here walk down Wensum St to

Tombland, where the market was originally located. 'Tomb' is an old Norse word for 'empty' – hence space for a market.

NORWICH CATHEDRAL

The focal point of the city, the Anglican **cathedral** (☎ 764385; admission free; ⏱ 7.30am-7pm May-Sep, 7.30am-6pm Oct-Apr) has retained the appearance and characteristics of a great Anglo-Norman abbey church more than any other English cathedral except Durham.

The foundation stone was laid in 1096, and the building took 40 years to complete. In 1463 it was made fireproof by means of a magnificent stone lierne vault (a kind of inside roof) that, with its sculpted bosses, is one of the finest achievements of English medieval masonry.

As you enter the cathedral through the western door, the first thing that strikes you is the length of the nave. Its 14 bays are constructed in yellow-beige stone. Above, on the amazing vault, stories from the Old and New Testament are carved into the bosses. Beyond the tower, which is richly patterned, is probably the most beautiful part of the cathedral – the eastern section.

At the eastern end, outside the War Memorial Chapel, is the grave of Edith Cavell, a Norfolk nurse who was shot by the Germans in Belgium during WWI for helping POWs to escape.

The cathedral close contains some handsome houses and the old chapel of the King Edward VI School (where Admiral Nelson was educated). Its current students make up the choir, which usually performs in at least one of the three services held daily here.

ST JULIAN'S CHURCH

Tucked away in a tiny alley is **St Julian's Church** (☎ 624738; St Julian's Alley; admission free; ⏱ 7.30am-5.30pm Apr-Sep, to 4pm Oct-Mar), where a shrine to Julian of Norwich is a centre for pilgrimage. Julian (also known as Juliana, 1342–c1416) wrote down her religious visions in a collection called *The Revelations of Divine Love*, which is unparalleled in English literature for its clarity and depth of perception. Although she was never beatified, she is still considered a saint because, on one occasion when she questioned her place in the world, God supposedly appeared to her and spoke the words 'All shall be well'. Pilgrims have been visiting her shrine for centuries,

though the cell where she wrote the book was torn down during the Reformation, and they have had to content themselves with a small chapel that was built after WWII.

OTHER MUSEUMS

About 200m north of the castle are three museums in the same area. The **Mustard Shop museum** (☎ 627889; 15 Royal Arcade; admission free; ⏱ 9.30am-5pm Mon-Sat, 11am-4pm bank holidays, closed Sun) tells the story of Colman's Mustard, a famous local product.

Nearby is **Bridewell Museum** (☎ 667227; Bridewell Alley; admission £4.95; ⏱ 10am-5pm Mon-Sat), which has surprisingly interesting displays of local industries throughout the past 200 years. Formerly a merchant's house, in the 14th century it served as an open prison for vagrants (a bridewell).

Strangers' Hall (☎ 629127; admission £2.50; ⏱ 9am-5pm Mon-Sat; tours per person admission £2.50, maximum 15 people, 11am, 1pm & 3pm Wed & Sat) is 250m west of here, along St Andrew's St and Charing Cross. It's a medieval town house with rooms furnished in period styles from Tudor to Victorian. Highlights include the stone vaulted undercroft, dating from 1320, the fine Georgian dining room and the Tudor great hall with its stone-mullioned window and screen.

Dragon Hall (☎ 663922; www.dragonhall.org; 115-123 King St; admission £2.50; ⏱ 10am-4pm Mon-Sat Apr-Oct, 10am-4pm Mon-Fri Nov-Mar) is another medieval town house with a superb crown-post roof and an impressive, timber-framed great hall. It's named for the intricately carved dragon that roars down from its ceiling beams.

SAINSBURY CENTRE FOR VISUAL ARTS

To the west of the city, on the university campus (a 20-minute bus trip from Castle Meadow), the **Sainsbury Centre** (admission £2; ⏱ 11am-5pm Tue-Sun) is remarkable both for the building itself and for the art it contains. It was designed by Norman Foster and is filled with an eclectic collection of works by Picasso, Moore, Bacon and Giacometti, displayed beside art from Africa, the Pacific and the Americas.

Sleeping

Most of the B&Bs and cheaper hotels are outside the ring road, along Earlham and Unthank Rds to the west, and around the train station. The closer the B&Bs along

Earlham Rd are to the centre, the more expensive they are.

By Appointment (☎ 630730; 25-29 St George's St; s/d from £70/95) One of our favourite hotels in all of eastern England, By Appointment may have an odd name, but the 15th-century listed building has some of the most beautifully appointed rooms you'll find anywhere in the region. Lodgings are above the restaurant – just *try* to resist the aromas in the kitchen. It's a small and well-loved place, so book ahead.

Beeches Hotel (☎ 621167; reception@beeches.co.uk; 2-6 Earlham Rd; s/d from £65/85; **P**) Luxury accommodation in three separate Grade II–listed Victorian houses, collectively known as the Beeches. They're all terrific, but try to get a room in the Plantation, if only because of its wonderful garden.

Norwich YHA Hostel (☎ 0870-770 5976; norwich@ yha.org.uk; 112 Turner Rd; dm from £10; ☯ Apr-Oct) Two miles from the train station on the edge of the city, this hostel runs the Rent-a-Hostel scheme from November to March, which caters to large groups only; phone for information. In addition to dorm beds, there are family rooms with two to six beds.

Georgian House Hotel (☎ 615655; reception@ georgian-hotel.co.uk; 32-34 Unthank Rd; s/d from £55/80; **P**) In a sprawling, elegant Victorian house opposite St John's Roman Catholic Cathedral, this 28-room boutique hotel features clean-lined, modern design in the rooms and a tree-lined hilltop location. The award-winning restaurant emphasises ecofriendly ingredients.

Maid's Head Hotel (☎ 209955; Tombland; s/d weeknights £100/120, weekends per person £47) This impressive, 700-year-old coaching inn just on the edge of the historic city centre has 84 comfortable, modern rooms and a friendly bar.

Other options we recommend:

Abbey Hotel (☎ 612915; 16 Stracey Rd; s/d £20/40) Our favourite in a row of B&Bs behind the station.

Edmar Lodge (☎ 615599; edmar@cwcom.net; 64 Earlham Rd; s/d from £35/40)

Lakenham Camping (☎ 620060; Martineau Lane, 1 mile south of the centre; pitches per person £5; ☯ Easter-Oct)

Eating

QUICK EATS & SELF-CATERING

There's a convenient **Tesco Metro supermarket** (Market Sq) for self-catering. **Zuckerman's Deli** (Unthank Rd) is also excellent for takeaway items – the sausage rolls are legendary.

Next door, the Unthank Kitchen does an incredible hangover-curing English breakfast (£3 to £5).

CAFÉS & RESTAURANTS

Walnut Tree Shades (☎ 620166; Old Post Office Court) This fabulous little restaurant in the city centre specialises in all things beefy; the steak Diane (£12.50) will have carnivores drooling.

Treehouse (☎ 763258; 14 Dove St; mains around £5 & £6.50; ☯ Mon-Sat) This excellent vegetarian restaurant above a health-food shop serves such delicacies as nut-and-moonbeam pâté. Main courses come in two sizes at two prices.

Kafe Da (☎ 622836; 18 Bedford St; dishes £4.50-7) A trendy café themed around international espionage – the subs are named after Bond movies, the sandwiches after Russian leaders. It turns into a cool bar at night.

Bedford's Brasserie & Bar (☎ 666869; 1 Old Post Office Yard; mains £6-7) Almost opposite Kafe Da, Bedford's menu features sautéed king prawns with chilli jam in a light puff pastry – not exactly your run-of-the-mill pub grub!

Briton Arms Coffee House & Restaurant (☎ 623367; 9 Elm Hill; mains £5-9) This lovely thatched cottage with its own little garden serves traditional English food as well as good coffee and cakes.

Waffle House (☎ 612790; 39 St Giles St; waffles £2.95-7) Oddly enough, one of the most popular late-night eateries in Norwich is this tiny café serving Belgian waffles with a selection of fillings.

Other recommendations:

Adlard's Restaurant (☎ 633522; 79 Upper St Giles St; 4-course dinner £35) Classic French cuisine, good for a splurge.

Aquarium (☎ 630090; 22 Tombland; mains around £9) English cuisine with French and Continental influences.

Caley's Tea Rooms (☎ 629364; Guildhall, Market Square) Some of the nicest chocolate in all of England.

Orgasmic Café (☎ 676650; 6 Queen St; mains around £6) Superb selection of wine by the glass.

Drinking

Adam & Eve's (Bishop Gate) This cute, tiny, sunken-floored stone pub is a haven for serious beer drinkers.

Ten Bells (76 St Benedict's St) This student-friendly pub has an instantly comfortable worn-in feel, with its ratty red velvet, eclectic signs and red phone booth in the corner.

Lillie Langtry (Unthank Rd) Another lively student hangout, this pub is one of several lined up in a funky little alternative neighbourhood near the university.

Entertainment
NIGHTCLUBS
Norwich's club scene is the only one in East Anglia to rival Cambridge. All of the nightclubs run from 9pm or 10pm to at least 2am.

Time (☎ 767649; Riverside; admission £2-5) About a mile west of town on the Yare is the biggest club in Norwich, with a capacity of 1700. The music is hard house and crowd-pleasing dance anthems. Admission varies depending on the night. Trainers and jeans are no-nos.

Several clubs line Prince of Wales Rd, including **Liquid** (☎ 611113; Prince of Wales Rd; admission £5), with a suitable soundtrack of techno and hard house, and **Mojo** (☎ 622533; 62 Prince of Wales Rd; admission £4), which features soul, break-beats, hip-hop and R&B.

THEATRE
St Andrew's and Blackfriars' Halls (☎ 628477; St Andrew's Plain) Once home to Dominican Blackfriars, this spookily Gothic-looking complex now serves as an impressive civic centre where concerts, antique and craft markets, the Music and Arts Festival and even the annual beer festival are held; there's also a café in the crypt.

Theatre Royal (☎ 630000; Theatre St) features programmes by touring drama and ballet companies. **Norwich Arts Centre** (☎ 660352; Reeves Yard, St Benedict's St) has a wide-ranging programme of drama, concerts, dance, cabaret and jazz. **Norwich Puppet Theatre** (☎ 629921; St James, Whitefriars; adult/child around £6/4) is popular, particularly with children.

Getting There & Away
National Express has a daily bus to London (£15, three hours). First Eastern Counties runs hourly buses to King's Lynn (1½ hours) and Peterborough (2 hours 40 minutes); and half-hourly buses to Cromer (1 hour). There are five buses daily to Bury St Edmunds (1½ hours) and an hourly service to Great Yarmouth (45 minutes).

There are hourly rail services to King's Lynn (40 minutes) and Ely (1¼ hours). To get to Cambridge you'll need to go via Ely.

AROUND NORWICH
Blickling Hall
There has been a manor house here since 1057 when Harald, earl of the East Saxons (later King Harald) built the first Blickling. In 1437 the house was bought by Geoffrey Boleyn and later inherited by his grandson Thomas, whose daughter Anne was born and raised here – at least, according to tradition; historians aren't so sure. Anne, of course, made the fatal mistake of marrying Henry VIII, which led to her execution in 1533, and it is said that on the anniversary of her execution a coach drives up to the house, drawn by headless horses, driven by headless coachmen and containing the queen with her head on her lap.

The current **house** (☎ 01263-733084; admission £7, garden only £4; ☼ hall 1-4.30pm Wed-Sun Apr-Jul, Sep & Oct, & Tue Aug, gardens 10.30am-5.30pm Wed-Sun Easter-Oct, 11am-4pm rest of year) was almost entirely rebuilt by Robert Lyminge at the behest of Sir Henry Hobart, James I's chief justice. It is filled with Georgian furniture, pictures and tapestries. There's an impressive Jacobean plaster ceiling in the long gallery. The house is surrounded by parkland offering good walks.

Blickling Hall is 15 miles north of Norwich. **Saunder's Coaches** (☎ 01692-406020) runs hourly buses here from Norwich bus station from June to August (£1.50, 20 minutes). Aylsham is the nearest train station, 1¾ miles away.

NORFOLK BROADS
Unmissable if you're in the area, the Norfolk Broads are a nature-lover's playground of navigable rivers, lakes, marshland, nature reserves and bird sanctuaries – 125 miles (200km) of lock-free waterways – in eastern Norfolk. The area, measuring some 117 sq miles (303 sq km), has national protected status, which is equivalent to being a national park. It is also an official Area of Outstanding Natural Beauty (AONB), a designation it easily lives up to with its wide expanses of open wilderness.

The scenery is more desolate than dramatic, which makes it ideal for bird-watching – there's not a lot to get between your binoculars and your feathered friends. The ecology of the area also means that it's a wonderful place for people who like being on or near the water. The habitat includes freshwater lakes, slow-moving rivers, water meadows, fens,

THE ORIGIN OF THE BROADS

For many years the origin of the Norfolk Broads was unclear. The rivers were undoubtedly natural, and many thought the lakes were, too – it's hard to believe they're not when you see them – but no-one could explain how they were formed.

The mystery was solved when records were discovered in the remains of St Benet's Abbey (on the River Bure). They showed that from the 12th century certain parts of land in Hoveton Parish were used for peat digging. The area had little woodland, and the only source of fuel was peat. Since East Anglia was well populated and prosperous, peat digging became a major industry.

Over a period of about 200 years approximately 1040 hectares were dug up. However, water gradually seeped through, causing marshes, and later lakes, to develop. The first broad to be mentioned in records is Ranworth Broad in 1275. Eventually, the amount of water made it extremely difficult for the diggers, and the peat-cutting industry died out. In no other area of England has human effort changed the natural landscape so dramatically.

bogs and saltwater marshes, and the many kinds of birds, butterflies and water-loving plants that inhabit them.

How Hill, a mere 12m above sea level, is the highest place in the Broads. Since there's nothing to impede the path of sea breezes, this is a good area for wind power. Many wind pumps (which look like windmills) were built to drain the marshland and to return the water to the rivers.

Orientation

The Broads form a triangle, with the Norwich–Cromer road, the Norwich–Lowestoft road and the coastline as the three sides.

Wroxham, on the A1151 from Norwich, and Potter Heigham, on the A1062 from Wroxham, are the main centres. Along the way there are plenty of waterside pubs, villages and market towns where you can stock up on provisions, and stretches of river where you can feel you are the only person around.

Information

The **Broads Authority** (☎ 01603-610734; www .broads-authority.gov.uk; Thomas Harvey House, 18 Colegate, Norwich NR3 1BQ) has details on conservation centres and Royal Society for the Protection of Birds bird-watching hides at Berney Marshes, Bure Marshes, Cockshoot Broad, Hickling Broad, Horsey Mere, How Hill, Ranworth, Strumpshaw Fen and Surlingham Church Marsh.

Getting Around

Blakes (☎ 01603-782911; www.blakes.co.uk) and **Hoseasons** (☎ 01502-501010; www.hoseasons.co.uk). operate boating holidays

Costs depend on the boat size, the facilities on the boat, the time of year and the length of the holiday. A boat for two to four people costs £525 to £850 (depending on the season and type of boat) for a week including fuel and insurance. Short breaks (three to four days) during the off season are much cheaper.

Many boat yards (particularly in the Wroxham and Potter Heigham areas) have a variety of boats for hire by the hour, half-day or full day. These include the traditional flat-bottomed boats known as wherries. Charges vary according to the season and the size of the boat; they start from £12 for one hour, £32 for four hours and £50 for one day.

No previous experience is necessary, but remember to stay on the right-hand side of the river, that the rivers are tidal, and to stick to the speed limit – you can be prosecuted for speeding.

If you don't feel like piloting your own boat, try **Broads Tours** Wroxham (☎ 01603-782207; the Bridge); Potter Heigham (☎ 01692-670711; Herbert Woods) who run 1½-hour **pleasure trips** (adult/child £5.80/4.20) from April to September, with a commentary.

GREAT YARMOUTH

☎ 01493 / pop 66,788

You'll either love Great Yarmouth or despise it, and it won't take long to make up your mind which. Norfolk's most popular seaside resort has gone the way of so many others – it's packed with amusement arcades, greasy spoon cafés and cheap B&Bs, and rivers of holiday-makers flow through its main streets toward the beach. If that spells 'ideal holiday' to you, you'll be in heaven; the vast beaches and long boardwalk demand strolling around with an ice-cream cone, checking out the scene. There is also a number of interesting buildings in the old town, and near the train station is a handy entry point to the Weaver's Way, a highly recommended walk that cuts through the Broads along the River Yare to Acle and then Potter Heigham. To find it, go around behind the train station and follow the tracks to the highway underpass; there's a bird-watching point and the beginning of the path just beyond it. The TIC sells a detailed map (75p).

The **TIC** (☎ 846345; ⏰ 9am-5pm Mon-Fri) is in the town hall in the centre of town. There's also **another office** (☎ 842195; Marine Pde; ⏰ 9.30am-5.30pm Easter–end Sep).

The **Elizabethan House Museum** (☎ 745526; South Quay; admission £2.70; ⏰ 10am-5pm Sun-Fri) was a merchant's house and now contains a display of 19th-century domestic life. The **Tolhouse Museum** (☎ 858900; Tolhouse St; admission £1.50; ⏰ 10am-5pm Mon-Fri, 1.15-5pm Sat & Sun) was once the town's courthouse and jail; prison cells can be seen, and there's a display covering the town's history. There's also a small **maritime museum** (Marine Pde) near the TIC. It has the same opening hours and admission prices as the Tolhouse.

The **Norfolk Nelson Museum** (☎ 850698; 26 South Quay; admission £2.50; ⏰ 10am-5pm Mon-Fri) opened in 2002 to celebrate the life and times of the one-eyed hero of Trafalgar, who was a regular visitor to Great Yarmouth (the town seems proud of having erected his statue, on the South Denes, in 1819 – beating London by 24 years).

Also worth checking out is the **Maritime Festival**, which takes place on the sensitively restored South Quay in September. Celebrating the town's rich seafaring heritage, it is a weekend-long shindig of music, crafts and visiting vessels.

There are numerous B&Bs up and down Trafalgar St, and **Great Yarmouth Youth Hostel** (☎ 0870-770 5840; fax 856600; 2 Sandown Rd; dm £10.25) is three-quarters of a mile from the train station, near the beach.

Great Yarmouth has bus and rail connections to Norwich: First Eastern Counties runs an hourly bus service (£2.85, 40 minutes); Wherry Lines runs trains roughly every half-hour (£4.30, 25 minutes) daily except Sunday, when there are hourly departures between 8.20am and 5.20pm only.

CROMER
☎ 01263

Seeming much more remote than Yarmouth, Cromer was the most fashionable resort on the coast during the late Victorian and Edwardian eras. It's now somewhat run down, but attractively so. With its elevated seafront, long sandy beach and scenic coastal walks, it's well worth visiting. Cromer has long been famous for its crabs, and they're still caught and sold here.

If you hear strange noises while you're strolling by the seaside, there's an explanation. During the 14th century the nearby village of Shipden was washed into the sea. In stormy weather, locals say, you can still hear the bells ringing from the submerged tower of the Church of St Peters.

The **TIC** (☎ 512497; ⏰ 9.30am-6pm Mon-Sat, 9.30am-5pm Sun mid-Jul–Aug, 10am-5pm Mon-Sat Sep–mid-Jul) is by the bus station.

Two miles southwest of Cromer, **Felbrigg Hall** (☎ 837444; admission £6.30; ⏰ 1-5pm Sat-Wed Mar-Oct) is one of the finest 17th-century houses in Norfolk. It contains a collection of 18th-century furniture; outside is a walled garden, orangery and landscaped park.

The TIC can point you to local accommodation, but one top choice is the **White Cottage** (☎ 512728; 9 Cliff Dr; s/d from £30/60), a family-run B&B just a short walk from the town centre, up the hill along the coastal path between the pier and the lighthouse. Rooms are plush, and the panoramic views are tremendous.

Cromer is one of the few coastal resorts with a train station linked to Norwich. There are 13 trains daily Monday to Saturday and six on Sunday (£3.40, 45 minutes).

CLEY MARSHES

Between Cromer and Wells, Cley Marshes is one of the top bird-watching places in Britain, with over 300 species recorded. There's a **visitor centre** (☎ 740008), built on high ground to give good views over the area. But probably the best spot for bird-watching is among the reeds, where there are some excellent hides.

WELLS-NEXT-THE-SEA
☎ 01328 / pop 2451

Set back from the sea, Wells is both a holiday town and a fishing port. It's a pleasant place, with streets of attractive Georgian houses, flint cottages and interesting shops.

The **TIC** (☎ 710885; fax 711405; Staithe St; ☺ 10am-5pm Mon-Sat, 10am-4pm Sun Easter–mid-Jul, Sep & Oct; 9.30am-6pm Mon-Sat, 9.30am-5pm Sun mid-Jul–Aug) can help with visitor inquiries.

The Coast Hopper bus goes through Wells approximately every two hours (on its way between Hunstanton and Sheringham). There's also a bus service to King's Lynn and Norwich stations.

A narrow-gauge steam railway runs 5 miles to **Little Walsingham**, where there are Catholic shrines and the ruins of an Augustinian abbey that have been an object of pilgrimage for almost 1000 years.

Wells YHA Hostel (☎ 0870-770 6084; fax 711748; Church Plains; dm £11.25) is a new hostel in a beautiful Victorian building.

AROUND WELLS-NEXT-THE-SEA

Situated in a 1200-hectare deer park 2 miles from Wells, **Holkham Hall** (☎ 710227; admission £6.50; ☺ 1-5pm Sun-Thu late May–Sep) is an extraordinarily grand Palladian mansion. The grounds were designed by Capability Brown. Admission includes the Bygones Museum (a small museum of local folklore and artefacts) and the park, which is open throughout the year.

Burnham Deepdale

☎ 01485

This gorgeous place actually consists of two villages – it includes the hamlet of Brancaster Staithe, which frequently causes some confusion. There's not much to either of the villages – it takes longer to say their names than to drive through them lengthwise. But that's not to say there's nothing to see. The area's stunningly beautiful and there's plenty to do, including all kinds of water sports, walking and cycling. Topping that, one of England's best backpacker hostels is here.

Picking up the Norfolk Coastal Path just across the main road from the Deepdale Granary (see later), you can go either east or west for as long as you like. If you head west, you'll soon reach **Northshore Sports & Leisure** (☎ 210236; the Boatyard, Brancaster Staithe), which can fulfil all your equipment needs, from kayaking to windsurfing.

The **TIC** (☎ 210256; ☺ 10am-4pm Thu-Mon) has plenty of information on activities and places to visit in the surrounding area, and also runs a free accommodation booking service. For general information on the area, go to www.burnhamdeepdale.co.uk or www.itnorfolk.co.uk.

The annual big event in town is the **Deepdale Jazz Festival** (☎ 210256; www.deepdalejazzfestival .co.uk; tickets £7-10), at the time of research being held in mid-June, featuring regional bands, beer and barbecue, among other things.

Marsh Barn (☎ 210036) is half a mile east of town, just off the A149 coast road. The four barns are used for a variety of local events, including art exhibitions, lectures and a jazz festival featuring local players that runs in late August.

A hostel and a half, **Deepdale Granary** (☎ 210 256; deepdaleinformation@deepdalefarm.co.uk; dm weekday/weekend £10.50/12.50) is a marvellous place spread across converted 17th-century stables and a barn. There's a good little coffee shop attached, camping in an adjoining field, laundry, lounges, a library, picnic tables and Internet access (£1 per hour). The management runs a wide variety of tours and is a good source of local information; it's worth popping in to the office for reconnaissance, whether you're staying at the hostel or not.

There are two pubs, both in Brancaster along the main road heading west: the **White Horse** (☎ 210262; www.whitehorsebrancaster.co.uk) is a more sedate, upscale place with a fine-food menu, while the **Jolly Sailors** (www.jollysailors .co.uk) is a more vivacious, late-night-drinking kind of pub, with a great outdoor patio and a small TV room for the kids.

The nearest train station is King's Lynn. Bus No 411 runs here (£1.40, 15 minutes) from Cromer.

KING'S LYNN

☎ 01553 / pop 40,921

Grown out of an unlikely combination of staunchly pious citizens and wild-and-woolly sailors, King's Lynn was once among England's most important medieval ports. Its location, about 3 miles from the sea on the River Great Ouse, made it a handy base for fishing fleets, and the number of religious devotees among its residents kept the fishing crews from getting out of hand. The old town is still a fascinating mixture of these elements, and Lynn is still a port today, though much less busy than it once was.

There are three market days a week: Tuesday (the major market, with everything

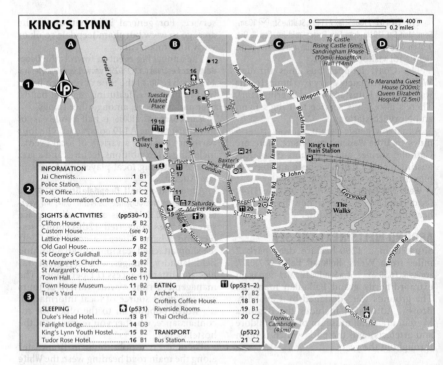

KING'S LYNN

0 —————— 400 m
0 —————— 0.2 miles

INFORMATION	
Jai Chemists...........................**1** B1	
Police Station........................**2** C2	
Post Office............................**3** C2	
Tourist Information Centre (TIC)..**4** B2	

SIGHTS & ACTIVITIES	(pp530–1)
Clifton House.........................**5** B2	
Custom House.....................(see 4)	
Lattice House........................**6** B1	
Old Gaol House.....................**7** B2	
St George's Guildhall..............**8** B2	
St Margaret's Church..............**9** B2	
St Margaret's House..............**10** B2	
Town Hall.........................(see 11)	
Town House Museum.............**11** B2	
True's Yard...........................**12** B1	

SLEEPING	(p531)
Duke's Head Hotel.................**13** B1	
Fairlight Lodge.....................**14** D3	
King's Lynn Youth Hostel.........**15** B2	
Tudor Rose Hotel..................**16** B1	

EATING	(pp531–2)
Archer's..............................**17** B2	
Crofters Coffee House............**18** B1	
Riverside Rooms....................**19** B1	
Thai Orchid.........................**20** C2	

TRANSPORT	(p532)
Bus Station..........................**21** C2	

To Castle
Rising Castle (6mi);
Sandringham House
(10mi); Houghton
Hall (14mi)

To Maranatha Guest
House (200m);
Queen Elizabeth
Hospital (2.5mi)

To
(Norwich;
Cambridge
(43mi))

from clothing to bric-a-brac to fish), Friday (with a limited selection of flowers and vegetables) and Saturday (a food market selling fish, fruit, flowers and vegetables). The Tuesday market takes place in the suitably named Tuesday Market Pl, while the Friday and Saturday markets are held in Saturday Market Pl, in front of St Margaret's Church. The markets open by 8am and usually run until 4pm, depending on the weather. In July there's the popular King's Lynn Festival of Music and the Arts.

Orientation

The old town lies along the eastern bank of the river. The train station is on the eastern side of the town. Uninspiring modern King's Lynn and the bus station are between them.

Information

Jai Chemists (☎ 772828; 68 High St; ☽ 9am-5.30pm Mon-Sat)

Police station (☎ 691211; St James Rd)

Post office (☎ 692185; Baxter's Plain; ☽ 9am-5.30pm Mon-Fri, 9am-12.30pm Sat)

Queen Elizabeth Hospital (☎ 613613; Gayton Rd)

TIC (☎ 819440; kings-lynn.tic@west-norfolk.gov.uk; ☽ 9.15am-5pm Mon-Sat, 10am-5pm Sun Apr-Oct, 10.30am-4pm Nov-Mar) In the Custom House (Purfleet Quay).

Sights

Little remains of the original buildings, but **St Margaret's Church**, founded in 1100 with a Benedictine priory, is impressive for its size (72m long) and contains two Flemish brasses that are among the best examples in the country. By the west door there are flood-level marks – 1976 was the highest, but the 1953 flood claimed more lives.

On the corner of St Margaret's Lane, and dating back to the 15th century, is a restored building that was once the warehouse or 'steelyard' of the Hanseatic League (the Northern European merchants' group). Now known as **St Margaret's House**, it is home to a number of civic offices. In theory, access is restricted to those offices alone, but you can wander in and have a look at the interior. If there's a group of you, you're better off seeking permission by calling the **Education League** (☎ 669200).

Across Queen St is the **town hall**, dating back to 1421. Next to it is the **Town House Museum** (☎ 773450; 46 Queen St; admission £2; ☙ 10am-5pm Mon-Sat, 2-5pm Sun May-Sep, 10am-4pm Mon-Sat Oct-Apr). Inside you will find exhibits charting life in the town from the Middle Ages up to the 1950s.

Next door the **Old Gaol House** (☎ 774297; admission £2; ☙ 10am-5pm Mon-Sat, 2-5pm Sun Easter-Oct, 10am-6pm Nov-Easter) is a tourist attraction with self-guided audio tours. The town's priceless civic treasures, including the 650-year-old King John Cup, can be seen in the basement. Last entry is at 4.15pm.

Further down Queen St is **Clifton House**, with its quirky barley-sugar columns and waterfront tower, which was used by merchants scanning the river for returning ships. Its interior is in dire need of restoration, so access is restricted to groups organised by the TIC.

Opposite the market square is **Purfleet Quay**, in its heyday the principal harbour. The quaint building with the lantern tower is the **Custom House** (housing the TIC), which dates back to 1683.

St George's Guildhall (☎ 767557) is the largest surviving 15th-century guildhall in England. It has served as a warehouse, theatre, courthouse and armoury (during the Civil War), and now contains art galleries, a theatre, a restaurant and a coffee house. This is the focal point of the annual King's Lynn festival.

At the end of King St is the spacious **Tuesday Market Pl**, which fulfils its original role once a week. It's bordered by old buildings, including the Corn Hall (1854) and the Duke's Head Hotel (1689).

Across Tuesday Market Pl on St Nicholas St is the **Tudor Rose Hotel** (see Sleeping), a late-15th-century house with some very interesting features, including the original main door. North of here, on the corner of St Ann's St, is **True's Yard**, where the two remaining cottages of the 19th-century fishing community that used to be here have been restored and now house a **folk museum** (☎ 770479; admission £2.50; ☙ 10am-5pm Apr-Sep, to 4pm Oct-Mar) detailing the life of a shellfish fisherman around 1850.

On the corner of Market Lane is an attractive building known as **Lattice House**, dating from the 15th century, which now houses a restaurant.

Festivals

The **King's Lynn Festival** – East Anglia's most important cultural gathering – was the brainchild of Lady Ruth Fermoy and offers a diverse programme of concerts and recitals of all kinds of 'serious' music, from medieval ballads to Jamaican jazz.

It usually takes place in the last week of July. There are also lectures and plays (Molière featured in the 2002 festival). Since 2001 the main festival has been preceded by the **Festival Too**, which usually takes place in and around Tuesday Market Pl and puts the spotlight squarely on rock and pop music.

For details of programmed events, you can contact the **administrative office** (☎ 767557; enquiries@klfestival.freeserve.co.uk) or the **box office** (☎ 764864).

Sleeping

Duke's Head Hotel (☎ 774996; Tuesday Market Pl; s/d from £55/95) This fine classical building overlooking the market is the town's top hotel. It has classy parlour sitting rooms, all furnished in antiques.

Tudor Rose Hotel (☎ 762824; kltudorrose@aol.com; St Nicholas St; s/d from £30/60) Tucked away just off the market square is this 15th-century house that has modern, well-appointed rooms in a historically interesting building with a well-preserved lobby/bar area.

Also recommended are the **Maranatha Guest House** (☎ 774596; fax 763747; 115-117 Gaywood Rd; s/d from £18/40), in a large, comfortable house east of the station; and the **Fairlight Lodge** (☎ 762234; 79 Goodwins Rd; s/d £20/35), a comfortable guesthouse with seven rooms, four with en suite. The complimentary biscuits in each room are homemade.

King's Lynn Youth Hostel (☎ 0870-770 5902; fax 764312; Thoresby College, College Lane; dm £9.25; ☙ 1 Jul-31 Aug & varied times rest of year) is excellently located. Call to check opening times for September to June.

Eating

Riverside Rooms (☎ 773134; lunch £8.25-13.95, dinner £14.95-18; ☙ lunch & dinner) This classy place right by the river, near the undercroft, serves upscale cuisine such as sea bass, lamb with apricots, and a scrumptious tomato and mozzarella tart.

Thai Orchid (☎ 767013; 33-39 St James St; lunch £6.95, evening mains from £6; ☙ lunch & dinner) The lunch buffet at this huge, atmospheric,

EASTERN ENGLAND

kitsch-clad place features a rotating selection of 15 classic Thai dishes.

Tudor Rose Hotel (☎ 762824; kltudorrose@aol.com; St Nicholas St; s/d from £30/60) has good-value pub grub in an antique-laden setting. **Archer's** (☎ 769177; Purfleet St; dishes £4-5.95; ☺ Mon-Sat) is a pleasant, friendly café with a good range of coffees. And **Crofters Coffee House** (King St; ☺ 9.30am-5pm Mon-Sat), in the guildhall undercroft at the Arts Centre, is recommended for teas or light meals; its patio offers a close-up view of the river action.

Getting There & Away

King's Lynn is 43 miles north of Cambridge on the A10.

First Eastern Counties runs an hourly bus service to Norwich (£4.85, 1½ hours) Monday to Saturday; on Sunday the service runs every two hours from 8.25am, with the last bus at 6.55pm.

There are hourly trains from Cambridge (£13.80, 50 minutes) and Norwich (£14.50, 45 minutes) to King's Lynn station.

AROUND KING'S LYNN
Castle Rising Castle

The amazingly well-preserved keep of this **castle** (☎ 631330; admission £3.75; ☺ 10am-6pm Apr-Oct, 10am-4pm Nov-Mar), built between 1138 and 1140, is set in the middle of a massive earthwork. It was once the home of Queen Isabella, who arranged the gruesome murder of her husband, Edward II, at Berkeley Castle in Gloucestershire. Watching the castle walls come into view as you pass through the stone gateway is genuinely transportive.

Bus No 411 runs here (£1.50, 19 minutes) every hour from King's Lynn bus station, 6 miles to the south.

Sandringham House

The Queen's country **pile** (☎ 772675; adult/child £6.50/4, grounds & museum only £4.50/2.50; ☺ 11am-4.45pm Apr-Sep unless royal family is in residence) is set in 25 hectares of landscaped gardens and lakes, and it's open to the hoi polloi when the court is not at home.

Queen Victoria bought the house and an 8000-hectare estate in 1862 so as to give her son, the Prince of Wales (later Edward VII), somewhere to call his official residence, but he wasn't altogether happy with the Georgian building. Over the next eight years, the house was redesigned in the style that would eventually bear his name.

The current crop of royals spends about three weeks a year here from mid-July to the first week in August, but they don't have the run of the whole estate. About half of the remaining 7975 hectares is leased out to farm tenants (a royal living doesn't pay for itself, you know), while the remaining hectares are managed by the Crown Estate as forestry.

The house itself is home to a museum that contains a collection of vintage cars, photographs from the last 100 years and other royal memorabilia. There are guided tours of the formal gardens on Friday and Saturday at 2pm.

There is also a yearly programme of special events, including a craft fair in September. Check with the office for details of upcoming events or write to Sandringham House, the Estate Office, Sandringham, Norfolk PE35 6EN.

First Eastern Counties bus No 411 (which also goes to Castle Rising Castle) runs here from King's Lynn bus station (£1.80, 25 minutes), 10 miles to the southwest.

Houghton Hall

Built for Sir Robert Walpole in 1730, **Houghton Hall** (☎ 01485-528569; admission £6.50; ☺ 1-5.30pm Thu-Sun Easter-Sep), in the Palladian style, is worth seeing for the ornate staterooms alone; you could build another halfdozen houses with the amount of decorative plasterwork in Houghton's interiors.

It's 14 miles northeast of King's Lynn. Last admission is at 5pm. Unfortunately, the house is not served by public transport; if you don't have your own wheels you'll have to get here from King's Lynn by taxi, which should cost £11 to £13. A reputable service in King's Lynn is **Ken's Taxis** (☎ 766166).

LINCOLNSHIRE

Lincolnshire suffers from a series of common misconceptions. It's generally thought of as flat, dull and strait-laced, when in fact those who've visited the county know that the landscape is quite varied and the people quite friendly. Nowhere is this more true than in the county capital, Lincoln. It's an exceedingly welcoming city that boasts one of the finest Gothic buildings in Europe, as well as a gorgeous old town in a hilltop setting full of drama.

Like the capital, the outlying areas of Lincolnshire are marked by evidence of their great success in the wool trade. The county is famous for its beautiful parish churches, standing cheek-by-jowl with solid, stone houses with red-tiled roofs to create a time-capsule effect that has attracted a number of film companies looking for an appropriate period setting in which to shoot.

The county consists of several distinct landscapes, from the hilly countryside of the western county to the flat marshlands of the east. The Lincolnshire Wolds, to the north and east of Lincoln, are composed of low, rolling hills and small market towns. To the southeast are the flat Lincolnshire Fens, fertile agricultural land reclaimed from the sea. The whole area is crisscrossed by a network of rivers and dykes, while the coastline to the east is marked by wide, sandy beaches, salt marshes, dunes and pools.

The gently varied landscape isn't the only reason Lincolnshire makes for inviting cycling and walking country. Even the weather seems to be friendly here: Lincolnshire receives only half the national average of rainfall, hence the county's slogan, 'the drier side of Britain'.

Activities

Lincolnshire is not renowned as a walking area, but if you want a long route from the sea to the Midlands in the footsteps of history, try the Viking Way, a 140-mile (225km) waymarked trail that runs from the Humber Bridge through the Lincolnshire Wolds to Oakham in Leicestershire. For a taster, you can focus on the section in the Lincolnshire Wolds and use the route as a base for a day walk.

Renting a bike in Lincoln, or bringing one with you, is an excellent idea. TICs stock sets of leaflets entitled *Lincolnshire Cycle Trails.*

Getting There & Away

Stamford and Lincoln are easily reached by bus from London. However, Lincolnshire is not quite on the well-trodden transport trail, and your best bet for getting here from the south is probably by train, although if you're planning to visit the county from Cambridge you'll most likely have to change in Peterborough.

Getting Around

For regional travel information, contact **Traveline** (☎ 0870-608 2608). Press option 4.

LINCOLN

☎ 01522 / pop 104,221

Lincoln is the sort of undervisited town where the staff at the tourist information centre seem pleasantly surprised whenever anyone steps through their doorway. Perhaps because they're not overrun by masses of tourists, the people of Lincoln are consistently friendly and welcoming. The place certainly rewards exploration; though you have to plough through some pretty drab and depressing suburbs to get to the good stuff, Lincoln has a well-preserved historic town centre and a cathedral that rivals the one at York. Regal and massive at the top of a hill, this 900-year-old mother church is the third-largest in England and one of the finest examples of Early English architecture in the country. Surrounding it, hidden inside the bland outskirts of town, is a compact medieval centre with some wonderful Tudor architecture and one of the steepest urban climbs this side of San Francisco. The presence of a university means that there are also plenty of young people around to keep the nightlife and pub scenes healthy.

History

For the last 2000 years, most of Britain's invaders have recognised the potential of this site and made their mark. Lincoln's hill was of immense strategic importance, giving views for miles across the surrounding plain. Communications were found to be excellent – below it is the River Witham, navigable to the sea.

The Romans established a garrison and a town they called Lindum. In AD 71 it was given the status of a colonia, or chartered town (Lindum Colonia); hence Lincoln. Gracious public buildings were constructed, and Lincoln became a popular place for old soldiers to spend their twilight years.

The Normans began work on the castle in 1068 and the cathedral in 1072. In the 12th century the wool trade developed, and wealthy merchants established themselves. The city was famous for the cloth known as Lincoln green, said to have been worn by Robin Hood. Many of the wealthiest merchants were Jews but, following the

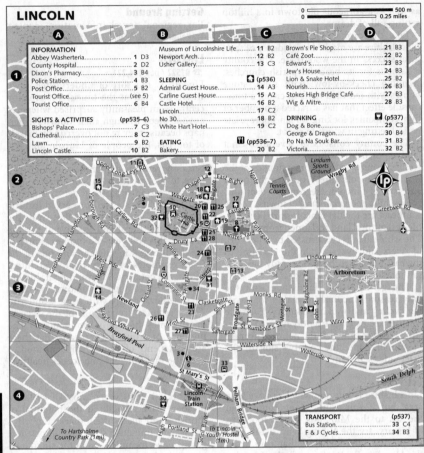

LINCOLN

0 — 500 m
0 — 0.25 miles

INFORMATION	Museum of Lincolnshire Life........**11** B2	Brown's Pie Shop.......................**21** B3
Abbey Washerteria.....................**1** D3	Newport Arch...............................**12** B2	Café Zoot...................................**22** B2
County Hospital...........................**2** D2	Usher Gallery................................**13** C3	Edward's.....................................**23** B3
Dixon's Pharmacy........................**3** B4		Jew's House................................**24** B3
Police Station...............................**4** B3	**SLEEPING** 🛏 (p536)	Lion & Snake Hotel....................**25** B2
Post Office....................................**5** B2	Admiral Guest House...................**14** A3	Nourish......................................**26** B3
Tourist Office.............................(see 5)	Carline Guest House...................**15** A2	Stokes High Bridge Café............**27** B3
Tourist Office...............................**6** B4	Castle Hotel.................................**16** B2	Wig & Mitre...............................**28** B3
	Lincoln..**17** C2	
SIGHTS & ACTIVITIES (pp535–6)	No 30..**18** B2	**DRINKING** 🍷 (p537)
Bishops' Palace............................**7** C3	White Hart Hotel.........................**19** C2	Dog & Bone...............................**29** C3
Cathedral......................................**8** C2		George & Dragon.......................**30** B4
Lawn...**9** B2	**EATING** 🍴 (pp536–7)	Po Na Na Souk Bar....................**31** B3
Lincoln Castle.............................**10** B2	Bakery...**20** B2	Victoria......................................**32** B2

TRANSPORT	(p537)
Bus Station...........................**33** C4
F & J Cycles..........................**34** B3

murder of a nine-year-old boy in 1255 for which one of their number was accused, they were mercilessly persecuted, and many were driven out.

During the Civil War the city passed from Royalist to Parliamentarian and back again, and prospered as an agricultural centre in the 18th century. In the following century, after the arrival of the railway, Lincoln's engineering industry was established. Heavy machinery produced here included the world's first tank, which saw action in WWI.

Orientation

The cathedral stands imperiously on top of the hill in the centre of the old part of the city, with the castle and most of the other attractions located conveniently nearby. Three-quarters of a mile down from the cathedral (a 15-minute walk) lies the new town, and the bus and train stations. Joining the two is the appositely named Steep Hill, and believe us, they're not kidding. Even locals stop to catch their breath.

Information

Abbey Washeteria (☎ 530272; 197 Monks Rd; per load £5.50)

County hospital (☎ 573103; off Greetwell Rd) Half a mile east of the visitor centre.

Dixon's Pharmacy (☎ 524821; 194 High St)

Police station (☎ 882222; West Pde)

Post office (☎ 526031; 90 Bailgate) Located next to the TIC.

TIC (tourism@lincoln.gov.uk) Main branch (☎ 873213; 9 Castle Hill; ☼ 9am-5.30pm Mon-Fri & 10am-5pm Sat & Sun); Cornhill branch (☎ 873256; 21 the Cornhill; ☼ 10am-5pm Mon-Sat)

Sights

LINCOLN CATHEDRAL

The superb **cathedral** (☎ 544544; www.lincolncath edral.com; admission £4; ☼ 7.15am-8pm Mon-Sat, 7.15am-6pm Sun Jun-Aug, 7.15am-6pm Mon-Sat, 7.15am-5pm Sun Sep-May) is the county's greatest attraction. Its three great towers dominate the city and can be seen from miles around. The central tower stands 81m high, which makes it the third-highest in the country after Salisbury Cathedral (123m) and Liverpool's Anglican Cathedral (101m). While this is impressive enough, imagine it twice as high, which it was until toppled by a storm in 1547.

Lincoln Cathedral was built on the orders of William the Conqueror, and construction began in 1072. It took only 20 years to complete the original building, which was 99m long with two western towers, but in 1185 an earthquake caused severe damage. Only the western front of the old cathedral survived. Rebuilding began under Bishop Hugh of Avalon (St Hugh), and most of the current building dates from the late 12th to late 13th centuries, in the Early English style.

The entrance is below the famous mid-12th-century frieze on the western front. Emerging into the nave, most people are surprised to find a substantial part of the cathedral empty, but this is actually how it would have looked back in 1250 when it was completed. Medieval cathedrals and churches, like mosques and Hindu temples today, did not have pews. This open area is now used for concerts and plays; services take place in St Hugh's choir. The stained glass in the nave is mostly Victorian, but the Belgian marble font dates back to the 11th century.

There are interesting stained-glass windows at each end of the transepts. The Dean's Eye contains glass that has been here since the 13th century; the glass in the Bishop's Eye dates from the 14th century. High above in the central tower, Great Tom is a 270kg bell that still sounds the hours.

St Hugh's Choir was the first section of the church to be rebuilt. The vaulting above is arranged at odd angles, but the canopied stalls of the choir are beautifully carved and over 600 years old.

The Angel Choir, named after the 28 angels carved high up the walls under the highest windows, was built as a shrine to St Hugh. Modern pilgrims search for the famous Lincoln Imp, a stonemason's joke that has become the city's emblem. The legend goes that this malevolent being was caught trying to chat up one of the angels and was turned to stone.

There are free one-hour tours of the cathedral at least twice a day; there are also less frequent tours of the tower (£4). You can listen to evensong in the cathedral daily except Wednesday at 5.15pm (3.45pm on Sunday), and sung Eucharist at 9.30am on Sunday.

BISHOPS' PALACE

Just south of the cathedral are the impressive ruins of the medieval **Bishops' Palace** (☎ 527468; admission £3.50; ☼ 10am-6pm daily Apr-Sep, to 5pm Oct-Mar), which, had it not been gutted by parliamentary forces during the Civil War, would still be one of Lincoln's most imposing structures. It was begun in 1150 and in its day was the administrative centre of the largest diocese in England. The East Hall range, with its superb vaulted undercroft, was built by Bishop St Hugh around 1200 as his private residence. The walled terrace garden is part of English Heritage's Contemporary Heritage Gardens scheme, and affords lovely views of the town below.

LINCOLN CASTLE

Begun in 1068, just four years before the cathedral, **Lincoln Castle** (☎ 511068; adult/child £3.50/2; ☼ 9.30am-5.30pm Mon-Sat, 11am-5.30pm Sun Apr-Sep, to 4pm daily Oct-Mar) was built over the original Roman town and incorporates some of the old Roman walls. As well as the usual views from the battlements you expect from a castle, the old prison is particularly interesting. Public executions used to draw crowds of up to 20,000 people, and took place in front of Cobb Hall, a horseshoe-shaped tower in the northeastern corner that served as the city's prison for centuries. The redbrick building on the eastern side replaced it and was used until 1878.

In the same building as the chapel, Lincoln's copy of the **Magna Carta** is on display. There are free tours of the castle at 11am and 2pm daily from April to September.

EASTERN ENGLAND

OTHER SIGHTS

The **Lawn** (☎ 873622; Union Rd; ♥ 9am-5pm Mon-Fri, 10am-5.30pm Sat & Sun; shorter hrs Nov-Feb) is a former lunatic asylum that now houses a concert hall and several exhibition areas. The **Sir Joseph Banks Conservatory**, in this complex, is a tropical glasshouse containing descendants of some of the plants brought back by this Lincoln explorer who accompanied Captain Cook to Australia.

A short walk up Burton Rd is the **Museum of Lincolnshire Life** (☎ 528448; adult/child £2/1.20; ♥ 10am-5.30pm May-Sep, 2-5.30pm Mon-Sat Oct-Apr). It's a fairly interesting museum of local social history – displays include everything from an Edwardian nursery to a WWI tank built here.

Newport Arch (Bailgate), built by the Romans, is the oldest arch in Britain that still has traffic passing through it.

As well as the black-and-white Tudor buildings on Steep Hill, **Jew's House** is of particular interest, being one of the best examples of 12th-century domestic architecture in Britain. It's now an upmarket restaurant (see Eating).

Located one block east of Jew's House is the **Usher Gallery** (☎ 527980; Lindum Rd; admission free; ♥ 10am-5.30pm Mon-Sat, 2.30-5pm Sun), the city's art gallery. Inside, the main focus is on the paintings and drawings of Peter de Wint (1784–1849) and on memorabilia associated with Lincolnshire-born Alfred Lord Tennyson (1809–92), the poet laureate. There are also temporary exhibitions and displays geared toward children.

Tours

Guided walking tours (adult £3, 1½ hours) from the TIC in Castle Hill take place at 11am and 2.15pm daily from June to September, and at weekends in June, September and October. Also leaving from the TIC is a 1¼-hour ghost walk (adult/child £3/2) at 7pm Wednesday, Friday and Saturday. **Guide Friday bus tours** (☎ 01789-294466; adult/child £6/2.50) explore the town daily from April to September.

Sleeping

BUDGET

Hartsholme Country Park (☎ 873577; Skellingthorpe Rd; site & 2 people £4-8; ♥ 31 Mar-31 Oct) This camping area is about 3 miles southwest of the train station. Take the R66 bus from the main bus station in the direction of Birchwood Estate; ask the driver to drop you off (it's about a 20-minute ride).

Lincoln Youth Hostel (☎ 0870-770 5918; fax 567424; 77 South Park Ave; dm £11, d £19; ♥ Feb-Oct, Fri & Sat Nov & Dec) This hostel provides good budget accommodation in various sized rooms.

MID-RANGE

Lincoln (☎ 530422; Eastgate; s/d from £60; P) Talk about your wild juxtapositions: directly across the street from the cathedral is this ultrachic, ultramodern 72-room hotel. Its amenity-jammed rooms have huge windows; ask for one that faces the cathedral. Don't be alarmed as the disco lights flash on and off when you walk up and down the hallway.

No 30 (☎ 521417; 30 Bailgate; s/d £25/45) There are just two rooms in this beautiful Georgian town house about 250m from the cathedral. It's an excellent choice, but be sure to book as early as possible, as it's always full.

Carline Guest House (☎ 530422; 1-3 Carline Rd; s/d £30/44) A bit more upmarket than No 30, this place has 12 individually appointed rooms, all with a private bathroom.

Admiral Guest House (☎ 544467; 16-18 Nelson St; s/d £25/38) One of several B&Bs just off Carholme Rd, this lovely 100-year-old house has really comfortable facilities. Unusually, smokers can puff away in their rooms.

TOP END

White Hart Hotel (☎ 526222; heritagehotels-lincoln .white-hart@forte-hotels.com; Bailgate; d £115; P) Near the cathedral, the White Hart is Lincoln's top hotel. It's a luxurious place with 48 beautifully appointed rooms.

Castle Hotel (☎ 538801; fax 575457; Westgate; s/d from £62/84; P) Directly across from the TIC, the fancy and comfortable Castle is in a restored 19th-century building.

Eating

Lincoln has a number of excellent restaurants with fine gourmet menus, but cheaper cafés are also in plentiful supply. There's also a good **bakery** (cnr Westgate & Bailgate; ♥ breakfast & lunch).

Jew's House (☎ 524851; Steep Hill; mains £9-12; ♥ lunch & dinner) Occupying a 12th-century building that's an attraction in its own right, this is Lincoln's top restaurant, serving astounding little installations of food sculpture that send foodies to the moon.

Brown's Pie Shop (☎ 527330; 33 Steep Hill; pies £8-12) Close to the cathedral and popular with tourists, this is the place to try out the Lincolnshire speciality – pies, with every filling you can imagine and then a few more. Rabbit pie with Dorset scrumpy costs £9, but there are cheaper options.

Lion & Snake Hotel (☎ 523770; Bailgate; burgers & pub food £2-5) Founded in 1640, the Lion & Snake is Lincoln's oldest pub. It's known for its real ale and inexpensive but really good homemade bar food.

Stokes High Bridge Café (☎ 513825; 207 High St; ☯ 9am-5pm Mon-Sat) This tea shop is hard to miss, as it's inside a 16th-century half-timbered building on the bridge over the River Witham, directly above the main shopping corridor – in other words, an ideal place to people-watch or gaze over the water. Lunches and teas are available.

Café Zoot (☎ 536663; 5 Bailgate; mains £4.95, specials £8) This sleek, techno-style café near the TIC serves creative, affordable lunches and excellent Continental cuisine, with a healthy number of vegetarian options.

Nourish (☎ 576277; 1 Newland; all mains around £2.50; ☯ 8am-3pm Mon-Fri, to 2pm Sat) This wonderful little café uses only organic ingredients. The quiche (£1.99) is particularly good.

Wig & Mitre (☎ 535190; 29 Steep Hill; mains around £13) Though it's nominally a pub, the Wig, near Brown's Pie Shop, behaves more like an upscale restaurant, with ambitious meals, a good wine list and a sophisticated candlelit atmosphere.

Edward's (☎ 519144; 238 High St; mains £7-9) At this large, welcoming bar-brasserie you can get everything from a coffee or a beer to a full meal.

Drinking

Victoria (6 Union Rd) Lincoln's most famous public house doesn't disappoint: it's a terrific bar with a huge selection of beers and just enough historic-pub bric-a-brac to seem warm, but not overdone or artificial. Every guided tour makes a stop at (or at least acknowledges) this historic place.

Dog & Bone (10 John St) This distinctive bar east of High St, just off Monks Rd, has a fine selection of ales.

George & Dragon (100 High St) One of the more popular pubs in town, what it lacks in original character it more than makes up

for in friendly ambience – though it can get very crowded at weekends.

Po Na Na Souk Bar (☎ 525828; 280-281 High St) Part of a vastly successful chain of clubs, Po Na Na is more serious about dancing than drinking. The tunes are deep, with a good mix of soulful house, eclectic funk and other esoteric sounds, set nicely against the vaguely Moroccan theme of the place.

Getting There & Away

Lincoln is 142 miles (229km) from London, 94 miles (151km) from Cambridge and 81 miles (130km) from York.

National Express runs a direct service between Lincoln and London (£17.50, 4½ hours) daily. Buses also run from Lincoln to Birmingham (£10.75, 2¾ hours) and Cambridge (£16.25, three hours; change at Peterborough).

Getting to and from Lincoln usually involves changing trains. There are hourly trains to Boston (£13.30, 1¼ hours) and Skegness (£15.60, two hours); change at Sleaford. There are also hourly trains to Cambridge (£30.10, 2½ hours); change at Peterborough and Ely. Trains run to Grantham (£8.70, 40 minutes) 20 times daily.

Getting Around

BICYCLE

You can rent everything from a three-speed to a mountain bike at **F&J Cycles** (☎ 545311; 41 Hungate), but 21 speeds are hardly an essential requirement for cycling in this flat county. An 18-speed costs £8 to £10 per day and up to £30 per week.

BUS

From the bus and train stations, bus No 51 runs past the youth hostel and Nos 7 and 8 link the cathedral area with the lower town (60p).

GRANTHAM

☎ 01476 / pop 34,592

Anyone old enough to remember the eventful reign of Lady Margaret Thatcher, who served as British Prime Minister from 1979 to 1990, will find a good example of her vision for Britain in the pleasant red-brick town where she was born. Baroness Thatcher lived at 2 North Pde, above her father's grocery shop; today it's a chiropractor's clinic. Another noteworthy inhabitant of Grantham was Sir Isaac Newton, who received his early education here. There's a statue of him in front of the guildhall – we're still waiting on the statue of the former Conservative prime minister.

The TIC (☎ 406166; Ave Rd; ☉ 9.30am-5pm Mon-Sat) is near the guildhall.

Until that commemorative statue comes around, the Iron Lady will have to content herself with a section devoted to her in the town's **museum** (St Peter's Hill; admission free; ☉ 10am-5pm Mon-Sat). Another section is devoted to Newton and frankly, unless you really want to see the famous handbag with which the former prime minister saluted the press after her 1979 electoral victory, it is by far the more interesting.

The town has an interesting parish church, **St Wulfram's**, with an 85m-high spire, the sixth-highest in England. It dates from the late 13th century. Inside there's a chained library, which Isaac Newton used while studying there.

Three miles northeast of Grantham on the A607 is **Belton House** (☎ 566116; bus Nos 601 & 609; admission £5.50; ☉ 1-5pm Wed-Sun Apr-Oct), one of the finest examples of Restoration country-house architecture. Built in 1688 for Sir John Brownlow, and set in a 400-hectare park, the house is known for its ornate plasterwork ceilings and woodcarvings attributed to the Dutch carver Grinling Gibbons.

Sleeping & Eating

Coach House (☎ 573636; coachhousenn@cwcom.net; per person £25; ✗) Just outside Belton House, this hotel is in a listed building with a large, pleasant garden – smokers will no doubt make use of it.

Red House (☎ 579869; fax 401597; 74 North Pde; s/d from £25/48) In another listed Georgian building in the town centre, the Red House has three en suite rooms.

Beehive (☎ 404554; Castlegate) This pub is best known for its sign – a real beehive full of live South African bees! The bees have been here since 1830, which makes them one of the oldest populations of bees in the world. Good, cheap lunches are available, and the bees stay away from the customers.

Getting There & Away

Grantham is 25 miles south of Lincoln. Lincolnshire Roadcar runs buses every hour between the two Monday to Saturday and

four times on Sunday (£2.80, one hour 10 minutes). It also runs a service (four daily, Monday to Saturday) to Stamford (£2.40, 1½ hours); National Express runs one bus daily Monday to Saturday.

By train (£8.70, 40 minutes), you'll need to change at Newark to get to Lincoln. There is at least one train per hour throughout the day. Direct trains run from London King's Cross to Grantham (£30, 1¼ hours) hourly throughout the day.

STAMFORD

☎ 01780 / pop 19,525

This beautiful town of stone buildings and cobbled streets was made a conservation area in 1967 and is one of the finest stone towns in the country. Its winding streets of medieval and Georgian houses slope gently down from the top of the hill to a riverside park that's ideal for a picnic.

The TIC (☎ 755611; 27 St Mary's St; ☉ 9.30am-5pm Mon-Sat year round, & 10am-3pm Sun Apr-Oct) is in the Stamford Arts Centre.

The **Stamford Museum** (☎ 766317; Broad St; admission free; ☉ 10am-5pm Mon-Sat year round, & 2-5pm Sun Apr-Sep) is certainly worth visiting. As well as displays charting the history of the town, there's a clothed model of local heavyweight Daniel Lambert, who tipped the scales at 336kg before his death in 1809 (see the boxed text below). After his death his suits were displayed in a local pub where Charles Stratton, better known as Tom Thumb, would put on a show by fitting into the suit's armholes. Hilarious, apparently.

LEICESTER'S WEIGHTIEST CITIZEN

Born in 1770, Daniel Lambert, the one-time keeper of Leicester Gaol, started life as a normal baby but soon began to tip the scales at ever more alarming totals. Despite eating only one meal a day, by 39 he weighed an astounding 52 stone 11lb (333kg), making him, as the *Dictionary of National Biography* puts it, 'the most corpulent man of whom authentic record exists'.

When he died in Stamford in 1809 one wall of the house had to be dismantled to remove the coffin, and 20 pallbearers were needed to carry it to the graveyard. A whole room in Leicester's Newarke Houses Museum is devoted to Lambert's memory.

Sleeping & Eating

George (☎ 750750; georgehotelofstamford@btInternet .com; 71 St Martin's St; s/d from £85/120) Nestled at the bottom of a hill where an elegant stone bridge crosses the river, the George is the top place to stay and is worth peeking inside even if it's out of your price range. It's a wonderful old coaching inn where the Burghley crowd used to rack up astronomical bills; parts of the building date back a thousand years. There's a cobbled courtyard and luxurious rooms with first-class amenities. There's also an excellent restaurant divided into several rooms; if you want anything fancier than upmarket pub grub, expect to pay at least £20.

St George's B&B (☎ 482099; 16 St George's Sq; s/d from £25/40) Not to be confused with the George hotel, this is a gorgeous 19th-century house with Victorian fireplaces and antiques. It also has a private garden.

Martin's (☎ 752106; fax 482691; 20 St Martin's Rd; s/d from £35/55) Another stellar B&B, Martin's is just beyond the bridge over the River Welland, only a couple of minutes' walk from the centre of town.

There are a number of historic pubs that also offer accommodation, including the beautiful, lace-curtained **Bull & Swann Inn** (☎ 763558; High St; s/d £35/45); good meals and real ale are available here, too.

Getting There & Away

Stamford is 46 miles from Lincoln and 21 miles south of Grantham.

National Express serves Stamford from London (£9.75, 2¾ hours) via Lincoln (£7.75, 1½ hours). Lincolnshire Roadcar operates four buses daily Monday to Saturday between Stamford and Grantham (£2.60, 1½ hours). National Express also runs one bus daily.

There are 15 trains daily to Cambridge (£13.90, 1¼ hours) and Ely (£8.70, 55 minutes). Norwich (£15.20, one hour 50 minutes) is on the same line, but there are fewer direct trains; you will most likely have to change at Ely.

AROUND STAMFORD
Burghley House

Just a mile south of Stamford, this immensely grand **Tudor mansion** (bur-lee; ☎ 752 451; www.burghley.co.uk; adult/child £7.80/3.50, 1 child free per paying adult; ☽ 11am-5pm Apr–early Oct) is the home of the Cecil family. It was built between 1565 and 1587 by William Cecil, Queen Elizabeth's adviser.

It's an impressive place with 18 magnificent staterooms. The Heaven Room was painted by Antonio Verrio in the 17th century, and features floor-to-ceiling gods and goddesses disporting among the columns; on the flip side, there's the stairway to Hell, with an equally fascinating painting depicting Satan as a giant cat-eyed uterus devouring the world. There are over 300 paintings, including works by Gainsborough and Brueghel; state bedchambers, including the four-poster Queen Victoria slept in; and cavernous Tudor kitchens. An exhibit in one of the lower hallways details the career of David Cecil, the Lord Burghley who was an Olympic athlete and part of the inspiration for the film *Chariots of Fire*.

It's a pleasant 15-minute walk through the park from Stamford train station. The **Burghley Horse Trials** take place here over three days in early September and are of international significance.

BOSTON
☎ 01205 / pop 35,124

A major port in the Middle Ages, Boston lies near the mouth of the River Witham, in the bay known as the Wash. By the end of the 13th century the town was one of the most important wool-trading centres in the country, exporting the fleeces of three million sheep annually. Boston's other claim to fame came in the 17th century, when it temporarily imprisoned a group of religious separatists looking to settle in the virtually unknown territories of the New World. These later became known as the Pilgrim Fathers, the first white settlers of the US. Word of their success made it back to the English Boston, whereupon a crowd of locals decided to sail across the Atlantic; there they founded a namesake town in the new colony of Massachusetts.

Today the Boston in Massachusetts wouldn't recognize its namesake; the English town is but a shadow of its former self. But it has retained much of its medieval appearance, down to the street grid, whereby the two main streets flank both sides of the river and are linked by small footbridges. It's an easy place to wander about in, and has a number of interesting sites.

The **TIC** (☎ 356656; Market Pl; ☽ 9am-5pm Mon-Sat year round) is under the Assembly Rooms on

Market Pl. Market days are Wednesday and Saturday; you can buy pretty much everything from a fish to a bicycle.

As you walk around the town, be sure to check out **Shodfriars Hall** (South St; not open to the public), a marvellous Tudor building that has been faithfully restored.

St Botolph's Church

In keeping with its high-flying status, the town ordered the construction of an impressive church in 1309: the result was **St Botolph's** (☎ 362864; church free, tower £2; ☼ 9am-4.30pm Mon-Sat, btwn services Sun) and its 88m-high tower – known as the Boston Stump because it doesn't come to a point. The fenland on which it's built was not firm enough to support a thin spire, hence the sturdy tower. Climb the 365 steps to the top to see (on a clear day) Lincoln, 30 miles away.

Inside there is a splendid 17th-century **pulpit** from which John Cotton, the fiery vicar of St Botolph's, delivered five-hour catechisms and two-hour sermons during the 1630s. By all accounts, it was he who convinced his parishioners to follow in the footsteps of the Pilgrim Fathers and emigrate.

Guildhall

It was from Boston that the Pilgrim Fathers made their first break for the freedom of the New World in 1607. They were imprisoned in the **guildhall** (☎ 365954; admission £1.50; ☼ 10am-5pm Mon-Sat & 1.30-5pm Sun May-Sep), where the cells that held them are now a fairly extensive visitor centre, with multimedia exhibits on the town's history and a eulogising display on the struggles of the Pilgrim Fathers.

Sleeping & Eating

Bramley House (☎ /fax 354538; bramleyhouse@ic24 .net; 267 Sleaford Rd; s/d from £20/40) An old 18th-century farmstead, Bramley House is about half a mile west of town along Sleaford Rd. It has nine comfortable rooms and also does pub grub.

There are many eateries dotted about town, but we recommend you check out **Maud's Tea Rooms** (☎ 352188; Maud Foster Windmill, Willoughby Rd; mains £5-8), about half a mile northeast of Market Pl. This is a fully functional mill, and the tearooms serve good vegetarian dishes. You can also buy the local produce: organic flour, not exactly your typical souvenir.

THE FENS

The Fens were strange marshlands that stretched from Cambridge north to the Wash and beyond into Lincolnshire. They were home to people who led an isolated existence fishing, hunting, and farming scraps of arable land among a maze of waterways. In the 17th century, however, the Duke of Bedford and a group of speculators brought in Dutch engineer Sir Cornelius Vermuyden to drain the Fens, and the flat, open plains with their rich, black soil were created. The region is the setting for Graham Swift's excellent novel *Waterland*.

As the world's weather pattern changes and the sea level rises, the Fens are beginning to disappear underwater again. It's estimated that by the year 2030 up to 400,000 hectares could be lost.

Getting There & Away

From Lincoln it's easier to get to Boston by train than by bus, but even that involves a change at Sleaford. Trains run from Lincoln hourly (1¼ hours).

SKEGNESS

☎ 01754 / pop 16,806

There's a particular craving that places like 'Skeggy' are engineered to cure. It's a hankering for candyfloss, fried foods, penny arcades and cheap funfair rides, for thousands of pasty optimists doing brave impressions of sunbathing regardless of the weather, for ice-cream-faced kids with kites and sandcastles. In other words, it's absolutely everything you want in a classic English seaside resort. Tens of thousands of Britons holiday here every year, mostly because it's cheaper than going to Spain, it's by the sea, and every night offers the chance for some brand of wild abandon – whether it's disco, bingo or bad cabaret. Virtually every inch of the Grand Pde, which skirts the 6-mile-long beach, is covered in amusement arcades, fish-and-chip shops, pubs, and B&Bs.

The **TIC** (☎ 764821; Grand Pde; ☼ 9.30am-5pm Apr-Sep, 10am-4pm Mon-Fri Oct-Mar) is directly opposite the **Embassy Centre** (☎ 768333), home of Skeggy's cabaret scene and the place to watch your favourite Abba tribute band in all its glory; shows usually kick off at around 7.30pm. From July to September, this stretch of beach is anointed with 25,000 light bulbs, which come on in the evening to celebrate the Skegness Illuminations.

B&Bs are not hard to find and are generally quite cheap, starting from around £18 per person. The TIC will help you find a room if you need one.

Skegness is pretty easy to get to by either bus or train. From Boston, Lincolnshire Roadcar runs five buses daily, Monday to Saturday (1¼ hours). **Brylaine Travel** (☎ 01205-364087) runs three daily along the same route. Tickets, however, are only valid on the service provided by the issuing company. From Lincoln, Lincolnshire Roadcar buses run hourly Monday to Saturday and five times on Sunday (1¾ hours).

There are 15 trains daily Monday to Saturday and eight on Sunday between Skegness and Boston (35 minutes).

LOUTH

☎ 01507 / pop 15,930

East Lincolnshire's largest market town, the largely Georgian Louth sits on the banks of the River Lud between the Wolds to the west and the marshes of the Lincolnshire coast. A curious fact about Louth is that it has two hemispheres – east and west – as the zero longitude line cuts right through the town.

Dominating the town is the soaring spire of **St James' Church** (☺ 10am-4.30pm Easter-Christmas), added to the medieval church between 1500 and 1515. The dramatic buttresses and battlements of the church exterior – described by Sir John Betjeman as 'one of the last great medieval Gothic masterpieces' – belie a fairly inconsequential interior, however, although the lovely wooden roof, built in the early 19th century, is undoubtedly a feature. You can climb the tower (£1.50) for marvellous views of the town and surrounding countryside.

The **TIC** (☎ /fax 609289; New Market Hall, off Cornmarket; ☺ 9am-5pm Mon-Sat) has all the information you'll need.

The most elegant street in town is Westgate, which is lined with Georgian houses. The mid-17th-century **church precincts** at No 47 and the grander No 45 are particularly handsome. Just opposite is Westgate Pl, and through the archway you'll find a row of terraced houses, one of which bears a plaque commemorating Tennyson's residence here between 1816 and 1820.

Sleeping & Eating

Priory (☎ 602930; fax 609767; Eastgate; s/d £45/69) In a magnificent building from 1818 is this simply gorgeous hotel, an all-white half-castle, half-residence – it's easily the top spot in town. For an extra £15 you can get dinner at the excellent restaurant.

Ramsgate Hotel (☎ 602179; 15 Ramsgate; s/d from £20/30) A less spectacular option, the Ramsgate has pretty, comfortable rooms and is very central.

Besides the Priory, Louth has a surprisingly good selection of restaurants. **Taipan Tai** (☎ 602332; 138 Eastgate; mains around £8) has a wonderful menu of Thai specialities. **Ferns** (☎ 603209; 40 Northgate; mains around £9) is a good choice if you're after solid English cuisine.

EASTERN ENGLAND

THE PILGRIMAGE OF GRACE

The revolt against Henry VIII's reformation of the church began in Louth in 1536. Deeply annoyed by Henry's plans to dissolve all of the monasteries and appoint new bishops to every diocese, northerners were pushed over the edge by Henry's minister Thomas Cromwell, who at the same time decided to pursue some fairly radical land-reform programmes in the northern counties. On 1 October, the crown commissioners arrived in Louth to fulfil Henry and Cromwell's orders, but they were attacked by an angry mob. What was a protest was now a full rebellion, later called the Pilgrimage of Grace. Lincoln was occupied, and the rebels demanded an end to dissolution, Cromwell's resignation and the dismissal of the newly appointed heretical bishops. Henry, however, was unmoved, and the rebellion petered out on 19 October.

Although the Louth rebellion was a bit of a damp squib, it inspired a more serious rebellion in Yorkshire by Robert Aske, a gentleman farmer who gathered 30,000 men, engaged the crown forces and forced Henry to consider the rebels' demands. He did, or pretended to, and Aske eventually disbanded his forces. The government reacted swiftly by arresting and executing the ringleaders in early 1537, and the rebellion was finally at an end.

Getting There & Away

Louth is 23 miles northeast of Lincoln, from where there are buses every couple of hours (£3.50, 45 minutes).

AROUND LOUTH
Saltfleetby-Theddlethorpe National Nature Reserve

Ten miles east of Louth along the B1200, which meanders its way through the Fens, is one of the most attractive **nature reserves** (☎ 01507-338611) in this part of the country. Spread over 5 miles of sand dunes and fresh- and saltwater marsh, it is best appreciated in early summer, when the stunning marsh orchids are in full bloom. In spring and autumn, migratory wildfowl flock to the reserve. Crisscrossing the whole area are dozens of trails, which help to keep your feet dry as you negotiate the myriad lagoons.

You'll need your own transport to get here. At the end of the B1200, take a right on to the A1031 and, about three quarters of a mile further on, follow the signs for the nature reserve.

Yorkshire

CONTENTS

Welcome to God's Own Country. Yorkshire folk are only half-joking when they talk about being heaven-blessed, so strong is their sense of 'national' pride. For Yorkshire was indeed a nation once, and while the Viking-governed Danelaw of the 9th century may be but the stuff of dusty annals, the sense of self that its history engenders has given Yorkshire a confident homogeneity you simply don't find anywhere else in England.

Round these parts, size *does* matter. Yorkshire is bloody huge, so big that it's split into four separate counties – South Yorkshire, West Yorkshire, North Yorkshire and the East Riding of Yorkshire. Topographers and administrators may quibble, but compass points matter far less than the place they're south, west, north or east *of*, at least in the minds of the people themselves. Maybe it's the landscape of dark moors and rocky outcrops, or the background of generations struggling to earn a living from the land or the factories – but whatever – Yorkshire folk shoot from the hip and never sit on the fence. Whether it's football, foreign wars, beer or just life in general, things are either great or terrible. There's no in-between.

Against this human story, the Yorkshire countryside is a magnificent backdrop, containing two of England's best national parks, beautiful countryside and a spectacular coastline. The cities, too, attract their share of visitors, with their museums, galleries, pubs and bars. If you make it to Yorkshire, consider yourself lucky; isn't it God's favourite place?

HIGHLIGHTS

- Going medieval in **York's** (p577) winding streets, awe-inspiring minster and fabulous museums
- Strolling down green valleys or hiking over high moors in the **Yorkshire Dales** (p563)
- Shopping, eating, drinking and dancing, then shopping some more in **Leeds** (p553)
- Weather-beaten **Whitby** (p602): a favourite with seadogs, sun-lovers and lackeys of the Prince of Darkness
- Riding steam trains on the **Settle–Carlisle Line** (p568)
- Going underground at the **National Coal Mining Museum for England** (p560) near Wakefield

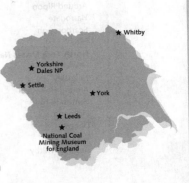

- POPULATION: 4.96 MILLION
- AREA: 5958 SQ MILES

Information

Yorkshire Tourist Board (☎ 01904-707070; www .yorkshirevisitor.com; 312 Tadcaster Rd, York YO24 1GS) has plenty of general leaflets and brochures. For more detailed information, contact the local Tourist Information Centres (TICs) listed throughout this chapter.

Activities

Within Yorkshire are high peaks, wild hills, tranquil valleys, farmland, moorland and a stupendous coastline. With this fantastic selection, not surprisingly, it's a great place for outdoor activities.

CYCLING

Cycling is a great way to see Yorkshire; there's a vast network of country lanes, although the most scenic areas are also attractive to car drivers, so even some minor roads can be busy at weekends. Options include:
North York Moors Off-road riders can avail themselves of the networks of bridlepaths, former railways and disused mining tracks now turned over to two-wheel use.
Whitby to Scarborough A traffic-free route that includes a disused railway line, and an effortless way to tour this rugged coastline.
White Rose Cycle Route A 120-mile (193km) cruise from Hull to York to Middlesbrough, via the rolling Yorkshire Wolds and the dramatic edge of the North York Moors, and a traffic-free section on the old railway between Selby and York. It is part of the National Cycle Network (p62).
Yorkshire Dales Great cycling in the quieter areas in the north around Swaledale and Wensleydale, and the west around Dentdale. The areas just outside the park, like Nidderdale, are also good. Also an excellent network of old 'drove roads' (formerly used for driving cattle to market) which wind across lonely hillsides, and tie in neatly with the narrow country lanes in the valley bottoms.

WALKING

For shorter walks and rambles, the best area is the **Yorkshire Dales**, with a great selection of hard and easy walks through scenic valleys or over wild hilltops, with even a few peaks thrown in for good measure. The **Yorkshire Wolds** hold hidden delights, while the quiet valleys and dramatic coasts of the **North York Moors** also have many good opportunities, although the broad ridges of the high moors can be a bit featureless and less attractive for keen walkers.

For general information get the *Walk Yorkshire* brochure from TICs or see www.walk yorkshire.com. All TICs stock a mountain of leaflets (free or up to £1.50) on local walks, and sell more detailed guidebooks and maps. At train stations and TICs, it's worth looking out for leaflets produced by companies such as Northern Spirit, detailing walks from train stations. Some tie in with train times, so you can walk one way and ride back.

Long-distance Walks

Cleveland Way A venerable moor-and-coast classic; details in the North York Moors section (p597).
Coast to Coast Walk England's No 1 walk, 190 miles (306km) across northern England eastwards from the Lake District, crossing the Yorkshire Dales and North York Moors. Doing the Yorkshire sections would take a week to 10 days and offers some of the finest walking of its kind in England.
Dales Way Charming and not-too-strenuous amble from the Yorkshire Dales to the Lake District (details in the Yorkshire Dales section, p564).
Pennine Way The Yorkshire section of England's most famous walk starts on day two and runs for over 100 miles (160km), via Hebden Bridge, Malham, Horton-in-Ribblesdale and Hawes, passing near Haworth and Skipton.
Wolds Way Beautiful but oft-overlooked walk that winds through the most scenic part of eastern Yorkshire (p572).

Getting There & Around

Yorkshire covers a large part of northern England, and a vast range of landscapes. From the Pennine Hills on the western side of the region (separating Yorkshire from age-old rival Lancashire), you can travel through the green valleys of the Yorkshire Dales, across the plains of the Vale of York and the rolling hills of the North York Moors and Yorkshire Wolds, to finally end at the dramatic east coast.

The major north–south transport routes – the M1 and A1 motorways and the main

---

YORKSHIRE DINING

You simply can't visit Yorkshire without indulging in a meal of local treats. Roast beef and Yorkshire pudding, with a light spread of horseradish sauce, is an absolute must (veggies are excused), followed by a Fat Rascal – a traditional teacake with currants and candied orange peel. To round it off, cut yourself a chunk of Wensleydale – one of England's best cheeses. What do you wash it all down with? A pint of Yorkshire bitter, of course – although make sure that it's pulled from a hand pump.

YORKSHIRE

YORKSHIRE

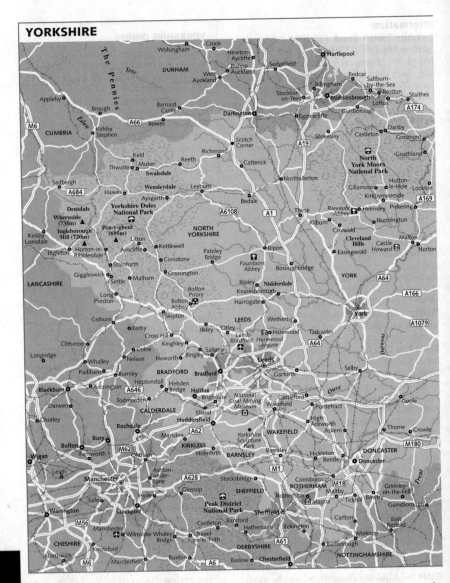

London to Edinburgh railway line – run through the middle of Yorkshire following the flat lands between the Pennines and the Moors, and serving the key cities of Sheffield, Leeds and York.

Yorkshire's main gateway cities by road and rail are Sheffield in the far south, Leeds for the west and York for the centre and north. If you're coming by sea from northern Europe, Hull (in the East Riding) is the region's main port. More specific details for each area are given under Getting There & Away in the separate sections throughout this chapter. For inquiries, the national **Traveline** (☎ 0870 608 2608) covers buses and trains all over Yorkshire.

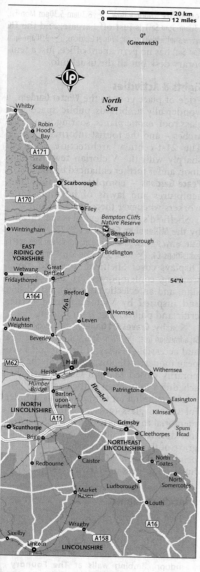

0   20 km
0   12 miles

service most cities and large towns in Yorkshire from London, the south of England, the Midlands and Scotland. More details are given under Getting There & Away in the individual town and city sections.

Bus transport around Yorkshire is frequent and efficient, especially between major towns. Services are more sporadic in the national parks but still perfectly adequate for reaching most places – particularly in the summer months (June to September).

TRAIN

The main line between London and Edinburgh runs through Yorkshire with at least 10 services per day, via York and Doncaster – where you might change to reach other places in Yorkshire. There are also direct services between the major towns and cities of Yorkshire and other northern cities like Manchester and Newcastle. One of England's most famous and scenic railways is the Settle–Carlisle Line (SCL), which crosses the Yorkshire Dales via a spectacular series of tunnels and viaducts. Trains start/end in Leeds, and Carlisle is a good stop on the way to Scotland (see p568). Call or check out **National Rail Enquiries** (☎ 08457 484950; www .nationalrail.co.uk) for timetable details.

SOUTH YORKSHIRE

South Yorkshire is virtually synonymous with Sheffield. And Sheffield is virtually synonymous with steel, most particularly the kind of steel you prod and poke food with. Indeed, having a 'Sheffield Steel' stamp on your cutlery was a mark of distinction for hundreds of years. Outside of the city, coal was the big industry, which was handy for the steel mills in and around Sheffield. Now that both industries have been consigned to history, the big question is: what is it about a bunch of old steel mills and coal pits that would make you want to come here?

The answer lies not in the mills or the pits (which are themselves unattractive), but in the wealth that was accrued as a result of them and, for those of a historical bent, in their significance as living museums of the past. Sheffield has a host of grand civic buildings built during the irrepressible Victorian Age that are well worth

BOAT

Details on passenger ferries to Hull from northern Europe are given in the main Transport chapter (see p750).

BUS

Long-distances buses and coaches run by **National Express** (☎ 08705 808080) regularly examining, while a host of museums has grown up looking to preserve the Industrial Age without having to relive it. Lastly, Sheffield's western outskirts brush up against the Peak District National Park, and the city serves as a handy gateway between the south and the north of England.

SHEFFIELD

☎ 0114 / pop 640,720

Mention Sheffield to anyone and chances are that they'll talk about steel, snooker or *The Full Monty*. Which is something of a PR problem, considering that the steel industry was more or less killed off in the 1980s – thanks to Thatcherism and the closure of the pits – while snooker, despite the immense national popularity of the world championships, is a game for those who believe that cigarettes and lager *do* have a part to play in sport. Which leaves *The Full Monty*, a feel-good movie sensation about six unemployed steelworkers (and, we presume, snooker fans) who turned to stripping to raise some cash. But the film has long since gone to DVD, so what is it about Sheffield these days?

Since the late 1990s, the city has worked hard to reinvent itself. Smart hotels and galleries are springing up, the whole centre is revelling in a major facelift, and several new attractions based on the industrial past are well worth a visit. On the entertainment side, there's a buzz that hasn't been seen for a long while, powered in no small way by an exuberant and ever-growing student population.

Orientation

Sheffield's bus and train stations are ringed by busy roads and grotty high-rise buildings so ugly that you might even consider turning around and getting out of here. Beyond them, however, are the city's most interesting bits, a central area around Church St, Tudor Sq, Fargate and a square called Barker's Pool. Just west of here Division St and Devonshire St have hip clothes and record shops, popular restaurants and trendy bars. A block north is West St, also pretty trendy.

Information

Handiest for all e-things is **Havana Internet Cafe** (☎ 249 5453; 32 Division St; ☎ 10am-6pm). The

post office (Norfolk Row; ☎ 8.30am-5.30pm Mon-Fri, 8.30am-3pm Sat) is just off Fargate, and the **TIC** (www.sheffieldcity.co.uk; Winter Gardens; ☎ 9.30am-4pm Mon-Sat) has no permanent office, just a temporary desk but all the usual info.

Sights & Activities

Pride of place goes to the **Winter Gardens**, a wonderfully ambitious public space with glass roof, exotic plants, soaring wood-clad arches – and the tourist information desk. The 21st-century architecture contrasts sharply with the Victorian **town hall** next door, and is further enhanced by the nearby **Peace Gardens** – complete with fountains, sculptures and lawns of lunching office workers whenever there's a bit of sun.

Sheffield's cultural revival is spearheaded by the **Millennium Galleries** (☎ 278 2600; Arundel Gate; www.sheffieldgalleries.org.uk; admission free, special exhibitions £4; ☎ 10am-5pm Mon-Sat, 11am-5pm Sun). Displays cover Sheffield steel and metalworking, contemporary art, craft and design, and an eclectic collection established and inspired by Victorian artist, writer, critic and philosopher John Ruskin.

Nearby, **Graves Art Gallery** (☎ 278 2600; Surrey St; admission free; ☎ 10am-5pm Mon-Sat) has a neat and accessible display of British and European modern art, plus works from the temporarily closed Mappin Gallery (which is scheduled to re-open at the end of 2005).

The **cathedral** on Church St has wonderful stained glass (ancient and modern), a memorial to the crew of the HMS *Sheffield* lost during the Falklands conflict and the grave of the earl of Shrewsbury, famous for being the jailer of Mary Queen of Scots and husband to Bess of Harwick (see p477).

ROCK CLIMBING

Sheffield is the capital of English rock climbing. All the real rock is in the nearby Peak District (p478), but if it's raining (or you need instruction) there are excellent indoor climbing walls at **The Foundry** (☎ 279 6331; 45 Mowbray St; adult/child £6.50/4; ☎ 10am-10pm Mon-Fri, plus 10am-6pm Sat & Sun Apr-Sep, 10am-8pm Sat & Sun Oct-Mar) and **The Edge** (☎ 275 8899; John St; adult/child £5.80/5; ☎ 10am-10.30pm Mon-Fri, 10am-8pm Sat & Sun). For online info, click onto www.sheffield climbing.com.

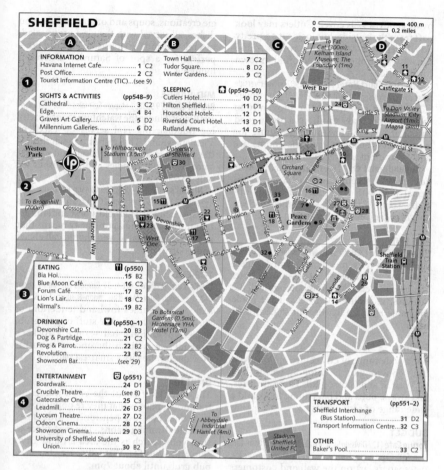

SHEFFIELD

INFORMATION	
Havana Internet Cafe	1 C2
Post Office	2 C2
Tourist Information Centre (TIC)	(see 9)

SIGHTS & ACTIVITIES	(pp548–9)
Cathedral	3 C2
Edge	4 B4
Graves Art Gallery	5 D2
Millennium Galleries	6 D2

Town Hall	7 C2
Tudor Square	8 D2
Winter Gardens	9 C2

SLEEPING	(pp549–50)
Cutlers Hotel	10 D2
Hilton Sheffield	11 D1
Houseboat Hotels	12 D1
Riverside Court Hotel	13 D1
Rutland Arms	14 D3

EATING	(p550)
Bia Hoi	15 B2
Blue Moon Café	16 C2
Forum Café	17 B2
Lion's Lair	18 C2
Nirmal's	19 B2

DRINKING	(pp550–1)
Devonshire Cat	20 B3
Dog & Partridge	21 C2
Frog & Parrot	22 B2
Revolution	23 B2
Showroom Bar	(see 29)

ENTERTAINMENT	(p551)
Boardwalk	24 D1
Crucible Theatre	(see 8)
Gatecrasher One	25 C3
Leadmill	26 D3
Lyceum Theatre	27 D2
Odeon Cinema	28 D2
Showroom Cinema	29 D3
University of Sheffield Student Union	30 B2

TRANSPORT	(pp551–2)
Sheffield Interchange (Bus Station)	31 D2
Transport Information Centre	32 C3

OTHER	
Baker's Pool	33 C2

Sheffield's prodigious industrial heritage is the subject of the excellent **Kelham Island Museum** (☎ 272 2106; Alma St; www.simt.co.uk; admission £3.50; ☾ 10am-4pm Mon-Thu, 11am-4.45pm Sun). The most impressive display is the 12,000-horsepower steam engine (the size of a house) that is powered up twice a day.

For a view of steel from an earlier era, go to **Abbeydale Industrial Hamlet** (☎ 236 7731; admission £3; ☾ 10am-4pm Mon-Thu, 11am-4.45pm Sun mid-Apr–Oct). It's 4 miles southwest of the centre on the A621 (towards the Peak District) and well worth a stop. In the days before factories, metalworking was a cottage industry, just like wool or cotton. These rare (and restored) houses and machines take you right back to that era.

Sleeping

Most of the central options cater primarily to the business traveller, which makes for cheaper weekend rates; there are, alas, no budget options in the city centre.

MID-RANGE

Houseboat Hotels (☎ 232 6556; www.houseboathotels .com; Victoria Quays, Wharfe St; d/q from £65/85) For a little watery luxury, kick off your shoes and relax on board your very own houseboat, which comes with its own self-catering kitchen and patio area. Available for groups of two or four only, guests are also entitled to use the gym facilities across the road at the Hilton.

Cutlers Hotel (☎ 273 9939; www.cutlershotel.co.uk; George St; s £38-52, d £52-62) Don't judge a book

YORKSHIRE

by its gaudy, 1970s cover: Cutlers may look naff from the outside, but inside it's a pretty tidy hotel with comfortable rooms – and the most central option you'll find in town for the price.

Riverside Court Hotel (☎ 273 1962; www.riverside court.co.uk; 4 Nursery St; s/d from £29/39) The riverside location and its relative proximity to the city centre make this hotel a pretty good choice if you don't want to get stung for a mid-week business rate; the rooms are fairly bland but utterly inoffensive.

Rutland Arms (☎ 272 9003; fax 273 1425; 86 Brown St; s/d from £24/37) A centrally located, fine traditional pub with a number of rooms upstairs, some of them en suite: they're clean and neat but pretty darn small.

TOP END

Hilton Sheffield (☎ 252 5500; www.hilton.co.uk; Victoria Quay; r £110) Pretty much what you'd expect from one of the world's best-known hotel chains: a top-class business hotel with all the facilities, including rooms that have made the name Hilton a byword for standardised luxury.

Eating

For a wide range of city centre options, you can't go wrong on Division St, Devonshire St, West St and Glossop Rd. There are cafés, takeaways, pubs and bars doing food, and a wide range of restaurants.

BUDGET

Forum Café (127 Division St; lunch about £5; ☑ 10am-1am Mon-Sat) Open and airy, with coffees, snacks, newspapers, art on the wall and customers who wander in from the vaguely alternative Forum Shopping Centre next door. In the evening, it's more bar-like, with lower lights and louder music.

Blue Moon Café (☎ 276 3443; 2 St James St; snacks £1-3, lunches £3-5; ☑ 7am-8pm Mon-Sat) Tasty veg-

gie creations, soups and other good-for-you dishes, all served with the ubiquitous salad, in a relaxed and very pleasant atmosphere – perfect for a spot of Saturday afternoon lounging.

MID-RANGE

Bia Hoi (☎ 279 9250; 1 Mappin St; mains £4-8; ☑ noon-7pm Mon-Sat) Under the watchful gaze of a pretty big Buddha, Bia Hoi serves up excellent Vietnamese and Thai dishes; a lunch thrill is the Siam Market menu, an all-you-can-eat smorgasbord of noodles and rice dishes for only £3.95.

Nirmal's (☎ 272 4054; 189 Glossop Rd; mains £5-8; ☑ noon-2.30pm & 6pm-1am) Gujarati cuisine is the speciality at Sheffield's best Indian restaurant. Its enduring popularity means that in order to get a table, you should call ahead and book one.

TOP END

Lion's Lair (☎ 263 4264; 31 Burgess St; mains about £12; ☑ noon-9pm Mon-Thu, noon-8.30pm Fri & Sat, noon-5pm Sun) Guinea fowl and tenderloin of springbok are hardly the stuff of pub grub, but this traditional bar – once a rocker's hangout – was given the once-over and is now one of the city's smartest eateries.

Drinking

The nice thing about the city's numerous traditional pubs is that they're popular with everyone, not just pensioners with questionable drinking habits. The best place to start your search is the area around Division and West Sts. Virtually every bar does pub grub until about 7pm.

Fat Cat (☎ 249 4801; 23 Alma St) One of Sheffield's finest pubs, the Fat Cat serves a wide range of real ales (some brewed on the premises) in a wonderfully unreconstructed interior. There are three bars (one non-smoking), good pub grub, a roaring fire in winter and – in the men's toilets – a fascinating exhibit on local sanitation. It's next door to the Kelham Island Museum.

Frog & Parrot (Division St) Home to the world's strongest beer, the 12%-strong 'Roger & Out', unsuspecting ale-heads saunter in looking to down the equivalent of a pint of fortified wine. Which is precisely why they only serve this particular brew in half-pint glasses – so that you have more than a 50/50 chance of walking out under your

---

TOP FIVE PUBS FOR A PROPER PINT

- **Fat Cat** (right; Sheffield)
- **Duck & Drake** (p557; Leeds)
- **Ye Olde Black Boy** (p574; Hull)
- **Ye Olde Starre** (p587; York)
- **Star Inn** (p599; Harome near Helmsley)

own steam. This no-frills popular pub also serves a range of less challenging beers.

Dog & Partridge (☎ 249 0888; 55 Trippett La) A no-nonsense Irish pub with a warren of cosy rooms, a fireplace to warm those places beer won't get to and traditional music in the evenings. It's a little bit of the Auld Sod in Sheffield, and a welcome bit it is too.

Devonshire Cat (49 Wellington St) A beer-lover's haven, this modern bar looks a bit bland, but one look at the wide selection of top-notch beers from around England and the world will explain its enduring popularity.

Revolution (Unit 1-2, West One, off Division St) The extraordinarily successful national chain bar has hit Sheffield with a bang. Its wide selection of vodkas and Soviet-theme design work a treat, but it begs the question: were bars ever this cool in the old USSR? It's doubtful.

Showroom Bar (7 Paternoster Row) Originally aimed at film fans, this terrific bar with its arty, hip clientele is one of the best night-time destinations in town. The ambience is good, and so is the food, but the service is horribly slow. Out of term-time the slothful moonlighting students go home and real bar-staff pour the drinks.

Entertainment

Sheffield has a good selection of nightclubs, a couple of top-notch theatres and venues that attract big names in music – both classical and popular. The weekly *Sheffield Telegraph* (75p, every Friday) is your key to unlocking Sheffield's entertainment scene.

NIGHTCLUBS

Gatecrasher One (☎ 279 6777; 112 Arundel St; admission £4-6) Sheffield's premier nightclub is the flagship for the renowned Gatecrasher crew; uplifting trance, house, pop and charty R & B sounds bellow out of the fabulous sound system.

The Leadmill (☎ 275 4500; www.leadmill.co.uk; 6-7 Leadmill Rd) Virtually every band to have appeared in the *New Musical Express* (NME) since the late 1970s has rocked the stage here and today's brooding breed keep the tradition very much alive; the rocker fan base has had to play nice and share its favourite venue with a number of club nights, the best of which is Saturday night's Sonic Boom, a postgig funk and Motown get-down.

The Boardwalk (☎ 279 9090; www.theboardwalk live.co.uk; 39 Snig Hill) This is an institution, and

---

> ### THE REWARDS OF A MISSPENT YOUTH
>
> Snooker – that really difficult game that makes pool look a cinch – doesn't quite generate the same interest as it used to in the late 1980s and early '90s, but April's World Championship has proved to be a stubborn exception. The BBC shows virtually every frame of snooker's top tournament, but TV doesn't capture the thrill of actually sitting in the audience at Sheffield's Crucible Theatre and watching the players do their thing live. Tickets for the championships are available from the theatre box office (☎ 249 6000).

excellent for live music; local bands, old rockers, up-and-coming stars, world music, the obscure, the novel and the downright weird – they all play here. No real music fan should miss checking what's on.

University of Sheffield Student Union (☎ 222 8500; Western Bank) A varied and generally good schedule of rock gigs and club nights – including appearances by some pretty class DJ names – make this a good spot to spend a night, not to mention the cheap lager.

THEATRE & CINEMA

The **Crucible** and **Lyceum** theatres on Tudor Sq share the same **box office** (☎ 249 6000). Both are home to excellent regional drama, and the Crucible's respected resident director draws in the big names; the Crucible is also home to the annual snooker world championships (see the boxed text above).

Showroom Cinema (☎ 275 7727; Paternoster Row) This the largest independent cinema in England, with a great mix of art-house, off-beat and not-quite-mainstream films on four screens. For everything else, there's the **Odeon** (☎ 272 3981; Arundel Gate).

Getting There & Away

For all travel-related info in Sheffield and South Yorkshire, call ☎ 01709-515151.

BUS

The bus station – called the Interchange – is just east of the centre, about 100m north of the train station. National Express services link Sheffield with most major centres in the north; there are frequent buses linking Sheffield with the Peak District via Leeds

(£4.50, 1¼ hours, hourly) and London (£14.50, four hours, eight daily).

TRAIN

Sheffield is served by trains from all directions: Leeds (£6.60, 30 minutes, hourly); London St Pancras (£52, around 10 daily, 2½ hours) via Derby or Nottingham; Manchester airport (£15.40, 70 minutes); Manchester Piccadilly (£11.40, one hour); and York (£12.20, 80 minutes).

Getting Around

Buses run every 10 minutes during the day (Monday to Saturday). Sheffield also boasts a modern Supertram that trundles through the city centre.

For a day of sightseeing, a South Yorkshire Peak **Explorer pass** (£6.25) is valid for one day on all of the buses, trams and trains of South Yorkshire and north Derbyshire. Buy passes on your first bus, or at the helpful **transport information centre** (9am-5pm Mon-Sat) just off Pinstone St.

AROUND SHEFFIELD

Northeast of Sheffield, just off the M1 motorway near Rotherham, it's well worth aiming for **Magna** (01709-720002; www.visitmagna.co.uk; Sheffield Rd, Rotherham; adult/child £8/6; 10am-5pm). An unashamed celebration of heavy industry and high technology, this science adventure centre is split into four main themes – earth, air, fire and water. You can stand in a tornado (or try to), mess around with kid-sized JCB mechanical diggers, see a video of steel being forged or blast away with water cannons. It advertises as fun for the whole family, but it's mostly for the kids.

From Sheffield, take bus No 69 (every 15 minutes Monday to Saturday, hourly Sunday; 20 minutes) towards Rotherham. It'll drop you at the door.

WEST YORKSHIRE

Best known for the textile industry that drove its economy and defined much of its landscape for centuries, West Yorkshire's reputation as a hard-bitten industrial region is only one part of the overall picture. West Yorkshire's *other* identity is softer, prettier and (thankfully for visitors) far more self-aware, although it wouldn't do in this no-nonsense, down-to-earth part of the world to suggest that West Yorkshire folk didn't eat nails for breakfast.

Take Leeds and Bradford, the region's biggest cities, now so big that they've more or less become one urban sprawl. Whereas the latter plods along its dour, industrious path without paying too much heed to how others view it, Leeds has spent the last 10 years at the urban beauticians, styling and grooming itself so as to look its absolute best. And it worked: in 2003 Leeds was voted the Best City in the UK by a national poll.

Beyond the cities, West Yorkshire is all about a landscape of bleak moorland separated by deep valleys dotted with old mill towns and villages. The wool and cloth industries that gave these places life have long since disappeared, but the relics of the past are still very much in evidence in the long rows of weavers' cottages and workers' houses built along ridges overlooking the towering chimneys of the mills in the valleys – landscapes so vividly described by the Brontë sisters, West Yorkshire's most renowned literary export.

Activities

CYCLING

West Yorkshire isn't great cycling country; many roads are too urban in flavour, and the hills are darned steep too. The **National Cycle Network** (see boxed text p62) in West Yorkshire includes the short but traffic-free Leeds to Shipley route, which mostly follows a canal-side path (passing Saltaire, covered in this section), with plans to extend to Bradford by 2005.

WALKING

The valleys and moors of West Yorkshire make good walking country, although the South Pennines (as this area's called) is wedged between the Peak District and the Yorkshire Dales, and has to defer to these areas in terms of sheer quality. The TICs all have leaflets and guidebooks on local walks, or see the main sections on the towns mentioned below, for more ideas. Hebden Bridge and especially Haworth make ideal bases for circular walks, with several long and short options.

The **Haworth to Hebden Bridge Path** is a popular trail that passes through quiet farmland and scenic wooded valleys.

The **Pennine Way** (p545), England's longest trail, follows the watershed through the area, and some good walks are possible following it for just a day or two.

Getting There & Around

The Metro is West Yorkshire's highly efficient train and bus network, centred on Leeds and Bradford – which are also the main gateways to the county. For transport details call **Metroline** (☎ 0113-245 7676; www.wymetro.com) or the national **Traveline** (☎ 0870 608 2608). MetroRover passes (£5) are good for travel on buses and trains after 9.30am on weekdays and all day at weekends. There's a thicket of additional Rovers covering buses and/or trains (see p751), plus heaps of useful Metro maps and timetables, all available at TICs.

LEEDS

☎ 0113 / pop 443,247

Leeds is one of the unrivalled success stories of the New Urban Revolution, that seemingly unassailable force that moves through punch-drunk postindustrial cities, overhauling, redesigning and rebranding them as the 'new something of somewhere.' In Leeds' case it's the 'Knightsbridge of the North', a shopping mecca whose counter is just getting longer. Its heart is lined with busy pedestrianised streets, packed with shops, restaurants, upstanding Victorian edifices and stunning arcades. From cutting edge couture to contemporary cuisine, Leeds will serve it to you on a plate…or in a stylishly designed bag. It's a see-and-be-seen place: shopping, eating, drinking and dancing are the main attractions, although it also boasts the impressive hardware of the Royal Armouries on its spruced-up canal bank.

Once pulsing with textile manufacturing and trade, this one-time driving industrial force is now pretty much dead, with memorials scattered over the city. Contemporary Leeds is the biggest financial centre in the country outside London, and, on a converse tip, has one of the biggest nightlife scenes. Many bars have late licences, lending the whole proceedings a relaxed flavour. Some legendary club nights have been honing their brand of hedonism for more than a decade, while new venues and versions pop up every time you blink.

The city is also a good base for excursions to Haworth, Hebden Bridge and Bradford.

Orientation

Most of the action takes place in the city centre, between Boar Lane to the south and The Headrow – the city's main drag – to the north. Briggate, which runs north–south between the two, is the focus of most of the shopping, while the best nightlife is concentrated in the warren of small streets at the western end of Boar Lane. In the last few years there has been a substantial waterfront development along both the River Aire and the Leeds–Liverpool Canal. It's best to explore the city centre on foot.

Information

Gateway to Yorkshire TIC (☎ 242 5242; www.leeds .gov.uk; The Arcade; ✆ 9am-5.30pm Mon-Sat, 10am-4pm Sun) In the train station.

Internet Exchange (☎ 242 1093; 29 Boar Lane; ✆ 9.30am-8pm Mon-Fri, 10am-7pm Sat, 11am-6pm Sun) Near the train station.

Leeds General Infirmary (☎ 243 2799) West of Calverley St in the city centre.

Post office (City Sq; ✆ 9am-5.30pm Mon-Sat)

Waterstone's (☎ 244 4588; 97 Albion St) Has a good selection of maps.

Sights & Activities

Home to a superb collection of 19th- and 20th-century British art, the **City Art Gallery** (☎ 247 8248; www.leeds.gov.uk/artgallery; The Headrow; admission free; ✆ 10am-5pm Mon, Tue, Thu-Sat, 10am-8pm Wed, 1-5pm Sun) is one of northern England's most important galleries. Heavyweights like Constable, Stanley Spencer and Wyndham Lewis are well represented alongside more recent arrivals like Antony Gormley, sculptor of the *Angel of the North* (p705). Pride of place, however, goes to the outstanding genius of Henry Moore (1898–1986), who graduated from the Leeds School of Art. The adjoining **Henry Moore Institute** (☎ 246 7467; www.henry-moore-fdn .co.uk; admission free; ✆ 10am-5.30pm, 10am-9pm Wed), in a converted Victorian warehouse, showcases the work of 20th-century sculptors from all over but not, despite the name, work by Moore.

Tucked away off northern Briggate is the redundant but lovingly nurtured **St John's Church** (☎ 244 1689; ✆ 9.30am-5.30pm Tue-Sat), a one-off masterpiece consecrated in 1634 – the first in the north of England following the Reformation. The gorgeous (and original) oak box-pews are certainly eye-catching,

LEEDS

INFORMATION	
Gateway to Yorkshire TIC	**1** B4
Internet Exchange	**2** B4
Leeds General Infirmary	**3** A3
Post Office	**4** B4
Waterstone's	**5** B3

SIGHTS & ACTIVITIES	(pp553–5)
City Art Gallery	**6** B3
Henry Moore Institute	**7** B3
Royal Armouries	**8** D5
St John's Church	**9** C3

SLEEPING	(pp555–6)
42 The Calls	(see 19)
Central Hotel	**10** C3
City Centre Hotel	**11** C3
Malmaison	**12** C5
Quebecs	**13** B4
Queen's Hotel	**14** B4

EATING	(p556)
Arts Café	**15** C4
Bibi's	**16** B4
Brasserie 44	(see 19)
Call's Grill	(see 19)
Fourth Floor Café	(see 42)
Georgetown	**17** C4
Little Tokyo	**18** C4
Pool Court	**19** D4
Sous le Nez en Ville	(see 13)
Tampopo	**20** B3

DRINKING	(p557)
Adelphi	**21** C5
Bar Fibre	(see 31)
Dr Wu's	**22** C4
Duck & Drake	**23** D4
Elbow Room	**24** C5
Guildford	**25** B3
Milo	**26** C4
Mook	**27** C4
MPV	**28** D4
Norman	**29** C4

Oslo	**30** C4
QC	**31** C4
Velvet	(see 29)
Whitelocks	**32** C4

ENTERTAINMENT	(pp557–8)
City Varieties	**33** C4
Grand Theatre & Opera House	**34** C3
HiFi Club	**35** C4
Mint Club	**36** C5
Mission	**37** C5
Space	(see 27)
Think Thank	**38** C4
Warehouse	**39** A4
West Yorkshire Playhouse	**40** D4

SHOPPING	(p558)
Corn Exchange	**41** C4
Harvey Nichols	**42** C4
Kirkgate Market	**43** C4
Victoria Quarter	**44** C4

TRANSPORT	(p558)
Central Bus Station	**45** D4

but they're only a temporary distraction from the intricate medieval design of the magnificent Jacobean screen that is without parallel in all of England.

Leeds' most interesting museum is undoubtedly the **Royal Armouries** (☎ 220 1940; www.armouries.org.uk; Armouries Drive; admission free; ✆ 10.30am-5pm), originally built to house

the armour and weapons from the Tower of London but subsequently expanded to cover 3000 years' worth of fighting and self-defence. It all sounds a bit macho, but the exhibits are as varied as they are fascinating: films, live-action demonstrations and hands-on technology can awaken interests you never thought you had, from jousting to Indian elephant armour. We dare you not to learn something. Catch bus No 95.

One of the world's largest woollen mills has been converted into the **Leeds Industrial Museum** (☎ 263 7861; adult/child £2/50p; ⏰ 10am-5pm Tue-Sat, noon-5pm Sun), which tells the story of Leeds' industrial past. Apart from the usual selection of working machinery, there's a particularly informative display on how cloth is actually made, beginning with the wool on the sheep's back. Take bus No 14, 66 or 67.

Leeds' most impressive medieval structure is the ruined-but-still-beautiful **Kirkstall Abbey** (☎ 263 7861; Abbey Rd; admission free; ⏰ dawn-dusk), founded in 1152 by Cistercian monks from Fountains Abbey in North Yorkshire. The dark, severe Norman ruins make for an evocative wander. Take bus No 50, 733, 737 or 757.

Across the road, the **Abbey House Museum** (☎ 230 5492; Abbey Rd; adult/child £3/1; ⏰ 10am-5pm Tue-Fri & Sun, noon-5pm Sat), once the Great Gate House to the abbey, contains meticulously reconstructed shops and houses to evoke Victorian Leeds. The impressive attention to detail is lit by flickering candlelike light. Children will enjoy it, and there are displays giving an interesting insight into monastic life as well.

The abbey and museum are off the A65, three miles northwest of the centre.

Festivals & Events

The last weekend in August sees 50,000 plus music fans converge on Bramham Park, 10 miles outside the city centre, for the **Leeds Festival** (www.leedsfestival.com), one of England's biggest rock music extravaganzas.

Sleeping

Budget options are virtually nonexistent in a city that caters unashamedly to the business market. Conversely, because it's a business destination, accommodation tends to be cheaper at weekends. There's a range of fairly basic B&Bs on Woodsley Rd, behind the University of Leeds, northwest of the centre. To get here, take bus No 56, 58 or 60.

MID-RANGE

City Centre Hotel (☎ 242 9019; fax 247 1921; 51 New Briggate; s/d from £29/55) Only a stone's throw from The Headrow, this fairly ramshackle hotel with pea-size bathrooms is a great op-

tion if you're looking for a bed after a night of clubbing and don't want the hassle of a taxi to the suburbs.

Central Hotel (☎ 294 1456; fax 294 1551; 35-47 New Briggate; s/d without bath £28/40, with bath £45/50) Like the adjoining City Centre Hotel, this friendly place is about as central as you'll get for the price, but don't expect much: the bathrooms are like Port-A-Loos or airplane toilets. Literally.

Glengarth Hotel (☎ 245 7940; fax 216 8033; 162 Woodsley Rd; s/d from £25/36) A converted family home with a dozen or so tiny rooms that are nevertheless quite comfortable. The breakfast is the best we had in town.

Butlers Hotel (☎ 274 4755; www.butlershotel.co.uk; 40 Cardigan Rd; s/d from £45/60) This fine hotel near Headingley cricket ground has a wide selection of rooms, from cluttered basics to 15 themed superior rooms decked with period furnishings, Jacuzzi baths and one – The Brontë Room – with a fab four-poster bed. Catherine Zeta-Jones stayed here when £1 million was a lot of money to her.

Other options around Headingley include the very friendly **Boundary Express** (☎ /fax 274 7700; 42 Cardigan Rd; d without/with bathroom £42/55) and **Trafford House & Budapest Hotel** (☎ 275 2034; fax 274 2422; 16-18 Cardigan Rd; s/d/tr from £32/49/70), both with rooms full of cricket memorabilia. The latter has rooms with good views of the cricket ground; three have balconies.

TOP END

Quebecs (☎ 244 8989; www.theetoncollection.com; 9 Quebec St; s/d/ste from £125/135/225) Victorian grace at its opulent best is the theme of our favourite hotel in town, a brilliant conversion of the former Victorian Leeds and County Liberal Club. The elaborate wood panelling and stunning heraldic stained-glass windows in the public areas are matched by the contemporary but equally luxurious design of the bedrooms. Two of the deluxe suites – the cutely named Sherbert and Liquorice suites – have dramatic spiral staircases.

42 The Calls (☎ 244 0099; www.42thecalls.co.uk; 42 The Calls; r £130-375) This snazzy boutique hotel in what was once a 19th-century grain mill is a big hit with the trendy business crowd, who love its sharp, polished lines and designer aesthetic. The smaller studio rooms are pretty compact indeed. Weekend rates start at £99; breakfast is not included.

Malmaison (☎ 398 1000; www.malmaison.com; Sovereign St; d/ste £129/165) Self-consciously stylish, this typical Malmaison property has a fabulous waterfront location and all of the trademark touches: huge comfy beds, sexy lighting and all the latest designer gear. The entrance is actually on Swinegate, but Sovereign St just sounds classier.

Queen's Hotel (☎ 243 1323; www.paramount-hotels .co.uk; City Sq; s/d from £75/100; P) This huge, Art Deco landmark right next to the railway station has been given a serious makeover and is once again a favourite with the business crowd. Rooms are extremely comfortable, but only the public spaces have retained their classy look.

Eating

In keeping with Leeds' overall rejuvenation, the city's reputation as a culinary centre is growing all the time. You won't have any problems finding good food here.

BUDGET

Arts Café (☎ 243 8243; 42 Call Lane; lunch mains about £5, dinner mains about £8; ☽ lunch & dinner) Local art on the walls and a bohemian vibe throughout make this a popular place for quiet reflection, a chat and a really good cup of coffee to wash down the excellent lunch-time sandwiches.

Norman (☎ 234 3988; 36 Call Lane; mains £5-8; ☽ lunch & dinner) The tasty Japanese noodle menu at one of the city's best bars is the reason to come here before nightfall; this place is as stylish by day as it is popular by night.

Tampopo (☎ 245 1816; 15 South Pde; mains £6-8; ☽ lunch & dinner Mon-Sat, lunch Sun) Masters of the art of conveyor-belt cuisine, Tampopo gets 'em in and out in virtually record time; between coming and going, diners tuck into tantalising noodle and rice dishes from Southeast Asia.

MID-RANGE

Little Tokyo (☎ 243 9090; 24 Central Rd; mains about £10-12; ☽ lunch & dinner Mon-Sat) Fans of genuine Japanese food should go no further than this superb restaurant, which serves a wide array of sushi and sashimi (including half-portions) and Bento box meals – those handy divided trays that serve the Japanese equivalent of a four-course meal.

Georgetown (☎ 245 6677; 24-26 Briggate; mains £8-13; ☽ lunch & dinner) Take a barely converted Victorian watchmaker's shop and turn it into a colonial-style dining room, complete with white linen tablecloths, crystal cut glass and fine bone china. Add a superb Malaysian-style menu and all of a sudden Leeds gets a little bit of Raffles of Singapore c 1930.

Bibi's (☎ 243 0905; 16 Greek St; mains £8-15; ☽ lunch & dinner Mon-Fri, dinner Sat & Sun) One of the city's most popular restaurants, Bibi's serves classic Italian dishes in a questionable setting – too many mirrors and white wicker furniture – but there's no need to argue with the cuisine. Nothing fancy, just good Italian nosh.

Sous le Nez en Ville (☎ 244 0108; Basement, Quebec House, 9 Quebec St; mains £12-18; ☽ lunch & dinner Mon-Sat) The name doesn't make a lot of sense (Under the Nose in Town?) but the expertly presented seafood certainly does at this excellent French restaurant below Quebecs Hotel.

Fourth Floor Café (☎ 204 8000; Harvey Nichols, 107-11 Briggate; mains from £11; ☽ 10am-6pm Mon-Wed & Fri, 9am-10pm Thu & Sat, noon-5pm Sun) A department store with a fancy restaurant? It could only be Harvey Nicks. It's called a café, but don't be fooled: the nosh here is the best of British, even if the portions would only satisfy the models in their catalogue.

TOP END

A trio of restaurants, side by side along The Calls, account for the top of the dining pile.

Pool Court (☎ 244 4242; 42 The Calls; mains about £18; ☽ noon-2pm & 7-10pm Mon-Thu, 7-10.30pm Fri, 7-11.30pm Sat) Leeds' top restaurant is a tiny little room that seats only 35 people (there's more room on the canalside terrace) but it's the only place in town to be blessed by the stars of Michelin. The cuisine is strictly Modern British.

Brasserie 44 (☎ 343232; 44 The Calls; mains about £12; ☽ lunch & dinner Mon-Fri, dinner only Sat) This top spot serves Modern British cuisine, which is pretty much anything Brits who like food would eat. The wide-ranging menu is sure to satisfy virtually every taste, although we're not at all convinced about the chintzy décor – leaf and leopard skin do not a good combination make.

Call's Grill (☎ 245 3870; 38 The Calls; steaks £12-20; ☽ dinner Mon-Sat) Although they do a couple of fish dishes and doff a cap to veggies, this place is really about red meat. Let your heart and wallet work a little overtime, because these steaks are divine.

Drinking

There are oodles of choices when it comes to getting a drink. The glammed-up hordes of party animals crawl the clusters of venues around Boar Lane and Call Lane, where bars are opening all the time. Most bars open till 2am, with an admission charge of £2 to £4, up to £6 at weekends. The more traditional pubs keep regular hours.

PUBS

Duck & Drake (☎ 246 5806; 43 Kirkgate) High ceilings, obligatory pub characters, real ales and regular, free live music – mostly jazz.

Whitelocks (☎ 245 3950; Turk's Head Yard) Great beer and good, old-fashioned décor in a very popular traditional pub dating from 1715. In summer, the crowds spill out into the courtyard.

Other recommendations include the **Adelphi** (☎ 245 6377; 3-5 Hunslet Rd), built in 1898 and hardly changed since and the **Guildford** (☎ 244 9204; 115 The Headrow), an attractive Art Deco classic.

BARS

Dr Wu's (☎ 242 7629; 35 Call Lane) Small and chock full of black leather seats, this grungy bar would slot comfortably into New York's East Village, and don't the punters just know it. The vibe is studied cool and the DJs play a suitable blend of eclectic (but always alternative) sounds.

Mook (☎ 245 9967; Hirst's Yard) Tucked away behind Call Lane, this stylish little bar was drawing in the city's cool kids at the time of writing. Maybe it was the excellent DJs, who play decks that are actually suspended from the ceiling, or the subdued lighting, which makes everyone that bit more beautiful.

MPV (☎ 243 9486; 5-8 Church St, Kirkgate) This wins our prize for weirdest looking bar in northern England. Four bright red, huge, Portakabins with glass fronts are as eye-catching a design as you'll ever see. Inside, DJs keep the crowd well entertained.

Norman (☎ 234 3988; 36 Call Lane) Lipstick-red seating, crazy-paving mirrors and a ferociously stylish crowd keep this super bar high up on the list of best boozers in town. The weekend DJs – playing mostly a mix of hip-hop, R & B and funk breaks – are uniformly top-notch.

QC (☎ 245 9449; Lower Briggate; ⏰ till 4am Mon-Sat) and **Bar Fibre** (☎ 200888; www.barfibre.com;

168 Lower Briggate) are almost interchangeable chrome-and-glass gay bars, next door to each other, both spilling out into the cannily named Queen's Court.

Other tips for a tipple:

The Elbow Room (☎ 245 7011; www.elbow-room.co.uk; 64 Call Lane) Pop art, purple pool tables and laid-back music.

Milo (☎ 245 7101; 10 Call Lane) Great bar for eclectic music, from reggae to electronica.

Oslo (☎ 245 7768; Lower Briggate) A trendy bar that is like a cave with a blue backlight.

Velvet (☎ 242 5079; 11-13 Hirst's Yard) Gay bar that can be pretty tough to get into if you're not arm-in-arm with a male model.

Entertainment

In order to make sense of the ever-evolving scene, get your hands on the monthly *Leeds Guide* (£1.70) or *Absolute Leeds* (£1.50).

NIGHTCLUBS

The tremendous Leeds club scene attracts people from miles around. In true northern tradition, people brave the cold wearing next to nothing, even in winter, which is a spectacle in itself. Clubs charge a variety of admission prices, ranging from £3 on a slow weeknight to £10 on Saturday.

HiFi Club (☎ 242 7353; www.thehificlub.co.uk; 2 Central Rd) This intimate club is a good break from the hardcore sound of four to the floor: if it's Tamla Motown or the percussive beats of dance-floor jazz that shake your booty, this is the spot for you.

Mint Club (☎ 244 3168; www.themintclubleeds.co.uk; 8 Harrison St) A small club with a big reputation, this usually packed venue generally offers up good house, breakbeats and techno.

Space (☎ 246 1030; Hirsts Yard) White-walled starkly modern venue that specialises in drum 'n' bass, hip-hop and grungy garage; it's incredibly packed at weekends.

Think Thank (☎ 234 0980; 2a Call Lane) The indie '90s are alive and well and rocking the floor at this sweaty little basement club, which throbs to the sounds of everything from the Beastie Boys to the Beatles.

Other danceterias:

Mission (☎ 0870 122 0114; www.clubmission.com; 8-13 Heaton's Ct) A massive new club that redefines the term 'up-for-it'.

Warehouse (☎ 246 8287; 19-21 Somers St) Home to the mixed bootie-shaker **Speed Queen** (www.speed queen.co.uk) featuring an outrageous crowd against a hi-energy soundtrack.

THEATRE & CINEMA

Culture vultures will find plenty to keep them entertained in Leeds.

City Varieties (☎ 243 0808; www.cityvarieties.co.uk; Swan St) This old-fashioned music hall features anything from clairvoyants to country music.

Grand Theatre & Opera House (☎ 222 6222; www .leeds.gov.uk/grandtheatre; 46 New Briggate) Hosts musicals, plays and opera, including performances by acclaimed **Opera North** (☎ 244 5326; www.operanorth.co.uk).

West Yorkshire Playhouse (☎ 213 7700; www.wy playhouse.com; Quarry Hill Mount) The Playhouse has a sturdy reputation for excellent live drama.

Hyde Park Picture House (☎ 275 2045; www.leeds cinema.com; Brudenell Rd) This Edwardian cinema shows a meaty range of art-house and mainstream choices. Take bus No 56 or 63 from the city centre.

SPORT

In 2004 the unthinkable happened: **Leeds United Football Club** (☎ 226 1000; www.leedsunited .com; Elland Rd) were relegated from the Premiership amid scandal, poor play and the threat of bankruptcy. But fans remain defiantly optimistic (things surely can't get any worse) and continue to pack the Elland Rd stadium; tickets are now just *slightly* easier to get. Take bus No 51, 52 or 54 from Kirkgate Market.

Headingley has been hosting cricket matches since 1890. It is still used for test matches and is the home ground of the **Yorkshire County Cricket Club** (tickets ☎ 278 7394; www .yorkshireccc.org.uk; test match from £25). Take bus No 74 or 75 from Infirmary St.

Shopping

Leeds' city centre has so many shopping arcades that they all seem to blend into one giant mall. Most of them are unremarkable, but the designer-ridden **Victoria Quarter** (☎ 245 5333) is worth visiting for aesthetic reasons alone. A handful of mosaic-paved, stained-glass roofed Victorian arcades have been beautifully restored (check out the County Arcade). Here, the biggest name is undoubtedly **Harvey Nichols** (☎ 204 8000; 107-11 Briggate), which has its usual selection of upmarket clothes.

Closer to earth, **Kirkgate Market** (☎ 214 5162; ☼ 9am-5pm Mon-Sat, 9am-1pm Wed; open-air market Thu-Tue), once home of Marks, who later joined Spencer, sells fresh produce and cheap goods.

The circular **Corn Exchange** (☎ 234 0363; ☼ 9am-6pm), built in 1865 to house the grain trade, has a wonderful wrought, armadillo-like lid, and is the place to come for one-off clothes, eclectic jewellery or records.

Getting There & Away

AIR

Eight miles north of the city via the A65, **Leeds-Bradford airport** (☎ 250 9696) offers domestic and charter flights, plus international flights to a few major European cities. The Airlink 757 bus operates every 30 minutes between the airport and the bus and train station (£1.80, 40 minutes). A taxi costs about £17.

BUS

National Express (☎ 0870 580 8080; www.national express.com) serves most major cities, including hourly services from London (£17.50, 4½ hours) and Manchester (£7, one hour).

Yorkshire Coastliner (☎ 01653-692556; www.york shirecoastliner.co.uk; coastliner freedom ticket adult £10 per day) has useful services linking Leeds, York, Castle Howard, Goathland and Whitby (Nos 840, 842 and X40), York and Scarborough (Nos 843, 845 and X45).

TRAIN

Leeds City Station has hourly services from London King's Cross (£65.20, 2½ hours), Sheffield (£6.60, 45 minutes), Manchester (£12.10, one hour) and York (£8.10, 30 minutes).

Leeds is also the starting-point for services on the famous Settle–Carlisle line. For more details see p568.

Getting Around

Metro buses go from the Central Bus Station and on or near City Sq. The various Day Rover passes (see p551) covering trains and/or buses are good for reaching Bradford, Haworth and Hebden Bridge.

AROUND LEEDS

A day out from Leeds opens up a fascinating range of options: stately splendour at Harewood, dust and darkness at the National Coal Mining Museum, or technology and poppadoms at Bradford, to name but a few. Places are listed roughly in order of distance from Leeds, first to the west and north, then to the south.

Bradford

☎ 01274 / pop 293,717

Only 9 miles west of Leeds but with suburbs so close that they effectively merge into one another, industrial Bradford is Leeds' closest neighbour and distinctly poorer cousin. Or so they will tell you in Leeds. Bradford may not have the same tourist-friendly plumage, but it has a kind of 'ugliness that could not only be tolerated but often enjoyed', according to its favourite cantankerous son, JB Priestley (1894–1984).

Thanks to its role as a major player in the wool trade, Bradford attracted large numbers of Bangladeshis and Pakistanis throughout the 20th century, who – despite occasional racial tensions – have helped reinvigorate the city and give it new energy. A high point of the year is a colourful celebration of Asian music and dance called the Mela, part of the annual Bradford festival which is held at the end of June.

SIGHTS

The top sight for any visit to Bradford is the **National Museum of Photography, Film & Television** (NMPFT; ☎ 202030; www.nmpft.org.uk; admission free, special events & cinemas adult/child £5/3; ☯ 10am-6pm Tue-Sun). Five exhibit-packed floors tell the story of the recorded visual image from 19th-century cameras and early animation to digital technology and the psychology of advertising. There's lots of hands-on stuff too; you can film yourself in a bedroom scene or play at being a TV newsreader.

The oft-overlooked **Colour Museum** (☎ 390955; Providence St; admission £1.50; ☯ 10am-4pm Tue-Sat) is a little gem, just a 10-minute walk from the centre. It tells the story of Bradford's wool-dying trade, and has a fascinating section on how our eyes perceive colour, including a display contrasting the visual sense of different species (what's blue to you isn't blue to Fido).

Bradford Industrial Museum (☎ 435900; Moorside Rd, Eccleshill; admission free; ☯ 10am-5pm Tue-Sat, noon-5pm Sun), 3 miles out of the centre, gives a hint of what a Yorkshire textile spinning mill was like at the peak of the Industrial Revolution. Other exhibits include various steam engines (sometimes working), transport from the last 100 years, and a horse-drawn tram to give a quick 'step back in history' round the car park.

EATING

Bradford is famous for its curries, so if you're still here in the evening, don't miss trying one of the city's hundred or so restaurants. A great help is the **Bradford Curry Guide** (http://website.lineone.net/~bradfordcurryguide) which sorts the rogan josh from the rubbish nosh.

Kashmir (☎ 726513; 27 Morley St; mains £4-5; ☯ evenings to 3am) Bradford's oldest curry house has top tucker, served with no frills or booze (it's BYO). Whatever you do, go for a table upstairs, as the soul-destroying, windowless basement has all the character of a public toilet. It's just around the corner from the NMPFT.

GETTING THERE & AWAY

Bradford is on the Metro train line from Leeds, with very frequent services every day.

Saltaire

A Victorian-era landmark, Saltaire was a model industrial village built in 1851 by philanthropic wool-baron and teetotaller Titus Salt. Overlooking the rows of neat honey-coloured cottages was the largest factory in the world at that time. Heating, ventilation and good lighting were high on Titus Salt's list of priorities, but there was no way on earth this sober humanitarian was going to give his workers somewhere to indulge in the demon drink, so the town had no pub.

The factory is now **Salt's Mill** (☎ 01274-531163; www.saltsmill.org.uk; admission free; ☯ 10am-6pm), a splendidly bright and airy cathedral-like building where the main draw is a permanent exhibition of work by local boy David Hockney (1937–). There are also shops of books and crafts, and a café.

Saltaire's **TIC** (☎ 01274-774993; www.visitsaltaire.com; 2 Victoria Rd; ☯ 10am-5pm) has maps of the village and runs free hour-long guided walks of the town throughout the year.

Saltaire is 9 miles west of Leeds centre, and 3 miles north of Bradford centre (effectively an outer suburb of Bradford). It's easily reached by Metro rail from both.

WORTH THE TRIP

For close to three centuries, West and South Yorkshire was synonymous with coal production; the collieries shaped and scarred the landscape, while entire villages grew up around the pits, each inhabitant and their descendants destined to spend their working lives underground. The industry came to a shuddering close in the 1980s, but the imprint of coal is still very much in evidence, even if there's only a handful of collieries left. One of these, at Claphouse, is now the **National Coal Mining Museum for England** (☎ 01924-848806; www.ncm.org.uk; Overton, near Wakefield; admission free; ☺ 10am-5pm), a superb testament to the inner workings of the coal mine.

Highlight of a visit is the tour underground; complete with helmet and head-torch you ride in a 'cage' almost 150m down, then follow passages all the way to the coal seam where massive drilling machines now stand idle. Former miners now work as guides, and explain the details – sometimes with a suitably authentic and almost impenetrable mix of local dialect and technical terminology.

Up on top, there are modern audiovisual displays, some fascinating memorabilia (including sketches by Henry Moore), plus exhibits about trade unions, strikes and the wider mining communities – only slightly over-romantic in parts. You can also stroll round the pit-pony stables (with their equine inhabitants also now retired) or the slightly eerie bath-house, totally unchanged since the miners scrubbed off the coal dust and emptied their lockers for the last time. There are also longer nature trails in the surrounding fields and woods.

The museum is about 10 miles south of Leeds, on the A642, which drivers can reach from the M1. By public transport, take a train from Leeds to Wakefield (at least hourly, 15 minutes), and then bus No 232 towards Huddersfield can drop you outside the museum (hourly, 25 minutes).

Harewood

There's only one reason to stop in Harewood, a tiny hamlet about 7 miles north of Leeds, and that is to visit the great park, sumptuous gardens and mighty edifice of **Harewood House** (☎ 0113-218 1010; www.harewood.org; admission £10, Sun & Bank Hols £11; grounds ☺ 10am-6pm, house 11am-4.30pm Feb–mid-Nov, house & grounds 10am-4pm mid-Nov–Jan). As an outing from Leeds you can easily fill a day here, and if you're heading for Harrogate, stopping off is highly recommended.

A classic example of a stately English pile, the house was built between 1759 and 1772 by the era's designer superstars, a team assembled by John Carr (who designed the exterior). Lancelot 'Capability' Brown laid out the grounds, Thomas Chippendale supplied the furniture (the largest commission he ever received, costing the unheard of amount of £10,000), Robert Adams designed the interior, and Italy was raided to create an appropriate art collection. The superb terrace was added 100 years later by yet another top name, Sir Charles Barry – he of the Houses of Parliament.

Many locals come to Harewood just to relax or saunter through the grounds, without even thinking of going inside the house. Hours of entertainment can be had in the **Bird Garden**, with many colourful species including penguins (feeding time at 2pm is a highlight), and there's also a boating lake, café and adventure playground. For more activity, there's a network of walking trails around the lake or through the parkland.

From Leeds, use bus No 36 (at least half-hourly Monday to Saturday, hourly on Sunday) which continues to Harrogate. Visitors coming by bus get half-price admission too (so hang on to your ticket). From the main gate, it's a two-mile walk through the grounds to the house and gardens. At busy times there's a free shuttle service.

HEBDEN BRIDGE

☎ 01422 / pop 4086

Unlike so many other textile-mill towns in this part of the world, Hebden Bridge didn't go gently into the good night when the industry disappeared; it raged a bit and then turned itself into an attractive little tourist trap with a slightly off-centre reputation. Besides the honest-to-God Yorkshire folk who have lived here for years, the town is home to university academics, die-hard hippies and a substantial gay community – all of which explains the inordinate number of craft shops, organic cafés and second-hand bookstores.

Above the town is the much older village of **Heptonstall**, its narrow cobbled street lined with 500-year-old cottages and the ruins of a

YORKSHIRE

beautiful 13th-century church. But it is the churchyard of the newer Methodist church that draws the curious visitors, for here is buried the poet Sylvia Plath (1932–63), wife of another famous rhymer, Ted Hughes (1930–98), who was born in these parts.

The **Hebden Bridge Visitor & Canal Centre** (☎ 843 831; Butlers Wharf, New Rd; ⌚ 9.30am-5.30pm Mon-Fri, 10.30am-5pm Sat & Sun mid-Mar–mid-Oct, 10am-5pm Mon-Fri, 10.30am-4.15pm Sat & Sun rest of year) has a good stock of maps and leaflets on local walks, including saunters in **Hardcastle Crags**, two unspoilt wooded valleys run by the National Trust (NT), 1½ miles northwest of town off the A6033. There are streams and waterfalls, and numerous walking trails, some of which link to the Pennine Way, and another which takes you all the way to Haworth.

Sleeping & Eating

High Greenwood Campsite (☎ 842287; £4.50) Basically just a large, sloping field with a block of facilities in a converted barn, this campsite about three miles northwest of town is reached on the lane that runs through Heptonstall. It's just off the footpath between Hebden Bridge and Haworth, near Hardcastle Crags, and the Pennine Way runs nearby too, so it's popular with walkers.

Mankinholes YHA Hostel (☎ 0870 770 5952; www.yha.org.uk; Todmorden; dm £10.60) A converted 17th-century manor house 4 miles southwest of Hebden Bridge, this hostel has limited facilities (no TV room) but it is very popular with walkers; the Pennine Way is only half a mile from here.

White Lion Hotel (☎ 842197; Bridge Gate; s/d from £28/40) A large 400-year-old coaching inn smack in the middle of town; the rooms in the converted coach house are that little bit more comfortable than the ones in the main house. Downstairs is a popular pub and a pretty good **restaurant** (mains £7-10) with a standard pub grub menu.

Crown Fisheries (Crown St; mains about £4; ⌚ 10am-6.30pm) A terrific chipper that serves up a great supper (fish, chips, bread and butter and tea), and also does takeaways.

Getting There & Away

Hebden Bridge is on the Leeds–Manchester Victoria Metro train line (services about every 30 minutes Monday to Saturday, hourly on Sunday, 45 minutes). Get off at Todmorden for the Mankinholes YHA Hostel.

HAWORTH

⌚ 01535 / pop 6078

As literary shrines go, only Stratford-upon-Avon can hold a candle to the quintessentially West Yorkshire village of Haworth, the 19th-century home of those bookish Brontë sisters, Emily, Anne and Charlotte. Here, in the handsome parsonage behind the church, a handful of literary classics were penned, including *Jane Eyre* and *Wuthering Heights*.

Even without the literary link, Haworth is worth a trip: the dark-stone houses of cobbled Main St, running steeply down from the parish church, provide a quintessential West Yorkshire view.

Information

The **TIC** (☎ 642329; www.haworth-village.org.uk; 2-4 West Lane; ⌚ 9am-5.30pm Apr-Sep, 9am-5pm Oct-Mar) has an excellent supply of information on the village, the surrounding area and, of course, the Brontës. Another good source of information is www.brontecountry.co.uk.

Main St is lined with cafés, tearooms, pubs and shops selling everything imaginable (and more) bearing the Brontë name. Handy stops might include: the **post office** (⌚ 9am-5.30pm Mon-Fri, 9am-12.30pm Sat); **Venables & Bainbridge**, selling used books, including many vintage Brontë volumes; and **Rose & Co Apothecary** (84 Main St), the beautifully restored druggist so favoured by Branwell Brontë.

Sights

Your first stop should be **Haworth Parish Church** (admission free), a lovely old place of worship, built in the late 19th century, on the site of the 'old' church that the Brontë

STEAM ENGINES & RAILWAY CHILDREN

Haworth is on the **Keighley & Worth Valley Railway** (KWVR; ☎ 645214; www.kwvr.co.uk; adult/child s £7/3.50, adult/child day rover £10/5) – which runs steam and classic diesel engines between Keighley and Oxenhope. It was here, in 1969, that the classic movie *The Railway Children* was shot; Mr Perks was stationmaster at Oakworth, where the Edwardian look has been meticulously maintained. Trains operate around hourly at weekends all year; in holiday periods they run hourly every day.

BAD LUCK BRONTËS

The Rev Patrick Brontë, his wife Maria and six children moved to Haworth Parsonage in 1820. On September 15, 1821, Maria died of cancer, after which her unmarried sister Elizabeth Branwell arrived from Penzance to help raise the children. Three years later, the eldest girl, Maria, was sent home from school on account of ill-health and died in May 1825, aged 11. A few weeks later, her younger sister Elizabeth arrived home sick from the same school and died, aged 10, on June 15. (Years later, Charlotte immortalised the school as the infamous Lowood in *Jane Eyre*.)

The double tragedy led the good reverend to keep his remaining family close to him, and for the next few years the children were home-schooled in a highly creative environment. The children conjured up mythical heroes and countries, and produced miniature home-made books. It was an auspicious start, at least for the three girls, Charlotte, Emily and Anne; the lone boy, Branwell, was more of a painter but he lacked his sisters' drive and discipline. After a short stint as a professional artist, he ended up spending most of his days in the Black Bull pub, drunk and stoned on laudanum obtained across the street at Rose & Co Apothecary. While the three sisters were setting the London literary world alight with the publication of three superb novels – *Jane Eyre*, *Wuthering Heights* and *Agnes Grey* – in one extraordinary year (1847), Branwell was fading quickly, and he died of tuberculosis on September 24, 1848. The family was devastated, but things quickly got worse. Emily contracted a cold at the funeral that also developed into tuberculosis; she never left the house again and died on December 19. Anne, who had also been sick, was next: Charlotte took her to Scarborough to seek a sea cure but she died on May 28 1849.

The remaining family never recovered. Despite her growing fame, Charlotte struggled with depression and never quite adapted to her high position in literary society. Despite her misgivings, however, she eventually married, but she too died, in the early stages of pregnancy, on March 31, 1855. All things considered, it's hardly surprising that poor old Patrick Brontë spent the remaining years of his life going increasingly insane.

---

sisters knew, which was demolished in 1879. In the surrounding churchyard, gravestones are covered in moss, or thrust to one side by growing trees, which gives the whole place a tremendous feeling of age.

Set in a pretty garden overlooking the church and graveyard, the **Brontë Parsonage Museum** (☎ 642323; www.bronte.info; admission £4.80; ☒ 10am-5.30pm Apr-Sep, 11am-5pm Oct-Mar) is where the Brontë family lived from 1820. Rooms are meticulously furnished and decorated, exactly as they were in the Brontë era, with many personal possessions on display. There's also a neat and informative exhibition, which includes the fascinating miniature books the Brontës wrote as children.

Walking

Haworth is surrounded by the moors of the South Pennines – immediately familiar to Brontë fans – and the TIC has leaflets on local walks to endless Brontë features. A 6½-mile favourite leads to Top Withins, a ruined farm thought to have inspired *Wuthering Heights*, even though a plaque clearly states that the farmhouse bore no resemblance to the one Emily wrote about. Other walks can be worked around the Brontë Way, a longer route linking Bradford and Colne via Haworth. Alternatively, the Pennine Way runs west of Haworth and can be followed south to Hebden Bridge (p560). There's also a direct walking route between Haworth and Hebden Bridge, via the scenic valleys of Hardcastle Crags.

Sleeping & Eating

Virtually every second house on Main St does B&B; they're mostly indistinguishable from each other but some are just that little bit cuter. There's little in the way of fine dining in Haworth, but many of the B&Bs also have small cafés that are good for a spot of tourist lunch – mediocre servings of local dishes and nice safe bets like sandwiches.

Old Registry (☎ 646503; www.oldregistry.com; 2-4 Main St; r £65-80) This is a favourite place in town, a stylishly rustic (or rustically stylish) hotel where each of the carefully themed rooms has a four-poster bed: the Blue Heaven room is just that – at least for fans of Laura Ashley's delphinium blue. We're just that little bit dramatic, so we loved the Stage Room, complete with theatrical memorabilia.

Rookery Nook (☎ 643374; 6 Church St; r £12.50-22) Almost attached to the church, this place has spacious rooms with New Age décor; the smaller, budget rooms are pretty cramped. Breakfast (£2.50 to £3.50) is served in the room.

Aitches (☎ 642501; www.aitches.co.uk; 11 West Lane; s/d from £35/50) A very classy Victorian stone bungalow with four beautiful rooms, each with wrought-iron beds and handsome furnishings.

Weaver's (☎ 643822; 15 West Lane; bar suppers £4-10, 3-course meal £20-25; ☉ Tue-Sat) Smart and stylish, with simply the best food in town and a menu featuring local specialities. Get there early to try the tasty two-course bar 'sampler' menu (£11).

Other options:

Apothecary Guest House (☎ 643642; www.theapothe caryguesthouse.co.uk; 86 Main St; s/d £20/40) Oak beams and narrow, slanted passageways lead to comfortable, airy rooms – even though some of the chintzy wallpaper is questionable.

Haworth Old Hall (☎ 642709; Sun St; snacks £3, salads £6, mains £6-10) A highly rated inn, with decent food, wine and beer, all served in convivial surroundings. The steak and ale pie is a classic. If you want to linger longer, comfortable doubles cost £50.

Haworth Tea Rooms (68 Main St; snacks £1-3, mains £4) A selection of healthy options including baked spuds and veggie nachos.

Haworth YHA Hostel (☎ 0870 770 5858; www.yha .org.uk; Longlands Drive, off Lees Lane; dm £11.80; ☉ Feb-Nov, Fri & Sat only Nov-Jan) A big old house with plenty of facilities, including a games room, lounge, cycle store and laundry. It's on the northeastern edge of town.

Old White Lion Hotel (☎ 642313; www.oldwhite lionhotel.com; West Lane; s/d from £48/68) Pub-style accommodation – comfortable if not spectacular – above an oak-panelled bar and highly rated restaurant (mains £10-13).

Getting There & Away

From Leeds, the easiest approach to Haworth is via Keighley, which is on the Metro train network. Bus No 500 runs between Keighley and Haworth (six daily, 15 minutes), and also serves Todmorden and Hebden Bridge. However, the most interesting way to get to Haworth from Keighley is via the KWV Railway (see p561).

YORKSHIRE DALES NATIONAL PARK

Comfortably wedged in between the Lake District to the west and the North York Moors to the east, the Yorkshire Dales (from the Viking word *dalr*, meaning 'valleys') is a marvellous area of high hills and moors, cut through by rugged stone walls and spotted with extravagant houses and the faded, spectral grandeur of monastic ruins.

The magnificent scenery aside, the national park is a walker's and cyclist's wonderland. Car drivers love it too, and as a result the roads can get extremely crowded. If you can't avoid busy summer weekends, try to come by bus or train, and even then it's well worth getting off the beaten track.

Orientation & Information

The 683-sq-mile (1769-sq-km) Yorkshire Dales National Park divides into two parts: in the north, two main valleys run west to east – broad expansive Wensleydale (home of the famous cheese) and narrow secretive Swaledale. In the south, the main valleys – Ribblesdale, Malhamdale, Littondale and Wharfedale – all run north–south and are the most popular areas for tourists.

The main Dales gateways are Skipton in the south, and Richmond in the northeast. Good bases in the park itself include Settle, Grassington and Hawes. All have excellent TICs (some are called park visitor centres), stocking a mountain of local guidebooks and maps, and providing accommodation details.

To the northwest and west, the towns of Kirkby Stephen and Kirkby Lonsdale can also make handy jumping-off points, although both these spots are outside the national park boundary, and actually in the county of Cumbria (despite definite Dales affiliations) – so they're covered in that chapter in this book.

The *Visitor* newspaper, available from TICs, lists local events and walks guided by park rangers, as well as many places to stay and eat. The official park website at www.yorkshiredales.org.uk is similarly useful.

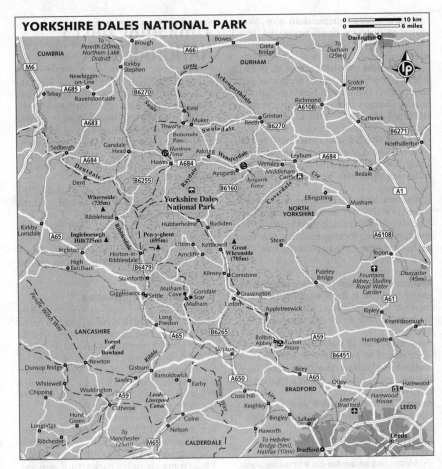

YORKSHIRE DALES NATIONAL PARK

Activities
CYCLING

Other than on busy summer weekends, this is excellent cycling country. Most roads follow the rivers along the bottom of the Dales so, although there are still some steep climbs, there's also plenty on the flat. TICs stock maps and leaflets with suggested routes (on-road and off-road) for a day or longer.

Just one example is the Yorkshire Dales Cycle Way, an energetic and exhilarating 130-mile (210km) loop, taking in the best of the park. Skipton is a convenient start, from where you ride up Wharfedale, then steeply over Fleatmoss to Hawes. From here turn east along Wensleydale to Aysgarth, then north over the wild hills to Reeth. The roads are steep but the scenery is breathtaking. Follow Swaledale westwards, through remote Keld and down to the market town of Kirkby Stephen. Then it's south to Sedbergh, and up beautiful Dentdale to pop out at Ribblehead. It's plain sailing now, through Horton-in-Ribblesdale to Stainforth, one more climb over to Malham, and finally back to Skipton for tea and medals.

WALKING

The Yorkshire Dales has a vast footpath network, with options for everything from easy strolls to challenging hikes; we suggest a few options throughout this section. Look out at TICs for leaflets on organised walks from train stations, notably on the

Settle–Carlisle Line. Serious walkers should equip themselves with *OS Outdoor Leisure Maps Nos 2, 10* and *30*.

Two of England's most famous long-distance routes cross the Dales. The Pennine Way goes through the rugged western half of the park. If you haven't got the three weeks required to cover all 259 miles (417km), a few days in the Dales, between Malham and Hawes for example, will repay the effort. The Coast to Coast Walk (a 190-mile/306km classic; p61) goes through lovely Swaledale in the northern Dales. Following the route for a few days is highly recommended – see p570.

Another long-distance possibility is the Dales Way, which begins in Ilkley, follows the River Wharfe through the heart of the Dales, and finishes at Bowness-on-Windermere in the Lake District. If you start at Grassington, it's an easy five-day 60-mile (97km) journey. A handy companion guide is *Dales Way* by Arthur Gemmell and Colin Speakman (1996, £4.99), available at most bookshops.

Sleeping

There are many villages in and around the park with a good range of hotels, B&Bs, hostels and campsites. Most rural pubs also do B&B. Walkers and hardy outdoor types can take advantage of camping barns. Usually owned by farmers, booking is organised centrally through the **YHA** (☎ 0870 870 8808). For details, TICs have a *Camping Barns in England* leaflet.

Getting There & Around

The main gateway towns of Skipton and Richmond are well served by public transport, and local bus services radiate out from there. Get hold of the very useful *Dales Explorer* timetable from TICs – as well as covering every bus in the region it contains maps, B&B listings, local information and an excellent selection of walks that tie in with bus services.

Going by train, the best and most interesting access to the Dales is via the famous Settle–Carlisle Line (p568). From the south, trains start in Leeds and pass through Skipton, Settle, and numerous small villages, offering unrivalled access to the hills straight from the station platform. Of course, if you're coming from the north, Carlisle is the place to get on board.

SKIPTON
☎ 01756 / pop 14,313

On the national park's southern edge is the busy market town of Skipton, once known as 'Sheeptown' – there's no guessing what was traded here. Monday, Wednesday, Friday and Saturday are market days on High St, bringing crowds from all over and giving the town something of a festive atmosphere. The **TIC** (☎ 792809; skipton@ytbtic.org.uk; 35 Coach St; ✹ 10am-5pm Mon-Fri, 9am-5pm Sat) is right in the middle of town.

Skipton Castle (☎ 792442; High St; admission £4.60; ✹ 10am-6pm Mon-Sat, noon-6pm Sun), at the top of the main street, is one of the best-preserved medieval castles in England – a fascinating contrast to the ruins you'll see elsewhere – and well worth a visit.

Sleeping & Eating

There's a strip of B&Bs just outside the centre on Keighley Rd. All those between Nos 46 and 57 are worth trying.

Westfield House (☎ 790849; 50 Keighley Rd; s/d from £25/40) This smallish house is deservedly popular on account of the friendly welcome. The rooms are all adequately comfortable.

Bizzie Lizzies (☎ 793189; 36 Swadford St; mains £5-6; ✹ lunch & dinner) This modern fish-and-chip restaurant overlooking the canal has won awards for quality, a rare thing for what is essentially deep-fried goodness. There's also an attached takeaway.

Of the pubs, **The Black Horse** (Coach St) is a large place with an outside terrace and meals daily, but our favourite is the **Narrow Boat** (Victoria St), a traditionally styled place with good beer, friendly service and bar food (not on weekends).

Getting There & Away

Skipton is the last stop on the Metro network from Leeds (at least hourly, 40 minutes). For heading into the Dales, see the boxed text p568. For Grassington, take bus No 72 (£4.30, six per day Monday to Saturday, 30 minutes) or No 67 (hourly, Sunday); most go via the train station.

BOLTON ABBEY

The tiny village and country estate of Bolton Abbey is about 5 miles east of Skipton, and the big draw here is the ruined church of **Bolton Priory** (admission free; ✹ 9am-dusk), a beautiful old place built in the 12th century. With soaring arches and huge windows looking frail against the sky, these grand remains have inspired artists such as Wordsworth and Turner, and part of the building is still used as a church today.

As well as the priory ruins, the main attraction here is the scenic River Wharfe, which flows through the grounds, and there's a network of footpaths and walking trails beside the river and through the surrounding area. It's very popular with families (part of the riverbank looks like a beach at weekends), and you can buy teas and ice creams in the Cavendish Pavilion, a short walk from the priory. Other highlights include the stepping-stones (with a large gap between two stones in the middle of the river, frequently forcing faint-hearted walkers to turn around and use the bridge) and The Strid, a narrow, wooded, picturesque gorge just upstream from the pavilion.

The shop and information centre in the village has leaflets (free) with walking maps and more details or you can check www .boltonabbey.com.

There are half-hourly buses from Skipton and Grassington Monday to Saturday; on Sunday there is only an hourly service from Skipton.

Sleeping
Devonshire Arms Hotel (☎ 01756-718111; www .thedevonshirearms.co.uk; s/d £160/220) As country house hotels go, this little mansion owned by the dukes of Devonshire – the 11th duke just passed on in 2004 – is actually like staying in one of their homes. The decoration of each bedroom was undertaken by the Duchess herself, and while her tastes might not be everyone's cup of tea, there's just no arguing with the quality and beauty of the furnishings; almost all of them were permanently borrowed from another of their properties, Chatsworth in Derbyshire.

GRASSINGTON
☎ 01756
The perfect base for south Dales jaunts, Grassington's handsome Georgian centre teems with walkers and visitors throughout the summer months, soaking up an atmosphere that – despite the odd touch of faux rustication – is as attractive and traditional as you'll find in these parts. It is 6 miles north of Skipton.

The **TIC** (☎ 752774; ⏰ 9.30am-5pm daily Apr-Oct, shorter hrs Nov-Mar) is at the big car park on the edge of town. There's a good stock of maps and guides, and a nice little display that puts the surrounding scenery in context.

Sleeping & Eating
There are several B&Bs along and just off Main St.

Devonshire Fell (☎ 718111; www.devonshirefell .co.uk; Burnsall; s/d from £75/115) The sister property to Bolton Abbey's Devonshire Arms Hotel (below left), this one-time gentleman's club for mill owners offers a substantially different aesthetic; here, the style is distinctly contemporary, with beautiful modern furnishings crafted by local experts. It's more like a big city boutique hotel than a rustic country property.

Ashfield House (☎ 752584; www.ashfieldhouse .co.uk; Summers Fold; r per person £38; ⏰ Feb-Nov only) A secluded 17th-century country house behind a walled garden with exposed stone walls, open fireplaces and an all-round cosy feel. It's just off the main square.

Dales Kitchen (☎ 753208; 51 Main St; mains about £5; ⏰ 9am-6pm) Classic Yorkshire munchies – rarebits, local sausage and, of course, Wensleydale – in a lovely tea rooms in the middle of town.

Getting There & Away
To reach Grassington, see p565. For onward travels the No 72 continues up the valley to the nearby villages of Kettlewell and Buckden.

AROUND GRASSINGTON
North of Grassington, narrow roads lead up the beautiful valley of Wharfedale. Drivers take the road on the west side of the river; if you're cycling, take the quieter east-side option. If you're walking, follow the charming stretch of the Dales Way long-distance footpath through a classic Yorkshire Dales landscape of lush meadows surrounded by dry-stone walls, with traditional field-barns dotting the hillsides.

About 7 and 11 miles respectively from Grassington, the villages of **Kettlewell** and **Buckden** make good places to aim for, between them offering a good choice of campsites, B&Bs, teashops and pubs (all doing food and accommodation). Favourite hostelries include the **Blue Bell Inn** and **The Racehorses** (which has a nice riverside garden) in Kettlewell, and the **Buck Inn** in Buckden. A few miles beyond Buckden, in the tiny settlement of Hubberholme, is the **George Inn**, also worth a stop.

Another option is a triangular route taking in Kettlewell, Buckden and the village of **Litton** in the little valley of Littondale, to the west of Wharfedale, where the **Queens Arms** is another fine historical inn.

Check at Grassington TIC about the local buses that trundle up and down Wharfedale daily in the summer months (weekends in winter) – ideal for bringing home weary walkers.

MALHAM
☎ 01729

At the northern end of the quiet and beautiful valley of Malhamdale, this small, traditional village is probably the most visited place in the valley, not only for its charm but also for the natural wonders nearby – all easily reached by foot.

The excellent **TIC** (☎ 830363; malham@ytbtic .co.uk; ☯ 10am-5pm Apr-Oct, Fri-Sun Nov-Mar) has the usual wealth of information, local walks leaflets, maps and guidebooks.

Walking

The 5-mile Malham Landscape Trail (the TIC has details) takes in **Malham Cove**, a huge rock amphitheatre that was once a waterfall to rival Niagara, and **Gordale Scar**, a deep limestone canyon with scenic cascades and the remains of an Iron Age settlement.

For something longer, you can follow various paths eastwards through remote farmland for anything between 6 miles and 11 miles to reach Grassington, or head west on a great 6-mile hike over the hills to Settle. An even better option is a two-day hike between Grassington and Settle via Malham.

The long-distance Pennine Way passes right through Malham, and you can go north or south for as many days as you like. A day's walk away is Horton-in-Ribblesdale, described later in this section.

Sleeping & Eating

Malham YHA Hostel (☎ 0870 770 5946; malham@yha .org.uk; dm/d £11.80/42; ☯ mid-Feb–Nov, Fri & Sat only Dec–mid-Feb) In the village centre is this purpose-built hostel; the facilities are top-notch and young children are well catered for.

Beck Hall (☎ 830332; www.beckhallmalham.com; s/d from £25/50; snacks about £4) This rambling 17th-century country house on the edge of the village is a favourite place to stay; of the 11 different rooms, we recommend the Green Room, with its old-style furnishings and four-poster bed. There's a rustling stream flowing through the garden and a nice tearoom.

SETTLE
☎ 01729 / pop 3621

The largish town of Settle is far too bustling to be really homely and quaint, but it retains enough of its traditional character to make it a worthwhile stop. Narrow cobbled streets lined with shops and decent pubs lead out from the central market square – that still sees stalls and traders every Tuesday. Access from the main A65 to the east is easy, and there are plenty of accommodation options.

The **TIC** (☎ 825192; settle@ytbtic.co.uk; Town Hall; ☯ 9.30am-5pm) has maps and guidebooks, and an excellent range of local walks leaflets (free).

Sleeping & Eating

Stainforth YHA Hostel (☎ 0870 770 5946; stainforth@ yha.org.uk; dm/d £11.80/42) A decent hostel in an old Georgian country house two miles north of Settle on the B6479 to Horton-in-Ribblesdale.

Golden Lion Hotel (☎ 822203; www.goldenlionhotel .net; Duke St; s/d £30/54; lunch mains about £6, evening £8-11) This handsome 17th-century coaching inn has 12 warm and comfortable rooms, an old-style pub and a pleasant restaurant that is one of the most popular in town.

Around the square are several cafés, including **The Shambles**, noted for filling fish-and-chip suppers (£5.90) and – in reference to the old Yorkshire saying that 'you don't bring now't into the world and you take now't out' – **Ye Olde Naked Man**, formerly an undertakers and now a bakery with cakes, snacks and ice cream.

Getting There & Away

The easiest way to get here is by train. From the south, trains from Leeds or Skipton heading for Carlisle (see the boxed text p568) stop at the station near the town centre; those heading for Morecambe (on the west coast) stop at Giggleswick, about 1½ miles outside town.

YORKSHIRE

THE SETTLE–CARLISLE LINE

The Settle–Carlisle Line (SCL) is one of the greatest rail engineering achievements of the Victorian era and takes passengers across some of the best countryside in northern England. The views from the windows are simply stunning. It was built between 1869 and 1875 after – as legend has it – the chairman of the Midland Railway Company drew a line across the Dales and declared 'that's where I'll have my railway!' He didn't care too much that the mountainsides weren't railway-friendly; *he* wasn't going to handle a blasting cap.

That job fell to 5000 navvies, who, armed with picks and shovels, performed Herculean tasks in simply atrocious conditions to get the railway built. They built 325 bridges, 21 viaducts and blasted 14 tunnels, retiring every night to filthy, smallpox-infested shanties along the newly laid tracks; nearly 200 workers died during the construction.

It served the national rail network very well until 1983, when British Rail announced that the line would close as part of their rationalisation of the network. The public outcry that ensued was enough to ensure its survival, and today it is a big tourist attraction (as well as a working railway) – which should keep it running for the time being.

The Journey

Trains run between Leeds and Carlisle via Settle about eight times a day. The first section of the journey from Leeds is along the Aire Valley, with a stop at **Keighley**, where the Keighley & Worth Valley Railway branches off to Haworth (of Brontë fame, p561). Next is **Skipton** – gateway to the southern Dales – and then your first sight of proper moors as the train arrives in the attractive market town of **Settle**. The train chugs up the valley beside the River Ribble, through **Horton-in-Ribblesdale**, across the spectacular Ribblehead Viaduct and then plunges through Blea Moor Tunnel, to pop out above Dentdale, where **Dent** station is one of the highest in the country. (Dent village is a couple of miles away down in the valley.) Next stop is **Garsdale** (just a few miles west of Hawes), then the train reaches its highest point (356m) at Ais Gill, before leaving the Dales behind and trundling down to **Kirkby Stephen**. The last halts are **Appleby** then **Langwathby,** just northwest of Penrith (a jumping-off point for the Lake District), then the train finally pulls into **Carlisle**. What a ride!

The Nuts & Bolts

The entire journey takes two hours and 40 minutes and costs £28 return (from Settle, the return fare to Carlisle is £16.80). Various hop-on hop-off passes for one or three days are also available. You can pick up a free SCL timetable – which includes a colour map of the line and brief details about places of interest – from most Yorkshire stations; for more information, contact **National Rail Enquiries** (☎ 08457 484950) or click on to www.settle-carlisle.co.uk or www.settle-carlisle-railway.org.uk.

AROUND SETTLE
Horton-in-Ribblesdale
☎ 01729

A favourite with walkers, cyclists and cavers, the little village of Horton is 5 miles north of Settle. Everything centres on the **Pen-y-ghent Cafe** (☎ 860333; ⏱ 9am-6pm Mon & Wed-Fri, 8am-6pm Sat & Sun), which serves up filling meals, home-made cakes and pint mugs of tea. The friendly owners sell maps, guidebooks and walking gear, and the café acts as the village **TIC** (horton@ytbtic.co.uk). Walkers on a long hike should avail themselves of the 'safety service', whereby they can register in and out. There's also a **post office shop** for groceries and takeaways.

SLEEPING & EATING
Horton is popular, so you're best bet is to book your accommodation in advance.

Golden Lion (☎ 860206; www.goldenlionhotel.co.uk; dm/s/d £8/20/45) Popular with walkers, the Golden Lion is a lively pub with dorms and basic private rooms upstairs, and three public bars downstairs where you can tuck into a bit of grub and wash it down with a pint of hand-pumped ale. They also do evening meals (three-courses £10) and make packed lunches (£5). Breakfast (£5.95) is not included.

Crown Hotel (☎ 860209; www.crown-hotel.co.uk; s/d from £27/55) Another popular rest stop with walkers, the Crown has a variety of basic rooms (with slightly over-the-top floral patterns) and a cosy bar that serves a range of meals.

Other options include: **Dub-Cote Farm Camping Barn** (☎ 860238; www.threepeaksbarn.co.uk; dm £8), a basic-but-lovely 17th-century stone barn half a mile southeast of the village, well equipped with self-catering facilities (BYO sleeping bag and pillow case); the **Knoll** (☎ 860283; s/d £22/40), a neat and efficient house near the village centre; and **Rowe House** (☎ 860212; s/d from £26/46), a nice homely option on the north side of the village.

The Three Peaks

The countryside north of Settle is dominated by the Three Peaks – Whernside (735m), Ingleborough (723m) and Pen-y-ghent (694m) – and the summits are linked by a long circular route that has been a classic walk for many years. The traditional start is the Pen-y-ghent Café in Horton-in-Ribblesdale and walkers try to complete the whole 25-mile route in under 12 hours. Others knock it off in six hours or less. You can also do just a section of the walk – for instance walking from Horton as far as Ribblehead, and returning by train – which is highly recommended.

HAWES

☎ 01969

Hawes is not particularly appealing but it's right at the heart of Wensleydale and is the best base for exploring the northern Yorkshire Dales. The main street and the narrow lanes off it are lined with old-style shops, some small supermarkets, banks with ATMs, outdoor shops, half a dozen pubs, even more cafés, a couple of smart restaurants, some basic fish-and-chip take-aways, endless craft and pottery studios, a laundrette and a post office…pretty much everything you'll need.

There's also the **Wensleydale Creamery Visitor Centre** (☎ 667664; admission £2; ☷ 9am-5.30pm), devoted to the production of the world-famous powdery-white cheese, but watching guys shovel tons of cheese around is only marginally interesting. You can taste it in the museum and then buy it in the shop, which is free to enter.

The **TIC** (☎ 667450; hawes@ytbtic.co.uk; ☷ 10am-5pm) shares the Old Station building with the **Dales Countryside Museum** (adult/child £3/free) –

> **THREE PEAKS CHALLENGE**
>
> Fancy a gruelling test of your endurance? Why not join the fell-runners on the last Sunday in April to complete the Three Peaks Challenge – 2004's winner did it in about 2½ hours. Cyclists have their chance to race like lunatics in the last week of September, racing over 38 miles and climbing 5000ft. Only cyclo-cross bikes are allowed – mountain bikes are a big no-no. For entry forms, contact **British Cycling** (www.britishcycling.org.uk).

---

a beautifully presented social history of the area. There's still an old train in the yard too.

About 1½ miles north of town is Hawes' other attraction, **Hardraw Force**, the highest above-ground waterfall in the country. For most of the year it's little more than a trickle on the rocks and not really worth the £1 'toll' you pay at the Green Dragon pub to walk up to it.

Sleeping & Eating

Bainbridge Ings Caravan & Camp Site (☎ 667354; www.bainbridge-ings.co.uk; car & 2 adults/hikers & cyclists £9/3.50) Pitches are around the edges of stone-walled fields located around a spacious farmhouse about half-a-mile east of town. Gas, milk and eggs are sold on site.

Hawes YHA Hostel (☎ 0870 770 5854; www.yha.org.uk; Town Head; dm £10.60) A modern place on the western edge of town, at the junction of the main A684 (Aysgarth Rd) and B6255.

Cocketts (☎ 667312; www.cocketts.co.uk; Market Pl; d from £60; 2-/3-course meal £14.95/16.95) The most stylish place in town is a handsome 17th-century stone house with eight pretty delightful rooms decorated in traditional style, two with four-poster beds.

Laburnum House (☎ 667717; www.stayatlaburnumhouse.co.uk; The Holme; s/d from £23/45) A quaint cottage in the centre, with a busy tearoom and terrace downstairs serving tea and scones (£2.50), hearty sandwiches (£3 to £5) and meals (£7). The rooms are decorated in various shades of blue.

Green Dragon Inn (☎ 667392; www.greendragoninn.fsnet.co.uk; Hardraw; s/d without breakfast from £18/36, with breakfast £25/43; mains about £5) About 1½ miles north of town is this 'famous' inn where you pay the fee for the nearby waterfall. It's terrific, with unspectacular but thoroughly comfortable rooms, good beer, home-cooked food and live bands at weekends.

There are plenty of pubs, including **The Fountain** (☎ 667206; Market Pl; bar food about £6). The traditional **White Hart** (Market Pl; pub grub about £7) is also good for a pint or a bar meal.

Getting There & Away

Hawes is a public transportation nightmare. From Northallerton, bus Nos 156/157 run to Hawes (four Monday to Friday, two hours) via Leyburn, where you can connect with transport to/from Richmond. On Sunday (March to October) there are buses to Hawes from Manchester (No X43) via Skipton and Grassington, and from Leeds (No 803). Between Hawes and the Lake District, bus No 112 runs to/from Kendal (twice daily, 90 minutes), very early in the morning and late in the evening, with a few extra services on some other weekdays. The TIC can advise on other bus services aimed at visitors.

RICHMOND
☎ 01748 / pop 8178

Psst. Tell everyone you know: Richmond is one of the most charming towns in England. Cobbled streets and alleyways, lined with Georgian buildings and old stone cottages, radiate from the large, cobbled market square, and give exhilarating glimpses of the surrounding hills and dales. To complete the scene, a massive ruined castle perches high on a rocky outcrop overlooking the town on one side and the rushing River Swale on the other. Get your camera out.

Orientation & Information

Richmond is east of the Yorkshire Dales National Park but makes a good gateway for the northern area. Centre of everything is Trinity Church Sq (with market day on Saturday). Just north of here, the **TIC** (☎ 850252; www.richmond.org.uk; Friary Gardens;

Victoria Rd; ☉ 9.30am-5.30pm Apr-Oct, 9.30am-4.30pm Nov-Mar) has the usual maps and guides, plus several leaflets (around 60p) showing walks in town and the surrounding countryside.

Sights

Top of the pile is the impressive heap that's left of **Richmond Castle** (EH; ☎ 822493; admission £3; ☉ 10am-6pm Apr-Sep, 10am-4pm Oct-Mar), founded in 1070 and one of the first castles in England since Roman times to be built of stone. It's had many uses through the years, including a stint as a prison for conscientious objectors during WWI (there's a small and sobering exhibition about their part in the castle's history). The best part of a visit is the view from the top of the remarkably well-preserved 30m-high tower; you can look down on the market place or over the surrounding hills.

Veterans and military buffs will enjoy the three floors of the **Green Howards Museum** (☎ 822133; Trinity Church Sq; adult/child £3/2; ☉ 10am-4pm Mon-Sat Feb-Nov, Sun also Apr-Oct), which pays tribute to the famous Yorkshire regiment.

In a totally different vein, **Richmondshire Museum** (☎ 825611; Ryder's Wynd; adult/child £1.50/1; ☉ 10.30am-4.30pm Easter-Oct) is a delightful little gem, with very informative staff and local history exhibits including an early Yorkshire cave-dweller, James Herriot's surgery, and informative displays on lead mining, which forever altered the Swaledale landscape a century ago.

Activities

West from Richmond walkers can follow paths along the River Swale, upstream and downstream from the town. A longer option is along the north side of Swaledale, following the famous long-distance Coast to Coast route (p61), all the way to Reeth. For a grand day out, take the first bus (£2.20) from Richmond to Reeth then walk back; the TIC has route and bus time details.

SOMETHING FOR THE WEEKEND

One of England's best-kept secrets is the elegant Georgian town of Richmond, a maze of cobbled streets guarded by the ruins of its massive **castle** (above).

Base yourself in the truly exceptional **Millgate House** (opposite), with a marvellous garden that will be hard to leave if the weather is in any way clement. On Saturday, explore the town itself, take in a museum or two and clamber about the ruins of the castle.

From the castle tower you will see the broad expanse of **Swaledale** (opposite), part of the northern section of the Yorkshire Dales National Park, which should be the focus of your Sunday activities.

Cyclists can also follow Swaledale: as far as Reeth may be enough, while a trip to Keld, then over the high wild moors to Kirkby Stephen is a more serious but very rewarding 33-mile undertaking.

Sleeping

King's Head Hotel (☎ 850220; www.kingsheadrichmond .co.uk; Market Pl; s/d from £69/95) Right on Market Pl, Richmond's fanciest hotel was once described by the painter Turner as 'the finest in Richmondshire'. That was a long time ago. It's still pretty fancy though; each of the traditionally furnished 30 bedrooms have wrought-iron or hardwood beds and plenty of comfort.

Willance House (☎ 824467; www.willancehouse .com; 24 Frenchgate; s/d £30/50) This is an oak-beamed, 17th-century house with four rooms that are small in size but bursting with cutesy character.

Frenchgate Hotel (☎ 822087; www.frenchgate hotel.com; 59-61 Frenchgate; s/d £42/75; P) A converted Georgian town house that is now a fine guesthouse with eight immaculate rooms. One of the bedrooms has a beautiful canopied bed, which fits somewhat snugly into the room (the others are equally compact). Downstairs there's a hospitable lounge with oak beams and an open fire.

There's a batch of pleasant places along Frenchgate, and several more on Maison Dieu and Pottergate (the road into town from the east). These include **Pottergate Guesthouse** (☎ 823826; 4 Pottergate), **66 Frenchgate** (☎ 823421; paul@66french.freeserve.co.uk; 66 Frenchgate) and **Emmanuel House** (☎ 823584; 41 Maison Dieu). Singles/doubles cost about £25/40.

Eating & Drinking

Trinity Church Sq and the surrounding streets have a huge choice of pubs, teashops, cafés and takeaways.

Frenchgate Café (☎ 824949; 29 Frenchgate; lunches about £4, evening mains £7-11; ⏰ 10am-10pm Tue-Sun) An all-meals-in-one kind of place, you can tuck into a tidy breakfast in the morning, a large sandwich or pasta dish at lunch and enjoy the delights of their quasi-Continental bistro menu in the evening.

A Taste of Thailand (☎ 829696; 15 King St; mains about £10; ⏰ dinner only) Does exactly what it says on the tin. An extensive menu of Thai favourites and a convenient BYO policy.

Surprisingly, despite a vast choice, few of the pubs in Richmond are up to much.

After extensive research, the best we found was the **Black Lion Hotel** (☎ 823121; Finkle St; bar food £5, mains in restaurant about £9), with cosy bars, low beams, good beer and food, plus B&B.

Getting There & Away

From Darlington (on the railway between London and Edinburgh) it's easy to reach Richmond on bus No 34 (£4.80, hourly, 30 minutes; four on Sunday). All buses stop in Trinity Church Sq.

SWALEDALE

West of Richmond, the River Swale flows through Swaledale – the quietest and least-visited of the Dales – with a wild and rugged beauty to contrast sharply with the softer, greener places further south. It's hard to imagine, but only a century ago this was a major lead-mining area. When the price of ore fell in the 19th century many people left Swaledale for good. Some went to England's burgeoning industrial cities, and others emigrated – especially to Wisconsin in the USA – leaving Swaledale almost empty, a legacy that remains today, with just a few small lonely villages scattered along its length.

Reeth

In the heart of Swaledale is the pretty village of Reeth – a great base for exploring Swaledale, with shops, cafés and some good pubs dotted around a large sloping green (Friday is market day). There's a **TIC** (☎ 01748-884059; reeth@ytbtic.co.uk) and many B&B options; one excellent choice is the **Arkleside Hotel** (☎ 01748-884200; www.arklesidehotel .co.uk; s/d from £56/82), made up of a converted row of old cottages just by the green.

To understand Swaledale's fascinating history, the dusty little **Swaledale Folk Museum** (☎ 01748-884373; admission £1; ⏲ 10.30am-5pm Easter-Oct) is well worth a look.

EAST RIDING OF YORKSHIRE

The only Yorkshire county to have retained the essence of its Viking name, the East Riding (from Old Danish *Thriding,* or third) was one of three administrative regions created by the conquering Danes in the 9th century – west and north ridings are now West and North Yorkshire.

Dominating the region is the no-nonsense port city of Hull, stolidly seated between the broad horizons of the rivers Humber and Hull; to the north is the market town of Beverley, with lots of 18th-century character, and an enormous medieval religious and cultural legacy.

The expanse of the River Humber, with its soaring, powerful bridge, flows to meet the sea by a flat, deserted coast and the strange protuberance of Spurn Head. Further north up the coast, there are some classic, small seaside settlements: Bridlington and the rather-more-restrained Filey, and beyond that the drama of the Flamborough cliffs and Bempton Cliffs Nature Reserve. Inland, the respite from the largely flat and nondescript drained marshland comes with the Yorkshire Wolds, an area of gently rolling chalky hills between Hull, York and the coast; it's an attractive area, in a low-key kind of way.

Activities

The Yorkshire Wolds are ideal for gentle walks and cycle tours. Whether you're on two feet or two wheels, the town of Beverley makes a good base, and the northern Wolds can also be easily reached from York.

The area's main long-distance walk is the 80-mile (130km) **Wolds Way**. This national

trail starts at Hessle, a riverside town 4 miles west of Hull, close to the Humber Bridge, and leads northwards through farmland, hills and quiet villages, to end at the tip of Filey Brigg, a peninsula on the east coast just north of the town of Filey. Billed as 'Yorkshire's best-kept secret', it takes five days, and is an excellent beginners' walk, as the landscape is not high and conditions not too strenuous.

The **Cleveland Way** (p597) also ends at Filey, and for a shorter walk in bracing sea air you can follow the Cleveland Way along a scenic stretch of coast northwards from Filey to Scarborough.

Getting There & Around

Hull is easily reached by rail from Leeds, York, Beverley, Filey and Scarborough, and is also the hub for regional bus services. There's a useful website at www.getting around.eastriding.gov.uk.

HULL

☎ 01482 / pop 301,416

This most curmudgeonly of English seaports, a hard-bitten city determinedly unaffected by the exotic trade that has passed through its docks, has in recent years begun to soften. Not much, mind you, but just enough for visitors to experience something other than the unforgiving air of a city that doesn't suffer much of anyone at anytime. Its full and proper name – Kingston-upon-Hull – seems like an unnecessary extravagance when plain old Hull will do, and it seems apt that jaundiced, rueful poet Philip Larkin (1922–85) presided over its university library for many years.

Orientation & Information

The Old Town of Hull, which retains a sense of the prosperous Victorian era, is bounded by Ferensway and Freetown Way and the Rivers Humber and Hull. Perched on the waterfront overlooking the Humber is the city's main attraction, a huge aquarium called The Deep. It's all walkable.

Central library (☎ 223344; Albion St) For Internet access.

Post office (57 Jameson St; ⏲ 9am-5.30pm Mon-Sat)

TIC (☎ 223559; www.hullcc.gov.uk; 1 Paragon St; ⏲ 10am-5pm Mon-Sat, 11am-3pm Sun)

Waterstone's (☎ 580234; 19-21 Jameson St) Best bookshop.

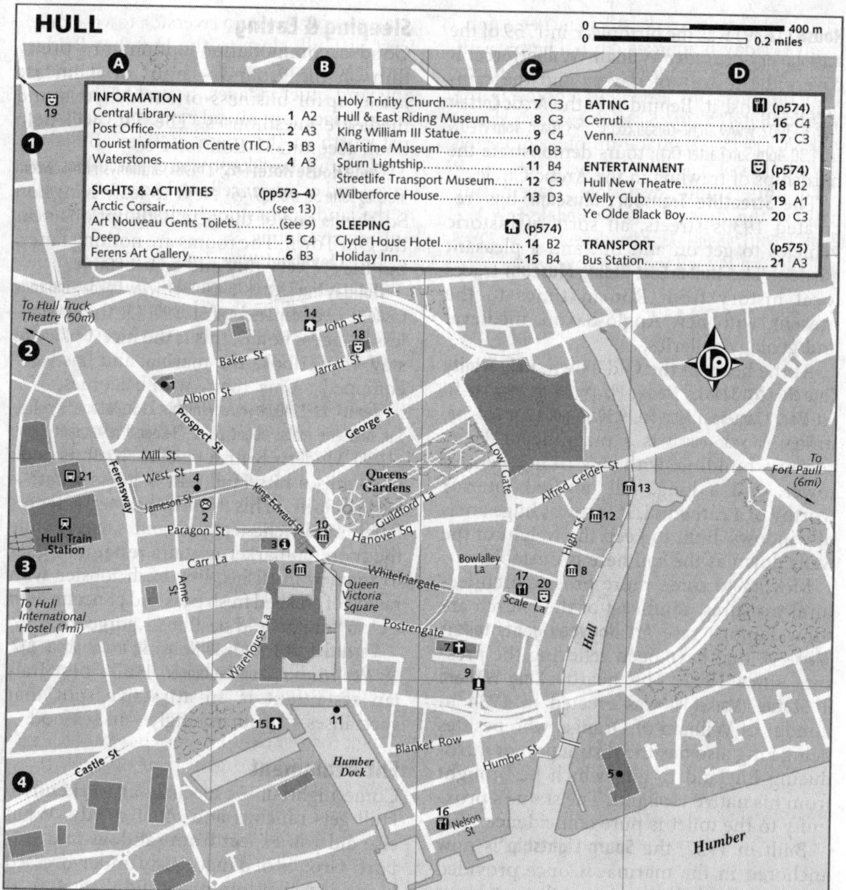
HULL
0 400 m
0 0.2 miles
A
B
C
D
1
2
3
4
INFORMATION
Central Library 1 A2
Post Office 2 A3
Tourist Information Centre (TIC) 3 B3
Waterstones 4 A3
SIGHTS & ACTIVITIES (pp573–4)
Arctic Corsair (see 13)
Art Nouveau Gents Toilets (see 9)
Deep 5 C4
Ferens Art Gallery 6 B3
Holy Trinity Church 7 C3
Hull & East Riding Museum 8 C3
King William III Statue 9 C4
Maritime Museum 10 B3
Spurn Lightship 11 B4
Streetlife Transport Museum 12 C3
Wilberforce House 13 D3
SLEEPING (p574)
Clyde House Hotel 14 B2
Holiday Inn 15 B4
EATING (p574)
Cerruti 16 C4
Venn 17 C3
ENTERTAINMENT (p574)
Hull New Theatre 18 B2
Welly Club 19 A1
Ye Olde Black Boy 20 C3
TRANSPORT (p575)
Bus Station 21 A3
To Hull Truck Theatre (50m)
John St
Baker St
Jarratt St
Albion St
Prospect St
George St
Mill St
West St
Ferensway
Jameson St
Paragon St
King Edward St
Queens Gardens
Guildford La
Hanover Sq
Low Gate
Alfred Gelder St
High St
To Fort Paull (6mi)
Hull Train Station
Carr La
Anne St
Whitefriargate
Queen Victoria Square
Bowlalley La
Scale La
To Hull International Hostel (1mi)
Postrengate
Warehouse La
Hull
Castle St
Humber Dock
Blanket Row
Humber St
Nelson St
Humber

The Deep

The colossal, angled monolith that is **The Deep** (☎ 381000; www.thedeep.co.uk; Tower St; admission £6; 🕑 10am-6pm) stands at the edge of the port, with great views across the Humber. Inside it's just as dramatic, as echoing commentaries and computer-generated interactives run you through the formation of the seas, and onwards. The largest aquarium contains 2.5 million litres of water (and 87 tonnes of salt) and even has a glass lift. To get a good view of the tank's seven different types of sharks, eels, rays and other watery dwellers, it's best (if more pedestrian) to take the stairs, as the lift ride is over no sooner than you start it. And it's rare you see a pod full of people zoom through a tank.

Other Sights

Hull has a remarkable collection of city-run **museums** (☎ 613902; www.hullcc.gov.uk/museums; 🕑 10am-5pm Mon-Sat, 1.30-4.30pm Sun). All share the same phone number and opening hours and are free unless otherwise stated.

The serene **Ferens Art Gallery** (Queen Victoria Sq), built in 1927, has a decent collection that includes works by Stanley Spencer and Peter Blake.

The dusty-feeling but interesting **Maritime Museum**, in the former dock offices (1871), celebrates Hull's long maritime traditions, and includes some daunting whale skeletons.

The well-preserved High St has some eclectic museums. Attractive, Georgian **Wilberforce**

House (1639) was the birthplace in 1759 of the antislavery crusader William Wilberforce. It covers the history of slavery and the campaign against it. Behind it is the **Arctic Corsair** (☎ 613902; www.arctic-corsair.co.uk; 10am-4pm Wed & Fri, 1.30-4pm Sun Easter-Oct); tours demonstrate the hardships of trawling in the Arctic Circle.

The **Streetlife Transport Museum** has recreated 1930s streets, all sorts of historic vehicles to get on and off, and a pleasant garden. The **Hull & East Riding Museum** traces local history from Roman times to the present, with new Anglo-Saxon, medieval and geology galleries.

At the heart of the Old Town, **Holy Trinity Church** (☎ 324835; Market Pl; 11am-2pm Tue-Fri Oct-Mar, 11am-3pm Mon-Fri, 9.30am-noon Sat Apr-Sep, services Sun year-round) is a magnificent 15th-century building with a striking central tower, and a long, tall, unified interior worthy of a cathedral. It features huge areas of windows, built to keep the weight of the walls down as the soil here is unstable.

Moving to some more prosaic architectural treasures, southeast of the church are some famous rare **Art Nouveau gents toilets** (Market Pl) that have been relieving the pressure since 1902. The nearby **King William III Statue** (Market Pl) was erected in 1734 in honour of William of Orange, who besides being king also has the distinction of introducing England to gin, which he brought from his native Holland. The statue's proximity to the toilet is pure coincidence.

Built in 1927, the **Spurn Lightship** is now anchored in the marina. It once provided guidance for ships navigating the notorious Humber estuary.

Around 6 miles east of the centre, along the A1033, **Fort Paull** (☎ 893339; www.fortpaull .co.uk; adult/child £4.50/3; 10am-6pm Apr-Oct, 11am-4pm Nov-Mar) is a grand, lavishly restored fort. The 1860s structure, with its underground labyrinths, is interesting, while stilted waxworks and warlike stuff document the fort's history from the AD 910 Viking landing onwards.

Walking

The TIC sells a brochure called *The Seven Seas Fish Pavement Trail* (40p), a delightful, historic self-guided tour of the Old Town, following fish shapes embedded in the pavement. Kids love it. Adults might prefer the *Hull Ale Trail* (40p), which needs no explanation.

Sleeping & Eating

Good accommodation options are pretty thin on the ground – most of them are made up of business-oriented hotels and mediocre guesthouses. The TIC will help book accommodation for free.

Clyde House Hotel (☎ 214981; anthonysmith@cwcom .net; 13 John St; s/d £27/45) Next to leafy Kingston Sq, this is one of the best B&B options near the Old Town. The rooms are nothing fancy, but they're very tidy and comfortable.

Holiday Inn (☎ 0870 400 9043; www.holiday-inn.com; Castle St; r weekday/weekend £120/90) Of the charmless business hotels, this is the nicest place to stay. It overlooks the marina, and has well-equipped rooms, many with balconies.

Venn (☎ 224004; www.venn.biz; 21 Scale Lane; Tue-Sat; brasserie mains about £8, 2-/3-course restaurant menu £32/38) Modern British cuisine in all its cool, posh guises hits Hull and – guess what? – sticks nicely. This trendy brasserie serves fancy sandwiches, pizzas and salads, while the more upmarket upstairs restaurant goes to town with dishes like fresh lobster with ravioli of crushed fresh peas and pancetta with a clear tomato and basil jus…gorgeous.

Cerruti (☎ 328501; 10 Nelson St; mains about £12; Mon-Fri lunch, Mon-Sat dinner) Hull's best Italian restaurant is an attractive spot that specialises – unsurprisingly – in seafood.

Entertainment

Come nightfall – especially at weekends – Hull gets raucous and often rowdy. What else did you expect from saltdogs in a seaport? Groups of dangerously under-dressed kids party like tomorrow didn't matter. If you're that pissed, it wouldn't.

Welly Club (☎ 326131, 221676; 105-7 Beverley Rd; admission free-£5; till 2am, closed Wed & Sun) Shake a leg to everything from ska to soul, and there's a Saturday residency by home-grown Steve Cobby of local heroes Fila Brazillia.

Ye Olde Black Boy (☎ 326516; 150 High St) A real old-fashioned boozer on a site dating from 1337, this place is smoke-stained and plush-seated in the great English pub tradition.

Hull Truck Theatre (☎ 323638; www.hulltruck .co.uk; Spring St) Home to acclaimed down-to-earth playwright John Godber, it presents vibrant drama, comedy and Sunday jazz.

Hull New Theatre (☎ 226655; www.hullnew theatre.co.uk; Kingston Sq) A traditional regional theatre hosting popular drama, concerts and musicals.

Getting There & Away

The bus station is on Ferensway, just north of the train station. National Express has buses to/from London (£21.50, 5¾ hours, two daily) and Manchester (£12.75, 4¼ hours, one daily). Both National Express and Bus No X46 run frequently to/from York (£6.25, 1¾ hours). Local services also leave from here.

The train station is west of Queen Victoria Sq, in the town centre. Hull has good rail links north and south, and west to York (£13.50, 1¼ hours, hourly) and Leeds (£13.10, one hour, hourly).

The ferry port is 3 miles east of the centre at King George Dock. A bus to/from the train station connects with the ferries. For details of departures, see p750.

AROUND HULL
Humber Bridge

The graceful, concrete and metal Humber Bridge swoops 1410m across the broad river – the world's third-longest single-suspension bridge – seemingly hung by fine threads. It has linked Yorkshire and Lincolnshire since 1981, opening up what was an often-overlooked corner of the country.

Near the base of the bridge on the north side is a small park with nature trails that run from the parking area all the way down to the riverbank. The park can be reached from the bridge access roads. The park is also home to the **Humber Bridge TIC** (☎ 01482-640852; 9am-5pm Mon-Fri, 9am-6pm Sat & Sun May-Sep, 10am-3pm Nov-Feb, 9am-4pm Mar, Apr & Oct). It handles information requests for all of the East Riding of Yorkshire and the Wolds Way and has a display documenting the construction of the bridge.

The bridge is a mile west of the small riverside town of **Hessle**, about 4 miles west of Hull and effectively an outer suburb. Bus Nos 66, 67 and 68 run regularly from Hull's centre (£2.10, 30 minutes) to Hessle, and this is also a stop for local trains on the line from Hull to Leeds, Doncaster and Sheffield.

Spurn Head

A narrow, hooked sandbank dangling off the coast on the north side of the Humber estuary, **Spurn Head** (admission per car £3) has a long military history and is an important nature reserve.

In 1804 gun batteries were built to meet the expected French; in following decades the fortifications were greatly expanded to meet various threats. By WWII there were guns of all sizes mounted in heavy concrete emplacements. After the war, the odds of some enemy force arriving in assault boats faded and the guns were removed, although remnants of the many concrete emplacements and roadways survive.

A benefit of the years of military use is that Spurn Head was spared commercial development. Today it is made up of large rolling sand dunes covered with various sea grasses. Most of the land is now part of the **Spurn National Nature Reserve**.

There are two TICs. One has a café and is at the end of the B1445 in Kilnsea, the last village on the mainland. Called the **Blue Bell Tea Room** (☎ 01964-650139; 11am-4.30pm Jul-Sep, 11am-5pm Sat & Sun Sep-Jun), it is close to the beach, and allows free camping on its grassy land. The other is run by the **Yorkshire Wildlife Trust** (10am-5pm Sat & Sun) and is a mile further south along the Spurn Head access road.

The single-track road to the point is 2½ miles long. There are many good walks, and at the tip of the head, you can see the spurting tides of the Humber as well as the busy shuttle boats used by the pilots of the many passing freighters.

Back in Kilnsea, along the B1445, the **Crown and Anchor** (☎ 01964-650276; s/d £34/50; mains £7-10) is a fine pub with good food, and a dramatic, isolated, waterside location.

Public transport to Kilnsea and Spurn Head is nonexistent. It's about 28 miles east of Hull. The flat roads are good for bikes.

BEVERLEY
☎ 01482 / pop 29,110

Thoroughly unspoilt Beverley merits far more attention than it has hitherto attracted. Beneath the magnificent medieval minster lies the handsome tangle of the town, literally brimming with exquisite Georgian and Victorian buildings.

Orientation & Information

Beverley is small and easily walked to from either the train or bus stations. There's a large market in the main square on Saturday.

Beverley Bookshop (☎ 0800 616394; 16 Butcher Row)

Post office (Register Sq; ◷ 9am-5.30pm Mon-Fri, 9am-12.30pm Sat)

Library (☎ 885355; Champney Rd; ◷ 9.30am-5pm Mon & Wed, 9.30am-7pm Tue, Thu & Fri, 9am-1pm Sat) Also has a small art gallery with changing exhibitions.

TIC (☎ 391672; beverley@ytbtic.co.uk; 34 Butcher Row; ◷ 9.30am-5.15pm Mon-Fri, 10am-4.45pm Sat, also 10am-2pm Sun Jun-Aug only)

Sights & Attractions

The third church to be built on this site (the first was constructed during the 7th century), the **minster** (☎ 868540; www.beverley minster.co.uk; admission by donation; ◷ 9am-5.30pm Mon-Sat May-Aug, 9am-5pm Sep-Oct & Mar-Apr, 9am-4pm Nov-Feb, also noon-4pm Sun year-round) dates from 1220, but construction continued for two centuries, spanning the Early English, Decorated and Perpendicular periods. Hailed for its unity of forms, the church has a magnificent Gothic perpendicular west front (1390–1420).

Inside, the nave is strikingly high. Extraordinary medieval faces and demons peer down from every possible vantage point, while expressive stone musicians play silent instruments. Note particularly the 10th-century *fridstol* (Old English for 'peace chair') which gave sanctuary to anyone escaping the law; the fruit- and angel-laden Gothic canopy of the Percy Tomb; the 68 medieval misericords (the largest collection in the country) and the late Norman font (c1170).

There's an interesting display showing the history of the minster and town. Check out the rebuilt treadwheel crane, where workers ground around like hapless hamsters to lift the huge loads necessary to build such medieval structures.

Doomed to play second fiddle to the mother church, **St Mary's** (☎ 865709; admission free; ◷ 9.15am-noon & 1.30-5pm Mon-Fri, 10am-5.30pm Sat & 2-5pm Sun Apr-Sep; 2-4.15pm Oct-Mar) is a glorious church, built in stages between 1120 and 1530. In the North Choir Aisle look out for a carving (c1330) thought to have inspired Lewis Carroll's White Rabbit. The West Front is considered one of England's finest (early 15th century).

Sleeping & Eating

Friary YHA Hostel (☎ 0870 770 5696; Friar's Lane; dm £10.60; ◷ Mon-Sat Easter–end Oct) Here's your chance to stay in a beautiful, restored 14th-century Dominican friary mentioned in Chaucer's *The Canterbury Tales*. This place might just have the best setting in town, only 100m southeast of the minster.

Beverley Arms (☎ 869241; www.regalhotels.co.uk; North Bar Within; s/d from £80/110) Beverley's top spot is a very elegant Georgian coaching house with all the trimmings, although we weren't overly impressed with the faux-antique furniture. Make sure to ask for a room in the old building, which has less of an ersatz feel about it.

Eastgate Guest House (☎ 868464; 7 Eastgate; s/d from £27/42, with bathroom £41/53) This relatively central B&B is highly recommended for sheer friendliness and relaxed atmosphere more than for the floral, simple rooms.

Number One (☎ 862752; www.numberone-bedand breakfast-beverley.co.uk; 1 Woodlands; s/d from £23/38) Three very comfortable rooms in a friendly, welcoming house located just west of the town centre.

Cerutti 2 (☎ 866700; Station Sq; mains £9-19; ◷ dinner only Mon-Sat) The only restaurant of note in town is unusually positioned inside the train station. Italian dishes of all kinds are on offer, without the seafood leanings of its sister restaurant in Hull.

White Horse Inn (☎ 861973; 22 Hengate; mains £7-8; ◷ lunch & dinner) Also known as Nellie's, this lovely, dimly lit place has rambling rooms, open fires and tables outside. There's regular live music and poetry.

Getting There & Away

The train station lies east of the town centre. The bus station is north on Sow Hill.

Bus No X46/X47 links Beverley with York (£3.60, one hour 10 minutes, hourly). There are frequent buses to Hull (Nos 121, 122, 246 and X46/X47, £2.10, 30 minutes).

There are regular trains to/from Scarborough via Filey (£11.10, 1½ hours). Trains to/from Hull (£3.80, 20 minutes) run at least hourly.

Details on boats to Hull from northern Europe are given in the main Transport chapter, p750.

BRIDLINGTON

☎ 01262 / pop 33,589

The little town of Bridlington presents a roll call of the English seaside's usual suspects, with all the tawdry charm that such diversions involve. The promenade has a small funfair, candyfloss, arcades, all-day breakfasts, palmists, lager specials and often windswept people. There's a long, sandy attractive beach.

The **TIC** (☎ 673474; 25 Prince St; ⏱ 9.30am-5.30pm Mon-Sat, 11am-3pm Sun) is near the north beach and has short-term parking at the front. It can book a vast array of rooms.

Bridlington is on the line from Hull to Scarborough with frequent trains to the former (£6.70, 45 minutes) and the latter (£4.40, 45 minutes).

AROUND BRIDLINGTON

As well as seaside towns, the coast of the East Riding of Yorkshire has long unpeopled stretches, and fine blustery cliff tops.

Bempton Cliffs Nature Reserve

The Royal Society for the Protection of Birds' **nature reserve** (☎ 01262-851179; pedestrian/car free/£3; visitor centre ⏱ 10am-5pm Mar-Nov, 10am-5pm Sat & Sun Dec & Feb) is a delightful place for non-twitchers too. Around 3 miles of paths (open at all times) skirt the top of the imposing chalk cliffs, which are home to more than 200,000 nesting sea birds – the largest colony in England – every spring and summer. There are many other feathered residents in place the rest of the year as well. The species flapping about include gannets, auks, guillemots, razorbills, kittiwakes and ever-popular puffins.

There is a good visitor centre with a small snack bar set back from the cliffs. Binoculars can be rented for £3 and there are usually volunteers on hand to provide guidance.

The reserve is a well-marked 1¼ miles from the village of Bempton and the B1229. By public transport, take one of the frequent trains on the Hull–Scarborough line and then walk.

Flamborough

The small village of Flamborough is 3 miles east of Bridlington. Fine views soar out from the milk-coloured cliffs at Flamborough Head, 2 miles east of the village.

Seabirds (☎ 01262-850242; Tower St; mains £5-12; ⏱ lunch & dinner) is a classic country pub with several rooms, open fires and a beer garden. The real ale selection is good and the seafood lunches and dinners excellent.

NORTH YORKSHIRE

The largest by far of Yorkshire's four counties, North Yorkshire is the most beautiful of the lot. Unlike much of northern England, the landscape is unmarked by the looming mills and mines that remain elsewhere – hallmarks of the Industrial Revolution. Here, sheep ruled the countryside from the Middle Ages onwards, and the fortunes made in this part of the world were made – literally – on their backs.

Those fortunes were used to construct the magnificent man-made monuments that dot the landscape, from the great houses and rich abbeys that sit ruined or otherwise in glorious isolation from the rest of the world to the towns and cities that share a particularly powerful sense of the past. Well-preserved buildings reflect their respective glory days, from the genteel spa of Harrogate, to the blowsy, dramatically situated resorts of Scarborough and Whitby, to the splendour of York.

Otherwise, the landscape has remained largely untouched, giving the land an untamed quality best experienced in North Yorkshire's two magnificent national parks – the Yorkshire Dales (p563) and North York Moors (p596).

Activities

The best walking and cycling is in the Yorkshire Dales (p563) and the North York Moors (p596).

Getting There & Around

The main gateway town is York and a web of buses and trains connect places in North Yorkshire. More specific details on the Yorkshire Dales and the North York Moors are given in those sections following. For county-wide information, call the national **Traveline** (☎ 0870 608 2608). There are various Explorer passes, and individual bus and train companies also offer their own saver schemes, so it's always worth asking for advice on the best deal when you buy your ticket.

YORK

☎ 01904 / pop 137,505

York is the kind of place that makes you wish – if only for an instant – that the Industrial Revolution never happened and reminds us of a world before the machines. A city of extraordinary cultural and historical wealth, its medieval spider's web of narrow streets is enclosed by a magnificent circuit of 13th-century walls. At its heart lies the immense, awe-inspiring minster, one of the most beautiful Gothic cathedrals in the world. The city's long history and rich heritage is woven into virtually every brick and beam; modern, tourist-oriented York – with its myriad museums, restaurants, cafés and traditional pubs – is a carefully maintained heir to that heritage.

Orientation

Compact and eminently walkable, there are five major landmarks to take note of: the wall enclosing the small city centre; the minster at the northern corner; Clifford's Tower at the southern end; the River Ouse

YORK: FROM THE BEGINNING

York – or the marshy area that preceded the first settlement – has been coveted by pretty much everyone that has ever set foot on this island. In the beginning there were the Brigantines, a local tribe that minded their own business. In AD 71 the Romans – who were spectacularly successful at minding everyone else's business – built their first garrison here for the troops fighting the poor old Brigantines. They called it Erboracum, and in time a civilian settlement prospered around what became a large fort. Hadrian used it as the base for his northern campaign, while Constantine the Great was proclaimed emperor here in AD 306 after the death of his father. After the collapse of the Roman Empire, the town was taken by the Anglo-Saxons who renamed it Eoforwic and made it the capital of the independent kingdom of Northumbria.

Enter the Christians. In 625 a Roman priest, Paulinus, arrived and managed to convert King Edwin and all his nobles. Two years later, they built the first wooden church; for most of the next century the city was a major centre of learning, attracting students from all over Europe.

The student party lasted until 866, when the next wave of invaders arrived. This time it was those marauding Vikings, who chucked everybody out and gave the town a more tongue-friendly name, Jorvik. It was to be their capital for the next 100 years, and during that time they put a rest to their pillaging ways and turned the city into an important trading port.

The next arrival was King Eadred of Wessex, who drove out the last Viking ruler in 954 and reunited Danelaw with the south, but trouble quickly followed. In 1066 King Harold II managed to fend off a Norwegian invasion-rebellion at Stamford Bridge, east of York, but his turn came at the hands of William the Conqueror a few months later at the Battle of Hastings.

Willie exercised his own brand of tough love in York. After his two wooden castles were captured by an Anglo-Scandinavian army, he torched the whole city (and Durham) and the surrounding countryside so that the rebels knew who was boss – the 'harrying of the north'. The Normans then set about rebuilding the city, including a new minster. From that moment, everything in York was rosy – except for a blip in 1137 when the whole city caught fire – and over the next 300 years it prospered through royal patronage, textiles, trade and the church.

No sooner did the church finally get built, though, than the city went into full recession. In the 15th century Hull took over as the region's main port and the textile industry moved elsewhere. Henry VIII's inability to keep a wife and the ensuing brouhaha with the church that resulted in the Reformation also hit York pretty hard. Henry did establish a branch of the King's Council here to help govern the north, and this contributed to the city's recovery under Elizabeth I and James I.

The council was abolished during Charles I's reign, but the king established his court here during the Civil War, which drew the devastating attentions of the Parliamentarians. They besieged the rabidly pro-monarchist York for three months in 1644, but by a fortunate accident of history their leader was a local chap called Sir Thomas Fairfax, who prevented his troops from setting York alight, thereby preserving the city and the minster.

Not much happened after that. Throughout the 18th century the city was a fashionable social centre dominated by the aristocracy, who were drawn by its culture and new racecourse. When the railway was built in 1839 thousands of people were employed in the new industries that sprung up around it, such as confectionary. These industries went into decline in the latter half of the 20th century, but by then a new invader was asking for directions at the city gates, armed only with a guidebook.

that cuts the centre in two; and the train station to the west. Just to avoid the inevitable confusion, remember that round these parts *gate* means street and *bar* means gate.

Information

American Express (☎ 676501; 6 Stonegate; ☺ 9am-5.30pm Mon-Fri, 9am-5pm Sat) With foreign exchange service.

Borders (☎ 653300; 1-5 Davygate; ☺ 9am-9pm Mon-Sat, 11am-5pm Sun) Well-stocked bookshop.

Internet Exchange (☎ 638808; 13 Stonegate; ☺ 9am-7pm Mon-Sat, 11am-6pm Sun)

Post office (22 Lendal; ☺ 8.30am-5.30pm Mon & Tue, 9am-5.30pm Wed-Sat)

This is York (www.thisisyork.co.uk)

Thomas Cook (☎ 653626; 4 Nessgate) A travel agent offering a full service.

TIC (☎ 621756; www.visityork.org; De Grey Rooms, Exhibition Sq; ☺ 9am-6pm Mon-Sat, 10am-5pm Sun Apr-Sep, 9am-5pm Mon-Sat, 10am-4pm Sun Oct-Mar) There's another branch at the train station.

York District Hospital (☎ 631313; Wiggington Rd) A mile north of the centre.

Sights

YORK MINSTER

The island's largest medieval cathedral – and easily Yorkshire's most important historic building – is the simply awesome **minster** (☎ 624426; www.yorkminster.org; adult/child £4.50/3, undercroft £3/2, minster & undercroft £6.50/4.50; ☺ 7am-6pm Mon-Sat, noon-6pm Sun Jan-Mar, Nov & Dec, to 6.30pm Apr, to 7.30pm May, to 8.30pm Jun-Aug, to 8pm Sep & to 7pm Oct; undercroft ☺ 10am-4.30pm Mon-Sat Jan, Feb, Nov & Dec, noon-6pm Mar, 10am-5.30pm Apr & Oct, 10am-6pm May & Sep, 9.30am-6.30pm Jun-Aug, from 12.30pm Sun) that dominates the city. Seat of the archbishop of York, the primate of England, it is second in importance only to Canterbury, home of the primate of *all* England (the two titles were given to settle a debate over whether York or Canterbury was the true centre of the church in England), but that's where Canterbury's superiority ends, for this is without doubt one of Europe's most beautiful Gothic buildings. If this is the only cathedral you visit in England, you'll still walk away satisfied.

The first church on the site was a wooden chapel built for Paulinus' baptism of King Edwin on Easter Day 627; its site is marked in the crypt. With deliberate symbolism, the church was built on the site of a Roman basilica, a vast central assembly hall; parts

THE YORK PASS

If you plan on seeing virtually everything in town, we strongly recommend the York Pass (one/two/three days adult £17/25/32, one/two/three days child £10/16/22); it grants you free access to every single pay-in sight in town, as well as free passage on a handful of tours, including the Citysightseeing bus tour (see Tours, p583). It is available at the TICs.

can be seen in the foundations. A stone church was started but fell into disrepair after Edwin's death. St Wilfred built the next church but this was destroyed during William the Conqueror's brutal suppression of the north. The first Norman church was built in stages to 1080; you can see surviving fragments in the foundations and crypt.

The present building, built mainly from 1220 to 1480, manages to represent all the major stages of Gothic architectural development. The transepts were built in Early English style between 1220 and 1255; the octagonal chapter house was built between 1275 and 1290 in the Decorated style; the nave from 1291 to 1340; and the west towers, west front and central, or lantern, tower were built in Perpendicular style from 1470 to 1472.

You enter from the south transept, which was badly damaged by fire in 1984 but has now been fully restored. To your right is the 15th-century **choir screen** depicting the 15 kings from William I to Henry VI. Facing you is the magnificent **Five Sisters Window**, with five lancets over 15m high. This is the minster's oldest complete window; most of its tangle of glass dates from around 1250. Just beyond it to the right is the 13th-century **chapter house**, a fine example of the Decorated style. Sinuous stonework surrounds a wonderful uninterrupted space. There are more than 200 expressive carved heads and figures.

Back in the main church, you should notice the unusually wide and tall nave, whose aisles (to the sides) are roofed in stone in contrast to the central roof, which is wood painted to look like stone. On both sides of the nave are painted stone shields of the nobles who met Edward II at a parliament in York. Also note the **dragon's head** projecting

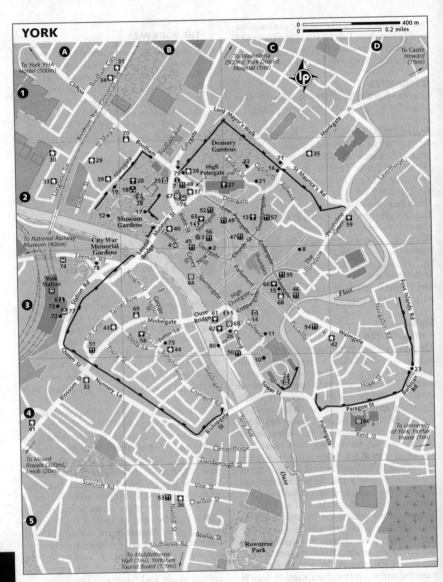

from the gallery – it's a crane believed to have been used to lift a font cover. There are several fine **windows** dating from the early 14th century, but the most dominating is the **Great West Window**, from 1338, with beautiful stone tracery.

Beyond the screen and the choir is the **lady chapel** and, behind it, the **high altar**, which is dominated by the huge **Great East Window** (1405). At 23.7m by 9.4m (78ft by 31ft) – roughly the size of a tennis court – it is the world's largest medieval stained-glass window and the cathedral's single most important treasure. Needless to say, its epic size matches the epic theme depicted within: the beginning and end of the world as described in Genesis and the Book of Revelations.

The minster's heart is dominated by the awesome **central tower** (adult/child £2.50/1; 10am-4.30pm Mon-Sat Jan, Feb, Nov & Dec, noon-6pm Mar, 10am-5.30pm Apr, Oct, 10am-6pm May & Sep, 9.30am-6.30pm Jun-Aug, from 12.30pm Sun) which is well worth climbing for the unparalleled views of York. You'll have to tackle a fairly claustrophobic climb of 275 steps and, most probably, a queue of people with cameras in hand. Access to the tower is near the entrance in the south transept, which is dominated by the exquisite **Rose Window** commemorating the union of the royal houses of Lancaster and York, through the marriage of Henry VII and Elizabeth of York, which ended the War of the Roses and began the Tudor dynasty (see p35).

Another set of stairs in the south transept leads down to the **undercroft**, where you'll also find the **treasury** and the **crypt**. These should on no account be missed. In 1967 the foundations were excavated when the central tower threatened to collapse; while engineers worked frantically to save the building, archaeologists uncovered Roman and Norman ruins that attest to the site's ancient history – one of the most extraordinary finds is a Roman culvert, still carrying water to the Ouse. The treasury houses

11th-century artefacts, including relics from the graves of medieval archbishops. The crypt contains fragments from the Norman cathedral, including the font showing King Edwin's baptism that also marks the site of Paulinus' original wooden chapel.

AROUND THE MINSTER

Owned by the minster since the 15th century, **St William's College** (637134; College St) is an attractive half-timbered Tudor building with elegant oriel windows built for the minster's chantry priests.

The **Treasurer's House** (NT; 624247; Minster Yard; admission £4; 11am-4.30pm Sat-Thu Apr-Oct) was home to the minster's medieval treasurers. Substantially rebuilt in the 17th and 18th centuries, the 13 rooms house a fine collection of furniture and supply a good insight into 18th-century life. The house is also the setting for one of the city's most enduring ghost stories: during the 1950s, a plumber working in the basement swore he saw a band of Roman soldiers walking *through* the walls; his story remains popular if unproven.

CITY WALLS

You can get onto the walls, built in the 13th century, via steps by **Bootham Bar** (on the site of a Roman gate) and follow them clockwise

YORKSHIRE

to Monk Bar, a walk offering particularly beautiful views of the minster. There are oodles more access points including off Station Rd and Monk Bar.

Monk Bar is the best-preserved medieval gate, with a small **Richard III Museum** (☎ 634191; www .richardiiimuseum.co.uk; admission £2; ☾ 9am-5pm Mar-Oct, 9.30am-4pm Nov-Feb) upstairs. The museum sets out the case of the murdered 'Princes in the Tower' and invites visitors to judge whether their uncle, Richard III, killed them.

Walmgate Bar is England's only city gate with an intact barbican (an extended gateway to ward off uninvited guests), and was built during the reign of Edward III.

MERCHANT ADVENTURERS' HALL

Built between 1357 and 1361, the outstanding **Merchant Adventurers' Hall** (☎ 654818; Fossgate; admission £2; ☾ 9am-5pm Mon-Thu, 9am-3.30pm Fri & Sat, noon-4pm Sun Apr-Sep, 9.30am-3.30pm Mon-Sat Oct-Mar) is one of the most handsome timber-framed buildings in Europe. This stunning building testifies to the power of the medieval guilds, which controlled all foreign trade into and out of York until 1830 – a handy little monopoly.

JORVIK

The much-trumpeted **Jorvik** (☎ 543403; www .vikingjorvik.com; Coppergate; adult/child £7.20/5.10; ☾ 10am-5pm Apr-Oct, 10am-4pm Nov-Mar) sounds terrific: a smells-and-all reconstruction of the original Viking settlement unearthed in this area during excavations in the late 1970s. A 'time-car' transports you 'back in time' and through what the town may have looked like, past groups of fibre-glass figures speaking a language derived from modern Icelandic. It is a bit of fun (for kids at least) but, except for the collection of actual artefacts scattered throughout, not altogether that fascinating. But, considering the crowds that queue up to get in to this museum, what the hell do we know? To cut the queue time considerably, book your tickets online – it only costs £1 more.

If you really want to get stuck into a bit of archaeology, check out the **Archaeological Resource Centre** (ARC; ☎ 654324; St Saviourgate; adult/child £4.50/4, with Jorvik £10.20/8.10; ☾ 10am-3.30pm Mon-Fri school term, 11am-3pm Mon-Sat school holidays) that is also run by the Jorvik people. It has various programmes that allow for hands-on exploration of archaeology.

CLIFFORD'S TOWER

There's precious little left of York Castle except for this evocative stone **tower** (EH; ☎ 646940; admission £2.50; ☾ 10am-6pm Apr-Jun & Sep, 9.30am-7pm Jul-Aug, 10am-5pm Oct, 10am-4pm Nov-Mar), a highly unusual figure-eight design built into the castle's keep after the original one was destroyed in 1190 during anti-Jewish riots. An angry mob forced 150 Jews to be locked inside the tower, but it wasn't enough, and the hapless victims took their own lives rather than be killed. There's not much to see inside but the views over the city are excellent.

YORK CASTLE MUSEUM

Near Clifford's Tower, this excellent **museum** (☎ 653611; admission £6; ☾ 9.30am-5pm) contains displays of everyday life, with reconstructed domestic interiors, and a less-than-homely prison cell where you can try out the condemned man's bed – in this case Dick Turpin's. There's a bewildering array of evocative everyday objects from the past 400 years, gathered together by a certain Dr Kirk from the 1920s onwards for fear that the items would become obsolete and disappear completely. He wasn't far wrong, which makes this place all the more interesting.

NATIONAL RAILWAY MUSEUM

Most railway museums are the sole preserve of lone men with dog-eared notebooks and grandfathers looking to bond with their grandchildren. While there's no shortage of either here, this **museum** (☎ 621261; www .nrm.org.uk; Leeman Rd; admission free; ☾ 10am-6pm) stands apart on account of its sheer size and incredible collection. Trainspotters and nostalgics will salivate at the massive gathering of engines and carriages from the past, but the attractions for regular folk are the gleaming carriages of the royal trains used by Queen Victoria and Edward VII; the speed-record-breaking *Mallard* (a mighty 2 miles a minute in 1938, still a record for a steam train); and a Series 'O' Japanese bullet train (1964–86), which you can sit in – it is a testament to the speed of technology that the train now appears a tad dated. Just next to it is a **simulator** (£3), which allows you to travel from London to Brighton in real time at supersonic speed – the journey takes four minutes. You can also wander around a vast annexe including the restoration workshops. Allow two hours to do the museum justice.

The museum is slightly out of the way (about 400m west of the train station), so if you don't fancy the walk, you can ride the **road train** (adult/child £1.50/50p; ☺ noon-5pm) that runs every 30 minutes between the minster and the museum.

OTHER SIGHTS

The **Museum Gardens** (☺ dawn-dusk) make a peaceful four-hectare city-centre oasis. Assorted picturesque ruins and buildings include the **Museum Gardens Lodge** (Victorian Gothic Revival) dating from 1874 and a 19th-century working **observatory**. The **Multangular Tower** was the western tower of the Roman garrison's defensive wall. The small Roman stones at the bottom have been built up with 13th-century additions.

The classical **Yorkshire Museum** (☎ 629745; adult/child £4/3; ☺ 10am-5pm) has some interesting Roman, Anglo-Saxon, Viking and medieval exhibits and good temporary exhibitions.

The ruins of **St Mary's Abbey** (founded 1089) date from 1270 to 1294. The ruined **Gatehall** was its main entrance, providing access from the abbey to the river. The adjacent **Hospitium** dates from the 14th century, although the timber-framed upper storey is a much-restored survivor from the 15th century; it was used as the abbey guesthouse. **St Mary's Lodge** was built around 1470 to provide VIP accommodation.

St Olave's Church (☺ 9am-5pm Mon-Fri) dates from the 15th century, but there has been a church dedicated to Norway's patron saint here since at least 1050.

Adjacent to Museum Gardens on Exhibition Sq is the 19th-century **York City Art Gallery** (☎ 551861; Exhibition Sq; admission free; ☺ 10am-5pm), which includes works by Reynolds, Nash, Boudin and Lowry.

Back inside the walls, the wonky lines inside **Holy Trinity** (☎ 613451; Goodramgate; ☺ 10am-5pm Tue-Sat May-Sep, 10am-4pm Oct-Apr) almost induce seasickness. The church was started in the 13th century and added to over the next 200 years. Rare 17th- to 18th-century box pews surround a two-tier pulpit.

If 18th-century Georgian houses are for you, then a visit to **Fairfax House** (☎ 655543; www.fairfaxhouse.co.uk; Castlegate; adult/child £4.50/1.50; ☺ 11am-5pm Mon-Thu & Sat, 1.30-5pm Sun, guided tours

11am & 2pm Fri late Feb–early Jan) should be on your itinerary. This exquisitely restored property was designed by John Carr (of Harewood House fame; see p560) and features the best example of rococo stucco work to be found in the north of England.

North of here, the quaintly cobbled **Shambles**, complete with overhanging Tudor buildings, hints at what a medieval street might have looked like if it was overrun with people told they have to buy something silly and superfluous and be back on the tour bus in 15 minutes. It takes its name from the Saxon word *shamel*, meaning slaughterhouse.

York Dungeon (☎ 632599; www.thedungeons.com; 12 Clifford St; adult/child £9.95/6.95; ☺ 10.30am-5pm Apr-Sep, 11am-4pm Nov-Jan, 10.30am-4.30pm Oct & Feb-Mar) is a series of exultantly gruesome historical reconstructions. For the especially hardened there's a lovely bit on the plague.

Tours

There's a bewildering array of tours on offer, from historic walking tours to a host of ever-competitive night-time ghost tours – pretty popular in what is reputed to be England's most haunted city.

BUS

York Citysightseeing (☎ 655585; www.city-sightseeing.com; day tickets adult/child £8/3.50) Two hop-on hop-off services calling at all the main sights; buses leave every 15 minutes from Exhibition Sq outside the main TIC.

BOAT

YorkBoat (☎ 628324; www.yorkboat.co.uk; Lendal Bridge; one-hr cruises adult/child £6.50/3.30; ☺ 10.40am, 12.10, 1.40 & 3.10pm Feb-Nov; ghost cruises adult/child £7.50/4; ☺ 6.30pm late Mar–Oct) Runs Ouse cruises from Lendal Bridge which depart King's Staith (behind the fire station) 10 minutes earlier. The obligatory ghost cruise runs nightly in high season from King's Staith.

WALKING

Association of Voluntary Guides (☎ 640780; 10.15am, also 2.15pm Apr-Oct & 6.45pm Jun-Aug) Free two-hour walking tours of the city from Exhibition Sq in front of York City Art Gallery.

Complete York Tour (☎ 706643) A walk around the city and the minster that can be adapted to your preferences. Call for details.

Ghost Hunt of York (☎ 608700; www.ghosthunt.co.uk; adult £4; ☺ 7.30pm) Award-winning and highly entertaining 75-minute tour beginning at the Shambles.

Original Ghost Walk of York (☎ 01759 373090; adult/child £3.50/2.50; ☼ 8pm) Ghouls and ghosts courtesy of a well-established group departing from the King's Arms pub by Ouse Bridge.

Roam'in Tours of York (☎ 07931 668935; www.roam intours.co.uk) History and specialist tours (adult/child £3/1) or you can take its DIY audio tour (£3.50).

Viking Walk (☎ 07796 772001; adult/child £3/2; ☼ 8.15pm Mon-Sat) Follow the fearsome but friendly Viking Gunhild on a tour of Jorvik. It's a bit of fun. Departures are from Exhibition Sq.

Yorkwalk (☎ 622303; www.yorkwalk.co.uk; adult/child £5/free) Offers a series of two-hour themed walks on an ever-growing list of themes, from the classics – Roman York, the snickelways (alleys) and City Walls – to specialised walks on chocolates and sweets, women in York, secret York and the inevitable graveyard, coffin and plague tour. Walks depart from Museum Gardens Gate on Museum St.

Festivals & Events

For a week in mid-February, York is invaded by Vikings once again as part of the **Jorvik Viking Festival** (☎ 643211; www.vikingjorvik .com; Coppergate), which features battle re-enactments, themed walks, markets and other bits of Nordic fun.

Sleeping

Beds are tough to find midsummer, even at the spiked prices of the high season. The TIC's efficient accommodation booking service charges £4, which might be the best four quid you spend in town.

Needless to say, prices go up the closer to the city centre you are. However, there are plenty of decent B&Bs on the streets north and south of Bootham, the northwest continuation of High Petergate; Grosvenor Tce, a handsome street along the railway tracks, is particularly full of them. Southwest of the town centre, there are B&Bs clustered around Scarcroft Rd, Southlands Rd and Bishopthorpe Rd.

BUDGET

York Backpackers (☎ 627720; www.yorkbackpack ers.co.uk; 88-90 Micklegate; dm/d from £13/34) In a Grade I Georgian building that was once home to the High Sheriff of Yorkshire, this large, well-equipped hostel has all the usual facilities as well as Internet access and a residents-only bar that serves cheap beer until 1am.

York Youth Hotel (☎ 625904; www.yorkyouthhotel .demon.co.uk; 11 Bishophill Senior; dm £12-15, s/d £25/44)

Offering the cheapest single rooms within the city walls, this is a good option for travellers who are on a budget but still want to stay close to the action.

York YHA Hostel (☎ 0870 770 6102/3; www.yha .org.uk; Water End, Clifton; dm £17) Once the Rowntree (Quaker confectioners) mansion, this handsome Victorian house in its own grounds is almost entirely self-contained – there's even a bar on the property. Most of the rooms are four-bed dorms. It's about a mile northwest of the TIC; turn left into Bootham, which becomes Clifton (the A19), then left into Water End. There's a riverside footpath from Lendal Bridge, but it's ill lit so avoid it after dark.

Fairfax House (☎ 434784; www.york.ac.uk; 99 Heslington Rd; ☼ Jun-Sep only) Part of the University of York, this ivy-clad building offers accommodation in standard, well-equipped rooms, but only outside of term. It is 2 miles southeast of the city. Take bus No 4.

MID-RANGE

Four High Petergate (☎ 658516; www.fourhighpeter gate.co.uk; 4 High Petergate; s/d £50/80) This stunning 18th-century house next to Bootham Bar has been converted into a gorgeous boutique hotel. Indonesian teak furniture, crisp white linen, flat-screen TV and DVD player are standard in all 14 bedrooms, even if the standard single and doubles are substantially more compact than the superior rooms. Highly recommended, for its class and location. The bistro next door is also excellent.

One3Two (☎ 600060; www.one3two.co.uk; 132 The Mount; s/d from £47.50/70; ℙ) This is how we would like all B&Bs to be. Five individually designed bedrooms, all with handcrafted teak beds (one has a particularly handsome four-poster), a flat-screen TV and DVD player, elegant old-fashioned bathrooms (but with all the modern amenities) and the kind of breakfast that a French-trained chef might put together. Pure luxury.

Dairy Guesthouse (☎ 639367; www.dairyguest house.co.uk; 3 Scarcroft Rd; s/d £32/50; ℙ) A wonderful Victorian home that has retained many of its original features, including pine doors, stained glass, and cast-iron fireplaces, but the real treat is the flower- and plant-filled courtyard, off of which are the cottage-style rooms. The name comes from the time when it served as a town dairy.

SOMETHING SPECIAL

Middlethorpe Hall (☎ 641241; www.middlethorpe.com; Bishopsthorpe Rd; s/d from £109/140; ℗) York's top spot is this breathtaking 17th-century country house set in 20 acres of parkland that was once the home of diarist Lady Mary Wortley Montagu. The rooms are spread between the main house, the restored courtyard buildings and three cottage suites. Although we preferred the grandeur of the rooms in the main house, every room is beautifully decorated with original antiques and oil paintings carefully collected so as to best reflect the period. The magnificent grounds include a white and walled garden and a small lake.

Jorvik Hotel (☎ 653511; www.jorvikhotel.co.uk; 50-52 Marygate; s/d from £36/60; ℗) This fine, family-run hotel just west of Museum Gardens has 23 comfortable – albeit slightly compact – rooms that are heavy on the floral patterns. There's also a pretty walled garden.

23 St Mary's (☎ 622738; www.23stmarys.co.uk; 23 St Mary's; s/d from £34/60; ℗) A smart and stately town house with handsome en suite rooms; some have hand-painted furniture for that country look, while others are decorated with antiques, lace and a bit of chintz.

Brontë House (☎ 621066; www.bronte-guesthouse .com; 22 Grosvenor Tce; s/d from £34/60) Five wonderful en suite rooms all decorated completely differently: particularly good is the double with a carved, 19th-century sleigh bed, William Morris wallpaper and assorted bits and bobs from another era.

Bar Convent (☎ 464902; www.bar-convent.org.uk; 17 Blossom St; s/d £37/56) England's oldest working convent (founded in 1686) offers B&B in basic rooms; only a handful are en suite. Despite the monastic comforts, there's a friendly, welcoming atmosphere about the place.

Other options:

Alcuin Lodge (☎ 632222; alcuinlodge@aol.com; 15 Sycamore Pl; d from £27) Pretty doubles in a cluttered Victorian house.

Arnot House (☎ 641966; www.arnothouseyork.co.uk; 17 Grosvenor Tce; s/d from £38/62; ℗) Four handsome if unexceptional rooms in a beautifully maintained Victorian house.

Briar Lea Guest House (☎ 635061; www.briarlea.co .uk; 8 Longfield Tce; s/d from £22/40) Clean, simple rooms and a friendly welcome in a house just off Bootham.

City Guesthouse (☎ 622483; www.cityguesthouse .co.uk; 68 Monkgate; s/d from £35/60; ℗) Very tidy house with meticulously arranged furniture and bric-a-brac; vegetarians catered for.

St Denys Hotel (☎ 622207; www.stdenyshotel.co.uk; St Denys Rd; s/d from £45/65) Slightly worn but still comfortable rooms. Good location inside the city walls.

TOP END

Judges Lodging Hotel (☎ 638733; judgeshotel@aol .com; 9 Lendal; s/d from £70/100) An elegant and excellent choice for central accommodation, this fine Georgian mansion has very tasteful rooms – despite one with a Queen Mother theme – in what was once the private home of an assizes judge.

Mount Royale (☎ 628856; www.mountroyale.co.uk; The Mount; r from £97; ℗ ⚲) A grand, William IV–listed building converted into a superb luxury hotel, complete with a solarium, beauty spa and outdoor heated tub and swimming pool. The rooms in the main house are gorgeous, but the best of the lot are the open-plan garden suites, reached via a corridor of tropical fruit trees and bougainvillea.

Dean Court Hotel (☎ 625082; www.deancourt -york.co.uk; Duncombe Pl; s/d from £90/120) With a commanding position directly across from the minster (you'll only get a church view from the superior rooms), this fine hotel has large, comfortable rooms, although we'd have to put a question mark next to some of the chintzy, pseudo-Georgian décor.

Eating

Eating well in York is not a problem – there are plenty of fine options throughout the centre; many of the city's pubs also do grub – they're listed in the Drinking section.

BUDGET

Betty's (☎ 659142; St Helen's Sq; sandwiches about £4.50, cream tea £6.50; ⏲ 9am-9pm) Afternoon tea, old-school style, in a Yorkshire institution. It's popular, the queues can get pretty long, but it's worth the wait. If you want the full treatment, go after 6pm, when a pianist adds a touch of class.

El Piano (☎ 610676; www.elpiano.co.uk; 15 Grape Lane; mains about £6; ⏲ 10am-1am Mon-Sat, noon-midnight Sun)

A vegetarian haven, this colourful, Hispanic-style spot has a lovely café downstairs and three themed rooms upstairs: check out the Moroccan room, complete with floor cushions.

Café Concerto (☎ 610478; 21 High Petergate; cakes £2-3, starters £4-6, mains £9.80-12.50; ☒ 10am-10pm) 'Music for your mouth' is the theme of this lovely café facing the minster. The walls are papered with sheet music, but it's the delicious food that makes the most noise – the chicken and avocado sandwich is sensational.

MID-RANGE

Siam House (☎ 624677; 63a Goodramgate; mains £7-10; ☒ lunch & dinner Mon-Sat, dinner only Sun) Delicious, authentic Thai food in about as authentic an atmosphere as you could muster up 6000km from Bangkok. The early bird, three-course special (£10.95) is an absolute steal.

Little Betty's (☎ 622865; 46 Stonegate; afternoon tea £10.25; ☒ 10am-5.30pm) Betty's younger sister is more demure, less frequented, but just as good; you go upstairs and back in time to what feels like the inter-war years – it's possible to spot a couple of Agatha Christie look-alikes. The afternoon tea would feed a small village.

Jinnah (☎ 659999; 105-7 Micklegate; dishes about £8; ☒ dinner only Mon-Sat, lunch & dinner Sun) This fine Indian restaurant is exceedingly popular for its creative cuisine as much as its all-you-can-eat buffet every day from 6pm and Sundays from noon.

Melton's Too (☎ 629222; 25 Walmgate; curries about £9; ☒ lunch & dinner) A very comfortable, booth-lined restaurant that purports to do modern Brit cuisine but actually serves up a terrific Thai green curry, which we highly recommend. It's the slightly scruffier younger brother to Melton's (see p586).

Rubicon (☎ 676076; 5 Little Stonegate; mains about £8; ☒ lunch & dinner) When a vegetarian restaurant can attract even the most avid carnivore with a tempting menu of imaginative dishes – why not try the cinnamon couscous and butternut squash with goat's cheese – served in a modern, airy room without ne'er a hippy wall hanging to be seen, it's bound to be a success.

Buzz Bar (☎ 640222; 20-24 Swinegate; bento boxes about £10; ☒ lunch & dinner) It was the owners' dream to open a Japanese restaurant-cum-trendy bar, and while the delicious bento box

meals are worth the struggle with the chopsticks, this place kind of falls between two stools, so it's neither restaurant nor bar.

Fiesta Mexicana (☎ 610243; 14 Clifford St; burritos £8.45; ☒ dinner) *Chimichangas, tostadas* and burritos served in a relentlessly happy atmosphere. Students and party groups on the rip add to the fiesta; it's not subtle or subdued, but when is Mexican food ever so?

TOP END

Blue Bicycle (☎ 673990; 34 Fossgate; mains £14-22; ☒ lunch & dinner) Once upon a time, this building was a well-frequented brothel; these days it serves up a different kind of fare to an equally enthusiastic crowd. French food at its finest, served in a romantic, candle-lit room, makes for a top-notch dining experience.

Melton's (☎ 634341; 7 Scarcroft Rd; mains £12-18; ☒ lunch & dinner Tue-Sat, dinner only Mon & lunch only Sun) Foodies come from far and wide to dine in one of Yorkshire's best restaurants. It tends to specialise in fish dishes but doesn't go far wrong with practically everything else, from Yorkshire beef to the asparagus risotto with pinenuts and herbs. There's an excellent lunch and early dinner set menu (£17).

Rish (☎ 622688; 7 Fossgate; mains £11-20; ☒ lunch & dinner) Hip Brit cuisine – basically traditional classics like Yorkshire fillet steak and bangers & mash given the modern once-over – served in a super-cool, contemporary room that has attracted critical kudos and customers in equal measure.

Drinking

With only a couple of exceptions, the best drinking holes in town are older, traditional pubs. In recent years, the area around Ousegate and Micklegate has gone from moribund to mental, especially at weekends.

Ackhorne (☎ 671421; 9 St Martin's Lane) Tucked away from beery, sloppy Micklegate, this locals' inn is as comfortable as old slippers. Some of the old guys here look like they've morphed into the place.

Black Swan (☎ 686911; Peasholme Green) A classic black-and-white Tudor building where you'll find decent beer, nice people and live jazz on Sundays. Nice.

Blue Bell (☎ 654904; 53 Fossgate) A tiny, tiny pub with décor dating from 1798 and a surprisingly contemporary crowd (read: lots of young people).

Casa (☎ 639971; 1a Lower Ousegate) This riverside bar with cracking views over the Ouse is our favourite of York's newer additions to the bar scene: it's very modern, with lots of blank white spaces, but not nearly as pretentious as it appears. It does, however, have a strict policy against sportswear.

King's Arms (☎ 659435; King's Staith; lunch about £5) York's best-known pub is a creaky place with a fabulous riverside location – hence its enduring popularity. A perfect spot for a summer's evening.

Ye Olde Starre (☎ 623063; 40 Stonegate) A bit of a tourist trap, but an altogether excellent pub that is popular with locals. It was used as a morgue by the Roundheads, but the atmosphere's improved since then. It has decent ales and a heated outdoor patio overlooked by the minster.

Entertainment

There are a couple of good theatres in York, a fairly interesting cinema, but as far as clubs are concerned, forget it: historic York is best enjoyed without them.

York Theatre Royal (☎ 623568; St Leonard's Pl) Stages well-regarded productions of theatre, opera and dance.

York Barbican Centre (☎ 656688; Barbican Rd) Big-name concerts in a partly pyramidal, modern building.

City Screen (☎ 541144; www.picturehouses.co.uk; 13-17 Coney St) Mainstream and art-house films.

Grand Opera House (☎ 671818; Clifford St) Despite its name puts on a wide range of productions.

Shopping

Coney St and its adjoining streets are the hub of York shopping, but the real treat for visitors are the second-hand and antiquarian bookshops, mostly clustered in two main areas, Micklegate and Fossgate.

Jack Duncan Books (☎ 641389; 36 Fossgate) Cheap paperbacks and unusual books.

Ken Spellman Booksellers (☎ 624414; 70 Micklegate) This fine shop has been selling rare, antiquarian and second-hand books since 1910.

Worm Holes Bookshop (☎ 620011; www.worm-holes .co.uk; 20 Bootham) Our favourite of York's dusty bookshops, with a decent and far-reaching selection of old and new titles.

Getting There & Away

BUS

The very useful **York Travel Bus Info Centre** (☎ 551400; 20 George Hudson St; ☼ 8.30am-5pm Mon-Fri) has complete schedule information and sells local and regional tickets. All local and regional buses stop along Rougier St, off Station Rd inside the city walls on the western side of Lendal Bridge.

National Express coaches also stop here as well as outside the train station. Tickets can be bought at the TICs. There are services to London (£22, 5¼ hours, four daily), Birmingham (£21.50, three hours, one daily) and Edinburgh (£28.50, 5½ hours, one daily).

CAR & MOTORCYCLE

You won't need a car around the city, but it comes in handy for exploring the surrounding area. Rental options include: **Europcar** (☎ 656161) by platform 1 in the train station which also rents bicycles and stores luggage (£4); **Hertz** (☎ 612586) near platform 3 in the train station; and **Practical Car & Van Rental** (☎ 624848; Tanners Moat) which is good for cheaper deals.

TRAIN

York train station is a stunning masterpiece of Victorian engineering. It also has plenty of arrivals and departures: Birmingham (£38, 2½ hours); Edinburgh (£38, 2½ hours, hourly); Leeds (£8.10, 50 minutes, hourly); London's King's Cross (£49, two hours, hourly); Manchester (£16.10, 1½ hours, six daily); and Scarborough (£9.30, 45 minutes).

Trains also go via Peterborough (£37, 1¾ hours, every 30 minutes), for Cambridge and East Anglia.

Getting Around

York is easily walked on foot. You're never really more than 20 minutes from any of the major sights or areas.

BICYCLE

The Bus Info Centre has a useful free map showing York's bike routes. If you're energetic you could pedal out to Castle Howard (15 miles), Helmsley and Rievaulx Abbey (12 miles) and Thirsk (another 12 miles), and then catch a train back to York. There's also a section of the Trans-Pennine-Trail cycle path from Bishopthorpe in York to Selby (15 miles) along the old railway line. The TICs have maps.

Two rental places are: **Bob Trotter** (☎ 622868; 13 Lord Mayor's Walk; rental per day £8), outside Monk Bar; and **Europcar** (☎ 656161; rental per day from £11).

BUS
The local bus service is provided by **First York** (☎ 622992), which sells a **day pass** (£2.20) valid on all of its local buses – although you'll hardly need it if you're sticking close to town. The Bus Info Centre has service details (see p587).

CAR & MOTORCYCLE
York gets as congested as most English cities in summer and parking in the centre can be expensive (up to £9 for a day); but most guesthouses and hotels have access to parking.

TAXI
Station Taxis (☎ 623332) has a kiosk outside the train station.

AROUND YORK
Castle Howard
Stately homes may be two a penny in England, but you'll have to try pretty damn hard to find one as breathtakingly stunning as **Castle Howard** (☎ 01653-648333; www.castle howard.co.uk; adult/child house & grounds £9.50/6.50, grounds £6.50/4.50; ☾ house 11am-4.30pm, grounds 10am-4.30pm mid-Mar–Oct), a work of supreme theatrical grandeur and audacity set in the rolling Howardian Hills with wandering peacocks on its terraces. This is one of the world's most beautiful buildings, and instantly recognisable for its starring role in *Brideshead Revisited* – which has done its popularity no end of good since the TV series first aired in the early 1980s.

When the earl of Carlisle hired his mate Sir John Vanbrugh in 1699 to design his new home, he was hiring a bloke who had no formal training and was best known as a playwright; luckily Vanbrugh hired Nicholas Hawksmoor, who had worked for Christopher Wren, as his clerk of works – not only would Hawksmoor have a big part to play in the house's design but the two would later do wonders with Blenheim Palace (p400).

If you can, try to visit on a weekday, when it's easier to find the space to appreciate this hedonistic marriage of art, architecture, landscaping and natural beauty. Wandering about the grounds, views open up over the hills, Vanbrugh's playful Temple of the Four Winds and Hawksmoor's stately mausoleum, but the great baroque house with its magnificent central cupola is an irresistible visual magnet. Inside, it is full of treasures, such as the chapel's Pre-Raphaelite stained glass.

Castle Howard is 15 miles northeast of York, 4 miles off the A64. It can be reached by several tours from York. Check with the TIC for up-to-date schedules. Yorkshire Coastliner has a useful bus service that links Leeds, York, Castle Howard, Pickering and Whitby (No 840). A day return from York costs £4.80, while a **Coastliner Freedom ticket** (adult/senior/family £10/7.50/26) is good for unlimited rides all day; buy tickets on the bus.

THIRSK
☎ 01845 / pop 9099
A handsome medieval trading town with tidy, attractive streets and a cobbled central square (Monday and Saturday are market days), Thirsk was made prosperous by its key position on two medieval trading routes: the old drove road between Scotland and York, and the route linking the Yorkshire Dales with the coast. That's all in the past, though: today, the town is all about the legacy of James Herriot, the wry Yorkshire vet adored by millions of fans of *All Creatures Great and Small.*

Thirsk does a good job as the real-life Darrowby of the books and TV series, and it should, as the real-life Herriot was in fact local vet Alf Wight, whose house and surgery has been dipped in 1940s aspic and turned into the incredibly popular **World of James Herriot** (☎ 524234; www.worldofjamesherriot .org; 23 Kirkgate; admission £4.85; ☾ 10am-6pm Apr-Oct, 11am-4pm Nov-Mar), an excellent museum full of Wight artefacts, a video documentary of his life and a re-creation of the TV show sets. It's all quite well done and you'll be in the company of true fans, many of whom have that look of pilgrimage on their faces.

Almost directly across the street is the less-frequented **Thirsk Museum** (☎ 527707; www.thirskmuseum.org; 14-16 Kirkgate; admission £1.50; ☾ 10am-4pm Mon-Wed, Fri & Sat), which manages to cram a collection of items from Neolithic times to the Herriot era into a tiny house where Thomas Lord (of Lord's Cricket Ground fame) was born in 1755.

Thirsk's **TIC** (☎ 522755; thirsk@ytbtic.co.uk; 49 Market Pl; ⏰ 10am-5pm Easter-Oct, 11am-4pm Nov-Easter) is on the main square.

Sleeping & Eating
The TIC books B&Bs and has a handy accommodation list.

The Three Tuns Hotel (☎ 523124; www.the-three-tuns-thirsk.co.uk; Market Pl; s/d from £45/65; mains from £6.50) A fairly imposing 18th-century coaching inn best known as having hosted the Wordsworths on their honeymoon in 1802. The bedrooms have changed somewhat since then, and today offer comfortable if unspectacular accommodation.

Getting There & Away
There are frequent daily buses from York (45 minutes).

Thirsk is well served by trains on the line between York and Middlesbrough. However, the train station is a mile west of town and the only way to cover that distance is on foot or by **taxi** (☎ 522473).

RIPON
☎ 01765 / pop 16,468
A small town with a huge cathedral, Ripon has winding streets and a broad, symmetrical market place lined by Georgian houses. Every evening at 9pm the Ripon Hornblower 'sets the watch' with a hoot of his horn by the central obelisk – a tradition that apparently dates from 886 when Alfred the Great gave the town a horn so as to sound the changing of the guard. These days, the ceremony is strictly for tourists. Much more interesting goings-on occur on Thursdays, when the busy market takes place.

Bus No 36 comes from Leeds via Harrogate every 20 minutes. The **TIC** (☎ 604625; Minster Rd; ⏰ 10am-1pm & 1.30-5.30pm Mon-Sat, 1-4pm Sun) is near the cathedral and has information on local walks, and will book accommodation.

Sights
Ripon Cathedral (☎ 602072; www.riponcathedral.org.uk; suggested donation £3, treasury £1; ⏰ 7.30am-6.30pm, evensong 5.30pm) is well worth exploring. The first church on this site was built in 660 by St Wilfred, and its rough, humble crypt

lies intact beneath today's soaring edifice. Above ground, the building dates from the 11th century, with its noble and harmonious Early English west front clocking in at 1220. Medieval additions have resulted in the medley of Gothic styles throughout, culminating in the rebuilding of the central tower – work that was never completed. It was not until 1836 that this impressive parish church got cathedral status. Look out for the fantastical creatures decorating the animated medieval misericords, believed to have inspired Lewis Carroll – his father was canon here (1852–68).

Until 1888 Ripon was responsible for its own peacekeeping, and this has resulted in a grand array of punishing attractions. **Law & Order Museums** (☎ 690799; 7-day combined ticket adult/child £5/free; ⏰ 11am-4pm Apr-Jun, 10am-4pm Jul & Aug, 1-4pm Sep, noon-3pm Oct) combine the **Courthouse Museum**, a 19th-century courthouse (recognisable from sappy TV series *Heartbeat*), the **Prison & Police Museum**, which includes the medieval punishment yard and the clammy cells where no-good Victorians ended up, and the **Workhouse Museum**, which shows the grim treatment of poor vagrants from the 19th century to WWII.

AROUND RIPON
Fountains Abbey & Studley Royal Water Gardens
Sheltered in the secluded valley of the River Skell are two of Yorkshire's most beautiful attractions and an absolute must on your northern itinerary. The strangely obsessive and beautiful formal **Studley Royal water gardens** were built in the 19th century so as to enhance the extensive ruins of the 12th-century **Fountains Abbey** (NT; ☎ 01765-608888; www.fountainsabbey.org.uk; abbey, hall & garden admission £5.50; ⏰ 10am-4pm Jan-Mar & Oct-Dec, 10am-6pm Apr-Sep). Together they create a breathtaking picture of pastoral elegance and tranquillity that have made them the most visited of all the National Trust's pay-in properties and Yorkshire's only World Heritage Site.

After falling out with the Benedictines of York in 1132, a band of rebel monks came here to what was then a desolate and unyielding patch of land to found their own monastery. Struggling to make it on their own, they were formally adopted by the Cistercians in 1135: by the middle of the 13th century the new abbey had become

---

THE WHITE MONKS

Founded at Cîteaux in Burgundy in 1098, the Cistercians were hardcore. They rejected the free-lovin', toga-party antics of those wild and crazy Benedictines in favour of an even more austere form of living: they lived in the most inhospitable parts of the kingdom and refused to wear underwear. Their habits were made of undyed sheep's wool – hence their nickname – and their diet was barely above starvation. Nobody complained either, because they were committed to long periods of silence and eight daily services. But with so much time given over to starving themselves in silent prayer, there was no room for work, so they ordained lay brothers who tilled their lands, worked their lead mines and tended their flocks of sheep. And so it was that their commitment to a super-disciplined 1st-century Christianity made them powerful and rich – and encouraged other orders like the Augustinians and their old nemesis the Benedictines to follow suit. The Scottish Wars and the Black Death threw an economic spanner in the works though, and they were eventually forced to lease their lands to tenant farmers and live off the proceeds. When Henry VIII went to war with the monasteries in 1536, he used their perceived greed and laziness as partial justification. Surely a case of king pot calling the white kettles black?

---

the most successful Cistercian venture in the country. It was during this time that most of today's ruins were built, including the church's nave and transepts, outlying buildings and the church's eastern end (the tower was added in the late 15th century).

After the dissolution (p35) the estate was sold into private hands and between 1598 and 1611 Fountains Hall was built with stone from the abbey ruins. The hall and ruins were united with the Studley Royal Estate in 1768.

The main house of Studley Royal burnt down in 1946 but the superb landscaping, with its serene artificial lakes, survives hardly changed from the 18th century. Studley Royal was owned by John Aislabie (once Chancellor of the Exchequer), who dedicated his life to creating the park after a financial scandal saw him expelled from parliament.

Fountains Abbey is 4 miles west of Ripon off the B6265. The **deer park** (admission free, car park £2) opens during daylight hours. **St Mary's Church** (☯ 1-5pm Apr-Sep) features occasional concerts. There are free one-hour **guided tours** (11am & 2.30pm Apr-Oct & 3.30pm Apr-Sep, garden 2pm Apr-Oct).

Public transport is limited to summer Sunday services; call for details of any buses that might be running.

HARROGATE
☎ 01423 / pop 85,128

Pretty, prim and immaculate, the Victorian spa town of Harrogate is pervaded by an old-fashioned Englishness that the local authorities have gone to great lengths to highlight and maintain. Once people flocked here for health cures, when sulphur water was all the rage, but now they head for its sweeter-smelling massive flower shows, which alongside frequent conventions have helped the town maintain its prosperity. Floral displays are at their height in spring and autumn, but there are extensive gardens all around town that make for a beautiful stroll at any time of year, and one that takes you back to another era – one with which many of the town's modern-day visitors were familiar as children.

Harrogate's most famous association is with Agatha Christie, who fled here incognito after her marriage broke down in 1926. The town's little-changed, lace-curtained façade appears an appropriate setting for the queen of quintessentially English crime to have sought some privacy.

The town is also close to the eastern edge of Yorkshire Dales National Park, and has many good hotels, B&Bs and restaurants. The glorious Turkish baths are not to be missed.

Orientation & Information

Harrogate is almost surrounded by gardens including the 80-hectare Stray in the south. The mostly pedestrianised shopping streets, Oxford and Cambridge Sts, are lined with smart shops and the **post office** (11 Cambridge Rd; ☯ 9am-5.30pm Mon-Sat). The **TIC** (☎ 537300; www .harrogate.gov.uk/tourism; Crescent Rd; ☯ 9am-5pm Mon-Sat, 10am-1pm Sun 9am-5pm Mon-Fri, 9am-4pm Sat Oct-Mar) is in the Royal Baths Assembly Rooms; staff can give information about free historical walking tours offered daily from Easter to October.

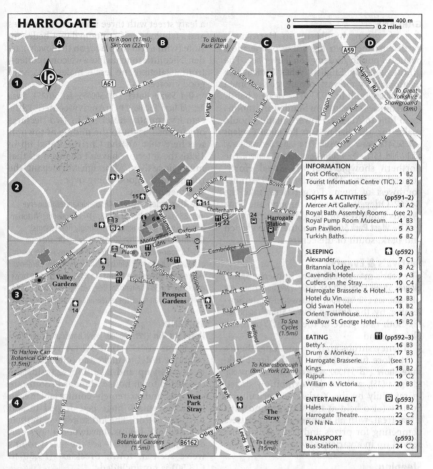

HARROGATE

0 — 400 m
0 — 0.2 miles

INFORMATION	
Post Office..................................	1 B2
Tourist Information Centre (TIC)..2	B2

SIGHTS & ACTIVITIES	(pp591–2)
Mercer Art Gallery.....................	3 A2
Royal Bath Assembly Rooms....(see 2)	
Royal Pump Room Museum.......	4 B3
Sun Pavilion.............................	5 A3
Turkish Baths...........................	6 B2

SLEEPING	(p592)
Alexander..................................	7 C1
Britannia Lodge.........................	8 A2
Cavendish Hotel.........................	9 A3
Cutlers on the Stray..................	10 C4
Harrogate Brasserie & Hotel......	11 B2
Hotel du Vin.............................	12 B3
Old Swan Hotel.........................	13 B2
Orient Townhouse......................	14 A3
Swallow St George Hotel............	15 B2

EATING	(pp592–3)
Betty's.....................................	16 B3
Drum & Monkey........................	17 B3
Harrogate Brasserie.............(see 11)	
Kings.......................................	18 B2
Rajput......................................	19 C2
William & Victoria.....................	20 B3

ENTERTAINMENT	(p593)
Hales.......................................	21 B2
Harrogate Theatre.....................	22 C2
Po Na Na..................................	23 B2

TRANSPORT	(p593)
Bus Station...............................	24 C2

Sights & Activities

THE WATERS

Take the plunge into the waters and the past in the fabulously tiled **Turkish Baths** (☎ 556746; www.harrogate.co.uk/turkishbaths; admission £12; ☽ 9am-9pm) in the Royal Baths Assembly Rooms. The mock Moorish facility is gloriously Victorian and offers a range of watery delights – steam rooms, saunas, and so on. A visit should last at least two hours.

There's a complicated schedule of opening hours that are at turns single sex and mixed pairs – call for more details. You can prebook a range of reasonably priced massages and other therapies.

Just around the corner is the ornate **Royal Pump Room Museum** (☎ 556188; Crown Pl;

admission £2; ☽ 10am-5pm Mon-Sat, 2-5pm Sun Apr-Oct, 10am-4pm Mon-Sat, 2-4pm Sun Nov-Mar), built in 1842 over the most famous of the sulphur springs. It gives an insight into how the phenomenon created the town and the illustrious visitors that it attracted, and there's a chance to tuck into some stinky spa water.

MERCER ART GALLERY

Another surviving spa building, the Promenade Room, is now home to this elegant **gallery** (☎ 556188; Swan Rd; admission free; ☽ 10am-5pm Tue-Sat, 2-5pm Sun), a stately space that hosts constantly changing exhibitions of visual art; throughout 2004 the main show was devoted to memories of childhood.

YORKSHIRE

GARDENS

A huge green thumbs-up to Harrogate's gardeners; the town has some of the most beautiful public gardens you'll ever see. The quintessentially English **Valley Gardens** are overlooked by the vast, ornate, glass-domed **Sun Pavilion**, built in 1933. The nearby bandstand houses concerts on Sunday afternoons from June to August. Flower-fanatics should make for the **Harlow Carr Botanical Gardens** (☎ 565418; www.rhs.org.uk; Crag Lane, Beckwithshaw; adult/child £5/1; ☼ 9.30am-6pm, dusk if earlier), the northern showpiece of the Royal Horticultural Society. The gardens are 1½ miles southwest of town. To get here, take the B6162 Otley Rd or walk through the Pine Woods southwest of the Valley Gardens.

The **West Park Stray** is another fine garden and park, south of the centre.

Festivals & Events

The year's main event is the immense **Spring Flower Show** (☎ 0870 758 3333; www.flowershow.org .uk; admission £10; late Apr), followed in late September by the **Autumn Flower Show** (admission £8). Both take place at the Great Yorkshire Showground.

If fancy shrubs aren't your thing, there's a lot more fun to be had at the **Great Yorkshire Show** (☎ 541000; www.greatyorkshireshow.org; admission £15), a three-day exhibition staged in mid-July by the Yorkshire Agricultural Society (also held at the showground). It's a real treat, with all manner of farm critters competing for prizes and last year's losers served up in a variety of ways.

Sleeping

BUDGET

Bilton Park (☎ 863121; biltonpark@tcsmail.net; Village Farm, Bilton; tent £10; ☼ Apr-Oct) A convenient campsite 2 miles north of town. Take bus No 201, 203 or 204 from the bus station.

MID-RANGE

Cutlers on the Stray (☎ 524471; www.cutlers-web .co.uk; 19 West Park; d from £80; Ⓟ) A touch of the Mediterranean comes to Yorkshire in the shape of this stylish boutique hotel and brasserie in a converted coaching inn. Yellows, creams and reds are used to great effect in the rooms, which are thoroughly modern in design. Some rooms have Stray views.

Britannia Lodge (☎ 508482; www.britlodge.co.uk; 16 Swan Rd; s/d £50/80; Ⓟ) A beautiful home on a leafy street with three immaculate doubles and a fabulous, self-contained two-bedroom suite (with a real fireplace) on the lovely garden. Nice little touches like a welcome coffee – from a cafetiere, no less – make this a very good choice.

Old Swan Hotel (☎ 500055; fax 501154; Swan Rd; s/d from £60/80; Ⓟ) An ivy-coated 18th-century country hotel set in two hectares of gardens – right in the middle of town. It was here that Agatha Christie holed up in 1926; the interiors haven't changed all that much since then. Although still elegant, the rooms need a good going over.

Other options:

The Alexander (☎ 503348; thealexander@amserve .net; 88 Franklin Rd; s/d £28/58; Ⓟ) Handsome Victorian mansion with immaculate, unstintingly floral rooms.

Cavendish Hotel (☎ 509637; 3 Valley Dr; s/d from £35/55, four-poster £70) Comfortable rooms with a touch of flounce, the best of which overlook the Valley Gardens.

Harrogate Brasserie & Hotel (☎ 505041; www.brass erie.co.uk; 28-30 Cheltenham Pde; s/d from £52/85) Has 14 stylish rooms, an excellent restaurant and frequent live jazz.

TOP END

Hotel Du Vin (☎ 856800; www.hotelduvin.com; Prospect Pl; r/ste from £95/145; Ⓟ ▣) A very stylish boutique hotel to make the other lodgings in town sit up and take notice. Inside the converted town house, standard rooms are spacious and extremely comfortable; each has a trademark huge bed draped in soft Egyptian cotton. The loft suites – with their exposed oak beams, hardwood floors and designer bathrooms – are the nicest rooms we've seen in town. Breakfast (£9.50 and £13.50) is not included.

Orient Townhouse (☎ 565818; www.orienttown house.com; 51 Valley Drive; s/d from £105/130) The Eastern flavours of this handsome town house don't extend much further than the duvet covers and the odd bit of decoration, but this fine guesthouse is an excellent choice if you're looking for a bit of pampering.

Swallow St George Hotel (☎ 561431; www.swal low-hotels.com; 1 Ripon Rd; s/d £55/100; Ⓟ ▣) Big Edwardian building across from the TIC with spacious albeit slightly characterless rooms. There's a health club and indoor pool.

Eating

BUDGET

Betty's (☎ 502746; www.bettysandtaylors.co.uk; 1 Parliament St; mains under £7; ☼ 9am-9pm) A classic tearoom dating from 1919, founded by a Swiss immigrant confectioner who got on a wrong train, ended up in Yorkshire and decided to stay. It heaves with scone groupies (tea and scones about £5). A pianist tinkles among the teacups from 6pm.

Harrogate Theatre (Oxford St; sandwiches about £5; 🕙 10am-6pm Mon-Sat) A grand old café that's popular at lunch time.

MID-RANGE

Drum & Monkey (☎ 502650; 5 Montpellier Gardens; mains about £8-11; 🕙 lunch & dinner Mon-Sat) Our favourite restaurant in town serves up mouthwatering seafood dishes to an enthusiastic and loyal clientele.

Harrogate Brasserie (☎ 505041; 30 Cheltenham Pde; 2-course meal £15; 🕙 dinner) There's more than a hint of New Orleans at this friendly, popular brasserie serving up some pretty good French cuisine. Photos of jazz greats adorn the red walls to complement the regular live performances.

William & Victoria (☎ 506883; 6 Cold Bath Rd; mains £8-16; 🕙 Mon-Fri lunch, Mon-Sat dinner) A dark and cosy, wood-lined wine bar that serves traditional British food.

Kings (☎ 568600; 24 Kings Rd; starters £5.50, mains about £13; 🕙 lunch & dinner Mon-Sat) A light and airy restaurant set in an old Victorian house offering inventive fish dishes and some succulent meat options.

Rajput (☎ 562113; 9-11 Cheltenham Pde; mains £6-9; 🕙 dinner) Tiptop Indian cuisine in a friendly, comfortable setting.

Entertainment

Hales (☎ 725571; 1-3 Crescent Rd) Have a decent pint of ale or some filling pub grub by flickering gaslight at this traditional pub.

Po Na Na (☎ 509758; 2 Kings Rd; free before 11pm; 🕙 10pm-2am Wed-Sat) Harrogate's only half-decent late bar-club, with a none-too outlandish soundtrack of funky stuff, from cheesy '70s disco to contemporary house.

Harrogate Theatre (☎ 502116; www.harrogatetheatre.com; Oxford St) Drama, comedy and music staged in Art Deco surroundings.

Getting There & Away

Trains serve Harrogate from Leeds (£5, 50 minutes, about half-hourly) and York (£5, 45 minutes, 10 to 12 daily).

National Express bus No 561 runs from Leeds (£2.75, 50 minutes, six daily). Bus No

383 comes from Ripon (£2.75, 25 minutes, four daily). Bus Nos 36 and 36A also run regularly between Ripon, Harrogate and Leeds.

SCARBOROUGH

☎ 01723 / pop 57,649

The doyenne of English seaside resorts, Scarborough is spectacularly set above two beautiful white-sand bays and is graced by a host of Georgian, Victorian and Edwardian buildings, topped by the hulk of a castle. It sounds very inviting, but once you're on the waterfront the seaside kitsch overwhelms what is left of Scarborough's more genteel side: neon-lit amusement arcades and casinos draw punters away from the donkey rides and tacky souvenir stands.

The town might have remained forever in medieval obscurity were it not for the announcement in 1620 that the waters were medicinal, making it one of the first places in England to popularise sea bathing. From the mid-18th century it was a successful seaside resort; it is the vestiges of that era that are most interesting about Scarborough today. Its renowned theatre is the base of England's popular playwright, Alan Ayckbourn, whose plays always premier here.

Orientation

Modern suburbs sprawl west of the town centre, which is above the old town and the South Bay. The town is on a plateau above the beaches; cliff lifts, steep streets and footpaths provide the links. The Victorian development to the south is separated from the town centre by a steep valley, which has been landscaped and is crossed by high bridges.

The main shopping street, Westborough, has a dramatic view of the castle rising in the distance. The North Bay is home to all the tawdry seashore amusements; the South Bay is more genteel. The old town lies between St Mary's Church, the castle and the Old Harbour.

Information

Complete Computing (☎ 500501; 14 Northway) For your Internet needs.

Laundrette (☎ 375763; 48 North Marine Rd)

Post office (11-15 Aberdeen Walk; 🕙 9am-5.30pm Mon-Fri, 9am-12.30pm Sat)

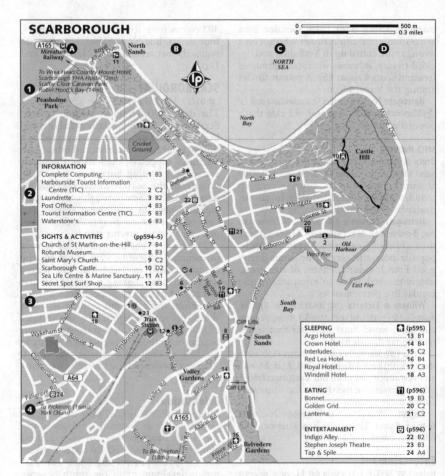

SCARBOROUGH

INFORMATION
Complete Computing.................................1 B3
Harbourside Tourist Information
  Centre (TIC)...2 C2
Laundrette..3 B2
Post Office..4 B3
Tourist Information Centre (TIC)........5 B3
Waterstone's..6 B3

SIGHTS & ACTIVITIES   (pp594–5)
Church of St Martin-on-the-Hill........7 B4
Rotunda Museum...................................8 B3
Saint Mary's Church.............................9 C2
Scarborough Castle.............................10 D2
Sea Life Centre & Marine Sanctuary..11 A1
Secret Spot Surf Shop.........................12 B3

SLEEPING   (p595)
Argo Hotel...13 B1
Crown Hotel..14 B4
Interludes...15 C2
Red Lea Hotel......................................16 B4
Royal Hotel..17 C3
Windmill Hotel.....................................18 A3

EATING   (p596)
Bonnet..19 B3
Golden Grid...20 C2
Lanterna...21 C2

ENTERTAINMENT   (p596)
Indigo Alley..22 B2
Stephen Joseph Theatre....................23 B3
Tap & Spile...24 A4

TIC (☎ 373333; www.discoveryorkshirecoast.com)
Valley Bridge Rd (Unit 3, Pavilion House ⏲ 9.30am-6pm
Apr-Oct, 10am-4.30pm Mon-Sat Nov-Mar); Harbourside
(⏲ 9.30am-6pm Apr-Oct, 10am-4.30pm Sun Nov-Mar)
Waterstone's (☎ 500414; 97-8 Westborough) For
books and magazines.

Sights & Activities

Scarborough is not exclusively about bingo,
buckets and burgers – there are a number
of sights to distract you from the beach and
its goings-on.

Battered **Scarborough Castle** (EH; ☎ 372451;
admission £3.20; ⏲ 10am-6pm Apr-Sep, 10am-4pm Thu-
Mon Nov-Mar) has excellent views across the
bays and the town. There's been some kind
of fortification here for nearly 2500 years,

but the current structure dates from the
12th century. Legend has it that Richard III
loved the views so much his ghost just keeps
coming back. More corporeal beings can
get to it via a 13th-century barbican.

Below the castle is **St Mary's Church**
(☎ 500541; Castle Rd; ⏲ 10am-4pm Mon-Fri, 1-4pm Sun
May-Sep), dating from 1180 and rebuilt in the
15th and 17th centuries, with some interesting 14th-century chapels. Anne Brontë is
buried in the churchyard.

Of all the family-oriented attractions
on the bays, the best of the lot is the **Sea
Life Centre & Marine Sanctuary** (☎ 376125; www
.sealife.co.uk; Scalby Mills; adult/child £7.50/5; ⏲ 10am-
6pm) overlooking North Bay. Here you can
explore the Jurassic seas, coral reefs and

the world of the octopus with aplomb. The rescue work done with woe-begone seals and sea turtles is quite uplifting.

The Pre-Raphaelite, high Victorian interior of the **Church of St Martin-on-the-Hill** (☎ 360437; Albion Rd; ☺ 7.30am-5.30pm) was worked on by Burne-Jones, Morris, Maddox Brown and Rossetti.

The **Rotunda Museum** (☎ 374839; admission £2.50; ☺ 10am-5pm Tue-Sun Jun-Sep, 11am-4pm Tue, Sat & Sun Oct-May) traces local matters from prehistory to the present, and has changing exhibitions on themes such as the seaside and pirates.

There are some decent waves out in the North Sea. The friendly **Secret Spot Surf Shop** (☎ 500467; www.secretspot.co.uk; 4 Pavilion Tce) can advise on conditions, recommend places for lessons and rent all manner of gear. The best time for waves is September to May.

See p604 for more information about the 20-mile Whitby–Scarborough Coastal Cycle Trail.

Sleeping

If something stays still long enough in town, it'll offer B&B; competition is intense and it's difficult to choose between places. In such a tough market, multi-night stay special offers are two a penny, which means that single-night rates are the highest of all.

BUDGET

Scarborough YHA Hostel (☎ 0870 7706022; fax 7706023; www.yha.org.uk; Burniston Rd; dm £10.25; ☺ Apr-Aug) This simply idyllic hostel in a converted water mill from around 1600 has comfortable four- and six-bed dorms as well as a lounge, self-catering kitchen and laundry. It is 2 miles north of town along the A166 to Whitby. Take bus No 3, 12 or 21.

Argo Hotel (☎ 375745; 134 North Marine Rd; s/d £20/40) Pleasant, small, floral rooms overlooking the cricket ground; it's especially popular with pensioners, who get a special discount in the off season.

Camping

Scalby Close Caravan Park (☎ 366212; Burniston Rd; pitches £8-12; ☺ Easter-Oct only) A small park about 2 miles north of town with plenty of pitches for vans and tents as well as five fixed holiday caravans for rent (£63 per night). The park has all the usual facilities. Take bus No 12 or 21.

MID-RANGE

Windmill Hotel (☎ 372735; www.windmill-hotel.co.uk; Mill St; s/d from £35/58; P) A beautifully converted 18th-century mill in the middle of town offers tight-fitting but comfortable doubles around a cobbled courtyard – the upstairs rooms have a small veranda.

Interludes (☎ 360513; www.interludeshotel.co.uk; 32 Princess St; s/d £34/60; P) Owners Ian and Bob have a flair for the theatrical, and have brought it to bear with incredible success on this lovely, gay-friendly Georgian home plastered with old theatrical posters, prints and other thespian mementos. The individually decorated rooms are given to colourful flights of fancy that can't but put a smile on your face. Children, alas, are not welcome.

Red Lea Hotel (☎ 362431; www.redleahotel.co.uk; Prince of Wales Tce; s/d £45/78; P ☀) An elegant terrace of six Georgian houses makes up this popular choice, which has large rooms rich in velvet drapes, lush carpets and king-size beds. Downstairs is a heated, kidney-shaped swimming pool and, next door, a small leisure centre with sauna, sunbeds and a gym.

TOP END

Wrea Head Country House Hotel (☎ 378211; www.englishrosehotels.co.uk; Barmoor La, Scalby; s/d £75/130) This fabulous country house about 2 miles north of the centre is straight out of *Remains of the Day*. The 20 individually styled bedrooms have canopied, four-poster beds, plush fabrics and delicate furnishings, while the leather couches in the book-cased, wood-heavy lounges seem fit for important discussions over cigars and expensive brandy.

Royal Hotel (☎ 364333; www.englishrosehotels.co.uk; St Nicholas St; s/d from £59/106) Scarborough's most famous hotel has a lavish Regency interior, grand staircase for Shirley Bassey–style entrances, and smart rooms, some with sea views. The perfectly comfortable but characterless rooms just don't compare with the grandeur of the public spaces.

Crown Hotel (☎ 373491; www.chariethotels.co.uk; Esplanade; s/d from £57/104; P ☀) This grand old hotel opened its nearly regal doors in 1845 and has been going strong ever since, changing constantly with the times. It looks fancy and Victorian, but inside it's just another comfortable business-style hotel. Rooms with sea views cost £10 extra.

Eating

Lanterna (☎ 363616; 33 Queen St; mains £12-18; ☾ Mon-Sat) A snug Italian spot that specialises in fresh local seafood as well as favourites from the Old Boot; it's the place to go for that special night out in Scarborough.

Golden Grid (☎ 360922; 4 Sandside; cod from £5.50; lunch & dinner Apr-Oct, to 5pm Nov-Mar) Who ever said fish and chips can't be eaten with dignity and grace has never set foot in the Golden Grid, which has been doling them out since 1883. It's bright and traditional, with starched white tablecloths.

Bonnet (☎ 361033; 38-40 Huntriss Row; mains from £5; café ☾ 9am-5.30pm, restaurant ☾ Fri & Sat dinner) An excellent tearoom, open since 1880, with delicious cakes, a serene courtyard, and adjoining shop selling handmade chocolates.

Drinking

Indigo Alley (☎ 375823; North Marine Rd) A small, welcoming pub with a good range of beers. Regular live jazz and blues and Monday theatre in a limpet-sized curtained-off space.

Tap & Spile (☎ 363837; 94 Falsgrave Rd) This relaxed pub has a few rooms and a good selection of Yorkshire ales.

Entertainment

Stephen Joseph Theatre (☎ 370541; www.sjt.uk .com; Westborough; tickets about £9) Stages a good range of drama. Renowned chronicler of middle-class mores Alan Ayckbourn premieres his plays here.

Getting There & Away

Reasonably frequent Scarborough & District buses (No 128) go along the A170 from Pickering (£4.80, one hour) and Helmsley (£5.50, 1½ hours). They leave from Westborough.

There are regular buses, Nos 93 and 93A (via Robin Hood's Bay), from Whitby (£4.80, one hour). No 843 arrives from Leeds (£13.80, eight to 12 daily) via York (£10).

There are regular trains from Hull (£10.40, one hour 20 minutes, hourly), Leeds (£17.20, one hour 20 minutes, six to eight daily) and York (£9.30, 45 minutes, hourly).

Getting Around

Victorian funicular lifts slope up and down Scarborough's steep cliffs to the beach daily from February till the end of October. Local buses leave from the western end of Westborough and outside the train station.

For a taxi call ☎ 361009; £4 should get you to most places in town.

FILEY

☎ 01723 / pop 6468

Filey is a quiet beach town with a respectable, vaguely refined air. Formerly a fishing village, since the 18th and 19th centuries it's been providing a more sedate and genteel alternative to its brasher neighbours, Bridlington and Scarborough. An important walking centre, it's the hub for the Cleveland Way, and the Wolds Way (p572) finishes here, at the dramatic coastal outcrop of Filey Brigg. Five miles of sandy beach offer ample scope for paddling weary feet. Murray St is lined with shops and links the train and bus stations to the beach.

Filey's **TIC** (☎ 518000; www.discoveryorkshirecoast .com; John St; ☾ 10am-6pm May-Sep, 10am-12.30pm & 1-4.30pm Oct-Apr) is well appointed and helpful, booking local accommodation.

Filey is served by trains on the line between Hull and Bridlington to the south and Scarborough to the north (every two hours). The bare-bones station is about a mile west of the beach. The town is 7 miles south of Scarborough on the A165. Bus Nos 120 and 121 come from Scarborough (30 minutes, hourly).

NORTH YORK MOORS NATIONAL PARK

The wild and often windswept expanse of the North York Moors is – in the lexicon of the Brontë fan – Heathcliff country: rolling whale-back hills cut by deep green valleys sheltering isolated farms and villages and the odd castle and ruined abbey. The ridge-top roads and high open moors afford terrific views of the dramatic countryside, while to the east the moors suddenly give way to an even more dramatic coastline of sheer cliffs, sheltered bays and long sandy beaches.

One of the principal glories of the moors is the vast expanse of heather, which flowers in an explosion of pink and mauve from July to early September. Outside the flowering season, the browns-tending-to-purple on the hills – in vivid contrast to the deep greens of the Dales – give the park its characteristic moody appearance.

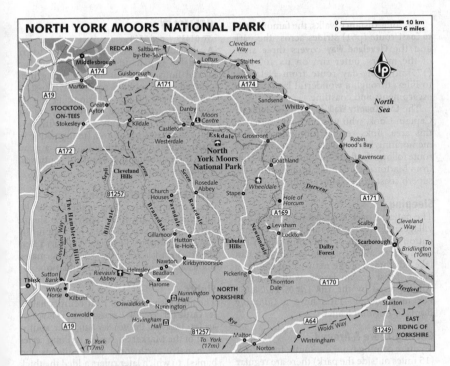

Orientation & Information

The park covers 553 sq miles (1432 sq km), with hills and steep escarpments forming the northern and western boundaries, and the eastern limit marked by the North Sea coast. The southern border runs roughly parallel to the A170 Thirsk–Scarborough road, and the main gateway towns are Helmsley and Pickering in the south, and Whitby in the northeast – all with good TICs. The national park also runs TICs (called visitor centres) at Sutton Bank, Danby and Robin Hood's Bay. Although outside the park, Scarborough is another good gateway (opposite).

The national park produces the very useful *Moors & Coast* visitor guide (50p), available at TICs, hotels etc, with information on things to see and do and an accommodation listing. The park website at www.moors .uk.net is even more comprehensive.

Activities

Several ideas for short walks and rides (from a few hours to all day) are suggested in this section, and TICs stock an excellent

range of walking leaflets (around 50p), as well as more comprehensive walking and cycling guidebooks.

CYCLING

Once you've puffed up the escarpment, the North York Moors make fine cycling country, with ideal quiet lanes through the valleys and scenic roads over the hills. There's also a great selection of tracks and former railways for mountain bikes.

WALKING

There are over 1400 miles (2300km) of walking paths and tracks crisscrossing the moors. The best walking opportunities are along the western escarpment and the cliff tops on the coast. The green and tranquil valleys are also ideal for a spot of relaxed rambling, although, for avid walkers, the broad ridges and rolling high ground of the moors can be a bit featureless after a few hours and for that reason this area is not as popular as the Yorkshire Dales or the Lake District – a plus if you're looking for peace and quiet.

YORKSHIRE

For long-distance walks, the famous **Coast to Coast** route (p61) strides across the park and the **Cleveland Way** covers three sides of the moors' outer rim on its 109-mile (175km), nine-day route from Helmsley to Filey, through a wonderful landscape of escarpments and coastline.

The **Cook Country Walk**, named for explorer Captain Cook, who was born and raised in this area, links several monuments commemorating his life. This 40-mile three-day route follows the flanks of the Cleveland Hills from Marton (near Middlesbrough), then the superb coast from Staithes south to Whitby.

Sleeping

The national park is ringed with towns and villages, all with a good range of accommodation – although options thin out in the central area. Walkers and outdoor fans can take advantage of the network of camping barns. Most are on farms, with bookings administered by the **YHA** (☎ 0870 870 8808). For more details TICs have a *Camping Barns in England* leaflet.

Getting There & Around

If you're coming from the south, from York (15 miles outside the park) there are regular buses to Helmsley, Pickering, Scarborough and Whitby.

From the north, head for Middlesbrough, then take the Esk Valley railway line through the northern moors to Whitby, via Grosmont and several other villages which make useful bases. A second line, the North Yorkshire Moors Railway (NYMR), runs through the park from Pickering to Grosmont. Using these two railway lines, much of the moors area is easily accessible for those without wheels.

The highly useful **Moorsbus** (www.moorsbus .net) operates on Sunday from May to October, daily from mid-July to late August or early September, and is ideal for reaching out-of-the-way spots. Pick up a timetable and route map from TICs. A standard Moorsbus day pass costs £2.50, and for £12.50 the pass covers you on the Esk Valley and NYMR trains too – a good deal if you plan to really make a day of it. Family tickets and one-off fares for short journeys are also available.

Call the national **Traveline** (☎ 0870 608 2608) for all public bus and train information.

HELMSLEY

☎ 01439 / pop 1559

A classic North Yorkshire market town, Helmsley is a handsome place made up of old houses and historic coaching inns centred on a cobbled square that hosts a market every Friday. Overlooking the lot is a fine Norman castle, and nearby are the superb ruins of Rievaulx Abbey. With several good walks in the area (many taking in historical sights), Helmsley makes a good base for exploring this beautiful southwest corner of the moors.

Orientation & Information

The centre of everything is the Market Pl; all four sides are lined with twee shops, cosy pubs and several cafés. The helpful **TIC** (☎ 770173; www.ryedale.gov.uk; ☯ 9.30am-5.30pm Mar-Oct, 10am-4pm Fri-Sun Nov-Feb) sells maps, books and helps with accommodation.

Sights

The impressive ruins of 12th-century **Helmsley Castle** (EH; ☎ 770442; admission £4; ☯ 10am-6pm Apr-Oct, 10am-4pm Thu-Mon Nov-Mar), just southwest of the Market Sq, have a striking series of massive earthworks (deep ditches and banks), to which later rulers added the thick stone walls and defensive towers – only one tooth-shaped tower survives today. In 2004 a new visitor centre and parts of the castle remains were opened, which include a partial reconstruction of an Elizabethan room.

Just outside the castle, **Helmsley Walled Garden** would be just another plant and produce centre, were it not for its dramatic position and its fabulous selection of flowers, fruits and vegetables – some of which are quite rare – not to mention the herbs, including 40 varieties of mint. If you're into horticulture with a historical twist, this is Eden.

South of the castle stretches the superb landscape of **Duncombe Park** with the grand stately home of **Duncombe Park House** (☎ 770213; www.duncombepark.com; house & grounds admission £6.50, park only £2; ☯ 11am-5.30pm Thu-Sun late Apr-Oct) at its heart. From the house and formal gardens, wide grassy walkways and terraces lead through woodland to mock-classical temples, while longer walking trails are set out in the parkland – now protected as a nature reserve. The house, ticket office

---

SOMETHING SPECIAL

Star Inn (☎ 770397; www.thestarathome.co.uk; Harome; mains £10-17; r £130-195; ☾ lunch & dinner Tue-Sat)
This thatched cottage pub about 2 miles south of Helmsley just off the A170 is like hitting the rustic gastro-jackpot. In the middle is the kind of pub you could happily get slowly sloshed in, but the only thing to tear you away is the Michelin-starred feast that awaits you in the dining room. Each dish is a delicious rendering of some local favourite with a flight of fancy to make it really special: how about Nawton-bred middle white pig casserole with baked apples, black pudding and sage & Somerset brandy cream? You won't want to leave, and the good news is you don't have to: the adjacent lodge has eight magnificent bedrooms, each decorated in classic but luxurious country style. If we could, we'd live here.

---

and information centre are 1½ miles south of town, an easy walk through the park. You could easily spend a day here.

Activities
Of the numerous walks in Duncombe Park, the 3½-mile route to Rievaulx Abbey is the real star. The TIC can provide route leaflets, and advise on buses if you don't want to walk both ways. This route is also the overture to the Cleveland Way (described under Activities, p597). Cycling to Rievaulx Abbey is also possible, but the roads are quite busy; a better option for cyclists is the network of quiet (and relatively flat) country lanes east of Helmsley.

Sleeping & Eating
Helmsley YHA Hostel (☎ 0870 770 5860; www.yha.org.uk; Carlton Lane; dm £10.60) This purpose-built hostel just outside the centre is a bit like an ordinary suburban home; its location at the start of the Cleveland Way means that it's virtually always full so book in advance.

There are a number of old coaching inns on Market Pl that offer B&B, half-decent grub and a pint (or more) of hand-pumped real ale. The **Crown Inn** (☎ 770297; fax 771595; Market Pl; mains £7-10; s/d £36/56) is a homely place that caters to an older, quieter clientele, while the **Feathers** (☎ 770275; feathershotel@aol.com; Market Pl; mains about £8; s/d from £42/65) has four-poster beds in some rooms and historical trimmings throughout.

Royal Oak (Market Pl) is the liveliest of the town's pubs, with good beer and bar-meals.

CAMPING
Wrens of Rydale (☎ 771260; wrensofryedale.fsnet.co.uk; Gale Lane, Nawton; car & 2 adults/hikers £9/7.50) Three acres of pristine parkland divided into sections for tents and caravans. This excellent campsite is 3 miles east of Helmsley, just south of Beadlam.

Getting There & Away
All buses stop in the Market Pl. From York to Helmsley, take bus Nos 31, 31A and 31X (£4.70, three per day Monday to Saturday, 1½ hours). Between Helmsley and Scarborough, bus No 128 (£5.70, hourly, 1½ hours; four on Sunday) goes via Pickering.

AROUND HELMSLEY
Rievaulx
The moors' most visited attraction is the famous remains of **Rievaulx Abbey** (EH; ☎ 798228; admission £4; ☾ 10am-6pm Apr-Sep, 10am-4pm Oct-Mar), about 3 miles west of Helmsley in the small eponymous village. Rievaulx (pronounced ree-voh) is everything a ruin should be: battered enough by the passage of time to give a venerable air, but with enough beautiful stonework, soaring pillars and graceful arches remaining so you can imagine how it looked in its 13th-century heyday.

The site is quite simply idyllic – a secluded, wooded valley overlooking fields and the River Rye – with a view pretty much as it was 900 years ago, when Cistercian monks first arrived. And it seems they enjoyed the scenery just as much as we do today: one abbot, St Aelred, famously described the abbey's surroundings as 'everywhere peace, everywhere serenity'. Perfect for a spot of contemplation. Or a picnic. Or both.

Near the abbey, **Rievaulx Terrace & Temples** (NT; ☎ 798340; admission £3.30; ☾ 10.30am-6pm Apr-Sep, 10.30am-5pm Oct-Nov) is a wooded escarpment once part of extensive Duncombe Park (p598). In the 1750s landscape-gardening fashion favoured a natural or gothic look, and many aristocrats had mock ruins built in their parks. The Duncombe family went one better, as their lands contained a

YORKSHIRE

medieval ruin – Rievaulx Abbey – and the half-mile-long grassy terrace was built, with classical-style temples at each end, so lords and ladies could stroll effortlessly in the 'wilderness' and admire the ruins in the valley below. Today, we can do the same, with views over Ryedale and the Hambleton Hills forming a perfect backdrop.

A visit to these two historic sites makes a great day out from Helmsley, but note that there's no direct access between the abbey and the terrace. Their entrance gates are about a mile apart and easily reached along a lane – steeply uphill if you're going from the abbey to the terrace.

Sutton Bank

Sutton Bank is a dramatically steep escarpment 8 miles west of Helmsley. If you're driving, this may be your entry to the North York Moors. And what an entry. The road climbs steeply up, with magnificent views westwards across to the Pennines and Yorkshire Dales. At the top, there's a **TIC** (☎ 01845-597426; 10am-5pm Apr-Oct, 11am-4pm Nov, Dec & Mar, 11am-4pm Sat & Sun Jan & Feb) with exhibitions about the moors, books and maps for sale, and handy leaflets on short walks to nearby viewpoints. If you don't have your own wheels, the Moorsbus service No M3 links Sutton Bank with Helmsley, from where all other parts of the park can be reached.

Coxwold

Coxwold is an immaculate village of golden stone with a serene sense of symmetry, nestling in beautiful countryside about 7 miles southwest of Helmsley. It may be in the north but it shouts middle England (it even *sounds* like Cotswold), and Yorkshire accents are pretty scarce hereabouts.

Apart from the quiet picture-postcard beauty of the place, the main attraction is the 15th-century **Shandy Hall** (☎ 01347-868465; admission gardens/house £4.50/2.50; gardens 11am-4.30pm May-Sep, house 2-4.30pm Wed, 2.30-4.30pm Sun May-Sep), home to ebullient eccentric Laurence Sterne (1713–68), author of *Tristram Shandy*. The house is full of 'Sterneana', with lots of information on this entertaining character who was seemingly the first to use the expression 'sick as a horse'.

Nearby is **Byland Abbey** (EH; ☎ 01347-868614; admission £2; 10am-1pm & 2-6pm Apr-Sep, to 5pm

Oct), the elegant remains of a fine Cistercian creation, now a series of lofty arches surrounded by open green slopes.

Your best bet for a decent and characteristic place to stay is the **Fauconberg Arms** (☎ 01347-868214; www.fauconbergarms.co.uk; Main St; mains £10-15; s/d £35/60), a cosy local in the heart of the village, with a fine continental-style menu in its elegant restaurant and four rooms furnished in simple (but comfortable) cottage style.

HUTTON-LE-HOLE
☎ 01751

A contender for best-looking village in Yorkshire, Hutton-le-Hole may sound odd but it's actually a wonderful collection of gorgeous stone cottages centred on a village green, an undulating grassy expanse with a stream creating a small valley that divides the village in two. The dips and hollows on the green might give the village its name – it was once called simply Hutton Hole, but posh wannabe Victorians added the Frenchified 'le', which the locals defiantly pronounce 'lee'. Its popularity as an understated tourist destination has tweeified the place somewhat, but it's lovely for a stroll and a streamside picnic.

The **TIC** (☎ 417367; 10am-5.30pm mid-Marearly Nov) has leaflets on walks in the area, including a 5-mile circuit to the nearby village of Lastingham.

The **Daffodil Walk** is a 2½-mile circular walk following the banks of the River Dove. As the name suggests, the main draws are the daffs, usually at their best in the last couple of weeks in April.

Attached to the TIC is the largely open-air **Ryedale Folk Museum** (☎ 417367; admission £3.25; 10am-5.30pm Mar-Nov), a constantly expanding collection of North York Moors buildings from different eras, including a medieval manor house, simple farmers' houses, a blacksmith's forge and a row of 1930s village shops. Demonstrations and displays throughout the season give a pretty fascinating insight into local life as it was in the past.

Sleeping & Eating

Hutton-le-Hole has a small choice of places to stay in the village itself, and the TIC can help with more suggestions if you want B&B on a farm in the surrounding countryside.

ALL ABOARD PLEASE!

Pickering is the southern terminus of the privately owned **North Yorkshire Moors Railway** (NYMR; ☎ Pickering Station 01751-472508, recorded timetable 01751-473535; www.northyorkshiremoorsrailway .com or www.nymr.demon.co.uk), which runs for 18 miles through beautiful countryside to the village of Grosmont. Lovingly restored steam locos pull period carriages, resplendent in polished brass and bright paintwork, and the railway appeals to train buffs and day-trippers alike. For visitors without wheels, it's excellent for reaching out-of-the-way spots. Even more useful, Grosmont is also on the main railway line between Middlesbrough and Whitby, which opens up yet more possibilities for walking or sightseeing.

Pickering, the railway, and the surrounding countryside can easily absorb a day. At all stations there's information about waymarked walks, lasting between one and four hours. Generally, there are four to eight trains daily between April and October. The full journey takes an hour, and tickets allowing you to get on and get off as much as you like cost £12 (children £5).

From Pickering the line heads northeast through a river valley, and the first stop is **Levisham station**, 1½ miles west of beautiful Levisham village, which faces Lockton across another steep valley.

Next along is **Newton Dale**, ideal for walkers heading for the impressive crater-like bowl in the hills called the Hole of Horcum (or the Devil's Punchbowl); it's a request stop only, so let the guard know if you want to get off here.

A few miles further is **Goathland**, a picturesque village surrounded by heather-clad moors. It attracts many visitors because of its status as 'Aidensfield' in the British TV series *Heartbeat*, and more recently was a set for the *Harry Potter* films. There are several good walks from the station, including along a pretty trail to Grosmont. If you want to halt for a while, there are several hotel and B&B options plus a campsite.

At the northern end of the line is the sleepy little village of **Grosmont** (pronounced gro-mont), although it comes alive when the steam trains pull across the level crossing on the main street. There are some B&B options here, plus a nice café and a pub doing food, and that's about it. All change please.

The Nuts & Bolts

You can start your train ride in Pickering, or in Grosmont, which is easily reached from Whitby by 'normal' train along the Esk Valley line (p602). A grand day out from Pickering combines the NYMR, the Esk Valley line between Grosmont and Whitby and the bus over the moors between Whitby and Pickering.

Burnley House (☎ 417548; www.burnleyhouse .co.uk; d £65) This handsome Georgian house is an excellent choice for stylish B&B and convivial atmosphere.

The Crown (bar meals £6-7) The village pub, this is a straightforward spot that's popular with locals and visitors.

The main street also boasts a handful of **teashops**, all offering drinks, snacks and lunches.

Getting There & Away

Hutton-le-Hole is 2½ miles north of the main A170 road, about equidistant from the market towns of Helmsley and Pickering. Moorsbus services (p598) through Hutton-le-Hole include No M3 between Helmsley and Danby (seven per day) and Nos M1 and M2 between Pickering and Danby (eight per day). Outside times when the Moorsbus runs, you'll need your own transport to get here. Alternatively catch bus No 128 along the A170, drop off at the junction east of Kirkbymoorside and walk the 2½ miles up the lane to Hutton-le-Hole.

PICKERING

☎ 01751 / pop 6616

The lively market town of Pickering has its charms – most notably the Norman castle and the fabulous North Yorkshire Moors Railway (see the boxed text above), for which Pickering serves as a terminus – but it is too big and bustling to keep you in thrall. It is, however, a handy staging post from which to explore the eastern moors.

The **TIC** (☎ 473791; www.ryedale.gov.uk; The Ropery; ⏰ 9.30am-5.30pm Mon-Sat, 9.30am-4pm Sun

Mar-Oct, 10am-4pm Mon-Sat Nov-Feb) has the usual details as well as all NYMR-related info.

Pickering Castle (EH; ☎ 474989; admission £3; ☼ 10am-6pm Apr-Sep, 10am-4pm Oct-Mar) is a lot like the castles we drew as kids: thick stone outer walls circling the keep, and the lot perched atop a high motte (mound) with great views of the surrounding countryside. Founded by William the Conqueror, it was added to and altered by later kings.

Sleeping & Eating

The White Swan Hotel (☎ 472288; www.white-swan .co.uk; Market Pl; mains £9-15; s/d from £80/140) The top spot in town successfully combines a smart pub, a superb restaurant serving local dishes with a continental twist and a luxurious little boutique hotel all in one. The stylish rooms come with DVD players, Penhaligon toiletries and those wide-head power showers that make you want to stay under them for hours.

There's a strip of similar B&Bs on tree-lined Eastgate (which becomes the A170 to/from Scarborough). Decent options include **Eden House** (☎ 472289; www.edenhousebandb .co.uk; 120 Eastgate; s/d £26/52), a pretty house with cottage-style décor, and flower- and plant-clad **Rose Folly** (☎ 475067; www.rosefolly.freeserve .co.uk; 112 Eastgate; s/d £25/50), with lovely rooms and a beautiful breakfast conservatory.

There are several cafés and teashops on Market Pl, and for drinks of another sort the **Bay Horse** (Market Pl) is a good no-nonsense pub.

Getting There & Away

Bus No 128 between Helmsley (40 minutes) and Scarborough (50 minutes) runs hourly via Pickering. Yorkshire Coastliner (Nos 840, 842 and X40) services run to/from York (£8.70, hourly, 70 minutes).

For train details, see the boxed text p598.

DANBY

☎ 01287

Danby is an isolated stone village deep in the moors at the head of Eskdale, where the surrounding countryside is particularly beautiful. It makes a good base, as the **Moors Centre** (☎ 01439-772737; www.moors.uk.net; ☼ 10am-5pm Apr-Oct, 11am-4pm Nov-Dec & Mar, 11am-4pm Sat & Sun Jan-Feb), the park headquarters, is just half a mile from the village, and has displays, information, a café, an accommodation-booking service and a huge range of local guidebooks, maps and leaflets as well as all the information you'll need on walking routes.

There are several short circular walks from the centre, but first on your list should be Danby Beacon; it's a stiff 2 miles uphill to the northeast, but the stunning 360° views across the moors sweeten the sweat.

The Duke of Wellington (☎ 660351; www.danby -dukeofwellington.co.uk; mains about £7; s/d from £30/60), a fine traditional pub – used as a recruitment centre during the Napoleonic Wars – serves good beer and meals; upstairs there are nine well-appointed rooms.

Getting There & Away

Using the delightful **Esk Valley Railway** (☎ 0845 748 4950; www.eskvalleyrailway.co.uk), access is easy: Whitby (£3) is 20 minutes east; Middlesbrough (£6) is 45 minutes west. There are four departures Monday to Saturday, two on Sunday.

WHITBY

☎ 01947 / pop 13,594

Of all of northern England's coastal resorts, none can hold a candle to Whitby for sheer charm. Colourful fishing boats crowd the busy harbour that leads to a winding maze of narrow medieval streets lined with restaurants and pubs, while breathtakingly perched atop one of the cliffs that hems the town in are the stunning remains of an ancient abbey. Like virtually every other coastal town with a beach, Whitby has its fair share of amusement arcades and other seaside paraphernalia, but unlike other resorts, they complement the town's overall aesthetic – in a traditional resort sort of way. It's all a far cry from the 18th century, when the town's most famous son, James Cook, was making his first forays to sea on his way towards becoming one of the best-known explorers in history.

Besides the caravan of ordinary sun worshippers and beachcombers that flood the town throughout the summer months, Whitby is popular with good-time girls and boys, retirees, hikers, bikers and even Goths – who flock here for two festivals honouring the king of the vampires: Bram Stoker set part of *Dracula* here (see the boxed text p604).

And finally there's the all-important matter of fish 'n' chips, and in Whitby you'll find the best in the *whole* country.

Orientation

Whitby is divided in two by the harbour and River Esk estuary. On the east bank (East Cliff) is the older part of town; the newer (19th-century) town grew up on the other side, West Cliff. An intriguing feature of Whitby is that many streets have two names. For example, Abbey Tce and Hudson St are opposite sides of the same street, as are West St and The Esplanade.

Information

Java Café-Bar (Flowergate) Internet access.

Laundrette (72 Church St)

Post office (8.30am-5.30pm Mon-Sat) Across from the TIC inside the Co-op supermarket.

TIC (☎ 602674; www.discoveryorkshirecoast.com or www.visitwhitby.com; Langborne Rd; 9.30am-6pm May-Sep, 10am-4.30pm Oct-Apr) A wealth of information on the town and the surrounding moors and coast.

Sights

There are ruins, and then there's **Whitby Abbey** (EH; ☎ 603568; admission £4; 10am-6pm Apr-Sep, 10am-4pm Thu-Mon Oct-Mar). Dominating the town, in a simply stunning location, this

ancient holy place dates from the 11th to 14th centuries, with huge solid pillars, soaring arches and gaping windows made all the more dramatic with the North Sea sky behind. Nearby, **St Mary's Church** (10am-5pm Apr-Oct, 10am-4pm Nov-Mar) has an atmospheric interior full of skewed and tilting galleries and box pews. You reach the abbey and the church via the famous 199 steps up the cliff side. Take time out to catch your breath and admire the fantastic view.

Cook-related links are a big deal in Whitby, but the best place to find out about the famous seafarer is at the **Captain Cook Memorial Museum** (☎ 601900; www.cookmuseumwhitby.co.uk; Grape Lane; adult/child £3/2; 9.45am-5pm Apr-Oct, 11am-3pm Sat & Sun Mar), a house once occupied by the ship-owner to whom Cook was apprenticed. Highlights include Cook's own maps and writings, etchings from the South Seas and a wonderful model of the *Endeavour*, with all the crew and stores laid out for inspection.

At the top of the cliff near East Tce, the **Captain Cook Monument** shows the great man looking out to sea, usually with a seagull

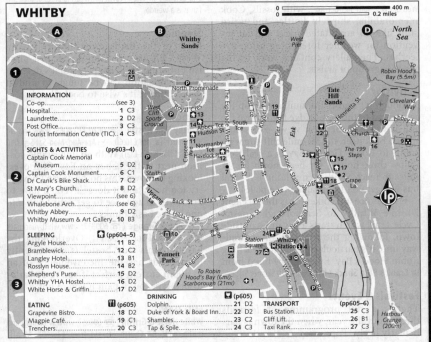

WHITBY

0 — 400 m
0 — 0.2 miles

INFORMATION	
Co-op	(see 3)
Hospital	1 C3
Laundrette	2 D2
Post Office	3 C3
Tourist Information Centre (TIC)	4 C3

SIGHTS & ACTIVITIES	(pp603–4)
Captain Cook Memorial Museum	5 D2
Captain Cook Monument	6 C1
Dr Crank's Bike Shack	7 C2
St Mary's Church	8 D2
Viewpoint	(see 6)
Whalebone Arch	(see 6)
Whitby Abbey	9 D2
Whitby Museum & Art Gallery	10 B3

SLEEPING	(pp604–5)
Argyle House	11 B2
Bramblewick	12 C2
Langley Hotel	13 B1
Rosslyn House	14 B2
Shepherd's Purse	15 D2
Whitby YHA Hostel	16 D2
White Horse & Griffin	17 D2

EATING	(p605)
Grapevine Bistro	18 D2
Magpie Café	19 C1
Trenchers	20 C3

DRINKING	(p605)
Dolphin	21 D2
Duke of York & Board Inn	22 D2
Shambles	23 C2
Tap & Spile	24 C3

TRANSPORT	(pp605–6)
Bus Station	25 C3
Cliff Lift	26 B1
Taxi Rank	27 C3

YORKSHIRE

WHITBY'S DARK SIDE

The famous story of *Dracula*, inspiration for a thousand lurid movies, was written by Bram Stoker while staying at a B&B in Whitby in 1897. Although most Hollywood versions of the tale concentrate on deepest, darkest Transylvania, much of the original book was set in Whitby, and many sites can still be seen today.

The events are remembered at Whitby's annual Gothic Festival (see Festivals & Events, p604). It's *Rocky Horror* at the seaside – the town is full of people in black, and the atmosphere is fun and relaxed, but quite bizarre.

The TIC sells an excellent *Dracula Trail* leaflet (60p), but you shouldn't miss the stone jetty in the harbour, where the Russian boat chartered by Dracula was wrecked as it flew in ahead of the huge storm. You'll need more imagination in the car park in front of the train station; this was once sidings for freight cars, and it's from here that Dracula left Whitby for London in one of his boxes of dirt.

After the town sites, you can climb the same 199 stone steps that the heroine Mina ran up when trying to save her friend Lucy. At the top of the steps is moody St Mary's Church, where Mina first saw Lucy sitting next to a suspicious black being. By that time, of course, it was too late. Cue music. The End.

perched on his head. Nearby is the **Whalebone Arch** (it's just that), remembering Whitby's days as a whaling port.

South of here, in a park overlooking the town, is the wonderfully eclectic **Whitby Museum & Art Gallery** (☎ 602908; Pannett Park; adult/child £3/1, art gallery admission free; ⌚ 9.30am-5.30pm Mon-Sat, 2-5pm Sun May-Sep, 10am-1pm Tue, 10am-4pm Wed-Sat & 2-4pm Sun Oct-Apr), with fossils, Cook memorabilia, ships in bottles and weird stuff like an amputated hand and an invention for weather forecasting using live leeches. The gallery contains work by the Staithes group of artists.

Activities

Although it's hardly tranquil, a walk up the main road to the new bridge high above the Esk is worth it for great views. For something a bit longer, the 5½-mile cliff-top walk south to Robin Hood's Bay is a real treat (allow three hours). Or head north for 11 miles to reach Staithes (five hours). A local bus will get you home again (see p606).

First choice for a bike ride is the excellent 20-mile Whitby to Scarborough Coastal Cycle Trail, which starts a few miles outside town, following the route of an old railway line. It's particularly good for reaching Robin Hood's Bay. Bikes can be hired from **Dr Crank's Bike Shack** (☎ 606661; 20 Skinner St).

Festivals & Events

There's a full programme of festivals throughout the year, when the town is particularly lively. Tops are:

Moor & Coast Festival (www.moorandcoast.co.uk; tickets £30) A traditional folk festival of music, dance and dubious Celtic art over the May Bank Holiday.

Musicport Festival (www.musicport.fsnet.co.uk; £67.50) A weekend-long world music festival in mid-October.

Whitby Gothic Weekends (www.wgw.topmum.co.uk; tickets £35) Goth heaven during the last weekends of April and October; anyone in town not wearing black or false fangs is a weirdo.

Sleeping

Most of the B&Bs are concentrated on West Cliff around Hudson St; if a place isn't offering B&B, chances are it's derelict. Accommodation can be tough to find at festival times; it's wise to book ahead.

BUDGET

Whitby YHA Hostel (☎ 0870 770 6089; www.yha.org.uk; Church La; dm £10.60; ⌚ Apr-Aug, Mon-Sat Sep-Oct, Fri & Sat Nov & Jan-Mar) With an unbeatable position next to the abbey on East Cliff overlooking the town, this hostel doesn't have to try too hard, and it doesn't. You'll have to book well in advance to get your body into one of the basic bunks.

Harbour Grange (☎ 600817; www.whitbybackpackers.co.uk; Spital Bridge; dm £11) Overlooking the harbour, this tidy hostel is conveniently located but has the inconvenience of an 11.30pm curfew; perfect if you're an early-to-bed type, but a pain if you're not.

MID-RANGE

White Horse & Griffin (☎ 604857; www.whitehorseandgriffin.co.uk; 87 Church St; s/d from £35/60) Walk

YORKSHIRE

through the suitably olde worlde frontage of this handsome 18th-century coaching inn and discover a boutique hotel with individually designed, super-stylish rooms that have managed to mix the best of tradition (antique panelling, restored period furniture, real flame fires) with the kind of sleek, contemporary lines and modern comforts you'd expect from a top-class guesthouse.

Shepherd's Purse (☎ 820228; www.shepherdspurse .co.uk; 95 Church St; s/d from £25/40) This place began life as a beads-and-baubles boutique in 1973, added a wholefood shop and vegetarian restaurant and now offers guesthouse accommodation. The plainer rooms that share a bathroom are perfectly adequate, but we recommend the en suite bedrooms situated around a lovely courtyard; each has a handsome brass or four-poster bed and nice pine furniture.

Langley Hotel (☎ 604250; www.langleyhotel.com; 16 Royal Cres; s/d £31/60; **P**) The whiff of Victorian splendour may have faded, but the panoramic views from West Cliff are as good as ever. The rooms are tidy and neat, if a little cramped.

Other options include **Bramblewick** (☎ 604 504; www.bramblewick.co.uk; 3 Havelock Pl; s/d £25/48; **P**), **Argyle House** (☎ 602733; 18 Hudson St; s/d £23/45) and **Rosslyn House** (☎ 604086; 11 Abbey Tce; s/d £22/45).

Eating & Drinking

For many visitors, Whitby cuisine extends no further than a fish-and-chip supper (served with peas, bread and tea), obtainable most everywhere for between £4 and £5 but preferred at the world's most famous chipper. If you want to keep your cholesterol in check, there are a few other options.

Magpie Café (☎ 602058; 14 Pier Rd; mains £7-10; lunch & dinner) The world's best fish and chips, or so the reputation would have it. They are bloody delicious, but the one downer is that the world and his wife knows about this place, and summertime queues can be off-putting.

Trenchers (☎ 603212; New Quay Rd; mains £7-10; ☽ lunch & dinner) Excellent fish and chips minus the reputation, Trenchers is your best bet if you want to avoid the queues. Don't be put off by the modern look.

Grapevine Bistro (☎ 820275; 2 Grape Lane; tapas about £4-6, mains £7-10; ☽ lunch & dinner) A highly rated Mediterranean-style place that serves mostly tapas plates but also lays on an evening menu of meat, fish and veggie dishes.

Shepherd's Purse (☎ 820228; 95 Church St; mains about £6) A veggie place behind a wholefood shop with the same name, with a great range of healthy, interesting snacks and meals, and a very nice courtyard.

Many pubs also serve food, including, of course, fish and chips or crab sandwiches, all for about £5 to £7. A good first choice is the popular **Duke of York** (Church St) at the bottom of the 199 steps, with plentiful food and a classic Whitby atmosphere, while next door the smaller **Board Inn** is another place with views, good beer and seafood. **The Dolphin** (Bridge St) has tables inside or out on the pavement, while **The Shambles** (Market Pl) is modern and spacious with huge picture windows overlooking the harbour. The **Tap & Spile** (☎ 603937; New Quay Rd) is a straightforward place with good local rock and folk bands.

Getting There & Away

Whitby is 230 miles (370km) from London and 45 miles from York.

CAPTAIN COOK – WHITBY'S FAMOUS (ADOPTED) SON

Although he wasn't actually born in Whitby, the town has adopted the famous explorer Captain James Cook, and since the first tourists got off the train in Victorian times, local entrepreneurs have mercilessly cashed in on his memory, as endless 'Endeavour Cafés' and 'Captain Cook Chip Shops' testify.

The young James Cook started his apprenticeship in 1746, working on Whitby 'cats' – unique, flat-bottomed ships carrying coal from Newcastle to London. Nine years later he joined the navy, and in 1768 began the first of three great voyages of discovery, during which he reached Australia. Cook returned to Europe with detailed charts, vast notebooks full of observations, numerous plant and animal samples, and a vast wealth of knowledge garnered from these long journeys. His ships on all three voyages, including the Endeavour, were based on the design of 'cats', and in this small but vital way Whitby played a part in world exploration and 18th-century scientific understanding.

Bus Nos 93 and 93A run to/from Scarborough (£3.40, one hour, hourly), and to Middlesbrough (about hourly), with fewer services on Sunday. Yorkshire Coastliner (Nos 840 and X40) runs between Whitby and Leeds (£8.60, seven per day, three hours) via Pickering and York.

If you're coming from the north, you can get to Whitby by train along the Esk Valley line from Middlesbrough (£10, four per day, 1½ hours). From the south, it's easier to get a train from York to Scarborough, then a bus from Scarborough to Whitby.

Getting Around

Whitby is a compact place and those 199 steps help burn off the fish and chips. But if you need one, there's a taxi rank near the TIC. The west cliff is also accessible via a lift (60p), which perishes the thought of clambering up the steep roads.

AROUND WHITBY
Robin Hood's Bay

Just 5 miles south of Whitby, Robin Hood's Bay has a lot more to do with smugglers than the Sherwood Forest hero, but this picturesque haven is well worth a visit, although like so many places it's very busy on summer weekends.

A single main street called New Rd winds through the old part of town, dropping steeply down from the cliff top to the sea. (There's compulsory parking at the top – don't even think about driving down as there's hardly room to turn at the bottom.) Off New Rd there's a honeycomb of cobbled alleys, secret passages and impossibly small houses. There are giftshops, teashops and a trail of pubs (it might be safer to start from the bottom and work your way up), many with seats outside, so this is an excellent place to just sit and watch the world go by.

Among the pubs, our favourite for ambience is the old **Dolphin**, the **Victoria Hotel** has the best beer and good food, and the **Bay Hotel** is notable for being the end of the famous **Coast to Coast long-distance walk** (p61). Some pubs do B&B and there are several other accommodation options – the TIC in Whitby (p603) can advise.

It's eminently possible to walk or cycle here from Whitby. Also, bus Nos 93 and 93A run hourly between Whitby and Scarborough via Robin Hood's Bay – the bus stop is at the top of the hill, in the new part of town.

Staithes

Tucked beneath high cliffs and running back along the steep banks of a river, the small fishing town of Staithes seems to hide from the modern world, focusing still on its centuries-old battle with the sea. It's a lot less touristy than Robin Hood's Bay: the houses are less prettified, you can see fishermen's jackets drying on lines, and seagulls the size of vultures swoop down the narrow alleys that lead off the main street.

The town's claim to fame is that explorer James Cook worked as a grocer here when a boy. Legend says that fishermen's tales of the high seas, and bad treatment by his master, led him to steal a shilling and run away to Whitby. The rest of the tale is told in great detail in the fascinating and lovingly maintained **Captain Cook & Staithes Heritage Centre** (admission £2.50; ⏰ 10am-5.30pm), packed to the gunwales with nautical relics.

Staithes is located 11 miles from Whitby. To get here, the buses on the Whitby-to-Middlesbrough run can drop you at the top of the hill. If you're feeling fit, walking one way and bussing the other makes for a great day out.

Northwest England

CONTENTS

The northwest is a generous slice of urban heaven. To some, the words sound like an impossible contradiction, but we urge you to think again. Crammed into its relatively tight confines you'll find one of the world's most pleasant cities; the birthplace of the world's best ever band, bar none; a picture-postcard town whose rich layers of history are revealed in its multi-tiered architecture; and the most eye-popping, stomach-turning rollercoaster we've ever been dizzy on. Life, music, history and hedonism. What more could you want? A bit of the world where humans haven't left their messy, mucky paw-prints, the urban cynics will say. Well, there's that too.

The northwest is best known as the engine-room of England's once-mighty industrial heartland. What's more impressive, though, is that this is the very place where the Industrial Revolution was born and raised into the overwhelming force of Capitalism; where, in Manchester, the world's first modern city was conceived; and where the endless possibilities of the Age of Reason were put through their original paces. Ancient Rome would have been proud of the accomplishment.

Perhaps the most compelling aspect of the northwest, however, is how it has embraced the future. The region has wholeheartedly embraced the revolutionary designs and styles of contemporary urban planning, a revolutionary ethos that seeks to combine the best of the past with a new vision, one that takes into account the indomitable desire of people to live well. Come and find out for yourself.

HIGHLIGHTS

- Admiring Manchester from the balcony of the **Godlee Observatory** (p616)

- Walking in Roman footsteps around **Chester's city walls** (p625)

- Getting queasy on the rollercoasters at Blackpool's **Pleasure Beach** (p643)

- Exploring the **Isle of Man** (p647) – not just for tax-dodgers and petrol-heads

- The **ferry across the Mersey** (p641): hum the song while enjoying the best views of Liverpool

- Browsing through the **Lady Lever Art Gallery** (p642) in Port Sunlight

■ POPULATION: 6.7 MILLION	■ AREA: 5473 SQ MILES

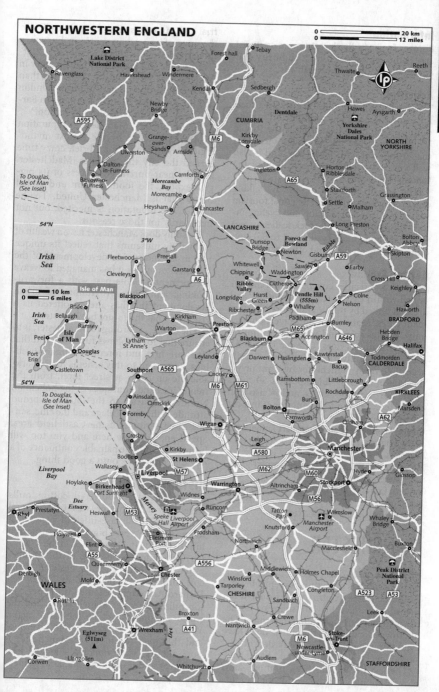

NORTHWESTERN ENGLAND

0 — 20 km
0 — 12 miles

Ravenglass

Lake District National Park

Hawkshead • Windermere
Forest hall • Tebay
Thwaite • Reeth

Newby Bridge
Kendal • Sedbergh
Dentdale
Hawes • Aysgarth

CUMBRIA
Kirkby Lonsdale
Yorkshire Dales National Park

A595

Grange-over-Sands • Arnside
Ulverston
NORTH YORKSHIRE

Dalton-in-Furness
Carnforth
Ingleton • A65
Horton-in-Ribblesdale

To Douglas, Isle of Man (See Inset)

Barrow-in-Furness
Morecambe Bay
Morecambe
Stainforth • Grassington

Heysham
Lancaster
Settle • Malham

54°N

3°W
LANCASHIRE
Long Preston

Irish Sea

Dunsop Bridge
Forest of Bowland
Newton • Gisburn • A59
Bolton Abbey

Fleetwood • Preesall
Whitewell • Waddington
Sawley • Earby
Skipton

Cleveleys
Garstang • A6
Chipping • Clitheroe
Cross Hill
Keighley

0 — 10 km
0 — 6 miles
Isle of Man
Blackpool
Ribble Valley
Longridge • Hurst Green
Pendle Hill (555m) ▲ • Colne
Nelson
Haworth

Irish Sea
Bride
Bellaugh • Ramsey
Kirkham
Ribchester • Whalley
Padiham • Burnley
BRADFORD

Peel
Isle of Man • Douglas
Warton
Preston
M65
Accrington • A646
Hebden Bridge
Halifax

Port Erin
Castletown
Lytham St Anne's
Blackburn
Darwen • Haslingden • Rawtenstall
Todmorden
CALDERDALE

54°N
Leyland
Chorley • Bacup
KIRKLEES

To Douglas, Isle of Man (See Inset)
Southport • A565
M6 • M61
Ramsbottom • Littleborough
Rochdale
Marsden

Ainsdale • Ormskirk
SEFTON • Formby
Wigan
Bury
Bolton
A62

Crosby
Leigh • A580
Farnworth
Oldham

Bootle
Kirkby • St Helens
Manchester

Liverpool Bay
Wallasey
Liverpool • M57
Warrington
M62 • M60
Hyde • Glossop

Hoylake
Birkenhead Port Sunlight
Widnes • Runcorn
Altrincham
Stockport

Dee Estuary
Heswall
Speke Liverpool Airport
Tatton Park
M56
Wilmslow
Whaley Bridge

Rhyl • Prestatyn
Frodsham
Knutsford
Manchester Airport
Buxton

Holywell
Ellesmere Port
Northwich
Macclesfield

Flint • A55
Queensferry
A556
Middlewich • Holmes Chapel
Peak District National Park

Denbigh
Chester
Winsford
Congleton • A523 • A53

WALES
Mold
Tarporley
CHESHIRE
Sandbach
Leek

Ruthin
Broxton
Nantwich • Crewe

Eglwyseg (511m) ▲
Wrexham • A41
Whitchurch
A6
Newcastle-under-Lyme

Corwen • Llangollen
Audlem
STAFFORDSHIRE

Information

Discover England's Northwest (www.visitnorthwest
.com) is the centralised tourist authority that
covers the whole of the northwest.

Activities

The northwest is predominantly an urban
area, and there are few walking and cycling
options. One main exception is the Ribble
Valley, which has decent walks including
the 70-mile (113km) **Ribble Way**, and is also
well covered by the northern loop of the
Lancashire Cycle Way.

The Isle of Man has top-notch walking
and cycling opportunities. Regional tourism
websites all contain walking and cycling information, and TICs all stock leaflets (free)
plus maps and guides (usually £1 to £5) covering walking, cycling and other activities.

Getting Around

The towns and cities covered in this chapter
are all within easy reach of each other, and
are well linked by public transport. The two
main cities, Manchester and Liverpool, are
only 34 miles apart and are linked by hourly
bus and train services. Chester is only 18
miles south of Liverpool, but is also easily
accessible from Manchester by train or via
the M56 motorway. Blackpool is 50 miles
to the north of both cities, and is also well
connected. Try the following for transport
information:

Greater Manchester Public Transport Authority
(www.gmpte.com) For extensive info on Manchester and
its environs.

Merseytravel (☎ 236 7676; www.merseytravel.gov.uk)
Taking care of all travel in Merseyside.

National Express (☎ 08705 808080; www.national
express.com) Extensive coach services in the northwest;
Manchester and Liverpool are major hubs.

MANCHESTER

☎ 0161 / pop 394,270

'Manchester has everything except a beach.'
Ex–Stone Roses frontman and local lad Ian
Brown may have his fair share of hometown pride, but he's not far wrong. The
uncrowned capital of the north does have
everything, or at least a pretty decent version of everything a city should have.

The last decade has been nothing short
of revolutionary for the world's first indus-

trial city, as it has transformed itself into
the envy of any urban centre in Europe, a
modern metropolis that has embraced 21st-
century style and technology like no other in
England. It is surely indicative of more than
just northern one-upmanship over London
and the south that Manchester looks to Barcelona as its main rival and inspiration.

To the outsider, Manchester's reputation
is best represented by the almost mytho-
logical nightlife that for a brief, crazy time
earned the city the moniker 'Madchester'
and the near-unrivalled success of its biggest export, the football team and global
brand that is Manchester United. To the
insider, the reputation is merited, but not
necessarily for those reasons.

Not only does Manchester have a wealth of
fascinating museums that reflect its unique
role in the pioneering developments of the
Industrial Age, but it has managed to weave
the mementos of its past with a forward-
looking, ambitious programme of urban
development that has already offered us a
vision of what the future holds in store.

The future, according to Manchester, is to
ensure that form follows function, and that
cities are first and foremost human dwellings. Testament to this belief is the remarkable life on show at street level, from the
trendy bars and boutiques of the bohemian
Northern Quarter to the loud-and-proud
attitude of the Gay Village and the chic, self-
possessed stylings of the Castlefield area.
Spend enough time here and you too will
be infected with the palpable confidence of a
city that knows it's onto a good thing.

HISTORY

Canals and steam-powered cotton mills
were how Manchester was transformed
from a small, disease-infested provincial
town into a very big, disease-infested
industrial city. It all happened in the 1760s –
in 1763 with the opening of the Bridgewater Canal between Manchester and the
coal mines at Worsley, and in 1769 when
Richard Arkwright patented his super cotton mill. Thereafter Manchester – and the
world – would never be the same again.
When the canal was extended to Liverpool
and the open sea in 1776, Manchester –
now dubbed 'Cottonopolis' – kicked into
high gear and took off on the coal-fuelled,
steam-powered gravy train.

MANCHESTER IN...

Two Days

Start your visit surrounded by the glorious Victorian trophies of the Industrial Age around **Albert Square** (p614). Jump onto a Metrolink tram and head south toward Salford Quays and its trio of top attractions, the **Imperial War Museum North** (p616), the **Lowry** (p616) and then the **Manchester United Museum** (p616). Pick a restaurant – **Yang Sing** (p620) will do to kick off the evening – find a bar and round the night off in a club. The next day, head toward **Castlefield Urban Heritage Park** (p615) before indulging in a spot of retail therapy around the **Millennium Quarter** (p623), breaking up the spendfest with a visit to **Urbis** (p615). Venture east and go alternative in the boutiques and off-beat shops of the **Northern Quarter** (p623).

Four Days

Follow the two-day itinerary and also tackle some of the city's lesser-known museums – the **Pumphouse People's History Museum** (p614), **Cheatham's Library** (p615) and the **Manchester Jewish Museum** (p617). Head south toward the university and tackle the **Manchester Museum** (p616) and **Whitworth Art Gallery** (p617). If it's a decent enough day, visit the **Godlee Observatory** (p616) before examining the riches of the **Manchester Art Gallery** (p614).

There was plenty of gravy to go around, but the good burghers of 19th-century Manchester made sure that the vast majority of the city's swollen citizenry (1801, population 90,000: 100 years later, two million) who produced most of it never got their hands on any of it. Their reward was life in a new kind of urban settlement, the industrial slum. Working conditions were scarcely better: impossibly long hours, child labour, work-related accidents and fatalities were commonplace. Mark Twain commented that he would like to live here because the 'transition between Manchester and Death would be unnoticeable'. So much for Victorian values.

The wheels started to come off the train toward the end of the 19th-century. The USA had begun to flex its own industrial muscles and was taking over a sizeable chunk of the textile trade; production in Manchester's mills began to slow down and then stop altogether. By WWII there was hardly enough cotton produced in the city to make a tablecloth. The city was rudely awoken from its economic sleep in 1996, when the blast of an IRA bomb spurred the authorities into beginning the programme of urban rejuvenation in evidence today.

ORIENTATION

Shoe power and the excellent Metrolink tram are the only things you'll need to get around the compact city centre. All public transportation converges on Piccadilly Gardens, just east of the cathedral. Directly north is the slightly decrepit but totally cool Northern Quarter, full of offbeat boutiques, hip cafés and fabulous record shops. A few blocks southeast is the Gay Village, centred on Canal St and, just next to it, Chinatown, basically a bunch of restaurants clustered around Portland St.

Southwest of the centre is Castlefield and Deansgate Locks, a super-trendy development that has successfully converted the 19th-century canalside industrial infrastructure into a groovy weekend playground for the city's fine young things. Further south again – and accessible via Metrolink – are the recently developed Salford Quays, home to the fab Lowry complex and the Imperial War Museum North. Nearby is the Old Trafford football stadium, where Scholesy, Giggsy, Keano and co earn their fabulous keep in Manchester United's famous red shirts.

INFORMATION
Bookshops
Cornerhouse Bookshop (☎ 200 1514; www.corner house.org/publications; 70 Oxford Rd) Art and film books, specialist magazines and kitschy cards.
Waterstone's Deansgate (☎ 832 1992); St Anne's Sq (☎ 837 3000)

Emergency
Ambulance (☎ 436 3999)
Police station (☎ 872 5050; Bootle St)
Rape Crisis Centre (☎ 273 4500)
Samaritans (☎ 236 8000)

MANCHESTER

INFORMATION
Cameolord Chemist	1 F4
Cornerhouse Bookshop	2 F5
Easy Internet Café	3 E2
Police Station	4 E3
Post Office	5 E3
Tourist Information Centre (TIC)	6 F3
Waterstone's	7 E2
Waterstone's	8 E2

SIGHTS & ACTIVITIES (pp614–7)
Castlefield Visitor Centre	9 C4
Central Library	10 E4
Chetham's Library & School of Music	11 F1
Godlee Observatory	(see 17)
John Rylands Library	12 E3
Manchester Art Gallery	13 F3
Manchester Buddhist Centre	(see 27)
Museum of Science & Industry	14 C4
Pumphouse People's History Museum	15 D3
Town Hall	16 E3
University of Manchester Institute of Science & Technology (UMIST)	17 G4
Urbis	18 F1

SLEEPING (pp618–9)
Castlefield	19 C4
Malmaison	20 H4
Midland	21 E4
Mitre	22 E1
Ox	23 C4
Rossetti	24 H3
YHA Manchester	25 C5

EATING (pp619–20)
Café And	26 G2
Earth Café	27 G2
Eighth Day	28 G6
El Rincón del Rafa	29 D4
Le Mont	(see 18)
Love Saves the Day	30 G2
Ox	(see 23)
Tampopo	31 E3
Yang Sing	32 F4

DRINKING (pp620–1)
Bar Centro	33 H2
Britons Protection	34 E5
Dukes 92	35 C5
FAB Café	36 F4
Kro 2	37 G6
Lass O'Gowrie	38 G5
Old Wellington Inn	39 F1
Peveril of the Peak	40 E5
Rain	41 E5
Temple of Covenience	42 F5

ENTERTAINMENT (pp621–3)
Band on the Wall	43 H1
Bridgewater Hall	44 E5
Cornerhouse Cinema	(see 2)
Club V	45 E3
Elemental	46 F4
Filmworks	(see 53)
G-Mex Exhibition Centre	47 E4
Green Room	48 F5
Jilly's Rockworld	49 F5
Library Theatre	(see 10)
Manchester Cathedral	50 E1
Manchester Opera House	51 D3
Manchester Roadhouse	52 H3
Music Box	(see 49)
Printworks	53 F1
Royal Exchange	54 E2
South	55 E3

SHOPPING (p623)
Affleck's Palace	56 G2
Harvey Nichols	57 E2
Oxfam Original	58 G2

TRANSPORT (pp624–5)
Bus Station	59 G3
Coach Station	60 G4
Travel Shop	61 G3

Blackfriars St

Salford Train Station

Bridge St

Wood St

Irwell St

Water St

Hardman St

Gartside St

Byrom St

Qu St

Lower Byrom St

Longworth St

14 / 15

Liverpool Rd

19 / 9

23

CASTLEFIELD

To Salford Quays, Lowry & Imperial War Museum North (1mi)

25 / Castlefield Basin

A56

G-Mex

35 / Castle St

Bridgewater Canal

Deansgate Train Station

Hewitt St

DEANSGATE LOCKS

Chester Rd

To Old Trafford; Lancashire County Cricket Club; Manchester Backpackers' Hostel; Old Trafford Lodge; Smiths Museum; Salford Boys Club; Manchester Gay Centre (2mi); Airport (12mi); Tatton Park (14mi)

Mancunian Way

A57

A6144

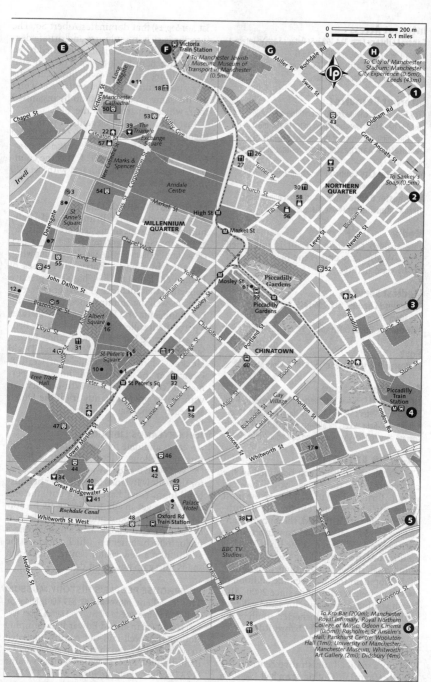

0 _____ 200 m
0 _____ 0.1 miles

To Manchester Jewish
Museum; Museum of
Transport in Manchester
(0.5mi)

To City of Manchester
Stadium; Manchester
City Experience (0.5mi);
Leeds (43mi)

To Sankey's
Soap (0.5mi)

NORTHERN
QUARTER

MILLENNIUM
QUARTER

Piccadilly
Gardens

Piccadilly
Gardens

CHINATOWN

Gay
Village

Piccadilly
Train
Station

BBC TV
Studios

To Kro Bar (200m); Manchester
Royal Infirmary; Royal Northern
College of Music; Odeon Cinema
(0.5mi); Rusholme; St Anselm's
Hall; Pankhurst Centre; Woolaton
Hall (1mi); University of Manchester;
Manchester Museum, Whitworth
Art Gallery (2mi); Didsbury (4mi)

Internet Access

Central Library (☎ 234 1982; St Peter's Sq; ☟ Internet access 1-6pm Mon-Sat; per 30 mins £1)
Easy Internet Café (8-10 Exchange St; ☟ 7.30am-10.50pm Mon-Sat, 9am-10pm Sun)

Internet Resources

City Life (www.citylife.co.uk) Everything you could possibly need to know about how to make the most of the city; the online extension of the excellent weekly mag.
Destination Manchester (www.destinationmanchester.com)
Manchester City Council (www.manchester.gov.uk) The city's official website.
Manchester Online (www.manchesteronline.co.uk)
Virtual Manchester (www.manchester.com)

Media

The superb *City Life* (£1.50) is published every Wednesday and is the best source of up-to-date listings.

Medical Services

Cameolord Chemist (☎ 236 1445; St Peter's Sq; ☟ 10am-10pm)
Manchester Royal Infirmary (☎ 276 1234; Oxford Rd)

Post

Post office (Brazennose St; ☟ 9am-5.30pm Mon-Fri)

Tourist Information

TIC (☎ 234 3157; www.manchester.gov.uk; Town Hall Extension, St Peter's Sq; ☟ 10am-5.30pm Mon-Sat, 10am-4.30pm Sun) Sells tickets for all sorts of guided walks which operate almost daily year-round and cost adult/child £5/4.

SIGHTS & ACTIVITIES

There's plenty to keep you occupied in the city centre, but these days you'll have to venture further afield to really make the most of the city's attractions. On the city's south-western edge is Castlefield, the hub of Manchester's industrial past and now an attractive heritage park. West across the River Irwell is Salford and the quays along the Manchester Ship Canal, site of an ambitious programme of development that has seen the addition of two heavyweight attractions since 2000. Also worth visiting are the museums and galleries of the University of Manchester, south of the city centre along and off Oxford Rd.

City Centre

The city's main administrative centre is the superb Victorian Gothic **town hall** (tours 2pm Sat, Mar-Sep; £4) that dominates Albert Sq. The interior is rich in sculpture and ornate decoration, while the exterior is crowned by an impressive 85m-high tower. You can visit the building on your own, but as it's the city's main administrative centre you won't get the same access as you do by organised tour, which departs from the TIC.

Just behind it, the elegant, Roman Pantheon lookalike **Central Library** (☎ 234 1900; St Peter's Sq; admission free; ☟ 10am-8pm Mon-Thu, 10am-6pm Fri & Sat) was built in 1934. It is the country's largest municipal library, with over 20 miles of shelves.

MANCHESTER ART GALLERY

A superb collection of British art and a hefty number of European masters are on display at the city's top **gallery** (☎ 235 8888; Mosley St; admission free; ☟ 10am-5pm Tue-Sun). The older wing, designed by Charles Barry (of Houses of Parliament fame) in 1834, has an impressive collection that includes 37 Turner watercolours, as well the country's best collection of pre-Raphaelite art. The new gallery features a permanent collection of 20th-century British art starring Lucien Freud, Francis Bacon, Stanley Spencer, Henry Moore and David Hockney. Finally, the Gallery of Craft & Design, in the Athenaeum, houses a permanent collection of pre–17th-century art, with works predominantly from the Dutch and early Renaissance masters.

JOHN RYLANDS LIBRARY

An easy candidate for top building in town, this marvellous Victorian Gothic **library** (☎ 834 5343; 35 Deansgate) was one hell of a way for the widow Rylands to remember her husband John. You'll have to wait until the end of 2005 to get inside to admire its breathtaking reading room and its fine collection of early printed books, as it's undergoing a major refurbishment – which includes the addition of a new visitor centre. All we can say is hurry up and get it done.

PUMPHOUSE PEOPLE'S HISTORY MUSEUM

This excellent **museum** (☎ 839 6061; Bridge St; adult/child £1/free, free to all Fri; ☟ 11am-4.30pm Tue-Sun) is housed in an old Edwardian pumping station with well-laid-out exhibits devoted to social history and the labour movement – including the desk at which Thomas Paine (1737–1809) wrote *Rights of Man* (1791).

URBIS

The stunning glass triangle that is **Urbis** (☎ 907 9099; City Park, Corporation St; admission free; ⏲ 10am-6pm) is a museum about how a city works and – often – doesn't work. The walls of the three floors are covered in compelling photographs, interesting statistics and informative timelines, but the best parts are the interactive videos, each of which tell stories about real people from radically different backgrounds and how they fare in Manchester. It's all well and good to theorise, but there's nothing like a real story to hammer home the truth. Homelessness, rootlessness and dislocation are major themes of urban living, and Urbis doesn't shy away from encouraging visitors to consider what it's like to sleep on a park bench.

CHETHAM'S LIBRARY & SCHOOL OF MUSIC

Beautiful **Chetham's** (☎ 834 7861; Long Millgate; admission free; ⏲ 9am-12.30pm & 1.30-4pm Mon-Fri) is the city's oldest complete structure (1421). It wouldn't be half as interesting were it not for the fact that during the mid–19th century two of its regular users were Messrs Marx and Engels, whose favourite seats were by the large bay window in the main reading room. The library is the only part of the building that is open to visitors, as the rest of it is a national school for young musicians.

Castlefield Urban Heritage Park

The heart of 19th-century industrial Manchester, a landscape of enormous, weather-stained brick buildings and rusting cast-iron relics of canals, viaducts, bridges, warehouses and market buildings, Castlefield has been successfully transformed into an interesting heritage park. Aside from the huge science museum, the big draw here is the Castlefield Basin. The Bridgewater Canal runs through it; in summertime thousands of people amble about the place and patronise its fine pubs and trendy restaurants. Start at the **visitor centre** (☎ 834 4026; enquiries@castlefield.org.uk; 101 Liverpool Rd; ⏲ 10am-4pm Mon-Fri, noon-4pm Sat & Sun)

MUSEUM OF SCIENCE & INDUSTRY

The city's largest **museum** (☎ 832 1830; Liverpool Rd; admission free; ⏲ 10am-5pm) comprises 2.8 hectares spread about two huge Victorian warehouses and the world's oldest passenger railway terminal. If there's anything you

---

THE MANCHESTER SMITHSONIAN

For many (including us), the best band to come out of Manchester was The Smiths. Fronted by the drole and laconic Morrissey and driven by the guitar genius of Johnny Marr, they are the city's most beloved musical treasure – adored by two separate generations of glumerati.

In June 2004, a small **museum** (☎ 876 5209; Salford Boys' Club, St Ignatius Walk, Salford) featuring band memorabilia, photographs and the like opened in a back room of the equally famous Victorian Salford Boys' Club, where Lord Baden-Powell began his scout movement in 1904 and where The Smiths were photographed for the gatefold sleeve of *The Queen is Dead*.

To get there, catch bus No 33 or 63 from city centre.

---

want to know about the Industrial (and post-industrial) Revolution and Manchester's key role in it, you'll find it among the collection of steam engines and locomotives, factory machinery from the mills, and the excellent exhibition telling the story of Manchester from the sewers up.

With over a dozen permanent exhibits, you could spend a whole day poking about the place, testing early electric-shock machines here and trying out a printing press there. In 2004 a new exhibit was added called Manchester Science, outlining the local inventions that changed the world. Did you know that Manchester was home to the world's first computer, a giant contraption called 'the baby', in 1948, or that the world's first submarine was built to the designs of local curate the Rev George Garrett in 1880? Neither did we.

Salford Quays

It seems that no 21st-century urban plan is complete without a docklands development; in Manchester's case the docks in question are the Salford Quays southwest of the city centre along the Ship Canal. Three major attractions draw in the punters and a shopping centre makes sure they have outlets to spend their money. It's a cinch to get here from the city centre via Metrolink (£1.80); for the Imperial War Museum North and Lowry it's the Harbour City stop.

IMPERIAL WAR MUSEUM NORTH

War museums generally appeal to those with a fascination for military hardware and battle strategy (toy soldiers optional), but the newest addition to the **Imperial War Museum** (☎ 877 9240; www.iwm.org/north; Trafford Wharf Rd; admission free; ⏱ 10am-6pm) takes a radically different approach. War is hell, it tells us, but it's a hell we revisit with tragic regularity.

The exhibits cover the main conflicts of the 20th century through a broad selection of displays, but the really effective bit comes every half hour, when the entire exhibition hall goes dark and one of three 15-minute films (*Children and War, Why War?* or *Weapons of War*) is projected throughout. Visitors are encouraged to walk around the darkened room so as to get the most of the sensory bombardment.

Although the audio-visuals and displays are quite compelling, the extraordinary aluminium-clad building itself is a huge part of the attraction and the exhibition spaces are stunning. It was designed by Daniel Libeskind (who in 2003 was granted the contract to replace New York's Twin Towers) and is made up of three separate structures, or shards, that represent the three main theatres of war: air, land and sea.

LOWRY

Directly across the canal from the war museum is a futuristic ship in permanent dock. No, not really, but the **Lowry** (☎ 876 2020; www .thelowry.com; Pier 8, Salford Quays; ⏱ 11am-8pm Tue-Fri, 11am-6pm Sun-Mon, 10am-8pm Sat) looks a bit like one. It caused quite a stir when it opened in 2000, but has proved an unqualified success, attracting over a million visitors a year.

The complex is named after one of England's favourite artists, LS Lowry, who is mostly noted for his industrial landscapes and impressions of northern towns, and it contains over 300 of his paintings and drawings. It also encapsulates two theatres (see p622), galleries, shops, restaurants and bars.

OLD TRAFFORD (MANCHESTER UNITED MUSEUM & TOUR)

Here's a paradox: the world's most famous and supported football club, beloved of fans as far apart as Bangkok and Buenos Aires, is the most hated club in England and has a smaller fan base in Manchester than its far less successful cross-town rivals, Manchester City. It's just jealousy, snigger dismissive United fans, who treat the **Old Trafford stadium** (Sir Matt Busby Way; ⏱ 9.30am-5pm) like holy ground and the stars that play there like minor deities. Such arrogance is enough to turn the rest of us into ABUs (Anyone But United) and make us smile when anyone else wins the championship.

But there's no denying that a visit to the stadium is one of the more memorable things you'll do here. We strongly recommend that you take the **tour** (☎ 868 8631; adult/child £9/6; ⏱ every 10 min, 9.40am-4.30pm except match days), which includes a seat in the stands, a stop in the changing rooms, a peek at the players' lounge (from which the manager is banned unless invited by the players) and a walk down the tunnel to the pitchside dugout, which is as close to ecstasy as many of the club's fans will ever get. It's pretty impressive stuff. The **museum** (admission £5.50; ⏱ 9.30am-5pm), which is part of the tour but can be visited independently, has a comprehensive history of the club and a state-of-the-art call-up system so you can view your favourite goals.

University of Manchester

About a mile south of the city, the University of Manchester is one of England's most extraordinary institutions, and not just because it is a top-class university with a remarkable academic pedigree and a great place to party. It is also home to a world-class museum and a superb art gallery.

MANCHESTER MUSEUM

If you're into natural history and social science, this extraordinary **museum** (☎ 275 2634; University of Manchester, Oxford Rd; admission free;

MORE MUSEUMS

If you can't get enough of annotated exhibits, Manchester has a number of other museums worth checking out.

The **Manchester Jewish Museum** (☎ 834 9879; 190 Cheetham Hill Rd; adult/child £3.25/2.50; ⏰ 10.30am-4pm Mon-Thu, to 5pm Sun; bus Nos 59, 89, 135 & 167 from Piccadilly Gardens), in a Moorish-style former synagogue, tells the story of the city's Jewish community in fascinating detail, including the story of Polish refugee Michael Marks, who opened his first shop with partner Tom Spencer at No 20 Cheetham Hill Rd in 1894.

Nearby, the wonderful **Museum of Transport in Manchester** (☎ 205 2122; Boyle St, Cheetham Hill; admission £3/1.75; ⏰ 10am-5pm Wed & Sat & Sun) is packed with old buses, fire engines and lorries built in the last 100 years.

The **Pankhurst Centre** (☎ 273 5673; 60-62 Nelson St; admission free; ⏰ 10am-5pm Mon-Fri) is the converted childhood home of Emmeline Pankhurst (1858–1928), a leading light of the British Suffragette Movement. It has displays on her remarkable life and political struggles.

⏰ 10am-5pm Mon-Sat, 11am-4pm Sun) is the place for you. It has galleries devoted to archaeology, archery, botany, ethnology, geology, numismatics, Oriental studies and zoology, but the real treat here is the Egyptology section and its collection of mummies. One particularly interesting section is devoted to the work of Dr Richard Neave, who has rebuilt faces of people who have been dead for over 3000 years, pioneering techniques that are now used in criminal forensics.

Take bus No 11, 16, 41 or 42 from Piccadilly Gardens.

WHITWORTH ART GALLERY

Manchester's second-most-important **art gallery** (☎ 275 7450; University of Manchester; Oxford Rd; admission free; ⏰ 10am-5pm Mon-Sat & 2-5pm Sun) has a wonderful collection of British watercolours. It also houses the best selection of historic textiles outside London and a number of galleries devoted to the work of artists from Dürer and Rembrandt to Lucien Freud and David Hockney.

All this high art aside, you may find that the most interesting part of the gallery are the rooms dedicated to wallpaper, proof that bland pastels and horrible flowery patterns are not the final word in home decoration.

MANCHESTER FOR CHILDREN

Urbis (p615) is always full of kids who find the interactive displays quite engaging, and the **Castlefield Urban Heritage Park** (p615) is the perfect all-day destination with a host of different activities and exhibits suited to younger visitors. Here, too, the canalside parks and walkways are pleasantly distract-ing. Manchester United's ground **Old Trafford** (opposite) is always popular with fans who are getting younger and younger, while the **Imperial War Museum North** (opposite), despite its sombre themes, is designed to engage the interest of kids barely into double figures.

City Life Kids (£3.50), available at the TIC and all bookshops in the city, is a comprehensive guide to virtually every aspect of family-oriented Manchester.

QUIRKY MANCHESTER

You don't have to work too hard to find oddity in Manchester: spend enough time on Piccadilly Circus and you'll know what we mean. However, for a different (and altogether fabulous) view of the city, climb to the parapet of the **Godlee Observatory** (opposite), a place virtually nobody ever goes to, a far cry from the alternative circus that is **Affleck's Palace** (p623), where in order to go unnoticed it's best if you look like Marilyn Manson or a really scruffy Kurt Cobain.

When you're done, you'll have to unwind with a pint in the **Temple of Convenience** (p620), a tiny basement pub with a terrific atmosphere located in…a former public toilet.

FESTIVALS & EVENTS

Manchester Irish Festival (www.manchesterirish festival.co.uk) Manchester's huge Irish community goes bonkers for a week in mid-March.

Manchester Pride (☎ 0871 230 2624; www.manches terpride.com) One of England's biggest celebrations of gay, bisexual and transgender life, held in late August.

Move (☎ 0870 405 0445; www.virgintrains.co.uk/move) Alternative music festival at Old Trafford Lancashire Cricket Ground in mid-July; The Cure headlined in 2004.

GAY & LESBIAN MANCHESTER

The city's gay scene is unsurpassed outside London, and caters to every taste. The useful *Gay & Lesbian Village Guide*, available from the TIC, lists numerous gay bars, clubs, galleries and groups. For other information, check with the **Manchester Gay Centre** (☎ 274 3814; Sydney St, Salford) and the **Lesbian & Gay Foundation** (☎ 235 8035; www.lgf.org.uk; ✆ 4-10pm). *All Points North* is a good free monthly paper covering the north of England and Scotland. The city's best pink website is www.gaymanchester.co.uk.

At the heart of it all is the Gay Village, centred on gorgeous Canal St. Here you will find bars, clubs, restaurants and hotels that cater almost exclusively to the pink pound.

The country's biggest gay and lesbian arts festival, It's Queer Up North (IQUP), takes place every two years – the next in spring 2006. **Manchester Pride** kicks off around the end of August each year and attracts over 500,000 people.

SLEEPING

Manchester's hotels cater mostly to the business traveller, but offer a dizzying range of deals, mostly at weekends, so prices can fluctuate wildly. We recommend that you use the TIC's accommodation service (£3) in order to find the kind of place you want for the best price. Remember that during the football season (August to May), rooms can be almost impossible to find if Manchester United are playing at home.

City Centre
BUDGET

YHA Manchester (☎ 839 9960; www.yha.org.uk; Potato Wharf; dm £19.50) This purpose-built canalside hostel is one of the best in the country, a top-class facility with four- and six-bed dorms, all en suite, as well as a host of good facilities, from a comfortable TV lounge to a laundry room. It's in the Castlefield area.

MID-RANGE

Castlefield (☎ 832 7073; www.castlefield-hotel.co.uk; 3 Liverpool Rd; s/d from £40/56; P 🗙) Another successful warehouse conversion that has resulted in a thoroughly modern business hotel overlooking the canal basin. It has spacious, comfortable rooms and excellent amenities, including a fitness centre and pool that is free to guests.

Mitre (☎ 834 4128; fax 839 1646; Cathedral Gates; s/d from £40/70) A stone's throw from the cathedral, this slightly old-fashioned place with comfortably Spartan rooms has found itself very much in demand over the last few years as Manchester's chic shopping district has grown up around it.

The Ox (☎ 839 7740; www.theox.co.uk; 71 Liverpool ...; ...44.95) Not quite your traditional B&B

(breakfast is extra), but an excellent choice nonetheless; nine oxblood-red rooms with tidy amenities above a fine gastro-pub (see opposite) in the heart of Castlefield. It's the best deal in town for the location.

TOP END

Malmaison (☎ 278 1000; www.malmaison.com; Joshua Hoyle Bldg, Auburn St; r Mon-Fri/Sat & Sun £129/99; 🖳) The Malmaison crowd just don't get tired of picking up designer awards, and this wonderfully stylish hotel across the street from the Piccadilly train station is no different. The rooms have all the Malmaison ingredients: huge beds dressed in fine fabrics and Egyptian cotton, slick art throughout and terrific power showers.

Midland (☎ 236 3333; www.themidland.co.uk; Peter St; d Mon-Fri/Sat & Sun from £110/80; 🖳 🗙) There could hardly have been a more suitably sumptuous setting for Mr Rolls to shake hands with Mr Royce than the lobby of this extraordinary Edwardian hotel just opposite the G-Mex Exhibition Centre. The luxury continues through the bars and dining room, but it all gets a little less dramatic in the bedrooms, which are the height of comfort but lacking that Edwardian panache. A £12 million refurb is about to get underway.

Rossetti (☎ 247 7744; www.aliashotels.com; 107 Piccadilly St; r from £105; 🖳) So long stevedore, hello Steven Dorff: this converted textile factory is now one of the city's coolest hotels. A favourite with showbiz celebs, it's a very stylish blend of original fittings and features with hip art and contemporary design. The loft-style bedrooms feature Moltini designer furniture from Italy, Monsoon showers and stacks of Aqua Sulis toiletries. If you want to go all out, go for one of the self-contained penthouse suites (£330). The super-cool, jeans-wearing staff appear casual, but the service is anything but.

Salford Quays
MID-RANGE
Old Trafford Lodge (☎ 874 3333; www.lccc.co.uk; Talbot Rd; r Mon-Fri/Sat & Sun from £59/49) Cricket fans will salivate at the thought of watching a first-class match from the comfort of their bedroom balcony; for the rest of us, this is a pretty good business hotel with decent amenities.

TOP END
The Lowry (☎ 827 4000; www.rfhotels.com; 50 Dearman's Pl, Chapel Wharf; s/d from £77/125) Simply dripping with designer luxury and five-star comfort, Manchester's top hotel has fabulous rooms with enormous beds, ergonomically designed furniture, walk-in wardrobes and bathrooms finished in Italian porcelain tiles and glass mosaic. You can also soothe yourself with a skin-brightening treatment or an aromatherapy head massage at the health spa.

Other Areas
BUDGET
Manchester Backpackers' Hostel (☎ 865 9296; 64 Cromwell Rd; dm £15) An very pleasant private hostel in Stretford, 2 miles south of the centre, with cooking facilities, a TV lounge and some doubles. It's a cinch to get to and from the centre via the Metrolink (Stretford stop).

University of Manchester/UMIST (☎ 275 2888; www.accommodation.man.ac.uk; Central Accommodations Office, The Precinct Centre, Oxford Rd; dm/d from £9/30; ☻ Jun-Sep) With over 9000 beds in a variety of rooms, from traditional residence halls to smart, modern flats spread throughout the campuses and suburbs, the university does a roaring summer trade. Call the office (9am to 5pm Monday to Friday) for details and bookings.

EATING
You'd have to go to London to find a bigger choice of cafés and restaurants. The most distinctive restaurant areas are Chinatown, in the city centre, and the southern suburb of Rusholme, on Wilmslow Rd (the extension of Oxford St/Rd), more commonly known as Curry Mile, with a concentration of Indian and Pakistani restaurants unsurpassed in

Europe. The Northern Quarter is the place to go for organic hippy shakes and inventive veggie cooking, while the city's fancy restaurants are pretty much spread all over. Many bars and pubs also do food; see Drinking p620. Below is but a small starter course.

BUDGET
Café And (☎ 834 1136; 74-76 High St; sandwiches £3; ☻ 9am-7pm Mon-Fri, 10am-7pm Sat, noon-5pm Sun) A trendy café, hip record store, contemporary art gallery and retro furniture shop all in one makes this your one stop for everything you might possibly need in the Northern Quarter. The toasties and wraps are delicious, but it's the excellent organic soups that kept us coming back for more.

Eighth Day (☎ 273 4878; 111 Oxford Rd; mains around £4; ☻ 9.30am-5pm Mon-Sat) New and most definitely improved after a major clean-up, the students' favourite environment-friendly hangout sells everything to make you feel good about your place in the world, from fair-trade teas to homeopathic remedies. The vegetarian- and vegan-friendly menu is substantial.

Love Saves the Day (☎ 832 0777; Tib St; house salad £5) The Northern Quarter's most popular café is a New York–style deli, small supermarket and sit-down eatery in one large, airy room. Everybody comes here – from crusties to corporate types – to sit around over a spot of lunch and discuss the day's goings on. A wonderful spot.

Earth Café (☎ 834 1996; www.earthcafe.co.uk 16-20 Turner St; chef's special £5.40; ☻ 10am-5pm Tue-Sat) Below the Manchester Buddhist Centre, this gourmet vegetarian café is working hard toward becoming the first 100% organic spot in town. The chef's special – a main dish, side and two salad portions – is generally excellent and always filling.

MID-RANGE
El Rincón del Rafa (☎ 839 8819; Longworth St; mains £9-12) Descend the steps into this basement restaurant and find yourself in a little corner of Spain, complete with mouthwatering tapas, bull-fighting posters and the kind of buzz more in keeping with Madrid than Manchester. It's always packed so book ahead.

The Ox (☎ 839 7740; 71 Liverpool Rd; mains £9-12; ☻ lunch & dinner) Manchester's only gastro-pub has elevated boozer-dining to a whole new level and earned plenty of kudos in the process.

The Brit nouveau cuisine – how's about an oven-roasted T-bone steak with tempura onion rings, beef-steak tomatoes and Portobello mushrooms – is complemented by an almost exclusively Australian wine list.

Tampopo (☎ 819 1966; 16 Albert Sq; mains from £7; ✆ lunch & dinner) Fast and furiously efficient, you'll be in and out of this Asian fusion canteen-style restaurant before you can learn the difference between the various *gorengs*. The food is uniformly excellent and well worth the 30-second wait.

Shere Khan (☎ 256 2624; 52 Wilmslow Rd; mains around £7; ✆ lunch & dinner Sun-Fri) Of the almost impossible selection of curry houses along the Curry Mile, we recommend this place above all others for its plush setting, unfailingly good cuisine, polite, friendly service and for the fact that their sauces can be found stocked in supermarkets all over the country.

TOP END

Le Mont (☎ 605 8282; Level 5 & 6, Urbis, City Gardens; 2-course lunch £14.95, 3-course dinner £24.95; ✆ lunch & dinner Mon-Fri, dinner only Sat) These days Robert Kisby's multiple-award-winning French restaurant on the upper floors of Urbis is all the rage; for the excellent cuisine, the fabulous views and the chichi Bollinger Bar – the only one outside London.

Yang Sing (☎ 236 2200; 34 Princess St; lunch mains around £9, dinner mains £16-22; ✆ lunch & dinner) A serious contender for best Chinese restaurant in England, Yang Sing attracts diners from all over with its exceptional Cantonese cuisine. From a dim sum lunch to a full evening banquet the food is superb, and the waiters will patiently explain the intricacies of each dish to punters who can barely pronounce them.

DRINKING

The current zeitgeist is the trendy café-bar with a wide selection of international beers and plenty of fancy, fruity cocktails, but the city has a boozer for every kind of thirst, from Bailey's to Boddington's. The Northern Quarter is full of trendy bars, while in recent years the Castlefield area has seen a mushrooming of chic watering holes. Otherwise, the area around Deansgate and Albert Sq has a mix of old-style pubs, designer dens and cheesy disco-bars. To make sense of it all, get a copy of the fortnightly *City Life* (£1.50), available most anywhere.

Bars

Bar Centro (☎ 835 2863; 72-74 Tib St; mains £5-8) A Northern Quarter stalwart, very popular with the bohemian crowd precisely because it doesn't try to be. Great beer, nice staff and a better-than-average bar menu make this one of the choice spots in the area.

FAB Café (☎ 236 2019; 111 Portland St) A place to check out if you're a big fan of *Thunderbirds*. The music is loud but best of all are the Thunderbirds models and puppets decorating the club. FAB Virgil!

Kro Bar (☎ 274 3100; 325 Oxford Rd; sandwiches £2.50, mains £5-8) The ice-cool hand of Scandinavian design is all over this terrific bar in the middle of student-land. An excellent bar menu packs them in at lunch while night-time DJs keep it going until closing. Its younger brother **Kro 2** (☎ 236 1048; Oxford Rd) is next to the BBC closer to the city, but it's not quite as classy as the original.

Ra!n (☎ 235 6500; 80 Great Bridgewater St) A rival to Dukes 92 (see Pubs) for best outdoor drinking, indoors it's both trendy newstyle bar and – downstairs – old-fashioned boozer, so whatever your mood, you'll find the right ambience in this former umbrella factory (there is logic to the name!).

Temple of Convenience (☎ 288 9834; Great Bridgewater St) This tiny basement bar with a capacity of about 30 has a great jukebox and a fine selection of spirits, all crammed into a converted public toilet. Hardly your bog-standard pub.

Pubs

Britons Protection (☎ 236 5895; 50 Great Bridgewater St; mains around £7) Whisky – 200 different kinds of it – is the beverage of choice at this liver-threatening, proper English pub that also does Tudor-style meals (boar, venison and the like). An old-fashioned boozer, no fancy stuff.

Dukes 92 (☎ 839 8646; 2 Castle St) Castlefield's best pub, converted stables that once belonged to the Duke of Bridgewater, has comfy, deep sofas inside and plenty of seating outside, overlooking Lock 92 of the Rochdale Canal – hence the name. If it's sunny, there's no better spot to enjoy a pint of ale.

Lass O'Gowrie (☎ 273 6932; 36 Charles St; mains around £6) A Victorian classic off Oxford St that brews its own beer in the basement. It's a favourite with students, old-timers and a clique of BBC employees who work just across the street in the Beeb's Manchester HQ. It also does good-value bar meals.

Other decent boozers include the **Old Wellington Inn** (☎ 830 1440; 4 Cathedral Gates), one of the oldest buildings in the city and a lovely spot for a pint of genuine ale, and **Peveril of the Peak** (☎ 236 6364; 127 Great Bridgewater St), an unpretentious pub with wonderful Victorian glazed tilework outside.

ENTERTAINMENT
Nightclubs

Having set the standard for how to party in the late 1980s and early 1990s, Manchester's club scene has mellowed substantially since those drug-fuelled halcyon days – even if paradoxically there's more choice today. Clubs host a forever-changing mixture of dance nights, so check *City Life* for what's on when you're in town. What follows is but a toe-poke in the vast ocean.

Music Box (☎ 236 9971; www.themusicbox.info; 65 Oxford St; admission £5-12; ☾ Wed-Sat) Deep in Jilly's Rockworld complex you'll find our favourite club in town and – judging by the queues – most everyone else's too. They come for the superb monthly club nights, like Mr Scruff's 'Keep it Unreal' and the dirty house of 'Stylus' as well as a host of terrific one-offs.

Sankey's Soap (☎ 661 9085; www.tribalgathering .co.uk; Jersey St, Ancoats; admission free-£10; ☾ Fri & Sat) With regulars like Danny Tenaglia, Sasha and Layo & Bushwacka in the box, hard-nose clubbers are in good hands when they trek out to the middle of Ancoats. Techno, breakbeats, tribal and progressive house.

South (831 7756; www.south-club.co.uk; 4A South King St; admission £5-6; ☾ Fri & Sat) An excellent basement club to kick off the weekend: Friday night is Rock 'n' Roll Bar, featuring everything from Ibrahim Ferrer to Northern Soul; and Saturday is Disco Rescue – that does exactly what it says.

Other clubs worth checking out include **Elemental** (☎ 236 7227; 69 Oxford St), popular for its mix of commercial and house nights, and **Club V** (☎ 834 9975; 111 Deansgate; admission £5; ☾ Fri & Sat) a great little basement club that moves to garage beats.

Cinemas

Cornerhouse (☎ 228 2463; www.cornerhouse.org; 70 Oxford St) Your only destination for good

arthouse releases; also has a gallery and café.

Filmworks (☎ 0870 010 2030; www.thefilmworks .co.uk; Printworks, Exchange Sq) Ultramodern 20-screen complex in the middle of the Printworks Centre; there's also an IMAX theatre.

Odeon (☎ 0870 505 0007; www.odeon.co.uk; 1 Oxford Rd) Chain cinema that shows only mainstream releases on its seven screens.

Theatre

Green Room (☎ 236 1677; 54 Whitworth St West) The premiere fringe venue in town.

Manchester Opera House (☎ 242 2509; www .manchestertheatres.co.uk; Quay St) West End shows and lavish musicals make up the bulk of the programme.

Library Theatre (☎ 236 7110; Central Library, St Peter's Sq) Old plays and new work in a small theatre beneath the Central Library.

Royal Exchange (☎ 833 9833; St Anne's Sq) Contemporary, interesting plays are standard at this magnificent, modern theatre-in-the-round.

Live Music
ROCK MUSIC

Band on the Wall (☎ 834 1786; www.bandonthewall .org; 25 Swan St) A top-notch venue that hosts everything from rock to world music, with splashes of jazz, blues and folk thrown in for good measure.

G-Mex Exhibition Centre (☎ 834 2700) A mid-size venue that hosts rock concerts by not-quite-super-successful bands as well as exhibitions and indoor sporting events.

Manchester Roadhouse (☎ 228 1789; www .theroadhouselive.co.uk; 8-10 Newton St) Local bands are put through their paces in front of a generally enthusiastic crowd.

MEN Arena (☎ 950 5000; Great Ducie St) Giant arena that hosts large-scale rock concerts (as well as being the home of the city's ice-hockey and basketball teams).

TOP FIVE MANCHESTER ALBUMS

- *Some Friendly* Charlatans
- *Pills Thrills & Bellyaches* Happy Mondays
- *Stone Roses* The Stone Roses
- *The Queen is Dead* The Smiths
- *Permanent* Joy Division

THE MADCHESTER SOUND

It is often claimed that Manchester is the engine-room of British pop. If this is indeed the case, then the chief engineer was TV presenter and music impresario Tony Wilson, founder of Factory Records – the label that in 1983 released New Order's ground-breaking *Blue Monday*, which successfully fused the guitar-driven sound of punk with a pulsating dance beat – to this day the best-selling 12" in British history.

When the money started pouring in, Wilson took the next, all-important step: he opened his own nightclub that would provide a platform for local bands to perform. The Haçienda opened its doors with plenty of fanfare but just wouldn't take off. Things started to turn around when the club started to embrace a brand new sound coming out of Chicago and Detroit: house. DJs Mike Pickering, Graeme Park and Jon Da Silva were the music's most important apostles, and when ecstasy hit the scene late in the decade, it seemed that every kid in town was 'mad for it'.

Heavily influenced by these new arrivals, the city's guitar bands took notice and began shaping their sounds to suit the clubbers' needs. The most successful was The Stone Roses, who in 1989 released *Fools Gold*, a pulsating hit with the rapid shuffle of James Brown's *Funky Drummer* and a druggie guitar sound that drove dancers wild. Around the same time the Happy Mondays, fronted by the laddish Shaun Ryder and the wacked-out Bez (whose only job was to lead the dancing from the stage), hit the scene with the infectious *Hallelujah*. The other big anthems of the day were *The One I Love* by The Charlatans, A Guy Called Gerald's *Voodoo Ray*, and *Pacific* by 808 State; all local bands and producers. The party known as Madchester was officially declared.

The party ended in 1992. Over-danced and over-drugged, the city woke up with a terrible hangover. The Haçienda went bust, Shaun Ryder's legendary drug intake stymied his musical creativity and the Stone Roses withdrew in a haze of post-party depression, not to be heard of again until 1994, when they released *Second Coming*, but it just couldn't match their eponymous debut album. They lasted another two years before breaking up. The fertile crossover scene – which had seen clubbers go mad at rock gigs and rock bands play the kind of dance sounds that kept the floor thumping until the early hours – virtually disappeared and the two genres withdrew into a more familiar isolation.

The next five years saw the rise of Manchester's most successful band, Oasis, whose *(What's the Story) Morning Glory* hit the shelves in 1995, selling more copies than all of the Manchester bands that preceded them. Despite their success and the in-your-face posturing of the Gallagher brothers, they were doomed to a limited run because they relied too much on the chord structures and infectious melodic lines created by The Beatles 25 years earlier. They're still going, but their one-time claim of being the most famous band in the world is sadly out of date.

Today, there is no such thing as Madchester. Eager to transcend the clichés that their success engendered, most of the city's musical talents refuse to be labelled as having any particular sound: jazzy house giant Mr Scruff, for instance, doesn't sound anything like the folksy guitar style of About a Boy or the funky hip-hop beats of Rae & Christian. There's plenty going on (in 2004 there were at least 20 different labels in the city), but it's reflective of an ever-changing, evolving and, most importantly, international scene.

Madchester is legendary precisely because it is no more, but it was a lot of fun. If you missed the party, you can get a terrific sense of what it was like by watching Michael Winterbottom's *24-Hour Party People* (2002), which captures the hedonism, extravagance and genius of Madchester's cast of characters, particularly Tony Wilson, played with uncanny accuracy by Steve Coogan.

CLASSICAL MUSIC

Bridgewater Hall (☎ 907 9000; www.bridgewater-hall .co.uk; Lower Mosley St) The world-renowned Hallé Orchestra has its home at this enormous and impressive concert hall, which also hosts a rich and varied programme of other events.

Lowry (☎ 876 2000; www.thelowry.com; Pier 8, Salford Quays) Two theatres – the 1750-capacity Lyric and 460-capacity Quays – host a diverse range of performances, from dance to comedy.

Manchester Cathedral (☎ 833 2220; Victoria St) A summer season of concerts by the Cantata Choir and ensemble groups.

Royal Northern College of Music (☎ 907 5555; www.rncm.ac.uk; 124 Oxford Rd) A full programme of extremely high-quality classical music and other contemporary offerings.

Sport

For most people, Manchester plus sport equals football, and football means Manchester United. That may be true everywhere else (which is why United are covered in the Sights & Activities section, p616) but not here – like all good northerners, most Mancunians are more comfortable supporting the scrappy underdog with the huge heart rather than the well-oiled soccer machine.

MANCHESTER CITY

Manchester's best-loved team is the perennial underachiever, Manchester City. In 2003 they moved to the spanking-new **City of Manchester stadium** (Sportcity, Rowsley St), where you can enjoy the **Manchester City Experience** (☎ 0870 062 1894; www.mcfc.com; adult/child £7.50/4.50), a tour of the ground, dressing rooms and museum before the inevitable steer into the kit shop. Tours must be booked in advance.

LANCASHIRE COUNTY CRICKET CLUB

Cricket is a big deal here, and the **Lancashire club** (☎ 282 4000; Warwick Rd), founded in 1816 as The Aurora before changing its name in 1864, is one of the most beloved of all England's county teams, despite not having won the county championship since 1930. The really big match in Lancashire's calendar is the Roses match against Yorkshire, but if you're not around for that one, the other games in the county season (admission £10 to £12), which runs throughout the whole summer, are a great day out.

International test matches are also played here occasionally.

SHOPPING

The huge selection of shops here will send a shopper's pulse into orbit; every taste and budget is catered for.

Millennium Quarter

The area around New Cathedral St, Exchange Sq and the impressive Triangle shopping arcade is the hot new shopping district, full of chi-chi boutiques and the queen of all department stores, **Harvey Nichols** (☎ 828 8888; 21 New Cathedral St).

Northern Quarter

Rag-trade wholesalers have given way to independent retailers stocking all manner of hip urban wear, retro fashions and other left-of-centre wear. At the heart of it all is **Affleck's Palace** (Oldham St), a four-storey warehouse full of outlets that Manchester's teenage Goths and the rest of the glumerati have turned into a social day out. The rest of the neighbourhood is full of great shops, including the marvellous **Oxfam Original** (☎ 839 3160; Unit 8, Smithfield Bldg, Oldham St), with terrific retro gear from the 1960s and '70s.

West End

Everything needs a catchy name, so the traditionally upmarket shopping area around St Anne's Sq, King St and Bridge St – full of attractive boutiques for designers both homegrown and international – is now called the West End.

SOMETHING FOR THE WEEKEND

A weekend is just about enough time to whet your appetite for Manchester's many delights. After you've checked into somewhere with a little bit of style – the **Rossetti** (p618) has more than enough, while the **Ox** (p618) offers affordable cool – do a little window browsing before grabbing a bite. Pick a bar, any bar, and keep going: there's an unhealthy choice of clubs if you're not that keen on a Saturday-morning start.

Saturday should be about a little sightseeing, and Manchester has something for literally every interest, from art to science and football. Break for dim sum at the fabulous **Yang Sing** (p620) and do some more, or devote the afternoon to some serious shopping. The evening should be about a meal, a drink and perhaps a concert – from rock to classical. Then, another drink and if you're really up for it, another club.

Saturday night should dictate the pace of Sunday. Brunch, a little browsing and a stroll along the canal bank will deplete the energy of some, while another full day's sightseeing will barely put a dint in others. If you didn't make it to the **Imperial War Museum North** (p616) on Saturday, get there today.

GETTING THERE & AWAY
Air
Manchester airport (☎ 489 3000; www.manchester airport.co.uk) is the largest outside London, served by 17 locations throughout Britain.

Bus
National Express serves most major cities almost hourly from Chorlton St coach station in the city centre. Destinations include Liverpool (£5.25, 1¼ hours), Leeds (£7, one hour) and London (£19, 4¾ hours).

Train
Manchester Piccadilly is the main station for trains to and from the rest of the country, although Victoria station serves Halifax and Bradford. The two stations are linked by Metrolink. Trains head to Blackpool (£10.45, half-hourly, 1¼ hours), Liverpool Lime St (£10.20, half-hourly, 45 minutes), Newcastle (£36, six daily, three hours) and London (£42, seven daily, three hours).

GETTING AROUND
To/From the Airport
The airport is 12 miles south of the city. A train to or from Victoria Station costs £3.10, a coach £2.70.

Public Transport
The excellent public transportation system can be used with a variety of **Day Saver tickets** (bus £3.30, bus & train £3.80, bus & Metrolink £4.50, train & Metrolink £5, bus, train & Metrolink £6.50). For

---

THE WAR OF THE ROSES
The War of the Roses was nothing more than a protracted quarrel between two factions, the House of Lancaster (whose symbol was a red rose) and the House of York (represented by a white one), over who would rule England.

It began with the Lancastrian Henry VI (1422–61 and 1470–71), who was terrific as a patron of culture and learning, but totally inept as a ruler, and prone to bouts of insanity. During the worst of these he had to hand power over to Richard, Duke of York, who served as protector but acted as king. Henry may have been nutty, but his wife Margaret of Anjou was anything but, and in 1460 she put an end to Richard's political ambitions by raising an army to defeat and kill him at the Battle of Wakefield. Round one to Lancaster.

Next it was the turn of Richard's son Edward. In 1461 he avenged his father's defeat by inflicting one of his own on Henry and Margaret, declaring himself Edward IV (1461–70 and 1471–83) as a result. One all.

But Edward's victory owed much to the political machinations of Richard Neville, Earl of Warwick – appropriately nicknamed 'the kingmaker' – but the throne proved an amnesiac and in time Eddie forgot his friends. In 1470 Warwick jumped ship and sided with the Lancastrians.' Edward was exiled and Henry, Margaret and Warwick were all smiles. Half-time and the score was two-one to Lancaster.

Edward came back strongly a year later. He first defeated and killed Warwick at the Battle of Barnet before crushing Henry and Margaret at Tewkesbury. Henry was executed in the Tower of London and Margaret ransomed back to France, where she died in poverty. Just to make sure, Edward also killed their son.

The Yorkists were back in the game, and Edward proved to be a good and popular king. When he died (apparently worn out by his sexual excesses), power passed to his brother Richard, who was to rule as regent until Edward's 12-year-old son came of age. Two months after the king's death, Richard arranged for the 'disappearance' of his nephew and he was crowned Richard III. The Yorkists, however, had scored an own goal, as when rumours of Dickie's dastardly deed became known, he was as popular as a bad smell. In 1485, the Lancastrians, led by the young Henry Tudor, defeated Richard at the Battle of Bosworth, leaving the fallen king to offer his kingdom in exchange for a horse. Final result: victory to Lancaster.

The coronation of Henry VII, and his subsequent marriage to Edward IV's daughter Elizabeth, put an end to the fighting and ushered in the Tudor dynasty, but it didn't end the rivalry.

They may not be fighting with swords and lances, but one of the great enmities in English football today is that between Lancashire's Manchester United – who wear red – and Yorkshire's Leeds United, who wear all-white.

inquiries about local transport, including night buses, contact the Greater Manchester Public Transportation Authority (GMPTE) **Travelshop** (☎ 228 7811; www.gmpte.com; 9 Portland St, Piccadilly Gardens; ◷ 8am-8pm).

BUS
Centreline bus No 4 provides a free service around the heart of Manchester every 10 minutes. Pick up a route map from the TIC. Most local buses start from Piccadilly Gardens.

METROLINK
There are frequent **Metrolink** (☎ 205 2000; www.metrolink.co.uk) trams between Victoria and Piccadilly train stations and G-Mex (for Castlefield) as well as further afield to Salford Quay. Buy your tickets from the platform machine.

TRAIN
Castlefield is served by Deansgate station with rail links to Piccadilly, Oxford Rd and Salford Crescent stations.

CHESHIRE

Largely agricultural Cheshire is all about farming and a rich Tudor heritage. Two-tone Friesian cows nuzzle the grasslands surrounding genuine black-and-white half-timbered farmhouses, not to be confused with the mock-Tudor monstrosities inhabited by the socceratis of Manchester and Liverpool – a lot of money and no taste goes a long way. For us mere mortals, however, handsome, gentle Cheshire is mostly about Chester.

CHESTER
☎ 01244 / pop 80,130
Marvellous Chester is one of England's most beautiful cities, a tidy collection of Tudor and Victorian buildings wrapped in an almost continuous 2-mile red sandstone wall originally built during Roman times, when, as Castra Devana, it was the largest Roman fortress on the island.

For much of the Middle Ages Chester was the northwest's most important port, but the gradual silting of the River Dee diminished its importance and by the 18th century it had been overtaken by Liverpool.

These days Chester ekes out a comfortable living as a major retail centre and tourist hotspot: they come, see and shop.

Orientation
Most places of interest are inside the walls where the Roman street pattern is relatively intact. From the Cross (the stone pillar which marks the town centre), four roads fan out to the four principal gates.

Information
Cheshire Constabulary (☎ 350000; Castle Esplanade)
Chester Royal Infirmary (☎ 365000; St Martin's Way)
Chester Visitors' Centre (☎ 351609; Vicar's Lane; ◷ 9.30am-5.30pm Mon-Sat, 10am-4pm Sun May-Oct, 10am-5pm Mon-Sat Nov-Apr)
i-station (☎ 401680; Rufus Ct; Net access per 30 mins £1)
Post office (2 St John St; ◷ 9am-5.30pm Mon-Sat)
TIC (☎ 402111; tis@chestercc.gov.uk; Northgate St; ◷ 9am-5.30pm Mon-Sat, 10am-4pm Sun May-Oct, 10am-5pm Mon-Sat Nov-Apr)

Sights & Activities
CITY WALLS
A good way to get a sense of Chester's unique character is to walk the 2-mile circuit along the walls that surround the historic centre. Originally built by the Romans around AD 70, they were altered substantially over the following centuries but have retained their current position since around 1200. The TIC's *Walk Around Chester Walls* leaflet (99p) is an excellent companion guide.

Of the many features along the walls, the most eye-catching is the prominent **Eastgate**, where you can see the most famous **clock** in England after London's Big Ben, built for Queen Victoria's Diamond Jubilee in 1897.

At the southeastern corner of the walls are the **wishing steps**, added in 1785; local legend claims that if you can run up and down these uneven steps while holding your breath your wish will come true. We question the veracity of this claim because our wish was not a twisted ankle.

Just inside Southgate, known here as **Bridgegate** (as it's at the northern end of the Old Dee Bridge), is the 1664 **Bear & Billet** pub, Chester's oldest timber-framed building and once a tollgate into the city.

On the western side of the walls lies the **Roodee**, Chester's ancient horse-racing track and still one of the country's most beautiful. There are races here during the summer.

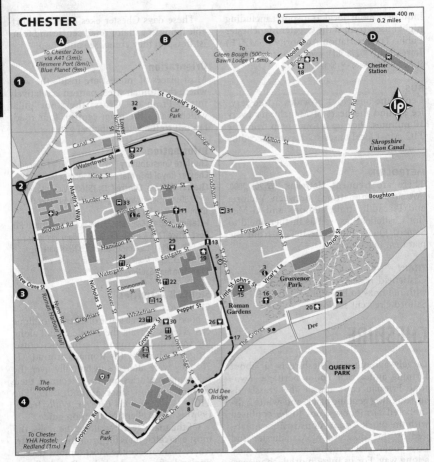

CHESTER

THE ROWS

Chester's other great draw is the **Rows**, a series of two-level galleried arcades along the four streets that fan out from the central Cross. The architecture is a handsome mix of Victorian and Tudor (original and mock) buildings that house a fantastic collection of individually owned shops. The origin of the Rows is a little unclear, but it is believed that as the Roman walls slowly crumbled, medieval traders built their shops against the resulting rubble banks, while later arrivals built theirs on top.

OTHER SIGHTS & ACTIVITIES

The **cathedral** (☎ 324756; donation £3; ☯ 7.30am-6.30pm) was a Benedictine abbey built on the remains of an earlier Saxon church dedicated to St Werburgh. The abbey was closed in 1540 as part of Henry VIII's dissolution frenzy, but was reconsecrated as a cathedral the following year. Although the cathedral itself was given a substantial Victorian facelift, the 12th-century cloister and its surrounding buildings are essentially unaltered and retain much of the structure from the early monastic years.

There are 1¼-hour **guided tours** (adult/child £2.50/1.50; ☯ 9.30am-4pm Mon-Sat), but they must be booked in advance.

The excellent **Grosvenor Museum** (☎ 402008; Grosvenor St; admission free; ☯ 10.30am-5pm Mon-Sat, 2-5pm Sun) is the place to go if you want to study Chester's rich and varied history, beginning with a comprehensive collection of Roman tombstones, the largest in the country. At the back of the museum is a preserved Georgian house, complete with kitchen, drawing room, bedroom and bathroom.

The **Dewa Roman Experience** (☎ 343407; Pierpoint Lane; admission £4.20; ☻ 9am-5pm), just off Bridge St, takes you through a reconstructed Roman street with the aim of showing you what Roman life was like.

The most complete set of genuine Roman remains are opposite the visitor centre, outside the city walls. Here is what's left of the **amphitheatre** (admission free), once an arena that seated 7000 spectators (making it the country's largest), now little more than steps buried in grass.

Adjacent to the amphitheatre is **St John the Baptist Church** (Vicars Lane; ☻ 9.15am-6pm), built on the site of an older Saxon church in 1075. It started out as a cathedral of Mercia before being rebuilt by the Normans. The eastern end of the church, abandoned in 1581 when St John's became a parish, now lies in peaceful ruin and includes the remains of a Norman choir and medieval chapels.

Steps at the back of the church lead down to the riverside promenade known as the Groves. Here you can hire different kinds of **boats** (per hr £5-7; ☻ 9am-6pm Apr-Sep) with pedals, oars or small engines. This is also the departure point for river cruises (see below).

Tours

The two tourist offices offer a broad range of walking tours departing from both centres. Each tour lasts between 1½ and two hours.
Ghosthunter Trail (adult/child £3.50/3; ☻ 7.30pm Thu-Sat Jun-Oct, Sat only rest of year) The ubiquitous ghost tour, looking for things that go bump in the night.
Pastfinder Tour (adult/child £4/3; ☻ 10.15am) 2000 years of Chester history

Roman Soldier Patrols (adult/child £4/3; ☻ 1.45pm Thu-Sat Jun-Aug) This tour of Fortress Deva is led by Caius Julius Quartus; perfect if you've kids in tow.

You can also take a cruise along the Dee; contact **Bithell Boats** (☎ 325394; www .showboatsofchester.co.uk) for details of its 30-minute and hour-long cruises up and down the Dee, including a foray into the gorgeous Eaton Estate, home of the Duke and Duchess of Westminster. All departures are from the riverside along the Groves and cost from £5 to £12.

City Sightseeing Chester (☎ 347452; www .city-sightseeing.com; adult/child £7/2.50, with boat tour £9.50/3.50; every 15-30 min Apr-Oct, weekends only Mar) offers open-top bus tours of the city, picking up from the TIC and the visitor centre; the additional river cruise is optional.

Festivals & Events

Held from mid-July to early August, the three-week **Summer Music Festival** (☎ 320700; www.chesterfestivals.co.uk) is a season highlight, featuring performances by all manner of stars both big and small. The **Chester Jazz Festival** (☎ 340005; www.chesterjazz.com; admission free-£8) is a two-week showcase from late August to early September.

Sleeping

If you're visiting between Easter and September, you'd better book early if you want to avoid going over-budget or settling for far less than you bargained for. Except for a handful of options – including the city's best – most of the accommodation is outside the city walls but within easy walking distance of the centre. Hoole Rd, a 10- to 15-minute walk from the centre and leading beyond the railway tracks to the M53/M56, is lined with low- to mid-price B&Bs.

TOP FIVE PUBS FOR A PINT

- **Philharmonic** (p639; Liverpool)
- **Temple of Convenience** (p620; Manchester)
- **Britons Protection** (p620; Manchester)
- **The Albion** (below right; Chester)
- **Rover's Return** (p649; Douglas, Isle of Man)

BUDGET

Chester YHA Hostel (☎ 0870 770 5762; www.yha.org.uk; 40 Hough Green; dm £14.50) In an elegant Victorian home about a mile from the city centre, this hostel has a variety of dorms that sleep from two to 10 people; there's also a cafeteria, a kitchen and a shop on the premises.

Brook St near the train station has a couple of good-value B&Bs from around £20 per person. The friendly and accommodating **Ormonde** (☎ 328816; 126 Brook St) and the comfortable **Aplas Guest House** (☎ 312401; 106 Brook St) are both less than five minutes' walk from the train station.

MID-RANGE

Bawn Lodge (☎ 324971; www.bawnlodge.co.uk; 10 Hoole Rd; s/d £30/50) Spotless rooms with plenty of colour make this charming guesthouse a very pleasant option. It's like staying with a favourite relative; no fuss but plenty of friendliness (and a delicious breakfast).

Grove Villa (☎ 349713; 18 The Groves; s/d from £25/45) You won't find a more tranquil spot in town than this wonderfully positioned Victorian home overlooking the Dee. The rooms have antique beds and great river views.

Redland (☎ 671024; 64 Hough Green; s/d from £45/70) The Victorian exterior belies the luxury inside, which is reminiscent of an earlier age. Each of the 13 individually styled (and named) rooms is exquisitely decorated with ornate antiques according to its period; we liked the Jacobean Room with its over-the-top four-poster bed.

TOP END

Green Bough (☎ 326 241; www.greenbough.co.uk; 60 Hoole Rd; r from £125) The epitome of the boutique hotel, this exclusive Victorian townhouse has individually styled rooms that are all dressed in the best Italian fabrics and wall-coverings, superb antique furniture and period cast-iron and wooden beds, including a handful of elegant four-posters. Modern touches include plasma-screen TVs, ministereos and a range of fancy toiletries.

Chester Grosvenor Hotel & Spa (☎ 324024; www.chestergrosvenor.com; 58 Eastgate St; s/d/ste from £110/140/180; P ✗ ⌨) The best hotel in town with the best location. The huge, sprawling rooms have exquisite period furnishings and modern conveniences such as ISDN lines; the spa (which is open to nonresidents) offers a range of body treatments, including Reiki, Lastone therapy, Indian head massage and four-handed massage.

Eating

There's no shortage of places to eat, but the quality of the fare is often barely above tourist-menu standard. Some pubs do great grub (see Drinking, below).

Francs (☎ 317952; 14 Cuppin St; mains £8-10; ☺ lunch & dinner) A very popular French bistro with a wide-ranging menu of salads, sandwiches and some excellent main courses direct from the French countryside.

Boulevard de la Bastille (Bridge St Row; sandwiches around £3) Our favourite café in town is also one of the most handsome, a very French place on the top tier of the Rows that is perfect for a *café au lait* and *pain au chocolat*.

Ruan Orchid (☎ 400661; 14 Lower Bridge St; 8-course banquet £16.95; ☺ lunch & dinner) Every conceivable Thai dish and concoction of curry is available at this lovely, intimate restaurant.

Katie's Tea Rooms (☎ 400322; 38 Watergate St; tea & scones £3; ☺ 9am-5pm Tue-Sat) Stone-walled tearooms located inside a historic building that is the place to go for a light lunch; after 5pm it turns into **MD's Restaurant** (2-course £10.50; ☺ dinner only Tue-Sat), a continental eatery with a pretty tasty menu.

Drinking

The Albion (☎ 340345; 4 Albion St; mains around £8) has no children, no music, and no machines or big screens (but plenty of Union Jacks). This 'family hostile' Edwardian classic is a throwback pub to a time when ale-drinking still had its own *rituals* – another word for ingrained prejudices. Still, this is one of the finest pubs in northwest England precisely because it doggedly refuses to modernise.

The Falcon (☎ 314555; Lower Bridge St; mains £4.95) is an old-fashioned boozer with a lovely atmosphere; the surprisingly adventurous menu offers up dishes like Jamaican peppered beef or spicy Italian sausage casserole. Great for both a pint and a bite.

Other good pubs include the **Boat House** (The Groves), with great views overlooking the river, and the **Boot Inn** (Eastgate Row), where 14 Roundheads were killed.

Alexander's Jazz Theatre (☎ 340005; Rufus Ct; admission £3-10, free before 10pm) is a combination wine bar, coffee bar and tapas bar.

Getting There & Away
BUS
The National Express bus station is just north of the city inside the ring road. Destinations include Birmingham (£9.50, 2½ hours, four daily), Liverpool (£5.75, one hour, three daily), London (£20, 5½ hours, three daily) and Manchester (£5.25, 1¼ hours, three daily).

For information on local bus services, ring the **Cheshire Bus Line** (☎ 602666). Local buses leave from the **Town Hall Bus Exchange** (☎ 602666). On Sunday and bank holidays a **Sunday Adventurer ticket** (adult/child £3.50/2.50) gives you unlimited travel in Cheshire.

TRAIN
The train station is a 15-minute walk from the city centre via Foregate St and City Rd, or Brook St. City-Rail Link buses are free for people with rail tickets, and run between the station and Bus Stop A on Frodsham St. Trains go to Liverpool (£3.50, 40 minutes, hourly), London Euston (£46.50, three hours, hourly) and Manchester (£10.20, one hour, hourly).

Getting Around
Much of the city centre is closed to traffic from 10.30am to 4.30pm so a car is likely to be a hindrance. Anyway, the walled city is easy to walk around and most places of interest are close to the wall.

City buses depart from the **Town Hall Bus Exchange** (☎ 602666).

Davies Bros Cycles (☎ 371341; 5 Delamere St) has mountain bikes for hire at £13 per day.

AROUND CHESTER
Chester Zoo
The largest of its kind in the country, **Chester Zoo** (☎ 380280; www.chesterzoo.org.uk; adult/child £12/9.50; ☉ 10am-dusk) is about as pleasant a

place as caged animals in artificial renditions of their natural habitats could ever expect to live. It's so big that there's even a **monorail** (adult/child £2/1.50) and a **waterbus** (adult/child £1.60/1.30) to get around in. The zoo is on the A41, 3 miles north of Chester's city centre. Bus Nos 11C and 12C (£2 return, every 15 minutes Monday to Saturday, half-hourly Sunday) run between the town hall and zoo.

Blue Planet Aquarium
They don't do things by halves around Chester, so you'll also find the country's largest aquarium, **Blue Planet** (☎ 0151-357 8804; www.blueplanetaquarium.com; adult/child £9.45/7; ☉ 10am-5pm Mon-Fri, 10am-6pm Sat & Sun), with 10 different kinds of shark, viewed from a 70m-long moving walkway that lets you eyeball them up close. Our researcher, three-year-old Max, assured us that one looked like Bruce from *Finding Nemo*. It's 9 miles north of Chester at junction 10 of the M53 to Liverpool. Bus Nos 1 and 4 run there every half-hour from the Town Hall Bus Exchange in Chester.

Ellesmere Port Boat Museum
Nearby, on the Shropshire Union Canal about 8 miles north of Chester is the superb **Ellesmere Port Boat Museum** (☎ 0151-355 5017; www.boatmuseum.org.uk; South Pier Rd; admission £5.50; ☉ 10am-5pm Apr-Oct, 11am-4pm Sat-Wed Nov-Mar), with a large collection of canal boats as well as indoor exhibits. Take Bus No 4 from the Town Hall Bus Exchange in Chester or it's a 10-minute walk from Ellesmere Port train station.

KNUTSFORD
☎ 01565 / pop 12,660
Fascinating Knutsford would be a typical lowland English market town if it wasn't for the eccentric philanthropy of Richard Watt (1842–1913), a millionaire glove manufacturer with his own personal vision of Mediterranean architecture. The weird and wonderful buildings that he commissioned for the town make it one of the most interesting places in Cheshire.

Although Watt's influence was certainly greater, Knutsford makes the biggest deal of its links with Elizabeth Cleghorn Gaskell (1810–65), who spent her childhood here and used the town as the model for *Cranford* (1853), her most noteworthy novel.

ROYAL MAY DAY

Since 1864 Knutsford has liked to go a bit wild on Royal May Day. The main festivities take place on the Heath, a large area of common land, and include Morris dancing, brass bands and a pageant of historical characters from fiction and fact. Perhaps the most interesting tradition is that of 'sanding', when the streets are covered in colourful messages written in sand. Legend has it that the Danish King Knut while crossing the marsh between Over and Nether Knutsford, scrawled a message in the sand wishing happiness to a young couple on the way to their wedding. The custom is also practised on weddings and feast days.

The **TIC** (☎ 632611; Toft Rd; ☼ 9am-5pm Mon-Fri, 9am-1pm Sat) is in the council offices opposite the train station.

The **Knutsford Heritage Centre** (☎ 650506; 90a King St; admission free; ☼ 1.30-4pm Mon-Fri, noon-4pm Sat & 2-4.30pm Sun) is a reconstructed former smithy that has plenty of information on Gaskell, including the *Cranford Walk Around Knutsford* (90p), a leaflet about her local haunts. The best displays, though, are on Watt and his quirky contributions to English architecture.

You can see the best example of these along King St, which is a fine example of the splendidly haphazard harmony of English urban architecture. The best examples are the **King's Coffee House** (meant to lure the men from the pubs) and the **Ruskin Reading Room** (Drury Lane).

The eye-catching **Gaskell Memorial Tower** incorporates the swanky **Belle Epoque Brasserie** (☎ 633060; www.thebelleepoque.com; 60 King St; mains £8-13; r from £65; lunch & dinner Mon-Sat), a *fin de siècle*-style restaurant that Oscar Wilde would look perfectly at home in. Upstairs are seven gorgeous rooms, each styled in accordance with the overall late–19th-century theme of the building.

Getting There & Away

Knutsford is 15 miles southwest of Manchester and is on the Manchester–Chester train line (Chester £7.65, 45 minutes; Manchester £3.55, 30 minutes). The train station is on Adams Hill, at the southern end of King St.

AROUND KNUTSFORD

The southern end of King St in Knutsford marks the entrance to the 400-hectare **Tatton Park** (NT; ☎ 01625-534400; www.tattonpark.org .uk; admission free; individual attractions adult/child £3/2 ☼ 10am-7pm). At the heart is a Regency **mansion** (☼ 1-5pm Tue-Sun Mar-Oct) and a wonderful Tudor **Old Hall** (☼ noon-4pm Sat & Sun Apr-Oct), a 1930s-style **working farm** (☼ noon-5pm Tue-Sun Mar-Oct, Sat & Sun Nov-Feb) and a series of superb Victorian **gardens** (☼ 10am-6pm Tue-Sun Apr-Sep, 11am-4pm Oct-Mar). The **Discovery Saver Ticket** (adult/child £4.60/2.60) allows you entry to any two attractions. Car admission to the park costs £3.90.

On Sunday bus No X2 links Tatton Park with Chester (one hour). At other times you'll need your own wheels.

NANTWICH

☎ 01270 / pop 13,450

Cheshire's second-best example of black-and-white Tudor architecture after Chester is the elegant town of Nantwich. The town was rebuilt after a devastating fire in 1583, thanks to a nationwide appeal (as well as a personal donation of £1000) by Elizabeth I, who deemed the town's salt production so important that she had to intercede to help.

Her generosity is proudly commemorated with a plaque on the appositely named **Queen's Aid House** (High St), itself a striking Tudor building.

The rest of the largely pedestrianised centre has plenty of fine examples of the black-and-white style, although it's a wonder how so many of them stay standing, such is their off-kilter shape and design.

Very few buildings survived the fire, most important of which is 14th-century **Church of St Mary** (☎ 625268; ☼ 9am-5pm), a fine example of medieval architecture.

Apart from salt, the town grew up around the production of cheese and leather, and all three are depicted in the **Nantwich Museum** (☎ 627104; Pillory St; admission free; ☼ 10am-4.30pm Mon-Sat Apr-Sep, Tue-Sat Oct-Mar).

The helpful **TIC** (☎ 610983; fax 610880; Church Walk; ☼ 9.30am-5pm Mon-Sat, 10am-4pm Sat, 11am-3pm Sun) is near the main square.

Sleeping & Eating

Crown Hotel (☎ 625283; www.crown-hotel.net; High St; s/d £60/78) There is barely a straight line in the place, but this gorgeous Tudor half-timbered hotel is easily top choice in town. The ground-floor **Casa Italiana** (mains £10-13) restaurant is a decent and popular spot that has every Italian dish on the menu.

Pillory House & Coffee Shop (☎ 623524; Pillory St; sandwiches £2.70) An old-style tearoom that serves sandwiches and inexpensive hot dishes – perfect for that quick lunch.

Getting There & Away

The **bus station** (Beam St) is 300m north of the TIC; there is an hourly bus from Chester (£4.10, 1 hour).

To get to Manchester, Chester or Liverpool, you'll have to change trains in Crewe (£1.60, 15 minutes, half hourly). The train station is about half a mile south of the centre.

LIVERPOOL

☎ 0151 / pop 469, 020

For far too long Liverpool has been dismissed as a city of smart-aleck scallies in shiny tracksuits, and for far too long Scousers have closed ranks and sent their critics packing with two fingers and a clever insult. Slagging has always been an Olympic sport around here, but these days you'll also get a handshake and a warm welcome to the European Capital of Culture 2008.

OK, so 2008 is still a few years away, but Liverpool is busy getting ready for the ball. Everywhere you look handsome old buildings are getting facials and brand-new ones are being built – often in place of those plain ugly ones that have scarred the cityscape since the 1960s. The once boarded-up buildings and warehouses of the city centre have been transformed into new shops, cafés and fancy apartments. Even Unesco was convinced, and in the summer of 2004 it declared the waterfront and docks a World Heritage Site.

And to those who would mock the city for its cultural pretensions, Liverpool will point to life beyond the Beatles – to the city's excellent art galleries and museums, to the fact that it has more listed buildings than any city besides London, to the city's rich and varied nightlife, but most of all, to the extraordinary sense of spirit and togetherness that is at the core of the Liverpool experience. It's hard to visit and not be infected.

HISTORY

Liverpool grew rich on the back of the triangular trading of slaves for raw materials. From 1700 ships carried cotton goods and hardware from Liverpool to West Africa, where they were exchanged for slaves, who in turn were carried to the West Indies and Virginia, where they were exchanged for sugar, rum, tobacco and raw cotton.

As a great port the city drew thousands of Irish and Scottish immigrants, and its Celtic influences are still apparent. However, between 1830 and 1930 nine million emigrants – mainly English, Scots and Irish, but also Swedes, Norwegians and Russian Jews – sailed from here for the New World.

The start of WWII led to a resurgence of Liverpool's importance. Over one million American GIs disembarked here before D-day and the port was, once again, hugely important as the western gateway for transatlantic supplies. The GIs brought with them the latest American records and Liverpool was thus the first European port of call for the new rhythm and blues that would eventually become rock and roll. Within 20 years, the Mersey Beat was *the* sound of British pop and four mop-topped Scousers had formed a skiffle band...

ORIENTATION

Liverpool is a cinch to get around. The main attractions are Albert Dock west of the city centre and the trendy Ropewalks area, south of Hanover St just west of the two cathedrals. Lime St Station, the bus station, the tourist office and the Cavern Quarter – a mecca for Beatles fans – lies just to the north.

The tourist office and many of the city's hotels have an excellent tearaway map with all of the city's attractions clearly outlined.

INFORMATION
Bookshops

Waterstones (☎ 708 6861; 14-16 Bold St)

Emergencies

Merseyside police headquarters (☎ 709 6010; Canning Pl) Opposite Albert Dock.

Internet Access

CaféLatte.net (☎ 709 9683; 4 South Hunter St; 9am-6pm; per 30 mins £1)
Planet Electra (☎ 708 0303; 36 London Rd; 9am-5pm; per 30 mins £1)

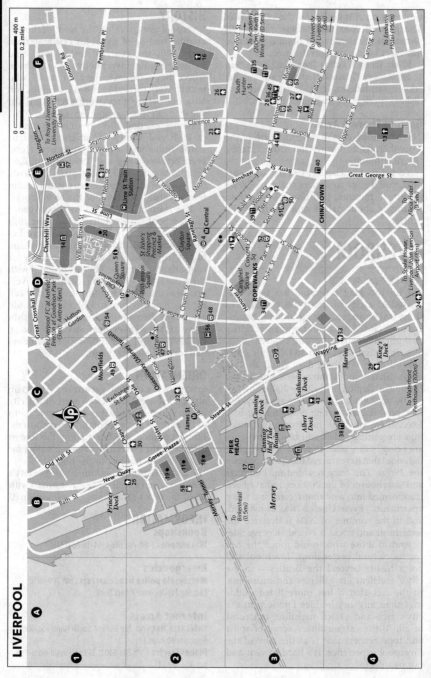

INFORMATION

CaféLatte.net........(see 28)
Mars Pharmacy........1 E1
Merseyside Police Headquarters........2 C3
Planet Electra........3 E1
Post Office........4 D2
TIC Albert Dock........(see 15)
TIC Queen Square Centre........5 D1
Waterstone's........6 D2

SIGHTS & ACTIVITIES (pp633–6)

Beatles Shop........7 D2
Beatles Story........8 C4
Beatles Tours Bus Stop........9 C4
Conservation Centre........10 D2
Cunard Building........11 B2
FACT........12 E3
Liverpool Cathedral........13 E4
Liverpool Museum & Planetarium........14 D1
Merseyside Maritime Museum........15 C3
Metropolitan Cathedral of Christ the King..16 F2
Museum of Liverpool Life........17 B3
Port of Liverpool Building........18 B2
Royal Liver Building........19 B2
St George's Hall........20 D1
Tate Liverpool........21 B3
Walker Art Gallery........(see 14)
Western Approaches Museum........22 C2
Yellow Duckmarine Tours........(see 9)

SLEEPING (pp637–8)

Aachen Hotel........23 E2
Campanile Hotel........24 D4
Crowne Plaza Liverpool........25 B2
Feathers........26 F2
Hope St Hotel........27 F3
International Inn........28 F3
Mersey Waterfront Apartments........29 C4
Racquet Club........30 C2
Trafalgar Warehouse Apartments........31 E1
Trials........32 C2
YHA Liverpool International........33 D4

EATING (pp638–9)

Colin's Bridewell........34 D3
Everyman Bistro........35 F3
London Carriage Works........(see 27)
Magnet Restaurant........36 F3
Other Place........37 F3
Pan-American Club........38 C4
Tea Factory........39 E3
Yuet Ben........40 E3

DRINKING (p639)

Baa Bar........41 D3
Baby Cream........42 C3
Blue Bar........43 C3
Hannah's........44 E3
Magnet........(see 36)
Philharmonic........45 F3
Ye Cracke........46 F3

ENTERTAINMENT (pp640–1)

Cavern Club........47 C2
Escape........48 D2
Everyman Theatre........(see 35)
G-Bar........49 C1
Garlands........(see 49)
Heebie Jeebies........50 E3
Masque........51 E3
Nation........52 D3
Philharmonic Hall........53 F3
Superstar Boudoir........54 D1
Unity Theatre........55 F3

TRANSPORT (pp641–2)

Bus Station & Parking........56 D2
National Express Coach Station........57 E1
Pier Head Ferry Terminal........58 B2

Internet Resources

Clubs in Liverpool (www.clubsinliverpool.co.uk) Everything you need to know about what goes on when the sun goes down.
Mersey Guide (www.merseyguide.co.uk)
Mersey Partnership (www.merseyside.org.uk) Guide to the greater Mersey area.
Merseyside Today (www.merseysidetoday.co.uk) The city and surrounding area.
TIC (www.visitliverpool.com)

Medical Services

Mars Pharmacy (☎ 709 5271; 68 London Rd) Open until 10pm nightly.
Royal Liverpool University Hospital (☎ 706 2000; Prescot St)

Post

Post office (Ranelagh St; 🕒 9am-5.30pm Mon-Sat)

Tourist Information

The TIC has three branches in the city. It also has an **accommodation hotline** (☎ 0845 601 1125).
Albert Dock TIC (☎ 0906 680 6886; Merseyside Maritime Museum; 🕒 10am-5pm)
Liverpool John Lennon Airport TIC(☎ 907 1057; Arrivals Hall; 🕒 4am-midnight Apr-Sept, 5am-11pm Oct-Mar)
Queen Square Centre TIC (☎ 0906 680 6886; 🕒 9am-5.30pm Mon-Sat, 10.30am-4.30pm Sun) The main branch.

SIGHTS

The wonderful Albert Dock is the city's biggest tourist draw and the key to understanding the city's history, but the city centre is where you'll find most of Liverpool's real day-to-day life.

City Centre

ST GEORGE'S HALL

Arguably Liverpool's most impressive building is **St George's Hall** (☎ 707 2391; www.stgeorgeshall.com), built in 1854 and the first European offering of neoclassical architecture. Curiously, it was built as law courts *and* a concert hall – presumably a judge could pass sentence and then relax to a string quartet. It is currently being refurbished and will open in 2005 with a brand-new visitor centre.

WALKER ART GALLERY

Touted as the 'National Gallery of the North', the city's foremost **gallery** (☎ 478 4199; www.liverpoolmuseums.org.uk/walker; William Brown St; admission free; 🕒 10am-5pm Mon-Sat, noon-5pm Sun) is Liverpool's answer to sneering critics who question its cultural credentials in the lead-up to 2008. The history of art from the 14th to the 20th centuries is covered in exquisite detail; strong suits are pre-Raphaelite art, modern British art, and sculpture.

LIVERPOOL MUSEUM

Natural history, science and technology are the themes of this sprawling **museum** (☎ 478 4399; www.liverpoolmuseums.org.uk/livmus; William Brown St; 🕒 10am-5pm Mon-Sat, noon-5pm Sun) whose exhibits range from birds of prey to space exploration. There's also a **planetarium** (admission £1), while an ongoing refurbishment will see the addition of an aquarium, a fancy new atrium and a hands-on discovery centre for kids both little and large. Consequently, certain exhibits may be closed when you visit.

LIVERPOOL IN...

Two Days

Head to the waterfront and explore the Albert Dock museums – the **Tate** (opposite), **Museum of Liverpool Life** (opposite) and **Merseyside Maritime Museum** (opposite) – before paying tribute to the Fab Four at the **Beatles Story** (opposite). Keep to the Beatles theme and head north toward the **Cavern Quarter** (see opposite) around Mathew St. Round off your evening with dinner at **London Carriage Works** (p639), a pint at the marvellous **Philharmonic** (p639) and wrap yourself in the crisp linen sheets of the **Hope Street Hotel** (p637). Night hawks can tear it up in the bars and clubs of the hip **Ropewalks** area (p640). The next day, explore the city's two **cathedrals** (below) and check out the twin delights of the **Liverpool Museum** (p633) and the **Walker Art Gallery** (p633).

Four Days

Follow the two-day itinerary but add in a **Yellow Duckmarine tour** (p636) to experience the docks from the water. Make a couple of pilgrimages to suit your interests: visit **Mendips** (opposite) and **20 Forthlin Rd** (opposite), the childhood homes of John Lennon and Paul McCartney respectively, now run by the National Trust; or walk on holy ground at **Anfield** (p640), home of Liverpool Football Club. Race junkies can head out to the visitor centre at **Aintree Racecourse** (p641), home of England's most beloved race, the Grand National.

CONSERVATION CENTRE

Ever wonder how art actually gets restored? Find out at this terrific **centre** (☎ 478 4999; www.liverpoolmuseums.org.uk/conservation; Old Haymarket; ☟ 10am-5pm Mon-Sat, noon-5pm Sun) housed in a converted railway good depot. Hand-held wands help tell the story, but the real fun is actually attempting a restoration technique with your own hands. Sadly, our trembling paws weren't allowed near anything of value – that was left to the real experts, whose skills are pretty amazing.

FACT

Proof that Ropewalks isn't all about booze and bars, this brand-new **media centre** (☎ 707 4450; www.fact.co.uk; 88 Wood St; ☟ galleries 11am-6pm Tue-Wed, 11am-8pm Thu-Sat & noon-5pm Sun, cinemas noon-10pm) – whose acronym stands for Film, Art & Creative Technology – is all about film and new media such as digital art. Two galleries feature constantly changing exhibitions and three screens show the latest arthouse releases. There's also a bar and café.

WESTERN APPROACHES MUSEUM

The **Combined Headquarters of the Western Approaches** (☎ 227 2008; 1 Rumford St; adult/child £4.75/3.45; ☟ 10.30am-4.30pm Mon-Thu & Sat Mar-Oct), the secret command centre for the Battle of the Atlantic, was abandoned at the end of the war with virtually everything left intact.

THE CATHEDRALS

The city's two cathedrals are separated by the length of Hope St. At the northern end, the Roman Catholic **Metropolitan Cathedral of Christ the King** (☎ 709 9222; off Mount Pleasant; ☟ 8am-6pm Mon-Sat, 8am-5pm Sun Oct-Mar) was completed in 1967 according to the design of Sir Frederick Gibberd after the original plans by Sir Edwin Lutyens, whose crypt is inside. It's a mightily impressive modern building that looks like a soaring concrete tepee, hence its nickname, Paddy's Wigwam.

At Hope St's southern end stands the neo-gothic **Liverpool Cathedral** (☎ 709 6271; www.liverpoolcathedral.org.uk; Hope St; voluntary donation £3; ☟ 8am-6pm), the life work of Sir Giles Gilbert Scott (1880–1960), whose other contributions to the world were the red telephone box and the power station in London that is now home to the Tate Modern. Size is a big deal here: this is the largest church in England and the largest Anglican cathedral in Europe. The central bell is the world's third-largest (with the world's highest and heaviest peal) while the organ, with its 9765 pipes, is probably the world's largest operational model.

There are terrific views of Liverpool from the top of the 101m **tower** (admission £3.25; ☟ 11am-3pm Mon-Sat).

Albert Dock

Liverpool's biggest tourist attraction is Albert Dock, 2¾ hectares of water ringed by a colonnade of enormous cast-iron columns and impressive five-storey warehouses that make up the country's largest collection of protected buildings, and now a World Heritage Site. A fabulous development programme has really brought the dock to life; here you'll find several outstanding museums and an extension of London's Tate Gallery, as well as top class restaurants and bars.

MERSEYSIDE MARITIME MUSEUM

The story of one of the world's great ports is the theme of this excellent **museum** (☎ 478 4499; admission free; ☟ 10am-5pm) and believe us, it's a graphic and compelling page-turner. One of the many great exhibits is Emigration to a New World, which tells the story of nine million emigrants and their efforts to get to North America and Australia – the walkthrough model of a typical ship shows just how tough conditions on board really were. But the real highlight is the Transatlantic Slavery exhibit, which pulls no punches in its portrayal of the shameful trade that made Liverpool rich and left us with the scourge of modern racism. This is heady stuff, and should on no account be missed.

MUSEUM OF LIVERPOOL LIFE

A celebration of Liverpool and its hardy history is on offer at this entertaining **museum** (☎ 478 4080; admission free; ☟ 10am-5pm) that looks at the city in all its guises; from its multiculturalism and advocacy of trade unionism to its role in the British Army and its unparalleled love of football. Liverpool life was always tough, it tells us, but Scousers have always managed to crack a smile and just keep going. If only real life were that simple.

TATE LIVERPOOL

Touted as the home of modern art in the north, this **gallery** (☎ 702 7400; admission free, adult/child £4/3 to special exhibitions; ☟ 10am-5.50pm Tue-Sun) features a substantial checklist of 20th-century artists across its four floors as well as touring exhibitions from the Mother Ship on London's Bankside. But it's all a little sparse, with none of the energy we'd expect from the world-famous Tate.

THE BEATLES STORY

Liverpool's most popular **museum** (☎ 709 1963; adult/child £7.95/5.45; ☟ 10am-6pm Mar-Oct, 10am-5pm Nov-Feb) won't illuminate any dark, juicy corners in the turbulent history of the world's most famous foursome – there's ne'er a mention of internal discord, drugs, Yoko Ono or the Frog Song – but there's plenty of genuine memorabilia to keep a Beatle fan happy. Particularly impressive is the full-size replica Cavern Club (which was actually tiny) and the Abbey Road studio where the lads recorded their first singles, while George Harrison's crappy first guitar (now worth half a million quid) should inspire budding, penniless musicians to keep the faith. The museum is also the departure point for the Magical Mystery and Yellow Duckmarine tours (see p636) as well as visits to Mendips and 20 Forthlin Rd (see boxed text below).

DOING THE BEATLES TO DEATH

Between March 1961 and August 1963, The Beatles played a staggering 275 gigs in a club on Mathew St called the Cavern, which was essentially a basement with a stage and a sound system. They shared the stage with other local bands who helped define the 'Mersey Beat', but it was John, Paul, George and Ringo who emerged into the sunlight of superstardom, unparalleled success and crass marketing.

Forty years later, the club is gone, the band has long broken up and two of its members are dead, but the phenomenon lives on and is still the biggest tourist magnet in town. The Cavern Quarter – basically a small warren of streets around Mathew St – has been transformed to cash in on the band's seemingly unending earning power: the Rubber Soul Oyster Bar, the From Me to You shop and the Lucy in the Sky With Diamonds café should give you an idea of what to expect. For decent memorabilia, check out **The Beatles Shop** (www.thebeatleshop.co.uk; 31 Mathew St).

True fans will undoubtedly want to visit **Mendips**, the home where John lived with his Aunt Mimi from 1945 to 1963, and **20 Forthlin Rd**, the rather plain terraced home where Paul grew up; you can only do so by prebooked **tour** (☎ 708 8574; £12; ☟ 10.30am & 11.20am Wed-Sun, Easter-Oct) from Albert Dock, just outside the Beatles Story. Visitors to Speke Hall (see p642) can also visit both from there.

If you'd rather do it yourself, the TICs also stock the *Discover Lennon's Liverpool* guide and map, and *Robin Jones' Beatles Liverpool*.

NORTHWEST ENGLAND

GAY & LESBIAN LIVERPOOL

There's no discernible gay quarter in Liverpool, with most of the gay-friendly clubs and bars spread about Dale St and Victoria St in Ropewalks. **Escape** (☎ 708 8809; 41-45 Paradise St) is still the city's overall best gay club, but it is being challenged by **Superstar Boudoir** (22-24 Stanley St). **Masque** (see p640) also runs at least one queer-friendly night a month.

G-Bar (☎ 255 1148; 1-7 Eberle St), in a small lane off Dale St behind Moorfields train station, is the city's premier gay bar, even though it attracts a mixed crowd; next door, **Garlands** (☎ 707 8385; 8-10 Eberle St) is earning rave reviews for excellent house nights.

North of Albert Dock

The area to the north of Albert Dock is known as **Pier Head**, after a stone pier built in the 1760s. This is still the departure point for ferries across the River Mersey (see p641), and was, for millions of migrants, their final contact with European soil.

Today this area is dominated by a trio of Edwardian buildings known as the 'Three Graces', dating from the days when Liverpool's star was still ascending. The southernmost, with the dome mimicking St Paul's Cathedral, is the **Port of Liverpool Building**, completed in 1907. Next to it is the **Cunard Building**, in the style of an Italian palazzo, once HQ to the Cunard Steamship Line. Finally, the **Royal Liver Building** (pronounced lie-ver) was opened in 1911 as the head office of the Royal Liver Friendly Society. It's crowned by Liverpool's symbol, the famous 5.5m copper Liver Bird.

LIVERPOOL FOR CHILDREN

The complex of museums on Albert Dock are extremely popular with kids, especially the **Museum of Liverpool Life** (p635) and the **Merseyside Maritime Museum** (p635), which has a couple of boats for kids to mess about on. The **Yellow Duckmarine Tour** (right) is a sure-fire winner, as is the **Conservation Centre** (p634), which gets everyone involved in the drama of restoration. Slightly older (and very old) kids – especially those into football – will enjoy the tour of Liverpool FC's **Anfield stadium** (p640) as it means getting your feet on the sacred turf.

QUIRKY LIVERPOOL

When a working public toilet is a tourist attraction, you know you have something special, and the men's loo at the **Philharmonic** (p639) is just that. The **Yellow Duckmarine tour** (above right), an amphibious exploration of Albert Dock, is a bit silly

but the guides are hilarious, while the **ferry across the Mersey** (p641) is something special – the tired commuters will give you more than a stare if you sing the song too loudly. The **Grand National Experience** (p641) at Aintree is proof that the English really do love their horses, while the concerts at the **Philharmonic Concert Hall** (p640) often throw up something completely different and avant garde instead of the Beethoven concerto you might expect.

TOURS

Magical Mystery Tour (☎ 709 3285; £11.95; ☽ 2.10pm year-round, plus 1.30pm Sat Jul-Aug; 2hr) Takes in all Beatles-related landmarks – their birthplaces, childhood homes, schools and places like Penny Lane and Strawberry Field – before finishing up in the Cavern Club (which isn't the original). Departures are from outside the Beatles Story on Albert Dock.

River Explorer Cruise (☎ 330 1444; adult/child £4.65/2.60; ☽ hourly 10am-3pm Mon-Fri, 10am-6pm Sat & Sun) Do as Gerry & The Pacemakers suggested and 'ferry 'cross the Mersey' on this 50-minute tour which illuminates the 850-year history of Liverpool as a port. Departures are from Pier Head ferry terminal.

Yellow Duckmarine Tour (☎ 708 7799; adult/child/family £9.95/7.95/29; ☽ from 11am) Take to the dock waters in a WWII amphibious vehicle after a quickie tour of the city centre's main points of interest. It's not especially educational, but it is a bit of fun. It leaves from Albert Dock, near the Beatles Story.

FESTIVALS & EVENTS

Africa Oye (www.africaoye.com) A free festival celebrating African music and culture in mid-June.

Aintree Festival (☎ 522 2929; www.aintree.co.uk) A three-day race meet culminating in the world-famous Grand National on the first Saturday in April.

Creamfields (☎ 0208 969 4477; www.creamfields .com) Alfresco dance-fest that brings some of the world's best DJs and dance acts together during the last weekend in August; 2004's headliners were the Chemical Brothers. It takes place at the Old Liverpool airfield in Speke.

Mathew Street Festival (☎ 239 9091; www.mathew streetfestival.com) The world's biggest tribute to the Beatles features six days of music, a convention and a memorabilia auction during the last week of August.

Merseyside International Street Festival (www .brouhaha.uk.com) A three-week extravaganza of world culture beginning in mid-July and featuring indoor and outdoor performances by artists and musicians from pretty much everywhere.

SLEEPING

There's been a small revolution in Liverpool; traditional, don't-try-too-hard B&Bs and bland chain hotels are being challenged by smart, independent boutique hotels and top-class international heavyweights. The result is that if you want even a modicum of character and quality you'll have to pay for it. Beds are tough to find when Liverpool FC are playing at home (it's less of a problem with Everton) and during the Beatles convention in the last week in August.

City Centre
BUDGET

International Inn (☎ 709 8135; www.internationalinn .co.uk; 4 South Hunter St; dm/d £15/36) A superb converted warehouse in the middle of uni-land: en suite, heated rooms with tidy wooden beds and bunks accommodate from two to 10 people. Facilities include a lounge, baggage storage, laundry facilities and 24-hour front desk. The staff are terrific and there's an Internet café next door.

Embassie Hostel (☎ 707 1089; www.embassie .com; 1 Falkner Sq; dm £13.50) Until 1986, this lovely Georgian house was the Venezuelan consulate; it has since been converted into a decent hostel that serves up free tea, coffee and toast at all times. There's also a TV lounge, a games room and a self-catering kitchen.

MID-RANGE

Aachen Hotel (☎ 709 3477; www.aachenhotel.co.uk; 89-91 Mount Pleasant; s/d from £28/46) A perennial favourite is this funky listed house with a mix of rooms, both en suite and sharing. The décor is strictly late '70s to early '80s – lots of flower patterns and crazy colour schemes – but it's all part of the welcoming, off-beat atmosphere.

Feathers (☎ 709 9655; www.feathers.uk.com; 119-125 Mount Pleasant; s/d from £60/90) A better choice than most of the similar-priced chain hotels is this rambling place, spread across a terrace of Georgian houses close to the Metropolitan Cathedral. The rooms are all comfortable (except for the wardrobe-sized singles at the top of the building) and all feature nice touches like full-package satellite TV, while the all-you-can-eat buffet breakfast is a welcome morning treat.

TOP END

Racquet Club (☎ 236 6676; www.racquetclub.org.uk; Hargreaves Bldg, 5 Chapel St; r £105) Eight individually styled rooms with influences that range from French country house to Japanese minimalist chic (often in the same room) make this new boutique hotel one of the most elegant choices in town. Antique beds, sumptuous Frette linen, free-standing baths and exclusive toiletries are all teasers to a pretty classy stay.

Trials (☎ 227 1021; www.trialshotel.com; 56 Castle St; s/d £115/130; P 🖳) Inside this converted Victorian building are 20 split-level suites primarily aimed at the business traveller but is excellent for the luxury-seeking holidaymaker. Jacuzzi baths and broadband Internet connection are standard. The hotel closed for a major refurb in January 2005 and won't reopen until June; standards (and prices) will undoubtedly go up.

SOMETHING SPECIAL

Hope Street Hotel (☎ 709 3000; www.hopestreethotel.co.uk; 40 Hope St; r/ste from £145/195) The new doyenne of luxurious Liverpool is this boutique hotel in the old London Carriage Works on the city's most fashionable street. The building's original features – heavy wooden beams, cast-iron columns and plenty of exposed brickwork – have been incorporated into a contemporary design inspired by the style of a 16th-century Venetian palazzo. King-sized beds draped in Egyptian cotton, oak floors with under-floor heating, LCD wide-screen TVs (with DVD players) and sleek modern bathrooms replete with a range of REN bath and beauty products are but the most obvious touches of class at this supremely cool address. Breakfast is not included, but can be enjoyed in the fashionable London Carriage Works restaurant on the ground floor (see p639).

APARTMENT LUXURY

If you want to live it up in self-catering style, you can opt for a luxury apartment along the waterfront or in the heart of town, which cost between £500 and £750 per week, including gas and electricity.

Trafalgar Warehouse Apartments (☎ 07715 118 419; Trafalgar Warehouse, 17-19 Lord Nelson St) Beautiful converted warehouses with solid wood floors, Jacuzzis and all the trimmings, close to Lime St Station.

Mersey Waterfront Apartments (☎ 487 7440; www.merseywaterfrontapartments.co.uk) Two luxury apartments on King's Dock.

Waterfront Penthouse (☎ 01695 727 877; www.stayinginliverpool.com) One luxury pad on Clippers Quay.

Alicia (☎ 727 4411; www.feathers.uk.com; 3 Aigburth Dr, Sefton Park; s/d from £67/94) This one-time wealthy cotton merchant's home is a sister hotel to the more central Feathers, but it's a far more handsome place. Most of the rooms have extra luxuries like CD players and Playstations. There's also a nice park on the grounds.

Around Albert Dock
BUDGET
YHA Liverpool International (☎ 0870 770 5924; www .yha.org.uk; 25 Tabley St; dm £19) It may look like an Eastern European apartment complex, but this award-winning hostel, adorned with Beatles memorabilia, is one of the most comfortable you'll find anywhere in the country. The en suite dorms even have heated towel rails and rates include breakfast.

MID-RANGE
Campanile Hotel (☎ 709 8104; fax 709 8725; cnr Wapping & Chaloner Sts; r £42; (P)) Functional, motel-style rooms in a purpose-built hotel next to Albert Dock. Great location and perfect for families – children under 12 stay for free.

TOP END
Crowne Plaza Liverpool (☎ 243 8000; www.cpliverpool.com; St Nicholas Pl, Princes Dock, Pier Head; r £115; (P)(🏊)) The paragon of the modern and luxurious business hotel, the Crowne Plaza has a marvellous waterfront location and plenty of facilities including a health club and swimming pool.

EATING
Liverpool's dining scene is getting better all the time. There are plenty of choices in Ropewalks, along Hardman St and Hope St, along Nelson St in the heart of Chinatown or slightly further afield in Lark Lane, near to Sefton Park, which is packed with restaurants.

City Centre
BUDGET
Everyman Bistro (☎ 708 9545; 13 Hope St; mains £4-7; 🕐 noon-2am Mon-Fri, 11am-2am Sat, 7-10.30pm Sun) Out-of-work actors and other creative types on a budget make this great café-restaurant beneath the Everyman Theatre their second home – with good reason. Great tucker and a terrific atmosphere.

Magnet Restaurant (☎ 709 1998; 41 Hardman St; meals around £6; 🕐 11am-3pm & 5-11pm Mon-Sat, 11am-4pm Sun) Liverpool's answer to a slum-trendy New York diner, complete with red leather booths, this is the best place in town for a late-night bite, especially if your night is only getting going.

MID-RANGE
Yuet Ben (☎ 709 5772; 1 Upper Duke St; mains £8-12; 🕐 5-11pm Tue-Sun) When it comes to best Chinese in town, you won't hear too many dissenting voices: Yuet Ben's Beijing cuisine usually comes out tops. The veggie banquet could bring round even the most avid carnivore. Get a seat by the window to eat in the shadow of Europe's largest Chinese gate.

Tea Factory (☎ 708 7008; 79 Wood St; mains £7-10; 🕐 11am-late) Who knew that cod 'n' chips could be so…cool? The wide-ranging menu covers all bases from typical Brit to funky finger foods like international tapas, but it's the room, darling, that makes this place so popular. Rock stars and the impossibly beautiful have found a home.

Keith's Wine Bar (☎ 728 7688; 107 Lark Lane; mains around £5; 🕐 11am-11pm) Friendly, bohemian and mostly vegetarian hangout with a sensational wine cellar that is the favourite resting place of the city's alternative lifestyle crowd.

The Other Place (☎ 707 0005; 29A Hope St; mains around £10) A more than able replacement for the Liverpool institution that was Becher's Brook, this elegant dining room serves British classics like bangers and mash and fancier dishes like confit of lamb shoulder. Book early.

TOP END

Colin's Bridewell (☎ 707 8003; Campbell Sq; lunch mains £8-9, dinner mains £16; ☺ noon-11pm) Top-notch British nosh *avec un* continental twist served in a converted police station – the booths are in the old cells; if prison food were this good, the crime rate would soar. It isn't as trendy as some of the city's newer offerings, but it's the insider's choice.

London Carriage Works (☎ 705 2222; 40 Hope St; 2/3-course meal £22/28; ☺ 8am-10pm Mon-Sat, 8am-8pm Sun) Paul Askew's award-in-waiting new restaurant is a super-cool reflection of Liverpool's current zeitgeist, A World in One City. Fashionistas, socceristas and the rest of the city's hip brigade share the large, open space that is the dining room – actually more of a bright glass box divided only by a series of sculpted glass shards – and indulge themselves in the marvellous menu with influences from every corner of the world.

Around Albert Dock

Pan-American Club (☎ 709 7097; Britannia Pavilion, Albert Dock; mains £12-22) A truly beautiful warehouse conversion has left us with this top-class restaurant and bar, easily one of the best dining addresses in town. Fancy steak dinners and other American classics can be washed down with drinks from the Champagne Lounge.

DRINKING

A recent survey has put Merseyside at the top of the All-England drinking league. It's official: Scousers love boozing. Health officials may be in despair, but Liverpool has pubs and bars to suit every imaginable taste. Most of the party action takes place in and around Ropewalks, the heart of which is Concert Sq. Unless specified, all the bars included here open until 2am Monday to Saturday, although most have a nominal entry charge after 11pm.

City Centre

Baa Bar (☎ 707 0610; 43-45 Fleet St) The first of Liverpool's style bars has weathered the fierce storm of new rivals with considerable aplomb. Packed virtually every night, it remains one of the city's favourite watering holes; the patio is perfect during the longer summer evenings.

Hannah's (☎ 708 5959; 2 Leece St) One of the top student bars in town. Try to land a table in the outdoor patio, which is covered in the event of rain. Late opening, a friendly, easygoing crowd and some pretty decent music make this one of the better places to get drunk in.

Magnet (☎ 709 6969; 39 Hardman St) Red leather booths, plenty of velvet and a suitably seedy New York dive atmosphere where Iggy Pop or Tom Waits would feel right at home. The upstairs bar is very cool but totally chilled out, while downstairs the dancefloor shakes to the best music in town, spun by up-and-comers and supported with guest slots by some of England's most established DJ names. It's two doors down from the eponymous diner (opposite).

Philharmonic (☎ 707 2837; 36 Hope St; no late opening) This extraordinary bar, designed by the shipwrights who built the *Lusitania*, is one of the most beautiful bars in all of England. The interior is resplendent with etched and stained glass, wrought iron, mosaics and ceramic tiling – and if you think that's good, just wait until you see inside the marble men's toilets, the only heritage-listed lav in the country.

Ye Cracke (☎ 709 4171; 13 Rice St; no late opening) Discreet and dilapidated, this atmospheric boozer is a favourite with pensioners and bohemians from the nearby college of art; in the early '60s these included John and Cynthia Lennon.

Albert Dock

Blue Bar (☎ 709 7097; Edward Pavilion) You don't need a Premiership contract to guarantee entry anymore, which means that mere mortals can finally enjoy the relaxed ambience of this elegant waterside lounge. So where have all the footballers gone? Downstairs, to the far more glam Baby Blue – a private members' bar.

Baby Cream (☎ 702 5823; Atlantic Pavilion) This super-trendy bar, run by the same crowd that created Liverpool's now-defunct-but-still-legendary Cream nightclub, is gorgeous and pretentious in almost equal measure. One pretty cool feature though is Creamselector – a set of touch screens where you can make your own compilation CD from a databank of over 2000 tracks (for a price) – it's like taking a piece of the famous nightclub home with you.

ENTERTAINMENT

There's always something going on in Liverpool these days – whether it's excellent fringe theatre, a performance by the superb Philharmonic or an all-day rock concert. And then there's the constant backbeat provided by the city's club scene, which pulses and throbs to the wee hours six nights out of seven. For all information, consult the *Liverpool Echo*.

Nightclubs

Most of the city's clubs are concentrated in Ropewalks, where they compete for customers with a ton of late-night bars; considering the number of punters in the area on a Friday or Saturday night, we're guessing there's plenty of business for everyone. Most clubs open at 11pm and turf everyone out by 3am.

Heebie Jeebies (☎ 708 7001; 80-82 Seel St; admission £3-6; ☺ Mon-Sat) Practically every musical style is on offer at this excellent nightclub, from '50s rock 'n' roll to skull-crushing techno. Thursday night's Mixed Bag is especially fun – and free.

Nation (☎ 709 1693; 40 Slater St/Wolstenholme Sq; admission £4-13) Formerly the home of Cream, England's most famous club night, Nation still draws them in – 3000 a night – from all over. You can relive a bit of Cream's teeth-shaking energy at the monthly Bugged Out! – the best techno night in town – or go for the up-for-it happy tunes of the weekly Wednesday Medication – a perennial favourite with students.

Masque (☎ 708 8708; 90 Seel St; admission £3-11; ☺ Mon-Sat) This converted theatre is home to our favourite club in town. The fortnightly Saturday Chibuku Shake Shake is one of the best club nights in all of England, led by a mix of superb DJs including Yousef (formerly of Cream) and superstars like Dmitri from Paris and Gilles Peterson. The music ranges from hip-hop to deep house – if you're in town, get in line.

Theatre

Most of Liverpool's theatres feature a mixed bag of revues, musicals and stage successes that are as easy on the eye as they are on the mind, but there is also more interesting work on offer.

Everyman Theatre (☎ 709 4776; Hope St) This is one of England's most famous repertory theatres and an avid supporter of local talent, which has included the likes of Alan Bleasdale.

Unity Theatre (☎ 709 4988; Hope Pl) Fringe theatre for those keen on the unusual and challenging; there's also a great bar on the premises.

Live Music

ROCK MUSIC

The Academy (☎ 794 6868; Liverpool University, 160 Mount Pleasant) This is the best venue to see touring major bands.

Cavern Club (☎ 236 1965; 8-10 Mathew St) 'The world's most famous club' is not the original basement venue where the Fab Four began their careers, but it's a fairly faithful reconstruction. There's usually a good selection of local bands, and look out for all-day gigs.

CLASSICAL MUSIC

Philharmonic Hall (☎ 709 3789; Hope St) One of Liverpool's most beautiful buildings, the Art Deco Phil is home to the city's main classical orchestra, but it also stages the work of avant garde musicians such as John Cage and Nick Cave.

Sport

Liverpool's two football teams – the Reds of Liverpool FC and the blues of Everton – are pretty much the alpha and omega of sporting interest in the city. There is no other city in England where the fortunes of its football clubs are so inextricably linked with those of its inhabitants. Yet Liverpool is also home to the Grand National – the world's most famous steeplechase event – that is run in the first weekend in April at the Aintree course north of the city (see boxed text opposite).

LIVERPOOL FC

England's most successful football club, **Liverpool FC** (☎ 263 9199; ticket office ☎ 220 2345; www.liverpoolfc.tv; Anfield Rd) epitomises the city's proud identity – even though it hasn't won the league championship since 1990. Virtually unbeatable for much of the 1970s and 1980s, the club is looking to a new generation of heroes like Steven Gerrard to fill the packed-but-dusty trophy cabinet.

The club's home is the marvellous Anfield but plans are afoot to relocate to a new, larger stadium a stone's throw away in Stanley Park before 2008. The experience of a live match

---

THE GRAND NATIONAL

England loves the gee-gees, but never more so than the first Saturday in April, when 40-odd veteran stalwarts of the jumps line up at Aintree to race across 4½ miles and over the most difficult fences in world racing. Since the first running of the Grand National in 1839 – won by the appositely named Lottery – the country has taken the race to heart and there's hardly a household that doesn't tune in, betting slips nervously in hand.

The race has captured the national imagination because its protagonists aren't the pedigreed racing machines that line up for the season's other big fixtures, the Derby and the Gold Cup: they're ageing bruisers full of the oh-so-English qualities of grit and derring-do, which they need in abundance to get over tough jumps like the Chair, Canal Turn and Becher's Brook, named after a Captain Becher who fell into it in 1839 and later commented that he had no idea water could taste so awful without whisky in it.

You can book **tickets** (☎ 522 2929; www.aintree.co.uk) for the Grand National, or visit the **Grand National Experience** (☎ 522 2921; adult/child with tour £7/4, without tour £3/2), a visitor centre that includes a race simulator – those jumps are very steep indeed. We recommend the racecourse tour, which takes in the stableyard and the grave of three-time winner Red Rum, the most loved of all Grand National winners.

---

is a memorable one, especially the sound of 40,000-odd fans singing 'You'll Never Walk Alone', but tickets are pretty tricky to come by. You may have to settle for a **tour** (☎ 260 6677; with museum adult/child £9/5.50; ⊙ every couple of hours except match days) that includes the home dressing room, a walk down the famous tunnel and a seat in the dugout or simply a visit to the **museum** (admission £5), which features memorabilia from Liverpool's glory years.

EVERTON FC

Liverpool's 'other' team are the blues of **Everton FC** (☎ 330 2400; ticket office 330 2300; www .evertonfc.com; Goodison Park), who may not have their rivals' winning pedigree but they're just as popular locally.

Tours (☎ 330 2277; adult/child £6.50/4.50; ⊙ 11am & 2pm Sun-Wed & Fri) of Goodison Park run throughout the year except on the Friday before home matches.

GETTING THERE & AWAY
Air

With the clever tagline of 'Above Us Only Sky', **Liverpool John Lennon Airport** (☎ 0870 750 8484; www.liverpoolairport.co.uk) serves a variety of destinations including Amsterdam, Barcelona, Dublin and Paris as well as destinations in the UK (Belfast, London and the Isle of Man).

Bus

The **National Express Coach Station** (☎ 0870 580 8080; Norton St) is 300m north of Lime St Sta-

tion. There are services to/from most major towns, including Manchester (£5.25, hourly, 1¼ hours), London (£20, seven daily, five to six hours), Birmingham (£9.50, five daily, 2¾ hours) and Newcastle (£17, three daily, 6½ hours).

Train

Liverpool's main station is Lime St. It has hourly services to most everywhere, including Chester (£3.50, 40 minutes), London (£55, three hours), Manchester (£10.20, 45 minutes) and Wigan (£6.10, 50 minutes).

GETTING AROUND
To/From the Airport

The airport is 8 miles south of the centre. **Arriva Airlink** (£1.50; 30 mins; 6am-11pm) bus Nos 80A or 180 departs from Paradise St Station every 20 minutes and **Airportxpress 500** (£2; 30mins; 5.15am-12.15am) buses run every half-hour from outside Lime St Station. A taxi to the city centre should cost no more than £12.

Boat

The famous cross-Mersey **ferry** (adult/child £1.10/ 90p) for Woodside and Seacombe departs from Pier Head Ferry Terminal, next to the Liver Building to the north of Albert Dock.

Car

You won't have much use for a car in Liverpool, and it'll end up costing you plenty in car park fees. If you must, there are parking meters around the city and a number of open and sheltered car parks. Car break-ins are a major problem, so leave absolutely nothing of value in the car.

Public Transport

Local public transport is coordinated by **Merseytravel** (☎ 236 7676; www.merseytravel.gov .uk). Highly recommended is the **Saveaway Ticket** (adult/child £3.70/1.90) which allows for one day's off-peak travel on all bus, train and ferry services throughout Merseyside. Tickets are available at shops and post offices throughout the city. The **bus station** (Paradise St) is in the centre.

MERSEYRAIL

Merseyrail (☎ 702 2071; www.merseyrail.org) is an extensive suburban rail service linking Liverpool with the Greater Merseyside area. There are four stops in the city centre: Lime St, Central Station (handy for Ropewalks), James St (close to Albert Dock) and Moorfields (for the Western Approaches Museum).

Taxi

Mersey Cabs (☎ 298 2222) operates tourist taxi services and has some cabs adapted for disabled visitors.

AROUND LIVERPOOL

PORT SUNLIGHT

Southwest of Liverpool across the River Mersey on the Wirral Peninsula, Port Sunlight is a picturesque 19th-century village created by the philanthropic Lever family to house workers in its soap factory. The main reason to come here is the wonderful **Lady Lever Art Gallery** (☎ 478 4136; off Greendale Rd; admission free; 🕒 10am-5pm) where you can see some of the greatest works of the Pre-Raphaelite Brotherhood, as well as some fine Wedgwood pottery.

Trains run from Liverpool's Lime St station to Port Sunlight.

SPEKE

A marvellous example of a black-and-white half-timbered hall can be visited at **Speke Hall** (NT; ☎ 427 7231; admission £6; 🕒 1pm-5.30pm Wed-Sun Apr-Oct, 1-4.30pm Sat & Sun Nov-Mar), six miles south of Liverpool in the plain suburb of Speke. It contains several priest's holes where 16th-century Roman Catholic priests could hide when they were forbidden to hold Masses. Any airport bus from Paradise St will drop you within a half mile of the entrance. Speke Hall can also be combined with a National Trust–run, 1½-hour **tour** (☎ 486 4006; with Speke Hall adult/child £12/free) to the childhood homes of both Lennon and McCartney (see the boxed text p635) – you can book at Speke Hall, at the Beatles Story or at the TIC.

LANCASHIRE

Lancashire has a bit of everything the north has to offer, from industry to isolation. In the south there's mighty Manchester – so big that it's administered separately to the rest of the county – whose workers traditionally flocked to the sea along the western coast, most notably to ever-popular Blackpool, the empress of tacky seaside resorts. Further north again is the handsome Georgian county town, Lancaster, while inland the Ribble Valley provides stunning scenery.

BLACKPOOL

☎ 01253 / pop 142,290

England's most popular resort is visited by more people than any other place in the country except for London: precisely the reason why Blackpool's tourist authorities, ably backed up by a huge chorus of the town's hoteliers, smile a knowing smile and go about their merry way every time the town gets a slagging for being tacky.

Blackpool epitomises tacky, but it does so with unparalleled success. Its not-so-secret formula is a clever combination of a time-tested, traditional British holiday by the sea with high-tech, 21st-century amusements that will thrill even the most cynical observer. Basically, Blackpool is all about pure, unadulterated fun.

Blackpool is famous for its tower, its three piers, its Pleasure Beach and its Illuminations, a successful ploy to extend the brief summer holiday season. From early September to early November, 5 miles of the Promenade are illuminated with thousands of electric and neon lights.

Orientation & Information

Blackpool is surprisingly spread out but can still be managed easily without a car –

trams run the entire 7-mile length of the seafront Promenade.

TIC Clifton St (☎ 478222; www.visitblackpool.com; 1 Clifton St; ☼ 9am-5pm Mon-Sat) North Pier (☎ 403 223; ☼ 9.15am-5pm, 10.15am-4.15pm Sun Apr-Sep)

Pleasure Beach

The main reason for Blackpool's immense popularity is the simply fantastic **Pleasure Beach** (☎ 0870 444 5566; www.blackpoolpleasurebeach .com; admission free; ☼ from 10am Apr-early Nov), a 16-hectare collection of over 145 different rides that attracts some 7 million visitors annually. As amusement parks go, this is the best you'll find anywhere in Europe.

The park's major rides include the Big One, the tallest and fastest rollercoaster in Europe, reaching a top speed of 85mph (137km/h) before hitting a near-vertical descent of 75m; the Ice Blast, which delivers you up a 65m steel tower before returning to earth at 80mph (130km/h); and, new in 2004, Bling, where riders are brought 40m into the air and then spun 360 degrees at 60mph – it's the perfect way to shift the contents of your stomach.

While the hi-tech modern rides will draw the biggest queues, spare a moment to check out the marvellous collection of old-style wooden rollercoasters known as 'woodies'. Here you can see the world's first Big Dipper (1923), but be sure to have a go on the Grand National (1935), whose carriages trundle along a 1½-mile long track in an experience that is typically Blackpool – complete with riders waving their hands (despite the sombre-toned announcement not to).

Rides are divided into categories and you can buy tickets for individual categories or for a mixture of them all. An unlimited ticket to all rides costs £30 for one day, £45 for two.

There are no set times for closing; it depends how busy they are.

Other Sights

Blackpool's most recognisable landmark is the 150m-high **Blackpool Tower** (☎ 622242; adult/child £12/10; ☼ 10am-11pm Apr-Oct, 10am-6pm Nov-Mar), built in 1894. Inside is a vast entertainment complex that should keep the kids happy, including a Dinosaur Ride, Europe's largest indoor jungle gym and a Moorish circus.

The highlight is the magnificent, rococo **ballroom**, with extraordinary sculptured and gilded plasterwork, murals and chandeliers. Couples still glide across the floor to the melodramatic tones of a huge Wurlitzer organ from 11am to 10pm every day.

Across from Pleasure Beach is **The Sandcastle** (☎ 343602; adult/child £7.95/6.50; ☼ from 10am daily May-Oct, Sat & Sun only Nov-Feb), an indoor water complex complete with its own rides.

Near the Central Pier is the state-of-the-art **Sealife Centre** (☎ 622445; New Bonny St; adult/child £7.50/5; ☼ 10am-8pm), which features eight-foot sharks and a giant octopus.

Sleeping

With over 2500 hotels, B&Bs and self-catering units, Blackpool knows how to put visitors up for the night. Even with so many places to stay, it is worth booking ahead during the Illuminations. If you want to stay close to the waterfront, prepare for a noisy, boisterous night; accommodation along Albert and Hornby Rds, 300m back from the sea, is that little bit quieter. The TIC will assist you in finding a bed.

Big Blue Hotel (☎ 0845 367 3333; www.bigblue hotel.com; Blackpool Pleasure Beach; r from £55; P) Cool, minimalist and very much a look into Blackpool's future, this hotel caters to 21st-century demands: smartly kitted-out rooms come with DVD players and computer games, while its location at the southern entrance of Pleasure Beach should ensure that everyone has something to do.

Old Coachhouse (☎ 349195; www.theoldcoach house.freeserve.co.uk; 50 Dean St; dinner £20; s/d from £40/70; P) A Tudor breath of fresh air is the south shore's oldest building, which has 11 handsome rooms; two have four-poster beds and beautiful garden views. A Japanese-style sun deck, a conservatory and an outdoor whirlpool complete the luxury.

Eating

Forget gourmet meals – the Blackpool experience is all about stuffing your face with burgers, doughnuts and fish and chips. Most people eat at their hotels where roast and three vegetables often costs just £4 a head.

There are a few restaurants around Talbot Sq (near the TIC) on Queen St, Talbot Rd and Clifton St. The most interesting possibility is the Afro-Caribbean **Lagoonda** (☎ 293837; 37 Queen St; mains £9), a friendly, no-nonsense eatery that serves up colourful (and often spicy) dishes with a tropical flavour.

Getting There & Away

BUS

The central coach station is on Talbot Rd, near the town centre. Destinations include Liverpool (£7.25, 1½ hours, one daily), London (£23.50, 6½ hours, five daily) and Manchester (£5.75, 1¾ hours, four daily).

TRAIN

The main train station is Blackpool North, about five blocks east of the North Pier on Talbot Rd. There is a direct service from Manchester (£10.95, 1¼ hours, half-hourly) and Liverpool (£11.60, 1½ hours, seven daily), but most other arrivals change in Preston (£5.05, 30 minutes, half-hourly).

Getting Around

A host of travel-card options for trams and buses ranging from one day to a week are available at the TICs and most newsagents. With more than 14,000 car-parking spaces in Blackpool you'll have no problems parking.

LANCASTER

☎ 01524 / pop 45,960

Although it dates back as far as Roman times, Lancaster's heyday was the 18th century, when it was an important port in the slave trade. The port is much quieter now, but the town's rows of handsome Georgian buildings make this a pleasant stopover on the way to the Ribble Valley.

Information

Post office (85 Market St; ☺ 9am-5.30pm Mon-Fri, 9am-12.30pm Sat)

TIC (☎ 841656; www.visitlancaster.co.uk; 29 Castle Hill; ☺ 9am-5pm Mon-Sat)

Lancaster Castle & Priory

Lancaster's imposing **castle** (☎ 64998; admission £4; ☺ 10am-5pm) was originally built in 1150. Later additions include the **Well Tower**, more commonly known as the Witches' Tower as it was used to incarcerate the accused of the famous Pendle Witches Trial of 1612, and the impressive, twin-towered **gatehouse**, both of which were added in the 14th century. Most of what you see today, however, dates from the 18th and 19th centuries, when the castle was substantially altered to suit its new role as a prison, which it remains today. Consequently, you can only visit the castle as part of a 45-minute **guided tour** (☺ every 30 min, 10am-4pm).

Immediately next to the castle is the equally fine **priory church** (☎ 65338; admission free; ☺ 9.30am-5pm), founded in 1094 but extensively remodelled in the Middle Ages.

Other Sights

The steps between the castle and the church lead down to the 17th-century **Judges' Lodgings** (☎ 32808; admission £2; ☺ 10.30am-1pm & 2-5pm Mon-Fri, 2-5pm Sat Jul-Sep, 2-5pm Mon-Sat Oct-Jun), once used by visiting magistrates and now home to a Museum of Furnishings by master builders Gillows of Lancaster (whose work graces the Houses of Parliament) and a Museum of Childhood with memorabilia from the turn of the 20th century.

A couple of other museums complete the picture: the **Maritime Museum** (☎ 64637; St George's Quay; admission £2; ☺ 11am-5pm Easter-Oct, 12.30-4pm Nov-Easter), in the 18th-century Custom House, recalls the days when Lancaster was a flourishing port at the centre of the slave trade; and the **City Museum** (☎ 64637; Market Sq; admission free; ☺ 10am-5pm Mon-Sat) has a mixed bag of local historical and archaeological exhibits.

Sleeping & Eating

Swallow King's Arms Hotel (☎ 32451; www.swallow -hotels.com; Market St; mains around £11; s/d £52/77; **P**) Lancaster's top hotel is a period house with modern, comfortable rooms and an all-round businesslike interior. Look out for the beautiful stained-glass windows, one of the only leftovers from the mid-19th century, when Charles Dickens frequented the place. The hotel restaurant is an excellent dining choice.

Otherwise, **Castle Hill House** (☎ 849137; gsut clif@aol.com.uk; 27 St Mary's Pde; s/d £27/42) is terraced Victorian house in the middle of town with comfortable, well-furnished rooms, while the **Wagon & Horses** (☎ 846094; 27 St Georges Quay; s/d £30/45) is a pleasant pub next to the Maritime Museum with five comfortable rooms upstairs; only one is en suite, but all have river views.

The **Old John of Gaunt** (☎ 32358; 53 Market St; mains around £5-6) is your one-stop for traditional pub grub, decent ale and live music.

Getting There & Away

Lancaster is on the main west-coast railway line and on the Cumbrian Coast Line.

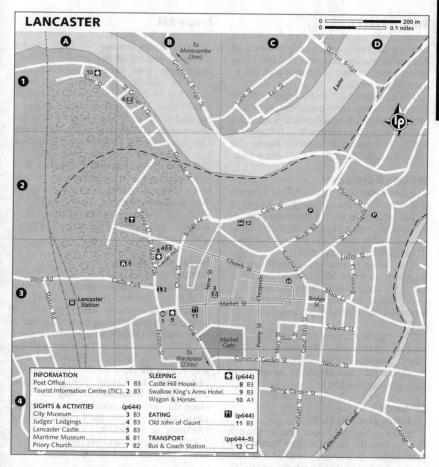

LANCASTER

0 _____ 200 m
0 _____ 0.1 miles

INFORMATION	
Post Office.........................1 B3	
Tourist Information Centre (TIC)..2 B3	

SIGHTS & ACTIVITIES	(p644)
City Museum.........................3 B3	
Judges' Lodgings...................4 B3	
Lancaster Castle....................5 B3	
Maritime Museum..................6 B1	
Priory Church.......................7 B2	

SLEEPING	(p644)
Castle Hill House....................8 B3	
Swallow King's Arms Hotel........9 B3	
Wagon & Horses...................10 A1	

EATING	(p644)
Old John of Gaunt................11 B3	

TRANSPORT	(pp644–5)
Bus & Coach Station..............12 C2	

Destinations include Carlisle (£19, one hour, hourly), Manchester (£11.05, one hour, hourly) and Morecambe (£1.45, 15 minutes, half-hourly)

MORECAMBE

☎ 01524 / pop 49,5700

Lancashire's *other* seaside resort was a mind-its-own-business fishing village until the middle of the 19th century, when the railway brought trains packed with mill workers and their families raring for some fun by the sea. Its popularity has irrevocably waned since WWII, however, when bolder and brasher Blackpool to the south became the west-coast resort for the bucket-and-spade brigade.

The **TIC** (☎ 582808; Old Station Bldgs; ⏰ 9.30am-5pm Mon-Sat year-round plus 10am-4pm Sun Jun-Sep) is on Central Promenade and runs a free accommodation service.

The old harbour has been refurbished and all that remains is the **stone jetty**, which is adorned with bird sculptures, a tribute to the glorious bay, which is considered the country's most important wintering site for birds. Sunsets here can be quite spectacular. Farther down the promenade is the town's most famous statue (by Graham Ibbeson) – of Ernie Bartholomew, better known as Ernie Morecambe, one half of comic duo Morecambe and Wise.

Trains run half-hourly from Lancaster (£1.45, 15 minutes), only 5 miles to the west.

RIBBLE VALLEY

Lancashire's most attractive landscapes lie trapped between the brash tackiness of Blackpool to the west and the sprawling urban conurbations of Preston and Blackburn to the south.

The northern half of the valley is dominated by the sparsely populated moorland of the Forest of Bowland, which is great for walks, while the southern half features the rolling hills, attractive market towns and ruins through which flows the River Ribble.

Walking & Cycling

The **Ribble Way**, a 70-mile (113km) footpath that follows the River Ribble from its source to the estuary, is one of the more popular walks in the area and passes through Clitheroe. For online information check out www .lancashirehillcountry.co.uk.

The valley is also well covered by the northern loop of the Lancashire Cycle Way; for more information about routes, safety and so on contact the **Blazing Saddles Mountain Club** (☎ 01442-844435; www.blazingsaddles .co.uk).

The TIC in Clitheroe (below) has three useful publications: *Bowlands by Bike* (free), *Mountain Bike Ribble Valley Circular Routes* (£2) and *Mountain Bike Rides in Gisburn Forest* (£1.50).

Clitheroe

☎ 01200 / population 14,700

The Ribble Valley's largest market town is best known for its impressive **Norman keep** (admission free; ☯ dawn-dusk), built in the 12th century and now standing sadly empty (although there are great views of the river valley below). The extensive grounds are home to the mildly interesting **castle museum** (☎ 424635; adult/child £2/50p; ☯ 11am-5pm May-Sep, Sat-Wed only Oct-Dec & Feb-Apr, closed Jan).

The **TIC** (☎ 425566; www.ribblevalley.gov.uk; 14 Market Place; ☯ 9am-5pm Mon-Sat, 9am-4pm Sun) has information on the town and surrounding area. **Pedal Power** (☎ 422066; Waddington Rd) has bikes for rent.

The 17th-century **White Lion Hotel** (☎ 426 955; 11 Market Pl; s/d from £21/35), opposite the TIC, has comfortable rooms, while **Halpenny's of Clitheroe** (☎ 424478; Old Toll House, 1-5 Parson Lane; mains around £5) is a traditional teashop that serves sandwiches and dishes like Lancashire Hot Pot.

Pendle Hill

The area's top attraction is Pendle Hill (558m), made famous in 1612 as the stomping ground of the Pendle Witches, 10 women who allegedly practiced all kinds of malefic doings until they were convicted on the sole testimony of a child and hanged. The tourist authority makes a big deal of the mythology surrounding the unfortunate women, and every Halloween a pseudo-mystical ceremony is performed here to commemorate their 'activities'.

If that wasn't enough, the hill is also renowned as the spot where George Fox had a vision in 1652 that led him to found the Quakers. Whatever your thoughts on witchcraft and religious visions, the hill, a couple of miles east of Clitheroe, is a great spot to walk to.

Forest of Bowland

☎ 01200

This vast, grouse-ridden moorland is somewhat of a misnomer. The use of 'forest' is a throwback to an earlier definition, when it served as a royal hunting ground. Today it is an Area of Outstanding Natural Beauty (AONB), which makes for good walking and cycling, including the **Pendle Witch Way**, a 45-mile walk from Pendle Hill to northeast of Lancaster that cuts right through the area, and the **Lancashire Cycle Way** that runs along the eastern border. The forest's main town is Slaidburn, about 9 miles north of Clitheroe on the B6478.

Other villages worth exploring are Newton, Whitewell and Dunsop Bridge.

Sleeping & Eating

The popular **YHA Youth Hostel** (☎ 0870 770 6034; www.yha.org.uk; King's House, Slaidburn; dm £10.60; ☯ Apr-Oct), a converted 17th-century village inn, was given the once-over in 2003. It is especially popular with walkers and cyclists.

More luxurious accommodation is limited. In Slaidburn, the wonderful 13th-century **Hark to Bounty Inn** (☎ 446246; www.harktobounty .co.uk; 3-course meal £15.95; s/d £29.50/59.50) has atmospheric rooms with exposed oak beams and, downstairs, an excellent restaurant that specialises in homemade herb breads.

Elsewhere, the stunning **Inn at Whitewell** (☎ 448222; fax 448298; Whitewell Village; s/d from £69/94) is a remarkable place set amid 1½ hectares of grounds. Once the home of the

Forest Keeper, it is now a superb guesthouse with a wonderfully eccentric feel. The gorgeous rooms have antique furniture, peat fires and Victorian clawfoot baths. The restaurant (mains around £11) specialises in traditional English game dishes.

Getting There & Around
Clitheroe is served by regular buses from Preston and Blackburn as well as hourly by train from Manchester (£6.45, one hour) and Preston (£5.10, 50 minutes). Once there, you're better off it you have your own transport, as there is only a Sunday bus service between Clitheroe and the rest of the valley villages.

ISLE OF MAN

Beloved of tax avoiders and petrol heads, the Isle of Man (*Ellan Vannin* in Manx) is a surprisingly beautiful place. It's thought of as a weird place by many mainlanders, most of whom have never actually seen the lush valleys, barren hills and rugged coastlines of the island, which make for great walking, cycling and driving. Anyone familiar with motor sports will know that the island is famous for its Tourist Trophy (TT) motorcycle races, which every May and June add 45,000 to the island's small population. The island's other great industry is tax avoidance – wealthy Brits can shelter their loot here without having to move to Monte Carlo or the Cayman Islands.

Home to the world's oldest continuous parliament, the Isle of Man enjoys special status in Britain, and its annual parliamentary ceremony honours the 1000-year history of the Tynwald (a Scandinavian word meaning meeting field). Douglas, the capital, is a run-down relic of Victorian tourism with fading B&Bs. The tailless Manx cat and the four-horned Loghtan sheep are unique to the Isles.

Orientation & Information
Situated in the Irish Sea, equidistant from Liverpool, Dublin and Belfast, the Isle of Man is about 33 miles long by 13 miles wide. Ferries arrive at Douglas, the port and main town on the southeast coast. Flights come in to Ronaldsway airport, 10 miles south of Douglas. Most of the island's historic sites are operated by Manx Heritage, which offers free admission to National Trust or English Heritage members. Unless otherwise indicated, **Manx Heritage** (MH; ☎ 648000; www.gov.im/mnh) sites open 10am to 5pm daily, Easter to October. The **Manx Heritage Pass** (adult/child £10/5) grants you free entry into four of the island's heritage attractions; pick it up at any of the TICs.

Walking & Cycling
There are plenty of walking trails. Ordnance Survey (OS) Landranger Map 95 (£5.99) covers the whole island, while the free *Walks on the Isle of Man* is available from the TIC in Douglas. The **Millennium Way** is a walking path that runs the length of the island amid some spectacular scenery. The most demanding of all walks is the 90-mile (145km) **Raad ny Foillan**, or Road of the Gull, a well-marked path that makes a complete circuit of the island and normally takes about five days to complete. Other routes are detailed under the relevant sections following.

There are six designated off-road cycling tracks on the island, each with varying ranges of difficulty.

The island is also home to the **International Cycling Week Festival**, which takes place in mid-July. It's a pretty serious affair, attracting top cyclists from around the world as well as enthusiastic Sunday racers. Check with the TIC in Douglas for details.

DOUGLAS
☎ 01624 / pop 22,200
All roads lead to Douglas, which is a bit of a shame, as the town isn't all that endearing. Still, it has the best of the island's hotels and restaurants – as well as the bulk of the finance houses frequented so regularly by tax-allergic Brits. The **TIC** (☎ 686766; Sea Terminal Bldg; ☼ 9.15am-7pm daily May-Sep, 9am-5pm daily Apr & Oct, 9am-5.30pm Mon-Fri & 9am-12.30pm Sat Nov-Mar) makes free accommodation bookings.

The **Manx Museum** (MH; admission free; ☼ 10am-5pm Mon-Sat) gives an introduction to everything from the island's prehistoric past to the latest TT race winners.

Sleeping & Eating
The seafront promenade is crammed with B&Bs. Unless you booked back in the 1990s, there's little chance of finding accommodation during TT week and the weeks each

ISLE OF MAN

To Belfast (85mi);
Stranraer (100mi);
(Summer Only)

Point of
Ayre

Road of the Gull

A10 — Bride

Andreas

Jurby

Ramsey
Bay

Irish
Sea

Sulby — Ramsey
A3
Churchtown

Bellaugh

Maughold

Kirk Michael

TT Circuit

A2

Snaefell
(620m)

A3

Isle of
Man

Laxey

A4

Peel

TT Circuit

Cregny
Baa

Baldrine

Patrick

St John's

Heritage Walk

Lonan
Church

Foxdale

Crosby

A1

Dalby

Douglas

Millennium Way

A5

To
Heysham
(65mi)

St Marks

Ballasalla

A5

Isle of Man
(Ronaldsway)
Airport

Port Erin

Chapel
Hill

Castletown

Cregneash

Port
St Mary

Calf
of Man

To
Liverpool
(75mi)

To Dublin (90mi);
(Summer Only)

0 ——— 10 km
0 ——— 6 miles

side of it. The TIC's camping information sheet lists sites all around the island.

Admiral House (☎ 629551; www.admiralhouse .com; Loch Promenade; mains around £8-10; s/d £40/75; P) A warm and elegant guesthouse overlooking the harbour near the ferry port with 23 spotless modern rooms. Plenty of bright reds and blues feature in the décor, a cheerful alternative to the worn look of a lot of other seafront B&Bs. In the basement, the smart **La Posada** is a good Spanish restaurant that does a delicious *paella*.

Claremont (☎ 698800; www.sleepwellhotels.com; 18-19 Loch Promenade; d/ste £90/125; 💻 P) The last word in contemporary business style in Douglas, the Claremont has very bright, airy rooms with all the latest gizmos – DVD players,

Internet connections and fancy TVs – as well as beautiful limestone bathrooms. The executive rooms have terrific harbour views.

Sefton Hotel (☎ 645500; www.seftonhotel.co.im; Harris Promenade; s/d from £79/96; P 🕱) Douglas' best hotel is an upmarket oasis with its own indoor water garden and rooms that range from plain and comfy to elegant and very luxurious – the rooms overlooking the water garden are superb, even better than the ones with sea views. You save up to 10% if you book online.

Spill the Beans (1 Market Hill; snacks around £1.50; ☷ 9.30am-6pm Mon-Sat) The most pleasant coffee shop in Douglas delivers proper caffeine kicks as well as cakes, buns and other sweet snacks.

Tanroagan (☎ 472411; 9 Ridgeway St; mains £9-15; ⏲ lunch & dinner Mon-Fri, dinner only Sat) The place for all things from the sea, this elegant eatery is the trendiest place in Douglas, serving fresh fish straight off the boats, given the merest of continental twists or just a spell on the hot grill. Reservations are recommended.

There are a few good pubs around, including the popular local hang-out **Tramshunter** (Promenade) and the originally named **Rover's Return** (☎ 676459; 11 Church St) specialising in the local brew Bushy Ales.

AROUND DOUGLAS

You can follow the TT course up and over the mountain or wind around the coast. The mountain route goes close to the summit of **Snaefell** (621m), the island's highest point. It's an easy walk up to the summit or take the electric tram from Laxey on the coast. The tram stops by the road where **Murray's Motorcycle Museum** (☎ 01624 613328; Bungalow Corner, Mountain Rd; adult/child £3/2; ⏲ 10am-5pm May-Oct only) displays motorcycles and TT memorabilia.

On the edge of Ramsey is the **Grove Rural Life Museum** (MH; adult/child £3/2). The church in the small village of **Maughold** is on the site of an ancient monastery; a small shelter houses quite a good selection of stone crosses and ancient inscriptions.

Describing the **Laxey Wheel** (MH; adult/child £3/2), built in 1854 to pump water from a mine, as a 'great' wheel is no exaggeration; it measures 22m across and can draw 250 gallons (1140L) of water per minute from a depth of 550m. The wheel-headed cross at **Lonan Old Church** is the island's most impressive early Christian cross.

CASTLETOWN & AROUND

At the southern end of the island is Castletown, a quiet harbour town that was originally the capital of the Isle of Man. The town is dominated by the impressive 13th-century **Castle Rushen** (MH; admission £4.25). The flag tower affords fine views of the town and coast. There's also a small **Nautical Museum** (MH; admission £3) displaying, among other things, its pride and joy *Peggy*, a boat built in 1791 and still housed in its original boathouse. A school dating back to 1570 in **St Mary's church** (MH; admission free) is behind the castle.

Between Castletown and Cregneash, the Iron-Age hillfort at **Chapel Hill** encloses a Viking ship burial site.

On the southern tip of the island, the **Cregneash Village Folk Museum** (MH; admission £3) recalls traditional Manx rural life. The **Calf of Man**, the small island just off Cregneash, is a bird sanctuary. **Calf Island Cruises** (☎ 832339; adult/child £10/5; ⏲ 10.15am, 11.30am & 1.30pm Apr-Oct weather permitting) run between Port Erin and the island.

Port Erin, another Victorian seaside resort, plays host to the small **Railway Museum** (admission £1; ⏲ 9.30am-5.30pm daily Apr-Oct) depicting the history of steam railway on the island.

Sleeping

Port Erin has a good range of accommodation, as does Port St Mary, across the headland and linked by steam train.

Aaron House (☎ 835702; aaron_house_iom@yahoo.com; the Promenade, Port St Mary; s/d £30/60) This splendid Victorian-style B&B has fussed over every detail, from the gorgeous brass beds and claw-foot baths to the old-fashioned photographs on the walls – it's like stepping back in time, minus the inconvenience of cold and discomfort. The sea views are sensational.

PEEL & AROUND

The west coast's most appealing town, Peel has a fine sandy beach but its real attraction is the 11th-century **Peel Castle** (MH; admission £3), stunningly positioned atop St Patrick's Island and joined to Peel by a causeway.

The excellent **House of Mannanan** (MH; admission £5; ⏲ year round) museum uses interactive displays to explain Manx history and its seafaring traditions.

A combined ticket for both costs £7.

Three miles east of Peel is **Tynwald Hill** at St John's, where the annual parliamentary ceremony takes place on 5 July.

Sleeping & Eating

Peel has several B&Bs, including the **Fernleigh Hotel** (☎ 842435; Marine Parade; rooms per person from £22), which has twelve decent bedrooms and prices include breakfast. For a better-than-average bite, head for the **Creek Inn** (☎ 842216 fax 843359; East Quay; mains around £7; r from £33), opposite the House of Mannanan, which serves Manx queenies and has self-catering rooms.

GETTING THERE & AWAY
Air

Ronaldsway Airport (☎ 01624 821600; Ballasalla) is 10 miles south of Douglas near Castletown.

Buses link the airport with Douglas every 30 minutes between 7am and 11pm; a taxi should cost you no more than £18. Airline contacts:

British Airways (☎ 0870 850 9850; www.britishair ways.com) From London Gatwick, Luton & Manchester.

Eastern Airways (☎ 01652-681099; www.easternair ways.com) From Leeds-Bradford, Bristol, Birmingham & East Midlands.

Emerald Airways (☎ 0870 850 5400; www.flyjem .com) From Liverpool.

EuroManx Airlines (☎ 0870 787 7879; www.euro manx.com) From Liverpool & London Stansted.

Flybe (☎ 0871 700 0535; www.3flybe.com) From London City, Jersey, Bristol & Birmingham.

Boat

Isle of Man Steam Packet (☎ 0870 552 3523; www.steam-packet.com; foot passenger single/return £15/25, car & two passengers £199 return) is a car ferry and hi-speed catamaran service from Liverpool and Heysham to Douglas.

GETTING AROUND

The island has a comprehensive bus service; the TIC in Douglas has timetables and fares.

Bikes can be hired from **Eurocycles** (☎ 624 909; 8A Victoria Rd; £12-18/day; ☼ Mon-Sat).

Petrol-heads will love the scenic, sweeping bends that make for some exciting driving – and the fact that outside the town there's no speed limit. Naturally, the most popular drive is along the TT route. Car-hire operators have desks at the airport; charging from £30 upwards per day.

There are several interesting **rail services** (☎ 663366; ☼ Easter-Sep) listed following; saver passes are available:

Douglas-Laxey-Ramsey Electric Tramway
(£6 return)

Douglas-Castletown-Port Erin Steam Train
(£7 return)

Laxey-Summit Snaefell Mountain Railway
(£6 return)

Cumbria & The Lakes

CONTENTS

Carved out by vast glaciers during the last Ice Age, the Cumbrian landscape is one of the most diverse and dramatic in England, from the wind-lashed cliffs of the coast and the green Eden Valley in the east to the silvery tarns and saw-tooth hills of the central Lakes. It's an area steeped in history, contested by Roman generals, Viking settlers, Scottish raiders and English kings – though present-day Cumbria has been in existence for barely 30 years, created in 1974 from the old counties of Cumberland and Westmorland. Cumbria is littered with reminders of its ancient past – prehistoric stone circles and ruined castles, tumbledown abbeys and medieval churches, cobbled villages and red-brick market towns – but the most obvious legacy has been left by Cumbria's generations of farmers, in the countless miles of dry-stone walls winding their way through the countryside.

These days, Cumbria is renowned as one of Britain's best places to experience the great outdoors. With a huge network of hiking trails, ranging from mountain ascents to woodland rambles, it's a world-class place for walking; but there are endless opportunities for cycling, sailing and rock climbing too. Book lovers can hit the literary trail in search of some of the area's famous characters – Beatrix Potter, Arthur Ransome, John Ruskin and, of course, one William Wordsworth – while gastrophiles can retire to one of the many fine pubs, inns and restaurants for some traditional Cumbrian cooking and a pint of local ale. Just don't forget to pack the compass.

HIGHLIGHTS

- Taking to the trails in the **Lake District National Park** (p655)
- Cruising the lakes of **Windermere** (p656), **Coniston** (p668) and **Derwent Water** (p673)
- Discovering the little-known lake of **Wast Water** (p671)
- Exploring the valleys of **Buttermere** (p678) and **Borrowdale** (p677)
- Admiring the outdoor sculptures of **Grizedale Forest** (p667)
- Following in the footsteps of Wordsworth and co at **Rydal Mount** (p664) and **Grasmere** (p665)
- Surveying the scene from **Helvellyn** (p679) and **Scaféll Pike** (p677)
- Travelling back in time amongst the ruins of **Furness Abbey** (p682)

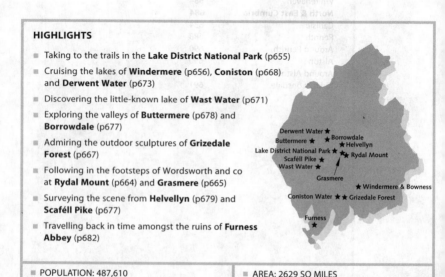

Derwent Water ★
Buttermere ★ ★ Borrowdale
★ Helvellyn
Lake District National Park ★ ★★ Rydal Mount
Scaféll Pike ★
Wast Water ★
Grasmere
★ Windermere & Bowness
Coniston Water ★ ★ Grizedale Forest
Furness
★

■ POPULATION: 487,610	■ AREA: 2629 SQ MILES

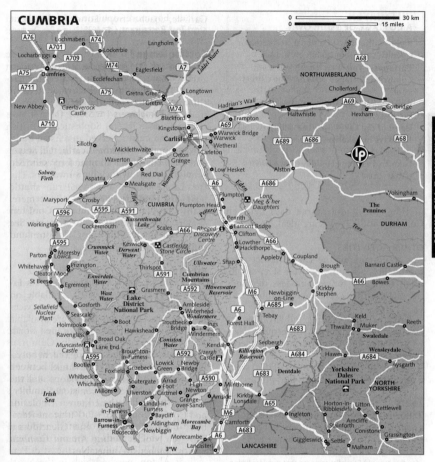

CUMBRIA

Activities

CYCLING

Cumbria is a good area for cycling, though the steep hills can be tough going. Keen cyclists could consider the waymarked 259-mile (432km) circular **Cumbria Cycle Way**. Another possibility is the 140-mile (225km) **Sea to Sea Cycle Route** (C2C) from Whitehaven or Workington, through the northern Lake District and North Pennines to Newcastle-upon-Tyne or Sunderland. Most people take five days to complete the route; the Cumbrian section makes a great weekend outing.

WALKING

For many, walking is one of Cumbria's main attractions. The region is crossed by a network of stunning footpaths and hiking trails. Outside the Lake District National Park, there are several other walking paths to be found along the often-overlooked Cumbria coast.

There's no official national trail through Cumbria, but one of Britain's most famous long-distance walks, the **Coast to Coast**, cuts west to east through the region towards the Yorkshire Dales and the North Yorkshire Moors. The total length is 191 miles (307km). The Cumbrian section, from St Bees to Shap, covers 82 miles (132km) and takes around five to seven days.

A more manageable option is the **Cumbria Way**, a 68-mile (109km), five-day route from Ulverston to Carlisle. If you're short

A COTTAGE OF YOUR OWN

If you're after some Cumbrian self-catering serenity, start your search on the Net:

Cottages 4 You (www.cottages4you.co.uk)
Cumbrian Cottages (www.cumbrian-cottages.co.uk)
Goosemire Cottages (www.lake-district-cottages.com)
Heart of the Lakes (www.heartofthelakes.co.uk)
Holidays in Lakeland (www.holidays-in-lakeland.co.uk)
Lakeland Cottage Holidays (www.lakeland-cottages.co.uk)

of time, the middle three days between Coniston and Keswick are ideal.

OTHER ACTIVITIES

The mountains of the Lake District offer top-quality rock climbing, from steep single-pitch routes to longer and less demanding classics that experienced climbers can tackle solo.

Unsurprisingly, sailing and kayaking are also popular pastimes. Windermere, Derwent Water and Coniston are considered the top spots.

Travel Information Centres (TICs) stock a selection of leaflets, maps and guides.

Tours

Tailor-made holidays and specialist tours are provided by many companies. For more England-wide tour companies see p753.
Cloudberry Holidays (☎ 017687-77257; www.cloudberry.co.uk) Specialist company that provides hiking trips for the YHA.
Mountain Goat (Map p657; ☎ 015394-45161; www.mountain-goat.com; Victoria St, Windermere) Half-day and full-day escorted tours (£14-28) of Cumbria and the Lake District in minivans.
Saddleback Trails (☎ 017684-86432) Small company arranging horse-riding holidays around the upper Eden Valley and northern Lake District.
2 Wheel Treks (☎ 01483 271 212; www.2wheeltreks.co.uk) Cycling tours around the Lake District.

Getting There & Away

There's a direct rail link from Manchester Airport via Preston and Lancaster to Barrow-in-Furness (2½ hours) and Windermere (2¼ hours). Carlisle has several bus services to Keswick. To both Windermere and

Carlisle, coaches from London take about 6½ hours, trains 3½ hours.

Getting Around

Traveline (☎ 0870 608 2608; www.traveline-cumbria.co.uk; ☼ 7am-8pm) provides travel information. TICs stock the free *Getting Around Cumbria* booklet, with timetables for buses, trains and ferries.

BOAT

Windermere, Coniston Water, Ullswater and Derwent Water all offer ferry services, providing time-saving links for walkers. The **Cross-Lakes Shuttle** (☎ 015394-45161) runs shuttle boats and minibuses between Windermere, Esthwaite Water, Grizedale and Coniston Water; cyclists and hikers are welcome. See the Windermere & Bowness, Coniston and Keswick sections for details.

BUS

The main operator is Stagecoach. Its **Explorer ticket** (1/4/7 days £8/18/25), available on the bus, give unlimited travel on services in Cumbria. Other day passes are available for specific areas or for use with First North Western trains.

Stagecoach operates some excellent buses, including No 555/556 (LakesLink) between Lancaster and Carlisle, which stops at all the main towns; No 505 (Coniston Rambler) linking Kendal, Windermere, Ambleside and Coniston; and No 517 (Kirkstone Rambler) between Bowness and Glenridding. The free booklet *Getting Around Cumbria* has comprehensive timetables.

CAR

Avoid bringing a car if you can, to help limit congestion and pollution in the area. The bus network is the best way of travelling around here, but you could conceivably use taxis. If you do take the taxi option, expect to pay £1.60 to £2 per mile, with a minimum charge of £2.30.

TRAIN

Aside from the Cumbrian Coast Line and the branch line from Oxenholme to Windermere, there are several steam railways. If you fancy a ride on a steam train, try the Ravenglass & Eskdale Railway (p683) or the Ambleside/Bowness to Haverthwaite Steam Railway (p658).

THE LAKE DISTRICT

I wander'd lonely as a cloud
That floats on high o'er dales and hills,
When all at once I saw a crowd,
A host, of golden daffodils…
    William Wordsworth
    from The Daffodils (1804)

Few regions in Britain can match the Lake District for rich, raw, unadulterated beauty. The surroundings are truly awe-inspiring: cloud-capped mountains divided by knife-edge ridges and plunging valley walls, mist-covered tarns and tree-fringed meadows, and deep, clear lakes studded with wooded islands and the reflections of craggy hill-tops. Little wonder that the 19th-century Romantics sought solitude and inspiration around the region's mountain tops and lake shores, but even in Wordsworth's day, there were concerns that the unique landscape could be ruined. Thankfully, the future of the Lakes was ensured when the area became Britain's largest national park in 1951.

Today, the Lake District is best known as the country's walking heartland, with routes ranging from relaxed day rambles to the classic mountain ascents of Skiddaw, Helvellyn and Scaféll Pike (the highest peak in England). It's a place to feed your soul – by bike or on foot, in country pubs or

CUMBRIA & THE LAKES

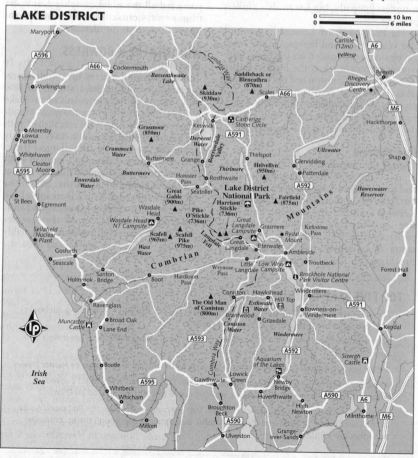

LAKE DISTRICT

fine-dining restaurants, in the great out-doors or on the literary trail – and every year, a hungry 14 million visitors pour in to taste the riches of the lakes for them-selves. In summer that cloudlike feeling may seem elusive, especially on weekends; but the western lakes are never as busy as their better-known cousins, and whatever the season, you'll be able to find solitude somewhere, whether it's at the bottom of a river valley or the crest of a hilltop trail.

Orientation

The Lake District is shaped in a rough star formation, with valleys, ridges and lakes radiating out from the high ground at its centre. The central area is crossed with countless footpaths, but few roads – a hikers' paradise.

The main bases are Keswick in the north and Windermere and Bowness in the south. Ambleside and Coniston are less hectic alter-natives. Windermere is the biggest, busiest lake. Ullswater, Coniston and Derwent Water lakes have a speed restriction of 10mph, and powerboats are banned on Grasmere, Crum-mock Water and Buttermere. Wast Water is the wildest and least accessible valley.

Information

The region's network of TICs stocks moun-tains of information on accommodation and exploring the Lake District, whether by bus, bike or on foot. The Windermere and Keswick branches are excellent; both have free local booking services. The national park runs nine TICs in the area, and a **visitor centre** (☎ 015394-46601; www.lake-district.gov.uk) at Brockhole, on the A591 near Windermere.

Hostels & Camping Barns

There are almost 30 YHA hostels in the Lakes. The YHA runs an **accommodation booking service** (☎ 015394-31117), and pro-vides shuttle buses linking Ambleside, Butterlip How, Elterwater, Hawkshead, Holly How and Langdale YHAs with Wind-ermere train station. For more information, call **Ambleside YHA** (☎ 015394-32304) or **Patter-dale YHA** (☎ 015394-31117; www.yhalakedistrict.org .uk). Within seven days of your intended arrival, you can make bookings for most Lake District Hostels through Patterdale YHA hostel.

The Lake District National Park Author-ity also administers several camping barns, costing around £4 per person per night; you need all the usual camping gear apart from a tent. Contact **Keswick information cen-tre** (☎ 017687-72645) for details.

WINDERMERE & BOWNESS
☎ 015394 / pop 7950

The shimmering waters of Windermere, the largest lake in England, stretch for 10½ miles across the southern half of the Lake District. The modern-day towns of Wind-ermere and Bowness were established with the arrival of the railway in 1847, quickly becoming the Lake District's largest trans-port centre, and a popular Victorian holi-day resort. Windermere is still the busiest and most commercial of the lakes. The streets are thronged with ice-cream sellers, souvenir stalls, chintzy tearooms and fish-and-chips shops, but despite the summer crowds, the lake itself remains undeniably beautiful, and is best appreciated aboard a lake cruise from Bowness Pier.

TOP FIVE LAKE DISTRICT BOOKS

- *The Lake District Walks* (Ordnance Survey Pathfinder Guides, Jarrold) – excellent guidebooks with extracts from Ordnance Survey (OS) maps
- *Complete Lakeland Fells* (Collins) – modern guide by local author Bill Birkett covering 120 popular routes
- *A Walk Round the Lakes* (Orion) – entertaining guide to the history of the Lakes by Hunter Davies
- *A Pictorial Guide to the Lakeland Fells* (Frances Lincoln Ltd) – Alfred Wainwright's seven-volume, hand-drawn series is the classic walking guide (though you'll need an OS map)
- *A Complete Guide to the Lakes* (Frances Lincoln Ltd) – Wordsworth wrote the first travel guide to the Lake District in 1810, and it's still a useful, descriptive read, though the accommoda-tion ideas are a little out of date

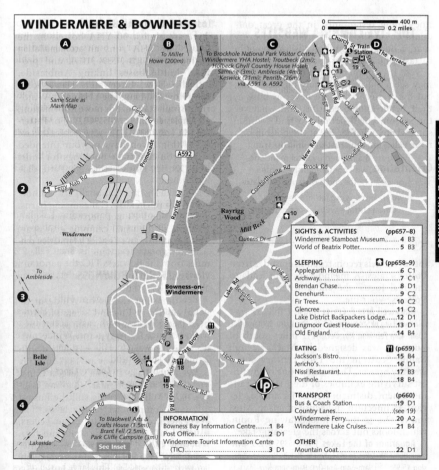

WINDERMERE & BOWNESS

SIGHTS & ACTIVITIES	(pp657–8)
Windermere Stamboat Museum.....4	B3
World of Beatrix Potter.................5	B3

SLEEPING	(pp658–9)
Applegarth Hotel...........................6	C1
Archway.......................................7	C1
Brendan Chase..............................8	D1
Denehurst....................................9	C2
Fir Trees.....................................10	C2
Glencree....................................11	C2
Lake District Backpackers Lodge......12	D1
Lingmoor Guest House...................13	D1
Old England...............................14	B4

EATING	(p659)
Jackson's Bistro...........................15	B4
Jericho's....................................16	D1
Nissi Restaurant..........................17	B3
Porthole....................................18	B4

TRANSPORT	(p660)
Bus & Coach Station.....................19	D1
Country Lanes.........................(see 19)
Windermere Ferry........................20	A2
Windermere Lake Cruises...............21	B4

OTHER	
Mountain Goat............................22	D1

INFORMATION	
Bowness Bay Information Centre.......1	B4
Post Office..................................2	D1
Windermere Tourist Information Centre	
(TIC)..3	D1

CUMBRIA & THE LAKES

Orientation

It's 1½ miles downhill from Windermere station to Bowness Pier. Buses and coaches leave from outside the train station. Bowness has the nicest places to eat, and is the livelier place to be in the evening.

Information

Brockhole National Park Visitor Centre (☎ 46601; www.lake-district.gov.uk; ✆ 10am-5pm late Mar-Oct) Flagship visitor centre 3 miles north of Windermere on the A591.
Post office (21 Crescent Rd; ✆ 9am-5.30pm Mon-Sat)
TIC Bowness Bay Information Centre (☎ 42895; bownesstic@lake-district.gov.uk; Glebe Rd; ✆ 9.30am-5.30pm Easter-Oct, 10am-4pm Fri-Sun Nov-Mar); Windermere (☎ 46499; windermeretic@southlakeland.gov.uk; Victoria St; ✆ 9am-6pm Apr-Jun & Sep-Oct, 9am-7.30pm

Jul & Aug, 9am-5pm Nov-Mar; Net access per 10min £1) Provides a free accommodation-booking service.

Sights

The **Windermere Steamboat Museum** (☎ 45565; www.steamboat.co.uk; Rayrigg Rd; admission £3.50; ✆ 10am-5pm mid-Mar–Nov) houses a marvellous collection of steam and motor boats, including the world's oldest mechanically powered vessel and the *Esperance*, which Arthur Ransome imagined as Captain Flint's houseboat in his work *Swallows and Amazons*. The museum also offers trips on a small steam launch (£5).

The **World of Beatrix Potter** (☎ 88444; www.hop-skip-jump.com; Crag Brow; adult/child £3.90/2.90; ✆ 10am-5.30pm Apr-Sep, 10am-4.30pm Oct-Mar) has

TOP FIVE CUMBRIA WEBSITES

■ www.golakes.co.uk – official website of the Cumbria Tourist Board

■ www.lake-district.gov.uk – the National Park Authority's official website

■ www.lakedistrictoutdoors.co.uk – walking routes, bike rides and safety tips provided by the Cumbria Tourist Board

■ www.lakedistrictwalks.com – great website maintained by local man John Dawson, with comprehensive route guides, photos and a distance calculator

■ www.ramblers.org.uk/info/regional /cumbria.html – website of the British Ramblers' Association

lots of models reconstructing episodes from Potter's tales. A meandering path leads to the real focus, the shop, where you can Potterise your life.

Blackwell Arts & Crafts House (☎ 46139; www .blackwell.org.uk; admission £4.75; ☉ 10am-5pm Apr-Oct, 10am-4pm Feb-Mar, Nov-Dec), 1½ miles south of Bowness, was designed by Mackay Hugh Baillie Scott in the 19th century for a wealthy brewer. The house is one of the finest surviving examples of the Arts & Crafts movement, distinguished by its simple, elegant architecture and sense of space. Most impressive is the White Drawing Room, which looks out across the gleaming lake.

Aquarium of the Lakes (☎ 015395-30153; www .aquariumofthelakes.co.uk; Lakeside, Newby Bridge; admission £5.95; ☉ 9am-6pm Apr-Oct, 9am-5pm Nov-Mar) is at the lake's southern end, and recreates over 30 freshwater habitats, including an underwater tunnel through Windermere's lakebed, complete with pike, Arctic char and diving ducks. As usual, though, the mischievous otters steal the show. The best way to arrive is by boat from Bowness or Ambleside (see Boat Trips, below).

Activities

BOAT TRIPS

Windermere Lake Cruises (☎ 015395-31188; www .windermere-lakecruises.co.uk) has a mixture of modern and old cruisers plying the lake from Bowness Pier. Regular boats run to Ambleside (adult single £6.75), Lakeside (single/return £4.60/6.85), and Ferry House

(£1.70/2.95), for Hawkshead and Hill Top. A Freedom of the Lake ticket allows unlimited cruises for 24 hours (£12), and 45-minute evening cruises are also available (£5, May to October).

Joint tickets tie in with the **Ambleside/Bowness to Haverthwaite Steam Railway** (☎ 015395-31594; return from Bowness £10.95, from Ambleside £14.90; ☉ Apr-Oct) and the **Aquarium of the Lakes** (return ferry & aquarium £11.75 from Bowness, £15.70 from Ambleside).

Motorboat hire costs around £15 per hour for two adults. Rowing boats cost £3 for an hour.

WALKING & CYCLING

Orrest Head, offering panoramic Lakeland views, is 2½ miles and a steep climb away. The path starts near the Windermere TIC. Another good viewpoint is **Brant Fell**, 2½ miles from the Bowness TIC; the panoramic views are worth the climb. Leaflets are available from local TICs.

Beatrix Potter's cottage at Hill Top (see p668) and the picturesque village of Hawkshead (see p667) are both easily accessible to walkers. Catch the ferry across Windermere; it's a 2-mile walk to Hill Top and another 2 miles to Hawkshead.

For bike hire, go to **Country Lanes** (☎ 44544; www.countrylanes.co.uk; per day £15; ☉ 9am-5pm Easter-Oct), in the train station.

Sleeping

BUDGET

Windermere YHA Hostel (☎ 43543; windermere@yha .org.uk; Bridge Lane, Troutbeck; dm £11.25; ☉ mid-Feb–Nov, weekends Nov–mid-Feb) This large hostel offers great lake views, 2 miles from the station. Take the A591 to Ambleside and turn right up Bridge Lane at Troutbeck Bridge. Bus Nos 555 and 559 run past Troutbeck Bridge.

Lake District Backpackers Lodge (☎ 46374; www .lakedistrictbackpackers.co.uk; High St; dm/d £12.50/30; 💻) A tiny hostel with small dorms in a converted slate-roofed house.

Brendan Chase (☎ 45638; brendanchase@aol.com; 1 & 3 College Rd; s/d £30/35-50; 🗙) From the floral furniture in the lounge to the HP sauce on the breakfast tables, this Edwardian guesthouse is everything a budget British B&B should be. The rooms offer few surprises, but the location is ideal for Windermere.

Park Cliffe campsite (☎ 31344; www.parkcliffe .co.uk; Birks Rd; sites £12-15.20) Fine wooded campsite with all mod cons, a bar and restaurant. It's midway between Windermere and Newby Bridge, off the A592; bus No 618 passes the turn-off, about half a mile away.

MID-RANGE

Applegarth Hotel (☎ 43206; www.applegarthhotel .co.uk; s/d £35/54-98; P ✕) Without doubt one of the finest residences in Windermere town, a detached house with many original Victorian features, including a wood-panelled lobby, 18 elegant bedrooms and the odd stained-glass window. Highly recommended.

Archway (☎ 45613; www.communiken.com/archway; 13 College Rd; s/d from £35/40; ✕) Plain, tasteful rooms in a Victorian terrace house, tucked away down a quiet side street away from the hustle and bustle of upper Windermere. Ask for one of the upper rooms with fell views.

Denehurst (☎ 44710; www.denehurst-guesthouse .co.uk; 40 Queens Dr; d £50-80; P ✕) The quaint rooms of this traditional Lakeland house are full of character; some offer wrought-iron bedsteads and oak-beamed attic ceilings. The varied breakfast menu includes eggs Benedict, French toast and American waffles.

The area around Queens Dr and Lake Rd is full of B&Bs, including **Glencree** (☎ 45822; www.glencreelakes.co.uk; d £40-60; P ✕), a handsome riverside Victorian house, and **Fir Trees** (☎ 42272; www.fir-trees.com; Lake Rd; d £46-84; P ✕), another welcoming Victorian residence further downhill towards Bowness.

TOP END

Holbeck Ghyll Country House Hotel (☎ 32375; www.holbeckghyll.com; Holbeck Lane; s/d £155/110-290) This country manor house was once the weekend hunting lodge of Lord Lonsdale; these days it's one of Windermere's finest country retreats. Set in private gardens overlooking the lake, the house offers richly furnished bedrooms, with more in a converted lodge nearby.

Miller Howe (☎ 42536; www.millerhowe.com; Rayrigg Rd; d £170-250) Reckoned by some to have the best views of any hotel in Windermere, this gorgeous Edwardian house is brimming with period character. The rooms are decorated with oil paintings, original furnishings and antique china, there's a conservatory with panoramic views over the gardens, and the restaurant is justly renowned.

SOMETHING SPECIAL

The Samling (☎ 31922; www.thesamling.com; Dove Nest; d £175-405; P ✕) Perhaps the most exclusive (and expensive) hotel in the Lake District, set in 67 acres of private grounds on a secluded hillside high above Windermere. The luxurious rooms scream style and good taste – guests can choose from private lounges, split-level balconies, A-framed attics or a private lodge.

To get here, head 2 miles north of Windermere towards Ambleside along the A591. Look out for the sign for Low Woods Sports centre; 300m further the turning for the hotel is on your right, up a very steep driveway.

Old England (☎ 42444; Church St; d £120-150) One of Windermere's oldest hotels, an ivy-covered lakeside mansion with plush rooms and a flavour of turn-of-the- century England.

Eating

Jericho's (☎ 42522; Birch St; mains from £16; ☽ dinner Tue-Sun) Nouveau cuisine hits the Lakes at this upmarket restaurant, run by a former head chef at Miller Howe. Choose from pan-seared turbot, wild mushroom risotto or Scotch beef fillet, delicately layered on huge plates.

Porthole (☎ 42793; 2 Ash St; mains £11-25; ☽ dinner Wed-Mon) A much-loved restaurant run by the same family for many years, offering classic Italian dishes and seafood in an intimate nautical-themed dining room. Look out for the ship's lantern above the doorway.

Jackson's Bistro (☎ 46264; St Martin's Pl; mains £9-16, 3-courses £12.95; ☽ dinner) A popular bistro, simply furnished with booths and wooden tables, serving French-inspired cooking such as Barbary duck breast or pork medallions in a Calvados and apple sauce.

Nissi Restaurant (☎ 45055; Crag Brow; mains £9-25; ☽ dinner Tue-Sun) This bright, cheerful Greek restaurant specialises in meze, but also has mains including moussaka and fried salt cod. Check out the bizarre Greek-themed mural in the main dining room.

Old England (☎ 42444; Church St; afternoon tea £10.95) Windermere's classiest spot for afternoon tea, served in a stately dining room or outside terrace, both with lake views.

CUMBRIA & THE LAKES

SOMETHING FOR THE WEEKEND

Start your weekend at the lavish **Holbeck Ghyll Country House Hotel** (p659), just outside Windermere. If you arrive in time, head to Bowness Pier for a sunset cruise on the lake and a smart supper at the renowned **Porthole restaurant** (p659) or **Jericho's** (p659).

On Saturday, head southwest to explore the sculptures of **Grizedale Forest** (p667) and John Ruskin's country estate of **Brantwood** (p668), or head north towards Ambleside for a brasserie lunch at **Lucy's on a Plate** (p664) and an afternoon visiting Wordsworth's houses at **Rydal Mount** (p664) and **Dove Cottage** (p665), both near Grasmere. For the second night, check in to the crenellated country manorhouse of **Langdale Chase** (p664), with its fine-dining restaurant; alternatively, head south for the country food and real ale at the **Mortal Man** (below) in Troutbeck.

On Sunday, swing westwards into the beautiful valley of **Langdale** (p669) for a morning's hike, surrounded by rolling fells and craggy mountains, and topped off with a pub lunch at the classic walkers' bar at the **Old Dungeon Ghyll Hotel** (p670) or the **Sticklebarn Tavern** (p670) nearby.

Getting There & Away
BUS
National Express buses run from Preston (£9.25, two hours, one daily) and on to Keswick (£7.25, 45 minutes). Service from London (£27, five hours 40 minutes, three daily) run via Lancaster and Kendal.

Local buses include No 555/556 to Lancaster (45 minutes, 13 daily Monday to Saturday, three on Sunday) via Kendal, and to Keswick (50 minutes, 13 daily Monday to Saturday, three on Sunday) via Ambleside and Grasmere.

Bus No 505 goes from Kendal (20 minutes) to Coniston (40 minutes) via Ambleside.

Bus No 599 links Grasmere, Ambleside, Brockhole, Windermere, Bowness and Kendal from April to October.

TRAIN
Windermere is on the branch line from Oxenholme (£3.25, 20 minutes, hourly), near Kendal, which connects with London Euston (£61.80, four hours, eight or nine daily Monday to Saturday, four on Sunday) to Glasgow.

Getting Around
Bus No 599 makes the 1½-mile journey from Bowness Pier to Windermere train station about every half-hour. You can call a taxi on ☎ 46664.

AROUND BOWNESS
Troutbeck
☎ 015394

This charming village is scattered across the hills, with flower-covered, whitewashed houses, crumbling barns and two great 17th-

century pubs. Beatrix Potter bred sheep here, at Troutbeck Park Farm.

A 17th-century yeoman farmer's house, the **Townend Farmhouse** (NT; ☎ 32628; admission £3; ♥ Tue-Fri & Sun Apr-Oct) has been in the same family for centuries and explores domestic life 300 years ago.

The **Mortal Man** (☎ 33193; www.themortalman .co.uk; s/d £50/70) is a rambling, three-storeyed pub, topped by tall chimneys and a gabled roof, which has been at the heart of Troutbeck village life for several centuries. It's still a fine place for a pint, either by the fireside bar or in the gorgeous beer garden, and the upstairs rooms all have fell views.

Troutbeck's other pub, the **Queen's Head** (☎ 32174; www.queensheadhotel.com; d £35-45), is a fine old 17th-century inn on the old coaching route between Windermere and Penrith. Its most notable feature is the carved oak chair on the first floor, used during a traditional mayoral ceremony dating back to Elizabethan times.

Bus No 517 stops outside the Queen's Head on its way from Windermere to Ullswater (12 minutes, three daily July and August, weekends only September to June).

KENDAL
☎ 01539 / pop 28,030

Kendal is known to most as the home of Kendal Mintcake – the high-energy snack made from sugar and peppermint oil that sustained Sir Edmund Hillary and Tensing Norgay on their ascent of Everest in 1953. Pre–mint cake, Kendal was founded by Norman barons, has been a market town since 1189, and was a wool and weaving centre from the Middle Ages to the 18th century – 'misbegotten knaves in Kendal-green' appear in *Henry IV Part I* – but its main attractions nowadays are its intriguing museums, an exceptional art gallery and a funky theatre and cinema complex.

Information

Dot Café (☎ 740313; ✆ 9.30am-5.30pm; Net access per 10min £1, per hr £5) On the first floor of Westmorland Shopping Centre.

Kendal Launderette (☎ 733754; Blackhall Rd; ✆ 8am-6pm Mon-Fri, 8am-5pm Sat & Sun)

Library (☎ 773520; Stricklandgate; ✆ 9.30am-5.30pm Mon & Tue, 9.30am-7pm Wed & Fri, 9.30am-1pm Thu, 9am-4pm Sat; Net access per 30mins £1)

Post office (75 Stricklandgate; ✆ 9am-5.30pm Mon-Fri, 9am-12.30pm Sat)

TIC (☎ 725758; kendaltown.org; Highgate; ✆ 9am-5pm Mon-Sat Nov-Easter, 10am-4pm Sun Easter-Oct) Inside the town hall.

Sights

Kendal Museum (☎ 721374; www.kendalmuseum.org .uk; Station Rd; admission £2.50; ✆ 10.30am-5.30pm Mon-Sat Apr-Oct, 10.30am-4pm Mon-Sat Nov-Mar) was founded in 1796 by a local natural history enthusiast, William Todhunter. Housed in a former wool warehouse, the museum displays local archaeological finds, explores the history of Kendal Castle, and has a fine natural history section filled with butterflies, insects and eerie stuffed animals. Alfred Wainwright, of *Pictorial Guide* fame, was honorary curator from 1945 to 1974, and his office and some possessions are still on show.

The **Museum of Lakeland Life** (☎ 722464; www .lakelandmuseum.org.uk; admission £3.50; ✆ 10.30am-5pm Mon-Sat Apr-Oct, 10.30am-4pm Mon-Sat Nov-Mar) is opposite the Abbot Hall Art Gallery. This atmospheric museum retraces the region's past using reconstructed buildings, including an Edwardian street scene, and exhibits on local industries such as spinning, mining and bobbin-making. One intriguing room recreates the study of Arthur Ransome, author of *Swallows and Amazons*.

Across the courtyard, the grand **Abbot Hall Art Gallery** (☎ 722464; www.abbothall.org.uk; admission £4.75; ✆ 10.30am-5pm Mon-Sat Apr-Oct, 10.30am-4pm Mon-Sat Nov-Mar) has a surprisingly rich collection, especially strong on watercolour landscapes and the work of local artists such as Daniel Gardner and George Romney. The gallery has links with the Tate, so it often has some superb temporary exhibitions.

There is a **combined ticket** (adult £7.50) available for Abbot Hall Art Gallery, the Museum of Lakeland Life and Blackwell Arts & Crafts House (in Windermere; p658). All the museums must be visited on the same day.

It's worth clambering up to the ruins of the 13th-century **Kendal Castle**, east of the river, once owned by the family of Katherine Parr (Henry VIII's last wife), and to **Castle Howe** – the remains of a Norman motte and bailey – to the west. At the lower end of town, the 12th-century **parish church** boasts five impressive aisles and several family chapels.

Activities

Kendal Climbing Wall (☎ 721766; www.kendalwall .co.uk; Mint Bridge Rd; adult £6) has a huge indoor wall and offers courses for all levels.

Sleeping

BUDGET

Kendal YHA (☎ 0870 7705893; kendal@yha.org.uk; 118 Highgate; dm £14.90; ✆ Mar-Aug & Dec-Jan, phone ahead at other times; ▯) Housed in part of the 19th-century brewery building, this hostel is a little cramped, but offers pool tables and Net access.

MID-RANGE

Lakeland Natural Vegetarian Guest House (☎ 733 011; Low Slack, Queens Rd; www.lakelandnatural .co.uk; s/d/f 39/66/89; Ⓟ ☒) A gorgeous detached Victorian house surrounded by landscaped gardens, linked with the Waterside Wholefoods café. The rooms are smart and simply furnished, and the best offer sweeping views over town. The vegetarian breakfast includes Californian muffins and homemade muesli.

Highgate Hotel (☎ 724229; www.highgatehotel .co.uk; 128 Highgate; s/d £30/48; Ⓟ ☒) Near the centre of town, this 18th-century townhouse once belonged to the town doctor, and now combines period character with all the mod cons (TV, hairdryers and en suite bathrooms). A small patio and garden area are available for guests' use.

Heaves Hotel (☎ 560396; www.heaveshotel.co.uk; Heaves; s/d from £33/58; Ⓟ ☒) A few miles south of Kendal, near Sizergh Castle, this wonderful family mansion is set in 10 acres of formal gardens and offers a taste of Cumbrian country living. Many of the rooms have four-poster beds, and there's a grand hallway, elegant lounge, and even a billiard room.

Bridge House (☎ 722041; www.bridgehouse-kendal .co.uk; s/d from £30/50) A quaint former stationmaster's house offering a couple of small traditionally decorated rooms, only one of which is en suite.

Other B&B options include **Headlands Hotel** (☎ 732464; 53 Milnthorpe Rd; s/d from £30/50; ✗), the pick of several standard guesthouses clustered along Milnthorpe Rd, and **Martindales** (☎ 724028; 9/11 Sandes Ave; s/d £30/50; ✗), a small, unassuming guesthouse near the train station with chintzy rooms and floral carpets to match.

Eating
CAFÉS
Waterside Wholefoods (☎ 729743; Kent View, Waterside; lunches £4-8; ✎ 8.30am-4.30pm Mon-Sat) Great vegetarian food served by the river, with a selection of sandwiches, chillis, soups and quiches, and a mouth-watering range of homemade cakes and organic teas to follow.

1657 Chocolate House (☎ 740702; www.thechoc olatehouse.co.uk; 54 Branthwaite Brow) For all things chocolaty, this Kendal institution is hard to beat. Upstairs, the frilly café sells cakes, teas and endless varieties of hot chocolate; downstairs, there's a homemade chocolate shop where you can pick up those all-important bars of mintcake.

RESTAURANTS
Green Room & Vats Bar (✎ from 10am Mon-Sat) Attached to the Brewery (above right), serving drinks and café food (salads, wraps, pizza and pasta £4 to £8) by day, and a more sophisticated menu by night.

Castle Dairy (☎ 730334; 26 Wildman St; 3 courses £19.95; ✎ lunch & dinner Tue-Sat, lunch Sun) Housed within the rough stone walls of the oldest house in Kendal, this homely restaurant specialises in regional country cooking – game pâté, poached egg florentine, braised venison and *coq au vin* are the order of the day.

Chang Thai Restaurant (☎ 720387; 54 Stramongate; mains £7-12; ✎ dinner Tue-Sun) An excellent Thai restaurant catering for Kendal's spicier side, with a varied menu based around regional curries, seafood and vegetarian dishes.

Paulo Gianni's (☎ 736581; 21a Stramongate; mains £6-8; ✎ lunch & dinner) A popular Italian restaurant, usually packed with office workers during happy hours (noon to 2pm and 5.30pm to 6pm) when pizza and pasta dishes are half price. There's a smart café-bar next door.

Drinking
There are lots of pubs in Kendal where you can down a few local ales – try the rambling **Burgundy's Wine Bar** (Lowther St), the traditional **Olde Fleece** (Highgate) or the **Ring O' Bells** (Kirkland Ave), which stands on consecrated ground.

For more contemporary drinking, **Mint** (☎ 734473; 48/50 Highgate) boasts steel fittings and stone flagstones, and turns into a popular nightclub at weekends. Light meals and free Internet access are available too.

Entertainment
Once a brewery that supplied much of Westmorland's beer, the excellent **Brewery** (☎ 725133; Highgate; www.breweryarts.co.uk) complex is now the focus of Kendal's arts scene, with two cinemas, a theatre, and regular programmes of film, dance and live music.

Getting There & Around
BUS
Useful buses include the No 106/107 from Kendal to Penrith (1¼ hours, eight daily Monday to Saturday) and No 505/505S from Windermere, Ambleside, Hawkshead and Coniston (two daily). No 555/556 stops at Kendal, Windermere, Ambleside, Grasmere and Keswick (five to 10 daily).

TRAIN
Kendal station is on the branch line to Windermere (£2.80, 15 minutes) from Oxenholme, 2 miles south of town, with regular trains from Carlisle (£13, one hour) and London Euston (£61.80, four hours).

AROUND KENDAL
Sizergh Castle
South of Kendal is **Sizergh Castle** (☎ 560070; admission £5.50, gardens only £3; ✎ gardens 12.30-5.30pm, castle 1.30-5.30pm Sun-Thu Apr-Oct), home of the Strickland family for over 700 years. Central to its construction is the 14th-century *pele* tower (fortified dwelling). Much of the interior is Elizabethan, including some stunning carved chimney pieces and the wood panelling of the Inlaid Chamber, sold to London's Victoria & Albert Museum during hard times, and returned after 100 years.

Sizergh Castle is 3½ miles south of Kendal along the A590. Bus No 555/556 from Grasmere, Ambleside, Windermere and Kendal runs past the castle every hour from Monday to Saturday.

Levens Hall

Two miles further south is **Levens Hall** (☎ 560321; www.levenshall.co.uk; bus No 555/556; house & garden £7.50, gardens only £5.80; ☺ gardens 10am-5pm, house noon-5pm Sun-Thu Apr–mid-Oct), another impressive Elizabethan manor built around a mid-13th-century *pele* tower. The beautifully kept house contains some wonderful paintings and Jacobean furniture, and an unusual leather-panelled dining room. The topiary garden (designed in 1694) could have come straight from *Alice in Wonderland*.

Levens Hall is 5 miles south of Kendal along the A6. Bus No 555/556 from Grasmere, Ambleside, Windermere and Kendal stops near the hall roughly every hour. Bus No 530 from Kendal to Grange also travels past the hall, but only runs on weekday afternoons.

AMBLESIDE
☎ 015394 / pop 3070

Ringed by hills and craggy peaks, Ambleside is one of the Lake District's main walking and climbing bases, and a thriving commercial centre. Its narrow cobbled streets are packed with B&Bs, teashops, quaint restaurants and rugged walkers taking a day's break from the fells, and though little of the old market town remains, the fine Victorian mansions and grey stone townhouses are crammed with Lakeland character. If you're planning on heading for the hills, Ambleside makes an excellent base camp.

Information

Laundromat (☎ 32231; Kelsick Rd; ☺ 10am-6pm)
Library (☎ 32507; Kelsick Rd; ☺ 10am-5pm Mon, Wed & Thu, 10am-7pm Tue & Fri; Net access per hr £2)
Post office (☎ 33267; Market Pl; ☺ 9am-5pm Mon-Fri, 9am-12.30pm Sat)
TIC (☎ 32582; www.amblesideonline.co.uk; Market Cross; ☺ 9am-5pm)

Sights & Activities

The **Armitt Museum** (☎ 31212; www.armitt.com; Rydal Rd; adult £2.50; ☺ 10am-5pm) explores Keswick's history, and has some interesting stuff on Lake luminaries, including John Ruskin and Beatrix Potter (though her early botanical drawings are strictly for the completist).

The TIC provides plenty of walks information. The **Loughrigg circuit** runs for 7 miles from the Rydal Rd car park to Grasmere Lake and back through woods, farmland and steep hills. For a shorter walk of 2 miles, head for the waterfall of Stockghyll Force, east of Ambleside. You can either head back to Ambleside through farmland or push on to Troutbeck, returning via Jenkyn's Crag, a rocky outcrop offering superb views of Windermere – a 7-mile round trip.

Ambleside is on the **Windermere Lake Cruises** route (p658).

Sleeping
BUDGET

Ambleside Backpackers (☎ 32340; www.english lakesbackpackers.co.uk; dm £13.50; P ✗ 💻) Good independent hostel with 72 beds in a converted cottage. If the dorms seem crammed, head for the wood-floored lounge and spacious dining room.

Ambleside YHA Hostel (☎ 0870 7705672; ambleside@yha.org.uk; Windermere Rd; dm £14.40; P ✗ 💻) A mile south of Ambleside, this huge lakeside house is one of the YHA's flagship hostels. The doubles are understandably popular; book well ahead.

Low Wray (☎ 32810; www.lowwraycampsite.co.uk; sites £10-14.50; ☺ Easter-Oct) A NT campsite 3 miles south of Ambleside on the western shore of Windermere. Catch bus No 505, then it's a 1-mile walk.

MID-RANGE

Church St and Compston Rd are packed with mid-range B&Bs.

Compston House Hotel (☎ 32305; www.comp stonhouse.co.uk; Compston Rd; d from £48; ✗) Ambleside's self-styled American B&B, where all the rooms are named after American states and decorated accordingly (think sunny Florida and maritime Maine). You can even order a stack of homemade pancakes for breakfast, complete with maple syrup.

Lakes Lodge (☎ 33240; www.lakeslodge.co.uk; Lake Rd; s/d £30/45-60; ✗ 💻) This unusual place offers a more modern B&B experience: laminate floors, purple and cream dining tables and sleek, understated bedrooms equipped with funky beds and DVD players.

Old Vicarage (☎ 33364; www.theoldvicarage.co.uk; Vicarage Rd; d £65-70; P ✗) No prizes for guessing who this ivy-clad Victorian house used to belong to; these days it's a lovely B&B surrounded by private gardens near Rothay Park. The chintzy wallpaper and frilly curtains are a touch old-fashioned, but it's still a comfortable choice.

TOP FIVE COUNTRY HOTELS

- **Langdale Chase** (below; Ambleside)
- **Old Dungeon Ghyll** (p670; Langdale)
- **The Samling** (p659; Windermere)
- **Eltermere Country House Hotel** (p669; Elterwater)
- **Holbeck Ghyll** (p659; Windermere)

3 Cambridge Villas (☎ 32307; www.3cambridgevillas .co.uk; Church St; s/d £20/45) Central townhouse with just a modicum of flounce.

Melrose Hotel (☎ 32500; www.melrose-guesthouse .co.uk; Church St; s/d £25-30/50-70) Pleasant, spacious rooms in a terraced house.

Mill Cottage (☎ 34830; www.millcottage-ambleside .co.uk; Rydal Rd; s/d £22-25/44-46) Patterned rooms above a teashop in a 16th-century building.

TOP END

Langdale Chase (☎ 32201; www.langdalechase.co.uk; d £130-188) A magnificent 19th-century lakeside mansion, embellished by crenellated turrets and stone verandas, once used as the setting for Alfred Hitchcock's *The Paradine Case*. Oak-panelled rooms, grand mahogany staircases, gorgeous rooms and a private boathouse are just the start.

Grey Friar Lodge Hotel (☎ 33158; www.cumbria -hotels.com; Clappersgate; d £56-116; P ⊠) A charming, ivy-covered Victorian house in private gardens near the River Brathay, near Ambleside in Clappersgate. The rambling rooms are filled with antiques and bric-a-brac, and most have four-poster beds and river views.

Eating & Drinking

Lucy's on a Plate (☎ 31191; www.lucysofambleside .co.uk; Church St; mains £7-14; ⏲ 10am-9pm) Lucy's started out as a specialist grocery, and has now expanded into this charismatic café-restaurant, furnished with rough wooden tables and old church chairs. Choose from the bistro-style menu or a blackboard of daily specials.

Lucy 4 (☎ 34666; 2 St Mary's Lane; tapas £4-8; ⏲ 5-11pm Mon-Sat, 5-10.30pm Sun) Lucy's latest venture is this laid-back wine bar and tapas restaurant. The twin levels are divided between smoking and nonsmoking areas.

Zeffirelli's Wholefood Pizzeria (☎ 33845; Compston Rd; pizza £5.50-7.45; ⏲ lunch & dinner) Great pizzas served in a dimly lit dining room or a buzzy garden room café. Zeffirelli's also runs the cinema next door; the 'Double Feature' menu includes cinema tickets and a two-course meal.

Glass House (☎ 32137; Rydal Rd; ⏲ lunch & dinner) This swish Mediterranean and British restaurant is housed in a three-storey conversion of a 16th-century watermill, with millwheels, cogs and machinery left intact.

Sheila's Cottage (☎ 33079; The Slack; ⏲ lunch & dinner) A much-respected restaurant along a quiet backstreet, serving homely country fare such as haddock risotto, fish pie and Welsh rarebit in the rustic dining room.

Ambleside also has a good selection of pubs and cafés.

Apple Pie (☎ 33679; Rydal Rd) Good choice for light lunches, afternoon cake & the house speciality, apple pie.

Golden Rule (☎ 32257; Smithy Brow) Popular pub with walkers, away from the tourist buzz.

Pippins (☎ 31338; 10 Lake Rd) Reliable café serving full English breakfasts, jacket potatoes, and sandwiches.

The Royal Oak (☎ 33382; Market Pl) Lively pub with outside tables, attracting a younger crowd.

Shopping

Compston Rd has enough equipment shops to launch an assault on Everest, with branches of **Rohan** (☎ 32946), **Hawkshead** (☎ 35255) and the **YHA Adventure Shop** (☎ 34284). The **Climber's Shop** (☎ 32297) hires out boots and other equipment.

Getting There & Around

Bus No 555 (and No 599 from April to October) regularly travels from Grasmere (20 minutes), to Windermere (15 minutes) and Kendal (45 minutes).

From April to October, No 505 runs from Coniston (35 minutes, 11 daily Monday to Saturday, six on Sunday), and from Kendal (30 minutes, twice daily Monday to Saturday, once on Sunday) via Windermere.

Bike Treks (☎ 31505; Compston Rd; half/full day £10/14) hires out bicycles.

AROUND AMBLESIDE
Rydal Mount

Wordsworth, the only poet laureate never to write a line of official verse, lived at **Rydal Mount** (☎ 33002; www.rydalmount.co.uk; admission £4.50, gardens only £2; ⏲ 9.30am-5pm Mar-Oct, 10am-4pm Wed-Mon Nov-Feb) from 1813 to 1850. After leaving Dove Cottage (opposite) in

A WATERY LITERARY TRAIL

William Wordsworth has done more than anyone to draw people to the Lakes, and despite being the author of one of the first holiday guides – *A Complete Guide to the Lakes* (1810) – he probably wouldn't be impressed by the area's thriving tourist industry (he campaigned against the railway link from Oxenholme to Kendal, finally managing to get the line drawn at Windermere). Wordsworth lived much of his life in Dove Cottage and Rydal Mount, both near Grasmere; you can also visit his boyhood home (Cockermouth), his school (Hawkshead), and his grave in St Oswald's churchyard (Grasmere).

Numerous other Romantic writers drew inspiration from the Lakeland scenery, including the visionary Samuel Taylor Coleridge and opium-eating Thomas De Quincey.

London-born Beatrix Potter first visited the Lakes on family holidays. She self-published her debut story, *The Tale of Peter Rabbit*, after being turned down by six publishers. The anthropomorphic tales of talking rabbits and house-proud hedgehogs quickly found worldwide success; the proceeds financed the purchase of Hill Top Farm in Near Sawrey, a rural village that inspired many of her illustrations. Later in life she became a passionate sheep farmer and an unlikely property magnate. Her original paintings are displayed at the Beatrix Potter Gallery (Hawkshead) and some early drawings are on display at Ambleside's Armitt Museum.

Leeds-born Arthur Ransome spent his boyhood summers by Coniston Water. After a summer teaching friends' children to sail, he was inspired to write the *Swallows and Amazons* series. A room at the Museum of Lakeland Life is dedicated to Ransome, and Windermere Steamboat Museum houses Captain Flint's houseboat.

The Victorian art critic and social campaigner John Ruskin moved to Coniston in 1872, and over the next 20 years constructed one of the country's great estates at Brantwood. His work is on display at the Ruskin Museum (Coniston), the Armitt Museum (Ambleside) and the Abbott Hall Gallery (Kendal).

search of space for his growing family, Wordsworth rented several houses around Grasmere, but only settled again with the discovery of this secluded house.

Set in a hectare of gardens (largely designed by Wordsworth, with formal terraces and a summerhouse in which to compose), the house is still owned by the poet's descendants. In contrast to the poky charm of Dove Cottage, Rydal Mount feels like a family home, and contains original furniture, manuscripts and possessions, including a cherub statue referenced in *The Excursion*, Wordsworth's pen, inkstand and picnic box, and a portrait of the poet by the American artist Henry Inman. On the top floor, you can wander around Wordsworth's study, from where it's just possible to glimpse Lake Windermere. Below the house, you'll find **Dora's Field**, planted with daffodils in memory of Wordsworth's beloved daughter, who died of tuberculosis.

The house is 1½ miles northwest of Ambleside, off the A591. Bus No 555 (and No 599 from April to October), between Grasmere, Ambleside, Windermere and Kendal, stops at the end of the drive.

GRASMERE
☎ 015394

Surrounded by woods, fells and jewel-green meadows, the slate-stone village of Grasmere is one of the most alluring in the Lakes. Though the village streets are crammed with tourists in summer, the quiet lake itself is undisturbed by motorboats, and there are countless walks leading into the countryside and woods nearby. For many years Grasmere was Wordsworth's adopted home; Dove Cottage and Rydal Mount are both nearby, ensuring a steady flow of poetry pilgrims. Wordsworth is buried under the yew trees of St Oswald's churchyard with his wife Mary and beloved sister Dorothy; nearby you'll also find the grave of Coleridge's son, Hartley.

The **TIC** (☎ 35245; Red Bank Rd; 9.30am-5.30pm daily Mar-Oct, 10am-3.30pm Sat & Sun Nov-Feb) has some great walking leaflets and can help with finding local accommodation.

Sights
Dove Cottage (☎ 35544; www.wordsworth.org.uk; adult £5.95; 9.30am-5.30pm), just off the A591 on the outskirts of Grasmere, is where

Wordsworth wrote many of his greatest poems. The white-walled, rose-covered cottage was once a pub, and the higgledy-piggledy ceilings, slate floors and roaring fireplaces are enormously atmospheric. It's often busy, but entrance is managed by timed tickets to avoid overcrowding, and an entertaining half-hour guided tour is included in the admission price. Thomas De Quincey, author of *Confessions of an Opium Eater*, lived here for several years after Wordsworth had left.

Next door, the **Wordsworth Museum** houses fascinating letters, journals and manuscripts by Wordsworth and his illustrious friends.

Sleeping
BUDGET
Butterlip How YHA Hostel (☎ 0870 7705836; gras mere@yha.org.uk; dm £11.90) North of the village, off Easedale Rd, this converted house set in private gardens makes a good base for exploring Grasmere and the lake.

Thorney How YHA Hostel (contact Butterlip How; dm £10.60; ☽ Apr-Oct) For more seclusion, head for this remote farmhouse, 15 minutes up-hill from Grasmere.

Grasmere Hostel (☎ 35055; www.grasmerehostel .co.uk; Broadrayne Farm; dm £14.50) An excellent independent hostel inside a former farm-house, offering en suite dorms and rooms and a Nordic sauna. It's a mile north along the A591; bus No 555 stops at the end of the road on request.

MID-RANGE & TOP END
How Foot Lodge (☎ 35366; www.howfoot.co.uk; Town End; d £52-60; ℗ ☒) Near Dove Cottage, this stately Victorian villa is owned by the Wordsworth Trust, and offers wonderfully plain rooms with views over the garden towards Grasmere Lake.

Beck Allans (☎ 35563; www.beckallans.com; College St; d £52-73; ℗ ☒) Though recently built, this handsome stone-walled house resembles a much older Lakeland property. Accom-modation is divided between smart rooms, self-catering apartments, and a charming wood-panelled 'showman's wagon' in the garden.

White Moss House (☎ 35295; www.whitemoss .com; Rydal Water; d £144-188, cottage £99pp; ℗ ☒) Tucked away on the road between Gras-mere and Windermere, this much-admired hotel occupies an elegant house that once

belonged to Wordsworth. There are five rooms in the main house, filled with trin-kets and antiques, and two further bed-rooms in a detached cottage.

Grasmere Hotel (☎ 35277; www.grasmerehotel.co.uk; Broadgate; d £70-100; ℗ ☒) Flouncy, expensive rooms in an imposing mansion alongside the River Rothay.

Harwood Hotel (☎ 35248; www.harwoodhotel.co.uk; Red Lion Sq; d from £59; ℗ ☒) Sweet rooms (some with lacy four-poster beds) above Harwood's Deli.

Riversdale (☎ 35619; www.riversdalegrasmere.co.uk; White Bridge; d £54-70; ℗ ☒) Simple B&B in a stone cottage on the edge of Grasmere village.

Eating
Dove Cottage Tea Rooms & Restaurant (☎ 35268; mains £9-13; ☽ tearooms 11am-5pm, restaurant dinner Tue-Sat) A quaint oak-beamed café-restaurant furnished with dried flowers and wooden tables, serving light lunches and cakes by day and a Mediterranean-flavoured menu in the evening.

Sara's Bistro (☎ 35266; 2 Broadgate; mains £10-12; ☽ lunch & dinner Tue-Sun) This cheery bistro serves 'chubbie' sandwiches (£3.50 to £4.50) and baguettes, burgers and salads at lunch-time, and more sophisticated dishes like poached salmon and oven-baked chicken after 6pm.

Sarah Nelson's Gingerbread Shop (☎ 35428; www.grasmeregingerbread.co.uk; Church Stile; ☽ 9.15am-5.30pm Mon-Sat) One of Grasmere's most fa-mous establishments, this minuscule cake shop has been trading in the old village schoolhouse since 1854. Follow your nose as you leave the churchyard.

Baldry's Tea Room (☎ 35301; Red Lion Sq; mains £4-7; ☽ Fri-Wed) This no-nonsense village café is a good spot for lunchtime sandwiches or afternoon tea, and also does a huge Baldry's breakfast (£4 to £6).

Travellers Rest Inn (☎ 35604; www.lakedistrict inns.co.uk; mains from £8-14; d £74-88; ℗ ☒) A much-refurbished 16th-century coaching inn on the edge of Grasmere village, with great pub food and comfortable rooms. The only drawback is the A591 running past its door.

Getting There & Away
Bus No 555 runs from Ambleside to Gras-mere (20 minutes), stopping at Rydal church and outside Dove Cottage. The seasonal No 599 runs from Kendal via Bowness (one hour, four daily April to October).

HAWKSHEAD

☎ 015394 / elevation 107m

With its quaint whitewashed buildings, cobblestone streets and countryside setting, Hawkshead is so immaculately picturesque it could have been constructed for the benefit of sightseers. Parking is provided on the outskirts of the village, so it's almost traffic-free. Wool has been the big money-spinner for Hawkshead from medieval times, and the Hawkshead Company is still a popular outdoor-clothing maker.

The **TIC** (☎ 36525; hawksheadtic@lake-district.gov.uk; ☻ 9.30am-5.30pm Apr-Oct, 9.30am-6pm Jul & Aug, 10am-3.30pm Fri, Sat & Sun Nov-Mar) is beside the main car park.

The **Hawkshead Grammar School** (admission £1; ☻ 10am-12.30pm & 1.30-5pm Mon-Sat, 1-5pm Sun Apr-Sep, 1-4.30pm Oct), across Main St from the TIC, was founded in 1585. Unused since 1909, the schoolhouse is set out much as it was when its most famous pupil, William Wordsworth, attended (1779–87). The curator is well informed about the alarming amount of classical schooling the pupils had to endure – probably what drove Wordsworth to carve his name so painstakingly on his desk.

The **Beatrix Potter Gallery** (NT; ☎ 36355; Red Lion Sq; admission £3; ☻ 10.30am-4.30pm Sat-Wed Apr-Oct) houses the original watercolours from her children's books in the former offices of her husband, solicitor William Heelis. Entry is by timed ticket.

Sleeping & Eating

Croft Camping & Caravanning (☎ 36374; www.hawkshead-croft.com; North Lonsdale Rd; sites £12-14.25; ☻ mid-Mar–mid-Nov) A pleasant, grassy campsite just east of the town centre,

Hawkshead YHA Hostel (☎ 0870 770 5856; hawkshead@yha.org.uk; dm £11.60; 💻) A mile south on the road to Newby Bridge, this fine Regency building overlooks Esthwaite Water. Bus No 505/506 passes here and stops in Hawkshead village.

Ann Tyson's Cottage (☎ 36405; www.anntysons.co.uk; Wordsworth St; s/d from £27.50/55; ✗) A delightful cob-walled cottage just off the main square, covered with colourful hanging baskets in summer. Wordsworth boarded here while attending school in Hawkshead, and all the rooms retain their traditional character.

Ivy House Hotel (☎ 36204; www.ivyhousehotel.com; Main St; d £102-106; P ✗) A superior B&B

with a touch of Kensington elegance – plush sofas and antique rugs in the sitting room, wooden four-poster beds and coloured cushions in the bedrooms upstairs. The main house has six rooms, and there are five more in the Mere Lodge behind.

The village pubs offer good food and accommodation; they include the flower-fronted **Queens Head** (☎ 36271; www.queenshead hawkshead.co.uk; Main St; s/d from £46.50/60; ✗) and the old **Kings Arms** (☎ 36372; www.kingsarmshawkshead.co.uk; The Square; s/d £38-43/66-76).

Minstrels Gallery (☎ 36423; The Square; lunches £4-8) Dating from the 15th century, this gorgeous little teashop is the top place in the village for light lunches and sticky treats.

Getting There & Away

Hawkshead is linked with Windermere, Ambleside and Coniston by bus No 505 (April to October). The **Cross-Lakes Shuttle** (☎ 015394-45161; No 525) climbs to Hilltop (10 minutes, ten daily July to September, weekends only April to June and November) before connecting with Windermere cruise boats to Bowness.

AROUND HAWKSHEAD
Grizedale Forest

Stretching out across the hills between Coniston Water and Esthwaite Water is Grizedale Forest, a dense woodland of oak, larch and pine; its name derives from the Old Norse for wild boar. Wandering through Grizedale today, it's hard to believe the forest has been mostly replanted by the Forestry Commission over the last hundred years; by the 19th century, the original woodland had almost disappeared due to the demands of local industry.

Since 1977 artists have been fashioning outdoor sculptures in the forest, and there are now more than 90 scattered throughout the park, including a wooden xylophone, a wave of carved ferns and a huge 'man of the forest'.

Even without its eccentric furniture, Grizedale Forest makes a great destination for walking and cycling. Mountain bikes can be hired from **Grizedale Mountain Bike Hire** (☎ 01229-860369; www.grizedalemountainbikes.co.uk; bikes half/full day £12/18; ☻ 9am-5pm Mar-Oct, Sat & Sun Nov-Feb), at the visitor centre, to tackle the 40 miles of marked cycle trails.

Grizedale Visitors Centre (☎ 01229-860010; www.grizedale.org; ☻ 10am-5pm Easter-Oct, 11am-4pm

Nov-Easter) provides information on trails and sells a guide to the forest sculptures (£3). There's also a café where you can refuel (doorstop sandwiches £3 to £4).

Grizedale Lodge (☎ 015394-36532; www.grizedale -lodge.com; s/d £45/60-95; P X) Right in the heart of the forest, this luxury B&B makes a great base. The rooms are tasteful and spacious, and the woodland views are stunning; in summer you can savour them over them over afternoon tea on the hotel's wooden veranda.

The Cross-Lakes Shuttle (☎ 015394-45161; Bus No 525) runs from Hawkshead to Grizedale (ten daily July to September, weekends only April to June and November).

Hill Top

Beatrix Potter wrote many of her best-known stories in this picture-postcard **farmhouse** (NT; ☎ 36269; adult £4.50; 10.30am-4.30pm Sat-Wed Apr-Oct) surrounded by a flower-filled garden and vegetable patch in the quiet village of Near Sawrey. Keep your eyes peeled during your visit – many of the buildings and furnishings found their way into her illustrations. Tickets are sold for set times; expect long queues during school holidays.

The house is 2 miles south of Hawkshead; bus No 505 (15 minutes, hourly) travels through the village, or you can catch the Cross-Lakes Shuttle (£2.20 from Hawkshead, four daily).

CONISTON
☎ 015394

Above the tranquil surface of Coniston Water, with its gliding steam yachts and quiet boats, looms the craggy, pock-marked peak known as the Old Man of Coniston (801m). The nearby village grew up around the copper-mining industry; these days, there are just a few sleepy streets, with two fine pubs and some tourist shops, making Coniston an excellent place for relaxing by the quiet lakeside.

Coniston is best known for the world-record speed attempts made on the lake by Sir Malcolm Campbell and his son, Donald, between the 1930s and 1960s. Tragically, after smashing the record several times, Donald was killed during an attempt in 1967, when his futuristic jet boat *Bluebird* flipped at around 320mph. The boat and its pilot were found in 2001; Campbell was buried in the cemetery near St Andrew's church.

Information

Summitreks (☎ 41212; www.summitreks.co.uk; 14 Yewdale Rd) Arranges outdoor activities and hires out walking gear, as well as bikes, kayaks and canoes (£14/15/20 per day).
TIC (☎ 41533; conistontic@lake-district.gov.uk; Coniston Car & Coach Park; 9.30am-5.30pm Easter-Oct, 10am-3.30pm Sat & Sun Nov-Easter)
Village Pantry (☎ 41155; Yewtree Rd; Net access per 30min £2)

Ruskin Museum

This fine town **museum** (☎ 41164; admission £3.50; 10am-5.30pm) explores Coniston's history, touching on copper mining, Arthur Ransome and the Campbell story. It's also an excellent introduction to John Ruskin, a great Victorian all-rounder, with displays of his writings, watercolours and sketchbooks.

Brantwood

Ruskin bought **Brantwood** (☎ 41396; www.brant wood.org.uk; admission £5.50; 11am-5.30pm mid-Mar–mid-Nov, 11am-4.30pm Wed-Sun mid-Nov–mid-Mar) in 1871 and spent 20 years expanding and modifying the house and grounds. The end result is undoubtedly the finest country estate in the Lake District, incorporating the lavish mansion and 250 acres of landscaped gardens, pastures and woodland. The house itself gives an insight into Ruskin's relentless intellect and prolific output, and there's a fine café (sandwiches £4 to £6) overlooking the lake. To see Brantwood at its best, it's essential to arrive by boat.

Activities
BOAT TRIPS

Rescued from dereliction by the NT, the steam yacht **Gondola** (☎ 63850; adult £5.50; five daily Apr-Oct), described by the *Illustrated London News* as 'a perfect combination of the Venetian gondola and the English steam yacht', was launched on Coniston Water in 1859. The luxurious saloons have been completely refurbished, and the boat runs like clockwork between Brantwood and Coniston Pier.

The modern **Coniston Launch** (☎ 36216; www .con istonlaunch.co.uk; north/south lake cruise £4/6) offers cruises on the lake. The North Lake boat calls at four jetties, including Brantwood; the South Lake cruise sails to Lake Bank at the lake's southern end. You can break your journey and walk to the next jetty.

Alternatively, the **Coniston Boating Centre** (☎ 41366; Coniston Jetty) hires out rowing and motor boats (per hour £11/5), canoes (two hours £10) and toppers/wayfarers (per hour £10/14).

WALKING

The popular climb to the summit of the **Old Man** (7½ miles, four to five hours) starts at St Andrew's Church in Coniston. On a clear day the views stretch to the Cumbrian coast and Windermere. Another walk from St Andrew's Church climbs through picturesque woods and farmland to **Tarn Hows**, an artificial lake backed by woods and mountains. Allow 2½ to three hours for the 5-mile walk. The TIC has leaflets on both walks.

Tarn Hows is one of the few upland tarns accessible by road. The **National Trust** (☎ 015394-35599) runs a free bus on Sunday (25 minutes, five daily May to October) between Coniston and Hawkshead (connecting with No 505), giving you a full day to explore the area.

Sleeping

Coniston Hall Campsite (☎ 41223; sites £8-15; ◷ Easter-Oct) A lovely lakeside campsite, a mile south of town.

Holly How YHA Hostel (☎ 0870 779 5770; conistonhh@yha.org.uk; Far End; dm £11.80; ◷ mid-Jun–Nov) A converted slate house set in private grounds near the village, with reasonable dorms and a few double rooms.

Coppermines YHA Hostel (☎ 0870 7705772; dm £10.60; ◷ daily Apr-Sep, Tue-Sat Sep-Oct) The former mine manager's house now makes a great hiking hostel, in a spectacular mountainside setting. Be warned – the access road is very rough.

Beech Tree Vegetarian Guest House (☎ 41717; Yewtree Rd; s/d from £30/40; P ✗) A dedicated vegetarian guesthouse with its own tree-shaded garden, located in the old town vicarage near the edge of the village. Some of the vibrant rooms share a bathroom; others have private showers.

Oaklands (☎ 41245; www.oaklandsconiston.co.uk; Yewdale Rd; s/d £25/45-50; P ✗) Across the road, this slate-walled private house has a homely family feel, with pastel-coloured rooms and bouncy pocket-sprung beds.

Coniston Lodge Hotel (☎ 41201; www.coniston -lodge.com; Station Rd; d £89.20; P ✗) An unusual modern hotel decorated as a country cottage. The plush rooms are named after mountain tarns, and there's a lovely wooden veranda where you can drink in the views.

Eating

Black Bull (☎ 41335; Yewdale Rd) This creaky, whitewashed free house is the town's oldest pub and the home of the Coniston Brewing company, which makes its own Bluebird beer.

Bluebird Café (☎ 41649; Lake Rd; lunches £4-6; ◷ breakfast & lunch) Delicious open sandwiches, jacket potatoes and cakes are served in this lakeside café. The outside terrace is usually packed on sunny summer days.

Sun Hotel (☎ 41248; www.thesunconiston.com; mains £8.50-16; s/d £35-50/70-80; P ✗) This gabled turn-of-the-century establishment is the most atmospheric inn in Coniston, just uphill from the village. There's an oak-beamed bar, a conservatory restaurant, and lots of photos of the Bluebird expedition – Donald Campbell had his headquarters here during his fateful campaign.

Getting There & Around

From April to October, Bus No 505 runs from Windermere (50 minutes, eight daily Monday to Saturday, six on Sunday) via Ambleside; it also runs from Kendal (one hour 10 minutes, two daily Monday to Saturday).

LANGDALE
☎ 015394

Jammed between soaring peaks and jagged valley walls, the green valley of Langdale contains some of England's finest walking, encompassing the Langdale Pikes, Elterwater and Dungeon Ghyll. The main road leads past Elterwater into the valley of Great Langdale, dwarfed by the Langdale Pikes. Another snaking, single-track road leads through Little Langdale over Wrynose and Hardknott

Passes to the coast – en route you'll stumble across some of the Lake District's finest country pubs and hotels.

Elterwater

Ringed by trees and rolling fields, the small, charming lake of Elterwater derives its name from the Old Norse for 'swan', after the colonies of whooper swans that migrate to its shores every winter. The nearby village later made its living from farming, quarrying and lacemaking; these days it's a popular walking centre, occupying a stunning spot on the Cumbria Way.

Nestling the other side of the bridge is **Elterwater YHA Hostel** (☎ 0870 7705816; elterwater@yha .org.uk; dm £10.60; ☺ daily Jul-Aug, phone ahead at other times; P ▣), a pretty slate-stone house.

A mile east of the village, **Langdale YHA Hostel** (☎ 0870 7705816; langdale@yha.org.uk; High Close, Loughrigg; dm £10.60; ☺ Mar-Oct; P ▣) is a beautiful, remote Victorian mansion in extensive gardens.

The **Britannia Inn** (☎ 37210; www.britinn.net; d £72-100; P ✗) is classic Lakeland inn, with comfy rooms, substantial food and pleasant tables overlooking the village green.

Elterwater is 3½ miles from Ambleside. Bus No 516 (20 minutes, five daily April to October) stops on the village green.

Great Langdale

With wonderful fell-walking opportunities, including Harrison Stickle (736m) and Pike o' Stickle (723m), the valley rolls on for another 3½ miles past Elterwater to the base of the wild Langdale Pikes.

Sticklebarn Tavern (☎ 37356; Great Langdale), 2½ miles from Elterwater, is a large country pub housed in a converted barn, offering live music, hearty hiking food (goulash,

three-bean chilli) and a huge patio beer garden with unparalleled fell views. Basic bunkhouse accommodation costs £10 per person; you'll need a sleeping bag.

Great Langdale Campsite (NT; ☎ 37668; langda lecamp@nationaltrust.org.uk; sites £10.50) occupies a tree-dotted, hill-backed spot. about a mile up the valley,

The ivy-clad **New Dungeon Ghyll Hotel** (☎ 37213; www.dungeon-ghyll.co.uk; d £84-98; P ✗) is dotted with stone chimneys and latticed windows, and is the perfect place for hikers looking for a luxurious night's sleep. The grand lounge is furnished with chaise longues and comfy armchairs, there's a dedicated walker's bar, and the plush bedrooms all have fell views. It's great value, too.

Bus No 516 (the Langdale Rambler) runs from Ambleside to the Old Dungeon Ghyll Hotel (30 minutes, five or six daily) from April to October.

Little Langdale

Separated from Great Langdale by Lingmoor Fell (459m), Little Langdale is a quiet village on the road to Wrynose Pass. There are many little-known walks nearby, and at the head of the valley is the **Three Shire Stone**, marking the traditional meeting point of Cumberland, Westmoreland and Lancashire.

Nestled into the valley, the cosy slatestone **Three Shires Inn** (☎ 37215; www.threeshires inn.co.uk; mains £7.50-11.25; d £70-94; P ✗) is well set up for walkers, and makes an ideal place to rest those weary bones. The restaurant serves delicious country cooking – the house special is Cumberland sausage with a Westmorland chutney – and the bright upstairs rooms all come with valley views.

Bus No 505/506 from Ambleside or Coniston stops at Skelwith Bridge nearby.

SOMETHING SPECIAL

Old Dungeon Ghyll Hotel (☎ 37272; www.odg.co.uk; s/d £41/82-88; P ✗) This famous old establishment is perhaps the Lake District's quintessential hotel, a favourite of many a famous climber and not-so-famous tourist over the last 100 years. It's a classic Lakeland inn, decked out with antique furniture, period features, solid wood doors and faded carpets. The snug, traditional rooms are endearingly old-fashioned, and though not all are en suite, the inspirational fell views can't be bettered anywhere else in the Lake District. The real heart of the hotel is in the Walker's Bar, with its roaring fire, white cob walls and hearty welcome after a long day's hike. There are many more luxurious hotels, but none of them can match the Old Dungeon Ghyll for charm and character.

The hotel is 7½ miles west of Ambleside. Bus No 516 from Ambleside stops outside the hotel five times daily, normally including Sundays from April to October.

CUMBRIA & THE LAKES

ESKDALE

The drive over the Wrynose and Hardknott Passes is breathtakingly beautiful, snaking through green mountains and glacial valleys on its way towards Eskdale and the Cumbrian coast. The grade reaches 1 in 4 in places – it's not uncommon to find some poor soul on the grassy verge with a burnt-out clutch. Both roads are usually impassable in winter.

Perched on a grassy spur above Eskdale is **Hardknott Castle Roman Fort**, the remains of a remote stronghold that once guarded the hilltop road. The 1.2-hectare site is a short walk from the road. It's still possible to make out the original outer walls, the commandant's house, granary store, and a couple of corner towers. A nearby level area was apparently the military parade ground.

Surrounded by fells and rocky crags, **Eskdale YHA Hostel** (☎ 0870 7705824; eskdale@yha.org.uk; Boot; dm £10.25; ☽ Mon-Sat Jun-Jun, Sep & Oct, daily Jul & Aug) is a converted farmhouse that offers a big lounge, kitchen and dining room (complete with open fireplace), and several good-sized dorms.

Nearby, the shoebox-sized village of **Boot** is huddled in the shadow of Scaféll Pike (978m), England's highest mountain. It's the closest settlement to Dalegarth station – the other end of the Ravenglass–Eskdale line (p683) – and makes a good walking base, far from the Lakeland crowds.

Hollins Farm Campsite (☎ 019467-23253; www.hollinsfarmcampsite.co.uk; adult/car £3/2; ☽ Mar-Oct) is a quiet, small and tree-lined campsite in the Esk valley.

Brook House Inn (☎ 019467-23288; www.brookhouseinn.co.uk; Boot; s/d £30/60-64; ℗ ✗) has comfortable rooms with pleasant views in a white-washed family-run hotel just outside Boot village.

Burnmoor Inn (☎ 0845 130 6224; www.burnmoor.co.uk; Boot; d £54-58; ℗ ✗) is another popular hiker's rest, offering nine plain rooms and a holiday cottage. The real draw is the excellent restaurant, serving wholesome favourites including Boot pie (steak and stout), game stew and giant Yorkshire pudding.

Woolpack Inn (☎ 019467-23230) A little way east of Boot, this cosy slate-roofed pub has two 'baas' split between walkers and normal drinkers (ie with no muddy boots or wet clothes).

WASDALE
☎ 019467

For a sense of the majesty and mystery of the Lakes, the remote valley of Wasdale is hard to beat. Hemmed in by some of the country's highest peaks (including Scaféll Pike and Great Gable), the wild lake of Wast Water is the deepest in the Lake District (79m). Backed by gravel-strewn walls of scree, and often blanketed in cloud and drifting mist, the lake can be a forbidding sight, especially in winter; but sudden breaks in the weather often transform the scene, lighting up the valley walls and bathing the lake in sunshine. It's much harder to get to than the other lakes, reached via the Hardknott Pass or from the coast.

Wast Water YHA Hostel (☎ 0870 770 6082; wastwater@yha.org.uk; Wasdale Hall; dm £10.60; ☽ Apr-Aug, Thu-Mon Feb-Mar & Sep-Oct, Fri & Sat Nov-Feb) is a 19th-century Gothic mansion on the lakeshore, 4 miles south of Wasdale Head.

Wasdale Head Campsite (NT; ☎ 26220; www.wasdalecampsite.org.uk; sites £10), a National Trust campsite, offers peace and solitude beneath the Scaféll Range.

Lingmell House (☎ 26261; www.wasdalehead.co.uk; d £56) is a wonderfully solitary granite house, with calm, simple rooms that contrast starkly with the views outside.

The **Barn Door Shop** (☎ 26384) sells maps and guides and oversees the useful Wasdale website (www.wasdaleweb.com). A short walk away is the tiny parish church; its cemetery is dotted with memorials to mountain walkers.

In the small settlement of Santon Bridge, 2½ miles southwest of Wast Water, the **Bridge Inn** (☎ 019467-26221; www.santonbridgeinn.com; s/d £45-55/55-70) is a whitewashed country inn that offers decent food and rooms, and

---

BIZARRE ENGLAND

The Bridge Inn at Stanton Bridge hosts the World's Biggest Liar competition every November in honour of Will Ritson, first landlord of the Wasdale Head Inn. Will used to regale customers with extravagant folklore, and past winners continue his mighty mendacious tradition. Members of the legal profession and politicians are barred from entering.

Alternatively, you could head for the World Gurning Competition, held in mid-September in Egremont, near St Bees. To gurn is to pull an ugly face; the challenge is believed to stem from the 12th century, when the lord of the manor handed out sour crabapples to his workers. Locally born Anne Wood won the trophy 24 years running till she was finally beaten in 2001.

---

hosts the World's Biggest Liar Competition each November (see the boxed text above).

The only public transport to Wast Water is the **Wasdale Taxibus** (☎ 019467-25308), which runs between Gosforth and Wasdale Head on Thursday, Saturday and Sunday – ring to book a seat.

COCKERMOUTH
☎ 01900 / pop 7450

Situated at the confluence of the Cocker and Derwent rivers, just outside the Lake District National Park, the small market town of Cockermouth has never received the same attention as its more famous neighbours, despite its proximity to the fells, some fine Georgian architecture and a clutch of intriguing museums (including Wordsworth's boyhood home). Consequently, the town makes a quiet and good-value base for exploring the northern reaches of the national park, especially the valleys of Buttermere and Borrowdale.

Information

Library (☎ 325990; Main St; ☼ 9.15am-7pm Mon & Wed, 9.15am-5pm Tue & Fri, 9.15am-12.30pm Thu, 9.15am-1pm Sat; Net access per 30min £1) You'll need to book for Net access.

Post office (South St; ☼ 8am-6pm Mon-Sat) Inside the Lowther Went shopping centre.

TIC (☎ 822634; email@cockermouth-tic.fsnet.co.uk; ☼ 9.30am-4.30pm Mon-Sat Apr-Jun & Oct, 9.30am-4pm Jan-Mar, Nov & Dec, 9.30am-5pm & 10am-2pm plus Sun Jul-Sep) Inside the town hall.

Sights

The handsome Georgian **Wordsworth House** (NT; ☎ 824805; Main St; £3.50; ☼ 11am-4.30pm Mon-Fri Apr-Oct, plus Sat Jun-Aug), built in 1745, was the birthplace of William Wordsworth and his sister Dorothy. Now operated by the National Trust, the house is furnished much as

it would have been in the 18th century, and contains Wordsworth memorabilia and some original furniture. There's a cosy café in the flagstoned kitchen, and the walled garden has a terrace running down to the riverbank, immortalised in Wordsworth's epic biographical poem *The Prelude*.

Perched by the River Cocker is **Jenning's Brewery** (☎ 821011; www.jenningsbrewery.co.uk; admission £4.50). The family-run firm has been churning out traditional ales and bitters on this site since 1874, and it's now possible to take a factory tour to see how the stuff is made. Tours last an hour and a half; phone ahead for times. Naturally, you couldn't leave without trying a brew or two: choices include traditional Cumberland Ale, Cocker Hoop, or the fantastically named Sneck Lifter.

Just down the street from Wordsworth House is the **Museum of Printing** (☎ 824984; Main St; admission £2.50; ☼ 10am-4pm Mon-Sat), crammed with exotic presses and equipment. If nothing else, it's certainly a lesson in how easy computers have made things.

Cumberland Toy & Model Museum (☎ 827606; www.toymuseum.co.uk; Banks Ct; admission £3; ☼ 10am-5pm Mar-Oct, 10am-4pm Feb & Nov) is run by a dedicated toy enthusiast, and its display cases are bursting with dusty doll's houses, train sets, Meccano models and other exhibits guaranteed to delight big and little kids alike.

Castlegate House Gallery (☎ 822149; www.castlegatehouse.co.uk; ☼ 10.30am-5pm Mon-Wed, 10.30am-5pm Fri & Sat, 2-5pm Sun), opposite **Cockermouth Castle**, exhibits local artists' work in Georgian surroundings, and modern sculpture in its walled garden. The castle itself dates from the 12th century, and is now a private residence.

Just outside town is the **Lakeland Sheep & Wool Centre** (☎ 822673; www.sheep-woolcentre.co.uk; Egremont Rd; adult £4; ☼ 9.30am-5.30pm, 4 shows Sun-Thu Mar-Nov), which houses the Western Lake

District Visitor Centre and puts on daily sheep-themed shows, including shearing, shepherding and dog-handling.

Sleeping
BUDGET
Cockermouth YHA Hostel (☎ 0870 770 5768; cockermouth@yha.org.uk; Double Mills; dm £9.50; ♈ Apr-Oct) has 26 beds in a 17th-century water mill on the southern edge of town. From Main St follow Station St, then turn left into Fern Bank Rd; the hostel is down a track off Fern Bank Rd.

Simple, good-value B&B options include the **Rook** (☎ 828496; www.therookguesthouse.gbr .cc; 9 Castlegate; s/d £20/32-36), a restored 17th-century townhouse with plain, snug rooms, and **Strathearn Guest House** (☎ 826749; www.smooth hound.co.uk/hotels/castlegate; 6 Castlegate; d from £40), which has old-fashioned accommodation in another period house across the road.

MID-RANGE & TOP END
Croft House (☎ 827533; www.croft-guesthouse.com; 6/8 Challoner St; s/d £32/47-50; P ✕) This lovingly converted Georgian house is the best B&B in town. The rooms are smartly decorated in a modern metropolitan style, with pine floors, subtle colours and contemporary furniture, and there's a daily changing breakfast menu that includes fruit salad and Spanish omelettes.

Allerdale Court (☎ 823654; www.allerdalecourthotel .co.uk; Market Pl; s/d £45-60/70-80; P ✕) In the heart of old Cockermouth, this cosy, traditional hotel offers a selection of rooms, the best of which have corner baths and four-poster beds, and two in-house restaurants: a relaxed Italian (mains £6 to £14) and a formal British dining room (set menu £18.95).

Trout Hotel (☎ 823591; www.trouthotel.co.uk; Crown St; s/d £59.95-149/109-169; P ✕) A plush, upmarket hotel in a former private mansion that once belonged to the Egremont Estate. The grand country-styled bedrooms range from spacious doubles to luxury suites, and the best have garden or riverside views.

Rose Cottage (☎ 822189; www.rosecottageguest .co.uk; s/d £35/50) Several flowery rooms in a pretty cottage B&B just outside town.

Eating & Drinking
Quince & Medlar (☎ 823579; 13 Castlegate; www .quinceandmedlar.co.uk; mains from £12.65; ♈ dinner Tue-Sat) If national awards and glowing reviews are anything to go by, this is probably the best vegetarian restaurant in England. Tuck into a sumptuous red onion tart or a timbale of broad beans and butternut squash in one of the wood-panelled dining rooms.

Cockatoo Restaurant (☎ 826205; 16 Market Pl; mains £11-15; ♈ lunch Wed-Mon, dinner Mon & Wed-Sat) Once a bog-standard fish-fry, the Cockatoo has recently been transformed into a modern bistro serving regional recipes and locally caught seafood – and the takeaway still does the best fish and chips for miles around.

Over the Top (☎ 827016; 36 Kirkgate; ♈ lunch & dinner Wed-Sat) A tiny, popular café furnished with wooden dressers and mismatched tables, usually crammed with a local crowd.

Bitter End (☎ 828993; Kirkgate) It might not be on quite the same scale as Jenning's, but this welcoming pub is Cumbria's smallest brewery, and serves a selection of excellent homemade ales and good lunchtime grub.

Getting There & Away
Bus No 600 travels to and from Carlisle (one hour, eight daily Monday to Saturday). Nos X5 and X4 between Workington, Keswick and Penrith also stop at Cockermouth (15 daily Monday to Saturday, six on Sunday).

KESWICK
☎ 017687 / pop 4990 / elevation 195m
Keswick is the Lake District's busy northern centre, a blue-slate market town jostling with B&Bs, pubs, cream-tea outlets and outdoor shops. The town is situated near the shores of Derwent Water, a glassy arc surrounded by fells and dense woodland, studded with five forested islands that could have fallen straight from the pages of *Swallows and Amazons*. Keswick was a centre of the graphite-mining industry in the 16th century; today it's an important walking base, with access to the Cumbria Way and countless trails crisscrossing the surrounding hills. It's also a great spot to get out on the water, either in a self-powered canoe or aboard a cruise boat.

Information
Keswick Launderette (☎ 75448; Main St; ♈ 7.30am-7pm)

Post office (☎ 72269; 48 Main St; ♈ 9am-5.30pm Mon-Fri, 9am-12.30pm Sat)

TIC (☎ 72645; www.keswick.org; Moot Hall, Market Pl; ♈ 9.30am-5.30pm Apr-Oct, 9.30am-4.30pm Nov-Mar)

U-Compute (☎ 72269; 48 Main St; ♈ 9am-5.30pm; per hr £2.99) Above the post office.

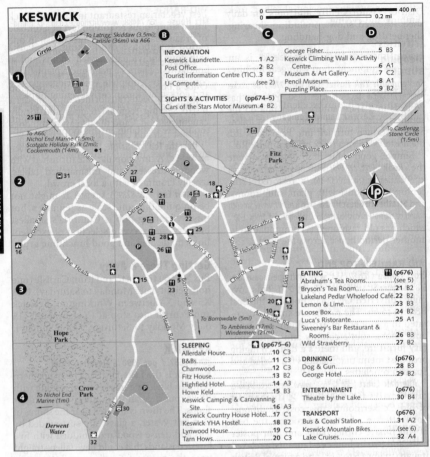

KESWICK

0   400 m
0   0.2 mi

INFORMATION
Keswick Laundrette..................1 A2
Post Office...............................2 B2
Tourist Information Centre (TIC)..3 B2
U-Compute............................(see 2)

SIGHTS & ACTIVITIES   (pp674–5)
Cars of the Stars Motor Museum..4 B2

George Fisher...........................5 B3
Keswick Climbing Wall & Activity
  Centre..................................6 A1
Museum & Art Gallery..............7 C2
Pencil Museum........................8 A1
Puzzling Place.........................9 B2

To Latrigg; Skiddaw (3.5mi);
Carlisle (36mi) via A66

To A66;
Nichol End Marine (1.5mi);
Scotgate Holiday Park (2mi);
Cockermouth (14mi)

To Castlerigg
Stone Circle
(1.5mi)

To Borrowdale (5mi)
To Ambleside (17mi);
Windermere (21mi)

To Nichol End
Marine (1mi)

EATING   (p676)
Abraham's Tea Rooms.............(see 5)
Bryson's Tea Room...................21 B2
Lakeland Pedlar Wholefood Café..22 B2
Lemon & Lime........................23 B3
Loose Box..............................24 B2
Luca's Ristorante.....................25 A1
Sweeney's Bar Restaurant &
  Rooms................................26 B3
Wild Strawberry......................27 B2

SLEEPING   (pp675–6)
Allerdale House......................10 C3
B&Bs.....................................11 C3
Charnwood............................12 C3
Fitz House..............................13 B2
Highfield Hotel.......................14 A3
Howe Keld.............................15 B3
Keswick Camping & Caravanning
  Site....................................16 A3
Keswick Country House Hotel....17 C1
Keswick YHA Hostel.................18 B2
Lynwood House.......................19 C2
Tarn Hows.............................20 C3

DRINKING   (p676)
Dog & Gun.............................28 B3
George Hotel..........................29 B2

ENTERTAINMENT   (p676)
Theatre by the Lake.................30 B4

TRANSPORT   (p676)
Bus & Coach Station.................31 A2
Keswick Mountain Bikes..........(see 6)
Lake Cruises...........................32 A4

Sights

People flock to the cult **Pencil Museum** (☎ 73 626; www.pencils.co.uk; Southy Works; admission £2.50; ☺ 9.30am-4pm) to pay homage to the humble pencil, which was first mass-produced in Keswick – attractions include a mine reconstruction, pencil sculptures and the dubious draw of the world's largest pencil. The museum is still attached to the Derwent Watercolour pencil factory, though the components are now imported from as far afield as Sri Lanka.

The classically Victorian **Museum & Art Gallery** (☎ 73263; Station Rd; admission £1; ☺ 10am-4pm Apr-Oct) displays original manuscripts from Wordsworth, Ruskin, Southey and Sir Hugh Walpole, and some fascinating

archaeological and natural history exhibits housed in old-fashioned glass cases.

Cars of the Stars Motor Museum (☎ 73757; www .carsofthestars.com; Standish St; admission £4; ☺ 10am-5pm) is a must-see for car junkies. Its fleet of celebrity vehicles includes Chitty Chitty Bang Bang, Herbie the Love Bug, a Batmobile, KITT from *Knightrider* and the Delorean from *Back to the Future*.

The **Puzzling Place** (☎ 75102; www.puzzlingplace .co.uk; Museum Pl; adult/child £3/2.50; ☺ 10am-6pm) will entertain older kids on a rainy day, with rooms devoted to holograms, optical illusions and gravity-defying trickery.

Keswick Climbing Wall & Activity Centre (☎ 72 000; www.keswickclimbingwall.co.uk; ☺ 10am-9pm), behind the Pencil Museum, organises outdoor activities including canoeing, abseiling, rock climbing and cycling.

Activities

George Fisher (☎ 72178; 2 Borrowdale Rd) is an outdoor-equipment shop with gear for hire.

BOAT TRIPS

Derwent Water has an excellent lake service run by the **Keswick Launch Company** (☎ 72263; www.keswick-launch.co.uk). From mid-March to November, regular boats call at seven landing stages around the lake: Ashness Gate, Lodore Falls, High Brandlehow, Low Brandlehow, Hawse End, Nichol End and back to Keswick. Boats leave every half-hour, clockwise and anticlockwise (return £5.70, 50 minutes); single fares are also available. The service operates six to eight times daily from December to mid-March. There's also an evening cruise at 7.30pm in summer, which includes a free glass of wine (one hour, £6.20, May to September).

Kayaks, windsurfers, rowboats and motor-boats are available from **Nichol End Marine** (☎ 73082; Nichol End).

WALKING

Keswick's youth hostels make useful bases for local hikes. Walkers could consider climbing to Skiddaw House YHA Hostel and Caldbeck along the Cumbria Way, or catching the launch to the lake's southern end (see Boat Trips, above) and walking up Borrowdale.

Sleeping

BUDGET

Keswick YHA Hostel (☎ 0870 770 5894; Kkeswick@yha .org.uk; Station Rd; dm £11; ☒ ⬚) A fine 91-bed hostel in a refurbished woollen mill beside the river. The small dorms are very pleasant, and some have balconies overlooking Fitz Park. Bike hire is also available.

Skiddaw House YHA Hostel (☎ 0870 7705754 via Carrock Fell YHA; skiddaw@yha.org.uk; Bassenthwaite; dm £7.75; ⊙ Apr-Oct) Twenty beds in a former shooting lodge behind Skiddaw, 6 miles from Keswick, and only accessible on foot (bring a torch).

Local campsites include **Scotgate Holiday Park** (☎ 78343; www.scotgateholidaypark.co.uk; adult/ car £4/2), a couple of miles from town (take bus No X5), and **Keswick Camping & Caravanning Club Site** (☎ 72392; Crow Park Rd; sites £15.35-18.35) near the lake.

MID-RANGE

Fitz House (☎ 74488; www.fitzhouse.co.uk; 47 Brundholme Tce; d £40-50) A splendid little B&B in a period townhouse overlooking Fitz Park, with four individually styled rooms and a holiday flat. There's a patio and a plant-filled conservatory, complete with fridge, glasses and corkscrew for an early-evening tipple.

Howe Keld (☎ 72417; www.howekeld.co.uk; 5-7 The Heads; s/d £33-35/46-70; ℗ ☒) Fifteen bright rooms are available in this popular guesthouse, renowned for its banquet breakfast (choices include homemade granola, air-cured bacon, Canadian pancakes and vegetarian rissoles).

Almost every house along Southey, Blencathra, Helvellyn and Eskin Sts offers B&B rooms. Top choices include **Charnwood** (☎ 74111; 6 Eskin St; d from £48), a listed Victorian residence with stencilled bedrooms; pastel-flavoured **Tarn Hows** (☎ 73217; www.tarnhows.co.uk; 3-5 Eskin St; s/d £25/52-26); slate-fronted **Lynwood House** (☎ 72398; www.lynwoodhouse.net; 35 Helvellyn St; d £42-46); and **Allerdale House** (☎ 73891; 1 Eskin St; d £40-50), a stone-walled townhouse covered in climbing roses.

TOP END

Highfield Hotel (☎ 72508; www.highfieldkeswick.co.uk; The Heads; d with dinner £100-126; ℗ ☒) The pick of the Victorian mansions along The Heads, with an impressive array of period features (turrets, bay windows, a grand veranda and even a converted chapel). The best rooms are front facing and have small balconies, with gorgeous views all the way to the lake.

WORTH THE TRIP

A mile east of Keswick stands **Castlerigg Stone Circle**, a mysterious loop of 48 stones believed to be between 3000 and 4000 years old, set on a hilltop surrounded by a brooding amphitheatre of mountains. The purpose of the circle is uncertain (current opinion is divided between a Bronze Age meeting place and a celestial timepiece), but one thing's for certain – those prehistoric builders certainly knew a good site when they saw one. The views in all directions are truly breathtaking.

The TIC has a good leaflet (50p) that outlines a 4-mile circular walk from the centre of Keswick.

Keswick Country House Hotel (☎ 0845-458-4333; www.thekeswickhotel.co.uk; Station Rd; d from £104/124; P ✗) A taste of turn-of-the-century grandeur is on offer at this huge, ornate hotel, set in formal grounds a little way out of town. The steepled, brick-built façade is impressive enough; inside you'll discover an elegant lounge, lavish bedrooms and a beautiful conservatory.

Eating

CAFÉS

Lakeland Pedlar Wholefood Café (☎ 74492; www .lakelandpedlar.co.uk; Hendersons Yard; mains £5-8; ☺ 9am-5pm) Excellent vegetarian café with wooden tables and a great Tex-Mex/organic menu. The veggie breakfasts and fair-trade coffee will set you up nicely for the day; homemade soups and sandwiches are available at lunchtime.

Bryson's Tea Room (☎ 72257; 42 Main St; meals £6; ☺ Apr-Dec, Mon-Sat Jan-Mar) One of the best-known bakeries in the Lakes now offers an upstairs café, serving salads, cakes and light lunches. Try the fruit cake and homemade florentines.

Wild Strawberry (☎ 74399; 54 Main St; mains £5.50; ☺ 10am-5pm) A classic English teashop with old wooden pillars, colourful lampshades and bone-china cups. The sticky toffee pudding, sandwiches and scones come recommended.

Abraham's Tearoom (☎ 72178; 2 Borrowdale Rd; mains around £5) An attic café tucked into the rafters of the George Fisher outdoor shop.

RESTAURANTS

Lemon & Lime (☎ 73088; 31 Lake Rd; mains £6-14; ☺ lunch & dinner) A new restaurant with a mix of international dishes (fajitas, Cajun red snapper, Thai green curry and Malaysian spicy noodles) served in the relaxed, light-filled dining room.

Luca's Ristorante (☎ 74621; High Hill; starters £3-7.50, mains £8-18; ☺ dinner Tue-Sun) An upmarket Italian restaurant housed in a former schoolhouse, offering classic dishes and more unusual fare (monkfish and salmon skewers, or spinach and ricotta *rotolo*).

Loose Box (☎ 772083; Kings Arms Courtyard; mains £5-6) A good choice for generous, authentic pizzas, attached to the Kings Arms Hotel.

Sweeney's Bar Restaurant & Rooms (☎ 772990; 18-20 Lake Rd; mains £7-12) A recently renovated English and Mediterranean restaurant with

leather sofas and contemporary cuisine; pleasant rooms are available upstairs.

Drinking

George Hotel (☎ 72076; 3 St John's St) This whitewashed pub (the oldest in Keswick) was once at the heart of a lucrative racket smuggling pencil materials; nowadays it's a great place to hide away a hearty pub lunch.

Dog & Gun (☎ 73463; 2 Lake Rd; mains around £6) Low-ceilinged and flagstone-floored, this town pub is another good spot for a pint of local ale.

Entertainment

Theatre by the Lake (☎ 74411; www.theatrebythe lake.com; Lakeside) The Lake District's only repertory theatre company stages new and classic drama is staged in its impressive purpose-built building on the shores of Derwent Water.

Getting There & Away

BUS

No 555/556 (the LakesLink) connects Keswick with Ambleside (40 minutes) Windermere (50 minutes) and Kendal (1½ hours) at least 10 times daily Monday to Saturday.

The X4/X5 travels from Penrith to Workington to Keswick (14 daily Monday to Saturday, six on Sunday).

Getting Around

Bikes can be hired from **Keswick Mountain Bikes** (☎ 75202; 1 Daleston Court) and **Keswick Climbing Wall & Activity Centre** (☎ 72000; www .keswickclimbingwall.co.uk) for £15 per day.

For taxis, call **Davies Taxis** (☎ 72676), **Keswick Taxis** (☎ 75585) or **Skiddaw Taxis** (☎ 75600).

BORROWDALE & BUTTERMERE VALLEYS

☎ 017687

Ringed by wooded hills, emerald-green valleys and stark granite outcrops, and dotted with little villages and isolated farmhouses, Borrowdale and Buttermere are among the most beautiful valleys in the Lake District. With thrilling access to some mighty peaks and low-level jaunts, they're a walker's dream, especially during the summer months; but the valleys are at their best in autumn, when the oaks and yew trees blaze with colour and the holiday crowds have left for home.

Borrowdale stretches for 6 miles from the northern end of Derwent Water to Honister Pass. Buttermere runs northwest from Honister Pass along the shores of Buttermere Lake and Crummock Water towards Cockermouth.

Borrowdale

Borrowdale's stunning position beside Derwent Water and its proximity to the peaks of Scaféll, Scaféll Pike and Great Gable make it popular with walkers.

Derwentwater YHA Hostel (☎ 0870 770 5792; derwentwater@yha.org.uk; Barrow House; dm £11.80; ✆ Feb-Nov, weekends Nov-Jan) is 2 miles from Keswick in an extraordinary setting overlooking the lake. This grand manor house was built by local notable Joseph Pocklington in the early 19th century; features include extensive grounds and a man-made waterfall.

Three miles from Keswick along the B5289, the impressive stone-fronted **Borrowdale Hotel** (☎ 77224; www.borrowdalehotel.co.uk; d £70-105; P ✗) occupies a wonderful position backed by woods and rocky peaks. The smart, wallpapered bedrooms all have good views and huge beds – the superior rooms are regal and worth the extra cost.

Borrowdale to Rosthwaithe

A couple of miles south of Borrowdale is the small village of **Grange-in-Borrowdale**. Nearby, the valley winds into the jagged ravine known as the **Jaws of Borrowdale**, a famous hiking spot with world-renowned views, especially from the 985-foot **Castle Crag**.

The next village south is **Rosthwaithe**, a rural hamlet scattered with stone cottages, slate-roofed farmhouses and a couple of country hotels.

Royal Oak Hotel (☎ 77214; www.royaloakhotel .co.uk; s/d £41/88-94; P ✗) was formerly an 18th-century farmhouse. This homely hotel has tiny windows, thick stone walls and a convincingly rustic feel.

For a touch more luxury, head next door to the **Scaféll Hotel** (☎ 77208; www.scafell.co.uk; d from £91; P ✗), where you'll find a lavish lounge, cocktail bar, an upmarket restaurant, and a selection of antique-filled bedrooms. Hikers and locals congregate in the Riverside Bar – the village's only pub.

Further into the village, the **Yew Tree Farm** (☎ 77675; www.yewtree-farm.co.uk; d £56-60; ✗) is a rambling, whitewashed farmhouse with an impressive claim to fame – one of its rooms put up Prince Charles during a covert hiking trip. Across the road, the **Flock Inn Tea Room** offers delicious home-baked cakes, flapjacks and scones.

Set at the head of Borrowdale Valley beside a bubbling river, **Borrowdale YHA Hostel** (☎ 0870 7705706; borrowdale@yha.org.uk; Longthwaite; dm £11.80; ✆ Feb-Dec) is a modern cedar-clad hostel that makes a great walking base and arranges outdoor activities.

Seatoller

The last stop before Honister Pass, Seatoller was originally a settlement for workers employed in the local slate quarries. These days, it's still a remote village, with just a few houses, a homely restaurant and a character-filled hotel.

Seatoller Barn Information Centre (☎ 77294; seatollertic@lake-district.gov.uk; ✆ 10am-5pm Apr-Nov) is Borrowdale's only TIC. It arranges local exhibitions and organised walks, and will help with finding accommodation.

Seatoller House (☎ 77218; www.seatollerhouse .co.uk; s/d £49.50/95; P ✗) is a charming 17th-century house that has accommodated weary travellers for the last 100 years. Two book-lined lounges, a tea bar and an excellent restaurant are available for guests' use, though most people find the cosy bedrooms offer more than enough comfort.

Next door, the quirky **Yew Tree Restaurant** (☎ 77634; mains £5-8; ✆ lunch Tue-Sun) serves up doorstop sandwiches, sumptuous cakes and hearty lunches in a low-ceilinged dining room, decorated with period photos and old cameras. There's an outdoor gear shop too.

GETTING THERE & AWAY

Bus No 79 – or 'the Borrowdale Rambler' – provides a regular service (at least hourly) from Keswick bus station to Seatoller.

From Easter to October No 77/77A – the Honister Rambler – makes the round trip from Keswick to Buttermere via Borrowdale and the Honister Pass four times daily.

Honister Pass

From Seatoller, Buttermere valley can be reached over the steep Honister Pass, one of the most productive slate-quarrying areas in the Lake District. It's possible to take a tour around **Honister Slate Mine** (☎ 017687-77230; www.honister-slate-mine.co.uk; £8.50; ✆ tours

10.30am, 12.30pm & 3.30pm Mar-Oct); less hardy souls can settle for buying slate ornaments in the attached gift shop.

Thanks to a couple of remote hostels, Honister makes a great base for an early-morning hike. A track to Great Gable starts nearby, and there are sweeping views from the top across the smoky, black-grey landscape, down into Buttermere valley. Bus No 77/77A stops here May to October.

Black Sail YHA (☎ 07711-108450; Ennerdale, Cleator; dm £10.60; ☷ Mar-Aug, Tue-Sat Sep-Oct) Isolated shepherd's bothy (cottage), 2½ miles west of Honister Pass and only accessible on foot.

Honister House YHA (☎ 0870 770 5870; Seatoller; dm £10.60; ☷ Jun-Aug, Thu-Mon Oct-Sep, weekends Nov) Basic hostel at the summit of the pass, housed in converted mine buildings.

Buttermere

The twisting road skirts around the edge of Buttermere lake, which shimmers at the centre of a circular crown of mountains, before reaching Buttermere village, 4 miles from Honister and 9 miles from Keswick. From Buttermere, the B5289 cuts north along the eastern shore of Crummock Water.

Buttermere YHA Hostel (☎ 0870 7705736; buttermere@yha.org.uk; dm £11.60) is a beautiful 70-bed slate house overlooking Buttermere Lake, with views of Red Pike and High Stile.

The old-fashioned **Fish Hotel** (☎ 70253; www .fish-hotel.co.uk; 2-night minimum stay d £124; ℗ ☒) was the pub that employed the famous 'Maid of Buttermere', an 18th-century beauty whose admirers included Wordsworth and Coleridge. These days the Maid may have gone, but there are still pleasant rooms, good beer and a roaring fire.

Luxurious accommodation right in the centre of Buttermere village, the **Bridge Hotel** (☎ 70252; www.bridge-hotel.com; £126-150 incl dinner; ℗ ☒) has a choice of standard rooms and some seriously lavish suites, complete with hill-view balconies and antique furniture.

GETTING THERE & AWAY

Bus No 77/77A services the Buttermere valley four times daily, Easter to October, departing from Keswick bus station.

ULLSWATER & AROUND
☎ 017684

Encircled by trees, patchwork fields and solid stonewalled villages, the silvery curve of Ullswater stretches for 7½ miles between Pooley Bridge and Glenridding and Patterdale to the south. Despite being the second-largest of the lakes, it's much less visited than Windermere and Derwent Water, though in summer it can get a little crowded along the western edge, especially at weekends. The eastern side is usually much quieter.

Ullswater 'Steamers' (☎ 82229; www.ullswater -steamers.co.uk; adult return £6.70-9.30) chug across the lake from Pooley Bridge to Glenridding via Howtown. Steamboats started plying the lake in 1859 but the current vessels, *Lady* (in operation since 1887) and *Raven* (since 1889), have been converted to conventional power.

Pooley Bridge
elevation 301m

With majestic mountains to the west, the serene village of Pooley Bridge nestles at the northern end of Ullswater, surrounded by green fields dipping down to the water's edge.

The **TIC** (☎ 86530; pooleybridgetic@lake-district .gov.uk; Finkle St; ☷ 10am-5pm Apr-Oct) can help with accommodation and enquiries. **Lakeland Boat Hire** (☎ 07773-671399; Lakeside) rents out motor boats for £15 to £20 per hour. Rowing boats cost from £10.

Park Foot Camping (☎ 86309; holidays@parkfootullswater.co.uk; Howtown Rd; sites £10-21.50) is a beautiful campsite on the edge of Ullswater, a mile south of Pooley Bridge.

Curiously resembling an Austrian alpine lodge, the 19th-century **Pooley Bridge Inn** (☎ 86215; www.pooleybridgeinn.co.uk; d £65-90; ℗ ☒) offers quaint, rustic-themed rooms, many with private front-facing balconies. The old stable courtyard has been converted into a fine alfresco restaurant.

Probably the oldest (and most luxurious) of the Lakeland country hotels, the **Sharrow Bay Country House Hotel** (☎ 86301; www.sharrow -bay.com; d £320-440) occupies a jaw-dropping lakefront setting and offers suitably grand rooms, furnished with antique armchairs, drapes and ostentatious bedsteads. There's a jetty, boathouse and private woodland, and the restaurant is nationally renowned.

If your budget won't stretch that far, head for the **Sun** (☎ 486205; mains £6-8), a fine village pub, for home-cooked pub grub and a sun-trap beer garden.

Glenridding
elevation 253m

Seven miles south from Pooley Bridge is the riverside town of Glenridding, the busiest of the villages near Ullswater. Forbidding Helvellyn (949m), the second-highest peak in the Lakes, looms up nearby, and Glenridding makes a great base for tackling the summit; more restful types can take to the lake aboard the Ullswater steamer. The nearby village of **Patterdale**, with its wind-worn slate and white houses, is also worth exploring.

Ullswater Information Centre (☎ 82414; glenriddingtic@lake-district.gov.uk; Beckside car park; ☼ 9am-6pm Apr-Oct, 9.30am-3.30pm Fri-Sun Nov-Mar) is a mine of information on local walks.

Gillside Farm Campsite (☎ 82346; www.gillsidecaravanandcampingsite.co.uk; adult/tent/car £4/1/1) is set among rugged foothills and is popular with walkers.

One and a half miles from Glenridding, the remote **Helvellyn YHA Hostel** (☎ 0870 770 5862; helvellyn@yha.org.uk; Greenside; dm £10.60; ☼ Jul-Aug, phone ahead at other times) is mainly popular with walkers setting out for Helvellyn. The rough road makes vehicle access tricky.

Completely refurbished in 2001, the old Lakeland-stone **Inn on the Lake** (☎ 82444; www.innonthelakeullswater.co.uk; s/d £65/118-170) now offers a selection of modernised rooms, ranging from richly decorated doubles to palatial four-poster suites; lake-view rooms are, not surprisingly, the most expensive.

Decent food and beer are served at the **Traveller's Rest** (☎ 82298; mains £6-10), a down-to-earth pub popular with folk from the campsite nearby.

Getting There & Around
Bus No 108 runs from Penrith to Patterdale, calling in at Pooley Bridge and Glenridding (six daily Monday to Saturday). Bus No 517 runs from Bowness Pier to Glenridding (three daily late-July to August, weekends only end-March to July).

CUMBRIAN COAST

It might not be the most conventionally beautiful stretch of shoreline in Britain, but the rugged Cumbrian coast has a wild, wind-battered grandeur all of its own. To the south is the broad, sandy sweep of Morecambe Bay, with some interesting

towns in the surrounding hills: gracious Grange, medieval Cartmel and bustling Ulverston. Northwards along the coast is Ravenglass, the starting point for *La'al Ratty*, a miniature steam train that chugs through the wilds of Eskdale, the gateway to remote Wast Water. Beyond the controversial nuclear power station of Sellafield is the seaside village of St Bees, which marks the beginning of the C2C walk, and further north, the historic port of Whitehaven – once the third largest in Britain.

Getting Around
The Cumbrian Coast railway line loops 120 miles from Carlisle to Lancaster (both on the main line between London and Glasgow). Trains run hourly, and a single costs £19. Phone ☎ 08457 484950 for full details.

The railway line's famous Carnforth station was immortalised in David Lean's 1945 film *Brief Encounter*, a classic of English restraint. The original clock still hangs near where Trevor Howard bumped into Celia Johnson.

GRANGE-OVER-SANDS
☎ 015395 / pop 4840

Overlooking the broad sweep of Morecambe Bay is the quiet seafront town of Grange-over-Sands, once one of Britain's most popular seaside resorts. During the 19th century, Edwardian gentry came in their droves to take in the invigorating sea air and stroll along the seafront promenade, and the town is dotted with reminders of its genteel golden age: ornamental gardens, elegant townhouses, and a selection of ridiculously grand hotels. Today, there's not much to keep you here unless you're after a peaceful haven for your twilight years.

Information
Library (☎ 32749; Grange Fell Rd; ☼ 9am-5pm Mon-Fri, 9am-1pm Sun)

Post office (☎ 34713; Main St; ☼ 9am-5pm Mon-Fri, 9am-12.30pm Sat)

TIC (☎ 34026; grangetic@southlakeland.gov.uk; Victoria Hall, Main St; ☼ 10am-5pm Easter-Oct)

Sleeping
Lymehurst Hotel (☎ 33076; www.lymehurst.co.uk; Kents Bank Rd; s/d £32-35/64-80; P ☒) The pick of several places along Kents Bank Rd, this converted Victorian house must have been

CUMBRIA & THE LAKES

QUICKSAND & THE QUEEN'S GUIDE

Before the railways arrived in Grange, the crossing over the sand flats of Morecambe Bay was the main route to the Lake District from the south of England. Cartmel monks moonlighted as guides for travellers, and horse-drawn coaches plied the route till 1857. It's still possible to walk across the flats at low tide, but only with the official Queen's guide (a role established in 1536), as the crossing is dangerous, fraught with unpredictable tides and quicksand – even experienced local fishermen have been known to lose carts, horses and tractors. The 8-mile crossing from Arnside to near Kents Bank train station takes around 3½ hours – contact the Grange TIC for details.

Remember that the fast-rising tides in Morecambe Bay are notoriously dangerous. In 2004, a group of Chinese cocklepickers was drowned by the incoming tide, and there have been many similar incidents down the years. The best – and safest – way to explore the bay is in the company of an experienced local guide.

---

a grand residence in its heyday; these days the rooms offer everything you'd expect from a British B&B.

Thornfield House (☎ 32512; www.grangeguesthouse.com; Kents Bank Rd; s/d from £27/45; P ⊗) Another decent option inside a detached townhouse, distinguished by its cosy bedrooms and bay views.

Grange Hotel (☎ 33666; www.grange-hotel.co.uk; Station Sq; s/d from £69/138; bay views add £10-35; P ⊗ ▢ ▣) Grange's former incarnation as an Edwardian holiday resort is made obvious by the concentration of huge hotels around town; this is one of the oldest and best, an Italianate mansion set in wooded gardens, offering lavish, luxurious rooms.

Eating

Hazelmere Cafe (☎ 32972; 1-2 Yewbarrow Tce; mains £6-9; ☯ 10am-5pm summer, 10am-4.30pm winter) Unsurprisingly for one of Cumbria's retirement hotspots, Grange is brimming over with cake shops and tearooms; this much-loved café is the best of the bunch, offering homemade cakes, sophisticated main meals (think venison sausage and Tuscan bean bake), and over 30 kinds of tea.

Higginsons (☎ 34367; Keswick House; Main St) For the finest pies, pasties and sausages for miles around, head for this renowned butcher's shop.

The Coffee Pot (☎ 33269; Main St; sandwiches £3-5) Opposite the TIC, this little tearoom is worth a look just for its views out across Morecambe Bay.

Getting There & Away

Both the train station and bus stop are just downhill from the TIC.

Bus No X35 from Kendal stops at Grange (five minutes, 14 daily) on its way to Barrow (50 minutes) via Ulverston.

Bus No 532 runs from Cartmel (30 minutes, four daily) from Monday to Saturday.

Grange is on the Cumbrian Coast Line, with frequent connections to Lancaster (£3.65, 25 minutes, hourly) and Carlisle (£21, 90 minutes, hourly). For a more scenic route, take the train from Kendal (£7.90, one hour, hourly).

AROUND GRANGE
Cartmel
☎ 015395

A mile west of Grange-over-Sands is the pretty, rural village of Cartmel. Most of the ivy-clad buildings and whitewashed houses (some of which date back to the Middle Ages) are clustered around its small market square, but the town is best known for its magnificent 12th-century church – one of the few priories to escape demolition during the dissolution of the monasteries under Henry VIII.

Cartmel Priory (☎ 36261; ☯ 9am-5.30pm May-Oct, 9am-3.30pm Nov-Apr) only avoided destruction thanks to its status as a parish church. Although much of the original glass was destroyed, the 45-foot-high 15th-century **east window** remains glorious, and on sunny days the church fills with intensely coloured light. The carved choir stalls date from 1440, and the church houses many tombs, including the 13th-century **Harrington tomb**, named after a local builder who reconstructed part of the church. Look out for the skulls and hourglasses carved in the floor – 17th- and 18th-century reminders of mortality.

Guided tours are available at 11am and 2pm on Wednesdays from May to October (£2), and there are concerts on summer Saturdays.

Cartmel Heritage Centre (☎ 36874; Market Sq; admission £2; ⏰ 10am-4pm Wed-Sun Easter-Halloween, 10am-4pm Sat & Sun in winter), located in the 14th-century priory gatehouse, has quirky displays including an inhouse clockmaker and reconstructions of the village smithy and a medieval privy.

Apart from the priory, Cartmel is also famous for its racecourse – the smallest in the country – which comes alive on the last weekend in May and in August.

Cartmel's other celebrated export is sticky-toffee pudding – the best is made at the **Cartmel Village Shop** (☎ 36201; www.sticky toffeepudding.co.uk; The Square; ⏰ 9am-5pm Mon-Sat, 10am-4.30pm Sun).

SLEEPING
Both of the village pubs offer B&B accommodation. Other choices include:

Bank Court Cottage (☎ 36593; d £50-55) A tiny family house reached through an arch by one of the bookshops on the square, with just two simple B&B rooms.

Prior's Yeat (☎ 35178; priorsyeat@hotmail.com; Aynsome Rd; s/d £32-24/52-56; P ✕) A detached Edwardian residence just outside the main village, with nicely furnished bedrooms and a peaceful setting.

Cartmel Caravan & Camping Park (☎ 36270; Wells House Farm; sites £8-12) A tranquil campsite just south of the village.

EATING
L'Enclume (☎ 36362; lenclume.co.uk; Cavendish St; mains £20-26, set menus £50-95) Tucked away in the shadow of the abbey, this fabulous fine-dining restaurant serves some of Cumbria's best cuisine – Bresse pigeon, roasted seabass, Challans duck and burnt cream pots – in an achingly tasteful dining room, furnished with overhead beams, slate sculptures and leather armchairs.

Cavendish Arms (☎ 36240; mains £6-13; s/d £35/50-55) The oldest pub in the village, an ivy-covered 16th-century inn with great food and its own excellent beer.

Kings Arms (☎ 36220; lunch £4-7, dinner £7-12) The village's second pub is in a pretty whitewashed building with a cobbled terrace on the square.

GETTING THERE & AWAY
Bus No 532 runs from Grange to Cartmel (30 minutes, four daily).

Holker Hall & Lakeland Motor Museum
Set in stately gardens, **Holker Hall** (☎ 58328; www.holker-hall.co.uk; admission £9.25, house & grounds £7.50, grounds only £4.75; ⏰ house 10.30am-4.30pm Sun-Fri, grounds 10am-6pm Mar-Oct) dates from the 16th century but is mainly a Gothic Victorian creation, furnished with stately drapery and grand woodcarving. There's a deer park, and the stables house the **Lakeland Motor Museum** (admission £8; ⏰ 10.30am-4.45pm), with truckloads of classic cars, as well as a replica of Donald Campbell's jetboat *Bluebird* (see p668; the original is in the National Motor Museum, p219).

ULVERSTON
☎ 01229
A century ago, the market town of Ulverston was a bustling centre for the local industries of tanning, cotton and iron ore. These days, the town runs at a more sedate pace, but it's still an attractive place to visit, especially on market days (Thursday and Saturday), when the cobbled streets fill up with stalls selling clothing, food and groceries. Ulverston hosts several annual festivals, and it's the official starting point for the Cumbria Way.

Information
Library (☎ 894151; Kings Rd; Net access per 30min £1)
TIC (☎ 587120; www.ulverston.net; County Sq; ⏰ 9am-5pm Mon-Sat)

Sights
Ulverston's most famous son is comedian Stan Laurel, who was born at 3 Argyle St in 1890. Fans will want to make the pilgrimage to the **Laurel & Hardy Museum** (☎ 582292; 4c Upper Brook St; admission £2; ⏰ 10am-4.30pm Feb-Dec), which has floor-to-ceiling memorabilia and shows some of their cinematic creations too.

The tower on top of Hoad Hill commemorates local hero Sir John Barrow (1764–1848), explorer and author of *Mutiny of the Bounty* (1831). The tiny 16th-century **yeoman's cottage** (☎ 585788; admission free; ⏰ 11am-4pm Sat, noon-4pm Sun) where he was born is usually open to the public at weekends.

Sleeping

Walkers Hostel (☎ 585588; www.walkershostel
.freeserve.co.uk; Oubas Hill; B&B £14) A cheery, eco-
friendly hostel geared towards the hiking
crowd, 10-minutes' walk from town on the
A590 to Kendal.

Trinity House Hotel (☎ 587639; www.traininghotel
.co.uk; Princes St; s/d £57/74-88). This fine Georgian
house – formerly the town rectory – is entirely
staffed by young people in training for local
hotel qualifications, so you can expect top-
notch rooms and four-star service at a very
reasonable price.

Lightburne Georgian Townhouse (☎ 01229
581930; www.lightburne.co.uk; 13 Princes St; s/d £30/55;
Ⓟ Ⓧ) A pleasantly refurbished townhouse
decked out with oriental rugs and antique
furniture. Some of the tastefully furnished
rooms overlook the back garden.

Other B&B choices include **Virginia House**
(☎ 584844; www.ulverstonhotels.com; 24 Queen St; s/d
£36/56; Ⓧ), a smart B&B in an imposing
Victorian gentleman's residence, and the
centrally-located **Rock House** (☎ 586879; www
.rock-house.info; 1 Alexander Rd; s/d £25/50; Ⓧ).

Eating & Drinking

King's (☎ 588947; 15-17 Queen St; mains £5-11;
Ⓧ lunch & dinner Mon-Sat) Ulverston's funkiest
café-bar serves up fresh, filling bistro food
in colourful surroundings, complete with
mirrors, stripped wood floors and pistachio-
and-pink walls.

Rustique (☎ 587373; off Brogden St; mains £8-15;
Ⓧ lunch & dinner Mon-Sat, 10-11.30am Sun) This
newly converted restaurant, down an alleyway opposite the old market hall, offers contemporary dining in a neutral-toned space;
sample dishes range from roast sea trout to
grilled swordfish with lemon pickle.

Hot Mango Café (☎ 584866; 27 King St; sandwiches
from £4.95; Ⓧ breakfast & lunch Tue-Sat) This buzzy

café is a good place to head for coffee and
light lunches (mainly warm baguettes,
sandwiches and salads).

Farmers Arms (☎ 584469; Market Pl; mains £6-10)
The pick of the town pubs for food and
local ale.

Getting There & Away

Regular trains from Carlisle (£24, two
hours) and Lancaster (£5.70, 40 minutes)
stop at Ulverston station, five minutes' walk
south of the centre. To reach Cartmel by
bus, you have to change at Grange (eight
daily Monday to Saturday).

AROUND ULVERSTONE
Conishead Priory

Two miles south of Ulverstone is **Conishead
Priory** (☎ 584029; www.manjushri.org.uk; admission
free, tours £2.50; Ⓧ 2-5pm Sat & Sun Easter-Oct). Originally a 12th-century leper colony, since
1977 it has been home to a Manjushri Buddhist Centre. The grand Victorian Gothic
house has been beautifully restored and
includes a 24-sq-metre Buddhist temple,
containing some of the largest Buddhist
statues in Europe. Tours begin at 2.30pm
and 3.45pm.

Bus No 11 makes regular trips from Ulverston to Barrow-in-Furness via the priory
(12 daily Monday to Saturday).

Furness Abbey

The rose-coloured ruins of **Furness Abbey** (EH;
☎ 823420; admission £3; Ⓧ 10am-6pm Apr-Sep, 10am-
5pm Oct; 10am-4pm Wed-Sun Nov-Mar) are hidden
away in the 'Vale of Deadly Nightshade',
1½ miles north of Barrow-in-Furness and
8½ miles from Ulverston. Founded in the
12th century by Savignac monks, and later
merged with the Cistercian order, the abbey
became one of the most powerful in the

WORTH THE TRIP

Perched on a small, windswept island off Cumbria's southern shoreline are the tumbledown remains
of **Piel Castle**, built in the 14th century by the monks of Furness Abbey as a defensive outpost,
and later used as a fortified warehouse for smuggling goods to Ireland. The landlord of the Ship
Inn is traditionally called the 'King of Piel', a tradition dating back to 1487, when Lambert Simnel
declared himself king on landing here.

Piel Island and the castle are accessible by ferry from Roa Island, 5 miles southeast of Barrow-
in-Furness. The **ferry** (☎ 835809 or 07799 761306) runs on weekends from April to September and
during school holidays – at other times, trips must be arranged in advance.

Bus No 11 runs to Ulverston from Barrow-in-Furness via Roa Island.

north of England, but in 1537 it became one of the first victims of the dissolution. Part of the north and south transept and the grand bell tower are still standing, and the atmospheric ruins are scattered with carved arches and elegant vaulting, hinting at the abbey's former grandeur.

An audio guide is included in the admission price. The small museum contains a collection of stone carvings, including two rare 13th-century effigies of armoured knights.

Bus No 6 or 6A from Ulverston to Barrow-in-Furness passes by the abbey on a regular basis.

RAVENGLASS & AROUND

It's difficult to imagine the tiny village of Ravenglass, a quiet cluster of seaside houses, 27 miles north of Barrow, as an important Roman port. The Romans were drawn to its sheltered harbour, but all that remains of their substantial fort are the walls of a 4th-century **bath house**, half a mile from the train station down a signposted track.

The main attraction in Ravenglass is the much-loved narrow-gauge **Ravenglass & Eskdale Railway** (☎ 01229-717171; www.ravenglass-railway.co.uk; adult £8.20), affectionately known as *La'al Ratty*, and originally built in 1875 to carry iron ore. The miniature trains chug along a beautiful 7-mile track into Eskdale and the foothills of the Lake District mountains. There's an interesting **museum** at the station, as well as the **Ratty Arms**, a family-friendly pub with good grub. A Wainwright booklet called *Walks from Ratty* (£1.50) is available from the railway.

A mile south of Ravenglass is **Muncaster Castle** (☎ 01229-717614; www.muncaster.co.uk; gardens adult £6, castle £2.50/1.50; ☉ gardens 10.30am-6pm, castle noon-5pm Sun-Fri), a grand crenellated castle dating from the 14th century and rebuilt in the 19th. Audio tours explore the castle's history and hauntings, and the huge grounds include an owl centre and an impressive maze.

The controversial **Sellafield Nuclear Power Plant**, a huge local employer, is 5 miles north of Ravenglass. There is a curiously popular **visitor centre** (☎ 019467-27027; www.sellafield.com; admission free; ☉ 10am-6pm Apr-Oct, 10am-4pm Nov-Mar) which houses Sparking Reaction, a huge-scale interactive exhibition created by the Science Museum in London.

Accommodation is almost nonexistent in Ravenglass. The most interesting place to stay locally is the former **Coachman's Quarters** (☎ 01229-717614; s/d £35/50-60; ℗), in the grounds of Muncaster Castle, which have been converted to provide spacious, comfortable double rooms.

Ravenglass is on the Cumbrian Coast Line, with frequent links north and south along the coast. Bus No 6 from Whitehaven stops at Ravenglass and terminates at Muncaster (70 minutes, five daily). Bus X6 travels the same route on Sunday (four daily).

ST BEES
☎ 01946

The windswept village of St Bees straggles out across the hills north of Sellafield, fronted by a sweep of white sand and rust-coloured rocks. Most of the village's rough stone houses and terracotta buildings are huddled along the main street, and apart from a couple of pubs and shops, there's not a great deal to see. Nearby clifftops are an important nesting site for seabirds, and much of the headland is taken up by the St Bees Head RSPB Nature Reserve. St Bees also marks the start of Alfred Wainwright's classic Coast-to-Coast Walk.

Sleeping & Eating
Fairladies Barn (☎ 822718; www.fairladiesbarn.co.uk; Main St; s/d £20-30/36-45; ℗ ☒) A large, converted 17th-century barn with 10 pleasant rooms within easy walking distance of the village pubs and shops. Self-catering flats are also available.

Queens Hotel (☎ 822287; Main St; s/d £35/50; mains £6.50) An ivy-covered, friendly free house in the village centre, offering good food, a conservatory and beer garden, and a selection of comfortable rooms, some with views.

French Connection (☎ 822600; Old Railway Station; mains £12-18; ☉ dinner Tue-Sun), Traditional French cooking served in the old station waiting room and booking office, with mains including monkfish wrapped in Parma ham and smoked-duck salad. Tapas is served from Tuesday to Thursday.

Getting There & Away
St Bees is on the Cumbrian Coast Line. Bus No 20 (25 minutes, six daily Monday to Saturday) is the most reliable bus from Whitehaven.

WHITEHAVEN

☎ 01946 / pop 25,980

The sleepy harbour of Whitehaven was once the third-largest port in England, and officially made its fortune exporting local coal and iron ore, though the town was also a mover and shaker in the slave trade. Following the decline of the coal and iron industries, many of the town's buildings fell into disrepair, but a recent facelift has spruced up the marina, and its pastel-painted Georgian houses fairly gleam along the waterfront. Whitehaven hosts a bi-annual maritime festival.

The main **TIC** (☎ 852939; tic@copelandbc.gov.uk; Market Pl; ☺ 9.30am-5pm Mon-Sat Apr-Oct, 10am-4.30pm Nov-Mar) is near the town centre. There's another small branch in the Beacon.

The **Beacon** (☎ 592302; www.thebeacon-white haven.co.uk; West Strand; admission £4.40, joint tickets with the Rum Story £7.50; ☺ 10am-5.30pm Tue-Sun Apr-Oct, 10am-4.30pm Nov-Mar) is a fine heritage centre overlooking the harbour. It shines a light on local mining, shipbuilding, trade and smuggling.

The **Rum Story** (☎ 592933; www.rumstory.co.uk; Lowther St; admission £4.95; ☺ 10am-5pm Apr-Sep, 10am-4pm Wed-Sun Oct-Mar), housed in an 18th-century warehouse, deals with the area's boozy connections. Intoxicating displays – complete with sounds and smells – explore the slave trade, the Royal Navy, prohibition and the jazz age.

Sleeping

Corkickle Guest House (☎ 692073; 1 Corkickle; s/d from £30/45; ✗) About 300m northeast of Corkickle train station, this quaint end-of-terrace townhouse is the best B&B in Whitehaven. There is a smart lounge and dining room, and the spick-and-span rooms are excellent value.

Georgian House (☎ 696611; www.thegeorgian househotel.net; 9-11 Church St; s/d £45/65; ✗) Located along one of Whitehaven's oldest Georgian streets, from the outside this looks like a quintessential sea-captain's residence; inside, it's a classy hotel with pine beds and fine rooms with a faint maritime feel.

Eating

Zest (☎ 696981; 8 West Strand; ☺ breakfast, lunch & dinner) A funky waterside restaurant with chrome seats, globe lights and a Continental atmosphere, serving ciabattas, wraps and salads. For more sophisticated eating, head for **Zest Restaurant** (☎ 692848; Low Rd; ☺ dinner Wed-Sat) in town.

Lime Lounge (☎ 693671; www.limelounge.co.uk; 9 Marlborough St; ☺ dinner Tue-Sun) A modern Mexican and tapas restaurant near the harbour, decked out with sleek wooden furniture and citrus-flavoured decor.

Henry Hornblowers (☎ 590492; Church St; mains £11-16; ☺ dinner Thu-Sun) Sophisticated British and fusion cuisine served in a listed building, decorated with a nautical theme. There's a special chargrill section and a Pacific Rim menu inspired by the chef's travels.

Getting There & Away

Whitehaven is on the Cumbrian Coast Line with hourly trains in each direction. Bus No 6/X6 travels to Ravenglass (one hour, four daily).

NORTH & EAST CUMBRIA

Though the dramatic landscapes of the central Lakes are undoubtedly Cumbria's main attraction, the rest of the county – dotted with small rural towns, wild moorland and wind-battered farms – is also well worth exploring, as well as the county's only city, Carlisle, best known for its impressive castle and red sandstone cathedral. South of Carlisle is the old market town of Penrith, which stands at the northern end of the lush Eden Valley. Northeast of Penrith is Alston, perched high in the North Pennines, and a good base for exploring the moors and Hadrian's Wall. The small town of Kirkby Lonsdale is in Cumbria's southeastern corner, close to the Yorkshire Dales National Park.

CARLISLE

☎ 01228 / pop 71,780

The solid redbrick town of Carlisle has been in the frontline of England's defences for the last thousand years. Sacked by the Picts, razed by the Vikings, battered by the Scots and terrorised by the Border Reivers (see opposite), its stormy location near the Scottish border has left it with a wealth of historical sights, including the massive sandstone castle and the remnants of the old town walls, as well as Cumbria's only cathedral. Nowadays, a small student population and the lively after-dark scene keep old Carlisle young at heart – but looking out from the castle ramparts or Hadrian's Wall nearby, it's not hard to imagine the bloodiness of bygone days.

Carlisle makes a good base from which to explore Northumberland, Hadrian's Wall and the Scottish Borders, as well as the Lake District.

History

A Celtic camp or *caer* (preserved in the name of Carlisle) provided an early military station for the Romans. After the construction of Hadrian's Wall, Carlisle became the Romans' administrative centre in the northwest. Following centuries of intermittent conflict between Picts, Saxons and Viking raiders, the Normans seized Carlisle from the Scots in 1092, and William Rufus began construction of the castle and town walls.

The English continued to develop Carlisle as a military stronghold throughout the Middle Ages, constructing the city walls, citadels and the great gates. During the Civil War, Royalist Carlisle was an important strategic base; the city was eventually taken, battered and starving, by the Roundhead Scottish army after a nine-month siege.

Peace only came to Carlisle with the Restoration. The city's future as an industrial centre was sealed with the arrival of the railways and the first cotton mills during the Industrial Revolution.

Orientation

From the M6, the main routes into town are London Rd and Warwick Rd. The train station is south of the city centre, a 10-minute walk from Town Hall Sq (also known as Greenmarket) and the TIC. The bus station is on Lonsdale St, about 250m east. Most of the town's B&Bs are dotted along Victoria Pl and Warwick Rd.

Information

@Cybercafé (☎ 512308; www.atcybercafe.co.uk; 8-10 Devonshire St; 🕑 8am-10pm Mon-Sat, 10am-10pm Sun; per hr £3)
Cumberland Infirmary (☎ 523444; Newtown Rd) Half a mile west of the city centre.

THE BORDER REIVERS

From the Middle Ages to the mid-16th century, the Scottish Borders (known as the Debatable Lands) were terrorised by the Reivers, feuding families who fought and robbed the English, Scots and each other, and struck fear into the hearts of the locals. For the Reivers, sheep rustling, looting, pillaging, highway robbery and homestead-burning became a way of life, and northern Cumbria, Northumberland, and the Scottish Borders are littered with small castles, keeps and *peles* (towers), designed to offer some protection against the Reivers' attacks.

It wasn't until James VI of Scotland succeeded Elizabeth I of England and united the two countries that order was finally reasserted. The Reivers are responsible for giving the words 'blackmail' and 'bereaved' to the English language.

Ottakar's (☎ 542300; 66 Scotch St; 9am-5.30pm Mon-Sat, noon-4pm Sun) Large chain bookshop stocking new titles and local books.
Police station (☎ 528191) Just north of Town Hall Sq off Scotch St.
Post office (20-34 Warwick Rd)
TIC (☎ 625600; historic-carlisle.org.uk; Greenmarket; 🕑 9.30am-5pm Mon-Sat Mar-Jun & Sep-Oct, 9.30am-5.30pm Mon-Sat Jul, 9.30am-6pm Mon-Sat Aug, 10.30am-4.30pm Sun Easter-Aug, Mon-Sat 10am-4pm Mon-Sat Nov-Feb; Net access per 15min £1) Offers a free accommodation booking service for personal callers.

Sights & Activities
CARLISLE CASTLE

English Heritage's brooding, rust-red **Carlisle Castle** (EH; ☎ 591922; admission £3.80; 🕑 9.30am-6pm Apr-Sep, 10am-4pm Oct-Mar) was built on the site of Celtic and Roman fortresses. The Norman keep was built in 1092 by William Rufus, and Mary Queen of Scots was briefly imprisoned here in 1568 after losing the Scottish throne. A maze of passages and chambers winds around the castle, and there are great views from the ramparts – you can even see some stones in the dungeon that prisoners licked to keep themselves hydrated. The castle also houses the **Kings Own Royal Border Regiment Museum**, which tells you all you'd ever want to know about Cumbria's Infantry Regiment. There are daily castle tours (£1.50; April to September).

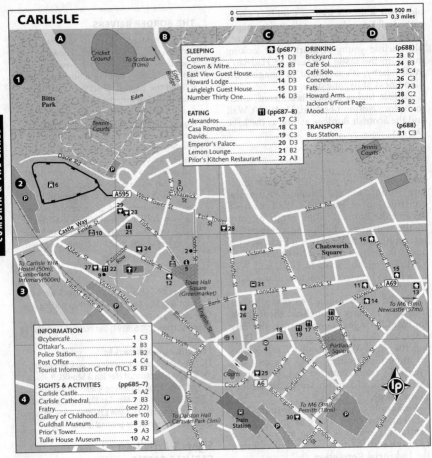

CARLISLE

SLEEPING 🏠 (p687)
Cornerways......................11 D3
Crown & Mitre..................12 B3
East View Guest House........13 D3
Howard Lodge...................14 D3
Langleigh Guest House.........15 D3
Number Thirty One.............16 D3

EATING 🍴 (pp687–8)
Alexandros.......................17 C3
Casa Romana.....................18 C3
Davids............................19 C3
Emperor's Palace................20 D3
Lemon Lounge....................21 B2
Prior's Kitchen Restaurant......22 A3

DRINKING (p688)
Brickyard.........................23 B2
Café Sol..........................24 B3
Café Solo.........................25 C4
Concrete..........................26 C3
Fats..............................27 A3
Howard Arms......................28 C2
Jackson's/Front Page.............29 B2
Mood..............................30 C4

TRANSPORT (p688)
Bus Station.......................31 C3

INFORMATION
@cybercafé.......................1 C3
Ottakar's.........................2 B3
Police Station....................3 B2
Post Office.......................4 C4
Tourist Information Centre (TIC)..5 B3

SIGHTS & ACTIVITIES (pp685–7)
Carlisle Castle...................6 A2
Carlisle Cathedral................7 B3
Fratry.......................(see 22)
Gallery of Childhood.........(see 10)
Guildhall Museum.................8 B3
Prior's Tower.....................9 A3
Tullie House Museum..............10 A2

CARLISLE CATHEDRAL

The city's red sandstone **cathedral** (☎ 548151; donation £2; 🕑 7.30am-6.15pm Mon-Sat, 7.45am-5pm Sun) was originally constructed as a priory church in 1122. During the 1644–45 siege by Parliamentarian troops, two-thirds of the nave was torn down to help repair the city wall and castle. Serious restoration didn't begin until 1853, but a surprising amount survives, including the east window and part of the original Norman nave.

Notable features include the fine 14th-century east window, the 15th-century misericords, the lovely Brougham Triptych in the north transept, and some ornate choir carvings.

Surrounding the cathedral are other priory relics, including the 16th-century **Fratry** (see p688) and the **Prior's Tower**.

TULLIE HOUSE MUSEUM

This excellent **museum** (☎ 534781; Castle St; www.tulliehouse.co.uk; admission £5.20; 🕑 10am-5pm Mon-Sat, noon-5pm Sun Apr-Oct, 10am-4pm Mon-Sat, 12-4pm Sun Nov-Mar) brings Carlisle's history to life with exhibitions exploring the foundation of the city, life under Roman rule, and the development of modern Carlisle. Highlights include an impressive reconstruction of Hadrian's Wall, and a lively audiovisual display on the **Border Reivers** (see boxed text p685).

The Millennium Gallery covers local geology and archaeology, and includes the

Whispering Wall, a glass wall that plays local stories through miniature speakers. Outside, there's a rotunda with great views of Carlisle Castle (which can be reached by an underground walkway from the museum), and a beautifully preserved Georgian townhouse containing the museum's **gallery of childhood**.

GUILDHALL MUSEUM

This small **museum** (☎ 532781; Greenmarket; ❍ noon-4.30pm Tue-Sun Apr-Oct; admission free) houses a modest local history collection. The most interesting exhibit is the building itself; constructed as a townhouse in about 1405, and later occupied by the trade guilds, it's now the last medieval structure in Carlisle.

Tours

Open Book Visitor Guiding (☎ 670578; www.great guidedtours.co.uk) offers tours of Carlisle and the surrounding area from April to September, including visits to Carlisle Castle and Hadrian's Wall.

Sleeping

BUDGET

Cornerways (☎ 521733; www.cornerwaysguesthouse .co.uk; 107 Warwick Rd; s/d £20-25/40-50; P ⊠) A listed Victorian townhouse on the corner of Warwick Rd and Hartington Pl, offering plain rooms with pine furniture and decorative bedspreads.

East View Guest House (☎ 522112; 110 Warwick Rd; s/d £25/45-50; P ⊠) On the other side of the road from Cornerways, this simple, no-frills B&B makes a good value base near the city centre. The nicest rooms are the larger doubles set back from the main road.

Carlisle YHA Hostel (☎ 0870 770 5752; dee .carruthers@unn.ac.uk; Bridge Lane; dm £14.50; ❍ Jul-Sep) Housed in the Old Brewery Residences (university halls), next to the castle; only open during the university's summer holidays.

MID-RANGE

Howard Lodge (☎ 529842; pat90howardlodge@aol .com; 90 Warwick Rd; s/d/tr £25-30/36-50/45-75; P ⊠) Another redbrick townhouse along Warwick Rd, offering chintzy comfort, pastel-shaded rooms and some attractive period features, including Victorian fireplaces and original cornicing.

Langleigh Guest House (☎ 530440; www.lang leighhouse.co.uk; 6 Howard Pl; s/d £26/47.50; P ⊠)

The pick of the mid-range B&Bs around Warwick Rd, arranged over several floors and impeccably restored in Victorian style, with ornate furniture, mirrors, tiled fireplaces and tasteful prints.

TOP END

Number Thirty One (☎ 597080; www.number31 .freeservers.com; 31 Howard Pl; s/d from £60/85; P ⊠) Half upmarket B&B, half hotel, this award-winning townhouse offers three luxurious bedrooms decorated in a quirky style (Mediterranean tones, pastel blues or Oriental baroque). From the bubbling fish tank in the kitchen to the lavishly decorated dining room, this is one B&B that simply oozes class.

Crown & Mitre (☎ 525491; www.crownandmitre -hotel-carlisle.com; English St; s/tw £79-90/90-105; P ⊠ ☎) The oldest, grandest hotel in town, housed in a splendid redbrick Edwardian building on the main square. The highlight is the impressive lobby, backed by the original staircase and stained-glass windows, but the plush, modern rooms are very respectable too.

Eating

Alexandros (☎ 592227; 68 Warwick Rd; meze £3-6, mains £9-14; ❍ dinner Mon-Sat) A homely Greek restaurant, with yellow-orange walls and maverick staff. Top dishes include mixed meze, chicken kebabs and chargrilled swordfish.

Emperor's Palace (☎ 402976; Warwick Rd; mains from £8; ❍ dinner Tue-Sun) A top-notch Chinese restaurant; takeaway is available, but discerning diners choose to eat in the main dining room surrounded by gilt Buddhas and Chinese screens.

Casa Romana (☎ 591969; 44 Warwick Rd; mains £5-18; ❍ lunch & dinner Mon-Sat) This simple Italian restaurant offers pizzas, pastas, and traditional meat and chicken dishes.

David's (☎ 523578; 62 Warwick Rd; mains £10-18; ❍ lunch & dinner Tue-Sat) Refined, modern British cuisine served in a smart converted townhouse, with a menu ranging from sautéed venison to roast cod in Parma ham.

Lemon Lounge (☎ 546363; 18 Fisher St; set menu £18; ❍ lunch & dinner Tue-Sat) Tucked down an alleyway near the cathedral, this lively Mediterranean-flavoured bistro serves light meals and good coffee, either in the snug dining room or a walled courtyard.

Prior's Kitchen Restaurant (☎ 543251; lunches £4-6; ☻ 9.45am-3 or 4pm Mon-Sat) Carlisle's most unusual dining experience can be found beside the cathedral in the Fratry (monks' dining room), where you'll find light lunches and afternoon tea served in a vaulted cellar.

Drinking

Locals save their energy for the weekends, and the bars south of the centre and around the cathedral get crammed.

Café Solo (☎ 631600; 1 Botchergate) A modern coffee bar with the requisite leather sofas and contemporary décor, which also does good lunchtime *paninis* (£4 to £6).

Café Sol (☎ 522211; 31 Castle St; ☻ 9.30am-6pm Mon-Wed, 9.30am-11pm Thu, to midnight Fri & Sat) Near the cathedral, the Solo's sister venue is decorated with Warhol-style prints and opens late at weekends. Sandwiches and coffee are served by day, beer and cocktails by night.

Jackson's/Front Page (☎ 596868; 4-8 Fisher St) This dingy bar/club is a Carlisle institution, and runs nights featuring anything from drum'n'bass to blues and karaoke.

Brickyard (☎ 512220; 14 Fisher St) Right next door, this is the best venue in town for gigs and live music, housed in the former Memorial Hall.

Fats (☎ 511774; 48 Abbey St; ☻ 11am-11pm) A funky, open-plan bar and one of the city's top nightspots, boasting exposed stone walls, slate floors, plush sofas and a smooth urban ambience.

Concrete (☎ 527400; 10-14 Lowther St; ☻ 10pm-2am Tue-Sat) A cutting-edge cellar club with barrel-vaulted brick ceilings, a sleek steel bar and a vaguely Egyptian vibe.

Mood (☎ 520383; www.mood.uk.com; 70 Botchergate; ☻ 11am-2am Mon-Sat, noon-12.30am Sun) Carlisle's contribution to the designer-bar genre; is it so-named because of the lurid purple-and-orange decor, or its staff's demeanour? Who cares – it's open till 2am.

Howard Arms (☎ 598941; Lowther St) For more traditional drinking, this quiet local pub offers a choice of rooms in which to nurse a real ale or two.

Getting There & Away
BUS

Carlisle is one of Cumbria's main transport hubs. Direct buses run by National Express include London (£28.50, seven hours, three or four daily – other services travel via Preston and Birmingham), Glasgow (from £14.50, two hours, 10 daily), Manchester (£20.50, three hours, three to five daily) and Bristol (£50.50, nine hours, one direct overnight service).

Useful local buses include No 555/556 (the LakesLink; 3¾ hours, three daily), which passes through Keswick, Grasmere, Ambleside, Windermere and Kendal on its way to Carlisle from Lancaster; No 104 (40 minutes, 13 daily Monday to Saturday, nine on Sunday), which connects Carlisle with Penrith; and AD122 (the Hadrian's Wall bus; six daily late May to late September), which connects Hexham and Carlisle in summer.

TRAIN
Regular trains run from London Euston (£72.80, four hours, nine to 11 daily).

Carlisle is the terminus for the following five scenic railways (☎ 08457 484950 for timetable details and information on Day Ranger passes):

Cumbrian Coast Line Follows the coastline to Lancaster (£19, 3½ hours), with views over the Irish Sea.

Glasgow–Carlisle Line The main route to Glasgow passes through spectacular Scottish landscape – the ScotRail route is the most scenic (£27, 1½ hours).

Lakes Line Branches off the main north–south line at Oxenholme near Kendal for Windermere (£15.50, 70 minutes).

Settle-Carlisle Line Cuts southeast across the Yorkshire Dales (£13.40, 1½ hours).

Tyne Valley Line Follows Hadrian's Wall to Newcastle-upon-Tyne (£11.20, 1½ hours).

Getting Around
TAXIS
Call **Radio Taxis** (☎ 527575), **Citadel Station Taxis** (☎ 523971) or **County Cabs** (☎ 596789).

PENRITH
☎ 01768 / pop 14,480
Like many of the towns on the fringes of the Lakes, stout, rosy-bricked Penrith has retained its traditional character as a market town and shopping centre. Many of the shops have their original façades, and the streets are lined with craft stores, bakeries and traditional grocers, as well as countless places to buy country clothing and hiking equipment. There's a Tuesday market in the central square. Penrith makes a good base for exploring the Eden Valley, the eastern lakes, and the North Pennines.

Information

Library (☎ 242100; St Andrew's Churchyard; ☽ Mon-Sat)

Map Room (☎ 891900; 4 Middlegate; ☽ 9.30am-5pm Mon-Fri, 9am-5pm Sat) Good for local maps and books.

TIC (☎ 867466; pen.tic@eden.gov.uk; Middlegate; ☽ 9.30am-5pm Mon-Sat, 1-4.45pm Sun) Information about the Eden Valley and accommodation booking service.

Sights

Penrith was once Cumbria's capital, and indications of its former importance are scattered around town. The plundered ruins of **Penrith Castle** (☽ 7.30am-9pm Easter-Oct, 7.30am-4.30pm Oct-Easter) occupy a park opposite the station. The 14th-century castle was built by William Strickland (later Bishop of Carlisle and Archbishop of Canterbury) to resist Scottish raids, one of which razed the town in 1345. The castle was later expanded by Richard, Duke of Gloucester – better known as Richard III – but fell into disrepair in the 16th century.

The 18th-century **St Andrew's Church** was built from the same local rust-red sandstone (Penrith means 'red fell'). Legend maintains that several worn, rounded stones in the churchyard belong to an Arthurian giant's grave, but the pillars are actually the weathered remains of Celtic crosses, while the central stones marked the graves of 10th-century chieftains.

The Penrith Beacon, constructed in 1719 on Beacon Fell, was once used to warn of border raids, and still offers great views. It can be reached from a path starting at Beacon Edge Rd.

The **Penrith Museum** (☎ 867466; admission free), inside the TIC, has some small displays on the town's history.

Sleeping

The best B&Bs are along Portland Pl; less expensive places are found along Victoria Rd.

Glendale Guest House (☎ 862579; www.glendaleguesthouse.com; 4 Portland Pl; s/d £36/55; ✗) A friendly and accommodating B&B, offering pastel rooms and flowery bedspreads in a typically Victorian house on Portland Pl. The huge breakfast includes Cumberland sausage, muesli and fresh fruit salad.

George Hotel (☎ 862696; www.georgehotelpenrith.co.uk; Devonshire St; s/d £49-64/86-142) Penrith's oldest hotel, a former coaching inn built from local sandstone. The wood-panelled lobby and dining rooms are filled with comfortable armchairs and faded photos, and the comfy bedrooms share the same old-world atmosphere.

Beckfoot Country House (☎ 713241; www.beckfoot.co.uk; nr Helton; s/d £38/76-90; ☽ Mar-Dec; Ⓟ ✗) Five miles south of Penrith, near the small village of Helton, this cosy manor house is set in peaceful wooded gardens with views over the fells. Rooms are spacious and plainly furnished, and there's a paddock behind the house for the owner's Shetland ponies.

Other B&Bs include **Brooklands** (☎ 863395; www.brooklandsguesthouse.com; 2 Portland Pl; s/d £30-35/55; ✗) and **Blue Swallow** (☎ 866335; www.blueswallow.co.uk; 11 Victoria Rd; s/d £30/50-60; ✗), the best of the budget guesthouses on Victoria Rd.

Eating

Costas Tapas Bar & Restaurant (☎ 895550; 9 Queen St; tapas from £4.50; ☽ Tue-Sun) A lively, splendidly tacky Spanish-themed bar, with waiting staff in full flamenco gear and huge portions of tapas.

Ruhm Gallery & Café (☎ 867453; www.ruhmgallery.plus.com; 15 Victoria Rd; lunches £4-8; ☽ 9am-5pm Mon-Sat, 10am-4pm Sun) A light, relaxed place to sip your morning coffee; it also does good sandwiches and *paninis*, and houses a small gallery of local artwork.

Gianni's Pizzeria (☎ 891791; 11 Market Sq; mains £5-8; ☽ Mon-Sat) Tucked away just off Market Sq, this is one of several decent Italian restaurants in Penrith. The rustic dining room is usually packed at weekends; main dishes include chicken and seafood, as well as generous helpings of pizza and pasta.

Getting There & Away

BUS

The bus station is northeast of the centre, off Sandgate. Bus No 104 runs between Penrith and Carlisle (£4.50, 45 minutes, 16 daily Monday to Saturday, nine on Sunday).

Bus No X4/X5 connects Penrith to the Lakes and the Cumbrian coast hourly Monday to Saturday and six times on Sunday, calling at Keswick and Cockermouth before terminating at Workington.

TRAIN

Penrith has frequent connections to Carlisle (£5.90, 20 minutes, hourly) and Lancaster (£10.60, 50 to 60 minutes, hourly).

CUMBRIA & THE LAKES

WORTH THE TRIP

The third-largest prehistoric stone circle in England, **Long Meg and Her Daughters** is a remote arrangement of 59 stones, 6 miles northeast of Penrith. Local legend maintains that the circle was once a coven of witches, zapped into stone by a local wizard. The circle is said to be uncountable (if anyone manages twice the spell will be lifted) and a terrible fate awaits anyone who disturbs the stones. Just outside the circle stands Long Meg herself, a 12ft red sandstone pillar decorated with faint spiral traces – another local legend says that the stone would run with blood if it were ever damaged. You'll need your own transport to get there.

The circle is about 10km northeast of Penrith, along a minor road about ¾ mile north of Little Salkeld, just off the A686.

AROUND PENRITH
Rheged Discovery Centre

Housed in the largest grass-covered building in Europe, Rheged (☎ 01768-686000; www .rheged.com; 1 film or attraction adult/child £5.50/3.90; ☽ 10am-6pm) is cunningly disguised as a Lakeland hill, 2 miles west of Penrith.

Built on a former quarry and rubbish site, the centre contains an Imax cinema and the Helly Hansen National Mountaineering Exhibition. The cinema shows four films: *Rheged, Mysteries of Egypt, The Living Sea* and *Everest*, a rip-roaring history of man's struggle against the world's highest mountain. Least successful is *Rheged*, which explores some of the region's myths and mysteries – expect dodgy costumes and ropey reconstructions aplenty.

The mountaineering exhibition includes memorabilia, photographs, illustrations and some stunning film footage. Most poignant is the collection of artefacts belonging to George Mallory (the British mountaineer who died climbing Everest in 1924), discovered when his body was found near the summit in 1999.

The frequent No X4/X5 bus between Penrith and Workington stops at the centre.

ALSTON

☎ 01434 / elevation 290m

Alston is an isolated town high in the North Pennines. The town's cluster of 17th-century buildings, with its hilly cobblestone streets and alleyways, has been used as a backdrop to films including *Oliver Twist* and *Jane Eyre*. Established around the area's mining industry, which faded in the 19th century, it claims to be the highest market town in England, despite no longer having a market.

The TIC (☎ 382244; alston.tic@eden.gov.uk; Town Hall; ☽ 10am-5.30pm Mon-Sat & 10am-4pm Sun Apr-Oct, 11am-2pm Mon-Sat Nov-Mar) is just south of the town square.

Sleeping & Eating

Single rooms book up quickly in summer as the town gets packed with lone railway lovers.

Alston YHA Hostel (☎ 0870 770 5668; The Firs; dm £10.60; ☽ May-Aug, Fri-Tue Mar-May & Sep-Oct) This modern hostel is just south of the town centre, and is popular with walkers on the Pennine Way and cyclists on the C2C route.

Nenthall Country House Hotel (☎ 381584; www .nenthallcountryhousehotel.co.uk; d £35-70; P X) A fine country manor built as a rural retreat by a local mine-owner, 2 miles east of Alston. Set in private landscaped grounds, the hotel offers a variety of spacious rooms, some with luxurious period furniture and four-poster beds, and a grand fire-lit lounge for guests' use.

Angel Inn (☎ 381363; Front St; d from £30) This 17th-century pub opposite the TIC offers filling pub grub and basic rooms with country side views.

Blueberry's Teashop (☎ 381928; Market Pl; meals £4-6) A great place for tea, cakes and traditional lunches such as boozy pie (steak and red wine), with colourful touches such as hand-knitted tea cosies.

Getting There & Away

Bus No 888 runs between Newcastle and Keswick via Alston and Penrith once daily (June to September). Bus No 680 runs from Nenthead to Carlisle via Alston twice daily, Monday to Saturday.

AROUND ALSTON

The narrow-gauge **South Tynedale Railway** (☎ 381696, talking timetable ☎ 382828; www.strps.org.uk; adult return £5) puffs from Alston to Kirkhaugh, along a route that originally operated from 1852 to 1976. It's a picturesque, high-level journey, following the River Tyne northwards; there and back takes 60 minutes.

The big attraction of nearby **Nenthead Mines** (☎ 382037; www.npht.com; £4, with mine trip £6.50) is a trip down the underground tunnels. There are 40 miles of them, but the one-hour guided tour takes in just a small section. Sturdy shoes and something warm are required; it's 10°C year-round and you will undoubtedly get dirty. Claustrophobics can check out the 98.4m illuminated shaft, and there are exhibitions on water power, and zinc and lead mining.

KIRKBY LONSDALE
☎ 01524

At the southeastern corner of Cumbria, just outside the Yorkshire Dales National Park, the old-world town of Kirkby Lonsdale is centred on its oblong marketplace, dotted with cafés and bakeries. From St Mary's

Church you can check out Ruskin's View over the river Lune (he proclaimed it 'one of the loveliest scenes in England').

The **TIC** (☎ 271437; 24 Main St; ☻ 9.30am-5pm Mon-Sat & 10.30am-4.30pm Sun Apr-Oct, 10.30am-4.30pm Thu-Sun Nov-Mar) is on the main street.

The **Royal Hotel** (☎ 271217; Marketplace; s/d £35/50; Ⓟ ✗), a fine Georgian-fronted inn on the town square, dates back to the 17th century. Several of the character-filled, small-windowed rooms are rumoured to be haunted by ghostly guests.

The **Snooty Fox** (☎ 71308; www.landmark-inns .co.uk/snootyfox; Main St; s/d £37/58; Ⓟ ✗) is a much-loved pub filled with quirky furnishings (old cavalry uniforms, gladiator costumes and weird ornaments) and the most interesting bedrooms in town.

Kirkby Lonsdale is 17 miles from Settle and 15 miles from Windermere. The nearest railway connection is at Oxenholme (12 miles). Bus No 567 runs from Kendal several times daily.

Northeast England

CONTENTS

Passionate, independent and isolated – Northeast England feels separated from the rest of the country. The vast, sprawling countryside is often empty and almost always remote, from the wind-lashed wilderness of Northumberland National Park and the long white-sand stretches of the coast to the gentle, heather-carpeted Cheviots and dark, brooding beauty of the North Pennines. Other parts of the country have fallen to civilisation's firm grip, but this defiant corner just refuses to give in.

It's not as if humans haven't tried. They have left their mark here since prehistory, although it took the indomitable Romans to really have a go; their legacy is the magnificent Hadrian's Wall, which served as their empire's northern frontier for nearly 300 years. Later arrivals, the Normans, weren't to be outdone: they built more castles here than anywhere else in the country, and in Durham they erected a cathedral that ranks among the finest in the world. Against their splendid backdrops, these marvellous constructions serve only to reinforce an impression of a landscape that hasn't changed all that much since the whole region was part of the ancient kingdom of Northumbria.

If you look closely, however, you will see that the landscape is run through with dark, menacing scars: dotted throughout are the rusting hulks of an industry that drove this region for nearly 700 years. Mining is all but defunct now, yet the cities it built are still very much alive, none more so than Newcastle, the biggest in the region and one of the most dynamic urban centres in England.

NORTHEAST ENGLAND

HIGHLIGHTS

- Gettin' doon in toon with a bottle of dog – aka taking on **Newcastle's wild nightlife** (p703)
- Walking the Roman walk along magnificent **Hadrian's Wall** (p715)
- Castle-spotting along the blustery white-sand beaches of **Northumberland** (p722)
- Fending off bird-shit attacks on puffin-, gannet- and seal-covered **Farne Islands** (p722)
- Going Norman in **Durham** (p705), a spectacular World Heritage Site
- Hiking to the top of **The Cheviot** (p730) in Northumberland National Park

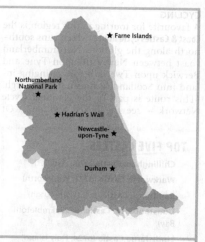

★ Farne Islands

Northumberland National Park ★

★ Hadrian's Wall

Newcastle-upon-Tyne ★

Durham ★

■ POPULATION: 2.5 MILLION   ■ AREA: 3320 SQ MILES

Orientation & Information

The Pennine Hills are the dominant geological feature, forming a north–south spine dividing the region from Cumbria and Lancashire in the west and providing the source of major rivers such as the Tees and the Tyne.

The major transport routes are east of this spine, from Durham northwards to Newcastle and Edinburgh. Newcastle is an important ferry port for Scandinavia. There's a northeast region website at www .thenortheast.com.

Activities

With the rugged moors of the Pennines and stunning seascape of the Northumberland coast, there's some good walking and cycling in this region. The scenery is beautiful in a wild and untouched way – quite different from the picture-postcard landscape of areas such as Devon or the Cotswolds. If you're out in the open be prepared for wind and rain at any time of year. But when the sun shines, you can't go wrong. More details on walking and cycling are given in the Outdoor Activities chapter, and suggestions for shorter routes are given throughout this chapter. Regional tourism websites all contain walking and cycling information, and Tourist Information Centres (TICs) all stock leaflets (free) plus maps and guides (usually £1 to £5) covering walking, cycling and other activities.

CYCLING

A favourite for touring in this region is the **Coast & Castles Cycle Route**, which runs south–north along the glorious Northumberland coast between Newcastle-upon-Tyne and Berwick-upon-Tweed, before swinging inland into Scotland to finish at Edinburgh. (This route is part of the National Cycle Network – see the boxed text p62.) Of course you can also do it north–south, or just do the northeast England section. The coast is exposed, though, so you should check the weather and try to time your ride so that the wind is behind you.

Another possibility is the 140-mile (230km) **Sea to Sea Cycle Route** (known as the C2C), which runs across northern England from Whitehaven or Workington on the Cumbria coast, through the northern part of the Lake District, and then over the wild hills of North Pennines to finish at Newcastle-upon-Tyne or Sunderland. This popular route is fast becoming a classic, and most people go west to east to take advantage of prevailing winds. You'll need five days to complete the whole route; the northeast England section, from Penrith (in Cumbria) to the east coast is a good three-day trip. If you wanted to cut the urban sections, Penrith to Consett is perfect in a weekend. The C2C is aimed at road bikes, but there are several optional off-road sections.

For dedicated off-road riding, good places to aim for in northeast England include Kielder Forest in Northumberland and Hamsterley Forest in County Durham, which both have a network of sylvan tracks and options for all abilities.

WALKING

The North Pennines are billed as 'England's last wilderness', and if you like to walk in quiet and fairly remote areas, these hills – along with the Cheviots farther north – are the best in England. Long routes through this area include the famous **Pennine Way**, which keeps mainly to the high ground as it crosses the region between the Yorkshire Dales and the Scottish border, but also goes through sections of river valley and some tedious patches of plantation. The whole route is over 250 miles (415km), but the 70-mile (117km) section between Bowes and Hadrian's Wall would be a fine four-day taster. If you prefer to go walking just for the day, good bases for circular walks include the towns of Alston (p690) and Middleton-in-Teesdale (p712).

Elsewhere in the area, the great Roman ruin of **Hadrian's Wall** is an ideal focus for walking. There's a huge range of easy loops taking in forts and other historical highlights. A long-distance route from end to end opened in 2003 and has already proved immensely popular, providing good options

TOP FIVE CASTLES

- **Chillingham Castle** (p730; Wooler)
- **Warkworth Castle** (p721; Warkworth)
- **Bamburgh Castle** (p723; Bamburgh)
- **Dunstanburgh Castle** (p722; Embleton Bay)
- **Lindisfarne Castle** (p724; Holy Island)

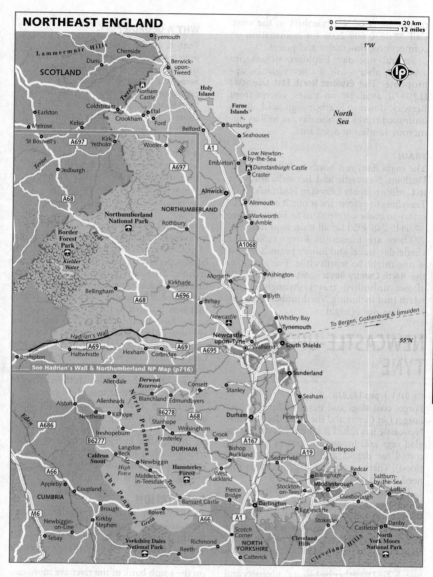

NORTHEAST ENGLAND

for anything from one to four days (see p716 for details).

The Northumberland coast has endless miles of open beaches, and little in the way of resort towns (the frequently misty weather has seen to that), so walkers can often enjoy this wild, windswept shore in virtual solitude. One of the finest walks is

between the villages of Craster and Bamburgh via Dunstanburgh, which includes two of the area's most spectacular castles.

Getting There & Around
BUS
Bus transport around the region can be difficult, particularly around the more

remote parts of Northumbria in the west. Call ☎ 0870 608 2608 for information on connections, timetables and prices.

Several one-day Explorer tickets are available; always ask if one might be appropriate. The **Explorer North East** (adult/child £5.75/4.75), available on buses, covers from Berwick down to Scarborough, and allows unlimited travel for one day, as well as numerous admission discounts.

TRAIN
The main lines run north to Edinburgh via Durham, Newcastle and Berwick, and west to Carlisle roughly following Hadrian's Wall. Travelling to or from the south, it may be necessary to make connections at Leeds. Phone ☎ 0845 748 4950 for all train inquiries.

There are numerous Rover tickets for single-day travel and longer periods, so ask if one might be worthwhile. For example, the **North Country Rover** (adult/child £61.50/30.75) allows unlimited travel throughout the north (not including Northumberland) any four days out of eight.

NEWCASTLE-UPON-TYNE

☎ 0191 / pop 189,870

Forget coal slags and never-ending slumps. Forget *Get Carter* and the bleak days of yore. Newcastle has tidied itself up, put on its best glad rags and invited the rest of the world round for drinks and some decent scran (food). There's a party going on and no-one need miss it.

There's something vaguely condescending about portraying Newcastle as a feet-on-the-ground kind of place that meets every difficulty with devil-may-care good humour and a knees-up good time. Problem is it's true, at least in part. Geordies (see the boxed text above right) are a fiercely independent bunch, tied together by history, adversity and that impenetrable dialect, the closest language to 1500-year-old Anglo-Saxon left in England. They are also proud, hard-working and indefatigably positive – perhaps their greatest quality considering how tough life has been.

Their city is a .eflection of all those characteristics. Raised and subsequently abandoned by coal and steel, Newcastle has matured into

WHY A GEORDIE?
Truth is, no one really knows for sure, not even the Geordies themselves. The most attractive explanation, at least here, is that the name was coined to disparage the townspeople who chose to side with the German Protestant George I against the 'Old Pretender', the Catholic James Stuart, during the Jacobite Rebellion of 1715. But a whole other school contends that the origins are a little less dramatic, and stem from Northumberland miners opting to use a lamp pioneered by George 'Geordie' Stephenson over one invented by Sir Humphrey Davy.

an elegant city of some grace and culture: a mammoth arts centre on the Tyne is but one of numerous excellent art galleries, while the latest superproject has seen world-renowned architect Sir Norman Foster leave his signature on a stunning new concert hall, the Sage Gateshead. The grand 19th-century streets that swoop down to the river from the city centre have been buffed and polished and are now as beautiful as any you'll see elsewhere in England, while down by the water the pace of development continues unabated under the shadows of Newcastle's recognisable features – the eclectic, cluttered array of the seven bridges that span the Tyne.

And then there's the nightlife, the alpha and omega of so many visits to the city. Geordies know how to party, and they do so with an irrepressible energy that borders on the irresponsible. Never mind the crazy amounts that people drink; how the hell do they survive the bitter cold wearing so little?

ORIENTATION
The River Tyne marks the boundary between Newcastle to the north and Gateshead to the south; it is also one of the focal points for visitors to the city. Frankly, there's very little to keep you in Gateshead – even the sights on the south bank of the river are more easily accessible by bridge from the northern side. North from the river is Newcastle's attractive Victorian centre, which the tourist authorities insist on calling Grainger Town, although the name elicits shrugs of uncertainty from locals. Jesmond is north of the city centre, and easily reached by bus or with the excellent Metro underground system.

Central Station (train) is to the south of the city centre. The coach station is on Gallowgate, while local and regional buses leave from Eldon Square and Haymarket bus stations.

Maps

The Ordnance Survey's Mini-Map (£1.50) is a handy foldaway pocket map of Newcastle, but not Gateshead. The **Newcastle Map Centre** (☎ 261 5622; www.newtraveller.com; 1st fl, 55 Grey St) supplies copious maps and guides.

INFORMATION
Bookshops

Blackwell's Bookshop (☎ 232 6421; 141 Percy St) A comprehensive range of titles.
Waterstone's (☎ 261 6140; 104 Grey St) There's another branch, also near Monument Metro, but this one is particularly finely housed.

Emergency

Police station (☎ 214 6555; cnr Pilgrim & Market Sts)

Internet Access

Internet Exchange (☎ 230 1280; 26-30 Market St) In the same gallery as the TIC, close to Monument Metro.

Laundry

Clayton Road Laundrette (☎ 281 5055; 4 Clayton Rd, Jesmond)

A NEWCASTLE TAXI RIDE   Fionn Davenport

While riding in a taxi, a foreign visitor was regaled by the driver on how fantastic Newcastle was. 'It's absolutely brilliant, gadgie, it's a canny toon; there's ne playce leik it. It's got the best nightlife in Europe, even better than Amsterdam, ya knaa what ah mean, leik?'

The visitor listened to the driver's enthusiastic plug of his home town and generally agreed, but mentioned that the previous evening (which was a Tuesday) was surprisingly quiet around town considering the mayhem of the weekend.

'That's reet gadgie,' replied the cabbie. 'Every night *except* Tuesday. On Tuesday nights toon is a proper shit-hole!'

Medical Services

Newcastle General Hospital (☎ 273 8811; Westgate Rd, off Queen Victoria St) A mile northwest of the city centre.

Money

Thomas Cook (☎ 219 8000; 6 Northumberland St) Has a bureau de change; it's just north of Monument.

Post

Main post office (35 Mosley St; ☉ 9am-5.30pm Mon-Fri, 9am-12.30pm Sat) In the city centre.

NEWCASTLE IN...

Two Days

Kick off your visit along the quayside, taking in the **Tyne bridges** (p699) and the remaining bits of 17th-century Newcastle, **Bessie Surtees' House** (p699), before crossing the Millennium Bridge and going to **Baltic** (p698). Wander back across and head toward the elegant Victorian centre, where you should pop into the **Laing Art Gallery** (p699) and the **Life Science Centre** (p699). Stop off in **Blake's Coffee House** (p702) for a pick-me-up. Work your way up to the **Trent House Soul Bar** (p703) and find that song you-love-but-haven't-heard-in-years on the incredible jukebox. And just keep going; everyone else is, so why shouldn't you?

The next day, if your head can take it, take the bus south through Gateshead to the **Angel of the North statue** (p705). Unfortunately, there's not much else going on here, so you'll have to head back into town. In the afternoon, take the Metro to Haymarket and explore the **museums** (p700) at Newcastle University.

Four Days

Follow the two-day itinerary and add a side-trip to **Bede's World** (p700) in the eastern suburb of Jarrow. In the afternoon, take a three-hour **sightseeing tour** (p701) along the Tyne. The next day, head for the Roman fort at **Segenundum** (p705), at the start of Hadrian's Wall. All the while, be sure to fuel your efforts; **Blackie Boy** (p703), a pub in the centre of town, is another great choice.

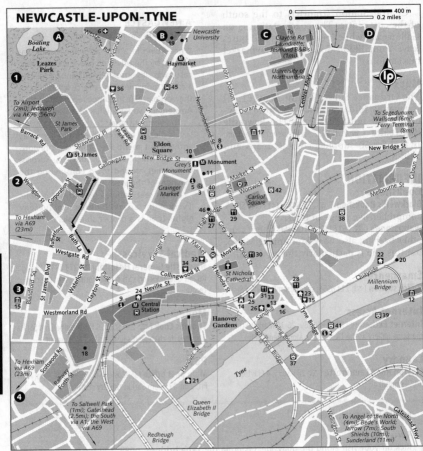

NEWCASTLE-UPON-TYNE

0 _____ 400 m
0 _____ 0.2 miles

Tourist Information

Gateshead Quays Visitor Centre (☎ 477 5380; St Mary's Church; ☽ 10am-4pm Sat & Sun) Information on Gateshead's attractions.

TIC (☎ 277 8000; www.newcastle.gov.uk; 132 Grainger St; ☽ 9.30am-5.30pm Mon-Wed, Fri & Sat, 9.30am-7.30pm Thu year round, plus 10am-4pm Sun Jun-Sep) Well stocked. There's also a convenient TIC at the **train station** (☎ 277 8000), and a desk at the **airport** (☎ 214 4422). All provide a free map, guide and accommodation list, and a **booking service** (☎ 277 8042).

SIGHTS
Tyne Quays

Newcastle's most recognisable attractions are the seven bridges that span the Tyne and some of the striking buildings that line it.

Along Quayside, on the river's northern side, is a handsome boardwalk that makes for a pleasant stroll during the day but really comes to life at night, when the bars, clubs and restaurants that line it are full to bursting. A really great way of experiencing the river and its sights is by cruise (see Tours, p701).

BALTIC – THE CENTRE FOR CONTEMPORARY ART

Once a huge, dirty, yellow grain store overlooking the Tyne, **Baltic** (☎ 478 1810; www.baltic mill.com; admission free; ☽ 10am-7pm Mon-Wed, Fri & Sat, 10am-10pm Thu, 10am-5pm Sun) is now a huge, dirty, yellow art gallery to rival London's Tate Modern. Unlike the Tate, there are no permanent exhibitions here, but the constantly rotating shows feature the work and installations of some of contemporary art's biggest show stoppers. The complex has artists-in-residence, a performance space, a cinema, a bar, a spectacular rooftop restaurant (you'll need to book) and a ground-floor restaurant with riverside tables. There's also a viewing box for a fine Tyne vista.

TYNE BRIDGES
The most famous view in Newcastle is the cluster of Tyne bridges, and the most famous of these is the **Tyne Bridge** (1925–28), built at about the same time as (and very reminiscent of) Australia's Sydney Harbour Bridge. The quaint little **Swing Bridge** pivots in the middle to let ships through. Nearby, **High Level Bridge**, designed by Robert Stephenson, was the world's first road and railway bridge (1849). The most recent addition is the multiple-award-winning **Millennium Bridge** (aka Blinking Bridge; 2002), which opens like an eyelid to let ships pass.

OTHER SIGHTS
The Tyne's northern bank was the hub of commercial Newcastle in the 16th century. On Sandhill is **Bessie Surtee's House** (EH; ☎ 269 1227; 41-44 Sandhill; admission free; 🕙 10am-4pm Mon-Fri), actually a combination of two 16th- and 17th-century merchant houses – all dark wood and sloping angles. Three rooms are open to the public. The daughter of a wealthy banker, feisty Bessie annoyed Daddy by falling in love with John Scott (1751–1838), a pauper. It all ended in smiles because John went on to become Lord Chancellor.

Just across the street is the rounded **Guildhall**, built in 1658.

City Centre
Newcastle's Victorian centre, a compact area bordered roughly by Grainger St to the west and Pilgrim St to the east, is supremely elegant and one of the most compelling examples of urban rejuvenation in England. At the heart of it is Grey St, lined with fine classical buildings and one of England's most handsome streets.

LIFE SCIENCE CENTRE
This excellent **science village** (☎ 243 8210; www.centre-for-life.co.uk; Scotswood Rd; admission £6.95; 🕙 10am-6pm Mon-Sat, 11am-6pm Sun), part of the sober-minded International Centre for Life (a complex of institutes devoted to the study of genetic science), is one of the more interesting attractions in town. Through a series of hands-on exhibits and the latest technology you (or your kids) can discover the incredible secrets of life. The highlight is the Crazy Motion Ride, a motion simulator that, among other things, lets you 'feel' what it's like to score a goal at St James' Park and bungee jump from the Tyne Bridge. There's lots of thought-provoking arcade-style games, and if the information sometimes gets lost on the way, never mind, kids will love it.

LAING ART GALLERY
The exceptional collection at the **Laing** (☎ 232 7734; www.twmuseums.org.uk; New Bridge St; admission free; 🕙 10am-5pm Mon-Sat, 2-5pm Sun) includes works by Kitaj, Frank Auerbach, Henry Moore and an important collection

---

THE VENERABLE BEDE

The fairly grim southeastern suburb of Jarrow is embedded in labour history for the 1936 Jarrow Crusade, when 200 men walked from here to London to protest against the appalling conditions brought about by unemployment.

But it is also famous as the home of the Venerable Bede, author of the *Ecclesiastical History of the English People* (see also p707). **Bede's World** (☎ 489 2106; www.bedesworld.co.uk; admission £4.50; ☻ 10am-5.30pm Mon-Sat, noon-5.30pm Sun Apr-Oct, noon-4.30pm Nov-Mar) comprises St Paul's Church, dating back to the 7th century, a museum, and many reconstructed medieval buildings. It's accessible via the Metro.

---

of paintings by John Martin (1789–1854), a Northumberland-born artist.

Outside the gallery is Thomas Heatherwick's famous **Blue Carpet** (2002) with shimmering blue tiles made from crushed glass and resin.

DISCOVERY MUSEUM

Newcastle's rich history is uncovered through a fascinating series of exhibits at this excellent **museum** (☎ 232 6789; www.twmuseums .org.uk; admission free; ☻ 10am-5pm Mon-Sat, 2-5pm Sun). The exhibits, spread across three floors of the former Co-Operative Wholesale Society building, surround the mightily impressive 30m-long *Turbinia*, the fastest ship in the world in 1897. The different sections are all worth a look; our favourites were the self-explanatory Story of the Tyne and the interactive Science Maze.

CASTLE GARTH KEEP

The 'New Castle' that gave its name to the city has been largely swallowed up by the railway station, leaving only the square Norman **keep** (adult/child £1.50/50p; ☻ 9.30am-5.30pm Apr-Sep, 9.30am-4.30pm Oct-Mar) as one of the few remaining fragments. It has a fine chevron-covered chapel and great views across the Tyne bridges from its rooftop.

University Museums

North of the city centre is Newcastle University, with an array of museums and galleries. Take the Metro to Haymarket.

The history of Hadrian's Wall and other things Roman is the subject of the **Museum of Antiquities** (☎ 222 7849; The Quadrangle; admission free; ☻ 10am-5pm Mon-Sat), on the main university courtyard. The small but well-stocked **Shefton Museum of Greek Art & Archaeology** (☎ 222 8996; www.ncl.ac.uk/shefton-museum; Armstrong Bldg; admission free; ☻ 10am-4pm Mon-Fri) has more ancient bric-

a-brac, while the well-known **Hatton Gallery** (☎ 222 6057; www.ncl.ac.uk/hatton; The Quadrangle; admission free; ☻ 10am-5.30pm Mon-Fri, 10am-4.30pm Sat) has a permanent collection of West African art, and houses interesting temporary displays.

Across Claremont Rd from the university grounds is the **Hancock Museum** (☎ 222 6765; www.twmuseums.org.uk; Barras Bridge; admission £2.50; ☻ 10am-5pm Mon-Sat, 2-5pm Sun), a traditional natural history museum with some remarkably large spiders, iguanas and creepy stuffed birds.

NEWCASTLE FOR CHILDREN

While Newcastle is generally friendly, this doesn't necessarily mean child-friendly. The city is not over-endowed with things for kids to do and places for them to be let loose in.

The two main exceptions are the **Life Science Centre** (p699) and the **Discovery Museum** (above left), which should entertain kids for the better part of a whole day.

The most popular park in town is **Leazes Park**, just north of St James Park, which has a rowing lake, but the nicest of all is **Saltwell Park** (☻ dawn-dusk), an elegant Victorian space behind Gateshead College and easily accessible by bus Nos 53 and 54 from the Gateshead Interchange. Pedestrians can get in through entrances on East Park Rd, West Rd, Saltwell Rd South, Saltwell View and Joicey Rd.

QUIRKY NEWCASTLE

Take in the David Lynch vibe at **Blackie Boy** (p703), where it's not all it appears to be. Pop your coins into the world's best jukebox at the **Trent House Soul Bar** (p703) for the stomping sound of Northern Soul (or a bit of rare ska, or whatever) and pretend that Britney Spears never released a record. Take a rowing boat onto the lake at **Leazes Park** – watch out for those fishing rods. Cross one of the **Tyne**

bridges (p698) on foot. Avoid the crumpled-up teenagers and pools of vomit on the **Tuxedo Royale** (p703) – a night on the Boat is a must for all comers to Newcastle's nightlife.

TOURS

The TIC has a wide range of hour-long **walking tours** (adult/child £3/2) running throughout the year, all departing from the main TIC. Some require advance booking; check with the TIC for details.

The best tours, however, are the three-hour sightseeing cruises run by **River Tyne Cruises** (☎ 296 6740/1; www.tyneleisureline.co.uk; adult/child £11/6; 2pm Sun May-early Sep) from Quayside pier (near Millennium Bridge, opposite Baltic).

SLEEPING

Party people and business folk make up most of Newcastle's overnight guests, which makes for very late nights or very early mornings. The latter will find a range of business hotels scattered through the city centre, while the former won't care that for the most part they're characterless comfort zones. The one factor, though, is price: you won't find a room in the centre for anything less than £60 to £70 – if you're looking for something cheaper you'll have to go north, to the handsome suburb of Jesmond, where the forces of gentrification and student power fight it out for territory. As the city is a major business destination, weekend arrivals will find that most places drop their prices for Friday and Saturday nights.

City Centre

With only one exception, the closer you get to the river, the more you'll pay.

MID-RANGE

Premier Lodge (☎ 0870 990 6530; www.premierlodge .com; Quayside; r from £28) With a superb location in the old Exchange Building, this budget chain is right in the heart of the action. If you're here for the party, you shouldn't care that your room has about as much flavour as day-old chewing gum – if all goes according to plan, you won't be spending much time here anyway!

TOP END

Malmaison (☎ 245 5000; www.malmaison.com; Quayside; d/ste Mon-Thu from £129/165, Fri-Sun from £99/140; P 💻) The affectedly stylish Malmaison touch has

been applied to this former warehouse with considerable success, although they could pull the brake on the quasi-poetic publicity. Big beds, sleek lighting and designer furniture flesh out the Rooms of Many Pillows.

Royal Station (☎ 232 0781; www.royalstationhotel .com; Neville St; s/d £75/90) The epitome of the elegant Victorian railway hotel, this 19th-century classic with its grand staircase and £25,000 chandelier was in the midst of a much-needed refurb throughout most of 2004, which aims to bring the fairly basic rooms up to contemporary scratch.

Waterside Hotel (☎ 230 0111; www.watersidehotel .com; 48-52 Sandhill, Quayside; s/d Mon-Thu from £64/78, Fri-Sun £50/68) The rooms are a tad small, but they're among the most elegant in town: lavish furnishings and heavy velvet drapes in a heritage-listed building. The location is excellent.

High-end business travellers have their choice of accommodation. Top of the heap are the **Copthorne** (☎ 222 0333; www.millennium hotels.com; The Close, Quayside; r Mon-Thu/Fri-Sun £155/129; P 💻 🏊), with its superb waterside location, and the **Vermont** (☎ 233 1010; www.vermont -hotel.com; Castle Garth; r £185; P 💻), whose style is mid-1930s Manhattan with new-millennium facilities.

Jesmond

The bulk of Newcastle's budget and mid-range accommodation is concentrated in the northeastern suburb of Jesmond, mainly on Osborne Rd. There are literally dozens of hotels and B&Bs along this street; below we recommend our favourites.

Catch the Metro to Jesmond or West Jesmond, or bus No 80 from near Central Station, or No 30, 30B, 31B or 36 from Westgate Rd.

BUDGET

Newcastle YHA Hostel (☎ 0870 770 5972; www.yha .org.uk; 107 Jesmond Rd; dm £11.80; ✆ daily Feb-Nov, Fri-Sun Dec & Jan) A nice, rambling place with small dorms that are generally full, so book in advance. It's close to the Jesmond Metro stop.

MID-RANGE

Adelphi Hotel (☎ 281 3109; 63 Fern Ave; s/d £25/50) Just off Osborne Rd is this attractive hotel with nice floral rooms that are clean and very neat – a rare thing around here for this price range.

Gresham Hotel (☎ 281 6325; www.gresham-hotel .com; 92 Osborne Rd; s/d from £45/68) Plenty of colours light up the rooms at this lovely hotel attached to the trendy Bar Bacca; it's extremely popular with weekend visitors who swear by the attentive-but-informal service.

Whites Hotel (☎ 281 5126; www.whiteshotel.com; 38-42 Osborne Rd; s/d £39/69) First impressions don't promise a great deal – the public areas are a bit tatty – but don't let that put you off; the bedrooms at this fine hotel are all uniformly modern and the service is first rate.

TOP END

New Northumbria Hotel (☎ 281 4961; www.new northumbria.co.uk; 61-69 Osborne Rd; s/d Mon-Thu from £75/85, Fri-Sun £55/80; ℗ ☐) Jesmond's top spot is a newish boutique hotel with all the trimmings, including huge rooms with designer furniture, big beds and fancy showers with those oversized heads that deliver water like a sandblaster.

EATING

Like the rest of the city, the dining scene is on the up. Although town abounds with crappy fast-food outlets and dodgy Chinese and Indian restaurants, a growing number of truly excellent restaurants serves a range of cuisines from pretty much everywhere. It's a far cry from pease pudding – a traditional Geordie dish made from peas and pickled pork. Many restaurants offer cut-rate early-bird specials and lunch deals.

City Centre

BUDGET

Blake's Coffee House (☎ 261 5463; 53 Grey St; breakfast £2-2.50, sandwiches £2; ✆ 9am-6pm) There is nowhere better than this high-ceilinged café for a Sunday-morning cure on any day of the week. It's friendly, relaxed and serves up the biggest selection of coffees in town, from the gentle push of a Colombian blend to the toxic shove of Old Brown Java. We love it.

MID-RANGE

Blackfriars Café (☎ 261 5945; Friar St; mains £9-13; ✆ lunch & dinner Tue-Sat, lunch only Sun) England's oldest purpose-built dining hall was the 12th-century refectory of the Dominican 'Black Friars', now a superb restaurant with an international menu ranging from Welsh rarebit to Thai beef. Thankfully, not one stone of this marvellous place has been changed.

Paradiso Café Bar (☎ 221 1240; 1 Market Lane; mains £7-11; ✆ lunch & dinner Mon-Sat, to 7pm Sun) Hidden away in a small alley off Pilgrim St is one of the city's most popular spots. Good food, a mellow atmosphere and a fabulous little balcony for alfresco action keeps this place full almost all the time.

Saque (☎ 230 2229; 46 Dean St; mains £8-10, early bird dinner 5.30-7pm £8.50; ✆ lunch & dinner) Here's something you don't see every day: an Indian restaurant – sorry, brasserie – that has wholeheartedly embraced modern design concepts (European minimalism) but still serves a traditional menu of subcontinental classics. Now if they could only knock off the rubbish muzak…

TOP END

Café 21 (☎ 222 0755; 19-21 Queen St; mains £13-17; ✆ lunch & dinner Mon-Sat) Simple but hardly plain, this elegant restaurant, all white tablecloths and smart seating, offers new interpretations of England's culinary backbone: pork and cabbage, liver and onions and a sensational Angus beef and chips.

Treacle Moon (☎ 232 5537; 5-7 The Side; mains £15-22; ✆ lunch & dinner) A truly international menu – how about roast rump of lamb or Malaysian curry? – in a beautifully contemporary setting: lots of deep purples, wood panels and plenty of glass.

Jesmond

There are plenty of dining options in Jesmond, but only one standout.

Pizzeria Francesca (☎ 281 6586; 134 Manor House Rd, Jesmond; mains £4-11.30) This is how all Italian restaurants should be: chaotic, noisy, friendly, packed cheek-to-jowl and absolutely worth making the effort for. Excitable, happy waiters and huge portions of pizza and pasta keep them queuing at the door – get in line and wait because you can't book in advance.

DRINKING

There are few places in England that pursue the art of the bevvie with the same untrammelled fervour as Newcastle. The brash and brazen tend to make for the bars around Bigg Market in short sleeves and short skirts, no matter what the weather is like. The slightly more sophisticated punters gravitate for the cooler bars along Quayside and Mosley St, while the traditional ale merchants have a handful of spit 'n' sawdust pubs to choose from.

We daren't even begin to list the pubs and bars in town, but here's a handful to start with. Get a bottle of dog and get doon.

Pubs

Blackie Boy (11 Groat Market) At first glance, this darkened old boozer looks like any old traditional pub. Look closer. The overly red lighting. The single bookcase. The large leather armchair that is rarely occupied. The signage on the toilets: 'Dick' and 'Fanny'. This place could have featured in *Twin Peaks,* which is why it's so damn popular with everyone.

Crown Posada (31 The Side) An unspoilt, real-ale pub that is a favourite with the more seasoned drinker.

Bars

Revolution (☎ 261 5774; Collingwood Chambers) This spectacularly successful chain has an outrageously lavish address in Newcastle, complete with marble-pillared interior and a suitably trendy crowd.

Thirty 3i8ht (☎ 261 6463; 38 Lombard St; mains £6-9) A stunning bar featuring big egg-capsule seating and a room dotted with cigarlike tables dominated by a plasma screen. Suitably refined food is served and there are regular DJs.

ENTERTAINMENT

Are you up for it? You'd better be, because Newcastle's nightlife doesn't mess about. There is nightlife beyond the club scene –

SOMETHING SPECIAL

Trent House Soul Bar (☎ 261 2154; 1-2 Leazes Lane) The wall has a simple message: 'Drink Beer. Be Sincere.' This simply unique place is the best bar in town because it is all about an ethos rather than a look. Totally relaxed and utterly devoid of pretentiousness, it is an old-school boozer that out-cools every other bar because it isn't trying to. And because it has the best jukebox in all of England – you could spend years listening to the extraordinary collection of songs it contains. It is run by the same folks behind the superb **World Headquarters** (see p704).

---

you'll just have to wade through a sea of staggering, glassy-eyed clubbers to get to it. For current listings pick up the monthly *North Guide* (£1.60) with good regional information, and the *Crack* (free) at the TIC or bookshops. Club admissions range from £3 to £12.

Live Music

Gateshead's once-forlorn riverside today boasts the Norman Foster–designed glass-and-chrome curves of the **Sage Gateshead** (☎ 443 4666; www.thesagegateshead.org; Gateshead Quays), which looks like a gigantic bottle lying on its side. When it's finished (sometime toward the end of 2004 or early 2005) it will be the home of the Northern Sinfonia as well as the main northeastern showcase for all other kinds of music, from popular to folk.

Nightclubs

Baja Beach Club (☎ 477 6205; Hillgate Quay) The cheesiest of all cheesy nightclubs, 'Badgers' (as its known here) has palm trees, surfing stuff, barmaids in bikinis and Top-40 slamming tunes for an over-enthusiastic crowd of hormonal, drunken revellers who will inevitably regret that snog-against-the-pillar but right now couldn't care less.

Foundation (☎ 261 8985; 57-59 Melbourne St) Warehouse-style club with a massive sound system, fantastic lighting rig and regular guest slots for heavyweight DJs from all over. If you want a night of hardcore clubbing, this is the place for you.

Tuxedo Royale (☎ 477 8899; Hillgate Quay) A rite of passage for all Geordies, 'the Boat' is like dancing on the cross-Channel ferry. It's cheesy, sloppy and full of drunken teenagers holding down vomit while spinning on the revolving dance floor. Sounds crap, but still packed.

World Heaquarters (☎ 261 7007; www.trent house.com; Curtis Mayfield House, Carliol Sq) Dedicated to the genius of black music in all its guises – funk, rare groove, dance-floor jazz, northern soul, genuine R&B, lush disco, proper house and reggae – this fabulous club is strictly for true believers, and judging from the numbers, there are thousands of them.

Sport

Newcastle United Football Club (☎ 201 8400; official www.nufc.co.uk, unofficial www.nufc.com; St James' Park, Strawberry Pl) is more than just a football team: it is the collective expression of Geordie hope and pride as well as the release for decades of economic, social and sporting frustration. Its fabulous ground, **St James' Park** (box office ☎ 261 1571) is always packed. Match tickets go on public sale about two weeks before a game or you can try the stadium on the day, but there's no chance for big matches, such as those against arch-rivals Sunderland.

Theatre

Theatre Royal (☎ 232 2061; www.theatre-royal-new castle.co.uk; 100 Grey St) The winter home of the Royal Shakespeare Company is full of Victorian splendour and has an excellent programme of drama.

GETTING THERE & AWAY
Air

Newcastle International Airport (☎ 286 0966; www.newcastleairport.com) is 7 miles north of the city off the A696. It has direct services to Aberdeen, London, Cardiff, Dublin, Belfast, Oslo, Amsterdam, Paris, Prague, Brussels and a number of destinations in Spain.

Boat

Norway's **Fjord Line** (☎ 296 1313; www.fjordline .co.uk) operates ferries between Newcastle, Stavanger and Bergen. **DFDS Seaways** (☎ 0870 533 3000; www.dfdsseaways.co.uk) operates ferries to Newcastle from Kristiansand in Norway, the Swedish port of Gothenburg and the Dutch port of Ijmuiden, near Amsterdam. For online ferry bookings, check out www .newcastleferry.co.uk.

Bus

National Express buses arrive and depart from the Gallowgate coach station. Destinations include Edinburgh (£14, 2¾ hours, four daily), London (£25, seven hours, six daily) and York (£11.25, 2½ hours, five daily). For Berwick-upon-Tweed (£4.50, two hours, five daily) take bus Nos 505, 515 and 525 from Haymarket bus station.

Local and regional buses leave from Haymarket or Eldon Square bus stations. For local buses around the northeast, don't forget the excellent-value Explorer North East ticket, valid on most services for £5.50.

Train

Newcastle is on the main rail line between London and Edinburgh. Services go to Alnmouth (for connections to Alnwick; £5.80, 20 minutes, four daily), Berwick (£11.80, 45 minutes, every two hours), Edinburgh (£35.50, 1½ hours, half-hourly), London King's Cross (£88, three hours, half-hourly) and York (£17, 45 minutes, every 20 minutes). There's also the scenic Tyne Valley Line west to Carlisle. See p717 for details.

GETTING AROUND
To/From the Airport & Ferry Terminal

The airport is linked to town by the **Metro** (£2.20, 20 min, every 15 min).

Bus No 327 (£3.20) links the ferry (at Tyne Commission Quay), Central Station and Jesmond Rd. It leaves the train station 2½ hours and 1¼ hours before each sailing.

There's a taxi rank at the terminal; it costs £14 to the city centre.

Car

Driving around Newcastle isn't fun thanks to the web of roads, bridges and one-way systems, but there are plenty of car parks.

Public Transport

There's a large bus network but the best means of getting around is the excellent underground Metro, with fares from 55p. There are also several saver passes. The TIC can supply you with route plans for the bus and Metro networks.

The **DaySaver** (£4, £3.20 after 9am) gives unlimited Metro travel for one day, and the **DayRover** (adult/child £4.20/2.10) gives unlimited travel on all modes of transport in the Tyne & Wear county for one day.

Taxi

On weekend nights taxis can be rare; try **Noda Taxis** (☎ 222 1888), which has a kiosk outside the entrance to Central Station.

AROUND NEWCASTLE

ANGEL OF THE NORTH

The world's most frequently viewed work of art is this extraordinary 200-tonne, rust-coloured human frame with wings (aka the Gateshead Flasher) towering over the A1 (M) about 5 miles south of Newcastle – if you're driving, you just can't miss it. Antony Gormley's most successful work is the country's largest sculpture at 20m high and with a wingspan wider than a Boeing 767. Bus Nos 723 and 724 from Eldon Square, or Nos 21, 21A and 21B from Pilgrim St, will take you there.

SEGEDUNUM

The last strong post of Hadrian's Wall was the fort of **Segedunum** (☎ 295 5757; www.tw museums.org.uk; admission £3.50; ☺ 10am-5pm Apr-Oct, 10am-3.30pm Nov-Mar) 4 miles east of Newcastle at Wallsend. Beneath the 35m tower (which you can climb for some terrific views) is an absorbing site that includes a reconstructed Roman bathhouse (with steaming pools and frescoes) and a fascinating museum that gives visitors a well-rounded picture of life during Roman times.

Take the Metro to Wallsend.

COUNTY DURHAM

Picturesque, peaceful villages and unspoilt market towns dot the lonely, rabbit-inhabited North Pennines and the gentle ochre hills of Teesdale. At the heart of it all is County Durham's simply exquisite capital, one of England's most visited towns and an absolute must on your northern itinerary.

Ironically, this pastoral image, so resonant of its rich medieval history, has only come back to life in recent years; for most of the last three centuries the county was given over almost entirely to the mining of coal and the countryside is punctuated with the relics of that once all-important industry, now slowly being reclaimed by nature. A brutal and dangerous business,

coal mining was the lifeblood of entire communities and its sudden end in 1984 by stroke of a Conservative pen has left some purposeless towns and an evocatively scarred landscape.

Durham has had a turbulent history, though it pales in comparison with its troublesome northern neighbour. To keep the Scots and local Saxon tribes quiet, William the Conqueror created the title of prince bishop in 1081 and gave them vice-regal power over an area known as the Palatinate of Durham, which became almost a separate country. It raised its own armies, collected taxes and administered a separate legal system that – incredibly – wasn't fully incorporated into the greater English structure until 1971.

Getting Around

The Explorer North East ticket (see p704) is valid on many services in the county.

DURHAM

☎ 0191 / pop 42,940

When you get off the train in Durham, keep your camera handy. Crammed onto a hilly peninsula in a bend of the River Wear is the enormous castle and, just behind it, England's most beautiful Romanesque cathedral, a masterpiece of Norman architecture that simply can't fail to impress. Surrounding it is a cobweb of cobbled streets that are usually full of upper-crust students, as Durham is also a posh university town. The university may not have the wizened prestige of Oxbridge – it was only founded in 1832 – but its terrific academic reputation and competitive rowing team make the disappointment of not getting into Oxford or Cambridge that bit easier to bear.

Once you've visited the cathedral, there's little else to do save walk the cobbled streets and find new spots from which to view Durham's main attraction. You can opt to visit as a day trip from Newcastle, which is recommended unless you plan to do some in-depth exploration of the surrounding county, in which case you could do far worse than base yourself here.

Orientation

Market Place, the TIC, castle and cathedral are all on the peninsula surrounded by the River Wear. The train and bus stations are

NORTHEAST ENGLAND

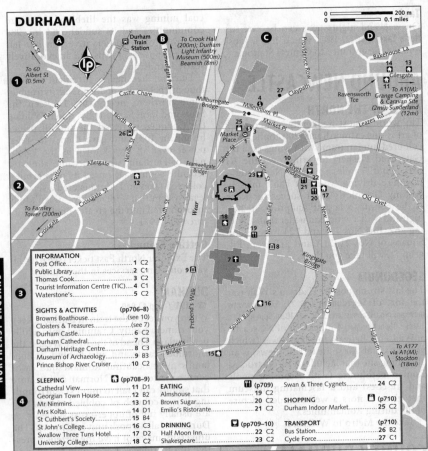

DURHAM

to the west on the other side of the river. Using the cathedral as your landmark, you can't really go wrong. The main sites are within easy walking distance of each other.

Information

Post office (Silver St; 9am-5.30pm Mon-Sat).

Public library (Millenium Pl; 9.30am-5pm Mon-Sat)
The only place in town to check email.

Thomas Cook (382 6600; 24-25 Market Pl)
Near the TIC.

TIC (384 3720; www.durhamtourism.co.uk; 2 Millennium Pl; 9.30am-5.30pm Mon-Sat, 10am-4pm Sun)
In the Gala complex, which includes a theatre and cinema.

Waterstone's (383 1488; 69 Saddler St) A good selection of books.

Sights
DURHAM CATHEDRAL

Durham's most famous building – and the main reason for visiting unless someone you know is at university here – has earned superlative praise for so long that to add more would be redundant; how can you do better than the 19th-century novelist Nathaniel Hawthorne, who wrote fawningly: 'I never saw so lovely a magnificent a scene, nor (being content with this) do I care to see better.' Let's not go nuts here. No building is *that* beautiful, but the definitive structure of the Anglo-Norman Romanesque style is still pretty amazing. We would definitely put it in our top church in England list – as do many others including Unesco, who declared it a World Heritage Site in 1986.

The **cathedral** (☎ 386 4266; www.durhamcath edral.co.uk; donation requested; ☻ 9.30am-8pm daily mid-Jun–Sep, 9.30am-6.15pm Mon-Sat & 12.30-5pm Sun Oct–mid-Jun; private prayer only 7.30am-9.30am Mon-Sat, 7.45am-12.30pm Sun year-round) is enormous and has a pretty fortified look; this is due to the fact that although it may have been built to pay tribute to God and to house the holy bones of St Cuthbert, it also needed to withstand any potential attack by the pesky Scots and Northumberland tribes who weren't too thrilled by the arrival of the Normans a few years before. Times have changed, but the cathedral remains an overwhelming presence, and modern-day visitors will hardly fail to be impressed by its visual impact.

The interior is genuinely spectacular. The superb nave is dominated by massive, powerful piers – every second one round, with an equal height and circumference of 6.6m, and carved in geometric designs. Durham was the first European cathedral to be roofed with stone-ribbed vaulting, which upheld the heavy stone roof and made it possible to build pointed transverse arches – the first in England, and a great architectural achievement. The central tower dates from 1262, but was damaged in a fire caused by lightning in 1429, and was unsatisfactorily patched up until it was rebuilt entirely in 1470. The western towers were added in 1217–26.

Built in 1175 and renovated 300 years later, the **Galilee Chapel** is one of the most beautiful parts. The northern side's **paintings** are rare surviving examples of 12th-century wall-painting and are thought to feature St Cuthbert and St Oswald. The chapel also contains the **Venerable Bede's tomb**. Bede was an 8th-century Northumbrian monk, a great historian and polymath whose work *The Ecclesiastical History of the English People* is still the prime source of information on the development of early Christian Britain. Among other things, he introduced the numbering of years from the birth of Jesus. He was first buried at Jarrow (p700), but in 1022 a miscreant monk stole his remains and brought them here.

The **Bishop's Throne**, built over the tomb of Bishop Thomas Hatfield, dates from the mid-14th century. Hatfield's effigy is the only one to have survived another turbulent time: the Reformation. The **high altar** is separated from **St Cuthbert's tomb** by the beautiful stone **Neville Screen**, made around 1372–80. Until the Reformation the screen included 107 statues of saints.

The cathedral has worthwhile **guided tours** (adult/child £3.50/free; call for times). Evensong is at 5.15pm from Tuesday to Saturday (Evening Prayer on Monday) and at 3.30pm on Sunday.

The **tower** (admission £2.50; ☻ 10am-4pm Mon-Sat Mar-Nov, 10am-3pm Dec-Feb) has 325 steps at the top of which is a splendid view.

Cloisters & Treasures

The monastic buildings are centred on the cloisters, which were heavily rebuilt in 1828. The west door to the cloisters is famous for its 12th-century ironwork. On the western side is a **monastic dormitory** (adult/child 80p/20p; ☻ 10am-3.30pm Mon-Sat, plus 12.30-3.15pm Sun Apr-Sep), now a library of 30,000 books and displaying Anglo-Saxon carved stones, with a vaulted undercroft that houses the Treasures and restaurant. A new addition is an **audiovisual display** (admission £1; ☻ 10am-3pm Mon-Sat Apr-Nov) on the building of the cathedral and the life of St Cuthbert.

The **treasures** (admission £2.50; ☻ 10am-4.30pm Mon-Sat, 2-4.30pm Sun) refer to the relics of St Cuthbert, but besides his cross and coffin, there's very little here related to the saint. The collection is made up mostly of religious paraphernalia from later centuries.

DURHAM CASTLE

Built as a standard motte-and-bailey fort in 1072, **Durham Castle** (☎ 374 3800; admission £3.50; ☻ tours only, on the hour 10am-12.30pm & 2-4pm Jun-Oct, 2-4pm Mon, Wed, Sat & Sun Nov-May) was the prince bishops' home until 1837, when it became the first college of the new university. It remains a university hall, and you can stay here (see p709).

The castle has been much altered over the centuries, as each successive prince bishop sought to put his particular imprimatur on the place, but heavy restoration and reconstruction were necessary anyway as the castle is built of soft stone on soft ground. Highlights of the 45-minute tour include the groaning 17th-century Black Staircase, the 16th-century chapel and the beautifully preserved Norman chapel (1080).

OTHER SIGHTS

Near the cathedral, in what was the St Mary le Bow Church, is the **Durham Heritage Centre** (☎ 386 8719; St Mary le Bow, North Bailey; admission £1.20; ⏰ 11am-4.30pm daily Jul-Sep, 2pm-4.30pm daily Jun, 11am-4.30pm Sat & Sun Apr, May & Oct), with a pretty crowded collection of displays on Durham's history from the Middle Ages to mining. It's all suitably grim, especially the reconstructed prison cells.

Durham and environs has other museums that may be of interest, including the small **Museum of Archaeology** (☎ 334 1823; Old Fulling Mill, The Banks; admission £1; ⏰ 11am-4pm daily Apr-Oct, 11.30am-3.30pm Fri-Mon Nov-Mar), located in a converted riverside mill building; and the **Oriental Museum** (☎ 334 5694; Elvet Hill; admission £1.50; ⏰ 10am-5pm Mon-Fri, noon-5pm Sat & Sun), 3 miles south of the city centre in the university campus. It has a good collection that ranges from fine Egyptian artefacts to a monster of a Chinese bed. Take bus No 5 or 6.

Crook Hall (☎ 384 8028; www.crookhallgardens .co.uk; Sidegate; adult/child £3.80/3; ⏰ 1-5pm Fri-Mon Easter, Sun May & Sep, Sun-Fri Jun-Aug) is a medieval hall with 1.6 hectares of charming small gardens, about half a mile north of the city centre.

Finally, if you really can't get enough of war and the uniforms people wear to fight them, you won't want to miss the **Durham Light Infantry (DLI) Museum** (☎ 384 2214; Aykley Heads; admission £2.50; ⏰ 10am-4pm), half a mile northwest of town. The history of Durham's County Regiment and its part in various wars from 1758 to 1968 is brought to life through anecdotes and poignant artefacts; there's a small art gallery with changing exhibitions.

Activities
BOATING

The **Prince Bishop River Cruiser** (☎ 386 9525; Elvet Bridge; adult £4; 2pm & 3pm Jun-Sep) offers one-hour cruises.

You can hire a rowing boat from **Browns Boathouse** (☎ 386 3779; per hr per person £3) below Elvet Bridge.

WALKS

There are superb views back to the cathedral and castle from the riverbanks; walk around the bend between Elvet and Framwellgate Bridges, or hire a boat at Elvet Bridge.

THE MINERS MARCH

In a tradition that dates to the end of the 19th century, the second weekend in July belongs to (now former) miners, who march from Market Pl to just past the Royal County Hotel on Old Elvet, where they are saluted by a dignitary of the British labour movement; the greatest cheer is usually reserved for Arthur Scargill, former head of the National Union of Mineworkers and the most vocal opponent of the Thatcher government that forced the closure of the pits. There's an inevitable nostalgia about the march these days, but in typical northern fashion everyone still manages to have a great time.

Guided walks (adult/child £3/free; 2pm Wed, Sat & Sun May-Sep; 1½ hrs) leave from Millennium Place – contact the TIC for details. **Ghost walks** (☎ 386 1500; adult/child £3/1; ⏰ 6.30pm Mon Jun-Sep, 8.30pm Jul & Aug; 1½ hrs) also drift around town.

Sleeping

The ace in the deck for Durham's hostellers is a cathedral view. Considering that the cathedral is the dominant building in town and visible from most everywhere, it's quality, not quantity, that is the real clincher. The TIC makes local bookings free of charge, which is a good thing considering that Durham is always busy with visitors: graduation week in late June results in accommodation gridlock.

Cathedral View (☎ 386 9566; www.cathedralview .com; 212 Gilesgate; s/d £50/70) This plain-fronted Georgian house has no sign, but inside it does exactly what it says on the tin. Six large rooms decorated with lots of cushions and coordinated bed linen and window dressings make up the numbers, but it's the three at the back that are worth the fuss: the views of the cathedral are superb. A small breakfast terrace with the same splendid vista is an added touch of real class.

Farnley Tower (☎ 375 0011; fax 383 9694; The Avenue; s/d from £50/68; P ✗) A beautiful Victorian stone building that looks more like a small manor house than a family-run B&B, it has 12 large, thoroughly modern rooms, some with stunning views of the cathedral and castle. The service is impeccable.

Georgian Town House (☎/fax 386 8070; 10-11 Crossgate; s/d from £55/70) A listed building smack in the middle of town, this B&B has large, airy rooms decorated in the true spirit of Laura Ashley: elaborate stencilling, plenty of pillows and fancy window dressings. It's close to the cathedral, so the rooms facing it have great views. There is also a small garden with flowers and a rockery.

60 Albert St (☎ 386 0608; www.sixtyalbertstreet .co.uk; s/d from £45/70; **P**) This tiny place has only three rooms – each stylishly restored with painted, cast-iron beds – which makes for truly attentive, individual service. The breakfast room is a Victorian showcase, with original antiques, polished wood floors and a beautiful fireplace.

Swallow Three Tuns Hotel (☎ 386 4326; www .swallowhotels.com; New Elvet; s/d from £95/100) A converted 16th-century coaching inn, the Three Tuns has plenty of 'olde worlde' feel – in the low-hanging ceilings, creaking passageways and heavy wooden beams throughout – until you get to the bedrooms, which are comfortable, modern and, well, a little bland. The rooms in the older section are larger than those in the new wing.

A couple of small, similarly priced B&Bs on Gilesgate may not offer much in the way of décor, size or cathedral view, but are worth a try if you're stuck:

Mrs Koltai (☎ 386 2026; 10 Gilesgate; s/d £20/38)

Mr Nimmins (☎ 384 6485; www.nimmins.co.uk; 14 Gilesgate; s/d £20/40)

Eating

Cheap eats aren't a problem in Durham thanks to the students, but quality is a little thin on the ground. Some pubs do good bar food; see Drinking, above right.

Almshouse (☎ 386 1054; Palace Green; dishes £3-7; ☽ 9am-5pm) Imaginative and satisfying snacks (how about spicy beef with red bean casserole and rice?) served in a genuine 17th-century house right on Palace Green. It's a shame about the interior, which has been restored to look like any old museum café.

Brown Sugar (☎ 454 2242; New Elvet; dishes £5-7; ☽ 7.30am-11pm Mon-Sat, 9am-10.30pm Sun) This trendy coffee shop-cum-bar is a favourite with university students, who fold into the over-size leather couches, nibble on a ciabatta sandwich (no ordinary bread here, mate) and talk about how much study they should be doing. A perfect hang-out.

Emilio's Ristorante (☎ 384 0096; 96 Elvet Bridge; pizza or pasta from £6.95; ☽ lunch & dinner Mon-Sat, dinner only Sun) Durham's top spot for pizza, pasta and other Italian staples has a wonderful location overlooking the Wear. Try the *malfatti al forno*, a kind of oven-baked ravioli filled with ricotta cheese and spinach.

Drinking

Durham may be a big student town, but most of them seem to take the whole study thing really seriously, because the nightlife here isn't as boisterous as you might expect from a university town. There is, however, a fistful of lovely old bars. The TIC has a bi-monthly *What's On* guide.

Half Moon Inn (New Elvet) Sports fans love this old-style bar for its devotion to the mixed pleasures of Sky Sports; we like it for its wonderful collection of whiskies and ales. There's a summer beer garden if you want to avoid the whoops and hollers of the armchair jocks.

Shakespeare (63 Saddler St) As authentic a traditional bar as you're likely to find in these parts, this is the perfect local's boozer, complete with nicotine-stained walls, cosy

---

UNIVERSITY ACCOMMODATION

Several colleges rent their rooms during the holidays (Easter and July to September). The rooms are generally modern and comfortable like most contemporary student halls. Phone ☎ 374 7360 or click on www.dur.ac.uk/conference_tourism/colleges.htm for more information.

St Cuthbert's Society (☎ 374 3364; 12 South Bailey; s/d £21/40) A few doors down from St John's, with similar student-style rooms.

St John's College (☎ 334 3877; 3 South Bailey; s/d £22/44) This college is right next to the cathedral; none of the rooms are en suite.

University College (☎ 374 3863; s/d with bathroom £35/64, s/d without bathroom £25/45) Smack on the Palace Green, this has the best location. Some rooms are available year round, such as the bishop's suite (per person £80), decked out with 17th-century tapestries.

snugs and a small corner TV to show the racing. Needless to say, the selection of beers and spirits is terrific. Not surprisingly, students love it too.

Swan & Three Cygnets (☎ 384 0242; Elvet Bridge; mains around £8) A high-ceilinged riverside pub with courtyard tables overlooking the river. It also serves some pretty good bar food, usually fancy versions of standard bar fare like bangers and mash.

Shopping

It's less about what you might buy and more about the place itself, but the Victorian **Durham Indoor Market** (☎ 384 6153; ⏱ 9am-6pm Mon-Sat) is worth a browse, if only for the motley collection of wares on sale, from fruit and veg to garden furniture.

Getting There & Away

BUS

The bus station is west of the river on North St. All National Express buses arrive here, while Bus No 352 links Newcastle and Blackpool via Durham, Barnard Castle, Raby Castle and Kirkby Stephen. Destinations include Edinburgh (£20, four hours, one daily), Leeds (£18.50, 2½ hours, three daily), London (£25, 6½ hours, four daily) and Newcastle (£2.25, 30 minutes, three daily).

TRAIN

There are services at least hourly to Edinburgh (£37.50, two hours), London (£88, three hours), Newcastle (£4.10 single, 20 minutes) and York (£17, one hour).

Getting Around

Pratt's Taxis (☎ 386 0700) charges a minimum of about £2.20. **Cycle Force** (☎ 384 0319; 29 Claypath) charges £16/8.50 per full/half day for mountain-bike hire.

AROUND DURHAM
Beamish Open-Air Museum

A great day out for visitors of all ages, **Beamish** (☎ 0191-370 4000; www.beamish.org.uk; admission Nov-Mar £4, Apr-Oct £14; ⏱ 10am-5pm Apr-Oct, 10am-4pm Tue-Thu, Sat & Sun Nov-Mar, last entry 3pm year-round) is a living, breathing, working museum that offers a fabulous, warts-and-all portrait of industrial life in the northeast during the 19th and 20th centuries.

You can go underground, explore mine heads, a working farm, a school, a dentist

and a pub, and marvel at how every cramped pit cottage seemed to find room for a piano. Don't miss a ride behind an 1815 Steam Elephant locomotive or a replica of Stephenson's Locomotion No 1.

Allow at least three hours to do the place justice. Many elements (such as the railway) aren't open in the winter – call for details.

Beamish is about 8 miles northwest of Durham; it's signposted from the A1(M) – take the A691 west at junction 63. Bus Nos 709 from Newcastle (50 minutes, hourly) and 720 from Durham (30 minutes, hourly) run to the museum.

BARNARD CASTLE
☎ 01833 / pop 6720

Barnard Castle, or just plain Barney, is a thoroughly charming market town packed with atmospheric pubs and antique shops, with a daunting ruined castle at its edge and an extraordinary French chateau on its outskirts. If you can drag yourself away, it is also a terrific base for exploring Teesdale and the North Pennines.

Staff at the **TIC** (☎ 690909; tourism@teesdale. gov.uk; Woodleigh, Flatts Rd; ⏱ 9.30am-5.30pm Easter-Oct, 11am-4pm Mon-Sat Nov-Mar) handle visitor inquiries.

Castle

Once one of northern England's largest castles, **Barnard Castle** (☎ 638212; admission £2.50; ⏱ 10am-6pm Easter-Sep, 10am-5pm Oct, 10am-1pm & 2-4pm Wed-Sun Nov-Mar) was partly dismantled during the 16th century, but its huge bulk, on a cliff above the Tees, still manages to cover more than two very impressive hectares. Founded by Guy de Bailleul and rebuilt around 1150, its occupants spent their time suppressing the locals and fighting off the Scots – on their off days they sat around enjoying the wonderful views of the river.

Bowes Museum

The 19th-century industrialist and art fanatic John Bowes didn't do things by halves, so when he commissioned a new museum to show off his terrific collection, the result was this extraordinary, Louvre-inspired French chateau 1½ miles west of town. Opened in 1892, the **Bowes Museum** (☎ 690606; www.bowesmuseum.org.uk; adult/child £6/free; ⏱ 11am-5pm) could give the V&A a run for its money, with lavish furniture and paintings by Canaletto, El Greco and Goya. The museum's most beloved exhibit, however, is the marvellous mechanical silver swan, operated at 12.30pm and 3.30pm.

Sleeping & Eating

Greta House (☎ 631193; 89 Galgate; s/d £35/50) This lovely Victorian home stands out for the little touches that show that extra bit of class – fluffy bathrobes, face cloths and posh toiletries. What really did it for us though was the stay-in service: a tray of lovely homemade sandwiches and a superb cheeseboard to nibble at from the comfort of bed.

Marwood House (☎ 637493; www.kilgarriff.demon .co.uk; 98 Galgate; s/d £27/48) Another handsome Victorian property with tastefully appointed rooms (the owner's tapestries feature in the décor and her homemade biscuits sit on a tray), but the standout feature is the small fitness room in the basement, complete with a sauna that fits up to four people.

Old Well Inn (☎ 690130; www.oldwellinn.co.uk; 21 The Bank; s/d from £48/60) You won't find larger bedrooms in town than at this old coaching inn, which makes it an excellent option for families – it even takes pets. It has a reputation for excellent, filling pub grub, although the service is somewhat lacklustre at times.

Getting There & Away

Bus No 352 runs daily between Newcastle and Blackpool via Durham, Bishop Auckland, Barnard Castle, Raby Castle and Kirkby Stephen.

AROUND BARNARD CASTLE

The ransacked, spectral ruins of **Egglestone Abbey** (☽ dawn-dusk), dating from the 1190s, overlook a lovely bend of the Tees. You can envisage the abbey's one-time grandeur despite the gaunt remains. They're a pleasant mile-walk south of Barnard Castle.

About 7 miles northeast of town is the sprawling, romantic **Raby Castle** (☎ 660202; www.rabycastle.com; admission £7; ☽ castle 1-5pm, grounds 11am-5.30pm Sun-Fri Jun-Aug, Wed & Sun May & Sep), a stronghold of the Neville family until it did some ill-judged plotting against the Crown in 1569 (the Rising of the North). Most of the interior dates from the 18th and 19th centuries, but the exterior remains true to the original design, built around a courtyard and surrounded by a moat. There are beautiful formal gardens and a deer park. Bus Nos 8 and 352 zip between Barnard Castle and Raby (20 minutes, eight daily).

BISHOP AUCKLAND

☎ 01388 / pop 24,770

The name's a giveaway, but this friendly market town 11 miles southwest of Durham has been the country residence of the bishops of Durham since the 12th century and their official home for over 100 years. The castle is just next to the large, attractive market square; leading off are small-town streets lined with high-street shops and a sense that anything exciting is happening elsewhere.

The **TIC** (☎ 604922; Market Pl; ☽ 10am-5pm Mon-Fri, 9am-4pm Sat year round, plus 1-4pm Sun Apr-Sep) is in the town hall on Market Pl.

The imposing gates of **Auckland Castle** (☎ 601627; www.auckland-castle.co.uk; adult/child £4/ free; ☽ 2-5pm Sun-Mon Easter-Jul & Sep, plus Wed Aug), just off Market Pl behind the town hall, lead to the official home of the bishop of Durham. It's palatial – each successive bishop extended the building. Underneath the spiky Restoration Gothic exterior, the buildings are mainly medieval. The outstanding attraction of the castle is the striking 17th-century chapel, which thrusts up into the sky. It has a remarkable partially 12th-century interior, converted from the former great hall. Admission is by guided tour only.

Around the castle is a hilly and wooded 324-hectare **deer park** (admission free; ☽ 7am-sunset) with an 18th-century deer shelter.

AROUND BISHOP AUCKLAND

One and a half miles north of Bishop Auckland is **Binchester Roman Fort** (Vinovia; ☎ 663089; www.durham.gov.uk/binchester; admission £1.60; excavations ☽ 11am-5pm Easter-Sep), or Vinovia as it was originally called. The fort, first built in wood around AD 80 and rebuilt in stone early in the 2nd century, was the largest in County Durham, covering 4 hectares. Excavations show the remains of Dere St, the main high road from York to Hadrian's Wall, and the best-preserved example of a heating system in the country – part of the commandant's private bath suite. Findings from the site are displayed at the Bowes Museum (opposite).

The stones of the abandoned Binchester Fort were often reused, and Roman inscriptions can be spotted in the walls of hauntingly beautiful **Escomb Church** (☎ 602861; admission free; 🕑 9am-8pm Apr-Sep, 9am-4pm Oct-Mar). The church dates from the 7th century – it's one of only three complete surviving Saxon churches in Britain. It's a whitewashed cell, striking and moving in its simplicity, incongruously encircled by a 20th-century cul-de-sac. If no-one's about, collect the keys from a hook outside a nearby house. Escomb is 3 miles west of Bishop Auckland (Bus No 86, 87 or 87A; 15 per day Monday to Saturday, 10 on Sunday).

Bus No 352 running from Newcastle to Blackpool passes through Bishop Auckland (daily March to November, Saturday and Sunday December to February), as does bus No X85 from Durham to Kendal (one on Saturday June to September).

You need to change at Darlington for regular trains to Bishop Auckland.

NORTH PENNINES

The western half of Durham county consists of fertile, rocky dales that run into the North Pennines. The Rivers Tees and Wear cut through the landscape, creating Teesdale to the south and Weardale to the north. Both are marked by ancient quarries and mines – industries that date back to Roman times. The wilds of the North Pennines, which only peter out just before Hadrian's Wall, are also home to the picturesque Derwent and Allen valleys, north of Weardale.

Teesdale
☎ 01833

From the confluence of the Rivers Greta and Tees to Caldron Snout at the source of the Tees, Teesdale is filled with woods, scattered unspoilt villages, rivers, waterfalls and sinuous moorland. There are huge numbers of rabbits bounding about, as if competing

---

TOP FIVE PUBS FOR A PINT

■ **Trent House Soul Bar** (p703; Newcastle)

■ **Allenheads Inn** (p714; Allen Valley)

■ **Ship Inn** (p722; Low-Newton-by-the-Sea, Embleton Bay)

■ **Ye Old Cross** (p721; Alnwick)

■ **Ship** (p724; Holy Island)

---

for a role in *Watership Down*. The Pennine Way snakes along the dale.

MIDDLETON-IN-TEESDALE

This tranquil, pretty village of white and stone houses among soft green hills was from 1753 a 'company town', the entire kit and caboodle being the property of the London Lead Company, a Quaker concern. The upshot was that the lead miners worked the same hours in the same appalling conditions as everyone else, but couldn't benefit from a Sunday pint to let off steam.

The existence of a typical Middleton family in the mid-19th century is the subject of **Meet the Middletons** (☎ 641000; Chapel Row; 🕑 11am-5pm), a small heritage centre in the middle of town. For everything else, including information on local walks, go to the **TIC** (☎ 641001; 🕑 10am-1pm & 2-5pm Apr-Oct, 10am-4pm Nov-Mar).

MIDDLETON TO LANGDON BECK

As you travel up the valley past Middleton toward Langdon Beck, 3 miles on is **Bowlees Visitor Centre** (☎ 622292; admission £1; 🕑 10.30am-5pm Apr-Oct, 10.30am-4pm Sat & Sun Nov-Feb), with plenty of walking and wildlife leaflets and a small natural-history display. A number of easy-going trails spread out from here, including one to the tumbling rapids of **Low Force**, a number of metre-high steps along a scenic stretch of river. One mile further on is the much more compelling **High Force** (adult/child £1.50/1, car park £2), England's largest waterfall, 21m (70ft) of almighty roar that shatters the general tranquillity of the surroundings. It's a sight best appreciated after a rainfall, when the torrent is really powerful.

The B6277 leaves the River Tees at High Force and continues up to **Langdon Beck**, where the scenery quickly turns from green rounded hills to the lonely landscape of the North Pennines, dotted with small chapels. You can either continue on the B6277 over the Pennines to Alston and Cumbria or turn right and take a minor road over the moors to St John's Chapel in Weardale.

Bus No 73 connects Middleton and Langdon Beck, via Bowlees and High Force, at least once a day Tuesday, Wednesday, Friday and Saturday. Bus Nos 75 and 76 serve Middleton from Barnard Castle several times daily.

SLEEPING & EATING

Cornforth & Cornforth (☎ 640300; www.cornforth
andcornforth.co.uk; 16 Market Pl, Middleton-in-Teesdale;
mains £5-6; s/d £25/44) Three absolutely gorgeous country-style rooms above a great
café are our choice for a place to stay (and
eat) in the village. The owners put a premium on organic, free-range produce and
it is reflected in the fresh, delicious food –
anyone for Teesdale grouse with a wild
blueberry hazelnut sauce?

Brunswick House (☎ 640393; www.brunswickhouse
.net; 55 Market Pl, Middleton-in-Teesdale; s/d £42/50) This
pretty Georgian house has a floral, fluffy
theme: nice quilted duvets and big pillows
with flowers all over them. Everything else
is painted white. Cute and comfortable.

High Force Hotel & Brewery (☎ 622222; www
.highforcehotel.com; Forest-in-Teesdale; s/d £26/60) This
former hunting lodge by the High Force waterfall is best known for the award-winning
beers brewed on the premises: Teesdale Bitter, Forest XB and Cauldron Snout – at 5.6%
it has a kick like a mule. Upstairs are six
decent enough bedrooms, while the bar also
serves food.

Langdon Beck YHA Hostel (☎ 0870 770 5910;
www.yha.org.uk; Forest-in-Teesdale; dm £10.60; ☒ Mon-
Sat Apr-Sep, Fri & Sat Nov, Tue-Sat early Feb-Mar, Sep-
Oct) Walkers on the Pennine Way are avid
fans of this hostel between High Force and
Langdon Beck. The hostel is also a good
base for short walks into the dales and the
Pennines, in particular to Cow Green Reservoir, the source of the Tees.

Weardale
☎ 01388

Sheltered by the Pennines, Weardale was once
the hunting ground of the prince bishops, but
for most of the 19th century it was primarily
a lead-mining centre, which has left the rust-
and olive-coloured patchwork moors pitted
with mining scars. There are splendid walks
in the surrounding countryside.

STANHOPE & IRESHOPBURN

Peaceful Stanhope is a honey-coloured town
with a cobbled marketplace – a good base
for windswept walks across the moors. Its
interesting church is Norman at the base,
but mostly dates from the 12th century.

The **TIC** (☎ 527650; durham.dales.centre@durham
.gov.uk; ☒ 10am-5pm Apr-Oct, 10am-4pm Mon-Fri, 11am-
4pm Sat & Sun Nov-Mar) has lots of information

on walks in the area, and there's a small
tearoom.

In **Ireshopeburn**, 8 miles on from Stanhope,
the **Weardale Museum** (☎ 537417; www.weardale
.co.uk; adult/child £1.50/50p; ☒ 2-5pm Wed-Sun May-Jul
& Sep, daily Aug) allows a glimpse into local history, including a spotless lead-mining family kitchen and information on preacher
John Wesley. It's next to **High House Chapel**,
a Methodist chapel (1760) that was one of
Wesley's old stomping grounds.

KILLHOPE

At the top of the valley, 13 miles from Stanhope, is a salutary example of just how bleak
miners' lives really were. In the **Killhope Lead
Mining Centre** (☎ 537505; admission £4.50, with mine
trip £6; ☒ 10.30am-5.30pm Apr-Oct), the blackened
machinery of the old works is dominated
by an imposing 10m-high water wheel that
drove a crushing mechanism.

In one of those unfortunate linguistic
ironies, 'hope' actually means 'side valley',
but once you get a look inside the place you'll
understand the miners' black humour about
the name. An absorbing exhibition explains
what life was like: poor pay, poorer living
conditions and the constant threat of illness
forced many workers into an early grave.
The most poignant records are those of the
washer boys – children employed in freez-
ing, backbreaking work. The mine closed in
1910 but you can visit its atmospheric underground network, as it was in 1878, on an
hour-long guided tour; wear warm clothes.

It's possible to buy a combined ticket for
the mine and the South Tynedale Railway
(see p690). From the mining centre it's another 7 miles up over the highest main road
in England (617m) and the North Pennines
and down into Alston.

Bus No 101 makes the regular trip up the
valley from Bishop Auckland to Stanhope
(10 daily). If you ring ahead, it will go on to
Killhope mid-morning and pick you up in
the afternoon. Call **Wearhead Motor Services**
(☎ 01388-528235) to arrange the service.

SLEEPING & EATING

Redlodge Guest House (☎ 527851; 2 Redlodge Cottages,
Market Pl, Stanhope; s/d £22.50/50) This friendly B&B
is in a stone house originally built in 1850 as
part of Stanhope Castle. The three bedrooms
are perfectly adequate, but they fill up quickly
as the town is the last stop on the C2C route

before cyclists push on to Sunderland. The single room is not en suite.

Queen's Head (☎ 528160; 89 Front St, Stanhope; mains £4.55-8) This handsome pub in the middle of Stanhope is a good spot for hearty pub grub.

Derwent Valley

Pretty Blanchland and Edmundbyers, two small, remote villages, are south of the denim expanse of the **Derwent Reservoir**, surrounded by wild moorland and forests. The 3½-mile-long reservoir has been here since 1967, and the county border separating Durham and Northumberland runs right through it. The valley's good for walking and cycling, as well as sailing, which can be arranged through **Derwent Reservoir Sailing Club** (☎ 01434-675258).

Nestling among trees, and surrounded by wild mauve and mustard moors, **Blanchland** is an unexpected surprise. It's a charming, golden-stoned grouping of small cottages arranged around an L-shaped square, framed by a medieval gateway. The village was named after the white cassocks of local monks – there was a Premonstratensian abbey here from the 12th century. Around 1721 the prince bishop of the time, Lord Crewe, seeing the village and abbey falling into disrepair, bequeathed the buildings to trustees on the condition that they were protected and looked after.

Another inviting, quiet village, **Edmundbyers** is 4 miles east of Blanchland on the B6306 along the southern edge of Derwent Reservoir.

It's 12 miles north of Stanhope and 10 miles south of Hexham on the B6306. Bus No 773 runs from Consett to Blanchland via Edmundbyers at least four times a day, Monday to Saturday.

SLEEPING & EATING

Lord Crewe Arms Hotel (☎ 01434-675251; www.lordcrewehotel.com; Blanchland; s/d £85/120; lunch £6-11, 4-course dinner £32) This glorious hotel was built as the abbot's lodge. It's a mainly 17th-century building, with a 12th-century crypt that makes a cosy bar. It has open fires, hidden corners, tall windows and superb food.

Edmundbyers YHA Hostel (☎ 0870 770 5810; www.yha.org.uk; Low House, Edmundbyers; dm £10.60; ☯ daily Jul-Aug, Wed-Sun Apr-Jun & Sep-Oct) A beautiful hostel in a converted 17th-century former inn. The hostel helps to serve walkers in the area and cyclists on the C2C route.

FLAMING ALLENDALE

Thought to be Viking or pagan in origin, the Baal Fire on New Year's Eve – a procession of flaming whisky barrels through Allendale, has certainly been taking place for centuries. The 45 barrels are filled with tar and are carried on the heads of a team of 'guisers' with blackened or painted faces – this hot and hereditary honour gets passed from generation to generation. The mesmerising procession, accompanied by pounding music, leads to a pile of branches, where the guisers chuck the scorching barrels to fire up an enormous pyre at midnight, doing their best not to set themselves alight.

Allen Valley

The Allen Valley is in the heart of the North Pennines, with individual, remote villages huddled high up surrounded by bumpy hills and heather and gorse-covered moors. It's fantastic walking country, speckled with the legacy of the lead-mining industry.

Tiny **Allendale** is a hamlet around a big open square. The quiet rural community hots up on New Year's Eve when the distinctly pagan and magical 'Tar Barrels' ceremony is performed (see the boxed text above). It's 7 miles from Hexham on the B6295.

Four miles farther south towards the Wear Valley is England's highest village, **Allenheads**, nestled at the head of Allen Valley. It really just consists of a few houses and a marvellously eccentric hotel (see below). There's a small **heritage centre** (☎ 685395; admission £1; ☯ 9am-5pm Apr-Oct) with some displays on the history of the village and surrounding area and access to a blacksmith's cottage and a small nature walk.

Bus No 688 runs up and down the Allen Valley from Hexham to Allenheads (stopping at Allendale Town; 30 minutes, five daily).

SLEEPING & EATING

Allenheads Inn (☎ 685200; www.theallenheadsinn.co.uk; Allenheads; mains around £7; s/d £27.50/48) An attraction in its own right, this 18th-century low-beamed pub has a quite extraordinary and bizarre collection of assorted bric-a-brac and ephemera, from mounted stag heads to Queen Mum plates. It's a friendly and highly recommended, creaky place to stay, and serves up hearty, tasty food as well.

HADRIAN'S WALL

What exactly have the Romans ever done for us? The aqueducts. Law and order. And this enormous wall, built between AD 122 and 128 to keep 'us' (Romans, subdued Anglo-Saxons) in and 'them' (hairy barbarians from Scotland) out. Or so the story goes. Hadrian's Wall, named in honour of the emperor that ordered it built, was Rome's single greatest engineering project, a spectacular 73-mile (118km) testament to ambition and the practical Roman mind. Even today, almost 2000 years after the first stone was laid, the sections that are still standing remain an awe-inspiring sight, proof that when the Romans wanted something done, they just knuckled down and did it.

It wasn't easy. When completed, the mammoth structure ran across the narrow neck of the island, from Solway Firth in the west almost to the mouth of the Tyne in the east. The section from Newcastle to the River Irthing was built of stone, and turf blocks were used on the section to Solway – roughly 3m thick and 4.5m high. A 3m-deep, 9m-wide ditch and mound were excavated immediately in front (except where there were natural defences). Every Roman mile (1.62 miles; even in measurement the Romans outdid us) there was a gateway guarded by a small fort (milecastle) and between each milecastle were two observation turrets. Milecastles are numbered right across the country, starting with Milecastle 0 at Wallsend and ending with Milecastle 80 at Bowness-on-Solway. Between each was a series of turrets, tagged alphabetically, so Milecastle 37 (a good one, see p719) was followed by Turret 37A, Turret 37B and then Milecastle 38.

A series of forts was developed as bases some distance south (and may actually predate the wall), and 16 actually lie astride it. The prime remaining forts on the wall are Cilurnum (Chesters), Vercovicium (Housesteads) and Banna (Birdoswald). The best forts behind the wall are Corstopitum, at Corbridge, and Vindolanda, north of Bardon Mill.

History

Emperor Hadrian didn't just order the wall built because he was afraid of northern invasion. Indeed, no part of the wall was impenetrable – a concentrated attack at any single point would have surely breached it – but was meant to mark the border as though to say that the Roman Empire would extend no further. By drawing an actual physical boundary, the Romans were also tightening their grip on the population to the south – for the first time in history, passports were issued to citizens of the empire, marking them out not just as citizens but, more importantly, as taxpayers.

But all good things come to an end. It's likely that around 409, as the Roman administration collapsed, the frontier garrisons ceased receiving Roman pay. The communities had to then rely on their own resources, gradually becoming reabsorbed into the war-band culture of the native Britons – for some generations soldiers had been recruited locally in any case.

Orientation

Hadrian's Wall crosses beautiful, varied landscape. Starting in the lowlands of the Solway coast, it crosses the lush hills east of Carlisle to the bleak, windy ridge of basalt rock known as Whin Sill overlooking Northumberland National Park, and ends in the urban sprawl of Newcastle. The most spectacular section lies between Brampton and Corbridge.

Carlisle, in the west, and Newcastle, in the east, are good starting points, but Brampton, Haltwhistle, Hexham and Corbridge all make good bases.

The B6318 follows the course of the wall from the outskirts of Newcastle to Birdoswald; from Birdoswald to Carlisle it pays to have a detailed map. The main A69 road and the railway line follow 3 or 4 miles to the south. This section follows the wall from east to west.

Information

Carlisle and Newcastle TICs are good places to start gathering information, but there are also TICs in Hexham, Haltwhistle, Corbridge and Brampton. The **Northumberland National Park Visitor Centre** (☎ 01434-344396; 🕑 9.30am-5pm Mar-May, Sep & Oct, 9.30am-6pm Jun-Aug) is off the B6318 at Once Brewed. There's a **Hadrian's Wall information line** (☎ 01434-322002; www.hadrians-wall.org) too. May sees a spring festival, with lots of re-creations of Roman life along the wall (contact TICs for details).

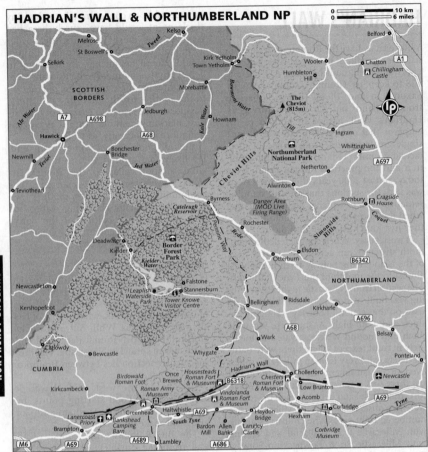

HADRIAN'S WALL & NORTHUMBERLAND NP

Walking & Cycling

Opened in May 2003, the **Hadrian's Wall Path** is an 84-mile (135km) National Trail that runs the length of the wall from Wallsend in the east to Bowness-on-Solway in the west. The entire route should take about seven days, giving plenty of time to explore the rich archaeological heritage along the way. Anthony Burton's *Hadrian's Wall Path – National Trail Guide* (Aurum Press, £12.99) available at most bookshops and TICs in the region, is good for history, archaeology and the like, while the recently published *Essential Guide to Hadrian's Wall Path National Trail* (£3.50) is a top guide to everyday facilities and services along the walk. If you're planning to cycle along it,

TICs sell the *Hadrian's Wall Country Cycle Map* (£3).

Getting There & Around

BUS

The AD 122 Hadrian's Wall Bus is a hail-and-ride, guided service that runs daily, June to September, between Wallsend and Bowness-on-Solway via Haltwhistle train station (four daily between Hexham and Carlisle). Bus No 185 covers the route the rest of the year (Monday to Saturday only).

West of Hexham the wall runs parallel to the A69, between Carlisle and Newcastle. Bus No 685 runs along the A69 hourly, passing near the youth hostels and 2 to 3 miles south of the main sites throughout the year.

The **Hadrian's Wall Rover** (adult/child 1-day £6/4, 3-day £10/6) is available from the driver or the TICs, where you can also get timetables.

TRAIN
The railway line between Newcastle and Carlisle (Tyne Valley Line) has stations at Corbridge, Hexham, Haydon Bridge, Bardon Mill, Haltwhistle and Brampton. This service runs daily, but not all trains stop at all stations.

CORBRIDGE
☎ 01434 / pop 2800
The mellow commuter town of Corbridge is a handsome spot above a green-banked curve in the Tyne, its shady, cobbled streets lined with old-fashioned shops. Folks have lived here since Saxon times when there was a substantial monastery, while many of the buildings feature stones nicked from nearby Corstopitum.

The **TIC** (☎ 632815; www.thisiscorbridge.co.uk; Hill St; ☼ 10am-1pm & 2-6pm Mon-Sat & 1-5pm Sun mid-May–Sep, 10am-1pm & 2-5pm Mon-Sat Easter–mid-May & Oct) is part of the library.

Corbridge Roman Site & Museum
What's left of the Roman garrison town of **Corstopitum** (EH; ☎ 632349; admission £3.50, incl museum; ☼ 10am-6pm Apr-Sep, 10am-4pm daily Oct, Sat & Sun Nov-Mar) lies about a half a mile west of the Market Place on Dere St, once the main road from York to Scotland. It is the oldest fortified site in the area, predating the wall itself by some 40 years, when it was used by troops launching retaliation raids into Scotland. Most of what you see here, though, dates from around AD 200, when the fort had developed into a civilian settlement and was the main base along the wall.

You get a sense of the domestic heart of the town from the visible remains, and the Corbridge Museum displays Roman sculpture and carvings, including the amazing 3rd-century Corbridge Lion.

Sleeping & Eating
Angel Inn (☎ 632119; www.theangelofcorbridge.co.uk; Main St; mains £12-16; s/d from £49/74) The fanciest place in town is this 17th-century inn that has been given a modern, stylish makeover. The restaurant is superb, with delicate renditions of classic meat (roast rack of lamb, beef medallions) and fish dishes

(pan-seared sea bass) winning plenty of kudos as far afield as Newcastle.

Town Barns (☎ 633345; off Trinity Tce; s/d £36/52; ☼ Apr-Oct) Romantic novelist Catherine Cookson used to own this handsome, spacious house with an appropriately sweeping staircase. The rooms are decorated in classic country-house style, with plenty of pillows and old wooden furniture.

Valley Restaurant (☎ 633434; Station Rd; mains £5.50-14; ☼ dinner Mon-Sat) This fine Indian restaurant in a lovely building above the station supplies a unique service as well as delicious food. A group of 10 or more diners from Newcastle can catch the train to Corbridge accompanied by a waiter, who will supply snacks and phone ahead to have the meal ready when the train arrives!

Getting There & Away
Bus No 685 between Newcastle and Carlisle comes through Corbridge, as does the half-hourly bus No 602 from Newcastle to Hexham, where you can connect with the Hadrian's Wall bus AD 122. Corbridge is also on the Newcastle–Carlisle railway line.

HEXHAM
☎ 01434 / pop 10,690
Famed for its fine Augustinian abbey, bustling Hexham is a handsome market town interlinked with cobbled alleyways. It is the most substantial of the wall towns, with more restaurants, hotels and high-street shops than anywhere between Newcastle and Carlisle. The **TIC** (☎ 652220; www.hadrian swallcountry.org; Wentworth Car Park; ☼ 9am-6pm Mon-Sat & 10am-5pm Sun mid-May–Oct, 10am-5pm Mon-Sat Oct–mid-May) is northeast of the town centre.

Sights
Stately **Hexham Abbey** (☎ 602031; ☼ 9.30am-7pm May-Sep, 9.30am-5pm Oct-Apr) is a marvellous example of early English architecture. Inside, look out for the Saxon crypt, the only surviving element of St Wilifrid's Church, built with inscribed stones from Corstopitum in 674.

The **Old Gaol**, completed in 1333 as England's first purpose-built prison, is the setting for the **Border History Museum** (☎ 652349; admission £2; ☼ 10am-4.30pm Apr-Oct, Mon, Tue & Sat Oct–mid-Nov). The history of the Border Reivers is retold along with tales of the punishments handed out in the prison.

Sleeping & Eating

Acomb YHA Hostel (☎ 0870 770 5664; www.yha.org
.uk; Main St; dm £8.20; ☺ Apr-Nov) Simple accommodation – basic bunks and functional
bathrooms – in a converted stable on the
edge of Acomb village, 2½ miles north of
Hexham and 2 miles south of the wall. Hexham can be reached by bus (Nos 745 and
880, frequently) or train.

West Close House (☎ 603307; Hextol Tce; s/d
from £20/40) This immaculate 1920s house,
in a leafy cul-de-sac off Allendale Rd (the
B6305) and surrounded by a beautiful
garden, is highly recommended for sheer
friendliness and comfort.

There are several bakeries on Fore St and,
if you turn left into the quaintly named
Priestpopple near the bus station, you'll
find a selection of restaurants.

Dipton Mill (☎ 606577; Dipton Mill Rd; mains around
£5-8) For sheer atmosphere, you can't beat
this superb country pub 2 miles out on the
road to Blanchland, among woodland and
by a river. It offers sought-after ploughman's lunches and real ale.

Getting There & Away

Bus No 685 between Newcastle and Carlisle
comes through Hexham hourly. The AD
122 and the winter-service No 185 connect
with other towns along the wall, and the
town is on the Newcastle–Carlisle railway
line (hourly).

CHESTERS ROMAN FORT & MUSEUM

The best-preserved remains of a Roman
cavalry fort in England are at **Chesters** (EH;
☎ 01434-681379; admission £3.50; ☺ 9.30am-6pm Apr-
Sep, 10am-4pm Oct-Mar), set among idyllic green
woods and meadows. They include part
of a bridge (complex and beautifully constructed) across the River North Tyne, an
extraordinary bathhouse and an underfloor

heating system. The museum has a large
collection of Roman sculpture. Take bus No
682 from Hexham.

HALTWHISTLE

☎ 01434 / pop 3810
The subdued market town of Haltwhistle,
basically one long street just north of the
A69, claims to be the centre of Britain.
Tough to argue, but the residents of Dunsop Bridge, 71 miles (114km) south of here,
do just that. Whatever the truth of it, Haltwhistle makes a good stop if you want to
get some cash and load up on groceries or
provisions. Thursday is market day.

The **TIC** (☎ 322002; ☺ 9.30am-1pm & 2-5.30pm
Mon-Sat, 1-5pm Sun May-Sep, 9.30am-noon & 1-3.30pm
Mon-Tue & Thu-Sat Oct-Apr) is in the train station.

Ashcroft (☎ 320213; www.ashcroftguesthouse.co.uk;
Lanty's Lonnen; s/d from £28/56) is a marvellous Edwardian home surrounded by beautifully
manicured, layered lawns and gardens
from which there are stunning views (also
enjoyed from the breakfast room). The
owners like their flowers so much they
decorated most of the house accordingly.
Highly recommended.

Bus No 685 comes from Newcastle (1½
hours) and Carlisle (45 minutes) 12 times
daily. Hadrian's Wall bus No AD 122 (four
daily June to early September) or No 185
(October to May) connect Haltwhistle with
other places along the wall. Bus No 681 heads
south to Alston (55 minutes, three daily
Monday to Saturday). The town is also on
the Newcastle–Carlisle railway line (hourly).

AROUND HALTWHISTLE
Vindolanda Roman Fort & Museum

The extensive site of **Vindolanda** (☎ 01434-
344277; www.vindolanda.com; admission £3.90, with Roman
Army Museum £5.60; ☺ 10am-6pm Apr-Sep, 10am-5pm
Feb-Mar & Oct-Nov) offers a fascinating glimpse

SOMETHING SPECIAL

Langley Castle (☎ 688888; www.langleycastle.com; s/d £99/109-£169/220) This 14th-century castle in four
hectares of woodland is the real deal minus the medieval privations. Live like one of the many nobles
associated with the castle's history in one of the grand rooms, with pointy four-poster beds and
window seats set in 2m-thick walls. Top of the heap is the fabulous Radcliffe Room, with a sunken
circular bath and a sauna – modern guests are better off than the room's namesake, Sir Edward, who
bought the Langley Estate in 1631 and pronounced himself the top aristocrat in Northumberland.
The rooms in the recently converted gate lodge also have canopied beds but aren't nearly as grand.
It's off the A686 (the road for Alston), off the A69 just before Haydon Bridge.

into the daily life of a Roman garrison town. The time-capsule museum displays leather sandals, signature Roman toothbrush-flourish helmet decorations, and countless writing tablets such as a student's marked work ('sloppy'), and a parent's note with a present of socks and underpants (things haven't changed – in this climate you can never have too many).

The museum is just one part of this large, extensively excavated site, which includes impressive parts of the fort and town (excavations continue) and reconstructed turrets and temple.

It's 1½ miles north of Bardon Mill between the A69 and B6318 and a mile from Once Brewed.

Housesteads Roman Fort & Museum

The wall's most dramatic site – and the best-preserved Roman fort in the whole country – is at **Housesteads** (EH; ☎ 01434-344363; admission £3.50; 10am-6pm Apr-Sep, 10am-4pm Oct-Mar). From here, high on a ridge and covering 2 hectares, you can survey the moors of Northumberland National Park, and the snaking wall, with a sense of awe at the landscape and the aura of the Roman lookouts.

The substantial foundations bring fort life alive. The remains include an impressive hospital, granaries with a carefully worked-out ventilation system and barrack blocks. Most memorable are the spectacularly situated communal flushable latrines, which summon up Romans at their most mundane.

Housesteads is 2½ miles north of Bardon Mill on the B6318, and about 3 miles from Once Brewed. It's popular, so try to visit outside summer weekends, or late in the day when the site will be quiet and indescribably eerie.

Other Sights

One mile northwest of Greenhead near Walltown Crags, the kid-pleasing **Roman Army Museum** (☎ 016977-47485; admission £3.50, with Vindolanda £6.50/4.30; 10am-6pm Apr-Sep, 10am-5pm Feb-Mar & Oct-Nov) provides lots of colourful background detail to wall life, such as how far soldiers had to march per day and whether they could marry.

On a minor road off the B6318 about 3 miles west of Greenhead is what's left of the **Birdoswald Roman Fort** (EH; ☎ 016977-47602; admission £3; 10am-5.30pm Mar-Oct), on an es-

HADRIAN'S WALL CIRCULAR WALK

Starting at Once Brewed National Park Centre, this walk takes in the most complete stretch of Hadrian's Wall. The walk is 7½ miles and takes approximately 4½ hours. The wall follows the natural barrier created by steep dramatic cliffs and the views north are stunning. Some parts of the wall are so well preserved that they have featured in films. You might recognise Milecastle 39, which acted Kevin Costner off the screen in *Robin Hood – Prince of Thieves*. The trail returns to the YHA hostel across swathes of farmland. The centre has a good map.

carpment overlooking the beautiful Irthing Gorge. A fine stretch of wall stretches from here to Harrow Scar Milecastle. About half a mile away, across the impressive river footbridge, is another good bit of wall, ending in two turrets and the meticulous structure of the **Willowford Bridge abutment**.

About 3 miles further west along the A69, just across the border in Cumbria, are the peaceful raspberry-coloured ruins of **Lanercost Priory** (EH; ☎ 016977-3030; admission £2.50; 10am-6pm Apr-Sep, 10am-4pm Thu-Mon Oct), founded in 1166 by Augustinian canons. Ransacked several times, after the dissolution it became a private house and a priory church was created from the Early English nave. The church contains some beautiful Pre-Raphaelite stained glass. The AD 122 bus can drop you at the gate.

Sleeping

Once Brewed YHA Hostel (☎ 0870 7705980; www.yha .org.uk; Military Rd, Bardon Mill; dm £11.80; Mar-Oct, Tue-Sat Nov-Feb) A modern and well-equipped hostel central for visiting both Housesteads Fort, 3 miles away, and Vindolanda, 1 mile away. Bus No 685 (from Hexham or Haltwhistle train stations) will drop you at Henshaw, 2 miles south, or you could leave the train at Bardon Mill 2½ miles southeast. The Hadrian's Wall bus drops you at the door June to September.

Greenhead YHA Hostel (☎ 016977-47401; www .yha.org.uk; dm £10.60; Jul-Aug, call to check other times) A converted Methodist chapel by a trickling stream and a pleasant garden, 3 miles west of Haltwhistle. The hostel is served by bus No AD 122 or 685.

Holmhead Guest House (☎ 016977-47402; www
.bandbhadrianswall.com; Thirlwall Castle Farm, Greenhead;
dm/s/d £9/41/62) Four fairly compact rooms in
a lovely remote old cottage; most of the space
is taken up by the big beds. All the rooms
have a shower rather than a bath. A barn was
recently converted into a large dorm room,
perfect for budget walkers and cyclists. It's
about half a mile north of Greenhead.

NORTHUMBERLAND

Northumberland feels like England's last
undiscovered frontier. Utterly wild and
stunningly beautiful, much of its rugged
interior has been preserved within the confines of a sparsely populated national park
dotted with fortified houses and friendly
villages. To the east is the magnificent,
pale, sweeping coast, punctuated by dramatic wind-worn castles, with tiny, magical
islands just offshore. To the west is Kielder
Water, a shockingly huge yet secluded lake,
with land on all sides enveloped by forest.
The most strikingly evocative part of
Hadrian's Wall slices through the south.

History
Northumberland takes its name from the
Anglo-Saxon kingdom of Northumbria
(north of the River Humber). For centuries
it served as the battleground for the struggle
between north and south. After the arrival of
the Normans in the 11th century, large numbers of castles and *peles* (fortified buildings)
were built and hundreds of these remain. All
this turmoil made life a tad unsettled till the
18th century brought calm. Today the land's
ferocious history has echoes all around the
sparsely populated countryside.

Getting Around
The excellent *Northumberland Public Transport Guide* (£1.50) is available from local
TICs. Transport options are good, with a
train line running along the coast from Newcastle to Berwick and on to Edinburgh.

ALNWICK
☎ 01665 / pop 7770
Northumberland's historic ducal town, Alnwick (ann-ick) is an elegant maze of narrow cobbled streets spread out beneath the
watchful gaze of a colossal medieval castle.

Not only will you find England's most perfect bookshop, but the overall quality of life
isn't half bad either: in 2003 Alnwick was
voted the best place to live in England by
Country Life.

The castle is on the northern side of
town and overlooks the River Aln. The
TIC (☎ 510665; www.alnwick.gov.uk; 2 The Shambles;
⊙ 9am-5pm Mon-Sat, 10am-4pm Sun) is by the marketplace, in a handsome building that was
once a butcher's shop.

There has been a market in Alnwick for
over 800 years. Market days are Thursday
and Saturday, with a farmers' market on the
last Friday of the month.

Alnwick Castle
The outwardly imposing **Alnwick Castle** (☎ 510
777; www.alnwickcastle.com; adult/child £7.50/free;
⊙ 11am-5pm Apr-Oct), ancestral home of the Duke
of Northumberland and a favourite set for
filmmakers, has changed little since the 14th
century. The interior is sumptuous and extravagant; the six rooms open to the public –
staterooms, dining room, guard chamber
and library – have an incredible display of
Italian paintings, including Titian's *Ecce
Homo* and many Canalettos. Magnificent
carving decorates the rooms, completed by
the Florentine-trained Alnwick school.

The castle is set in parklands designed by
Lancelot 'Capability' Brown. The woodland
walk offers some great aspects of the castle,
or for a view looking up the River Aln, take
the B1340 towards the coast.

The **Alnwick Garden** (☎ 510777; www.alnwick
garden.com; adult/child £4.50/free; ⊙ 10am-7pm Jun-Sep,
10am-6pm Apr-May & Oct, 10am-4pm Nov-Jan, 10am-5pm
Feb-Mar) is an attempt to recreate the grandeur
of the castle's 19th-century formal garden,
but is very much a work in progress.

Sleeping & Eating
White Swan Hotel (☎ 602109; fax 510400; Bondgate
Within; s/d from £65/110; Ⓟ) Alnwick's top address is this 300-year-old coaching inn right
in the heart of town. Its rooms are all of a
pretty good standard, but this spot stands
out for its dining room, which has elaborate
original panelling, ceiling and stained-glass
windows filched from the *Olympic*, sister
ship to the *Titanic*.

A row of handsome Georgian houses
along Bondgate Without offer several
worthwhile options that all charge around

SOMETHING FOR THE WEEKEND

Country Life says it's one of the nicest places to live in England, but Alnwick, the historic ducal town of Northumberland, works well for the weekend too. The **White Swan Hotel** (opposite) in the middle of town is the perfect base. On Saturday, visit the **castle** (opposite) – but don't miss the market, which has been running for 800 years. Also not to be missed is a pilgrimage to **Barter Books** (below), arguably the best bookshop in the country and a browser's dream. For dinner, **Bibby's** (below) is a good choice. Round off the evening with a pint in **Ye Old Cross** (below).

Sunday should be about exploring the surrounding area. **Warkworth Castle** (below) is only a few miles away, while further on up the coast (only six miles from Alnwick) is the little sea village of **Craster** (p722), famous for its kippers. A short walk from here is **Dunstanburgh Castle** (p722) and **Embleton Bay** (p722), a wonderfully idyllic spot that reveals the best of Northumberland's windswept coastline.

£25 per person, including **Lindisfarne Guest House** (☎ 603430; 6 Bondgate Without) and the **Teapot** (☎ 604473; 8 Bondgate Without), which has the largest teapot collection in town.

Bibby's (☎ 602607; 14 Bondgate Within; mains £8-15; ⏱ lunch & dinner) Head chef Michael Bibby used to serve precision-balanced meals to the footballers of Newcastle United, but these days he's letting it all hang out at his wonderful new restaurant at the end of a small lane off Bondgate Within. You won't find anything fancy here, just solid lip-smackers like pan-friend loin of pork with rice and a particularly good spaghetti Bolognese, which is surprisingly difficult to get just like Mamma made it.

Alternatively, a number of atmospheric pubs also do a good line in grub. The **Market Tavern** (☎ 602759; 7 Fenkle St; stottie £5), near Market Sq, is the place to go for a traditional giant beef stottie (bread roll), while **Ye Old Cross** (☎ 602735; Narrowgate; mains around £6) is good for a drink and is known as 'Bottles', after the dusty bottles in the window: 150 years ago the owner collapsed and died while trying to move them and no-one's dared attempt it since.

Shopping

One of the country's largest second-hand bookshops is the magnificent, sprawling **Barter Books** (☎ 604888; www.barterbooks.co.uk; Alnwick Station; ⏱ 9am-7pm), housed in a Victorian railway station with coal fires, velvet ottomans and reading (once waiting) rooms. You could spend days in here.

Getting There & Away

There are regular buses from Newcastle (Nos 501, 505 and 518, one hour, 28 per day Monday to Saturday, 18 on Sunday). Bus No 518 has 10 to 14 daily services to the attractive towns of Warkworth (25 minutes) and Alnmouth (15 minutes), which has the nearest train station. Bus Nos 505 and 525 come from Berwick (45 minutes, 13 daily Monday to Saturday). The **Arriva Day Pass** (£4.10) is good value.

WARKWORTH
☎ 01665

Biscuit-coloured Warkworth is little more than a cluster of houses around a loop in the River Coquet, but it makes for an impressive sight, especially if you arrive on the A1068 from Alnwick, when the village literally unfolds before you to reveal the craggy ruin of the enormous 14th-century castle.

A 'worm-eaten hold of ragged stone', **Warkworth Castle** (EH; ☎ 711423; adult £3; ⏱ 10am-6pm Apr-Sep, 10am-4pm Oct, Sat-Mon only Nov-Mar) features in Shakespeare's *Henry IV* Parts I and II and will not disappoint modern visitors. Yes, it is still pretty worm-eaten and ragged, but it crowns an imposing site, high above the gentle, twisting river.

Tiny, mystical, 14th-century **Warkworth Hermitage** (EH; admission £2; ⏱ 11am-5pm Wed & Sun Apr-Sep), carved into the rock, is a few hundred yards upriver. Follow the signs along the path, then take possibly the world's shortest ferry ride. It's a lovely stretch of water and there is **rowing boat hire** (adult/child per 45 min £2.50/2; ⏱ Sat & Sun May-Sep).

Sun Hotel (☎ 711259; www.rytonpark-sun.co.uk; 6 Castle Tce; mains s/d from £49/75) Fourteen huge, country-style bedrooms above a cosy bar and elegant restaurant that serves local dishes given the French treatment. There are excellent views of both the castle and the river.

NORTHEAST ENGLAND

The Greenhouse (☎ 712322; 21 Dial Pl; mains £6.95-13; ◷ lunch & dinner Mon & Wed-Sat, lunch only Sun) Right in the centre of the village is this café-bistro that serves great coffee, cakes and more substantial fish and meat dishes on large pine tables.

Bus No 518 links Newcastle (1½ hours, hourly), Warkworth, Alnmouth and Alnwick. There's a train station on the main east-coast line, about 1½ miles west of town.

CRASTER
☎ 01665

Sandy, salty Craster is a small sheltered fishing village about 6 miles north of Alnwick that is famous for its kippers. In the early 20th century, 2500 herring were smoked here *daily*; these days, its mostly cigarettes that are smoked, but the kippers they do produce are excellent.

The place to buy them is **Robson & Sons** (☎ 576223; 2 for around £7), which has been stoking oak sawdust fires since 1865. For fish facts and other info, call into the **TIC** (☎ 576007; Quarry Car Park; ◷ 9.30am-5.30pm Apr-Oct, 9.30am-4.30pm Sat & Sun Nov-Mar).

You can also sample the day's catch – crab and kipper pâté are particularly good – and contemplate the splendid views at the **Jolly Fisherman** (☎ 576218; sandwiches £2-4).

Bus No 401 or 501 from Alnwick calls at Craster (30 minutes, around five daily). A pay-and-display car park is the only place in Craster where it's possible to park your car.

Dunstanburgh Castle

A dramatic one-mile walk along the coast from Craster is the only path to the striking, weatherbeaten ruins of yet another atmospheric **castle** (EH; ☎ 576231; admission £2; ◷ 10am-6pm Apr-Sep, 10am-4pm Oct-Mar, Thu-Mon only Nov-Mar). High on a basalt outcrop, the haunting sight of the ruins can be seen for miles along this exhilarating stretch of shoreline.

Dunstanburgh was once one of the largest border castles. Started in 1314, it was strengthened during the War of the Roses, but then left to rot. Only parts of the original wall and gatehouse keep are still standing; it was already a ruin by 1550, so it's a tribute to its builders that so much is left today.

You can also reach the castle on foot from Embleton.

EMBLETON BAY

From Dunstanburgh, beautiful Embleton bay, a pale wide arc of sand, stretches around to the endearing, sloping village of **Embleton**. The village has the seaside **Dunstanburgh Castle Golf Club** (☎ 01665-576562) and a cluster of houses. Bus No 401 or 501 from Alnwick calls here too.

Past Embleton, the broad vanilla-coloured strand curves around to end at **Low-Newton-by-the-Sea**, a tiny whitewashed, National Trust–preserved village with a fine pub. Behind the bay is a path leading to the **Newton Pool Nature Reserve**, an important spot for breeding and migrating birds such as black-headed gulls and grasshopper warblers. There are a couple of hides where you can peer out at them. You can continue walking along the headland beyond Low Newton, where you'll find **Football Hole**, a delightful hidden beach between headlands.

Sleeping & Eating

Sportsman (☎ 01665-576588; Embleton; s/d £30/60) This large, relaxed place, set up from the bay, has a wide deck out the front and a spacious, plain wooden bar. The rooms are nothing to shout about, but the views from them are, and the bar serves good food.

Ship Inn (☎ 576262; Low-Newton-by-the-Sea; mains around £8, bar food £4-6) Our favourite pub in all of Embleton Bay is this wonderfully traditional ale house with a large open yard for fine weather, although it would take a real dose of sunshine to tear you away from the cosy interior. The menu puts a particular emphasis on local produce, so you can choose from local lobster (caught 50m away), Craster kippers or perhaps a good ploughman's lunch made with cheddar from a local dairy?

Blink Bonny (☎ 01665-576595; Christon Bank; mains around £6) Named after a famous racehorse, this typical stone country pub is a cut above the average. A huge open fireplace, oak panelling everywhere and a menu that puts a heavy accent on seafood – the lobster is particularly recommended – plus traditional music at weekends; what more could you want?

FARNE ISLANDS

One of England's most incredible sea-bird conventions is to be found on a rocky archipelago of islands about three miles offshore from the undistinguished fishing village of **Seahouses**. There's a **TIC** (☎ 01655-720884; Seafield Rd; ☺ 10am-5pm Apr-Oct) near the harbour in Seahouses and also a **National Trust Shop** (☎ 01665-721099; 16 Main St; ☺ 10am-5pm Apr-Oct) for all island-specific information.

The best time to visit the **Farne Islands** (NT; ☎ 01665-720651; admission £4.80, £3.80 Apr & Aug-Sep; ☺ 10.30am-6pm Apr & Aug-Sep, Inner Farne also 1.30-5pm May-Jul, Staple also 10.30am-1.30pm May-Jul) is during breeding season (roughly May to July), when you can see feeding chicks of 20 species of sea bird, including puffin, kittiwake, Arctic tern, eider duck, cormorant and gull. This is a quite extraordinary experience, for there are few places in the world where you can get so close to nesting sea birds. The islands are also home to England's only colony of grey seals.

To protect the islands from environmental damage, only two are accessible to the public: Inner Farne and Staple Island. Inner Farne is the more interesting of the two, as it is also the site of a tiny chapel (1370, restored 1848) to the memory of St Cuthbert, who lived here for a spell and died here in 687.

Getting There & Away

There are various tours, from 1½-hour cruises to all-day specials, and they get going from 10am April to October. Crossings can be rough, and may be impossible in bad weather. Some of the boats have no proper cabin, so make sure you've got warm, waterproof clothing if there's a chance of rain. Also recommended is an old hat – those birds sure can ruin a head of hair!

Of the operators from the dock in Seahouses, **Billy Shiel** (☎ 01665-720308; www.farne-islands.com; 3-hr tour adult/child £10/8, all-day tour with landing £20/15) is recommended.

BAMBURGH
☎ 01668

Bamburgh is all about the castle, a massive, imposing structure high up on a basalt crag and visible for miles around. The village itself – a tidy fist of houses around a pleasant green – isn't half bad, but it's really just about the castle, a solid contender for England's best.

Bamburgh Castle (☎ 214515; www.bamburghcastle.com; admission £5; ☺ 11am-5pm Apr-Oct) is built around a powerful Norman keep and played a key role in the border wars. It was

restored in the 19th century by the great industrialist Lord Armstrong (who also turned his passion to Cragside; see p728). The great halls within are still home to the Armstrong family. It's just inland from long open stretches of empty white-sand beach, ideal for blustery walks.

The **Grace Darling Museum** (☎ 214465; by donation £1; ☺ 10am-5pm) has displays on Bamburgh's most famous resident, lighthouse keepers in general and the small boats they rescued people in. Grace was a local lass who rowed out to the grounded, flailing SS *Forfarshire* in 1838 and saved its crew in the middle of a dreadful storm. She became the plucky heroine of her time – a real Victorian icon.

Sleeping & Eating

Bamburgh Hall (☎ 214230; cresswell@farming.co.uk; r £60) This magnificent farmhouse built in 1697 has only one room, but we highly recommend it for the sheer pleasure of the views, right down to the sea, and the huge breakfast, served in the very dining room where the Jacobite officers met during the rebellion of 1715.

Victoria Hotel (☎ 214431; www.victoriahotel.net; Front St; mains around £12; s/d £52.50/95) Overlooking the village green is this handsome hotel with bedrooms decorated with quality antiques and – in the superior rooms – handcrafted four-posters. Here you'll also find the best restaurant in town, with a surprisingly adventurous menu where, for instance, chorizo is preferred over Cumberland sausage.

Greenhouse (☎ 214513; www.thegreenhouseguesthouse.co.uk; 5-6 Front St; s/d from £26/52) With four large modern rooms with power showers and a mix of views (Rooms 1 and 2 overlooking

NORTHEAST ENGLAND

the front are best), this is a decent option, although they are loath to sell a room as a single during the summer.

The **Copper Kettle** is the place to be for tea and you can stock up for a picnic at the **Pantry**.

Getting There & Away

Bus No 501 runs from Newcastle (£4.20, 2¼ hours, two daily Monday to Saturday, one Sunday) stopping at Alnwick and Seahouses. Bus Nos 401 and 501 from Alnwick (£3.70, four to six daily) take one hour.

HOLY ISLAND (LINDISFARNE)

☎ 01289

There's something unearthly, almost otherworldly about Holy Island. For one, this small island (two square miles) is tricky to get to, as it's connected to the mainland by a narrow, glinting causeway that only appears at low tide. It's also fiercely desolate and isolated, barely any different from when St Aidan came to what was then known as Lindisfarne to found a monastery in 635. As you cross the empty flats to get here, it's not difficult to imagine the marauding Vikings that repeatedly sacked the settlement between 793 and 875, when the monks finally took the hint and left. They carried with them the illuminated *Lindisfarne Gospels* (now in the British Library in London) and the miraculously preserved body of St Cuthbert, who lived here for a couple of years but preferred the hermit's life on Inner Farne. A priory was re-established in the 11th century but didn't survive the dissolution in 1537.

It is this strange mix of magic and menace that attracts the pious and the curious; during summer weekends the tiny fishing village, built around the red sandstone remains of the medieval priory, is swarming with visitors. The island's peculiar isolation is best appreciated midweek or preferably out of season, when the wind-lashed, marum-covered dunes offer the same bleak existence as that taken on by St Aidan and his band of hardy monks.

Whatever you do, pay attention to the crossing-time information, available at TICs and on noticeboards throughout the area. Every year there is a handful of go-it-alone fools who are caught midway by the incoming tide and have to abandon their cars.

Sights

Lindisfarne Priory (EH; ☎ 389200; admission £3.50; ☺ 10am-6pm Apr-Oct, 10am-4pm Nov-Mar, Sat & Sun only Nov-Jan) consists of elaborate red and grey ruins and the later 13th-century St Mary the Virgin Church. The museum next to these displays the remains of the first monastery and tells the story of the monastic community before and after dissolution.

Twenty pages of the luminescent *Lindisfarne Gospels* are on view electronically at the **Lindisfarne Heritage Centre** (☎ 389004; Marygate; adult/child £2.50/free; ☺ 10am-5pm), which also has displays on the locality.

Also in the village is **St Aidan's Winery** (☎ 389230), where you can buy the sickly-sweet Lindisfarne Mead, cleverly foisted upon unsuspecting pundits as an age-old aphrodisiac.

Half a mile from the village stands the tiny, story-book **Lindisfarne Castle** (NT; ☎ 389244; adult £4; ☺ noon-3pm Apr-Oct), built in 1550, and extended and converted by Sir Edwin Lutyens from 1902 to 1910 for Mr Hudson, the owner of *Country Life* magazine. You can imagine some decadent parties have graced its alluring rooms – Jay Gatsby would have been proud. Its opening times may be extended depending on the tide. A **shuttle bus** (☎ 389236) runs here from the car park.

Sleeping & Eating

It's possible to stay on the island, but you'll need to book in advance.

Open Gate (☎ 389222; theopengate@theopengate .ndo.co.uk; Marygate; s/d £32/54) This spacious Elizabethan stone farmhouse with comfortable rooms caters primarily to those looking for a contemplative experience. There is a small chapel in the basement and a room full of books on Celtic spirituality, and there are organised retreats throughout the year.

Ship (☎ 389311; Marygate; s/d/t from £46/60/80) Three exceptionally comfortable rooms – one has a four-poster – above an 18th-century public house known here as the Tavern. There's good local seafood in the bar.

Getting There & Around

Holy Island can be reached by bus No 477 from Berwick (Wednesday and Saturday only, Monday to Saturday July and August). People taking cars across are requested to park in one of the sign-posted car parks (£4 per day). The sea covers the causeway and cuts the island off from the mainland for about five hours each day. Tide times are listed at TICs, in local papers and each side of the crossing.

BERWICK-UPON-TWEED
☎ 01289 / pop 12,870

England's northernmost city is a salt-crusted fortress town that has the dubious honour of being the most fought-over settlement in Europe after Jerusalem: between 1174 and 1482 it changed hands 14 times between the Scots and English. Although it has been firmly English since the 15th century, it retains its own peculiar identity, as though the vagaries of its seesaw history have forced it to look inwards and not trust anyone but its own.

Indeed, Berwick's biggest attraction is its massive ramparts, built during Elizabethan times and still virtually complete, encircling the town centre. You can walk the entire circuit, taking in some stunning views across the town, river and sea. The town's turbulent history is well documented in its museums. Otherwise, there's little to do here save perhaps go watch Berwick Rangers, the only English football team to play in the Scottish League (sadly, the low-level 2nd division in 2004–5).

Orientation & Information
The fortified town of Berwick is on the northern side of the Tweed; the three bridges link with the uninteresting suburbs of Tweedmouth, Spittal and Eastcliffe.

The **TIC** (☎ 330733; www.berwick-upon-tweed.gov .uk; 106 Marygate; ☼ 10am-6pm Easter-Jun, 10am-5pm Jul-Sep, 10am-4pm Mon-Sat Oct-Easter) is helpful. Access the Net at **Berwick Backpackers** (☎ 331481; 56-58 Bridge St).

Sights & Activities
Berwick's superb **walls** (EH; admission free) were begun in 1558 to reinforce an earlier set built during the reign of Edward II. They represented the most state-of-the-art military technology of the day and were designed both to house artillery (in arrowhead-shaped bastions) and to withstand it (the walls are low and massively thick, but it's still a long way to fall).

You can walk almost the entire length of the walls, a circuit of about a mile. It's a must, with wonderful, wide-open views.

Only a small fragment remains of the once mighty **border castle**, by the train station. The TIC has a brochure (40p) describing the main sights.

Designed by Hawksmoor, **Berwick Barracks** (EH; ☎ 304493; The Parade; admission £3; ☼ 10am-6pm Apr-Oct, 10am-4pm Oct-Mar, closed Mon-Tue Nov-Mar) are the oldest purpose-built barracks in Britain (1717) and now house an eclectic collection of museums on soldiery and the general history of the town.

The original jail cells in the upper floor of the town hall (1750–61) have been preserved to house the **Cell Block Museum** (☎ 330900; admission £2; ☼ tours 10.30am & 2pm Mon-Fri Apr-Oct), devoted to crime and punishment, with tours taking in the public rooms, museum, jail and belfry.

Recommended are one-hour **guided walks** (adult/child £3/free; ☼ 10am, 11.15am, 12.30pm & 2pm Mon-Fri Apr-Oct) starting from the TIC.

Sleeping
There are plenty of B&Bs around the town, most of which offer fairly basic but comfortable rooms; the TIC can assist in finding one.

Berwick Backpackers (☎ 331481; www.berwick -backpackers.co.uk; 56-58 Bridge St; dm/s/d £10/14/32) This excellent hostel, basically a series of rooms in the outhouses of a Georgian home around a central courtyard, has one large comfortable dorm, a single and two doubles, all en suite. It also has Net access. Highly recommended.

No 1 Sallyport (☎ 308827; www.1sallyport-bedand breakfast.com; Bridge St; r £70-90) Three magnificent rooms make this the top choice in town. The Master Suite is a country-style Georgian classic complete with a wood-burning stove; the Manhattan Loft, crammed into the attic, makes the minimalist most of the confined space; but the real treat is the Smugglers' Suite, with a separate sitting room complete with widescreen TV, DVD players and plenty of space to lounge around in.

Castle Hotel (☎ 307900; ringers.home@virgin.net; 103 Castlegate; s/d from £35/55) When in doubt, it's all about location. This handsome old hotel directly across from the train station – and the first building you see upon arrival – is a bit grey around the temples and not quite as grand as when LS Lowry used to stay (it was his favourite), but the rooms are still in good nick.

Eating & Drinking
Good dining is a little thin on the ground, but there are a few exceptions.

Café 52 (☎ 306796; 50-52 Bridge St; mains £4-7; 9am-10pm Mon-Sat) Next door to the hostel, this fine little café with a tasty bistro-style menu is a local pioneer in the establishment of a café culture; it's the only place in town where you can sit around over a cup of good coffee.

Magna Tandoori (☎ 302736; 39 Bridge St; mains £6-12; ⏰ lunch & dinner Mon-Sat, dinner only Sun) There's nothing much in this handsome Georgian room to suggest an Indian restaurant, but the huge menu, chock-full of dishes, makes this the best of its kind in town.

Barrels Alehouse (☎ 308013; 56 Bridge St) Elvis and Muhammad Ali grace the walls of this fine pub, where you'll also find real ale and vintage Space Invaders. There's regular live music in the atmospherically dingy basement bar.

Getting There & Away
BUS
Berwick has good links into the Scottish Borders; there are buses west to Coldstream, Kelso and Galashiels. Bus Nos 505, 515 and 525 go to Newcastle (2¼ hours, five daily) via Alnwick. Bus No 253 goes to Edinburgh (two hours, six daily Monday to Saturday, two Sunday) via Dunbar.

TRAIN
Berwick is almost exactly halfway between Edinburgh (£13.10, 50 minutes) and Newcastle (£13.10, 50 minutes) on the main east-coast London–Edinburgh line. Half-hourly trains between Edinburgh and Newcastle stop in Berwick.

Getting Around
The town centre is compact and walkable; if you're feeling lazy try **Berwick Taxis** (☎ 307771). **Tweed Bicycles** (☎ 331476; 17a Bridge St) hires out mountain bikes for £17 a day.

AROUND BERWICK-UPON-TWEED
Norham Castle
Six and a half miles southwest of Berwick on a minor road off the A698 are the pinkish ruins of **Norham Castle** (EH; ☎ 01289-382329; admission £2; ⏰ 10am-6pm Apr-Sep). An imposing, battered keep (12th to 16th century) rises high on rocks above the green tiling

of fields and a swerving bend in the River Tweed. It was originally built by the prince bishops of Durham in 1160 to guard a crossing on the river.

Bus No 23 regularly passes Norham Castle from Berwick train station on its way to Kelso in Scotland (seven daily Monday to Saturday).

Etal & Ford
The pretty villages of Etal and Ford are part of a 6075-hectare working rural estate set between the coast and the Cheviots, a lush and ordered landscape that belies its ferocious, bloody history.

Etal (*eet*-le) perches at the estate's northern end, and its main attraction is the roofless 14th-century **castle** (EH; ☎ 01890-820332; admission £3; ⏰ 10am-6pm Apr-Sep, 10am-5pm Oct). It was captured by the Scots just before the ferocious Battle of Flodden, and has a striking border warfare exhibition. It is 12 miles south of Berwick on the B6354.

About 1½ miles southeast of here is **Ford**, where you can visit the extraordinary **Lady Waterford Hall** (☎ 01890-820524; admission £1.75; ⏰ 10.30am-12.30pm & 1.30pm-5.30pm Apr-Oct, other times by appointment), a fine Victorian schoolhouse decorated with Biblical murals and pictures by Louisa Anna, Marchioness of Waterford. The imposing 14th-century **Ford Castle** is closed to the public.

If you're travelling with kids, we recommend a spin on the toy-town **Heatherslaw Light Railway** (☎ 01890-820244; adult/child £5/3; hourly 11am-3pm Apr-Oct, to 4.30pm mid-Jul–Aug), which chugs from the Heatherslaw Corn Mill (about halfway between the two villages) to Etal Castle. The 3½-mile return journey follows the river through pretty countryside.

SLEEPING & EATING
Estate House (☎ 01890-820668; www.theestatehouse .supanet.com; Ford; s/d £27.50/55) This fine house near Lady Waterford Hall has three lovely bedrooms (all with handsome brass beds) overlooking a colourful, mature garden. An excellent choice; the owners have a plethora of local information.

Black Bull (☎ 01890-820200; Etal) This is a whitewashed, popular place and is Northumberland's only thatched pub. It serves great pub food and pours a variety of well-kept ales.

SOMETHING SPECIAL

Coach House (☎ 01890-820293; www.coach house crookham.com; Crookham; dinner £19.50; r £27-58) This is an exquisite guesthouse spread about a 17th-century cottage, an old smithy and other outbuildings. There is a variety of rooms, from the traditional (with rare chestnut beams and country-style furniture) to contemporary layouts flavoured with Mediterranean and Indian touches. The food, beginning with an organic breakfast, is absolutely delicious and the equal of any restaurant around.

GETTING THERE & AWAY

Bus No 267 between Berwick and Wooler stops at both Etal and Ford (six daily, Monday to Saturday).

Crookham & Around

Unless you're a Scot or a historian, chances are you won't have heard of the Battle of Flodden, but this encounter between the Scots and the English in 1517 – which left the English victorious and the Scots to count 10,000 dead – was a watershed in the centuries-old scrap between the two. A monument 'to the brave of both nations' surmounting an innocuous hill overlooking the battlefield is the only memorial to the thousands used as arrow fodder.

The battlefield is 1½ miles west of Crookham, on a minor road off the A697; Crookham itself is 3 miles west of Ford. Bus No 710 between Newcastle and Kelso serves these parts (two daily Monday to Friday).

NORTHUMBERLAND NATIONAL PARK

Truly the last great English wilderness is encompassed within the lonely, grand landscape of Northumberland National Park. With a mere 2000 inhabitants spread across its 398 sq miles, the park is a natural wonderland, with spiky moors of autumn-coloured heather and gorse, the soft swells of the Cheviot Hills, and deep colossal Kielder Water, skirted by endless acres of forest. Even the negligible human influence has been benevolent: the finest sections of

Hadrian's Wall run along the park's southern edge and the challenging landscape is dotted with prehistoric remains and fortified houses – the thick-walled *peles* that were the only solid buildings constructed here until the mid–18th century.

Orientation & Information

The park runs from Hadrian's Wall in the south, takes in the Simonside Hills in the east and runs into the Cheviot Hills along the Scottish border. There are few roads.

For information, contact the **Northumberland National Park** (☎ 01434-605555; www.nnpa.org .uk; Eastburn, South Park, Hexham). There are visitor centres at Wooler (p729), Rothbury (p728) and Once Brewed (p715), as well as **Ingram** (☎ 01665-578890; ingram@nnpa.org.uk; ⏰ 10am-5pm Apr-Nov). All the TICs handle accommodation bookings.

Walking & Cycling

The most spectacular stretch of the **Hadrian's Wall Path** (see p716 for details) is between Sewingshields and Greenhead in the south of the park.

There are many fine walks into the Cheviots, frequently passing by prehistoric remnants; contact the Ingram, Wooler and Rothbury TICs for information.

Though at times strenuous, cycling in the park is a pleasure; the roads are good and the traffic is light in this part of Northumberland. There's off-road cycling in Border Forest Park.

Getting There & Around

Public transport options are limited, aside from buses on the A69. See the Hadrian's Wall section (p716) for access to the south. Bus No 808 (55 minutes, two daily Monday to Saturday) runs between Otterburn and Newcastle. Postbus No 815 and Bus No 880 (45 minutes, eight daily Monday to Saturday, three on Sunday) runs between Hexham and Bellingham. National Express No 383 (three hours, one daily, £19) goes from Newcastle to Edinburgh via Otterburn, Byrness (by request), Jedburgh, Melrose and Galashiels.

BELLINGHAM

☎ 01434

The small, remote village of Bellingham (bellin-jum) is a pleasant enough spot on the banks of the Tyne, surrounded by beautiful, deserted countryside on all sides. It is an excellent base from which to kick off your exploration of the park.

The **TIC** (☎ 220616; Main St; ☿ 9.30am-1pm & 2-5pm Mon-Sat, 1-5pm Sun Apr-Oct, 2-5pm Mon-Sat Nov-Mar) handles visitor inquiries.

There's not a lot to see here save the 12th-century **St Cuthbert's Church**, unique because it retains its original stone roof, and **Cuddy's Well**, outside the churchyard wall, which is alleged to have healing powers on account of its blessing by the saint.

The **Hareshaw Linn Walk** passes through a wooded valley and over six bridges, leading to a 9m-high waterfall 2½ miles north of Bellingham (*linn* is an Old English name for waterfall).

Sleeping & Eating

Bellingham's on the Pennine Way; book ahead for accommodation in summer. Most of the B&Bs are clustered around the village green.

Bellingham YHA Hostel (☎ 0870 770 5694; www.yha.org.uk; Woodburn Rd; dm £9.30; ☿ Tue-Sat mid-Apr-Oct, daily Jul & Aug) A cedarwood cabin with spartan facilities on the edge of the village, the hostel is almost always busy, so be sure to book ahead. There are showers, a cycle store and a self-catering kitchen on the premises.

Lyndale Guest House (☎ 220361; www.lyndale guesthouse.co.uk; beds from £20) The bedrooms in this pleasant family home just off the village green are modern and extremely tidy; it's a bit like visiting a really neat relative.

Pub grub is about the extent of the village's dining; recommended is the **Black Bull** or the **Rose & Crown**.

ROTHBURY

☎ 01669 / pop 1960

The one-time prosperous Victorian resort of Rothbury is an attractive, restful market town on the River Coquet that makes a convenient base for the Cheviots.

There's a **TIC & visitor centre** (☎ 620887; Church St; ☿ 10am-5pm Apr-Oct, 10am-6pm Jun-Aug).

The biggest draw in the immediate vicinity is **Cragside House, Garden and Estate** (NT; ☎ 620 333; admission to all £8, estate & garden £5.50; house ☿ 1-5.30pm Tue-Sun Apr-Sep, 1-4.30pm Oct, estate & garden ☿ 10.30am-7pm & 11am-4pm Wed-Sun Nov-Dec), the quite incredible country retreat of the first Lord Armstrong. In the 1880s the

house had hot and cold running water, a telephone and alarm system, and was the first in the world to be lit by electricity, generated through hydropower.

The Victorian mansion and gardens are well worth exploring. The latter are huge and remarkably varied. They feature from lakes and moors and one of the world's largest rock gardens. Visit in May to see myriad rhododendrons.

The estate is 1 mile north of town on the B6341; there is no public transport to the front gates from Rothbury – try **Rothbury Motors** (☎ 620516) if you need a taxi.

High St is a good area to look for a place to stay

Katerina's Guest House (☎ 602334; Sun Buildings, High St; www.katerinasguesthouse.co.uk; s/d from £36/50) Beamed ceilings, stone fireplaces and canopied four-poster beds make this one of the nicer options in town, even though the rooms are a little small.

Other similarly priced options include **Alexander House** (☎ 621463; s/d £30/45) and the **Haven** (☎ 620577; Back Crofts; s/d £27/50), up on a hill.

Food options are limited to pub grub. For takeaway you could try the **Rothbury Bakery** (High St) for pies and sandwiches or **Tully's** (High St) for flapjacks.

Bus No 416 from Morpeth (30 minutes) leaves every two hours Monday to Saturday and three times on Sunday.

KIELDER WATER

Built to quench the thirst of the northeast, Europe's largest artificial lake holds 200,000 million litres and has a shoreline of 27 miles. Not to be outdone on the superlative front, Kielder Forest is the largest in England, with 150 million rather uniform spruce and pine trees. Today the lake is the setting for one of England's largest outdoor-adventure playgrounds, with water parks, cycle trials, walking routes and plenty of bird-watching sites, but it's also a great place to escape humanity: you are often as much as 10 miles from the nearest village. In summer, however, your constant companion will be the insistent midge: bring strong repellent.

The **Tower Knowe Visitor Centre** (☎ 0870 240 3549; www.kielder.org; ☿ 10am-5pm Jun & Sep, 10am-6pm Jul-Aug, 10am-4pm Oct-Apr), near the southern end of the lake, has plenty of information on the area, with lots of walking leaflets and maps, a café and a small exhibition on the history of the valley and lake. *Cycling at Kielder* and *Walking at Kielder* are useful leaflets available from any of the area's TICs (£2 each). They describe trails in and around the forest, their length and difficulty.

Sights & Activities

Most of the lake's activities are focused on **Leaplish Waterside Park** (☎ 0870 240 3549), a few miles north of Tower Knowe. It is a purpose-built complex with a heated outdoor pool, sauna, fishing and other water sports as well as restaurants, cafés and accommodation.

The **Birds of Prey Centre** (☎ 01434-250400; www .birdsofprey.com; admission £3.50; ☯ 10.30am-5pm Mar-Oct) is also located here, with owls, falcons and hawks flapping about; the birds are flown twice daily from April to September.

The **Osprey** (☎ 01434-250312; 4 per day Easter-Oct, adult/child £5.50/3.50) is a small cruiser that navigates the lake and is the best way to get a sense of its huge size.

At the lake's northern end, 6 miles on from Leaplish and 3 miles from the Scottish border, is the sleepy village of **Kielder**.

Kielder Castle (☎ 01434-250209; admission free; ☯ 10am-5pm Apr-Oct, 10am-6pm Aug, 11am-4pm Sat & Sun Nov-Dec) was built in 1775 as a hunting lodge by the Duke of Northumberland. It now houses a Forestry Enterprise information centre – with countless maps and leaflets.

Sleeping & Eating

Leiplish Waterside Park (☎ 0870 240 3549; campsite per person £4.50, cabin £50, Reiver's Rest dm/d £14/30; ☯ Apr-Oct) The water park offers three distinct types of accommodation. The small campsite (12 pitches) is set among trees; the Reiver's Rest (formerly a fishing lodge) has en suite doubles and two dorms that all share a kitchen and a laundry, while the fully self-contained log cabins offer a bit of waterside luxury, complete with TVs and videos. The catch is that the cabins can only be rented for a minimum of three nights.

Kielder YHA Hostel (☎ 0870 770 5898; www.yha .org.uk; Butteryhaugh, Kielder Village; dm £11.80; ☯ Apr-Oct) This well-equipped, activities-based hostel on the lake's northern shore has small dorms and a couple of four-bed rooms.

Gowanburn (☎ 01434-250254; s/d £20/40) Probably the most remote B&B in England is Mrs Scott's fabulous spot on the eastern side of the lake at Gowanburn, accessible by a nar-row road from Kielder village. The iron-grey lake spreads out before the house, the welcome is warm and the breakfast's fantastic.

Falstone Tea Rooms (☎ 01434-240459; Old School House, Falstone) Has filling all-day breakfasts for £3.65.

Getting There & Around

From Newcastle, bus No 714 (adult/child return £5.50/3.50, 1½ hours) goes directly to Kielder on Sundays and bank holidays, May to October. The bus leaves in the morning, turns into a shuttle between the various lake attractions and returns in the afternoon. Bus No 814 (adult/child £2.50/1.25, two daily Monday to Friday term time, one hour) arrives from Otterburn, calling at Bellingham, Stannersburn, Falstone, Tower Knowe Information Centre and Leaplish; the bus begins in Bellingham from June to September (Tuesday and Friday only). **Postbus No 815** (☎ 01452-333447; 2 daily Mon-Fri, 1 Sat) runs between Hexham train station and Kielder on a similar route along the lake and makes a detour to Gowanburn and Deadwater in the morning.

Kielder Bikes (☎ 01434-250392; Castle Hill; bike hire adult/child £18/10; ☯ 10am-6pm Easter-Sep) is opposite Kielder Castle. If no-one's around, there's an excellent long-distance doorbell.

WOOLER

☎ 01668 / pop 1860

The harmonious, stone-terraced town of Wooler owes its sense of unified design to a devastating fire in 1863, which resulted in an almost complete reconstruction. It is an excellent spot to catch your breath in, especially as it is surrounded by some excellent forays into the nearby Cheviots (including a clamber to the top of The Cheviot, at 814m the highest peak in the range) and is the midway point for 65-mile (105km) St Cuthbert's Way running from Melrose in Scotland to Holy Island on the coast.

The **TIC** (☎ 282123; www.wooler.org.uk; Cheviot Centre, 12 Padgepool Pl; ☯ 10am-5pm Mon-Sat, 10am-4pm Sun Jul-Aug, 10am-4pm Apr-Oct, 10am-5pm Mon-Sat Jul-Aug, Sat & Sun only Nov-Mar) is a mine of information on walks in the hills.

Walking

A popular walk from Wooler bus station takes in **Humbleton Hill**, the site of an Iron Age hill fort and the location of yet another battle between the Scots and the English (1402). It's immortalised in Shakespeare's *Henry IV* and the *Ballad of Chevy Chase* (no, not *that* Chevy Chase). There are great views of the wild Cheviot hills to the south and plains to the north, merging into the horizon. The well-posted, 4-mile trail returns to Wooler. It takes approximately two hours.

A more arduous hike leads to the top of **The Cheviot**, 6 miles southeast. The top is barren and wild, but on a clear day you can see the castle at Bamburgh and as far out as Holy Island. It takes around four hours to reach the top from Wooler. Check with the TIC for information before setting out.

Sleeping & Eating

Black Bull (☎ 281309; 2 High St; mains around £6; s/d £25/38) A 17th-century coaching inn that has retained much of its traditional character, this is probably the best option in town; it also does decent pub grub.

Tilldale House (☎ 281450; tilldalehouse@freezone.co.uk; 34-40 High St; s/d from £22/40) has comfortable, spacious rooms that work on the aesthetic premise that you can never have enough of a floral print.

Wooler YHA Hostel (☎ 0870 770 6100; www.yha.org.uk; 30 Cheviot St; dm £10.80; ☿ Mon-Sat Apr-Jun, Tue-Sat Sep, Fri & Sat Mar) A 46-bed hostel with all the normal amenities.

Getting There & Around

Wooler has good bus connections to the major towns in Northumberland. No 464 comes from Berwick (50 minutes, five per day Monday to Saturday) and No 470 (six per day Monday to Saturday) or 473 (eight per day Monday to Saturday) come from Alnwick. Bus No 710 makes the journey from Newcastle (1½ hours, Wednesday and Saturday).

Cycle hire is available at **Haugh Head Garage** (☎ 01668-281316; per day from £12.50) in Haugh Head, 1 mile south of Wooler on the A697.

AROUND WOOLER
Chillingham Castle

One of England's most interesting medieval castles is **Chillingham** (☎ 01668-215359; www.chillingham-castle.com; admission £5; ☿ 1-5pm Sun-Fri

Easter-Sep), steeped in history, warfare, torture and, inevitably, ghosts: it is reputed to be one of the country's most haunted places, with ghostly clientele ranging from a phantom funeral to Lady Mary Berkeley in search of her errant husband.

The current owner, Sir Humphrey Wakefield, has gone to great lengths to restore the castle to its eccentric, noble best after a 50-year fallow period when the Grey family (into which Sir Humphrey married), who have owned the place since 1245, were forced to abandon it because they couldn't afford the upkeep.

Well done, Sir H. Today's visitor is in for a real treat, from the extravagant medieval staterooms that have hosted a handful of kings in their day to the stone-flagged banquet halls, where many a turkey leg must surely have been hurled to the happy hounds. Belowground, Sir Humphrey has gleefully restored the grisly torture chambers, which have a polished rack and the none-too-happy face of an Iron Maiden. There's also a museum with a fantastically jumbled collection of objects – it's like stepping into the attic of a compulsive and well-travelled hoarder.

In 1220, 148 hectares of land were enclosed to protect the herd of **Chillingham Wild Cattle** (☎ 01668-215250; adult/child £3/1; park ☿ 10am-noon & 2-5pm Mon & Wed-Sat, 2-5pm Sun Apr-Oct) from borderland raiders; this fierce breed is now the world's purest. They were difficult to steal, as they cannot herd and apparently make good guard animals. Around 40 to 60 make up the total population of these wild white cattle (a reserve herd is kept in a remote place in Scotland, in case of emergencies).

It's possible to stay at the medieval fortress in the seven apartments designed for guests, where the likes of Henry III and Edward I once snoozed. Prices vary depending on the luxury of the apartment; the **Grey Apartment** (£75) is the most expensive – it has a dining table to seat 12, or there's the **Tower Apartment** (£56), in the Northwest Tower. All of the apartments are self-catering.

Chillingham is 6 miles southeast of Wooler. Bus No 470 running between Alnwick and Wooler stops at Chillingham (six daily Monday to Saturday).

Directory

CONTENTS

Country-wide practical information is given in this directory. For details on specific areas, flip to the relevant regional chapter.

ACCOMMODATION

Accommodation in England is as varied as the sights you visit, and – whatever your budget – is likely to be your main expense. The wide choice is all part of the attraction (from hip hotels to basic barns, tiny cottages to grand castles) and we make numerous recommendations throughout this book. To help you choose, most Sleeping sections are divided into three price bands: budget (under £20 per person per night), mid-range (£20 to £50) and top end (over £50).

B&Bs & Guesthouses

The B&B ('bed and breakfast') is a great British institution. Basically, you get a room in somebody's house, and at smaller places you'll really feel part of the family. Larger B&Bs may have four or five rooms and more facilities. 'Guesthouse' is sometimes just another name for a B&B, although they can be larger, with higher rates.

In country areas, your B&B might be in a village or isolated farm; in cities it's usually a suburban house. Wherever, facilities usually reflect price – for around £15 per person you get a simple bedroom and share the bathroom. For around £25 you get extras like TV or 'hospitality tray' (kettle, cups, tea, coffee), and a private bathroom – either down the hall or en suite.

B&B prices are usually quoted per person, based on two people sharing a room. Solo travellers have to search for single rooms and pay a 20% to 50% premium. Some B&Bs simply won't take single people (unless you pay the full double-room price), especially in summer.

Here are some further B&B tips:

- Advance reservations are always preferred, and are essential during popular periods.
- If you're on a flexible itinerary, places with spare rooms hang up a 'Vacancies' sign.
- Many B&Bs are nonsmoking or only allow smoking in the lounge.
- Rates may rise at busy times and differ from those quoted in this book.
- If a B&B is full, owners may recommend another place nearby (possibly a private house taking occasional guests, not in tourist listings).
- In cities, some B&Bs are for long-term residents or people on welfare; they don't take passing tourists.
- Most B&Bs cater for walkers and cyclists, but some don't; let them know if you'll be turning up with dirty boots or wheels.
- Some places reduce rates for longer stays (two or three nights); others require a minimum two nights at weekends.
- Most B&Bs serve enormous breakfasts; some also offer packed lunches (around £3) and evening meals (around £10).

■ If you're in a hurry, B&Bs may give you a discount for not having breakfast (possibly saving £5), but this is unusual. Bed-only rates are more common at ferry ports.

■ When booking, check where your B&B actually is. In country areas, postal addresses include the nearest town, which may be 20 miles away – important if you're walking! For those on foot, some B&B owners will pick you up by car for a small charge.

Bunkhouses & Camping Barns

A bunkhouse is a simple place to stay, handy for walkers, cyclists or anyone on a budget in the countryside. They usually have heating, stoves and basic showers, but you provide the sleeping bag and possibly cooking gear. Most charge £7.50 to £10 per person per night.

Camping barns are even simpler: usually converted farm buildings, providing shelter for walkers and visitors to country areas. They have sleeping platforms, a cooking area, and basic toilets outside. Take everything you'd need to camp except the tent. Charges are around £4 per person.

Camping

The opportunities for camping in England are numerous – great if you're on a tight budget or simply enjoy fresh air and the great outdoors. In rural areas, camping grounds (called campsites in England)

range from farmers' fields with a tap and a basic toilet, costing around £2 per night, to smarter affairs with hot showers and many other facilities, charging £5 or more per person.

Hostels

There are two types of hostel in England: those run by the Youth Hostels Association (YHA), and independent hostels. There are hostels in rural areas, towns and cities, and they're aimed at all types of traveller – whether you're a long-distance walker or touring by car – and you don't have to be young or single to use them.

YHA HOSTELS

YHA hostels once had an austere image, but today they're a great option for budget travellers. Some are purpose-built, but many are in cottages, country houses – even castles. Facilities include showers, drying room, lounge and an equipped self-catering kitchen. Many hostels also have twin or four-bed family rooms, some with private bathroom. Boarding-school dorms and queues for cold showers are a thing of the past.

To stay, you must join the YHA (£14 per year; £7 for under-18s) or another Hostelling International (HI) organisation. Charges vary – small hostels cost around £10, larger hostels with more facilities are £13 to £19. London's excellent YHA hostels cost around £25. Meals (optional) cost about £4 for breakfasts and packed lunches,

---

ACCOMMODATION CONTACTS

An excellent first stop is **Stilwell's** (www.stilwell.co.uk), a huge user-friendly database of accommodation for independent tourists, with holiday cottages, B&Bs, hotels, campsites and hostels. Stillwell's is not an agency – once you've found what you want, you deal with the cottage or B&B owner direct.

Recommended guidebooks include the annually published *Good Hotel Guide* and the *Which? Good Bed & Breakfast Guide*. Both are genuinely independent (hotels have to be good – they can't pay to get in). Back on the web, agencies include **Bed & Breakfast Nationwide** (www.bedandbreakfastnationwide.com) and **Hoseasons Country Cottages** (☎ 01502-502588; www.hoseasons.co.uk).

For details on hostels, contact the **YHA** (☎ 0870 770 8868, 01629-592700; www.yha.org.uk). The YHA website also has information about camping barns. The **Independent Hostel Guide** (www.independenthostelguide.co.uk) covers hundreds of hostels in England and beyond, and is by far the best listing available. It's also available in book form (£4.95) at hostels or direct from the website.

If you're planning to camp extensively, it's worth joining the **Camping & Caravanning Club** (☎ 024-7669 4995; www.campingandcaravanningclub.co.uk), which owns over 90 campsites and lists thousands more in the excellent and invaluable *Big Sites Book* (free to members). Annual membership costs £29 and includes discounted rates on club sites and various other services.

and around £6 for good-value three-course dinners.

Hostels tend to have complicated opening times and days, especially out of tourist season, so check these before turning up. Smaller rural hostels may close from 10am to 5pm. Reservations are usually possible, and you can often pay in advance by credit card.

INDEPENDENT HOSTELS

England's independent and backpackers hostels offer a great welcome. In rural areas, some are little more than simple bunkhouses (charging around £5), while others are almost up to B&B standard, charging £15 or more.

In cities, backpackers hostels are perfect for young budget travellers. Most are open 24/7, with a lively atmosphere, good range of rooms (doubles or dorms), bar, café, Internet and laundry. Prices are around £15 for a dorm bed, or £20 to £35 for a bed in a private room.

Hotels

A hotel in England can be a simple place with a few rooms or a huge country house with fancy facilities, grand staircases, acres of grounds and the requisite row of stag-heads on the wall. Charges vary as much as quality and atmosphere, with singles/doubles costing £30/40 to £100/150 or beyond. More money doesn't always mean a better hotel – whatever your budget, some are excellent value while others overcharge. Throughout this book, we guide you to the best choices.

Chain hotels along motorways depend on business trade, so offer discount weekend rates and often a flat charge (eg £40 for a twin-bed room and private bathroom). In London and other cities you can find similar places – motorway-style, but in the centre of town – that can be very good value, although lacking a tad in atmosphere. Look out for new arrival EasyHotels, with no-frills airline-style rates and rooms, which may possibly revolutionise the bargain-accommodation scene.

Pubs & Inns

As well as selling drinks, many pubs and inns offer B&B, particularly in country areas. Staying in a pub can be good fun – you're automatically at the centre of the community – although accommodation

varies enormously, from stylish suites to threadbare rooms aimed at (and last used by) 1950s commercial salesmen. Expect to pay around £15 per person at the cheap end, around £30 for something better. A major advantage for solo tourists is that pubs are more likely to have single rooms.

If a pub does B&B, it normally does meals – served in the bar or in a smarter restaurant. Breakfast may also be served in the bar the next morning – not always enhanced by the smell of stale beer and ashtrays.

Rental Accommodation

If you want to slow down and get to know a place better, renting for a week or two can be ideal. Choose from neat town apartments, quaint old houses or converted farms (although always called 'cottages'), all with bedrooms, bathroom, lounge and equipped kitchen.

At busy times (especially July and August) you'll need to book ahead, and cottages for four people cost from around £200 to £300 per week. At quieter times, £150 to £180 is more usual, and you may be able to rent for a long weekend.

University Accommodation

Many universities offer student accommodation to visitors during July and August vacations. You usually get a functional single bedroom with private bathroom, and self-catering flats are also available. Prices range from £10 to £30 per person.

SOMETHING FOR THE WEEKEND?

England has a huge choice of hotels and cottages, but if you thirst for even more variety, contact the **Landmark Trust** (☎ 01628-825925; www.landmarktrust.org.uk), an architectural charity that rents historic buildings; your options include medieval castles, Napoleonic forts and 18th-century follies.

Another option is **Distinctly Different** (www.distinctlydifferent.co.uk), specialising in unusual, bizarre or even vaguely risqué accommodation. Can't sleep at night? How about a former funeral parlour? Need to spice up your romance? Then go for the converted brothel or the 'proudly phallic' lighthouse. Feeling brave? We have just the haunted inn for you, sir.

Back safely down to earth with the final option: the **National Trust** (NT; www.nationaltrust.org.uk) has over 300 holiday cottages and 80 B&Bs, many on NT-owned working farms or the land of stately homes owned or run by the NT.

ACTIVITIES

This section covers a selection of activities that you might tie in with your travels around England. The two most popular activities, walking and cycling, are covered on p52. For more ideas see p753.

Fishing

Fishing is enormously popular in England, but it's highly regulated. Many prime stretches of river are privately owned, with exclusive fishing. There's a fishing club on the idyllic trout-filled River Itchen in Hampshire where it's rumoured even Prince Charles had to join the waiting list.

If you want to try your luck, the best place to cast around for information is a local Tourist Information Centre (TIC). The staff can direct you to local clubs or places offering fishing for a day or two, such as stocked reservoirs that allow public access or smart hotels with private lakes or stretches of river.

Even on rivers that can be freely fished, everyone needs a licence – available from post offices (from £3 per day to £60 for the season) or from the website of the **Environment Agency** (www.environment-agency.gov.uk/fish).

Golf

Golf may be 'a good walk spoilt', but a few rounds on a scenic course is a fine way to see the English countryside. Golf courses fall into two main categories, private and public. Some exclusive private clubs admit only golfers who have a handicap certificate from their own club, but most welcome visitors. Public courses run by town or city councils are open to anyone.

A round on a public course will cost around £10 (more at weekends). Private courses average around £40. Top-end hotels may have arrangements with nearby courses which get you reduced fees or guaranteed tee-off times. If you need to hire, a set of golf clubs costs from £10 per round.

A very good starting point for golfers from overseas is the **Golf Club of Great Britain** (☎ 020-8390 3113; www.golfclubgb.co.uk); this friendly organisation can advise on where to play and arranges regular tournaments.

Horse-riding & Pony Trekking

There's a theory that humans are genetically programmed to absorb the world at walking pace. It's all to do with our nomadic ancestors, apparently. Add the extra height, and seeing England from horseback is a highly recommended way to go.

Across the country, riding centres cater to all levels of proficiency, especially in national parks and other rural areas. Generally, pony trekking is aimed at novice riders. If you're more experienced in equestrian matters, most centres have horses available.

For more information, ask at local TICs. Many riding centres advertise in nationalpark newspapers (available free from hotels, TICs and local shops). A half-day pony trek costs around £15, a full day £20 to £30. Serious riders pay higher rates for superior mounts. The **British Horse Society** (☎ 08701 202244; www.bhs.org.uk) publishes *Where to Ride*, which lists riding centres throughout the UK.

Rock Climbing & Mountaineering

There are indoor climbing competitions at various venues, but for the outdoor noncompetitive side of things, England's main centre for long multipitch routes is the Lake District; there are some fine short routes here as well. Other popular climbing areas are the Peak District and Yorkshire Dales.

England also offers the exhilaration of sea-cliff climbing, most notably in Cornwall. Nothing makes you concentrate more on finding the next hold than waves crashing 30m below!

The website of the **British Mountaineering Council** (☎ 0870 010 4878; www.thebmc.co.uk) covers indoor climbing walls, access rules (don't forget, all mountains and outcrops are privately owned; see p59 and p64), competitions and so on.

British climbing grades are different from those in the USA and continental Europe; there's a conversion table at www.rockfax.com/publications/grades.html.

Sailing & Windsurfing

England has a nautical heritage and sailing is a very popular pastime, in everything from tiny dinghies to ocean-going yachts. In recent years there's been a massive surge in windsurfing too. Places to sail in England include the coasts of Norfolk and Suffolk, Southeast England (eg, Brighton, Eastbourne and Dover), Devon, Cornwall, and the Solent (the stretch of water between the Isle of Wight and the south coast – and one of the most popular sailing areas in Britain). There are also many inland lakes and reservoirs, ideal for training, racing or just pottering.

Your first port of call for any sailing or windsurfing matter should be the **Royal Yachting Association** (☎ 0845 345 0400; www.rya.org.uk). This organisation can provide all the details you need about training centres where you can learn the ropes, improve your skills or simply charter a boat for pleasure.

Surfing

If you've come from the other side of the world, you'll be delighted to learn that summer water temperatures in England are roughly equivalent to winter temperatures in southern Australia (approximately 13°C). But as long as you've got a wetsuit, there are many excellent surf opportunities. England's huge tidal range means there's often a completely different set of breaks at low and high tides.

The best places to start are Cornwall and Devon, where the west coast is exposed to the Atlantic; from Land's End to Ilfracombe there's a string of surf spots. Newquay is the English surf capital, with all the trappings from Kombi vans to bleached hair.

The main national organisation is the **British Surfing Association** (☎ 01637-876474; www.britsurf.co.uk); its website has news on approved instruction centres, courses, competitions and so on. Another good site is www.britsurf.org, with comprehensive links and reports from around Britain. Combine it with *Surf UK* by Wayne Alderson, a comprehensive guidebook covering almost 400 breaks.

BUSINESS HOURS

Most offices, businesses, shops, banks and post offices operate from 9am to 5.30pm, Monday to Friday. Shops keep the same hours on Saturday, while Sunday hours are around 11am to 4pm. London and large cities have 24-hour convenience stores. In smaller towns, shops tend to close at weekends and for lunch (normally 1pm to 2pm), and in country areas on Wednesday or Thursday afternoon too.

When you're sightseeing, large museums and major places of interest are usually open every day. Some smaller places will open just five or six days per week, usually including Saturday and Sunday, but may be closed on Monday and/or Tuesday. Much depends on the time of year too – places of interest will open daily in high season, but may open just at weekends (or keep shorter hours) in quieter periods.

For something to eat, restaurants in England open either for lunch (about noon to 3pm) *and* dinner (about 7pm to 10pm in smaller towns, up to 11pm or midnight in cities), or they might open for lunch or dinner only – depending on the location. Restaurants are usually open every day of the week, although some may close on Sunday evening, or all day Monday.

Cafés and teashops also vary according to location. In towns and cities, cafés may open from 7am, providing breakfast for folk on their way to the office or building site, but close mid-afternoon. Others stay open until 5pm or 6pm. In country areas, cafés and teashops will open in time for lunch, and may stay open until 7pm, catering to tourists leaving stately homes or hikers down from the hill.

In winter months in country areas, café and restaurant hours will be cut back, while some places may close completely from October to Easter.

Pubs in towns and country areas usually open daily from 11am to 11pm, although some may shut from 3pm to 6pm. In cities, some pubs enjoy longer hours, or have been reclassified as clubs so the fun can keep going until 2am or later.

Throughout this book, many restaurants and cafés are listed and reviewed, and we indicate if they're open for lunch or dinner or both, but precise opening times and days are given only if they differ markedly from the pattern outlined here.

CHILDREN

Travel with children can be fun, and kids are a great excuse if you secretly yearn to visit railway museums or ride the scariest roller coaster in the country. Many national parks and resort towns organise activities for children, especially in the school holidays (see p739 for dates), and local TICs are another great source of information on kid-friendly attractions. To help you further we've also included boxes such as 'London For Children', 'Manchester for Children' and so on in the big-city sections.

Some hotels welcome kids (with their parents) and provide cots, toys and babysitting services, while others prefer to maintain an adult atmosphere, so you need to check this in advance. Likewise restaurants – some will have crayons and highchairs, and not mind if the menu ends up on the floor; others firmly say 'no children after 6pm'. Pubs and bars ban under-18s, unless they're specifically 'family-friendly' places (and many are, especially those serving food).

On the sticky topic of dealing with nappies while travelling, most museums and historical attractions have very good baby-changing facilities (cue old joke: I swapped mine for a nice souvenir), as do smart department stores. Elsewhere, you find facilities in motorway service stations and city centre toilets – although the latter can sometimes be a bit on the grimy side.

Breastfeeding in public remains controversial, but if done modestly is usually considered OK. For more advice see www.babygoes2.com – packed with tips, advice and encouragement for parents on the move.

CLIMATE CHARTS

England's changeable weather is discussed on p13. These charts give the figures:

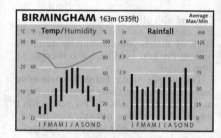

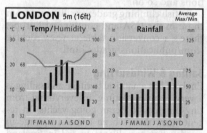

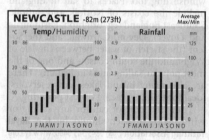

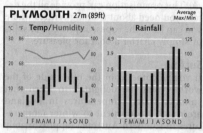

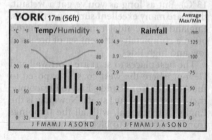

CUSTOMS

The UK has a two-tier customs system – one for goods bought in another EU country where taxes and duties have already been paid, and the other for goods bought duty-free outside the EU. Below is a summary of the rules; for more details see www .hmce.gov.uk or under Customs Allowances at www.visitbritain.com.

Duty Free

If you bring duty-free goods from *outside* the EU, the limits include 200 cigarettes, 2L of still wine, plus 1L of spirits or another 2L of wine, 60cc of perfume, and other duty-free goods (including beer) to the value of £145.

Tax & Duty Paid

There is no limit to the goods you can bring from *within* the EU (if taxes have been paid), but customs officials use the following guidelines to distinguish personal use from commercial imports: 3000 cigarettes, 200 cigars, 10L of spirits, 20L of fortified wine, 90L of wine and 110L of beer – still enough to have one hell of a party.

DANGERS & ANNOYANCES

England is a remarkably safe country, considering the wealth disparities you'll see in many areas, but crime is certainly not unknown in London and other cities, so you should take care – especially at night. When travelling by tube, tram or urban train service, choose a carriage containing lots of other people. It's also best to avoid some deserted suburban tube stations at night; a bus or taxi can be a safer choice.

Pickpockets and snatchers operate in crowded public places, so make sure your bag is safe. Money and important documents are best out of sight and out of reach rather than in a handbag or shoulder bag.

In large hotels, don't leave valuables lying around; put them in your bag or use the room safe if there is one. There's no harm doing the same at city B&Bs too; in rural areas there's less risk. In hostels with shared dorms, keep your stuff packed away and carry valuables with you. Many hostels provide lockers, but you need your own padlock.

If you're driving, remove luggage from the car when parking overnight in cities and

---

SATURDAY NIGHT HEAVER

In cities and towns, the sight of bleary-eyed lads desperately ordering four pints of beer 15 minutes before closing time may be a sign of trouble ahead; England's archaic pub laws mean groups of liquored-up 'lager louts' are all tossed onto the streets shortly after 11pm, so brawls are not unknown. Recent liberalisation of the rules (allowing pubs to stay open longer or reclassify as 'clubs' – with the same result) may ease the pressure, but does nothing for the splattered evidence of too much ale and vindaloo that decorates the pavements next morning. The solution: keep a low profile on Saturday night, give drunken yobs a wide berth – and watch where you step.

---

towns. The same applies even in some apparently safe rural locations. While you're out walking in the countryside, someone may well be walking off with your belongings. Where possible, look for secure parking areas near TICs.

Minicabs

In large cities, avoid unlicensed minicabs unless you know where you're going. Tricks include driving round in circles, then charging an enormous fare. Use a metered taxi or phone a reputable minicab company and get an up-front quote for the ride.

DISABLED TRAVELLERS

If you happen to be in a wheelchair, use crutches or just find moving about a bit tricky, you're unlikely to find too many problems in England. All new buildings have wheelchair access, and even hotels in grand old country houses often have modern lifts, ramps and other facilities added. Smaller B&Bs and guesthouses are often harder to adapt, so you'll have less choice here. In cities, new buses have low floors for easy access, as do many long-distance trains. If they don't, just have a word with station staff and they'll be happy to help.

Useful organisations and websites include the following:

All Go Here (www.allgohere.com)

Disability UK (www.disabilityuk.com) Excellent resource, includes details of shopmobility schemes.

Good Access Guide (www.goodaccessguide.co.uk)

Holiday Care Service (☎ 0845 124 9971, 020-8760 0072; www.holidaycare.org.uk) Publisher of numerous booklets on UK travel.

Royal Association for Disability & Rehabilitation (RADAR; ☎ 020-7250 3222; www.radar.org.uk) Publishes titles include *Holidays in Britain and Ireland*.

Tripscope (☎ 08457 585641, 0117-939 7782; www.tripscope.org.uk)

ELECTRICITY

The standard voltage throughout England is 240V, and equipment rated at 230V to 240V will work. Plugs have three square pins.

EMBASSIES & CONSULATES
British Embassies

Below is a selection; for a complete list of Britain's diplomatic missions (embassies, consulates and high commissions) overseas, see the website of the **Foreign & Commonwealth Office** (www.fco.gov.uk), which also lists foreign embassies in the UK.

Australia (☎ 02-6270 6666; www.uk.emb.gov.au; Commonwealth Ave, Yarralumla, ACT 2600)

Canada (☎ 613-237 1530; www.britainincanada.org; 80 Elgin St, Ottawa, Ontario K1P 5K7)

France (☎ 01 44 51 31 00; www.amb-grandebretagne .fr; 35 rue du Faubourg Saint Honoré, 75383 Paris Cedex 8)

Germany (☎ 030-204 570; www.britischebotschaft.de; Wilhelmstrasse 70, 10117 Berlin)

Ireland (☎ 01-205 3700; www.britishembassy.ie; 29 Merrion Rd, Ballsbridge, Dublin 4)

Japan (☎ 03-5211 1100; www.uknow.or.jp; 1 Ichiban-cho, Chiyoda-ku, Tokyo 102-8381)

Netherlands (☎ 070-427 0427; www.britain.nl; Lange Voorhout 10, 2514 ED The Hague)

New Zealand (☎ 04-924 2888; www.britain.org.nz; 44 Hill St, Wellington 1)

USA (☎ 202-588 6500; www.britainusa.com; 3100 Massachusetts Ave, NW, Washington, DC 20008)

Embassies in England

A selection of foreign diplomatic missions in London is given below. This will be of use to tourists from overseas, but remember that they won't be much help if you're in trouble for committing a crime locally. Even as a foreigner, you are bound by the laws of England.

Australia (☎ 020-7379 4334; www.australia.org.uk; Strand, WC2B 4LA)

Canada (☎ 020-7258 6600; www.canada.org.uk; 1 Grosvenor Sq, W1X 0AB)

France (☎ 020-7073 1000; www.ambafrance.org.uk; 58 Knightsbridge, SW1 7JT)

Germany (☎ 020-7824 1300; www.german-embassy .org.uk; 23 Belgrave Sq, SW1X 8PX)

Ireland (☎ 020-7235 2171; 17 Grosvenor Pl, SW1X 7HR)

Japan (☎ 020-7465 6500; www.uk.emb-japan.go.jp; 101 Piccadilly, W1J 7JT)

Netherlands (☎ 020-7590 3200; www.netherlands -embassy.org.uk; 38 Hyde Park Gate, SW7 5DP)

New Zealand (☎ 020-7930 8422; www.nzembassy .com/uk; 80 Haymarket, SW1Y 4TQ)

USA (☎ 020-7499 9000; www.usembassy.org.uk; 24 Grosvenor Sq, W1A 1AE)

FESTIVALS & EVENTS

Countless festivals and events are held around the country all year. Below is a selection of biggies that are worth tying in with your travels. In addition, towns and villages have annual fairs or fêtes, and many of these are listed in the regional chapters.

JANUARY
New Year Celebrations (January 1, city centres nationwide) Get drunk and kiss strangers as the bells chime midnight. The biggest crowds are in London's Trafalgar Square.

FEBRUARY
Jorvik Viking Festival (York) Horned helmets galore, plus mock invaders and Viking longship races.

MARCH
University Boat Race (London) Traditional rowing contest on the River Thames, between Oxford and Cambridge University teams.

Crufts Dog Show (Birmingham) Highlight of the canine year. Top dogs abound.

APRIL
Grand National (first Saturday in April, Aintree, Liverpool) The most famous horse race of them all, with notoriously high jumps.

MAY
FA Cup Final (early May, Cardiff or Wembley) Gripping end to venerable football tournament.

Brighton Festival (Brighton) Lively and innovative three-week arts feast. See p199.

Bath International Music Festival (mid-May to early June, Bath) Top-class classical music and opera, plus jazz and world music, with art-full Fringe attached. See p277.

Chelsea Flower Show (late May, London) Blooming marvellous.

Glyndebourne (end May to August, Lewes, Sussex) World-class opera in country-house gardens. See boxed text p195.

JUNE

Beating Retreat (early June, London) Military bands march down Whitehall.

Derby Week (early June, Epsom, Surrey) Horse-racing and people-watching.

Trooping the Colour (mid-June, London) Whitehall again; bearskins and pageantry for the Queen's birthday parade.

Royal Ascot (mid-June, Ascot, Berkshire) More horse-racing, more people-watching, plus outrageous hats. See boxed text p157.

Wimbledon – Lawn Tennis Championships (late June, London) Two weeks of rapid-fire returns.

Glastonbury Festival (late June, Pilton, Somerset) Huge open-air musical happening, with hippy roots. See p287.

Royal Regatta (late June/early July, Henley-on-Thames, Oxfordshire) Premier rowing and social event. No hippies here. See p403.

Mardi Gras Pride in the Park (June/July, London) Loud and proud, one of Europe's largest gay and lesbian festivals.

JULY

Hampton Court Palace International Flower Show (early July, London) Does exactly what it says on the tin.

Cowes Week (late July, Isle of Wight) Yachting spectacular.

International Flying Display (late July, Farnborough, Surrey) World's largest aeroplane show.

Womad (late July, Reading) Global gathering of world and roots music.

York Early Music Festival (late July, York) Medieval choirs and concerts.

AUGUST

Notting Hill Carnival (late August, London) Spectacular multicultural feast, Caribbean style.

Reading Festival (late August, Reading, Berkshire) Three-day open-air rock, pop and dance extravaganza. See p158.

Leeds Festival (late August, Leeds, Yorkshire) The Reading of the North, and just as good.

OCTOBER

Horse of the Year Show (Birmingham) Top show-jumping event.

NOVEMBER

Guy Fawkes Day (5 November) Bonfires and fireworks around the country.

DECEMBER

New Year Celebrations (31 December) That's another year gone! Get ready for midnight – see January.

FOOD

For a flavour of England's cuisine, see the Food & Drink chapter. For a real taste, visit some of the restaurants we recommend throughout this book. Most Eating sections are divided into three price bands: budget (under £10), mid-range (£10 to £20) and top end (over £20).

GAY & LESBIAN TRAVELLERS

England is a generally tolerant place for gays and lesbians. London, Manchester and Brighton have flourishing gay scenes, and in other sizable cities (even some small towns) you'll find communities not entirely in the closet. That said, you'll still find pockets of homophobic hostility in some areas.

For info, listings and contacts, see monthly magazines (and websites) *Gay Times* (www.gaytimes.co.uk) and *Diva* (www.divamag.co.uk). Another useful source of information is the **Lesbian & Gay Switchboard** (☎ 020-7837 7324; www.llgs.org.uk; ☺ 24hr). See also the boxes of specific gay and lesbian information in the sections on major cities throughout this book.

HOLIDAYS

In England and Wales, most businesses and banks close on official public holidays (hence the quaint term 'bank holiday').

New Year's Day 1 January
Easter (Good Friday to Easter Monday inclusive) March/April
May Day first Monday in May
Spring Bank Holiday last Monday in May
Summer Bank Holiday last Monday in August
Christmas Day 25 December
Boxing Day 26 December

If a public holiday falls on a weekend, the nearest Monday is usually taken instead.

On public holidays, some small museums and places of interest close, but larger attractions specifically gear up and have their busiest times, although nearly everything closes on Christmas Day. Generally speaking, if a place closes on Sunday, it'll probably be shut on bank holidays as well.

Following is a rough list of the main school holidays:

Easter Holiday Week before and week after Easter
Summer Holiday Third week of July to first week of September
Christmas Holiday Mid-December to first week of January.

DIRECTORY

There are also three week-long 'half-term' school holidays – usually late February (or early March), late May and late October. At school-holiday times, especially in the summer, roads and resorts get busy, and prices go up.

INSURANCE

Travel insurance is highly recommended for all overseas visitors to England; for details about health insurance, see p745. Car insurance is covered on p752.

INTERNET ACCESS

Places with Internet access are reasonably common in England, but you won't find them on every corner. We've listed Internet cafés where they exist in the cities described. In the bigger cities access costs around £1 per hour; out in the sticks you can pay up to £5 per hour. Public libraries often have free access, but only for 30-minute slots.

If you're planning to use your laptop to get online, your connection cable may not fit in English sockets – although adaptors are easy to buy at electrical stores in airports or city centres.

LEGAL MATTERS
Drugs

Illegal drugs are widely available, especially in clubs. All the usual dangers apply and there have been much-publicised deaths associated with ecstasy. The government reclassified cannabis in 2002: possession remains a criminal offence, but the punishment for carrying a small amount is usually a warning. Dealers face far stiffer penalties, as do people caught with any other 'recreational' drugs.

Driving Crimes & Transport Fines

Drink-driving is a serious offence. For more information, and details about speed limits and parking rules, see p752.

On buses and trains (including the London Underground), people without a valid ticket for their journey may be fined on the spot.

MAPS

For a map of the whole country, a road atlas is handy – especially if you're travelling by car. The main publishers are Ordnance Survey (OS) and Automobile Association

---

LEGAL AGE

The age of consent in England is 16 (gay and straight). You can also get married at 16 (with permission from parents), but you'll have to wait two years for the toast – you must be over 18 to buy alcohol. Over-16s may buy cigarettes, so you can have a celebratory smoke instead.

You usually have to be 18 to enter a pub or bar, although the rules are different if you have a meal. Some bars and clubs are over-21 only, so you won't see many highchairs – although there may be a lot of school uniforms around.

(AA), with atlases in all sizes and scales. If you plan to use minor roads, you'll need a scale of about 1:200,000 (3 miles to 1 inch). Most road atlases cost £7 to £10 and are updated annually, which means old editions are sold off every January – look for bargains at motorway service stations.

For more detail, the OS *Landrangers* (1:50,000) are ideal for walking and cycling. OS *Explorer* maps (1:25,000) are even better for walking in lowland areas, but can sometimes be hard to read in complex mountain landscapes. Your best choice here is the excellent specialist series produced by Harvey Maps (www.harveymaps.co.uk), covering mountain areas and national parks, plus routes for hikers and bikers.

MONEY

The currency of England (and Britain) is the pound sterling. Other currencies are not accepted if you're buying goods and services, except for a few places in southern England which take Euros. A guide to exchange rates is given on the inside front cover, and there are some pointers on costs in the Getting Started chapter.

ATMs

Debit or credit cards are perfect companions – the best invention for travellers since the backpack. You can use them in most shops, and withdraw cash from ATMs (often called 'cash machines') – which are easy to find in cities and even small towns. But ATMs aren't fail-safe, and it's a major headache if your only card gets swallowed, so take a back-up.

Credit Cards

Visa, MasterCard, AmEx and Diners credit cards are widely accepted in England, and are good for larger hotels, flights, long-distance travel, car hire etc. Smaller businesses, such as pubs or B&Bs, often only take cash or cheque.

Moneychangers

Finding someone to change your money (cash or travellers cheques) into pounds is never a problem in cities, where banks and bureaus compete for business. Be careful using bureaus, however; some offer poor rates or levy outrageous commissions. You can also change money at some post offices – very handy in country areas.

Paper money comes in £5, £10, £20 and £50 denominations, although £50s can be difficult to change because fakes circulate.

Tipping & Bargaining

In restaurants you're expected to leave around 10% tip, unless the service was unsatisfactory. (It might be already added to your bill but you still don't have to pay it if the food or service was bad). The same might apply at the smarter cafés and teashops. Taxi drivers also expect tips (about 10%, or rounded up to the nearest pound), especially in London. It's less usual to tip minicab drivers. Toilet attendants (if you see them loitering) may get tipped around 50p.

In pubs, when you order drinks at the bar, or order and pay for food at the bar, tips are not expected. If you order food at the table and your meal is brought to you, then a tip may be appropriate – if the food and service have been good, of course.

Bargaining is rare, although occasionally encountered at markets. It's fine to ask if there are student discounts on items such as theatre tickets or books.

Travellers Cheques

Travellers cheques (TCs) offer protection from theft, so are safer than wads of cash, but are not used much in England as credit cards and ATMs become the method of choice for most travellers. If you do prefer TCs, note that they are rarely accepted for purchases (except at large hotels), so for cash you need to go to a bank or bureau.

POST

Although queues in main post offices can be long, the Royal Mail delivers a good service. Within the UK, first-class letters cost 28p and usually takes one day; 2nd-class (21p) up to three days. Airmail costs are 27p to EU countries, 47p for other European countries and 47p for Americas or Australasia (up to 10g). For details on all prices, see www.royalmail.com

RADIO & TV

The BBC is a venerable institution, with several channels dominating national radio. Foreigners are amazed that public service broadcasting can produce such a range of professional, innovative, up-to-date and stimulating programmes. All this – and without adverts too!

Music station BBC Radio 1 (98.8MHz FM) plays everything from syrupy pop to underground garage, with a predominantly young audience and some truly inane presenters. When you're too old for this, turn to Radio 2 (88–92MHz FM); it plays favourites from the 1960s to today, plus country, jazz and world music, with presenters who also got too old for Radio 1.

BBC Radio 3 (91.3 MHz FM) offers predominantly classical music, but also goes into roots and world, while media gem Radio 4 (93.5MHz FM, 198kHz LW) offers a mix of news, comment, current affairs, drama and humour. Radio 5 Live (693kHz MW), aka 'Radio Bloke', provides a mix of sport and talk.

Alongside the BBC are many commercial broadcasters. Every city has at least one music station, while national stations include pop-orientated Virgin Radio (1215Hz MW) and pleasantly nonhighbrow classical specialist Classic FM (100–102MHz FM).

Turning to TV, Britain produces some of the world's best programming, with the BBC once again leading the way, although with competition from cable and satellite channels some shows tend to be dumbed down as ratings are chased.

There are five free-to-air 'terrestrial' (ie not cable or satellite) TV channels – BBC1 and BBC2 are publicly funded and don't carry advertising; ITV and Channels 4 and 5 are commercial stations. Of these, BBC2 and Channel 4 generally have the most interesting programming. Whatever

DIRECTORY

channel you watch, things get better after about 9pm.

TELEPHONE

England's famous red phone boxes can still be seen in city streets and especially in conservation areas, although soulless glass cubicles are more common these days. Either way, public phones accept coins, and usually credit cards. Minimum charge is 20p. To save hunting for change, prepaid British Telecom (BT) Phonecard Plus cards (£3, £5, £10 or £20) are widely available from post offices and newsagents.

Codes or numbers starting with ☎ 0500 or ☎ 0800 are free; ☎ 0845 is local-call rate; ☎ 0870 is national-call rate; ☎ 0891 or ☎ 0906 is premium rate, and should be specified by the company using the number (ie in their advertising literature), so you know the cost before you call.

Codes for mobile phones (cellphones) usually start with ☎ 07 – more expensive than calling a land line.

International Calls

To call outside the UK dial ☎ 00, then the country code, the area code (you usually drop the initial zero) and the number. For country codes, see the inside front cover of this book. Direct dialled calls to most overseas countries can be made from most public telephones, and it's usually cheaper between 8pm and 8am Monday to Friday and at weekends. You can usually undercut BT international rates by buying a phonecard (usually denominated £5, £10 or £20) with a PIN that you use from any phone by dialling an access number (you don't insert it into the machine). There are dozens of cards, usually available from city newsagents – with rates of the various companies often vividly displayed.

To make reverse-charge (collect) calls, dial ☎ 155 for the international operator. It's an expensive option, but what the hell – the other person is paying!

To call England from abroad, dial your country's international access code, then ☎ 44 (the UK's country code), then the area code (dropping the first 0) and the phone number.

Local & National calls

Local calls are within 35 miles and are cheaper than national calls. All calls are cheaper from 6pm to 8am Monday to Friday, and from midnight Friday to midnight Sunday. From private phones, rates vary between telecom providers. From BT public phones the weekday rate is about 5p per minute; evenings and weekends it's about 1p per minute.

For the operator, call ☎ 100. For directory inquiries, a host of agencies compete for your business and charge from 10p to 40p; numbers include ☎ 118 192, ☎ 118 118 and ☎ 118 811.

Mobile Phones

Around 40 million Britons now have the facility to tell their loved ones they're 'on the train'. The terse medium of text-messaging is a national passion – with a billion messages sent monthly. Phones in the UK use GSM 900/1800, which is compatible with Europe and Australia but not with North America or Japan (although phones that work globally are increasingly common).

Even if your phone works in the UK, because it's registered overseas, a call to someone just up the road will be routed internationally and charged accordingly. An option is to buy a local SIM card (around £30), which includes a UK number, and use that in your own handset (as long as your phone isn't locked by your home network).

A second option is to buy a pay-as-you-go phone (from around £50), which comes with its own telephone number. To stay in credit, you simply buy 'top-up' cards at newsagents or filling (petrol) stations.

TIME

Wherever you are in the world, time is measured in relation to Greenwich Mean Time (GMT, or Universal Time Coordinated – UTC – as it's more accurately called), so a highlight for many visitors to London is a trip to Greenwich and its famous line dividing the western and eastern hemispheres.

To give you an idea, if it is noon in London, it is 4am on the same day in San Francisco, 7am in New York and 10pm in Sydney. British summer time (BST) is Britain's daylight saving; one hour ahead of GMT from late March to late October.

TOURIST INFORMATION

Before leaving home, check the comprehensive and wide-ranging websites VisitBritain (www.visitbritain.com) and VisitEngland (www.visitengland.com), covering all the angles of national tourism, with links to numerous other sites. Details about local and regional websites and tourist organisations are also given at the start of each main chapter throughout this book.

Tourist Offices Abroad

VisitBritain's main overseas offices are listed below. Those with an office address can deal with walk-in visitors. For the others it's phone or email only. As well as information, they can help with discount travel cards, often available only if you book before arrival in England.

Australia (☎ 02-9021 4400; www.visitbritain.com/au; 15 Blue St, North Sydney, NSW 2060)
Canada (☎ 1 888 847 4885; www.visitbritain.com/ca)
France (☎ 01 58 36 50 50; www.visitbritain.com/vb3-fr-fr)
Germany (☎ 01801-46 86 42; www.visitbritain.com/de; Hackescher Markt 1, 10178 Berlin)
Ireland (☎ 01-670 8000; www.visitbritain.com/ie; 18-19 College Green, Dublin 2)
Japan (☎ 03-5562 2550; www.visitbritain.com/jp; 1F Akasaka Twin Tower, Minato-ku, Tokyo 107-0052)
Netherlands (☎ 020-689 0002; www.visitbritain.com/nl)
New Zealand (☎ 0800 700741; www.visitbritain.com/nz)
USA (☎ 800 462 2748; www.travelbritain.org; 551 Fifth Ave, New York, NY 10176)

Local Tourist Offices

Every English city and town has a Tourist Information Centre (TIC), with free leaflets, books and maps for sale, and loads of advice on places to go and things to see in the local area. Full details are given throughout the book. TICs have incredibly friendly staff, and they can also help with booking accommodation. Some TICs are run by national parks and often have small exhibitions about the area.

Most TICs keep regular business hours, while in popular tourist areas they open daily year-round. Smaller TICs close from October to March.

VISAS

If you're a European Economic Area (EEA) national, you don't need a visa and may live and work in England freely. Citizens of Australia, Canada, New Zealand, South Africa and the USA are given leave to enter England at their point of arrival for up to six months, but are prohibited from working. (If you intend to seek work, see p744.)

English immigration authorities are tough, and if they suspect you're coming to England for more than a holiday, you may need to prove that you have funds to support yourself, details of any hotels or local tours booked, or personal letters from people you'll be visiting. Having a return ticket helps too.

Visa and entry regulations are always subject to change, so it's vital to check with your local British embassy, high commission or consulate before leaving home. For more information, check www.ukvisas.gov.uk or www.ind.homeoffice.gov.uk.

HISTORY TIPS

Membership of the National Trust (NT) and English Heritage (EH) is valuable if you plan to visit many historic sights, as this gives you free entry to properties, reciprocal arrangements with other heritage organisations (in Wales, Scotland and beyond), maps, information handbooks and so on. You can join at the first NT or EH site you visit. If you are a member of a similar organisation in your own country, this may get you free or discounted entry at NT and EH sites in England.

National Trust (☎ 0870 458 4000; www.nationaltrust.org.uk) protects hundreds of historic buildings (normally around £5 to enter) plus vast tracts of land with scenic importance. Membership costs £36 per year (£16.50 for under-26s, and £50 to £65 for families). Alternatively, a NT touring pass gives free entry to NT properties for seven-day or 14-day periods (£16/20); families and couples get cheaper rates.

English Heritage (☎ 0870 333 1181; www.english-heritage.org.uk) is a state-funded organisation, responsible for the upkeep of numerous historic sites. Some are free, while others cost £1.50 to £6. Annual membership costs £34 per adult, £58 per couple (£38 for seniors). Alternatively, an Overseas Visitors Pass allows free entry to most major EH sites for seven/14 days (£15/19).

We have included the relevant acronym (NT or EH) in the information brackets after properties listed throughout this book.

WEIGHTS & MEASURES

England is in transition when it comes to weights and measures, as it has been for the last 20 years – and will be for 20 more. Most people still use 'imperial' units of inches, feet, yards and miles, although mountain heights on maps are given in metres only.

For weight, many people use pounds and ounces, even though since January 2000 goods in shops must be measured in kilograms. And nobody knows their weight in pounds (like Americans) or kilograms (like the rest of the world); Brits weigh themselves in stones, an archaic unit of 14 pounds.

When it comes to volume, things are even worse: most liquids are sold in litres or half-litres, except milk and beer, which come in pints. Garages sell petrol priced in pence per litre, but measure car performance in miles per gallon. Great, isn't it?

In this book we have reflected this wacky system of mixed measurements. Heights are given in metres (m) and distances in miles, with kilometre (km) equivalents given where necessary. For conversion tables, see the inside front cover.

WOMEN TRAVELLERS

The occasional wolf whistle or groper on the London Underground aside, solo women will find England fairly enlightened. There's nothing to stop women going into pubs alone, for example – although you may feel conspicuous. Restaurants may assume you're waiting for a date unless you specify a table for one, but once you've clarified, it's no big deal.

The contraceptive pill is available free on prescription in England, as is the morning-after pill (also on sale at chemists). Most big towns have a Well Woman Clinic that can advise on general health issues; find its address in the local phone book.

Safety is not a major issue, although commonsense caution should be observed in big cities, especially at night. Hitching is always unwise. Should the worst happen, most cities and towns have a Rape Crisis centre, where information or counselling is free and confidential; see www.rapecrisis.org.uk for details.

WORK

Nationals of most European countries don't need a permit to work in England, but everyone else does. If this is the main purpose of your visit, you must be sponsored by an English company. For more details on regulations, see p743.

If you're a Commonwealth citizen with a UK-born parent, a Certificate of Entitlement to the Right of Abode allows you to live and work in England free of immigration control. If one of your grandparents was born in the UK you may be eligible for an Ancestry Employment Certificate allowing full-time work for up to four years.

Commonwealth citizens under 31 without UK ancestry are allowed to take temporary work during their holiday, but need a Working Holiday Entry Certificate – which must be obtained in advance and is valid for four years. You're not allowed to engage in business, pursue a career (evidently serving in bars doesn't count) or work as a professional athlete or entertainer. Au pair placements are generally permitted.

Full-time students from the USA can get a six-month work permit; the **British Universities North America Club** (☎ 020-7251 3472; www.bunac.org) can provide advice and assistance. For more advice, www.workingholidayguru.com is a handy site aimed mainly at Australians coming to Europe. Another good source is weekly *TNT Magazine,* available free in London – or see www.tntmagazine.com.

TRACE THE ANCESTORS

If you're a visitor with ancestors who once lived in England, your trip could be a good chance to find out more about them. You may even discover long-lost relatives. Here are a few guidelines to get you started.

Start at the **Family Records Centre** (☎ 0870 243 7788; www.familyrecords.gov.uk; 1 Myddelton St, London EC1R 1UW). This helpful department of the Public Records Office (PRO) is used to ancestor-hunters and has publications (available by post) outlining the process. You'll need a passport as ID to see original records. Documents referring to individuals are closed for 100 years to safeguard confidentiality.

The **Association of Genealogists & Researchers in Archives** (www.agra.org.uk) lists professional researchers, who (for a fee) can search for ancestors or living relatives on your behalf.

Health <small>Dr Caroline Evans</small>

CONTENTS

England is a healthy place to travel, and the National Health Service (NHS) provides an excellent service, free on the point of delivery, which – although Brits may complain – is better than most other countries offer. Across the country, hygiene standards are high (despite what your nose tells you on a crowded tube train) and there are no unusual diseases to worry about. Your biggest risks will be from overdoing activities – physical, chemical or other.

BEFORE YOU GO

No immunisations are mandatory for visiting England.

European Economic Area (EEA) nationals can obtain free emergency treatment in England on presentation of an E111 form, validated in their home country. Reciprocal arrangements between the UK and some other countries around the world (including Australia) allow their residents to receive free emergency medical treatment and subsidised dental care at hospitals, general practitioners (GPs) and dentists. For full details, see the overseas visitors section of the Department of Health's website: www.publications.doh.gov.uk.

Regardless of nationality, anyone will receive free emergency treatment at Accident & Emergency departments of NHS hospitals. Travel insurance, however, is advisable as it offers greater flexibility over where and how you're treated, and covers expenses for emergency repatriation.

Chemists and pharmacies can advise on minor ailments such as sore throats and earache. In large cities, there's always at least one chemist open 24 hours.

Internet Resources

Lonely Planet's website (www.lonelyplanet.com) has links to the World Health

Organization (WHO) and the US Centers for Disease Control & Prevention. Other good sites include the following:

www.who.int/ith WHO International Travel and Health.
www.ageconcern.org.uk Advice on travel for the elderly.
www.mariestopes.org.uk Women's health and contraception.
www.mdtravelhealth.com Worldwide travel health recommendations, updated daily.

IN TRANSIT
Deep Vein Thrombosis (DVT)

Deep Vein Thrombosis (DVT) refers to blood clots that form in the legs during plane flights, chiefly because of prolonged immobility. The longer the flight, the greater the risk. The chief symptom is swelling or pain in the foot, ankle or calf. When a blood clot travels to the lungs, it may cause chest pain and breathing difficulties.

To prevent DVT on long flights you should walk about the cabin, contract leg muscles while sitting, drink plenty of fluids and avoid alcohol.

Jet Lag

To avoid jet lag (common when crossing more than five time zones), try drinking plenty of nonalcoholic fluids and eating light meals. Upon arrival, get exposure to natural sunlight and readjust your schedule (for meals, sleep and so on) as soon as possible.

IN ENGLAND
Water

Tap water in England is always safe unless there's a sign to the contrary (eg on trains). Don't drink straight from streams in the countryside – you never know what's upstream.

Sunburn

In summertime in England, even when there's cloud cover, it's possible to get sunburnt surprisingly quickly – especially if you're on water. Use sunscreen, wear a hat and cover up with a shirt and trousers.

Women's Health

Emotional stress, exhaustion and travel through time zones can contribute to an upset in the menstrual pattern. If using oral contraceptives, remember some antibiotics, diarrhoea and vomiting can stop them from working.

If you're already pregnant, travel is usually possible, but you should always consult your doctor. The most risky times for travel are the first 12 weeks of pregnancy and after 30 weeks.

Transport

CONTENTS

GETTING THERE & AWAY

London is an international transport hub, so you can easily fly to England from just about anywhere in the world. On flights to/from Ireland and mainland Europe, the recent emergence of budget or 'no-frills' airlines has increased competition – and reduced fares.

Your other main option between England and mainland Europe is ferry, either port-to-port or combined with a long-distance bus trip – although journeys can be long and savings not huge compared to budget airfares. International trains are much more comfortable, and the Channel Tunnel allows direct services between England, France and Belgium.

Getting from England to Scotland and Wales is easy. The bus and train systems are fully integrated and in most cases you won't even know you've crossed the border. Passports are not required (although some Scots and Welsh may think they should be!)

AIR
Airports
London's Heathrow and Gatwick are the two main airports for international flights, though some transatlantic planes zip direct to regional airports like Manchester

and Birmingham. These airports are also served by numerous scheduled and charter flights to and from continental Europe and Ireland; other airports include Luton and Stanstead (near London), Newcastle, Bristol, Southampton, Nottingham East Midlands and many more, including the new, neatly tagged Robin Hood Doncaster Sheffield Airport – destined to be a major northern entrepôt.

HEATHROW
Some 15 miles west of central London, **Heathrow** (LHR; ☎ 0870 000 0123; www.baa.com/main/airports/heathrow) is the world's busiest international airport. It has four terminals, with a fifth under construction and a sixth mooted. Make certain you know which terminal your flight is departing from as airlines and flights can shift around the airport.

Heathrow can feel chaotic and crowded so allow yourself plenty of time to get lost in the labyrinth of shops, bars and restaurants. Each terminal has competitive currency-exchange facilities, information counters and accommodation desks.

There are **left-luggage facilities** at Terminal 1 (☎ 8745 5301), Terminal 2 (☎ 8745 4599), Terminal 3 (☎ 8759 3344) and Terminal 4 (☎ 8745 7460). They open from 5am to 11pm, and charge £3.50 for up to six hours, or £4 per day. All can forward baggage.

For inquiries and flight information phone ☎ 0870 000 0123. There is no booking fee at the London Underground **Hotel Reservation Service** (☎ 8564 8808), which can help book rooms near the airport, although the service on the arrivals floor charges £5.

GATWICK
Smaller, better-organised **Gatwick** (LGW; ☎ 0870 000 2468; www.baa.com/main/airports/gatwick) is 30 miles south of central London. North and South Terminals are linked by a monorail, which takes two minutes. Charters, scheduled airlines and no-frills carrier Easyjet fly from Gatwick.

Airlines
Most of the world's major airlines have services to/from England, including the

following (with their UK contact and reservation numbers):

Aer Lingus (☎ 0845 084 4444; www.aerlingus.com)
Air Canada (☎ 0871 220 1111; www.aircanada.ca)
Air France (☎ 0845 359 1000; www.airfrance.com)
Air New Zealand (☎ 0800 028 4149; www.airnew zealand.co.nz)
Alitalia (☎ 0870 544 8259; www.alitalia.com)
American Airlines (☎ 08457 789 789; www.american airlines.com)
British Airways (☎ 0870 850 9850; www.ba.com)
British Midland (☎ 0870 607 0555; www.flybmi.com)
Cathay Pacific (☎ 020 8834 8888; www.cathaypacific .com)
Continental Airlines (☎ 01293-776464; www.con tinental.com)
Delta Air Lines (☎ 0800 414767; www.delta.com)
El Al Israel Airlines (☎ 020-7957 4100; www.elal.co.il)
Emirates (☎ 0870 243 2222; www.emirates.com)
Iberia (☎ 0845 850 9000; www.iberia.com)
KLM-Royal Dutch Airlines (☎ 08705 074 074; www.klm.com)
Lufthansa Airlines (☎ 08708 377 747; www.luft hansa.com)
Qantas Airways (☎ 08457 747 767; www.qantas .com.au)
Scandinavian Airlines (☎ 020-8990 7159; www.scan dinavian.net)
Singapore Airlines (☎ 0870 608 8886; www.singa poreair.com)
South African Airways (☎ 0870 747 1111; www.flysaa.com)
United Airlines (☎ 08458 444 777; www.united.com)
Virgin Atlantic (☎ 0870 380 2007; www.virgin -atlantic.com)

Budget airlines flying between England and other European countries can offer real bargains. Fares vary according to demand, and are best bought online. The only downside is that some no-frills airlines land at minor airports a considerable distance from the centre of the city they claim to serve. Main players:

EasyJet (☎ 0870 600 0000; www.easyjet.com)
Ryanair (☎ 0871 246 0000; www.ryanair.com)
Virgin Express (☎ 0870 730 1134; www.virgin-express .com)

To save trawling several sites, services such as www.skyscanner.com and www.lowcost airlines.org have information on many scheduled airlines.

Charter flights are another option. You can buy seat-only deals on the planes that

---

DEPARTURE TAX

Flights within the UK, and from the UK to EU destinations, attract a £10 departure tax. For other international flights from the UK you pay £20. This is usually included in the ticket price.

---

carry tourists between, for example, England and numerous Mediterranean resorts. Contact high-street travel agencies, or specialist websites such as www.flightline.co.uk and www.cheapflights.co.uk.

Tickets

You can buy your airline ticket from a travel agency (in person, by phone or on the Internet), or direct from the airline (the best deals are often available online only). Whichever, it always pays to shop around. Internet travel agencies such as www.travelocity.com and www.expedia.com work well if you're doing a straightforward trip, but for anything slightly complex there's no substitute for a real live travel agent who knows the system, the options, the special deals and so on.

The best place to start your search for agencies or airlines is the travel section of a weekend newspaper. Scan the advertisements, phone a few numbers, check a few websites, build up an idea of options, then take it from there. Remember, you usually get what you pay for: cheaper flights may leave at unsociable hours or include several stopovers. For quick and comfortable journeys, you have to fork out more cash.

Australia & New Zealand

To England from the southern hemisphere is a very popular route, with a wide range of fares from about A$1500 to A$3000 return. From New Zealand it's often best to go via Australia. Round-the-world (RTW) tickets can sometimes work out cheaper than a straightforward return. Major agencies include the following:

AUSTRALIA
Flight Centre (☎ 133 133; www.flightcentre.com.au)
STA Travel (☎ 1300 733 035; www.statravel.com.au)

NEW ZEALAND
Flight Centre (☎ 0800 243544; www.flightcentre.co.nz)
STA Travel (☎ 0508 782 872; www.statravel.co.nz)

Canada & the USA

There is a continuous price war on the world's busiest transcontinental route. Return fares from the east coast to London range from US$300 to US$600. From the west coast, fares are about US$100 higher. Major agencies include the following:

USA
Flight Centre (☎ 1866-WORLD 51; www.flightcentre.us)
STA Travel (☎ 800 781 4040; www.statravel.com)

CANADA
Flight Centre (☎ 1888-967 5355; www.flightcentre.ca)
Travel CUTS (☎ 866 246 9762; www.travelcuts.com)

LAND

Bus

You can easily get between England and numerous cities in Ireland or mainland Europe via long-distance bus. The international bus network **Eurolines** (www.eurolines .com) connects a huge number of destinations; the website has links to bus operators in each country, and gives contact details of local offices. In England, you can book Euroline tickets on the phone or at the website of **National Express** (☎ 08705 808080; www.national express.com), and at many travel agencies.

Bus travel may be slower and less comfortable than going by train, but it's usually cheaper, especially if you're under 25 or over 60. Some sample single fares (and approximate journey times) are: Amsterdam to London €50 (10 hours); Barcelona €125 (24 hours); Dublin €30 (12 hours). Frequent

---

WARNING

The information in this chapter is particularly vulnerable to change: fares are volatile, schedules change, rules are amended and special deals come and go. You should get opinions, quotes and advice from as many airlines and travel agencies as possible, and make sure you're 100% clear on each ticket's benefits and restrictions, before parting with your hard-earned cash. You should also be fully aware of visa regulations and security requirements for international travel. The details given in this chapter should be regarded as pointers and are not a substitute for your own up-to-date research.

---

special offers can bring these fares down, but it's still worth checking the budget airlines. You may pay a similar fare and knock a large chunk off the journey time.

Train

CHANNEL TUNNEL SERVICES

The Channel Tunnel makes direct train travel between England and continental Europe a fast and enjoyable option. High-speed **Eurostar** (☎ 08705 186 186; www.eurostar.com) passenger services hurtle at least 10 times daily between London and Paris (3 hours), and London and Brussels (2.5 hours), via Ashford and Calais. A new high-speed rail link on the English side will be complete in 2007 and slice another 30 minutes off the journey.

You can buy tickets from travel agencies, major train stations or direct from Eurostar. The normal single fare between London and Paris/Brussels is £149, but advance deals can drop to around £100 return, or less. Seniors and under-25s get reductions. Bicycles must be in a bike bag.

Your other option is **Eurotunnel** (☎ 08705 353535; www.eurotunnel.com). You drive to the coast (Folkestone in England, Calais in France), drive onto a train, get carried through the tunnel, and drive off at the other end. The trains run about four times hourly from 6am to 10pm, then hourly. Loading and unloading is one hour; the journey takes 35 minutes. You can book in advance direct with Eurotunnel or pay on the spot (cash or credit card). A car (and passengers) costs around £200 return, but there are often cheaper promotional fares.

TRAIN & FERRY CONNECTIONS

As well as Eurostar, many 'normal' trains run between England and mainland Europe. You buy a direct ticket, but get off the train at the port, walk onto a ferry, then get another train on the other side. Routes include: Amsterdam to London (via Hook of Holland and Harwich); Brussels to London (via Ostende and Dover); and Paris to London (via Calais and Dover). Single fares are about £50, but cheaper deals are usually available.

Travelling between Ireland and England, the main train-ferry-train route is Dublin to London, via Dun Laoghaire and Holyhead. From southern Ireland, ferries sail between Rosslare and Fishguard or Pembroke (Wales), with train connections on either side.

SEA

The main ferry routes between England, Ireland and mainland Europe include Holyhead to Dun Laoghaire (Ireland), Dover to Calais (France), Dover to Ostende (Belgium), Harwich to Hook of Holland (Netherlands), Hull to Zeebrugge (Belgium) and Rotterdam (Holland), Portsmouth to Santander or Bilbao (Spain), and Newcastle to Bergen (Norway) and Gothenberg (Sweden), but there are many more.

Competition from Eurotunnel and no-frills airlines has forced ferry operators to offer constant discounted fares, although options vary massively according to time of day or year. The best cross-channel bargains are return fares – often much cheaper than two singles; sometimes cheaper than *one* single! If you're a foot passenger, or cycling, you've got more flexibility. If you're driving a car, planning ahead is worthwhile: as well as the usual variants (time of year etc), fares depend on the size of car and the number of passengers. On longer ferry trips, the fare might include a cabin.

Main ferry operators (and their UK contact numbers):

Brittany Ferries (☎ 08703 665 333; www.brittany -ferries.com)

Fjord Line (☎ 0191-296 1313; www.fjordline.co.uk)

Hoverspeed (☎ 0870 240 8070; www.hoverspeed.co.uk)

Irish Ferries (☎ 08705 171717; www.irishferries.com)

P&O Ferries (☎ 08705 202020; www.poferries.com)

Speedferries (☎ 01304-203000; www.speedferries.com)

Stena Line (☎ 08705 707070; www.stenaline.com)

Another option is www.ferrybooker.com – an online agency covering all sea-ferry routes, plus Eurotunnel.

GETTING AROUND

For getting around England by public transport, your main options are train and bus: services between major towns and cities are generally good, although expensive compared to other European countries. Delays are frequent too, especially on the rail network, but these tend to afflict commuters rather than visitors: if your journey from London to Bath runs 30 minutes late, what's the problem? You're on holiday!

As long as you have time, with a mix of train, coach, local bus, the odd taxi, walking and occasionally hiring a bike, you can get almost anywhere without having to drive. You'll certainly see more of the countryside than you might slogging along grey motorways, and in the serene knowledge that you're doing less environmental damage. Having said that, in some rural areas the bus services can be patchy, so a car can often be handy for reaching out-of-the-way spots.

Public Transport Information (www.pti.org.uk) is a very useful website covering services nationwide (although some areas are better represented than others), with numerous links to help plan your journey.

AIR

England's domestic air companies include British Airways, British Midland, EasyJet and Ryanair, but flights aren't really necessary for tourists. Even if you're going from one end of the country to the other (eg London to Newquay or Newcastle) trains compare favourably with planes, once airport down-time is factored in. Pricewise, you might get a bargain air fare, but with advance planning trains can be cheaper.

BICYCLE

England is a compact country, and getting around by bicycle is perfectly feasible – and a great way to really see the country – if you've got time to spare. For more ideas see p61.

BUS & COACH

If you're on a tight budget, long-distance buses and coaches are nearly always the cheapest way to get around, although they're also the slowest (sometimes by a considerable margin).

In England, long-distance express buses are called coaches, and in many towns there are separate bus and coach stations. Make sure you go to the right place!

National Express (☎ 08705 808080; www.national express.com) is the main operator, with a wide network and frequent services between main centres. Fares are very reasonable (eg London to York £22, and special-offer 'fun fares' can be as low as £1).

Also offering fares from £1 is **Megabus** (www.megabus.com), which operates a budget airline-style service between about 20 main destinations around the country. Go at a quiet time, book early, and your ticket will be very cheap. Book later, for a busy time and…you get the picture. Along the same lines is **EasyBus** (www.easybus.co.uk) – due for launch in late 2004.

For information about short-distance and local bus services see p752.

Bus Passes & Discounts

National Express offers Discount Coach-cards to full-time students, under-26s and people over 50. Proof and a passport photo are required. Cards cost £10, and get you 25% to 50% off standard adult fares. Families and disabled travellers also get discounts.

For touring the country, National Express also offers Brit Xplorer passes, which allow unlimited travel for seven days (£70), 14 days (£120) and 28 days (£190). You don't need to book journeys in advance with this pass; if the coach has a spare seat – you can take it. This deal is only available to non-Brits though.

CAR & MOTORCYCLE

Travelling by private car or motorbike, you can be independent and flexible, and reach remote places. For solo budget travellers a downside of car travel is the expense, and in cities you'll need superhuman skills to negotiate heaving traffic, plus deep pockets for parking charges. But if there's two of you (or more), car travel can work out cheaper than public transport.

Motorways and main A-roads are dual carriageways and deliver you quickly from one end of the country to another. Lesser A-roads, B-roads and minor roads are much more scenic and fun, especially in northern England, as you wind through the country-side from village to village; ideal for car or motorcycle touring. You can't travel fast, but you won't care.

Petrol costs around 80p per litre. Diesel is slightly cheaper. Note also that fuel prices rise the further you get away from regional centres.

Hire

Compared to many countries (especially the USA), hire rates are expensive in England; you should expect to pay around £250 per week for a small car (unlimited mileage).

Rates rise at busy times, and drop at quiet times (especially at EasyRentacar, where you also get better rates for advance reservations, and special offers can drop to £3 per day). Some main players:

Avis (☎ 08700 100 287; www.avis.co.uk)
Budget (☎ 08701 565656; www.budget.com)
EasyRentacar (☎ 0906 333 3333; www.easycar.com)
Europcar (☎ 0870 607 5000; www.europcar.co.uk)
Hertz (☎ 0870 844 8844; www.hertz.co.uk)
National (☎ 0870 400 4502; www.nationalcar.com)
Sixt (☎ 08701 567567; www.e-sixt.co.uk)
Thrifty (☎ 01494-751600; www.thrifty.co.uk)

Many international websites have separate pages for customers in different countries, and the prices for a car in England on, say, the UK pages can be cheaper or more expensive than the same car on the USA or Australia pages. The moral is – you have to surf a lot of sites to find the best deals.

Your other option is to use an Internet search engine to find small local car-hire companies in England who can undercut the big boys. Generally those in cities are cheaper than in rural areas. See under Getting Around in the main city sections for more details, or see a rental broker site such as **UK Car Hire** (www.uk-carhire.net).

Motoring Organisations

Large motoring organisations include the **Automobile Association** (☎ 0800 600 0371; www.theaa.com) and the **Royal Automobile Club** (☎ 0800 722822; www.rac.co.uk); annual membership starts at around £40, including 24-hour breakdown assistance. A greener alternative is the **Environmental Transport Association** (☎ 01932-828882; www.eta.co.uk); it provides all the usual services (breakdown assistance, roadside rescue, vehicle inspections etc) but *doesn't* campaign for more roads.

Parking

England is small, and people love their cars, so there's often not enough parking space to go round. Many cities have short-stay and long-stay car parks; the latter are cheaper though maybe less convenient. 'Park and Ride' systems allow you to park in a satellite car park and then ride to the centre on the regular buses provided for an all-in-one price.

Yellow lines (single or double) along the edge of the road indicate restrictions. Find

TRANSPORT

the nearby sign that spells out when you can and can't park. In London and other big cities, traffic wardens operate with efficiency; if you park on the yellow lines at the wrong time, your car will be clamped or towed away, and it'll cost you £100 or more to get driving again. In some cities there are also red lines, which mean no stopping at all. Ever.

Purchase

If you're planning a long tour around England you may want to buy a vehicle. You can find a banger for £300, and a reasonable car for around £1000. If you want a campervan, expect to pay at least £2000 for something reliable. For more ideas prices, pick up *Autotrader* magazine, or look at www.autotrader.co.uk.

To be on the road, all cars require:

■ a Ministry of Transport (MOT) safety certificate, valid for one year
■ third-party insurance – shop around, but expect to pay at least £300
■ a registration form ('log book') signed by both the buyer and seller
■ a 'tax disc' – £88/160 for six months/one year (less for engines under 1100cc).

It saves loads of hassle to buy a vehicle with a valid MOT certificate and tax disc; both remain with the car through change of ownership. Third-party insurance goes with the driver rather than the car, so you'll still have to arrange this.

Road Rules

A foreign driving licence is valid in England for up to 12 months. If you plan to bring a car from Europe, it's illegal to drive without (at least) third-party insurance. Some other important rules are:

■ drive on the left (!)
■ wear fitted seat belts in cars
■ wear crash helmets on motorcycles
■ give way to your right at junctions and roundabouts
■ always use the left-side lane on motorways and dual-carriageways, unless overtaking (although so many people ignore this rule, you might think it wasn't law)
■ don't use a mobile phone while driving unless it's fully hands-free (another rule frequently flouted).

Speed limits are 30mph (48km/h) in built-up areas, 60mph (96km/h) on main roads, and 70mph (112km/h) on motorways and dual carriageways. Drinking and driving is taken very seriously; you're allowed a blood-alcohol level of 80mg/100mL and campaigners want it reduced to 50mg/100mL.

All drivers should read the *Highway Code*. It's often stocked by TICs, and available online at www.roads.dft.gov.uk/road safety (and, incidentally, often around No 7 in national nonfiction bestseller tables).

HITCHING

Hitching is not as common as it used to be in England. Travellers should understand that they're taking a small but potentially serious risk, and we don't recommend it. If you decide to go by thumb, note that it's illegal to hitch on motorways; you must use approach roads or service stations.

LOCAL TRANSPORT

English cities usually have good local public-transport systems, although buses are often run by a confusing number of separate companies. The larger cities have tram and underground rail services too. TICs can provide information, and more details are given in the city sections throughout this book.

Bus

All cities have good local bus networks, and in rural areas popular with tourists (especially national parks) there are frequent bus services from Easter to September. Elsewhere in the countryside, bus timetables are designed to serve schools and industry, so there can be few midday and weekend services, or buses may link local villages to a market town on only one day each week.

For information about local bus travel, contact the national **Traveline** (☎ 0870 608 2608; www.traveline.org.uk). By phone, you get transferred automatically to an advisor in the region you're phoning *from*; for details on another part of the country you may have to be transferred to another assistant.

Once you're on the spot, double-check at a Tourist Information Centre (TIC) before planning your day's activities around a bus that you later find out only runs on Thursdays after a full moon.

BUS PASSES

If you're taking a few local bus rides in a day of energetic sightseeing, ask about day-passes (with names like Day Rover, Wayfarer or Explorer), which will be cheaper than buying several singles. If you plan to linger longer in one area, three-day passes are a great bargain. Often they can be bought on your first bus, and may include local rail services. Passes are mentioned in the regional chapters, and it's always worth asking ticket clerks or bus drivers about your options.

POSTBUS

A postbus is a van on usual mail service that also carries passengers. Postbuses operate in rural areas (and some of the most scenic and remote parts of the country), and are especially useful for walkers and backpackers. For information and timetables contact **Royal Mail Postbus** (☎ 08457 740 740; www.postbus.royalmail.com).

Taxi

There are two main sorts of taxi: the famous black cabs (some carry advertising livery in other colours these days), which have meters and can be hailed in the street; and minicabs, which can only be called by phone. In London and other big cities, taxis cost £2 to £3 per mile. In rural areas, it's about half this, which means when it's Sunday and you find that the next bus out of the charming town you've just hiked to is on Monday, a taxi can keep you moving. If you call **National Cabline** (☎ 0800 123444) from a landline phone, the service will pinpoint your location and transfer you to an approved local company.

TOURS & ACTIVITY HOLIDAYS

If your time is limited or you prefer to travel in a group, a tour can be a great way to get around – especially if it's combined with an activity. This section suggests some England-wide tours and holidays, while local choices are listed in the relevant chapters. Many national parks organise activity days or weekends, concentrating on wildlife and outdoor stuff like landscape painting or drystone walling. For more information or ideas, enquire at local TICs or have a look at the suggestions on www.visitbritain.com.

Acorn Activities (☎ 08707 405055; www.acorn activities.co.uk) Themed tours and day trips from abseiling to yachting, via cycling, silversmithing and much more.

Backpacker Co (☎ 020-8896 6070; www.backpacker .co.uk) Day trips to classic English sporting events, and tours further afield.

Black Prince Holidays (☎ 01527-575115; www.black prince.com) Canal boats for hire from bases across Britain, for three days, a week or more. Traditional on the outside, modern on the inside.

British Trust for Conservation Volunteers (☎ 01302-572244; www.btcv.org) Environmental working holidays, for weekends or longer.

Contiki (☎ 020-8290 6422; www.contiki.com) Fun-packed bus tours of Britain.

Contours (☎ 017684-80451; www.contours.co.uk) Self-guided walking tours on long-distance paths. Routes, accommodation and baggage transfer is all arranged; you travel when and as fast as you like.

Country Lanes (☎ 01425-655022; www.countrylanes .co.uk) Guided and self-guided cycling and walking tours throughout England.

Road Trip (☎ 0845 200 6791; www.roadtrip.co.uk) Minibus tours for backpackers – trips for one, three or five days, with optional activities.

YHA (☎ 0870 770 8868; www.yha.org.uk) Massive range of walking tours, guided or self-guided, group or independent, long-distance paths to weekend rambles, and activity holidays (caving, climbing, horse-riding, mountain-biking, kayaking and countless others) for people of all ages, plus active family breaks – including paint-ball weekends to work out all those issues.

TRAIN

For long-distance travel around England, trains are generally faster and more comfortable than coaches, but can be more expensive, although with discount tickets they can be competitive – and they often take you through beautiful countryside. Train services are run by about 20 different operating companies (for example, First Great Western runs from London to Bath, and GNER covers the East Coast line), while track and stations are run by Network Rail. For passengers this system can be confusing, but information and ticket-buying services are increasingly centralised.

Your first stop should be **National Rail Enquiries** (☎ 08457 484950, 020-7278 5240; www.national rail.co.uk), the nationwide timetable and fare information service. By phone, once you've checked times and fares, you then have to contact the relevant train operator to actually buy the ticket (for the cheaper advance-purchase tickets), or you can buy on the spot at stations (but advance-purchase discount tickets are usually not available here). The website has direct links to the individual operators and to two centralised ticketing services: www.thetrainline.com and www.Qjump.co.uk. The National Rail website also has special offers, plus real-time links to station departure boards, so you see if your train is on time (or not).

Classes

There are two classes of rail travel: 1st and standard (often called 2nd class). First class costs around 50% more than standard and, except on very crowded trains, is not really worth it. However, at weekends some train operators offer 'upgrades': for an extra £10 (£15 for long journeys) on top of your standard class fare you can enjoy more space and legroom in 1st class.

Costs & Reservations

For short journeys (under about 50 miles), it's best to buy tickets on the spot at rail stations. You may get a choice of express or stopping service – the latter is obviously slower, but can be cheaper, and may take you through charming countryside or grotty suburbs.

For longer journeys, on-the-spot fares are always available, but tickets are much cheaper if bought three days before travel (and even cheaper with more notice). Advance purchase gets you a reserved seat too. The cheapest fares are nonrefundable though, so if you miss your train you're stuck.

ALL THE FUN OF THE FARES

On coaches and especially trains, passengers are frequently faced with a bewildering array of ticket types and prices. Throughout this book we give the price for single tickets (unless otherwise specified) bought on the day you travel, outside peak times – ie outside 7am to 9.30am and 4pm to 6pm on weekdays, and about 4pm to 8pm on Friday and Sunday evenings.

If you plan your itinerary at least three days ahead, and buy tickets in advance, you'll make considerable savings on the prices we quote here.

Return fares can be anything from double the single price to only very slightly more (for example, a London to York 'saver' single train fare is £65; a return is £66).

If you have to change trains, or use two or more train operators, you still buy one ticket – valid for the whole of your journey. The main railcards are also accepted by all operators.

If you buy by phone or website, you can have the ticket posted to you (UK only), or collect it at the originating station on the day of travel, either at the ticket desk (get there with time to spare, as queues can be long) or via automatic machines.

For short or long trips, fares are usually cheaper outside 'peak' travel times (ie not when everyone else is trying to get to or from work). It's worth avoiding Fridays and Sundays too, as fares are higher on these busy days.

Following are the main fare types. The varying prices of London to York tickets are given by way of example.

Open Single/Return Available on the spot. No restrictions. Valid for a month. (London–York single/return £69/138.)

Day Return Valid any time on the day specified. Cheaper than an open return.

Cheap Day Single/Return Available on the spot. Valid only on the specified day, but has time restrictions (eg no travel before 9.30am).

Saver Single/Return Available on the spot. Return valid for one month. More restrictions (eg no peak travel). (London–York single/return £65/66.)

SuperSaver Available on the spot. Cheaper than Saver, but even more restrictions (eg no peak or weekend travel).

SuperAdvance Must be bought before 6pm on day before travel, but only a limited number of seats available, so can sell out. Buy further ahead if possible. Valid for one month, but you must fix your return-journey date. (London–York single/return £49/50.)

Apex Must be bought at least seven days in advance. Valid for one month and requires a fixed return date. Limited seats are available, so you must book well ahead to get this fare. (London–York single/return £37/38.)

Children under five travel free; those aged between five and 15 pay half price, except on tickets already heavily discounted.

Train Passes

Local train passes usually cover rail networks around a city (many include bus travel too), and are mentioned throughout this book.

For country-wide travel, BritRail passes are good value, but only for visitors from overseas and they *cannot be bought in England*. They must be bought in your country of

BIKES ON TRAINS

Bicycles can be taken on most train journeys for £1 to £3, but space limitations and ridiculously complicated advance-booking regulations often makes this difficult, especially on long-distance journeys. It really seems as if they don't want customers, although with persistence you can usually get where you want. Start with **National Rail Enquiries** (☎ 08457 484950; www.nationalrail .co.uk) and have a big cup of coffee or stress-reliever handy.

On local trains and shorter trips in rural areas there's generally much less trouble; bikes can be taken free of charge on a first-come-first-served basis. Even so, there may be space limits. A final warning: when railways are being repaired, cancelled trains are replaced by buses – and they won't take bikes.

origin from a specialist travel agency. There are many BritRail variants, each available in three different versions: for England only; for the whole of Britain (England, Wales and Scotland); and for the UK and Ireland. Below is an outline of the main options, quoting adult prices. Children's passes are usually half price (or free with some adult passes), and seniors get discounts too. For about 30% extra you can upgrade to first class. Other deals include a rail pass combined with the use of a hire car, or travel in Britain combined with one Eurostar journey.

BRITRAIL CONSECUTIVE

Unlimited travel on all trains in England for four, eight, 15, 22 or 30 days, for US$149/215/325/400/485. Anyone getting their money's worth out of the last pass should earn some sort of endurance award.

BRITRAIL FLEXIPASS

These passes mean you don't have to get on a train every day to get full value. Your options are four days of unlimited travel in England within a 60-day period for US$189, eight in 60 for US$275, or 15 in 60 for US$415.

ALL LINE ROVERS

If you don't (or can't) buy a BritRail pass, an All Line Rover gives unlimited travel anywhere on the national rail network (£338/515 for seven/14 days), and can be purchased in England, by anyone.

INTERNATIONAL PASSES

Eurail passes are not accepted in England, and InterRail passes are only valid if bought in another mainland European country.

RAILCARDS

If you're staying for a while, railcards cost £20 (valid for one year, available from major stations) and get you a 33% discount on most train fares. On the Family and Network cards, children get a 60% discount, and the fee is easily repaid in a couple of journeys. Proof of age and a passport photo may be required. For full details see www .railcard.co.uk.

Disabled Person's Railcard Costs £14. Cannot be bought at stations, but they can give you an application form; or from the website. Call ☎ 0191-281 8103 for more details.

Family Railcard Covers up to four adults and four children travelling together.

Network Card If you're concentrating on southeast England (eg London to Dover, Weymouth, Cambridge or Oxford) this card covers up to four adults travelling together outside peak times.

Senior Railcard For anyone over 60.

Young Person's Railcard You must be between 16 and 25, or a full-time UK student.

TRANSPORT

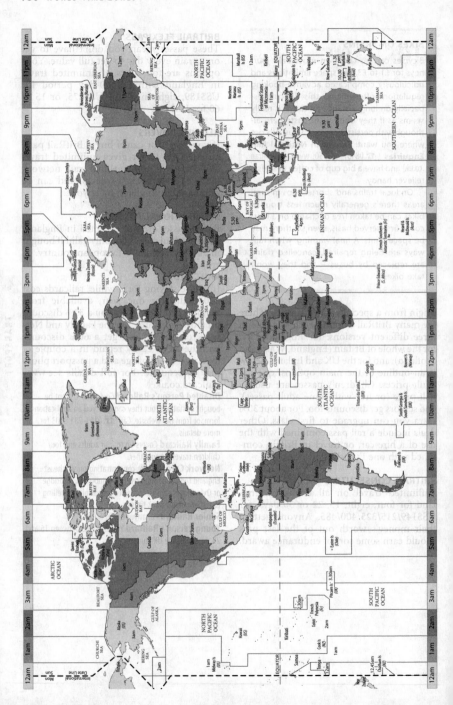

Glossary

agister – someone paid to care for stock
aka – also known as
almshouse – accommodation for the aged or needy

bailey – outermost wall of a castle
bairn – baby (northern England)
banger – old, cheap car
bangers – sausages
bap – bun
bar – gate (York, and some other northern cities)
barbican – extended gateway in a castle designed to make entry difficult for unwanted guests
beck – stream (northern England)
bent – not altogether legal
bevvied – drunk
bevvy – drink (originally from northern England)
bill – restaurant check
billion – the British billion is a million million (unlike the American billion – a thousand million)
biscuit – cookie
bitter – beer
black pudding – type of sausage made from dried blood and other ingredients
blatherskite – boastful or talkative person (northern England)
bloke – man
bodge job – poor-quality repair
bonnet (of car) – hood
boot (of car) – trunk
bridleway – path that can be used by walkers, horse riders and cyclists
Brummie – native of Birmingham
bum – backside (not tramp, layabout etc)
bus – local bus; see also *coach*
BYO – bring your own

caff – cheap café
cairn – pile of stones marking path, junction or peak
canny – good, great, wise (northern England)
capital – head of column
cenotaph – tomblike monument, memorial to person/s whose remains lie elsewhere
cheers – goodbye; thanks; also a drinking toast
chemist – pharmacist
chine – valley-like fissure leading to the sea (southern England)
chips – deep-fried potatoes or fries
circus – junction of several streets, usually circular
clunch – chalk (used in connection with chalk walls in building)

coach – long-distance bus
coaching inn – inn along a stagecoach route where horses were changed in the days before trains and motor transport
coasteering – adventurous activity that involves making your way around a rocky coastline by climbing, scrambling, jumping or swimming
cob – mixture of mud and straw for building
cot – crib
couchette – sleeping berth in a train or ferry
courgette – zucchini
court – courtyard
crack – good conversation, or good times (anglicised version of Gaelic 'craic')
cream tea – cup of tea and a scone with jam and cream
crisps – potato chips
croft – plot of land with adjoining house worked by the occupiers

dear – expensive
DIY – do-it-yourself, ie home improvements
dolmen – chartered tomb
donkey engine – small (sometimes portable) engine to drive machinery
dosh – money, wealth
dough – money
downs – rolling upland, characterised by lack of trees
dram – whisky measure
duvet – doona

EH – English Heritage
en suite room – hotel room with private attached bathroom (ie shower, basin and toilet)
Essex – derogatory adjective (as in 'Essex girl'), meaning tarty, and identified with '80s consumerism
EU – European Union
evensong – daily evening service (Church of England)

fag – cigarette; also boring task
fagged – exhausted
fanny – female genitals, not backside
fell race – tough running race through hills or moors
fen – drained or marshy low-lying flat land
fiver – five-pound note
flat – apartment
flip-flops – thongs
footpath – sidewalk

gaffer – boss or foreman
gate – street (York, and some other northern cities)

ginnel – alleyway (Yorkshire)
graft – work (not corruption)
grand – one thousand
greasy spoon – cheap café
grockle – tourist
gutted – very disappointed
guv, guvner – from governor, a respectful term of address for owner or boss; can sometimes be used ironically

hart – deer
hammered – drunk
HI – Hostelling International (organisation)
hire – rent
hosepipe – garden hose
hotel – accommodation with food and bar, not always open to passing trade
Huguenots – French Protestants

inn – pub with accommodation

jam – jelly
jelly – jello
jumper – sweater

kippers – salted and smoked fish, traditionally herring
kirk – church (northern England)

lager lout – see *yob*
lass – young woman (northern England)
ley – clearing
lift – elevator
lock – part of a canal or river that can be closed off and the water levels changed to raise or lower boats
lolly – money; can also mean candy on a stick (possibly frozen)
lorry – truck
love – term of address, not necessarily to someone likeable

machair – grass- and wildflower-covered sand dunes
mad – insane, not angry
manky – low quality, rotten, mouldy
Martello tower – small, circular tower used for coastal defence
mate – friend of any gender; also term of address, usually male-to-male
midge – mosquito-like insect
motorway – freeway
motte – mound on which a castle was built

naff – inferior, in poor taste
nappies – diapers
neeps – turnips (northern England)
NT – National Trust
NYMR – North Yorkshire Moors Railway

oast house – building containing a kiln for drying hops
off-license ('offie') – carry-out alcoholic drinks shop
OS – Ordnance Survey
owlers – smugglers

p (pronounced 'pee') – pence (ie 2p is 'two p' not 'two pence' or 'tuppence')
pargeting – decorative stucco plasterwork
pete – fortified house
pint – beer (as in 'let me buy you a pint')
pimms – popular English spirit mixed with lemonade, mint and fresh fruit, drunk by the pitcher in summer
piscina – basin for priests to wash their hands
pissed – drunk (not angry)
pissed off – angry
pitch – playing field
ponce – ostentatious or effeminate male; also to borrow (usually permanently)
pop – fizzy drink (northern England)
postbus – minibus that follows postal delivery routes, carrying mail and passengers
provost – mayor
punter – customer

queue – line
quid – pound

ramble – short easy walk
rebud – heraldic device suggesting the name of its owner
reiver – warrior (northern England)
return ticket – round-trip ticket
roll-up – roll-your-own cigarette
RSPB – Royal Society for the Protection of Birds
RSPCA – Royal Society for the Prevention of Cruelty to Animals
rubber – eraser; also (and less commonly) condom
rubbish bin – garbage can
rugger – rugby

sarnie – sandwich
sarsen – sandstone boulder, a geological remnant, usually found in chalky areas (sometimes used in Neolithic constructions for example at Stonehenge and Avebury sites)
sett – tartan pattern
shag – have sex; also a tough or tiring task
shagged – tired
sheila-na-gig – Celtic fertility symbol of a woman with exaggerated genitalia, often seen carved in stone on churches and castles. Rare in England, found mainly in the Marches, along the border with Wales.
shout – to buy a group of people drinks, usually reciprocated
shut – partially covered passage
single ticket – one-way ticket

sixth-form college – further-education college
Sloane Ranger – wealthy, superficial but well-connected young person
snicket – alleyway (York)
snog – long, drawn-out kiss (not just a peck on the cheek)
spondulicks – money
SSSI – Site of Special Scientific Interest
stone – unit of weight equivalent to 14lb or 6.35kg
subway – underpass (for pedestrians)
sweet – candy

ta – thanks
tatties – potatoes
thwaite – clearing in a forest (northern England)
TIC – Tourist Information Centre
ton – one hundred (slang)
tor – pointed hill (Celtic)
torch – flashlight
Tory – Conservative (political party)
towpath – path running beside a river or canal, where horses once towed barges
trainers – tennis shoes or sneakers
traveller – nomadic person (traditional and new-age hippy types)
tron – public weighbridge
twit – foolish (sometimes annoying) person
twitcher – obsessive birdwatcher
twitten – passage, small lane
tube – London's underground railway

underground – London's underground railway (subway)

VAT – value-added tax, levied on most goods and services, currently 17.5%
verderer – officer upholding law and order in the royal forests

wanker – stupid/worthless person (offensive slang)
wide boy – ostentatious go-getter, usually on the make
wolds – open, rolling countryside

YHA - Youth Hostels Association
yob – hooligan

GLOSSARY OF RELIGIOUS ARCHITECTURE

abbey – monastery of monks or nuns or the buildings they used
aisle – passageway or open space along either side of a church's *nave*
ambulatory – processional *aisle* at the east end of a cathedral, behind the altar

apse – semicircular or rectangular area for clergy, traditionally at the east end of the church

baptistry – separate area of a church used for baptisms
barrel vault – semicircular arched roof
boss – covering for the meeting point of the ribs in a *vaulted* roof
brass – memorial common in medieval churches consisting of a brass plate set into the floor or a tomb
buttress – vertical support for a wall; see also *flying buttress*

campanile – free-standing belfry or bell tower
chancel – eastern end of the church, usually reserved for choir and clergy
chantry – *chapel* established by a donor for use in their name after death
chapel – small, more private shrine or area of worship off the main body of the church
chapel of ease – *chapel* built for those who lived too far away from the parish church
chapter house – building in a cathedral *close* where the dean meets with the chapter; clergy who run the cathedral
chevet – *chapels* radiating out in a semicircular sweep
choir – area in the church where the choir is seated
clearstory – see *clerestory*
clerestory – a wall of windows above a church's *triforium*
cloister – covered walkway linking the church with adjacent monastic buildings
close – buildings grouped around a cathedral
collegiate – church with a chapter of canons and prebendaries, but not a cathedral
corbel – stone or wooden projection from a wall supporting a beam or arch
crossing – intersection of the *nave* and *transepts* in a church

flying buttress – supporting *buttress* in the form of one side of an open arch
font – basin used for baptisms, usually towards the west end of a church, often in a separate *baptistry*
frater – common or dining room in a medieval monastery

lady chapel – *chapel*, usually at the east end of a cathedral, dedicated to the Virgin Mary
lancet – pointed window in Early English style
lierne vault – *vault* containing many tertiary ribs

minster – church connected to a monastery
misericord – hinged choir seat with a bracket (often elaborately carved) that can be leant against

nave – main body of the church at the western end, where the congregation gather

presbytery – eastern area of the *chancel* beyond the choir, where the clergy operate

GLOSSARY

precincts – see *close*

priory – religious house governed by a prior

pulpit – raised box where the priest gives sermons

quire – medieval term for *choir*

refectory – monastic dining room

reredos – literally 'behind the back'; backdrop to an altar

rood – archaic word for cross (in churches)

rood screen – screen carrying a *rood* or crucifix, which separates the *nave* from the *chancel*

squint – angled opening in a wall or pillar to allow a view of a church's altar

transepts – north–south projections from a church's *nave*, which is often added at a later date than the original construction. It gives the whole church a cruciform (cross-shaped plan).

triforium – internal wall passage above a church's *arcade* and below the *clerestory*; behind the triforium is the 'blind' space above the side *aisle*

undercroft – vaulted underground room or cellar

vault – roof with arched ribs, usually in a decorative pattern; see also *barrel vault* and *lierne vault*

vestry – robing room, where the parson keeps his robes and puts them on

Behind the Scenes

THIS BOOK

This third edition of *England* was commissioned in Lonely Planet's London office and prepared in the Mebourne office. It was researched by David Else (coordinating author), Etain O'Carroll, Becky Ohlsen, Oliver Berry, Martin Hughes, Fionn Davenport and Sam Martin.

THANKS from the Authors

David Else First, massive thanks must go to my wife Corinne, who kept me topped up with coffee during late-night writing sessions, and read through all my drafts to make sure the final chapters were ready for those eagle-eyed editors at LP, Kate James and John Hinman, whose input and feedback was also appreciated. Although my name goes down as coordinating author of this book, I couldn't have done without the input (and, in some cases, company) of the other authors on this team, so hearty thanks to Fionn, Becky, Oliver, Sam, Etain and Martin. Thanks also to the specialists in arts, music, sport and literature who helped me get my facts straight: Heather Dickson, Lydia Cook, Sarah Johnstone, Kate Whateley, John Else, Tom Cook, Tom Hall and Tom Parkinson. And finally, thanks to Alan Murphy and Amanda Canning, commissioning editors at LP, for ideas, guidance, inspiration, sausage and chips, the occasional joke and several soothing beers, all along the way.

Etain O'Carroll Huge thanks to all the patient staff at TICs around my area for answering endless questions and queries, and special thanks to staff in Ironbridge Gorge, Tetbury and Porlock for giving me so much time. Sincere thanks also to Julian Owen,

music editor for *Venue* magazine for his boxed text on the Bristol music scene, and to Glyn Whiting in Pembridge for the local low-down. Thanks also to Adrian Southgate, Pauline Rogers, Ian Sinclair, Frances Rogers and Peter and Sheila Baseby for suggestions on additions to the text and as always, giant thanks to Mark for getting me through what seemed like an endless mountain of paper.

Becky Ohlsen Thanks to David Else, Alan Murphy and Amanda Canning at LP, Matt McNally in Norwich, Anne and Richard Symonds and Phil Jones in Castleton, Zach Hull and Patrick Leyshock of the Sang-Froid Riding Club, Pete Wild, Steve Aylett, John Graham, and everyone in all the tourist offices, museums and pubs who gave me such great travel tips.

Oliver Berry Special thanks go once again to Susie Berry, for love, listening and long-distance phone calls; to the staff of Britain's tourist offices, especially the ladies of Whitehaven; to the characters I met along the way; to Trevellas for long afternoons and late-night fires; to WW and SC for shining a light; and to The Hobo, my constant travelling companion. Thanks also to my Lonely Planet partners Alan Murphy, who gave me the chance to write about my favourite places, and David Else, who kept the show on the road.

Martin Hughes Thanks to Kirsti, Jeremy, Jane, Sean, Ardal, Melanie, Amanda, Emma, Marco, Gianfranco and Zola. Also, big thanks to Amanda, Fiona and Tom in the London office, for their time, effort and expertise.

Sam Martin Big, big, big thanks to Rob and Holly Burr, whose generous spirit and tiny London flat made this trip possible. Cheers to Phil and his car (but not his driving). Best to Richard in Broadstairs, the two Virginia commune dwellers and everyone else who selflessly offered tips and guidance for a Texan in England. Biggest thanks of all go to Denise for all her hard work – I couldn't have done it without you – and to the mighty Ford, whose charm sparked many a conversation on the road.

Fionn Davenport England is a terrific country, full of friendly, helpful who made my job a hell of a lot easier. If you met me along the way and succumbed to my pestering ways, I hope you remember me and my gratitude for your guidance. Pestering is a travel writer's lot, it seems, and the staff at LP bore the brunt of a lot of it, not least Alan Murphy, Amanda Canning, Kate James et al. Thanks guys and let's do it again sometime. Thanks to Laura Fraser, without whom England just isn't the same. Finally, a big thanks to my occasional travel mate and constant soul mate, Libby McCormack, who made even the greyest day seem sunny.

CREDITS

This edition was commissioned and developed in Lonely Planet's London office by Amanda Canning and Alan Murphy. The project manager was Rachel Imeson. Editing was coordinated by Kate James and Suzannah Shwer with assistance from Tom Smallman, John Hinman, Sarah Bailey, Emily Coles, Michelle Coxall and Jackey Coyle. Cartography was coordinated by Simon Tillema, with assistance from Piotr Czajkowski, Joelene Kowalski, Jody Whiteoak, Kusnandar, Tony Dupcinov, Jolyon Philcox and Andrew Smith. Managing the editing and cartography were Melanie Dankel and Mark Griffiths. Jacqui Saunders chose the colour images and Jacqueline McLeod laid the book out with help from Kaitlin Beckett. The cover was designed by Radek Wojcik. Dan Caleo input the cross references. Kate McDonald, Sally Darmody, Adriana Mammarella and Sonya Brooke checked the layout.

THANKS from Lonely Planet

Many thanks to the following travellers who used the last edition and wrote to us with helpful hints, useful advice and interesting anecdotes.

A Nicholas Anchen, Kaare Arkteg **B** Matt Bassett, Roger Bielec, Robert Braiden, M Ter Brugge **C** Helen Cardrick, Tim Clack, Alison

Columbine, Thomas Culetto **D** Edward Darran, Kate Darwent, Leisa Drury **E** Jim Edwards, Kirsten Elliott, Hanne Espolin Johnson **F** Mr & Mrs Fyvie **G** Scott Gaeckle, Megan Gibbons, Nicole Glaser, Dan Glass, Marcus Gomm **H** Amanda Hargraves, Wendy & Mike Harper, Stephen Harvey, John Hesketh, Babs Hodgin, Natalie Holmes, Victoria Hughes, Russell Huntington, James Hyde **J** Paul Jackson **K** Noa Kamrat, Nina Kessing, Pia Kokkarinen **L** Leroy Latta, Heather Lawson, John Lloyd **M** Andrew Mark, Ash Mather, Sarah McDonald, Audrey Moran, Kay Mould **O** Arthur Owen, Katie Owens **P** Shalom S Paul, Mike Pavasovic, Kate & Bob Perrett **R** Karlmarx Rajangam, Karl Raven, William Reeves, Stephane Reynolds, Craig Richmond, James Roberts, Stuart Roberts, Stan Rolfe, Cameron Ryan **S** Maria & Colin Sanders, Hubert Segain, Steve Senkiw, Janet Shipperlee, Ruth Shwer, Greg Stephenson, Michelle Stevenson **T** Kellie Tainton, Paul Trigg **V** Herma & Olix Vermeulen, Kristina Vogt **W** Andrew Wenrick, Laura Wood

ACKNOWLEDGMENTS

Many thanks to the following for the use of their content:

Globe on back cover © Mountain High Maps 1993 Digital Wisdom, Inc.

London Underground Map © 2003 London Transport Museum

Index

000 Map pages
000 Location of colour photographs

000 Map pages
000 Location of colour photographs

INDEX

INDEX

INDEX

INDEX

INDEX

INDEX

000 Map pages
000 Location of colour photographs

MAP LEGEND

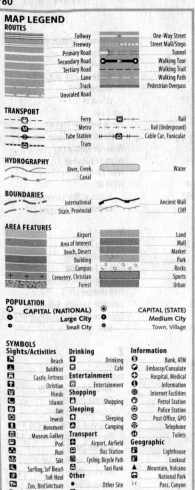

ROUTES

Tollway	One-Way Street
Freeway	Street Mall/Steps
Primary Road	Tunnel
Secondary Road	Walking Tour
Tertiary Road	Walking Trail
Lane	Walking Path
Track	Pedestrian Overpass
Unsealed Road	

TRANSPORT

Ferry	Rail
Metro	Rail (Underground)
Tube Station	Cable Car, Funicular
Tram	

HYDROGRAPHY

River, Creek	Water
Canal	

BOUNDARIES

International	Ancient Wall
State, Provincial	Cliff

AREA FEATURES

Airport	Land
Area of Interest	Mall
Beach, Desert	Market
Building	Park
Campus	Rocks
Cemetery, Christian	Sports
Forest	Urban

POPULATION

CAPITAL (NATIONAL)	CAPITAL (STATE)
Large City	Medium City
Small City	Town, Village

SYMBOLS

Sights/Activities
Beach, Buddhist, Castle, Fortress, Christian, Hindu, Islamic, Jain, Jewish, Monument, Museum, Gallery, Pool, Ruin, Sikh, Surfing, Surf Beach, Trail Head, Zoo, Bird Sanctuary

Eating
Eating

Drinking
Drinking, Café

Entertainment
Entertainment

Shopping
Shopping

Sleeping
Sleeping, Camping

Transport
Airport, Airfield, Bus Station, Cycling, Bicycle Path, Taxi Rank

Other
Other Site, Parking Area, Picnic Area

Information
Bank, ATM, Embassy/Consulate, Hospital, Medical, Information, Internet Facilities, Petrol Station, Police Station, Post Office, GPO, Telephone, Toilets

Geographic
Lighthouse, Lookout, Mountain, Volcano, National Park, Pass, Canyon, River Flow, Waterfall

LONELY PLANET OFFICES

Australia
Head Office
Locked Bag 1, Footscray, Victoria 3011
☎ 03 8379 8000, fax 03 8379 8111
talk2us@lonelyplanet.com.au

USA
150 Linden St, Oakland, CA 94607
☎ 510 893 8555, toll free 800 275 8555
fax 510 893 8572, info@lonelyplanet.com

UK
72–82 Rosebery Ave,
Clerkenwell, London EC1R 4RW
☎ 020 7841 9000, fax 020 7841 9001
go@lonelyplanet.co.uk

Published by Lonely Planet Publications Pty Ltd
ABN 36 005 607 983

© Lonely Planet 2005

© photographers as indicated 2005

Cover photographs by Lonely Planet and Getty Images: Angel of the North statue, Newcastle-upon-Tyne, Antony Edwards (front); sunbathers on deckchairs near Brighton pier, Christer Fredriksson (back). Many of the images in this guide are available for licensing from Lonely Planet Images: www.lonelyplanetimages.com

Printed through Colorcraft Ltd, Hong Kong.
Printed in China